UNM - GALLUP

P9-CKO-473   69 0

ENCYCLOPEDIA OF SEMIOTICS

ENCYCLOPEDIA OF
SEMIOTICS

Paul Bouissac

Editor in Chief

OXFORD UNIVERSITY PRESS

New York   1998   Oxford

OXFORD UNIVERSITY PRESS

Oxford   New York
Athens   Auckland   Bangkok   Bogotá
Buenos Aires   Calcutta   Cape Town   Chennai
Dar es Salaam   Delhi   Florence   Hong Kong   Istanbul
Karachi   Kuala Lumpur   Madrid   Melbourne   Mexico City
Mumbai   Nairobi   Paris   São Paulo   Singapore
Taipei   Tokyo   Toronto   Warsaw
and associated companies in
Berlin   Ibadan

Copyright © 1998 by Paul Bouissac

Published by Oxford University Press, Inc.,
198 Madison Avenue, New York, New York 10016
http://www.oup-usa.org

Oxford is a registered trademark of Oxford University Press

All rights reserved. No part of this publication may be reproduced,
stored in a retrieval system, or transmitted, in any form or by any means,
electronic, mechanical, photocopying, recording, or otherwise,
without the prior permission of Oxford University Press.

Library of Congress Cataloging-in-Publication Data

Encyclopedia of semiotics / Paul Bouissac, editor in chief.
p.   cm
Includes bibliographical references and index.
1. Semiotics—Encyclopedias.   I. Bouissac, Paul.
P99.E64   1998   401',41'03—dc21   98-23092 CIP
ISBN 0-19-512090-6

Printing (last digit): 9 8 7 6 5 4 3 2 1

Printed in the United States of America
on acid-free paper

Contents

◆

Editorial Board

vii

Preface

ix

ENCYCLOPEDIA OF SEMIOTICS

Directory of Contributors

653

Index

657

Editorial Board

EDITOR IN CHIEF

Paul Bouissac
Professor of French, University of Toronto

EDITORIAL COMMITTEE

Göran Sonesson
Associate Professor of Semiotics, Lunds Universitet

Paul J. Thibault
Associate Professor of English, Università di Venezia

Terry Threadgold
Professor of English, Monash University

ADVISORY BOARD

M. Philip Bryden
Professor of Psychology, University of Waterloo (deceased)

Teresa de Lauretis
Professor of History of Consciousness, University of California, Santa Cruz

Frantisek W. Galan
Professor of Comparative Literature, Vanderbilt University (deceased)

Mart R. Gross
Professor of Zoology, University of Toronto

Marlene Posner-Landsch
Professor of Semiotics and Communication Theory, Freie Universität Berlin

Lorraine Weir
Professor of Comparative Literature, University of British Columbia

Preface

◆

The twentieth century has witnessed an increasing fragmentation of knowledge into a multitude of disciplines and specialties. At the same time, integrative visions have arisen in an effort to make sense of the flood of information generated by the modern intensification of formal and empirical research. Semiotics represents one of the main attempts—perhaps the most enduring one—at conceiving a transdisciplinary framework through which interfaces can be constructed between distinct domains of inquiry. Other endeavors, such as the unified science movement of the 1930s or cybernetics and general systems theory in the 1950s and 1960s, met with only limited success. By contrast, semiotics remains a credible blueprint for bridging the gaps between disciplines and across cultures, most likely because of its own intellectual diversity and pluridisciplinary history, as well as its remarkable capacity for critical reflexivity. Cultural theory, one of its most powerful offshoots, similarly transcends traditional boundaries between academic and political domains, sexual and epistemological spheres, and economic and symbolic orders.

Informed by the degree to which these endeavors permeate both scholarly and popular discourse, this volume is designed primarily to provide a handy reference work for students of all ages who want to improve their proficiency in the languages and concepts of semiotics and cultural theory. Its goal is to explain the historical development of these systems of thought and critical approaches within their scientific and philosophical contexts. But semiotics and its outgrowths are not a closed chapter in the history of ideas. The dynamic of this fundamental, overarching inquiry keeps upsetting the epistemological landscape inherited from two centuries of disciplinary marshaling. It opens channels of communication among faculties and traditions, builds pressure on artificial partitions, connects levels, constructs interfaces, and awakens the mind to serial, lateral, and holistic thinking. Hence, it is difficult to map exhaustively this movement, which cannot be equated with a single theory, a homogeneous academic culture, or a normative set of principles. It forms, rather, a moving configuration of projects, all rooted in their respective intellectual traditions, but all aiming at a still-elusive understanding of the ways in which signs linguistically and otherwise convey, or create, meanings in a wide range of social and cultural contexts.

In the 1950s, when semiotics emerged from centuries of philosophical and linguistic speculations to formulate its own epistemological agenda, the perception of the landscape was much simpler. Two streams had sprung in the recent past. There was, on the one hand, in the wake of logical positivism and behaviorism, the ambitious blueprint of Charles Morris for a general science of signs. This endeavor was based on some models extrapolated from the profuse and provocative theorizing of the American scientist and philosopher Charles Sanders Peirce (1839–1914). On the other hand, there existed a parallel undertaking inspired by the mostly oral tradition coming from the Swiss linguist Ferdinand de Saussure (1857–1913), whose innovative views on the nature and functioning of language had spawned several schools in Europe. Like Peirce, Saussure had envisioned the daunting project of a science of signs, which he had called semiology. Both Saussure and Peirce considered themselves pioneers of a science-to-be that was destined to encompass, and restructure, a vast array of disciplines and to open new horizons to human knowledge. Such was the somewhat simplistic perception of the double intellectual genealogy that was held by most of those who, imbued with a deep sense of epistemological optimism, started the construction of modern semiotics as the second half of the twentieth century unfolded.

The picture is quite different some fifty years later, principally as a result of three distinct developments. First, historians of ideas have traced back some of the most basic notions of semiotics, under many other names, to a much longer and richer speculative tradition that is not restricted to the Western civilizations. In the meantime, unpublished manuscripts by Peirce and Saussure have come to light, revealing more complex and problematic systems of thought than earlier interpretations suggested. Second, the early models of twentieth-century European and American semiotics have come under intense scrutiny from both within and outside their respective paradigms. As a result, new models have emerged and new questions have been raised, shifting the whole field toward a more critical semiotics, whose variety of discourses often takes the prefix "post-" to symbolize the framing of earlier theories within more challenging perspectives. This semiotic turn has precipitated epistemological crises in the social sciences, and has forced a drastic rethinking of their very foundations. The impact of this radical questioning on the social construction of knowledge has triggered a heated debate with the empirical sciences. In the process, the borderline between theory and politics has been blurred. Third, advances in the information sciences, the cognitive neurosciences, and evolutionary biology have encroached upon the traditional domains of semiotics and borrowed parts of its terminology, thus facilitating the construction of promising interfaces and giving rise to disciplinary hybrids such as biosemiotics, neurosemiotics, zoosemiotics, sociobiology, and memetics.

It is this complex, dynamic situation that the present volume endeavors to picture and document. An encyclopedia of semiotics and cultural theory cannot be a mere inventory of concluded biographies and completed theories. To be true to its object, it must reflect not only the achievements but also the uncertainties and anxieties of its practitioners. A full century of theorizing on signs, structures, signification, representation, communication, and meaning has led to hypotheses conceived within, or in dialogue with, the main intellectual paradigms of the century—phenomenology, psychoanalysis, Marxism, structuralism, evolutionism, and information theory among them. The questions raised, debated, and still unsolved continue to engage the mind and motivate reflection and research. The reader will discover that most of the articles in this volume are problem-oriented rather than dogmatic. The points of entry variously are technical terms, names of schools of thought, authors and scholars, book titles, and general or specific domains of application. But it should be kept in mind that this volume is not meant to be a *Who's Who* of semiotics and cultural theory. It focuses on ideas and problems rather than on the individuals who have formulated them. It is also selective in its choice of the domains of application, offering illustrative probes rather than attempting an exhaustive review of the many topics that have now been tackled by semioticians of all persuasions.

The guiding principles for the elaboration of this encyclopedia have been to be comprehensive, problem-oriented, and user-friendly. The three hundred articles forming this work cover a wide range of topics and present a balanced view of the various theoretical and methodological approaches to the study of signs, communication, and culture that have been produced throughout the twentieth century. Forays into non-Western philosophical and linguistic traditions, such as Chinese theories of representation, Buddhist semiotics, and Indian semantics, add a global dimension to this work. The articles have been written by some one hundred international specialists in a language free of jargon, easily accessible to an educated audience, without oversimplifying the challenging ideas and novel perspectives that are the salt and spice of a thoughtful life. Differences and polarizations have been described, but none of the articles has been construed as a polemical piece. The contributors have endeavored, however, to indicate in the conclusion of their articles the problematic nature of some notions or assumptions that are at the core of the theoretical concepts and methods considered. More generally, they have pointed to still unexplored directions of research or thought so as to reflect closely the dynamic nature of today's critical semiotics and cultural theory, and to engage the reader's reflection and creativity. Each article is followed by a carefully chosen bibliography.

Using this encyclopedia in a constructive way is made easy through the cross-references that are listed at the end of each article. For instance, the article ALTHUSSER refers to DISCOURSE ANALYSIS, FOUCAULT, MARX, MATERIALIST SEMIOTICS, and ROSSI-LANDI. Any of these new points of entry further expands the network of relevant topics. Turning from ALTHUSSER to DISCOURSE ANALYSIS, one is then led further to BAKHTIN, BOURDIEU, CONVERSATION, CULTURAL CHANGE, DIALOGISM, DIALOGUE, HABERMAS, and KRISTEVA. Note that this system of cross-references is not circular: no two articles in the volume refer only to each other. Thus, this knowledge base is alive with an infinity of potential paths that the reader can explore, discovering at each trip a new horizon. In addition, there is a fine-grained analytical index through which the reader can not only check whether a particular topic is the subject of an article, but also identify all the articles in which an author, a work, or a concept are treated in some detail.

This one-volume *Encyclopedia of Semiotics* appears in a rich environment of reference works and handbooks, published in English or English translations, which it will complement in many useful ways. The three-volume *Encyclopedic Dictionary of Semiotics* (1986) remains an important knowledge resource that the present volume does not duplicate, notably with respect to the rich philosophical, psychological, and logical traditions that led to modern semiotics. Winfried Noeth's *Handbook of Semiotics* (1990), translated with revisions from the original German edition (1985), is a single author's encyclopedic work effectively organized in chapters, somewhat in the form of an advanced textbook. Finally, the monumental *Semiotik/Semiotics: Ein Handbuch zu den zeichentheoretischen Grundlagen von Natur und Kultur/A Handbook of the Sign-Theoretic Foundations of Nature and Culture,* whose first volume appeared in 1997, will provide researchers with a hefty and systematically structured mass of semiotic discussions and references, approximately equally divided between German and English. Other semiotic publications of an encyclopedic nature, but in a more specialized sense, include *Semiotics and Language: An Analytical Dictionary* (1982), a work translated from the French, which expounds the key concepts of Greimassian semiotics, also known as the Paris School; *Selected Concepts in Semiotics and Aesthetics: Material for a Glossary* (1978), which appeared in the McGill University series Studies in Communication; and *Semiotica Indica: Encyclopaedic Dictionary of Body-Language in Indian Art and Culture* (1994), a two-volume illustrated work in English comprising more than five thousand entries listed in Sanskrit alphabetical order (with a notional index in English), whose scope extends beyond body-language to other forms of nonverbal communication and their symbolism in the Indian tradition.

Obviously, the scope of this new *Encyclopedia of Semiotics*—which extends beyond the spectrum of topics covered by previously published works of the same kind—could not have been achieved without the input of an editorial board representing a wide range of disciplines. I would like to acknowledge in particular the editorial advice provided by Professors Göran Sonesson, Paul Thibault, and Terry Threadgold at various stages of the completion of this work. My thanks also go to Gary Kuris, who, as vice-president of Garland Publishing, initiated this project in the early 1990s and provided stimulating encouragement at the beginning of a lengthy process; Professor Edward A. Walker for his editorial assistance in the earlier phase of this project; and, last but not least, Andrea Kovacs, who with unfailing patience entered in our database the numerous successive versions of the articles as they were edited, restructured, completed, condensed, or expanded in a constant dialogue with their authors. Her perceptive feedback greatly contributed to the overall reader-friendliness of the text. I wish to conclude by stating that since the project was taken over by Oxford University Press, it has been a sheer pleasure to work with Mark Mones and Jeffrey Edelstein, development editor and managing editor, respectively, of Oxford's Scholarly and Professional Reference Department, to bring this book to publication.

This work is dedicated to Thomas A. Sebeok, Distinguished Professor Emeritus of Linguistics and Semiotics at Indiana University, whose crucial role in the conceptual and social construction of modern semiotics on a global scale is widely recognized, and from whom, over some twenty years of collaboration, I have learned whatever I know of the arduous art of scholarly editing.

BIBLIOGRAPHY

Bellert, I., and P. Ohlin. *Selected Concepts in Semiotics and Aesthetics: Material for a Glossary.* Studies in Communication. Montreal: McGill University, 1978.
Bouissac, P. "The Golden Legend of Semiotics." *Semiotica* 17.4 (1976): 371-384.
Bouissac, P. "Praxis and Semiosis: the 'Golden Legend' Revisited." *Semiotica* 79.3-4 (1990): 289-306.
Greimas, A. J., and J. Courtés. *Semiotics and Language: An Analytical Dictionary.* Translated by L. Crist, D. Patte, et al. Bloomington: Indiana University Press, 1982.
Noeth, W. *Handbook of Semiotics.* Bloomington: Indiana University Press, 1990.

Posner, R., K. Robering, and T. A. Sebeok, eds. *Semiotik/Semiotics: Ein Handbuch zu den zeichentheoretis-chen Grundlagen von Natur und Kultur/A Handbook on the Sign-Theoretic Foundations of Nature and Culture*, vol. 1. Berlin: Walter de Gruyter, 1997.

Sebeok, T. A., ed. *Encyclopedic Dictionary of Semiotics*, 3 vols. Berlin: Mouton de Gruyter, 1986.

Shukla, H. L., *Semiotica Indica: Encyclopedic Dictionary of Body-Language in Indian Art and Culture*, 2 vols. New Delhi: Aryan Books International, 1994.

—PAUL BOUISSAC

January 1998

ENCYCLOPEDIA OF SEMIOTICS

A

ABACUS. A mechanical device for making arithmetic calculations, the abacus is a precursor to and a very primitive form of a computer in that it supports simple calculations such as counting. It was developed in ancient times and has been used in many countries all over the world.

The word *abacus* is a Latin derivation from the Greek *abax,* which designates a flat surface, specifically a table on which reckoning was performed by manipulating pebbles or other small objects according to certain rules. There is archaeological evidence that the abacus method of reckoning goes back to the earliest known civilizations. This artifact can be seen as the first evidence of human semiotic conceptualization since it is based on easily manipulable objects that can stand for any countable items and whose value depends on their relative position at a given time in a structured space. The rules of manipulation of these entities are designed to produce as an output information that would not be available otherwise or that would be available only through the lengthy and painstaking process of manipulating the actual items. The abacus method of reckoning also allows one to perform operations on virtual quantities irrespective of whether or not these quantities correspond to real objects. The word *calculus* comes from the Latin word for pebble and refers to the use of pebbles in the earliest forms of abacus reckoning.

Versions of the abacus small enough to be held in one hand have been found in Roman archaeological sites. It is in such form, on various scale, that the abacus was used until the advent of modern calculators. This kind of abacus consists of a frame set with rods of wire on which balls or beads can be moved. Each wire represents a place value (e.g., in the decimal system 1, 10, 100, 1000 . . .). The number of beads on one wire represents the number in the respective place value (e.g., five beads in the 10 place value represent 50). By moving the beads from one end to another, any number can be represented within a certain range.

The abacus can be used as a device for adding up numbers by moving around beads representing the numbers. This can be compared to the process of adding up two or more numbers by hand. First one adds the lowest place value. Then the higher place values follow (taking into account the carryover). The resulting configuration of beads on the abacus represents the sum of these numbers. There exist different rules and forms for representing numbers and for adding them up.

[*See also* Algorithm; Artificial Intelligence; Computer; *and* Turing.]

BIBLIOGRAPHY

Pullan, J. M. *The History of the Abacus.* London: Hutchinson, 1969.

—MARKUS PESCHL

ABDUCTIVE REASONING is the process of adopting an explanatory hypothesis, which according to Charles Sanders Peirce (1839–1914) is the first stage of any scientific inquiry and interpretive strategy. As a process of finding premises, it is the basis of the reconstruction of causes and intentions, as well as the invention of theories. Motivated by the observation of a surprising fact or an anomaly that frustrates an expectation, abductive reasoning is a strategy for solving problems and discovering relevant premises.

Since, for Peirce, the "mind is a sign developing according to the laws of inference," semiosis, the infinite process of interpretation of signs, is structured as an argumentation. Thinking and reasoning are based on abductive, deductive, and inductive inferences, aiming at establishing beliefs, habits, rules, and codes.

In his early article "Deduction, Induction, and Hypothesis" (1878), Peirce describes the three modes of inference as different syllogistic forms. In his "Lectures on Pragmatism" (1903), abduction, deduction, and induction are conceived of as interacting aspects with different epistemological functions. Deduction determines the necessary consequences, relying on logical coherence between the premises and the conclusion. Induction is aiming at empirical coherence between the premises and experience, in order to derive a provable generalization. Yet induction only classifies the data, while abductive reasoning furnishes the reasoner with a problematic theory explaining the causal relation among the facts. From the abductive suggestion, which synthesizes a multitude of predicates, "deduction can draw a prediction which can be tested by induction."

Abductive reasoning is "inference to the best explanation." It has the logical form of an inverse *modus ponens* (rule of inference) and is reasoning "backward" from consequent to antecedent. Therefore, Peirce calls it also "retroductive reasoning." From a logical point of view, reasoning backward is not a valid form of inference. It is conjectural or presumptive thinking, aiming at matching pragmatic standards of plausibility, guided by the reasoner's "guessing instinct." However, Peirce claims that abduction is logical inference because it can be represented in "a perfect definite logical form": "The surprising fact, C, is observed; but if A were true, C would be a matter of course; hence, there is reason to suspect that A is true."

With this concept of abductive reasoning as a "logic of discovery," Peirce tries to reformulate the Kantian question of how synthetic reasoning is possible at all. The notion of abductive inference becomes a fundamental issue for the evolution of knowledge. In his "Lectures on Pragmatism," Peirce states that the question of pragmatism "is nothing else than the question of the logic of abduction." Since it is the "only kind of reasoning which supplies new ideas, the only kind which is, in this sense, synthetic," it must be by abductive reasoning that we have the capacity "to learn anything or to understand phenomena at all." Even perceptual judgments are to be regarded as "extreme cases" of abductive inferences. As an "act of insight" that "comes to us like a flash," abduction is also associated with creative and aesthetic experiences such as contemplation, daydreaming, and play of thought, which Peirce calls "musement."

The question of the status of abductive reasoning as a major aspect of the "logic of discovery" is a controversial issue in the philosophy of science and epistemology. Norwood R. Hanson (1965) differentiates between two aspects in the rational process of hypothesis selection: first, reasons for accepting a hypothesis, and second, reasons for entertaining a hypothesis in the first place. While the former highlights the problem of logical coherence, the latter stresses pragmatic relevance.

In Karl Popper's notion of the "logic of science," growth of knowledge is due to a procedure by "trial and error." On the one hand, the ability to solve problems depends on "the creative ability to produce new guesses, and more new guesses" (Popper, 1979). On the other hand, the task of a logic of science is to engage a critical discussion of the methods and the logical criteria of hypothesis falsification and elimination. The Peircean account of abductive inference denies the possibility of making a sharp distinction between the "context of discovery" and the "context of justification."

Peirce describes the evolution of knowledge by analogy with the Darwinian model of evolution. The "selection" of hypotheses is performed by a partly inborn, partly learned "guessing instinct" that has developed as a part of the universe and has evolved under the influence of its laws. Therefore, Peirce states that abduction is "nothing but guessing." In order to make "fair guesses," abductive inference links the reasoner's "guessing instinct" with the rational "principle of economy," which is the "leading consideration" in abduction. The "economy of research" aims at maximal plausibility for the hypothesis and the maximal efficiency of the process of hypothesis formation and hypothesis testing. Therefore, "the simpler hypothesis in the sense of the more facile and natural, the one that instinct suggests, that must be preferred."

Besides its importance to epistemology, the model of abductive inference had an impact on linguistics, hermeneutics, and artificial intelligence. Noam Chomsky used the notion of guessing instinct and abductive inference to explain language acquisition as a process of limiting the class of admissible hypotheses that are submitted to "corrective action" (Chomsky, 1968).

Massimo Bonfantini and Giampaolo Proni suggested interpreting the abductive guessing instinct not only as a "natural insight" but also as an insight in our cultural background (Bonfantini and Proni, 1983). As Umberto Eco points out, the abductive "logic of interpretation" could also become a model for hermeneutic processes (Eco, 1990).

More recently, the concept of abduction as "reasoning to the best explanation" has been introduced and discussed in the field of artificial intelligence (van der Lubbe, 1993). Expert systems aim at simulating the process of reasoning and emulating the human faculty to deal with uncertain information in a very efficient way. The question, however, is how abductive inference as a pragmatic strategy of reasoning can be implemented in expert systems and whether artificial intelligence as a computational automatism can make creative guesses.

[*See also* Artificial Intelligence; Peirce; *and* Semiosis.]

BIBLIOGRAPHY

Bonfantini, M., and G. Proni. "To Guess or Not to Guess." In *The Sign of the Three: Dupin, Holmes, Peirce,* edited by U. Eco and T. A. Sebeok, pp. 119–134. Bloomington: Indiana University Press, 1983.

Chomsky, N. *Language and Mind.* New York: Harcourt, Brace and World, 1968.

Eco, U. *The Limits of Interpretation.* Bloomington: Indiana University Press, 1990.

Hanson, N. "Notes Toward a Logic of Discovery," In *Perspectives on Peirce: Critical Essays on Charles Sanders Peirce,* edited by R. J. Bernstein, pp. 43–65. New Haven: Yale University Press, 1965.

Lubbe, J. van der. "Human-like Reasoning under Uncertainty in Expert Systems." In *Signs, Search, and Communication: Semiotic Aspects of Artificial Intelligence,* edited by R. J. Jorna, B. van Heusden, and R. Posner, pp. 113–133. Berlin and New York: Mouton de Gruyter, 1993.

Peirce, C. S. "The Logic of Abduction." In *C. S. Peirce, Essays in the Philosophy of Science,* edited by V. Tomas, pp. 235–255. New York: Liberal Arts Press, 1957.

Peirce, C. S. *Collected Papers.* Vols. 1–6, edited by C. Hartshorne and P. Weiss; vols. 7–8, edited by A. W. Burks. Cambridge, Mass.: Harvard University Press, 1931–1935, 1958. Discussions of abductive reasoning can be found in the following sections: 1.74, 2.777, 3.516, 5.145, 5.171, 5.188, 5.196, 5.600, 6.458, 6.469, 6.477, 7.46, 7.219.

Popper, K. *Objective Knowledge: An Evolutionary Approach.* Oxford: Oxford University Press, 1979.

Thagard, P. *Computational Philosophy of Science.* Cambridge, Mass.: MIT Press, 1988.

—UWE WIRTH

ABÉLARD, PIERRE (1079–1142), French theologian and philosopher. Born and schooled in Brittany, Abélard studied in Paris under the philosophers of nominalism and realism of the beginning of the twelfth century. He soon rebelled against his masters and began to teach his personal theory of conceptualism.

Abélard's reflections on the nature of language focused on the relationship between words and things. A word first refers to the idea of a thing, and we know the thing through this idea. For Abélard, language is invented; it is a human institution. His theory of signification is based upon the correspondence between ideas and things and on the capacity of words to generate ideas.

Abélard distinguishes between senses, imagination, and intellect. From the world of senses and things, we proceed to the world of the imagination, which transcends the world of normal space and time and enables us to reflect upon and constitute incorporeal, pure forms: the ideas or the concepts of things. These ideas are based on and derived from the things, but in the process of reflection and intellection they acquire independent statuses. Socrates as Socrates is a specific, individual thing. But Socrates as a man corresponds to the idea of man—the being of man—which is not a thing. The word *man,* according to Abélard, is the result of a certain mental activity rather than an adequate translation of the nature of the thing. Thus, language is not a natural given but is derived from human reflection. Through language, we do not deal directly with the empirical world. To signify is to generate intellections, and these intellections play a mediating role between the mind and the world; things can exist only by themselves, separately, independently. The idea of being a man is perceived and reflected upon in several different men, but it has no substance. It designates a universal noun. The universal is not a thing.

Abélard's originality in his time was that he was neither an Aristotelian nominalist nor a Platonistic realist. His process of intellection has its point of departure in the world of the senses and constitutes a conceptual domain in which it is possible to keep the two poles of words (signs) and things (objects) in a certain relation through the mediation of intellection.

The words of language are signs whose signification or correspondence with things depends upon how the things are understood, perceived, and reflected upon in both their specificity and their universality. The Abélardian process of intellection consists of first abstracting a given characteristic or feature of a thing; for instance, perceiving wood as soft, then observing the same softness in cotton, stone, drink, voice, and so on until the intellect constructs the idea of softness independent of all empirical softnesses found in specific things. From the world of the senses, we rise to the conceptual world, which enables us to comprehend our universe, which is both visible and invisible, for softness is separated from the things only intellectually. In the empirical world, this separation is not possible. These analogous conceptual forms, these pure forms, enable us, however, to comprehend the truth of the physical forms. This understanding of our sign system as constructed images or abstracted forms is generally considered a unique contribution by Abélard.

The Abélardian sign has a certain psychological import. Moreover, these intellections follow the doctrine of multiplicity: the mode of signification depends upon the manner in which the objects are conceived. And Abélard insists that there is an essential difference between the mode of conceptualization and the mode of existence. Abélard compares his conceptual signs or mental images with the previsions of the artist. Just as a sensorial experience cannot be confused with the object experienced, intellection is also not to be confused with the form of the object that it conceives. It is entirely a mental activity, and this intellectually constituted form is a fictive and imaginary reality that the mind constructs when and how it wants.

The vision of an artist takes a definitive form, but however perfect a given statue, for instance, might be, it does not correspond exactly to the pure form of the conceptual construct. Hence, multiple or endless forms can be created without exhausting the intellection of the mental image. The pure, incorporeal, invisible conceptual form allows ceaseless creativity in innumerable empirical forms. Abélardian signs that generate intellection thus not only take into account forms that already exist but also those that might exist one day. The relationship between the physical image and the mental image is dialectical; it is situated at the crossroads of epistemology and creativity.

In his *Dialectica* (112.2) Abélard distinguishes six modes of signification: imposition (the word *man* is imposed by convention on the mortal, rational animal); determination (nouns—e.g., *reason, man*—determine certain qualities in a substance through contextual disambiguation); generation (words generate intellection); exclusion (what designates a definite noun is in some sense designated by a corresponding indefinite noun, as *nonman* helps define *man*); designation (following the characteristics of the subject or the coexistence of acts); logical consecution (The statement "A is the father of B," implies a logical reciprocity, "B is the son of A"). The sixth mode is one of Abélard's most important contributions to the theory of semiotics. It concerns primarily his analysis of the interrelationship of the Holy Trinity, specifically of Father and Son, or God and Jesus. The problematics of this thesis concern the concept of hierarchy or equality in this very complex relationship. Abélard argued that this relationship is due to logical consecution. Father and son derive their being from each other. A being before the birth of its son cannot rightly be called father. It is the birth of the son that bestows on him the status of fatherhood. There is no father without son or son without father. This relationship is reciprocal, mutually dependent, and simultaneous. Hence, the question of hierarchy does not arise. While this proposition of logical consecution solved the riddle of the relationship between God and Jesus Christ, the ecclesiastical authorities did not feel comfortable with this theory of signification, for it abolished the concept of hierarchy not only in the divine context but also in all other social, cultural, and religious contexts. For example, a man and a woman become husband and wife reciprocally and simultaneously. They derive their husbandhood and wifehood from each other. Then they have a child, and it is the birth of the child that bestows on them the appellations of *father* and *mother*. Conceptually, the father and the child or the mother and the child give birth to each other in logical consecution. If this argument is extended to all domains of social, political, and religious relations, it abolishes all hierarchical parameters, and no order established on hierarchical relations can accept such a logic. Hence, Abélard was excommunicated, and his books were burned by the ecclesiastical authority in Rome in 1140.

Abélard extended his arguments to the study of the sacred texts. He showed that not only had different Fathers of the Church contradicted each other on specific theological issues but at times the same theologian made contradictory statements in different contexts. While the ecclesiastical authorities were upset at this heretical presentation, Abélard demonstrated that a specific proposition does not correspond to the reality of the object; it refers to the reality of the composition of the words. This correspondence is with the state of the object, the way in which the object is understood. In other words, both the author and the reader are in a certain dialectical relationship with the text. Both are engaged in generating corresponding intellection. The creative and the analytical processes are two sides of the same coin.

With respect to the existence of genres and species, Abélard claimed that words signify the things that really exist, like the signification of singular nouns. In this sense they exist, but in another sense they constitute a "pure and naked intellection." The next question is whether genres and species are corporeal or incorporeal. That is, Are they bodies or not? Are they sensible or not? Are they separated—discrete—or not? Abélard replies that the universal nouns are corporeal with reference to the nature of things and incorporeal with reference to their manner of signification, for they signify things separated but do not do so separately.

For Abélard, a word has two aspects. As *vox* (sound), it is a phonetic, physical entity. As *sermo* (sense), it is a signified, a conceptual construct. Its intellection depends upon how it is conceived by the one who enunciates it and how it is perceived by the one who listens to it. Communication thus takes place between two thinking beings, and the field of signification is constituted in the dialectics of the two corresponding intellections. *Voces* (sounds) differ from one language to another; hence, they are arbitrary. The *sermones* (senses), however, are due to individual impositions and individual intellection; hence, language is a human institution.

The conceptualism of Abélard thus deals with four planes (words, intellections, ideas, things) at the same time. Words generate intellections that create ideas of things. Epistemology and creativity are integrated within the same conceptual construct.

[*See also* Medieval Semiotics; *and* Realism and Nominalism.]

BIBLIOGRAPHY

Gill, H. S. *Mental Images and Pure Forms: The Semiotics of Abelardian Discourse.* Delhi: Bahri, 1991.
Jolivet, J. *Arts du langage et théologie chez Abélard.* Paris: Vrin, 1969.
Luscombe, D. E. *The School of Peter Abelard: The Influence of Abelard's Thought in the Early Scholastic Period.* London: Cambridge University Press, 1969.
Minio-Palnello, L. *Twelfth-Century Logic: Texts and Studies.* Rome: Edizioni di Storia et Letteratura, 1956–1958.
Tweedale, M. *Abailard on Universals.* Amsterdam: North Holland, 1976.

—Harjett Singh Gill

ACTANTIAL MODEL. *Actant* is a term that was introduced into narratology and semiotics in 1966 by Algirdas Julien Greimas as a synonym for Vladimir Propp's *sphere of action* governed by a dramatis persona in the Russian folktale (1928) and for Etienne Souriau's *function* subsumed by the "character in situation" in drama (1950). It was borrowed from the work of the syntactician Lucien Tesnière (1959), where it refers to a linguistic notion corresponding to an abstract, semantic category similar to Charles Fillmore's concept of deep-structure case or role (1968).

The actant is any of the six constant or invariant roles maintained by characters in the narrative deep structure; it is opposed to the actors or variable roles that the characters assume in the unfolding of the story on the surface level. Each actant is claimed to be the opposite of another such that three pairs are obtained: (1) Subject versus Object, (2) Sender versus Receiver, and (3) Helper versus Opponent. The set of six interrelated actants forms the actantial model and provides one possible principle of textual coherence and one principle of the organization of the semantic universe into smaller microuniverses: textual summaries, smaller narratives, scenes, or situations. Since we can foreground or bring into perspective a very small number of roles in any such scene, the actantial set is sufficient to account for the organization of a microuniverse. In fact, the semantic microuniverse can become or be defined as a meaningful whole only insofar as it can manifest itself as an actantial structure.

The three pairs of actants also form an elementary narrative configuration, which Greimas represents spatially. The actants are fixed along vertical and horizontal axes in a functional network of syntactic and semantic relations:

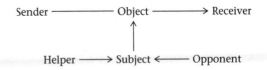

The positional value of the Object is doubly defined by the convergence of the actantial axes: both as an "object of desire" sought by the Subject and as an "object of communication" situated between the Sender and Receiver. In addition to these four primary actants, we also have two secondary actants, the Helper and Opponent, who play auxiliary and adversary roles in the action of the subject by facilitating or blocking the realization of the Subject's desire.

The actantial model has three sources: Propp, Souriau, and Greimas's extrapolation and refinement of Tesnière's case grammar, which in France was known as an area of structural syntax. Greimas, however, gives his hypothesis on linguistic actants primacy by sequence and next seeks confirmation in the textual units of Propp and Souriau, to which he refers generically as "actants of the Russian folktale" and "actants in the theater." His choice of the term *actant* to refer to both sentential and textual categories indicates his wish to find a constellation of sentential roles and match it with the constellation of textual roles and, second, for the sentence constellation to form the nucleus and the theoretical grounding for the textual constellation. His retention of the terms *subject* and *object,* even though redefined semantically to mean things wholly other than grammatical units, also attests to the same dual aim. Greimas intends to make the semantic structure of the sentence imprint itself on the larger text and discourse. The rationale behind the primacy given to the sentence rests on the supposition that the number of roles in the sentence cannot be greater than the number of roles in a text or microuniverse: "Since 'natural' discourse cannot increase the number of actants nor widen the syntactical grasp of meaning beyond the sentence, it must be the same within every microuniverse" (1966; English trans., 1983).

It is important to remember that the extrapolation Greimas talks about and practices is a top-down one, from the text down to the sentence, that holds the inventories of Propp and Souriau as models while seeking and extrapolating a mirror image in the sentence. Moreover, the linguistic or sentential set of actants is the smallest of the three sets, consisting of only two actantial categories in the form of binary oppositions, (1) subject versus object and (2) sender versus receiver. Thus, out of the three sources used to generate the actantial model, the linguistic constellation of actants carries the least evidentiary weight

and does not support the myth surrounding the model that maintains it was derived from sentence structure. Greimas himself recognizes that his refinement of Tesnière's linguistic actants "fails" in the mirror match he attempts between the sentential and textual constellations of roles (1966). But with the similarities he has already established, he presents the actantial model in the end as an inference from Propp's and Souriau's inventories and as a construction that "takes the syntactical structure of natural languages [i.e., the sentence] into account" (1966). The wording here, if not elsewhere, is very cautious with regards to the actual contribution of sentence linguistics to the actantial model.

Propp's *Morphology of the Folktale* (1928) is the pioneering work that established the norms of structural narratology and text semiotics in the search for isolating the minimal units of narrative and specifying the ways and principles in which these units combine. Propp introduced the basic distinction between constant and variable elements of content and applied it to a collection of one hundred Russian folktales, obtaining striking results for the plotline as well as the constellation of basic roles that he called spheres of action. Functions, as the minimal units of action, serve as the stable, constant elements, whereas the characters vary. All tales are of one type and manifest an identical sequence of thirty-one functions. Grouping these functions together yields a nuclear constellation of a limited and finite number of roles for the folktale, aptly described as spheres of action, since the roles are condensations of action. Seven basic spheres of action are present in the tale and are, once again, constant and invariant, whereas the characters performing them are variable. These are, in the order given by Propp: (1) the villain; (2) the donor; (3) the helper; (4) a princess (a sought-for person) and her father; (5) the dispatcher; (6) the hero; and (7) the false hero.

While the linguistic actants carried the least weight in evidence for the invention of the actantial model, Propp's spheres of action provided the most rigorous and compelling evidence, and the third source, Souriau's dramatic functions, operated more or less as a collateral backup. Souriau's constellation of theatrical roles has not been as influential as Propp's constellation, partly because it is not based on any analysis of plays and hence remains mere speculation. In the pursuit of the universality of an actantial model, Souriau's constellation was necessarily useful since it extended the possible application of actants to another genre, that of drama. It was useful also in the sense that it corroborated, even if loosely and subjectively, Propp's results, which were achieved with a passion for scientific precision. On the other hand, Souriau's vivid discussions of the actant are not to be underestimated for their clarity, their insight, and their evocative power.

By comparing and reworking the three actantial inventories, Greimas aims to go beyond the notion of a simple list by searching for the structure (the relations among actants) and by interpreting the meaning of the activity attributed to actants. It is not the individual actants nor a list of them that matter but the semantic structure that interrelates them. Whatever difficulties were encountered in this task stemmed from the concurrent drive to improve upon the logic and rigor of Propp's methods and to exceed him in universality, transcending every genre and every humanistic discipline.

In order to see the operational value of the model for the analysis of texts and the order in which it is applied, we shall begin with the following equivalences set up between the actants and the spheres of action in the Russian folktale.

Subject	hero
Object	a princess (a sought-for person)
Sender	dispatcher and father of sought-for person
Receiver	hero
Opponent	villain and false hero
Helper	donor and helper

The syntagmatic order of the actants, based on Propp's sequence of functions and Greimas's analysis of it elsewhere, may be reconstructed as follows. Starting with a situation of villainy or lack, the hero (Subject) is approached by the dispatcher (the initial Sender) with a request or command. Misfortune or lack is made known to the Subject (for example, the abduction of a princess) and he or she is allowed to go or is dispatched. Thus, the Subject sets out on a quest which is to find the goal or Object, which becomes the Object of desire in the final position of the tale. The donor and helper enable the Subject to acquire the means, know-how, and power to confront the Opponent (or anti-Subject) and come out victorious. The tale reaches its peak in this event in which the initial misfortune or lack is liquidated. The hero has succeeded in finding the Object of his or her

quest. The next dramatic spring of the tale is a demand of recognition due to the Subject. The final and judicial Sender (say, the father of the princess) judges, sanctions, and rewards the Subject's deeds, which are acknowledged socially or made known. The Subject is, in this case, married to the princess and ascends the throne. The object of desire is here the same as the object of communication, and the exchange between the Subject and the final Sender is that of a gift and countergift. The father returns the daughter to the Subject and gives her to him in marriage. The Subject is the ultimate Receiver.

Unlike the full example of actantial analysis, which takes the syntagmatic order of the text into account, Greimas's examples are intentionally made very simple so that they read like lists with no explanation (1966). The lists, however, are no longer lists of confusedly parallel fates but networks of relations that start with the primary axis of desire, the relation between the Subject and Object. The actantial model may be applied to many other types of text besides the folktale: novels, philosophies, law, ideologies, advertising, business, all semantic microuniverses. Thus, for a philosopher of the classical age whose Object is the desire to know, the actants of his drama of knowledge are distributed in the following manner:

Subject	philosopher
Object	world
Sender	God
Receiver	humanity
Opponent	matter
Helper	spirit

The most generalized interpretation of the actantial structure emphasizes the extent to which meaning is akin to purposive action and involves a person's ongoing transaction with the outside world. The two major actantial axes, Subject-Object and Sender-Object-Receiver, are viewed (1) on the individual level, as the relation of a person with the object of his or her desire and the embedding of that object within the structures of interhuman communication, or (2) on the social level, as the relation of a person to work that produces object-values and puts them into circulation within the framework of a structure of exchange. The originality of this basic, universal, plotlike constellation lies in the way it construes the social context as the exchange and circulation of object-values.

[See also Actants; Greimas; Narratology; and Russian Formalism.]

BIBLIOGRAPHY

Budniakiewicz, T. *Fundamentals of Story Logic: Introduction to Greimassian Semiotics.* Amsterdam and Philadelphia: John Benjamins, 1992.

Fillmore, C. J. "The Case for Case." In *Universals in Linguistic Theory,* edited by E. Bach and R. Harms, pp. 1–88. New York: Holt, Rinehart, and Winston, 1968.

Greimas, A. J. "Reflections on Actantial Models." In *Structural Semantics* (1966), chapter 10. Translated by D. McDowell, R. Schleifer, and A. Velie. Lincoln: University of Nebraska Press, 1983.

Greimas, A. J. *On Meaning: Selected Writings in Semiotic Theory.* Translated by P. Perron and F. Collins. Minneapolis: University of Minnesota Press, 1987.

Hénault, A. *Narratologie, sémiotique générale.* Paris: Presses Universitaires de France, 1983.

Hendricks, W. O. "Prolegomena to a Semiolinguistic Theory of Character." *Poetica* 7 (1977): 1–49.

Nef, F. "Case Grammar vs. Actantial Grammar." In *Text vs. Sentence,* edited by J. Petöfi, vol. 2, pp. 634–653. Hamburg: Helmut Buske Verlag, 1979.

Propp, V. *Morphology of the Folktale* (1928). Austin and London: University of Texas Press, 1968.

Souriau, E. *Les deux cent mille situations dramatiques.* Paris: Flammarion, 1950.

Tesnière, L. *Eléments de syntaxe structurale* (1959). Paris: Klincksieck, 1965.

—THERESE BUDNIAKIEWICZ

ACTANTS. Introduced as a term into semiotics by Algirdas Julien Greimas in 1966, actants are constant or invariant roles maintained by characters in the deep structure of a narrative. Greimas's actual model consists of six actants that form three pairs of relations: Subject versus Object, Sender versus Receiver, and Helper versus Opponent. Each of these pairs will be treated in turn.

Subject versus Object. Although the actantial categories of subject and object were borrowed in part from structural syntax (Tesnière, *Eléments de syntaxe structurale,* 1959), they have been redefined by Greimas within the context of his narrative theory. The linguistic notion of transitivity that connects the subject and object on the sentence level was converted on the textual level into a relation that proves to be either partially or totally outside the domain of syntax; namely, one of desire and teleology. (The actant is spelled here with the first letter capitalized when it refers to the narrative and textual actant and lowercased when it refers to the sentential-case role.)

In the model, the axis of desire ties the Subject and Object, and this desire is manifested as a quest. The relation is also the manifestation of a goal-oriented aim conceived as being broadly teleological. Identifying the Object, which in practical analysis is often hidden or obscure, consists, then, in looking for what is the aim of the Subject's quest, what the Subject wants. In the table of equivalences Greimas posits among the three inventories, he equates the Subject with Vladimir Propp's hero and the Object with Propp's sought-for person and Etienne Souriau's representative of the desired good, of the orienting value. In fact, the actantial model treats the Subject as nothing other than a substitute for hero or protagonist and the Object as a substitute for goal or objective.

Considering that Greimas often illustrates the Subject-Object relation by means of sentences such as "Peter hits Paul" that use a transitive action-process verb—the subject in the semantic role of agent, the object in the role of patient—it is difficult to see how these semantic cases could overlap with the actants in the folktale or those in the dramatic play. Yet Greimas takes the analysis of Propp's and Souriau's textual actants as empirical evidence confirming his hypothesis on sentential roles. The semantic cases of the sentential subject and object, the agent and patient, were abandoned, it seems, from the very beginning, especially the patient. The narrative Subject was later recognized as being both agent and patient, but neither of these sentential roles was considered pertinent to its characterization.

Although the semantic roles of agent and patient were abandoned, the notational nomenclature was, however, retained and used to provide cover terms for distinctive categories of a textual nature. This use of syntactic apparatus has the unintended effect of confusing and obscuring the problems at issue. As it turns out, the way the actantial model is applied, the textual actants are not like the sentential roles, but the reverse obtains: The sentential roles are claimed to be like the textual actants. More fundamentally, syntactic structure is redefined as being like the structure of simple narrative. The concealed solution proposed to resolve the unsuspected difficulties involved in linking the two types of organization—sentential-case and textual-actantial—can be characterized as an example of "truthful equivocation."

The analogy with syntactic-semantic theory is restricted solely to vocabulary divorced from the attendant conceptual machinery of the theory of sentence syntax; on close examination, the parallel appears to be no more substantial than this. Since the model was developed to account for texts or semantic microuniverses and constitutes a formalization of Propp's and Souriau's textual-narrative categories, throwing the model back onto the sentence in order to suggest the universality of the model does not invalidate the postulation or hypothesis with respect to texts. Thus, it should be clear that the verbal mismatch does not provide any counterevidence against the actantial model but does question the linguistic derivation and naming.

Sender versus Receiver. The Sender and Receiver are the more problematic actants, and they can be grasped only within the context of all of Greimas's works from 1966 to 1979; that is, by taking more than the original 1966 version of the actantial model into account and by recontextualizing explanatory comments made later. Sender and Receiver are problematic only in their derivation and in the "equivalence" postulated to exist between the sentence constellation and the text constellation. However, if we suspend the issue of theoretical and technical rigor and look at the "equivalence" of actant and role as a rhetorical device, then we can see the concepts emerge as hermeneutic notions. As was shown with Subject and Object, it seems best to view the equivalence between the structure of the narrative and that of the sentence as a mere analogy or an interesting metaphor, useful for expository purposes.

The only example of correspondences between the textual actants and the sentential roles Greimas gives in his "extrapolation" of sentence linguistics is "Eve gives an apple to Adam," where Eve, the sender, transmits the object of communication, the apple, to Adam, the receiver. One of the points emphasized at the sentence level is the coalescence—called the syncretic manifestation—of two actants into one actor or the concretization of one actant in several distinct actors. Eve is the point of departure of a double relation, one established between *Eve* and *apple* (subject versus object) and another between *Eve* and *Adam* (sender versus receiver), Eve being at the same time the subject and the sender. In Souriau's inventory, the actantial pair Sender versus Receiver is said to be clearly marked and to correspond to the Arbiter, Awarder of Good, and the virtual Beneficiary of Good.

In Propp's inventory, they are less obvious. The Sender is concretized into two distinct actors, the dispatcher and the father of the sought-for person, while the Receiver is fused completely with the hero (Subject), having no separate sphere of action. The activity of both of these Senders is interpreted as being that of one "who charges the hero with a mission," and this is their identifying semantic trait (Greimas, *Sémantique structurale*, 1966).

Based on these correspondences and the research that followed it, the general meaning of the axis of communication on which the Sender communicates an object to the Receiver receives in the actantial model three specific senses that are highlighted in different segments of the story, beginning, middle, or end: (1) the Sender sends the hero on the quest, and the object is the mission to accomplish; (2) the Sender is the Arbiter who judges whether the hero has accomplished the mission; (3) the Sender is the Awarder of Good who has the power to reward or punish the hero. Only in the last sense is the Sender a giver in the way that Eve was with the apple. So, although communication is usually associated with the verbs *to say* and *to know* and *to give* and *to have*, this is not the predominant meaning in the actantial model.

In radical contrast to the sentence, the Sender functions at a hierarchically superior position to the Subject-Receiver and is characterized by its preestablished power and syntagmatic position, which precedes that of the Subject-Receiver. Due to the asymmetry in the respective status between Sender and Receiver, which is none other than a power differential between them, the Sender and Receiver actants operate at a different level than the Subject-Object actants. They are connected intimately insofar as the Sender is the power that activates the hero to start out on the quest and provides the support for attaining the object of desire. Both the Sender and Subject are agents in a general sense, but the Sender's action embeds and controls the action of the Subject, as illustrated by the sentence "The Sender hired the Subject-hero to do (something)."

In sense (1) of the communication axis, the Sender makes or persuades the subject-hero to do something with the implicit promise that he or she will give the object of communication to the Receiver. The Subject-Receiver accepts the proposal freely. A negotiation is struck between them, or, as Greimas would say, a contract is made, such that a double exchange will take place between them: first an exchange of commitments, followed by a reciprocity of programs of execution. In the initiating phase of communication, however, the Sender is clearly a manipulative trustee of values who seeks to endorse them in programs of action. He or she exercises a cognitive and persuasive action that aims at provoking the action of the Receiver. The Sender is the instigator of the action and the promoter responsible for the action executed by the Receiver-Subject.

The Sender, or any other actant, need not appear as an anthropomorphic being or human actor. Unlike the term *character* that *actant* replaces, it applies not only to human beings but also animals, objects, or concepts. Even though the Sender, as described above, suggests an active intervention and participation, in many cases it is not a character but an abstraction in terms of the context precipitating the Subject-hero's action. The Sender's sphere of action can then be identified with the efficient or propelling factor, the cause, the influence, or the prime mover that moved the Subject to act as he or she did. It represents the locus of those values that activate and cause the Subject-hero to do what he or she wants. Thus, in Gustave Flaubert's novel *Madame Bovary* (1856), Romantic literature influences Emma Bovary to act as she does and to seek happiness in love affairs. There are, of course, other causes to Emma's behavior, such as the class structure of nineteenth-century bourgeois society, which limits her fate, and this points to the need for flexibility in applying the model.

In senses (2) and (3) of the communication axis, which are manifested in the final position of the tale, the Sender brings in its share of the exchange and the contractual contribution. The Sender is a judge of the conformity of actions with respect to an axiology of reference. He or she has to judge whether the object of the quest has been attained and whether the object-value is really in the hands of the Receiver and also must judge the Subject (the protagonist) on the basis of his or her performance and sanction him or her both cognitively (the recognition) and pragmatically (the reward).

From the syntagmatic point of view, Propp's narrative schema presents itself in its whole as a double pathway of the Sender, of which the two segments— initial and final—frame and mount the pathway of the Subject. Two figures of a Sender, the initial, manipulative Sender and the final, judicial Sender are thus joined paradigmatically into one arch-actant in the actantial model. If the model is to be applied cor-

rectly, the two reciprocal figures must be kept in mind and their connection established, since the judicial Sender sanctions the hero's performance, which was originally dispatched by the manipulative Sender.

Helper versus Opponent. The Helper and Opponent were derived by Greimas from Propp and Souriau and have no parallel in sentence structure. The Helper gives help to the hero by acting in the direction of desire or facilitating communication. Conversely, the Opponent creates obstacles by opposing either the realization of desire or the communication of the object. Greimas thus coalesces two Proppian spheres of action into a single actant, fusing the donor and helper into the actant Helper and uniting the villain and the false hero in the actant Opponent. The term *helper* comes from Propp, and the term *opponent* from Souriau.

These actants are not of the same primary nature as the others insofar as they participate in an incidental and subordinate fashion to the quest of the hero. Although they might be numerous in a story and contribute much to the intrigue, they function as auxiliary and adversary forces in the action. For that reason, Greimas sees them as circumstantial participants rather than true actants. They are compared to adjectives qualifying a noun and to adverbs modifying a verb, describing the ease of ability in carrying out the action or the level of difficulty. Hence, they can be seen as forms of internal or external power and, at the polar opposite, inner or external barricades to the use of that individualized power. Expressions such as *effortlessly* or *with the greatest of difficulty* illustrate this salient feature. In Greimas's actantial model of 1973, the Helper and Opponent have been renamed positive and negative auxiliants, respectively, and eliminated from the model.

An Opponent is a true actant and no longer an auxiliant when he or she is also a quester like the Subject and has aims that are at cross-purposes with those of the Subject. In this case, the Opponent attains the status of anti-Subject and represents the major antagonist in the story. The evolution of the Opponent into the anti-Subject took place when applied semiotics found it useful to project any actant onto the semiotic square and split it into four actantial positions (actant, antiactant, nonactant, nonanti-actant). This formulation highlights the fact that an anti-Subject is always an Opponent for the Subject but not every opponent is an anti-Subject. An opponent who is only a momentary obstacle or who incidentally runs into conflict with the Subject is an auxiliant.

The most characteristic situation of a story, as revealed in the Proppian folktale, is a polemical one: a situation of conflict containing contradictory ties between hero and villain, Subject and anti-Subject. The quest of the Subject is threatened or prevented by the other Subject. On the program of the first, the second is an Opponent or anti-Subject, as is the first on the program of the second. The two protagonists, the Subject and anti-Subject, are in opposition to each other and confront each other. Of the two actions that are thus opposed, one must succeed and the other must fail. The struggle between them will result in a situation where a victorious Subject acquires an object-value that was withheld by the anti-Subject. In this manner, the conflict and confrontation manifest the existence of two "narrative programs" and two actantial structures that are partially overlapping and fully correlated. The crossing of the two chained and superimposed programs splits the narrative into a dual narrative; their opposition to each other makes the narrative not only dual but polemical.

Given that Propp lists the villain first in his folktale inventory and that the order of the list is important, there is no doubt that he viewed the villain as the major antagonist and not as a mere auxiliary figure. Therefore, the question arises: why did Greimas first dilute the force of the Proppian villain into the auxiliant Opponent and then, ten years later, reinstate it to full actantial status by means of the anti-Subject? If the point of the actantial model was to interrelate the confused miscellany of actants, then why grant the anti-Subject another autonomous actantial structure, separate from the Subject and doubling it? These issues point to problems in the derivation of Greimas's model, its well-formedness, and its inner consistency throughout the various stages of its development. More important, the problems were not ignored, as corrective measures were taken in continuous attempts to requestion, rethink, and resolve the issues involved by shifting the ground of investigation and challenging formulations that were once considered certain and well established. All these innovations and reorganizations of the theory attest to the intellectual vitality and creative flexibility of the semiotic project, constantly open to self-renewal rather than holding fast to a seemingly definite and fixed body of knowledge.

[See also Actantial Model; Greimas; Narratology; Paris School; and Semiotic Square.]

BIBLIOGRAPHY

Greimas, A. J. "A Problem of Narrative Semiotics: Objects of Value." In *On Meaning: Selected Writings in Semiotic Theory.* Translated by P. Perron and F. Collins, pp. 106–120. Minneapolis: University of Minnesota Press, 1987.
In addition, see the works cited in the bibliography to the preceding entry.

—THERESE BUDNIAKIEWICZ

ACTING. In theater, the actor is the key element in the complex network of signs that constitutes theatrical performance. It is through the body and the person of the actor that all the contributing systems of meaning (visual, vocal, spatial, fictional) are activated; the actor is the principal medium through whom the dramatic text functions in relation to the audience. The study of acting according to semiotic principles is still relatively undeveloped, but it is already evident that semiotics can greatly assist the exploration of precisely what it is that actors do and how their performances function to construct and communicate meanings.

The Czech critic Otakar Zich (1879–1934) was the first to attempt a structural theory of the actor's signifying process and, while his 1931 book on the aesthetics of dramatic art has still not been translated into English, his ideas underpin work done by the Prague School in the 1930s and subsequently and still provide the basis for a semiotics of acting. For Zich, the actor's performance consists of three principal components: the performer's personal characteristics; an immaterial dramatic character, residing in the consciousness of the audience; and a third, intermediate term, the stage figure, an image of the character that is created by the actor, costume designer, director, and others as a kind of technical object or signifier. (See summary in Quinn, 1990.)

The semiotics of acting is concerned with relations set up between these three terms and between each of them and the spectator, who is the other vital element in the communicative event. An analytical chart involving all four terms reveals the complexity of what is occurring in theatrical performance.

Actor ——————— Stage Figure
Actor ——————— Character
Actor ——————— Spectator
Stage Figure ——— Spectator
Character ——— Spectator
Character ——————— Stage Figure

Performance genre and historical, social, and cultural factors affect relations at every level of this analytical process, and the notion of celebrity or notoriety, which is so frequently an attribute of the actor, also intervenes to problematize these relations. It is evident, for example, that the relationship between actor and character varies radically in different periods and cultures. For instance, in some traditions, the actor is seen as possessed by the character; but for Bertolt Brecht (1898–1956) the critical distance between the two is essential. The extent to which the actor draws on his or her own emotions in the construction of the character's responses is still a vexed question for some moralists. In postmodern performance, the relation between actor and stage figure is dominant, and in the work of some groups the actor/character relation is virtually excluded, but it is significant that when the spectator is brought into the equation, character tends to reassert itself, even in the most radically postmodern performance.

There are five major expressive and signifying systems utilized by the actor in the construction of stage figure and character that need to be addressed in any semiotic theory of acting. The actor is both a sign and a producer of signs, and the situation of the analyst is complicated by the need to allow for the actor's own subjectivity. The use of the terms expressive and signifying is an attempt to indicate this, and although some modes of performance foreground one at the expense of the other, both are always present and functioning to some degree.

1 and 2. *Linguistic* and *paralinguistic.* In the theater, the linguistic system necessarily includes the paralinguistic variables, as the verbal is always vocalized, and paralinguistic features might replace or override the linguistic message. In some forms of theater, such as mime, the linguistic component is absent; in others, like *kabuki,* it is the responsibility of specialized performers; and in still others, the linguistic or paralinguistic material is so dominant that the actor's body is almost obliterated as an expressive medium.

3. *Facial.* The importance of the actor's face and its expressive powers is a constant throughout theater history, though the emphasis varies in importance and the expressivity of the face can be extended or modified through makeup, lighting, or the use of masks. Theater architecture is a factor in this (in many eighteenth- and nineteenth-century theaters, the actor's faces could be seen clearly by only a small fraction of the audience), and the use of neutral masks in some forms of mime is a means of transferring spectator attention from the face to the body as a whole. Recent studies (Fitzpatrick and Batten, 1991) indicate that the actor's face is overwhelmingly the primary site of audience attention in the contemporary theater.

4. *Kinesic.* The expressive qualities of the human body, transformed or made more explicit through costume or its absence, are another constant, and here it might be necessary to introduce categories such as *gestural* and *corporeal* in order to define more accurately the ways in which the actor has refined his or her expressive powers in response to social and cultural factors and to acknowledge the extent to which the body is fragmented and reconstructed in performance. In some genres, the emphasis has been focused on the upper body, arms, and hands; at other times, big arm movements have been judged melodramatic and the emphasis has been concentrated on face and hands; and some performance modes demand that the whole body become expressive.

5. *Proxemic.* The actors' movements within the presentational space are a further crucial aspect of theatrical signification. These movements are used by actors and directors to construct meaningful spatial groupings, to articulate emotional or dramatic progression, and to point up significant relations between characters, between stage figures and props or elements of decor, and between character, and fictional places. This aspect of the performance is the means by which the performance space is fully activated, and it is an important element in the spectator's construction of meaning.

All these signifying systems are derived from behavior that occurs and is meaningful in the world outside the theater. Generic and historical factors affect the extent of the divergence between acting and everyday behavior and also determine the "markers" of theatricality, but all the signifying systems involved in acting can function only in relation to their functions in the world outside the theater. A good deal of work has been done by behavioral sociologists, cultural anthropologists, and others on expressive behaviors, and this work is extremely useful for the study of acting. Indeed, one of the problems confronting semioticians in this field is the extent to which the constitutive elements of acting have already been theorized in other contexts and have already developed analytical strategies and methods of notation.

The current task for a semiotics of acting is to select analytical strategies and concepts from a variety of disciplines, to devise appropriate methods of notation that will not swamp the analyst with so much data that conclusions become impossible, and to bring together what has been fragmented by this plurality of disciplinary practices within the unifying perspective of performance—that is, expressive and signifying behaviors undertaken by one group of people for another group for their mutual pleasure and potential enlightenment.

[See also Ekman; Face; Nonverbal Bodily Sign Categories; Prague School; and Theater.]

BIBLIOGRAPHY

Deak, F. "Structuralism in Theatre: The Prague School Contribution." *The Drama Review* (December 1976): 83–94.

Fisher-Lichte, E. *The Semiotics of Theater.* Translated by J. Gaines and D. L. Jones. Bloomington: Indiana University Press, 1992.

Fitzpatrick, T., and S. Batten. "Watching the Watchers Watch: Some Implications of Audience Attention Patterns." *Gestos* 12 (1991): 11–31.

McAuley, G. "The Actor's Work with Text in Rehearsal and in Performance." In *Reader Response to Literature: The Empirical Dimension,* edited by E. Nardocchio. Berlin and New York: Mouton de Gruyter, 1992.

Pavis, P. "Problems of a Semiology of Theatrical Gesture." *Poetics Today* 2. 3 (1981): 65–93.

Pavis, P. "Acting: Explication of Gesture or Vectorisation of Desire?" *Assaph* C:8 (1992): 87–112.

Quinn, M. L. "Celebrity and the Semiotics of Acting." *New Theatre Quarterly* 22 (1990): 154–161.

Schmid, H., and A. Van Kesteren, eds. *Semiotics of Drama and Theatre.* Amsterdam: John Benjamins, 1984.

Veltrusky, J. "Contribution to the Semiotics of Acting." In *Sound Sign and Meaning,* edited by L. Matekja, pp. 553–606. Michigan Slavic Contributions. Ann Arbor: University of Michigan, 1976.

—GAY MCAULEY

ADVERTISING. Since the 1960s, advertising has been one of the main areas of research in applied semiotics. The semiotics of advertising first developed as a critical instrument for the analysis of ideological meanings in advertising messages. It soon became an interdisciplinary forum at the crossroads of marketing, communication, and consumer research.

Denotation, Connotation, and Ideology. Foundations in semiotic advertising research were first laid by Roland Barthes in *Elements of Semiology* and "Rhetoric of the Image" (1967). This semiological approach is characterized by the application of principles and methods of structuralist linguistics—with concepts such as system, structure, pertinence, distinctiveness, segmentation, and combination—to the visual, verbal, and symbolic messages in advertising. Barthes's main tool of investigation was what he took to be Louis Hjelmslev's semantic dichotomy of denotation versus connotation. Since denotation is the literal or core meaning of a sign and connotation refers to secondary meanings associated with it, the theory of connotation appeared to be a most appropriate tool for the discovery of "hidden" layers of meaning in the advertising message. For Barthes, an illustrated advertisement conveys a denotational meaning in the form of a noncoded iconic message. In particular, he sees the photographic image of the product as a denotational "message without a code." At a second level of interpretation, we find connotational meanings in the form of a coded iconic or symbolic message based on our associated cultural knowledge. In advertising and in the mass media in general, the signifiers of connotative signs amalgamate into systems of connotations that form the rhetoric of advertising.

The idea of an ideologically "innocent" primary layer in the denotational message was, however, abandoned in later semiotic research. In *S/Z* (1970), Barthes himself calls the assumption of denotative primacy an illusion and argues that denotation, instead of being primary, is no more than the final result in a series of connotations associated with a message. It ensues that not even an "informative" pictorial representation of a commercial product in an advertisement can be a purely denotational message. The product, being part of the system of commodities, is already a sign coded in several connotational ways before it appears in a specific advertisement. Utilitarian, commercial, and sociocultural meanings are among the typical connotations associated with the message of the product.

The Coded Message. The semiotic theory of codes has been the basis of several studies of advertising. Since codes are the systems of knowledge underlying all cultural communication processes, the theory of codes has been considered as another key to deciphering the hidden messages of advertisements. Barthes first distinguished between an uncoded message, the photographic image of the "real" objects, and two coded messages: the verbal message, depending on the code of language, and the coded iconic or symbolic visual message. The problem inherent in this distinction is the same as the one in the denotation-connotation dichotomy discussed above.

Umberto Eco, in his *Struttura assente* (1968), speaks of advertising codes with double registers, one verbal and one visual, and distinguishes five levels of visual codification: (1) the iconic level, similar to Barthes's uncoded iconic message; (2) the iconographic level, based on historical, cultural traditions and genre conventions; (3) the tropological level, with the visual equivalents of rhetorical figures; (4) the topic level, with the premises and topoi of argumentation; and (5) the enthymematic level, with the actual structure of the visual argumentation—that is, an incomplete syllogism that is implied by the juxtaposition of images. In these various fields of coding, research in rhetorical figures in the verbal and visual advertising messages has been particularly intensive.

Text-Semiotic Studies. Text-semiotic studies of advertising have been carried out in the tradition of structuralism, structural semantics, and semiolinguistics. An investigation of semantic deep structures that aims at the discovery of semantic universals in advertising is Varda Langholz-Leymore's *Hidden Myth* (1975). Her text-semiotic approach follows Claude Lévi-Strauss's model of the structural analysis of myths and A. J. Greimas's structural semantics. According to this study, advertising is a mediator between the concrete (the product) and the abstract (the signs). The semantic characteristics of the advertisement appear as a binary structure in which an opposition between the positive properties of the advertised product and the negative properties of competing products are explicitly or implicitly contrasted. The two products and their positive/negative properties form a twofold sign of which the former are the signifiers and the latter are the signifieds. Within this twofold sign, an equivalence relation holds between the two opposed products and their two qualities. The analysis of these binary oppositions leads to the conclusion that advertising, just as myth, is concerned with finding answers to universal human problems such as those of life/death, happiness/misery, war/peace, and hate/love. These universal themes are present with the same regularity in the deep structures of both advertising and myth, but because advertising works with simpler means, it appears as a degenerate form of myth.

Several studies have been conducted within the framework of Greimas's semiolinguistics, describing actantial and narrative constellations in advertising and extending the search for the semantic core of advertisements from binary oppositions to constellations in the form of the semiotic square. Thus, Jean-Marie Floch (1990) interprets the discourse of advertising in terms of a fourfold typology of values: practical valorization, concerning the use value of a product; its opposite, utopian valorization, representing basic existential values concerning identity and life; playful valorization, the negation of practical values in the form of luxury; and critical valorization, the negation of existential values, concerning such commercial aspects as cost and benefit of the product.

Indexical Semiosis. Peirce's fundamental distinction between iconic, indexical, and symbolic signs has been applied fruitfully to the study of advertising. Pictorial representations of the product and its consumers, comparisons, metaphors (Forceville, 1995), and other signs referring to their object by similarity belong to the domain of the icon in advertising. Symbols appear in the language, brand names, trademarks, and visual logos. In its most prototypical function, however, the advertiser's attempt to draw the consumer's attention toward the product implies an act of pointing, which as been seen as the sign type of an index.

Indexical semiosis also takes place in the subtler strategies of meaning attribution and image creation. These processes can be described as indexical-feature transfer. Instead of showing the positive features of the product iconically, which is often impossible, the product is represented in contiguity with valuable objects, film stars, or similar entities whose desirable attributes are well known. By means of this contiguity relation a semantic transfer occurs. The well-known features of the "valuable," "famous," or "desirable" object or personality become associated with the less well known commercial product. This feature transfer implies an indexical-sign relation: The features transferred to the product refer to it as an index. Most connotations with which products are associated in an advertising campaign are generated by this process of indexical semiosis.

Functions of the Advertising Message. An influential paradigm in the study of the pragmatic dimension of advertising has been Roman Jakobson's model of the six communicative functions. These functions can serve as the basis for a typology of advertising messages. In informative advertisements, the focus is on the referential function of the message. The expressive function predominates in messages representing an emotionally involved advertiser. Advertisements operating on the basis of the conative or appellative function focus on the potential consumer whom they want to persuade, advise, or invite to acts of consumption. When the phatic function predominates, the advertisement aims at creating or maintaining contact with the consumer. The metalinguistic function predominates in advertisements focusing on the name, sometimes the change of the name of a product. The poetic function focuses on the code that is used in a particularly creative way in communicating the message.

Despite the multiplicity of semiotic means and strategies, advertisements are messages with an invariant pragmatic and semantic core. No advertisement can be successful if it fails to convey the message of the product (referential core) and when it does not have some appeal to purchase it (conative core). These core messages belong to the consumer's general cognitive frame of the text genre. Even when the core messages of an advertisement are masked in the textual surface structure, the consumer will use his or her general text-pragmatic knowledge as a substitute. Purchase appeal and other references to the economic interests of the advertiser are especially and typically subject to a strategy of occultation. For example, instead of advising the consumer to buy the product, the advertiser will recommend *enjoying* it.

Advertising is thus a text type that is interpreted by the consumer on two levels: the level of an overt or surface message and the level of a hidden message. The hidden message in this sense is not about any subliminal meaning (as described by some advertising psychologists) but about the economic realities of selling and buying. These realities are hidden only in the surface text; they are not unknown to the consumer. Reference to the economic interests of the advertiser is avoided in the overt message because it seems to be detrimental to the effects of persuasion. Therefore, a typical conflict exists between the contents of the overt and the hidden messages in advertising.

Approaches and Perspectives. The state of the art in semiotic advertising research has been reviewed by David Mick (1988). Besides several monographs and volumes of collected papers (Henny, ed., 1986; Umiker-Sebeok, ed., 1987, Larsen et al., eds. 1991), special issues of the journals *Recherches sémiotiques/Semiotic Inquiry* 8.3 (1988) and the *International Journal of Research in Marketing* 4.3-4 (1988) have been dedicated to the subject.

Semiotics contributes to advertising research both with respect to methodology and to the object of investigation. Concerning the latter, semiotics expands the analytic horizon from the verbal message in the narrower sense to the multiplicity of codes used in persuasive communication. Concerning the former, semiotics, as the theory of signs and communication, provides the theoretical tools for the analysis of advertisements. Besides explicitly semiotic approaches, there are implicitly semiotic approaches to the subject, such as Erving Goffman's seminal study of nonverbal communication, "Gender Advertisements" (1976). In the field of marketing and consumer research, approaches relevant to semiotics are those which study the selling, purchasing, and consumption of products as a process of communication or as symbolic activity—for example, symbolic consumption research and consumer aesthetics.

[*See also* Jakobson's Model of Communication; Logo; Mass Communication; Mythologies; Myths; Rhetoric of the Image; Semiosis; Signs; *and* Trademark.]

BIBLIOGRAPHY

Bachand, D., and C. Cossette, eds. "Images du marketing/Marketing Iconics." Special issue of *Recherches sémiotiques/Semiotic Inquiry* 8.3 (1988).

Barthes, R. *Elements of Semiology.* Translated by A. Lavers and C. Smith. New York: Hill and Wang, 1967.

Barthes, R. *S/Z.* Translated by R. Miller. New York: Hill and Wang, 1975.

Barthes, R. "Rhetoric of the Image." In *Image-Music-Text,* translated by S. Heath, pp. 32–51. London: Fontana, 1977.

Eco, U. *La struttura assente.* Milan: Bompiani, 1968.

Floch, J.-M. *Sémiotique, marketing et communication.* Paris: Presses Universitaires de France, 1990.

Forceville, C. *Pictorial Metaphors in Advertising.* London: Routledge, 1995.

Goffman, E. "Gender Advertisements." *Studies in the Anthropology of Visual Communication* 3.2 (1976): 69–153.

Henny, L., ed. *The Semiotics of Advertisements.* Aachen: Rader, 1986.

8

♦ AESTHETICS

Langholz-Leymore, V. *Hidden Myth: Structure and Symbolism in Advertising.* New York: Basic Books, 1975.

Larsen, H.-H., et al., eds. *Marketing and Semiotics.* Copenhagen: Nyt Nordisk Forlag, 1991.

Magariños de Morentín, J. A. *El mensaje publicitario.* Buenos Aires: Hachette, 1984.

Mick, D. G. "Contributions to the Semiotics of Marketing and Consumer Behaviour." In *The Semiotic Web 1987,* edited by T. A. Sebeok and J. Umiker-Sebeok, pp. 535–584. Berlin: Mouton de Gruyter, 1988.

Nöth, W. "Advertising, Poetry and Art." *Kodikas/Code* 10 (1987): 53–81.

Nöth, W. "The Language of Commodities: Groundwork for a Semiotics of Consumer Goods." *International Journal of Research in Marketing* 4 (1988): 173–186.

Umiker-Sebeok, J., ed. *Marketing and Semiotics.* Berlin: Mouton de Gruyter, 1987.

Williamson, J. *Decoding Advertisement.* London: Marion Boyars, 1978.

—WINFRIED NÖTH

AESTHETICS is a branch of philosophy that concerns either the nature of beauty (whether natural or artistic) or the nature of art (whether beautiful or not). Aesthetics is sometimes understood to encompass any rigorous and philosophical contemplation of the arts; taken in this sense, aesthetics developed in the West out of the discussions of dramatic, rhetorical, and musical performance forms in Plato and Aristotle and led to a great diversity of perspectives. In this first framework, the semiotics of art is simply one among various approaches. Aesthetics is understood alternatively in a narrower sense that takes Immanuel Kant's (1724–1804) *Critique of Judgment* (1790) as its point of origin and Alexander G. Baumgarten's (1714–1762) elaboration of aesthetics as the first specialized study of it. This narrower perspective, with its distinct emphasis on beauty, is the one that creates controversy within semiotics.

As a topic in semiotics, aesthetics suggests at least three questions: (1) Are works of art always and necessarily signs? (2) If artworks and artistic performances are indeed signs, can they be characterized as a distinct class of signs on strictly semiotic criteria as opposed to sociological or psychological criteria? (3) What is the impact on our fundamental notions of semiotics if we consider art as a field within the domain of semiosis?

1. Is the artwork a sign? In the Kantian tradition, art is understood to embody an essence that does not reduce to representation but that we may identify as its beauty. This essence is always held to be a perceptible quality. The difficulties of this opinion are easy to specify: What is beautiful—indeed, what counts as art to one person or one epoch or one culture—might not be beautiful or artistic to another. No one succeeds in giving an objective account that can separate beautiful or artistic objects from those that are not. These difficulties are not sufficient, however, to vitiate the idea. The supposition of a special artistic quality is not entirely different in principle from the supposition of qualities in general.

While it might seem obvious that qualities have representational functions, the philosophical problems of understanding consciousness itself are linked directly to the impossibility of accounting for qualities entirely in terms of their representational functions. If there is something more to the experience of art than understanding all its referential meanings, however broadly we construe the latter, then it is not clear that an artwork is primarily a sign. The problem is not trivial, for it involves our whole conception of the relation of signs to experience.

2. Is the artistic sign a distinct type? The reconciliation of the Kantian tradition—taken here to refer to the orientation sketched above—with a semiotic perspective was first attempted in the Prague School of the 1930s. The ground for a synthesis was the idea of sign function that descends from the work of Karl Bühler (1879–1963) on language. In this sense, a function is the purpose fulfilled by a sign, such as providing information about the emitter of a sign or about the object to which a sign refers.

The concept of function provided a wider framework for the sign than Saussurean analysis did but was compatible with it. In this framework, the referential and structural dimensions of the sign system captured by Saussure's theory were taken as a partial description that needed to be complemented by analysis of other expressive, emotional, and psychological values transmitted by any sign. While there was no quick consensus on the exact number and distribution of sign functions, the notion of a distinct aesthetic function figures throughout this development, receiving a very elaborate exposition in Jan Mukařovský's work and later a precise structural formulation in Roman Jakobson's essay on linguistics and poetics (1960).

In this school of thought, the aesthetic function of a sign is identified with the value the sign acquires for itself or as the sign's self-reference. While these explicit definitions can be readily dismissed as opaque or tautological, it is implicit in their elaboration by Jakobson and others that the aesthetic function involves a foregrounding of internal structural arrangements within the sign. This focus is achieved on the one hand through specific structural characteristics and on the other in the positioning of the sign with respect to cultural systems of value.

The structural analysis stresses three factors: the heightened artifice of symmetries of all sorts, departures from stylistic norms, and transformation of the sign's logical character. Jakobson's statement that "the poetic function transposes the axis of selection onto the axis of combination" epitomizes this last strategy. The cultural analysis stresses the relativity of aesthetic valuation. Whereas structural analysis affirms that art as subclass of signs is intrinsically distinct, cultural analysis disagrees: The precious manuscript becomes a fish wrap or vice versa, depending only on social values. While this perspective is a commonplace today, it was not so in the 1930s when papers presented to the Prague Linguistic Circle first exploited that vantage point to validate oriental arts, folk arts, avant-garde forms, and neglected periods of the arts' histories; furthermore, the theory of the norm and its social function brings to the relativist perspective certain subtleties that still merit restudy.

3. *How does aesthetics impact semiotics?* Jakobson observed in his "Glance at the Development of Semiotics" (1980) that explicitly semiotic studies did not deal with the arts before the twentieth century. Following the work of the Prague School, semiotic theory has been reshaped by its effort to comprehend the problems of artistic semiosis, though not reshaped systematically. Do different media admit equivalent modes of structure as signifiers or vehicles? Do different media have different domains of reference? Can the concept of sign as an ontological category be abstracted from the function of reference? Jacques Derrida's approach to semiotics might be characterized as generalizing the aesthetic problem of stylistics to establish a new vista on philosophical foundations (1978).

The first two of the questions above lead to the precise differentiation of the capacities of different media for structure and reference: auditory versus visual, temporal versus atemporal, verbal versus nonverbal, and so on. These questions have a considerable history and distribution in philosophy, but it is noteworthy how concrete some of the Prague School analyses appear when compared with the idealistic essentialism of the aesthetics in the works of G. W. F. Hegel and even in the works of as late and different an aesthetic philosopher as Susanne Langer (1953).

Structuralist orientations do not come fully to grips with the differences between a structured system (such as language) and a structured object (such as a poem). The exclusive interest of structuralism in patterns of difference is a further handicap in accounting for a realm of experience in which sensation plays a diverse and positive role. Finally, the preponderant bias toward binarism in structuralism—all minimal distinctions in a message depend on two-choice situations—is prejudicial to artistic analysis. One need go no further than the common musical scales of five and seven notes to see that. Charles Sanders Peirce's "semeiotic" is suggestive but equally inadequate for coming to grips with the details of artistic transactions. Peirce seems to have understood aesthetic experience only as a matter of feeling. While his global framework is general enough to encompass the arts, he does not help us understand in any concrete way the variety of interactions of intellectual and affective processes in art, and he fails to shed light on the relations of part to whole that are so delicate and essential in art. The more recent development of a "semiotics of culture"—particularly in the work of Jurij Lotman (1975, 1990), with its deep roots in Russian formalism and Prague School semiotics and its comprehensive grasp of later ideas—is deeply informed by aesthetic data and aesthetic concerns but is still centered on verbal art. Lotman's work on cinema offers a promise, not yet realized, that the arts can teach semiotics how to build a foundation that is truly anterior to linguistics.

One traditional focus of aesthetic theory has remained entirely outside the pale for semiotic scholarship but is also neglected by other contemporary approaches to the analysis or appreciation of art: the phenomenon of beauty. The Pythagorean search for a numerical explanation, which finds its latest outlet in speculations on turbulence and fractals, seems a neighbor if not a denizen of semiotic exploration. Could some interaction of semiotic and biological perspectives reopen the question? Our understanding of the brain physiology of visual and auditory perception, however coarse it might seem now in relation to our knowledge of artistic structure, has already advanced to an extent that it invites us to recast some of that knowledge. Manfred Clynes's (1978) research on algorithmic representations of musicality and expressivity is suggestive of new openings for a neurosemiotics of art. See also the volumes edited by Ingo Rentschler et al (1988) and Gerald Cupchik and László János (1992).

[See also Arnheim; Art; Clynes; Jakobson; Moscow-Tartu School; Music; Prague School; and Russian Formalism.]

BIBLIOGRAPHY

Baumgarten, A. G. *Reflections on Poetry.* Translated with the original text in Latin, by Karl Aschenbrenner and William B. Holther. Berkeley: University of California Press, 1954.

Baumgarten, A. G. *Aesthetica* (1750). Hildesheim: G. Olms, 1961.

Bühler, K. *Sprachtheorie.* Jena: Fischer, 1934.

Clynes, M. *Sentics: The Touch of the Emotions.* Garden City, N.Y.: Anchor Press/Doubleday, 1978.

Cupchik, G., and L. János, eds. *Emerging Visions of the Aesthetic Process: Psychology, Semiology, and Philosophy.* Cambridge: Cambridge University Press, 1992.

Derrida, J. *The Truth in Painting* (1978). Translated by Geoff Bennington and Ian McLeod. Chicago: University of Chicago Press, 1987.

Jakobson, R. "Closing Statement: Linguistics and Poetics." In *Style in Language,* edited by T. A. Sebeok, pp. 350–377. New York: John Wiley and Sons, 1960.

Jakobson, R. "Glance at the Development of Semiotics." In *The Framework of Language,* edited by I. R. Titunik and L. Matejka, pp. 1–30. Michigan Studies in the Humanities. Ann Arbor: University of Michigan, 1980.

Langer, S. K. *Feeling and Form: A Theory of Art Developed from Philosophy in a New Key.* New York: Charles Scribner's Sons, 1953.

Lotman, J. *Theses on the Semiotics of Culture.* New York: Humanities Press, 1975.

Lotman, J. *Universe of the Mind: A Semiotic Theory of Culture.* Translated by A. Shukman. Bloomington: Indiana University Press, 1990.

Mukařovský, J. *On Poetic Language,* translated and edited by John Burbank and Peter Steiner. Lisse: The Peter de Ridder Press, 1976.

Rentschler, I., B. Herzberger, and D. Epstein, eds. *Beauty and the Brain: Biological Aspects of Aesthetics.* Basel: Birkhäuser Verlag, 1988.

—DAVID LIDOV

AFFORDANCE as a term was coined by James J. Gibson (1904–1979) to stand for perceptible proper-ties of an object that indicate its relevance to the observer. The object can provide aid or support or, quite the reverse, a threat. In either case, Gibson contended, its potential was evident in informative patterns of light or sound or other perceptible energies.

Affordances have an important role in Gibson's theory of perception, which defends realism (the thesis that the world can be perceived accurately and reliably). Gibson wished to reject the traditional idea that matters of beauty and value were only in the eye and mind of the beholder. He proposed that the beholder selects from the potential uses of objects in the environment and that this selection can be based on visible properties that accurately reflect the capacity of the object to serve the desired function. Similarly, life-threatening events can be detected by perceptual means, their unpleasant affordances being indicated to the observer by sensory information. While different observers might notice quite different affordances, this is not due to the affordances being merely in each observer's mind. Each affordance is objective, and attention can be paid to it or not, depending on the needs of the observer and the specifics of the situation at hand. Meanings found in the world are both subjective and objective, Gibson insisted, in the sense that they can be perceived accurately, though appropriate sensitivity and attention are necessary.

An important implication of Gibson's theory is that the perceptual information for an affordance can be represented. Accordingly, the information can be made to come from an artificial source such as a picture or model that does not actually possess the affordances being represented. One cannot find shelter in an enclosure depicted in a flat picture. Similarly, a wax apple only looks ripe and edible. It appears to offer sustenance, but it does not do so in fact. Gibson's point is that affordances exist in natural and many artificial circumstances, but their information can be artificially copied to make it appear as though objects are stronger or weaker, more or less worthwhile, or more or less beneficial than they actually are. The existence of misleading information for affordances in some cases should not mislead us into thinking that affordances and information for them are always untrustworthy. Close observation obtains more information about an object or a terrain and will generally enable the perceiver to distinguish the false from the real. For example, misinformation for affordances occurs, Gibson noted, when a transparent surface is not noticed and the observer tries to walk through a glass door, or when quicksand is perceived as firm.

Gibson's belief that the useful properties of the environment can be perceived accurately in terms of the observer's own body scale has stimulated considerable research on practical matters, such as visual judgments of pathways. Stairs with various riser heights can be walked up efficiently if the riser height fits the observer's leg length and strength: Most observers can make accurate estimates of the ease with which various riser heights can be used. Doorways can be in keeping with our stature or unduly narrow, and research indicates observers have an appreciable ability to detect at a distance whether a passageway fits their body or the vehicle they are driving.

[See also Biosemiotics; Gibson; Umwelt; and Vision.]

BIBLIOGRAPHY

Gibson, J. J. *The Senses Considered as Perceptual Systems.* Boston: Houghton Mifflin, 1966.

Gibson, J. J. *The Ecological Approach to Visual Perception.* Boston: Houghton Mifflin, 1979.

Konczak, J., H. J. Meeuwsen, and M. E. Cress. "Changing Affordances in Stair Climbing: The Perception of Maximum Climbability in Young and Older Adults." *Journal of Experimental Psychology: Human Perception and Performance* 18 (1992): 691–697.

—JOHN M. KENNEDY

ALGORITHM. In a general sense, an algorithm is an instruction (or a sequence of instructions) according to which a process has to occur. More specifically, a computer program is an instance or an implementation of an algorithm. This instruction has to be formulated in such a precise way so that it can be performed by an operator that is capable of interpreting and executing the algorithm's instructions. Examples of algorithms are the rules for adding and subtracting two or more numbers, for playing board games, for cooking according to recipes, and so on. Normally, an algorithm instructs the executive device (usually a human, a computer, or any machine that can interpret and execute instructions) step-by-step or which action to take. In general, an algorithm solves a class of problems. The selection of a specific problem is determined by the parameters that act as an input for the algorithm. Furthermore, an algorithm has to (1) be deterministic—that is, the same initial conditions and the same input have to lead always to the same result or output (otherwise it would be a stochastic algorithm); (2) terminate—that is, the execution of the algorithm has to come to a stop and a result within finite time.

In terms of computer science, an algorithm specifies step-by-step how the input data are transformed into output data in order to solve a certain problem. The following conditions have to be fulfilled for an algorithm to be successful: (1) there has to be a precise description of the problem or situation that one wants to solve and represent; (2) the algorithm has to specify the way of solving this problem in "atomic" and unambiguous steps (e.g., basic instructions of a programming language); (3) there has to exist an interpreter and execution mechanism that is capable of unambiguously interpreting and executing the algorithm's instructions. Turing machines are such mechanisms. Although it would be possible to physically build such a machine, it is not very economical. The von Neumann computer architecture is one example (which is found in most of today's PCs) of how the abstract concepts of a Turing machine can be realized physically. Any program running on such a machine is an example of an algorithm: The instructions of the program are interpreted and executed by the processor. In this process, already existing data are used for controlling the flow of instructions, and new data are created that will influence the future flow of instructions and the algorithm's output.

Consider the following example of an algorithm: The problem is to compute the factorial of a number n. The factorial $n!$ can be defined as a function: $N1 = f(n) = 1*2*3*4* \ldots *n$ (with $n > 0$). There are different ways that this problem can be described and solved: (1) description in everyday language: to compute N1 multiply the sequence of numbers 1, 2, 3, 4, $\ldots$, n with each other; (2) a more formal description written in the programming language BASIC:

```
10 INPUT N
20 RESULT = 1
30 IF N<= 1 THEN GOTO 100
40 I = 2
50 RESULT = RESULT*1
60 I = I + 1
70 IF I > N THEN GOTO 100 ELSE GOTO 50
100 PRINT RESULT
100 END;
```

(3) as a recurrent function:

$$f(0) = 1$$
$$f(x+1) = (x+1)*f(x);$$

(4) in a PASCAL-like program (the most elegant solution):

```
function factorial (n:integer):integer
factorial: = (if n = 0 then 1 else n*factorial (n − 1).
```

This example illustrates that in most cases there exists a variety of algorithms to describe and solve a given problem and that one algorithm can be instantiated in different forms (e.g., in different programming languages).

[*See also* Abacus; Artificial Intelligence; Computer; Knowledge Representation; *and* Turing.]

BIBLIOGRAPHY

Church, A. *Introduction to Mathematical Logic*. Princeton: Princeton University Press, 1956.
Harel, D. *Algorithmics: The Spirit of Computing*. Reading, Mass.: Addison Wesley, 1992.
Kozen, D. *The Design and Analysis of Algorithms*. New York: Springer-Verlag, 1992.
Wilson, S. W. "The Genetic Algorithm and Simulated Evolution." In *Artificial Life*, edited by C. Langton. Reading, Mass.: Addison Wesley, 1989.

—MARKUS PESCHL

ALLEGORY encompasses messages expressed in manners other than plain speaking. The term is derived from the Greek *allos* (other) and *agoreuein* (to speak in a public forum). It is a figure of rhetoric and semiotic praxis that in its major manifestations is peculiar (though not exclusive) to fiction and other imaginative forms and that asserts that the ultimate signification of a text is different from what the words mean literally. In the context of medieval theology, allegory was one of four possible interpretations of a text, particularly a biblical one (see figure), but outside the theological framework it denotes any level of meaning that is other than literal. Allegory thus lies on that axis of signifying modes that bifurcates direct denotation by introducing an intermediate term between sign and meaning. The two poles of this axis are simile and enigma; between the two are such devices as fable, metaphor, irony, and riddle; allegory has been categorized by some theorists as a more elaborate form of metaphor. From the nearest

pole to the farthest, the defining characteristic of the axis is that the ultimate meaning becomes increasingly unclear.

The purpose of allegory and similar modes is essentially comparative and explicative, to equate one domain of experience with another, with a view to illuminating that which the readers do not know ("My lady's eyes") by reference to something that they do ("are nothing like the sun"). The purpose of allegory, however, is not only cognitive and instructive. Because the new term introduced is habitually drawn from the realms of the aesthetic and sensory experience, the use of the device can also be pleasurable for the reader. And in direct proportion to the increasing ambiguity of the intended meaning, there is increasing delight experienced in the act of deciphering, so that in the figure of the enigma the act of unlocking the meaning might be more important than the meaning itself. Discovering allegorical meanings confers on the reader the status of an initiate, someone who possesses the perspicacity to see through the "veils," which is the metaphor once used by poets to describe the way they hid one meaning behind another. It follows that the first semiotics of allegory and similar modes of discourse relate to the degree of determination of the sign and to the emotions connected with problem solving and with admission to an elite.

The term *allegory* appeared only in late antiquity, but the concept—designated by the Greek *hyponoia*, literally the "subconscious" but by extension a "hidden meaning or sense"—had been in use from the time of the earliest exegeses of Homer in the sixth and fifth centuries BCE. Although the root meaning of *allegory* denotes the enunciating subject's intention—that is, the deliberate embedding of meanings in a text whose material structure (or message) is only an objective correlative of those meanings—the original thrust of the concept was hermeneutic. *Allegory* designated not what the text said but what the addressee wanted it to say. The aim and effect of allegorizing was to replace the ideas of the author by others more acceptable to a later generation of readers. Disliking the immoral stories told about the gods in the *Iliad*, rationalist Periclean Greeks explained them away as picturesque modes of talking about the forces of nature (Bolgar, 1954). Later generations of allegorists (Hellenistic Greeks of late antiquity, European and Byzantine Christians of the early and late Middle Ages) claimed similarly that the myths of

Homer and Ovid were euhemeristic accounts of dei-
fied humans or were astrological in intent or contained in veiled terms an account of the Christian
revelation. At different points in history, earlier allegorical readings were disputed by later readers, who
substituted their own hermeneutic for that of their
predecessors. Semiotically, then, allegory raises the
issue of what has been called the "limits of symbolism": what, in fact, are the semantic confines of any
sign or set of signs? Beyond what point can a given
reading be considered impossible?

From the point of view of hermeneutics, allegory
is a means of recuperation, a way of replacing distasteful meanings with others that are edifying and
that thus assure than an aesthetically pleasing text
(or an unavoidable one such as the Bible) can also be
seen as instructive and hence readable in the prevailing intellectual or religious context. The most famous of these allegorical readings is undoubtedly
Saint Paul's explanation of Abraham's fathering and
subsequent banishment of Ishmael. The story, told in
Genesis 16 and 21, is interpreted by Paul in *Galatians*
4.22–30 as an allegory of God's two convenants to
man, to Moses on Sinai and through Christ at
Jerusalem, since Abraham's polygamy and subsequent cruelty to his child and the child's mother
were otherwise inconsistent with first-century
Christianity.

Recuperative allegory is generally metaphorical in
nature. The literal meaning of the story, whether fictional or protohistorical, is dismissed as inoperative;
the words in which it is told are deprived of reference and become a merely "poetic" expression of
the meaning that the interpreter has discovered.
Renaissance humanists rejected the narrow recuperative readings of their medieval predecessors, favor-
ing instead a metonymical approach whereby the
allegorical reading stood alongside the literal, thereby
conserving the text as text and not merely as sign.
The notion that the text might be a metonymy of its
allegory was undoubtedly fostered by the fourfold interpretation of Scripture that was current in the later
Middle Ages and whose formulation is often attributed to Dante. In this hermeneutical system, the
allegorical was the second of four consecutive or simultaneous readings of the Old and New Testaments,
the others being the historical (or literal), the tropological (or applied), and the anagogical (or mystical).
The progression is thus from the cognitive (knowing
the facts) to the doctrinal (the allegory is the set of

principles for which the facts are interpreted to stand)
thence to the pragmatic (the moral action that the
allegory teaches) and finally to the symbolic (an extrapolation of the historical event from the particular to the general, from the accidental to the
universal, from the human to the divine). Projected
onto a semiotic square, these readings assume the following relation:

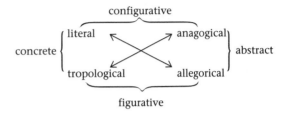

Hermeneutic allegorizing assumes the author of
the text intended it to have such other meanings as
we might discover there. And there are, indeed, texts
that display signs of such intentions; the thirteenth-
century French *Roman de la rose* and the seventeenth-century English *Pilgrim's Progress* by John
Bunyan are the best known and most literal examples. In these works, the key to the intention lies in
the names of the characters and places, which do
not correspond to readers' normal experience of
nomenclature and toponymy. In subtler texts,
names or events might still seem so obviously motivated or so lacking in likelihood that the allegory
is clearly willful. In short, intended allegory will be
marked by decreased mimesis, since the determining criterion will not be the imitation of an action
but the fidelity to an abstraction. Some theorists
have even argued that allegorical writing is incompatible with truth, on the grounds that an action
that is mimetically impossible cannot denote possibility on the level of meaning. Allegory is hence also
an act of enunciation, as its name implies, but in
this case the author's decision to mark the text in
such a way as to facilitate the passage from the apparent to the real meaning is subjective and therefore not accessible to semiotic analysis. That is, a
writer might believe that sign x will be read as signifying y, but his assumption might be unfounded
within the cultural context in which his work is received. The converse is also true, with authorially
unmotivated signs being read as allegories, whether
by individuals or by a collectivity. The semiotics of
allegory is thus a semiotics of reading, not of writing, except in a limited number of cases.

Whether enunciative or hermeneutic, the supplementary or substituted meanings of a text are labeled "hidden," "deeper," or "higher," but they are always elsewhere than in the literal meaning of the words, either behind, below, or above that meaning. Semiotically, allegory is thus also spatial and distributive. It presumes that the artifacts of the imagination possess planes or levels and that sets of signs identified on the most visible of these are really just the signifying counterparts of signifieds that are to be sought on other planes or levels and that will convey their "real" meanings. An allegorical text hence initially appears to be produced by the connotative potentiality of each of its individual terms. It follows that allegory is not semantic (i.e., determined by the positive and negative poles of all the text's lexemes), nor is it metaphorical in the Jakobsonian sense of the term (i.e., decipherable by virtue of the text's standing for the dictionary definitions of the sum of its terms). It functions, however, metonymically, in the sense that a text has allegorical meaning by virtue of the mutual interaction of its set of signifiers. The network of signs observable at the textual level is believed or intended to replicate an equivalent network existing in another domain of experience. This is not the same thing as the passage from virtual to actual described by Greimas (i.e., from abstract relations to a narrative articulation of those relations). The allegorical meaning of a text is mimetic and referential, replicating in the domain of ideas and feelings the structure of events. The movement is hence the opposite of the virtual-actual transition.

This notion of levels or planes of signifying and signification raises in turn the problem of the transfer from one to the other(s). On the basis of what evidence can a reader surmise that an artifact has a meaning beyond the literal one? By what devices can authors or artists arrange their creations so as to encourage and permit a reader to pass from the literal plane to the other intended meaning? The answers to these questions lie perhaps in the field of Peircean semiotics. A text that is mimetic in the Aristotelian sense is marked by iconicity. Any disruption of the iconicity may hence be taken as an indexical sign that another meaning is intended and that the attempt to read the original configuration as purely literal must be abandoned. Semiotically speaking, allegory is the process whereby icon evolves into symbol.

[*See also* Denotation and Connotation; Greimas; Iconicity; Indexicality; Isotopy; Jakobson; Metaphor; Metonymy; Peirce; Poetics; *and* Semiotic Square.]

BIBLIOGRAPHY

Bolgar, R. R. *The Classical Heritage and Its Beneficiaries: From the Carolingian Age to the End of the Renaissance.* London and New York: Cambridge University Press, 1954.

Dupriez, B. *A Dictionary of Literary Devices: Gradus, A–Z.* Translated and adapted by Albert W. Halsall. Toronto and Buffalo: University of Toronto Press, 1991.

Lausberg, H. *Handbuch der literarischen Rhetorik: Eine Grundlegung der Literaturwissenschaft.* 2d rev. ed. Munich: Max Hueber Verlag, 1973.

Lewis, C. S. *The Allegory of Love.* Oxford: Clarendon Press, 1936.

Lubac, H. de. *Exégèse médiévale: Les quatre sens de l'ecriture.* 2 vols. Paris: Aubier, 1959.

Madsen, D. L. *Rereading Allegory: A Narrative Approach to Genre.* New York: St. Martin's Press, 1994.

Preminger, A., and T. V. F. Brogan, eds. *The New Princeton Encyclopedia of Poetry and Poetics.* Princeton: Princeton University Press, 1993. See pages 12–15.

Weinberg, B. *A History of Literary Criticism in the Italian Renaissance.* 2 vols. Chicago: University of Chicago Press, 1991.

—JOHN MCCLELLAND

ALPHABET. Any sign system comprising symbols or letters representing individual sounds of speech is termed an alphabet. There is a distinction between script—any visual representation of spoken language—and an alphabet, which is based on a phonetic representation of each phoneme. An alphabet is therefore a specific type of script.

The earliest known script is Sumerian cuneiform (c.3500 BCE), one of a number of scripts that developed independently in areas such as Mesopotamia, India, China, Egypt, Crete, and Syria between about 3500 and 1500 BCE. The common factor behind the development of written language appears to be the growth of urban settlements and the need to record the economic and administrative exchanges involved in trade, taxation, law, and other aspects of urban society.

The early scripts are primarily pictorial or logographic, using three main types of logograms. The first type is a pictogram, where there is an iconic relationship between signifier and signified: a picture of a tree means *tree*. The second type is an ideogram where the signifier and signified are connected by conventional association: a picture of a sun might mean *sun* or, by extension, *bright* or *day*. The third type is the syllabic sign or rebus: abstract words for which there is no obvious pictogram are broken down into syllables for which pictograms can be found— for example, *kingship* could be written using pictograms of a king and a ship.

Rebus writing led to the appearance of syllabaries, symbols representing a consonant and a following sound, which were incorporated into the earliest written languages. Logograms representing monosyllabic words were used to represent syllables, as in Sumerian, where the logogram for *ti,* meaning "arrow," was used to represent the syllable *ti* wherever it occurred. So identical syllables came to be written with identical logograms, regardless of the original meaning of the logogram. The phonetic value of a symbol began to override its semantic value.

Syllabaries therefore introduced the process of phonetization, the crucial step between logographic writing and an alphabet. Each logogram acquired a phonetic value independent of the meaning of the logogram when it was used to represent a whole word. The logograms now had a dual function: as representations of specific referents and as phonetic symbols representing syllables of speech.

The implications of this change were considerable. Syllabaries enabled written languages to become more flexible, to be written down more quickly, and to be memorized more easily. Unlike a language based mainly on logograms, which has to have a huge number of characters, a language using symbols to represent syllables can increase its vocabulary without increasing the number of symbols.

The alphabet was derived from syllabaries, and there is some disagreement as to whether the earliest form of the alphabet, developed by western Semitic peoples during the second millennium BCE, was in fact an alphabet or a syllabary. The Semitic alphabet consisted of consonants only, with the vowel sounds implied by the consonantal symbols. Unlike a syllabary, the symbols of the Semitic alphabet were only phonetic symbols; the semantic function, as signs representing a whole word, had disappeared. This introduced the basic distinction between logographic scripts and the alphabet.

When the Greeks took over the Phoenician version of the Semitic alphabet by the eighth century BCE, they added five vocalic symbols, since vowel sounds were phonetically more significant in Greek than in the Semitic languages. This is generally regarded as the decisive moment when an alphabet came into being as a complete phonetic system, transferable from one language to another. The English word *alphabet* is formed from the first two letters of the Greek alphabet, *alpha* and *beta,* names derived from the Phoenician and Semitic alphabets.

The Greek alphabet was inherited by the Romans, via the Etruscans, in the mid-seventh century BCE and was gradually adapted to meet the phonetic requirements of Latin. By the third century BCE, the Roman alphabet consisted of twenty-one letters and was almost perfectly phonemic. The remaining five letters (*j, u, w, y, z*) were added over the ensuing centuries in response to borrowing from Greek and phonological differences between Latin and its descendant languages. The modern English alphabet was not fixed until the era of large-scale publishing began in the early nineteenth century.

The two most important stages in the development of the alphabet, then, were (1) phonetization, or the use of symbols to represent phonemes rather than material referents; and (2) the addition of vowel symbols to the consonantal alphabet.

Since there are only twenty-six letters in the alphabet but many more individual phonemes in spoken English, the alphabet is not a direct phonetic transcription of speech. Many letters, individually or in combination, represent more than one phoneme, and many modern standard spellings are either the result of convention rather than phonetic accuracy or preserved earlier pronunciations (e.g., *night,* of which all consonants were once pronounced).

Although the alphabet is used as the medium of written language, the letters themselves can convey meaning apart from their phonetic function in words. Like other forms of script, the letters work as nonverbal signs in contexts such as punctuation, orthography, mathematics, and visual art.

In printed texts, upper- and lowercase letters and italics conventionally suggest tones of speech. The letters *a, b, c,* and so on indicate the order of items, while various forms of upper- and lowercase letters convey the meaning of mathematical and chemical formulas. In manuscripts, the shape and form of the letters provide information to paleographers, even if they cannot understand what the words mean. On blocks of stone, carved letters signify a memorial inscription, whether or not the viewer can understand what has been inscribed. The alphabet itself can be foregrounded in written texts, as in alphabet books, calligraphy, or illuminated manuscripts.

The alphabet is therefore a signifying code whose letters can convey meaning quite separately from the words formed by those letters. It is a system of signs whose meanings are constructed by context and convention.

[See also Code; Number Representation; and Phoneme.]

BIBLIOGRAPHY

Coulmas, F. *The Writing Systems of the World.* Oxford: Basil Blackwell, 1989.

Diringer, D. *The Alphabet: A Key to the History of Mankind.* 2 vols. London: Hutchinson, 1968.

Gelb, I. J. *A Study of Writing.* Chicago: University of Chicago Press, 1952.

Goody, J. *The Interface between the Written and the Oral.* Cambridge: Cambridge University Press, 1987.

Healey, J. F. *The Early Alphabet.* Berkeley: University of California Press, 1990.

Ong, W. J. *Orality and Literacy.* London: Methuen, 1982.

—HELEN FULTON

ALTHUSSER, LOUIS (1918–1990), French philosopher who was a Communist Party theorist during the 1960s and 1970s. Like Ferruccio Rossi-Landi (1928–1985) in Italy, Althusser was part of the Eurocommunist attempt to deal with the crisis of Marxism. Both sought to shift Marxism out of a deterministic materialism and into a concern with language and subjectivity.

Althusser sought to initiate a rereading of Marx in *For Marx* (1965) and *Reading Capital* (with Etienne Balibar, 1979). Althusser proposed that one could periodize Marx: that there were two Marxisms, separated by an "epistemological break." The young Marx was a humanist concerned with alienation and an essentially Hegelian-derived concern with the unfolding of the human spirit, albeit in material terms. According to Althusser, the young Marx operated in a prestructuralist methodological framework. He proposed that after the "break" Marxism had shifted into being a science and that dialectical materialism was the science of structures. Althusser claimed that this shift into structuralism represented an elimination of the notions of human subject and human agency. The humanist idea of an active human subject was,

according to Althusser, replaced by the notion of humans as the bearers of structures.

For Althusser, Marx was concerned primarily with developing a science for the analysis of material structures. Althusser accepted the inherent validity of Marx's materialist structuralism but recognized that Marxism's growing methodological crisis was an outcome of materialist determinism. Althusser's attempt to solve this methodological crisis was ingenious: he attempted to expand the Marxist method such that the structuralist method devised by Marx for a materialist application could be isolated and reused upon nonmaterialist, subjective phenomena. Structural Marxism, a "school" that effectively modified the Marxist understanding of ideology, was born. It was a Marxism with concerns that overlapped to a considerable extent the concern of semiotics, because Althusser ultimately sought to locate ideology within structures of meaning. It was a Marxism that effectively sought to explain domination and exploitation in terms strongly similar to the semiotic notion of the "prison house of language" (Jameson, 1972).

For Althusser, ideology functions to secure domination by one class in society. However, ideology works at the level of subjective structures or language, through a process Althusser called interpellation. This is a far cry from Marx's materialist explanation of ideology. Althusser saw individuals as positioned by language in "imaginary relationships" with their real conditions of existence. Reality was hidden within a process of semiosis. Insofar as language interpellates people, it succeeds in constituting them as individuals who accept their roles within existing relations of production. For Althusser, it was the role of the ideological state apparatus (ISA)—such as schools, media, church, family, political parties, and cultural/sporting bodies—to produce these structures of meaning.

Althusser's reformulation of the concept of ideology created an unanticipated problem for Marxist theory. Within his formulation, communist societies will presumably also, of necessity, have ISAs. So communist societies will also have an ideology that serves to interpellate citizens. In the original Marxist formulation, ideology would disappear once exploitative economic structures were done away with. No such possibility exists in the Althusserian formulation, because once human beings are merely the bearers of structures, there can be no escape from such structures. In Althusser's antihumanism there is no escape from ISAs. Hence, there is no end to ideology because there is no escape from the endless chain of ISA-produced semiosis.

For Althusser, the task of Marxism—as the science of structure—was to expose this ideology. If for Marx the task was to reveal the "reality" of materialist exploitation and domination, for Althusser it was to reveal the "reality" of ISA or "subjective" domination. Althusser's aim was to produce a "scientific" method that would enable people to identify and understand the structures of meaning (ideology) that imprisoned them. For Althusser, science is a form of production—a practice distinct from other practices, including ideological practices. By extension, Marxism as science is, for Althusser, not an ideology. However, in this antihumanist formulation, Marxism has no solution. Althusserian Marxism might expose ideology, but it cannot end it. Ultimately Althusser's structuralist turn served merely to exacerbate Marxism's crisis by introducing methodological incoherence (especially in *Reading Capital*). For Marxism, the Althusserian moment was a wrong turn that was to prove highly destructive, and by the mid-1970s its time had passed.

[*See also* Discourse Analysis; Foucault; Marx; Materialist Semiotics; *and* Rossi-Landi.]

BIBLIOGRAPHY

Althusser, L. *Lenin, Philosophy and Other Essays*. London: Verso, 1971.

Althusser, L. *For Marx* (1965). London: Verso, 1979.

Althusser, L., and E. Balibar. *Reading Capital*. London: Verso, 1979.

Calinicos, A. *Althusser's Marxism*. London: Pluto Press, 1976.

Hirst, P. "Althusser and the Theory of Ideology." In *On Law and Ideology*, pp. 40–74. London: Macmillan, 1979.

Jameson, F. *The Prison-House of Language: A Critical Account of Structuralism*. Princeton: Princeton University Press, 1972.

—Eric Louw

ANATOMY OF CRITICISM

(1957) was Northrop Frye's (1921–1990) attempt to provide a coherent system for the study of poetic structure. The four essays that comprise the book (originally titled "Structural Poetics") set out in detail the framework of interpenetrating contexts in which literature might be understood.

The first two essays deal, in a very broad way, with aspects of literary history. Frye believed that any understanding of literary history had to be based on something more than social history, and this belief in the autonomous authority of verbal culture led him to seek a context for the discussion of literary history proper to the nature of literature itself. In his view, literary history in the West has evolved according to a modal sequence of five stages, which are defined by the decline in the hero's power and in freedom of action. In the age of myth, the god's power and his freedom of action are unlimited; in the age of romance, the hero is superior in degree to other human beings and to his environment; in epic and tragedy, the hero is superior in degree to other human beings but not to his environment; in the age of realism or the low mimetic, the hero becomes a character and is "one of us," superior neither to others nor to his environment; and, finally, in the ironic age, the character, in power and freedom of action, is inferior both to ourselves and to his environment.

In his second essay, Frye applies a similar five-part scheme to the symbolic modes of literary works, which move through literal, descriptive, formal, archetypal, and apocalyptic stages. The pull in literature away from myth and toward more realistic and ironic forms of fiction or language involves what Frye calls displacement: the adaptation of myth to increasingly realistic rules of narrative plausibility. However, Frye does not see this movement as ultimately a demythologizing one. The final context of all fictional modes, even the most realistic, is the shaping power of myth.

Thus, Frye's third essay opens with a consideration of the metaphoric structure of imagery and then proceeds to a discussion of myth as the basis of narrative structure. Frye classifies imagery according to a cosmological scheme, with the vegetable, animal, and mineral worlds providing apocalyptic images of the garden, the sheepfold, and the city, respectively. In their extension, these organizing metaphors—primarily biblical and Christian in their provenance—account for the global structure of imagery in Western literature. The discussion of imagery is the basis of what is perhaps the most influential section of the *Anatomy of Criticism*, the elaboration of the four *mythoi* or story types: comedy, romance, tragedy, and irony.

An important influence in Frye's quest for a unifying narrative principle was the group of classicists writing in the early decades of this century, including Gilbert Murray, Francis Cornford, and Jane Harrison, whose analysis of Greek rituals based on the myth of the dying god revealed the structure of tragedy and comedy. For Frye, this myth has four aspects—*agon, pathos, sparagmos,* and *anagnorisis*—that correspond to the four *mythoi* or archetypal plots that are the radicals of all possible stories. The *agon,* or conflict, corresponds to romance, which is the sequence of adventures undertaken by the hero. *Pathos,* or suffering and death, corresponds to tragedy and the mutual deaths of hero and monster. *Sparagmos,* or "tearing to pieces," corresponds to the disappearance of the hero in irony and satire. And *anagnorisis,* or discovery, corresponds to comedy and the recognition of the resurrected hero, who rises in triumph with a new society forming around him. In Frye's view, the logic of the structures, conventions, and patterns of imagery that we find in literary works is derived from the complete form of this myth, which, found in a variety of forms in Western mythologies, always manifests the same general shape: the disappearance and return of a divine being. The various story forms that we find in literature, then, are episodes, adding up to one complete narrative structure (which we can only infer and reconstruct hypothetically). One of Frye's favorite illustrations of the importance of a story's shape is the Gospels narrative, in which the tragedy of Christ's crucifixion must be seen as only an episode in a larger cosmic structure that is resolved in a final rebirth and recognition scene.

In the elaborate and detailed analysis of rhetoric and genre in the fourth and last essay, Frye isolates four root genres in literature, which he ascribes to different verbal rhythms: epos, or the rhythm of recurrence; prose, or the rhythm of continuity; drama, or the rhythm of decorum; lyric, or the rhythm of association. For a more specific analysis, he turns to the previous discussion of *mythoi* and charts the specific forms of epic, prose, drama, and lyric as they appear at different points on the "story wheel."

Anatomy of Criticism placed Frye's theoretical views at the center of a growing interest in critical and literary theory in the 1950s and 1960s. Structuralist critics such as Tzvetan Todorov and Gerard Genette were to recognize the obvious relevance of his ideas to intellectual developments in continental Europe.

[*See also* Frye; Narratology; *and* Poetics.]

BIBLIOGRAPHY

Darham, R. *Northrop Frye and Critical Method.* University Park, Pa.: Pennsylvania State University Press, 1978.
Frye, N. *Anatomy of Criticism: Four Essays.* Princeton: Princeton University Press, 1957.
Hamilton, A. C. *Northrop Frye: Anatomy of His Criticism.* Toronto: University of Toronto Press, 1990.
—JOSEPH ADAMSON

ANICONIC VISUAL SIGNS. There are signs that are conveyed visually without being iconic as well as iconic signs that are nonvisual, since the sign function known as iconicity simply means that the thing serving as expression shares at least some properties with the thing corresponding to the content. The concept of aniconicity was first introduced by T. A. Sebeok (1979) as the "complementary obverse" of iconicity. It is formed by prefixing the ancient Greek *a/an* ("without") to the term to be negated, as in *amoral* or *anaesthesia.*

Among aniconic visual signs, some are strongly codified, such as punctuation signs, syllabic and phonetic writing systems, ideograms, Morse, Braille, and the modern signs for numbers. Other examples of true aniconic signs are some of the signs for chemical substances and compounds used by the alchemists, some hobo signs, and many traffic signs (Aicher and Krampen, 1977; Liungman, 1991).

Decorative patterns and so-called abstract painting represent instances of aniconic visual signs that are less codified. Flags often function as aniconic visual signs. For example, the maritime flag code consists of different combinations of a round ball, a triangular pennant, and a square flag. It is also true of national flags, even though their colors may be iconic with respect to some aspects of the environment characterizing the country they represent (Weitman, 1973). Aniconic visual signs are usually purely conventional signs. In the same way, garments may become aniconic visual signs of different ethnic groups, of different degrees of adherence to fashion, and even of political convictions (Sonesson, 1993).

Even when movement is added, some visual configurations are aniconic. This is normally not the case in the theater, where persons represent persons and objects objects. Even in the "poor theater," which uses minimal means of representation, objects normally have some abstract properties in common with what they represent (e.g., a chair representing a person has a dominant vertical extension).

Mime is, of course, largely iconic, although, as Ferdinand de Saussure observed, it has a "rudiment of convention." Gestures of the kind accompanying natural conversation are often iconic, even when they are not pictorial, representing abstract spaces, positions, and movements. The latter probably applies to a lesser degree to more formalized gesture systems, such as that used by the North American Indians and the different varieties of sign language employed by the deaf, in particular, of course, those corresponding to the alphabet. The coded gestures used by policemen to regulate traffic are mostly non-iconic, as are very codified systems of dancing, such as the classical dance of India. On the other hand, to the extent that they do carry meaning, other visually prominent kinds of behavior, such as classical ballet, sports, and acrobatics, seem to be predominantly iconic.

It therefore appears that there are rather few aniconic signs conveyed by the visual mode. Although visuality and iconicity do not mutually imply each other, they certainly seem to be intrinsically related. Perhaps the predominance of visual perception in the human world makes iconicity a more convenient way of creating visual signs. Indeed, the study of aniconic visual signs often leads to discovering the limits or relativeness to their aniconicity, thus making the investigation of this kind of signs particularly challenging.

In the course of history, iconic signs tend to become more or less aniconic. This process, known as "deiconization" or "conventionalisation" (Wallis, 1975), has been observed often in the case of Chinese and Egyptian glyphs and other forms of "picture writing," as well as in many gesture systems. What is usually meant, however, is that signs that start out as detailed pictures, reproducing very closely the visual properties of the content object, are transformed into more distant renderings of a few important details of the content, sometimes ending up as mere mnemonic devices. This is better termed schematization (Krampen, 1988). The opposite process, pleromatization, is observed in children's drawings and to some extent in petroglyphs. In the latter case, however, a modification from a nonpictorial to a pictorial kind of iconicity might be more common (Sonesson, 1994).

[See also Arbitrariness, Principle of; Icon; Iconicity; Ideograms; Number Representation; Pictorial Semiotics; and Postage Stamps.]

BIBLIOGRAPHY

Aicher, O., and M. Krampen. *Zeichensysteme der visuellen Kommunikation.* Stuttgart: Verlagsanstalt Alexander Koch, 1977.

Krampen, M. *Geschichte der Strassenverkehrzeichen.* Tübingen: Narr, 1988.

Liungman, C. G. *Dictionary of Symbols.* Santa Barbara: ABC-Clio, 1991. Revised as *Thought Signs: The Semiotics of Symbols—Western Ideograms* (Amsterdam and Tokyo: IOS Press, 1995).

Mallery, G. *Sign Language among North American Indians Compared to That among Other Peoples and Deaf-Mutes* (1881). The Hague and Paris: Mouton, 1972.

Sebeok, T. A. "Iconicity." In *The Sign and Its Masters,* pp. 107–127. Austin and London: University of Texas Press, 1979.

Sonesson, G. "The Multiple Bodies of Man: Project for a Semiotics of the Body." *Degrés* 21. 74 (1993): d1–42.

Sonesson, G. "Prolegomena to the Semiotic Analysis of Prehistoric Visual Displays." In *Semiotica* 100.3–4 (1994): 267–331.

Studnick, F. "Traffic Signs." In *Semiotica* 2.2 (1970): 151–172.

Wallis, M. *Arts and Signs.* Lisse and Bloomington: Peter de Ridder Press and Indiana University Press, 1975.

Weitman, S. R. "National Flags." In *Semiotica* 8.4 (1973): 328–367.

—CARL G. LIUNGMAN and
GÖRAN SONESSON

ANIMAL. Allegorical depictions of animals in artworks, fables, and myths have produced a global archive of folkloric wisdom, ranging in subjects from moral imperatives to the nature of sexuality and desire. Philosophical discourse has employed the figure of the animal as a means of determining the specificity of human existence, while religious practices and narratives have frequently located the animal form—through sacrificial rites and the belief in the transmigration of souls or reincarnation, for example—as a means of exposing mankind to the metaphysical realm. The medical, biological, and psychological sciences, among other branches, have relied on animal experimentation to understand, by analogy, the nature of humankind's physical and psychological place in the world.

Aristotle (384–322 BCE) is credited with having produced the first systematic study of biology, exceeding the confines of a mere taxonomy and pushing philosophical as well as scientific inquiry into a new era. In his work, Aristotle began to articulate a theory that saw every aspect of the phenomenal world as a kind of collective sign that points with every manifestation toward the structure of being. Among the enormous range of subjects that Aristotle covered, animals occupy a prominent position, often providing an occasion for Aristotle to reflect on ethics, society, language, and the very constitution of human existence. In *Politics,* for example, Aristotle argues that while animals are endowed with the ability to communicate such feelings as pleasure and pain, the greater power of speech is reserved for human beings. In turn, the communication of thoughts, Aristotle insists, forms the basis of an ethical existence. By denying animals the capacity for true speech, Aristotle's dialectical reasoning put into play an axiom that remained with the philosophical tradition until the nineteenth century: namely, that human identity is established in contradistinction to the animal by the divide of language.

Alongside the philosophical path charted by Aristotle, another classical tradition adamantly included animals within the domain of language. Most notably, natural historians Plutarch (c.50–120 CE) and Pliny the Elder (23–79 CE) and later Michel de Montaigne (1533–1592) adhered to a school of thought that George Boas (1891–1980), a founder of the discipline of the history of ideas, calls "theriophily"—the belief that animals are capable of rational thought and behavior. According to Boas, the theriophilist holds that not only are animals reasonable, they are actually more rational, more ethical, and happier than human beings. Maintained as a critique of the Western dogmatic rationalism that posited the superiority of human beings, theriophilists from the cynic Diogenes of Sinope (c. 412–323 BCE) to the poet Walt Whitman (1819–1892) situated the animal within the larger semiotic framework of instinctual, sensual, and natural signification.

The notion that human beings represent the highest form of life on earth survived from antiquity and was reinforced by such allegorical narratives as the biblical account of Adam lording over and naming the beasts in *Genesis* 1.28 and 2.19. The modern era's most vociferous call for the segregation of human and animal existence appears in *Discours de la méthode* (1637) by the philosopher and mathematician René Descartes (1596–1650). In Descartes's view, con-

sciousness and the language it engenders establish an existential threshold between human beings and animals. Animals are likened to automata, capable of mimick-ing speech but unable to engage in the dynamic of an authentic language that sustains consciousness. In banishing the animal to the underworld of consciousness—to the unconscious—Descartes not only propelled the momentum of modernity and its humanist mythologies but inadvertently laid the groundwork for future excavations of the unconscious. Criticizing Descartes's suppression of the animal from the realm of consciousness, semiotician Charles Sanders Peirce (1839–1914) wrote: "Descartes was of the opinion that animals were unconscious automata. He might as well have thought that all men but himself were unconscious." The ramifications of Descartes's segregation of the human and animal worlds extend beyond the immediate confines of philosophy, implicating the discourses of cognition and communication in a variety of scientific and social disciplines. The impact of Descartes's essential duality still persists in contemporary discourse.

In the twentieth century, for example, Martin Heidegger (1889–1976) extended the Cartesian line of thought to the limits of metaphysics. Trying to think the essence of being, or *Dasein,* Heidegger articulated the concept of "world," which is the capacity to know things "as such." Heidegger associated world-forming skills with language, which he called "the house of being." Because for Heidegger human beings alone are capable of using language, only mankind experiences the plenitude of the world, while animals, plants, and things stand apart, at varying degrees of distance from the world. Interestingly enough, Heidegger wavers over the specific question of an animal world, arguing at times that animals are "worldless" (*weltlos*) and at others that they are merely "poor or lacking in world" (*weltarm*). Nonetheless, without language, an animal's relation to things in the world is, in Heidegger's words, like words that have been crossed out. The animal world is thus represented as a world under erasure. That is, animals experience things but not "as such": they are unable, Heidegger reasons, to signify the things with which they interact. Heidegger's approach is in contrast with the notion of *Umwelt* that had been introduced by his contemporary, biologist Jakob von Uexküll (1864–1944), in order to establish scientifically the world-forming capacity of animals.

The persistence of Cartesian duality and metaphysics during the modern era notwithstanding, the nineteenth century saw dramatic shifts in the semiotics of the animal. The theory of evolution put forth by Charles Darwin (1809–1882), for one, struck at the stability of the Cartesian taxonomy. The notion of a continual flux, a continuum of organic life, in many ways eroded the edifice of Descartes's ontology. Darwin's invocation of instinct and genetic adaptation opened the possibility of another site of communication. The idea of a perpetual becoming that informs Darwin's thought questions the origin and integrity of biological species and influenced a generation of theorists who incorporated the Darwinian dynamic into their thought, including Sigmund Freud (1856–1939), Henri Bergson (1859–1941), and John Dewey (1859–1952). And while evolution did not resolve the Cartesian dilemma, it added a new dimension to the debate concerning animal ontology and facilitated a dialogue between philosophy and biology, metaphysics and the natural sciences.

Concerning the function of language, Darwin himself sought to restore language to the organic order of things, speculating in *The Descent of Man* (1871) that languages, like species, are prone to the laws of evolution—to the struggle for survival and the possibility of extinction. Darwin's "naturalization" of language reintegrated the function of communication into the exigency of being, suggesting the finite vitality of language in determining the contours of existence. In fact, Darwin's claim returned the conception of language, or *logos,* to its classical origins in philosophy. Apropos of Darwin's linguistics, Jacques Derrida remarked upon the essential connection between the sign of language (logos), and that of life (*zoon*) in Plato's *Sophist* where, Derrida explains, "*Logos* is a *zoon*"; "*Logos,* a living, animate creature, is thus also an organism that has been engendered.... In order to be 'proper', a written discourse *ought* to submit to the laws of life just as a living discourse does." Derrida argues that the origins of logos are embedded in zoon and that one cannot entirely eliminate the trace of life from the materiality of discourse (Derrida, 1981, p. 79).

Following the advent of the Darwinian revolution, the movement to reintegrate the animal into the semiotics of language began to gain momentum. At the end of the nineteenth century, Freudian psychoanalysis and its unconscious topographies signaled a critical point of contact between the human and animal worlds. Acknowledging his debt to Darwin, Freud incorporated evolutionary thought in his attempts to articulate the properties of the unconscious: "Biological research," Freud wrote, "robbed man of his peculiar privilege of having been specially created, and relegated him to a descent from the animal world, implying an ineradicable animal nature in him" (Freud, 1920, p. 296).

For Freud, the radical alterity of the unconscious exposes mankind to its ineradicable animal nature, dissolving the sovereignty of the human subject. The powers of hypnosis, which Freud and Josef Breuer (1842–1925) emphasized in their 1895 *Studies on Hysteria,* can be traced to their origins in experiments by Jesuit scholar Athanasius Kircher (1601–1680) and physician Anton Franz Mesmer (1734–1815) in "animal magnetism." Seizing upon the apparently uncanny ability of animals to communicate without language, both Kircher and Mesmer had attempted to unravel and harness these powers. The quasi-scientific and parapsychic experiments of the two eventually entered the fold of psychoanalytic practice in the form of hypnosis. Freud and other early psychoanalysts believed that hypnosis facilitated a communion with the unconscious, with the ineradicable trace of the animal other. What emerges from the unconscious is, according to Freud, of an animal nature: "Perversions," he wrote, "regularly lead to zoophilia and have an animal character" (Freud, 1985, p. 223).

The Freudian intervention, the effects of which are still being absorbed and contested, led to a revolution in the conception of language. No longer a mere representation of consciousness, language in the wake of psychoanalysis came to be seen as a form of consciousness that carries with it an intrinsic unconscious dimension. Rather than establishing the divide between human and animal being, language now introduced the ineradicable trace of the animal into the human world. This, in turn, profoundly affected the practice of literature, evoking the suppressed relation between logos and zoon. Speaking to the irrepressible animality that explodes in the corpus of Franz Kafka (1883–1924), for example, Walter Benjamin wrote: "Because the most forgotten alien land is one's own body, one can understand why Kafka called the cough that erupted from within him 'animal.' It was the most advanced outpost of the great herd" (Benjamin, 1969, p. 142).

Elsewhere in the space of modernity, the eruption of the animal as a sign began to be felt. In the field of graphic representation, physiologist Etienne-Jules Marey (1830–1904) and photographer Eadweard James Muybridge (1830–1904) developed similar series of photographic studies of animal movement in the late nineteenth century. In entirely separate institutional and aesthetic contexts, Marey and Muybridge captured on film the previously imperceptible dynamic of animal locomotion, Marey using a revolving photographic plate and Muybridge a line of still cameras. Besides participating in the evolution of photographic animation or cinema, Marey's and Muybridge's depictions of animal movement introduced dramatic new views of the animal body, profoundly influencing developments in twentieth-century art and industry.

Postmodern and poststructuralist theories have opened new venues for reassessing the semiotics of the animal. Following the work of literary modernists such as Lewis Carroll (1832–1898), Akutagawa Ryunosuke (1892–1927), and Franz Kafka, whose novels and stories feature speaking animals, contemporary theorists such as Gilles Deleuze and Félix Guattari, Jacques Derrida, Donna Haraway, and Vicki Hearne have challenged many of the tenets of classical philosophy, including the exclusion of the animal from language. A new focus on the reconfigured animal has yielded new approaches to the semiotics of ontology. Since the advent of evolution, psychoanalysis, and deconstruction, the animal sign has come to encompass a far greater range of significance than that determined by questions of language and consciousness, extending into the semiotics of ethics, feminism and gender studies, and technology. Indeed, the animal sign in contemporary theoretical discourse has facilitated a hybridization of many traditionally separate fields. In this sense, the function of the figure of the animal in modernity can be seen as truly epistemic.

[*See also* Allegory; Biosemiotics; Meme; Memetics; Sebeok; Umwelt; *and* Zoosemiotics.]

BIBLIOGRAPHY

Benjamin, W. "Franz Kafka: On the Tenth Anniversary of His Death." In *Illuminations* (1934), edited by H. Arendt and translated by H. Zohn, pp. 111–140. New York: Schocken, 1969.

Boas, G. "Theriophily." In *Dictionary of the History of Ideas*, pp. 384–389. New York: Scribners, 1973.

Deacon, T. *The Symbolic Species*. New York: W. W. Norton, 1997.

Deleuze, G. and F. Guattari. *Kafka: Toward a Minor Literature*. Translated by Dana Polan. Minneapolis: University of Minnesota Press, 1986.

Derrida, J. *Dissemination*. Translated by B. Johnson. Chicago: University of Chicago Press, 1981.

Freud, S. *A General Introduction to Psycholanalysis,* edited and translated by J. Riviere. New York: Doubleday, 1920.

Freud, S. *The Complete Letters of Sigmund Freud to Wilhelm Fliess, 1887–1904,* edited and translated by J. M. Masson. Cambridge, Mass.: Belknap Press, 1985.

Haraway, D. *Primate Visions: Gender, Race, and Nature in the World of Modern Science.* New York: Routledge, 1989.

Haraway, D. *Simians, Cyborgs, and Women: The Reinvention of Nature.* New York: Routledge, 1991.

Hearne, V. *Adam's Task: Calling Animals by Name.* New York: Alfred A. Knopf, 1987.

Lippit, A. M. "Afterthoughts on the Animal World." In *Modern Language Notes* 109 (1994): 786–830.

Salisbury, J. *The Beast Within: Animals in the Middle Ages.* New York: Routledge, 1994.

Sebeok, T. A., ed. *How Animals Communicate.* Bloomington: Indiana University Press, 1977.

Uexküll, J. von. *Theoretical Biology.* Translated by D. L. Mackinnon. New York: Harcourt Brace, 1926.

—AKIRA LIPPIT

APARTHEID. The National Party of the Republic of South Africa coined the word *apartheid* as an electoral slogan in 1948. The word means apartness or separateness in Afrikaans. From 1948 until the mid-1980s, apartheid was the official ideology of Afrikaner nationalism. During this period, it grew into an elaborate sign system and a sophisticated sociopolitical machine premised upon both a subjective belief in racial and cultural segregation and the material (economic) interests of white Afrikaners.

The ideology of apartheid had both subjective and objective underpinnings. Subjectively, apartheid was premised upon the nationalist belief that racial, linguistic, and cultural differences should be the fundamental organizing principle in society. According to the apartheid sign system, different "types" of people should be kept separate. Each "group" should have its own national territory and infrastructure (schools, government, media, and cultural bodies). Apartheid policy divided South Africa into ten black "nations" and three nonblack "nations." Apartheid institutionally entrenched each of these thirteen divisions. White Afrikaners, especially from the early 1980s onward, justified apartheid by saying that they were merely giving to other nations what they demanded for themselves—namely, cultural autonomy and *eiesoortigheid* (ownness).

A common pejorative meaning ascribed to apartheid was that of an irrational belief in racism. But apartheid was never merely a subjectivity or irrational racist belief structure. Apartheid, as ideology, was a subjective process "inhabiting" the realm of ideas: it was a racist belief and language system that was processed and reproduced in institutions including the schools, universities, courts, and media. But as a language (system of signs), apartheid was also always intertwined dialectically with an objective economic dynamic; apartheid always had a material base.

If apartheid during the 1950s and 1960s utilized a fairly overt racist sign system premised on *blanke baasskap* ("white supremacy"), this began shifting after the 1976 Soweto riots. Beginning in the early 1980s, apartheid underwent a linguistic reform and encompassed the notions of "separate group identities," "cultural difference," and "minority rights." Race-based "influx control" laws, which curtailed the movement of blacks into "white areas" were dropped in favour of deracialized laws dealing with "orderly urbanization." The resultant semantic shifts, however, produced little improvement in the lives of black people. The government could declare that "apartheid is dead," but it remained alive on the ground.

The reformed sign system of "separate development" (or "multinational development") proposed that there was no longer a horizontal separation between South African "peoples" (as opposed to "people") within the reformed system. Rather, it was claimed that South Africa was a country of "minorities" (thirteen different "peoples"). Reformed apartheid apparently represented the vertical separation of these groups. In terms of this discourse, white people no longer occupied a privileged position in a hierarchial pecking order. Instead, it was claimed that the different peoples were merely separated so that the "groups" could develop parallel to each other. This offered the supporters of apartheid a comfortable ideology that served to semantically erase the repressive nature of apartheid.

The apartheid planners undertook a great deal of semantic engineering around this "separate development" notion and then disseminated their new sign system via the media and educational infrastructure that they controlled. But the reform was more than semantic. By the mid 1980s, the National Party had

engineered into existence three nonblack "own affairs" administrations and ten black nations, each with its own territorial "homeland," government, citizenship, police, school system, codified language, radio stations, and, in some instances, even separate armies and universities. Millions of black people worked for these separate black administrations and so developed a material interest in maintaining the apartheid system.

The apartheid sign system was, in effect, "materialized" into the political and social practices of multiple minibureaucracies across South Africa. Eventually, there were fourteen ethnically based bureaucracies (often with overlapping jurisdictions). Culture and ethnic-based sign systems were codified and then naturalized within the country's educational and media machinery. Many South Africans, white and black, internalized this apartheid discourse. Hence, separate black "tribal" nationalisms even began to emerge, parallel to Afrikaner nationalism. This was especially the case between the Zulu and Tswana. (Some of the violence of the 1990s was linked to this resultant tribal nationalism.) So the sign system of reforming apartheid was ultimately tied to the material interests of a patronage system through which Afrikaner nationalism retained its hegemony by coopting both whites and blacks into a well-paid apartheid bureaucracy. By the 1980s, apartheid served the material interests of white and black state bureaucrats, as did the more substantial reforms during the 1990s.

Despite massive efforts, the National Party never succeeded in stabilizing apartheid. It proved to be economically, socially, politically, and linguistically unworkable. The way in which the meanings within the apartheid sign system had to be continually modified was but one indication of how crisis ridden the system was. From 1984 until 1990, a massive and violent revolt against the apartheid system developed. In 1989, the National Party, under President F. W. De Klerk, finally told white voters in its election manifesto that apartheid had to be dismantled because it was unworkable. In February 1990, De Klerk initiated the first real reform of apartheid that went beyond mere semantics.

[See also Althusser; Discourse Analysis; *and* Materialist Semiotics.]

BIBLIOGRAPHY

Adam, H., and H. Giliomee. *The Rise and Crisis of Afrikaner Power.* Cape Town: David Philip, 1979.

De Klerk, W. *The Puritans of Africa: A Story of Afrikanerdom.* Harmondsworth, England: Penguin, 1976.

Louw, P. E., and K. Tomaselli. "Semiotics of Apartheid: The Struggle for the Sign." *European Journal for Semiotic Studies* 3.1–2 (1991): 99–110.

Louw, P. E. "Language and National Unity in a Post-Apartheid South Africa." *Critical Arts* 6.1 (1992): 52–60.

O'Meara, D. *Volskapitalisme: Class, Capital and Ideology in the Development of Afrikaner Nationalism.* Johannesburg: Ravan, 1983.

—ERIC LOUW

ARBITRARINESS, PRINCIPLE OF. One of the tenets of Ferdinand de Saussure's theory of linguistic signs, the principle of arbitrariness has been the source of confusion and controversies. Saussure introduced it in the first chapter of his *Course in General Linguistics* (1916). The initial definition of the linguistic sign is of a psychological nature: There is an associative link "in the brain" that brings together a concept and an acoustic image. This formulation is oriented to concrete, individual uses of signs in the speech circuit. Saussure then insists on the intimate and two-way nature of this link. How, then, is this relationship arbitrary? These two perspectives can be accounted for by the fact that the overall system of relations—not the relation internal to the individual sign—constitutes the general condition for the particular internal relationships that hold between any given signified and signifier in the system. For Saussure, the former is external to the given sign relation, acting on it from the outside; the latter, on the other hand, is internal to it. After this initial twofold definition, Saussure proceeds with terminological clarifications and specifies that "the link unifying signifier and signified is arbitrary or, even more, since we understand by the sign the total result of the association of a signifier with a signified, we can say more simply: *the linguistic sign is arbitrary*" (Saussure, 1971, p. 100; emphasis in original).

The introduction of the term *arbitrary* in the second definition is also accompanied by a further critically important terminological shift: Saussure begins to use the more abstract terms *signifier* (*signifiant*) and *signified* (*signifié*) instead of *acoustic image* and *concept* to designate the two components of the sign relation. The linguistic sign is now seen as occurring not in the speech circuit that connects individuals but in the overall, necessarily more abstract system of relations, *langue.*

Saussure privileges the system-based view of the linguistic sign. The "arbitrariness of the sign" is taken to be axiomatic. In saying this, Saussure refers not to the internal relationship that unifies signifier and signified per se but to the result of that relationship: the sign taken as a whole. He then makes it clear that the principle of arbitrariness refers to the "collective habits," "the convention," or "the rule," all of which fix this relation for all speakers of a language.

Saussure's brief discussion of two possible counterexamples to the principle of arbitrariness—onomatopoeia and exclamation—is less a concession to the possibility of exceptions to the arbitrariness principle and more a decision to exclude such phenomena from the theoretically privileged domain of *langue.* For Saussure, such expressions "are never organic elements of a linguistic system" (1971, 101) because *langue* is a system of purely internal relations of value. To the extent that onomatopoeic words are truly imitative and not, therefore, conventional, they are motivated by extralinguistic phenomena that do not fall within the province of *langue.* Thus, the purely system-based criterion of arbitrariness is compromised. It is ironic that Saussure, in order to preserve his *langue*-based notion of arbitrariness, marginalized the phenomena that provide the merest glimpse of the motivated character of all signs in the social processes of semiosis. These processes always entail motivated contact between the semiotic and the material.

The presumed arbitrariness of the internal link that constitutes the signifier/signified relation has remained an influential idea ever since and in ways that go well beyond linguistics itself. This has caused some misunderstanding as Saussure's methodological privileging of the abstract system of sign-types—*langue*—did not lead him to inquire into the social basis of meaning making. The principle of arbitrariness as stated by Saussure has generated an ongoing debate among linguists concerned with the evolutionary origins of language and sociosemioticians who consider that most signs in their contexts of use are functionally motivated rather than arbitrary.

[*See also* Linguistic Motivation; Saussure; Sign; *and* Signification.]

BIBLIOGRAPHY

Hodge, R. G. Kress. *Social Semiotics.* Cambridge: Polity, 1988.
Lee, B. "Peirce, Frege, Saussure, and Whorf: The Semiotic

Mediation of Ontology." In *Semiotic Mediation: Sociocultural and Psychological Perspectives,* edited by E. Mertz and R. J. Parmentier, pp. 99–128. New York and London: Academic Press, 1985.

Saussure, F. de. *Course in General Linguistics* (1916). Translated by Roy Harris. London: Duckworth, 1971.

—PAUL J. THIBAULT

ARCHITECTURE. In addition to providing functional space (shelters for living, working, or storing goods; defensive works; temples, etc.), human-made constructions can be, and most often are, endowed with symbolic values. The capacity of architecture to convey meaning makes it a relevant object of inquiry for semiotics. The dual aspect of buildings—functional and symbolic—was noted as early as the first century CE by the Roman architect Marcus Vitruvius Pollio in his treatise *De Architectura.* Following the Stoics' doctrine of signs, Vitruvius distinguished "that which signifies" from "that which is signified" (1.3.3), a general distinction that Vitruvius considered applicable to architecture inasmuch as the architect makes visible the invisible through a quasi-magical creation of meaningful monuments that cause wonder in the viewer's mind.

This complex process of signification encompasses visionary conception, creative design, coding of instructions given to the actual builders through blueprints, and interpretation by the users. The outcome of this process is the built environment that characterizes each culture through its technology, style, values, and ideology. Spacing, structures, proportions, and decorations are among the factors contributing to such results and play an important part in the socialization of developing individuals. This signifying potential was first addressed in modern semiotic terms in the 1930s by Jan Mukařovský, who was working from the point of view of the Prague School's structural functionalism. It became the focus of academic and professional attention during the 1960s and 1970s, a time when the semiotics of architecture received institutional sanction in the form of university courses and specialized journals.

A variety of approaches have been used in order to provide a theoretical basis for the obvious capacity of buildings to produce meaningful effects. In the wake of structural linguistics, which was hailed at that time as a "pilot science" and was introduced in many disciplines in the form of descriptive models, architecture was construed as a "language" and the built environment envisioned as sets of "messages" and "texts." Architecture as communication or as a language became a popular topic for semiotic speculations. The perceived analogy led to further extrapolations that attempted to identify the visual or tactile equivalents of the functional parts and relations of linguistic communication. For instance, Italo Gamberini (1961) considered the constitutive elements of architecture (e.g., floors, roofs, walls, pillars and beams, etc.) as analogous to classes of words in language, while Renato De Fusco (1967) equated the exterior of a building with the signifier and the interior with the signified, and Umberto Eco (1972) suggested that building elements denote their function (e.g., the door is the signifier and the function of communicating between two rooms is the signified).

Many semioticians embraced a componential-analysis approach, striving to categorize units and elucidate their hierarchy and combinatory rules. In this context, an important issue was to decide whether, like language, architecture was endowed with duality of patterning (or double articulation)— that is, whether it was possible to identify a finite set of meaningless units (equivalent to phonemes) whose combinations produced meaningful units (equivalent to morphemes). Ferruccio Rossi-Landi (1975) claimed that there were "homologies of production" between artifacts and language, the former involving several levels ranging from raw material to geometrical configurations that played a functional part in more complex organizations equivalent to sentences and finally to larger compositions similar to discourse. In the same vein, Donald Preziosi (1979) proposed a hierarchy of architectonic sign types with three levels, each of which he subdivided into various categories of minimal and maximal units. He also assessed the communicative potential of architecture with respect to the six functions charted by Roman Jakobson (1960) in his model of linguistic communication.

These efforts toward a componential and functional analysis of architectonic systems generated technical terminologies using the vocabulary of geometry, topology, or rhetoric and coining neologisms in which the ending *-eme* indicated the assumed semiotic functionality of a type of unit. For instance, *archemes* (from the Greek word meaning primacy or origin) designated the primal units of an architectonic system, functionally equivalent to linguistic phonemes; *choremes* (from the Greek word for space or spot) suggested the spatial equivalent of linguistic morphemes; *urbemes* (from the Latin word for city or town) applied to more complex meaningful units such as houses, whose clusters form settlements. Redefined terms, borrowed from other disciplines, included words such as *distinctive features, figures, forms, cells, matrices,* and *templates.* None of these conceptual nomenclatures appears to have gained currency in either architecture or semiotics.

The semiotics of architecture was initiated typically by semioticians who were not professional architects but were trained as art historians, philosophers, or linguists. However, some architects, in search of a theoretical basis for their discipline and its teaching, looked toward American or European semiotic theories as promising approaches and took an active part in the elaboration of analytical strategies developed over the years in dialogue with semioticians. For instance, the Argentinian architect Cesar Jannello (1918–1985), the founder, in 1968, of the Institute of Architecture in Buenos Aires, introduced the formal teaching of architectonic semiotics to the faculty of architecture. Mainly based on the general concepts and models elaborated by Louis Hjelmslev and A. J. Greimas, Jannello's theory of spatial delimitation starts with a theory of design configurations (classes of relations among elements and their morphological operations on space) rather than of geometric figures, which are conceived as autonomous static entities, and denotative representations, which are merely analogic. The end result is a generative system that prescribes variants of paradigmatic and syntagmatic relations. Claudio Guerri (1988), a disciple of Jannello who expounded his theory in English, also introduced some Peircean concepts in this dynamic system. Max Bense relied exclusively on Peirce to deal with architecture in the context of his semiotic aesthetics (1973). Others drew their generative models directly from Noam Chomsky's theory of syntax (e.g., Pierre Boudon, whose programmatic article on the semiotics of place appeared in *Semiotica* in 1973) or endeavored to apply the Hjelmslevian principles of Greimas's structural semantics to architectural topology (e.g., Manar Hammad and his architect colleagues in Groupe 107 whose analyzed architectural blueprints as language between 1973 and 1976).

In England, Geoffrey Broadbent, an early exponent of the language analogy, presented a critical assessment of the field in 1977 and eventually found in Peirce and Charles Morris conceptual tools better suited to a theorization of architecture in the context of a multisensory perception of space (1993). The latter article is symptomatic of a renewed interest in a more inclusive semiotic conceptualization of architecture, following a decade-long crisis caused by the linguistic-model fallacy and the shortcomings of its constraining formalism. Research rooted in evolutionary ecology, anthropology, and a better understanding of spatial cognition provides a promising basis for a semiotic approach to architecture and design (e.g., Egenter, 1994).

[*See also* Cultural Landscape; Distance; Mindscape; Space; *and* Urban Semiotics.]

BIBLIOGRAPHY

Ashihara, Y. *The Hidden Order: Tokyo through the Twentieth Century.* Tokyo: Kodansha International, 1989.

Bense, M. "Architectursemiotik." In *Wörterbuch der Semiotik,* edited by M. Bense and E. Walther. Cologne: Kiepnheuer and Witsch, 1973.

Boudon, P. "Recherches sémiotiques sur le lieu." *Semiotica* 7.3 (1973): 189–225.

Broadbent, G. "A Plain Man's Guide to the Theory of Signs in Architecture," *Architecture Design* 47.7–8 (1977): 474–482.

Broadbent, G. "Buildings as Symbols of Political Ideology." In *Semiotics 1980,* edited by M. Herzfeld and M. D. Lenhart, pp. 45–54. New York: Plenum, 1982.

Broadbent, G. "The Multi-Sensory Perception of Space." *VS. Quaderni di studi semiotici* 65–66 (1993): 143–168.

Broadbent, G., R. Bunt, and C. Jencks, eds. *Signs, Symbols and Architecture.* Chichester: John Wiley and Sons, 1980. See pages 11–68 for U. Eco's article "Function and Sign: The Semiotics of Architecture."

De Fusco, R. *Architettura come mass-medium.* Bari: Dedalo, 1967.

Eco, U. "A Componential Analysis of the Architectural Sign/Column." *Semiotica* 5.2 (1972): 97–117.

Egenter, N. *Architectural Anthropology: Semantic and Symbolic Architecture.* Lausanne: Structura Mundi, 1994.

Gamberini, I. *Analisi degli elementi costitutivi dell'architettura.* Florence: Coppini, 1961.

Guerri, C. F. "Architectural Design and Space Semiotics in Argentina." In *The Semiotic Web 1987,* edited by J. Umiker-Sebeok and T. A. Sebeok, pp. 389–419. Berlin: Mouton de Gruyter, 1988.

Hammad, M., M. Miaille, E. Provoost, C. Renaudin, and M. Vernin. *Sémiotique des plans en architecture.* 2 vols. Paris: Groupe 107, 1973–1976.

Jakobson, R. "Concluding Statement: Linguistics and Poetics." In *Style in Language,* edited by T. A. Sebeok, pp. 350–377. Cambridge, Mass.: MIT Press, 1960.

Krampen, M. *Meaning in the Urban Environment*. London: Pion, 1979. Part 1 provides an excellent overview of the semiotics of architecture from the late 1950s to the late 1970s.

Mukařovský, J. *Aesthetic Function, Norm, and Value as Social Facts* (1936). Translated by M. E. Suino. Michigan Slavic Contributions. Ann Arbor: University of Michigan, 1970.

Preziosi, D. *Architecture, Language, and Meaning: The Origins of the Built World and Its Semiotic Organization*. The Hague and Paris: Mouton, 1979.

Preziosi, D. *The Semiotics of the Built Environment*. Bloomington: Indiana University Press, 1979.

Rossi-Landi, F. *Linguistics and Economics*. The Hague: Mouton, 1975.

Vitruvius. *The Ten Books on Architecture*. Translated by M. H. Morgan. New York: Dover, 1960.

—PAUL BOUISSAC

ARNHEIM, RUDOLPH (b. 1904), pioneer in the semiotics of visual arts. Trained in the methods of scientific research at the Psychological Institute of the University of Berlin at a time when empirical research on perception was conducted under the founders of Gestalt psychology (Wolfgang Köhler, Max Wertheimer, and Kurt Koffka Lewin), Arnheim published, in 1928, his doctoral thesis on the analysis of facial expressions and graphological data. However, his multidisciplinary mind, stimulated by the cultural context of the Weimar Republic, embraced a wide range of research interest. He wrote *Film as Art* (1932), a book that anticipates a semiotic theory of the components and syntax of cinematographic language. Forced into exile by Nazism, he worked in Italy and England in media-related positions before moving to New York in 1940. Foundation grants allowed him to pursue his research on the content analysis of *roman radiophonique* (*Radio, an Art of Sound*, 1972) and to apply the theory and methods of Gestalt psychology to visual arts, a much more complex domain than the usually simple patterns used in psychological experiments.

In *Art and Visual Perception* (1954), Arnheim opened the way to the empirical study of works of art and introduced new analytical concepts in the domains of art history and psychology. As the first professor of the psychology of art at Harvard University, Arnheim endeavored to prove that thought could articulate itself through purely visual means—hence the title of his book, *Visual Thinking* (1971). As he stated later in *My Life in the Art World* (1984), he "could not find any operation of thought which was not already contained in what artists do when they look."

His approach is characterized by the construction of a theoretical and methodological interface between science and the visual arts. For instance, he addresses the issue of artistic evolution in terms of concepts borrowed from contemporary physics such as entropy and dissipative structures. His numerous articles, however, bear the mark of the rigorous empirical training he had acquired in his formative years, albeit with the occasional indication of epistemological anxiety: "My own analysis of the formal parameters ... had given me some insight into the particular functions of such devices as balance or parallelism or dynamic tension, but it also seemed to me to fall short of the meaning of any work of art as a whole" (1992). Thus, the scientific analysis of chromatic contrasts in a painting by Matisse could betray the artist by focusing on a mere aspect of his work. This is why he decided to shift his vantage point from a purely scientific perspective, which is by necessity eccentric with respect to art, toward a view from within art and to look for the principles that painting, sculpture, architecture, and other arts have in common. This approach, which he characterized as phenomenological and cognitive, leads to a higher degree of abstraction because of the generality or universality it attempts to reach in its understanding of art. The purview is global, in accordance with the Gestalt inspiration of the enterprise, rather than analytical or fragmentary.

For instance, using the traditional art-historical concept of composition, Arnheim dealt with the specific dynamism of architectural forms in *The Power of the Center* (1988), noting the universality of focal constructions as overall organizations of architectural systems of forces and tensions with respect to the complementary opposition between center and periphery.

Surprisingly, Arnheim does not make reference to semiotics in his work in spite of the fact that he consistently addressed typically semiotic issues and referred explicitly to basic semiotic concepts such as *signifier* and *signified* (e.g., 1992). This seems to be characteristic of the generation of the 1950s, among which prominent theoreticians of visual art such as Pierre Francastel, Meyer Shapiro, Hubert Damish, and Arnheim himself showed extreme skepticism toward the linguistic dependency that appeared to mark the first attempts to establish visual semiotics. Arnheim's contribution to semiotics has been precisely to curtail unwarranted and unjustified extrapolation from linguistics to the visual arts.

[*See also* Aesthetics; Art; Cinema; *and* Pictorial Semiotics.]

BIBLIOGRAPHY

Arnheim, R. *Art and Visual Perception.* Berkeley: University of California Press, 1954.

Arnheim, R. *Visual Thinking.* Berkeley: University of California Press, 1971.

Arnheim, R. *Radio, an Art of Sound.* New York: Da Capo, 1972.

Arnheim, R. *Toward a Psychology of Art.* Berkeley: University of California Press, 1972.

Arnheim, R. *The Dynamics of Architectural Form.* Berkeley: University of California Press, 1977.

Arnheim, R. *The Power of the Center.* Berkeley: University of California Press, 1982.

Arnheim, R. *My Life in the Art World.* Ann Arbor: University of Michigan Press, 1984.

Arnheim, R. *New Essays on the Psychology of Art.* Berkeley: University of California Press, 1986.

Arnheim, R. "Is It Science?" In *To the Rescue of Art: Twenty-Six Essays,* pp. 175–194. Berkeley: University of California Press, 1992.

—FERNANDE SAINT-MARTIN

ART. Can works of art be defined by any intrinsic properties that do not exist in objects that are not artworks? In contrast to aesthetic theories that have aimed at the discovery of such properties in objects of art, semiotic approaches to aesthetics consider an artwork not as an object but as a sign, a signifier whose production and reception are specific processes of semiosis. On this basis, semiotic aesthetics has both developed its own theories of art and aimed at a reinterpretation of traditional theories of aesthetics from a semiotic point of view. Apart from their common foundation in the theory of signs, widely divergent approaches to art are encompassed by semiotic aesthetics.

From the point of view of the history of semiotics, the following schools of semiotic aesthetics can be distinguished:

1. *Classical semiotic aesthetics.* Its foundations have been laid by Alexander G. Baumgarten and Gotthold E. Lessing (Wellbery, 1984). Baumgarten, in his *Theoretische Ästhetik* (1750), explicitly postulated semiotics as a branch of aesthetics. Lessing's *Laokoon*

(1766) presents a theory of mimesis in the poetic and pictorial arts.

2. *Peircean semiotic aesthetics.* Although aesthetics is not a central topic in the philosophy of Charles Sanders Peirce, his writings deal with aesthetic problems at several points (Kaelin, 1983) and have become the foundation of Max Bense's Stuttgart School of semiotic aesthetics (see the journal *Semiosis*).

3. *Morris's semiotic aesthetics.* Beginning in his "Aesthetics and the Theory of Signs" (1939), Charles Morris developed a behaviorist theory of semiotic aesthetics that characterizes art as an iconic sign of value (Morris and Hamilton, 1965).

4. *Prague School aesthetics.* The structuralist theory of art developed by the Prague School is a functional theory that defines the essence of art within the pragmatic dimension of semiosis (Matejka and Titunik, eds., 1976). A dominant figure of this school of aesthetics is Jan Mukařovský (1936). Important contributions to Prague School aesthetics were also made by Roman Jakobson (Winner, 1987).

5. *Glossematic aesthetics.* The theory of art developed in the framework of Louis Hjelmslev's glossematics has been applied primarily to the field of literary semiotics. Its key to the nature of the aesthetic sign is the theory of connotation.

6. *Structuralist semiotics of art.* In French structuralist semiotics, there was discussion about the analogies between art and language in various papers entitled "Is Art Language?" (e.g., Dufrenne, 1966). However, this discussion is mainly restricted to the semiotics of painting.

7. *Semiotics of art of the Moscow-Tartu School.* With roots in Russian Formalism, glossematics, and cybernetics, the semiotics of the Moscow-Tartu School has developed the theory of art as a secondary semiotic system constructed on the model of language (Lotman, 1970).

8. *Information-theoretical aesthetics.* Mathematical approaches to the study of art have been adopted in the framework of Max Bense's Stuttgart School of semiotic aesthetics and in part also in studies of Moscow semioticians. These approaches to the arts pursued the goal of defining such aesthetic phenomena as originality, innovation, or harmony in terms of mathematical concepts such as order, symmetry, complexity, probability, information, and entropy.

9. *Eco's semiotics of art.* Umberto Eco's aesthetics is based on his theory of codes and of the open message.

10. *Goodman's symbol theory of art.* Nelson Goodman's philosophy of art has been hailed by some as one of the most exciting advances in semiotic aesthetics, whereas others have criticized it as being inadequate to the purpose of providing a theory of art. Goodman does not himself call his aesthetics a semiotics of art, but this might be only a terminological question.

11. *Semiogenetic theory of art.* The evolutionary perspective of art has its roots in ethology and zoosemiotics. Thus, Thomas A. Sebeok, in *The Play of Musement* (1981), has studied prefigurations of visual art and music in animals, and Walter Koch (1984) has developed a semiogenetic theory of the evolution of art from nature to culture. In this perspective, Sebeok sees rudiments of art in morphological parallelisms in nature, to which he ascribes a biological survival value because the pleasure associated with the perception of such aesthetic objects facilitates the essential survival tool of environmental object classification. In the evolution of animal behavior, Koch sees prefigurations of art in behavioral delays and diversions that occur in courting rituals, displacement activities, and other forms of behavioral ritualizations whose biological function is one of enhancing primary gratification.

From the point of view of semiotic systematics, the main semiotic approaches to art can be assigned to the domains of semantics, pragmatics, and the theory of aesthetic codes.

Semantics of Art. According to the semantic approaches to semiotic aesthetics, the work of art is a sign that derives its aesthetic quality from a particular kind of meaning or mode of reference. The specific proposals that have been made in this respect are quite diverse and even incompatible. Some argue that the artwork is replete with meaning, being polyfunctional or polysemous. Others argue that art is empty, so to speak, in its semantic dimension. They propose a theory of aesthetic self-referentiality, according to which the sign refers to nothing but itself. Still others seek the essence of art in its iconicity, the mode of reference based on likeness. Precursors or even implicitly semiotic theories of this kind include the classical theories of art as mimesis and the various representational theories of art in philosophical aesthetics.

Art in the Peircean semiotic framework. Peirce's semantic specification of the sign in the icon-index-symbol trichotomy has been adopted by many semi-

otic aestheticians in their definitions of art, but no agreement has been reached as to which type of sign characterizes best the essence of art. The best-known application of the Peircean trichotomy to aesthetics is probably Morris's interpretation of art as an iconic sign. However, the theory of iconicity of art did not remain undisputed. Some authors, among them Goodman, have argued that the relation of the aesthetic sign to its object is symbolic, since it represents by means of conventionality.

From a still different point of view, the work of art is also indexical. In his *Collected Papers*, Peirce describes the indexical nature of art as follows: "Works of sculpture and painting can be executed for a single patron and must be by a single artist. A painting always represents a fragment of a larger whole. It is broken at its edges. . . . In such a work individuality of thought and feeling is an element of beauty" (1.176). The categories of exemplification or ostension by which others have characterized art are also modes of indexicality in the Peircean sense.

The different definitions of art as iconic, indexical, or symbolic are only incompatible when the aesthetic sign is assigned exclusively to one of the three types. Peirce himself would have rejected a definition of art based on a simple specific type of sign-object relation. In his view, art is characterized by a harmony in the conjunction of all three types of sign: "The most perfect of signs are those in which the iconic, indicative and symbolic characters are blended as equally as possible" (4.448).

A further semantic specification of art in terms of Peircean semiotics arises in the definition of art with respect to its interpretant. From this point of view, Bense, in his *Semiotische Ästhetik* (1971), characterizes the work of art as a rheme, a sign of "qualitative possibility" that does not affirm anything. This definition of art is related closely to the theory of interpretative openness of art. As to the nature of the sign vehicle (Peirce's representamen), art is polyfunctional. In the interpretation of Bense, a work of art is a *sinsign* (an individual object) because of its creative-innovative nature, but with respect to its materiality the artwork functions as a *qualisign* (a quality), and with respect to its conventional characteristics, the artwork is a *legisign* (a type) (Peirce, 1955, pp. 115–119).

Morris's theory of aesthetic iconicity. The theory of the iconic character of art has a precursor in the classical theory of mimesis. Morris (1939) gave this ancient theory a new interpretation. In his definition, art evinces the two criteria of iconicity and value. An iconic sign, according to Morris, is one whose designatum can be apprehended directly, because the sign vehicle and its designatum have some properties in common. In contrast to icons, such as common pictures, the aesthetic icon is a sign whose designatum is a value. This concept of value is central to Morris's semiotics, and he defines value as a property of an object relative to an act of interest by the perceiver. Thus, the aesthetic sign exists only in a process of interpretation, and hence the semantic definition of art has a necessary counterpart in its pragmatic dimension.

The theory of aesthetic iconicity seems to contradict the assumption of aesthetic autonomy, which is the ground of the theory of aesthetic self-referentiality in the tradition of the *l'art pour l'art* aesthetics. While the former is based on a criterion of reference, the latter seems to refute the very idea of a referential object. Morris, however, argued that his theory of aesthetic iconicity could solve even this paradox. Since in aesthetic signs "there is the direct apprehension of value properties through the very presence of that which itself has the value it designates, . . . aesthetic perception is tied to the work itself and does not use this merely as a springboard for evoking reveries and recollections" (1939, p. 420). The paradox of aesthetic self-reference or of "disinterested interest" is thus "accounted for in the fact that in the apprehension of the iconic sign there is both a mediated and an immediate taking account of certain properties." Morris later modified his position somewhat in response to criticism of the concept of iconicity. For details see Morris and Hamilton (1965).

Goodman's symptoms of art. Nelson Goodman has developed an important contribution to semiotic aesthetics in his book *Languages of Art* (1976). His theory of art is a strictly cognitive one. It is thus an antithesis to expressive theories of art such as Susanne Langer's in *Feeling and Form* (1953), which develops the thesis that art is the creation of forms symbolic of human feelings. Goodman, by contrast, argues that there are "languages of art" and that works of art are like utterances in a system of symbols. In particular, works of art have certain referential functions, such as representation, description, exemplification, and expression. By exemplification as opposed to denotation, Goodman describes a mode of reference that also characterizes the difference between showing and telling. Exemplification includes expression, which Goodman defines as metaphorical or figurative exemplification. In exemplification, a symbol refers to properties that the symbol itself evinces or possesses. A sign by exemplification is both iconic (by having features in common with its referential object) and indexical (since the referential object is present in the act of semiosis).

On the basis of these semiotic distinctions, Goodman distinguishes five "symptoms" of art, partly referring to the syntactic, partly to the semantic dimension of semiosis. These symptoms are: (1) syntactic density (the symbols lack finite articulation or differentiation); (2) semantic density (the symbols are differentiated by minimal differences); (3) syntactic repleteness (relatively many features of the symbols are significant); (4) exemplification; and (5) multiple and complex reference. Goodman, however, is cautious not to call his symptoms criteria of art and argues that these symptoms "are neither a necessary nor a sufficient condition for, but merely tend in conjunction with other such symptoms to be present in, aesthetic experience" (1976, p. 252). He proposes that the question "What is art?" should be replaced by the question "When is art?" to remind the aesthetician of the necessary pragmatic conditions under which objects actually function as works of art.

Pragmatics of Art. According to the pragmatic theories of art, the specifically aesthetic character of the artwork cannot be sought in its referential function or in its syntactic structure. Instead, the work of art is considered to be referentially autonomous or even self-referential, and its aesthetic quality is defined as arising from an act of aesthetic attention, a specific semiotic attitude in the process of aesthetic reception. Among the first who developed a semiotic aesthetics on this basis were the Prague School structuralists. In semiotic poetics, Jakobson held similar views of aestheticness.

The pragmatic theory of art has its roots in the tradition of the *l'art pour l'art* aesthetics. An early explicit formulation of the doctrine of aesthetic autonomy was given by Augustine of Hippo, who defined beauty as something that pleases in itself. In Immanuel Kant's *Critique of Judgment* (1790), the exclusion of references in aesthetic experience is implied in his classical criteria of "disinterested pleasure" in the perception of art and of "purposiveness without purpose" as a function of art. It was precisely this ideal of the detachment of art from its referential (and social) context that caused sociologists such as Pierre Bourdieu to develop an anti-Kantian aesthetics. However, the traditional theories of aesthetic autonomy did not maintain that the artwork excludes reference in principle. The argument is rather that the specifically aesthetic nature of art is not in its referential function.

Jan Mukařovský gave a first outline of his semiotic theory of art in his article "Art as a Semiotic Fact" (1934) and in his book *Aesthetic Function* (1936). The aesthetic or autonomous sign function, according to this theory, is defined in contrast to the communicative function of signs. Both functions might be present in a work of art (e.g., in a realistic painting), but only the autonomous function constitutes the specificity of art. The essence of art does not lie in communication. While the communicative sign refers to something distinctively existing, the autonomous sign is without any documentary authenticity although it refers globally to the reality of a given social context. Hence, the autonomy of art is not explained by a lack of reference but by the fictionality of its reference. This is a still rather moderate version of the theory of aesthetic autonomy. More radical variants of this theory of art have gone further by defining the aesthetic sign as autotelic or self-referential.

A basic feature of the aesthetic function is its "ability to isolate an object" and to "cause maximal focus of attention on a given object" (Mukařovský, 1936, p. 21). These are the characteristics that in the poetics of the Russian Formalist and Prague Schools have been described by the principles of estrangement, deautomatization, and foregrounding. With special reference to the visual arts, Mukařovský emphasizes that the difference between a natural object and an object of art is essentially "based on the way in which the perceiver approaches it" (1936, pp. 230–231). The perceiver can even approach objects of nature aesthetically and thus discover features of art in nature.

Aesthetic Codes. The concept of code, originally derived from information theory, has been adopted in semiotic aesthetics as a tool for the description of creativity in terms of a deviation from a system of given norms. Two influential theories of art based on a theory of codes are those of Umberto Eco and Jurij Lotman.

Within the theory of codes developed in Eco's *Struttura assente* (1968) and *Theory of Semiotics* (1976),

innovative messages are generated in a process of coding and overcoding. The aesthetic code is the result of a dialectic between a conventional code and an innovative message. By their innovative character, aesthetic messages infringe the rules of their genres and thus negate the code, but at the same time the new message creates a new aesthetic code. Thus, the work of art violates and strengthens the code by transforming and completing it. In *A Theory of Semiotics*, Eco describes the process of aesthetic innovation as one of overcoding—that is, the creation of new rules on the basis of preestablished ones. Aesthetic overcoding generates a semiotic "surplus" on the levels of content and expression. Through this surplus, the text becomes open to multiple interpretations.

In *Opera aperta* (1962), Eco develops his aesthetics of the open work of art. Because of its ambiguity and the plurality of cultural codes, the aesthetic message has the character of an "empty form" into which the interpreter inserts meaning. The openness is a challenge to the interpreter to try to fill this form with meaning. However, there is a "logic of the signifier" that counteracts this openness. This opposite principle is the requirement of interpretative fidelity to the message according to the rules of the conventional code. In this way, the dialectic of code and message in art is paralleled by the dialectic between the openness of the work in relation to its closure due to conventional coding.

Lotman's semiotics of art is a theory of the plurality of artistic codes based on models of information and communication theory. Like any other message, the artistic message can be decoded only on the basis of a common code shared by both the sender and the receiver. In literature, for example, this code consists of a standard language but also of the traditional literary conventions, which have become codified in normative poetics and rhetoric. Messages generated from only these common codes follow an aesthetics of identity.

Aesthetically innovative messages, by contrast, are based on an aesthetic of opposition. The receiver tries to decipher the innovative message on the basis of a code that is different from the creator's code. As a result, the text is either recoded by the receiver (which might even involve its aesthetic destruction when the text is treated as nonaesthetic) or it is interpreted as an artistic text, which requires the creation of an as-yet-unknown aesthetic code. In this case, the receiver recognizes in the course of decoding that he or she has to work out a new code for deciphering the message. This new aesthetic code can be either the author's code or a transformation of it. Such transformations often occur as "creolizations"—that is, as assimilations with other codes of the interpreter. Therefore, the artistic text might acquire different meanings for sender and receiver. Even fortuitous elements of the text might be interpreted as meaningful. Lotman calls this "the ability of an artistic text to amass information" (1970, p. 25).

[See also Aesthetics; Arnheim; Bense; Eco; Gombrich; Goodman; Lotman; Moscow-Tartu School; Peirce; and Prague School.]

BIBLIOGRAPHY

Bense, M. Semiotische Ästhetik. Baden-Baden: Agis Verlag, 1971.

Dufrenne, M. "L'art est-il langage?" Revue d'esthétique 19 (1966): 1–43.

Eco, U. Opera aperta. Milan: Bompiani, 1962.

Eco, U. A Theory of Semiotics. Bloomington: Indiana University Press, 1976.

Goodman, N. Languages of Art. Indianapolis: Hackett, 1976.

Kaelin, E. F. "Reflections on Peirce's Aesthetics." In The Relevance of Charles S. Peirce, edited by E. Freeman, pp. 224–237. LaSalle, Minn.: Hegler Institute, 1983.

Koch, W. A. "Art: Biogenesis and Semiogenesis." Semiotica 49 (1984): 283–304.

Langer, S. Feeling and Form: A Theory of Art Developed from Philosophy in a New Key. New York: Charles Scribner's & Sons, 1953.

Lotman, J. The Structure of the Artistic Text (1970). Ann Arbor: University of Michigan Press, 1977.

Matejka, L., and R. I. Titunik, eds. Semiotics of Art: Prague School Contributions. Cambridge, Mass.: MIT Press, 1976.

Morris, C. W. "Esthetics and the Theory of Signs" (1939). In Writings on the General Theory of Signs, pp. 415–433. The Hague: Mouton, 1971.

Morris, C. W., and D. J. Hamilton. "Aesthetics, Signs, and Icons." Philosophy and Phenomenological Research 25 (1965): 356–364.

Mukařovský, J. "Art as a Semiotic Fact" (1934). In Structure, Sign and Function, edited and translated by J. Burbank and P. Steiner, pp. 82–88. New Haven: Yale University Press, 1977.

Mukařovský, J. Aesthetic Function, Norm, and Value as Social Facts (1936). Ann Arbor: University of Michigan, 1970.

Peirce, C. S. "Logic as Semiotic: The Theory of Signs." Philosophical Writings of Peirce, edited by J. Buchler, pp. 98–119. New York: Dover, 1955.

Sebeok, T. A. The Play of Musement. Bloomington: Indiana University Press, 1981.

Wellbery, D. E. Lessing's Laokoon: Semiotics and Aesthetics in the Age of Reason. Cambridge: Cambridge University Press, 1984.

Winner, T. G. "The Aesthetic Semiotics of Roman Jakobson." In Language, Poetry, and Poetics, edited by K. Pomorska, pp. 257–274. Berlin: Mouton de Gruyter, 1987.

—WINFRIED NÖTH

ART AND ILLUSION (1960) is an influential work by Ernst Gombrich (b. 1909) that emphasizes the conventional context of art-historical discourse.

In his introduction, Gombrich presents his psychology of perception and pictorial representation as a way to go beyond the old opposition between seeing and knowing, and he locates the traditional problem in the conventions, distortions, and transformations of mimesis. Art historians had been somewhat dismissive of this question of representation in image making and image reading. By revealing conventions in our conception of nature, Gombrich defines a learning process of mapping and correcting, through perceptual trial and error, bearing upon the problems of cognition that generated stylistic change. Searching for a rational explanation for these changes, he presupposes art as a distinct category with its own history and claims that aesthetic experience has to be seen as a cultural rather than a natural category.

Posing the representation of reality as a permanent subject matter, Gombrich's perceptual psychology of art then describes the history of stylistic evolution as one of options for or against possible forms. In putting forward his basic theoretical contentions and his empirical arguments for a psychological history of forms that could be integrated into a historical process when tested against the natural object, Gombrich ranges over the history of art, noticing particularly the ancient Greeks, those inventors of the mimetic principle; the medieval conceptual and logical schemata referring to universals and particulars; Chinese painters; the classical imagist masters of the Italian Renaissance and the Baroque such as Leonardo da Vinci and Rembrandt; and the Impressionists' and the Cubists' radical departures from representations of objective reality. He reexamines these accomplishments that have helped us raise the veil of illusion, question the notions of truth and stereotype, and stress the optical ambiguities of the third dimension.

Through numerous examples of the use and abuse of conventionalized graphic signs such as Villard de

Honnecourt's heraldic thirteenth-century copy of a "real" lion, Albrecht Dürer's portrayal of a rhinoceros covered with imbricated plates to signal and suggest the roughness of his skin, or John Constable's technique of contrasting tones to depict and transcribe onto canvas the presence of light in an English landscape, Gombrich explains that as addressees, we succeed in understanding the semantics of these pictorial representations, however stylized, by way of a codified system of expectations. Also, by an analysis of caricatural documents and the means of commercial artists, he seeks to further clarify the beholder's share. Outlining the perceptual conditioning imposed by current iconic codes on the interpreting viewer, he adds that, progressively, this iconic representation might even become more true than the natural experience as we look at things, read the image created, and probe reality through the colored glasses of conventional cultural habits and content.

To the historical students of the visual image and to visual semioticians such as Umberto Eco, René Lindekens, Hartmut Espe, to name but a few, Gombrich's experiences concerning a child's hobbyhorse or the Wivenhow park photographs are still of relevance today because they drew attention to and showed for the first time how the context of action, which to that point had been strangely excluded from our understanding of the representational status of these images, created specific conditions of illusionism. In this sense, perception must always be regarded as an active process, conditioned by our expectations and adapted to situations. Gombrich thus showed that naturally recognizable imitation or similarity between an artistic image and its object is also a matter of previously culturally conditioned convention and narrative. He succeeded in elucidating and correcting the traditional model of an ever more perfect duplication of nature in art and defined a new discipline offering a series of practical demonstrations. In later papers (1981), Gombrich revised his more extreme conventionalist stance in *Art and Illusion,* finally claiming—following the psychologist James Gibson—that pictorial illusionism does have a certain naturalistic, biologically induced, basis.

[*See also* Aesthetics; Art; Gibson; Gombrich, *and* Pictorial Semiotics.]

BIBLIOGRAPHY

Arnheim, R. *Art and Visual Perception: A Psychology of the Creative Eye.* Berkeley: University of California Press, 1954.

Arnheim, R. *Visual Thinking.* Berkeley: University of California Press, 1971.

Bryson, N. *Vision and Painting: The Logic of the Gaze.* New Haven and London: Yale University Press, 1983.

Gibson, J. J. *The Perception of the Visual World.* Boston: Houghton Mifflin, 1950.

Gombrich, E. H. *Art and Illusion: A Study in the Psychology of Pictorial Representation.* A. W. Mellon Lectures in the Fine Arts, 1956. Bollingen Series 35. Princeton: Princeton University Press, 1960.

Gombrich, E. H. "The Sky Is the Limit: The Vault of Heaven and Pictorial Vision." In *Perception: Essays in Honor of James J. Gibson,* edited by R. B. Macleod and H. L. Pick Jr., pp. 84–94. Ithaca, N.Y.: Cornell University Press, 1975.

Gombrich, E. H. "Image and Code: Scope and Limits of Conventionalism in Pictorial Representation." In *Image and Code,* edited by W. Steiner, pp. 11–43. Detroit: University of Michigan Press, 1981.

Goodman, N. *The Languages of Art: An Approach to a Theory of Symbols.* New York: Bobbs-Merrill, 1968.

Read, H. *Icon and Idea: The Function of Art in the Development of Human Consciousness.* London: Faber and Faber, 1955.

—MARIE CARANI

ARTICULATION. A division into parts, articulation refers in semiotics to two different but intimately connected topics: the componential structures of signifying terms and the divisions imposed on experience by signs. The term *articulation* entered semiotics through Ferdinand de Saussure's linguistics. He pointed out the felicitous etymology from the Latin *articulus* (joint, division). The theory of articulation in linguistics is well developed but narrowly specialized. Its three most outstanding achievements are the concept of double articulation, distinctive-features theory, and descriptions of marking or markedness. In the absence of a more general theory, other branches of semiotics have borrowed these linguistic notions with only limited success. The possibility of articulation in any domain of signs depends on the physical characteristics of its medium and the biological characteristics of the perception and performance channels involved as well as the structural characteristics of semiotic practices. No area of study in semiotics is more promising with respect to the growth of testable knowledge and the opportunity for productive synthesis than the general study of articulation. While we must have recourse to comparisons with language to organize what we know at this stage, it is possible to suggest additional perspectives.

Linguistic and Nonlinguistic Articulation. The French linguist André Martinet (1967) claimed that double articulation was distinctive of language, but his assertion is not based on detailed comparative analyses of contrasting modalities. He is necessarily correct in the sense that it is always possible to note features of linguistic double articulation that are not shared by other media, but for the features he himself emphasized parallels can be proposed.

The double articulation—or duality of patterning (Hockett, 1958)—of language is evinced by the successive division of the stream of speech into parts by two entirely independent criteria. The first articulation identifies units of reference or smallest meaningful segments (for instance, *trees* can be divided into *tree* and *s,* the latter being a phoneme indicating the plural). In Saussure's view and according to the common tenets of structuralism, this articulation is at one and the same time a division of the speech continuum and a division of the material continuum of experience. The second articulation is the division of the resultant entities of the first articulation on the basis of phonemic equivalence (for instance, *tree* as opposed to *free*).

Few other semiotic media offer the precise adherence to such a scheme that language does (though Louis Prieto [1966] cites examples from technical codes), but instances of comparable structures abound. A mosaic picture allows a similar analysis, first by images and then by tessellation, as do much of van Gogh's painting and some styles of Chinese watercolor painting in which the brush strokes (sortable by type, color, and direction) provide a second articulation. Like phonemes, the tessellation and brush strokes do not refer to a represented object, but they exhibit dimensions of patterning that are essential to perception of the visual sign as a whole. What we cannot assert is that such schemes are fundamental to visual semiosis. In John Constable's paintings, for instance, we see only a depiction (a reference) with parts that refer to parts of the object (as in the first articulation of language); in the work of Piet Mondrian or Jackson Pollock, we see articulated elements that have no references (like those of the second articulation of language). Indeed, the most prominent articulatory characteristic of visual semiosis is just this flexibility. Music is particularly difficult to assess from this point of view. The hierarchy of narrative forms in general, although multilayered, does not include a stratum like the phonic in language, whose signification, if any, functions on an order completely different from that of the larger parts.

The theory of distinctive features in linguistics reduces its sound elements to complexes of binary values, all of which indicate the presence or absence of one of a small number of characteristics, such as voicing or nasalizing. Descriptions with similar structures, sometimes invoking contraries rather than simple presence or absence, are possible for a wide range of structures. They were adapted by Claude Lévi-Strauss as a key element of his structural anthropology (1968). What is exceedingly difficult to judge in many cases is whether the oppositions ascribed really inhere in the original system of articulation or are features of a particular linguistic description. Doubt on just this score has dogged the reception of the century's most ambitious project in analysis by oppositional schemata, that of Algirdas Julien Greimas (1983). While neurophysiology and experimental psychology have both offered strong support to the idea that binary oppositions are fundamental to human information processing, every caution must be exercised in attributing such structure to higher-level constructs.

Outside linguistics, the idea of a distinctive-feature description need not in principle be restricted to variables of binary value. Music theorists have long celebrated the "parametric" description of notes according to pitch, register, and duration, represented as values in small, finite, but not binary scales of measure.

The theory of marking emerged within and complemented distinctive-feature theory. This theory demonstrates that binary oppositions in semiotic structures tend to be asymmetric functionally and psychologically. Roman Jakobson and more recently Michael Shapiro (1983) have employed the theory of marking to establish a fundamental link between syntactic and semantic relations through the principle that marked signifiers align with marked signifieds. Though originally conceived as a tool to explain details of phonology and syntax, the concept of marking continues to find broad application, as for example in critiques of cultural sexism or studies of reference in music (Hatten, 1994). Markedness relations in psychology are amenable to statistical study, as in Salus and Salus (1978).

Extrasemiotic Factors. It must be emphasized that articulation does not arise simply as a property of structure but emerges in the negotiation of structural factors with biological and physical ones. In language, the capacity of the vocal tract and the auditory pathway are determining features. The eye could not possibly make use of "octave equivalence" (frequency doubling) in the electromagnetic spectrum, as the ear does in the acoustic, because the eye's color range is just under an octave, while the ear takes in about ten octaves. Odors and sounds have immediately perceptible beginnings but not endings. (Beginnings of silences at the ends of sounds are perceptible when structured appropriately.) Further differences between channels develop at higher levels of cognitive processing. Differences such as these, many of which can be explored experimentally, limit the transferability of articulatory schemes across media.

Content Articulation. The most subtle and most difficult aspect of articulation theory is its comprehension of signified content. Starting again with language, Saussure seems to assert that the divisions of experience represented by words are strictly a function of the way words divide up their own space. This view typifies structural linguistics and is echoed in the Sapir-Whorf hypothesis. It cannot be entirely correct, for the extreme interpretation would deny that the genetic biases of visual perception, for example, and the brute attributes of nature play any role at all in the construction of our semantic schemes. A more balanced interpretation of the principle holds that the articulatory patterns of language or any other semiotic system project patterns on fields that are never tabulae rasae and that there can be negotiation between systems of content and systems of expression. If so, we are led to ponder how the patterning of content can be conceived other than through the language that brought it to our attention in the first place. From the standpoint of articulation theory (as opposed to that of structural semantics), no higher ground is available to offer a neutral perspective, but we can sometimes study the intersections of distinct articulatory systems, such as the linguistic and the visual or the musical and the kinaesthetic. In some other cases, we are at a loss for any such analytic standpoint. The articulation of time by tense seems to grow out of language alone.

Articulatory Structures. In the absence of any consensually established scheme for an overview of articulation structures independent of linguistics, the discussion that follows is an experimental effort to indicate a territory where study is needed and should be productive. References are provided to mathematical rather than linguistic precedents.

Articulatory phenomena do not come into view in relation to simple, single signs but with systems of signs or complex signs that have a systematic aspect. A problem of terminology arises with this fact. We must decide, somewhat arbitrarily, whether the minimal parts or features of signs that participate in articulatory systems (e.g., the phonemes of language or individual tiles of a mosaic) are themselves to be called signs or something else. At first view, they do not, at least in isolation, seem to "mean" anything. There is a heuristic advantage to perusing the opposite idea that they do signify relations and differences, but that path will not be pursued here. Louis Hjelmslev suggested the term *figurae* for these infrasemiotic components. It is not necessary to settle the underlying question, as we may adopt the term *elements* without prejudice: elements of an articulatory system might or might not be signs.

Semiosis has recourse to five principal articulatory categories: (1) oppositions; (2) systems of boundaries and regions; (3) systems of representatives; (4) systems of vectors; (5) hierarchies.

1. *Systems of oppositions* align elements in binary relations. This type of articulation is particularly characteristic of language and of social objects supported primarily by language. Opposition is an old topic in philosophy (Aristotle identified seven types). Note that any system reduced to oppositions of positive and negative terms leaves as its residue or kernel another articulatory system that is not so reduced. Such kernel elements are nasalization, voicing, and so on for phonemes and horizontal, vertical, diagonal, and so on for chess moves. These are systems of vectors. Oppositional schemes are modeled in formal logic.

2. *Systems of boundaries and regions* of appropriate continua include physical surfaces and time. We can speak here of a dual articulation (not to be confused with the double articulation or dual patterning of language.) The surface of the earth is articulated by a system of boundaries in which the elements are lines of latitude and longitude. These represent lines of division, not the regions that result. In the case of latitudes, there is a complementary system of climatic zones that names regions but not boundaries; for longitude, the system of time zones also names regions. Politically, landmasses are divided into regions. Normally, political boundaries are not named except secondarily, as a product of the regions, such as "the

U.S.-Canadian border." The elements of a clock face correspond to boundaries, which does not imply, of course, that we think of them as infinitesimal. "I'll meet you at two o'clock" varies in its intention of precision from speaker to speaker but always has some margin. Our precise articulation of time switches to regions for periods longer than a day; regions within the day (morning, evening) tend to be a bit vague. Boundaries and regions are modeled in topology.

3. *Systems of representatives* are articulatory structures in which elements that are logically or physically like boundaries or approximations of boundaries function as regions. Colors and musical pitches can compose such systems. A box of crayons or a palette of paints selected from the continuum of colors tends (unless it is very limited) to represent the entire continuum, though this depends on many factors. The case is clearer for melody. Movement between adjacent notes is heard as connected; the absence of the pitches that would sound if a violinist slid his finger from one note to the next is not felt as a skipped space in the scale. A thermometer imposes a system of representatives on temperature. Money, considered as an articulation of economic value, is also a system of representatives. Representatives are studied in conjunction with set theory.

4. A *system of vectors* is not semiotic in origin. It borrows the singularities of the physical world or the biological channels that convey it. The variables of the distinctive features of a language are vectors and find their source in the articulatory capabilities of the phonetic tract. Odors are vectors; each is particular. Vectors are associated with scalars, which articulate their value. These can be oppositions, simply positive or negative in a binary scheme, or there can be systems of representatives as precise as the pitches of notes or as vague as descriptions of odors or tastes (mild, intense, etc.). In a vector system, the number of elements is important to the quality of the articulation. The fewer vectors there are, the more autonomous and articulate the system appears. The model is linear algebra.

5. The *hierarchies* of articulation are based on inclusion. The most salient seem to be hierarchies of disjunct elements in which parts do not overlap and inclusion relationships can be illustrated by tree graphs. However, there are other hierarchical structures. The tonal hierarchy of music is best construed

in terms of regions (intervals) and boundaries (notes)—conjunct parts because each boundary joins two regions. This type of hierarchy also occurs in dance (with positions and motions) and narrative (with situations and actions). Theories of lattices and graphs provide a model.

[*See also* Binarism; Distinctive Features; Hjelmslev; Markedness; Music; Opposition; Pictorial Semiotics; Semiosis; *and* Whorf.]

BIBLIOGRAPHY

Greimas, A. J. *Structural Semantics*. Translated by D. McDowell, R. Schleifer, and A. Velie. Lincoln: University of Nebraska Press, 1983.

Hatten, R. *Musical Meaning in Beethoven: Markedness, Correlation, and Interpretation*. Bloomington: Indiana University Press, 1994.

Hockett, C. *A Course on Modern Linguistics*. New York: Macmillan, 1958.

Lévi-Strauss, C. *Structural Anthropology*. Translated by C. Jacobson and B. Schoepf. New York: Basic Books, 1968.

Martinet, A. *Elements of General Linguistics*. Chicago: University of Chicago Press, 1967.

Prieto, L. *Messages et signaux*. Paris: Presses universitaires de France, 1966.

Salus, M., and P. Salus. *Cognition, Opposition, and the Lexicon*. Toronto Semiotic Circle Monographs, no. 3. Toronto: Victoria University, 1978.

Shapiro, M. *The Sense of Grammar: Language as Semeiotic*. Bloomington: Indiana University Press, 1983.

—DAVID LIDOV

ARTIFICIAL INTELLIGENCE. As a discipline, artificial intelligence (commonly referred to as AI) has fuzzy boundaries and no clear definition; its goals are practical: "making computers smart" or "building machines capable of performing intelligent behavior and/or cognitive tasks." Such goals apply to many different situations in our everyday lives: language understanding, generating language and texts, any kind of problem solving from puzzles to scientific discoveries, analyzing visual images in fractions of seconds, planning and learning, representing any kind of knowledge, and so on. Most of these tasks obviously require some form of modeling of semiotic competence.

AI was first conceived of by Alan Turing (1912–1954), who adumbrated the construction of computers and proposed a test that could decide whether a machine is thinking or not. The machine passes the Turing test if a human interacting with a computer believes that the observed communication is being conducted between two humans. AI was "officially" launched in 1956 at a conference at Dartmouth College, at which leading experts in the fields of computer science, psychology, linguistics, and cybernetics met and outlined the program of artificial intelligence.

As computer-programming languages, hardware, and software progressed at a fast pace, AI attracted abundant research funds, which made it possible to build the powerful computers that AI needed to test its hypotheses. This momentum led to the creation of chess-playing programs, theory-proving programs, and the simulation of simple cognitive tasks. Around the same time, cognitive psychology developed quite similar concepts for the simulation and explanation of cognitive abilities. Its compatibility with AI's theories brought scientists from both fields to close cooperation.

Having expanded greatly in terms of theoretical improvement, resources, and applications, AI now influences both the academic world and everyday life. Three semiotically relevant themes dominate the theoretical basis of AI:

1. *Knowledge representation.* To exhibit "intelligent" behavior, an artificial or natural cognitive system must have knowledge about its environment. The different forms in which this knowledge is "stored" in the system (computer) are called principles or methods of knowledge representation. In traditional AI, the form of symbolic representation has become very important; it says in short that all knowledge can be represented in symbolic/propositional structures. Allen Newell and Herbert Simon's Physical Symbol Systems Hypothesis (Newell and Simon, 1976; rev. Newell, 1980) is the most extreme position in this approach. There are several forms of symbolic knowledge representation such as rules, frames, scripts, and semantic networks. The connectionist approach offers an alternative, however, proposing that knowledge is represented implicitly in the connection weights that determine the system's behavioral dynamics without the mediation of any symbols.

2. *Knowledge manipulation and inference.* If we have a certain domain and its representation in a representational space, we can execute operations on these structures. In the case of symbolic representation, we are manipulating symbols according to certain rules and algorithms (e.g., we can draw inferences on the given facts and rules or in a semantic network). In the case of connectionist networks, activations spread through the network and generate patterns of activations that lead to the externalization of behavior.

3. *Simulation.* From the first two propositions, we can conclude that the concept of simulation plays an extremely important role in AI. By *simulation* we mean that a problem, knowledge domain, task, or other issue is first transformed into a representational space. This construct or formal structure of relations acts as a kind of model of reality; we can apply an inference algorithm or rules to this model and change parameters, derive new parameters or symbols, and so on. This process can be compared to the simulation of, say, a flight of an airplane. The models that are used there exist only in the representational space of the computers but are so realistic that most pilots learn to fly on such simulators. Similarly, a certain aspect of our world or knowledge domain can be mapped to a formal knowledge-representation structure, and simulations in the form of inference programs can be executed over this structure. Reality is simulated in the dynamics of an artificial representational space. The results are "brought back to reality" by an act of interpretation by the user.

These three concepts represent the basis for AI, its methods, and applications, such as the creation of expert systems. In general, expert systems represent the most important commercial application of AI.

Basic research in AI is related closely to cognitive science, as its main interest lies in the investigation and the study of intelligent behavior. This implies an interdisciplinary cooperation between cognitive psychology, linguistics, and computer science. Nevertheless, computer science is dominating the process of research, as most models are based on and constrained by computer-science methods, such as certain knowledge-representation or reasoning techniques or hardware constraints.

In AI, a number of problems remain unsolved or unaddressed.

1. *Methodological problems.* Traditional AI has clearly reached its limits in our days. The reason for this can be found in a lack of methodology and in rather product-oriented basic research. AI has become a typical field of engineering in which each solution that solves a given problem in an appropriate manner counts as a solution to the problem. Such a strategy would be acceptable from an engineering

perspective if AI researchers do not try to "expand" it from claims about very small and formal domains to claims of explaining cognitive processes and general problem solving. Such claims can hardly be justified by traditional methods of knowledge representation and manipulation.

2. *Lack of interdisciplinarity.* Due to the strong product orientation, no truly interdisciplinary cooperation has been established. Thus, while we might achieve quite interesting and good results in very specific problems, we will not achieve a deeper or more general understanding of cognitive processes.

3. *Focus on optimization.* As an implication of AI's product-oriented strategy, we can find almost no basic research in the field. What is being called basic research is more or less the addition of new features and the adapting and optimizing of existing methods and strategies. There are no quantum leaps or revolutions (in the sense of Thomas Kuhn's paradigm shifts) to be expected. This is due also to the pseudointerdisciplinary structure and to the lack of interest in achieving deeper understanding of very general and epistemological problems, such as knowledge or language per se. This leads us to the next point:

4. *Lack of philosophical/epistemological background.* Most AI researchers neglect or even ignore philosophical and epistemological issues in their field. Only when a discipline has reached its limits do some people start asking why there are problems that cannot be solved with the traditional methods. In many cases, philosophy or epistemology can show the reasons for the failure of a certain approach or mechanism. It has turned out, especially in the question of knowledge representation, that epistemology has a very long tradition that could be quite helpful in avoiding dead ends in research.

5. *Naive assumptions about knowledge representation.* We can find very often quite naive assumptions about knowledge and its representation in traditional AI; take, for instance, the symbolic approach—it never reflects one of the central questions in the context of knowledge representation: How can knowledge or the meaning of a symbol evolve or change? It assumes implicitly that there is a given meaning and thus pushes back the interesting process of symbolization onto the user. Another example is the rather naive view of knowledge representation as the result of a process of mapping from the environment to the knowledge-representation structure; an iso- or homomorphic relation between these two domains is assumed. These assumptions about knowledge representation lead to the problems and limits of traditional AI. These limits concern, for instance, the very important representations of common sense or implicit knowledge.

Without considering alternative methods in an interdisciplinary context that is also interested in achieving a deeper understanding of cognitive processes, it seems that AI will find it difficult to solve these problems.

[*See also* Algorithm; Computer; Connectionism; Cybernetics; Expert Systems; Knowledge Representation; *and* Turing.]

BIBLIOGRAPHY

Boden, M. A., ed. *The Philosophy of Artificial Intelligence.* New York: Oxford University Press, 1990.

Newell, A. "Physical Symbol Systems." In *Cognitive Science* 4 (1980): 135–183.

Newell, A., and H. A. Simon. "Computer Science as Empirical Inquiry: Symbols and Search." (1976) In *Mind Design,* edited by J. Haugeland, pp. 35–46. Cambridge, Mass.: MIT Press, 1981.

Winston, P. H. *Artificial Intelligence.* 2d ed. Reading, Mass.: Addison-Wesley, 1984.

—MARKUS PESCHL

ARTIFICIAL LANGUAGE, like "natural language" is generally regarded as a self-explanatory term. Like many divisions of nature from culture, however, natural and artificial languages form a somewhat ambiguous opposition. A straightforward interpretation might be this: The rules of a natural language are intuitive or instinctive and unconscious; an artificial language is one formed and controlled by deliberated, explicit, conscious rules. There certainly are languages that meet this criterion for artificiality, but it is not clear that any languages are known in which the rules are purely intuitive or unconscious.

It is possible for an artificial language (a calculus) to be meaningless—to have no semantic dimension—in the limited sense that it generates propositions that do not predicate anything about anything. However, artificial languages, at least the most prominent ones, such as Boolean algebra and generative grammar, do represent something in that they are constructed as models or experiments. The project of artificial language remains psychologically ambitious. Noam

Chomsky's mathematical models of language are in themselves artificial languages that in some interpretations, purport to simulate the human brain.

Nelson Goodman (1968) has constructed notational systems formally as a class of maximally articulate artificial languages with explicit, formal rules. In summary form, the chief principles are these: (1) A notational system has a finite vocabulary of "characters" (we could substitute *signs* or *elements*). Characters are abstract. They are what Charles Sanders Peirce would call *legisigns* or *types*. (2) Each character can be represented by "inscriptions" (*tokens, vehicles*). Technically, the point of Goodman's formulation is to reconstruct the type-token relation, which he finds unclear in Peirce's exposition. Kari Kurkela finds a parallel imprecision in Goodman's version, which he attempts to remedy in his *Note and Tone* (1986). (3) Given any one inscription, there must be no ambiguity about which character it stands for. For example, this requirement is met by printed letters (inscriptions) with respect to the twenty-six characters of the alphabet; however, handwritten letters cannot be guaranteed to qualify, since it might be unclear whether my handwritten inscription is an *a* or a *d* and, by a further rule, we may not appeal to context.

Goodman calls the preceding constraints syntactic; the following are semantic: (1) Each character must represent a class of objects. (2) The classes of objects must not overlap. (3) Given any object, there must be no ambiguity concerning which class it belongs to and which character can represent it. To continue the same example, the normal English alphabet represents sounds, but the classes of sounds do overlap, disqualifying the alphabet as a notation for sound. The *o* in *got* and the *a* in *father* are not clearly distinct. The phonetic alphabet is designed to avoid such ambiguity, and it is intended as a notation in Goodman's sense.

Goodman's definition represents an idealized type. A notational system is a combinatorial system that represents another combinatorial system. Notations must represent strictly articulated objects. There are not many pure cases, but we can review a few candidates.

Digits as a notation for integers might fit the bill but not when they are used to notate the real numbers because of the requirement for finite decidability. Decimal 17, binary 10001, and Hex 11 are either representations of the same number by different compound representamina (forms) in different digital-notation systems (a "realist" view) or they represent each other (a "nominalist" view). Integers can be notated because they are distinct and nonoverlapping. The digits are also distinct, and they are of finite types. Given an expression in digits in a particular system, there is no ambiguity about which integer it represents.

Goodman's paradigm case of a notational system is musical notation, which is explicit regarding pitches and rhythms. When a note on paper is drawn properly, there is no ambiguity concerning which pitch it represents. Assuming that the instrument that plays the note is roughly in tune, there is no ambiguity as to whether or not a note played is a note represented by the note on paper. Only the pitches and durational relations of music allow strict notation, for these, subsumed by systems of representatives, have a fully articulated vocabulary. Loudness does not. There are written terms for loudness (*p* [piano], *pp*, *f* [forte], *ff*). Those terms meet the syntactic criteria—we can tell them apart—but they do not meet the semantic criteria since their meanings are vague. Musical notation is as true an example of an artificial language as FORTRAN, BASIC, or CPLUS. Music per se, however, is not, though European classical music developed under the influence of notation and is much the different for it.

Goodman asks why music can be notated but painting cannot. His answer concerns syntactic articulation. Paintings do not normally resolve into combinations of distinct objects from a finite vocabulary, like the notes of music or the syllables of speech. On the other hand, he takes dance notation to be potentially as influential as musical notation. He holds that dance, like music and unlike painting, is composed of combinations of elements from a discrete, finite vocabulary. His argument that dance and music have this characteristic hinges on his analysis of the fact that we can recognize performances in either medium as instances of particular compositions. I can walk into the hall and say, "That is Beethoven's Fifth" or "That is *Giselle*." Ballets and musical compositions are what he calls allographic works. I recognize them despite glitches and other differences so long as the performances comply with the composed combinations of vocabulary elements. In these terms, paintings are autographic, in that ultimately the reproduction can not substitute for the original. With musical compositions and dances, every performance, good or bad, stands in relation to the conceptual construction on its own; there is not one "original."

Goodman's comparison of dance and musical notations neglects to consider that musical notation has reference to a system of representatives that had already been impressed on singing by the influence of instruments. Dance styles have vocabularies that also establish a system of representatives for movement, but the widely practiced system of notation developed by Rudolph Laban (1879–1958) is not keyed directly to any such system. It is vectorial and hinges on the perception of angles with unspecified precision. Laban's notation does not appear to meet Goodman's requirements for a notational system.

The notation of a text is a model of the text, but not all models are notations. We speak of a sign as a model when (1) the representamen is constructed entirely from a vocabulary of known elements and known relations; (2) we understand the resemblance of the representamen to the object to be such that we can learn about the object by studying the representamen alone; and (3) the actual connection between the representamen and object is immaterial.

A musical notation is a model for a performance. A blueprint is a notational model for a house. The conductor's beat is a nonnotational model for a symphonic performance. A photograph is not a model, first because we do not know all its elements. For example, in a black-and-white photograph, the various grays and the various shapes cannot be assumed to be known. The second criteria is satisfied: We can learn about the photographed object from the photograph. The third criteria, however, is not: Our reliance on the photograph results from its physical derivation; the actual connection between model and object is not immaterial. The mathematical equation for an ellipse is truly a model (whether correct or not) for an orbit. In general we speak of theories as models for their objects. Diagrams aspire to the status of models.

[See also Articulation; Blissymbolics; Diagrams; Goodman; Number Representation; Peirce; Realism and Nominalism; and Type and Token.]

BIBLIOGRAPHY

Goodman, N. Language of Art. Indianapolis: Bobbs-Merrill, 1968.

Kurkela, K. Note and Tone: A Semantic Analysis of Conventional Music Notation. Helsinki: Suomen Musiikkitieteellinen Seura Musikvetenskapliga Sälskapet i Finland, 1986.

Laban, R. Choreutics: The Language of Movements, a Guidebook to Choreutics, edited by L. Ullmann. Boston: Plays, 1974.

—DAVID LIDOV

ARTIFICIAL LIFE. The field known as artificial life (AL) is the study of biology through the attempt to create life by artificial means. Many researchers believe that artificial creations—such as synthetic chemicals, robots, and most of all computers—have evolved to a level of complexity such that the quest to achieve human-made life is worth a serious consideration. Artificial creations are already capable of exhibiting, singly, many attributes once restricted to natural biological entities; humans can create things that "flock," "explore their environments," "parasitize a host," "communicate," "decode messages," "compete for limited resources," "reproduce," "evolve by mutation and selection," and so on. Of course, any one of these attributions can be challenged as being too metaphorical. For instance, some might argue that the "flocking" of robots is too different from the natural behavior of birds to be properly called flocking. Few would want to argue that the possession of any *one* of these attributes is sufficient to endow an artificial system with life. But these objections notwithstanding, a critical mass of researchers are attempting to create life artificially with more technological credibility than at any time in the past.

Given the early stage of development of this discipline, it would be premature to start with a detailed definition of its object. It is rather a set of research programs that interface with semiotics or biosemiotics, since AL presupposes some kind of artificial semiosis. At this point, we can point to a few generally agreed-upon observations.

First, AL can be seen as complementing biology—particularly theoretical biology—in two interrelated ways: whereas traditional biology is concerned primarily with the analysis of living organisms and biological phenomena, artificial life is concerned with the *synthesis* of lifelike behavior in various media, and whereas traditional biology studies life as we know it (the carbon chain–based entities we find on earth), artificial life strives to explore the possibilities of life as it could be. As science identifies characteristics that purport to be general characteristics of or phenomena related to living things, AL explores the full range of mechanisms that can give rise to such phenomena, regardless of whether those mechanisms are like those that we find in our own particular biopshere.

Second, AL shares many superficial similarities and some philosophical methodologies with artificial intelligence. This affinity is sometimes characterized in the form of an analogy: "artificial life is to biology as artificial intelligence is to psychology." Both fields depend heavily on computational models of their phenomena of interest. Both attempt through synthesis to expand domains of study traditionally analyzed by biology and psychology. AL has as a goal the creation of human-made biological entities, while artificial intelligence has as a goal the creation of human-made psychological entities. Both fields place a lot of weight on the assumption that through the attempt to create artificial examples of normally natural phenomena we will at the very least come to a better understanding of those natural phenomena.

Just as is sometimes done in artificial intelligence debates, it seems reasonable to distinguish between "weak" and "strong" versions of the goals of AL. The weak version holds that computers, robots, and other physical experiments, if appropriately designed, provide science with powerful tools with which to formulate and test biological theories. Thus, AL would be on par with statistics, electron microscopy, or any other field that develops new techniques and formalisms useful for advancing biological science. The strong version adds to the weak version the claim that computers, robots, and other physical experiments, if appropriately designed, actually could be biological systems. According to this stronger thesis, AL has as its goal the extension of the number of entities in the world that can be considered truly biological. Following the claim that AL studies life as it could be, the ultimate goal of AL is the creation of new, human-made life.

Third, since we now have a schema with which to approach the large amount of work being done under the rubric of AL, we can divide the field up into several rough subdisciplines. Two areas of research will be considered here. The first, genetic algorithms, pertains to the weaker thesis and attempts to complement the areas of traditional biology that involve evolutionary theory. The second, computational biology, belongs to the stronger thesis and seeks to create "life in a computer." In trying to instantiate life in a medium (computer memory) not usually associated with genuine biological phenom-

ena, this area of AL hopes to expand the empirical basis upon which biology is based. These two general projects can give an idea of the potential of this new, developing discipline.

Genetic algorithms make it possible to test models of evolutionary behavior. There are still many open questions in theoretical biology about the roles played by many of the characteristics of natural evolution. For instance: What are the comparative advantages and disadvantages of sexual and asexual reproduction? How did sexual reproduction arise in the first place? What roles do the large amount of apparent redundancy and "junk" DNA play in evolutionary dynamics? What is the importance of genetic diversity to population dynamics? Can there be too much diversity or too little? How does something resembling cooperation come into existence in a system characterized by Darwinian selection? These are merely a few of the interesting evolutionary questions for theoretical biology. Important progress has been made with traditional experimental-biology approaches, but AL offers a new arena within which answers can be formulated and approached.

The term *genetic algorithm* refers to a set of formalisms based on the concept of evolution by natural selection. Although research on generic algorithms predates the conception of artificial life proper, it has become one of the main areas of concentrated research that can be considered under this rubric. The advantage to biology resulting from the use of genetic-algorithm formalism lies in the ability to crisply pose questions of interest. What are the relative advantages of the various genetic operators (point mutation, crossover, etc.) present in biological systems? One might begin by designing a genetic algorithm that exhibits the identified features of some version of natural evolution and some natural but arbitrary set of initial conditions. The relative contributions of each of the genetic operators can then be explored by generating multiple runs of the genetic operators. What happens with the rate of mutation turned up or turned off? What happens if you disallow crossover? Genetic algorithms hold out the interesting possibility of answering questions such as these, both for computer simulations and for the real biological phenomena they model. But the goal of artificially creating new forms of life is more daunting.

In recent years, a most intriguing phenomenon that blurs the distinction between computers and biology has appeared: the computer virus. These small bits of computer code, which come in a variety of forms and can affect their computer hosts in a variety of ways, have begun to plague computer users the world over as they spontaneously replicate from machine to machine, wreaking havoc or causing mirth. The use here of a biological metaphor is eerily appropriate. Biological viruses, themselves occupying an uncertain position relative to the line between living and not living, consist primarily of small strings of genetic code that inject themselves into organisms in order to take over their hosts' energy resources for the purposes of further replication of the virus's own code. The appropriateness of the biological metaphor when referring to the behavior of certain fragments of computer code points to the increasing complexity of computational environments. As the power of computational technology has increased, the idea of attempting to replicate biological phenomena within the physical spaces enclosed by modern computers has become more and more feasible.

Perhaps the most interesting attempt in this domain is the research begun by Thomas Ray with his Tierra simulator. Using Tierra, Ray has evolved a variety of computer "organisms" that compete for processor time and space in the RAM (the high-speed computer memory) of a computer, which can be thought of as the "environment" within which Ray's putative artificial organisms exist. To keep from begging the crucial question, we will refer to these bits of code as stringlets. These stringlets are short strings of zeros and ones that Tierra (which is akin to an operating system) can execute. Before describing an imaginary run of Tierra, a few details need to be discussed. First, Tierra includes a subprogram called the "reaper," which culls off a percentage of the population whenever it gets above a certain level. The stringlets, when they first come into existence, are placed on the bottom of a list kept by the reaper. The reaper removes the members of the population who are listed at the top of the list. Stringlets can move themselves down the list by properly executing code or up the list by improperly doing so. As in the real world, no stringlet can escape the reaper forever. The second detail is that variation is introduced into the stringlet population in three ways. Tierra will occasionally (1) flip a random bit in the RAM; (2) randomly introduce an error when copying a string of code; and (3) randomly flip a bit in a stringlet when reading that bit during execution. So, like genetic algorithms, Tierra contains all the basic elements of

natural selection: a large population of entities that must compete for limited resources in order to make copies of themselves—copies that may be imperfect due to the possibility of mutation.

A sample run might go like this: the RAM is "inoculated" by placing into it a handcrafted, eighty-instruction-long stringlet. This "ancestor" has been designed to be a relatively efficient replicator in the Tierra environment. When the run begins, the RAM soon begins to fill up with copies of the ancestor, and the reaper begins culling the population. As mutations occur, different stringlets begin to appear, but as most of these mutations are nonbeneficial, they generally fail to thrive (that is to say, most mutations lead to stringlets that are unable to replicate themselves). Eventually, a "successful" mutant appears, say a forty-five-instruction-long "parasite" that, when located next to an ancestor, can trick that stringlet into replicating the *parasite* instead of itself. The parasites and their ancestor hosts then enter a predator-prey cycle as each population places a check on the population level of the other; that is, until a mutant of the ancestor appears that is immune to the parasites' trick. Tierra can continue indefinitely in this fashion as newer and more complicated stringlets evolve in competition with others for the limited resources it doles out.

Ray's work is important for several reasons. First, it demonstrates concretely something that has been suggested by the emerging sciences of complexity for many years: that systems of even relatively simple interacting entities can exhibit complex and dynamic behavior without perturbations introduced from outside the system. When confronted with a system exhibiting some stable behavior for a long period of time that then moves into a highly unstable behavioral state, our commonsense response is to look for some external cause that somehow "kicked" that system into the new behavioral regime. If we see extended periods of slow evolutionary change in the fossil record, for example, punctuated by relatively short periods of fast change (e.g., the Cambrian "explosion" or a "mass extinction" event), our first impulse is to look for causes external to the system (such as the impact of a large meteor or comet). Tierra is an example of a system that exhibits often highly erratic behavior resulting entirely from the *internal* dynamics of the interacting parts that make up the system. The search for internal systemic causes of nonlinear behavior in Tierra might lend help to others who investigate this phenomena in other biological and ecological settings, be it explosive disease epidemics or the sudden onset of fibrillation in heart muscle.

Second, as an example of artificial life, Tierra raises important philosophical questions for theoretical biology. Exactly what is the biological status of Ray's stringlets? When writing of the results of AL research, there is generally a liberal use of scare quotes. Are these legitimate? If so, on the basis of what do we make attributions of *organism, living, evolution,* and other such terms to observed phenomena?

A proponent of the stronger AL thesis would be quick to point out that my characterization of Tierra's stringlets is misleading. They are not strings of zeros and ones but a physical pattern of high and low voltages that humans often *interpret* as zeros and ones. If we could peek into the working memory of a computer running the Tierra simulator, what we would see is an initially random scattering of high and low voltages that begins to change as one particular pattern of high and low voltages (what we call the "ancestor") replicates itself. The proponent of strong AL would argue that it is the particular properties (such as replication) of physical patterns that are what life is all about. A system such as Tierra is at least a candidate to be an AL system because it has properties like those of a test tube containing replicating bacteria, even though the two systems are different in many of the details of their makeup.

No doubt this field will see a lot of changes in its composition and concerns as it progresses over the following years. As computers and other artificial media become more complex and capable of supporting more complicated phenomena, AL is sure to grow. The issues discussed in this field are sure to become more and more important as our power to biologically engineer the life we find around us increases.

[*See also* Algorithm; Autopoiesis; Evolution; Meme; *and* Memetics.]

BIBLIOGRAPHY

Boden, M. A., ed. *The Philosophy of Artificial Life.* Oxford: Oxford University Press, 1995.

Emmeche, C. "A Semiotical Reflection on Biology, Living Signs, and Artificial Life." *Biology and Philosophy* 6 (1991): 325–340.

Emmeche, C. *The Garden in the Machine: The Emerging Science of Artificial Life.* Translated by Steven Sampson. Princeton: Princeton University Press, 1994.

Goldberg, D. *Genetic Algorithms in Search, Optimization, and Machine Learning.* Reading, Mass.: Addison-Wesley, 1989.

Holland, J. H. *Adaptation in Natural and Artificial Systems.* Ann Arbor: University of Michigan Press, 1975.

Holland, J. H. "Genetic Algorithms." *Scientific American* (July 1992): 66–72.

Langton, C. G., ed. *Artificial Life: The Proceedings of an Interdisciplinary Workshop on the Synthesis and Simulation of Living Systems.* Santa Fe Institute Studies in the Sciences of Complexity, vol. 6. Redwood City, Calif.: Addison-Wesley, 1989.

Langton, C. G., ed. *Artificial Life III.* Santa Fe Institute Studies in the Sciences of Complexity, vol. 17. Redwood City, Calif.: Addison-Wesley, 1994.

Langton, C. G., C. Taylor, J. D. Farmer, and S. Rasmussen, eds. *Artificial Life II.* Santa Fe Institute Studies in the Sciences of Complexity, vol. 10. Redwood City, Calif.: Addison-Wesley, 1991.

Varela, F. J., and P. Bourgine, eds. *Toward a Practice of Autonomous Systems: Proceedings of the First European Conference on Artificial Life.* Cambridge, Mass.: MIT Press, 1992.

—BRIAN L. KEELEY

AUGUSTINE OF HIPPO (354–430), often known as the last of the church fathers—those early Christian writers, both Greek and Latin, who established the foundations of Christianity in literary and intellectual history—and the first of the medievals who, cut off from Greek learning for centuries after the collapse of the Roman empire, developed in Europe an indigenously Latin civilization and intellectual culture out of which eventually emerged the so-called modern world (Gilson, 1949).

Semiotic historiography can follow this conventional periodization. Augustine was the first to articulate explicitly the idea of sign as it has come to form the basis for semiotics in the contemporary sense. This seminal role has been described variously (Manetti, 1993; Beuchot, 1986) but probably best by Umberto Eco, Roberto Lambertini, Costantino Marmo, and Andrea Tabarroni (1986), who stated that Augustine was the first to propose a "general science" or "doctrine" where sign becomes the genus of which words and natural symptoms are both species.

To understand Augustine's contribution on its own terms, one must look directly at the definition of sign he proposed and understand something of the context in which he proposed it. For this purpose, looking at the sources of influence on Augustine, such as the Stoics or rhetoricians of classical Roman antiquity, is only marginally helpful. For Augustine is important not for the way in which he assimilated his sources but for the way in which he transformed them with the explicit idea that the sign transcends the ancient distinctions between nature and culture and between reality and imagination in order to be able to mediate the structuring of human experience. Before Augustine, there were only natural signs. After Augustine, there are conventional signs as well.

Augustine makes his revolutionary proposal in *De doctrina christiana* (c.397–426), whose context is as much religious and theological as it is philosophical. In book 1, Augustine opens with the distinction between signs and things, saying he will devote book 1 to the consideration of things and book 2 to the consideration of signs. Indeed, when he comes to the second book, he begins the discussion with what he intends to be a perfectly general definition of sign: "A sign is a thing which, over and above the impression which it makes on the senses, makes another come into thought."

Despite this beginning on a note promissory of a general semiotics in precisely the sense never dreamed of by ancient thought and sought anew in postmodern contemporary developments, a very curious thing happens. No sooner has Augustine enunciated what we would call a semiotic point of view (the treatment of things purely in terms of their signifying function) than he closes it down again by narrowing his consideration to some very specific religious and theological concerns. Thus, he begins with a whole series of distinctions covering practically the entire range of semiotic phenomena: natural versus conventional signs, signs as they function in animal cognition versus their function in human cognition, words and groans, and flags. But he distinguishes all these phenomena only in order to exclude them as being not germane to his more limited immediate purpose, which is to develop the specific case of the conventional signs instituted by God, namely, the words of Scripture and the sacraments. The opening distinctions establish the semiotic point of view and sweep over the horizon of prelinguistic, linguistic, and postlinguistic semiotic phenomena, but when the dust settles, far from developing this standpoint or vindicating its foundations, Augustine leaves us with no more than a definition that, however it might be justified ultimately, hangs in the thin air of pure presupposition. The further discussion of sign throughout Augustine's vast writings leaves

many paradoxes for the Latins to wrestle with, having always at their center "a constantly alive, burning and inevitable problem" (Beuchot, 1986).

Eventually, the Latin age that Augustine opened responded directly to the challenge posed by Augustine's general definition, and the last four and half centuries of the so-called medieval period occupied itself with, among other things, the theoretical foundations and ultimate presuppositions of the general notion of sign originally proposed by Augustine. But Augustine himself did not take up the project and indeed showed a profound ambivalence toward the role of signs in human experience, as exhibited by his celebrated little book *De magistro* (On the Teacher, c.388–391). This essay divides into two parts. The first part proves that everything is learned through signs, whereas the second part proves that in reality nothing is learned through signs but only through the illumination of Christ ("the teacher") within the soul.

This ambivalence is not unrelated to the acceptance by the medievals of Augustine's original definition of sign in general, as it served to bring the Scriptures of Christian revelation and the sacraments of Christian religious practice into a focus that facilitated rational discourse about the Christian life. After all, the centuries following Augustine were not only "dark ages" brought on by the collapse of Greek and Roman education; they were also an age of faith in which the primary concern was less with questions of epistemology and nature and more with questions of faith and salvation.

In this context, it was enough that Augustine's understanding of the sign sufficed to encompass the Scriptures and provide as well a basis for the development of sacramental theology. For just as the words of Scripture are in their visible and audible aspects material structures that on being perceived convey thought to something other than the noises heard or marks seen, so, too, are the sacraments perceptible materials that convey to the soul something beyond. As "an outward sign instituted by Christ to give grace," a sacrament is a manifest species of Augustine's sign. This fact, together with Augustine's authority as the "last of the Church Fathers," readily explains the inclusion of Augustine's definition of *signum* in Peter Lombard's *Sentences* (c.1150), the compilation of patristic views that became the basis of theological studies in the medieval university from the twelfth century till the end of the Latin age.

The fourth book of Lombard's *Sentences*, wherein Augustine's definition is incorporated, became the focus of what is in effect the "high semiotics" of the Latin age—namely, sacramental theology as it developed continuously right down to the present day and to a great extent even across the post-Reformation denominational lines of competing Christian sects. For that specifically religious phase of historical-theoretical semiotic development, as for many others (see Sullivan, 1963), Augustine stands astride the split of Renaissance Christianity into Catholic and Protestant as a kind of governing figure over the thinking of both sides. In the matter of semiotics, his influence among the Latins resonates no less in treatises of Clemens Timpler (1616) and Christoph Scheibler (1617) than in those of the Conimbricenses and the *Tractatus de signis* of John Poinsot.

At its very opening point in the work of Augustine, therefore, medieval semiotics envisions two lines of thinking as possibly unified: the ancient one, according to which signs are found only within phenomena of nature, and the Augustinian one, according to which signs are found in cultural phenomena as well. But how the ancient view can be thus assimilated through a general notion of sign such as Augustine has proposed is a complex matter about which Augustine's own work left his successors to wonder and ponder in detail. One of the results of such wonderment and pondering is the whole story of medieval semiotics. Another of the results is the taking up again of Augustine's proposed theme and the threads of the medieval development that worked out its foundational requirements in the work of C. S. Peirce, a principal fountainhead of contemporary semiotic development. But to Augustine belongs the credit of having first conceived of the sign in a general sense that makes semiotics as a unified inquiry possible in the first place.

[*See also* Medieval Semiotics; Poinsot; Semiosis; *and* Sign.]

BIBLIOGRAPHY

Beuchot, M. "Signo y lenguaje en San Agustín." *Dianoia* 32 (1986): 13–26.

Eco, U., et al. "Latratus Canis or: The Dog's Barking." In *Frontiers in Semiotics*, edited by J. Deely, B. Williams, and F. Kruse, pp. 63–79. Bloomington: Indiana University Press, 1986.

Gilson, E. *Introduction à l'étude de Saint Augustin*. 3d ed. Paris: Vrin, 1949.

Manetti, G. "Augustine." In his *Theories of the Sign in Classical Antiquity*, translated by C. Richardson, pp. 157–168. Bloomington: Indiana University Press, 1993.

Sullivan, J. E. *The Image of God: The Doctrine of St. Augustine and Its Influence*. Dubuque, Iowa: Priory Press, 1963.

—JOHN DEELY

AUTOPOIESIS. A transliteration of a Greek word meaning "self-making," the term *autopoiesis* was introduced to semiotics in 1973 by the Chilean biologists Humberto R. Maturana and Francisco J. Varela to name the self-producing organization that is unique to living things. The aim of the theory of autopoiesis is to specify precisely the organization that is necessary and sufficient for a system to be a living system. According to the theory, living systems have a self-producing or autopoietic organization: a living system is defined as a network of processes that simultaneously produce and realize that same network as a unity.

The motivating question about the nature of life is of course an old one in philosophy and biology, going back at least to Aristotle. A comparatively recent ancestor is the nineteenth-century debate between vitalism and mechanism. The vitalists held that life activities could not be understood simply within the framework of efficient or mechanical causality; inherent in such activities is a nonmaterial and nonmechanical animating force. The mechanists, on the other hand, claimed that life could be understood in purely material and mechanical terms.

Maturana and Varela begin from uncompromisingly mechanist premises: no forces or principles not found in the physical universe are to be adduced at any point in the theory. Moreover, living systems are to be treated as machines in a certain abstract sense. Usually, one thinks of a machine as a concrete hardware system with various material components. But at a more abstract level, a machine can be specified entirely in terms of the processes carried out by the components and the relations among those processes. At this level, no reference need be made to the actual (for example, physical or chemical) nature of the components and relations that realize the processes. This level provides what Maturana and Varela call the organization of the machine (the relations that constitute the machine and determine the interactions and transformations it can undergo). One can, however, also talk about the actual nature of the components and their relations—for example, their physical and chemical constitution. This level gives what they call the structure of the machine. The task that Maturana and Varela set for themselves, then, is to specify the particular organization that a system must have if it is to be deemed alive.

Their fundamental claim is that autopoiesis is necessary and sufficient to characterize the organization of living systems: "The autopoietic organization is defined as a unity by a network of productions of components which (i) participate recursively in the same network of productions of components which produced these components, and (ii) realize the network of productions as a unity in the space in which the components exist" (Varela, Maturana, and Uribe, 1974).

The basic idea in this definition is that an autopoietic system exhibits a certain kind of homeostasis—that is, it maintains some of its variables constant or within a limited range of values. In an autopoietic system, the system's own defining network of relations is the fundamental invariant. Thus, the theory of autopoiesis builds on the classical idea of homeostasis but extends it in two significant directions. First, it makes every reference to homeostasis internal to the very system itself through the mutual interconnection of processes; second, it posits this mutual interconnection of processes as the very source of the system's identity or, in biological terms, of its individuality.

There are six criteria for determining whether a system has an autopoietic organization. The system must: (1) have an identifiable boundary; (2) have constitutive elements or components; (3) be a mechanistic system in the sense that the interactions and transformations of its components are determined entirely by the properties and relations of the components; (4) be self-bounded in the sense that relations among the components determine the system's boundary; (5) have a boundary whose components are produced by the interactions of the components of the system; (6) have components that are produced entirely by the interactions and transformations of the components themselves.

It can now be seen how the theory of autopoiesis transforms the idea of mechanism and in so doing moves beyond the conceptual framework of the classical mechanism-vitalism debate. Within the framework provided by autopoiesis, it turns out the vitalists

were wrong that there is no mechanistic explanation of the autonomy of the living, but they were right (and the mechanists wrong) that biological phenomena are not reducible to physics and chemistry. On the one hand, living systems are claimed to be physical autopoietic machines. But introduced into the mechanist framework is an idea that was not available to the nineteenth-century mechanists nor even to classical cybernetics and systems theory: the idea of an organizationally closed, circular concatenation of processes that generates and maintains itself. Furthermore, contrary to the classical mechanist position, the theory of autopoiesis implies that biological phenomena are not reducible to physics and chemistry. Autopoiesis is defined at the level of organization, not structure.

The notion of autopoiesis has had an influence in many fields. In biology, it figures prominently in research on the origins of life and in attempts to model the basic mechanisms of life with simple synthetic chemical systems. It has been invoked by Lynn Margulis in her work on the Gaia theory (Margulis and Sagan, 1997). It has also emerged as one of the central ideas in the new discipline of artificial life, an interdisciplinary combination of computational science, the theory of complex dynamical systems, and theoretical biology. Outside biology, it has figured in a surprisingly wide range of disciplines, from cognitive science and computer design to social and legal theory as well as family therapy. Of particular relevance to semiotics is Varela's development of a formal "calculus for self-reference," based on the British mathematician G. Spencer Brown's "laws of form," to model certain aspects of autopoiesis. These formal developments have found their way into semiotics through the work of Floyd Merrell (1991). One topic has been especially prominent in the wide-ranging discussion and debate about autopoiesis: are there, or can there be, different types of realization of the autopoietic organization? In particular, can there be higher-order realizations of autopoiesis at, for example, the multicellular level, the level of the biosphere, or social levels?

These questions have been discussed extensively by Maturana and Varela, though their writings seem to contain different positions on the issue. In their most recent collaborative work, Maturana and Varela (1987) use the term *metacellulars* to refer to systems that contain cells as structural components, and they call such systems second-order autopoietic systems.

Second-order autopoietic systems thus include multicellular organisms, colonies, and societies, since all contain cells as structural components, though the patterns of relation are fundamentally different in each case. They then raise the question: Are some metacellulars autopoietic unities in their own rights—that is, are they also first-order autopoietic systems? They decide to leave the question open because although the molecular processes involved in single-cell autopoiesis are known in great detail, there is no comparable body of knowledge that describes how the components and relations in an organism (let alone in a colony or society) make it an autopoietic unity (if it is one). Varela's position, on the other hand, as detailed in his 1979 book *Principles of Biological Autonomy,* seems clear: he holds that the notion of autopoiesis applies properly only to the cell. A phenomenon is biological to the extent that it depends on cellular autopoiesis, but higher-order systems such as multicellular organisms, insect colonies, and animal societies are described as having an autonomous but not autopoietic organization. An autonomous organization is defined as any operationally closed network of processes that constitutes the system as a unity in the domain in which the processes exist. Autonomy thus becomes the generic concept under which autopoiesis falls as a particular species.

[*See also* Artificial Life; Biosemiotics; Cybernetics; Gaia Hypothesis; *and* Semiosis.]

BIBLIOGRAPHY

Fleischaker, G. R. "Autopoiesis: The Status of Its System Logic." *BioSystems* 22 (1988): 37–49.

Margulis, L., and D. Sagan. *Slanted Truths: Essays on Gaia, Symbiosis, and Evolution.* New York: Springer-Verlag, 1997.

Maturana, H. R., and F. J. Varela. *Autopoiesis and Cognition: The Realization of the Living.* Boston Studies in the Philosophy of Science, vol. 42. Dordrecht: D. Reidel, 1980. Contains the English version of the original 1973 paper in Spanish, "Autopoiesis and the Organization of the Living."

Maturana, H. R. and F. J. Varela. *The Tree of Knowledge: The Biological Roots of Human Understanding.* Boston: New Science Library, 1987.

Merrell, F. *Signs Becoming Signs: Our Perfusive, Pervasive Universe.* Bloomington: Indiana University Press, 1991.

Mingers, J. *Self-Producing Systems: Implications and Applications of Autopoiesis.* New York: Plenum Press, 1994.

Varela, F. J. *Principles of Biological Autonomy.* New York: Elsevier North Holland, 1979.

Varela, F. J., H. R. Maturana, and R. Uribe. "Autopoiesis: The Organization of the Living Systems, Its Characterization and a Model." *BioSystems* 5 (1974): 187–196.

Varela, F. J., and P. Bourgine, eds. *Toward a Practice of Autonomous Systems: Proceedings of the First European Conference on Artificial Life.* Cambridge, Mass.: MIT Press, 1992.

—EVAN THOMPSON

B

BAKHTIN, MIKHAIL M. (1895–1975), Russian cultural and literary theorist whose life and works remain the object of controversies. Several key episodes in his life are shrouded in mystery, and the textual history of his works is extremely complicated due in part to the political context in which they were written.

Born in Orel, Russia, Bakhtin studied classics, literature, and philosophy at Saint Petersburg University. He then spent two years teaching secondary school in Nevel in western Russia, where he became part of a group of intellectuals that included Valentin Nikolaevich Voloshinov. Their activities involved organizing concerts and public lectures.

In 1919, Bakhtin published a two-page article entitled "Art and Answerability," a brief, abstract consideration of one's relationship to art and life, in which he contends that individuals have a moral responsibility to make connections between their lives and their experiences of art. In 1920, Bakhtin moved to Vitebsk, Byelorussia, a lively cultural center where several artists (including Casimir Malevich and Marc Chagall) and intellectuals such as Pavel Nikolaevich Medvedev (1891–1938) and Ivan Ivanovich Sollertinskij (1902–1944) also lived. What was later known as the Bakhtin Circle was formed, with Bakhtin providing the main intellectual inspiration. In his writings of the 1920s, Bakhtin does not seem to have made any explicit statements about the Russian Revolution or the political and religious issues of his time.

In 1924, Bakhtin returned to Saint Petersburg (Leningrad), where he led a difficult material existence working at the Historical Institute, giving private lectures, and doing some consulting for the state publishing house. During the early 1920s, he continued to be at the center of a circle of intellectuals (Voloshinov, Medvedev, and others) and wrote an extended essay on moral responsibility and aesthetics. It was published in Russian in two fragments after his death, under the titles "Toward a Philosophy of the Act [or Deed]" and "Author and Hero in Aesthetic Activity" (1920–1923). These can be seen as participating in one of the central philosophical debates of the time on neo-Kantianism. (Other essays of the early 1920s seem to have been lost.) Kant's views involved negotiating philosophically the split between the world (the realm of objects) and the mind (the world of concepts). Some of Bakhtin's contemporaries and teachers, who had been influenced by the neo-Kantianism in vogue in Germany at the turn of the century, attached great importance to the transcendental or idealist aspect of Kant's synthesis of the world/mind split. Bakhtin's early work, which is also informed by a keen interest in physics and physiology and which emphasizes questions of perception and materiality, can be seen as an attempt to go against the idealist trends of neo-Kantianism.

"Author and Hero in Aesthetic Activity" is a speculative, erudite work that explores ethical and aesthetic acts in axiological terms (i.e., in terms of values). Bakhtin wrote it during a period of intense literary debate in Russia about not only neo-Kantianism but formalism, a new and complex approach to literature that tended to schematize literary works and to see them primarily as the sum of their devices or techniques rather than in historical or sociological terms. Also prominent during this time were other literary movements such as symbolism, futurism, and a sociological approach based in Marxism. "Author and Hero," written in five sections, deals with broad philosophical questions: how do the parts of a work relate to the whole? what is the nature of one's relation to another person? what is the nature of an author's relation to fictional characters? The focus of the essay shifts back and forth between considerations about literature and life in general in an effort to develop an overall conceptual framework within the field of aesthetics. The first three parts of the essay explore the "spatial form" of the hero, the "temporal whole" of the hero, and "the whole of the hero as a whole of meaning." The fourth section examines the "problem of the author," and this is followed by a concluding section. At times descriptive and at others prescriptive, Bakhtin sees the relation between authors and heroes (and between egos and others) as dynamic, conflictual, and constantly evolving (or open-ended). He prefers authors who allow their characters "a surplus of aesthetic being"—that is, authors who allow their heroes to appear to speak for themselves in an independent way, as opposed to authors who use characters as a means of expressing their own personal opinions. Such a view, when applied to the realm of human relations, insists on the fundamental, concrete, simultaneous necessity of other people without whom the establishment of one's identity would be impossible.

In 1924, Bakhtin wrote a polemical essay on poetics, "The Problem of Content, Material, and Form in Verbal Art," in an effort to go beyond Kant's categories and in opposition to the formalists. Bakhtin insists on the necessity of accounting for perception or cognition in a unified aesthetics, at the same time accusing the formalists of a rudimentary psychologism.

Bakhtin's celebrated book on Fyodor Dostoevsky was published in 1929 as *Problems of Dostoevsky's Creative Works* and then substantially revised and published in 1963 as *Problems of Dostoevsky's Poetics*. Dostoevsky is the creator of the polyphonic novel, a novel in which a plurality of distinct, unmerged voices and consciousnesses (including those of the author) exist not in aesthetic harmony but in conflict. This is one kind of antiformalist, anticanonical dialogism that Bakhtin also develops in his later essays on the novel. Dostoevsky's novel is not a genre but rather a particular novelistic form that can be traced back to the Menippean satires and beyond. One of the most frequently cited chapters of this book is the final one, "Discourse in Dostoevsky," in which Bakhtin presents a typology of double-voiced discourses. The Russian word for discourse (*slovo*) can mean both the utterance and the word. Bakhtin discusses such literary devices as stylization, parody, and polemic as examples of double-voiced discourse. His focus is thus on the multiple and equally powerful positions that can coexist in a text (polyphony) and the types of language (or utterance) at an author's disposal.

During the 1920s, three books, now known as the "disputed texts," appeared in print: *Freudianism: A Critical Sketch* (1927) and *Marxism and the Philosophy of Language: Basic Problems in Sociolinguistics* (1929) were published under the name of V. N. Voloshinov; *The Formal Method in Literary Study: A Critical Introduction to Sociological Poetics* (1928) appeared

under the name of P. N. Medvedev. These three works might in fact have been written in large part by Bakhtin, and their content can be seen as complementary to the works published under Bakhtin's own name. The book on Freudianism is a detailed critique of Freud's theories of the human subject. *Marxism and the Philosophy of Language* uses Marxist terminology to develop a semiotic theory of language in opposition to both Russian formalism and French linguistics (especially that of Ferdinand de Saussure and Charles Bally). Bakhtin rejects Saussure's distinction between *langue* and *parole*, focusing rather on the utterance as the proper object of linguistic study. Utterance, Bakhtin holds, is language in a state of struggle because it is used by speakers in everyday situations and one only speaks out of dissent. *The Formal Method* engages in a study of the many weaknesses of formalism, which lacks a sociological basis for its theoretical framework.

Bakhtin was arrested in 1929, perhaps because of alleged activity in the underground Russian Orthodox Church. Originally sentenced to ten years in a labor camp on the Solovetski Islands, Bakhtin ended up spending six years in internal exile in the town of Kustanay, Kazakhstan, where he worked on a collective farm as a bookkeeper. During the 1930s, he wrote several largely theoretical studies of the novel, including "Discourse in the Novel" (1934–1935), "The *Bildungsroman* and Its Significance in the History of Realism" (1936–1938), and "Forms of Time and the Chronotope in the Novel" (1937–1938). Bakhtin defined the novel not in terms of rigid rules but as a dynamic, innovative, antigeneric force ("novelization"), whose influence could be traced throughout literary history. The novel thus represents the centrifugal forces of language that enter into a conflictual relationship with centripetal or codifying forces. At the beginning of the 1930s, he also wrote two controversial prefaces to an edition of the collected works of Leo Tolstoy. He apparently produced a study of Goethe and the bildungsroman in the 1930s; what survives of it is included in *Speech, Genres, and Other Late Essays* (1986). The works that Bakhtin wrote during the 1930s are a development of the theory of the novel first elaborated in *Problems of Dostoevsky's Creative Works*. At the center of these works is dialogism, both a theory of language and a theory of literature in general.

Bakhtin moved to Saransk in 1936 to take up a professorship at the Mordovia Pedagogical Institute, where he taught Russian and world literature until his retirement in 1961. In 1940 and 1941, Bakhtin produced more works on the novel: "From the Prehistory of Novelistic Discourse" (1940), *Rabelais in the History of Realism* (a thesis submitted to the Gorky Institute; 1940), and "Epic and Novel: Toward a Methodology for the Study of the Novel" (1941). Although the thesis was rejected originally, Bakhtin revised it for publication in 1965 under the title *The Work of François Rabelais and Popular Culture during the Middle Ages and the Renaissance*. In this work, Bakhtin develops the concept of the carnivalesque as well as a new understanding of the human subject as a social force acting in history. Carnival is seen as a ritualized time and space in which it is impossible to maintain distinctions between observers and performers.

From the 1950s until his death, Bakhtin wrote and published essays on a diversity of topics and revised some earlier unpublished manuscripts: "The Problem of Speech Genres" (1952–1953), "The Problem of the Text in Linguistics, Philology, and the Human Sciences: An Experiment in Philosophical Analysis" (1959–1961), "On the Revision of the Dostoevsky Book" (1961), "Rabelais and Gogol" (1970), "Response to a Question Put by the Editorial Board of *Novy Mir*" (1970), and others. This later work (especially that on speech genres) has been used in the field of pragmatics to develop historically informed speech-act theories.

During most of his life, Bakhtin seems to have been uninterested in having his work published. It was only in his later years that he was persuaded to bring out several manuscripts and to revise earlier published work. His reputation as a major twentieth-century cultural philosopher and critical thinker was established only after his death.

Much work remains to be done in the field of Bakhtin studies. The genealogy and genesis of his concepts require much more investigation than has been carried out so far. The relationship of his ideas to those of other thinkers such as György Lukács, Walter Benjamin, Erich Auerbach, and Leo Spitzer needs to be examined, as does his influence on poststructuralist thought.

[*See also* Communication; Dialogism; Dialogue; *and* Rabelais and His World.]

BIBLIOGRAPHY

Bakhtin, M. M. *The Dialogic Imagination: Four Essays by M. M. Bakhtin*. Edited by M. Holquist, translated by C. Emerson and M. Holquist. Austin: University of Texas Press, 1981.

Bakhtin, M. M. *Problems of Dostoevsky's Poetics*. Edited and translated by C. Emerson. Minneapolis: University of Minnesota Press, 1984.

Bakhtin, M. M. *Rabelais and His World*. Translated by H. Iswolsky. 2d ed. Bloomington: Indiana University Press, 1984.

Bakhtin, M. M. *Speech, Genres, and Other Late Essays*. Edited by C. Emerson and M. Holquist, translated by Vern W. McGee. Austin: University of Texas Press, 1986.

Bakhtin, M. M. *Art and Answerability: Early Philosophical Essays*. Edited by M. Holquist and V. Liapunov, translated and with notes by Vadim Liapunov, supplemental translations by K. Brostrom. Austin: University of Texas Press, 1990.

Bakhtin, M. M. *Toward a Philosophy of the Act*. Edited by V. Liapunov and M. Holquist, translated by V. Liapunov. Austin: University of Texas Press, 1993.

Clark, K., and M. Holquist. *Mikhail Bakhtin*. Cambridge, Mass.: Harvard University Press, 1984.

Hirschkop, K., and D. Shepherd, eds. *Bakhtin and Cultural Theory*. Manchester: Manchester University Press, 1989.

Morson, G. S., and C. Emerson. *Mikhail Bakhtin: Creation of a Prosaics*. Stanford: Stanford University Press, 1990.

The following journals have published special issues on Bakhtin: *The University of Ottawa Quarterly* 53.1 (1983); *Critical Inquiry* 10.2 (1983); *Etudes françaises* 20.1 (1984); *L'Imagine riflessa* 7.1/2 (1984); *Studies in Twentieth Century Literature* 9.1 (1984); *Critical Studies* 1.2 (1989), 1 (1990); *Bakhtin Newsletter* 1 (1983), 2 (1986), 3 (1991); *Discours social* 3.1–2 (1990).

—ANTHONY WALL and CLIVE THOMSON

BARTHES, ROLAND (1915–1980), French semiologist, narratologist, critic, and essayist whose multifaceted and productive career spanned four decades. Barthes's first book, *Le degré zéro de l'écriture* (Writing Degree Zero, 1953), explored the ideological significance of the choice of a mode of writing. The second, *Michelet par lui-même* (1954), was a phenomenological description of selected "existential thematics" pertaining to sensations and substances at work in the imaginative histories of nineteenth-century French historian Jules Michelet (1798–1894). In the early 1950s, Barthes began production of his "little mythologies of the month" for a periodical, *Les lettres nouvelles*, later collected as *Mythologies* (1957). As France was becoming a consumer society, Barthes decoded manifestations of the dominant bourgeois ideology in semiological terms. Myth is a metalanguage, a second-order semiological system built upon a first-order linguistic system, about which it speaks. "Myth is a type of speech," Barthes claimed, which gives to historical contingencies a natural justification. Barthes claimed that myths are consumed as if they were factual rather than semiological. The mythologist studies the processes by which this distortion occurs. In the study of popular culture, *Mythologies* had important precursors in Louis Aragon's *Le paysan de Paris* (Paris Paysant, 1926), Walter Benjamin's *Einbahnstrasse* (One-Way Street, 1926), and Marshall McLuhan's *The Mechanical Bride* (1951).

Barthes scholars divide his career into two parts. The first was committed to the parallel scientific practices of semiology and narratology. Barthes's trademark analysis of "staggered" systems, introduced in the "little mythologies," matured over ten years through *Eléments de sémiologie* (1964) and *Système de la mode* (The Fashion System, 1967). Barthes's simple double system (linguistic and mythical) had its switching point in the first system's signs, which became the signifiers of the second mythological metalanguage. In *Eléments de sémiologie*, Barthes complicated his model's amplification of a first system by adding a further switching point, defined in terms borrowed from Hjelmslev's glossematics. The first-order system of expression-relation-content became the plane of expression for a connotative semiotics and the plane of content for a metalanguage or semiotics of semiotics. Barthes then reconfigured as a triplex the complex ensemble of denotation and connotation: an initial real system, a second metalanguage (denotation), and a third level of connotation.

When Barthes turned to the systems of a written fashion in *Système de la mode*, he elaborated a stacked and staggered quadruplex model whose signification of fashion was explicit and a triplex model whose signified was implicit. The first of two levels of denotation is a real vestmental code in which a reference is represented through a verbal element whose signifier is clothing and whose signified is fashion. The second denotative system is terminological and amplified metalinguistically, having the sign of the first system's verbal elements as its signified, whose signifier or substance is the sentence or proposition. On the remaining connotative levels, the transition to the third system called the connotation of fashion is itself amplified connotatively since what is noted

simply is the signifier (corresponding to second system's sign sentence or proposition) of the signified *fashion*. All such "worldly utterances," Barthes claimed, signified fashion, thereby building into his model a high degree of generality and redundancy. In the fourth rhetorical system, the sign of notation/fashion becomes the signifier of the phraseology of a specific magazine whose signified is its vision of the world. In a system whose signifieds are implicit, Barthes emphasized that the vestmental code absorbs notation into the details of a garment's features, and there is only one level of connotation (rhetorical).

Barthes laid the theoretical groundwork for a science of literature in his 1966 seminal essay "Introduction à l'analyse structurale des récits" (in Barthes, 1977b, pp. 79–124). For Barthes, beyond a linguistics of the sentence lay a linguistics of discourse whose object is the language of narrative. Narrative is the object of the structuralist science of narratology, and literature is the privileged vehicle of narrative. By 1970, with the publication of *S/Z*, a study of the short story "Sarrasine" by Honoré de Balzac (1799–1850), Barthes's scientist period had ended. Structural analysis was displaced by a gradual, textual analysis. Aiming beyond both sentences and narratives, Barthes posited a new, plural, intertextual object, marked by his ambivalent attachments to structuralist conceptions in an ostensibly poststructuralist book. The Balzacian text consists of *lexias*, units of reading, relying upon five codes (proaïretic, hermeneutic, semic, cultural, and symbolic). The "voices" of the five codes speak contrapuntally, and Barthes is concerned with producing their multivalent structuration rather than rigorously reproducing their structures. Although "Sarrasine" was in Barthes's terms a readerly, classic text with a limited plurality, it served him well as the object of a writerly—freely plural, active compositional—encoding of a text such as *S/Z*.

The concept of "zero degree" recurred throughout Barthes's oeuvre in new configurations of absences. In *L'empire des signes* (The Empire of Signs, 1970) Barthes read Japan as a "fictive nation" perfused with "empty signs." The features from which Barthes formed a system were signifiers whose signifieds remained hidden from him. This opacity was underwritten by the radically exotic character of his empire of signs and his refusal to merge with it. Barthes found emptiness everywhere: The shimmering signifiers of Japanese food were without depth but rich in surface effects; haiku exempted itself from meaning. These same concerns carried over into Barthes's study of the *Logothetes*—founders of languages that said nothing—in *Sade/Fourier/Loyola* (1971). Just as Japanese boxes and packages deferred for Barthes what they concealed, Charles Fourier's writing was driven forward by its incessant delays toward the promise of an exposé; Ignatius Loyola's invention of a language adequate to deciphering God's will reverentially accepted God's silence and the delay of his signs; the Sadean voyage and rhetorical portraits taught and painted nothing. Barthes's fascination with systems without centers was strikingly postmodern.

The "second Barthes" wrote reflective and aphoristic texts. *Le plaisir du texte* (The Pleasure of the Text, 1973) theorized pleasure (*jouissance*) in the theory of the text and refined Barthes's voluptuary tastes for the anisotropic features of both traditional and new forms of writing. This hedonistic style was marked by repeated invocations, in *Fragments d'un discours amoureux* (A Lover's Discourse: Fragments, 1977a) and *La chambre claire* (Camera Lucida: Reflections on Photography, 1980), of the embodied knowledges of a fractured body. Having transcended the technical demands of narrative analysis and disavowed the orthodoxies of literature, Barthes turned to autobiography, treating himself "as an effect of language," in *Roland Barthes par Roland Barthes* (Roland Barthes on Roland Barthes, 1975). By 1977, when Barthes accepted the chair of literary semiology at the Collège de France, semiology had become for him an artistic rather than a scientific activity in which one savored and followed the leads of signifiers, nourishing rather than mining them, as so many fictions.

Selected interviews with Barthes spanning twenty years appeared posthumously in *Le grain de la voix* (The Grain of the Voice, 1981). Barthes's journal entries illumining his gay sexuality in *Incidents* (1987) have recently focused critical attention on biographical issues and the reconsideration of his earlier theoretical claim: "I have no biography."

[*See also* Denotation and Connotation; Elements of Semiology; Hjelmslev; Introduction to the Structural Analysis of Narratives; Metalanguage; Mythologies; *and* Rhetoric of the Image.]

BIBLIOGRAPHY

Works by Barthes

Writing Degree Zero (1953). Translated by A. Lavers and C. Smith. London: Jonathan Cape, 1967.

Michelet (1954). Edited by R. Barthes and translated by R. Howard. New York: Hill and Wang, 1987.

Mythologies (1957). Translated by A. Lavers. London: Jonathan Cape, 1972.

Elements of Semiology (1964). Translated by A. Lavers and C. Smith. New York: Hill and Wang, 1968.

The Fashion System (1967). Translated by M. Ward and R. Howard. Berkeley: University of California Press, 1990.

The Empire of Signs (1970). Translated by R. Howard. New York: Hill and Wang, 1982.

S/Z (1970). Translated by R. Miller. New York: Hill and Wang, 1975.

Sade/Fourier/Loyola (1971). Translated by R. Miller. New York: Hill and Wang, 1976.

The Pleasure of the Text (1973). Translated by R. Miller. New York: Hill and Wang, 1975.

Roland Barthes by Roland Barthes (1975). Translated by R. Howard. New York: Hill and Wang, 1977a.

Image-Music-Text. Essays selected and translated by S. Heath. London: Fontana, 1977b.

A Lover's Discourse: Fragments (1977). Translated by R. Howard. New York: Hill and Wang, 1978.

Camera Lucida: Reflections on Photography (1980). Translated by R. Howard. New York: Hill and Wang, 1981.

The Grain of the Voice: Interviews 1962–1980 (1981). Translated by L. Coverdale. New York: Hill and Wang, 1985.

Incidents (1987). Translated by R. Howard. Berkeley: University of California Press, 1992.

Other Works

Aragon, L. *Paris Paysant* (1926). Translated by S. W. Taylor. London: Jonathan Cape, 1971.

Benjamin, W. *Einbahnstrasse* (1926). Berlin: Suhrkamp, 1955.

Bensmaïa, R. *The Barthes Effect: The Essay as Reflective Text.* Translated by P. Fedkiew. Minneapolis: University of Minnesota Press, 1987.

Compagnon, A. "The Two Barthes." Translated by James McGuire and Didier Bertrand. In *Signs in Culture: Roland Barthes Today*, edited by S. Ungar and B. R. McGraw. Iowa City: University of Iowa Press, 1989.

Lavers, A. *Roland Barthes: Structuralism and After.* London: Methuen, 1982.

McLuhan, M. *The Mechanical Bride.* Boston: Beacon Press, 1951.

Ungar, S. *Roland Barthes: The Professor of Desire.* Lincoln: University of Nebraska Press, 1983.

—GARY GENOSKO

BASEBALL. Although Americans consider the sport of baseball their national pastime, it has long been popular well beyond the United States, throughout much of Latin America and in Asia,

Taiwan, the Philippines, and Japan, where the game was introduced by missionaries and teachers. The Japanese have developed a passion for baseball that rivals that of the Americans.

In several senses, baseball is a distinctively "odd" field sport. There is hardly an even number associated with baseball: no quarters, no midfield, no halftime and (in its American version) the game does not allow for tie scores. Even the apparent regularity of the diamond-shaped infield is divided into three bases plus home plate.

While the bases are squares, home plate is pentagonal in shape. Rather than a halftime break, baseball provides its fans with a "seventh-inning stretch." The normal team (exclusive of pinch hitters, pinch runners, or designated hitters) comprises nine players. The game (unless there is a tie) is nine innings long. Its smaller rhythmic units are also odd. Baseball's distinctive rhythm is a kind of waltz where "one-two-three" at bat means "you're out" while the same rhythm in running brings you back home. Asymmetries shape the game's time, its space, and its fundamental rules of play.

The key to the semiotic unity of baseball is the structural asymmetry by which a fixed beginning is poised against an open and contingent end. This structural asymmetry is an important aspect of baseball's organization of time. Baseball is not so much a slow game as one that unfolds in alternating pulses. Long periods of inactivity are punctuated by sudden bursts of dramatic action. This alternation permits spectators to withdraw periodically into "domestic" pursuits (eating, scorekeeping, analyzing the game, or even sleeping) even as the game is being played. This alternation of attention, mimicking the "home" and "away" alternation of baseball play, probably contributes to the high degree of mental (as opposed to kinesthetic) engagement fans have with the sport. And it makes unnecessary a halftime break from the game, common in other field sports.

Baseball time is controlled notably by the contingency of events rather than by the clock. Baseball time is "inning time." A game normally ends when the visiting team has played at least nine innings at bat and play has produced a difference in score between the teams. Baseball has several theoretically endless or open moments. A game that produces no asymmetry in score can go on without limit. A team can theoretically have an endless inning at bat, in which their opponents fail to produce the required three outs to "retire the side." And the batter faces the possibility of an endless "at bat" in which he keeps "fouling off" pitches, producing an interminable standoff between pitcher and batter.

While these limitless moments are only theoretical possibilities in baseball, they affect how the sport is perceived. Baseball is repeatedly associated with the power to overcome time and to reunite estranged generations and eras through a mystical evocation of the recuperative power of the ball field. Baseball is America's nostalgic game, with an ability to fold the past back into the present (the uniforms of baseball tend to reproduce styles of times past). Baseball's capacity to bridge generations for American men is an important reason why fathers value playing catch with their sons.

Baseball is the only sport in the United States that fields organized teams throughout a person's entire life cycle. Baseball's ideal "endless summer" is a dimension not only of a particular season but also of one's life. From the T-ball leagues for the very young through a chain of teams in Little League, Pony League, and Babe Ruth League, from high school to college to men's and women's softball leagues, baseball is the sole sports idiom that can encapsulate an entire biography. For reasons of symbolism as well as physiology, Old Timer's Day only makes sense in baseball.

Baseball's open-ended time frame is complemented by its insistent fixing of its beginnings. The asymmetry of baseball time is linked to the tension between open ends and closed beginnings. Within the game itself, the start of play is always marked ritually. This need to demarcate clearly baseball's beginnings must have been behind the creation of a mythical American starting point for baseball.

The orchestration of space in baseball parallels closely its asymmetrical organization of time. Unique among field sports in America, baseball eschews the symmetrical rectangular playing space for a kind of wedge-shaped field. The ball field is defined by an "inner zone" (from which the game gets its "innings") that is measured precisely and is identical in every park. At the apex of this "infield" is "home plate," also called the "bag" or the "dish." The three bases and home plate define a ninety-foot square, while the pitcher's mound is exactly sixty feet, six inches from home plate, the result of an early surveyor's error that became standardized for all professional fields.

By contrast with the precisely standardized infield, baseball's outfield is not governed by such fixed dimensions. Outfield distances are governed by minimum but not maximum dimensions. From home plate to the outfield fence, as measured along the foul lines, a professional field must measure at least 250 feet (325 feet for parks built after 1958). And from home plate to the center-field fence, on a line drawn through second base, must measure at least 400 feet. Owners are free in baseball to change the shape of the outfield to suit the hitting style of their team, a practice some have called "marrying the field to the team." As with time in baseball, there are no outer limits in the constitutive rules governing baseball space.

The most basic realization of baseball's asymmetrical form is the fact that in baseball a team never faces directly the opposing team. The game juxtaposes a "field" of coordinated players against individual players either at bat or running the bases. In fact, the team at bat is kept out of sight, in a below-ground "dugout," so that only an individual player faces the fielding team.

Most baseball players have two alternating personas: a defensive role in the field and an offensive one at bat. The "home" area of play is the locus of individuated action, while the outer field is the focus of more socially coordinated play.

The ideological foundations of this opposition are built into the terms used to speak about the game. Fielders are "playing" their positions, while batters and runners "are" what they do. One never "plays batter," one "bats" or "is up at the plate." Moreover, the closer a fielder comes to playing at home, the more he is considered an offensive rather than a defensive role. Thus, pitchers have an "essential" status like batters (one never plays pitcher), and catchers do not "play" home plate in the way that a fielder "plays the outfield" or "plays third base."

The key asymmetry underlying those of time and space in baseball is the opposing of individual action (at home) and social interaction (in the field). Baseball thus orchestrates a set of complex and problematic relations between communitarian values and those of American individualism, engaging them in a kind of dialogue. Baseball's fascination with statistics is probably linked to its romance with individuated action, and the democratic fondness for reducing qualitative distinctness to quantitative comparison. In this way, the quantification of base-

ball is equivalent to the American passion for polls and market surveys by which everything can be reduced to common terms and compared.

The basic action structure of baseball differs from that of most field sports. Most have a common, basic game plan. The aim is for one team to move across a field of defenders with the goal of placing an object (a ball or a puck) in their goal space at the opposite end of the field.

In baseball, by contrast, offensive strategy is to separate the ball and the player by as much territory as possible. In baseball, it is the player who scores (by coming home) and not the ball. Even when a home run is hit out of the park, the score is not made by the ball but by the player's making his way unimpeded around the bases and returning home again. Unlike other field sports, whenever the ball catches up with the runner in baseball, the runner is in danger of being "out."

The action of baseball can be conceived of as a series of individuals who attempt to leave home and make a circuit through a social field marked by obstacles. It is not getting to the field itself that scores, however, but returning safely home. Baseball is a telling of a mythic journey of conquest, where a lone hero sets out on a perilous adventure, with the hope of returning home with newfound wealth or wisdom.

Baseball, in its organized tension between social cooperation and heroic individuals, also reflects a deep ambivalence about the relation between rules and personal assertiveness. Though baseball's umpires control all play, and their decisions are never overruled, highly stylized conventions of arguing with the umpire by players and managers are part of the game. Team members will even risk being ejected from the game to carry on the ultimately fruitless ritual of facing down the umpire. "Kill the umpire" is a classic American baseball expression. From the earliest years of Little League play, baseball models for American boys a tradition of questioning authority, even as they grudgingly learn that in baseball there is no alternative to acceding to the umpire's rulings.

Important features of baseball's semiotics remain to be studied. Several works have been written comparing Japanese baseball to its American model, but relatively little has been written about how baseball's forms have been adapted to other cultural settings. No careful semiotic comparison of baseball and English cricket has ever been published. The analysis here of the organization of time, space, and action in baseball has been largely from the perspective of the spectator. Much remains to be studied about how baseball is experienced from other perspectives, such as those of the television viewer and, of course, the players themselves.

[*See also* Cultural Knowledge; *and* Sport.]

BIBLIOGRAPHY

Angell, R. *The Summer Game.* New York: Viking Press, 1972.
Candelaria, C. "Baseball in American Literature: From Ritual to Fiction." Ph. D. diss., University of Notre Dame, 1976.
Frank, L. *Playing Hardball: The Dynamics of Baseball Folk Speech.* New York: Peter Lang, 1983.
Gordon, P. H., *Diamonds Are Forever: Artists and Writers on Baseball.* San Francisco: Chronicle Books, 1987.
Novack, M. *The Joy of Sports: End Zones, Bases, Baskets, Balls, and the Consecration of the American Spirit.* New York: Basic Books, 1976.
Voigt, D. Q. *America Through Baseball.* Chicago: Nelson Hall, 1976.
Whiting, R. *The Chrysanthemum and the Bat: Baseball Samurai Style.* New York: Dodd, Mead, 1977.

—BRADD SHORE

BATESON, GREGORY (1904–1980), American anthropologist, philosopher, and ecologist. Born in Cambridge, England, the son of William Bateson, a famous but controversial biologist, young Gregory matured with an advanced understanding of the philosophical and scientific aspects of evolution. Although he decided to become an anthropologist, a profound understanding of evolutionary biology remained with him all his life. So too, did his father's anti-Darwinian stance.

Bateson is best remembered among anthropologists for producing one of the first ethnographic films, which he made together with his wife, Margaret Mead, in Bali between 1936 and 1938. He is also known for his book on the Iatmul of New Guinea, *Naven* (1936), in which he wrestled with epistemological problems of ethnographic representation. At the time, theories of functionalism provided a formula enabling anthropologists to write systematic accounts of local culture without worrying too much about the relations between subject and object, self and other, observer and the observed. By contrast, *Naven*, as its subtitle—*A Survey of the Problems Suggested by a Composite Picture of the Culture of a New Guinea Tribe Drawn from Three Points of View*—indi-

cates, took the relationship of observer to observed as its central focus.

Naven discusses how ethnographic method gave rise to fallacies of misplaced concreteness—a term Bateson borrowed from the English philosopher Alfred North Whitehead—that derive from hiding points of view. This occurs in the first instance when ethnographers gather information from informants, for informants always have points of view though ethographers might not label them as such but treat them as scientific data. Then, a second level of hidden reference occurs, as the observer-scientist calls such evidence true, real, and objective, even though such attributions are invariably derived from the scientist's own labeling of the evidence.

In the postwar period, Bateson drew upon what he called "logical types" in order to understand how hidden viewpoints relate to patterns of social interaction and give rise to dysfunctional communication among family members in a therapeutic setting. Logical typing was a procedure derived by Bertrand Russell to overcome problems of paradox in logical generalization. Russell introduced logical types in order to save the mathematics of set theory (cf. George Boole's *An Investigation of the Laws of Thought*, 1854), which Russell believed was subject to self-referential paradox. In Bateson's thinking, logical types were a means for investigating the many levels of references and the structure of reflexiveness that order recursive patterns of communication. *Metaset*, a concept Russell devised in order to ban logical paradox, became Bateson's *metacontext*, a means through which hidden patterns of generalization could be uncovered. Bateson developed other expressive terminology for discussing these hidden patterns of abstraction such as *context markers* to discuss the marking of context; *punctuation* to discuss perception of the pattern of relations among communicators in communicative exchange; and *double bind* to express the operational embodiment of paradox in systems of communication. Family therapists who tried to apply Bateson's ideas found his perspective difficult to assimilate.

Bateson's fundamental premise is that mind is different from the territory that mind maps and that therefore dilemmas of choice are typical of the processes of abstraction (mapping) that occur in mental relations. These occur together with semantic confusion, miscommunication of meaning, circular logic, and pathological misapprehension. All these features indicate that the study of communication has to be predicated on assumptions quite different from those originating in sixteenth-century Western natural science (such as the separation of mind from body or substance) and carried over to social science through the materialism and positivism of the nineteenth century. In this respect, key assumptions of information theory and applied cybernetics required redefinition. For example, the theorems of information theory pay little or no attention to meaning except as an adjunct to the elimination of noise in a channel. Bateson held that noise has its analogue in playfulness, helping create responses from which a new game (cf. Wittgenstein's concept of the "language game") could be played; noise is always a preprevision against the occurrence of unknowns. During the 1950s and 1960s, Bateson wrestled with epistemological issues of reflexiveness in information (*Steps to an Ecology of Mind*, 1972), while in the 1970s he began to enlarge the scope of his central ideas by melding them into a discussion of evolution (*Mind and Nature: Their Necessary Unity*, 1979).

Bateson's study of communicative order occurred in three phases. In the immediate postwar period, Bateson was among the founders of cybernetics, a new science concerned with the operation, control, and epistemology of circular causal systems in natural order, artificial intelligence, and robotics. The second phase was marked by *Communication: The Social Matrix of Psychiatry* (1951), which Bateson wrote with psychiatrist Jurgen Ruesch. This book employed a matrix of ideas drawn from psychology, sociology, and anthropology in order to refute the dominance of behaviorism in psychology and the moral determinism of sociology and anthropology, trends that had produced what Bateson saw as an unnecessary split between the disciplines of psychology and social science. Since psychological and sociological organization both exhibit feedback—that is, their systemic organization is both nonlinear and circularly causal—psychological and sociological inquiries must accord with these systemic characteristics. In a third phase, Bateson published numerous papers with his research team on a communicative approach to pathologies of mind, especially on schizophrenia and the phenomenon of the double bind.

Some of Bateson's work on pathology in family systems appears in *Steps to an Ecology of Mind*. What emerges from *Steps* is an ecological approach to systems thinking: living systems or subsystems are in-

terrelated with their environment through multiple levels of interrelationship, as parts to wholes and wholes to parts. Without including all levels of interrelationship, it is impossible to discuss how any system survives.

Other papers of this period argue that communicative order is both paralinguistic and paralogical. Formal linguistics seemed to concentrate upon a single form of coding: digital coding considered either as general codes permitting semantic selections, associated subcodes constraining dialects, or the codes of discourse, formal tests, and statements created through digital coding. Understanding the wider domain of communication required much more than knowing permutations of the discrete elements upon which formal linguistics lavished its attention. Bateson discusses various types of coding, the feature of each code (he identified about seven) being that they are not reducible to another, nor are they opposed to the other. Each has its own characteristics or logical type. Analogue codes are continuous forms of coding in which the term *not* does not appear. Iconic codes organize information into pictorial or auditory images from a very large number of digital bits. Most common errors arising from iconic coding lie in giving excessive credibility to iconic images while forgetting to acknowledge the synthetic process entailed in organizing complex masses of bits. No camera ever "saw" an image.

Bateson considers boundary conditions in a synthetic field of coding from several perspectives. The figure-ground boundary, for example, is the result of introducing a digital distinction into the analog continuum of differences in a perceptual field. Human dreaming exemplifies an interesting intermediate space between the iconic coding of animals and the verbal coding of human speech; this is also the case in human myth. Another perspective addresses boundaries between the processes of cognition and the processes of perception: Bateson proposed that the boundary between these two processes encapsulates neither what is "inside" (cognitive processes in the brain) nor what is "outside" (perceived patterns of nature). Rather, the boundary arises through interrelated processes of communication—the ideas of communicators, for example, which are themselves "meta" to the processes through which individual perception and cognition take place. These metaprocesses generate their own embodiments. One of Bateson's most important legacies for semiotic and communication studies was to point out that embodiment of communication does not occur only in the body, in a physical sense of brain or corporeal sensitivity, but lies in it *plus* the generated pattern of relations among communicators. This is why both perceptual and cognitive illusions are commonplace in all systems of communication and why beliefs about falsification or its opposite, trust, are such important characteristics of all patterns of communicative exchange. Bateson identifies the matrix of embodiment, together with communicators' beliefs and preconceptions and systemic patterns of self-correction, as the relational field of communicative interaction.

Another of Bateson's interests is to develop ways in which an observer can abandon explanation based on efficient causality. The latter is always predicated on relations between cause and effect at a single level of analysis, usually that of energy, "need," or "work." His interest in metaphor arose from this, as he believes metaphor must somehow provide the means for occidental civilization to escape from the tyranny of quantity and quantification. He finds metaphor essential to all comparison and to all thought, for by metaphor Bateson means not only the juxtaposition of linguistic universals but all forms of dreams, drama, art, and humor—indeed any way in which a correspondence of form occurs between something mentioned and some other thing mentioned. The total network of interlocking and interdependent metaphors constitutes the skeleton and microscopic connective tissue of our thinking about which action shall be compared with what else. Moreover, bad metaphor poisons the well of human thinking. In its broadest dimensions, the subject matter of metaphor is relationship, but the effect of metaphor occurs at an interface of levels of description where metaphor is a mapping using analogies with a vengeance but concealing its own "as ifness." For this reason, use of metaphor can induce vicious circularities, for metaphor requires a double description—both a relation reference and a conceptual reference—in order to unravel its significance: schizophrenics, for example, are often unable to distinguish or frame metaphor as metaphor.

Bateson resigned from practice and research in family therapy in the mid-1960s. He began to pursue some of his father's ideas, substituting his own knowledge of information theory and cybernetics for his father's deductions about rhythms and resonance in biological variation and symmetry. A considerable portion of Gregory Bateson's ideas about a communicative grounding of order in nature appeared a year before his death in *Mind and Nature* (1979). The book is a general attack on those biologists who, while recognizing that genetics belong to a field of information, treat the information characteristics of genes in the same terms as they treat energy in physicochemical bits. To Bateson's way of thinking, it is sheer perversity to consider any communicative field, whether of genetics or of a field of ideas, in the same terms as its material substrate. While all ideas have a material carrier, the communicative characteristics of the one cannot be reduced to the characteristics of the other. Furthermore, although organisms evidently require a positive energy budget in order to survive, their primary order in nature is communicative and not energy related. No energy-centered explanation—that is, one that focuses on the inputs and outputs of metabolism—can account for morphological differences in biological forms, nor can materialist explanation account for intelligence in nature. Moreover, the repeated use of free-energy metaphors in mainstream biology divides organism from environment, much as the same metaphors divide the relations of mind and body in Western epistemology.

Bateson sought a correspondence between ideas in culture and the communicative order of nature, hence the importance of his expression "ecology of mind." All thought, evolution, ecology, life, and learning occur in systems that are an aggregate of interacting parts or components. Interaction between parts is triggered by a difference, which is a nonsubstantial phenomenon located neither in a specific space nor in an identifiable moment of time. In contrast to the billiard-ball interactions of the material world—an identifiable series of temporally successive events—communicative relationship between two parts (a sender and a receiver) or between self at time 1 and the same self at time 2, requires some third component, a "receiver" ready to respond to a difference or a change. Without this condition of readiness, a change will not take place because it will not be understood. All effects of difference are transforms, coded versions of events that preceded them. Their rules of transformation are comparatively stable, and it is these we can trace rather than tracing through successive events of coding and recoding.

Many of Bateson's ideas about ecology appeared posthumously. Initially, he had used the term *ecology* as a metaphor for the logic of interrelationships he was trying to describe. From 1975 onward, he began to speak about a new and as-yet-unnamed holistic science that he termed an epistemology of recursion, synonymous with an ecology of mind. Aspects of this holistic epistemology appear in *Angels Fear: Toward an Epistemology of the Sacred* (1987), written with his daughter Mary Catherine Bateson, while other aspects appear in another set of essays called *A Sacred Unity: Further Steps to an Ecology of Mind* (1991), edited by his archivist, Rodney Donaldson. Other ideas remain buried in unpublished letters, interviews, and transcripts of talks lodged in his archive. His posthumous work contains evident shifts in direction. The term *sacred* appears in both titles, and as he uses it, it is a metaphor about biospheric integration that presupposes a surface or topology on which a new science of aesthetics and consciousness could be mapped. Since Bateson rejects any form of transcendental explanation, the metaphor does not propose a return to spirituality; rather, he argues that aesthetics can provide a shortcut toward resolving our ecological dilemmas. Though aesthetics is often considered to be a question of individual judgment or taste, Bateson states that the processes of perception through which aesthetic sensibility is generated are by no means subjective but epistemological. He spoke of an active aesthetics, both as a medium through which humanity could begin to understand the unity of the biosphere and as a medium capable of transforming prevailing epistemology. He looked forward to a situation in which an aesthetic understanding of "the patterns which connect"—patterns vastly transformed from Darwinian notions of competitive fitness and the moral injunctions stemming therefrom—would yield, recursively, transformed conceptions of science. Only a holistic science, incorporating an active aesthetics into its modes of explanation, can avoid the lethal contradictions that our dominant materialist epistemology is steadily driving humanity toward.

As mounting evidence of stress in humanity's relations with its natural environment fosters a wide-ranging discussion of the unity and integrity of the biosphere, the epistemology behind Bateson's metaphors—based on the premises of a communicative rather than a materialistic or energy-focused order—is becoming much better understood.

[*See also* Biosemiotics; Communication; Cybernetics; Double Bind; Information; Russell; Umwelt; *and* Wittgenstein.]

BIBLIOGRAPHY

Bateson, G. *Naven*. Cambridge: Cambridge University Press, 1936.
Bateson, G. *Steps to an Ecology of Mind*. New York: Ballantine, 1972.
Bateson, G. *Mind and Nature: A Necessary Unity*. New York: Dutton, 1979.
Bateson, G. *A Sacred Unity: Further Steps to an Ecology of Mind*. Edited by R. Donaldson. New York: Cornelia and Michael Bessie Books, 1991.
Bateson, G., and M. C. Bateson. *Angels Fear: Toward an Epistemology of the Sacred*. New York: Macmillan, 1987.
Bateson, G., and J. Ruesch. *Communication: The Social Matrix of Psychiatry*. New York: Norton, 1951.
Bateson, M. C. *Our Own Metaphor: A Personal Account of a Conference on Conscious Purpose and Human Adaptation*. New York: Knopf, 1972.
Bateson, M. C. *With a Daughter's Eye: A Memoir of Margaret Mead and Gregory Bateson*. New York: Morrow, 1984.
Berger, M. M., ed. *Beyond the Double Bind: Communication and Family Systems, Theories, and Techniques with Schizophrenics*. New York: Brunner/Mazel, 1978.
Boole, G. *An Investigation of the Laws of Thought*. London: Walton, 1854.
Brockman, J. ed. *About Bateson: Essays on Gregory Bateson*. New York: John Dutton, 1977.
Harries-Jones, P. *A Recursive Vision: Ecological Understanding and Gregory Bateson*. Toronto: University of Toronto Press, 1995.
Keeney, B. P. *Aesthetics of Change*. New York: Guilford, 1983.
Lipset, D. *Gregory Bateson: The Legacy of a Scientist*. Englewood Cliffs, N.J.: Prentice Hall, 1980.
Wilden, A. *The Rules Are No Game: The Strategy of Communication*. London and New York: Routledge and Kegan Paul, 1987.
Wilder, C. M., and J. B. Weakland, eds. *Rigor and Imagination: Essays from the Legacy of Gregory Bateson*. New York: Praeger Scientific, 1981.

—PETER HARRIES-JONES

BAUDRILLARD, JEAN (b. 1929), French critical thinker whose work is read largely as postmodern theory in the English-speaking world. Baudrillard began his career in the early 1960s as a book reviewer for *Les Temps modernes*. Trained as a Germanist, he translated into French major works by the German playwright Peter Weiss, writings by Bertolt Brecht, Friedrich Engels, and social anthropologist Wilhelm

E. Mühlmann, among others. From 1967 to 1973, Baudrillard was associated with the sociology of urbanism group associated with the journal *Utopie*, and in 1975 he joined the founding editorial board of the cultural-theory journal *Traverses*, based at the Centre Georges Pompidou in Paris.

In his first two major studies, *Le système des objets* (The Systems of Objects, 1968) and *La société de consommation* (The Society of Consumption, 1970), he argued that social life is mediated and radically alienated by a controlled logic of merchandise in which consumption has nothing to do with reality and the satisfaction of needs. Modern consumers are "cyberneticians" engaged in a "calculus of objects" that have been liberated from their functions and materiality. Baudrillard's central claim is that objects have become signs whose value is determined by a disciplinary cultural code. In this code, the idea of the relation between signs is consumed. Modern monopolistic production produces the signs of differentiation that establish social standing and personalization, thus fully integrating the consumer into the system. Like Henri Lefebvre (1968), Baudrillard used structuralist method to criticize the structural logic of consumer society, but unlike Lefebvre he claimed that revolution was impossible at the level of a total system that thinks and speaks of itself through consumption.

In a series of books published in the 1970s, Baudrillard elaborated and criticized key concepts from his first studies. *Pour une critique de l'économie politique du signe* (For a Critique of the Political Economy of the Sign, 1972) described the collapse of the parallel orders of production and consumption into a general political economy. By demonstrating the homology between material and sign production, Baudrillard was able to define the stage at which commodities are produced immediately as signs and signs as commodities. Use value, exchange value, and sign-exchange value converge in two-sided "object forms" integrated into a functional syntax and controlled by a code that determines their circulation.

In *Le miroir de la production* (The Mirror of Production, 1973), Baudrillard abandoned Marxism, arguing that its categories mirror the capitalist mode of production and are uncritically dependent upon bourgeois political economy. Marxism is a "repressive simulation" of capitalism and therefore incapable of describing life before and after the era of production and of presenting a genuine revolutionary alternative. Baudrillard criticized structural Marxist anthropology because it projects its own categories, without critically transforming them, onto primitive societies. This criticism was made necessary for his theory of primitive societies based upon "symbolic exchange," a concept he adapted from Georges Bataille's notion of a general antiproductivist economy of expenditure (1933) and Marcel Mauss's analysis of the potlatch and the gift (1925).

Baudrillard invests precapitalist societies with principles that cannot be recouped by any economic or semiological logic of value. Eschewing ethnographic detail, Baudrillard defines symbolic exchange as an incessant cycle of giving and receiving at odds with accumulation, scarcity, production, necessity, surplus, and even survival. Accordingly, commodities and signs are produced and consumed under the illusion of "symbolic participation." The political economy of the sign reproduces the exploitative power relations of capitalism, themselves unwittingly mirrored by Marxism.

Baudrillard developed his concepts of simulation and symbolic exchange in *L'échange symbolique et la mort* (Symbolic Exchange and Death, 1976), where he claims that a "structural revolution of value" has abolished and surpassed Ferdinand de Saussure's and Karl Marx's laws of value. Baudrillard explains the social and historical mutations leading to this new era of simulation in a model of three orders of simulacra. In *La transparence du Mal* (The Transparency of Evil, 1990), he added a fourth order. Simulacra emerge from the annihilation and subsequent higher-order reproductions of reference to the real in a pure structural system whose terms trade indeterminably among themselves. Each order has a law (natural, market, structural, fractal), a dominant form (counterfeit, production, simulation, proliferation), displays certain semiotic features (arbitrariness, seriality, codification, viral metonymy), and suggests the successive predominance of different types of signs (corrupt symbol, icon, linguistic sign, index).

The sure and referential symbols of an endogamous society were corrupted by the emergence in the Renaissance of arbitrary signs freed from their referential obligations. These exogamous signs counterfeited an extrasystemic referent as they played together "democratically." With the Industrial Revolution, the extermination of reference made possible the machinic replication of serial signs. These iconic simulacra were dull, repetitive, and operational. In the postindustrial era of simulation, mechanical reproduction gave way to a universal semiotics operating according to the metaphysical models of the code. Conceived in terms of their reproducibility and given the impertinence of the referent, the signs of this order are simulations of second-order iconic simulacra. Today, Baudrillard adds, a fourth fractal order has emerged. The simulation of the simulation of reference has imploded into an uncontrollable metonymic and "viral" proliferation in all directions to infinity. Promiscuity reigns in an unstable condition of transsignification and transversal contamination that erases all distinctions and differences. Baudrillard exploits Benoit Mandelbrot's concept of the fractal (1975) and concepts from biology but without, he thinks, transposing them from their disciplines to his description of the fourth order's "Xerox degree of culture" because they, too, are subject to universal commutation.

In L'échange symbolique, Baudrillard also criticized Sigmund Freud's idea of wit, linguistic interpretations of Saussure's anagrams, and, most controversially, the fetishistic disjunction of life and death through symbolic exchange. His goal was to reclaim death from its "social exile," making it a condition of social being in a reciprocal symbolic relation between the living and the dead. No longer an end nor an individual fatality mourned through melancholy, death is a "gift" received from the cultural Thanatos system, one which must be returned to it as a radical "countergift" if death is to become a symbolic act, breaking the system's control over it.

In L'effet Beaubourg (1977) and A l'ombre des majorités silencieuses (In the Shadow of the Silent Majorities, 1982), Baudrillard elaborated further symbolic countergifts based upon the potlatchlike behavior of the masses. They return the gifts of culture and the simulations of the social by bringing their critical mass to bear upon the Beaubourg and by the pathological manipulation and sumptuary hyperconsumption of signs. During this period, Baudrillard turned his critical concepts of symbolic reversibility and cancellation against Michel Foucault's analyses of power and sexuality in Oublier Foucault (Forget Foucault, 1977).

Baudrillard gave symbolic exchange a new face in De la séduction (Seduction, 1979), although the principle of seduction retained all the features he had invested in the radical alterity of primitive societies. Seduction is still recoverable today despite being transfigured and simulated in a universe incommensurable with the primitive world. Seduction is symbolically effective because it replaces production and challenges "representative signs" bound to transcendent meanings by means of "ritual signs" establishing symbolic pacts. Free from the dictates of an abstract digital code, these signs bind themselves together so strongly that their "senseless unfolding" leaves no room for meaning. Seduction is an agonistic, nondiacritical, antisemiological principle.

Baudrillard renewed his interest in objects in Les stratégies fatales (Fatal Strategies, 1983). Since then, he has published mostly sociological diaries, including Amérique (America, 1986), Cool Memories 1980–85 (1987) and Cool Memories II (1990), and La guerre du golfe n'a pas eu lieu (The Gulf War Did Not Take Place, 1991). In delineating all the senses of "fatality," Baudrillard theorized a world of wily objects potentiating their passions, fulfilling their destinies, and thwarting the subject's will to know them. Baudrillard's theoretical debts to the theaters of Antonin Artaud (1896–1948) and Alfred Jarry (1873–1907) are much in evidence here in the cruel "revenge of things" and the "pataphysical delicacy" of a world he thinks must be seen in the place of the traditional one at whose center subjectivity once stood.

Baudrillard's concern with a postmodern world of simulacra that uncontrollably hyperrealize themselves has manifested itself in his equally extreme style of theorizing. His guiding principle that only a response equal to or greater than the message issued by the system can in theory effectively challenge it has been especially influential among art critics and critical theorists. However, Baudrillard's long-standing critical engagement with signs has been insufficiently analyzed, although therein lie his most perspicacious and disputatious claims to date.

[See also Code; Critique of the Political Economy of the Sign, For a; Postmodernism; and Poststructuralism.]

BIBLIOGRAPHY

Works by Baudrillard

The Systems of Objects (1968). Translated by J. Benedict. London: Verso, 1996.

La société de consommation, ses mythes, ses structures. Paris: S.G.P.P., 1970.

For a Critique of the Political Economy of the Sign (1972). Translated by C. Levin. Saint Louis: Telos Press, 1981.

The Mirror of Production (1973). Translated by M. Poster. Saint Louis: Telos, 1975.

Symbolic Exchange and Death (1976). Translated by I. H. Grant. London: Sage, 1993.

L'effet Beaubourg: Implosion et dissuasion. Paris: Galilée, 1977.

Forget Foucault (1977). Translated by S. Lotringer. New York: Semiotext(e), 1987.

Seduction (1979). Translated by B. Singer. Montreal: New World Perspectives, 1990.

Simulacra and Simulation (1981). Translated by S. Glaser. Ann Arbor: University of Michigan Press, 1994.

In the Shadow of the Silent Majorities (1982). Translated by P. Foss, J. Johnston, and P. Patton. New York: Semiotext(e), 1983.

Fatal Strategies (1983). Translated by P. Beitchman and W.G.J. Niesluchowski. London: Pluto, 1990.

America (1986). Translated by C. Turner. London: Verso, 1988.

Cool Memories 1980–85 (1987). Translated by C. Turner. London: Verso, 1990.

Cool Memories II (1990). Translated by C. Turner. London: Verso, 1996.

The Gulf War Did Not Take Place (1991). Translated by P. Patton. Bloomington: Indiana University Press, 1995.

Other Works

Bataille, G. "The Notion of Expenditure" (1933). Translated by A. Stockl. In *Vision of Excess: Selected Writings, 1927–1939.* Minneapolis: University of Minnesota Press, 1985.

Frankovits, A., ed. *Seduced and Abandoned: The Baudrillard Scene.* Glebe, New South Wales: Stonemoss Services, 1984.

Gane, M. *Baudrillard, Critical and Fatal Theory.* London: Routledge, 1991.

Gane, M. *Baudrillard's Bestiary, Baudrillard and Culture.* London: Routledge, 1991.

Genosko, G. *Baudrillard and Signs.* London: Routledge, 1994.

Kellner, D. *Jean Baudrillard: From Marxism to Postmodernism and Beyond.* Stanford: Stanford University Press, 1989.

Lefebvre, H. *Everyday Life in the Modern World* (1968). Translated by S. Rabinovitch. New York: Harper and Row, 1971.

Mauss, M. *The Gift* (1925). Translated by I. Cunnison. Glencoe, Ill.: Free Press, 1954.

Pefanis, J. *Heterology and the Postmodern: Bataille, Baudrillard, and Lyotard.* Durham, N.C.: Duke University Press, 1991.

Stearns, W., and W. Chaloupka, eds. *Jean Baudrillard: The Disappearance of Art and Politics.* New York: St. Martin's Press, 1992.

—GARY GENOSKO

BENJAMIN, WALTER (1892–1940), German essayist, literary critic, and philosopher whose fragmentary collection of writings refuse to unite into a system of thought. Benjamin's recurring theme, however, is that every mode of signification must be understood in relation to the historical conditions that produced it. For Benjamin, the history of sign production does not unfold in a continuous and rational progression. Rather, history is a sequence of unconnected fragments, where Europe's "cultural treasures" collect in a vast heap of ruins. Even in his personal history as recounted in *Berliner Chronik* (A Berlin Chronicle, 1932)—a recollection of his upbringing in an upper-middle-class Jewish family—he presents the past as "moments and discontinuities" that cannot be fully recovered in the present and thus undermines the very notion of autobiography. His doctoral dissertation, "Der Begriff der Kunstkritik in der deutschen Romantik" (The Concept of Art Criticism in German Romanticism, 1919), also concerns fragments, in this case scattered texts on the philosophy of art by Friedrich Schlegel and Novalis.

In his only complete book-length work of criticism, *Ursprung des deutschen Trauerspiels* (Origin of the German Tragic Drama, 1925), Benjamin practices what he calls "philosophical criticism," the task of which is to transform historical content—the raw material of every work of art—into philosophical truth. Philosophy, however, cannot approach truth itself because truth cannot be grasped objectively in order to be studied. Truth resides in ideas, and ideas inhabit a world of their own that shapes the world of human experience without belonging to it. To describe the relation between ideas and the objects of experience, Benjamin resorts to a simile: "Ideas are to objects as constellations are to stars." Like constellations, ideas have a "discontinuous structure" but hold unconnected entities together. Therefore, any work of criticism that aims to represent ideas in their constellations has to mimic their discontinuity because the form of philosophical discourse is not to be distinguished from its content.

Ideas structure reality by naming it. Since they act only when they are uttered, ideas are something linguistic. Although everyday language obscures the creativity of names, philosophical criticism works to "redeem" them in their truth, rescuing the name from its profane meanings and recovering its sacred power to shape the world. Philosophical criticism is a redemptive semiotics that recalls that every empirical phenomenon has its "origin" in an idea. An origin is the form in which an idea interrupts the course of history. It is not a beginning but a setting into play, and there are as many origins as there are ideas.

Benjamin developed his thesis that language communicates only itself in his essay "Über die Sprache überhaupt und über die Sprache des Menschen" (On Language as Such and on the Language of Man, 1916). He rejects the "bourgeois" notion that words are signs that transfer facts from one person to another. For him, nothing is communicated through language, yet the "linguistic being" of things is communicated *in* language. Everything, moreover, has its own language: There is a language of nature that is nameless and unspoken, just as, according to Genesis, there is a language of God that made the world by naming it. Humanity speaks God's language but names things in order to know them not to create them. Knowing is an act of translation that transforms things by lifting them from the nameless language of nature into the human language of names. Sculpture and painting, for example, are languages that translate things into intelligible forms. The claim that translation is the transformation of one language by another receives extended treatment in "Die Aufgabe des Überstezers" (The Task of the Translator, 1921).

"Einbahnstrasse" (One-Way Street, 1926) uses fragments of prose to translate the language of things into a language of social analysis. These fragments take their titles from the names of objects and the slogans of street signs—for example "Filling Station," "Gloves" and "Post No Bills." By transforming urban objects into prose commentary, Benjamin began to read the city as if it were a literary text.

This shift in his work coincides with his turn toward Marxism. Benjamin's "undialectical" version of Marxism found expression in his vast, unfinished "Passagen-Werk" (Arcades Project, 1927–1940), a set of fragments that translate the political and cultural cityscapes of nineteenth-century Paris into the language of historical materialism. He tries in particular to show how urban life imprinted itself on the work of Charles Baudelaire at a time when innovations in the means of production gave rise to new social forms that created the conditions for new modes of signification. For example, the literary supplements, or feuilletons, that began appearing in Paris newspapers in the late 1830s provided a venue for the development of the serial novel. The world exhibitions fostered the worship of commodities, and the entertainment industry reconceived the working classes as such commodities. The advent of the iron frame in architecture led to the construction of ar-

cades: pedestrian avenues closed to traffic and roofed with glass—the precursors of today's malls. The idler (*flâneur*) who wandered among the displays of goods, seeking out the hidden motives of passersby, protested implicitly against new specializations in the division of labor and was the prototype of the modern detective. In "Über einige Motive bei Baudelaire" (On Some Motifs in Baudelaire, 1939), Benjamin cites the city dweller's everyday contact with the crowd to explain why the experience of shock lies at the center of Baudelaire's work. This sort of shock is what Benjamin calls on writers to deliver to literary traditions in "Der Author als Produzent" (The Author as Producer, 1934). The duty of the socialist author is to fracture that tradition by transforming the forms and techniques of literary production. This "functional transformation"—an idea first advocated by Brecht—makes literature itself a ground for revolution.

While thus declaring that transformation is a matter of personal responsibility, "Das Kunstwerk im Zeitalter seiner technischen Reproduzierbarkeit" (The Work of Art in the Age of Mechanical Reproduction, 1935) acknowledges that change often occurs in ways that artists can neither predict nor control. Nineteenth-century innovations in techniques of reproduction—particularly photography and film—transformed the experience of art in a way that Benjamin calls "the decay of aura." Since aura is an effect of distance, a work that possesses an aura must be unique and remain inaccessible to its audience. Benjamin insists that aura has a ritual function and makes itself available for use in cults, and he defines fascism, with its Führer cult, as a modern ritual that manipulates art for reactionary ends. Yet film and photography make it possible to generate endless copies of a work of art, thereby depriving it of its aura. The mass-produced artwork therefore puts itself at the disposal of socialist politics. Photographs, which have the power to stir their viewer, move the masses to action, while film puts the viewer in the position of the critic, the arbiter of what is right.

In "Über den Begriff der Geschichte" (Theses on the Philosophy of History, 1940), Benjamin argues that the moment when the oppressed class bursts into revolutionary action is a moment of redemption. Revolution is an explosive instant when the Messiah arrives to break history apart. Benjamin's messianism, which he also sketches in his "Theologisch-politisches Fragment" (Theologico-political Fragment, 1920–1921), dispenses with the notion of history as a causal series of successive events in "homogeneous empty time." Benjamin's "historical materialism" breaks up the linear time of historicism into discrete instants of messianic time: "the time of the now," in which the present is not a transition from past to future but a point where the oppressed class gathers its resolve to break the continuum of history and bring time to a halt. To prepare the way for the Messiah, the oppressed class does not direct its gaze forward to the future liberation of its grandchildren but back toward the humiliations of its ancestors. Revolution gains its energy from a memory that recalls that cultural artifacts are not timeless human treasures but concrete signs of the misery of the people who produced them. By amassing signs of past wrongs, the oppressed pack every second of the present with an explosive charge. Benjamin attempts to justify the irruption of messianic violence in "Zur Kritik der Gewalt" (Critique of Violence, 1921).

Benjamin committed suicide in 1940 in Port Bou, France, after he was told he would be handed over to the Nazis. Benjamin's work was largely ignored until a German edition of his writing appeared in 1955. The fragmentary "Passagen-Werk," perhaps Benjamin's major achievement and one of the great Marxist texts, has only begun to attract sustained critical attention.

[See also Barthes; Deconstruction, and Postmodernism.]

BIBLIOGRAPHY

Benjamin, A., and P. Osborne, eds. *Walter Benjamin: Destruction and Experience*. London and New York: Routledge, 1994.

Benjamin, W. *Illuminations: Essays and Reflections*. Edited by H. Arendt, translated by H. Zohn. New York: Schocken Books, 1968.

Benjamin, W. *Berliner Chronik*. Frankfurt: Suhrkamp, 1970.

Benjamin, W. *Origin of the German Tragic Drama*. Translated by John Osborne. London: NLB, 1977.

Benjamin, W. *Reflections: Essays, Aphorisms, Autobiographical Writings*. Edited by P. Demetz, translated by E. Jephcott. New York: Schocken Books, 1978.

Buck-Morss, S. *The Dialectics of Seeing: Walter Benjamin and the Arcades Project*. Cambridge, Mass., and London: MIT Press, 1989.

Cohen, M. *Profane Illumination: Walter Benjamin and the Paris of Surrealist Revolution*. Berkeley: University of California Press, 1993.

Eagleton, T. *Walter Benjamin, or Towards a Revolutionary Criticism*. London and New York: Verso, 1981.

McCole, J. *Walter Benjamin and the Antinomies of Tradition*. Ithaca, N.Y.: Cornell University Press, 1993.

Scholem, G. *Walter Benjamin: The Story of a Friendship*. Translated by H. Zohn. Philadelphia: Jewish Publication Society of America, 1981.

Witte, B. *Walter Benjamin: An Intellectual Biography*. Translated by J. Rolleston. Detroit: Wayne State University Press, 1991.

Wolin, R. *Walter Benjamin: An Aesthetic of Redemption*. New York: Columbia University Press, 1982.

—CHRISTOPHER BRACKEN

BENSE, MAX (1910–1990), German scientist and philosopher. The founder of the "Stuttgart School"—probably more an intellectual movement than a coherent semiotic school—Max Bense was a controversial scholar and teacher. His entire work is shaped by his formative years of studying physics as well as mathematics, chemistry, and geology. Under the supervision of Oskar Becker, he wrote a dissertation on quantum mechanics and relativity (1937). His postdoctoral work is on a spiritual history of mathematics (1946). In light of this background, Bense's writings in philosophy, aesthetics, semiotics, text theory, and even his atheistic literature, political articles, and his poetry appear as a continuation of his scientific work. Indeed, his ambition was to establish a scientific foundation for those areas of the humanities in which he became interested. This ambition frequently led him to create "circles" and publications dedicated to his program.

Bense contributed powerful ideas to contemporary semiotics, but their significance is best appreciated in the broader context of his heterogeneous work. As an existential rationalist, he very early refuted speculative philosophy. Under the influence of the then-emerging fields of information theory and cybernetics, he proceeded, as did Abraham A. Moles (1920–1993), with a very ambitious project for a new aesthetics that emphasized the mathematical and technical foundations of what he defined as creative processes and the resulting artifacts. His work, entitled *Aesthetica* (1954), in some ways parallels that of the founder of aesthetics, Alexander Baumgarten (1714–1762). Semiotic considerations that Baumgarten only enunciated but never elaborated became a major theme of Bense's work. Modeled after Claude Shannon and Warren Weaver's syntactic model of communication (1949) and heavily indebted to information theory, Bense's information aesthetics contains both a quantitative aesthetics and a semiotic aesthetics. Within quantitative aesthetics, ideas taken from Christian von Ehrenfels (1859–1932) on Gestalt degrees (1916) and George D. Birkhoff (1884–1944) on aesthetic measure as a relation between order and complexity (1933) are transformed into quantifiers that describe and measure aesthetic states. But Bense's real breakthrough is in his semiotic thought.

Bense stated correctly that there are no specific aesthetic signs but rather aesthetic functions fulfilled in given contexts of interpretation. Firmly anchored in reality, Bense was obsessed with how much of the object represented in an artwork is present and identifiable as such in the work. Here he introduced the notion of semiotic information: the degree of presence of the object in the material embodiment of signs participating in a work of art. The inverse of semiotic information is semioticity, or the degree of independence of the object from its representation. Later on, semioticity was to define the conventional nature of aesthetic artifacts.

It is no accident, though quite paradoxical, that Bense's semiotic attempt unfolds within a Peircean framework, the terminology of which he adopted in view of its resonance with his own vocabulary. Moreover, Peirce's scientific background made him literally a model for Bense. Remarkably, Bense converted the dynamic thought fundamental to Peirce's semiotics, and best embodied in the notion of semiosis, into a structuralist posture to which Bense remained captive in the end. Peirce offered the scheme of typology; Bense filled the cells and looked further for a semiotic calculus. Finally, he discovered this calculus in the form of the semiotic matrix and matrix operation, especially the so-called inverse matrix that translates sign typologies back into the realm of the object represented. This achievement needs more than acknowledgment. It is indeed exciting to conceive of a universal semiotics as powerful and effective as, say, calculus or information theory.

As has been pointed out in articles and lectures dealing with Bense's contribution to contemporary aesthetics, the effort goes counter to the implicit assumption of Peirce's semiotics, which is that of infinite sign processes. This explains why Bense kept changing the terminology of his aesthetic semiotics. For a while, the aesthetic condition was represented by an iconic supersign displaying aestheticity. Later, art seemed to have an iconic appearance—an indexical reality—but a symbolic existence. And again, further down the road of his brilliant but undisciplined research, art was represented by a very well defined Peircean rhematic-indexical-legisign whose formulation he justified thus: Art is open-ended (the rhematic character); it is intentional and singular (the indexical aspect); and it is conventional (the legisign). What seems to escape this obsession with typologies is the elementary concern with the interpretant dimension of each sign.

A direction of investigation inspired by Bense that deserves more attention than provided until now is that of generative procedures. Bense is the author of the innovative idea of generative aesthetics, and in this capacity he wrote quite impressively about what it takes to program a machine for generating artifacts endowed with aesthetic characteristics. Under his direction, research was carried out in Germany that was much ahead of research done in other countries; exhibitions, in which semiotic aspects were discussed ardently, embodied these investigations.

Bense contributed quite a bit more to the interest in and exercise of semiotics in Germany and in the countries where his students became active (notably Brazil). Text semiotics, which in his view is the analytical classification of texts from an aesthetic and semantic viewpoint, and semiotic models applied to design, education, photography, and visual communication were the subjects of many of his publications. He can be credited with major advances in visual semiotics; and within this concern, he stimulated attempts toward applied semiotics in product design, architecture, and visual communication. But probably the most lasting legacy of Bense's semiotic work remains embodied in the course of study he initiated at the University of Stuttgart and in the work of his many colleagues and students. Among those whose work in semiotics he influenced decisively are Elisabeth Walther, Hans Brög (in the field of art education), Manfred Schmalriede (the Gestalt aspect), Siegfried Maser (design), Frieder Nake (generative procedures), Borek Sipek (architecture), Georg Kiefer (environment), and T. A. Schulz (Peircean semiotics). He edited the journal *Semiosis* (founded in 1976) and organized semiotic seminars at the University of Stuttgart.

[See also Aesthetics; Art; Cybernetics; Information; Peirce; *and* Semiosis.]

BIBLIOGRAPHY

Works by Bense

Quantenmechanik und Daseinsrelativität. Cologne: Verlag Kiepenheuer und Witsch, 1938.

Konturen einer Geistesgeschichte der Mathematik. Hamburg: Classen and Coverts, 1946–1949.

Technische Intelligenz. Stuttgart: Deutsche Verlagsanstalt, 1949.

Plakattwelt. Stuttgart: Deutsche Verlagsanstalt, 1952.

Aesthetica: Metaphysische Beobachtungen am Schönen. Stuttgart: Deutsche Verlagsanstalt, 1954.

Theorie der Texte. Cologne: Verlag Kiepenheuer and Witsch, 1962.

Semiotik. Allgemeine Theorie der Zeichen. Baden-Baden: Agis-Verlag, 1967.

Einführung in die informationstheoretische Ästhetik. Hamburg: Rowohlt, 1969.

Zeichen und Design: Semiotische Ästhetik. Baden-Baden: Agis-Verlag, 1971.

Semiotische Prozesses und Systeme in Wissenschaftstheorie und Design, Ästhetik, und Mathematik. Baden-Baden: Agis-Verlag, 1975.

Other Works

Baumgarten, A. G. *Aesthetica* (1750). Hildesheim, Germany: G. Olms, 1961.

Birkhoff, G. D. *Aesthetic Measure.* Cambridge, Mass.: Harvard University Press, 1933.

Ehrenfels, C. von. *Foundations of Gestalt* (1916). Munich: Philosophia Verlag, 1988.

Shannon, C. E., and W. Weaver. *The Mathematical Theory of Communication.* Urbana: University of Illinois Press, 1949.

—MIHAI NADIN

BHARTṚHARI (fifth century), Indian philosopher and grammarian. Bhartṛhari belongs to the grammatical school of classical Indian tradition, which includes Pāṇini, Kātyāyana, and Patañjali as his illustrious predecessors. Most contemporary scholars believe that he lived in the fifth century, though an account of the Chinese traveler Yijing suggests a period two centuries later. Bhartṛhari also figures in Sanskrit literature as a major poet.

Bhartṛhari's reputation today as a major philosopher of language is next only to that of Pāṇini as a grammarian. His seminal work in this domain is *Vākyapadīyam* (On Sentences and Words), which is divided into three sections or *kāṇḍas* that scholars refer to as "Brahmakāṇḍa," "Vākyakāṇḍa," and "Padakāṇḍa" or "Prakīrnakāṇḍa."

Vākyapadīyam begins with a lengthy discourse on the metaphysical issues concerning language. The focus here is the linguistic basis of the ultimate reality or *brahman*. The source of these speculations is the prevalent idea that the universe is in the nature of sound or word (i.e., *śabdabrahma*). Section 2 contains Bhartṛhari's philosophy of grammar, presenting his arguments on the relationship between sentences and words, between the sequenceless and the se-

quential, between the universal and the particular, and between form and meaning. Section 3 is a detailed two-part discussion of the properties or categories of words such as *jāti* (universal/class), *dravya* (substance), *bhūyodravya* (another class of substance), *sambandha* (relation), *guṇa* (quality), *dik* (position/direction), *sādhana* (means/accessories of action), *kriyā* (action), *kalā* (time), *puruṣa* (person), *sāṃkhya* (number), *upagraha* (aspect), *liṅga* (gender), and *vṛtti* (complex word formations, each of which are made up of meaningful elements and give an integrated meaning that is somewhat different from those of the parts). This chapter is called "Padakāṇḍa" or "Prakīrṇa" (Miscellany). According to K. Raghavan Pillai (notes to Bhartṛhari, 1971), Bhartṛhari's authorship of the third *kāṇḍa* is disputed by some scholars of the tradition.

"Brahmakāṇḍa" is a treatise on the metaphysics and ontology of the form and meaning aspects of language. Among the philosophical speculations presented here, Bhartṛhari regards the form of the word as the result of eternal transformations of the *śabdabrahma* (the primordial and eternal word or sound). Meaning is also understood as a dynamic process involving the particular instantiation or activation of the *śabdabrahma* by way of a spontaneous emergence or "bursting forth" (*sphoṭa*) of meaning in the intellect (*pratibhā*) of the speaker or hearer. *Sphoṭa* is the main concept of the meaning in the Brahmanic tradition and refers to the spontaneous transformation of the undifferentiated (semantic) part of language into the differentiated (sound) part (*dhvani*), or perhaps even the reverse.

The main aspect of Bhartṛhari's metaphysics is the constancy and the omnipresence of transformations in the universe. Both the word and the world are the result of the eternal transformations or apparent differentiations of a cosmic unity (the *śabdabrahma*). (The ultimate principle of the *brahman* is the sound-word, referred to as *śabdatattva*). From an eternalist perspective, these transformations and differentiations are unreal and illusory. Time, as one of the elements of the unchanging cosmic unity, is the material force that produces these transformations, which are in turn perceived and cognized as actions of particular things. The *śabdabrahma* is initially differentiated into its mental and material media, and the force of time (*kalāśakti*) affects both these aspects.

In the ever-differentiating domain of the world, there are essentially two kinds of transformations af-

fected by the power of time, namely birth or manifestation and death or hiding. More specifically, there
are six kinds of transformations in the world: birth,
existence, change, increase, decrease, and death. The
transformations between the intellect and its verbal
manifestation involve at least three stages: *parā* (eternal), *paśyanti* (mental/transcendental), and *madhyamā* (mediatory/phonemic). The fourth stage
(*vaikharī*) is that of differentiated (phonetic) speech.

One of Bhartṛhari's central assumptions is that the
"word in the intellect" is the "cause" of the manifest
word. The intellect is believed to be undifferentiated
and therefore sequenceless, in contrast to the spoken
word. The meaning of the spoken word could be an
object "which is connected to some action."

It is difficult to say whether Bhartṛhari's notion of
sphoṭa coincided with the word in the intellect or
with the spontaneous bursting forth of the recognition of meaning. Both probably have roles in the
grasping of meaning. If this view is correct, then we
can think of the word-in-the-intellect aspect of *sphoṭa*
as a kind of deep mental schema (in the Kantian
sense) and the flashlike understanding as akin to the
"spontaneous synthesis" supposed by Kant. The latter connection has, in fact, been proposed by T. R. V.
Murti (see Coward, 1980:67). The key point is that
meaning apprehension involves an internal mental
representation of the word, which is ultimately linked
to the eternal word. Thus, Bhartṛhari does attribute
some innate linguistic knowledge to the newborn
child; just as the infant has the ability to breathe or
to make the simplest of movements (which no one
has taught it), so it is the possessor of a thread of the
eternal knowledge.

The relation between the word in the intellect and
the spoken word is construed not as the relation between the internal and the external but as that between the fixed and static on the one side and the
mobile and the dynamic on the other. A comparison
is made with the apparent movement of a static thing
when reflected in moving water. There is also a more
telling comparison with the structure of sensation
(i.e., sense-perceiving organs) and the perceived objects. *Sphoṭa*, or the meaning in the mind, grasps the
sound form just as the sense organs perceive the
sensed objects.

As an *Anvitabhidhānavādin* (one who argues that
the undivided sentence has meaning, opposed to the
Abhihitanvayavādins, who grant meaning to individual words), Bhartṛhari affirms that only the sen-

tence—not the words, which do not signify anything
in the world—can completely express "reality."
Consequently, reality is expressible only in the form
"it exists," implying that linguistic expressions must
be compounded with an existential verb. Further, the
verb—designed to denote an action—constitutes the
essential and minimal content of a sentence.

The concept of "action," the unifying pivot of the
meaning of a sentence, represented by a verb, is central to the Indian grammatical tradition. Bhartṛhari's
preferred definition of the sententially represented
action is the following: "Whenever something, finished or unfinished, is presented as something to be
accomplished [i.e., *sādhya*], then it is called ⟨action⟩
because of its having acquired the form of sequence."
He also favors Patañjali's definition, per which "action is the distinctive mode of behavior of the accessories," and seems to be rejecting another view
wherein "action is that moment immediately after
which the result is produced" (e.g., in cooking, there
is a critical moment that separates the cooked state
from the raw state).

The fact that action is something that has the form
of parts arranged in sequence entails that it cannot
be perceived directly. It can be inferred only by the
mind. *Vākyapadīyam* (3.8.4) states: "What is called action is a collection of parts produced in a sequence
and mentally conceived as one and identical with the
parts which are subordinated to it (i.e., the whole)."
The argument here is that since an action can be infinitely divided into its temporal subparts, it cannot
be perceived directly but only inferred. In cooking,
the subparts, including the transformation of the raw
into the cooked state, are subject to unified inference.

An important principle that Bhartṛhari shares with
the other grammarians and not with the logicians
(Naiyāyikas) is that for the grammarian, reality is understood only through speech and language, and it
is understood only in the form in which it is presented by speech. Language cannot describe the intrinsic nature of things, although we know of the
world only in the form in which words present it.
Bimal Matilal (1990) has suggested that from this perspective, knowing is "languageing."

Bhartṛhari rejects the existence of individual word
meanings as an illusion. Only the undifferentiated
meaning of a sentence is real. The sentence meaning
is not a concatenation of word meanings as argued
by the Mīmāmsā philosophers and others; rather, it
is to be understood in terms of a "complex cogni-

tion." Bhartṛhari compares this complex cognition with that of the cognition of a picture (citrajñāna). Thus, in his top-down analysis, the apparent word meanings are the result of rather artificial analysis. The relationship between sentence meaning and word meaning is compared to that between a picture and its component parts and colors.

Bhartṛhari's views on the sentence and its meaning may be summarized as follows: The sentence represents and reveals at least a fragment of the eternal activity in the universe, presented from the point of view of the speaker. The verb highlights the specific character of this activity, expressed through the accessories and means and their qualities. These accessories in action are referred to in the grammatical context as kārakas (a factor of action; actant). Bhartṛhari's conception of the kāraka, a key term in Indian grammatical literature, can be understood as follows. A sentence represents and reveals the accomplishment of an action. Means and accessories (sādhana) are the power (śakti) of a thing to accomplish actions. The difference in the powers of objects is relative to the form that speakers subjectively impose on them. Each object that is involved in any action and at any time is seen as having a particular means or power for that time. The particular help rendered to the action is expressed by the case markers. Kāraka is that which helps in the accomplishment of an action by assuming different forms (thus, kāraka is different from the logicians' notions of hetu [cause] and lakṣana [sign], which are relatively more based in the world). It is claimed that an object can have any one of six different powers responsible for action. These six powers correspond to the six kārakas: kartā (actor), karma (the object or goal), karaṇa (instrument), adhikaraṇa (the location of action), sampradāna (the destination), and apadāna (the source of action). These correspond roughly to the nominative, accusative, instrumental, locative, dative, and ablative notions of Latin-based grammars, but the philsophical underpinnings are very different.

[See also Actantial Model; Actants; Burke; Catastrophe Theory; and Meaning].

BIBLIOGRAPHY

Bhartṛhari. The Vākyapadīya. Translated and with notes by K. Raghavan Pillai. Delhi: Motilal Banarasidass, 1971. Critical texts of cantos 1 and 2.

Bhartṛhari. The Vākyapadīya. Translated by K. A. Subramania Iyer. Poona: Deccan College Postgraduate and Research Institute, 1971. Chapter 3, part 1.

Bhartṛhari. The Vākyapadīya. Translated by K. A. Subramania Iyer. Delhi: Motilal Banarasidass, 1974. Chapter 3, part 2.

Bhartṛhari. The Vākyapadīya: Kāṇḍa II. Translated and with notes by K. A. Subramania Iyer. Delhi: Motilal Banarasidass, 1977.

Coward, H. C. The Sphoṭa Theory of Language: A Philosophical Analysis. Delhi: Motilal Banarasidass, 1980.

Matilal, B. The Word and the World: India's Contribution to the Study of Language. Oxford: Oxford University Press, 1990.

Murti, T. R. V. "Some Thoughts on the Philosophy of Language in the Indian Context." Journal of Indian Philosophy 2 (1974): 321–331.

Scharfe, H. Grammatical Literature, vol. 5, fasc. 2, History of Indian Literature. Edited by J. Gonda. Wiesbaden: Otto Harrassowitz, 1977.

Staal, J. F., ed. A Reader on Sanskrit Grammarians. Delhi: Motilal Banarasidass, 1985.

Subramania Iyer, K. A. Bhartṛhari: A Study of Vākyapadīya in the Light of Ancient Commentaries. Poona: Deccan College Postgraduate Research Institute, 1969.

—FRANSON MANJALI

BINARISM is the characteristic feature of systems that are based on pairs of oppositions. The Latin bini, from the same root as duo (two), means "two by two," "twofold," and "double." The adjective binarius applies to any object characterized by some form of duality.

The linguistic concept of binary opposition has its basis in the Cours de linguistique générale (Course in General Linguistics, 1916), in which Ferdinand de Saussure proposes a more abstract level of analysis of the sounds of language than that which had hitherto characterized the study of speech sounds. Saussure bases his analysis on what he calls the "articulatory act." This is an important descriptive principle since acoustic units alone cannot be the basis of the description. These must be linked to what Saussure refers to as the "chain of movements in phonation" (1971, p. 65), claiming that to each sound corresponds an articulatory moment. Thus, the first descriptive units that are obtained by segmenting the spoken chain are called phonemes.

Saussure's overriding concern is to establish general principles of analysis. These principles leave aside those acoustic "nuances" that do not make a categorical difference so as to discover the underlying principle of the sound system. Saussure is less interested in what these phonemes consist of, positively speaking, than in those "negative factors" that have a "differentiating value." First, Saussure proposes four principles for specifying phonemes: expiration, oral articulation, vibration of the larynx, and nasal resonance. He then excludes expiration on the grounds that it is a "positive factor" that is present in all acts of phonation. Consequently, it has no differentiating value, though all the remaining terms do. Saussure proposes the schema of the possible variations shown in figure 1.

Putting aside oral articulation for the moment, the four vertical columns indicate whether the four types of sound are differentiated by laryngeal or nasal vibration. Noting that sounds were generally classified according to the "place of their articulation" in the vocal apparatus, Saussure proposes a different and far more general schema, which he bases on the principle of oral articulation: *all* vocal sounds are classifiable in terms of the opposition between "complete closure and maximal openness." The opposition between these two new terms constitutes the two extremes of a hypothetical space in relation to which Saussure classifies seven categories of sounds. Thus, "it is only within each category," Saussure claims, "that we distribute the phonemes into diverse types according to their own place of articulation" (1971, p. 70). This shows that he had discovered the categorical nature of phonetic perception and the topological basis of the organization of these categories.

The main thrust of Saussure's proposals is directed against a science of the sounds of language that takes single, isolable sounds as its point of departure. His theory is concerned with "relations of internal dependency" between sounds in a given sequence. But when two sounds are combined, these relations of internal dependency entail reciprocal constraints whereby "there is a limit to the variations in one with respect to the other." This implicates more general "relations and rules," which it is the business of the linguist to discover. There is, then, as Saussure argues, a place for "a science which takes as its point of departure the binary groups and sequences of phonemes" (1971, p. 78). This science will consider such binary groups to be "like algebraic equations; a binary group implicates a certain number of mechanical and acoustical elements which reciprocally condition one another."

In his pioneering study, the *Principles of Phonology* (1939), Nikolaj Trubetzkoy clearly formulated the distinction between phonology and phonetics as modern linguists understand it. Trubetzkoy quite explicitly distances himself from Saussure, who attached little importance to "the distinction between the study of sound pertaining to *parole* and the study of sound pertaining to *langue*." It was Trubetzkoy, along with Roman Jakobson and Sergej Karcevskij, who first made the modern distinction between phonetics and phonology at the first international congress of linguists in the Hague in 1928. Trubetzkoy retains the crucial Saussurean concept of opposition, but in so doing he abstracts this from the material medium in which sounds are made. Phonologically distinctive oppositions are those oppositions of sound that distinguish the meaning of one word from some other word in the same language. Trubetzkoy calls such oppositions the meaning-differentiating functions of sound. Not all oppositions of sound are distinctive in this way. Such oppositions are said to be phonologically nondistinctive.

In English, the opposition between the phonemes /n/ and /ŋ/, as in the words *sin* and *sing*, is phonologically distinctive. A further example is the phonological opposition between the singular and the

FIGURE 1. *Saussure's Schema of Possible Varieties of Speech Sounds.* The schema has been adapted slightly to approximate modern notational conventions. Key: lg = laryngeal vibration; nv = nasal vibration; + = presence of feature; − = absence of feature.

	1 Voiceless Sounds	2 Voiced Sounds	3 Voiceless Nasal Sounds	4 Voiced Nasal Sounds
a	Expiration	Expiration	Expiration	Expiration
b	Oral articulation	Oral articulation	Oral articulation	Oral articulation
c	[−lg]	[+lg]	[−lg]	[+lg]
d	[−nv]	[−nv]	[+nv]	[+nv]

plural morphemes /ʊ/ and /i:/ in the words *foot* and *feet*. On the other hand, the phonological oppositions among the phonemes /z/, /iz/, and /s/, which realize the plural morpheme in words such as *bananas*, *horses*, and *cats*, are phonologically nondistinctive. Each of these occurs in phonologically distinct groups, but they all realize the same meaning of plurality. For this reason, they are not meaning differentiating in the Trubetzkoy analysis. Thus, /iz/ occurs after sibilant and affricative consonants; /s/ occurs after voiceless consonants; and /z/ occurs in all other possible phonological environments, such as after voiced sounds.

Each member of an opposition is what Trubetzkoy defines as a "phonological (or distinctive) unit." The smallest phonological unit is the phoneme. The meaning Trubetzkoy gave to this term is different from the Saussurean use. The phoneme cannot be further analyzed into still smaller distinctive units. Trubetzkoy points out that phonemes are not the "building blocks out of which individual words are assembled." Rather, a word, which is a phonic entity, is a gestalt: a functionally defined configuration in which phonemes are the distinctive marks.

Trubetzkoy's framework is a structural-functional one that is concerned with the distribution of phonological forms in phonemic configurations. The particular distributions are functions of the phonological systems of a given language. Trubetzkoy's concept of the phoneme means that it is a kind of phonological category. Thus, regularities in the phonetic organization of the language differentially realize phonological categories.

A phonological category is defined along two dimensions: the paradigmatic and the syntagmatic axes. Phonologists use the first of these to specify the nature of the phonetic regularities that realize a given phoneme. This is where the concept of binary opposition is important. Phonologists say that a given phoneme either has or does not have a given feature. They specify the presence or the absence of a feature by using the "+" and "−" signs. For example, the notation [+ consonantal] means that a given phoneme is consonantal; vowels are nonconsonantal. The notation [+ tense] means a phoneme is tense, as opposed to lax—acoustically speaking, the steady-state portion of the sound is lengthened as opposed to reduced [+ lax].

Phonologists developed a matrix form of representation in order to represent the interaction of the paradigmatic and syntagmatic dimensions. The paradigmatic dimension is represented by a series of vertical rows. The syntagmatic dimension is represented horizontally. This dimension specifies the actual sequence of phonemes as they occur in a word. These are the functionally related parts that make up the whole gestalt (word).

As shown in figure 2, Noam Chomsky and Morris Halle use numbers to express the stress contour of a word. The first vertical row shows the binary specification of features for the initial phoneme /i/ in the word *inn*. The phoneme comprises the bundle of features specified. Phonologists specify these features as a binary opposition between the presence or absence of that feature (see above). Thus, the phoneme /i/: (1) is nonconsonantal; (2) is vocalic; (3) has second-degree nasality; (4) is nontense; (5) has first-degree stress; (6) is voiced; (7) is continuant.

Unlike Saussure, the Chomsky-Halle analysis, which follows in the tradition first proposed by Trubetzkoy and Jakobson, has no basis in the material reality of sound substance. It is a purely abstract representation. It makes no reference to the "articulatory act" in Saussure's sense. Chomsky and Halle

FIGURE 2. *Phonetic Matrices for the Words* Inn *and* Algebra. (From Chomsky and Halle, 1968, p. 165.)

	(a) *inn*		(b) *algebra*						
	i	n	œ	l	g	e	b	r	œ
consonantal	−	+	−	+	+	−	+	+	−
vocalic	+	−	+	+	−	+	−	+	+
nasal	2	+	−	−	−	−	−	−	−
tense	−	−	−	−	−	−	−	−	−
stress	1	−	1	−	−	4	−	−	4
voice	+	+	+	+	+	+	+	+	+
continuant	+	−	+	+	−	+	−	+	+

claim a perceptual (not articulatory) reality for these features.

Roman Jakobson and Morris Halle (1956) make a clear-cut distinction between the semantic level of language and what they call its feature level. The first involves meaningful units of varying degrees of complexity; these range from morpheme to discourse. The feature level is the phonological level. On this level, the units and their combinations serve merely to differentiate and to "cement" or "partition" or otherwise highlight the meaningful units on the first level. They have no meaning of their own. Two observations are in order. First, Jakobson and Halle follow the structuralists' separation of the phonology from the materiality of sound substance. Second, they suggest that distinctive features on both the phonological and the semantic levels entail a choice between the two terms of some binary opposition.

The Jakobson-Halle account presents us with a number of significant departures from Saussure's position. Saussure did not project the binary principles of organization that he discovered in the signifier onto the level (stratum) of the signified. Further, Saussure considered both levels to be meaning making (value producing). Thus, the structuralists' account of binary oppositions, as witnessed in the work of some of its key exponents, involves a radical recontextualization of Saussure's conception. In the structuralists' account, this entailed: (1) a clearcut distinction between form (phonology) and meaning (semantics). This is not the same as Saussure's conception of the relationship between signifier and signified, which Saussure envisaged as a single meaning-making complex; and (2) the projection of the principle of binary oppositions from phonology onto semantics. This move has important consequences for the subsequent development of this principle.

Structural semanticists adopted and further developed the techniques of distinctive-feature analysis of phonological oppositions. They attempted to analyze meaning in its minimal semantic units. By analogy with the work that phonologists had carried out, semanticists sought to "decompose" meaning itself into binary oppositions of distinctive features. A vast literature characterized this endeavor. Depending on specific allegiances or traditions, these attempts were referred to as "componential analysis" or "combinatorial semantics," to name just two. Likewise, structural semanticists variously called the minimal units of meaning that they analyzed "semes" or "sem-

emes." The partial parallelism with the term *phoneme* reflects this interest in minimal units of meaning, which they sought to define as binary oppositions of semantic features. Broadly speaking, there were two main approaches. The first was concerned with the psychological reality of the units so identified. Exponents of this approach include Manfred Bierwisch (1970) and Jerold Katz (1966). This perspective is concerned with the universal conceptual substance of language, which semanticists of this persuasion see as organized in terms of a finite number of semantic components. They believe these to be independent of the semantic structure of particular languages.

The second perspective is interested in metalinguistic questions and has its basis in Louis Hjelmslev's proposals concerning the structured organization of the vocabulary of language (1959). These semanticists attempted to organize this as a closed system of items, in accordance with the principles Hjelmslev had developed for the analysis of grammar. Exponents of this approach include Luis Prieto (1964) and Algirdas Julien Greimas (1966).

The following examples express the basic principles of this approach. Consider the proportionalities man:woman::stallion:mare. This reads: "man is to woman as stallion is to mare." In other words, the two terms in the first pair share features that are not shared by the two terms in the second pair and vice versa. According to structural semanticists, the two pairs of terms have a number of distinctive semantic features (or semes or sememes) in common. By a process of factorization (Lyons, 1968), it is possible to determine the minimal semantic features that compose the meaning of the word. Thus:

man :	woman ::	stallion :	mare
[+ human]	[+ human]	[+ equine]	[+ equine]
[+ male]	[+ female]	[+ male]	[+ female]
[+ adult]	[+ adult]	[+ adult]	[+ adult]

As with the phonological analysis, structural semanticists represent each feature as a binary contrast between the presence or absence of some feature. Lyons (1968, p. 472) points out that this type of analysis has a long history and did not necessarily originate with the structural approach to semantics in the twentieth century. The same principles occur in the traditional method of definition whereby a genus is divided into species and the species into subspecies. Yet the most direct influence on the structural semanticists remains the phonological theory that Trubetzkoy and Jakobson pioneered. The principles of structural semantics have proved widely influential. There have been applications and further developments in disciplines such as anthropology, psychology, sociology, philosophy, and logic. Researchers in these areas took up the principles of structural semantics in their quest for the "underlying" conceptual or cognitive structures of particular cultures.

A number of theoretical and methodological problems remain unsolved. First, structural semanticists believed that it was the properties of the conceptual substance that somehow characterized word meanings. Second, the widespread interest in the techniques and claims of structuralist semantics outside mainstream linguistics occurred at a time when linguists showed little interest in the relationship of lexis to grammar. This led to a general failure, both within and outside linguistics, to understand that lexis and grammar are related. Third, this failure meant that ad hoc and ultimately tautologous descriptions of a restricted set of vocabulary items effectively replaced the analysis of the only domain in which the structural principles of cognition are evidenced: the categorical organization of lexicogrammatical form.

The French anthropologist Claude Lévi-Strauss adopted the phonemic principle of binary oppositions in his analysis of myth, explicitly acknowledging his debt to the work of Trubetzkoy and Jakobson. Yet he also claimed his analysis of "mythemes" to be on a higher level than that of phonemes and sememes (Lévi-Strauss, 1972). In his analyses, he proposed oppositions between categories such as raw and cooked, life and death, male and female, and nature and culture.

Anthony Wilden (1981) has effectively criticized Lévi-Strauss's use of binary oppositions by pointing out that many so-called binary oppositions are, in fact, hierarchical and conflictual. Some relations are true oppositional ones; many others are not. The concept of the binary opposition can have the effect of reducing a hierarchical and hence nonsymmetrical relationship to a symmetrical and oppositional one. In a genuine hierarchical relation, Wilden argues, one term is dependent on another. Lévi-Strauss's opposition between "nature" and "culture" is a good illustration of this: Culture is dependent on the higher-order system of material and ecosystemic relations and processes in the natural environment;

thus, nature and culture are not two discrete entities opposed to each other. There are continual exchanges of matter, energy, and information that cross-couple the two in a unified system of relationships of various orders of complexity. In other words, Wilden shows that the real nature of the material and social relations involved is flattened out as if it were a single level and symmetrical one between two opposing sides. Wilden's wider point is that Lévi-Strauss, in raising binary oppositions from a methodological to an ontological status, ends up reproducing, probably unconsciously, the principles of domination and exploitation that characterize capitalist socioeconomic relations. In raising binary oppositions to the status of an ontology, Lévi-Strauss accords these a universal status insofar as the binary opposition, along with the categories of mythical thought he analyzes, come to be seen as universal categories of mind. He fails to appreciate these as ethnocentric projections onto non-Western cultures of his own reified and digitalized ontological categories of Western thought.

For example, in his analysis of the role of the trickster in North American mythology, Lévi-Strauss (1972, pp. 224–225) poses the following question: Why is this role almost invariably assigned to either the coyote or the raven? To answer this question, Lévi-Strauss reorganizes these myths by using the matrix representation developed by structural phonologists. To each vertical column, he assigns a number of binary oppositions, whose relations constitute a mytheme. The columns are to be read as a progression going from left to right. According to Lévi-Strauss, the elements in each column combine to generate the elements in the next rightmost column. Thus, the initial binary opposition between life and death is replaced by two equivalent terms: agriculture and warfare. A third term—hunting—mediates these two. In the third and final column, herbivorous animals and beasts of prey replace the previous pair. The third term that mediates this new pair is carrion-eating animals (such as coyotes and ravens).

Lévi-Strauss makes no hierarchical distinctions between levels in his analysis. His concept of the mytheme is an explicit appropriation of the structural phonologists' notion of the phoneme, but these phonologists excluded meaning from this level of their analysis. Lévi-Strauss, however, admits meaning into his analysis, though the only meanings are those that the binary oppositions between the mythemes have already defined. Lévi-Strauss replicates the digital (discrete, discontinuous) mode of analysis that phonologists had applied to the phonological level but applies it at all levels. In effect, the analysis "flattens out" the levels so that they resemble the type of digital organization mentioned earlier. Lévi-Strauss does not connect the meanings he identifies to the higher-order cultural relations and processes that define what the meaning of something is. He has no theory of context; he projects the context-free assumptions that the structural phonologists made about phonological oppositions onto the level of meaning itself.

In recent years, poststructuralist and feminist theorists have extensively critiqued the theory of binary oppositions, especially the structuralist appropriation of it as a theory of meaning. What Lévi-Strauss projects as universal schemata of meaning resemble the "self-conscious subject" that Georg Wilhelm Friedrich Hegel (1770–1831) analyzes in his *Phenomenology of Mind* (1807). This is a universalist and masculine subjectivity that constantly pits itself against the other in a life-and-death struggle for existence. In this oppositional logic, the two subjects must, in order to survive, "bring their certainty of themselves, the certainty of being for themselves, to the level of objective truth" (Hegel, 1967, p. 232). In order to sustain this struggle so that the two self-consciousnesses do not simply negate each other, Hegel suggests the need for a "middle term." In this way, the mutual "giving" and "taking"—that is, the competitive social basis of the relation—is upheld. What Lévi-Strauss reproduces is the universalist and masculine ontology of the self as strongly insulated from the other. Self and other here reproduce the logic of the digital code of discrete, discontinuous oppositions between the two. It is a logic of struggle, control, domination, and production. It is the logic of capitalist socioeconomic relations raised to the status of an ontology and of a scientific method.

The structuralist appropriation of the concept of binary oppositions involved two strategic recontextualizations. In the first, the structural phonologists asserted that the principle of the binary opposition is the fundamental organizing principle of phonology. Saussure, in contrast, postulated an interstratal view of the way in which the less abstract and material sound substance is reconstrued or recontextualized by the value-producing differences that are intrinsic to the more abstract and higher level of phonological form (the signifier). This was a thoroughly hierarchical and hence contextual theory of the way phonological form categorizes significant differences in sound substance. As the relevant parts of the *Course in General Linguistics* show, there is, in turn, a further reconstrual of these differences at the still more abstract level of value-producing forms on the level of the signified. The structural phonologists, in cutting off phonological form from the materiality of sound substance, recontained the notion of binary opposition in a relatively closed or context-free theory of oppositions on the same level of abstraction. Saussure had understood in principle that there was an exchange of matter, energy, and information between the sound substance and phonological form.

A second recontextualization occurred when the structural semanticists projected the same baggage of assumptions onto the level of meaning. This led to the frequently unconvincing and circular character of many of these analyses on account of the context-free assumptions imported from phonology. It was but a small step to the raising of these principles to full-blown ontological status in Lévi-Strauss's structural analysis of myth.

[*See also* Distinctive Features; Lévi-Strauss; Number Representation; Opposition; Poststructuralism; Semiotic Terminology; *and* Structuralism.]

BIBLIOGRAPHY

Bierwisch, M. "Semantics." In *New Horizons in Linguistics*, edited by John Lyons, pp. 166–184. Harmondsworth, England: Penguin, 1970.

Chomsky, N., and M. Halle. *The Sound Pattern of English*. New York and London: Harper and Row, 1968.

Greimas, A. J. *Structural Semantics* (1966). Translated by D. McDowell, R. Schleifer, and A. Velie. Lincoln: University of Nebraska Press, 1983.

Harris, R. "Translator's Introduction." In Saussure, 1983 (below), pp. ix–xvi.

Hegel, G.W.F. *Phenomenology of Mind* (1807). Translated by J. B. Baillie. New York: Harper and Row, 1967.

Hjelmslev, L. "Pour une sémantique structurale." *Travaux du Cercle Linguistique de Copenhague* 12 (1959): 96–112.

Jakobson, R., and M. Halle. "Phonology in Relation to Phonetics." In *Manual of Phonetics*, edited by B. Malmberg, pp. 411–449. Amsterdam: North-Holland, 1956.

Katz, J. L. *The Philosophy of Language*. New York: Harper and Row, 1966.

Lévi-Strauss, C. *Structural Anthropology*. Translated by C. Jacobson and B. G. Schoepf. Harmondsworth, England: Penguin, 1972.

Lyons, J. *Introduction to Theoretical Linguistics*. Cambridge: Cambridge University Press, 1968.

Prieto, L. J. *Principes de noologie: Fondements de la théorie fonctionelle du signifié.* Janua Linguarum, series minor, 35. The Hague: Mouton, 1964.

Saussure, F. de. *Cours de linguistique générale* (1916). Edited by C. Bally and A. Sechehaye. Paris: Payot, 1971.

Trubetzkoy, N. S. *Principles of Phonology* (1939). Translated by C.A.M. Baltaxe. Berkeley: University of California Press, 1969.

Wilden, A. "Semiotics as Praxis: Strategy and Tactics." *Recherches sémiotiques/Semiotic Inquiry* 1.1 (1981):1–34.
—PAUL J. THIBAULT

BIOSEMIOTICS. The study of living systems from a semiotic perspective, biosemiotics is not a subdiscipline of biology but rather constitutes a theoretical frame for it. The term *biosemiotics* was used in Russian semiotic literature by Yuri Stepanov as early as 1971 but did not appear in international literature until it was introduced by the American linguist and semiotician Thomas A. Sebeok in 1986. According to biosemiotics, all processes that take place in animate nature at whatever level, from the single cell to the ecosystem, should be analyzed and conceptualized in terms of their character as sign processes. This does not deny any of the well-established physical and chemical laws; it is simply claimed that life processes are part of—and are organized in obedience to—a semiotic dynamic. Biosemiotics, then, is concerned with the sign aspects of the processes of life itself, not with the sign character of the theoretical structure of life sciences. Biosemiotics, however, is still in a state of vagueness, and a diversity of interests and viewpoints have come to express themselves under its umbrella, as witnessed by the collection of articles edited by Thomas A. Sebeok and Jean Umiker-Sebeok in 1992.

The beginnings of biosemiotics can be traced back to its roots in the work of the Estonian-born German biologist Jakob von Uexküll (1864–1944). In 1926, Uexküll founded the Institut für Umweltforschung at Hamburg University, where he studied the phenomenal world (*umwelt*) of animals—that is, the worlds around animals as they themselves perceive them. This research program not only greatly influenced Konrad Lorenz (1903–1989)—making Uexküll thus indirectly a founder of ethology—but at the same time introduced a new set of semiotic conceptual tools. The semiotic nature of Uexküll's biology has been reviewed by his son Thure von Uexküll (1982) and by Sebeok (1979).

In 1963, Sebeok suggested the term *zoosemiotics* to account for the study of animal behavior (ethology), and this may be seen as the inauguration of modern biosemiotics, which is essentially concerned with the interpretation of nature's sign universe in the context of the semiotic tradition of Charles Sanders Peirce (1839–1914). Peirce saw the sign as the connective element not only in all experience and thought but in the universe at large. From a biosemiotic perspective, the life sphere is permeated by sign processes (semiosis) and signification. Whatever an organism senses also means something to it—food, escape, sexual reproduction, and so on—and all organisms are thus born into a semiosphere: a world of meaning and communication defined by sounds, odors, movements, colors, electric fields, waves of any kind, chemical signals, touch, and other sensations. The semiosphere poses constraints or boundary conditions to the umwelts of populations, which are forced to occupy specific semiotic niches; that is, they have to master a set of visual, acoustic, olfactory, tactile, and chemical signs in order to survive the semiosphere. And it is entirely possible that the semiotic demands on populations are often a decisive challenge to success. Organic evolution has to do, probably more than with anything else, with the development of ever more sophisticated means for surviving in the semiosphere.

In addition to Sebeok, Gregory Bateson (1904–1980) and Thure von Uexküll (b. 1908) were among the pioneers of biosemiotics. Bateson did not himself use the concept of biosemiotics, but his whole scientific project dealt with communication between animals, people, and machines. And his conception of evolution and thought as two related mind processes fits nicely into the biosemiotic set of ideas. Thure von Uexküll has further developed the umwelt theory and used it as a basis for a biosemiotic understanding of psychosomatic medicine (Uexküll, 1986). He also constructed a semiotic theory of natural levels ranging from the cell, which constitutes the lowest level (a "semiotic atom"), through vegetative semiosis (phytosemiotics) and animal semiosis (zoosemiotics) to human sign systems, such as language, that allow for the capacity to represent absent objects and possible worlds.

There is an important distinction in biosemiotics between endosemiotics and exosemiotics: Endosemiotics is concerned with sign processes that take place inside organisms, while exosemiotics deals with sign processes between organisms. The latter is by far the better-studied area since it covers disciplines such as ethology, sociobiology, and behavioral ecology. Exosemiotics may be concerned with, for instance, pheromone emission by insects, alarm calls in birds, the dances of cranes, or even cultural greeting rituals. An area of special interest to exosemiotics is interspecific communication (Bouissac, 1993). More research needs to be done in this area within the framework of semiotics.

Endosemiotics has only recently been subject to detailed studies (Uexküll, 1986; Hoffmeyer, 1997). While the semiotic aspects of phenomena such as the songs of birds, threat behavior in baboons, or camouflage colors in butterflies are intuitively rather obvious, the processes going on under the skin have been described traditionally by the well-developed conceptual systems of biochemistry and physiology, in which the binomial or dyadic cause-effect model is generally believed to be sufficient. But this is clearly not satisfactory if, as biosemiotics claims, the biochemical and physiological processes are organized according to their semiotic functions in integrated organisms.

Millions of so-called receptors capable of recognizing specific signal molecules in the cell environment are located in the membranes of each of our cells. These receptors function as communication channels through which our cells, tissues, and organs are persistently communicating with each other within the body. Especially interesting is the recent discovery that receptors on the surface of immune cells are capable of decoding the messages exchanged among nerve cells and vice versa. The psychosomatic integration of the nervous system, the immune system, and the endocrinological system in a healthy organism is the result of this gigantic semiotic interaction among many thousand billions of cells, each of which is capable of interpreting a limited range of molecular signs. Disease may be seen then as the result of erroneous communication among our body parts. We fall ill because our cells cannot quite succeed in uniting to create us.

Another important distinction in biosemiotics is between horizontal semiotics and vertical semiotics. Horizontal semiotics is concerned with sign processes unfolding in the spatial or ecological dimension and comprises most of endo- and exosemiotics. Vertical semiotics studies the temporal or genealogical aspects of biosemiotics—that is, heredity: the transmission of

messages between generations through the interdependent processes of reproduction and ontogenesis. From a semiotic point of view, this transmission is based on an unending chain of translations of the hereditary messages back and forth between the digital code of DNA and the analog code of the organism. A crucial but often overlooked fact about this process is that DNA does not contain the key to its own interpretation. In a way, the molecule is hermetic. In the prototype case of sexually reproducing organisms, only the fertilized egg "knows" how to interpret it—that is, how to use its text as a kind of receipt specifying how to construct the organism through the integrated processes of cell division, differentiation, and migration. The interpretant of the DNA message is buried in the cytoskeleton of the fertilized egg (and the growing embryo), which again is the product of history—that is, of the billions of molecular habits acquired through the evolution of the eukaryotic cell in general and the successive phylogenetic history of the species in particular.

Life, then, exhibits a nontrivial semiotic interaction between two coexisting messages: the analogically coded message of the organism itself and its redescription in the digital code of DNA. This principle has been termed *code duality* (Hoffmeyer and Emmeche, 1991). As analogically coded messages, the organisms recognize and interact with each other in the ecological space while, as digitally coded messages, they are passively carried forward in time between generations after eventual recombination through meiosis and fertilization in sexually reproducing species. The essence of heredity is "semiotic survival."

The joint emergence on our planet of life and code duality brought us from the sphere of difference to the sphere of distinction, which is defined by information in the sense of Bateson's famous definition: "a difference which makes a difference" (Bateson, 1970), which itself is in fact quite close to a *sign* in Peirce's sense. Sebeok's prophecy that "a full understanding of the dynamics of semiosis may in the last analysis turn out to be no less than the definition of life" is worth mentioning in this connection (Sebeok, 1979).

In its most radical version, biosemiotics sees itself as "general semiotics" while traditional semiotics studying human sign systems is seen as just a special part thereof called anthroposemiotics. This understanding might be coupled eventually to a cosmological vision of evolution as a general tendency of our universe to strengthen the autonomy of the semiotic sphere relative to the physical sphere on which it depends. In the system that is the earth, this might further be seen as a trend in organic evolution toward the formation of species with increasingly sophisticated umwelts or, in other words, toward a general growth of semiotic freedom, a trend that has reached its temporarily richest expression in the art, religion, and science of human cultures.

[*See also* Artificial Life; Autopoiesis; Chemical Communication; Gaia Hypothesis; Koch; Receptors; Sebeok; Umwelt, *and* Zoosemiotics.]

BIBLIOGRAPHY

Bateson, G. "Form, Substance, and Difference: Nineteenth Annual Korzybski Memorial Lecture" (1970). In G. Bateson, *Steps to an Ecology of Mind*, pp. 448–464. New York: Ballantine Books, 1972.

Bouissac, P. "Ecology of Semiotic Space: Competition, Exploitation, and the Evolution of Arbitrary Signs," *The American Journal of Semiotics* 10 (1993):145–166.

Hoffmeyer, J. *Signs of Meaning in the Universe.* Bloomington: Indiana University Press, 1997.

Hoffmeyer, J., and C. Emmeche. "Code-Duality and the Semiotics of Nature." In *On Semiotic Modelling*, edited by M. Anderson and F. Merrell, pp. 117–166. New York: Mouton de Gruyter, 1991.

Sebeok, T. A. *The Sign and Its Masters.* Austin: University of Texas Press, 1979.

Sebeok, T. A., and J. Umiker-Sebeok, eds. *Biosemiotics: The Semiotic Web 1991.* Berlin and New York: Mouton de Gruyter, 1992.

Uexküll, T. von. "Introduction: Meaning and Science in Jacob von Uexküll's Concept of Biology." *Semiotica* 42 (1982):1–24.

Uexküll, T. von. "Medicine and Semiotics." *Semiotica* 61 (1986):201–217.

—JESPER HOFFMEYER

BLASON POÉTIQUE. A French Renaissance literary genre related to the emblem, the *blason poétique* (poetic blazon) normally consists of a series of short descriptive poems by one or several authors and is collectively devoted to the enumeration of noteworthy aspects or qualities of a person, thing, or activity, typically with the intention of praising or blaming. The *blason poétique* derives from the heraldic practice of blazon, which is the orderly and rigorous description of coats of arms. In France as in other countries of western Europe, heraldic blazon reached a peak of fanciful elaboration in the fifteenth and early sixteenth centuries, often characterized as much by the invention and description of imagined arms for illustrious historical, mythological, legendary, and biblical personages as by the wish to remain faithful to an already well established set of indigenous heraldic traditions. Many of the verse descriptions of these imagined coats of arms—those of the Virgin Mary, for example—are couched in verse and apply traditional color symbolism from heraldry and popular culture to the delineation of the moral qualities of the personage in question.

At the same time, however, the word *blason* is used in Middle French to denote in general terms a speech, more particularly one of praise or of blame. From this practice of poetical description of invented arms, it is thus but a short step, particularly given the predilection in the sixteenth century for illustrated books, to the application of the same rhetorical techniques of enumeration and amplification to the description not of arms but of persons and things. Just as the herald blazons an achievement of arms, so does the poet in the *blason anatomique* come to celebrate the various parts of his loved one's body by devoting one or more short poems to each part in turn. While the *blason poétique* remains analogous to the heraldic blazon, at least in its early development, it is clearly very different from its antecedent in a number of ways. The poets who wrote *blasons anatomiques* aimed not so much to identify as to celebrate their lovers, and the collaborative nature of many *blasons poétiques* certainly differs from that of the heraldic blazon.

The *blason poétique* is thus more clearly allied to other illustrated literary and quasi-literary genres popular during the sixteenth and early seventeenth centuries, such as the emblem, the device or *impresa*, the *figures de la bible*, and the *Totentanz* or *danse macabre*. Like those genres, it requires the combination—indeed, the fusion—of picture and text in order to function at its best (in all but the first editions of the *blasons anatomiques*, each body part is illustrated by a woodcut; like them, it rapidly declined in importance and popularity in the latter part of the sixteenth and early years of the seventeenth century.

Unlike the emblem book, which is a moralizing genre, the *blason poétique* tends to be amatory or satirical in inspiration and expression, and so it is not surprising that many poets who had little or nothing to do with emblem books, such as Clément Marot (1495–1544), took part in collections of *blasons*.

Many emblem authors also composed *blasons* of various sorts, however, and Gilles Corrozet's (1510–1568) *Blasons domestiques*, a book of poems devoted to enumerating and describing the many different parts of the home and the activities proper to each, are among the most elaborate examples of the genre. As the sixteenth century wore on, the *blason anatomique* gave way increasingly to other sorts of *blason* that were frequently religious, propagandist, or satirical in nature; among these were the *contre-blasons anatomiques*, which emphasized, often in the most vituperative terms, the vileness rather than the loveliness of the female human body. The *blason* is thus connected intimately with the *querelle des femmes* (the debate on women) and the whole question of misogyny in the sixteenth century.

With the passage of time, the word *blason* came to be applied first to any sort of poem of praise or blame that relied on techniques of enumeration and subsequently to many unillustrated works, frequently individual rather than serial or collective in nature, whose only connection with the sixteenth-century *blason poétique* lay in their attempt to paint a verbal picture of a person or object. In the period of its decline, the *blason* was thus perhaps related more closely to the witty enigma than to the moralizing emblematic literature of the previous century.

[*See also* Blazon; Emblem; Heraldry; *and* Poetics.]

BIBLIOGRAPHY

Pike, R. E. "The 'Blasons' in French Literature of the Sixteenth Century." *Romanic Review* 27 (1936):223–242.

Saunders, A. *The Sixteenth-Century Blason Poétique*. University of Durham Publications. Bern and Las Vegas: Peter Lang, 1981.

Tomarken, A., and E. Tomarken. "The Rise and Fall of the Sixteenth-Century French Blason." *Symposium* 29 (1976):139–163.

Wilson, D. Bruce. *Descriptive Poetry in France from Blason to Baroque*. Manchester and New York: Manchester University Press and Barnes and Noble, 1967.

—DAVID GRAHAM

BLAZON. The description of coats of arms that are coded expressions of genealogy and social status, the blazon occupies a central place in heraldry and is governed by a set of rules that were for the most part strictly laid down in the sixteenth century, several centuries after the bearing of arms became common. Just as the requirement that all arms must be both unique and easily recognizable has resulted in traditional heraldic rules governing the content, disposition, and coloring of the various elements contained in a coat of arms, so is blazon tightly circumscribed by rules intended to ensure that descriptions of arms are uniform, clear, and consistent. Only thus can heralds plausibly guarantee the re-creation of only a single style of arms based on reading a given blazon.

The origins of blazon are no doubt in the sheer proliferation of coats of arms in the late twelfth and early thirteenth centuries and in the rise in popularity of tournaments as a form of knightly recreation, which occurred about a hundred years after the first arms began to be borne (c. 1250). By that time, armor had evolved to the point where no knight could be recognized or identified except by the arms he bore (including those painted not only on his shield but on his surcoat and on the bards of his horse) and by the ornamental crest affixed to his helmet. In consequence, it became crucial for heralds, whose functions had come to include the organization and conduct of tournaments, to be able to announce the identity of each knight prior to his entrance into the lists; to facilitate this requirement, they compiled what in England came to be called "occasional rolls" of arms, in which descriptions of the arms of all knights present at a special occasion or competing in a given tournament could be recorded. Heralds also compiled "ordinary rolls," containing blazons organized by their central geometric motif or "ordinary," which a herald faced with an unfamiliar coat of arms could consult in order to identify its bearer. Other rolls of arms, often less well executed, gather paintings and descriptions of coats of arms by locality ("local rolls").

For this system to function smoothly, it was essential that a given blazon should generate the re-creation of one and only one set of arms and that all heralds blazoning a given coat of arms should proceed in such a way as to generate the same text. In other words, the conventional mapping of the visual and verbal codes had to be made to coincide at as many points as possible and necessarily at certain points deemed crucial to any coat of arms: the items displayed on the shield (or "charges"), their disposition or placement on it, and their coloring. Heralds thus restricted themselves to a highly codified and stylized technical vocabulary derived from Old French and observed syntactic conventions governing the order in which the various parts of a shield should be described. In blazon, certain key terms stand alone in their own right while others are never found in isolation but only bound to main terms as descriptors; still others, including many prepositions, function as "field designators" (Brault, 1972) to separate the parts of the blazon from one another.

By visualizing a shield as having been painted in layers, the blazon proceeds by describing those layers in the order of their painting. Thus, the field or base color (or colors) of the shield is named first of all; the "ordinary" or basic identifying geometric shape (such as a cross, a horizontal, a vertical, or diagonal stripe, or a chevron) is named and its color mentioned; then all the other charges are named, and their number, position, and color given; the border, if any, is described; any part added to the shield so as to overlie the border, such as a canton in an upper corner, is mentioned; finally, any ephemeral addition to the shield, such as a mark of difference, is named. After the shield itself, as the central element of the arms, has been fully blazoned, any heraldic additions such as a helmet, crest, or mantle is described; last of all, the herald gives the details of the base (or "compartment") on which the shield stands and of the figures ("supporters") on either side of the shield, if they are present. However, the blazon leaves some artistic license in the domains that do not pertain to the distinctive features of the system, such as decorative flourishes, the exact size and shape of some charges, and minor variations in color such as "diapering," by which an otherwise unrelieved field or charge is varied by executing on it a nonheraldic repeating pattern in a darker shade of the same color.

[See also Aniconic Visual Signs; Blason Poétique; Emblem; Heraldry; Logo; and Trademark.]

BIBLIOGRAPHY

Brault, G. J. Early Blazon: Heraldic Terminology in the Twelfth and Thirteenth Centuries with Special Reference to Arthurian Literature. Oxford: Clarendon Press, 1972.

Franklyn, J. Heraldry. South Brunswick, N.Y.: A. S. Barnes and Company, 1968.

Franklyn, J., and J. Tanner. An Encyclopaedic Dictionary of Heraldry. Oxford: Pergamon Press, 1969.

Galbreath, D. L. Manuel du blason. Edited by Léon Jécquier. Lausanne: SPES, 1977.

Pastoureau, M. Traité d'héraldique. Paris: Grands Manuels Picard, 1979.

Thiébaud, J.-M. Petit dictionnaire des termes du blason. Lons-le-Saunier: Marque-Maillard, 1982.

—DAVID GRAHAM

BLISSYMBOLICS. An artificial visual signs system, Blissymbolics was invented by the Austrian Charles Bliss (1897–1985). Originally named Karl Blitz, Bliss himself used the term *semantography* (Bliss, 1965). Although it is nowadays used mainly, even exclusively, as a communication aid in the rehabilitation of aphasics and other severely speech-impaired persons, Blissymbolics was conceived as a kind of visual Esperanto that would permit communication between speakers of different languages and thus further international understanding and world peace (McDonald, 1980). In its origins, then, Blissymbolics was not very different from the kind of universal-language projects that have proliferated since the seventeenth century. In his later years, Bliss cooperated with the Blissymbolics Communication Institute in Toronto, founded in 1975, though it developed and disseminated his system for only more practical and limited purposes.

There has been no serious semiotic study of Blissymbolics thus far. Its signs refer to concepts rather than words to the extent that no phonetic elements—and thus no rebus constructions—are employed. Naturally, the choice of concepts might have been influenced by the Indo-European language background of Bliss and later contributors to the system. However, even if the sign "$\| = 2$" which means "similar sound" (e.g., *flour* written as "similar sound to flower") is used abundantly, Blissymbolics resembles ideographic writing systems.

This impression is also borne out by the fact that the system contains determinatives or classifiers, just like all historically evolved visual-sign systems connected with language (i.e., ^ transforms something into an "action"). Compound signs are formed either by superimposition (a chair on a wave form means *toilet*; the line of the sky with a nose below means *air*, and when an arrow for direction is added the total meaning becomes *wind*) or as sequences, which can take the form of something resembling a possessive construction (*house* + *to* + *knowledge* means *school*) or simple concatenations (*radio* is *thing* followed by *ear* and *electricity*). Syntax seems to be derived largely from English.

The fact that many aphasics, who cannot at all (or to only a limited extent) make use of spoken or ordinary written language, do actually manage to learn Blissymbolics is not only humanely gratifying but also theoretically enlightening. In the first place, it means that severely language-impaired persons still retain some general semiotic competence, although they are unable to convey it by direct or indirect verbal means (Sonesson, 1992). On the other hand, the same fact undoubtedly points to some semiotically relevant differences between the two systems.

The fact that Blissymbolics actually works has sometimes been explained by the assumed iconicity of the system (for which Muter, 1986, furnishes some experimental support). On the contrary, other experts in the field (e.g., Sawyer-Woods, 1987) claim that the system fails to be iconic to any appreciable degree. Both parties, however, clearly base their arguments on a restricted concept of iconicity, identifying it with a similarity of perceptual appearance between the expression and the content of the sign—that is, with the pictorial sign function.

There certainly are some genuine aniconic signs among those employed in Blissymbolics: thus, for instance, ^ for action, ˅ for evaluation, and 5 for plural seem rather arbitrary. It is true that the first sign suggested to Bliss the forming of volcanic cones, but this can hardly be counted as anything more than an idiosyncratic association and even so would account only for some subclass of the meaning of the sign, which would then have to be derived indexically, with the indexical viewpoint being selected rather arbitrarily.

Many signs of Blissymbolics are iconic of other, more commonly known signs, some of which are themselves arbitrary, such as digits, musical notes, the equivalence sign, and the question mark. Other signs recycled by Bliss are the familiar shapes of a heart and a star, which might have some rudiment of pictoriality, although in their received forms they are essentially conventional.

Some other signs are iconic—and, indeed, pictorial—in the same way as verbal metaphors and compound words, respectively. In the first case, the sign may be said to be iconic of a real-world object, although it is used to signify something different. The sign for *time,* for instance, resembles a clock (actually an analog clock, a subclass of clocks used today), but it means *time.* The relationship between time and a clock is, of course, indexical, but it is also arbitrary, first because clocks are not recognized in all human civilizations and, second, because other indexical relationships could have been singled out.

The second case is found more clearly in compound signs. Thus, the combination of a mouth and a note meaning *song* is relatively arbitrary, because other combinations are conceivable. This is also true of compound words in verbal language, which Saussure said were "relatively motivated," although the elements entering into the combination were not, in the case of language, themselves iconic.

Blissymbolics signs depicting objects of the perceptual world are clearly what Mieczyslaw Wallis (1975) would have called "schemata" (outline) rather than "pleromata" (full)—that is, they depict relatively few perceptual properties of the objects in question. Martin Krampen (1988) observes rightly that there is a continuous scale from highly schematic to highly pleromatic pictures and that this scale is independent of the one going from high degrees of iconicity to total conventionality, as are the corresponding processes of historical change. It should be noted, however, that decreasing pictoriality does not necessarily mean decreasing iconicity.

In addition to mere depictions, Blissymbolics contains at least two types of iconic signs. It is possible, for instance, that the figures signifying *man* and *woman,* like similar figures employed to indicate men's and women's washrooms, do not so much depict trousers and skirts—just as some prehistoric petroglyphs do not show a penis and a vagina, respectively—but exemplify generally perceived properties of masculinity and femininity. Indeed, rounded, closed shapes as well as triangles pointing upward have been shown universally to indicate femininity, whereas the opposite shapes stand for masculinity (Sonesson, 1994).

Many signs of Blissymbolics are iconic with respect to human ecology: the signs for the earth (a line below) and the sky (a line above) and for other positions and directions (a point inside or outside a square, etc.). The same observation applies to the square as a signifier for an object.

The presence of these different kinds of more or less pleromatic and otherwise abstract iconicity might account for the relative success of Blissymbolics as a communication tool for the language impaired. However, it also suggests some grounds for the claim made increasingly today that where Blissymbolics fails other sign systems—such as the computer-implemented card system C-VIC (Steele et al., 1989), which is not only overwhelmingly pictorial (like Otto Neurath's ISOTYPE) but also pleromatic and geared to context-bound communication—might succeed.

[*See also* Aniconic Visual Signs; Artificial Language; Icon; Iconicity; Ideograms; Index; *and* Indexicality.]

BIBLIOGRAPHY

Bliss, C. *Semantography*. Sydney: Semantography Publications, 1965.

Krampen, M. *Geschichte der Strassenverkehrzeichen*. Tübingen: Narr, 1988.

McDonald, E. T. *Teaching and Using Blissymbolics*. Toronto: Blissymbolics Communication Institute, 1980.

Muter, P. "Blissymbolics, Cognition, and the Handicapped." In *Communication and Handicap*, edited by E. Hjelmquist and L. G. Nilsson, pp. 233–252. Amsterdam: North Holland, 1986.

Neurath, O. *BASIC by ISOTYPE*. London: Kegan Paul, Trench, Trubner, 1937.

Sawyer-Woods, L. "Symbolic Function in a Severe Non-Verbal Aphasic." *Aphasiology* 1.3 (1987): 287–290.

Sonesson, G. "The Semiotic Function and the Genesis of Pictorial Meaning." In *Center/Periphery in Representations and Institutions: Proceedings of the Conference of the International Semiotics Institute, Imatra, Finland, July 16–21, 1990*, edited by E. Tarasti, pp. 156–211. Imatra: Acta Semiotica Fennica, 1992.

Sonesson, G. "Prolegomena to the Semiotic Analysis of Prehistoric Visual Displays." *Semiotica* 100.2–4 (1994): 267–331.

Steele, R., et al. "Computer-Based Visual Communication in Aphasia." *Neuropsychologia* 27.4 (1989): 409–426.

Wallis, M. *Arts and Signs*. Bloomington: Indiana University Press, 1975.

—GÖRAN SONESSON

BOGATYRËV, PËTR GRIGOR'EVIČ (1893–1971),

Russian folklorist and literary scholar, a co-founder of the Moscow Linguistic Circle in 1915 and an active member of the Prague Linguistic Circle from 1928 onward. Bogatyrëv studied under the historical-philological faculty of Moscow University (1912–1918); after lecturing at Saratov University (1919–1921), he returned to Moscow, where he directed a theater while teaching at the Higher Technical School. From 1922 until 1939, he lived in Czechoslovakia, where in 1930 he defended a doctoral thesis at Bratislava University on Subcarpathian folklore. In 1940, he was appointed professor at the Institute of Philosophy in Moscow, then at Moscow State University; his study *Czech and Slovak Folk Theater* (*Lidové divadlo české a slovenské*) was accepted as his doctoral dissertation in 1940. In addition to his work at the university, Bogatyrëv headed the Section of Folklore at the Institute of Ethnography of the Soviet Academy of Sciences from 1943 to 1949. From 1952 to 1959, Bogatyrëv worked at Voronež University and from 1958 to 1963 at the Institute of World Literature. From 1964 until his death, he taught again on the philological faculty of Moscow State University.

Bogatyrëv and Roman Jakobson met in August 1914 when they both were students standing in line to register for classes; they immediately planned common fieldwork projects and soon started collecting and publishing dialectological and folklore materials from Russian provinces (1914–1916); they also founded a linguistic circle at Moscow University. This discussion group led to the foundation of the Moscow Linguistic Circle in 1915, which fostered heated debates on the semiotic problems of the relations between folklore and literature in 1919 and 1920. Bogatyrëv insisted on and demonstrated the possibility of a rigorous typology of folklore narratives, a task later fulfilled by Vladimir Propp with fairy tales. From the early 1920s, Bogatyrëv's studies were influenced strongly by Ferdinand de Saussure's emphasis on synchronic studies in linguistics and by a focus on dynamic elements in the synchronic view of folklore. He was particularly engaged by the constant change of both form and function in folklore and the competition between different, even opposite, functions related to one and the same folklore event. On the basis of the material collected during several expeditions to Carpathian Russia, Bogatyrëv published his study *Magical Acts, Rituals, and Beliefs in Subcarpathian Russia* (1929). In further applications of "functional structuralism" to ethnographic studies, Bogatyrëv published "The Christmas Tree in Eastern Slovakia" (1932–1933), "Costume as Sign" (1936), and the subsequent book on this topic, *The Functions of Folk Costume in Moravian Slovakia* (1937). Bogatyrëv described how one and the same object may serve different functions in varying contexts and how different objects may fulfill one and the same function. He also reflected on the problem of functional hierarchy, contending that the consideration of the separate functions of an object is not sufficient and that the structural unity of an object is more than the mere sum of its elements. Bogatyrëv focused upon the problem of the dominant and secondary functions, the possibility and laws of their changes, and what he termed the "function of the structure of functions": On the one hand, the loss of a particular function might lead to the loss of other functions; on the other hand, secondary functions that might predate the others can eventually guarantee the survival of a given phenomenon. In brief, the concept of "polyfunctionality" pertains to the dynamic change of the hierarchy of functions.

Several of Bogatyrëv's structuralist works from the late 1930s were devoted to folk theater. In his study of the functions of folk costume, Bogatyrëv distinguished two functional varieties of the costume: It functions as a material object and as a sign at the same time. In theater, all theatrical phenomena are signs of signs or signs of material objects. Together with subsequent studies by Jindřich Honzl and Jiří Veltruský these works laid the foundations for modern semiotics of theater. During the last 30 years of his life in Russia, Bogatyrëv became one of the most important experts in Slavic folklore.

[*See also* Prague School; Russian Formalism; *and* Theater.]

BIBLIOGRAPHY

"Bibliografija naučnych rabot i perevodov P. G. Bogatyrëva" In P. G. Bogatyrëv, *Voprosy teorii narodnogo iskusstva*, pp. 523–542. Moscow, 1971.

Bogatyrëv, P. G. *Actes magiques, rites et croyances en Russie Subcarpatique.* Paris: Institut d'études Slaves, 1929.

Bogatyrëv, P. G. *The Functions of Folk Costume in Moravian Slovakia* (1937). The Hague: Mouton, 1971.

Matejka, L., and J. R. Titunik, eds. *Semiotics of Art: Prague School Contributions.* Cambridge, Mass.: MIT Press, 1976.

—PETER GRZYBEK

BOURDIEU, PIERRE (b. 1930), French ethnographist and cultural sociologist whose interest has focused on the social practices of everyday life and whose work has been influential in related fields of educational sociology, critical linguistics, and cultural studies. Bourdieu sees all social phenomena as organized semiotically by codes, rules, symbols, images, language, and signifying systems. Culture and society, therefore, can be analyzed in terms of theories of signification and signifying practices. Although Bourdieu is not a semiotician by either disciplinary or theoretical orientation, his theoretical and empirical work has focused on the semiotic representations of individuals, groups (i.e., social classes), and institutions (e.g., schools).

In his early ethnographic account of the Algerian Kabyle, (1973, 1979), Bourdieu examined how the cultural organization of time, space, persons, and social relations and identities among the Kabyle was structured in a symbolic and cultural order of mean-

ing. Influenced by Claude Lévi-Strauss's structuralism, Bourdieu interpreted the Kabyle's culture and social system as organized primarily around binary oppositions of meaning, ritual and symbolism, social relations and practices. The most fundamental opposition and basic difference, according to Bourdieu, is that of sex and gender. Sexual difference is real and biological (natural), whereas gender difference is a socially constructed, symbolic order of meaning (cultural). The symbolic meanings, rituals, and values attached to sexual difference in complex gender systems provide a core cultural distinction and means of classification not only among the Kabyle but for all cultures.

Social practices in everyday life are coded symbolically and embodied in real, material bodies. Bourdieu's early recognition of the cultural and theoretical importance of the body and embodied difference is the key to his later conceptualization of the "habitus" (as embodiment of "cultural goods" and symbolic value) and more indirectly of his concepts of "cultural capital," "symbolic violence," and his later work on language and "symbolic power."

Educational sociology in the late 1970s and 1980s utilized the concepts of cultural capital and symbolic violence to explain how schooling reproduces social class differences through the differential pedagogical treatment that children receive, depending on the kinds of cultural capital they bring with them from home. By *cultural capital* Bourdieu means certain kinds of legitimate and relevant knowledge a pupil brings to school that the school variously values or devalues. Closely associated with cultural capital is symbolic capital, which is the prestige, honor, and social status associated with family background and bestowed on the child. In Bourdieu's early studies of the class-stratified French education system, economic and social capital are seen to be indexed by the father's occupational and educational status, which in turn enables financial privilege or imposes constraints, and by class-related social relations with others of similar social and economic access and resources. Bourdieu thus suggests that in the "social space" of the school each child brings a set of social and symbolic goods that signify class background and that interact with the middle-class attitudinal and behavioral codes and knowledges of the school. Pupils present their selves through a range of semiotic significations; these include dress, speech patterns, language use, attitudes toward learning and the discourse of schooling, parental involvement in schools, the family car, and the school lunches mothers prepare for their children. The cultural capital derived from the "pedagogic action" of home and community is embodied in the child's habitus and interacts with the discourse of schooling articulated by and in the interests of the dominant groups. Those whose cultural capital and habitus align with the school culture will succeed academically, whereas those whose cultural goods signify "deficit" will be systematically excluded. The pivotal factor in determining cultural and class reproduction is the discourse of schooling, which includes the symbolism and meanings of mostly abstract curricular knowledges, routinized learning, school rituals, and culture.

Bourdieu and Passeron (1977) term the imposition through mass schooling of rules, codes, meanings, and constraints defined by the ruling class on subordinate classes "symbolic violence." The pedagogic work and authority of schooling legitimates its own discourse and practices by producing consumers of its own symbolic product (e.g., credentialing). Since all modern schooling concerns symbolic rather than practical mastery of curricular knowledge (i.e., scientific and literary "elite" knowledge), only those socialized into elite culture and the corresponding habitus will have the cultural and symbolic capital, the appropriate discipline and attitude to education, to achieve symbolic mastery of the discourse in which they are reared. Children with inadequate cultural capital become prey to the symbolic violence of the significations of an agenda-setting cultural elite.

Bourdieu and Passeron believe that subordinated classes largely accept the legitimacy and "fairness" of meritocratic education and the symbolic value of credentials. Working-class children's failure to succeed in such a system is legitimated through inferior credentials, which certify an alleged lack of academic ability that in turn perpetuates their economic and social disadvantage. This limits their demand for higher education, which thereby remains the domain of the very privileged groups who defined schooling practice and knowledge in the first place.

This institutionalized process of cultural differentiation and exclusion reproduces the class and power relations of a stratified society. Although Bourdieu and Passeron's study centered on the French educational system, their concepts have been used widely in Anglo-American educational sociology to reveal the hidden curriculum of the school's selection and distribution of cultural knowledge and of the cultural endowments and semiotic information embodied in pupils' habitus.

Bourdieu's theory of language differs little from current sociolinguistic and poststructuralist accounts: He views language as socially constructed and as constructing the social world and actors' experience of that world. Since for Bourdieu the cultural classifications of differences are central to social order and practices, language is fundamental and central to the production of those differences and of social life. The "linguistic habitus" and "linguistic capital" of persons reflect the differential distribution and cultural valorization of cultural goods that have symbolic and economic value on the "linguistic market." For instance, in official and formal settings, culturally dominant speech patterns have more exchange and cultural value than culturally subordinate and marginalized speech. As Bourdieu and Passeron argued in *Reproduction in Education, Society and Culture*, the symbolic violence of educational knowledge, language, and practices penalizes those with "inadequate" linguistic capital. Pedagogic authorities act upon the semiotics of pupils' and parents' linguistic and cultural cues by rewarding those with appropriate resources. Language performance, for Bourdieu, is not so much indexical of linguistic competence but indicative of wealth, class background, and social status. Speakers bring to the linguistic market different linguistic capital that, through the habitus, predisposes them to certain expressive modes and competencies. The contextual demands of the linguistic market set certain rules within which speakers negotiate their linguistic productions. Sites within the linguistic market (e.g., academic debate or shopping) have different market conditions that censor some forms of speech and sanction others. Upper-class speakers, according to Bourdieu, have a linguistic habitus that enables them to negotiate fluently and with "distinction" most formal linguistic occasions. Working-class speakers, by contrast, have more limited linguistic repertoires and must contend with the censorship of formal linguistic exchanges as well as self-censorship of "inappropriate" expression.

Bourdieu maintains that linguistic relations are always relations of power and also, by definition, social relations. Social life is accomplished through language that makes the social world intelligible. Linguistic utterances are to be seen not only in terms of their illocutionary force in getting things done but, rather, as signifiers of difference and social location. Linguistic variation signifies difference of linguistic capital, class origin, gender, authority, educational capital, and so on. Finally, because the language of formal political and institutional sites corresponds to the linguistic capital of culturally, socially, and economically dominant groups, the legitimacy of power—"symbolic power"—is embedded in those institutions and persons with the authority to define valued linguistic capital. Closely aligned to Antonio Gramsci's concept of hegemony (1985), Bourdieu argues that symbolic power exercised noncoercively through language is seen by subordinate groups as legitimate because they do not recognize it as arbitrary. Instead, it is seen as natural and naturalized across a range of formal institutions from schooling to the welfare office. And, as Bourdieu has argued since the 1970s, schooling is probably the most important institutionalized mechanism in naturalizing the arbitrary distinctions of difference. Since schooling is concerned centrally with language and since it is a social experience all citizens must pass through by law, the differential distribution and certification of class-based cultural resources affirms the seemingly natural and silent operations of symbolic violence. For Bourdieu, the social semiotics of language use and its reception (or exchange value) on the open market of the social field constitute a central aspect of social, cultural, and economic reproduction.

Social practice, for Bourdieu, is not a process of passive socialization and internalization of rules and values but a kind of bricolage by which individuals neither consciously nor unconsciously negotiate themselves and the world in a marketplace of constraints and possibilities, limits and opportunities. Bourdieu's politically significant and original contribution to a social semiotics, then, lies in the theoretical and methodological link he provides between microsociologies of the body, subjectivity, and experience and more traditional sociologies of culture and social structure. Bourdieu's work highlights the social production of the semiotics of everyday life, which provides an analytically useful corrective to contemporary semiotic and cultural studies that remain focused almost exclusively on text. His meticulous analyses of the semiotic-signification systems of private and public social life in traditional and modern Western societies have enabled him to map the semiotically coded interconnections of social and educational stratification, cultural production and consumption, and individual and collective (re)production.

[*See also* Cultural Difference; Cultural Knowledge; *and* Habitus.]

BIBLIOGRAPHY

Bourdieu, P. *Outline of a Theory of Practice* (1972). Translated by R. Nice. Cambridge: Cambridge University Press, 1977.

Bourdieu, P. "The Berber House." In *Rules and Meanings*, edited by M. Douglas, pp. 98–110. Harmondsworth, England: Penguin, 1973.

Bourdieu, P. *Algeria 1960*. Translated by R. Nice. Cambridge: Cambridge University Press, 1979.

Bourdieu, P. *Distinction: A Social Critique of the Judgement of Taste* (1979). Translated by R. Nice. London: Routledge and Kegan Paul, 1984.

Bourdieu, P. *Language and Symbolic Power* (1989). Translated by G. Raymond and M. Adamson. Cambridge: Polity, 1991.

Bourdieu, P., and J.-C. Passeron. *Reproduction in Education, Society and Culture* (1970). Translated by R. Nice. London: Sage, 1977.

Calhoun, C., E. Lipuna, and M. Postone, eds. *Bourdieu: Critical Perspectives*. Chicago: University of Chicago Press, 1993.

Gramsci, A. *Antonio Gramsci: Selections from Cultural Writings*, edited by D. Forgacs and G. Nowell-Smith, translated by W. Boelhower. Cambridge, Mass: Harvard University Press, 1985.

—CARMEN LUKE

BRØNDAL, VIGGO (1887–1942), Danish linguist and language philosopher. Brøndal received a traditional education in philology but showed an early concern for theoretical problems. The Danish philosopher Harald Høffding introduced him to the theory and history of philosophical categories, which was to be the basis of his theory of structural linguistics. This background made him receptive to the ideas of the prestructuralists (such as Antoine Meillet) during his studies in Paris (1912–1913). He read Ferdinand de Saussure's *Cours de linguistique générale* immediately after its publication as he was proofreading the final version of his sociologically oriented thesis on language history (*Substrater og Laan i Romansk og Germansk*, 1917). Elements from Saussure were footnoted in his book.

In 1928, Brøndal was appointed professor of Romance languages at the University of Copenhagen, where he taught until 1942. Louis Hjelmslev and

Brøndal soon became the main figures in Danish structural linguistics. Brøndal was in close contact with the Prague Linguistic Circle, especially Roman Jakobson, and was active in establishing the Copenhagen Linguistic Circle in 1931. He founded *Acta Linguistica* with Hjelmslev in 1939.

The basic problem Brøndal addressed in his linguistics was the relationship between thought and language. He elaborated a universal grammar that united linguistics and logic along the principles of modern structural linguistics. For Brøndal, Saussure's structural linguistics was such an attempt. The grammatical doctrine of Brøndal is outlined in his major work, *Ordklasserne* (1928), and in "Langage et logique" (1937) and "Linguistique structurale" (1939), both reprinted in *Essais de linguistique générale* (1943, with Brøndal's annotated bibliography). His universal grammar was supposed to contain all the principles for the deduction of the specific elements of language at different levels and for their relations to nonlinguistic facts, as far as those elements and those relations could express the relation between language and thought. Both the universal and the language-specific grammars contain four dimensions: morphology, syntax, symbolic, and logic. The two latter dimensions cover the linguistic expression and the linguistic content, respectively.

Although a convinced structural linguist, Brøndal never defended the idea of language as a purely immanent structure. His favorite image of language is of it as a geometry by which we turn the world into meaning and, in doing so, act upon both our own position and the structure of the world. This indissoluble relation between language and reality, subject and object, mind and matter *is* our reality. To be valid, the theory must answer the question of how human beings relate to the world through a linguistically determined consciousness, not merely describe an immanent formal structure. The core of Brøndal's theory is a reinterpretation of Aristotle's philosophical categories. From this outset, Brøndal proposes a synthesis of classical and modern linguistics in an ambitious attempt at comprehending human reality on the basis of language universals, integrating the concepts of the logic and the linguistic philosophies of Scholasticism, the school of Port-Royal, G. W. Leibniz, and Wilhelm Humboldt as well as Edmund Husserl's phenomenology and the relational logic of logical positivism.

Brøndal's work on a universal grammar focuses on morphology and merely sketches semantics (*Praepositionernes theori*, 1940) and syntax (*Morfologi og syntax*, 1932). He deals only sporadically with phonology and phonetics—that is, the symbolic dimension in his theory. Brøndal was not particularly concerned with the concept of sign. His ultimate purpose was to find the basic features of language that maintained it as an intentional phenomenon in the phenomenological sense used by Franz Brentano and Husserl. He saw the essence of language as object oriented and constitutive of the human relation to the world. But Brøndal's concepts derive from the same philosophical context as the concept of sign and are primarily the Aristotelian categories—substance, quantity, quality, and relation—revised to referred to the four generic categories *relatum, descriptum, descriptor,* and *relator*. These categories are the basic elements for the construction of a grammar.

The requirements of structural linguistics helped Brøndal to define the categories in necessary and sufficient interrelationship for morphological and syntactical purposes. But he also developed a set of specific relative categories, especially symmetry, transitivity, and connectivity, from the logical relations of modern logical theory, mainly for semantic purposes. All the categories articulate different ways of relating objects and consciousness. Furthermore, both set of categories are organized according to a series of structural principles derived from the doctrine of language as a structure of differences and similarities.

Like his concept of universal grammar and the concept of intentionality, Brøndal's idea of structural law is influenced by Husserl's *Logische Untersuchungen* (1900–1901), an influence reinforced by his discussions with Jakobson on Husserl's concept of founding (*Fundierung*), which establishes the hierarchical relationships between the elements of a totality. Every element of language is integrated in the grammatical structure on a qualitative and a quantitative basis: qualitatively, it is defined by the double dichotomy of morphology versus syntax and symbol versus logic; quantitatively or formally, it is defined by the structural principles for differences and similarities between elements. Thus, the defining notions of Brøndal's doctrine cover that area which in other theories is defined by notions developed in connection with the sign.

In *Ordklasserne*, Brøndal tries to characterize the specificity of a given totality (the morphology of a language) from the presence and absence of its constituents (the word classes). This analysis is made on the basis of two structural principles: the principle of symmetry, which says that every system of word classes has a tendency to balance manifest contrasts, and the principle of continuity, which says that every system of word classes has a tendency to realize elements of mediation between manifest contrasts. These principles are employed to determine the possible or necessary manifestation or non-manifestation of word classes in the grammar of a given language in relation to the total inventory of word classes in the morphology of the universal grammar.

Later, Brøndal improved his analysis of structural regularities in generalizing them to include all parts and levels of grammar. When developing the principle of symmetry, Brøndal sets up six forms of relation, which indicate the formal possibilities of the manifestations of a given element: positive, negative, neutral, complex, positive-complex, and negative-complex. These forms were applied by, among others, A. J. Greimas (1917–1992) in his structural semantics, following the generalizing intention of Brøndal.

Brøndal also developed the principle of continuity to include the two interdependent concepts of compensation and variation. They are logically inferior to the forms of relation and the categories, and they presuppose the existence of elements already defined qualitatively by the categories and quantitatively by the forms of relation. On this basis, they create a link between the qualitative and the formal characteristics of the grammatical units: if, in a given language, a grammatical element (e.g., a word class) is formally defined as complex, then the internal differentiation of the class will be more restricted than the internal differentiation of an element of less complex definition (positive, negative, or neutral). This is called the principle of compensation. If, in a given language, two elements or groups of elements receive almost the same qualitative or formal definition (e.g., nouns and adjectives, prepositions and prefixes), then the internal differentiation of the two elements or groups of elements will be different. This is called the principle of variation. These two structural regularities are set forth in greatest detail in *Praepositionernes theori.*

[See also Copenhagen School; Greimas; and Hjelmslev.]

BIBLIOGRAPHY

Brandt, P. A., ed. *Linguistique et sémiotique: Travaux du cercle linguistique de Copenhague* 22 (1989).

Brøndal, V. *Essais de linguistique générale* Copenhagen: Munksgaard, 1943. Includes contributions in English and French.

Larsen, S. E. "A Semiotician in Disguise." In *The Semiotic Web '86,* edited by Thomas A. Sebeok and J. Umiker-Sebeok, pp. 47–102. Berlin: Mouton de Gruyter, 1987. Contains a complete annotated bibliography of Brøndal's works and a complete bibliography of works on Brøndal.

Larsen, S. E., ed. "Actualité de Brøndal." *Langages* 86 (1987).
—SVEND ERIK LARSEN

BUDDHISM. How is communication explained by Buddhism? What are the characteristics of signs? What are their statuses and functions? In what ways does semiosis—the cultural practice of creation and interpretation of signs and transmission of knowledge—occur? Further, which strategies concern the discursive transposition of Buddhist religious experience? What kind of relationship connects cosmology, ontology, soteriology, and semiotic concepts and practices within the Buddhist *episteme*? All these questions are relevant to the interpretation of cultures in which Buddhism developed, since Buddhist philosophical reflection on sign and related practices probably constituted their predominant semiotic paradigm (or at least part of it) for many centuries.

Buddhist Philosophy of Language. Debates concerning philosophical problems on language occupy a large part of Buddhist theoretical reflection.

According to Buddhist phenomenologies (*abhidharma, yogācāra*), language is not a *dharma* (a constitutive entity of reality) in itself but a combination of three different *dharma*s: phonemes, words, and sentences. These three linguistic *dharma*s have a peculiar nature in that they are different from material entities, from mind—considered by Buddhism as pure consciousness—and from mental factors, which are affective and intentional states. Every concrete activity of thought is a manipulation of syllables or phonemes into words or sentences, the only structures of ordinary language endowed with meaning. For this reason, linguistic *dharma*s belong to a group of incorporeal entities, neither material nor mental.

Buddhist thought conceives of language as the main tool for building up and articulating phenomenal reality. The fourth ring in the chain of conditioned causation (*pratītya-samutpāda*), known as names-forms (*nāma-rūpa*), represents the inextricable interdependence of cognitive processes and external reality, phenomena and discriminating mind, names and things of the ordinary world of suffering.

Linguistic descriptions of the world have no absolute truth value; language is an instrument of fallacious knowledge, for it creates reality as perceived and constructed in ordinary states of consciousness through categorization and conceptualization of perceptual data and their semantic articulation. For the *yogācāra* epistemology, a radical constructivism, language has the function of articulating a world of illusion through the power of semiotic "seeds" (*bīja*). Nonenlightened people consider their own ordinary image of the world to be true and corresponding to reality since they attribute to the objects characteristics peculiar to linguistic expressions (autonomy, immutability, homogeneity). Such confusion of ontology with epistemology, of reality with its linguistic descriptions and mental images is called *avidyā* (ignorance) in Buddhism. Epistemologic ignorance is the first cause of existential suffering. Therefore, there is an absolute gap separating language from true reality. The tradition of the great Indian philosopher Nāgārjuna (c.150–250 CE) in particular developed systematically this philosophical position (Murti, 1955).

According to a traditional doctrine quoted in some Buddhist texts, ordinary language is made up by words that are (1) related to superficial aspects of phenomena; (2) uttered in dreams; (3) conditioned by fallacious attachment to wrong ideas; and (4) forever conditioned by the seeds of suffering. Buddhist linguistic speculation thus had to face the question of the status of the word of the Buddha. Did the Buddha contribute to the suffering and delusion of sentient beings by speaking words devoid of truth? Doctrinal matters of pedagogy, epistemology, and soteriology were at stake here that also affected speculations on the nature of the Buddha and the status of his historical manifestations. Obviously, it was not possible to deny completely the value of the word of the Buddha, because this would have meant the self-destruction of Buddhism. Thus, a distinction was made between the wisdom of the Buddha and the signs that convey it, and the word of the Buddha was given a peculiar status. Texts such as the *Diamond Sutra*, the *Vimalakīrti Nirdeśa Sūtra*, and the *Laṅkāvatāra Sūtra* sanction in an inevitably paradoxical way the ineffability of the wisdom of the Buddha in human ordinary language.

This sanction of ineffability can be interpreted in two ways, both very interesting for the semiotician: (1) the Buddha does not speak and conveys his experience in a nonlinguistic way because ultimate communication through language is not possible; this view was later developed in particular by some Chan and Zen currents, which rigorously attempted to deconstruct and dissolve every semiosic practice; (2) the Buddha uses a peculiar language consisting in special systems of signs, which it is possible to know and understand. These opposite positions both presuppose a theory of communication and a semiotics of initiatory transmission of meaning. In spite of doctrinal differences, all Buddhist traditions agree upon the basic assumption that the Buddha explained many different doctrines in consideration of the circumstances, contexts, and the competence and salvational needs of the audience.

The first sanction of ineffability (communication through language is impossible) was developed by the tradition ascending back to Nāgārjuna and was aimed at the attainment of emptiness through an incessant deconstruction of meaning. The second option (the Buddha speaks a different, higher form of language) could yield in turn two different interpretations: (1) the language of the Buddha is a mere *upāya* ("skillful means"), an expedient devoid of absolute value but necessary in order to help humans attain a truth transcending every language (this is the doctrinal position of most Buddhist schools); (2) absolute truth can be communicated, and the Buddha speaks peculiar words of a nonordinary language in order to lead sentient beings to salvation. This is the basic assumption of the teachings of esoteric or tantric Buddhism. In both cases, a systematic manipulation of linguistic signs was put into practice in order to bring language beyond its limits and force it to speak the absolute (see Grapard, 1987; Rambelli 1991).

The Indian religious experience attributes major importance to a set of words called *mantra*, used in meditation and in rituals (Alper, 1989). This peculiar kind of words has been exploited also in Mahāyāna Buddhism as tools for meditation (*dhāraṇī*) or as amulets. The profoundest teachings of the Buddha were thought to have been transmitted by this kind of "twilight language" or "intentional language" (*saṃdhābhāsā* or *saṃdhyābhāsā*), comprehensible only to those endowed with superior faculties.

In any case, theoretical and ritual problematics of mantras were not developed clearly by Mahāyāna Buddhism, which tends on the contrary to present language as a provisional means (*upāya*); the absolute principle of *tathatā* ("thusness"; absolute reality) remains beyond language and signification.

Tantric Buddhism, especially in its East Asian forms, has developed systematically the doctrines and practices of the absolute language, which it identified with *mantra*s and *dhāraṇī*s. The word of the Buddha was considered to be a reality in itself, which cannot be reduced to mere expression of an individual thought: It was the objective expression, the double of reality as experienced after enlightenment. As the great Japanese monk Kūkai (774–835) wrote, only if language and reality are closely and deeply related can the Buddha show the way to salvation through his teachings (Hakeda, 1972). The esoteric Japanese Buddhist notion of *hosshin seppō* (the preaching of the Buddha in its absolute modality of existence) is based on the identity of language and reality (Rambelli, 1994a).

However, for the attainment of the goals of esoteric Buddhism (becoming Buddha in this very body [*sokushin jōbutsu*] and obtaining worldly benefits [*genze riyaku*], it is not enough to simply postulate the deep identity of language and reality: such identity must be evident from the structure of language itself. This is the only way for Tantric symbolic practices to have efficacious and instantaneous results. It is not surprising, then, that Tantric Buddhism devoted great efforts to the rearticulation and remotivation of signs in order to give them the status of microcosms (doubles of the enlightened universe).

As far as Japanese esoteric Buddhism is concerned, Kūkai was the first who explicitly outlined the fundamentals of an esoteric semiotics. Kakuban (1095–1143), by developing Chinese ideas of his time, opened the way for the introduction of mantric expressions into a complex network of correlations. Sanskrit letters were correlated to natural elements, parts of the human body, stars, orientations, seasons, and so forth. Meditation on these microcosmic letters produced a "symbolic" assimilation of the whole cosmos within the ascetic's body. Kakuban was able to condense in the mantric expressions the whole esoteric knowledge of his time, turning each linguistic unit into a minimal *maṇḍala*.

According to esoteric Buddhist teachings, language is true because once its ordinary laws have been deconstructed, it becomes iconic and thus—for a fundamental postulate of esoteric logic—identical to what it speaks of. Theoretical identity is confirmed by processes of remotivation that concern not just the sounds of language but also writing and the forms of sentences and texts.

Buddhist Semiotics. A systematic study of Buddhist semiotics has yet to be undertaken. Until now, only a few scholars have tackled aspects of Buddhist cultures with a semiotic eye, among them Allan Grapard (1992), Stanley Tambiah (1970), Alexander Piatigorsky (1984), and Bernard Faure (1991, 1993). There are multifarious Buddhist semiotic ideas and practices, for they developed in a wide variety of cultural, historical, and social contexts. Buddhism established two basically different kinds of semiotics: One is related to what could be called "ordinary" semiosis; the other describes the interactions with reality in altered (ritual and meditative) states of consciousness. Only the most basic elements of Buddhist semiotics, common to a large part of the Buddhist universe of discourse, will be outlined here.

One of the most striking characteristics of the Buddhist canon is its heterogeneity; even the doctrines traditionally attributed to the teaching of the historical Buddha Śākyamuni are often in overt contradiction with one another. The Buddhists gave such doctrinal heterogeneity a pragmatic and communicational meaning. One of the core notions of Buddhism, in fact, is that the Buddha taught many different doctrines according to the faculties and possibilities of comprehension of his audience. This is in accordance with Indian cosmology and psychology, which recognize various levels of existence and stages in the development of consciousness: to each stage correspond a certain truth and a certain set of doctrines. Therefore, Buddhist exegesis presents interesting semiotic features, such as different levels of truth and a semiotics of textual cooperation.

Numberless Buddhas are believed to be preaching the Law at the same time to multitudes of beings living in countless world systems that make up the Buddhist cosmos; each Buddha is teaching the Dharma using a particular language, and verbal language is just the most unsophisticated. The semiotician is confronted here with two problems: the semiotic status of these languages and the unifying principle of all cosmic discourses.

In Mahāyāna Buddhism, the Buddha is no longer simply a historical person, the teacher, or the enlightened one; he is transformed into a manifestation of the universal principle of enlightenment, a silent, eternal, numinous presence, called *Dharmakāya* (the body of the dharma). This transformation made the universal Buddha the ultimate subject of all discourses, the universal principle of articulation of discursivity. This is shown in many texts where the Buddha says nothing until the epilogue but silently empowers the characters in the text to talk and explain difficult doctrines.

Perhaps the most influential Buddhist model of semiosis was developed within the Indian *yogācāra* epistemologic tradition by Asaṅga (fourth century), Vasubandhu (fourth and fifth centuries), and later by Indian, Chinese, Korean, Japanese, and Tibetan monks. The principles of this school are very subtle and complicated. *Yogācāra* epistemology emphasized the connections between three different layers of psychophysical reality: the material world, the mind, and the perceptive, intellective, and volitional activities connecting them. The outside world is not considered to be endowed with an independent existence. Organized in categories, it is not independent from the mind articulating them. Semiosis (and knowledge) is thus a complex process of interaction between various levels and functions of mind with a supposedly "outside" world through the mediation of senses. Each one of the six sense functions (sight, hearing, taste, smell, touch, intellect) perceives qualities among six perceptual fields in the "outside" world (visible objects, sounds, flavors, perfumes, tactile qualities, the thinkable). Perceptual data of experience (preceding the attribution of a name) are elaborated further by six sense consciousnesses corresponding to each of the six sense functions. The sixth consciousness in particular unifies data, attributes names, and formulates judgments.

These six superficial consciousnesses are based on another consciousness, called *mano-vijñāna*, which is the center of the "I consciousness," creating the distinction between subject and object. But this process is possible because of the existence of a still deeper consciousness, the *ālaya-vijñāna*, the store of sign seeds, which acts recursively on perception and volition and on the interaction of the mind with the world. *Ālaya-vijñāna* has usually been described by modern scholars as a kind of unconscious or subconscious, but it is perhaps more accurate to consider it as the center of semiosis. It contains the seeds of all perceptions, objects, thoughts, deeds, volitions;

past experiences influence future ones, and future experiences reorganize the deposit of seeds. In this way, time and *karma* receive a semiotic foundation.

The basic tenets of the *yogācāra* epistemology are that only the mind exists and that the world is the result of the articulating activity of the mind (*vijñapti-mātratā*). The image a person has of the ordinary world is ultimately nothing else than a transformation of *ālaya-vijñāna*. External reality is nonexistent because the objects are created by consciousness through a complex work of articulation and organization. Usually described as a form of idealism, this view seems rather to be closer to constructivism. In any case, it should be remembered that according to the *yogācāra* school, mind and consciousness are also nonexistent from the point of view of enlightenment, and everything is not different from emptiness, which is at the same time semiosic potentiality and mirrorlike quiescence.

Yogācāra semiotics posits two different kinds of signs: signs as characteristics of the objects (*lakṣaṇa* and *nimitta*) and signs as cognitive and passional potentialities stored in *ālaya-vijñāna* (*bīja*). *Lakṣaṇa* is the name of signs characterizing the essence of things (such as the thirty-two marvelous marks of the Buddha body) and has positive overtones. *Nimitta* are superficial, external characteristics of things.

The power of *ālaya-vijñāna* to create all things is compared with the generative power of vegetal seeds. Actually, the power of *ālaya-vijñāna* depends on the existence of semiotic seeds called *bīja*. There are two kinds of *bījas*: (1) linguistic and karmic seeds: The phenomenal existence of the subject and the outside world is related closely to the language that articulates it; linguistic seeds sown by good or bad actions are called karmic seeds and affect the subject's becoming; (2) innate *bījas* (such as the seeds to become a Buddha) and newly produced *bījas* (seeds sown after experience). Seeds produce the phenomenal world, but at the same time the phenomenal world affects the *ālaya-vijñāna*, where it sows new seeds. Production of new *bījas* depends on perceptual and cognitive contact with *lakṣaṇas* and *nimittas*; but at the same time, the recognition of objects consists in the identification of *lakṣaṇas* and *nimittas* through *bījas* stored in the *ālaya-vijñāna*.

The production of new seeds is called *perfuming* (*vāsanā, abhyāsa, bhāvanā*). As a strong perfume lingers on a dress, so do the impressions of experienced things remain in the consciousness and affect the mind and the body. Through the power of *karma*, the cognitive and affective contents of phenomena perfume the knower's *ālaya-vijñāna* and produce new *bīja*s, which in turn give rise to more phenomena. This recursive circuit of subject and object generates the ordinary world, and semiosis, as a discriminatory process articulating the world, is the cause of ignorance, attachment, illusion, and suffering.

Buddhism posits the existence of two radically different cognitive modalities corresponding to two different semiotic models: one is ordinary, discriminative, and basically fallacious, the other is contemplative, integrating, and undifferentiated. Ordinary knowledge (*jñāna*) is considered fallacious because it confuses a presumed ontological reality of the universe with the ordinary psychomental phenomena and processes (modalities and functions of the mind) that create that reality. On the contrary, true and absolute knowledge, described in many different ways by Buddhist schools, is called *prajñā* or *bodhi*. It is the product of the practice of *yoga*, resulting in altered (nonordinary) states of body, mind, and language. Usually translated as *enlightenment*, true knowledge has often been ascribed by Western scholars to the various phenomena of irrationality and mysticism and its theoretical semiotic relevance has been overlooked.

Such an absolute knowledge implies radical transformation of the human cognitive apparatus. *Ālaya-vijñāna* is transformed through the practice of *yoga* from an ideative device, source of illusion and suffering, into pure mind, a clear mirror reflecting everything without formulating interpretations or judgments. The more superficial consciousness apparatus becomes the agent of good and pure actions. In this way, ordinary consciousness can turn into the instrument for the attainment of Buddhahood and liberation from suffering.

Once the human cognitive apparatus has been transformed into the supreme mirrorlike wisdom, semiosis (as the activity of creation, interpretation, and transmission of signs) is brought to an end by the attainment of emptiness. What remains is only the reiteration of cosmic processes and the reflection of the absolute and undifferentiated realm of essence performed through *yoga*. Buddhist texts describe this condition that defies human possibilities of comprehension through the metaphor of Indra's Net: each pearl reflects all the other pearls without interpreting or modifying them. The Buddhist universe in its absolute modality is made of reflections reflecting reflections in a cosmic interplay of pure light.

Buddhism in Semiotics. Since the late 1970s, Buddhist concepts and metaphors have been met more and more frequently in semiotic discourses. It is less a systematic phenomenon than a transversal attitude fragmented across scattered texts and in the usages of many authors within the general ambit of the new cognitive sciences (constructivism, cognitivism, complexity, artificial intelligence), in which traditional boundaries between "hard" and human sciences, between physics, biology, psychology, and semiotic disciplines, are blurred.

Although fragmentary and in many respects still superficial (and fashionable), the introduction of Buddhist concepts in semiotic discourses is a significant symptom of an epistemological crisis in scientific research. The "new sciences," having distanced themselves from the tradition of modern science and its dualistic postulates, need new models of reality and new descriptions of the world to accommodate their critical approaches. A significant number of thinkers are resorting more or less explicitly to Buddhism in their searches for new metaphors and concepts.

Roland Barthes (1970) was perhaps the first to introduce into semiotics Buddhist concepts such as *kū* (emptiness) and *satori* (enlightenment). Although very simplified, these concepts borrowed from Zen Buddhism entered Barthes's own personal semiotic discourse aimed at bringing language to a stop ("*arrêter le langage*"), in a quest for what he called the zero degree of semiotics. Barthes's peculiar interpretation of the "empire of signs" had a significant impact in Japan. In spite of the shortcomings of his interpretation of Zen, Barthes contributed to the semiotic problematization of concepts such as emptiness and enlightenment, usually considered only from a religious point of view.

Buddhism has been associated also with the practices of deconstruction. Some scholars have pointed to methodological affinities between the treatments of language by Jacques Derrida and Nāgārjuna. Robert Magliola (1984) has shown how the study of Buddhist deconstructionist doctrines can be useful also for the creation of a postmodern Christian theology.

Douglas Hofstadter (1979) used Zen Buddhism as a paradoxical tool to solve logical apories related to systemic recursiveness and to formulate hypotheses on the problem of mind and consciousness. Buddhist metaphors and concepts appear to be important for the development of a new epistemological paradigm. For instance, the cosmology of the new sciences is often described with metaphors drawn from "oriental" thought, after the groundbreaking work of Fritjof Capra (1975), although the category of "oriental thought" itself is very problematic.

Criticism of classical ideas of rationality and the study of different cognitive modalities (Matte Blanco, 1975; Morin, 1986) seem to be inspired by Indian *yoga* and Buddhist thought. According to Ignatio Matte Blanco, for instance, there are two ways to understand the world: one is asymmetrical and dividing, the other is symmetrical and unifying. This is very close to Buddhist psychological and epistemological theories.

Humberto Maturana and Francisco Varela (1987) are the authors of a radical and semiotically grounded theory of living entities emphasizing the continuity of knowledge with the perceptive and biological structures of beings. Their recursive theory of knowledge is significantly similar to Buddhist *yogācāra* epistemology, although they never mention it.

Floyd Merrel (1991), using Peirce's theme of unlimited semiosis as a starting point, attempts to outline a theory of semiotics suitable to the "new" cosmology. According to Merrell, who describes the cosmos as an incessant semiosic flow, there is no way to talk about objective reality because everything that exists in our world "can be no more than semiotically real." To sketch his semiotic cosmology, Merrell resorts also to Buddhist metaphors and concepts such as emptiness and Indra's net (see above).

Francisco Varela relies extensively on works from Confucian, Taoist, and Buddhist traditions in his elaborations of a project of ethics for a new society. According to Varela, Buddhist doctrines of no self and nondualism can offer an interesting contribution to a dialogue with cognitive science. For instance, the doctrine of no self can help to explicate the fragmentation of the self revealed by cognitivism and connectionism; Buddhist nondualism, especially that of Nāgārjuna's tradition, complements the conceptions of Maurice Merleau-Ponty (1908–1961) and also more recent ideas on knowledge as enaction.

The penetration of Buddhism into semiotics, epistemology, and ethics is by no means a surprise. Since the 1970s, Buddhism has been taking root in Western countries and is flourishing as an autonomous tradition. This is perhaps similar to what happened many centuries ago in China and in the other countries of East and Southeast Asia, when many forms of Buddhism spread and started to interact with those cultures, producing new and richer ideas and practices.

[*See also* Barthes; Mandala; Mantra; *and* Zen Gardens.]

BIBLIOGRAPHY

Buddhist Philosophy of Language

Alper, H. P., ed. *Mantra*. Albany: State University of New York Press, 1989.

Conze, E., ed. *Buddhist Wisdom Books: The Diamond and the Heart Sutra*. London: Unwin, 1958. Revised edition published in 1988.

Gómez, L. O. "Buddhist Views on Language." In *The Encyclopedia of Religion*, edited by M. Eliade, vol. 8, pp. 446–451. New York: Macmillan, 1987.

Grapard, A. G. "Linguistic Cubism: A Singularity of Pluralism in the Sanno Cult." *Japanese Journal of Religious Studies* 14.3 (1987):211–234.

Hakeda, Y. *Kūkai: Major Works*. New York: Columbia University Press, 1972.

Kajiyama Y. *Kū no shisō: Bukkyō ni okeru kotoba to chinmoku* (The Philosophy of Emptiness: Language and Silence in Buddhism). Kyoto: Jinbun Shoin, 1983.

Kunjunni Raja, K. *Indian Theories of Meaning*. Madras: Adyar Library and Research Centre, 1963.

Luk, C., ed. *Vimalakirti Nirdesa Sutra*. Berkeley and London: Shambhala, 1972.

Murti, T. R. V. *The Central Philosophy of Buddhism* (1955). London: Unwin, 1987.

Rambelli, F. "Re-Inscribing Maṇḍala: Semiotic Operations on a Word and Its Object." *Studies in Central and East-Asian Religions* 4 (1991):1–24.

Rambelli, F. "The Semiotic Articulation of Hosshin seppō." In *Esoteric Buddhism in Japan*, edited by I. Astley, pp. 17–36. Copenhagen: Seminar for Buddhist Studies, 1994a.

Rambelli, F. "True Words, Silence, and the Adamantine Dance." *Japanese Journal of Religious Studies* 21.4 (1994b): 373–405.

Suzuki, D. T., ed. *The Lankavatara Sutra*. London: Routledge, 1932.

Buddhist Semiotics

Faure, B. *The Rhetoric of Immediacy: A Cultural Critique of Chan/Zen Buddhism*. Princeton: Princeton University Press, 1991.

Faure, B. *Chan Insights and Oversights: An Epistemological Critique of the Chan Tradition*. Princeton: Princeton University Press, 1993.

Grapard, A. *The Protocol of Gods: A Study of the Kasuga Cult in Japanese History*. Berkeley: University of California Press, 1992.

Piatigorsky, A. *The Buddhist Philosophy of Thought*. London and Totowa, N.J.: Curzon Press and Barnes and Noble Books, 1984.

Piatigorsky, A., and D. B. Zilberman. "The Emergence of Semiotics in India." *Semiotica* 17.3 (1976):255–265.

Tambiah, S. J. *Buddhism and the Spirit Cults in North-East Thailand*. Cambridge: Cambridge University Press, 1970.

Buddhism in Semiotics

Barthes, R. *The Empire of Signs* (1970). Translated by R. Howard. New York: Hill and Wang, 1982.

Capra, F. *The Tao of Physics*. Berkeley: Shambhala, 1975.

Hofstadter, D. R. *Gödel, Escher, Bach: An Eternal Golden Braid*. New York: Basic Books, 1979.

Magliola, R. *Derrida on the Mend*. West Lafayette, Ind.: Purdue University Press, 1984.

Matte Blanco, I. *The Unconscious as Infinite Sets: An Essay in Bi-Logic*. London: Duckworth, 1975.

Maturana, H., and F. J. Varela. *The Tree of Knowledge*. Boston: Shambhala, 1987.

Merrell, F. *Signs Becoming Signs: Our Perfusive, Pervasive Universe*. Bloomington: Indiana University Press, 1991.

Morin, E. *La méthode 3: La connaissance de la connaissance/1*. Paris: Seuil, 1986.

Varela, F., E. Thompson, and E. Rosch. *The Embodied Mind: Cognitive Science and Human Experience*. Cambridge, Mass.: MIT Press, 1991.

—FABIO RAMBELLI

BURKE, KENNETH D. (1897–1993), American critic and literary theorist who developed dramatism, a method of linguistic and conceptual analysis that treats language and thought primarily as modes of action rather than means of conveying information. All verbal acts are to be considered as symbolic action, and dramatism thus views literature and language as species of symbolic action.

For Burke, the realm of symbolic action comprises three levels. First is the level of dream, in which unconscious or subconscious factors in a text play a compensatory or therapeutic role. An obsessive pattern of engrossments and avoidances expresses itself as a cluster of interrelated images, which in turn implies a cluster of interrelated ideas. Images are thus supersaturated with ideas, and Burke suggests that we should take Sigmund Freud's key terms—condensation and displacement—as overall categories for the analysis of the text as dream. Events have a tendency to become metaphoric or metonymic representatives of other events. Condensation, the image as more than itself—a combining of several images or ideas into one—works along the metaphoric or vertical axis of meaning, whereas displacement, the image as other than itself, works along the metonymic or horizontal axis of meaning. For Burke, as for Jacques Lacan, the unconscious is structured like a language, and the critic is its cryptologist. However, the text as dream is not the essence of the literary act. It would be as great an error to regard dream as the originary cause of the literary act as it would be to disregard the rich suggestiveness of psychoanalytic interpretation.

The second level, that of prayer, pertains to the communicative, audience-oriented functions of a text. It has a rhetorical dimension and induces attitudes and actions to the extent that rhetoric deals with the arousal and fulfillment of expectations. For Burke, meaning has a dual nature: On the level of dream, it is primarily the product of an author and the property of a text, whereas on the level of prayer it is primarily the response and interpretation of a reader.

The third level, chart, concerns the realistic sizing up of situations that is sometimes explicit, sometimes implicit, in verbal strategies. The symbol is the "verbal parallel to a pattern of experience" (1931) and has realistic content insofar as it encompasses the situation it represents. The encompassment is necessarily imperfect because human beings have no nonsymbolic or nonlinguistic access to the structure of reality. Although representation cannot be anchored ontologically in some transcendental signified or objective frame of reference, it has a causal efficacy of its own in its power to induce attitudes and actions. To expose the epistemological fraud that representation often perpetrates is not to negate the force of its ideological and social consequences. Representation does its work of power in the world and subserves a pragmatic and realistic function. In *A Grammar of Motives* (1945) and *A Rhetoric of Motives* (1950), Burke elaborates the chart/prayer/dream triad into a more sophisticated scheme: grammar, rhetoric, and the symbolic.

Burke has a grammar in the Aristotelian sense of a set of verbal terms of categories by means of which a discourse can be analyzed. His dramatistic grammar centers on observations of this sort: For there to be an act, there must be an agent. Similarly, there must be a scene in which the agent acts. To act in a scene, the agent must employ some means or agency, and there cannot be an act, in the full sense of term, unless there is a purpose. Burke labels these five terms the dramatistic pentad. His aim is to show how their designated functions operate in the imputing of motives.

The grammar is a series of blanks to be filled out when one imputes motive to action, and any statement of motives involves the dramatistic pentad. The agent, however, need not be a human being. Anticipating Greimas, Burke insisted that even conceptual "terms are *characters* . . . an essay is an attenuated play. . . . Names are shorthand designations for certain fields and methods of action" (1937, pp. 311–312). The grammar blanks offer opportunities for disposition and transposition, and dialectic explores the combinatory, substitutive, and transformational possibilities, which, of course, are endless. But Burke's point is that any statement of motives must deal with the five terms he has isolated, even if it foregrounds one and backgrounds others. The grammatical resources are principles, and the various philosophies are casuistries in that they seek to apply these principles to particular cultural situations. Burke attempts an ingenious casuistry of his own, taking major philosophic systems as cases and developing their distinctive characters in terms of their variant stresses upon one or another of the terms of his dramatistic pentad.

As a method of discourse analysis, dramatism is protostructuralist to the extent that structure in all kinds of texts can be accounted for by the combinatory potential of terms of the pentad. It is antistructuralist, however, to the extent that every grammar of motives implies a rhetoric of motives. Since every dialectic transposes and disposes the terms of the pentad in a uniquely constitutive fashion with a uniquely exhortative attitude, every dialectic implies a rhetoric of action. Though vulgar Marxists might see the historical and economic scene as determinative of acts and attitudes that agents engage in, their scenic grammar embraces a program of social change that urges the strategic deployment of linguistic and political agency for the purpose of revolution.

In contrast to grammar's attempt to furnish an exhaustive inventory of textual expression, rhetoric's function is to counteract the alienation that is endemic to every social order wherein debilitating differences of race, gender, education, ethnicity, class, education, wealth, and so forth prevail. Through the operations of identification, rhetoric seeks to overcome these differences by inducing cooperation and community. Nevertheless, there is an obvious sense in which every identification rhetoric induces implies a concomitant dissociation and vice versa. Although rhetoric involves the formation of identity and the establishment of community, it is predicated upon division and difference. If identification and consubstantiality were really possible, there would be no need to induce them.

Division and difference, then, create the need for identification and consubstantiality, giving rise to what Burke calls a rhetoric of courtship (use of suasive devices) between individuals who occupy different rungs on the social ladder. The hierarchic motive is all pervasive, and "the vocabularies of social and sexual courtship are so readily interchangeable, not because one is a mere 'substitute' for the other, but because sexual courtship is intrinsically fused with the motives of social hierarchy" (1950, p. 217). Burke calls the attempt to extricate the motives of social hierarchy concealed in literary representations socioanagogic criticism.

The real of the socioanagogic involves the ways in which things of the senses are secretly emblematic of motives in the social order. Burke explores the theoretical implications of this approach in "What Are the Signs of What? (A Theory of 'Entitlement')" (1966). Burke reverses the slogan of naive verbal realism—words are the signs of things—into its socioanagogic counterpart: things are the signs of words. Words, he suggests, possess a spirit peculiar to their nature as words, and the so-called things of experience are the materializations of this spirit. Since verbal spirits are symbolized enigmatically in nonverbal things, their derivation comes from both the forms of language and the group motives that language possesses by reason of its nature as a social product.

The symbolic, which Burke associates with poetics per se, is grounded in the proposition that "a work is composed of implicit or explicit 'equations' (assumptions of 'what equals what'), in any work considered as one particular structure of terms or symbol system" (1941, p. 8). There are also dissociations or agons (what versus what), and this apposition and opposition of terms unfolds so as to effect dramatic resolution and dialectical transformation (what leads to what). The symbolic, then, should take at least three factors into account: associative clusters, dramatic alignments, and narrative progressions.

All told, then, there is symbolic action as designation (the grammatical), as communication (the rhetorical), and as expression (the symbolical). These levels, however, are interdependent. Burke's general approach might be called pragmatic in the sense that he assumes that a work's structure is described most accurately by thinking always of the work's function. Form is function. What a text is is what a text does.

A case in point is Burke's 1939 essay "The Rhetoric of Hitler's 'Battle,' " in which he brings his critical arsenal to bear on *Mein Kampf*. Burke sees Nazism as the materialization and perversion of a religious pattern, particularly in regard to its projective device of the scapegoat—"the 'curative' unification by a fictitious devil function" (1941, p. 218)—and to its ritual of rebirth: the compensatory doctrine of inborn superiority whereby Aryans are born again into the purity of their ancestral blood. Focusing on the dialectical relationship between literary strategy and extraliterary situation, Burke examines Hitler's use of sexual symbolism, of the imagery of blood, pollution, and disease, and of the rhetoric of identification and dissociation. According to Hitler's twisted dream, Germany is a dehorned Siegfried; its masses are feminine and desire to be led by a domineering male; this male must overcome the rival Jewish male, a seducer who would poison Aryan blood by intermingling with the folk. An associative cluster emerges. Blood poisoning, syphilis, prostitution, incest, and so on are equated materially with the infection of Jewish blood and spiritually with the infection of Jewish ideas. Burke's point is to show how imagery and ideation, rhetoric and grammar, sustain each other in Hitler's sinister and nightmarish text. Because of Hitler's resistance to a purely environmental account of socioeconomic problems, his grammar of motives systematically elevates agent at the expense of scene. The superagent is none other than Hitler himself, the self-styled living incarnation of Aryan will to power. Although it takes a great deal of sophistical ingenuity to distinguish benign Aryan superindividualism from malign Jewish individualism, these are the only factors that really matter in Hitler's diagnosis of and remedy for Germany's woes. The extrinsic causal factors that have in large measure shaped and determined the socioeconomic scene are disregarded completely. This truncated grammar of motives makes for a concomitant rhetoric of motives: a rhetoric of identification that induces the people to see themselves as consubstantial with their leader and a rhetoric of dissociation that induces the people to alienate themselves from the Jews, which makes pos-

sible the brutal victimization of them. Hitler's psychotic dream, rife with its obsessive images and fanatical hatreds, is thereby converted into a grammar of the agent and a rhetoric of persecution. He spontaneously evolves his cure-all on the grammatical and rhetorical levels in response to inner compulsions on the symbolic level. The perverse genius of *Mein Kampf* resides in its provision of "a noneconomic interpretation of economic ills" (1941, p. 204).

Burke's dialectical model of the relationship between ideology, language, culture, and history gave way in the 1950s to a perspective on language that Burke eventually codifies as logology (1961). Burke's central claim is that because theology deals with ultimate terms par excellence, it is uniquely qualified to provide the sorts of analogies that yield insight into the internal logic of symbol systems in particular and of language in general. Logology, words about words, discovers in theology, words about God, the drive toward perfection in all discourse. Burke calls the movement in language toward higher and higher levels of generalization and abstraction the entelechial motive, *entelechy* being Aristotle's term for the force that impels an entity to attain the kind of perfection appropriate to the kind of thing it is. Theology strives toward God—language toward god terms. Hence, there is a terminological compulsion in all discourse to rigorously track down the manifold implications of its god terms. Language, Burke observes wryly, is rotten with perfection. Like any twentieth-century citizen, he is all too familiar with the obscenity of final solutions and so cannot view perfectionism from anywhere other than an ironic standpoint.

Ultimately, for Burke, words are agents of power: They are value-laden, ideologically motivated, and morally and emotionally weighted instruments of persuasion, power, purpose, and representation. As a form of symbolic action in the world, literature is linked inextricably to society; it is not a privileged form of language that exists in its own separate and autonomous sphere. Resolutely opposed to specialized professionals who "take the division of our faculties in our universities to be an exact replica of the way in which God himself divided up the universe" (1941, p. 303), Burke, for the greater part of his career, was viewed as an interdisciplinary maverick and relegated to the margins of serious academic discourse. Since the 1980s, however, critics and theorists have begun to acknowledge that Burke's dramatistic and logological theory of literature and language, which was largely developed from 1930s to the 1960s, adumbrates the linguistic and rhetorical turn in the human sciences and has a significant role to play on the contemporary scene.

[*See also* Discourse Analysis; Grammar of Motives, A; Greimas; *and* Language as Symbolic Action.]

BIBLIOGRAPHY

Burke, K. *Counter-Statement.* Berkeley: University of California Press, 1931.

Burke, K. *Permanence and Change: An Anatomy of Purpose.* Berkeley: University of California Press, 1935.

Burke, K. *Attitudes Toward History.* Berkeley: University of California Press, 1937.

Burke, K. *The Philosophy of Literary Form: Studies in Symbolic Action.* Berkeley: University of California Press, 1941.

Burke, K. *A Grammar of Motives.* Berkeley: University of California Press, 1945.

Burke, K. *A Rhetoric of Motives.* Berkeley: University of California Press, 1950.

Burke, K. *The Rhetoric of Religion: Studies in Logology.* Berkeley: University of California Press, 1961.

Burke, K. *Language as Symbolic Action: Essays on Life, Literature, and Method.* Berkeley: University of California Press, 1966.

Burke, K. *Dramatism and Development.* Barre, Mass.: Clark University Press, 1972.

—GREIG HENDERSON

C

◆

CARTOGRAPHY. As a field relevant to semiotics, cartography can be studied from two points of view: functional, if the intention is to place the signs of map symbolism into perspective by considering the contexts of their creation and of their use; and structural, if the sign universe of map symbolism and its organization are described and treated as given. Naturally, the contexts of production influence the structure of map symbolism to some extent.

Functional Cartography. The signs that underlie mapping and map reading must be considered in the contexts of their creation and their use. At least six topics are of interest: the concepts and percepts that function, respectively, as contents and as expressions; sign production; the influence of reality and of sign use on the structural characteristics of the signs; map use; and the links between map symbolism and natural language.

1. *Conveyable contents.* In principle, all information that relates to places in earth space can be conveyed. To map it, one must render the location of each place through some coordinate transformation. The stock of conveyable concepts is inexhaustible. For instance, there is an indeterminable number of observed and conceivable shapes of lakes. Further, by virtue of coordinate transformations, all of them can be expressed formally, including those that have not been encountered before.

2. *The expression material.* Comprising all visible items that can be inscribed intentionally on the map face, expression material includes marks used in other fields of signification (figurines, emblems, writing). These marks usually enter the map as expressions (not as mere material)—that is, they are already coupled to meanings. The expression material has an autonomous perceptual order that is frequently put to service in signification. Outside the map face, writing is used largely for explanations.

3. *Sign production.* The most obvious process of sign production is transcription, or the selection of graphic items and their assignment to contents (which are here taken as given). At the level of min-

imal signs, the mapmaker has some freedom of transcription; coding conventions are introduced and specified in annotations (legend, projection statement, etc.), but the relative freedom of transcription permits the representation of many varied mappable phenomena by reusing a limited stock of graphic means. This is most noticeable in the rendering of the plan-free information and makes for economy of sign production. In response to the requirements of sign use, cartographic practice has given rise to various and partly incompatible principles of transcription, the two principal ones of which are standardization and homology. Under standardization, the aim is to fix the expression of a given content unit for all (or at least many) maps; this is practically useful only within specified thematic domains, such as weather charts or stratigraphic maps. Homological transcription focuses not on items but on relations. The code, therefore, regulates the links between expression and content not just for individual signs but rather for whole systems of signs. In transcribing the plan information, homology is usually brought about automatically through coordinate transformation; in rendering plan-free contents, it must be deliberately created. (This is the most frequent way of extending iconicity to the mapping of plan-free information.) Either way, the autonomous perceptual organization of the expression material is put to service in signification.

Apart from transcription, sign production in mapping comprises at least the selection and structuring of the information that one wants to convey (thus, mapping has a cognitive import) and, further, the stylistic aspects of the choice of expression material. These processes afford the mapmaker some leeway, and his actual choices and their results are again amenable to semiotic interpretation.

4. *Reality.* Although maps may show fictitious situations or be used to deceive, they are most often intended to serve as sources of factually correct information about actual places. But they are not completely faithful to facts (owing to projection, generalization, and several other factors). Therefore, a map user must routinely assess the fidelity of a map, which requires factual or world knowledge and metasemiotic information about mapping procedures.

5. *Map use.* Maps are made to be read. A competent mapmaker transcribes information with a view to the intended map-reading operation(s). For example, if area sizes are to be compared visually, one must choose a projection that does not, or not greatly, misrepresent the relative sizes of areas. In geography, one often wants to read several map entries at the same time in order to derive new knowledge, especially about spatial distributions. Such map-reading tasks normally presuppose a homological transcription. The important homology principle, then, is at least in part a response to requirements of map use. That is, such requirements influence the very organization of the sign system of a map, imparting to it the character of a constructed language.

6. *Map symbolism and natural language.* Finally, writing is in several ways bound up with map symbolism and contributes to signification: first, most code components in the individual map are introduced via written language by annotations in the map margins; second, place-names and numbers are written into the map face because they cannot be conveyed adequately by graphic means. By contrast, certain contents are expressed by graphic-plan traits only (e.g., the many shapes of existing lakes) because they cannot be rendered verbally with comparable accuracy.

Structural Cartography. The discipline of structural cartography deals with graphic models that, whatever other traits and functions they have, represent a space (typically that of the earth's surface) by means of space. The most common and best known of these models is the map, a metrically determinate plan representation. The linguistic study of such models as cartographic semiotics (or cartosemiotics) started in the 1960s with several pioneering works, among which the 1967 study *Semiology of Graphics* by the French scholar Jacques Bertin is most widely known.

As in other fields of semiotics, there are various theoretical frameworks, but the basic ideas and research results of different authors are largely comparable. The terminology, however, is not yet well developed and is in part provisional. Mapping and map use are based on a system of graphic signs or "map symbolism" usually called "map language."

Recent syntheses have been contributed by Charles Hussy (1995), A. A. Lyutyy (1988), Ján Pravda (1990), and Hansgeorg Schlichtmann (1985; developed further in Pravda, Schlichtmann, and Wolodtschenko, 1994). C. Grant Head (1991) has reviewed a major part of the literature.

Map symbolism comprises spatial and nonspatial components (more specifically, plan and plan-free ones) on both the content side and the expression side. The partly spatial nature of the map, in turn, makes for some problems of semiotic analysis, as cartographers view space either as a continuous collection of points or as divided into segments.

The sign inventory of a map comprises images and artifacts. On the one hand, the map face shows an assemblage of plan images of objects, the shapes and spatial arrangements of which are derived ultimately from factual traits. Thus, some features of the signs are influenced by the objects represented (even though these objects are given to us through concepts). On the other hand, map signs have been created primarily as conventional tools of communication. This languagelike or artifactual component of map symbolism is better understood than the part with iconic character.

The rendering of plan images implies that the plan information—both units and relations—is largely iconic. The mapmaker might deliberately extend this iconicity to the conveyance of plan-free information. In map symbolism, a complex expression can be analyzed only into meaningful units; the functions of signification, distinction, and emphasis are served by the same perceivable elements or at least by elements of the same kind. There are signs at several levels of complexity. Taxonomies proposed by various authors, in spite of differences in detail, show an encouraging core of agreement. Two different types of signs are recognized: units of the "artifactual" kind (topemes and minimal signs) that are stable in that they are isolated once and for all according to consistent criteria (which is familiar from the study of language); and focus units that are not given a priori but filtered out from a complex of images according to a chosen focus (as one does when interpreting paintings or photographs).

In an expanse of earth space, the mapmaker conceptually and graphically singles out objects that occupy space and are located; these can also be conceived of as places with certain characteristics. Each such place is the referent of a topeme or localized sign. From the mapmaker's point of view, a topeme is the smallest complete entry on a map. Its content is the complex concept of an object (e.g., a wheat field) taken together with the location of that object. Its expression normally contains a single, visually unitary mark, the position of which conveys the object's location. The unity of a topeme, then, is established by a graphic or expression-related criterion, not by a content-related one. The topeme expression occupies a segment of map space; seen from the expression side, the topeme is a segmental unit.

A topeme is a syntagm. It can be analyzed into minimal signs, comparable to monemes (minimal units of meaning) in language; Pravda (1990) speaks of map morphemes. In a map of field crops, if *wheat* is expressed by the color yellow, then *wheat* and yellow together constitute a minimal sign, the unity of which can in principle be determined by a commutation test. The expression of a minimal sign can be defined either as a signifying trait of a mark (e.g., yellow) or as a segmental item, a symbol, that carries such a trait (e.g., a yellow patch). Though the second view is more frequent in the literature, the first tends to yield simpler analyses and has been adopted here. The two views of space mentioned earlier enter into the conception of the topeme. If a city is mapped by an area symbol, then the corresponding place is a segment in discrete space and it is treated as undifferentiated; the content "city" is associated with the place as a whole and is the content of a single minimal sign. But to say that a place has one location is only a convenient simplification (at least if location is described by point coordinates); actually, each point within this place has a location (and each point in the area symbol has a position). Thus, the topeme contains many minimal signs made up of location and position values. Such a set of adjacent points with traits assigned to them (here location and position values, respectively) is a field or, more often, a section of a field. In order to account for field sections, the unity of the topeme above has been based on a graphic criterion.

A map user may isolate any part of the assemblage of images within the map face under a focus of interpretative interest. The resulting sign is a focus unit. Like a topeme, it is a segmental item. Empirically, it is most often a structured complex of topemes. The content of such a complex might be "cluster of farmsteads," for example, or "valley bottom with meandering river, oxbow lakes, and backswamps" (for simplicity, location and other items of plan infor-

mation are disregarded here). Focus units of this type have been tentatively likened to text units in language (Schlichtmann, 1985). In other cases, a focus unit coincides with one topeme, with part of one (e.g., the image of the Gaspé Peninsula as part of the image of North America), or with a set of such parts (e.g., a section cut out of a bundle of contour lines, their collective shape indicating a landslide). A typology of focus units would include the descriptive models of spatial organization that are familiar in geography (distribution area, point pattern, network, mosaic, etc.). Different foci may coexist in an interpretation; thus, the identified space segments may overlap. Further, smaller units may be contained in larger ones (e.g., administrative or other regions) and such units are ranked in a hierarchy. But while there are constant criteria to assign the two ranks of minimal sign and topeme, no such criteria apply to focus units; rather, a hierarchical rank is contingent on the problem under study. Finally, although it is up to the map user to establish focus units, the mapmaker might employ graphic means to direct the reader's structuring attention to a specific space segment. For example, by mapping for selective perception (in the sense used in Bertin, 1983), one guides the interpreter to recognize distribution areas, an aim that is frequent in geographic mapping.

The sign system of a map is based on several code components that are mostly established before mapping and map use. But some of the expression-content links are set up only in map interpretation. This holds especially where visual-plan characteristics of objects are reproduced. A damned reservoir in a valley, a cutoff meander, or a crater lake usually have diagnostic shapes, and these, once they are learned, function as sign contents. Often, they are learned not in the field by looking at the objects themselves but in map interpretation by looking at their images. Where one cannot get a total view of an object (e.g., the continent of Africa), its spatial traits become known only through an imaging model (cartographic or otherwise). Thus, the representation functions as a source of new factual knowledge. One may learn to read a given symbol not just as "(some) object with shape as depicted" but as "reservoir" or "Africa." In this case, a more specific rule is added to the code, based on the learning of diagnostic object traits, and so the code is fully elaborated only after the map has been made.

Syntax is understood here in a wide sense as a combinatorics of signs. Two kinds of syntax are distinguished, a local and a supralocal one. The local syntax pertains to the combination of minimal signs within topemes; these minimal signs contain plan-related and plan-free content and expression traits, which are associated with places. The supralocal syntax covers the arrangement of topemes (which are segmental units) and their integration into larger configurations. While the supralocal syntax in effect models the spatial combination of objects, the local syntax does not generally do so. If one disregards the complication of a topeme corresponding to a field section, the place represented by a topeme is a segment of discrete space and is treated as homogeneous or as the smallest object recognized. If an area symbol indicates the built-up area of a town, then any objects within the town (streets, houses, parks) as well as their arrangement are irrelevant and hence not shown. The corresponding space segment on the map face is freed up for the use of graphic means that convey information about the place as a whole (e.g., the number of inhabitants or the dominant economic function). The local syntax can, in principle, be studied like the syntax of sentences in a natural language. In either case, one can find combination plans that are artifacts of the sign system—that is, primarily human creations. In the supralocal syntax, by contrast, a combination pattern ultimately reflects a factual arrangement of objects in space.

Some combinational aspects, finally, come into view only if all entries on a map face are considered, such as the fact that a map brings together contents under different themes (Pravda, 1990). Since in the extreme case all topemes on a map unite into one focus unit, such aspects could perhaps be accommodated in a supralocal syntax. This point needs further study.

Within a map's relational order, minimal signs and larger, segmental units must be kept apart. Minimal signs are amenable to an analysis that reveals an order by syntagmatic and paradigmatic relations. One can describe the order of the contents and ask whether and how it influences that of the expressions. As for syntagmatic relations, there is little scope for such influence. But paradigmatic relations of contents are very often replicated on the expression side: The organization of the expressions is homologous (isomorphic) to that of the contents. If yellow expresses *wheat* and pink expresses *barley*, then the expressions *yellow* and *pink* are related in the way the respective contents *wheat* and *barley* are; they have something

in common and are different (but not ranked). Homology is a form of iconicity; it pertains not to units but to relations between units.

Segmental units (topemes and configurations of such) are organized by various spatial and nonspatial relations. Their order remains to be explored in detail. It belongs to the image component of map symbolism and thus ultimately reproduces a factual order. It is not yet clear whether and to what extent the notions of syntagmatic and paradigmatic order are fruitful in this field of study. Further, the supralocal combinatorics, in contrast to the local syntax, are governed by homology insofar as spatial content relations are replicated by spatial relations between expressions.

[*See also* Code; Cultural Landscape; Distance; Iconicity; Space; Structuralism; Structure; Urban Semiotics; *and* Zen Gardens.]

BIBLIOGRAPHY

Bertin, J. *Semiology of Graphics: Diagrams, Networks, Maps* (1967). Translated by W. J. Berg. Madison: University of Wisconsin Press, 1983.

Head, C. G. "Mapping as Language or Semiotic System: Review and Comment." In *Cognitive and Linguistic Aspects of Geographic Space*, edited by D. M. Mark and A. U. Frank, pp. 237–262. Dordrecht: Kluwer, 1991.

Hussy, C. *La carte: Un modèle, un langage.* Geneva: Université de Genève, 1995.

Lyutyy, A. A. *Yazyk karty: Sushchnost', sistema, funktsii.* Moscow: Institut geografii, Akademiya nauk SSSR, 1988.

Palek, B. "The Map: The Signs and Their Relations." *Semiotica* 59. 1–2 (1986): 13–33.

Pravda, J. *Základy koncepcie mapového jazyka.* Bratislava: Geografick ústav, Slovenská adadémia vied, 1990. Includes an English-language summary.

Pravda, J., H. Schlichtmann, and A. Wolodtschenko. *Cartographic Thinking and Map Semiotics.* Bratislava: Geografick ústav, Slovenská akadémia vied, 1994. Also published as *Geographia Slovaca* 5.

Schlichtmann, H. "Characteristic Traits of the Semiotic System 'Map Symbolism.'" *Cartographic Journal* 22 (1985): 28–30.

—HANSGEORG SCHLICHTMANN

CARTOONS, as objects of historically oriented studies, have generally been analyzed for content, with the drawings treated as indexes of social attitudes that might otherwise be difficult to recover. The cartoons themselves have usually been presented as the most suitable means for the author's purpose but as not intrinsically interesting objects of semiotic investigation. Thus, political caricature has not been fully theorized as a form of expression with distinctive features. Some have sought to create a theory of caricature in relation to political structures (e.g., Streicher, 1967), but critics noted that there was insufficient evidence to justify any generalizations (Coupe, 1969). Cartoons have been found to be strongly affected by political regimes and by whether they were produced in times of peace or of war because of the variable impact of censorship. The cultural production of cartoons has been examined by Charles Press (1981) among others. The technical aspects include the limitations imposed by the available materials and the change from expensive artisanal to cheap mass production. The organizational aspects include the nature of the political regime, the working conditions of cartoonists, and the kinds of markets faced by the magazines and newspapers that publish the drawings. Syndication and local monopoly ownership have tended to move cartoonists from subordinate members of the editorial team to the status of columnists.

In semiotically oriented cartoon research, as in visual semiotics generally, there are those who emphasize content and those who attribute more importance to expression. Geneviève Dolle (1975) sought to explain political humor in terms of multiple significations along the plane of expression. Mike Emmison and Alec McHoul (1987) showed how the national economy as a persona had gradually emerged in British caricature. Ray Morris (1993) considered cartoons as a form of symbolic political action along both planes, finding that the expression reinforced the content, as, for example, the foolishness of politicians was contrasted with the constructiveness of business executives. This research also illustrated the usefulness to the analysis of cartoons of Mikhail Bakhtin's work on carnival.

As a political art, cartoons have tended to pay more attention to the plane of content than to that of expression. While cartoonists pride themselves on developing distinct individual styles, they recognize that the quick communication of a message is paramount. If the "skimmer" cannot get the point of the drawing in a few seconds, it is a failure. This applies equally to the nonsatirical forms of the genre. As a result, such works are much more likely than paintings to be open to ready translation into a verbal message.

Cartoons are in many respects very simplified, by comparison with classical artworks. They rarely if ever use color, their use of tones is very restricted, and a plain white background is almost universal. There are rarely as many as four significant personae in any one drawing, with the exception of crowd scenes where distinctions among the background figures are very slight. They usually occupy too small a space to be elaborate compositions. Even their satirical use of metaphor and multiple signifiers or signifieds to produce comic effects are frequently subordinated to the need for rapid communication. However, there is at least one aspect that endows cartoons with their own kind of complicity: they tend to selectively deform the features of the persons they portray. The cognitivist David Perkins has studied the laws of such deformations (1975).

Cartoons are a promising area of study, posing less formidable challenges for semiotic analysis than other, more complex artforms. Their plane of expression, in particular, deserves more systematic attention in light of the work that Peter Golding and Graham Murdock (1979), among others, have done on the ideological influence of the plane of expression within the media. Recent work on newspaper photography also offers a promising area for comparisons.

Little attention has been paid to the mechanisms by which cartoons generate laughter. Some drawings could be described aptly as visual gags, pointing up amusing similarities in shape between disparate signifiers or portraying the ambiguities that evoke mirth. Editorial cartoons often rely on humor in commenting on domestic affairs, but on international relations, poverty, the nuclear threat, and environmental damage they are usually deadly serious. To define cartoons exclusively in terms of humor would exclude the substantial moralizing element that underlies caricature and, indeed, satire generally.

Efforts to liberate visual semiotics from the hegemony of its verbal counterpart have tended to focus debate on a binary opposition between verbal and visual language. The usual practice of cartoonists, however, undermines this by including captions beneath or labels within drawings, for example, either by according complementary functions to the picture and the words or by letting one contradict or subvert the other. The ratio of verbal to pictorial space varies widely: while the latter dominates in most modern cartoons, their predecessors often littered their drawings with extensive commentaries and allusions. It would be more fruitful to see the verbal and the visual either as polar extremes along a continuum or, better, as two related but distinct dimensions.

[See also Comics; Face; Hjelmslev; and Pictorial Semiotics.]

BIBLIOGRAPHY

Beniger, J. R. "Does Television Enhance the Shared Symbolic Environment? Trends in Labeling of Editorial Cartoons, 1948–1980." *American Sociological Review* 48.1 (1983): 103–111.

Coupe, W. A. "Observations on a Theory of Political Caricature." *Comparative Studies in Society and History* 11.1 (1969): 79–95.

Dolle, G. "Rhétorique et supports de signification iconographiques." *Revue des sciences humaines* 159 (1975): 343–359.

Emmison, M., and A. McHoul. "Drawing on the Economy: Cartoon Discourse and the Production of a Category." *Cultural Studies* 1.1 (1987): 93–114.

Golding, P., and G. Murdock. "Ideology and the Mass Media: The Question of Determination." In *Ideology and Cultural Production*, edited by M. Barrett et al., pp. 198–224. London: Croom Helm, 1979.

Meyer, K., et al. "Women in July Fourth Cartoons: A Hundred-Year Look." *Journal of Communications* 30.1 (1980): 21–30.

Morris, R. N. "Visual Rhetoric in Political Cartoons: A Structuralist Approach." *Metaphor and Symbolic Activity* 8:3 (1993): 195–210.

Morris, R. N. *The Carnivalization of Politics*. Montreal: McGill-Queen's University Press, 1995.

Perkins, D. "A Definition of Caricature: Caricature and Recognition." *Studies in the Anthropology of Visual Communications* 2.1 (1975): 1–24.

Press, C. *The Political Cartoon*. Rutherford, N.J.: Fairleigh Dickinson University Press, 1981.

Streicher, L. S. "On a Theory of Political Cartooning." *Comparative Studies in Society and History* 9.4 (1967): 427–445.

—RAY MORRIS

CASSIRER, ERNST (1874–1945), German philosopher who taught in Berlin, Hamburg, Oxford, and Göteborg before emigrating to the United States in 1941, where he held visiting professorships at Yale and Columbia Universities until his death. In Cassirer's rich trove of ideas pertinent to semiotics, there are a few that qualify him as a visionary. Today, his name is associated with those who are making the networked world a captivating reality. Cassirer

himself—more a classicist than an innovator—would probably be confused by seeing his philosophy conjured up in the analysis of multiuser dungeons (MUDs), which involve dialogue between virtual personae that are embodied in textual expressions. Cassirer's work is also referred to by scholars involved in the semiotic issues of representation as they try to emulate human intelligence. Still, Cassirer's work in semiotics remains little known, although some modern semioticians (Jurij Lotman, Roland Barthes, and Umberto Eco among them) have pursued themes and notions that bear his imprint: symbolic expression, the study of the myth, and culture as a semiotic system.

Cassirer's work makes up a large body of philosophic elaborations that is almost Renaissance-like in scope, starting with his dissertation, *Descartes' Critique of Mathematical and Natural Scientific Knowledge* (University of Marburg, 1899) and culminating with *The Philosophy of Symbolic Forms*, the fourth and final volume of which was published posthumously. His oeuvre is difficult, with many digressions, and covers philosophic subjects ranging from themes originating in ancient Greek philosophy to the subjects of existentialism, positivism, and epistemology.

Commentators on his work place Cassirer between neo-Kantianism (probably in view of the influence of his mentor, Hermann Cohen, head of the Marburg school) and phenomenology. (He takes a position close to that of Edmund Husserl in supporting a logic free of psychological components). The focus of his inquiry is on knowledge, although his philosophic interrogation expands into the study of myth, language, art, religion, humanities, and the theory of science, and he provides generous amounts of historic context for the objects of his investigations. Cassirer is preoccupied with the constitution of knowledge and its expression, and accordingly his territory is not the object domain but the metadomain.

In Cassirer's view, philosophy and science evolve from myth. Nevertheless, the mythical world is of extreme richness and is therefore more dynamic than that of our theories and infinitely more impregnated with emotional qualities. "Science, the last step in man's mental development" appears to Cassirer as both the "highest and most characteristic attainment of human culture" and the expression of a particular condition summed up in what he called *animal symbolicum*, by which human beings are understood as symbolic animals.

For Cassirer, the symbolic and the semiotic are equivalent. This conception leads him to the popular assumption that all signs are symbols. While not eager to further differentiate in the realm of signs (as many of his illustrious contemporaries did), he nevertheless set the foundation for what later became the obsession with semiotics as a universal science. Robert Hertz (1881—1915) and Hermann von Helmholtz (1821–1894) were his precursors in defining symbols as objects of scientific inquiry: "These symbols are so constituted that the necessary logical consequences of the image are always images of the necessary natural consequences of the imagined objects." Transcending the functional level of existence (the world of signals, receptors, and effectors), the symbolic system is an artificial realm: "The fundamental concepts of each science, the instruments with which it propounds its questions and formulates its solutions, are no longer regarded as passive images of something, but as symbols created by the intellect itself."

Significance (*Prägnanz*, which in German involves also pithiness, precision, and meaningfulness) is correlative to the symbolic form. It is an aspect of symbolic activity and one of its goals. A symbolically significant experience (such as cause, time, or space) conveys meaning and becomes part of self-consciousness. Symbolic significance is a relational notion.

In this vein, Cassirer's semiotic elaborations become visionary, and this contribution makes his work attractive to current researchers in artificial intelligence and other fields of advanced scientific inquiry. Unfortunately, his contribution has been of less interest to semioticians, who at times appear more concerned with justifying the implicit legitimacy of their endeavors than with the significance of semiotics for those working outside it. Cassirer is quite blunt in observing that "science does not mirror the structure of being," thus continuing the post-Kantian critical examination of how knowledge is attained and of its significance.

Cassirer carries through a notion of symbolic productivity that resonates in today's attempts to build effective computational procedures rooted in constructivist philosophy:

The logic of things, i.e., of the material concepts and relations on which the structure of science rests, cannot be separated from the logic of signs, for the sign is no mere accidental cloak of the idea, but its necessary and essential organ. It serves not merely to communicate a complex and given thought process, but is an instrument, by means of which this content develops and fully defines itself. . . . Consequently, all truly strict and exact thought is sustained by the symbolic and semiotics on which it is based. (1960–1964, vol. 1, p. 85)

It would be risky, however, to construe these speculations as a comprehensive foundation for modern cognitive sciences. Rather, we should see them as parts of a conceptual structure, subject to further refinement. Cassirer's work bears the burden of those who illuminated his thinking, from Giambattista Vico, Johann Gottfried Herder, Hermann von Helmholtz, Georg Simmel, and Hermann Cohen to Albert Einstein. Cassirer in turn influenced many of the scholars who gave modern semiotics its own legitimacy. M. I. Kagan, who was influential within what became the famous circle around Mikhail Bakhtin, upon returning from Germany identified Cassirer as an influence on his philosophy of language. It is probably too late for some of Cassirer's less-appreciated ideas to further advance the field. Nevertheless, some of his writings will continue to be read as almost prophecies that have been borne out: "Physical reality seems to recede in proportion as man's symbolic activity advances. Instead of dealing with things themselves, man is in a sense constantly conversing with himself. He has so enveloped himself in linguistic forms, in artistic images, in mythical symbols or religious rites that he cannot see or know anything except by the interposition of this artificial medium" (1962, p. 25). Our current world is, indeed, one in which the "tangled web of experience" is expanding as we continue to "weave the symbolic net" of our interconditioning and interdependency. More than a semiotic awareness of symbolic forms, Cassirer made possible a cognitive self-awareness based on semiotic assumptions.

[*See also* Barthes; Burke; Cultural Knowledge; Eco; Lotman; Metalanguage; Metaphor; Myths; *and* Whorf.]

BIBLIOGRAPHY

Cassirer, E. *Language and Myth.* Translated by S. K. Langer. New York: Dover, 1946.

Cassirer, E. *The Problem of Knowledge: Philosophy, Science, and History since Hegel.* Translated by W. H. Wogloms and C. W. Handel. New Haven: Yale University Press, 1950.

Cassirer, E. *The Philosophy of Symbolic Forms.* Translated by R. Manheim. 4 vols. New Haven: Yale University Press, 1960–1964.

Cassirer, E. *An Essay on Man: An Introduction to the Philosophy of Human Culture.* New Haven: Yale University Press, 1962.

Cassirer, E. *An Annotated Bibliography.* New York: Garland, 1988.

Verene, D. P., ed. *Symbol, Myth, and Culture: Essays and Lectures of Ernst Cassirer, 1935–1945.* New Haven: Yale University Press, 1979.

—Mihai Nadin

CATASTROPHE THEORY. French mathematician René Thom's natural, realist philosophy is governed by the two central principles of structural stability and morphogenesis. The importance of catastrophe theory (CT) to linguistics and semiotics—an issue Thom himself has expounded—comes from the fact that it is most directly concerned with structures. The theory has essentially to do with the effect of local (quantitative, micro) variations on the global (qualitative, macro) structure. Catastrophe theory involves the description of the sudden, abrupt discontinuities induced by the continuous local perturbations of a system. As per Thom's theorem, "the number of qualitatively different configurations of discontinuities that can occur depends not on the number of state variables, which is generally very large, but on the control variables, which is generally very small. In particular, if the number of control variables is not greater than four, then there are only seven types of catastrophes, and in none of these more than two state variables are involved" (Saunders, 1980, p. 3). The seven elementary catastrophes are fold, cusp, swallowtail, butterfly, elliptic umbilic, hyperbolic umbilic, and parabolic umbilic, each of which has a corresponding topology.

For Thom, the universe is characterized by constant and incessant interactional dynamism in the physical and biological domains. This infinite flux is not, however, to be taken as universal chaos. The process can be grasped in terms of structures that are at least momentarily stable. The stable structures are the interactionally dynamic morphologies that come to be and disappear. Thus, the universe does not consist of things but of the constant creation and destruction of stable forms—in other words, a continuous process of morphogenesis, which denotes the appearance of organic forms during the course of

evolution; in more general terms, it denotes "any process creating (or destroying) forms" (Thom, 1983, p. 14). These forms do not vary infinitely, however, since their possible variety is constrained drastically by the four dimensions of space and time in the natural world. We can identify a restricted set of morphologies arising from basic physical and biological interactional dynamics. These are the archetypal morphologies assumed to be universally valid and extensive across the physical, biological, cognitive, and linguistic domains.

Correlative to the understanding of the universe as consisting of forms that are continuous, dynamic, irreducibly gestaltlike, and defined by their stability of structure, Thom's notion of meaning integrates its physical and cognitive aspects without setting up an exclusively linguistic level. The central problem that Thomian semantics addresses is that of the gap that arises between the physical reality and its phenomenological presentation. This gap, referred to as the "scission between phenomenology and physics" stems from the fact that though the physical world is perceived in its essential continuum, (i.e., as a totality of things and their relations), its description in language suffers some sort of a fracturing, an inevitable discretization by means of apparently disjoined lexical elements. For Thom, the syntax that is primarily a means of recapturing this continuum is generated from a semantic level that is also the deep conceptual syntax. His approach, based on a study of "interactional morphologies," is intended to develop an appropriate formalization of the semantic syntax of natural languages.

The importance of archetypal morphologies for linguistic theory comes from how they account for deep syntax in a deductive manner. The surface structures defined in terms of the formal combinatorics of the syntactic categories (noun, verb, etc.) do not capture the interactional dynamism that characterizes the semantic level. Meaning has its source in the real physical/biological occurrences that emerge as surface linguistic structures via the archetypal morphologies. This is what Jean Petitot (1985) has called the "morphogenesis of meaning."

Thom's basic claim is that there is a mediation between the physical, the cognitive, and the linguistic domains that can be understood in terms of morphological organization, or rather through the morphologies of interaction. The latter, rather than belonging to any one of the domains, are "rooted in the a priori of physical objective." The basic aim of the morphological approach in linguistics is to develop an ontologically adequate formalization of the semantic syntax of natural language.

A strictly geometricotopological analysis of language has yielded for Thom a set of eighteen archetypal morphologies that are the space-time schematisms or graphs of basic biological or physical interactive dynamics. These are claimed to be the perceptually relevant natural "deep structures" for the syntax and semantics of the otherwise discretized linguistic forms and their combinatorics. Wolfgang Wildgen (1982) and Jean Petitot (1989) have preferred to call these morphologies "semantic archetypes" and "actantial graphs," respectively.

Following Jakob von Uexküll (1864–1944), Thom believes that basic concepts originate as a function of the biological self-regulation involving the prey, the predator, and the (sexual) partner. The more complex concepts are built upon these: "The logos of living beings has served as the universal model for the formation of concepts." These biologically founded and linguistically valid concepts play the role of actants in the interactions represented by the verb, which is the organizing center—that is, the event that distributes the actantial places. Verbs are identified by their own structural stability as events. They have as their sources and models the simulation of elementary actantial interactions realizable in space-time. Perceptually, these interactions are constrained by the four dimensions of space-time.

It is possible to describe the morphogenesis of sentence structures by projecting the actant(s) on a substratum space and by assuming their "inflections" according to the increase in the number of actants and the evolution of interactions over time. For instance, a zero-valent verb such as *to rain* denotes an event that occupies the entirety of the perceptual space. An univalent verb such as *to go* evokes a real agent's action that is continuous in time, while a bivalent verb involves interactions, and hence its graph—obtained from the cusp catastrophe—shows a discontinuity (at the zone of interaction) that separates the earlier parts of the event from the later ones. Thom's example of such a verb is *to capture*, whose actantial graph is:

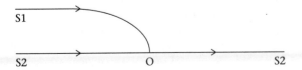

This indicates the paths in time of the two actants S1 and S2 and O, the point of interaction.

Besides *capture* or *domination*, the above schema can account for a wider range of actual actions such as *enter*, *eat*, or being subject to gravity. From such observations, Thom suggests that the core of language is structured like biology and even like physics. The morphologies are arranged in ascending order of verbal valences and hence of topological complexity. (See Thom [1983] for his complete list.)

Applying CT to Algirdas Julien Greimas's semiotic square, Petitot has suggested that the relations associated with the privative and qualitative binary oppositions (i.e., the axes of contrariness and contradiction) could be schematized by means of the catastrophes of minimal complexity of conflict and bifurcation (called the "fold"), respectively. This shift, he thinks, is in tune with the inherent topological potential of the square and involves the abandonment of a purely logicocombinatory method that is unsuitable for a properly structural method. The morphogenesis of the square can be modeled by a procession of elementary catastrophes.

Moreover, in Greimas's actantial model of the narrative transformations, the cusp catastrophe—and thus its associate morphology of *capture*—can account for the conversion of a disjunctive subject-object (S ∪ O) relation into a conjunctive one (S ∩ O). As regards the metapsychological dimension of desire that defines the subject-object relationship of the interaction (i.e., intentionality), Petitot notes that the archetypal morphologies are indeed the actantial schematisms that are isomorphic with the biological structures of predation and sexuality.

More recently, applications of CT have been proposed in models of connectionist cognitive science, especially to address the problems of constituency in cognitive grammar and visual perception.

[*See also* Actantial Model; Biosemiotics; Connectionism; Greimas; Morphology; Narratology; Semiotic Square; Thom; *and* Umwelt.]

BIBLIOGRAPHY

Petitot, J. *Morphogenèse du sens*. Paris: Presses universitaires de France, 1985.

Petitot, J. "On the Linguistic Import of Catastrophe Theory." *Semiotica* 74.3–4 (1989): 179–209.

Petitot, J. "Morphodynamics and Attractor Syntax: Constituency in Visual Perception and Cognitive Grammar." In *Mind as Motion: Explorations in the*

Dynamics of Motion, edited by R. F. Port and T. van Gelder, pp. 227–281. Cambridge, Mass.: MIT Press, 1995.

Saunders, P. T. *An Introduction to Catastrophe Theory.* Cambridge: Cambridge University Press, 1980.

Thom, R. *Structural Stability and Morphogenesis: An Outline of a General Theory of Models.* Reading, Mass. Benjamin, 1975.

Thom, R. *Mathematical Models of Morphogenesis* (1980). Translated by W. M. Brookes and D. Rand. New York: Horwood Wiley, 1983.

Wildgen, W. *Catastrophe Theoretic Semantics.* Amsterdam: John Benjamins, 1982.

Zeeman, E. C. "Catastrophe Theory." *Scientific American* 236:.4 (1976): 65–83.

—FRANSON MANJALI

CHEMICAL COMMUNICATION. There is an enormous range of applications of selective chemical recognition in nature that serve diverse purposes such as stimulation of nerves and muscles, growth, defense, marking of territory, and sexual attraction. In all these cases, specific chemical agents are used as a means of communication to elicit a desired response. Unlike speech communication, however, chemical communication can be extremely limited in the amount of useful information it conveys since selective chemical recognition by a receptor site provides no structural information about a chemical agent (an analyte); rather, the binding process simply indicates the presence and relative concentration of a species of interest. This lack of information places restrictions on the quality and reliability of analyses and on the use of chemicals for development of a language. The physical basis of the primary processes associated with chemical communication can be identified in order to explore the quality of the information and communication available from selective chemical binding.

Interfacial chemical processes provoke selective and nonselective responses and intrinsically set limits on the transduction of structural information and operational characteristics such as sensitivity, speed, reversibility, and stability. It is clear that a signal develops because of the presence of alterations in a receptor's structure or environment (complex formation, product evolution), yet it is not clear how such a signal can be used to deduce structural information about the analyte. The general consensus in biochemistry seems to be that receptor selectivity is directly proportional to the binding energy; however,

this is misleading in the analytical context since selective binding does not necessarily provide an analytical signal and might in fact provide no signal or even interference to the desired analytical signal. In an analytical context, the term *selectivity* applies to the experimentally observed generation of an analytical signal, which is not necessarily equivalent to thermodynamic selectivity. Although it is true that a receptor will thermodynamically select the site (ligand) with which it can bind most strongly, it is possible that a receptor will bind strongly to different ligands, some of which might not produce analytical signals. Also, the binding energy associated with a ligand might provide an analytical signal by altering the function of the protein in ion or solute transport. This latter possibility introduces a further complexity to the discussion of the development of an analytical signal and indicates that selective binding based on statistical probability can confuse the relationships between the recognition and the development of an analytical signal.

In a practical experiment, recognition of the selective binding of a receptor can be derived from detection of the extent that the available receptor sites are occupied or from detection of a secondary biological signal induced by an analyte that acts as an agonist (i.e., a ligand that induces a biological response when binding to the receptor). Occupancy forms the basis of most arguments of information theory, yet accurate information about analyte binding is often derived from a secondary process of biological signal generation induced by an agonist (analyte) (Fraga et al., 1978).

In bimolecular recognition, the energies responsible for binding can be low in order to allow for reversibility; therefore, the strength of binding is not a good index of degree of selectivity or signal generation. In protein-protein and protein-ligand interactions, there are considerable losses in rotational and translational degrees of freedom associated with binding.

The analytical goal for a chemoreceptive system is the selective and sensitive detection of molecular species within complicated matrices without sample preparation; this demands that analytical recognition must be derived from the charge, size, and three-dimensional steric charge distribution at the reactive surface of an analyte. The availability of distributed potential contact points in three dimensions for a larger organic analyte indicates that such molecules intrinsically contain more information for molecular recognition than is available for small molecules or ions.

Formal calculation of the quantity of information contained in a particular molecular structure has been proposed, and information indexes can be calculated by using structural features of functional group distribution, molecular-symmetry elements, electron delocalization, and various combinations of the above. General indexes of molecular complexity that combine the information indexes on atomic composition, type and total amount of chemical bonds, and symmetry and conformations and give an indication about the variety of these structural elements in a structure were proposed by Steven H. Bertz (1981).

Theoretical information indexes find use in the classification of compounds, quantitative structure-property and structure-activity correlations, computer processing, and retrieval of chemical information. Information indexes are not absolute properties of molecules but have only a relative value, and, although they are related to atomic and molecular properties, the relation can be complicated. The information content of an analyte—or alternatively the information that defines the selectivity of a receptor—can be related directly to the size and three-dimensional complexity of the molecule. This only indicates that information is available, however, and does not indicate how binding is optimally achieved nor how this binding process can lead to a direct analytical signal.

It is interesting and perhaps important to chemoreception that a multidimensional approach to signal collection can indirectly provide structural information and improve the reliability of the analysis. Arrays of partially and differently selective sensors can provide binding data that might infer the presence of particular molecular species or functional groups. This chemometric approach to the elimination of interferences is based on knowledge of the action of each receptor in the presence of each chemical component in the system. Such calibration would likely be unsuitable in "real" analyses when new species are present, which can completely obviate any validity in an analysis unless the detection and processing system can adapt to the new mixtures of signals. This is where the process of learning becomes significant, as exemplified by the case of an oenophile who can learn to distinguish wines by differences in odors and flavors.

[*See also* Biosemiotics; Information; Receptors; *and* Umwelt.]

BIBLIOGRAPHY

Agosta, W. C. *Chemical Communication: The Language of Pheromones*. New York: W. H. Freeman, 1992.

Bertz, S. H. "The First General Index of Molecular Complexity." *Journal of the American Chemical Society* 103 (1981): 3599–3601.

Burton, R. *The Language of Smell*. London: Routledge and Kegan Paul, 1976.

Classen, C., D. Howes, and A. Synnott. *Aroma: The Cultural History of Smell*. London and New York: Routledge, 1994.

Fraga, S., K. M. S. Saxena, and M. Torres. *Biomolecular Information Theory*. Elsevier: Amsterdam, 1978.

Raming, K., et al. "Cloning and Expression of Odorant Receptors." *Nature* 361 (28 January 1993): 353–356.

Roper, S. D., and J. Atema, eds. *Olfaction and Taste IX*. New York: New York Academy of Science, 1987.

Stoddart, D. M. *The Scented Ape: The Biology and Culture of Human Odour*. Cambridge: Cambridge University Press, 1990.

—ULRICH J. KRULL

CHINESE IDEOGRAMS. The word *idéogramme* was used first by the French linguist Jean-François Champollion in 1822 to refer to Egyptian symbols: the French word *idéographique* was used to refer to Egyptian hieroglyphic writing and Chinese script. The English word appeared in the same year and was probably a transliteration from the French. Both *ideographs* and *ideograms* have been later applied loosely and wrongly to Chinese writing systems in general. In a stricter sense, these two interchangeable terms designate written signs that directly represent "ideas" with or without phonetic mediation. Hence the popular notion that the Chinese writing system is "motivated" or, in Louis Hjelmslev's terminology, a "pleremic" (semantically full) script as opposed to a "cenemic" (semantically void) script, such as English.

Nina Catach (1986) observes that Chinese writing fully displays "the whole range of semiological possibilities of writing" because this essentially "pleremic system endowed with cenemic complementary procedures" epitomizes writing's paradoxical nature of encompassing both autonomy from and complementarity with speech. The minimal components of Chinese writing are graphemes, commonly understood as "strokes." The strokes in themselves are cenemic but often become motivated as a result of retroactive semanticization or iconization. From the lowest graphemic level are derived graphemic compounds, or morphographemes, known as "radicals"; from these are derived the still higher level of graphs known as "characters" (*wen* or *zi*), whose combinations are graphic strings (*ci*), moving toward a unique "graphosyntax" (*ju*). The relation between morphographemes and graphs is not invariably linearly unidirectional, as in speech, but reciprocal. Just as a grapheme can be elevated to the higher morphographemic and sometimes graphic levels, a graph can be "degenerated," so to speak, into a morphographeme. It is not surprising that degradation sometimes even involves the condensation of a chain of action (syntax) in one graphic unit.

A major difference between speech and writing is that, unlike phonemes, graphemes per se are not pronounceable. As to semantics, in speech only the lexical level is pleremic, but in Chinese writing almost all levels are pleremic, including the extreme case where a graphic sign or word contains only one grapheme. The syntactic uniqueness of Chinese writing has to do with its scarcity of grammatical morphemes, such as tense and aspect markers, articles or demonstratives, number, genitive or case markers, classifiers, coverbs, clause linkers, and complementizers or subordination markers.

The system specificity of Chinese writing manifests itself in the principles that govern the distribution of elements on various levels and their integration into the global structure. One such structural principle is differentiation. Graphemic elements are produced in order to distinguish a new character from an existing one. According to traditional interpretation, consensus enabled the scribe to draw a circle to stand for the sun. Since the same sign was already in use to signify "closure," a diacritical dot or short line was added to the center of the circle for the sake of differentiation. This kind of makeshift device is more conventional than realistic and hence puts the assumption of motivation into question.

In the second century BCE, Chinese lexicographers had already developed a classification system in which the then relatively unified script was divided into six categories, concerning respectively the relation between form (including morphographeme and morphophoneme) and meaning and between one graph and another. These six categories can be regrouped into four according to the structure and function of the graphic sign: pictogram, ideogram, phonogram, and hypergram.

The pictogram is a simple character (*wen*) that is intended and agreed upon to resemble metonymically the shape of an object. As such, it is semantically full but can lend itself as a morphographemic or semantic unit to form graphic signs of a higher order. Following the Peircean trichotomy, one could call it an iconic sign, though it does not directly resemble its original but is an abstract and stylized representation. Like all graphic signs, it can be thus considered symbolic in that it requires shared knowledge among people who accept the sign as such. Paradoxically, this conventionally at once ensures and undermines the pictogram's representational function. The undermining function is especially evident when the pictogram lends itself as a morphographeme to form a complex sign such as an ideogram or is loaned to represent (visually) a morphophoneme, morpheme, or lexia that does not have a graphemic and graphic sign of its own. In both cases, the iconic sign either is transformed into an indexical sign or is appropriated as a symbolic sign.

As its name suggests, the ideogram signifies an idea, a concept, or a quality that usually does not have a referent or an existence in itself. There are two types of ideogram: the simple one and the compound one, depending on the level of its component (i.e., whether it is a morphographeme or a graph). Subtype 1 consists of pictograms appropriated not to represent the objects they refer to but to signify a quality inherent in the objects. Subtype 2 includes graphs where constituent graphemes enter into a relationship that indicates position, direction, and quality rather than a real or imagined object. Therefore, they can be regarded as a type of indexical sign.

Unlike icons, all these indexes represent abstract concepts. While these cannot conceivably be iconicized in an alphabetical language, in Chinese they are based mostly on icons as constituents. Some graphs of this subtype are borrowed from pictograms with modifications. For example, two diacritical graphemes in the shape of dots are added under the human icon's stretched arms to form a new graph meaning *armpits*. Later on, because of the graph's phoneticization and grammaticalization, both iconic and indexical functions were lost, and a new homophonous graph was coined to stand for the armpits. Similar cases are the modifications of the iconic *tree* into *treetop* and *root*. Both involve an iconic sign of tree, but the additional grapheme in the form of a short horizontal line on top or below the tree icon introduces a new spatial relation.

The indexization of iconic signs can be also seen in the more abstract compound ideogram that is formed by at least two individual iconic or indexical signs, both of which are pleremic. The new graph, however, might carry a phonological value completely alien to that of either morphographeme. The ideogram denoting brightness or dawn is a compound of two pictograms visualizing the sun and the moon, both having been reduced to the lower status of morphographeme in the new graph. While the semantic values are retained, the phonological values are completely lost.

Two subtypes of compound ideogram can be identified. Subtype 1 is the reduplication of a single pictogram to form an ideogram. When the pictogram denoting a tree is duplicated and thus degraded from the status of graph to morphographeme, it becomes the ideogram representing a grove; when triplicated, it represents a forest. What differentiates the tree, the grove, and the forest is the increase not only in morphographemic quality but also in the indexical spatial relation. Such examples confirm Peirce's description of the index as involving an icon of a peculiar kind, not resembling its object but modifying it. Moreover, this specific iconic sign serves as a good example to illustrate Peirce's first trichotomy of sign, according to which a sign in itself can be a mere quality (qualisign), an actual existence (sinsign), or a law (legisign). In the examples above, all the three tree icon–based graphs contain the quality of treeness; as sinsign, each involves a qualisign or several qualisigns, and the reduplication establishes them as legisigns. There is no syncategorical element among the morphographemes, which is replaced by spatial orientation; the iconic sign repeats itself and situates the replicas in a given space to generate the concept it denotes. In the compound ideogram, the sign might have more than one object, as the compound sign represents a set of objects, the explanation of the sign itself, and the relationship among the components. This is especially true of subtype 2 of the compound ideogram.

Subtype 2 denotes an event rather than a quality, what Ernest Fenollosa describes as a "verbal idea of action." Such ideograms exhibit the tendency toward a special type of graphosyntax; instead of using phonetic signs to suggest temporality, the ideogram suggests the

succession of events through spatial arrangement of its pictorial morphographemes. This unique graphosyntax is not displayed on the horizontal axis, nor does the method of combination constitute linear syntagmata. While the iconic sign observes the metaphorical principle of equivalence and selection in the relation between the representamen and object, the indexical sign observes the metonymic principle of combination and contiguity. Grammatical indexes in English (e.g., demonstratives, deictics) have the potential of forming syntax, but Chinese graphemic and graphic indexes show how metaphors (a type of icon according to Peirce) in their paradigmatic relations join to produce a third metaphor that either belongs to the same paradigm or forms another, more inclusive paradigm on a higher (i.e., graphemic → graphic; graphic → graphosyntactic) level. Therefore, the procedure from pictogram to ideogram is not the distribution of paradigmatic elements on the syntagmata but the integration of one paradigm with another of a higher order.

The third category of graphic sign is the compound phonogram whose method refers to the use of one graph as a morphographeme of another new graph to indicate the sound of the latter. When thus used, it is known in English as a phonetic. The other morphographeme that signifies meaning is conveniently called the signific. Most scholars agree that this type of character was a later development. It shows the trespassing of speech on writing or the marriage of the two. The phonogram can be also divided into a few subtypes according to different degrees of representationality and conventionality. The most popular type is iconic, in which one morphographeme is visual and the other auditory. For example, the archaic pictogram for a bird stands for the general class of bird. In order to differentiate among kinds of birds, such as chicken, duck, and goose, an additional morphographeme used as phonetic is added to the graph, now degraded to a morphographeme and serving the function of signific. This newly introduced phonetic has been desemanticized, such as the famous example cited by Sergei Eisenstein (1898–1948). Eisenstein (1949) poetically glosses a compound ideogram consisting of an *ear* signific and a *door* phonetic as "the picture of an ear near the drawing of a door = to listen" without knowing that the *door* has lost its semantic value. When originally pleremic iconic signs have been desemanticized, iconic signs are changed into symbolic signs. Conventionalization transforms all the iconic and indexical signs into symbolic ones that signify, as Peirce observes, "only by virtue of [their] being understood to have that signification."

The tendency toward arbitrary symbolization can be seen best in the last category of graphic unit, which, lacking a better term, can be provisionally called, following Saussure's analysis of the anagram, the hypergram. The word is thus used in the sense that another graph has been superimposed on an existing graph or a graph is loaned from an anterior graph. The hypergram is governed by the principle of appropriation, which allows individual graphs to bear secondary meanings, either by conventional extension of ideas or as direct loans. Sometimes, the signific of a graph is loaned to coin new graphs; other times, the phonetic is loaned; there are still other occasions when the whole graph is loaned by virtue of homophonicity. This multiplication of characters and usages is accelerated by grapho- and phonosyntaxization. Grammatically, most deictics, anaphoras, prepositions, and conjunctions that contribute to characters' distribution on the axis of syntax fall into this category.

From the perspective of Peircean semiotics, the four categories of archaic Chinese script can be subsumed by the trichotomy of signs, and the process from the iconic through the indexical to the symbolic corresponds to the historical development of Chinese script. While all the four categories have come to be regarded as signs through the empirical and pragmatic operations of the interpretant, the relationships among the sign, its object, and interpretant are different. The sign's symbolization leads finally to the Peircean propositional logic of grammar that deals with meaning and truth.

[See also Alphabet; Arbitrariness, Principle of; Iconicity; Indexicality; Linguistic Motivation; Peirce; and Writing, Ethnography of.]

BIBLIOGRAPHY

Catach, N. "The Grapheme: Its Position and Its Degree of Autonomy with Respect to the System of the Language." In New Trends in Graphemics and Orthography, edited by G. Augst, pp. 1–10. Berlin: Walter de Gruyter, 1986.
Creel, H.G. "On the Nature of Chinese Ideography." Toung pao 32 (1936): 85–161.
Defrancis, J. The Chinese Language: Fact and Fantasy. Honolulu: University of Hawaii Press, 1984.
Derrida, J. Of Grammatology. Translated by G. Chakravorty Spivak. Baltimore: Johns Hopkins University Press, 1974.
Eisenstein, S. Film Form: Essays in Film Theory. Edited by J. Leyda. New York: Harvest–Harcourt Brace Jovanovich, 1949.
Fenollosa, E. "The Chinese Written Character as a Medium for Poetry." In Instigations, edited by E. Pound, pp. 357–388. New York: Boni and Liveright, 1920.
Géfin, L. K. Ideogram: History of a Poetic Method. Austin: University of Texas Press, 1982.
Hjelmslev, L. Essais linguistiques. Travaux du Cercle Linguistique Copenhague, 12. Copenhagen: Akademisk Forlag, 1959.
Starobinski, J. Words upon Words: The Anagrams of Ferdinand de Saussure. Translated by O. Emmt. New Haven: Yale University Press, 1979.
Yau, Shun-chiu. "Elements Ordering in Gestural Languages and in Archaic Chinese Ideograms." Cahier de linguistique Asie orientale 3 (March 1978): 51–65.

—HAN-LIANG CHANG

CHINESE ONTOLOGICAL REALISM. Nearly all major Chinese philosophical schools since ancient times have been concerned with the relationship between words and realities that from the modern perspective constitutes an important aspect of semiotic studies. Of all those who contributed to this field, one line of thinkers stands out in the sense that they were concerned with the relationship beween word and reality not for its moral and political significance (as in Confucianism) nor for its metaphysical import (as in Daoism) but for the epistemological aspect of the dichotomy itself.

The earliest name usually associated with this line of thinking is Mozi (479–438? BCE), who advocated a mimesis theory of meaning. According to him, words and realities are distinct categories, but the two can be unified because the former are derived from the latter. The most quoted aphorism from the texts of Mozi in relation to this topic is "yi ming ju shi," where ju means "to imitate or represent," shi means "extralinguistic realities," and ming indicates words that are used to imitate or represent.

The philosophical discussion of the relationship between verbal signs and extralinguistic realities reached a high point during the subsequent period of the Warring States (403–222 BCE). Unlike their predecessors and successors in the history of Chinese philosophy, scholars of this historical period as a whole showed a concentrated interest in the problem of the correspondence between names and realities, for which they were given the collective title "the School of Names." Among them were Gongsun

Longzi (380–? BCE) and Xunzi (298–238 BCE), whose actual texts were not only known to their contemporaries but also preserved and therefore read and studied by later generations. Gongsun Longzi holds the belief that all things in the world appear in particular shapes and substances, and as such they are given different names. To know whether the meaning of a word corresponds to its reality or not, we have to know the conditions that give rise to it. As he puts it in chapter 6 of his *On Names and Realities,* "A name is to designate a reality. If we know that this is not this and know that this is not here, we shall not call it ['this']. If we know that that is not that and know that that is not there, we shall not call it ['there']."

On the word-reality relationship, Xunzi is probably the most systematic of all the ancient Chinese philosophers. He was born in a historical era that witnessed an epidemic of "discrepancies between words and realities," a situation that drove him to write his famous tract *On the Rectification of Names.* According to this work, the motivations for rectifying names are epistemological as well as political. On the one hand, there is a need to distinguish the higher from the lower in terms of social status; on the other hand, we must discriminate different states and qualities of things. "When the distinctions between the noble and the humble are clear and similarities and differences [of things] are discriminated, there will be no danger of ideas being misunderstood and work encountering difficulties or being neglected." From there, Xunzi proceeds to discuss the theoretical possibility of achieving linguistic universality, which is a line of argument very similar to that proposed by his Greek counterpart Aristotle (384–322 BCE). They both hold that names or words are symbols of mental impressions, and Xunzi argues that although forms and colors are distinguished by the eye, sounds and tunes are heard by the ear, sweetness and bitterness are differentiated by the mouth, freshness and foulness are smelled by the nose, and pain and comfort are felt by the skin, in the end the information we acquire through all these senses have to be processed by the mind, for it is because the mind collects knowledge that it is possible to know sound through the ear and form through the eye. Nevertheless, the collection of knowledge depends on the natural organs first registering it, and "the organs of members of the same species with the same feelings perceive things in the same way. Therefore things

are compared and those that are seemingly alike are generalized. In this way they share their conventional name as a common meeting ground." Finally, Xunzi lays down what he calls "the fundamental principle on which names are instituted": When things are similar, they ought to be given the same name; when things are different, they ought to be given different names. When a simple name is not sufficient, a compound name ought to be used.

After Xunzi, the discussion of the word-reality relationship gradually moved away from the center of Chinese intellectual speculations and never regained its position of dominance over other areas of human concerns till the present century, when Western epistemology as an important branch of the social sciences was introduced into China through Marxist philosophy. This does not mean, however, that Chinese curiosity in this respect ended with the period of the Warring States. On the contrary, the debate about the word-reality relationship continued sporadically throughout the history of Chinese thought. One important example is Ouyang Jian (267?–300 CE), who picked up the same topic four and a half centuries later and whose expositions further completed the realist theory of meaning in ancient China. In his best-known essay, *On the Exhaustive Capacity of Language*, he propounds a purely instrumental theory of the verbal sign. Continuing the realist theme but pushing it to its ontological extreme, he argues that

without heaven speaking, the four seasons run all the same; without sages talking, the differences among things still exist. Shapes of the circle and the square show themselves before they are given names; colors of white and black are apparent before they receive appellations. So names do not add anything to things; nor can language modify the nature of things. However, in their efforts to rectify names, sages past and present cannot achieve their aim without the help of words. Why? Because without words the nature of things formulated in the mind cannot be differentiated. If there are no words to express thoughts, there will be no communication; if there are no names, there will be no differentiation of things. Differentiation classifies things that are different from one another and communication in language makes possible the expression of thoughts. In their origin, things do not have natural names; nor do thoughts command fixed words. To differentiate among actualities, different names are employed; to communicate thoughts, words are created. Names change as things do and words alter as thoughts do, just as echoes to sounds and shadows to bodies.

What is spelled out there in simple but emphatic terms by Ouyang Jian are two important principles of the realist theory of meaning. First, independent of verbal signs, there exist ultimate qualities of things and states of events in the extralinguistic world. Second, meanings of words or other expressions of human language are derivative and secondary in the sense that they are only reflections of extralinguistic actualities that are captured in language and then passed on to others.

If situated in the context of the global history of semiotics, Ouyang Jian's text acquires a further dimension of intertextual and intercultural significance. Its example of the self-existing circle can be linked to Plato's seventh epistle, where the nature of the circle is also conceived as a prelinguistic "form" which is then represented imperfectly either in language or in painting. The second example of prelinguistic color differentiation has even greater relevance to modern Western semiotics, for the formation of color terms in language not only furnishes a point of departure for Saussurean linguistics in its attack on traditional linguistics but also becomes one of the most debated issues in twentieth-century linguistic scholarship.

Although contemporary Chinese philosophy of language professes to be an application of Marxist philosophy to the study of language, on a deeper level it remains as much an heir to its native tradition of ontological realism. To a great extent, it still assumes the independent existence of an extralinguistic world, natural as well as social. That is, to most contemporary language theorists in China, the essential characteristics of things exist in themselves and would exist even if there were no words to reveal them. However, there is one important difference between the ancient and the modern. Unlike their ancient predecessors, modern language philosophers are more acutely aware of the trap of word-reality dualism where the correspondence between the two cannot be guaranteed logically. For this reason, they try to insert into the dichotomy a third element, human cognition, that is capable of achieving linear progression. In a wordless world, they argue, actualities of things are available for dis-

covery, but such discovery is made possible by the formation of human consciousness after millions of years of evolution. Whereas consciousness reflects reality, language is the means that makes it possible. Humans use words to designate surrounding objects and phenomena, their connections and relations, and so on. Words in a way substitute for objects, representing them in the human consciousness, but they also record the abstract activity of human thinking. This means that words and phrases are the result of a generalized cognition based on sensations and perceptions engendered by the impact on the human sense organs of the objects and phenomena of reality. Furthermore, the process of cognition is an endless one, in the course of which human thought draws closer to the essence of the things of the extralinguistic world. From this perspective, the form of a language expression, due to its close connection with human consciousness, ultimately communicates the essential nature of whatever is denoted by it.

[See also Linguistic Motivation; Marx; Meaning; Realism and Nominalism; Reference; and Whorf.]

BIBLIOGRAPHY

Chan, Wing-Tsit, trans. and ed. *A Source Book in Chinese Philosophy.* Princeton: Princeton University Press, 1973.
Fung, Yu-lan. *A History of Chinese Philosophy.* 2 vols. Translated by D. Bodde. Princeton: Princeton University Press, 1952–1953.
Gao Mingkai. *On Language.* Beijing: Science Publisher, 1963.
Jiang Ghozhu. *A History of Chinese Epistemology.* Zhengzhou: Henan People's Press, 1989.

—ERSU DING

CHIROGRAPHY. One of the two categories of picture signs proposed by the psychologist James J. Gibson (1904–1979), chirography (resulting from the traces of a hand or a handheld tool) is distinct from photography (produced by the action of luminosity on a sensitive surface).

Chirographic pictures, like photographic ones, are largely indexical in that they are indexicalities (which in some cases become indexes) of all the forces that contribute to producing them. Developmental psychology suggested that the marks a toddler makes on paper are accidental traces of motor activity that are at that point experienced as rewarding in themselves; only at about the age of eighteen months, with the emergence of the semiotic function, will the child react with disappointment when no strokes and dots result from the contact of marker with paper, and only at three years will she or he refuse to draw in the air (Gardner, 1973). What was at first accidental substance becomes the very form of the act. Thus, chirographic pictures are indexical in origin; only later does iconicity come to the fore.

If chirography can be defined first by contrast with photography, a deeper understanding requires situating this category of visual signs in a broader array of semiotic processes. "Hard icons" (Maldonado, 1974) are signs that are related to what they depict through direct traces (X-ray pictures, hand stencils on cave walls, acoustic pictures produced by ultrasound, silhouettes, nuclear-bomb impressions, thermograms, and ordinary photographs). The real contiguity between the picture and its referent is here taken to guarantee the cognitive value of the picture. Hard icons are not, however, simply signs that are both indexical and iconic, for that is true also of chirographs; there must be coincidence between their indexical and iconic grounds.

According to another classification (Gubern, 1987), chirographic pictures, such as drawings, are distinct from technographic pictures (photography, cinematography, and video). All hand-produced pictures are based on similarity, as they depend on the "hand-eye-system" (Gibson, 1980), whereas all machine-made pictures are derived indexically. For instance, technography includes both pictures produced by instruments such as the physionotrace, an eighteenth-century device for making drawings from silhouettes, and synthetic pictures (computer graphics). The latter, however, actually upset the distinction between chirography and technography, since they look exactly like photographs but are mediated by similarity rather than derived by contiguity.

Espe (1983) has proposed a threefold division of graphics, comprising all kinds of manipulations of two-dimensional surfaces: photographics, chirographics, and typographics (the production of markings on surfaces by the use of standardized implements). However, in desktop publishing, destandardized typefonts can vary along a number of parameters (size, obliqueness, etc.) thus bringing them closer to being chirographic pictures, and, conversely, handprints found on cave walls are standardized, contiguity based, and yet not machine produced.

Contrary to photography, chirography has not

been studied semiotically as such: If anything, it dissolves into the traditional categories of drawing and painting. But, obviously, an adequate classification of chirographs in relation to other picture signs or other tracings on surfaces remains a task for the future.

[*See also* Gibson; Iconicity; Index; Indexicality; *and* Photography.]

BIBLIOGRAPHY

Espe, H. "Realism and Some Semiotic Functions of Photographs." In *Semiotics Unfolding: Proceedings of the Second Congress of the International Association for Semiotic Studies, Vienna 1979*, vol. 3, edited by T. Borbé, pp. 1435–1442. Berlin, New York, and Amsterdam: Mouton, 1983.
Gardner, H. *The Arts and Human Development*. New York: Wiley and Sons, 1973.
Gardner, H. *Artful Scribbles*. New York: Basic Books, 1980.
Gibson, J. "A Prefatory Essay on the Perception of Surfaces versus Perception of Markings on a Surface." In *The Perception of Pictures*. Volume 1: *Alberti's Window*, edited by M. Hagen, pp. xi–xvii. New York: Academic Press, 1980.
Gubern, R. *La mirada opulenta: Exploración de la iconosfera contemporánea*. Barcelona: Gustavo Gili, 1987.
Maldonado, T. *Vanguardia e razionalità*. Torino: Einaudi, 1974.
Moles, A. *L'image—communication fonctionelle*. Brussels, Casterman, 1981.

—GÖRAN SONESSON

CINEMA. Semiotic studies of cinema started in France in the 1960s and can be divided into two phases. The earlier phase (1964–1974) is linked to the theories and methods of structural linguistics, with a readily identifiable debt to the work of Ferdinand de Saussure and Louis Hjelmslev. The later phase (1975–1980) is linked to psychoanalysis (chiefly Sigmund Freud and Jacques Lacan), with a shift in emphasis from the film construed as text to its reception by the audience. During both phases, the most influential theoretical texts have been written by the French linguist and semiotician Christian Metz (1931–1994).

Metz's earliest writings on cinema stemmed from his reaction to the film theorist and historian Jean Mitry's two-volume *Esthétique et psychologie du cinéma* (The Aesthetics and Psychology of the Cinema, 1965). For Metz, Mitry's study was the great synthesis of the humanistic film theory of the time, but it also marked the end of an era. Following Hjelmslev and Roland

Barthes, Metz proceeded to address a recurring issue of humanist scholarship: the often offhanded remark that cinema was a "language" with its own syntax and grammar. By strategically demonstrating that in cinema there is no exact equivalent of the word (the briefest shot being the equivalent of at least a sentence) and that there is no such thing in film as the double articulation (phoneme/moneme) of language, Metz dismissed past generalizations about cinema as a language. He nevertheless conceded that as a system of communication or a medium of expression, cinema offered peculiar characteristics suited to study under the umbrella of semiotics. Cinema would thus be subjected to a more scientific approach than previous scholars had allowed. Metz's own rigorous writings on film theory proved that the study of cinema could be as challenging as that of other disciplines.

Metz's approach distinguishes five materials of expression in film: photographed moving images, photographed words, recorded voice, sound effects, and music. His semiotic discussions of film rely on the terminology of Barthes's *Eléments de sémiologie* (Elements of Semiology, 1964), with emphasis on the familiar pairings of, for instance, signifier and signified, denotation and connotation, and paradigm and syntagma. However, Metz and others have added extensively to the terminology pertinent to film studies. The filmic text is regularly referred to as a *récit* (tale) (often even when the narrative status of the film discussed is debatable); the word *diégèse* (diegesis), reintroduced by Etienne Souriau (1950) into the French language to refer to all stated and implied elements of a film's fictional universe, was even later borrowed from film semiotics by literary narratologists such as Gérard Genette (1965, 1969). With such concepts in place, the semiotician can undertake the systematic description, segmentation, or analysis of a filmic text or a portion thereof.

For film semioticians, the status of the shot as the smallest signifying unit in the text is of unequivocal importance. Not only is a shot of a cat the equivalent of the sentence, "Here is a cat," but it also conveys the textual specificity of the filmed cat: whether it is black or white, moving or reclining, contented or angry, even, perhaps, whether it is domestic or wild. The referent in a film is never just lexical (as is the dictionary word *cat*).

The paradigms of filmic expression are often identified in opposing pairs such as fixed shots/traveling shots or pans; brief shots/long takes; close-ups/long

or establishing shots. In addition, all the alternatives that fall between these extremes can be found along the paradigmatic axis. For instance, the medium shot and the so-called *plan américain* (or three-quarter shot) and variations thereof are neither as close as the close-up nor as distant as the long shot. Each shot consists of a combination of visual (and in sound cinema auditory) elements selected from an endless number of filmic paradigms. Of course, while the vertical paradigmatic axis involves the notion of selection of messages, the syntagmatic axis organizes the messages along a horizontal *déroulement* or flow. The syntagmatic axis in film analysis is linked clearly to the process of editing.

The dominant subject of discussion for film semioticians is the notion of the filmic code. If a text is an ensemble of signifying elements (*signifiants*), then codes are functioning simultaneously to create the signified meaning (*signifié*). For the conditioned filmgoer, a white Stetson on a cowboy in a traditional Western is more than a white hat: It identifies the cowboy as the hero, whereas a black Stetson identifies the villain. Articles of clothing such as hats, along with a multitude of other signifying elements from the everyday world (food, automobiles, hairstyles, furniture, etc.) are referred to as nonspecific codes, a term which encompasses all the codes found in other art forms, such as dialogue (from the theater), underlit or overlit shots (from photography), printed narration (from literature), perspective (from painting), and so on. As a result, the specific codes (which relate exclusively to film) are relatively few in number. Among them are such techniques as rapid cutting, undercranked and overcranked shots, traveling shots, dissolves, rack-focus shots, and zoom shots.

Distinctions are made between syntactical codes, such as codes of punctuation (the straight cut, the dissolve, the fade-out) and semantic codes (conveying content), but many codes are versatile enough to perform both functions. The shot/reverse shot, for instance, is a semantic code inasmuch as it shows the relationship between two individuals who exist in the diegesis. It is also a syntactical code because of the importance of editing to its very existence. While codes are sometimes classified as either denotative or connotative, it is generally recognized that the spectator automatically responds first to the connotations of filmic signifiers and must, in fact, make an effort to delve below the connotative finish to isolate the core of raw denotative representation.

Film semioticians engage primarily, then, in the study of codes, whether the various codes in one particular filmic text or one particular code over a large body of films. In the latter case, the corpus to be studied is most often limited according to some relationship among the filmic texts of a common filmmaker, a common genre, a common country of origin, or a common historical period. For instance, Metz chose to study the American classical cinema (from roughly 1932 to 1959) as completely as possible in an attempt to define and describe what he hoped was the most strategic narrative code of the period. The result was his influential identification of eight kinds of filmic segments that form the great syntagma system or *la grande syntagmatique*. A classic American film's syntagmatic axis is structured from the continuous and contiguous union of autonomous segments of film selected from the eight paradigmatic structural options identified in *la grande syntagmatique*. Metz believed that by identifying the code of film montage as more important than others, he would demonstrate the value of semiotics to film analysis.

The second phase of film semiotics was introduced to English-language readers in 1975. The key text is Metz's *Le Signifiant imaginaire* (The Imaginary Signifier, 1981). Metz's emphasis on the parallels between the spectator's dreamlike state while motionless watching a film in a darkened room and the content and perceived "projection" of actual dreams and daydreams in the brain evokes questions of spectatorial identification. Jean-Louis Baudry's contemporaneous articles complement Metz's ideas and, in fact, insist even more strongly than Metz does on the association between Lacan's mirror phase in an infant's development and the *dispositif* or screening position of a filmgoer. This phase of film semiotics carries its psychoanalytical implications to the conclusion that filmmakers and psychoanalysts alike are capable of hypnotizing their subjects and consciously do so.

Other psychoanalytical approaches to cinema study examine the film as a symptom of some psychoanalytical phenomenon in the director. One "psychoanalyzers" Federico Fellini through his work, or, like Dominique Fernandez, one reconstructs Sergei Eisenstein's psychobiography through his films. Textual studies like Raymond Bellour's analysis of Alfred Hitchcock's *North by Northwest* emphasize the manner in which the signifiers arouse or release in the spectator hidden, archetypal, psychoanalytical patterns or resources.

The semiotic approach to film study has had considerable impact on the whole discipline. Prior to Metz, film theory was not only less rigorous but even frequently impressionistic and subjective. Semiotic discussion is designed to eschew any consideration of personal preferences such as those applied by practitioners of what is now called the auteur theory. Film discussions with a mimetic or esthetic thrust are rejected in favor of strong clinical-analytical discourse. For a semiotician, all films are equally worthy of discussion, provided the discussion focuses on the functions of the film's signifiers.

In general, in spite of their original aspirations toward absolute scientific precision, the French film semioticians and their followers have had to settle for a not-unenviable rigor, which is best exemplified in their various film analyses. The most important body of analysis is doubtless that of Bellour, collected in his *L'Analyse du film*. Other seminal analyses are those of *Muriel* by Michel Marie, Marie-Claire Ropars, and Claude Baiblé; of *October* by Ropars, Michèle Lagny, and Pierre Sorlin; of *M* and *The Most Dangerous Game* by Thierry Kuntzel; of *Touch of Evil* by Stephen Heath; of *The General Line* by Jacques Aumont; of *Stagecoach* by Nick Browne; and, of course, Metz's own analysis of *Adieu Philippine*—a film not from the American classical period that he nevertheless used to illustrate *la grande syntagmatique*.

While the majority of these film analyses are from France, film semioticians of major importance have been operating in Great Britain, Italy, the former Soviet Union, the United States, and elsewhere. These theorists, however, have not necessarily been working in the field of film analysis, nor have they always been homogeneous in their interests. For instance, Noel Burch is a film theorist who is sometimes linked with the semioticians even though his important work is more appropriately classified as formalist. Similarly, working as earnestly as, if with less impact than, the Saussurean and Lacanian-influenced Metz have been the Bahktin-inspired Jurij Lotman and the Peirce-oriented Gilles Deleuze. Michel Colin, who discussed film primarily from the standpoint of models borrowed from transformational grammar, is grouped loosely with the practitioners of semiotics. Even Jacques Derrida has been formally adopted as a film semiotician by Peter Brunette and David Wills.

From the preceding list, it is clear that, especially since 1980, the semiotics of cinema has in some theorists' minds and hands escaped its formerly

Metz-prescribed parameters. But while each of these individual theorists can find at least a few adherents to vouch for their authenticity as film semioticians, there is little argument about the global indebtedness to semiotics of two tangential schools of film scholars: the narratologists and the feminists. But even in these groups, few of their practitioners can be classified unequivocally as semioticians.

Some of the most influential studies to result even indirectly from the film-semiotics movement have been in the realm of film narratology. Particularly noteworthy scholarship has been produced by David Bordwell, Edward Branigan, Nick Browne, André Gaudreault, François Jost, and Sarah Kozloff, to name only a few. The sources of their theories have been as varied as Aristotle, Emile Benveniste, Wayne Booth, Seymour Chatman, Gérard Genette, Roman Jakobson, Plato, Gerald Prince, Victor Šklovsky, and Jurij Tynianov. Their studies have introduced or renewed in critical discourse the use of such words as *mimesis* and *diegesis*, *fabula* and *syuzhet*, *shifters*, *monstration*, and *narratee*. Their theories are constantly profiting from debate and fine-tuning.

A rich vein of semiotic film analysis has been tapped by the vigorous group of feminist theorists of whom Laura Mulvey became the acknowledged seminal force with her 1975 article, "Visual Pleasure and Narrative Cinema." The article is indebted to work done by some French semioticians (Jean-Pierre Oudart and Daniel Dayan, for instance) on the montage phenomenon known as the suture. It deals primarily with notions of the female spectator confronted with signifiers created by male filmmakers for male audiences. Mulvey evokes questions of voyeurism, eroticism, fetishism, and patriarchy in what soon became an effective call to arms for female (and a few male) theorists. Some of Mulvey's numerous followers studied during the 1970s in the famous Paris Film Programme under Metz, Bellour, Aumont, Marie, and Burch. As a collective, these women later disseminated the writings of their French instructors through the pages of the pacesetting journal *Camera Obscura*, which they founded in California.

The semiotic study of sound in cinema was largely ignored until the late 1970s. Since then, the subject has received close attention, most notably from Michel Chion, Daniel Percheron, Elizabeth Weis, John Belton, and Rick Altman. Ben Andrews reanalyzed *Adieu Philippine*, taking into account the film's soundtrack. Marxist inroads into film semiotics for a time seemed to be guiding the future of the discipline, but the years have proved that theorists such as Julia Kristeva and Louis Althusser have had relatively little lasting impact on film analysis. Nevertheless, the relation of filmic signifiers to the expression of any number of ideologies remains a permanent focus of semiotic discussion. Naturally, cinema semiotics has not escaped discussions of the self-reflexive text, intertextuality, and transtextuality.

Throughout the 1980s and early 1990s, rumors of the death of film semiotics abounded. This might well have resulted from the inactivity of Christian Metz in film studies during most of the period, along with looser interpretations of what constituted legitimate semiotic methodologies. In fact, this period witnessed a renewed interest in film history as a backlash against what many saw as the hyperevolution of film theory. The new concern for painstaking methodology in film history might, however, be at least partially attributable to the lessons film scholars learned from the practice of semiotics. As for studies in the pure theory of film semiotics, published works have indeed become rarer. But film analyses from a semiotic perspective continue to be written, and the work done by feminists and narratologists has never been livelier.

[*See also* Barthes; Code; Elements of Semiology; Film Semiotics; Grande Syntagmatique, La; Lacan; Metz; Narratology; *and* Photography.]

BIBLIOGRAPHY

Altman, R., ed. *Yale French Studies* 60 (1980). Special issue on "Cinema/Sound."

Andrew, D. *The Major Film Theories: An Introduction.* New York and Oxford: Oxford University Press, 1976. The continuation of this book is his *Concepts in Film Theory* (New York and Oxford: Oxford University Press, 1984).

Brunette, P., and D. Wills. *Screen/Play: Derrida and Film Theory.* Princeton: Princeton University Press, 1989.

Genette, G. *Figures of Literary Discourse* (1965). Translated by A. Sheridan. New York: Columbia University Press, 1981.

Genette, G. *Narrative Discourse* (1969). Translated by J. E. Lewin. Oxford: Basil Blackwell, 1980.

Heath, S. *Questions of Cinema.* Bloomington: Indiana University Press, 1981.

Lotman, J. *Semiotics of Cinema.* Translated and with a foreword by M. E. Suino. Ann Arbor: University of Michigan Press, 1976.

Metz, C. *Film Language: A Semiotics of the Cinema.* Translated by M. Taylor. New York and Oxford: Oxford University Press, 1974.

Metz, C. *The Imaginary Signifier.* Translated by A. Guzzetti et al. Bloomington: Indiana University Press, 1981.

Mitry, J. *The Aesthetics and Psychology of the Cinema* (1965). Translated by C. King. Bloomington: Indiana University Press, 1997.

Mulvey, L. *Visual and Other Pleasures.* Bloomington: Indiana University Press, 1990.

Souriau, E. *Les Deux cent mille situations dramatiques.* Paris: Flammarion, 1950.

Stam, R., R. Burgoyne, and S. Flitterman-Lewis. *New Vocabularies in Film Semiotics: Structuralism, Poststructuralism, and Beyond.* New York: Routledge, 1992.

Wollen, P. *Signs and Meaning in the Cinema.* Bloomington: Indiana University Press, 1972.

Wollen, P. *Readings and Writings: Semiotic Counter Strategies.* London: Verso, 1982.

—C. D. E. TOLTON

CLYNES, MANFRED (b. 1925), Austrian-born American neurophysiologist and engineer who was also trained as a musician and became for a while a noted concert pianist. Clynes's experimental studies in neurobiology were inspired by his own observations of musical expression and depended on the ingenious exploitation of computer recording and averaging of waveforms. He developed a desktop instrument for this purpose more than a decade before desktop computers were available. Clynes's work since the mid-1970s has developed applications of the same instrumentation to analyze aspects of musical performance rhythm bearing on musicality and style.

In biocybernetic articles that appeared in the 1960s and in succeeding publications (e.g., Clynes, 1977), Clynes provided a complex set of hypotheses and experimental measurements regarding expressions of emotion, as well as extensive suggestions relating these to musical expression. Despite their novelty, Clynes's experiments have so far failed to attract a wide professional response.

There is no consensual theory of emotions. Among important differences in competing theories are whether the theories conceive emotions as comprising a finite "lexicon" of distinct elements or as a continuous spectrum and the extent to which the range of emotions is viewed as genetically set or culturally determined. Clynes's theory portrays emotion as determined genetically and as referencing a neurologically defined finite lexicon. On the basis of his specific experimental methodology, Clynes isolates and describes a group of fixed time patterns for neu-

romuscular activation associated with different emotions. His cross-cultural studies indicate that the patterns are biologically rather than culturally determined.

The experimental studies employ a pressure transducer ("sentograph") that allows the subjects' touch on a relatively rigid button to be transcribed by a computer as a waveform. A typical experimental procedure, which lasts about twenty-five minutes, requires the subject to sit in a restful position with her or his finger on the sentograph button. The session is divided into eight parts. At the beginning of each part, a recorded voice names a particular emotion ("no emotion," "anger," "hate," "grief," "love," "sex," "joy," "reverence"), and during the following three minutes or so the subject hears a series of between twenty and forty soft taps at irregular intervals. At each tap, the subject voluntarily presses the button according to the general instruction that the motion should be executed with the precise expressive intent to convey the designated emotion. In other words, a gestural articulation is prescribed, but its particular inflection must be determined by the subject. The subject is encouraged to believe that an expressive inflection can be discovered by trial, but no indication of what the inflection might be is provided. Responses are recorded and averaged by computer.

It is characteristic of this methodology that in the course of the experimental session the subject induces fantasy-emotion states and that the clarity of these contemplative states increases with practice. As in art, the emotion is not necessarily situational although the subject might imagine situations. Clynes's chief finding through experiments such as these is that with unguided practice the expressive patterns selected by most subjects tend to converge on a shape that is distinct for each of several different emotions but the same for most subjects.

Clynes calls these shapes "sentic forms" (same root as *sentiment*). Sentic shapes are temporal patterns of fixed duration that describe the growth and decay of muscular effort. The quickest is anger, which reaches a peak in a fifth of a second. Those of grief and reverence need a full second to reach their peak and recover still more slowly. The shapes traced as computed averages are easily accommodated by intuitive descriptions: anger flashes; hate jabs; grief droops; love (parental) caresses; sex thrusts; joy skips. The graphs are reproduced in figure 1. Clynes does not claim to have found all the sentic forms.

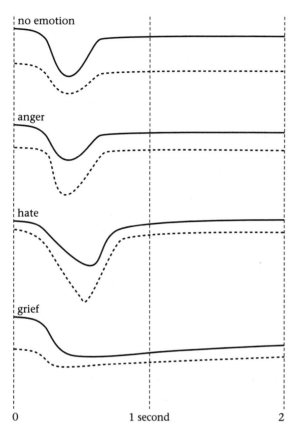
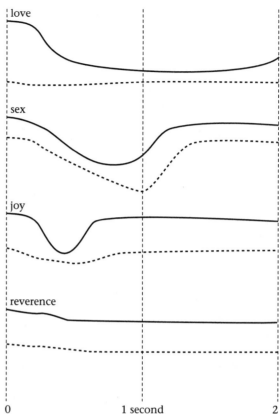

Figure 1. *Clynes's Sentic Forms.* (After Clynes, 1969.)

The work and the results entail a number of mutually interdependent hypotheses, including, inter alia:

1. The sentic form is a unit of neuromuscular behavior that is correlated biologically with a state of mind and body. The behavior has a set duration and time pattern for the growth and decay of its effort and might occur several times while the state continues. The state has no set duration. "Feeling" is the appearance of this state in consciousness.

2. The correlation of feeling state with gestural behavior is fixed and involuntary. The correlation can be suppressed to some extent but not fundamentally rearranged. You cannot accurately fake the behavior without feeling the state.

3. The patterns are transforms of independently triggered molar actions (single voluntary impulses); the patterns can in principle be expressed by any voluntary motor muscles as a transformation of an underlying intentional action.

4. When one person performs a gesture expressive of a sentic form it reinforces the feeling of the person who performs it; tends to induce imitation in the person who perceives it; and tends to arouse the same feeling in the perceiver. So long as mimicry is aroused, it may be repressed externally without loss of the attendant feeling.

5. Intensity of feeling is correlative with the precision with which innate gestural forms are executed rather than with other quantities such as amplitude, frequency, and speed.

6. Up to a point, repetition intensifies the feeling if the timing is appropriate. Rhythmically regular repetition discharges the feeling.

7. Emotion expression, though anchored in an innate lexicon of forms, is a developing skill that will be self-taught in appropriate situations.

8. Combinations of some of these sentic forms are possible.

9. Any art medium can convey the trace of some

sentic forms, and the sentic form, so conveyed, retains its capacity to trigger the attendant feeling.

In *Sentics* (1977), Clynes provides several examples of musical figures that he identifies as representing sentic shapes. The identifications are supported by a variation of the experimental technique described above in which musicians express inflections on the sentograph while fantasizing performances. It is not possible to prove that a particular sentic shape is called for by a particular musical figure, but the experimental apparatus allows musicians to display their intuitions within the vocabulary of the theory.

The gesture hypothesis offers to bring several heterogeneous and puzzling phenomena within the comprehension of explanatory biological paradigms. These include aspects of creative intuition, aspects of cross-cultural communication in the fine arts, the proven effectiveness of some nonverbal pedagogies, and the capacity of art to introduce us to realms of feeling that we have not previously experienced in so-called real life. If we understand artistic talent as involving, among other things, the ability to tap certain innate biological patterns, we can deal with these phenomena wih more sobriety.

[*See also* Artificial Language; Music; *and* Nattiez.]

BIBLIOGRAPHY

Clynes, M. "Toward a Theory of Man: Precision of Essentic Form in Living Communication." In *Information Processing in the Nervous System*, edited by K. N. Leibovic and J. C. Eccles, pp. 177–206. New York: Springer Verlag, 1969.
Clynes, M. "Biocybernetics of the Dynamic Communication of Emotions and Qualities." *Science* 170 (1970): 764–765.
Clynes, M. *Sentics: The Touch of Emotions.* New York: Doubleday, 1977.
Clynes, M. *Music, Mind, and Brain: The Neuropsychology of Music.* New York: Plenum Press, 1982.

—DAVID LIDOV

CODE. The notion of code in semiotics refers to (1) a set of shared rules of interpretation, and (2) a meaning-making potential.

The first view models communication as follows: The Sender (S) of a message has an idea, thought, or piece of information in mind. S wishes to transmit this to someone. S encodes this as a message in a suitable medium of expression. S transmits the message to the Receiver (R). R perceives the message and seeks to extract (decode) S's thought from the message. R does this by applying rules of interpretation in order to infer S's thoughts or intentions. Insofar as R guesses correctly, R has decoded the message that S transmitted. S and R have communicated successfully.

The salient features of this model are that there are two minds, respectively housed in S and R, separate from each other. The two minds think thoughts. The material means of expression is the medium in which S's thoughts are encoded for transmission to R. The medium, then, exercises no shaping influence on the thoughts so transmitted. The medium of expression is a neutral vehicle for packaging and conveying thoughts. For the communication to come off successfully, S and R must share a common code. R applies the rules of the code to the message so as to make correct interpretations concerning the thoughts that S wished to communicate.

This model was influential in the development of semiotics in the 1960s and 1970s; it derives from the first generation of research in information theory (Shannon and Weaver, 1949) and cybernetics (Ashby, 1956). The code is a context-free set of rules for the encoding, transmission, and decoding of information. The theory sought to define information transmission in quantitative and statistical terms, using the closed system and mechanistic-cybernetic models of the time.

Early developments in semiotics incorporated these insights with varying degrees of literality or with attempts to modify them. One problem was the theoretical status of the semiotic means of expression, that is, language. Is language in the mind or in the material world? Do we think in language, or is language a neutral medium for transmitting essentially nonlinguistic concepts, ideas, and thoughts, and so on which language "processes" as information? How can R get at S's thoughts if these are separate from R's—namely, in S's mind—and not the same as the language used to transmit them? How do S and R know when they share the "same" thoughts and thus when they have communicated successfully?

At its crudest and most reductionist, this model refers to the communication of messages in a purely mechanistic (nonhuman) system: A signal is the stimulus emitted from a source; it is conveyed by a channel to a destination, where it produces a response. Umberto Eco (1976) distinguished such communication systems from the systems of signification that semiotics studies. The latter require rules of interpretation (a code), which R uses to interpret what S's thoughts are. Eco argues that semiotics is concerned with the latter. Nevertheless, the mechanistic model retains a powerful hold on theories of human communication. One reason for this might be the privileged focus on the mind of the individual. For Noam Chomsky (1965), a generative grammar is a system of rules for relating signals to their semantic representations. Chomsky claimed that this pairing of signal and semantic representation corresponds to the idealized competence of the speaker-hearer. This competence specifies the underlying mental mechanisms that make this pairing process possible. This model continues to exert influence.

A code may pair phonetic and semantic representations of sentences (Chomsky), or it may couple "present entities with abstract units" (Eco). It is essentially a set of rules or conventions of interpretation, whether these are mental (competence) or social (convention). Expression is that which conveys the extrasemiotic information or which provides a means of storing this information in a visible and durable form. Written language is an example of the latter. But the transcoding of speech into writing significantly transforms the structures of the former. This poses a problem for the view that claims that code is a mechanism for pairing expressions and contents. In focusing on the encoding-decoding and transmission processes, it has less to say about the ways in which semiotic codes make and enable meanings. It says little about how meanings come about as effects of the specific medium and its code.

The second view of code in semiotics maintains that code and medium have a significant meaning-making potential in their own rights. Readers of this article have learned how to construe shared ways of making sense of the black marks printed on the page or the sound waves that vibrate in the air when we speak to each other. The black marks on the page or the sound waves in the air are used in regular, patterned ways. They signal patterns of difference to which we have learned to attach significance through our community's shared ways of making meaning. Not all possible patterns of difference are recognized as important for a community's shared ways of acting and meaning. In a given community, only some patterns of differences, out of all the possible patterns that might have occurred, have significance. This is because every community has its shared ways of making meanings with the patterns to which it attaches significance—language, visual codes, kinesic codes, gestural codes, music, and so on. To make meanings with a given semiotic code is to use a system of socially shared meanings.

Code, in this view, is a semiotic resource—a meaning potential—that enables certain kinds of meanings to be made (in language, in the ways we dress, in our eating rituals, in the visual media, and so on) while others are not, or at least in that code. This view differs from the previous one in two important ways: First the internal-design features of the code—its grammar—have a significant potential for constructing meanings. Code is not, then, a simple pairing mechanism. Instead, the formal differences intrinsic to the code's internal design are already potentially meaning making. Second, there is no dichotomy between code and behavior or use. This view goes back to Ferdinand de Saussure's (1916) *langue*-based view of grammar as a system of value-producing differences that are intrinsic to its internal design. Gregory Bateson's view (1951) of codification as a multilevel and hierarchical system of contextualizing relations is also important. Saussure made a methodological decision to separate code (*langue*) from individual use (*parole*). His privileging of the former as the object of linguistic science did not allow him to see the systematic relationship between code as a meaning-making resource and the socially shared ways of making meaning in a community. Louis Hjelmslev's reworking of this distinction (1943; rev. ed., 1961) in terms of system (code) and process (text) and further developments of this (e.g., Halliday, 1984) go in this direction.

As a sign system, a code does not operate on single items but on the systems of paradigmatic oppositions that are intrinsic to its internal design. A code is a system of signs with content and expression. A simple example is the traffic-light code, as in figure 1.

The relation between content and expression is one of realization, which is an interstratal relationship: Contents both realize and are realized by expressions. Thus, content and expression are strata in a stratified coding system. Typically, the level of content is more abstract than the level of expression. Content and expression do not designate an a priori disinction between two distinct domains. Instead, content is interpreted in and through the expression, depending on the way in which the code constrains both the exchange of information and the behavior of the participants. In the traffic-light code, this information is constrained in the act of construing a given content, say, "stop" in a given unit of expression, [red]. In so doing, the code constrains or mediates the kind of information that may be exchanged between the two strata. At the same time, it also constrains the possible behaviors of the participants in the system.

Content is more abstract than expression because the code imposes a boundary distinction on the phenomenal continuum of differences in the expression. At this more concrete level, the continuum of differences—light waves—is construed, abstracting away from the physical medium of transmission, as the meaningful differences [red], [amber], and [green]. Participants can then reconstrue these differences as meaningful distinctions according to the code in operation. Codes provide a semiotic space in which meaningful differences in phenomenal reality are reconstrued as conscious acts of meaning or signs. The traffic-light code enables its users to construe a phenomenal, perceptual event—a red light, for example—as an act of meaning, which impacts upon the consciousness of the user. The code enables its users to attend selectively to phenomenal/material reality as defined by meaningful differences. In so doing, the code transforms such events into acts of meaning (signs). A sign is not something already given; it is made and construed in and through the material and semiotic potentialities of the code.

Generally speaking, Hjelmslev's "plane of content" (or Saussure's "concept") has been thought of in purely ideational terms, as if the sign were the realization of this one kind of meaning. But Gregory Bateson, Bronislaw Malinowski, and Michael Halliday have shown that signs always minimally comprise two kinds of meaning simultaneously. Bateson (1951) refers to these as the "report" and "command" dimensions of every communicative act; Malinowski (1923) calls them the "reflection" and "action" dimensions; while Halliday (1984) terms them the "ideational" and "interpersonal" dimensions. These refer to two fundamental modes of meaning present in any act of semiosis. In a minimal semiotic code, such as the traffic-light system, the paradigmatic opposition between the two basic modes of meaning combines with a further opposition between two basic domains of experience, intersubjective (you and me) and objective (others). The code does not simply construe single phenomenal/material events as signs; it is, minimally, a two-dimensional semiotic space, constituting a system of signs.

FIGURE 1. *Traffic-Light Code.* Note: ↘ means *realizes* and *is realized by.*

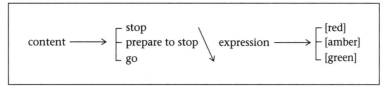

FIGURE 2. *Paradigmatic (Systemic) Oppositions in Traffic-Light Code Seen as Semiotic Space for Making Meanings.*

mode of interaction / domain of mutual understanding	action/command	reflection/report
you and me	you must stop; I must stop, etc.	you and I know that [red] means *stop*, etc.
others	he/she/they must stop, etc.	he/she/they know that [red] means *stop*, etc.

The traffic-light code has just one realization cycle. A given expression, say, [red], means that this phenomenal level projects both modes of meaning—the active and the reflective, in Malinowski's terms—in a single, two-dimensional construct. For example, a red traffic light impacts upon the consciousness of a motorist. He or she construes it as a sign that simultaneously reports or reflects upon a state of affairs at the same time that the motorist construes it as an appropriate mode of action and interaction in relation to some addresser. The two modes of meaning are realized simultaneously in the same expression. The conceptual and psychic bias in the Western conception of the sign has tended to look on semiosis as an individual mode of consciousness rather than a form of social interaction. The code both enables and constrains the potential for such forms of consciousness and their related forms of social interaction. The code is a systemic potential that makes socially meaningful acts possible. Such acts (signs) are simultaneously a social mode of consciousness (knowledge) and a social mode of interaction with some culturally specific other (action). The sign is not the property of an individual consciousness. Instead, the code makes possible intersubjective structures of recognition in and through which signs emerge.

In the traffic-light code, the content plane is tied directly to the phenomenal plane of experience. In such a code, expressions are the discrete phenomenal units [red], [amber], and [green]; they do not combine to form larger units. Language and many other complex semiotic codes bring the two planes, as shown in the traffic-light code, into relations with a more abstract level of grammatical organization. The organizational principles and functions of this stratum have been worked out most extensively in the case of language. Recent research shows that analogous principles are at work in semiotic codes as diverse as music and the visual.

Interstratal relationships are a key design feature of all semiotic codes. They are based upon the principle of redundancy (Bateson). The meanings of "stop," "prepare to stop," and "go" are both realized by and realize the expressions [red], [amber], and [green]. This means that these contents "redound with" their respective expressions. If the meaning "stop" is realized, then we can predict the expression [red], and so on. Redundancy relations are symmetrical at all levels of organization in the code. This means that [red] realizes "stop," and "stop" is real-

ized by [red]. Both semiotic points of view are simultaneously true.

The paradigmatic nature of the code shows that there is no simple or direct pairing of expressions and contents. Instead, there is a second-order, or metaredundancy, relation which says that [red], [amber], and [green] redound not with "stop," "prepare to stop," and "go" but with the redundancy of these expressions with the two sets of paradigmatic oppositions in the code. Thus, [red], [amber], and [green] are redundant with the redundancy of action/reflection and you and me/others with "stop," "prepare to stop," and "go."

The traffic-light code is a relatively closed system. In more complex semiotic codes, the grammar permits a purely abstract level of organization between the two levels we have seen here. This means that the content is no longer directly dependent on the phenomenal, which greatly increases the relative semiotic freedom of a code to evolve historically, as well as to interact with constantly changing "external" states and processes. A code is a dynamic, open system; there is a constant exchange of matter, energy, and information between a code and its environment(s). The code is a generative process. It is not, in the second view, an abstract, underlying competence that explains the user's "performance." Code is a meaning-making potential that expands and renews itself through the ongoing exchange with its environment, which is its use.

The cognitive bias in the Western tradition's ways of talking about codes and the signs they make possible tends to privilege the more explicit, obvious, and segmentable regularities of meaningful social actions. Signs are said to have this or that conceptual content on the basis of the regularities so segmented. Analysts tend to resort to a priori classification of types of coded cultural content. At the same time, they overlook the ways in which signs are also and simultaneously deployed in the structuring of situationally specific social actions. Such functions elude an analysis based on the assignment of a priori conceptual categories derived from an abstract system of types. These are seen as belonging to the code; situationally specific ways of constructing socially meaningful interactions are not. This dichotomy persists in much semiotic theory; a "pragmatic" level of action, seen as constitutively separate from conceptual meaning, is exported out of the systemic potential of the code. Alternative lines of research indicate that this most recent manifestation of the code/behavior dichotomy can be resolved.

[*See also* Bateson; Communication; Eco; Hjelmslev; *and* Saussure.]

BIBLIOGRAPHY

Ashby, W. R. *An Introduction to Cybernetics*. London: Chapman and Hall, 1956.

Bateson, G. "Information and Codification: A Philosophical Approach." In *Communication: The Social Matrix of Psychiatry*, edited by J. Ruesch and G. Bateson, pp. 168–211. New York and London: Norton and Company, 1951.

Chomsky, N. *Aspects of the Theory of Syntax*. Cambridge, Mass.: MIT Press, 1965.

Eco, U. *A Theory of Semiotics*. Bloomington and London: Indiana University Press, 1976.

Halliday, M. A. K. "Language as Code and Language as Behaviour: A Systemic-Functional Interpretation of the Nature and Ontogenesis of Dialogue." In *The Semiotics of Culture and Language*. Vol. 1, *Language as Social Semiotic*, edited by R. P. Fawcett et al., p. 3–35. London and Dover, N.H.: Frances Pinter, 1984.

Hjelmslev, L. *Prolegomena to a Theory of Language* (1943). Rev. English ed. Translated by F. J. Whitfield. Madison and London: University of Wisconsin Press, 1961.

Malinowski, B. "The Problem of Meaning in Primitive Languages" (1923). Supplement 1 to C. K. Ogden and I. A. Richards, *The Meaning of Meaning*. New York: Harcourt Brace and World, 1959.

Saussure, F. de. *Course in General Linguistics* (1916). Translated by R. Harris. London: Duckworth, 1983.

Shannon, C. E., and W. Weaver. *The Mathematical Theory of Communication*. Urbana: University of Illinois Press, 1949.

—PAUL J. THIBAULT

COEVOLUTION occurs when two sets of organisms evolve together in such a way that the evolution of the one set affects the evolution of the other and conversely; moreover, there is a feedback relationship between the two groups (that is, the effects that they have on each other are not independent). Hence, two predators living side by side but evolving in response to different prey would not count as coevolution. Nor would a predator living on and evolving in response to some prey count as coevolution, unless the prey evolved in response to that predator's predation. Coevolution can occur within a species or across species, with organisms of radically different kinds evolving together.

Assuming with today's evolutionists that natural selection is the main force for evolutionary change and that its result is organisms that are adapted toward survival and reproduction, it is convenient to distinguish two kinds of coevolution: "arms races" and "mutual cooperation." In arms races, two lines of organisms compete against each other, with at least one side trying to exploit the other for its own ends but with both sides having equally to protect themselves against the other's counterattacks. A classic case (and the first example of the working of natural selection given by Charles Darwin in the *Origin of Species* [1859]) is that of the wolf that chases the deer. The deer has to evolve into a faster runner, and so the wolf likewise must evolve in a speedier animal. (It is perhaps odd to think of the deer's speed as a counterattack, but this is what it is to a starving wolf.) In mutual cooperation, we have members of two groups working for their mutual benefit. An equally classic case (also discussed by Darwin) is that of the plant that evolves so as to attract insects (to the end of its own fertilization) and the insect that evolves so as to fertilize plants (to the end of its own food gathering).

Although communication is not an absolutely essential part of coevolution—an invertebrate developing a thicker shell is not communicating with the fish that attempts to eat it with its ever sharper teeth nor conversely—as a matter of empirical fact, communication is crucial to both kinds of coevolution. An angler fish trying to tempt its prey into its mouth is sending a message to that prey, even as the prey is evolving in such a direction that it can better distinguish real food from the apparent. A normally ferocious predator signals to its cleaner fish that all is safe as the cleaner fish evolve better ways of telling the predator that for once it is in its interests to shut off its attack mechanisms.

There is, however, a crucial difference in the nature of communication in the two forms of coevolution. In the arms race instance, there is little or no reason to think that the interactions themselves will regulate the strengths of the signals being used. Obviously, there are exceptions, as when subtlety is needed for deceit, and there will be overall limits based on physiology as well as costs, but generally the stronger the better. In the case of mutual cooperation, since both sides benefit, subject to efficiency, one can reduce signals to a minimum.

Making the point, John Krebs and Richard Dawkins write: "The distinction . . . can be illustrated by an analogy with human communication: contrast the Bible-thumping oratory of a revivalist preacher with the subtle signals, undetected by the rest of the company, between a couple at dinner party indicating to one another that it is time to go home. The former bears the hallmark of signalling designed for persuasion, the latter of a conspiratorial, cooperative whisper" (1984, p. 391).

As always in nature, there will be variations on the divisions and methods, including cases that are on the borderline (certain kinds of parasite/host interaction, for instance). The crucial point is that coevolution is widespread, it shows the workings and results of selection pushing toward adaptive optima, and communication is a crucial factor both as cause and as effect.

BIBLIOGRAPHY

Darwin, C. R. *The Origin of Species* (1859). Harmondsworth, England: Penguin, 1968.

Feldman, M. W., and L. L. Cavelli-Sforza. "Cultural and Biological Evolutionary Processes, Selection for a Trait under Complex Transmission." *Theoretical Population Biology* 9.2 (1976): 238–259.

Krebs, J. R., and R. Dawkins. "Animal Signals: Mind-Reading and Manipulation." In *Behavioural Ecology: An Evolutionary Approach*, edited by J. R. Krebs and N. B. Davies, pp. 380–402. 2d ed. Oxford: Blackwell Scientific Publications, 1984.

Lumsden, C. J., and E. O. Wilson. *Genes, Minds, and Culture: The Coevolutionary Process.* Cambridge, Mass.: Harvard University Press, 1981.

—MICHAEL RUSE

COMICS. Spatial sequences formed by graphically separated but structurally related static images, comics may integrate written messages in order to specify descriptive or narrative information and dialogues. Because comics display images and narrate stories at the same time, the conventions of this medium belong to iconographic and narrative codes, and its study is relevant to visual semiotics and to narratology. On the other hand, since they usually include written messages, comics typically combine iconic and linguistic codes. The comics appear as a new form of representation of the graphic narrative space in modern Western culture that implements the iconization of diegetic temporality.

The reading order of comics corresponds to chronological progression and is ruled by the linearity of the Western writing. This compulsory directionality has been called the line of indicativity. Each pictorial unit in the sequence is called a frame and represents a delimited diegetic space (e.g., a landscape) and a variable duration, which is the time required to perform the action depicted in it. Each static pictogram represents in fact a durative instant. Each consecutive frame represents a different and ulterior phase of the descriptive/narrative structure. The frame within which a written text is inscribed is called a lexipictogram—that is, a reading unit comprising image and words.

The frames can adopt very different configurations and sizes and offer diverse optical scales of the items represented in them. The pictorial elements integrated in a frame may be ruled by different iconographic codes and subcodes. The scenographic code, for instance, is relevant to the representation and denotation of a diegetic scenic space (e.g., a meadow, a street, a planet). The identity of the characters acting in this scenic space is usually denoted by strongly cultural stereotypes, such as the hero, the villain, the rich man, the housewife, the drunkard, and the vagabond. The codification of these stereotypes is often based on a metonymic representation of their moral attributes and social position through physical and visible features—such as body shape and posture, clothing, and accessories—many of which have connotative functions. These stereotyped characters express themselves and behave using simultaneously linguistic and nonverbal codes. The facial and mimic codes are very important. The facial language through which emotions are expressed is based on the interaction of graphic signs representing the eyebrows, the eyelids, the eyes, the lips, and other facial elements. Not all these graphic elements are equally relevant. It is generally agreed that the eyebrows are the dominant feature in organizing the emotional expression of a face, but some hyperbolic conventions can be used—such as the teeth drawn in a canine way—to express anger. The mimetic codes can refer to social codes of urbanity, psychological codes of emotional expression, or to individualized codes of idiosyncratic validity. An important part of the gesture symbolism of the comics' characters comes from the codes of representations of body language in ancient academic painting and in the theater. However, some symbols are specific to the modern art of the cartoonist, such as horizontal circles drawn above a head to indicate dizziness or vertigo.

A semiotic peculiarity of the comics is the presence and interaction of iconic and written elements in the same frame. A special terminology has been developed for descriptive purposes: characters' spoken words are inscribed in a delineated blank surface called a locugram (*balloon* in the terminology of the cartoonist), with a connecting line to the face of the speaker, a derivation from the phylacteries used in some medieval paintings. The delimiting line of the locugram is called the perigram, and the line of its configuration can vary to express metaphorically or metonymically the coolness, anger, or other qualities and emotions of the character, in the same way as the lettering of the inscribed text can be connotated by a variety of graphic stylizations. The thoughts or dreams of characters are usually expressed with iconic representations in psychopictograms (or dream balloons), with perigrams similar to clouds located over their heads. A vast repertory of ideograms have been invented to represent the sensations and feelings of characters. Many of these ideograms, called sensograms, are iconic transcriptions of culture-dependent verbal expressions (e.g., a "bright idea" might be expressed by an electric bulb; a log might mean "to sleep like a log"; a broken heart might refer to "a love that breaks one's heart"). Idiomatic phrases such as the French "voir trente-six chandelles" (see stars; literally, to see thirty-six candles) can be shown pictographically by several burning candles. Other iconic symbols include kinesic signs or mobilgrams located behind or in front of moving elements to indicate directionality, speed, or impact. Among the written messages also appear inarticulated sounds from persons or animals. Comics have produced a vast repertory of onomatopoeiae, often coming from phonosymbolic English words (e.g., *smack, bang*), rendered graphically with redundant plastic values, a device that inspired many pop artists.

The lexipictographic nature of the comics explains the complexity of the semiotic conventions of this medium. These conventions have been formalized mainly since 1896, when the journalistic series "The Yellow Kid," created by the American cartoonist Richard F. Outcault, established the principles of the modern comics, based on three elements: (1) the sequence of frames; (2) a permanent character along the series; (3) the use of locugrams. But not all the conventions that are pertinent to the humorous genre, drawn with a caricaturesque style, are equally pertinent to the epic or sentimental genres, drawn with a more naturalistic style.

The sequence of lexipictograms of a comic strip can be displayed in many different modes. It can be printed in a full page, in a half page, in one single strip, and in color or black and white. It can appear daily or weekly, completing an autonomous episode every time or in a serialized structure to be continued in the next issue. All these options are relevant to the strategies of the montage (or editing) of the frames that builds the narrative continuity by means of the formal discontinuity of the lexipictograms. This discontinuity digitalizes the analogic flow of iconized temporality with a serialization of the present tense crystallized in each frame for the reader. In 1906, the American cartoonist Winsor McCay experimented with the formal discontinuity of the pictograms by making the scenic space shown at the right border of a frame continue graphically at the left border of the next frame. The architectures of montage became more elaborated when, by the end of the 1920s, the serialized structure derived from the complexity of the intrigues of novels and feature films was adopted by this medium.

Much has been written about the analogy between comics and cinema, supported in part because of their practical interactions in the cultural industries but also because they share common elements of expression, ranking from the optical viewpoint of the visual field selected with a frame to the narrative structures (parallel actions, flashbacks, subjective viewpoints, etc.) and some laws of the art of editing the images, motionless pictograms in a frame in one case and dynamic shots in the other, and therefore imposing on comics a much more elliptic narrative structure. But the evident analogies tend to overlook the many semiotic differences between them. Not only are the differences between static and mobile image very important, but in the cinema the perception of the images and dialogues is simultaneous, while in the comics it is consecutive since the acoustic medium is entirely coded graphically.

Interest in the semiotic analysis of the comics started in the mid-1960s in Europe. In France, a special issue of *Communications* (1976) was devoted to the topic. In other contributions, Umberto Eco (1994) focused on visual metaphors; Roman Gubern (1972) and Pierre Fresnault-Deruelle (1972) proposed a comprehensive semiotic framework for analyzing this medium and its codes. Content analysis has also been applied to comics as a way to critically scrutinize the various ideologies conveyed through this popular medium (e.g., Barker, 1989).

[*See also* Cartoons; Cinema; Face; Pictorial Semiotics; *and* Stereotype.]

BIBLIOGRAPHY

Barbieri, D. *I linguaggi del fumetto*. Milan: Bompiani, 1990.

Barker, M. *Comics: Ideology, Power, and the Critics*. Manchester: Manchester University Press, 1989.

Berger, A. A. *The Comic-Stripped American: What Dick Tracy, Blondie, Daddy Warbucks, and Charlie Brown Tell Us about Ourselves*. New York: Walker, 1973.

Coma, J., and R. Gubern. *Los Comics: Una mitologia del siglo*. Barcelona: Plaza Janés, 1988.

Eco, U. *Apocalypse Postponed*. Edited by R. Lumley. Bloomington: Indiana University Press, 1994.

Fresnault-Deruelle, P. *La bande dessinée, essai d'analyse sémiologique*. Paris: Hachette, 1972.

Gasca, L., and R. Gubern. *El discurso del comic*. Madrid: Cátedra, 1988.

Gubern, R. *El lenguaje de los comics*. Barcelona: Penínula, 1972.

Inge, T. *Comics as Culture*. Jackson: University Press of Mississippi, 1990.

Reynolds, R. *Safe Heroes: A Modern Mythology*. Jackson: University Press of Mississippi, 1994.

—ROMAN GUBERN

COMMUNICATION. The etymology of *communication* (Latin, *communicare*, to share material goods or ideas, meanings, information) indicates some form of transfer in a reciprocal or unidirectional mode (to communicate *with* versus to communicate *to*). In modern English, *communication* applies both to the general and selective circulation of messages and to their technological means of conveyance. Moreover, it can refer either to the process of communication or to its products.

Studies of communication are in some respects equivalent to semiotics. However, the different histories of the two terms have meant that there is both overlap and discrepancy between them. Communication theory can be taken to refer to alternative brands of semiotics, or semiotics can be understood as a specific set of theories of communication. Each can be used as the perspective from which to critique or supplement the limitations of the other. For instance, *communication* markedly emphasizes agency and process, while semiotics usually focuses on the signs and their relations. However, various traditions in semiotics and linguistics

(social semiotics, discourse analysis, poststructuralism) have attempted to retheorize their discipline to take account of process and social action in ways that have been influential in contemporary semiotics.

Communication comprises at least four distinct notional themes that have significant theoretical implications from the point of view of semiotics.

Linear Models of Communication. Communication studies, especially as it developed in the United States after the 1950s, relied on linear models of communication to study modern mass-communication systems. In its most extreme form, it was labeled the "bullet theory" of communication, since it represented the processes of mass communication as acting like a series of bullets fired by senders aiming to reach their designated targets with pelletlike messages. Bias was studied as a measurable deflection of messages from a publicly available standard of truth. Media effects were studied in how they impinged on audiences presumed to be largely passive in their responses, capable only of simple actions like switching the TV on or off or buying a product (or voting for a politician) or not. Variation was studied, following classic stratification theory, to reveal the differences attributable to class, gender, age, and ethnicity. "Effective communication" (communication that reached its intended target) was something that could be learned and taught.

This positivist model of communication and the paradigm with which it was associated gave communication studies a dubious reputation among semiotically informed students of the mass media. Semioticians investigate more complex relationships and mediations between a message and its referent than the simple facts of truth or bias. For most brands of semiotics, interconnections of systems of signs lead to a systemic lack of perfect fit between signs and referents that is not a deliberate effect of a particular text but a recurring feature, expressing the historically constituted conditions of the coding system or ideological tendencies that are shared by senders and receivers. However, the effects model did contain its own implicit semiotic theory, and its object of study was relevant to general semiotics: the form and function of sign systems operating in technologically advanced mass societies. *Communications* is still a valid term for referring to much of what is studied by semiotics, and this has been reflected in the increasing use, under other names, of semiotic theories applied to the mass media in departments of communications studies.

Reciprocal and Participatory Models of Communication. In the Saussurean tradition, verbal language was considered an exemplary code, and *langue* rather than language (text or communication) was the primary object for semiotics (semiology). *Language* in this sense referred essentially to a collective product, expressing the collective will and common knowledge of a whole language community. The term *community*, a cognate of *communication*, carries much the same ideology of solidarity and identity, constructed by language as a precondition for communication. But, by definition, actual acts of communication (utterances, discourse) were not considered a relevant topic for semiotics by Saussure.

However, within language-oriented branches of semiotics, the issue of communication has been productive, if not always foregrounded through that term. The tradition in anthropological linguistics, shaped by George Boas, Edward Sapir, and Benjamin Lee Whorf, for instance, implicitly addressed the problem of communication. The so-called Sapir-Whorf hypothesis proposes essentially that communication is impossible across different languages because each language is totally embedded in a specific linguistic and cultural complex that tightly binds the language community together and makes it practically impenetrable. Within a language community, communication is assumed to occur perfectly and universally, just as is the case in Saussurean semiotics.

Structuralist linguistics was criticized independently by Jürgen Habermas (1976) and Dell Hymes (1971), both of whom used the term *communication* in similar ways. For both, the target was Noam Chomsky's notion of "competence," which was a restatement of the abilities assumed to underpin the knowledge implied by Saussure's concept of *langue*. They proposed the term *communicative competence* to refer to the knowledge that underpins successful communicative behaviors and that must include more than a knowledge of the language. Communicative competence exceeds mere grammatical proficiency and includes a knowledge of what can be said on what occasions by whom and to whom. These are discursive rules governing discursive practices, sensitive to the functions and contexts of communication, not just abstract linguistic rules governing the well-formedness of sentences in texts. There are even times when it is socially inappropriate to produce full and correct grammatical utterances. *Communication* in this sense still includes the consensus ideology that

is part of the semantic field of the term. This competence was construed as part of a contract linking speakers and hearers as equal individuals in a given community.

In the 1920s, Valentin N. Voloshinov critiqued Saussurean linguistics and proposed that the basic unit for analysis should be utterances—that is, semiotic exchanges and acts of communication as irreducibly social acts (1930). This proposal led to later developments such as speech-act theory and discourse analysis and has become the founding premise of social semiotics. Voloshinov's work has two main implications for a semiotic retheorization of the concept of communication. First, the taken-for-granted basis of individual acts of communication is intrinsically ideological, ultimately serving the interests of the dominant classes. In a similar vein, Michel Pêcheux (1975) later drew attention to the "unsaid" in discourse as the site where ideology is at its most potent. Second, Voloshinov stressed that social meanings are the product of continual struggle and renegotiation, so that the signs of language are typically multiaccented and so interpreted differently by different contending classes. This opens up the possibility that the shared basis of understanding that underpins individual acts of communication is often or even typically in dispute to a degree that itself is often kept from view, so that the perfect communication assumed by most communications analysis is merely ideological.

Umberto Eco (1979) has analyzed this kind of situation from a semiotic point of view through the concept of "aberrant coding," which refers to the situation where readers of a text interpret it with a different code than that used by those who constructed it. This concept provides a new way of semiotically theorizing the discrepancies found by empirical research in the effects model, related to different class, gender, or race positions in communications studies. There is now an increasing recognition that the distinctive role and activity of readers and other consumers of text is an important semiotic phenomenon. As a result, "communication failure" or "communication breakdown" can be analyzed as sites of sociosemiotic processes involving different codes, purposes, or strategies.

Communication as Process and Product. Communication as a product is closely equivalent to a text or message, but it has no technical sense in either semiotics or communication theory. As a

process, communication is the chain of events linking the production, reception, and circulation of messages and meanings. In this sense, it can be compared
usefully to the different senses of the word *semiosis*
in Charles Sanders Peirce's theories, where it refers
primarily to the process by which signs are constituted in transactions linking repesentamens with objects and with a third element that Peirce called
interpretants. In this scheme, the representamen is
the sign that is used to represent an object or idea,
while the interpretant is the idea or meaning created
by the original sign in the mind of another. The concept of the interpretant, then, assigns a decisive role
to the communication process in semiosis. Peirce emphasized that semiosis is unlimited, so that meaning
is continually being made and remade as signs circulate in discourse.

Peirce's concept of semiosis refers primarily to the
processes of signification, an inherently social process
involving participants in acts of communication.
Semiosis thus refers to all the processes involved in
the production, reception, and circulation of meanings, including signification, representation, and
communication.

Communication as Material Process. *Communication* can refer to systems that transport people and
material goods from one place to another, such as
roads and railways, and to material systems that
transfer messages, such as telephone and telegraph
systems, mail services, and so on. With the rapid development of computerized technologies, the sophistication of material networks of communication
has increased dramatically. These developments have
been and will be decisive influences on contemporary life in advanced societies. Theorists of the postindustrial and the postmodern have drawn attention
to the importance of these phenomena for understanding the contemporary conditions of semiosis.

But as early as the 1950s and 1960s, Harold A.
Innis (1951) and Marshall McLuhan (1964) began to
theorize the interdependence of technological developments in transport systems and in the mass media.
McLuhan talked of the media as "extensions of man,"
seeing an equivalence between forms of technology
that transported bodies or goods from one part of the
globe to another and forms that transported images
of goods or bodies. Innis was concerned with the way
that communication systems such as railways transformed the conditions of social existence and the nature of social identity.

Neither carried out their theorizations under the
rubric of semiotics because semiotics at that time
seemed not to be concerned with the material and
technological conditions and consequences of semiosis. Within an extended notion of the scope and
tasks of semiotics, this division of labor has come to
seem less justified. The communications industries
require analysis from political, economic, and technological points of view, as well as from what had
traditionally been the semiotic point of view. Insofar
as social semiotics includes the material, social, and
technological bases of the social production of meaning within its purview, it is forced to take on for analysis this new set of objects that seems to grow in
complexity and scope every decade. However, this extension of social semiotics has not yet been achieved
on a significant scale. In this respect, the ambiguities
of the term *communication* still contain important
challenges and provocations for the development of
semiotics.

[*See also* Code; Linguistic Relativism; Mass
Communication; Multimodality; Speech Act Theory;
and Whorf.]

BIBLIOGRAPHY

Crowley, D., and D. Mitchell, eds. *Communication Theory Today.* Stanford: Stanford University Press, 1994.
Eco, U. *The Role of the Reader: Explorations in the Semiotics of Texts.* Bloomington: Indiana University Press, 1979.
Gerbner, G. "Toward a General Model of Communication." *Audio Visual Communication Review* 4.3 (1956): 171–199.
Gumbrecht, H. U., and K. L. Pfeiffer, eds. *Materialities of Communication.* Stanford: Stanford University Press, 1994.
Habermas, J. *Communication and the Evolution of Society* (1976). Translated by T. McCarthy. Boston: Beacon Press, 1979.
Hymes, D. *On Communicative Competence.* Philadelphia: University of Pennsylvania Press, 1971.
Innis, H. A. *The Bias of Communication.* Toronto: University of Toronto Press, 1951.
McLuhan, M. *Understanding Media: The Extensions of Man.* New York: McGraw-Hill, 1964.
O'Sullivan, T., J. Hartley, D. Saunders, M. Montgomery, and J. Fiske. *Key Concepts in Communication and Cultural Studies.* 2d ed. London and New York: Routledge, 1994.
Pêcheux, M. *Language, Semantics, and Ideology* (1975). Translated by H. Nagpal. New York: St. Martin's Press, 1982.
Shannon, C. E., and W. Weaver. *The Mathematical Theory of Communication.* Urbana: University of Illinois Press, 1949.
Voloshinov, V. N. *Marxism and the Philosophy of Language*

(1930). Translated by L. Matejka and I. R. Titunik. New York: Seminar Press, 1973.

—ROBERT HODGE

COMPUTATIONAL NEUROSCIENCE. A discipline that combines methods and concepts from computer science and neuroscience to achieve a better understanding of brain and cognitive processes, computational neuroscience seeks to explain how chemical and electrical signals process information in the nervous system and how their representational function is achieved. Nervous systems are interpreted as information-processing systems whose dynamics can be simulated on computers.

There are two possible strategies to address the field's fundamental questions: The bottom-up strategy is a kind of reductionism that contends that so-called higher-level cognitive abilities cannot be understood unless the underlying basic processes of each neuron, synapse, gate, and other components are understood. In its extreme form, the goal is to explain cognition in terms of physics; The top-down strategy holds that the actual realization of cognitive processes in the neural substratum is irrelevant to understanding cognition. The physical realization of the cognitive system itself remains more or less a black box; its organization is described speculatively by an artificially constructed mechanism (symbol manipulation). Thus, superficially observed linguistic behavior, for example, is used to explain internal processes that are responsible for generating this superficial behavior. Most models in artificial intelligence suggest such an approach.

Neither strategy can lead to a satisfactory explanation of the very complex phenomenon of cognition. They mutually constrain each other in developing theories. However, the top-down perspective cannot be sustained in the domains in which empirical evidence for the mechanisms generating these higher-level cognitive functions can be found. As the eliminative materialists suggest, top-down explanations will be replaced by neuroscientific theories after neuroscience has developed further. But for the present, we are far from having theories or a full understanding that could explain complex cognitive phenomena. That is why we have to work from both sides toward a joint result.

A twofold approach is taken in computational neuroscience: on the one hand, empirical results play a crucial role. Experiments on real "wet ware" are the basis for most theories about neurons, synapses, neurotransmitters, and other parts. On the other hand, computational simulation experiments are performed in which theories about neural processes are transformed into more or less abstract models that can be simulated on computers. An interesting, fruitful, and mutually stimulating interaction has evolved between these two approaches: neuroscience provides basic theories about certain aspects of neurons, neural networks, and synaptic processes; computer science tries to model and simulate them. It is much easier to change parameters in the models than in biological tissues. This sometimes leads to interesting new hypotheses that can be tested by neuroscience. The results can in turn provide new input for computer science. The computational approach itself speculatively develops ideas and concepts (e.g., for learning in neural structures), which can form fruitful inputs for neuroscience. Coupling between these two disciplines achieves a better understanding by mutual stimulation and verification.

Computational neuroscientists do not use computers only in their experiments for collecting, transforming, and computing empirical data; they also use them as mechanisms, which themselves generate results. As neuroscientific models are quite complex, it is impossible to predict their behavior purely intuitively. Their implicit dynamics must be made explicit by simulating them on computers.

Computational neuroscience differentiates between two classes of brain models that are relevant to empirical semiotics (Sejnowski, Koch, and Churchland, 1990): the realistic brain models try to simulate neural processes at the cellular level (e.g., in the synaptic gap or inside a neuron). But the more parameters that are added, the more complex the model and its behavioral dynamics become. Adding more parameters could produce a degree of complexity as intractable as the natural nervous system itself. Moreover, since these models require a lot of computational power to simulate only very small components of neural systems, current technology and its constraints do not provide the means to simulate higher cognitive functions. The alternative to the complexity and limitations of realistic brain models is simulations that capture only the very basic features of natural neural structures, such as parallel processing, local processing, and a high level of interaction between simple processes and spreading activations. Complex global behavior emerges as a result of interaction between many simple local processes. The most prominent exponent of simplified brain models is the class of models known as connectionist or parallel distributed processing (PDP).

Assuming that cognition is the result of neural processes and that these processes can be treated as information processes, the approaches taken in computational neuroscience promise to be fruitful. An important step that has to be taken is to consider also epistemiological concepts; they are especially important in investigating the problems of knowledge representation and language. However, the basic question remains: are human brains capable of understanding themselves?

[See also Artificial Intelligence; Connectionism; and Cybernetics.]

BIBLIOGRAPHY

Baumgartner, P., and S. Payn, eds. *Speaking Minds: Interviews with Twenty Eminent Cognitive Scientists.* Princeton: Princeton University Press, 1995.
Churchland, P. M. *A Neurocomputational Perspective—The Nature of Mind and the Structure of Science.* Cambridge, Mass.: MIT Press, 1989.
Churchland, P. S. *Neurophilosophy: Toward a Unified Science of the Brain.* Cambridge, Mass.: MIT Press, 1986.
Churchland, P. S., and T. J. Sejnowski. "Neural Representation and Neural Computation." In *From Reading to Neurons*, edited by A. M. Galaburda, pp. 217–250. Cambridge, Mass.: MIT Press, 1989.
Churchland, P. S., and T. J. Sejnowski. *The Computational Brain.* Cambridge, Mass.: MIT Press, 1992.
Rumelhart, D. E., and J. L. McClelland. *Parallel Distributed Processing: Explorations in the Microstructure of Cognition. Volume 1, Foundations.* Cambridge, Mass.: MIT Press, 1986.
Sejnowski, T. J., C. Koch, and P. S. Churchland. "Computational Neuroscience." In *Connectionist Modeling and Brain Function*, edited by S. J. Hanson et al., pp. 5–35. Cambridge, Mass.: MIT Press, 1990.

—MARKUS PESCHL

COMPUTER. If it were distinguished only by its number-crunching ability, the computer would be no more than a better abacus. From a semiotic perspective, such a device would be relevant in regard to automating operations corresponding to a well-defined category of signs, such as those that represent quantities in some way. That quantities can be represented iconically, indexically, or symbolically is a matter of cultural record, as is the fact that there are many number systems (e.g., binary, decimal, and hexadecimal). Nevertheless, the type of representation is relevant for defining the ever-changing cognitive condition of the human being. Some representations are very close to what they represent; others tend to become more general or to reach increasing levels of abstraction.

Many types of devices have been built over time in order to accommodate the ever-growing need for calculations posed by practical tasks of augmented complexity or by theoretical endeavors. These devices embody literally human knowledge of numbers: at the end of the nineteenth century in England, the word *computer* applied to people who carried out astronomical calculations professionally. They also embody understandings of proportions and rules for addition and subtraction in that their physicality and their functionality are interdependent. The degree of abstraction implicit in the reality of a machine, which logic and mathematics advanced as such machines became increasingly abstract, fundamentally affected this physical limitation. Before the first computer was ever built, computers had already been conceived of as theoretical machines able to process on a symbolic level. The Turing machine, the archetype of the modern computer, is such a theoretical construct.

On the object level, there are at least three aspects of computers that have semiotic relevance; computation, interface (the interaction between persons and computers), and networking (the integration of machines and programs in an underlying structure facilitating human interaction). On a metalevel, semiotically relevant aspects pertain to: representation, understanding (the semantics of computation), and learning of self-awareness (self-organization in pursuit of lifelike properties such as adaptation, self-learning, awareness, self-criticism, and immunity). These lists are not exhaustive.

Computers are basically semiotic engines. Regardless of their implementation, as digital computers or as devices working in any number system, computers process symbols. Embodied in a computer are a logic (Boolean in current computer technology), data (today almost exclusively in digital format), and instructions (in the form of programs). Semiotically, this meeting of logic, signs, and operations can be described as semiosis (i.e., sign processes), which in principle is open-ended. The logic is embedded in the hardware and reflected in the structure and function of the programming language. Programs can also be at least partially embedded in matter (in particular in the silicon chips), although they are written as "applications" and provided in the form of instructions. The data to which logic is applied and upon which operations are carried out stands for measurements, thoughts, emotions, and so on. As a semiotic engine, the computer is fed by the inexhaustible energy of sign-based human activities, interactions included.

Such descriptions could not shed much light on the subject of computers and computation if they were only yet another attempt to capture for semiotics a field of inquiry and practical application to which semiotics itself has contributed little or nothing. But the intellectual history of computers does not start with silicon. The magnificent semiotic project of Gottfried Wilhelm Leibniz (1646–1716) articulated the goal of a *calculus ratiocinator*; many other projects, such as those by Ramón Lull (1232–1316), Blaise Pascal (1623–1662), John Napier (1550–1617), and others prepared the stage for the applications pursued by Charles Babbage (1792–1871) that he embodied in his analytical engine. Charles Sanders Peirce (1839–1914), who himself probably became involved in the attempt to build contraptions able to support sign processes, discussed the semiotic significance of such attempts and suggested a complete set for performing any sign calculus through the operations of insertion, omission, and substitution. Joseph-Marie Jacquard (1752–1834), Herman Hollerith (1860–1929), Howard Aiken (1900–1973), and J. W. Manchly (1907–1980), for instance, constructed such machines. Others, such as Norbert Wiener (1894–1964), Herbert Simon (b. 1916), Allen Newell, Vannevar Bush (1890–1974), and Marvin Minsky (b. 1927), to name only a few, gave them their underlying semiotic identity. In the process of dedicating a great deal of effort to designing languages suitable for programming, computer science appropriated the convenient semiotic distinction of syntax, semantics, and pragmatics.

Not too many computer scientists and even fewer semioticians have recognized the need for integrating semiotic considerations into the current dynamics of technological change. They are aware that semiotic considerations proved very useful in approaching the fundamental problem of interface (the iconic interface is the better-known example of this application) and in the design of computer-supported interactions, such as the ones pertinent to the networked world. Vannevar Bush will probably be remembered less for his technological genius, embodied in the differential analyzer (an analog computer built in 1930 at the Massachusetts Institute of Technology) and more for his anticipation of non-linear-thinking applications such as those embodied by the World Wide Web. Semiotic engineering, too, is in the process of gaining well-deserved legitimacy.

Computation as a semiotic substratum and supported by semiotic considerations is only part of the ongoing efforts to deal with issues of human intelligence, virtual reality, and artificial reality. Semiotics has little if anything to contribute to implementations of neural networks, algorithms, parallel processing, and similar issues. The significance of semiotics becomes apparent, however, in addressing notions of appropriateness (which signs optimally support a certain human endeavor), distinction (which features and which correlations support processes such as pattern recognition and image understanding), and integration (design and implementation of multimedia expressions). Multimedia, in that it unites various data types, is a computational challenge. But it is even more a semiotic experience of a type different from that embodied in the processing of single, homogeneous data types.

What generally qualifies the semiotic approach is dedication to the entire effort of computation—that is, a commitment to ensuring the coherence of the integrated sign processes that are facilitated and carried through computationally. A good interface will never automatically guarantee the success of a program. A good program (as relative as this is in a world of rapidly successive versions) that has difficult interactions will perform only at a percentage of its potential. A coherent, integrated semiotic strategy extends to everything that supports and defines the activity. In some way, such a semiotic strategy is the metaprogram that unites software, data flow, input/output performance, connectivity, process and human interface, cultural and social acceptance, and learning.

As a still young technology in a phase of rudimentary evolution, computers maintain the semiotic engine on a level still detached from the application at hand, rather than as part of it. The challenge probably lies in the integration of computers into human pragmatics in order to make them appear as extensions of human intellect and skill. At that level, the semiotic engine should display awareness of the sign processes and should be able to initiate semioses appropriate to the goal pursued.

[*See also* Abacus; Artificial Intelligence; Computer-Mediated Communication; Icon; Index; Interface; Metalanguage; Number Representation; Semiosis; *and* Turing.]

BIBLIOGRAPHY

Anderson, P. B. *A Theory of Computer Semiotics.* Cambridge: Cambridge University Press, 1990.

Aspray, W. *Computer: A History of the Information Machine.* HarperCollins, 1996.

Bush, V. "As We May Think." *Atlantic Monthly* 176.1 (1945): 23–35.

Nadin, M. *The Civilization of Illiteracy.* Dresden: Dresden University Press, 1997.

Winograd, T., and F. Flores. *Understanding Computers and Cognition: A New Foundation for Design.* Reading, Mass.: Addison-Wesley, 1986.

—MIHAI NADIN

COMPUTER-MEDIATED COMMUNICATION. A new form of human communication made possible by links between personal and mainframe computers, modems, and telecommunication lines, computer-mediated communication transpires in "cyberspace," an abstract, disembodied space consisting only of information and electronic pulses, in which the ordinary coordinates of physical space and time are suspended. "The Net" (for "network" or "network of networks") has become a meeting place for millions of people. Remarkable new forms of "virtual culture" are now developing in this intensely semiotic domain of human interaction. At the present time, messages are still mainly typed and textual, although graphics and sound and video clips are increasingly being added. The technology for video conferencing—oral, computer-mediated face-to-face communication including visual images in real time—exists.

Interpreted broadly, the term *computer-mediated communication* includes not only person-to-person and person-to-group communication but also person-to-computer contacts in which individuals access files or interact with programs on remote computers. Global computerization is breaking down the traditional distinction in print culture between the solo-authored, decontextualized written text and the face-to-face personal conversation. Thus, within minutes or hours of examining a document via the World Wide Web—a system of links between digital files of text, sound, or graphics, effortlessly accessed by most computers around the globe—a person can contact its author(s) by electronic mail (e-mail) and begin a dialogue.

While corresponding through e-mail can be seen as a mere acceleration of time-delayed communication, group communication based on the basic e-mail mode puts large numbers of individuals in intense synchronous interaction. Discussion-list messages are posted to a central address and automatically distributed to the personal accounts of all other subscribers. In some groups, a moderator edits and distributes messages in batches.

Synchronous modes enable individuals logged on simultaneously to "chat" by typing messages to each other in real time. For instance, just as face-to-face speakers hear their interlocutors formulating their messages as they are spoken, when the "talk" function is activated on the Unix operating system, two individuals can read each other's messages as they are being typed. In addition to specialist or lobbyist networks, there are real-time, collective role-playing fantasy games of long duration in which individuals develop fictional personae, either of the same or the opposite sex, and interact in virtual rooms.

Early research conducted in the late 1970s was concerned with the effects of the new medium on organizational functioning, efficiency, and hierarchical relationships. Many perceived the medium as cold, anonymous, and lacking in "social presence" because of "reduced bandwidth" and the absence of nonverbal cues such as facial expression. Alongside this ongoing research tradition, newer approaches focusing on the linguistic, playful, and expressive aspects of computer-mediated communication are of greater interest to students of semiotics, discourse analysis, sociolinguistics, folklore, and anthropology.

Digital writing is strikingly dynamic, playful, and even speechlike and challenges currently held beliefs among folklorists and students of rhetoric, oral literature, and the history of literacy about the uniqueness of oral culture. Oral culture is believed, for example, to be agonistically toned, whereas writing, subject to processes of decontextualization, supposedly neutralizes this component of human interaction. Yet even in ordinary e-mail, both private and person-to-group, we find a striking prevalence of sudden flare-ups of anger and insult, known in cyberculture as "flaming."

Descriptive studies of the language of e-mail identify "oral" features (e.g., slang, expressions such as "well" and "OK," fragmentation, and a tolerance for misspellings that resemble the dysfluencies of ordinary speech); "written" features (e.g., ellipsis, note taking, lists); and uniquely digital features, including the use of "emoticons," which are typographic symbols used to convey information usually communicated by tones of voice.

Some researchers argue that this language is an emergent new register of English, which is in a state of transition from the norms and practices of print culture to those of the emergent computer culture. It reflects much confusion on the part of writers, who bring to basic e-mail and discussion groups experience with many precomputer genres of oral and written communication, including the face-to-face conversation, the telephone conversation, the business letter, the personal letter, the telegram, the postcard, the ritual greeting card, and the intraoffice memo. In comparison with paper-based written messages, the text of the electronic message carries a particularly heavy semiotic burden. Aspects such as the shape and size of paper or quality of handwriting are not available to supplement the linguistic channel. E-mail messages automatically come with a memo-like computer-generated header that includes the sender, date, and subject line. This is a generalized use of the format of the traditional intraoffice memo. Whereas in the intraoffice memo no personal greeting was considered necessary and writers proceeded directly to the body of their message, e-mail writers—mainly communicating globally and not just within organizations—often add personally chosen greetings and other openings, though practices are far from standard.

Synchronous, descriptive studies of the language and generic features of e-mail messages do not suffice to identify the sources of confusion as individuals adapt to the new medium or to document the crystallization of emergent new norms. Diachronic studies are necessary to answer such questions as: how are practices in private e-mail and related modes crystallizing over time? To what extent is the communication style of today's initiates like that of the pioneers of e-mail technology in the 1970s? Are newcomers merely initiated into a pattern already set by pioneers or have important changes occurred? In what ways are the lines of demarcation between the decontextualized business letter and the contextualized personal letter becoming blurred in the new medium, and why is this happening? Does the medium encourage more rapid movement toward a personal, expressive style between a given pair of business correspondents than would happen in extended exchanges of business letters? To what extent are such developments also the product of a general cultural trend toward a preferred oral style of writing?

Playfulness flourishes particularly in the synchronous modes, which in effect become textual playgrounds. Individuals play with language, writing, and the computer keyboard, as well as with their own identities, the frames of interaction, and even with the commands of the computer programs that make their interactions possible. There are important affinities between computer-based, spontaneous playfulness and real-world, written genres such as graffiti and comics, on the one hand, and with face-to-face genres such as charades, carnivals and masked balls, parties, shows, and improvisational theater on the other. Yet most of what happens on-line consists only of typed, interactive text—letters and typographic symbols on a computer screen—created by geographically dispersed persons who cannot see one another and who might never meet. In real-world carnivals, masks and costumes liberate participants; here, the ephemeral, nonmaterial medium, the typed text, and the prevalent use of nicknames provide the mask. (See figure 1.)

In synchronous modes, writing becomes performance: participants invite others to pay special attention to how their messages are packaged. Typed, on-line improvisation sometimes reaches virtuoso heights, with participants handing out compliments to one another. Although improvisational performance predominates in synchronous modes, there are also experiments with scripted performance. A group calling themselves the Hamnet Players is experimenting with on-line theater through Internet relay chat (IRC), virtual cast party included. They have scripted outrageous parodies of *Hamlet* and *Macbeth* called "Hamnet" and "PCbeth," respectively, juxtaposing Shakespeare's canonical plots and poetry with clever puns, speed-writing conventions, obscenity, and IRC computer jargon. At a signal from the artistic director, persons already "in disguise" in

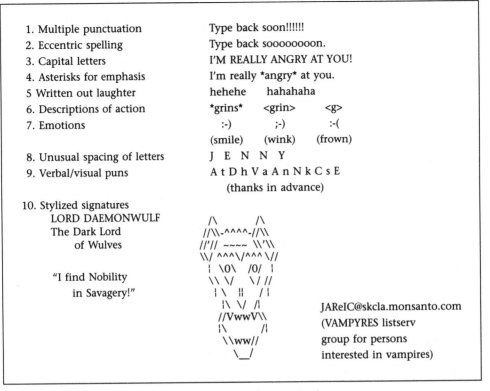

FIGURE 1. *Play with Typography in Computer-Mediated Communication.*

their regular IRC identities change their "nicks" (nicknames) to the names of the characters they are about to "play." The performance is semiotically most interesting and most complex when players improvise on their scripted roles. Their aspirations go beyond having fun; they seek to develop a new form of performance art.

In the coming decade, there will be extensive research on the long-term social implications of computer-mediated communication. Among the many issues to be studied are what criteria we can use to evaluate the quality of "community" in cyberspace, as well as what the effects of extended participation on individual well-being are. Are low-risk virtual relationships being substituted for real-world relationships, or are people enriching their real-world experiences with new forms of social interaction and behavior? While social isolates might escape into cyberspace instead of cultivating real-world ties, friends and family can now keep in touch on a daily basis at low cost. Thus, this medium might prove to strengthen weak extended-family and community ties among geographically dispersed persons who

kept in touch in the past only by the occasional letter or telephone call, supplemented by infrequent reunions at holiday or birthday times. It is already clear that cyberspace is not an entirely benign place: sexual harassment, racism, deception, arrangements for and depictions of the molestation of children, and so on are common and difficult to manage, if not impossible to control. It remains to be seen whether we can contain such problems and, at the same time, preserve the openness of the emergent culture of cyberspace.

[*See also* Communication; Conversation; Flaming; *and* Mass Communication.]

BIBLIOGRAPHY

Aycock, A. "Virtual Play: Baudrillard Online." *Arachnet Electronic Journal on Virtual Culture* 1.7 (1993). Electronic manuscript available from listserv@kentvm.kent.edu (file aycock v1n7).

Benedikt, M., ed. *Cyberspace: First Steps.* Cambridge, Mass.: MIT Press, 1991.

Bolter, J. D. *Writing Space: The Computer, Hypertext, and the History of Writing.* Hillsdale, N.J.: Lawrence Erlbaum, 1991.

Curtis, P. "Mudding: Social Phenomena in Text-Based Virtual Realities." *Intertrek* 3(1992): 26–34. Also available as an electronic manuscript via anonymous ftp from parcftp.xerox.com/pub/MOO/papers, DIAC92.{ps, txt}.

Danet, B., L. Ruedenberg, and Y. Rosenbaum-Tamari, "'Hmmm. . . Where's All That Smoke Coming From?' Writing, Play and Performance on Internet Relay Chat." In *Network and Netplay: Virtual Groups on the Intenet*, edited by S. Rafaeli, F. Sudweeks, and M. McLaughlin, pp. 41–76. Cambridge, Mass.: AAAI/MIT Press, 1998.

Ferrara, K., H. Brunner, and G. Whittemore. "Interactive Written Discourse as an Emergent Register." *Written Communication* 8.1 (1991): 8–33.

Meyer, G., and J. Thomas. "The Baudy World of the Byte Bandit: A Postmodernist Interpretation of the Computer Underground." In *Computers in Criminal Justice*, edited by F. Schmalleger. Bristol, Ind.: Wyndham Hall, 1990. Also available as an electronic manuscript via anonymous ftp from eff.org/pub/cud/papers/baudy.world.

Murray, D. E. *Conversation for Action: The Computer Terminal as Medium of Communication.* In Pragmatics and Beyond, new series 10. Amsterdam and Philadelphia: John Benjamins, 1991.

Raymond, E. S., ed. *The New Hackers' Dictionary.* With assistance and illustrations by G. L. Steele, Jr. Cambridge, Mass.: MIT Press, 1991.

Rheingold, H. *The Virtual Community: Homesteading on the Electronic Frontier.* Reading, Mass.: Addison-Wesley, 1993.
—BRENDA DANET

CONNECTIONISM. Known also as parallel distributed processing (PDP) or neural computation, connectionism endeavors to simulate the processes taking place in a network of neurons on a very abstract level; connectionist models are simplifying models of the brain. Simulating these "neurally inspired" or brainlike models on the computer might lead to a deeper understanding of cognitive processes (Rumelhart, 1989). This computational approach differs from conventional computer programs in which information is stored more or less (linguistically) explicitly and can be retrieved via an address by an algorithm (changing, storing, duplicating, deleting, etc.) operating on these representations. Empirical evidence from neuroscience shows that no symbol, proposition, sentence, or algorithm (in the traditional sense) can be found in the brain. There must be an alternative, more basic, mechanism for the representation and processing of knowledge. The goal of the connectionist approach is to construct an abstract model of the neural processes taking place in the brain. For a detailed discussion, see Rumelhart and McClelland (1986) and McClelland and Rumelhart (1986); a short introduction is given in Rumelhart (1989).

The basic components of connectionist systems include a set of processing units that model single neurons; the processing takes place inside each unit u_i. All units are working in parallel and completely locally. Units that are "connected" to the environment are called input or output units. External stimuli can enter the network via input units; output units are connected to an output device transforming the activations into a behavioral output. All other units that do not interact directly with the environment are referred to as hidden units.

At each time t each unit u_i has a certain activation $a_i(t)$, which is a function of the inputs stemming from the units which are connected to u_i. All these activations taken together represent the current state or the pattern of activations of the connectionist network at t. This state is always determined by the previous state (especially if the network has a recurrent architecture), by the stimuli coming from the environment, and by the values of the synaptic weights connecting the units. The dynamics of these activations "generate" the global behavior of the PDP network.

Further crucial concepts of connectionism include:

1. *Pattern of connectivity.* The units are connected to each other via synaptic weights w_{ij}; that is, the value of w_{ij} determines the influence of unit's u_i output on unit u_j. There are positive as well as negative weights connecting units. Hence, a whole network of connections (weights) is built up that determines the behavior of the network by controlling the flow of activations. The set of weights implicitly represents the knowledge of the network and determines its behavioral dynamics; that is, they determine how the activations can spread through the network and, thus, how the network behaves.

2. *Learning rule.* The flow of activations can be called the first-order dynamics of a PDP network; changing weights is a kind of second-order dynamics in a network as it changes its behavioral dynamics. A learning rule changes the connection strengths between the units and, thus, the knowledge being represented in the network. That is why this process of changing weights is referred to as learning. The second-order dynamics changes the first-order dy-

namics by developing, destroying, or changing the values of existing weights. Donald Olding Hebb (1949) was the first to realize that learning in neural structures could relate to a change in the network's architecture and thus in its behavioral dynamics.

We can differentiate between two main classes of learning algorithms: associative and classificatory. The goal of associative (supervised) learning is to train the network in such a way that it learns to associate different inputs with certain output patterns. Input and output patterns can be, for instance, sensory input, linguistic items, behavioral events, and so on. There is an external teacher who presents the input/output pairs and who computes the degree of error (i.e., the difference between the desired and the actual output) in order to change the weights in such a way that they will generate a better result in the next step of processing. In other words, the goal is to learn the mapping from one pattern to another pattern of activations. As observers, we can interpret this behavior as the learning of associations. By contrast, the goal of the classification paradigm is to discover regularities in the environment without an external teacher. The classification of the stimuli in the environment is done by the network itself and is the result of the statistical regularities in the presented stimuli.

3. *Environment*. In most cases, the importance of the environment being connected to the artificial neural network is not sufficiently stressed. But if we are interested in adequately understanding cognitive processes and knowledge representation in neural structures, the environment plays an important role therein. It is not only the environment per se, but also how the PDP network is linked to it—whether via a symbol system, via various positioned and linked sensors and effectors, or through a closed-feedback loop between the system and its environment—that has a strong influence on the structure of knowledge representation, which is not reduced to linguistic categories but rather to dynamic patterns.

4. *Periphery*. The periphery (the sensory and motor system), plays an important role as it is responsible for coding and decoding "external" stimuli and neural activations. A lot of the knowledge being represented in the whole system can be found here.

5. *Context of interpretation or semantic embedding*. From an epistemological perspective, the context of interpretation is of special interest because it determines the semantics and the kind of knowledge said to be represented in the system. Generally speaking, any connectionist network can be interpreted as an abstract transformation mechanism that maps patterns of activation (i.e., vectors) from the input to the output. It is only in the process of interpreting these activations that this transformation (and thus the knowledge) has a meaning or semantics.

6. *Neural architecture*. Neural networks can have either feedforward architectures, in which the flow of activations goes in only one direction from the input units to the output units, or recurrent architectures, in which there are internal-feedback connections. The latter sort of architecture entails that the network has its own dynamics, as it is interacting not only with the stimuli coming from the environment but also with its own activations. Both kinds of networks show complex emergent behaviors, due to the large number of quite simple processes taking place in the single units, the parallel structure of these processes, and their massive connectivity. Hence, interaction of a large number of simple local processes can cause complex global behaviors. (Figure 1 gives a more formal description of a PDP network.)

The connectionist processing and learning paradigm has many implications. Due to its associative processing mechanism (an input pattern triggers an association), it has a content-addressable memory. Graceful degradation is another feature that is typical of natural and artificial nervous systems; if small parts of the network are damaged, this has only small effects on its overall performance. Learning is based on a process of self-organization on a prelinguistic level. The possibility of learning makes PDP networks even more interesting for two reasons: First, learning determines the structure of knowledge representation. Second, we can learn a lot from these simulations for the natural nervous systems' dynamics, as well as for epistemological questions concerning the problem of knowledge representation. From a philosophy of science perspective, there is an interesting interaction between simulated and empirical results in that they can be used systematically to develop new empirical theories in the field.

Connectionist networks also offer some interesting applications and features, such as the simulation of associative memory, pattern- and picture-recognition tasks, language processing, the simulation of simple neural circuits, robot control, pattern completion, graceful degradation, constraint satisfaction, soft-rule application, fault tolerance, and others.

FIGURE 1. *Description of a PDP Network.*

Let us assume a network N that has n units u_i connected to each other via weights w_{ij}. The weight's value w_{ij} represents the influence of unit u_i on unit u_j. The whole set of weights could be represented by a weight matrix WN having n rows and n columns. Thus, a fully connected network is possible. The set of weights is referred to as the architecture of the network; the values of the weights determine the flow of activations and, hence, the dynamics of the network's behavior. If the weight $w_{ij} = 0$, no connection between unit u_i and u_j is established. The weights' values are unidirectional. Each unit u_j computes its activation a_j at each time t. Which rules are responsible for these computations?

At first, the netto input is computed:

$$net_j(t) = \sum_i w_{ij} o_i$$

The outputs o_i of the connected units are multiplied by the weights (influences) w_{ij} (both can have positive or negative values). These products are summed up and represent the netto input net_j. This net_j is transformed into the activation a_j by an activation function $f(net_j)$. In this example we are assuming that the activation equals the output of the unit.

The activation (output) function is typically a linear (threshold) or sigmoid function. The sigmoid function could look like this:

$$f(net_j) = \frac{1}{1 + e^{-net_j}}$$

Each unit computes these steps in parallel and locally. The result is an emergent process of spreading activations. We cannot focus on technical (hardware and software) issues here. So far, we have discussed, how activations are—from a more formal point of view—spreading through a network. Let us take a short look at the learning rules now; as has been mentioned the learning rules are changing the weights incrementally:

$$w_{ij}^{new} := w_{ij}^{old} + \Delta w_{ij}$$

Hence, the value we are interested in is Δw_{ij}. In the most simple case, the Hebb rule (1949) is applied: If unit u_i and u_j are active, then strengthen their weight. Another learning rule represents the delta rule or Widrow-Hoff rule (Rumelhart and McClelland 1986; Rumelhart 1989). A value t_j represents the "teaching input" (i.e., the desired output) given by an external teacher.

$$\Delta w_{ij} = \eta(t_j - o_j)o_i$$

In this case, there is an external teacher presenting an input and verifying the output. If there is a difference between the desired output t_j and the actual output o_j, the weights are changed according to the rule above; a more general rule for networks with more than two layers is the generalized-delta rule; which has become one of the most important learning rules in technical and commercial applications; it is, however, biologically implausible. There are several other learning strategies based on statistical methods, such as competitive learning and the Hopfield learning algorithm and others; we cannot focus on them in detail here. (Hinton, 1987, has a good and detailed overview of the most common learning rules.) The point of interest here is the basic idea behind all learning techniques. They ae all based more or less on D. O. Hebb's idea of slightly changing the weights in order to stabilize the dynamics of the network. Many very small and local changes cause a global change in the behavior of the PDP network.

From a philosophical and epistemological perspective, connectionist networks have interesting implications for our understanding of knowledge and knowledge representation in both natural and artificial cognitive systems. This epistemological dimension might lead to major revisions in philosophy of science, philosophy of mind, and epistemology (P. M. Churchland, 1991, 1995). From a semiotic perspective, artificial neural networks are of special interest, as they offer the possibility of explaining and simulating the process of sign and symbol formation. This can be done by connecting a neural network via sensors and effectors to an environment. In an artificial-lifelike simulation (Langton, 1995), the network can interact with its environment and other neural networks. Consequently, it could establish a symbollike language for communication. A symbol is understood in this context as a neural-activation pattern that refers to another pattern in the environment or the neural system. The relation(s) between these patterns can be learned by applying one learning algorithm that changes the weights and thus the relations between the processing units. Unlike symbol systems, the network can operate on a so-called subsymbolic or presymbolic level, which enables processing without referring to explicit and already existing symbols.

[*See also* Artificial Intelligence; Artificial Life; Computational Neuroscience; Error Back-Propagation; *and* Knowledge Representation.]

BIBLIOGRAPHY

Bechtel, W., and A. Abrahamsen. *Connectionism and the Mind: An Introduction to Parallel Processing in Networks.* Cambridge, Mass.: Basil Blackwell, 1991.

Churchland, P. M. "A Deeper Unity: Some Feyerabendian Themes in Neurocomputational Forms." In *Beyond Reason*, edited by G. Munevar, pp. 1–23. Amsterdam: Kluwer, 1991.

Churchland, P. M. *The Engine of Reason, the Seat of the Soul: A Philosophical Journey into the Brain.* Cambridge, Mass.: MIT Press, 1995.

Hebb, D. O. *The Organization of Behavior.* New York: Wiley, 1949.

Hertz, J., A. Krogh, and R. G. Palmer. *Introduction to the Theory of Neural Computation.* Redwood, Calif.: Addison-Wesley, 1991.

Hinton, G. E. *Connectionist Learning Procedures: Technical Report CMU-CS-87-115.* Pittsburgh: Carnegie-Mellon University Press, 1987.

Langton, C. G., ed. *Artificial Life.* Cambridge, Mass.: MIT Press, 1995.

McClelland, J. L., and D. E. Rumelhart. *Parallel Distributed Processing, Explorations in the Microstructure of Cognition.* Volume 2, *Psychological and Biological Models.* Cambridge, Mass.: MIT Press, 1986.

Rumelhart, D. E. "The Architecture of Mind: A Connectionist Approach." In *The Foundations of Cognitive Science*, edited by M. I. Posner, pp. 133–159. Cambridge, Mass.: MIT Press, 1989.

Rumelhart, D. E., and J. L. McClelland. *Parallel Distributed Processing, Explorations in the Microstructure of Cognition.* Volume 1, *Foundations.* Cambridge, Mass.: MIT Press, 1986.

—MARKUS PESCHL

CONNOTATION. *See* Denotation and Connotation.

CONVERSATION comprises both verbal and nonverbal face-to-face interaction. It is useful to distinguish "natural" conversation from a variety of "contrived" forms of conversation.

Natural conversation, the spontaneous communicative exchange of verbal and nonverbal signs between at least two interactants, constitutes an intricate semiotic behavior. Its degrees of subtlety and complexity depend on the variety of channels used (face-to-face, telephone, Internet), the interaction components, and the personal, social, and cultural factors involved. Contrived conversation is developed in theatrical performances in which the participants' motives and the artificially coded messages are not genuine. More crucial from a sociophysiological and even culture-specific point of view is the investigation of reduced-interaction conversation—that is, conversation with or among the disabled, when one or more communicative channels are impeded either by causes external to the person or by severe physical impairment such as deafness, blindness, paralysis, amputations, or different temporary malfunctions. The most critical ones are, of course, those caused by permanent curtailment of their interactive capabilities, as they may be unable to complete, either as emitters or receivers, the basic structure language-paralanguage-kinesic interactions and therefore cannot code or decode messages through mutually complementary (i.e., supporting, emphasizing, contradicting) channels, as fully functional interactants do.

For the microanalysis of natural conversations, eight basic types of semiotic behavior can be differentiated, singly or jointly; these are displayed verbally and nonverbally, including silence and stillness; and as feedback by other somatic signs and even by extrasomatic message-conveying means such as the manipulation of objects.

1. *Initial behaviors.* Initial turn claiming by one or more of the interactants can be displayed verbally or nonverbally. Spontaneous initial-turn taking is typical on the part of one or more participants, the attempts of the others having failed. Failed spontaneous initial-turn-taking is characterized by a first phase comprising the spontaneous turn-taking behaviors followed by the actual failure phase in which the aborted verbal, paralinguistic, and kinesic interventions come to a halt, the kinesic ones typically losing strength until they disappear into a listener's state. Initial turn offering, with or without initial turn claiming, is typical of any interactant willing to become a listener, thus granting a more legitimate status to the first speaker. Granted initial-turn taking is, therefore, the logical next step (unless failed turn taking occurs), the speaker acquiring his turn according to the prescribed ritual.

2. *Turn-change behaviors.* *Turn-taking* is an umbrella term for a set of structural alternatives. While *taking* may rightfully signify the straightforward beginning of a new speaker's speech, it should also be understood as a gradual move that can be broken down into several stages, preferably alternating with some complementary speaker's behavior. Virtually any conversational behavior consists of a "prebehavior" anticipating or leading to it, a central defining one that constitutes the truly regulatory act, and a "postbehavior" or residual act. For instance, the listener does not always make a claim by passing abruptly from a state of passive listening to the claiming behavior but can go through a preparatory phase, a "preclaiming," during which lip moistening or parting, a slight postural shift, or brow raising occur. At this point, the claim may still be aborted, resulting in abandoned turn claiming; otherwise, the appropriate turn-claim behavior will then be displayed. But even if the speaker has granted the turn, the listener's claim will still be noticeable until the actual preopening or turn-taking behavior through a "postclaiming" phase signaled by muscle tonus, eye contact, and posture. Turn claiming is shown when the listener wants to say something, the speaker indicates that she or he is willing to relinquish her or his turn through turn offering, or when the speaker displays a turn-preclosing behavior. Turn offering on the part of the speaker might avoid the claim and elicit the listener's turn taking. Turn preopening is a distinct intermediate step by the listener between the claiming and the speaker's yielding, followed by the actual opening instead of other structural alternatives listed above. Turn granting is a very brief, mostly nonverbal signal by the speaker to acknowledge the listener's turn claiming prior to the actual yielding (e.g., a smile), which permits her or him to conclude her or his turn while "reserving" the future speaker's turn; this can appear within different sequences. Turn yielding is the step preceding the listener becoming the speaker, as is turn-offering if the turn has not been given already through offering, thus precluding any yielding, and often after turn granting. Turn taking is the expected fluent and legitimate way of acquiring the turn when the listener takes the floor because the speaker has offered it, granted it, or yielded it. Sometimes, perhaps because the claiming failed, he or she just decides to speak up through turn suppressing or by claiming and taking the turn in rapid succession without waiting for the speaker's yielding.

3. *Secondary turn-change behaviors.* Turn holding is often displayed by the speaker as a counterrule after the listener's claim, beyond what is felt to be the limit of the turn. Turn-claim suppressing, another counterrule, can be displayed by the speaker (e.g., "Let me finish") or by any listener against the one claiming the turn. Turn suppressing is another unacceptable way of becoming speaker and is done often through actual interruption, as are turn opening and turn taking if they are not preceded by the speaker's turn yielding. Turn relinquishing occurs when the speaker simply stops, after which the turn can be taken without any preambles or through interlistener offering or by claiming it. Turn opening occurs after the turn has been relinquished or yielded to the claim by the previous speaker, simply granted, or right after having claimed it. Absent turn claiming is a not unusual situation in which the speaker, after a brief pause perhaps, resumes speaking if there is no turn claiming. Failed turn claiming, on the other hand, is caused by the speaker ignoring any claiming cues. Absent turn taking after having been claimed, even preopened, might cause a break in the conversation, after which the original speaker resorts to turn resumption, unless another speaker takes the turn.

4. *Listener's speaker-directed behaviors.* The listeners' feedback and secondary behaviors are more numerous than those of the speaker because they remain free to use different forms of communication, of which the most important is feedback. Listeners' feedback, often an interesting culture-specific behavior, is the only permissible and desirable type of intermittent (and simultaneous) verbal or nonverbal activity on the part of the listener and one which, if lacking, will produce anxiety, depending on the varying cultural tolerance for silence, since it contributes to the normal development of the conversation. Besides the basic expected responses of attention or inattention, interest or disinterest, and approval or disapproval, there are many others (pleasure or displeasure, surprise, realization, embarrassment, etc.) displayed through language and silence, kinesics and stillness, chemical reactions (e.g., tears), dermal messages (e.g., blushing, blanching, gooseflesh), and thermal ones (rises and falls in body temperature). What in general has not been recognized about the complexity of feedback is that any of the listener's

conscious or unconscious feedback might respond not only to the speaker's simultaneous (or virtually so) verbal or nonverbal activity but to the preceding one, or even as anticipation of something that has not been said or done.

5. *Listener's secondary behaviors.* The listener's secondary behaviors include verbal or nonverbal requests for clarification or supplementary information; requests for different volume; verbatim repetition of the speaker's last statement to indicate the listener's attitude (e.g., amusement, adulation), an interesting sociocultural behavior quite common on the part of the younger or inferior person; brief restatement of the speaker's preceding thought; simultaneous conclusion, in which the listener anticipates what the speaker is going to say; sentence completion—not true simultaneous speech but the termination of the sentence begun by the speaker, whether she or he actually finishes it (but without constituting interruption) or the listener is providing the lacking words (e.g., during word searching, thought, hesitation); interruptions that truly break the flow of the speaker's delivery because of their disruptive quality; and prompting signals, aimed at monitoring or controlling the speaker's performance by instructing her or him to say, not say, or do something, such as introduce someone (e.g., with throat clearing or eye contact).

6. *Interlistener behaviors.* Typically, interlistener behaviors are displayed in a low key—that is, with whispered language and paralanguage and with subdued, though perhaps tense, kinesics and need hardly any explanation: interlistener feedback about the speaker but not speaker directed; interlistener turn offering, turn claiming, turn granting, claim suppressing; and prompting signals that are similar to the speaker-directed ones, instructing one to pay attention, to keep quiet, and so forth.

7. *Speaker's secondary behavior.* Displayed during her or his turn, the speaker's secondary behaviors serve to maintain the proper back-channel communication during the ongoing conversation. They include sender's counterfeedback to the auditor's feedback, which the speaker can convey kinesically (e.g., through smiles, gaze) without interrupting the verbal message but also by repeating successful words, with an acknowledging pause as performers use, and so on; feedback request, typical also of performers but common in conversation (e.g., "nd' stand?" "Mm?"); turn preclosing after technically relinquishing the floor or as a preyielding signal by accelerating speech tempo, gazing at the listener, and so forth; turn closing, indicated by relaxation of posture or postural shift, lip moistening, and some idiosyncratic or culture-specific behaviors; and turn resumption after either the speaker has been disrupted momentarily or due to the listener's failure to take the floor.

8. *Acoustic and visual pauses.* Voluntary or involuntary pauses in conversation are paralinguistic, kinesic, or both. The most important aspects of pauses (which are far from semiotic or communicative voids, as various types of signs other than verbal may occur) still await cultural and cross-cultural research, including: the possible cooccurrence of sound and stillness or silence and movement; the slowdown of movement at the onset of the acoustic gap and how it picks up again at the end of the pause; the costructuration of a paralinguistic or kinesic pause with preceding, simultaneous, and succeeding behaviors and other activities; the intensity and duration of pauses; how paralinguistic or kinesic pauses can be filled with other somatic activities (e.g., tear shedding, blushing); how the absent sound or movement still communicates through that very absence (zero sign) or through the meaningful characteristics of silence and stillness discussed earlier; the conversational functions of a single (silence/stillness) or double (silence and stillness) pause; those with which speaker and listener can help each other; their negative functions (e.g., a manipulative, anxiety-creating silence); and the important differentiation between voluntary (attitudinal) and involuntary pauses.

The most common acoustic and visual pauses are due to the *absence of turn-claiming* and turn taking, turn offering, and turn opening before the actual beginning of the new speaker's turn; preturn ending, anticipating the actual turn-closing sentence, which allows the future speaker to get ready; turn ending, a brief transition between different speakers; turn relinquishing or turn yielding without the turn being taken immediately by a new speaker; transitional pauses (a whole research subject) between different parts of a topic, different topics, or whole turns, displayed variously according to psychological, socioeducational, and cultural variables and not just paralinguistic or kinesic but supported by smoking, flicking real or imaginary lint, preening behaviors, and others; task-performing pauses (another important cultural topic), which can have transitional purposes but also have the principal intention of doing the things just mentioned and others (e.g., changing glasses, shifting posture, arranging clothes) though they can function as powerful flow-disrupting manipulators through which we can regulate an encounter; somatic-function pauses, which can also be manipulative or truly used for the purpose of clearing one's throat, blowing one's nose, yawning, scratching, spitting (all very much conditioned by culture); feedback-seeking pauses; hesitation with various forms according to age (hence, interesting in developmental studies), sex, personality, and other factors; within this category but worth studying on their own are the pauses caused by word searching, memory searching, and thought searching; thinking pauses (all with paralanguage, stillness, squinting, lip biting, etc.): manipulative pauses; external-interference pauses (a doorbell or a telephone, etc.); and emotional pauses, during which speed is interrupted.

Further research in this area should address the development of conversational skills (i.e., of each type of turn-changing rules and counterrules, of increasingly sophisticated feedback behaviors, of controlled and uncontrolled pauses, etc.), the various deficiencies in those skills in traumatized patients and in the various forms of reduced interaction. Research could also investigate the hampering of conversational fluency by crowding, subordinate position, and social tension or the very fluent conversational repertoires of socialites.

[See also Communication; Computer-Mediated Communication; Gossip; and Nonverbal Bodily Sign Categories.]

BIBLIOGRAPHY

Duncan, S., and D. W. Fiske. *Face-to-Face Interaction: Research, Methods, and Theories.* New York: Wiley, 1977.

Jefferson, G. "A Case of Precision Timing in Ordinary Conversations." *Semiotica* 9.1 (1973): 47–96.

Kendon, A. *Studies in the Behavior of Face-to-Face Interaction.* Lisse: Peter de Ridder Press, 1977.

Poyatos, F. *Body Language and the Social Order.* Englewood Cliffs, N.J.: Prentice-Hall, 1972.

Poyatos, F. *New Perspectives in Nonverbal Communication: Studies in Cultural Anthropology, Social Psychology, Linguistics, Literature, and Semiotics.* Oxford: Pergamon, 1983. See especially chap. 7.

Poyatos, F. *La communicación no verbal, 1: Cultura, lenguaje y conversación.* Madrid: Ediciones Istmo, 1993. See especially chap. 7.

Schegloff, E., and H. Sacks. "Opening Up Closings." *Semiotica* 8.4 (1973): 289–327.

Schiffrin, D. *Discourse Markers.* Cambridge: Cambridge University Press, 1987.

Schiffrin, D. "The Principle of Intersubjectivity in Communication and Conversation." *Semiotica* 80.1–2 (1990): 121–151.

West, C., and D. H. Zimmerman. "Conversation Analysis." In *Handbook of Methods in Nonverbal Behavior Research,* edited by K. R. Scherer and P. Ekman, pp. 506–541. Cambridge and Paris: Cambridge University Press and Editions de la Maison des Sciences de l'Homme, 1982.

—FERNANDO POYATOS

COPENHAGEN SCHOOL is the name usually given to the structuralist movement in Danish linguistics that developed in the early 1930s around Viggo Brøndal and Louis Hjelmslev. Both Brøndal and Hjelmslev attended the First International Congress for Linguists in The Hague in 1928 and were impressed by the presentation of the structuralist theses of the Prague School and their almost instant international impact. The same year, Brøndal, who had just published *Ordklasserne* (Word Classes), returned to Copenhagen as a professor of Romance philology after several years in Paris, and Hjelmslev published his *Principes de grammaire générale* (Principles of General Grammar).

In the early 1940s, after Brøndal's death, the Copenhagen School became identified with the glossematic theory of Hjelmslev, who published his seminal *Omkring sprogteoriens grundlaeggelse,* of which an English translation titled *Prolegomena to a Theory of Language* appeared in 1953. In the late 1950s, new trends in linguistics shifted the focus of Danish linguists toward T G (transformational generative) grammar. The Copenhagen School has contributed greatly to the development of European semiotics.

The first crucial event was the founding in 1931 of the Cercle Linguistique de Copenhague in cooperation with the Cercle Linguistique de Prague. The circle was characterized by a structuralist orientation marked by the contrasting theoretical approaches of Brøndal and Hjelmslev. It became the focus of discussions bearing on fundamental questions of linguistics. A series of working groups made periodic reports to the plenary forum of the circle. The grammatical and phonological groups were the most active.

The first outcome of these activities was the publication, mostly in French, of the *Bulletin du Cercle Linguistique de Copenhague* (1934–1941, 1944–1965, and 1965–1966), which featured a great variety of topics treated by Danish and foreign contributors who took part in the scientific discussion of linguistic problems. The second major event was the Fourth International Congress for Linguists (Copenhagen, 1936), with Otto Jespersen and Brøndal as the main organizers. The third and most important result of the circle's activities was the foundation of the journal *Acta Linguistica* (1939), coedited by Hjelmslev and Brøndal, which immediately reached an international readership. (The journal has been published under the title *Acta Linguistica Hafniensia* since 1966.) The first four issues featured a series of seminal papers critically addressing the debate on the sign in Saussurean and post-Saussurean linguistics, clarifying the structuralist position and opening epistemological, pragmatic, and philosophical perspectives. From the semiotic point of view, this is the turning point of the activities of the circle. Here, linguistics and semiotics become inextricably linked.

After the tenth anniversary of the circle in 1941 and the death of Brøndal in 1942, Hjelmslev became the unchallenged leader of the Copenhagen School. With his *Prolegomena* as the basic text, the glossematic theory defined the basic questions asked by the school and shaped the guiding principles for concrete linguistic investigations. When *Acta Linguistica* resumed publishing when World War II was nearly over, Hjelmslev was the only editor, and he wrote an editorial with a clear glossematic orientation. Also in 1944, the *Travaux du Cercle Linguistique de Copenhague* resumed publication. Three volumes are of special importance for semiotics: *Recherches structurales* (vol. 5, 1949), celebrating Hjelmslev's fiftieth birthday, contains a series of substantial Danish and international contributions to the glossematic debate; Henning Spang-Hanssen's *Recent Theories on the Nature of the Language Sign* (vol. 9, 1954) presents a glossematic interpretation of the linguistic sign with respect to competing theories; *Essais linguistiques* (vol. 12, 1959) reprints Hjelmslev's essential articles to honor his sixtieth birthday and shows the development of the glossematic theory from the 1930s. Frans Gregersen (1992) provides the most complete account of the Copenhagen School.

The linguistic and semiotic relevance of the Copenhagen School is based both on the works it published and on the intellectual and scientific agenda it promoted. In spite of their differences, both Brøndal and Hjelmslev envisioned a scientific linguistics that was founded on explicit theoretical grounds and that reflected explicitly on the constitution of its object, in both the epistemological and methodological senses. In doing so, they distanced themselves from theoretically naive, positivist, and purely philological preoccupations with language.

However, both approaches show basic unsolved linguistic and semiotic problems. Hjelmslev's method-oriented formalism is combined with a somewhat latent knowledge that a complete methodological explicitness is impossible (because indefinables will always interfere) and that nonformal irregularities exist in the very heart of language. Brøndal's philosophy-oriented linguistics has a precise and comprehensive goal but no clear analytical procedures. When the nonlinguistic constitution of the object is a precondition for linguistic analysis, the immanent description is only half of the linguist's legitimate and necessary task. But then, the whole analysis will have to change every time a critical new detail comes to light.

Brøndal and Hjelmslev made the Copenhagen School address all the crucial questions of modern linguistics and gave it a general perspective that opened new theoretical possibilities for semiotics. Through their differences, they showed the range of the very notion of structure in science, from the deep epistemological sense to its more superficial, methodological aspect. Their demonstration of the applicability of the nature of structure to specific problems in linguistics and semiotics—that of the notion of sign among others—proved to be very influential.

[*See also* Brøndal; Hjelmslev; Prague School; Recent Theories on the Nature of the Language Sign; Recherches Structurales 1949.]

BIBLIOGRAPHY

Gregersen, F. *Sociolingvistikkens (u)mulighed*, 1–2 (The [Im]possibility of Sociolinguistics). Copenhagen, 1992. This book includes a summary in English and an extensive bibliography.

Hjelmslev, L. *Essais linguistiques*. Travaux du Cercle Linguistique de Copenhague, vol. 12. Copenhagen: Nordisk Sprog- og Kulturforlag, 1959.

Hjelmslev, L. *Prolegomena to a Theory of Language*. Translated by F. J. Whitfield. Madison: University of Wisconsin Press, 1961.

—SVEND ERIK LARSEN

COSERIU, EUGEN (b. 1921), Romanian linguist whose work in the history of linguistics and language theory has contributed significantly to the development of modern semiotics. Most notably, he has clarified the history of semiotic notions and written on innovative distinctions that improve upon structuralist dichotomies and on original perspective in the conception of language as a system.

Born in Mihaileni, Romania, and educated in Iasi, Coseriu was exposed to many cultures. After his doctoral work in language (Rome, 1944) and philosophy (Milan, 1949), he taught at the universities of Montevideo, Coimbra, Bonn, Frankfurt, Strassbourg, and Tübingen. He remained interested throughout his academic career in how languages work. Many of his articles focus on structural-semantic aspects related to Romance languages, (Romanian in particular). The experience of this inquiry was, for those not aware of the complexity of his mother tongue, surprising. Although relatively few in number, articles dealing with words in Romanian (as well as some of the many languages in which Coseriu is fluent) are contributions to one of the most disputed aspects of linguistics, and by extension of semiotics: the relation between words and the things they name. Coseriu is well aware of Cratylus's position in Plato's dialogue of that name, according to which there is a physical relation to be accounted for, but he opts for a very nuanced theory of arbitrariness (1967) in which Hermogenes's position in the dialogue is understood within the Aristotelian conception of language. The notion of sign, as generalization of the word, is derived from a linguistic perspective that dominates Coseriu's entire contribution to semiotics.

Other contributions of his to the history of semiotic ideas have been in the area of understanding the model of language in the works of ancient philosophers; in particular, he has demonstrated that this pre-Peircean model is also triadic. He has also analyzed some of the major contributions to semiotic concepts made by, among others, Christian Wolff (1679–1754), under the influence of G. W. Leibniz (1646–1716), and Johann Heinrich Lambert (1728–1777) as well as some of the relevant linguistic contributions to semiotics by Wilhelm von Humboldt (1767–1835) and Pierre-Nicholas Bonamy (1694–1770).

Witness and participant to the post-Saussurean structuralist attempt to define a language theory, Coseriu tested major anthropological and cultural hypotheses in various linguistic contexts. Hjelmslev's sign theory underwent such a test (1962), and as a result Coseriu advanced a more dynamic definition of the dichotomy of form and substance. The same can be said in regard to his differentiation between the Saussurean *signifiant* and *signifié* and even more of his better understanding and use of the dichotomy between synchronism and diachronism. At this juncture, his critical contributions turn into an original perspective.

What in Hjelmslev's work was the complementary dichotomy between system and text becomes in Coseriu's theoretic contributions a dynamic interplay between a revised notion of system and norm. System, in his conception, is more than the sum of all functional structures of language: it contains, in addition, all possible structures that can result from the rules of a language. The potentiality thus introduced ensures its dynamics. The concept of norm reflects precisely the fact that not all that is possible is actually realized. In many ways, Coseriu opens a perspective different from that of Chomsky's dichotomy between competence and performance. Indeed, the norm is a collective instantiation of the system. The individual concrete realization of the norm is the word containing, above and beyond the norm, the expressive originality of speaking individuals. Intent upon reconciling the dichotomy between synchronism and diachronism, Coseriu advances in his model the hypothesis of language functioning synchronically while being constituted diachronically. The result, a coherent structural semantics, markedly different from A. J. Greimas's, is a sort of distillation of historic, methodic, and conceptual contributions.

This original model influenced a number of researchers in fields as diverse as the language of gestures (Meo-Zilio, 1961, acknowledges this influence) and the semiotics of theater (Fischer-Lichte, 1992, distinguishes between theatrical code as a system, norm, and speech). It is likely that more semiotic contributions inspired by Coseriu's writings will be produced in the future.

[*See also* Arbitrariness, Principle of; Hjelmslev; Signification; *and* Synchronic and Diachronic.]

BIBLIOGRAPHY

Coseriu, E. *Sistema, norma, y habla (con un resumen en alemán).* Montevideo, 1952.

Coseriu, E. *Sincronía, diacronía, e historia: Il problema del cambio lingüístico.* Montevideo, 1958.

Coseriu, E. *Teoría del lenguaje y lingüística general.* Madrid, 1962.

Coseriu, E. "Pour une sémantique structurale." *Travaux de linguistique et de littérature* 2.1 (1964): 139–186.

Coseriu, E. "L'arbitraire du signe: Zur Spätgeschichte eines aristotelischen Begriffes." *Achiv für das Studium der neueren Sprachen und Literaturen* 204 (1967): 81–112.

Coseriu, E. *Die Geschichte der Sprachphilosophie von der Antike bis zur Gegenwart: Eine Übersicht.* 2 vols. Tübingen, 1969–1972.

Fischer-Lichte, E. *The Semiotics of Theater.* Translated by J. Gaines and D. L. Jones. Bloomington: Indiana University Press, 1992.

Meo-Zilio, G. *El lenguage de los gestos en el Río de la Plata.* Montevideo: Imprimaría Libertad, 1961.

—MIHAI NADIN

COURSE IN GENERAL LINGUISTICS (*Cours de linguistique générale*, 1916).

Ferdinand de Saussure (1857–1913) was a professor of Sanskrit and of the comparative grammar of Indo-European languages at the University of Geneva when he agreed in 1906 to succeed Joseph Wertheimer as the chair of general linguistics in the same university. Saussure gave three cycles of lectures on the subject of general linguistics between 1906 and 1911. He did not again return to this subject, and in the remaining two years of his life he dedicated himself to a number of problems in Germanic languages and mythology and to the study of Chinese.

After Saussure's death, Charles Bally and Albert Sechehaye, with the help of Albert Reidlinger, worked on the compilation and the publication of the only source that existed for the texts of the *Cours de linguistique générale* (*CLG*) as we know it today: the notes taken by the students who followed Saussure's lecture. A first edition was published in Paris in 1916. Rudolf Engler's important critical edition was published in 1967. Engler's edition is a work of textual scholarship that brings together all of the variant source material and systematically compares it with the edition published by Bally and Sechehaye. Another important source of information about the manuscripts on which *CLG* is based is Robert Godel's *Les sources manuscrites du cours de linguistique générale de F. de Saussure* (1957). Currently, two English-language translations are available: those by Wade Baskin (1959) and Roy Harris (1983). It is doubtful that either of these provide entirely satisfactory solutions for the English reader to the terminological problems documented by Engler and Godel.

The intellectual significance of Saussure's text is often characterized as Copernican. This should not be taken to mean, however, that Saussure alone in-vented either the field of general linguistics or the concept of the linguistic sign. Eugen Coseriu (1958) pointed out that a number of the key concepts in *CLG* such as the distinction between *langue* and *parole* are to be found in works by a number of Saussure's contemporaries and predecessors. These include scholars such as Hans Georg Canon von der Gabelentz, Anton Marty, Franz N. Finck, and Wilhelm von Humboldt. Furthermore, the concept of the sign itself has a long history in the Western grammatical tradition, going back to the Sophist's concern with grammar and rhetoric, the linguistic theories of Plato and Aristotle, the post-Aristotelian Stoics, and the medieval grammatical theories of the Modistae. However, with *CLG*, Saussure is generally credited for having founded twentieth-century structural-functional studies of language and other sign systems.

CLG gives voice to a number of discourses that are woven together and positioned in relation to each other so as to produce the realignment of linguistic theory that Saussure sought to achieve. Saussure's text takes up, responds to, and variously aligns itself with Aristotle's explanation of the sign in terms of *psyche* and *physis*; Jean-Jacques Rousseau's conception of the social contract; Emile Durkheim's sociological theory; the marginalist theory of political economy of the Lausanne school, especially Vilfredo Pareto's separation of the notion of utility from value in that framework; the naturalistic perspective on grammar of the German School of linguistics known as the Neogrammarians; and the nineteenth-century philological tradition of historical comparative linguistics.

Saussure's influence was strong in the first half of the twentieth century. The Soviet semiotician Valentin N. Voloshinov articulated an important critique of Saussure's failure to provide an adequate account of the social determination of sign systems and sign use (1928). Some of the most important early developments of the guidelines Saussure laid down for a structural-functionalist approach to the study of linguistic form and function were elaborated further in the years immediately preceding and following Saussure's death. Vilém Mathesius, an important early exponent of the Prague School of linguistics, articulated a powerful deconstruction of the Saussurean notion of a static synchronic linguistics in his paper "On the Potentiality of the Phenomena of Language" (1911). Mathesius argues that Saussure's notion of synchrony is unable to account for variability, or what Mathesius calls "static oscillation" or "instability at the given period" in language. Mathesius proposes both a critique as well as a further development of the Saussurean distinction between synchronic and diachronic linguistics. Eugen Coseriu's study *Sincronia, diachronia e storia* (1958) is a major reexamination of the Saussurean opposition between synchronic and diachronic studies of language.

Saussure's influence on the Prague School was profound. A good example is Nikolaj S. Trubetzkoy's seminal study *Principles of Phonology* (1939), which starts from the Saussurean premise that oppositions of sound on the phonological stratum differentiate meaningful distinctions on other levels in the linguistic system.

In his *Prolegomena to a Theory of Language* (1943), Louis Hjelmslev proposes a systematic reinterpretation of Saussure's opposition between *langue* and *parole*. Hjelmslev reworks this opposition such that process (text) is the manifestation of system. Hjelmslev further draws out the implications of the Saussurean conception of the linguistic sign; in particular, he produces a more fully articulated view of stratification, which is the core of the Saussurean conception of the sign relation. The influence of these developments continues to be relevant in the linguistic theories of, for example, Sydney M. Lamb and Michael Halliday.

The impact of *CLG* in the first half of the twentieth century, roughly speaking, can be characterized as a further development of disciplinary specializations in structural-functionalist linguistics. The more recent developments and critiques of Saussurean thought have taken place in the broadly defined thematic regions that pass under the rubrics of structuralism and poststructuralism. This has involved the further recontextualizing of *CLG* in relation to a wide range of otherwise discrete disciplines, such as anthropology, ethnology, media studies, narrative theory, music, and architecture. See, for example, the commentaries of Jonathan Culler (1976), Terence Hawkes (1977), and Richard Harland (1987).

The structuralist reading further develops the ontology that Saussure's notion of *langue* leaves implicit. Thus, *langue* is seen by the structuralists as providing the general systemic condition for human experience and subjectivity. The structuralists claim that underlying and unconscious systems of signification and their rules of orderliness constitute the general ways of seeing and doing of the individual members of a given cultural order. Claude Lévi-Strauss, for instance,

explicitly locates these abstract systems and rules in the pregiven and universal structures of the human mind. Roland Barthes's *Elements of Semiology* (1964) is a vigorous attempt within the structuralist tradition to give substance to Saussure's appeal for the development of a more general science of signs, or semiology.

The leading exponent of the poststructuralist problematization of Saussure is Jacques Derrida, who in *Of Grammatology* (1967) undertakes a complex interrogation of the problematic character of the signifier-signified distinction, especially in relation to Saussure's discussion of the distinction between speech and writing. Derrida's analysis has had widespread influence within the fields of literary criticism and narrative theory, though work in this field has moved considerably away from close readings of Saussure's actual text.

[*See also* Arbitrariness, Principle of; Binarism; Deconstruction; Langue and Parole; Linguistic Motivation; Poststructuralism; Saussure; Synchronic and Diachronic.]

BIBLIOGRAPHY

Aristotle. "On Interpretation." In *The Organon*, edited by H. P. Cooke and H. Tredennick, pp. 114–179. London and Cambridge, Mass.: Heinemann and Harvard University Press, 1955.

Barthes, R. *Elements of Semiology* (1964). Translated by A. Lavers and C. Smith. New York: Hill and Wang, 1967.

Coseriu, E. *Sincronia, diacronia e storia: Il problema del cambio linguistico* (1958). Translated into Italian by P. Mura. Turin: Boringhieri, 1981.

Culler, J. *Ferdinand de Saussure*. London: Fontana, 1976.

Derrida, J. *Of Grammatology* (1967). Translated by G. Chakravorty Spivak. Baltimore and London: Johns Hopkins University Press, 1976.

Harland, R. *Superstructuralism: The Philosophy of Structuralism and Post-Structuralism*. London and New York: Methuen, 1987.

Hawkes, T. *Structuralism and Semiotics*. London: Methuen, 1977.

Mathesius, V. "On the Potentiality of the Phenomena of Language" (1911). In *Praguiana: Some Basic and Less Known Aspects of the Prague Linguistic School*, selected, edited, and translated by J. Vachek and L. Dusková, pp. 3–43. Amsterdam and Philadelphia: John Benjamins, 1983.

Saussure, F. de. *Course in General Linguistics*. Translated by W. Baskin. New York and London: McGraw-Hill, 1959.

Saussure, F. de. *Cours de linguistique générale*. Edited by R. Engler. Wiesbaden: Otto Harrassowitz, 1967.

Saussure, F. de. *Cours de linguistique générale*. Edited by C. Bally and A. Sechehaye. Paris: Payot, 1971.

Saussure, F. de. *Course in General Linguistics*. Translated by R. Harris. London: Duckworth, 1983.

Voloshinov, V. N. *Marxism and the Philosophy of Language* (1928). Translated by L. Matejka and I. R. Titunik. New York: Seminar Press, 1973.

—PAUL J. THIBAULT

CRITIQUE OF THE POLITICAL ECONOMY OF THE SIGN, FOR A. Jean Baudrillard's third book, *For a Critique of the Political Economy of the Sign* (1972) continues his earlier structural analyses of the system of object-signs and the ideological genesis of needs in consumer society but takes a critical turn with regard to his methods of analysis. Its eleven essays contain key hypotheses on the limits of structuralist method and the metaphysical faults of Marxian political economy, semiology, and communication theory.

This is Baudrillard's most systematic book because it moves toward a general theory, as summarized in a table of conversions between Marxian political economy and semiology. Following his homological structuration of the commodity and the sign, whose mutation into an "object form" means ultimately that both "are abolished as specific determinations" in what he calls semiurgic society, the table formalizes conversions and reconversions among four logics of value: use value, economic-exchange value, sign-exchange value, and symbolic-exchange value.

Each logic has its own operational principle (utility, equivalence, difference, ambivalence), its own specific determinations (functional, commercial, structural, psychical), and its own forms (instrument, commodity, sign, symbol). The table is interpreted in three clusters: production and consumption (use value and economic-exchange value); transfiguration (use value and economic-exchange value in relation to sign-exchange value); and, most important, transgression (the first three values in relation to symbolic exchange). The first cluster expresses the mutual dependence of the processes of production and consumption in classical and Marxist political economy. The second group entails the systematic identity of material and sign production in virtue of Baudrillard's equation of the commodity and the sign (the structural relation of implication between economic-exchange value over use value equals that of the signifier over the signified, hence economic exchange

is to the signifier as use value is to the signified). The determinations and principles of use value and economic-exchange value are redefined by the coded differential positions and rules of combination by which object signs are manipulated for different kinds of profit (social, aesthetic, etc.). The conversions of transgression indicate the passage from the domain of economic and semiological value to the symbolic, while the reconversions describe the reductive revaluing of symbolic exchange through its reinstrumentalization as a commodity or a sign.

Baudrillard includes symbolic exchange among the other values, although it stands "beyond" all value, in order to define general political economy. Symbolic exchange is virulently antisemiological, and in the wake of its violent "effraction" (break and entry) into the sanctuary of value by means of revolutionary consumptive practices "signs must burn." Baudrillard analyzes the ideological process that defines the contemporary social order in terms of the "semiological reduction" of symbolic relations based upon a transparent, concrete, agonistic, ambivalent, and obligatory pact between persons sealed by an absolutely singular symbol (such as a wedding ring and other ritual objects). When the symbol is reified as a sign whose value emanates from the system, its ambivalence becomes a structural equivalence, rendering social relations of production and consumption abstract and opaque. The symbolic is Baudrillard's revolutionary anthropological antidote to the political economy of the sign, and it challenges signs from the perspective of what they attempt to expel and annihilate.

Central to Baudrillard's critique is his insight into structural form as revealed through the homology between commodity and sign. Exchange value and the signifier have a "strategic value" that is greater than the "tactical value" of use value and the signified. Binary oppositive structuration is never symmetrical since each antecedent term produces its own "alibi" as its consequent term. Use value and the signified are "effects" or "simulation models" of their antecedent terms. They are produced respectively by Karl Marx's analysis of commodity fetishism in terms of exchange value alone, while semiolinguistics privileges the signifier as its principle of circulation and regulated interplay. For Marx use values were "incomparable" and thus not implicated in the abstract logic of equivalence pertaining to exchange value, but for Baudrillard they have a specific code of their own, especially in relation to symbols. Similarly, Baudrillard's signified-referent pairing lacks the metaphysical status and autonomy afforded to it in the tripartite division of signifier-signified-referent precisely because it does not exist "beyond" the shadow of signification.

Baudrillard theorizes that the exclusion of the referent in Saussure's separation of the sign (signifier-signified) from the world entails a "metaphysical representation of the referent." Baudrillard demonstrates this by criticizing Émile Benveniste's relocation of the arbitrariness of the signifier-signified relation to that between the sign (signifier-signified) and the referent. This relocation is possible only by reviving the sign's initial separation from the referent and by repairing it with what Baudrillard calls the "supernatural" provision of motivation. (It matters little whether motivation is affirmed or denied.) Motivation parallels the concept of need in political economy; need is a function of the capitalist system, just as motivation is a function of the sign system. Baudrillard concludes that arbitrariness analyzes nothing whatsoever.

Baudrillard then applies his critique to the Left's faith in revolutionary praxis to effect a critical reversal of the media by liberating its "fundamentally egalitarian" nature perverted by capitalism. The Left fails to analyze the "ideological matrix that communication theory embraces" and thus accepts uncritically a theory that simulates a genuine exchange based on personal and mutual responsibility. Baudrillard demonstrates these shortcomings by focusing on Roman Jakobson's model of communication. Baudrillard hypothesizes that agency has passed into the code that terrorizes communication by positioning the sender and receiver in an "abstract separateness" and privileging the sender. Jakobson's "phatic function," for instance, is for Baudrillard evidence of the distance between the poles and a critical fiction akin to motivation. Jakobson's model reproduces social relations based upon the power of the media to give what cannot be returned except by the simulacral detour of a response (a poll or referendum). Under the guise of admitting ambiguity and even polyvocality, the model excludes an ambivalent exchange between persons. Baudrillard claims that it is the code that speaks, since it dictates the unidirectional passage of information and guarantees the legibility and univocality of the message. The model is therefore ideological rather than scientific and objective.

[*See also* Baudrillard; Binarism; Jakobson's Model of Linguistic Communication; Marx; Materialist Semiotics; *and* Semiurgy.]

BIBLIOGRAPHY

Baudrillard, J. *For a Critique of the Political Economy of the Sign* (1972). Translated by C. Levin. Saint Louis: Telos, 1981.

D'Amico, R. *Marx and the Philosophy of Culture.* Gainesville: University Presses of Florida, 1981.

Giradin, J.-C. "Toward a Politics of Signs: Reading Baudrillard." Translated by D. Pugh. *Telos* 20 (1974): 127–137.

Levin, C. "Baudrillard, Critical Theory, and Psychoanalysis." *Canadian Journal of Political and Social Theory* 8.1–2 (1984): 35–52.

—GARY GENOSKO

CULTURAL DIFFERENCE. The complexity of each of the terms in the phrase *cultural difference* has evoked considerable debate. Raymond Williams (1958) places *culture* among the most complicated words in the English language, noting the intricacies of the word's etymological history. He also attributes *culture*'s difficulty to the quite disparate meanings that it conjures in different intellectual disciplines. In this regard, *difference* enjoys an equally nuanced and controversial existence. Through its foundation in Saussurean semiology, structuralism sought to bring the concepts of culture and difference together. As a consequence, there is some resonance within the field of semiotics between the troubling paradox that marks the inherent identity of the sign and the equally problematic nature of the phrase *cultural difference*.

In the *Course in General Linguistics* (1916), Ferdinand de Saussure argued that meaning is produced through a relational system of differences, a diacritics of form whose "sense" is shared by a community of language speakers. In an attempt to illustrate the arbitrary nature of the sign—that is, that the sign is not anchored to a real world of substance—Saussure ventured several examples dependent upon the language differences that separate one community of speakers from another. He compared, for instance, the idea of sister to the sound *s-ö-r* in French; similarly, he noted that the idea of ox has as its signifier *b-ö-f* in French, which turns to *o-k-x* (*Ochs*) across the German border. This exercise in translation was meant to illustrate that the representation of an idea is arbitrary. As the fact of different language attests, an idea can be evoked just as readily by a variety of different sounds.

However, by installing one common signified (idea) as the anchor for various signifiers (sounds), Saussure inadvertently returned to the logic of nomenclature that he had opposed elsewhere. These examples cut across the grain of Saussure's larger thesis, which insists that signifiers and signifieds are inseparable, mutually constitutive, and derive their meanings from the larger language system in which they are embedded. In order to identify and explain the inner workings of one language system, Saussure seemed compelled to compare it with information internal to another. Saussure repeated this "mistake" when he routinely confused the signified with material reality itself. Later commentators on the *Course*, such as Roman Jakobson and Émile Benveniste, tried to purge Saussure's work of such contradictions only to reproduce them in their own work in more subtle guises.

This confusion is inescapable because the process of translation must interpret difference through comparison. Consequently, the result is always contaminated by an undeclared standard of measurement that, ironically, can only recognize difference through what is identical or similar. Translation renders differences equivalent by removing the density of connections that animate a specific unit of meaning. If a language system is indeed self-referential and autonomous such that translation is always a mistranslation, then the implied problem of relativism looms large within Saussure's argument. Despite appearances, interpretation can never really escape the boundaries of a particular language system.

This problem raises a number of questions about the relationship between language and culture. Such questions are powerfully engaged in the work of Edward Sapir (1884–1939), a linguist and anthropologist whose research in the 1920s formed the beginning of structural linguistics in the United States. Although cut adrift from European developments in linguistics by the disruptions of World War I, Sapir's studies of Native American languages were in many ways consistent with the implications of Saussure's thesis. Sapir argued that language entails a structuring principle that predisposes a community of speakers to perceive the world through very particular "points in the pattern" of their language.

Like Saussure before him, Sapir argued that "the worlds in which different societies live are distinct worlds, not merely the same world with different labels attached" (1949, p. 162). Sapir went further than this, however, suggesting that speakers find it difficult to hear certain distinctions in other languages if the distinctions are foreign to the phonemic structure of their own language. According to this view, language mediates reality in a way that constitutes its very perceptibility. This line of research was developed further by Sapir's student Benjamin Lee Whorf. Based largely on his studies of the Hopi language, Whorf argued that grammatical structures within language, such as tense, have a structuring effect on the way a culture conceptualizes time and space. Consequently, different cultures (language communities) inhabit different configurations of time and space.

This is a radical claim and one that finds more recent expression in the work of American anthropologist Marshall Sahlins. In his provocative essay "Colors and Cultures" (1976), Sahlins proposes that culture conditions color perception. He warns, however, against those who would test this claim by appealing to a universal referent. The bind of a relativist position, as Saussure's confusions illustrate, is that proof of the system's internal coherence and the relativity of its worldview cannot be determined from a position outside that system. Sahlins summarizes this dilemma by asking, "How then to reconcile these two undeniable yet opposed understandings: color distinctions are naturally based, albeit that natural distinctions are culturally constituted?" (1976, p. 22).

Across the Atlantic, Saussure's linguistic legacy was developed further by Roman Jakobson, among others, and adapted by French anthropologist Claude Lévi-Strauss. At the time of their meeting in New York, both scholars were émigrés as a result of World War II. Lévi-Strauss adopted the diacritical, synchronic analysis of Saussurean linguistics and applied it to the broad arena of cultural and social life. Although there has been some debate as to whether the complexity of the linguistic unit, with its double articulation, can actually be transposed onto anthropological data in this way, Lévi-Strauss nevertheless offers an important and provocative perspective on the nature and structure of cultural material. He also went some way toward envisioning the promise of Saussure's "semiology," a science of semiotics in which linguistics, as Saussure himself put it, "will circumscribe a well-defined area within the mass of anthropological facts" (1974, p. 16).

After studying data from tribal societies, Lévi-Strauss argues that there is an underlying structure that articulates the logic of kinship ties, marriage arrangements, eating habits, the spatial arrangements of village and domestic life, the cosmology of myths, and, indeed, all aspects of social, political, and cultural endeavor. Focusing on the presence/absence binary that underpins the Saussurean analysis of phonology, Lévi-Strauss argues that the symbolic order of cultural diversity is figured similarly through binary pairs; culture versus nature, right versus left, male versus female, sacred versus profane, and so on. Lévi-Strauss insists that this compulsion to divide the world into a binary order is not peculiar to tribal societies and is also evident in so-called complex societies, although the contents of the categories are different for each group. For Lévi-Strauss, the origin of the variations in this common design can be traced back to the repository of the human mind. According to this form of structural anthropology, cultural difference is a specific articulation of a universal property that defines the human condition. In other words, relativism is displaced within structuralism because the problematic nature of cross-cultural translation is not conceded.

By reading social and cultural data through the relational interdependence of its terms, Lévi-Strauss questioned the atomism of traditional forms of anthropology, which had focused only on the terms themselves. However, this important intervention suffered from the same conceptual impasse as Saussurean linguistics did. The heuristic necessity to freeze the system or structure in time and to delimit it as an autonomous entity severs language and culture from the dynamics of its own history. Furthermore, structuralism also forecloses any critical discussion about the nature of the interpreting subject. Lévi-Strauss's work certainly implicates the human subject within the dynamic process of difference and transformation that is structuration. But if the subject is subjected, constructed by, and constrained within regimes of differentiation, then the unity of the interpreting subject is also called into doubt. As a consequence, the universalism of structuralism's transcendental perspective is open to critique precisely because the interpreting subject must be located culturally.

The acknowledgment that the interpreting subject is implicated in cultural production heralds a battery of provocations and difficulties that might be gathered loosely under the banner of poststructuralism. Psychoanalysis has been an important and useful approach to the analysis of subject formation, especially as it has been developed by Jacques Lacan's rereading of Sigmund Freud through Saussurean linguistics. Lacan's "literalization of the subject" is enabled by reinterpretation of the Saussurean sign that treats the signifier as autonomous. Lacan's approach places great emphasis on the bar that restricts access by the signifier to the signified. The subject, likened to a signifier by Lacan, slides along a chain of signifiers and never arrives at a final signified; consequently, the subject is never unified. The subject is constituted in a metonymic structure of displacement whose motor, Lacan tells us, is nothing but desire.

Lacan's analysis of the systemic production of difference (as "otherness") has been extremely influential in refiguring the politics of sexual, racial, and cultural equity. Feminists such as Juliet Mitchell, Jacqueline Rose, Julia Kristeva, Luce Irigaray, Jane Gallop, and Elizabeth Grosz have used the work of Freud and Lacan to analyze the inherent masculinism within theories of the subject. Although these theorists are by no means a homogeneous group, each addresses the political and ethical ramifications that attend the production of sexual difference; further, each writer argues that the very notion of equity presumes a masculine norm against which "the feminine" will always be found wanting. The economy through which the other is both feminized and denigrated in the same movement has wider ramifications for all marginal and disempowered subjects. For example, woman was "the dark continent" for Freud, just as Africa and "the primitive other" were sexualized by Western imperialism as entities inviting conquest and penetration. Given that these sexualized and racialized relations produce the very notions of what constitutes identity and difference, the representation of cultural difference has become increasingly problematic. This is why recent writers such as Homi K. Bhabha, Trinh-T. Minh-ha, bell hooks, and Stuart Hall, among many others, seek ways of reinscribing otherness as something that exceeds its diminished value as negativity and lack.

Another poststructuralist approach to the question of cultural difference is exmplified in the work of Gayatri Chakravorty Spivak. Her collection of essays, *In Other Worlds* (1987), takes up the generalized notion of textuality in Jacques Derrida's work and ideas from recent feminist and Marxist interventions in order to explore the problems of representation and postcolonialness. Whereas Lacan's notion of language was restricted to its sense of speech and writing, Derrida's work extends, reinscribes, and displaces the conventional notions of language and text such that they include whatever they would define themselves against. Through Spivak's analysis, conventional notions of where political action or being takes place are provocatively refigured. The representation of cultural difference marks a political complexity whose implications have no simple resolution. Spivak's "way forward" continually underlines its provisional nature and argues that an interpreter's complicity with oppressive structures of representation has to be used and refashioned rather than simply condemned and discarded.

Recent debates around the nature of cultural difference have taken advantage of the broad reach of interdisciplinary material, leading to a loose category of research and inquiry often referred to as cultural studies. This cluster of writings and authors is hybrid in its theoretical allegiances and in the eclecticism of its approach. This, coupled with the diversity of its subject matter, explains why cultural studies is often regarded as a disciplinary synonym for postmodernism in much contemporary literature.

Cultural studies in Britain during the 1960s and 1970s was based at the Birmingham Centre for Contemporary Culture Studies. Although heavily indebted to Marxism, cultural studies became possible only with the critique of Marx's base/superstructure model of society. According to classical Marxist theory, the ultimate determinant of change is located in the economic base of a society, while culture, assigned to the society's "superstructure," is a passive reflection of the forces and relations of economic production. The first move of cultural studies, then, is to grant culture a significant degree of productive efficacy and address the workings of culture on the level of the everyday. Where previously *culture* had been defined by "ruling-class culture"—that is, to the commodification of an elite class's aesthetic tastes in literature and the arts—the Birmingham Centre sought to pluralize the notion of culture and question the assumption that some people "have culture" while others lack it. The diversity of popular culture—the internal differences within one culture that are class specific, age and sex specific, inflected by sexual orientation, race, ethnicity, and geographical location—has become the stuff upon which many

cultural critics now focus their attention. A prominent example of this sort of work is Dick Hebdige's *Subculture: The Meaning of Style* (1979).

Yet these new topics of analysis have also brought new theoretical approaches whose ramifications have split British cultural studies down the middle. Referred to as the "two paradigms" debate following an article by Stuart Hall, the dispute derives from the impact of structuralism in general and the work of Louis Althusser in particular, together with the critique of the unified subject found in psychoanalysis. The importance of these linguistically based theories has been rejected by many critics because the dissolution of the humanist subject seems to erase agency and thereby forfeit the possibility of individual action toward political change. Poststructuralists counter such criticism by explaining that although agency is erased as a causal origin of action, its analytical worth is not discarded but rather made more complex. This split between what Hall calls the culturalist and structuralist positions has emerged in more recent form within American cultural studies, with culturalism gaining dominance over a structuralism informed by Continental philosophy.

The notion of cultural difference refers to both cross-cultural and intracultural differences. The representation of this diversity and the political asymmetries involved have led some critics to focus on the practice of representation itself. In ethnographic studies, the principal practice involved is writing. Postmodern interventions in ethnography, such as the anthology *Writing Culture* (Clifford and Marcus, 1986) offer insights from cultural critics and anthropologists about the politics of representing otherness. Ethnography, they suggest, needs to abandon prose styles that pretend to maintain objectivity and instead explore literary, poetic, and experimental writing genres that capture more faithfully the fieldwork experience. This critique of ethnography, as well as the culturalist approach to cultural studies, tends to confine the question of representation to a question of adequacy. The assumption here is that representation is a practice, an act that represents people and their lifeworlds through the mediation of writing. According to this view, certain writing genres are more faithful than others to the life experiences they describe. Mikhail Bakhtin's notion of "the dialogical" is often invoked as a way to better represent the relationship between the ethnographic subject and the researcher. However, the actual complexity of

Bakhtin's work has yet to be addressed in any form of ethnography, and proposed solutions to the problem of representation have as yet remained in the realm of abstract possibility. Against this, poststructuralist approaches to diference do not perceive the difficulty of its representation in terms of mediation's tendency to be inaccurate. Rather, the problem of the interpreting subject aside, representation is granted a constitutive force within poststructuralism, a force whose economy is politically inflected and whose consequences are material.

Michel Foucault's notion of discourse underscores this complexity in a different way. This notion appears to metamorphose throughout Foucault's work, changing from its linguistic sense of sentence multiplication in speech and writing to include the entire diversity of representational regimes that both constrain and produce objects as knowable. In the genealogies, this might also include regimes of the gaze and of touch, architectural plans, and so on. Foucault argued that discourse constitutes its object as a material entity. He sought to displace the structuralism of Marxism and its depth/surface, base/superstructure model by insisting that power and knowledge are joined together in discourse. Foucault's work is particularly relevant to the question of cultural difference, since a nexus of power and knowledge implies that all forms of discourse—whether traditional forms of anthropology, experimental "new ethnography," or the study of popular culture—constitute rather than merely describe their objects. For Foucault, discourse is not simply repressive, alienating, and inherently denying the truth of a subject who is otherwise excluded or misrepresented; rather, to be the subject *of* knowledge is to be subject *to* knowledge, constituted within a network of power relations that have material effects.

As elaborated in the work of Edward Said and Johannes Fabian, the Foucauldian approach insists that cultural difference is produced discursively. Said (1979) discusses the production of the Orient as the West's other, a sexualized place of fantasy and fear that remains forever burdened by this projected identity. Fabian (1983) discusses the way that different cultures, especially tribal cultures, are represented if they occupy the dead weight of historical time past, as if they are not living cultures with a contemporary identity but a timeless repetition of the West's own transcended origins. Tzvetan Todorov explores similar themes in *The Conquest of America: The Question of the Other* (1982). Within a Foucauldian analysis, attempts to repair the errors of representation become a much more problematic endeavor. The truth itself becomes a product of discursive regimes of power, such that any sense of absolute arbitration is no longer possible. Current engagements with the question of cultural difference now seek to acknowledge the ramifications of these complexities.

[*See also* Binarism; Jakobson; Kristeva; Lacan; Lévi-Strauss; Postcolonialism; Poststructuralism; Saussure; Structuralism; *and* Whorf.]

BIBLIOGRAPHY

Clifford, J., and G. E. Marcus, eds. *Writing Culture: The Poetics and Politics of Ethnography*. Berkeley: University of California Press, 1986.

Fabian, J. *Time and the Other: How Anthropology Makes Its Object*. New York: Columbia University Press, 1983.

Ferguson, R., M. Gever, T. M. Trinh, and C. West, eds. *Out There: Marginalization and Contemporary Cultures*. Cambridge, Mass.: MIT Press, 1990.

Foucault, M. *Power/Knowledge: Selected Interviews and Other Writings, 1972–1977*. Edited by C. Gordon. New York, Pantheon Books, 1980.

Hebdige, D. *Subculture: The Meaning of Style*. New York and London: Methuen, 1979.

Lévi-Strauss, C. *Structural Anthropology*. Translated by C. Jacobson and B. Grundfest Schoepf. London: Allen Lane, 1968.

Sahlins, M. "Colors and Cultures." *Semiotica* 16.1 (1976): 1–22.

Said, E. *Orientalism*. New York: Vintage, 1979.

Sapir, E. *Selected Writings in Language, Culture, and Personality*. Edited by D. G. Mandelbaum. Berkeley: University of California Press, 1949.

Saussure, F. de. *Course in General Linguistics* (1916). Edited by C. Bally and A. Sechehaye. Translated by W. Baskin. London: Fontana Collins, 1974.

Spivak, G. C. *In Other Worlds: Essays in Cultural Politics*. New York and London: Methuen, 1987.

Todorov, T. *The Conquest of America: The Question of the Other* (1982). Translated by R. Howard. New York: Harper and Row, 1984.

Williams, R. *Culture and Society*. London: Chatto and Windus, 1958.

—VICKI KIRBY

CULTURAL KNOWLEDGE varies as to how widely and deeply it is shared within a community. Some forms of cultural knowledge are shared by all members of a group and provide the bases for their shared worldview. This is foundational knowledge and is likely to be learned by infants as part of primary socialization. Foundational knowledge is intersubjective in that it provides a shared framework of knowing upon which most subjective or personal knowing rests.

Contextually distributed forms of knowledge are shared widely but assigned to very specific cultural domains. How to order food in a fast-food restaurant is an American example of such contextually delimited knowledge. Other kinds of cultural knowledge are not fully shared but are socially distributed forms of knowledge related to particular subgroups within a society. Personal knowledge is based on an individual's experience, though it is commonly filtered through culturally standardized models and thus becomes an individual version of cultural knowledge. Even the fantasies of deranged individuals or shamans tend to be culturally recognizable.

Much of our shared knowledge is very limited in detail and comprises what might be termed interface knowledge, which is the minimum knowledge one must have to engage successfully in a cultural domain. Shopping engages interface knowledge in that the shopper must share with the seller a minimum knowledge of how to begin and conclude transactions. Yet the buyer's knowledge of the business is generally far more restricted than that of the seller.

Cultural knowledge also varies in its degree of explicitness. Knowledge is stratified in layers of decreasing consciousness, a fact of great significance for culture theory. Much of our stock of cultural knowledge is tacit knowledge in that it is taken for granted as necessary background to everyday life and is therefore not fully conscious knowledge. While tacit knowledge might under special circumstances come to the surface of awareness, it normally remains preconscious. The more foundational the knowledge, the less it will be open to fully consciousness awareness. Successful negotiation of our everyday worlds requires the placing on background of basic knowledge structures. The study of primary socialization is in part the study of how such knowledge structures become tacitly known.

Focal knowledge, by contrast, is readily available to consciousness. Thus, though the basic cultural script for shopping usually remains tacit, the shopper is more fully aware of such issues as what items are on sale, what is out of stock, and which particular items he or she wants to buy.

Finally, strategic knowledge is the awareness of changing circumstances and a deliberate calculation of appropriate responses. Any shopper who has engaged in bargaining for a desired good must shift to strategic knowledge in order to bargain successfully. It is important to stress that cultural knowledge differs along a gradient of consciousness so that we can speak only of relative tacitness and relatively focal knowledge under specific circumstances. An "ecological" approach to human knowledge needs to characterize the distribution of cultural knowledge in terms of relative tacitness.

In recent years, cognitive science has resurrected schema theory as a way to understand thinking. The mind understands experiences by engaging specific models or schemata through which perception is mediated. Even presumably basic perceptions such as vision or sound are mediated by models. Cultural anthropology has borrowed the idea of schema as a way to relate the objective properties of social institutions to the individual mind. Such institutions are understood as cultural models or cultural schemata and are the basis of cultural cognition. Cultural models come in many forms, and cognitive anthropologists are only beginning to explore the psychological and semiotic implications of different kinds of cultural models. The formulation of an adequate theory of cultural models and their formal properties is one of the most important priorities for psychological and symbolic anthropology. Some of the most important kinds of cultural models are scripts; cultural scenarios; checklists; recipes; verbal formulas; metaphors; taxonomies; prototypes; kinesthetic-image schemata; action sets; and olfactory models.

Cultural scripts tend to be specific to common social situations in which people need to rely on a scripted framework to guarantee smooth interactions. Examples of cultural scripts are "ordering food at a restaurant," "bargaining with a car salesman" or, even, "having an argument with a spouse." While the particulars of these interactions are contingent and responses can be invented on the fly, the general form of the interactions tends to follow a well-defined cultural pattern. Cultural scripts are part of recognizable occasions or situations within a culture. These occasions or cultural scenarios are familiar because they fit general models of occasion types. For most people, everyday life is a series of reenactments because most events can be subordinated to a general model of a cultural scenario.

Checklists are scripts that involve ordered lists of objects or activities that people must engage with or perform repeatedly in the same way. Airline pilots employ checklists prior to takeoff as a way to guarantee that everything is in order in the cockpit. The ritualized reading of such lists is a strategy for trying to guarantee the completion of a crucial task without error.

Recipe knowledge is task oriented like a checklist, but it involves more extensive procedures. Any complex cultural task—like making a tool or the persistent stalking of a game animal—might become standardized in a culture and remembered as a rigid sequence of actions. Recipe knowledge permits successful techniques to be repeated and transmitted to others without having to be rediscovered each time. Some recipes are verbal, while others (like threading a needle) are complex kinesthetic-image schemata (see below).

Human languages all contain verbal formulas that encapsulate a wide range of important cultural knowledges. Verbal formulas take many forms, such as proverbs, nursery rhymes, clichés, and memory aids ("Thirty days hath September . . ."). Verbal formulas often employ poetic resources such as alliteration, rhythm, and rhyme to promote their memorability. Everyday speech is full of metaphors, many of which are not obvious even to the speaker. For instance, metaphors that treat time as a manipulable substance underlie such common sentences as "I don't have *much time* left," "I make $6.50 *per hour*," and I'll see you *at* 8 tonight." The structuring of discourse through metaphor models is a form of tacit knowledge of great importance for understanding the semiotics of culture.

One of the best-studied kinds of cultural model is the taxonomy. Taxonomic models are kinds of knowledge trees underlying much human classification of ordinary experiences. Taxonomies are employed when individuals classify phenomena by the formula "*x* is a kind of *y*." Taxonomies define a wide variety of cultural and cognitive domains. Examples from taxonomic domains from Western culture include clothes, vehicles, colors, diseases, and persons. The classical model of category formation assumes well-defined categories with perfectly distributed semantic components or traits. If classification followed classical models, every object of perception would be defined unambiguously by a taxonomy. But in real-world classification, many phenomena do not fit in this classical model and are only ambiguously classifiable. Such phenomena define fuzzy sets rather than classical categories.

While early research into classification presumed that humans employed culturally specific taxonomies to divide up the world, interest shifted in the 1970s to the role of prototypes in human classification. Prototype models for basic categorizing have been well studied by cognitive psychologists. When we understand something by means of a prototype model, we attempt to compare a novel object or event to a "typical" or "characteristic" form already familiar to us. Many of these prototype models are culturally specific; a robin is is a good prototype model of a bird for most Americans but not likely for members of a tropical culture. Sometimes prototype models are derived from average cases, while in other cases very prominent individuals or events (key exemplars) assume the role of prototype models. Cultural heroes, origin myths, and sacred acts are common cultural-prototype models. Prototype models are the basis of much of our classifying experiences into general categories.

While many cultural models employ language forms, others do not. A kinesthetic-image schema is a cultural model embodied literally. Conventional bodily positions, aspects of muscle tone, or posture or movement can be powerfully infused with cultural meaning. Kinesthetic-image schemata are important ways in which social rank and social relations are modeled. Bowing, sitting postures, stylized ways of movement, and rules controlling physical proximity between individuals in social settings are all important forms of cultural knowledge. Simple, stylized body movements can become integrated into a co-ordinated exchange. When such action sets become standardized, they become cultural models. Action sets appear to be a very basic way in which individuals coordinate relationships. The most primitive action set is undoubtedly the peekaboo game enacted by infants and their caregivers. Hand shaking, clapping games among children, mutual bowing, and embracing are other examples of culturally salient action sets. Complex action sets often in conjunction with other kinds of models form what we normally refer to as ritual.

Kinesthetic-image schemata point up the important role of nonverbal cultural models. It is likely that poorly verbalized senses such as smell are exploited as cultural resources and have a great importance in shaping human experience. Culturally specific orchestrations of senses such as smell, taste, or touch can engage individual understanding in particularly profound ways because they are preintellectual. Incense, perfumes, or oils can create culturally specific olfactory models whose effects on our understanding are as powerful as they are hard to express in words. Olfactory models have not received adequate attention from scholars, probably because scholars, more comfortable with linguistically encoded models, lack the conceptual tools to adequately describe models orchestrated by smell, taste, or touch.

There is a long tradition in anthropology and the philosophy of culture of attempting to characterize the differences between cultural traditions in global terms with significant semiotic and cognitive implications. This is the venerable issue as to whether different kinds of cultural traditions define distinct "modes of thought." One of the earliest and most misunderstood advocates of this global approach to culture and mind was Lucien Lévy-Bruhl (1857–1939). Employing the evolutionary framework common to Victorian anthropology, Lévy-Bruhl distinguished between the scientific thought of so-called civilized peoples and the emotional thought of so-called primitive peoples. Primitive thought for Lévy-Bruhl was prelogical because it employed the principle of "participation," which recognized the projection of mind and intention into what we think of as inanimate matter. Lévy-Bruhl made the crucial error of distinguishing between kinds of humans rather than between modes of thought and cultural representation. His work is thus not taken seriously by modern anthropologists.

It is interesting, however, that the kinds of distinctions Lévy-Bruhl was struggling to articulate have turned up many times in modern writings in more acceptable forms. Semiotic studies of cultural forms have repeatedly suggested a dualistic framework for classifying cultural symbols. For the philosopher Susanne Langer (1895–1986), the relevant distinction is between discursive and presentational forms (1953). Discursive forms as represented by ordinary language have the power to represent almost anything, while presentational forms (such as music or visual arts) can directly present powerful experiences but lack the ability to analyze or comment on them.

For Gregory Bateson (1972) and Anthony Wilden (1972), the key distinction is between analogic and digital codings of cultural forms. Analogic codings

(such as ritual) are constrained to mimic the contours of that which they seek to represent. Digital codings (such as language or numbers) transform experiences into a new but flexible coding where they can be manipulated. British linguist Basil Bernstein once distinguished between restricted and elaborated codes in language. He was interested in class differences in speech resources in Britain, but his distinctions have more general relevance to a semiotics of culture. Restricted codes constrain the freedom of expression but encode a strong relationship of speaker to context or to an authority. Elaborated codes permit the speaker considerable flexibility of expression and consequently less dependence on context for conceptualizing. For example, speech forms dependent upon clichés and verbal formulas are, in Bernstein's terms, highly restricted codes. By contrast, speech forms that employ a wide range of vocabulary, few clichés, and a high proportion of relative clauses constitute a form of elaborated discourse.

These three dichotomies all point to a common distinction in the fundamental semiotic resources of cultural symbols. A semiotic approach to culture suggests that anthropologists need to clarify the nature and cognitive status of these sorts of distinctions. A cognitively oriented semiotics of culture needs to study the relation between what is culturally coded and how it is coded. These general distinctions between analog and digital codings or presentational and discursive forms provide a promising starting point for an integration of cognitive anthropology and semiotics.

[See also Bateson; Bourdieu; Cultural Difference; Culture, Semiotics of; Cultureme; Douglas; Ethnoscience; Habitus; Haptics; Leach; Myths; and Paroemiology.]

BIBLIOGRAPHY

Bateson, G. *Steps to an Ecology of Mind.* Novato: Calif.: Chandler Publishing Company, 1972.

Geertz, C. *Interpretation of Cultures.* New York: Basic Books, 1973.

Haskell, R. *The Psychology of Metaphoric Transformation.* Norwood, N.J.: Ablex Publishing Corporation, 1987.

Lakoff, G. *Women, Fire, and Dangerous Things: What Categories Tell Us about the Mind.* Chicago: University of Chicago Press, 1987.

Langer, S. *Feeling and Form: A Theory of Art.* London: Routledge and Kegan Paul, 1953.

Lévy-Bruhl, L. *Primitive Mentality.* Translated by L. A. Clare. Boston: Beacon Press, 1966.

Obeyesekere, G. *The Work of Culture.* Chicago: University of Chicago Press, 1990.

Shweder, R., and R. LeVine, eds. *Culture Theory: Essays of Mind, Self, and Emotion.* Cambridge: Cambridge University Press, 1984.

Turner, V. *The Forest of Symbols.* Ithaca, N.Y.: Cornell University Press, 1967.

Wilden, A. *System and Structure.* London: Tavistock Press, 1972.

—BRADD SHORE

CULTURAL LANDSCAPE. The most general definition of the cultural landscape is "the natural landscape as altered by human activity." Thus defined, the landscape can be studied from many points of view in addition to the semiotic. Clarence Glacken (1967) has shown that there is a history, one that extends almost as far back as writing itself in the Western tradition, of statements that express the opinion that the changes people make to the physical environment are evidence of the "triumph" of human beings or "civilization" over nature. However, when considering any attempt at reading the landscape, it is necessary to distinguish between the state of mind of the transmitter (i.e., the person or persons who create a particular landscape) and of the receiver (i.e., those who read it). With that caution in mind, we note that the classical writings Glacken cites, together with their oriental counterparts, are the oldest record of the belief that a particular cultural landscape might embody messages that could be read by those who had the eyes to see.

Dating from the same period, we have evidence of buildings that were intended to house the activities by means of which ordinary mortals were to make reliable contact with the gods. Judging by what we know from later periods, there can be no doubt that the architectural form, the orientation, and the location of such buildings can all safely be presumed to embody statements of belief with respect to the relations of the people with the divine. In the case of the cathedrals of medieval Europe, the iconography—the code in which the beliefs were expressed—has been deciphered. With varying degrees of completeness, the same can be said of the temples, mosques, and other holy places of the world's many religions.

When the painters of the Italian Renaissance invented or discovered perspective, they initiated a dialectical process that took many generations to work out. Equipped with the new technique, artists began to paint pictures of rural landscapes in a style of conventional realism. For a painting to be called realistic according to the usages of everyday speech, someone who knows either the painting or the scene it depicts will recognize the other as the scene depicted or as a painting of that scene, respectively. In other words, there is a fairly high degree of isomorphic correspondence between the impact on the retina of the two visual fields. For the artists of the sixteenth and seventeenth centuries, however, it was normal to paint naturalistic landscapes that were in fact products of the artists' imaginations. The qualification *conventional* is added to show that there were conventions, themselves inspired by classical literature, as to what painted landscapes ought to look like.

If the development of that genre of painting is taken to be the thesis, the antithesis developed in England in the eighteenth century as existing tracts of countryside were reshaped chiefly by the removal of "inappropriate" elements (quite often including the houses in which people who lacked the power needed to protect their homes were living) and their replacement with elements deemed appropriate— which is to say, ones whose presence gave to that piece of countryside an appearance that rendered it a suitable subject for a painting of the fashionable type; thus inscribing social forces on landscape.

If the great landowners of England are the first agents to reshape extensive tracts of countryside in pursuit of an ideal rather than for utilitarian purposes, it is among the scholars of the same period that we find the first conscious attempts at what with hindsight we can call semiotic analysis. Both those who sought theoretical explanations of the artistic process underlying painting and those who sought to explain the spatial organizations of cities occasionally argued that there were parallels between artifactual expressions organized in space and the structures of verbal expression.

Landscape as modified nature together with the built environment can convey information in a wide array of domains. The information embodied in the architectural form of a building is transmitted by predominantly arbitrary conventions, as in the case of large edifices intended to house both religious activity (cathedrals, mosques, temples, etc.) and the offices of central government (palaces, legislatures, etc.). In the case of clusters of buildings forming all or large parts of individual settlements, information is carried by means of the spatial pattern composed by the buildings, the streets on which they stand, and often the wall or other boundaries that frame the settlement. The extent to which transmitters are conscious of the techniques they are using is often open to debate. Within this typology, we should include only those settlements where, in order to be able to interpret the message, the receiver must either be a member of the same culture as the transmitter or have acquired an understanding of it equivalent to theirs.

Information can be also transmitted by the form of the building, which itself is a direct consequence of its function. In considering cases of this type, it is assumed that the function of the building is to make it possible for the transmitter to attain some utilitarian goal. The most common case consists of those buildings where the function of the building is to control or even prevent entrance to and egress from it. Such buildings range along a continuum from forts, castles, and prisons to the residences of most towns and cities—indeed, any building where the openings in the exterior walls can be shut, with control available only on the inside or only to the residents or owners. Other cases involve buildings designed to facilitate the observation of activities carried on within them, such as athletic stadiums or Jeremy Bentham's panopticon. An arbitrary element is present in all such cases, but once the class is understood, the occurrence in different cultures can be inferred with some confidence. Since the 1950s, several semioticians have devoted much effort to showing that there are parallels between the formal relations of words and sentences in verbal discourse and the relations of components to buildings and of buildings to yet larger units of the landscape. So far, successes have been partial and those in two ways: first, the identification of formal parallels has been limited to the specific cases studied by individual scholars; general methods have not been found. Second, the ratio of information obtained to effort required to establish the validity of the interpretation (as measured by the length of published text and the density of the special terminology involved) to the information obtained is low. Notwithstanding these criticisms, the work along these lines of Amos Rapoport (1982), Martin Krampen (1979), and Donald Preziosi (1979), among others, commands respect. In an alternative approach, information is transmitted by a mode that is equivalent to figurative speech, but the reading of the information can

then be purely idiosyncratic rather than intended to unravel a formal generative system.

The feature that distinguishes the extensive body of writings that fall under this approach is that little or no attempt is made to justify the reading. The receiver simply asserts, for example, that "une contrée devient à la longue une médaille frappée à l'effigie d'un peuple" (a country eventually becomes a medal engraved with the portrait of its people). Though Vidal de la Blache, who wrote these words in 1903, is credited with the foundation of modern human geography in France and is widely perceived as a precursor of contemporary humanistic geography, this statement of his has not merely been taken by geographers to be a metaphor; rather, metaphors themselves are now taken to be "poetic." In other words, they are perceived as being decorative rather than as conveying significant meaning.

It is not only geographers who have dismissed metaphors as uninteresting; most social scientists have done the same. Despite this general hostility toward figurative speech, a number of scholars have offered interpretations of buildings or of whole landscapes that have commanded wide respect: Sigfried Giedion (1967), Lewis Mumford (1964), William George Hoskins (1955), John B. Jackson (1979), Charles Jencks (1984), and Paul Wheatley (1971) are probably the best known. Their writings are persuasive at the time of reading, and it is reasonable to believe that their examples were influential in inspiring the search for formal parallels between the "texts" formed by landscapes and verbal texts.

Combining insights from cybernetics, neuropsychology, linguistics, structuralism, and developmental psychology, it can be argued persuasively that the spontaneous form of human thought is the creation of images that function as models of the environment (widely understood) of the thinking individual. It might be helpful to think of these models as being more like gestalts than like the monistic concepts that the term *image* suggests. This view forms the core of the biostructuralism advocated by Charles Laughlin and Eugene d'Aquili (1974). They argue that, beginning in infancy, individuals work their ways through a four-stage process. First, they create gestalt models of the environment. Next, they manipulate the models in order to predict how their relationships with the environment will change if they behave in particular ways. Third, they compare what happens against what they have predicted. Finally, providing the individuals survive the consequences of their misinterpretations, they modify their models in the light of what happened.

Putting it in other words, the act of thinking, in this view, consists of the operation of neurognostic structures—bioelectronic structures formed by and between the neurons of the brain. Neurogenetic structures extend from relatively simple types that contain the data of long-term memory to the vastly more complex ones that function in effect as programs that control the data of memory. Each newborn child comes equipped with a relatively small number of programs (e.g., those that control the beating of the heart) and what Laughlin and d'Aquili call the "seeds" of others that will, under normal circumstances, evolve into those that control overt behavior, including speech, as well as all those necessary for the functioning of the adult brain. The control programs that evolve during infancy endure for the remainder of life. Examples include those needed to place the lips and tongue in the positions needed to generate the sounds used in language. Control over voicing and pitch must also be programmed in this way, of course.

When the ability to form gestalt models is considered in the light of evolutionary pressures, it is reasonable to argue that the critical capacity is that of forming accurate representations of the environment. The basic capacity involved is that of making judgments of the similarity or dissimilarities between items in memory and objects perceived in the environment (in other words, classification). Given the ability to make such judgments and to express them in speech, we can now argue that everything else in human intelligence follows through the elaboration, refinement, and proliferation of gestalt models. As a striking instance of this proposition, George Lakoff and Mark Johnson (1980) have shown that it is not necessary to postulate an innate concept of causation. Because this concept can be expressed in a single word, it is easy to think that it cannot be reduced to yet simpler components. However, as Lakoff and Johnson show, it is a complex gestalt model that infants could form through the repeated experience of manipulating objects within their reach.

When it comes to the capacity for logical argument, a similar situation prevails. In the form associated with adult life, it is not innate. All that the infant can do is judge whether two objects are like

or unlike or whether an object is similar or not to a gestalt model. With that power comes metaphorical thought; that is, the form of thought we call metaphorical is among the spontaneous capacities that come with our genes. In the words of Lakoff and Johnson; "Our ordinary conceptual system, in terms of which we think and act, is fundamentally metaphorical in nature" (1980, p. 3). They go on to consider a wide range of metaphors and argue that it is partly through their use that we organize our strategies for dealing with the world. It is noteworthy that they offer no explanation of either why we do this nor why certain metaphors appear to be quasi-universal features, occuring in most languages. They do claim that their explanation of human understanding rests on an experiential base, but they admit: "We do not know very much about the experiential bases of metaphors" (1980, p. 19).

That deficiency can be overcome in the case of some key metaphors by incorporating the biogenetic structuralism of Laughlin and d'Aquili and focusing attention on infancy and early childhood. During those years, the following elements are associated: children learn their mother tongue through interaction with the adults on whom they depend; that language not only contains expressions relating to essential needs but also incorporates statements of value; as values do not exist in material form, the statements are necessarily metaphorical; during the period when they are building up the gestalt models and control programs associated with the ability to speak their mother tongue, children have certain physically necessary relations with the adults upon whom they depend.

For instance, let us consider metaphors of height, which are commonly used as signs for (positive) values. We can now see why: first, when infants are small, their brains form fundamental programs and data banks of speech and value; second, they do so by absorbing from the specifically linguistic elements in their environment forms of speech in which height is used as the code for positive value. Because the conditions are found worldwide, the joint operation of the Laughlin-d'Aquili and Lakoff-Johnson processes allow us to predict that in all cultures, not just in those where English is spoken, height will be used as a metaphor for value. Drawing on Laughlin and d'Aquili, though independent of Lakoff and Johnson, Sitwell (1981) argued that metaphors of height, centrality, and durability are routinely found embodied in buildings and settlements as signs of the values held by the people responsible for those particular built environments. In the case of height, research reviewed by Ellis (1992) not only cites evidence derived from controlled observations that confirms the strength of the association with power and status but also provides further theoretical justification on the basis of strategies for mate selection used by heterosexual women.

Not the least interesting feature of these metaphors of the landscape is the fact that they hold across the boundary separating traditional societies from free-enterprise, market-driven ones. This can be shown easily by considering the case of the joint operation of height and centrality to mark the location of the most important operations carried on in both sets of societies. In the case of Western societies, it is generally maintained that tall buildings are found in the central districts of our cities because of the operation of market forces on real-estate values. That is true, but it is not the whole truth. In order that anyone should want to build the skyscrapers that house the key operations that provide the economic energy that powers the world of business, it is first necessary that people believe that the primary goals of life are the creation of material goods and the pursuit of personal wealth. The towers that scraped the skies of societies whose goals were set by the values associated with traditional religions were those of churches, temples, and mosques. The commercial towers of our cities were not built until after the value systems of traditional societies were abandoned and replaced by those of modern times. Once the profit-making capacity of land bought and sold in a free market had become a socially legitimized value, commercial towers made financial sense, provided that they were located at the centers of central places (which is the geographers' name for our large cities).

While there is still plenty of scope for further research into the ways in which metaphors of height, centrality, and durability have been embodied in specific landscapes, there are far greater opportunities in examining the interrelations of metaphors with the capacity of the individual to identify with others. Though identification is a psychological process, psychologists have paid little attention to it. It does, however, play a central role in the theory of Peter Berger and Thomas Luckmann (1966) relative to how societies are formed and construct the social realities that then shape subsequent generations. The results of this process have been revealed in a number of preindustrial societies in the analyses of Claude Lévi-Strauss and more recently by Fiske (1983), who discusses modern urbanized societies. Moreover, both of these scholars discuss instances where sets of conceptual binary oppositions are reproduced in the landscape. Such research might perhaps be reconciled with that of Mark Gottdiener (1995). In his sociosemiotics he argues for the adoption of Charles Sanders Peirce's approach, with its obligation to include a material referent in theoretical analysis. His reading of the landscape formed by the giant shopping malls of North America is relatively accessible to the nonspecialist.

[See also Architecture; Cultureme; Distance; Image and Picture; Mindscape; Pictorial Semiotics; Space; Urban Semiotics; and Zen Gardens.]

BIBLIOGRAPHY

Berger, P. L., and T. Luckmann. *The Social Construction of Reality: A Treatise in the Sociology of Knowledge.* New York: Doubleday, 1966.

Ellis, B. J. "The Evolution of Sexual Attraction: Evaluative Mechanisms in Women." In *The Adapted Mind: Evolutionary Psychology and the Generation of Culture,* pp. 267–288. New York: Oxford University Press, 1992.

Fiske, J. "Surfalism and Sandiotics: The Beach in Australian Popular Culture." *Australian Journal of Cultural Studies* 1 (1983). Republished in John Fiske, *Reading the Popular* (Boston: Unwin Hyman, 1989) as "Reading the Beach," pp. 43–76.

Giedion, S. *Space, Time, and Architecture.* Cambridge, Mass.: Harvard University Press, 1967.

Glacken, C. J. *Traces on the Rhodian Shore: Nature and Culture in Western Thought from Ancient Times to the End of the Eighteenth Century.* Berkeley: University of California Press, 1967.

Gottdiener, M. *Postmodern Semiotics: Material Culture and the Forms of Postmodern Life.* Oxford: Blackwell, 1995.

Hoskins, W. G. *The Making of English Landscape* (1955). Harmondsworth, England: Penguin, 1986.

Jackson, J. B. *The Interpretation of Ordinary Landscapes: Geographical Essays.* Edited by D. W. Meinig. New York: Oxford University Press, 1979.

Jencks, C. *The Language of Postmodern Architecture.* New York: Rizzoli, 1984.

Krampen, M. *Meaning in the Urban Environment.* London: Pion, 1979.

Lakoff, G., and M. Johnson. *Metaphors We Live By.* Chicago: University of Chicago Press, 1980.

Laughlin, C., and E. d'Aquili. *Biogenetic Structuralism.* New York: Columbia University Press, 1974.

Mumford, L. *The Highway and the City.* New York: The American Library, 1964.

Preziosi, D. *The Semiotics of the Built Environment.* Bloomington: Indiana University Press, 1979.

Rapoport, A. *The Meaning of the Built Environment: A Nonverbal Communication Approach.* Beverly Hills, Calif.: Sage, 1982.

Sitwell, O. F. G. "Elements of the Cultural Landscape as Figures of Speech." *Canadian Geographer* 25 (1981): 167–180.

Wheatley, P. *The Pivot of the Four Quarters: A Preliminary Enquiry into the Origins and Character of the Ancient Chinese City.* Chicago: Aldine, 1971.

—O. F. G. SITWELL

CULTURE, SEMIOTICS OF. For anthropologists, the term *culture* refers to any conventional arrangements communities use as adaptations to their surroundings. Whereas genetic adaptations are controlled and transmitted organically through DNA, cultural adaptations are invented and learned conventions transmitted between individuals and generations by language and other shared symbolisms. *Culture* is a kind of umbrella term that covers a multitude of learned, conventional adaptations. Clearly, no one has ever exhaustively documented the complete range of cultural forms for even a single community.

A semiotic approach to culture views culture as a knowledge system. From this perspective, cultural forms have both symbolic and cognitive dimensions. As symbolic forms, culture comprises a set of objectively observable public institutions. A particular kind of handshake, a set of kinship terms, a method of preparing sago, an origin myth, an arrangement of house space, a conception of femaleness are all examples of possible cultural conventions. As a cognitive construct, culture comprises forms of knowledge embodied in cognitive models or schemata. It is by means of cultural schemata that objective cultural forms become available to the mind as one of its constituting features. Culture thus has a kind of double life as an objective social fact in the world and as a dimension of subjective experience. A semiotic view of culture invites us to bridge these perspectives.

Semiotic approaches to culture focus on culture as a set of meaning systems rather than as a set of purely functional strategies. Cultural institutions are assumed to have distinctive formal properties as sign systems or codes. A semiotics of culture assumes that meaning entails shared symbolic forms. It presumes, moreover, that what we know is dependent on how we know it. The formal character of cultural codes is intrinsic to cultural meaning. Culture has been treated as a kind of knowledge in at least seven distinctive theoretical traditions: symbolic analysis; structuralism; cybernetics; Peircean analysis; psychoanalytic analysis; ethnoscience; and discourse analysis. While each approach is represented in relatively "pure" fashion by particular scholars, it is important to recognize that anthropologists often move opportunistically among these traditions as they seek ways to analyze cultural materials.

1. Symbolic analysis is associated with the work of David Schneider, Clifford Geertz, and Victor Turner. Drawing on seminal works of Max Weber and Emile Durkheim and on Ruth Benedict's notion of culture as symbolic patterns, symbolic analysis deals with culture viewed as a coherent assemblage of symbolic productions. Symbolic anthropologists explicate clusters of key cultural symbols and their meanings and uses. Cultural institutions are treated as analogues to texts in literary analysis. The aim of symbolic analysis is thus to "open up" the text analogues to hermeneutic analysis by exploring the various meanings of key symbols as revealed in different cultural contexts. Symbolic analysis focuses on the explication of important cultural domains such as kinship categories, concepts of person, gender, space, and time.

2. Structuralism is a theoretical tradition associated with French anthropologist Claude Lévi-Strauss and the Swiss linguist Ferdinand de Saussure. Like symbolic analysis, structuralism treats cultural forms as text analogues. Structuralists take the linguistic analogy more literally, however, and have borrowed their analytic techniques from structural linguistics, especially from structural phonologists of the Prague School. Structuralists distinguish between surface features of cultural forms and the underlying deep structure. It is the stable and more universal deep-structural forms that structuralism seeks to uncover in its approach to cultural forms.

Structuralists tend to assume that cultural productions are compromise formations. Culture reflects the attempts of minds to resolve existential dilemmas by proposing contradictions in the form of binary oppositions and then proposing symbolic mediations of those oppositions. Of particular importance for Lévi-Strauss is the distinction between nature and culture (1963). In contrast to the cultural relativism of symbolic analysis, structuralism tends toward the discovery of universal symbolic processes and symbolic forms. It is also strongly rational in its attention to conceptual dualisms and intellectualist in its focus on logical structures rather than on everyday acts and meanings.

3. *Cybernetics* was introduced into anthropology through the work of Gregory Bateson. Bateson was influenced by work in the emerging fields of cybernetics and information science, particularly that of Norbert Weiner. A cybernetic approach to cultural analysis treats culture as an information system aimed at maintaining a social system within an adaptive set of parameters. Viewed in this way, culture becomes a symbolic dimension of human ecology, a way of regulating relations of people to one another and to their environments.

Bateson's early work focused on rituals in New Guinea, which he treated as a set of messages for the standardization of male and female ethos. Roy Rappaport used Bateson's approach to analyze the function of a ritual complex in New Guinea as a regulator of warfare, population size, and food resources (1967). Cybernetic analysis also stresses symbolic interaction as a form of cultural learning. Social institutions are seen as embodying significant cultural messages that serve to inculcate and reinforce significant kinds of relationships.

4. *Peircean analysis* derives from the semiotic theory of Charles Sanders Peirce. Peirce outlined an elaborate framework for the analysis of signs. While few anthropologists have exploited the full range of his complex schemata of cultural analysis, Peirce's distinctions between iconic, indexical, and conventional signs have proved very useful for anthropologists. Iconic signs (such as maps or pictures) are those in which there is a relationship of formal similarity between a signifier and its referent. They are metaphoric in structure. Indexical signs (as smoke is to fire) point to (or index) their referents as symptoms rather than as analogues. Indexical signs thus establish metonymic rather than metaphorical relations. Finally, conventional signs (Peirce called them legisigns) stand for referents only by virtue of a conventional agreement of a community. Peirce's schema has an important advantage over Saussure's notion of arbitrary signs in that Peirce recognized that only some signifiers were arbitrarily related to their referents. His framework points out a range of connections between signifier and signified and different degrees of what linguists call symbolic motivation. While purely conventional signs are not motivated, iconic and indexical signs are. Peirce provides a firm basis for a theory of symbolic motivation.

5. *Psychoanalytic analysis* of culture derives from Sigmund Freud's seminal work on dream symbolism. Psychoanalytically oriented anthropologists treat cultural forms as culturally constituted defenses, subject to the same sort of symbolic analysis as the psychological fantasies of individuals. Psychoanalysis shares with structuralism the assumptions that cultural forms are compromise formations and that they embody hidden meanings. Psychoanalytic analysis presumes that the content of collective (i.e., cultural) representations will reflect the same sort of problems (mainly Oedipal) that analysis reveals for individual mental life. Moreover, cultural and personal symbols are understood to be subject to the same kinds of symbolic processes, such as repression, condensation, reaction formation, projection, and denial.

In recent years, in an influential series of books and papers using data from Sri Lanka, Gananath Obeyesekere has attempted to revise the psychoanalytic approach to cultural symbolism in the direction of cultural relativism. For Obeyesekere (1990), "psychogenetic" symbols are those that have originated in someone's psyche but have lost their personal force and become conventionalized as purely public symbols. "Personal symbols," by contrast, retain a powerful link with the individual psyche even as they employ expressive forms recognizable to members of the individual's community.

6. *Ethnoscience* studies the way in which different languages map specific domains of experience through terminological systems. Ethnoscience focuses on domains of experience that linguistically are highly encoded in elaborate terminologies. Kin terms, color terms, disease classifications, and plant and animal classifications are favorite subjects of ethnoscience.

Because ethnoscience treats cultural knowledge only insofar as it is modeled by vocabulary terms, it is yet another variant on the text analogue of culture. As an approach to cultural semiotics, it bears close relations to prototype theory and category theory in cognitive psychology. Ethnoscience understands culture as a set of linguistic models, organized hierarchically as taxonomies. Taxonomies are defined in relation to a set of semantic components that might be present in different combinations in different terms of a set. For example, kin terms might be broken down into semantic primitives such as gender, lineality, generation, sex, seniority, and so on. Like distinctive features in the production of language sounds, these primitives may be represented as either present or absent, so that each term becomes a bundle of binary features.

Practitioners of ethnoscience are split on how universal they assume these semantic primitives are. More universalist models presume a common stock of semantic primitives that are distributed differently in different language communities. More relativist versions of ethnoscience recognize that the very semantic components themselves might vary from culture to culture and that one may not even presume equivalent domains for comparison.

7. *Discourse analysis* treats cultural forms as the contingent and ongoing production of speech and writing. Rather than seeking to discover in cultural institutions timeless and hidden structures of meaning, discourse analysis understands bits of narrative in everyday discourse as the constitutive units of culture. This view of culture has been shaped strongly by what has come to be called poststructuralism. Of great importance here is the work of writers such as Mikhail Bakhtin, Michel Foucault, Anthony Giddens, and Pierre Bourdieu. Discourse analysis understands cultural meaning as negotiated, unstable, and always contested. For this reason, "dialogue" replaces text as the key metaphor for culture.

Central to traditional semiotic approaches to culture is the notion of worldview. Worldview presumes that reality is at least in part a cultural construction. It assumes that members of distinct cultural groups live in distinct life worlds. A worldview includes complex, specific understandings of such basic components of reality as time, space, causality, person, gender, origins, life, and death. A worldview provides for members of a community a shared horizon of expectations and a framework for anticipating and interpreting experience.

Yet the nineteenth-century idea of worldview (weltanschauung) raises a set of important issues for a semiotics of culture. How coherent, in fact, is a worldview? Does each culture contain only one? Is a

worldview shared equally among all members of a community? Or does any given account of reality within a culture presume other, contested visions that might not be given full expression in public culture? These issues are important for any semiotic theory of culture. They suggest that cultural knowledge can be shared within a community in different ways and to different degrees. Anthropology has yet to develop an adequate conception of cultural knowledge to handle these issues. While culture presumes some degree of shared knowledge, it is evident that cultural forms are not all shared in the same way or to the same degree.

[*See also* Bateson; Cultural Knowledge; Cybernetics; Discourse Analysis; Douglas; Ethnoscience; Foucault; Leach; Lévi-Strauss; Peirce; Structuralism; *and* Turner.]

BIBLIOGRAPHY

Barth, F. *Ritual and Knowledge among the Baktamen of New Guinea.* New Haven: Yale University Press, 1975.

D'Andrade, R. G. "Cultural Meaning Systems." In *Culture Theory: Essays on Mind, Self, and Emotion,* edited by R. Schweder and R. LeVine, pp. 88–119. Cambridge: Cambridge University Press, 1987.

Daniel, E. V. *Fluid Signs.* Berkeley: University of California Press, 1984.

Feld, S. *Sound and Sentiment: Birds, Weeping, Poetics, and Song in Kaluli Expression.* Philadelphia: University of Pennsylvania Press, 1982.

Fernandez, J. W., ed. *Beyond Metaphor: The Theory of Tropes in Anthropology.* Palo Alto: Stanford University Press, 1991.

Hanson, F. A. *Meaning in Culture.* London: Routledge and Kegan Paul, 1975.

Holland, D., and N. Quinn, eds. *Cultural Models in Language and Thought.* Cambridge: Cambridge University Press, 1987.

Lévi-Strauss, C. *Structural Anthropology.* Translated by C. Jacobson and B. G. Schoepf. New York: Basic Books, 1963.

Lévy-Bruhl, L. *The Notebooks on Primitive Mentality.* Translated by P. Riviere. Oxford: Basil Blackwell, 1975.

Lotman, Y. *Universe of the Mind: A Semiotic Theory of Culture.* Translated by A. Shukman. Bloomington: Indiana University Press, 1990.

Munn, N. "Visual Categories: An Approach to the Study of Representational Systems." *American Anthropologist* 68 (1966): 936–950.

Obeyesekere, G. *The Work of Culture: Symbolic Transformation in Psychoanalysis and Anthropology.* Chicago: University of Chicago Press, 1990.

Rappaport, R. *Pigs for Ancestors: Ritual in the Ecology of a New Guinea People.* New Haven: Yale University Press, 1967.

Shore, B. *Culture in Mind: Cognition, Culture, and the Problem of Meaning.* Oxford: Oxford University Press, 1996.
—BRADD SHORE

CULTUREME. Any portion of cultural behavior apprehended in signs of symbolic value that can be broken down into smaller units or amalgamated into larger ones is referred to as a cultureme. This term was coined by Fernando Poyatos (1976), who developed this microanalytic method for the systematic analysis of a culture within any discipline.

Most cultural patterns are not the same in urban societies as in rural ones. For instance, people behave and communicate differently in differing circumstances. Besides the realm of social interactions, the urban and the rural worlds form distinct sensorial environments that sometimes diverge radically in the ways they are perceived. Both aspects offer two principal domains: exterior and interior. These dichotomies yield a grid of the four basic zones—urban-exterior, urban-interior, rural-exterior, and rural-interior—that constitute the four basic culturemes. Through them, a given culture can be characterized, albeit in a rather impressionistic way.

After differentiating these four basic zones, it becomes apparent that any culture that has reached a certain degree of complexity offers two more broad domains in each of the above basic areas: the people's artifactual and natural environments, which not only shape their behaviors but are in turn shaped (culturized) by those behaviors. For instance, the study of greeting behaviors between pedestrians in urban settings depends on aspects of the artifactual environment, such as the width or narrowness of the streets, that condition the frequency and nature of the greetings. These two broad environmental and behavioral subdivisions of each of the four basic culturemes constitute primary culturemes. An analysis in terms of these eight basic categories allows for an intermediate level of study between the comprehensive basic zones and the progressively finer presentation of the more specific stages that offer a deeper understanding of culture. We might examine urban-interior culture in the United States or Spain without specifying various settings for a general overview of the more active manifestations of a culture, as contrasted with the more static, human-created ones: proxemics in closed spaces, loudness of voice and other obvious paralinguistic features, and so on. Here

there is a need for some kind of structural framework. We could apply the linguistic framework proposed by Edward Hall (1959)—"isolates," "sets," and "patterns"—but at this stage we would not require units below patterns (e.g., the social function of porches in the Spanish small-town square); we would recognize certain sets (clapping or hissing as a beckoning signal for a waiter in a Spanish sidewalk café) but hardly any isolates (such as the position of the hands in clapping for the waiter). This stage can be experienced as part of the acculturation process through either systematic learning or observation. At this point, there are two methodological options: classification by topics, referring either to settings (the street, the park, the bus stop, the sidewalk café) or to social patterns (general proxemic behavior, clothes); or the sensible-intelligible approach through which we perceive culture sensorially (e.g., smells, sounds, kinesthetic experiences) and intellectually (e.g., uses of time, employer-employee relations). As soon as we initiate a process of acculturation (a term applicable not only to an immigrant or a diplomat but also to a traveler and a participant-observer doing fieldwork), we are also starting a process of involvement that may vary considerably cross-culturally. At first, we do not acknowledge any hierarchy or classification of sensory perceptions but simply sense them in a sort of cultural amalgam. At the same time, our culturally shaped intellect begins to discern cultural patterns (Hall's sets), such as the characteristics of the customer-waiter relationship.

Much more refined analysis comes from breaking down each primary cultureme into as many settings as we can find in a given culture—such as the home, the church, the school, the bar, the restaurant, the square, the stadium—as long as we do not ignore their interrelationships, each of them being now a secondary cultureme that naturally can also be approached through the various sensible and intelligible channels. This systematic progression toward a finer and finer apprehension of various cultural subsystems is similar to the process of observational learning in acculturation. For example, studies of the home (within "urban-interior-environmental") would outline the layout of the rooms, the proxemic arrangement of formal and informal space, and so on until at the very end of "visual perception" we could deal, for instance, with peripheral vision as a perceptual modality in a single cultureme: that is, as "visual culture in the home"; later, as a "derived culrureme," an even more critical study could deal exclusively with "peripheral visual perception as related to spatial arrangement," also as a separate cultureme in itself. Similarly, we might study "postural behavior in a working class home," but we could hardly do it competently without first considering the general behavior of the laborer's class in the home as a setting (secondary cultureme) and then the visually perceived patterns in that setting (tertiary cultureme), both behavioral (kinesics, proxemics, etc.) and environmental (style and arrangement of furniture, temperature). Later, we might address the kinesic repertoire (derived cultureme 1) and finally the kinesic repertoire in the same setting (derived cultureme 2), from which we could go into postures displayed by the same people in front of certain other people and so on. We should not, therefore, bypass secondary, tertiary, and derived culturemes—for instance, trying to carry out a minute analysis of "eye contact at the table between upper-class hosts and middle-class guests" without progressively studying first their kinesic behavior in such a situation (derived cultureme 1), their general kinesic repertoires (derived cultureme 2), the other visually perceived systems such as proxemics (tertiary cultureme), and the urban-interior human behavior of those two groups in the home (secondary cultureme). It is at this level of secondary culturemes, however, that we begin to identify certain interrelationships among different cultural systems and subsystems (paralinguistic, kinesic, behavior in face-to-face interaction, proxemics, gender values, etc.), while some borderlines between various subcultures within the same culture, geographically as well as socially, begin to show themselves more distinctly.

In this progressive probing of cultural layers in search of signs and sign complexes, there is a breakdown of each secondary cultureme into smaller tertiary culturemes, thus limiting the span of our analysis but adding substantially to its depth. Here the sensible-intelligible approach allows for an even more systematic classification because each sensible or intelligible compartment is analyzed as a separate unit—for instance, "urban-interior-behavioral-acoustic: the home" or "kinesic behavior in the urban American home." It is at this stage, when we have gone as far as isolating not only the various settings against which people develop a great number of behaviors at different levels but also those behaviors, that we may identify with a reasonable amount of

accuracy two important elements: (1) cultural systems, since after observing, for instance, the urban-interior-human-visual culture as reflected in the home, the school, the church, the university, the theater, the funeral parlor, the barbershop, and elsewhere, we have enough material to deal with systems such as furniture or proxemic arrangement of interior spaces across one whole culture; and (2) subcultures, both geographical (horizontally) and social (vertically). After studying "urban-interior-environmental-visual culture in the home" as one single cultureme in different areas of the country, the differences and similarities will usually stand out quite clearly. At the same time, we can differentiate the interior or their respective kinesic repertoire of the upper-class home from one of the working class. If we acknowledge Hall's categorizations of cultural units, we realize that sets and patterns become more obvious—the types of chairs, of pictures on the walls that constitute certain norms in upper- or middle-class homes—while isolates (i.e., the typical brass or silver reproduction of *The Last Supper* hanging in many Italian or Spanish middle- and lower-class dining rooms) are generally not identified until later on.

Derived phases come after this point, when, pursuing our progressive analysis, we can once more break down the last unit we isolated, a tertiary cultureme such as "urban-interior-environmental-visual: the home," into smaller ones. We could focus on each manifestation of that communicative modality, in this case the visual: clothes, kinesics, and proxemics (previously included with a tertiary cultureme), each of which is an individual derived cultureme. Kinesics, for instance, would specify the behavior in the living room, at the table, and elsewhere, thus offering the possibility for finer further analysis. The first type of derived cultureme concentrates on specific areas, such as "kinesics at the table," which would refer to formal or informal meals according to the social status of both hosts and guests. Thus, should we require more critical distinctions, we would go into a more specific category. "Kinesic behavior of upper-class hosts and guests" or "upper-class hosts and middle-class guests" would now be dealt with as second-level derived culturemes. Formal and informal encounters around the table would also display characteristic social techniques: table manners, silverware, individual plates or just a large one in the center, use of glasses or a common container, use of napkins, and so on.

On an even further subdivided level would be

"upper-class eye contact behavior at the table." For the sake of orderliness, within the area of human behavior, separate levels of derivation can be assigned to language, paralanguage, kinesics (movement), proxemics (space), chronemics (time). Each time we deal with a different cultureme, such as "eye contact," it is possible to build up a whole class—for instance, "eye-contact behavior in exteriors and interiors in urban and rural settings"—made up of segments carefully and progressively analyzed at different levels. In addition, the relationships between different systems, which began to appear after the analysis of tertiary culturemes, can now be studied in great detail: "relationship between eye contact and proxemic behavior at the table according to social status" in a given culture; "relationship between proxemics and architecture"; "relationship between kinesthetic involvement and architectural style"; "relationship between peripheral vision and architectural style"; and many others.

[See also Conversation; Cultural Knowledge; Habitus; and Nonverbal Bodily Sign Categories.]

BIBLIOGRAPHY

Hall, E. T. The Silent Language. New York: Doubleday, 1959.
Poyatos, F. "Analysis of a Culture Through Its Culturemes: Theory and Method." In The Mutual Interaction of People and Their Built Environment, edited by A. Rapoport, pp. 265–274. World Anthropology Series, edited by A. Rapoport. The Hague: Mouton, 1976.
—FERNANDO POYATOS

CULTURGEN. A notion introduced by Charles Lumsden and Edward O. Wilson in their Genes, Mind, and Culture: The Coevolutionary Process (1981), culturgen denotes any particular item of culture. More formally, Lumsden and Wilson define it as "a relatively homogeneous set of artifacts, behaviors, or mentifacts (mental constructs having little or no direct correspondence with reality) that either share without exception one or more attribute states selected for their functional importance or at least share a consistently recurrent range of such attribute states within a given polythetic set." Lumsden and Wilson stress that this is a broad term, analogous to (although certainly not identical with) the terms used by many other authors interested in the evolution of culture and covering things as well as beliefs and behaviors. It would therefore encompass Richard

Dawkins's "meme," but since this is a purely mental notion analogous to the physical gene, a culturgen could extend out beyond into the world of spatiotemporal objects, such as humanmade artifacts.

To understand fully the notion of a culturgen, one must see it as embedded in the particular theory of gene-culture coevolution endorsed by Lumsden and Wilson, in which the key concept is that of an "epigenetic rule." They contend that animals—especially the higher ones, such as Homo sapiens—are born with certain innate dispositions to think and behave in predetermined, biologically advantageous ways. These dispositions or rules are, as it were, hardwired into our brains, and they direct us to act and think in certain preset fashions. The precise content of the epigenetic rules is given by the culturgens, which are shifted, formed, and organized according to the particular situations in which individual organisms find themselves. Thus, for instance, there might be a certain biological advantage to recognizing an in-group/out-group division, with some people being regarded as friends, relatives, sexual partners, or whatever. This division is kept in place by the epigenetic rules, but the actual content is a function of the culturgens.

Critics have complained that the notion is too broad to be truly meaningful, to which the authors reply that at least it enables one to aim for a truly integrated coevolutionary theory—with genetics and culture as partners—unlike, say, the meme-based theory of Dawkins, in which the memes seem to have lives of their own, irrespective of the biological state of affairs. Dawkins might not deny this but equally might not regard it as a criticism, arguing that the point of culture is that it does take on a life of its own, irrespective of biological constraints.

Signaling and language form an important part of Lumsden and Wilson's coevolutionary theory, and they believe that it is precisely inasmuch as animals (humans particularly) have been able to take crude signs (culturgens of a primitive nature) and build them into powerful methods of information transfer (culturgens of a sophisticated nature) that culture itself has been able to push forward the progressive upward climb begun by biological evolution. Indeed, for Wilson, that humans have been able to transcend the downward path of social evolution, from the "highest" colonial organisms through the social insects down to the higher mammals, is one of the overpowering facts of evolution. Thanks to the culturgens, as guided by the epigenetic rules, humankind has reversed this decline and scaled the highest "pinnacle" of sociality.

[*See also* Coevolution; Cultureme; Dawkins; Evolution; Meme; *and* Memetics.]

BIBLIOGRAPHY

Dawkins, R. *The Selfish Gene.* Oxford: Oxford University Press, 1976.
Dennett, D. *Darwin's Dangerous Idea.* New York: Simon and Schuster, 1995.
Lumsden, C. J., and E. O. Wilson. *Genes, Mind, and Culture.* Cambridge, Mass.: Harvard University Press, 1981.
Lumsden, C. J., and E. O. Wilson. *Promethean Fire: Reflections on the Origin of Mind.* Cambridge, Mass.: Harvard University Press, 1983.
Ruse, M. *Taking Darwin Seriously.* Oxford: Blackwell, 1986.
Wilson, E. O. *Sociobiology: The New Synthesis.* Cambridge, Mass.: Harvard University Press, 1975.

—MICHAEL RUSE

CYBERNETICS. One of the basic disciplines in modern natural sciences and epistemology, cybernetics has provided some of the most powerful conceptual tools for the development of computers and theories of dynamic systems. Derived from the ancient Greek verb *kubernētēs* (pilot), cybernetics—the science of control and communication in organisms and machines (Wiener, 1948)—deals with systems at a very abstract level and has been applied beyond the domains of the natural and computer sciences, such as in the study of complex systems in general. It has been important input for the elaboration of the semiotics of communication in the 1960s and 1970s both in the United States (e.g., Bateson, 1967) and in the Soviet Union (e.g., Shaumyan, 1971; Ivanov, 1965). Its models have also been influential in narratology (e.g., Todorov, 1969). W. Ross Ashby (1956) was one of the most important exponents in this field.

Mechanisms and machines in the most general sense are the focus of cybernetics. Every physical system can be treated as a cybernetic system. Cybernetics is concerned with the abstract relationships between the system's components, with the state transitions and with the system's dynamics rather than with the actual physical realization of a machine.

1. *States.* Each system consists of components that interact with each other according to certain rules. The current state $s(t)$ of a system at a time t is the whole pattern of states of the single components. At each point in time, any system finds itself in a certain state. The set of states can be interpreted as the system's variables, which have a certain value at time t. The state of a system is determined by its history and by the inputs entering the system.

2. *State transition.* State transitions describe the process of changing states from time t to time $t + \delta$. They are the system's rules, which determine its behavior and dynamics. They can be described in form of rules: "If system is in state $sx(t)$ and input ik is present, then change to state $sy(t + \delta)$." The whole set of state transitions describes implicitly the system's dynamics. In most cases, such as in the nervous system, we do not have the full description of all possible states and state transitions. Generally speaking, most time in neuroscience is spent in finding out exactly these rules (transition tables) by making experiments, opening the "black box" of the brain, and trying to specify its behavior. The state transitions determine the system's dynamics—thus, a machine moves along a certain behavioral trajectory until it is perturbed by some change in input. These concepts provide the basis not only for a better understanding of machines and physical systems but also for modern computer science; state transitions can also be interpreted as rules defining an automaton, which is the conceptual basis for all computers.

Cybernetics focuses also on the coupling of two or more systems, introducing the concept of feedback. Studying this phenomenon is one of the main points of interest in cybernetics, as it turns out that most systems are recurrent or feedback systems. If the number of interacting entities in a given problem increases, it can be shown that the problem becomes very quickly incomprehensible. This is why our nervous system, which consists of about 10^{11} highly interactive neurons, is so difficult to understand.

Another issue raised by Ashby in his book is the problem of modeling. The process of developing a model from experimental data is central to most disciplines and especially computer science and cognitive science, where models, which can be simulated on computers, have to be found for making predictions and explanations of certain phenomena. The main problems occur in finding the relevant parameters and the set of state transitions (i.e., the relations between the parameters). It is the scientist's responsibility to find an appropriate set of parameters in order to create a functioning model. But, from a philosophy of science perspective, there is a dilemma in that the scientist chooses the set of variables so as to fit either the model or the observed phenomena. This is not always an easy decision—especially if the observed phenomena are already theory laden. In any case, the cybernetician (as with most scientists) observes a phenomenon, tries to extract the relevant variables, and comes up with a set of rules describing the dynamics of the model as well as (hopefully) the phenomenon. The goal is to find a homomorphism between the observed entities (and their behavior) and the models (and their dynamics). It is clear that each model has to be a simplification, but it is by no means clear which simplifications are appropriate. The variety of models generated by narratology bears witness to these difficulties.

Ashby also tackles the problem of communication and information. His explanations, based on the concepts discussed above, follow the traditional pattern of argumentation. In the last part, he addresses the concept of control. His main claim is that the aim of control is to find a stable state or equilibrium between two or more interacting systems, whereby each system follows its own dynamics and is perturbed by the outputs of the other systems. We have to find mechanisms that lead to a stable relationship between these entities. These concepts have interesting implications for semiotics and our understandings of language and culture since symbols, languages, and semantic systems can be understood as stable states in this kind of interaction.

[*See also* Bateson; Computer; Feedback and Feedforward; *and* Structure.]

BIBLIOGRAPHY

Ashby, W. R. *An Introduction to Cybernetics.* London: Chapman and Hall, 1956.

Bateson, G. "Cybernetic Explanation." *American Behavioral Scientist* 10.8 (1967): 29–32.

Farrington, G. H. *Fundamentals of Automatic Control.* London: Chapman and Hall, 1957.

Ivanov, V. V. "The Role of Semiotics in the Cybernetic Study of Man and Collective" (1965). In *Soviet Semiotics,* edited and translated by D. P. Lucid, pp. 27–38. Baltimore: Johns Hopkins University Press, 1977.

Shaumyan, S. K. *Principles of Structural Linguistics.* Translated by J. Müller. The Hague: Mouton, 1971.

Shaumyan, S. K. *A Semiotic Theory of Language.* Bloomington: Indiana University Press, 1987.

Todorov, T. *Grammaire du Décaméron.* The Hague: Mouton, 1969.

Wiener. N. *Cybernetics, or Control and Communication in the Animal and the Machine.* New York: Wiley, 1948.

—MARKUS PESCHL

D

◆

DAOISM. What is commonly called "Daoism" or "Taoism" (Chinese, *daojiao* or *daojia*) is a nebula of texts, lineages, traditions, rituals, beliefs, practices, and sacred places; it is scattered over the entire East Asian region and developed over almost twenty-four centuries. Its most famous text is the *Daodejing* (*Tao Te Ching*), attributed to a mythical Laozi (or Lao Tzu). This work, whose oldest known version was written probably toward the end of the third century BCE, is a short and elusive collection of aphorisms, sayings, and proverbs. The *Daodejing* was the object of several hundred commentaries in Chinese and is one of the most translated books in the world. Other well-known Daoist texts are the *Zhuangzi* (*Chuang Tzu*) and the *Huainanzi*. Daoism cannot be reduced to any single text. Perhaps the *Daodejing* can be better described as a reservoir of metaphors, images, and ideas that need other texts in order to be developed, interpreted, understood, and actualized. The plurality of Daoism is represented by the Daoist Canon, a vast collection of philosophical texts, ritual instructions, talismans, genealogies, stories, and the like.

Despite their wide usage of metaphors and symbolic objects, their frequent discussions of language and extensive commentarial activity, the Daoists tended to deny any value to ordinary language and cognitive modalities. The best-known Daoist texts emphasize the need to separate oneself from language and cognitive activity and point to an ineffable and unconditioned entity called *dao*, and the state of primordial chaos (*hundun*) associated with it (Girardot, 1983; Kohn, 1991, pp. 124–137). The Dao is explicitly constructed as a nonsemiotic entity: "The Way [Dao] is concealed and has no name" (*Daodejing*, 3); the Dao is "eternally nameless" (*ibid.* 76); it is "the amorphous," "the form of the formless, the image of nonentity" (*ibid.* 5), as the space of potentiality that precedes and grounds differences, signs, and language. An ineffable and a-semiotic entity such as the Dao, however, is definitely worth the interest of the semiotician since it confronts the mind with the notion of a nonsemiotic primordial reality that can be

characterized as an enlightenment in which the manipulation of special symbols emancipates the mind from the alienating effects of signs. The image of the "uncarved block," used to represent the return to the primordial chaos in a process of "unsignifying," an undoing of ordinary signification, is central to the Daoist discourse.

The scriptures (*jing*) are held to be spontaneous and unconditioned revelations or manifestations of the cosmic essence; talismans (*tianfu* or simply *fu*), the nuclei of scriptures, are graphs, often incomprehensible, written in a calligraphic style resembling that of archaic official documents of the state; registers (*lu*) list the members of specific Daoist lineages, from the heavenly beings who revealed the scriptures venerated by the lineages and the human ascetics who found them, down to the present members of the community of faithfuls. Talismans and scriptures are archaic and meaningless without extensive commentaries, which amount to translations in religious or philosophical language of the spiritual essence of the Dao. Texts function mainly as ritual objects and must accordingly be ritually employed: handed down from master to disciple as symbols of spiritual achievement, legitimacy, and orthodoxy; manipulated as amulets—condensations of cosmic power—used to communicate directly with the deities through chanting or by sending them back to the Invisible world through a fire sacrifice.

The Daoist masters developed the notion that the Dao—an entity so elusive that it transcends ordinary knowledge and perception—manifests itself spontaneously, and can be "understood" in a nondiscursive way only by those who have prepared their minds-bodies to receive such a revelation. How does the Dao manifest itself? The most cogent manifestation of the Dao is probably in written form, particularly in the so-called "cloud seals" (*yunzhuan*) that form the core of the Heavenly talismans (*tianfu*) and sacred texts.

The sacred texts of Daoism (*jing*, usually translated as "classics") are not primarily doctrinal treatises, but condensed form of the cosmic breath-energy (*qi*) that permeates the universe, the pneumatic "matter" out of which all things and beings are made. According to Daoism's cosmology, in the beginning this primordial *qi* filled the Void. The Breath gradually and spontaneously congealed into invisible light rays and "solidified" further to form, even before the creation of the world, immense "cloud-seal" characters (*yun-zhuan*), still nebulous but more concrete. Interestingly, these cloud-seals resemble and appear to be imitations of the ancient Chinese scripts used in divination and in official documents. The cloud-seals emitted light and sound. Ages later they were written down by the gods or heavenly scribes on jade or gold tablets and preserved in the celestial palaces or in the sacred mountains. Their transcription into human writing happened only much later, when Heaven revealed them to the chosen Daoists in the form of clouds, usually in the context of a visitation from a divine messenger. The chosen human beings copied and transmitted them. A revelation of talismans and registers of the gods lay often at the basis of the establishment of a new Daoist tradition; initiation involved the conferral of a register of gods (*lu*), a set of scriptures central to a specific revelation, a list of related prohibitions, vestments, talismans, spells, and sacred charts (Benn, 1991).

Talismans (*fu*) consist of incantatory sounds and pictures that must be written down and recited in every religious function. Prayers, invocations, and summonses addressed to spirits and deities are also written down every time they are needed. The act of writing itself is thus an important component of the ritual. Talismans, and more generally scriptures (most of which are basically expanded talismans), play several functions in the interaction with the invisible world of Daoist deities and cosmic forces. They are also used as mediative supports to enact a transformation in the practitioner who thereby becomes an Immortal (*xianren*), a Daoist saint, and therefore acquires power to control unruly deities. Furthermore, in a less informed and noninitiatory usage, talismans are believed to release a protective power by virtue of their status as embodiments, traces of cosmic forces.

Fu are not necessarily written down in ink on paper. Often they lack a permanent material form: they may be written in the air by incense, clouds, the priest's sword, or his right hand in the "sword gesture" (Lagerwey, 1987, p. 267). In some rituals, talismans were drawn into consecrated water, which was used for purifying ablutions and later swallowed by the priest (Robinet, 1997, p. 141). Others were burned and then the ashes were consumed by the adept. Since the talismans are not linguistic expressions but semiotic configurations of the primordial, cosmic energy of the gods or other spiritual principles, once ingested their power would permeate the adept, thus making him able to transform himself and the external reality in an efficacious way. In some traditions, certain talismans are deemed so sacred and numinous that they are not even written down (Schipper, 1993, p. 88); instead, a brush and ink are set before a blank sheet of paper in the most sacred part of the ritual space, and this is enough to release their power in this world (Dean, 1993, p. 47).

The initiatory usage of talismans is a complex drama involving the body and the mind of the adept. Even when the talismans are written down materially (either on paper, in water, or in the air with a sword), they have first been created by the adept in meditation combining breathing techniques and visualization. Meditation reproduces the cosmic conditions for the renewed revelation of the talismans, and at the same time operates an interiorization of the talismans and their power. In other words, the body-mind of the adept becomes a microcosm in which the original manifestation of the talisman is reproduced. The adept, then, as the embodiment of the primordial cosmic energy, by writing the talisman makes it visible to the human beings in a process similar to that of the gods who triggered the initial revelation to the ancient masters by displaying their copy of the primordial talismans in the clouds.

These powers are purported to harmonize individuals, society, and the cosmos, to achieve immortality, and to avoid perils and political enemies (Robinet, 1997, p. 90), but also to gain more concrete worldly benefits, such as easy childbirth, success in love, and healing; some eschatological movements even claimed that only the possessors of certain talismans will survive the final armageddon (Robinet, 1997, p. 162).

The source of the talisman's power can be located in the talisman's nature as a seal and in the ancient Chinese theories about language that constitute the foundation of the usage of seals. A seal is a name signed to give force to an order or a covenant. Like a personal signature, it completely engages its author, to whom it is related by a deep and close metonymy: the seal is the trace of its author's innermost intention and essence. Today the sacred writings of Daoism are still handed down from master to disciple in an initiation ritual accompanied by an oath witnessed by the gods. Moreover, when used as certificates of initiation, talismans incorporated the vital spirit from the master's body, as well as their original cosmic force. Talismans have never lost their nature as seals in a contract between humans and gods, in which they represent the essence of each party. In other words, *fu* are the visual and sonic form of cosmic energies—they are the signatures, as it were, the "true names" of these energies. For example, a talisman known as the *Map of the True Form of the Five Sacred Mountains* is based on the relief of China's great sacred mountains, of which it is a sort of map. When the talisman is actualized in meditation, it enables the adept to travel through the labyrinth of the mountain and to encounter the gods and immortals who live there (Schipper, 1993, p. 173). Knowledge of talismans was related to the ability to control the forces of which they are a semiotic configuration.

The emphasis on talismans is related to the particular status of writing in China. In China, writing is traditionally considered not a mere transcription of speech, but a faithful representation of reality (Staal, 1979), of which it reveals the innermost patterns, their "true forms." Natural entities have not only forms, but also sounds, and the knowledge of the correct pronunciation is essential. In Daoist ritual, when the texts are chanted by the ritual specialists, they are also believed to be sung by the gods in the heavens (Robinet, 1997, p. 126).

As pointed out by John Lagerwey (1987, p. 155), a Daoist talisman is a "symbol" in the etymological sense of the word: *fu* is the term designating each of two halves of an object representing a contract between two parties (gods and masters), or two different modalities of a sacred entity (a landscape, or gods, or cosmic powers); in Daoism the two halves are the written configuration of a divine energy—and the energy itself. A legitimate line of transmission ensures the correctness of the model of the written half that the priest or the adept copies. However, the power of the talisman depends on its reunification with the other, invisible half. What kind of semiosis is implied by this kind of talismanic communication with the realm of invisible potencies? In a way, a talisman stands for something else—its hidden part, a god, a sacred place, or even the primordial cosmic breath. However, these entities are not "signified" by the talisman, since there is no proper "signified" corre-

sponding of the talismanic signifier—the talisman *is* those entities, to which it must be reunited, in order to be effective, through ritual action. As a coagulation of the cosmic breath, the talisman is in itself a microcosm or, as Giorgio Raimondo Cardona calls it, a *pentaculum,* a magical object constructed around an interplay between macro- and microcosm that ensures the control over cosmic forces (Cardona, 1981, p. 181). As Cardona explains, this particular form of writing is a model that reproduces cosmic forces and events but does not hide anything: that which it stands for is not absent, but present in the materiality of writing itself. No interpretive strategies develop to explain the talismans—or if they do, these explanations are just provisional efforts to show the cosmic structure of the talisman and its function in ritual. Talismans are not made to be interpreted, but to be used in order to produce certain effects. This is a case of a sort of "illocutive" act (a manipulation of language in order to produce certain effects in the world), but one that pertains not to "speech" but to "writing"—if it is possible to suggest a theory of the illocutionary and perlocutionary effects of *written* speech acts (Cardona, 1981, pp. 176–178).

The Daoists use talismans in order to overcome the limitations of language and signs vis-à-vis the absolute and unconditioned Dao. In this respect, Daoism is similar to certain Buddhist traditions in East Asia (in particular, esoteric Buddhism), which attempted to represent the absolute realm of Buddhahood in semiotic fashion. The Buddhists developed a theory and a practice of secret signs, in particular the *siddham* characters, treated as minimal *maṇḍala*s (representations of the enlightened universe), which presuppose a complex underlying semantic system. The Daoist use of talismans, however, is very different from Buddhist attitudes toward sacred language. The Daoists did not emphasize a secret system of meaning (even though it could not be completely absent), but considered their talismanic signs as condensation of the primordial cosmic forces. Talismans operate outside of semiosis proper; they do not stand for something that is absent; on the contrary, when they are deployed in ritual through evocation (drawn on various mediums), ingestion, or oblation, they manifest and reveal the presence of the fundamental cosmic forces.

Because of their status, talismans provide a cosmic legitimacy of power and authority. Their model is that of the imperial regalia and the symbols of imperial power. Accordingly, the investiture of a Daoist master is comparable to that of an emperor. This fact makes of Daoism a very ambiguous discourse, in which the distinctions between center (the emperor and the core apparatus of the Chinese imperium) and periphery (local traditions, oppositional discourses and movements, people, classes, and places without status in the Confucian state) are continuously relativized, blurred, deconstructed. Daoism's ambiguous relation with the imperium could result in turning certain Daoist lineages into religious arms of the state, thus contributing to the further permeation of its apparatuses and ideologies in peripheral regions. On the other hand, it is true that many influential Daoist traditions, based on revelations of cosmic texts, developed into revolutionary movements that, in a few occasions, succeeded either in defeating the ruling dynasty or in establishing their own political system. Kenneth Dean suggests that, even though the imperial system and its imagery were pervasive and came to inform every aspect of premodern Chinese society, Daoism provided at least the possibility to "react . . . to this architectonic of the state by scrambling the codes" (1993, p. 184). Because of its fundamental emphasis on process, change, and localized power, and its distrust of language and master narratives, Daoism was able to appropriate the imperial and bureaucratic metaphors and other preexisting intellectual systems (*yinyang* dialectics, the cosmology of systematic correspondence, divination, etc.) and the practices related to them, but used them in different ways and to different purposes. Instead of focusing on the state, the "despotic signifier," the ultimate mediator between local and cosmic instances, Daoism empowers representatives of specific local areas and thus provides a terrain for the proliferation of different and often contradictory representations of spiritual, political, and intellectual power. The strategic deployment of talismans and other "cosmic" texts, while pointing to the limits of ordinary language and thus of dominant discourses, can also provide oppositional and revolutionary alternatives to the despotism of the center.

[*See also* Buddhism; Mandala; Mantra; Semiotic Terminology; Speech Act Theory; *and* Yi Jing.]

BIBLIOGRAPHY

Bell, C. "The Ritualization of Texts and the Textualization of Ritual in the Codification of Taoist Liturgy." *History of Religions* 27.4 (1988): 366–392.

Benn, C. D. *The Cavern-Mystery Transmission: A Taoist Ordination Rite of A.D. 711.* Honolulu: University of Hawaii Press, 1991.

Cardona, G. R. *Antropologia della scrittura.* Turin: Loescher, 1981.

Dean, K. *Taoist Ritual and Popular Cults of South-east China.* Princeton: Princeton University Press, 1993.

Girardot, N. J. *Myth and Meaning in Early Taoism: The Theme of Chaos (hun-tun).* Berkeley: University of California Press, 1983.

Kohn, L. *Taoist Mystical Philosophy: The Scripture of Western Ascension.* Albany: N.Y.: State University of New York Press, 1991.

Lagerwey, J. *Taoist Ritual in Chinese Society.* New York: Macmillan, 1987.

Lao Tzu (Laozi). *Tao Te Ching (Daodejing).* Translated by Victor H. Mair. New York: Bantam Books, 1990.

Rambelli, F. "The Semiotic Arcitulation of *Hosshin Seppo*: An Interpretive Study of the Concepts of *Mon* and *Monji* in Kukai's *Mikkyo*." In *Esoteric Buddhism in Japan,* edited by Ian Astley, pp. 17–36. Copenhagen: Seminar for Buddhist Studies, 1994.

Robinet, I. *Taoism: Growth of a Religion.* Stanford University Press, 1997.

Schipper, K. *The Taoist Body.* Berkeley, University of California Press, 1993.

Seidel, A. "Imperial Treasures and Taoist Sacraments: Taoist Roots in the Apocrypha." In *Tantric and Taoist Studies in Honor of R. A. Stein,* edited by Michel Strickmann, pp. 291–371. Mélanges chinois et bouddhiques, 21. Brussels: Institut Belge des Haute Études Chinoises, 1983.

Staal, F. "Oriental Ideas on the Origin of Language." *Journal of the American Oriental Society* 99.31 (1979): 1–14.

Strickmann, M. *Le Taoïsme du Mao Chan, chronique d'une révélation.* Paris: Institut des Hautes Études Chinois du Collège de France, 1981.

—FABIO RAMBELLI

DARWIN, CHARLES ROBERT

DARWIN, CHARLES ROBERT (1809–1882), author of *Origin of Species* (1859), which established the idea of evolution, for which he also provided a mechanism, natural selection, or as he later called it—following Herbert Spencer—the survival of the fittest. Starting from the Malthusian claims that population numbers will always outstrip food supplies and that there will be a consequent struggle for existence, Darwin went on to argue that success in the struggle will be, on average, a function of the features peculiar to the winners (the fittest). If we combine this natural form of selection—with its analogy to the selection practiced by animal and plant breeders to develop better or more desirable forms—with the assumption that variation in heritable features or characteristics is unending, then over time we will have full-blown evolution.

Darwin's mechanism addresses a problem that he thought faced any student of the organic world, namely that of design. How is it that organisms function as well as they do? Rather than invoke an all-powerful designing god, Darwin tried to put the full burden on the working of the mechanisms of natural selection. In short, Darwin did not deny the natural theologian's emphasis on the adapted nature of the organic world; rather, he gave a naturalistic, non-miraculous alternative explanation of adaptations.

For obvious reasons, Darwin's main concern in his various evolutionary writings was with physical adaptations, like arms and legs and the organs of reproduction—from an evolutionary viewpoint, there is little point to an organism if it does not reproduce. He was concerned also to show, in the face of objections by Alfred Russel Wallace, the codiscoverer of natural selection that selection works always and only for the benefit of the individual. Darwin was a staunch opponent of suppositions of group selection.

From the start, Darwin realized the importance of behavior, including communication—understood in the broad sense of the transmittal of information—between organisms. He realized also that despite the individualistic nature of selection, enlightened self-interest might come into play, and organisms might find it in their evolutionary interests to cooperate or work together. Obviously, such cooperation, almost of necessity, will demand communication.

Darwin himself was interested in communication at all levels and of all kinds. In work on orchids, he discussed how plants develop parts that attract insects seeking food and mates in order that the plants themselves might get fertilized. In work on insectivorous plants, he discussed how plants deceive unsuspecting insects, for instance, who are attracted by a smell that simulates that of rotten meat. In animal-animal communicative interactions, crossing species boundaries, Darwin did less personal original work, but he was highly appreciative and supportive of the findings of others (e.g., Henry Walter Bates, who showed how certain palatable butterflies mimic the markings of others, thus tricking predators into thinking that they are poisonous, distasteful, and thus as unsuitable as those that they copy).

Darwin was always insistent that the only true key to understanding communication, whether true or false, is the benefit it bestows on the communicator. The instrument of communication evolves solely for the benefit of the communicator. Darwin's truly seminal work on communication, however, was centered on interactions between members of the same species, and it came primarily as he worked out the implications of a secondary mechanism of evolution that he proposed: sexual selection. This was a long-standing notion and arose directly from the analogy with artificial selection that sparked the initial move to natural selection. Breeders select not only for those characteristics that are useful (like thicker wool or fleshier rumps) but also for those features they find beautiful (like the feathers of birds) or otherwise desirable in a nonutilitarian fashion (like the fighting spirit of bulls and cocks). Darwin supposed, therefore, that in nature individuals compete not just for survival and consequent reproduction but for reproduction itself. Sexual selection involves two reproductive types of selection: selection for male combat—such as when two males fight for access to females—and selection for female choice, where females choose the most attractive males, such as much-befeathered peacocks.

Although sexual selection was introduced into Darwin's writings as early as natural selection, it lay essentially undeveloped until Darwin wrote on the human species in *The Descent of Man* (1871). Challenged by Wallace to explain the evolution of certain human characteristics that seem to have no direct connections with natural selection, Darwin turned in earnest to sexual selection and in the process provided some of his most important discussions of communication. In both male combat and female choice, the need to transfer information is crucial. The whole point is that the male is trying to put across a message to the female. But information transfer is needed in male combat also. Initially, it might well be in the interests of both combatants to pass on information to the other, such as "I have antlers that are much bigger and stronger than yours, so don't waste the time and effort of either of us in trying to take me on" or "I have antlers that are much smaller than yours so don't think that I am about to threaten you." One can think of similar situations right through to the mating of the most successful male.

As Darwin applied sexual selection to humanity, he started to realize that humans demand an even more extended view of evolution's workings than he had thought previously. For a start, the divisions of sexual selection were clearly not as fixed as he had implied. Although Darwin usually saw the combat/choice versions separated cleanly by the male/female divide, he had never held to this absolutely, and humankind really showed that information transfer in sexual relations goes in all directions. Males are certainly as much into choice as females.

Pursuing the broader perspective, Darwin was led to incorporate studies of emotions and communication, studies that had occupied him for many years—from the time of the birth of natural selection and, coincidentally, the time when he married and when he started to raise a family. In his publications, *The Descent of Man* led straight to the writing of *The Expression of the Emotions in Man and Animals* (1872), which deals in depth with the ways in which various emotions are shown by animals and by humans and their significance from the point of view of evolution.

It seems fair to say that yet another mechanism was thought really significant here, the (now-discredited) Lamarckian idea of heritable acquired characters. Darwin believed that we start to show certain emotions and that these can then be fixed through habit and transference to new generations. What is significant, however, is that Darwin saw how what at first might be entirely involuntary motions, with or without immediate adaptive significance, could be exaggerated or otherwise modified. Thus, they might take on a purely symbolic significance, adaptively signaling to an observer the state of mind of the performer. Language is clearly important in human communication, but, determined always to show humans' oneness with the rest of the organic world, Darwin stressed again and again how we, like the animals, communicate virtually with our whole bodies and not just with our larynges.

[*See also* Biosemiotics; Coevolution; Dawkins; Evolution; Koch; Sebeok; Trivers; *and* Zahavi.]

BIBLIOGRAPHY

Browne, J. *Charles Darwin: Voyaging. Volume 1 of a Biography.* New York: Knopf, 1995.

Campbell, B. *Sexual Selection and the Descent of Man.* Chicago: Aldine, 1972.

Darwin, C. *On the Origin of Species.* London: John Murray, 1859.

Darwin, C. *The Descent of Man.* London: John Murray, 1871.

Dawkins, R. *The Selfish Gene.* Oxford: Oxford University Press, 1976.

Richard, R. J. *Darwin and the Emergence of Evolutionary Theories of Mind and Behavior.* Chicago: University of Chicago Press, 1987.

Ruse, M. *The Darwinian Revolution: Science Red in Tooth and Claw.* Chicago: University of Chicago Press, 1979.

Ruse, M. *Darwinism Defended: A Guide to Evolutionary Controversies.* Reading, Mass.: Benjamin/Cummings Publishing, 1982.

Ruse, M. *Taking Darwin Seriously.* Oxford: Blackwell, 1986.

—MICHAEL RUSE

DATABASE. Computer systems that provide well-structured forms in which huge amounts of data can be stored, retrieved, and manipulated, databases are, in most cases, central pools of data that are accessed by different programs and applications. For instance, a database that holds all the data of a library might be organized in records such that each record corresponds to one book. Each book has certain features, such as an author, a title, number of pages, the location in the library, key words, and each record contains entries on all these features. We have to differentiate between the abstract definition of such a record as thus described and an instantiation of such a record. The latter is one of thousands of references to a particular book, whereas there is only one definition of the record. The process of "filling" the variables of a record with actual data is called instantiation. After collecting all the bibliographical data of a library and transferring them into the computer by instantiating records, a well-structured collection of data of the library—a database of all of books—is available. Normally, a database provides an interface via a kind of programming language or a graphical user interface so that a certain set of operations can be executed on the database. One basic operation is to search and retrieve certain records which fulfill criteria, such as having a certain author or containing certain key words.

The retrieving process is not limited to the fulfillment of only one exact match with a certain variable in the record. It is possible to search in certain ranges, such as "find all books that have been published between the years 1993 and 1995." The retrieving process is not limited to criteria in one variable but can be combined with other variables such as "find all books that have been published between the years 1989 and 1992 or before 1965 and have the author *x*." As the records do not hold data of only bibliographical interest, the librarian or other user can access via his program the price of the books or other statistics.

One can not only read these data but also write to them: instantiating a new record (that is, computationally registering a new book) is a basic writing routine. It is not only possible to write whole records but also to change values in existing variables; if a book is lent to someone, the field that holds the person's name will be filled. This name will be erased after the book has been returned.

If many persons are using the same database, some problems can occur: first, there is the problem of access—who can access which data, who is allowed to read which parts of the records, who is allowed to write to the records, and so on. These are very difficult questions concerning the security and privacy of data; a database is in most cases the heart of many offices, industrial structures, and research labs. If someone has access to these data, he or she could easily abuse them or even change them. The second problem is the access to writing on the same record. Think, for instance, of the following situation. Two persons want to book a flight from New York to Los Angeles at the same time. There is only one seat left on this particular flight. There has to be a mechanism in the database program that does not allow both parties to write to the same record (the particular seat) at the same time.

There are further interesting applications of databases if two or more of them are joined. This can allow cross-referencing. Another interesting development is the combination of databases with expert systems: with a huge amount of data accessible, the expert system and its rule-application module has access to a large knowledge base. In many cases, this increases performance, as the system is more likely to find rules that fit in the large amount of data and thus find solutions more quickly.

[See also Artificial intelligence; Expert Systems; and Knowledge Representation.]

BIBLIOGRAPHY

Date, C. J. An Introduction to Data Base Systems. 5th ed. Reading, Mass.: Addison-Wesley, 1990.

Rishe, N. Database Design Fundamentals. Englewood Cliffs, N.J.: Prentice-Hall, 1988.

—MARKUS PESCHL

DAWKINS, RICHARD (b. 1941), British evolutionist whose landmark book The Selfish Gene (1976) argues that the overriding mark of the organic world is its designlike nature. Unlike theologians, however, Dawkins locates a naturalistic causal explanation in the Darwinian mechanism of natural selection.

But, taking the argument a step further than was possible for Charles Darwin, who wrote at a time when little was known of the nature of heredity, Dawkins argues that the locus of selection must be that of the individual gene. This is not to deny, as Dawkins fully recognizes, that the genes must come packaged, as it were, and it is these packages—survival machines or vehicles (better known to us as individual organisms)—that interact with the outside world, whether organic or inorganic. But it is the genes, the replicators, that ultimately survive or fail in the struggle for existence, and it is these that are therefore necessarily selected or not.

Following the modern tendency to locate struggles at the lowest, most "reductionist," level, Dawkins contends that genes give rise to features, "adaptations," which redound always to the benefit of the individual, defined at the gross level as vehicle and at the refined level as replicator. Hence, Dawkins's metaphor of the selfish gene, which holds simply that selection promotes the benefit of the individual. It has never been Dawkins's claim that the organism itself must and will always act in a selfish manner. Indeed, Dawkins—who was trained by Nikolaas Tinbergen as an ethologist—has always argued that at the physical, behavioral level, altruism and reciprocation might at times be by far the best tactics for survival.

To this latter end, Dawkins played a key role in popularizing John Maynard Smith's notion of an "evolutionary stable strategy" (ESS), whereby it can be shown that in a group situation selection promotes paths of individual behavior that can rest in equilibrium with the behaviors of others. Although an ESS might lead to aggression—like the strategy of always attacking an opponent, following if he or she flees, and running away if he or she attacks—Dawkins stressed (with Maynard Smith) that often, especially with conspecifics, the pertinent ESS might lead to cooperation, as in the case of refraining from taking advantage of an injured rival because you, too, might be or become just such a rival.

Naturally, this interest in ESSs led Dawkins, both in The Selfish Gene and in his later works The Extended Phenotype (1982) and The Blind Watchmaker (1986), to detailed study of communication. With fellow ethologist John Krebs, he has been much interested in the theory of signaling, drawing a major distinction between signaling as manipulation and signaling as mind reading. Much communication is of the straightforward variety, as when an organism draws attention to itself or its needs—a chick begging a parent, for instance. But some communication goes beyond this to the stage where one actor is trying to force or trick another into some action—manipulation. Note that this does not necessarily just concern animals but can extend to plants also. In the case of mind reading, the organism is trying to figure out the behavior of another in order to exploit it for its own ends. "The mind-reader is able to optimize its own behavioral choices in the light of the probable future responses of its victim. A dog with its teeth bared is statistically more likely to bite than a dog with its teeth covered. This being a fact, natural selection or learning will shape the behavior of other dogs in such a way as to take advantage of future probabilities, for example by fleeing from rivals with bared teeth."

Here, as elsewhere in the organic world, Dawkins sees much scope for the action of arms races, where lines coevolve by trying to take advantage of and better the adaptations of competitors. This leads to a kind of progress, including progress in communication (done for whatever reason), and although Dawkins warns always against believing in some kind of absolute progress that culminates with the human species, he does admit that humans have, through culture, taken communication to hitherto unknown heights. Indeed, to account for humankind, Dawkins has proposed a whole new level of evolution above that of the genes, which he calls the evolution of the memes. Hence, "we are built as gene machines and cultured as meme machines, but we have the power to turn against our creators. We, alone on earth, can rebel against the tyranny of the selfish replicators."

[See also Darwin; Evolution; Manipulation; Meme; Memetics; and Zahavi.]

BIBLIOGRAPHY

Cronin, H. The Ant and the Peacock. Cambridge: Cambridge University Press, 1991.

Dawkins, R. The Selfish Gene. Oxford: Oxford University Press, 1976.

Dawkins, R. The Extended Phenotype: The Gene as the Unit of Selection. Oxford: W. H. Freeman, 1982.

Dawkins, R. The Blind Watchmaker. London: Longman, 1986.

Hull, D. "The Naked Meme." In Learning, Development and Culture: Essays in Evolutionary Epistemology, edited by H. C. Plotkin, pp. 273–327. Chichester, England: Wiley, 1982.

Maynard Smith, J. The Evolution of Sex. Cambridge: Cambridge University Press, 1978.

Maynard Smith, J. Evolution and the Theory of Games. Cambridge: Cambridge University Press, 1982.

Maynard Smith, J. Games, Sex, and Evolution. New York: Harvester and Wheatsheaf, 1988.

Ruse, M. "Evolution and Progress." Trends in Ecology and Evolution 8.2 (1993): 55–59.

Ruse, M. Monad to Man: The Concept of Progress in Evolutionary Biology. Cambridge, Mass.: Harvard University Press, 1996.

—MICHAEL RUSE

DEBUGGING is the process of testing computer programs. Even if a program is syntactically correct (i.e., if in the parsing process an executable program has been generated by the compiler), it is not guaranteed that it is also semantically correct—that is, that it produces the expected results. That is why intensive testing is necessary before a piece of software can be made public. Many unexpected errors that cannot be foreseen in the process of programming can occur because most large programs have such complex structures that it is not possible to predict their detailed behavior.

Software engineering has provided quite powerful tools (called debuggers) for detecting and correcting bugs in programs. Normally, a program's results are tested with different sets of input data (especially with "critical" data that tests the limits of the program system). From these protocols, one can try to reconstruct the errors in some procedure or subroutine. A more convenient approach is provided by a debugger, which offers the possibility of tracing the behavior of a program. This means that the programmer has full access to all values of the variables and to the current and next step of code at any point in time. This helps determine quickly what is wrong in a procedure. Debuggers offer access to all structures of the program ranging from complex variable structures to single bits in a central-processing unit's registers. He or she can introduce "breakpoints" in the programs that enable him or her to stop the execution of the program at exactly one point. The current variable status can then be checked in any detail at this point. Finding errors with a debugger thus is much easier than endless testing and guessing where an error might occur.

[*See also* Artificial Intelligence; Computer; Cybernetics; *and* Expert Systems.]

BIBLIOGRAPHY

Myers, G. J. *The Art of Software Testing.* New York: Wiley, 1979.

—MARKUS PESCHL

DECONSTRUCTION. A theoretical and ethical activity that came to prominence in philosophy and literary criticism during the 1960s, deconstruction is not merely a method of criticism but a process already at work within systems of concepts. The task of deconstructionists is to bring pressure to bear on the internal contradictions that underlie a given conceptual order, showing that it is undermined and fractured by the very principles that ground and support it.

It is customary to locate the origin of this approach in the philosophy of Jacques Derrida who in 1967 published three influential collections of essays: *De la grammatologie* (Of Grammatology, 1976), *L'écriture et la différence* (Writing and Difference, 1987), and *La voix et le phénomène* (Speech and Phenomena and Other Essays on Husserl's Theory of Signs, 1973). However, in *Mémoires: Pour Paul de Man* (Mémoires: For Paul de Man, 1986), Derrida denies his originary status, arguing instead that deconstruction exists in several forms radiating from a number of institutions, languages, and traditions. Indeed, deconstruction has made its mark throughout the humanities and social sciences, sparking innovations in such diverse fields as architecture, religious studies, anthropology, and legal studies.

Four decades earlier, Martin Heidegger had promised to undertake the destruction (*Destruktion*) of the history of Western ontology in *Sein und Zeit* (1927; published in English as *Being and Time*, 1962). His aim was not to tear down the ontological tradition but to uncover the forgotten structures that make it possible. In particular, Heidegger noted that Western philosophy has consistently neglected the question of Being, even though a precomprehension of the meaning of Being structures every philosophical epoch. Though Heidegger never published his destruction of ontology, in his later writings he argued that Western philosophy, which he referred to as metaphysics, was coming to a close. For Heidegger, the task of thinking at the end of philosophy was to think the difference between beings (the sum of what is) and Being itself—the self-concealing event that makes beings present in the world yet itself remains unthought.

For Derrida, deconstruction is a practice of thinking that inhabits the closure of Western metaphysics. Like Heidegger, Derrida characterizes metaphysics as the general system of concepts that has structured Western thought since Greek antiquity. It would be wrong, though, to view Derrida as a disciple of Heidegger or anyone else, for Derrida's work draws its resources from every text it deconstructs.

In "Signature événement contexte" ("Signature Event Context," 1972), Derrida notes that every metaphysical concept belongs to a system of predicates that defines it. Metaphysics is a system of signifying systems in which concepts acquire meaning in relation to other concepts, but no concept is metaphysical in itself. What *is* metaphysical is the system that imposes its order on its component elements. Metaphysics holds its elements in place not by virtue of a natural law but through an arbitrary application of force. It is a system of hierarchical oppositions in which one term dominates another, setting speech above writing, the human over the animal, man over woman, Europe over the non-European. The act of deconstruction displaces the metaphysical order by reversing the nonconceptual forces that hold its concepts in a system of subordination.

As Derrida points out, notably in *De la grammatologie*, the hierarchical structure of metaphysics is built on the premise that being is a mode of presence and nonbeing a mode of absence. In metaphysics, everything that is is assumed to be present to reason, thought, and consciousness—what Derrida calls *logos*. The *logos* is the ground that determines the interpretation of the concept of Being in each epoch of philosophy. The term *logos* itself names a historical constant that has assumed a number of particular forms over time. No matter what form it takes, though, metaphysics remains a logocentrism because it posits human reason as the ground on which Being manifests itself in its plenitude.

Derrida argues that within logocentrism the concept of truth finds its condition of possibility in the subordination of the sensible to the intelligible. Logocentrism assumes that thought is a universal language capable of offering a true representation of things, while spoken words are sensuous substitutes that represent thoughts to others. Writing is thus seen as a substitute for speech. Whether written or spoken, every word or sign has two components: a sensible form (the signifier) and an intelligible content (the signified).

Under logocentrism, the sign's intelligible content is conceived of as existing independently of the sensible signifier that represents it. Language, therefore, points toward an intelligibility that exceeds it: an infinite or transcendental signified. As Derrida points out, however, every signified acquires its meaning only by referring to a signifier that defines it, and this second signifier refers to a signified that, in an infinite process of dissemination, defines itself by referring to yet another signifier. Since the signified is itself another signifier, a sign's intelligible content does not escape the play of sensible marks. Nevertheless, in metaphysics, spoken signifiers are held to be superior to written ones because speech is assumed to stand in immediate proximity to thought. Writing is construed as the representation of spoken representation, the signifier of a signifier. Although nothing is considered lost in the transition from thought to speech, the representation of speech by writing debases thought, bringing the intelligible down to the level of the sensible. Phonetic language provides an ideal mode of communication, while graphic script constitutes a fall from the absolute presence of the signified. Logocentrism is therefore a phonocentrism and, in a paradoxical way, phonocentrism is a powerful form of ethnocentrism. For even as the Western tradition sets speech above writing, it insists that cultures possessing a system of writing are superior to oral cultures.

To displace the foundational structures of phonocentrism, Derrida argues that all signifying practices, including speech and writing, have their source in an "arche-writing" (from the Greek *archē*, "beginning"), which cannot be understood in terms of presence and absence. In "La différance" (1967), Derrida explains this prior form of writing by recalling Ferdinand de Saussure's insight that language is a system of differences without positive terms. For Saussure, what enables a signifying mark to stand for something else—to signify—is the difference that distinguishes that mark from all other signifiers. A structural law requires every signifier to relate itself to something other than itself, for whenever it presents itself a signifier bears within itself the "trace" of other signifiers belonging to both the immediate context and others. Signification would be impossible without this "hinge" that simultaneously allows signifiers to be strung together in a continuous discourse yet holds them apart to ensure that each unit of that discourse has a discrete meaning and function.

Yet as Derrida also notes, the same signifier can be repeated in different texts and at different places in the same text only because it is already other than itself. A signifier that is absolutely unitary, that does not differ from itself, could only be written once. A signifier can be grafted into an infinite number of contexts precisely because it functions in the absence of its author, its reader, and the things and ideas it signifies. Hence, every signifier, whether spoken or written, is a nonpresent, nonabsent "remainder" cut off from origin, destination, meaning, and reference. It is because speech and writing share the same structure of potential iteration that Derrida describes them as two modes of a general writing that is logically prior to speech and script and makes them possible, much as Being lays the ground for individual modes of being.

By arguing that the structure of the signifier implies a relation to the other, Derrida binds his work to the philosophy of Emmanuel Levinas, who understands the ethical relation as a responsibility toward an other who remains absolutely other. Derrida's brand of deconstruction is above all an ethical practice, a bulwark against totalitarian regimes of thought that reduce differences by collapsing the other into the same.

Paul de Man also uses deconstruction to reveal the disjunctions that structure seemingly "monadic totalities." In *Allegories of Reading* (1979), he defines the text as a site where incompatible yet interdependent systems of grammar and rhetoric conflict. Grammar is the set of rules for combining signifiers into technically correct utterances, yet it functions independently of meaning and reference. Rhetoric is the system of tropes and figures that ties the text to the nonverbal world, but the system of reference established by rhetoric gives the text mutually contradictory referents. Instead of clarifying the text's relation to its world, then, rhetoric confronts the reader with paradoxes that remain undecidable, generating further questions and producing more text instead of helping the reader map the text onto its apparently intended object. De Man says *rhetoric* is another name for literature, while literature is a mode of allegory that dramatizes its own undecidability by simultaneously affirming its ability to refer and showing that reference is impossible. Literature is therefore the discourse that deconstructs itself.

[*See also* Buddhism; Postmodernism; *and* Post-structuralism.]

BIBLIOGRAPHY

Works by Derrida

Of Grammatology (1967a). Translated by G. C. Spivak. Baltimore: Johns Hopkins University Press, 1976.

Speech and Phenomena and Other Essays on Husserl's Theory of Signs (1967b). Translated by D. B. Allison. Evanston: Northwestern University Press, 1973.

Writing and Difference (1967c) Translated by A. Bass. Chicago: University of Chicago Press, 1978.

"Signature Event Context" (1972). Translated by A. Bass. *Glyph* 1 (1977): 172–197.

Mémoires: For Paul de Man. Translated by C. Lindsay, J. Cullen, and E. Cadava. New York: Columbia University Press, 1986.

Other Works

Culler, J. *On Deconstruction: Theory and Criticism after Structuralism.* Ithaca, N.Y.: Cornell University Press, 1982.

De Man, P. *Allegories of Reading: Figural Language in Rousseau, Nietzsche, Rilke, and Proust.* New Haven and London: Yale University Press, 1979.

Gasché, R. *The Tain of the Mirror: Derrida and the Philosophy of Reflection.* Cambridge, Mass.: Harvard University Press, 1986.

Heidegger, M. *Being and Time* (1927). Translated by J. Macquarrie and E. Robinson. New York: Harper and Row, 1962.

Johnson, B. *The Critical Difference: Essays in the Contemporary Rhetoric of Reading.* Baltimore and London: Johns Hopkins University Press, 1980.

Kamuf, P., ed. *A Derrida Reader: Between the Blinds.* New York: Columbia University Press, 1991.

Norris, C. *Deconstruction: Theory and Practice.* London and New York: Routledge, 1982.

Taylor, M.C. *Deconstruction in Context.* Chicago: University of Chicago Press, 1985.

Ulmer, G. L. *Applied Grammatology: Post(e)-Pedagogy from Jacques Derrida to Joseph Beuys.* Baltimore: Johns Hopkins University Press, 1985.

—CHRISTOPHER BRACKEN

DEIXIS.

DEIXIS. Semiotics and linguistics distinguish two reference-defined categories each of verbal and non-verbal expressions: indexical ones and representational ones. The former are usually designated by the generic term *deixis* (a transliteration of the Greek, which is the nominal form corresponding to the verb *deiknumai,* "to show," "to point"); the latter are instances derived from the general notion of modeling. This distinction arises from the facts that some linguistic expressions have their meaning determined strictly by the situation in which they are used and that when taken out of such situations, these linguistic forms are, so to speak, empty. They have no referential autonomy, unlike an expression such as "the blue book," which conveys to the mind the virtual presence of an object of the world endowed with a set of qualities and determinations. The determinations of *I, you, here* and *now,* for example, in the normal use of language, vary with each situation, a characteristic that Otto Jespersen (1922) captured by categorizing these linguistic forms under the metaphorical term *shifter,* thus indicating that their contents shift as situations change. Roman Jakobson (1963) also employs this term. By contrast, representation defines those linguistic expressions whose meanings are determined with relative independence from the situations in which they are produced. Within a linguistic community, there is a consensus that, assuming that the speaker is correctly informed and does not lie, a sentence such as "New York is east of Chicago" conveys information concerning an actual state of the world, regardless of the situation in which the statement is produced. This representative capacity to convey information about something not present by means of a conventional arrangement of signs, linguistic or other, is designated by the term *modeling.* The speaker or source purports to represent a state of the world that is independent of the immediate situation and that is a possible state of the world or of a possible world. Naturally, this clear-cut conceptual distinction between indexical and referential or representational expressions can be shown to be actually blurred in concrete instances of linguistic communication, as both kinds of expression are blended in the pragmatics of discourse and as there are several levels of integrated conventions in a given linguistic community. Even the most explicit and objective statements require some cognitive framework and situational assumptions in order to be understood fully. This distinction does nevertheless stand on theoretical and empirical grounds, and there is, indeed, a great deal of phylogenetic, ontogenetic, and neuropsychological evidence that deixis and representation describe markedly different types of symbolic behavior (e.g., Nespoulous, 1981; Petitto, 1987).

This distinction does not apply only to the verbal domain but to the nonverbal as well: gestures can point to objects or mimic their shapes or functions, as graphic marks can model an itinerary or simply indicate presence. Within a text, demonstratives and personal pronouns refer to other elements of the text (the cotext) or to the situation (actual or implied) of the context of the enunciation. Inasmuch as all instances of discourse are instances of enunciation, the notion of pure representation remains a semiotic utopia or an ideological strategy.

[*See also* Discourse Analysis; Indexicality; Pragmatics; Semiotic Terminology; *and* Speech Act Theory.]

BIBLIOGRAPHY

Bouissac, P. "Deixis vs. Modeling in the Phylogeny of Artistic Behavior." In *Origins of Semiosis,* edited by W. Noeth, pp. 405–418. Berlin: Walter de Gruyter, 1994.

Brown, S. *Speakers, Listeners, and Communication: Explorations in Discourse Analysis.* Cambridge and New York: Cambridge University Press, 1995.

Clark, H. H. *Using Language.* Cambridge: Cambridge University Press, 1996.

Duchan, J. F., G. A. Bender, and L. E. Hewitt, eds. *Deixis in Narrative: A Cognitive Science Perspective.* Hillsdale, N.J.: Lawrence Erlbaum Associates, 1995.

Fuchs, A. *Remarks on Deixis.* Heidelberg: J. Groos, 1993.

Jackobson, R. "Shifters, Verbal Categories, and the Russian Verb" (1963). In *Selected Writings,* vol. 2, *Word and Languages,* pp. 130–147. The Hague: Mouton, 1971.

Jespersen, O. *Language: Its Nature, Development, and Origin.* London: Allen and Unwin, 1922.

Klein, W. "Local Deixis in Route Directions." In *Speech, Place, and Action: Studies in Deixis and Related Topics,* edited by R. J. Jarvella and W. Klein. New York: John Wiley, 1982.

Nespoulous, J.-L. "Two Basic Types of Semiotic Behavior: Their Dissociation in Aphasia." In *The Neurological Basis of Signs in Communication Processes,* edited by P. Perron, pp. 101–125. Toronto: Toronto Semiotic Circle Monograph, 1981.

Petitto, L. A. *From Gesture to Symbol: The Relationship between Form and Meaning in the Acquisition of Personal Pronouns in American Sign Language.* Bloomington: Indiana University Linguistics Club Dissertations, 1987.

—PAUL BOUISSAC

DE LAURETIS, TERESA (b. 1938), Italian-born American gender theorist and film semiotician. De Lauretis's critical interest in materialist semiotics as well as poststructuralism and psychoanalysis set her apart from most feminist writers in the American tradition.

Her first book, *Alice Doesn't* (1984) operates in constant dialogue with Umberto Eco's semiotics, reformulating his questions and answering in ways that redefine the field in her own terms. This dialogue articulates what de Lauretis calls the "contradiction of feminist theory itself": the fact that it is always both excluded from discourse and imprisoned within it so that the only way to challenge it is from within, by "displacing oneself within it" and rewriting the voice of the master from somewhere else—a different text, a contradictory position. The strategies associated with the speaking position are indeed crucial in feminist theory. One of de Lauretis's tasks has been to theorize the excluded feminine experience, to semioticize it so that it becomes readable within the frameworks that have excluded it.

De Lauretis began by showing that in the 1960s and 1970s feminist film criticism had first used the Marxist critique of ideology to explain how the dominant traditions of narrative cinema operated to keep woman "in her place." Using the semiotic notion that language and other systems of signification (visual or iconic systems) work through coded systems of signs, this approach theorizes the way in which the image of "woman in place" is constructed through the codes of filmic representation. At the time, psychoanalysis had also become a dominant discourse in cinema studies (Metz, 1981), and de Lauretis was critical of this subordination of cinema to language. Consequently, her work with Stephen Heath (1985) has a more materialist and Foucaldian inflection. The cinematic apparatus is understood in both its historical and ideological forms as a relation between the technical and the social. It spans the industrial, the economic, and a range of technologies that comprise machines of the visible, none of which is separate from the making of meaning or from ideology.

For de Lauretis, the central questions are how men and women are addressed by cinema and film; whether they are addressed differently; how perception and vision might be connected; how the perception of signs as visual images might be related to the construction of gendered subjectivity; and, finally, how socially constructed meanings might become gendered subjects. Neither the structural-linguistic model on which classical semiology is based nor the psychoanalytic model are adequate to answer these questions. The former excludes any consideration of gender; the latter does allow a subjectivity constructed in language but explains that subject in terms of processes dependent on the instance of castration and thus predicated on what can only be a male subject. Both are inadequate because they are founded on unacknowledged premises of sexual difference. Even a feminist psychoanalytic view of film, which is doomed from the start to see woman as only the support for a masculine subject's projection and identification—that is, the object of a male gaze (Mulvey, 1989)—remains inadequate.

Against this position, de Lauretis endeavored to demonstrate that meaning was nowhere near as fixed nor so binary, the cinematic apparatus and narrative not so monologic, and the question of visual pleasure not so clear-cut, not so inevitably masculine and based in biology, as the psychoanalytic story would have it. To displace the psychoanalytic feminist view then, and in a sense to speak from "outside" it, she relies on Eco's (1979b) theory of sign production, finding it useful to appropriate his rewriting of the classical system-based and static code of classical semiology—an account that had already been soundly critiqued in work on film. For Eco, whose work derived from that of Louis Hjelmslev and Charles Sanders Peirce, the sign was a sign function, a transient and processual correlation of expression form and content form. The content was a culturally pertinent semantic unit. This made it possible to think of semantic fields as systems of cultural units to some extent independent of the systemic organization of sign vehicles or expression forms. Culture as a semantic system could then be conceived not as a single system but as a "hypercode, a complex system of subcodes" involving many codes or networks of correlations across the planes of content and expression. Most important, it was possible for a sign to become the expression form for another content, an interpretant in a process of what Eco called, after Peirce, "unlimited semiosis." The move from sign to sign through a series of interpretants allowed exchanges of meaning between the verbal, the visual, the corporeal, and so on. But there is still, however, no sign of a gendered subject of semiosis, and that is why de Lauretis undertook to rewrite Eco. She turned first to the ways in which cinema binds fantasy to images and "institutes for the spectator, forms which are unequivocally social."

De Lauretis drew on the physiologist Colin Blakemore (1973) and again on Eco (1979b), using the concept of mapping that is common to them both, to reframe, in nonpsychoanalytic terms, the notion of visual pleasure. According to Blakemore, the human perceptual apparatus does not copy reality but symbolizes it, effecting "a mapping of visual space on to the substance of the brain." Moreover, perception appears to be coded and therefore "predictive." Mapping is used by Eco to theorize the way in which the process of semiosis operates in what he calls "invention": the making of new meanings, mapping pertinent features from one material continuum to another. For Eco, this process is always a mapping from a perceptual model to a semantic model to a unit of expression. It was this working of perception and signification that interested de Lauretis in her development of a theory of the spectator.

Her argument is twofold. First, Laura Mulvey's psychoanalytic arguments that perception is based on biology cannot be maintained. Second, since every (re)production is still embedded in a speech act, it can never be separate from a process of enunciation that involves the whole history of the speaking subject—memory, desire, pain, expectations, and so on. Thus, just as there is no semiosis without subjectivity, there is no perception without semiosis, and the semiosis at work in sensory perception is corporeal, inscribed in "the human body and the film body." She calls this extremely complex process that she has constructed—making meaning, not transmitting it—imaging. It can be reduced to neither the linguistic nor the iconic. It involves different codes and modalities of sign production and includes the production of difference through the interaction of the social and these complex mechanisms for perception and signifying mechanisms.

In theorizing the female subject of semiosis, de Lauretis contests the feminist position that sees feminist experience as an untheorized "nearness to nature, the body, or the unconscious." This formulation targets the work of Julia Kristeva in particular, as well as Eco's refusal to consider either consciousness or the embodied and gendered nature of the subject of semiosis in his theory of semiotics. In the materialist tradition within which Eco is working, testable cultural products include the traces of "real" subjects in texts but do not include embodied consciousness or sexually differentiated bodies. Similarly, while Eco finds in Peirce the missing link between semiosis and reality—human action—that human action "must be excised of its psychological, psychic and subjective component" (de Lauretis, 1984).

De Lauretis's critique also relates discussions of production and consumption to an opposition between high and popular culture in the work of Eco, Kristeva, and others (1984, p. 178). First, de Lauretis contests the typical representation of the consumer as passive, arguing that the interpreter or user of signs is also the producer of meaning because she is the "body in whom the significate effect takes hold." She is careful not to conflate the reader and writer, as Barthes had effectively done (1975), pointing to the critical differences between enunciation and reception and all the issues of address and power surrounding the question of "who speaks to whom and why." She then compares the Lacanian concept of the subject constructed in language—the subject that is always divided from itself at the moment of utterance, split between the enunciation and the enounced—to the Peircean subject that is also divided from itself by means of its relation to a chain of interpretants. "As each interpretant results in habit or habit-change, the process of semiosis comes to a halt, fixing itself provisionally to a subject who is but *temporarily* there" (1984, p. 180). She sees this fixing as related to the Lacanian suture, but she notes that the suture is "bad" both in Lacanian psychoanalysis and in Louis Althusser's theory of ideology, whereas the process that joins the subject to the social in Peirce is neither good nor bad. *Suture* carries connotations of delusion, imaginary closure, and false consciousness. De Lauretis asks whether consciousness has to be always already false consciousness or whether the opposition in Lacan between the truth of the unconscious and the deception of the conscious might not be the discursive product of a "cold war" in which Eco's contrary refusal to countenance the subjective in the social also participates.

Her next step is to revalue the social spaces of everyday life as sites for the production and changing of meaning. The gendering of the bodies who participate in these everyday activities involves the solidarity of habit and belief that is consequent upon a body that is implicated physically in the production of meaning. Habit is the crystallized form of past muscular and mental effort, but the overdetermination of meaning, perception, and experience that folds the subject and reality into one another also potentially involves a continual modification of consciousness and thus the possibility of social change.

The path of semiotics that de Lauretis adumbrates in her discussion of Eco's refusal of Kristeva's "subject in process" has proved effective. Semiotics has in many places become transformed into cultural studies as a result—a paradigm that is now as skeptical of linguistic and literary analyses of signifying practices as de Lauretis was in 1983. Her work was the forerunner of new theories of the female subject and the feminist and heralded new work on the reception and the audiences of texts.

A decade later, de Lauretis's *The Practice of Love* (1994) signals the development of a new interdisciplinary formation of queer theory and gay and lesbian studies out of the cultural studies that was semiotics. It marks another division between those areas and post- and neocolonial studies, both of which have raised issues that this feminism cannot any longer pretend to speak for. Forms of oppression such as race, ethnicity, and class have made it clear that feminism cannot be based simply on gender oppression and, indeed, that white intellectual feminists are in these cases often the oppressors, not the oppressed.

These are salient issues that have emerged since de Lauretis did her groundbreaking work in writing into existence the female subject of semiosis. What should not be forgotten is that that subject is potentially rewritable and that without it some of these other issues might never have been speakable.

[*See also* Cinema; Eco; Feminist Theories; Film Semiotics; Kristeva; Lacan; *and* Metz.]

BIBLIOGRAPHY

Barthes, R. *S/Z* (1970). Translated by R. Miller. New York: Hill and Wang, 1975.

Blakemore, C. "The Baffled Brain." In *Illusion in Nature and Art*, edited by R. L. Gregory and E. H. Gombrich, pp. 1–26. New York: Scribner, 1973.

De Lauretis, T. *Alice Doesn't: Feminism, Semiotics, Cinema*. Bloomington: Indiana University Press. 1984.

De Lauretis, T. *Technologies of Gender: Essays on Theory, Film, and Fiction*. Bloomington: Indiana University Press, 1987.

De Lauretis, T. *The Practice of Love: Lesbian Sexuality and Perverse Desire*. Bloomington: Indiana University Press, 1994.

De Lauretis, T., and S. Heath, eds. *The Cinematic Apparatus*. New York: St. Martin's Press, 1985.

Eco, U. *Lector in Fabula*. Milan: Bompiani, 1979a.

Eco, U. *The Role of the Reader*. Bloomington: Indiana University Press, 1979b.

Grosz, E. *Sexual Subversions: Three French Feminists*. Sydney: Allen and Unwin, 1989.

Metz, C. *The Imaginary Signifier*. Bloomington: Indiana University Press, 1981.

Mulvey, L. "Visual Pleasure and Narrative Cinema." In her

Visual and Other Pleasures, pp. 14–26. Bloomington: Indiana University Press, 1989.

Threadgold, T. "Language and Gender." *Australian Feminist Studies* 3 (1988): 41–70.

—TERRY THREADGOLD

DENOTATION AND CONNOTATION. The correlated terms *denotation* and *connotation* cover at least four conceptual distinctions, some of which themselves comprise several varieties, yet all may be seen as different ways of carving up a particular semantic domain made up of the expression and content of the sign function along with a portion of the empirical world corresponding to the content (that is, the referent). Consistent with the views of Ferdinand de Saussure (1857–1913) and Louis Hjelmslev (1899–1965), content is considered to be a mentality, or more precisely an intersubjective one, whereas the referent is taken to be something that might be encountered in the empirical world—at least potentially—through direct perception. Given these preliminaries, the four basic distinctions can be adequately derived, but, unlike the terms, the resulting concepts are not mutually exclusive and are often confused in the literature.

The Logical Distinction. In logic and philosophy, *denotation* has the same meaning as *extension* in that it refers to the object or class of objects subsumed by a concept. Similarly, *connotation* is another term for *intension* or *comprehension,* meaning the list of all properties characterizing a concept or only those properties conceived of as the necessary and sufficient criteria for ascribing some object to the concept, or the properties that permit us to pick out the objects that fall under the concept. The distinction between *extension* and *comprehension* was first introduced by the French grammarians and philosophers Antoine Arnauld (1612–1694) and Pierre Nicole (1625–1695) in their 1662 treatise *La logique, ou L'art de penser* (Logic, or the Art of Thinking), usually referred to as the Port Royal logic, from the name of the convent where they resided, whereas the use of the terms *denotation* and *connotation* probably derives from John Stuart Mill (1806–1873), whose *System of Logic* (1843) develops a theory of meaning (Garza Cuarón, 1978).

Intension and extension are sometimes identified respectively with what Gottlob Frege (1848–1925) termed *Sinn* and *Bedeutung* (1892) in writing that various intensions may correspond to a single extension:

for instance, "the morning star" and "the evening star" (Venus), "equilateral triangle" and "equiangular triangle," "the vanquisher of Austerlitz" and "the vanquished of Waterloo" (Napoleon), and other pairings employ the same extensions but different intensions. If the intension is taken to contain all properties common to the objects in the extension, then all terms having the same extension will also have the same intension (Kubczak, 1975). For instance, both the morning star and the evening star could be described as a particular star that can be seen shortly before the rising and shortly before the setting of the sun. If this is indeed the content of both terms, it is difficult to explain the fact that, in many contexts, one of the terms cannot be exchanged for the other. Kubczak concludes that in linguistic signs intensions do not contain full information about the objects to which they refer. An alternative explanation was suggested by Edmund Husserl (1859–1938) and spelled out in further detail by Aron Gurwitsch (1964): according to this analysis, the conceptual *noema* (from the ancient Green *nous,* meaning thought or mind)—that is, the intension—does in fact contain all elements found in the object but is organized each time into a particular thematic hierarchy (Husserl, 1970).

The Stylistic Distinction. Also originating in the Port Royal logic, the stylistic distinction treats connotation as *idées accessoires* (subsidiary ideas). The German grammarian Karl Otto Erdmann (1858–1931) in 1900 distinguished between *Hauptbedeutung, Nebensinn,* and *Gefühlswert.* Erdmann apparently thought that the core meaning, which he believed conceptual in nature, could be distinguished from subsidiary-meaning aspects on one hand and emotional values and ambience on the other; as the distinction is nowadays stated, the latter two notions are amalgamated. Wilbur Urban (1939), Raymond Firth (1957), and Charles K. Ogden and Ivor A. Richards (1927) circulated his concept in the English-speaking world, translating the first term as *denotation* and conflating the latter two terms as *connotation.*

According to this conception, a demarcated portion of the content domain corresponds point by point to an object in the perceptual world, such as it would appear in a completely "objective" account; the other part, the residue, has no equivalent in the real-world object but is added to the content by the sign or the sign users. The features of the first part are supposed to be cognitive or conceptual, thus permitting the identification of the real-world object; the features of the other part are said to be emotive or expressive, and it is never made clear whether they are part of the intersubjective content of the sign, are contributed by the sign producer, or result from the reaction of the sign receiver. Moreover, the cognitive meaning is taken to be more important than the rest, perhaps because cognition is postulated to carry more importance than emotion.

Hjelmslev's Distinction. According to Hjelmslev (1943), connotation is a particular configuration of languages and opposed in this respect not only to denotation but also to metalanguage. A connotational language is a language (a system of signs), whose plane of expression is another language, which means that it is the inversion of a metalanguage, the content plane of which is another language. Contrary to both of the latter, denotational language is a language, none of which's planes form another language. Thus, denotation is a relation that serves to connect the expression and the content of a sign, whereas connotation and metalanguage both relate two separate signs, each with its own expression and content.

Hjelmslev gives various examples of connotations such as different styles, genres, dialects, national languages, and voices. In a telling example, he suggests that while he is speaking Danish and denoting different contents, he is connoting the Danish language. In a parallel fashion, a person speaking in a foreign tongue will all the time be connoting "I am a foreigner." In many languages, the use of an /r/ produced with the tip of the tongue or with the uvula indicates and thus connotes different geographical origin. In analyzing these and other examples, we see that semiotic connotations reside in the choice from a set of alternatives of a particular expression to stand for a given content or of a particular variant to realize the invariant expression.

Hjelmslev's connotations have often been compared to some of those mentioned by Leonard Bloomfield (1933), which depend on the social and geographical origin of the speaker or are associated with improper or intensified versions of more normal signs. There is certainly a similarity in the kind of contents invoked, but for Hjelmslev what is important to connotation is not the particular contents or kinds of contents conveyed but the formal relationships that they presuppose.

Even if some particular kinds of content are really associated with connotational language, there is cer-

tainly nothing in Hjelmslev's text to suggest that these should have something to do with emotion, contrary to what has been taken for granted by those who identify Hjelmslev's connotation with the stylistic one. Henning Spang-Hanssen (1954), himself a collaborator of Hjelmslev, observes that emotive signs do not contain only connotations nor do all emotive signs contain them. Indeed, four-letter words certainly connote their being "four-letter words," but this effect is produced quite independently of the reactions of the audience and of the degree of emotion with which the words are used.

Hjelmslev's formal theory of connotation is much more complex than most commentators have realized. Thus, it can be demonstrated, for instance, that Hjelmslev distinguished connotations stemming from the form of denotational language, in which the units of connotation and denotation are identical, from those derived from such language's substance, where the matter serving as the vehicle of the two signs is segmented differently. As soon as we delve deeper into the text, we will also discover that Hjelmslev's examples embody a theory that is narrower, if not simply different, from the one conveyed by his definitions, and we will encounter reasons to doubt that connotational language, interpreted in this way, can really be considered a mirror image of metalanguage, as ordinarily understood.

Eco's Distinction. Although Umberto Eco claims to take the notion of connotation from Hjelmslev, he has turned it into something rather different. The first time he employs the term, Eco (1968) produces a heterogeneous list of phenomena that seems to include logical connotation, stylistic connotation, and much else, which he then describes as the total sum of cultural entities brought up before the receiver's mind. In a later text, however, Eco (1976) defines connotation as "a signification conveyed by a precedent signification," which rather suggests what logicians call a contextual implication—the context being offered by some kind of "meaning postulate" defined in a particular sign system. More recently, Eco (1984) observes that what he calls the second level of the connotational system is based on inference.

To illustrate his idea of connotation, Eco asks us to imagine a dike provided with an alarm system in which the sign AB denotes danger, the sign AD insufficiency, and so forth. In the context of the dike, danger is known to result from the rise of water above a determinate level, whereas insufficiency indicates that the water level is too low. We are also acquainted with the fact that in the first case it will be necessary to let some portion of the water out and that in the latter case some amount of water must be allowed to enter the system. The sign AB, then, denotes danger and connotes evacuation (and then no doubt also high water level), and the sign AD denotes insufficiency while connoting the entering of the water into the system (and low water level). Given the stock of accessible knowledge, all these facts could be said in the context of the dike to imply each other.

In spite of its multiple layers of meaning, this case does not confirm Hjelmslev's model, as Catherine Kerbrat-Orecchioni (1977) observes, since it is only the content of denotation, not the whole sign, that is transformed into the expression of connotation. But there is really no reason at all to expect that Eco's example should confirm Hjelmslev's model, since, in spite of using the same term, they are concerned with different phenomena. Indeed, as a close reading of Hjelmslev's text will show, Eco's connotations would be symbols to Hjelmslev and could in some cases be conveyed indirectly by connotational languages.

No doubt we could look upon Hjelmslevian connotation as a particular case of implication—that is, as an implication resulting from the peculiar relation between the expression and content of a sign. It is, however, an implication involving signs, not mere content parts, and that is what is essential to Hjelmslev's conception.

[*See also* Barthes; Frege; Pictorial Semiotics; *and* Rhetoric of the Image.]

BIBLIOGRAPHY

Arnauld, A., and F. P. Nicole. *The Art of Thinking* (1662). Translated by J. Dickoff and P. James. Indianapolis: Bobbs-Merrill, 1964.
Bloomfield, L. *Language*. New York: Allen and Unwin, 1933.
Eco, U. *La struttura assente*. Milan: Bompiani, 1968.
Eco, U. *A Theory of Semiotics*. Bloomington: Indiana University Press, 1976.
Eco, U. *Semiotics and the Philosophy of Language*. Bloomington: Indiana University Press, 1984.
Erdmann, K. O. *Die Bedeutung des Wortes*. Leipzig: E. Avenarius, 1900.
Firth, R. *Papers in Linguistics, 1934–1951*. London: Oxford University Press, 1957.
Frege, G. *Translations from the Philosophical Writings of Gottlob Frege*. Translated by P. Geach and M. Black. Oxford: Blackwell, 1966. This edition includes a translation of "Sinn und Bedeutung" (1892) on pages 56–78.
Garza Cuarón, B. *La connotación: Problemas del significado*. Mexico City: El Colegio de México, 1978.
Greimas, A. J. *On Meaning*. Translated by P. J. Perron and F. Collins. Minneapolis: University of Minnesota Press, 1987.
Gurwitsch, A. *The Field of Consciousness*. Pittsburgh: Duquesne University Press, 1964.
Hjelmslev, L. *Prolegomena to a Theory of Language* (1943). Translated by F. J. Whitfield. Madison: University of Wisconsin Press, 1961.
Husserl, E. *Logical Investigations*. Translated by J. N. Findlay. New York: Humanities Press, 1970.
Kerbrat-Orecchioni, C. *La connotation*. Lyon: Presses Universitaires de Lyon, 1977.
Kubczak, H. *Das Verhältnis von Intention und Extension*. Tübingen: Narr, 1975.
Mill, J. S. *A System of Logic: Ratiocinative and Inductive*. 2 vols. London: Longmans and Green, 1843.
Ogden, C. K., and I. A. Richards. *The Meaning of Meaning: A Study of the Influence of Language upon Thought*. London: Kegan Paul, 1927.
Rössler, G. *Konnotation: Untersuchungen zum Problem der Mit- und Nebenbedeutung*. Wiesbaden: Steiner Verlag, 1979.
Sonesson, G. *Pictorial Concepts: Inquiries into the Semiotic Heritage and Its Relevance for the Analysis of the Visual World*. Lund: Lund University Press, 1989.
Spang-Hanssen, H. *Recent Theories on the Nature of the Language Sign*. Copenhagen: Nordisk Sprog- och Kulturforlag, 1954.
Urban, W. M. *Language and Reality: The Philosophy of Language and the Principles of Symbolism*. London: Allen and Unwin, 1939.

—GÖRAN SONESSON

DIAGRAMS. Visuospatial representations of concepts and their relations, diagrams offer the opportunity to regard all the parts of a system simultaneously, which is one key to their cognitive power. Simultaneity is a perceptual construct of consciousness. We know that the brain, like a computer, has to take in its data from the world in relatively small bits and that it builds up a picture of "now" that encompasses a lot more of that data than it grasps simultaneously. The visual sense is privileged in this regard: hearing, for example, has less capacity to detach itself from the flow of time. Diagrams hold steady for consciousness a complex of relations that otherwise would seem to flow by in temporally elusive thought, exceeding the grasp of comprehension. What we should discern through this analysis is that the clarity provided by diagrams is both perceptual and logical.

As a class of sign vehicles, diagrams are heterogeneous but endowed with a few common traits: they are usually in two dimensions and two colors. They favor straight lines, distinct borders, right angles, and circles or parts of circles. A roughly drawn diagram is generally intended to be seen as a sketch that could be rendered more strictly with a compass and straightedge. Diagrams have a tone of formality that recalls the elements of plane geometry, so they tend as a class to connote the articulatory power of artificial languages. There are some technical diagrams, like diagrams of transformational groups in linear algebra and computer-programming flowcharts, that do achieve precision. Perhaps the best known are Venn diagrams, which illustrate addition and intersection of classes. But frequently, we use diagrams to make our ideas look better than they are.

Two diagrams, just like two sentences, may be synonymous. For example, in figure 1, it is easy to think of diagram A as synonymous with B, and it is fairly easy to extend the synonymy to C, though the presentation here is a bit perverse. Of course, it all depends on what we are representing. These three diagrams might be of the same sentence and fully synonymous. On the other hand, there is no reason in principle why different meanings could not be assigned to the open and closed lines of A and B. Diagramming is an open game. Still, the possibility of synonymy is obvious, and therefore we should look, if we can, from the vehicle to the underlying logic that forms the ground of these representations.

In the absence of universal conventions, it is impossible to state what constitutes the grounds of all visual diagrams, but there are some recurrent traits. Typically, line segments in diagrams represent relations such as inclusion, dominance, cause, or choice between the objects represented at their endpoints. Such visual elements as connecting lines, dividing lines, horizontal or vertical alignment, and proximity or separation tend to represent such nonvisual relations as cooccurrence, temporal order, inclusion, and category affiliation. Diagrams readily suggest relations that we cannot explicate. Representing ideas by diagrams gives us a feeling of control over them and suggests that we can play with them. Even if the feeling is largely illusory, the effect is significant: it shows how a finite combinatorial system (e.g., a system with lines and dots as its vocabulary) creates its own semiotic universe, how ready we are to enter it, and how formal systems lead to free play.

Diagrams resemble notational systems but rarely are fully articulate. While diagrams in general are vague, mathematics constructs some special types that are formally explicit (Capobianco, 1989), such as graphs that can be used as notations. The concrete visual realization of these graphs, however, lies outside the mathematical theory. A graph, as a mathematical object, is defined most economically as a list of points and a list (drawing on the first) of pairs of points. The pairs of points are often represented visually by lines joining labeled endpoints. If the pairs are ordered, the lines are directed (like arrows). Commonly, such points are called vertices, nodes, or dots and the lines are called arcs, branches, or lines. Every line connects two dots; two or more lines can be connected at one dot.

As a notational system, graph theory allows us to pin down the distinctions among types of hierarchies. A succession of lines, each connected to the next, forms a path between the extreme vertices of the succession. If a graph has one and only one path between any two dots, the graph is called a tree graph. In figure 2, if there is more than one path, the graph is a type of net graph. Graph A is a tree graph. Graphs B and C are equivalent net graphs—that is, taken as representamens, they are potentially synonymous. Tree graphs can notate a componential hierarchy ascribed to sentences but not all the componential hierarchies commonly ascribed to music. If we take graphs seriously as cognitive models, then different

FIGURE 1. *Synonymy in Diagrams.*

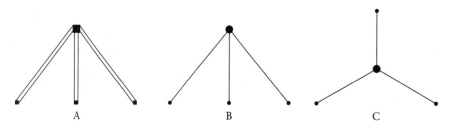

A   B   C

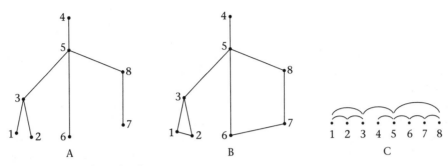

FIGURE 2. *Tree and Net Graphs.*

sorts of comprehension are suggested for music and language in adapting these different models.

[*See also* Articulation; Artificial Language; Peirce; Pictorial Semiotics; *and* Vision.]

BIBLIOGRAPHY

Capobianco, M. F. "What Is a Graph? Three Possible Anwers." In *Graph Theory and Its Applications: East and West,* edited by M. F. Capobianco, et al. Annals of the New York Academy of Sciences, vol. 576. New York: New York Academy of Sciences, 1989.

Roberts, D. D. *The Existential Graphs of C. S. Peirce.* The Hague: Mouton, 1973.

—DAVID LIDOV

DIALOGISM. A widely accepted semiotic principle, dialogism asserts that all language inevitably enters into dialogue with the words of others: all utterances are interrelational, all meanings interactive. Originally a theory of language conceived by Mikhail Bakhtin in the 1920s, dialogism has implications also for the understanding of texts, cultural theory, and the notion of subjectivity. Dialogism, then, is fundamental to the way in which language functions at every level of society. If every word, every sentence is to some extent defined by or against other words and the words of others, no utterance exists as a wholly self-determined, totally fixed entity: there is no pure monologism.

That Bakhtin developed the notion of dialogism in Stalinist Russia explains its social and political dimensions. What might appear today to be a benignly relativistic theory emerged as a radical, if somewhat strategically oblique, theoretical position. The oppositional and subversive element in Bakhtin's work—his celebration of the resistance of the unofficial, the

antiauthoritarian, and the improper—did not go unnoticed by Soviet censors. This accounts for the difficulty he encountered in getting his work published and in fact resulted in his political exile. But Bakhtin was not silenced completely. His linguistic and literary theory critiques the social and historical tendency for certain utterances—certain "speech genres," literary genres, and discourses—to attempt to be as authoritative and unitary as possible. Authoritative discourses—the enshrined words of legal, religious, and military institutions—attempt to limit the polysemic impulses of language. Bakhtin's point is that meanings cannot be fixed or made absolute and that the desire for order and stability is inevitably defined against the persistent residual otherness of anarchy, irresolution, and multiplicity.

The philosophical basis of dialogism is outlined in Bakhtin's "Discourse in the Novel" (1934). This theoretical framework indicates the many different levels to which the dialogue principle applies: official and unofficial, formal and informal, the artistic and the everyday. Very simply, Bakhtin asserts that there are "two embattled tendencies in the life of language"—the centripetal and the centrifugal—and that these forces confront each other in the utterance (Bakhtin, 1981). On the one hand, language is a shared medium through which we convey information and ideas; on the other hand, it is the locus of the social struggle inherent in all utterances. How, then, is Bakhtin able to offer this conflict-based account of the way communication functions and malfunctions as something positive? Bakhtin proceeds to examine the way "authoritative discourses" seek to impose their truth upon us, in contrast to the open and negotiable process of meaning making he calls "internally persuasive discourse." In very broad terms, fascist or totalitarian discursive regimens are contrasted against more democratic, noncoercive discourses.

There is a close connection between dialogism and what Bakhtin calls heteroglossia (from ancient Greek, literally meaning "different tongues") in referring to the social context of dynamic interaction between socially stratified and subculturally differential utterances in which discourses are formed and circulate. With the emerging influence in the academy of cultural studies, the tendency has been increasingly to refer to discourse outside of the novel, and this broad semiotic understanding of dialogism has subsumed much of what Bakhtin refers to as heteroglossia.

An understanding of dialogism as being not only *dialog-ic* but also *dia-logic* reiterates Bakhtin's assertion of the way language functions in a doubling, pluralistic fashion. Understood in this way, dialogism undercuts the hegemonic assumption of a singular, rational form of logic. Bakhtin does not accept the linear, teleological trajectory of simplistic dialecticism, particularly the assumption that synthesis is actually ever realizable. Final and absolute agreement is not possible. Even the self cannot coincide with itself, since one's sense of the self is essentially a dialogic configuration. Bakhtin describes the construction of subjectivity in this way: "The ideological becoming of a human being . . . is the process of selectively assimilating the words of others" (1981, p. 341). Subjectivity, therefore, can be understood as a process of semiotic or discursive constitution and reconstitution. Any sense of selfhood and identity that we possess, then, is fabricated out of the words of others.

The material and ideological nature of any utterance, any sign, is argued most strongly in a text Bakhtin is thought to have either published under Valentin Voloshinov's name or at least strongly influenced, *Marxism and the Philosophy of Language*. In this text, Voloshinov criticizes both subjective individualism and objective abstraction. Communication is grounded in dialogism, for the "word is a two-sided act. It is determined equally by whose word it is and for whom it is meant. As word, it is precisely the product of the reciprocal relationship between speaker and listener, addresser and addressee" (1986, p. 86). Voloshinov goes on to emphasize the philosophical logic underpinning this dialogic principle by asserting that "each and every word expresses the *one* in relation to the *other*."

These ideas build on Bakhtin's earlier reference to

the "social multiaccentuality" of the sign, which signals the importance of contextuality in reading signs, words, and utterances. The very same utterance might have different meanings, depending on intonation, orientation, and evaluative accent. And, of course, the meaning-making process itself is a dynamic relationship between addresser and addressee—a much more negotiable process than it appears at first. Multiaccentuality relates to Bakhtin's claim that the utterance is a site of struggle: as much as meanings are shared, they are also contested, tension filled, and contradiction ridden. We never simply repeat the words of others: when we take them on ourselves, we invest them with our own inflections and accent them differently. Thus, while a good deal of deterministic force is imposed upon us as we enter language and culture (centripetal forces), we make our own space within these social constraints (centrifugal impulses). This is not to mask the differential magnitude of various regimes of power but simply to assert that control is not totalizable and that absolute power is a fiction.

While Bakhtin's dialogism is seen as contributing to a materialist sociolinguistics, many critics have also pointed to the connection between his ideas and poststructuralism (e.g., the sense of a decentered self and the potent[ial] instability of meanings). Julia Kristeva signals this deconstructionist thrust: "More than binarism, dialogism may well become the basis of our time's intellectual structures" (1986, p. 59). The focus has since shifted from the fiction of structural polarities to the struggle for meaning in between the multiplicity of forces that seek to control it. In other words, there are no authoritatively singular meanings, but there is no absolute free play of signification either. More recently, Bakhtin's ideas have also informed postcolonial theory not only through his account of the carnivalesque and the obvious relevance this has for people living under colonial rule but also through his identification of discursive power relations, which has informed analyses of colonial discourse. An important part of Bakhtin's work is his deconstruction of myths of linguistic and cultural purity, superiority, and authenticity. See, for example, the account of the way the "alien, foreign word" is tied inextricably to the formation of social and political hegemonic "unity" (Voloshinov, 1986).

[*See also* Bakhtin; Dialogue; Inner Speech; Kristeva; Postcolonialism; *and* Poststructuralism.]

BIBLIOGRAPHY

Bakhtin, M. M. "Discourse in the Novel" (1934). In *The Dialogic Imagination,* edited by M. Holquist, translated by C. Emerson and M. Holquist, pp. 259–422. Austin: University of Texas Press, 1981.

Bakhtin, M. M. *Problems of Dostoevsky's Poetics.* Edited and translated by C. Emerson. Manchester: Manchester University Press, 1984.

Bakhtin, M. M. *Speech Genres and Other Late Essays.* Edited by C. Emerson and M. Holquist, translated by V. W. McGee. Austin: University of Texas Press, 1986.

Hitschkop, K. "Is Dialogism for Real?" *Social Text* 30 (1992): 102–113.

Holoquist, M. *Dialogism: Bakhrin and His World.* London and New York: Routledge, 1990.

Kristeva, J. "Word, Dialogue, and Novel." In *The Kristeva Reader,* edited by T. Moi, pp. 34–61. Oxford: Basil Blackwell, 1986.

Maranhao, T., ed. *The Interpretation of Dialogue.* Chicago: University of Chicago Press, 1990.

Morson, G. S., and C. Emerson. *Mikhail Bakhtin: Creation of a Prosaics.* Stanford: Stanford University Press, 1990.

Voloshinov, V. N. *Marxism and the Philosophy of Language.* Translated by L. Matejka and I. R. Titunik. Cambridge, Mass.: Harvard University Press, 1986.

—JOHN FIELDER

DIALOGUE. A structured exchange of messages, both verbal and nonverbal, dialogue is the primary semiotic mode in the construction of all social systems. Minimally, a social system consists of a dyad (two interacting individuals), such as the mother-infant dyad. To function appropriately as a member of a dyad, each individual must anticipate the likely responses of the other. This ability—based partly on built-in biological constraints—is learned through a shared developmental history of message exchanges with others in a given semiotic system. It depends on the social scripts and discourse genres that members learn through their participation in these interactions.

Dialogue structures and processes are not specific to the human species. Evidence of dyad membership, indicating the individual's membership in a higher-order social system, is found in other social mammals (e.g., wolves, dolphins, and primates). The social mammals participate in dyad structures that enable them to recognize and respond to others as individual members of a social system. They have been mutually socialized through their participation in communicative interactions.

The dialogue mode of interaction emerges in the very earliest stages of human infant behavior, well before the protolinguistic stage. Typically, this is around the age of five to eight months (Halliday, 1990). Studies of the exchange of face-to-face expressions between mother and infant show that these take on dialoguelike structures around the age of about thirteen weeks (Kaye, 1984). The increasing ability of the infant to coordinate his or her "turn" in the ensuing exchange does not appear to be entirely inborn; it is also the result of the infant's insertion into a higher-order social system, the mother-infant dyad. Kaye's research on face-to-face interactions between mother and infant points to the phase that Trevarthen (1979) identifies as primary intersubjectivity. The coordinated exchange of facial expressions functions as a dialogic "turn." This elementary nonlinguistic but signifying interaction—the mother-infant dyad—is the beginning of intersubjectivity. It is through such dialogues that the infant is recruited into the structures and processes of the social system. The infant, in learning to reciprocate the mother's facial expressions, completes an implicit social structure. This results in the emerging awareness that the phenomenal and material world can be construed and organized in terms of a you and a me. Dialogue structures and processes are not necessarily linguistic, though they are always semiotic. They provide the central organizing concepts in the infant's joint construction with others of the social system, and they afford the fundamental semiotic resource in all forms of learning and instruction (Bateson, 1973). Learning can only occur through situationally specific dialogues involving implicit structures and rules regarding exchange and cooperation.

Halliday (1984) has provided an account of how the sociosemantics of exchange is made grammatical and expressible in English in a number of basic speech-act types: statement, question, offer, and command. The research focus is thus on how these forms are deployed in dialogue to make and negotiate meanings. A given speech act is one speaker's contribution to the signifying interaction in and through which meanings are exchanged. A given speech act is always tied to a response or potential response known as its finalization (Bakhtin, 1986). Dialogue is organized in terms of such basic semantic interactants, which Bakhtin described as the primary genres out of which more complex types are constructed. It is through such local acts of finalization that some determinate shape and temporality is given to the social situations negotiated in the ongoing exchange of meanings in dialogue. Finalization does not always occur as an immediate response to the initiating speech act; the completion of the dialogue might be near or far in time.

The grammatical and semantic resources of small-scale exchange are deployed to construct larger dialogue structures, such as spoken and written texts, situationally specific occasions of discourse. A dyad is a minimal instance of a jointly constructed signifying act. The focus is on the socially shared and constructed action formations that are built up from the sign systems—the semiotic resources—of a culture. Different types of semiotic actions select from and use these sign systems in different ways, such as in the writing of a love letter, the conducting of a history lesson, the buying of goods and services, and the making of a news broadcast. All of these are different kinds of action formation, but they all entail a regular and recognizable deployment of the available sign systems to enact socially meaningful forms of dialogue.

Dialogue begins with the joint construal of shared experiences of the environment. In the first instance, these are present simultaneously to both parties, who construe the experience as a joint signifying act in the exchange process. At a later stage, this evolves into the ability to construe as meanings experiences from which one of the parties to the interaction was absent (Halliday, 1990). The infant develops the ability to talk about experiences that another did not take part in. After the event, the experience is construed dialogically as a shared act of meaning—perhaps a shared memory—in which both can participate. The basic mode is still dialogic, not monologic. This is so of all forms of social semiosis—both verbal and nonverbal, both spoken and written language.

[See also Conversation; Dialogism; and Gossip.]

BIBLIOGRAPHY

Bakhtin, M. M. "The Problem of Speech Genres" (1952–1953). In Speech Genres and Other Late Essays, edited by C. Emerson and M. Holquist, translated by V. W. McGee, pp. 60–102. Austin: University of Texas Press, 1986.

Bateson, G. "The Logical Categories of Learning and Communication." In Steps to an Ecology of Mind, pp. 250–279. London and New York: Paladin, 1973.

Halliday, M. A. K. "Language as Code and Language as Behaviour: A Systemic-Functional Interpretation of the Nature and Ontogenesis of Dialogue." In The Semiotics of Culture and Language, vol. 1, Language as Social Emiotic, edited by R. P. Fawcett et al., pp. 3–35. London and Dover, N.H.: Frances Pinter, 1984.

Halliday, M. A. K. "The Place of Dialogue in Children's Construction of Meaning." In Proceedings of the Third International Conference "Dialogue Analysis," edited by S. Stati. Bologna: Pátron, 1990.

Kaye, K. The Mental and Social Life of Babies: How Parents Create Persons. London: Methuen, 1984.

Riegel, K. "The Temporal Organization of Dialogues." In Foundations of Dialectical Psychology, pp. 85–110. New York and London: Academic Press, 1979.

Trevarthen, C. "Communication and Cooperation in Early Infancy: A Description of Primary Intersubjectivity." In Before Speech: The Beginning of Interpersonal Communication, edited by M. Bullowa. Cambridge: Cambridge University Press, 1979.

Voloshinov, V. N. Marxism and the Philosophy of Language. Translated by L. Matejka and I. R. Titunik. New York and London: Seminar Press, 1973. This volume was published originally in Russian under the title Marksizm filosopfija jazyka (Leningrad: Academica, 1930).

—PAUL J. THIBAULT

DISCOURSE ANALYSIS is a term with a complex history within semiotics and cultural theory. The general meaning of *discourse*, "language in use," derives from its definition within linguistics to mean "connected speech or writing" above the level of the sentence. Zellig Harris (1952) was the first to argue that the formal methods of linguistics could be used to describe connections between sentences rather than just the structure within sentences. He used invented data to describe the formal properties of connected speech, but other researchers in this field have worked with naturally occurring talks and texts and focused on the contextual and social functions of such texts, not just their purely formal properties (e.g., Halliday and Hasan, 1989). This particular focus on discourse entailed a move away from the elucidation of formal systems (*langue*) toward the study of actual speech events in contexts, although it fell short of actually examining the processes of production and reception of texts.

Norman Fairclough (1992a), in his selective survey of current approaches to discourse analysis, divides them into the critical and the noncritical. The former attempts to show how discourse is shaped by power relations and ideologies and constructs identities, social relations, and systems of knowledge; the latter merely describes discursive practices and includes text linguistics, applied linguistics (pragmatics, sociolinguistics), and the empirical sociological approach to discourse as conversation. The empirical approaches involve largely sociological forms of analysis that have taken discourse to mean human conversation. There have been several approaches, including that of the Birmingham School (Sinclair and Coulthard, 1975), that worked toward a general descriptive system for analyzing discourse in the classroom, concentrating on the transaction and the structures of exchanges within it. One of the most productive works in conversational analysis has been that of Harvey Sacks (1935–1975), based on the approach of Harold Garfinkel's *Studies in Ethnomethodology* (1967)—a sort of empirically based poetics of ordinary talk. Other classic works in the field include Sacks, Emanuel Schegloff, and Gail Jefferson on turn taking and correction in conversation (1974); Gillian Brown and George Yule (1983) on topic organization in conversation; and work on such topics as nonvocal aspects of the interaction such as gaze and gesture (Goodwin, 1981) and the analysis of other institutional modes of discourse such as that of the courtroom (Matoesian, 1993) or the psychotherapeutic interview (Labov and Fanshel, 1977). Gregory Matoesian's work in particular makes connections between conversational analysis and critical-discourse analysis, looking at the issue of talk and power in rape trials. Dorothy Smith's use of ethnomethodological and conversational analysis in her attempts to write a feminist sociology (1990) extends the analysis of exchanges to the dialogism between written texts in the construction of the everyday and gendered relations of ruling and power. In the process, Smith again demonstrates the potential for using these kinds of analysis to support other politically committed forms of discourse analysis that are not based in such well-grounded analysis of linguistic discursive features.

The critical approaches are based on an integration of the work of social theorists such as Antonio Gramsci, Louis Althusser, Michel Foucault, Jürgen Habermas, and Anthony Giddens with work in critical linguistics using Halliday's systemic functional grammar. Critical linguistics was developed by a group based at the University of East Anglia in the 1970s (Fowler, 1981). Though influenced mostly by

Michael Halliday, they also used stylistic methods borrowed from generative-transformational linguistics and derived some inspiration from the work of Roland Barthes and early French semiotics. It is also important to recognize, through the work of Halliday, the influence of Prague School linguistics and semiotics, British structuralist-functionalist anthropology, the work of the educational sociologist Basil Bernstein (whose later work [1990] is specifically on pedagogic discourse), and the much earlier work of the linguists Edward Sapir (1921) and Benjamin Lee Whorf (1956). This intertextual and discursive history needs to be thought of as still operating, albeit at a distance, in the work on discourse of this school of linguists. Critical linguistics reads the meanings in texts as the realization of social processes, seeing texts as functioning ideologically and politically in relation to their contexts. Less attention was paid to the production and interpretation of texts, and the relationship between textual features and social meanings was assumed to be self-evident. There was also a Marxist top-down view of ideology and power and an emphasis on social structure rather than social action, social reproduction rather than social transformation.

The work of the group that came to be known as social semioticians in Australia included some of the same people—Michael Halliday, Ruqaiya Hasan, Gunther Kress, and Robert Hodge—and worked with some of the same ideas, but in the Australian context there was a strong influence from poststructuralism and French structuralism and semiotics as well as from the work of semioticians such as Umberto Eco and from a variety of feminisms, so that what Halliday had called a theory of language as social semiotic became, in the work of this group, something quite other by the early 1990s. There was a concern to rethink functional linguistics in the light of Foucault's work on discourse, institutions, and power, Bakhtin's writings on heteroglossia and dialogism, the work of psychoanalytic feminisms on the unconscious, and the questions of the body and subjectivity derived from a number of sources including Pierre Bourdieu. A new focus on processes of textual interpretation and production emerged, and the importance of intertextuality and subjectivity in those processes as discursive processes involving struggle and change was foregrounded.

Fairclough (1992a) has debated with forms of discourse analysis that are derived from text linguistics, a term first used in the 1950s by Eugen Coseriu and taken up later by Ulrich Weinreich (1967), Teun van Dijk (1972), and Robert de Beaugrande (1980). This project's history lay in poetics, stylistics, and narratology and whose goal was to read the social effects of a text through a linguistic analysis. In its most formal mode, text linguistics attaches itself to the logical and philosophical tradition of John Searle et al. (1980) and John Austin (1962). This approach has now redefined itself as discourse analysis, for instance in the journal *Discourse and Society.*

At the same time as the term *discourse* is used in an increasing variety of ways, it has come to carry a very different set of connotations and determinations since the work of Foucault. Fairclough (1989, 1992b) has worked extensively on the discursive analysis of the construction of social relations in the kinds of genres of social interaction singled out by Foucault's work, looking at the construction of social relations and of the self in the medical interview or the conversational anecdote, exploring the construction of reality in various regimes of power and discourse, such as the literature on prenatal care and the discourses of corporate culture. He has taken up the issues of power, knowledge, discourse, and subjectivity that Foucault's earlier work foregrounded, seeking to explore these issues in actual textual and social practice but seeing Foucault's concept of power as too structuralist and therefore rejecting it. Fairclough's most recent work has been concerned with exploring three major tendencies of an international and perhaps transnational kind—what he calls democratization, commodification, and technologization, the latter a term he uses to describe the use of discourse to effect social change (social engineering).

[*See also* Althusser; Bakhtin; Bourdieu; Conversation; Cultural Difference; Dialogism; Dialogue; Foucault; Habermas; *and* Kristeva.]

BIBLIOGRAPHY

Austin, J. L. *How to Do Things with Words.* Cambridge, Mass.: Harvard University Press, 1962.

Beaugrande, R. de. *Text, Discourse, and Processes.* Norwood, N.J.: Ablex, 1980.

Beaugrande, R. de, and W. Dressler. *Introduction to Text Linguistics.* London: Longman, 1981.

Bernstein, B. *The Structure of Pedagogic Discourse.* London and New York: Routledge, 1990.

Brown, G., and G. Yule. *Discourse Analysis.* New York: Cambridge University Press, 1983.

Coseriu, E. *Textlinguistik.* Tübingen: Narr, 1980.

Dijk, T. A. van. *Some Aspects of Text Grammar.* The Hague: Mouton, 1972.

Dijk, T. A. van. *Handbook of Discourse Analysis.* London: Academic Press, 1985.

Fairclough, N. *Language and Power.* London: Longman, 1989.

Fairclough, N. "Discourse and Text: Linguistic and Intertextual Analysis within Discourse Analysis." *Discourse and Society* 3.2 (1992a): 193–217.

Fairclough, N. *Discourse and Social Change.* Cambridge, Mass.: Polity Press, 1992b.

Fairclough, N. *Critical Discourse Analysis: The Critical Study of Language.* London: Longman, 1995.

Fowler, R. *Literature as Social Discourse: The Practice of Linguistic Criticism.* London: Batsford Academic and Education, 1981.

Fowler, R. *Language in the News: Discourse and Ideology in the Press.* London: Routledge, 1991.

Garfinkel, H. *Studies in Ethnomethodology.* Englewood Cliffs, N.J.: Prentice-Hall, 1967.

Goodwin, C. *Conversational Organization.* New York: Academic Press, 1981.

Halliday, M. A. K., and R. Hasan. *Language, Context, and Text: Aspect of Language in a Social-Semiotic Perspective.* Oxford: Oxford University Press, 1989.

Harris, Z. S. "Discourse Analysis." *Language* 28 (1952): 1–30.

Labov, W., and D. Fanshel. *Therapeutic Discourse: Psychotherapy as Conversation.* New York: Academic Press, 1977.

Matoesian, G. M. *Reproducing Rape: Domination through Talk in the Courtroom.* Chicago: University of Chicago Press, 1993.

Sacks, H. *Lectures on Conversation (1964–72).* 2 vols. Edited by G. Jeferson. Oxford: Blackwell, 1995.

Sacks, H., E. A. Schegloff, and G. Jefferson. "A Simplest Systematics for the Organization of Turn-Taking in Conversation." *Language* 50 (1974): 696–785.

Sapir, E. *Language* (1921). New York: Harcourt, 1949.

Searle, J., F. Kiefer, and M. Bierwisch, eds. *Speech Act Theory and Pragmatics.* Boston: D. Reidel, 1980.

Sinclair, J. M., and M. Coulthard. *Toward an Analysis of Discourse: The English Used by Teachers and Pupils.* London: Oxford University Press, 1975.

Smith, D. *The Conceptual Practices of Power: A Feminist Sociology of Knowledge.* Toronto: University of Toronto Press, 1990.

Weinreich, U. *Languages in Contact.* The Hague: Mouton, 1967.

Whorf, B. L. *Language, Thought, and Reality.* New York: Wiley, 1956.

—TERRY THREADGOLD

DISTANCE. Space is used to encode social meanings that govern interpersonal relationships. Edward

Hall (1975) has labeled this kind of code *proxemics*—that is, the semiotics of distance or degrees of proximity. The simplest form of proxemic code uses different distances between people to encode social relationships such that greater physical distance signifies greater social distance. A code of this form would be fully motivated. In practice, purely physical proxemic codes do not exist in isolation in any society. Social space is always mapped in complex ways to encode relationships of power and solidarity by using different supplementary coding systems.

One motivated meaning of distance is as a measurement of solidarity, such that great distance signifies low solidarity (hostility, suspicion, etc.) and closeness the opposite. However, distance can also signify the scope of power, so that those with power express it by claiming large amounts of space. This is itself a motivated signifier. If someone enters the space of a powerful person without due permission, then that act is typically interpreted as a denial of status and an offense against solidarity. Closeness can thus signify either close intimacy or life-threatening hostility, depending on how the relationship is perceived by participants (who might not encode it in the same way).

There is, then, an inherent instability in this apparently most simple of coding systems, and this instability is the key to the properties of the numerous systems that are built on it. In order to disambiguate the important meaning of power, space is used to provide other signifiers of this dimension. Some of the most common motivated signs of power pertain to height, movement, size, and symmetry. Height is a common signifier of power, achieved either by raising the powerful (e.g., on a platform) or by artificially depressing the height of the nonpowerful, such as through bowing and curtsying. But sometimes power is signified by its apparent opposite, as for instance by remaining seated while the nonpowerful stand to attention. Similarly, movement often signifies the ability of the powerful to do what they like, while the nonpowerful signify their weakness through limited mobility. But some other times, a lack of need to move signifies power. For these reasons, the systems that encode power are often very different from one society to another. What is required behavior in one culture is transgressive behavior in another. This fact leads people to conclude that these codes are highly arbitrary, as they indeed are, but this arbitrariness derives in no small degree from inherent contradictions in the basic motivated code.

A further source of instability in this set of codes comes from the fact that distance between people is a material fact that can have a number of causes and therefore a number of distinct meanings. If distance can be chosen freely by all parties, then it may be taken to encode an agreed meaning. However, distance might be affected by physical constraints, so that people find themselves closer to each other than either or both would prefer (as with people jammed together in an elevator) or so that the distance is constructed unilaterally by one participant (e.g., a "pushy" salesperson). For this reason, secondary coding systems are required to adjust to or correct the meanings implied by the actual physical distance. These typically include a large conventional component, although they often draw in similar ways on a common repertoire of motivated signifiers.

Among these secondary codes, direction of gaze and bodily posture provide a set of signifiers that is probably universal. Turning aside the head or body normally signifies that the physical distance is too close to express the social meaning at issue. Averting the gaze (with or without turning the face away) has the same meaning. These signifiers can act to override the signifiers of physical distance (as people on a crowded subway gaze ahead fixedly to signify that they are not close in spite of the proximity of their bodies), or they can act to provide a complex running commentary on the meaning of the relationship as it is being negotiated with words and bodies (as in flirting).

There are important cultural differences in what is accepted or required with such signals. For instance, aversion of eye contact might be interpreted as proper modesty in one cultural system but as shiftiness and dishonesty in another. However, such differences are constituted by two distinct components: the meanings projected by the coding system (e.g., direct gaze signifies intimacy) and a set of rules about who is allowed to express intimacy to whom (e.g., what are the required or forbidden levels of intimacy with strangers, with older people, and with persons of the other sex). It is theoretically possible for two societies to have coding systems that are identical but rules of intimacy that are opposites, so that the same behavior might have an identical meaning encoded in it about relationships but have the opposite social value. In practice, cultural differences can be expected to include both factors but in different proportions; the task of addressing cultural differences of this kind needs to make the distinction.

In the semiotics of film, the role of the look or the gaze has been investigated extensively, especially by feminist theorists who observe the way in which females and their bodies are represented as objects for the male gaze. The same is true of female nudes in art. The gaze constructs a relationship between the object as represented and the position of the spectator, and since spectators are always looking, they are always being positioned and their relationship to the objects in the frame of representation constantly constructed by the act of looking. Developments in the history of art such as perspectivism and antiperspectivism can be understood semiotically in the same terms. Renaissance illusionism, for instance, constructed a unitary observer placed centrally outside the frame with mathematical precision. Prosceniumarch theater similarly constructed an ideal audience with a privileged and detached point of view on the action of the play. Movements in art or theater that attack these conventions (e.g., Cubism in art, street theater) challenge the typical construction of the spectator and the social relations of power and solidarity that constitute the dominant tradition.

Many rules of etiquette (e.g., shaking hands, embracing, kissing, standing up or sitting down, sitting next to someone) are secondary signifiers of spatial meanings, encoding these primary social meanings in bodies and behaviors. A rule of etiquette such as one about aversion of gaze encodes both a piece of meaning and the relationships that it is designed to express. In a similar way, subtle variations in performance of a basic rule of etiquette can signify important differences of meaning. For example, there are a number of different forms of kissing in Anglo-Saxon society: mutual kiss into empty space behind the ear (social greeting of older relatives), peck on the cheek (more intimate version of this), kiss on the lips (sexual intimacy), and "deep kiss" (intense sexual intimacy). Similarly, handshakes in Anglo-Saxon societies can range between soft and firm grip, bodies close or distant, accompanied by a hand grasp to forearm, upper arm, or shoulder, and so on. There are also other variations, such as ritual handshakes, that encode specific meanings while still encoding basic relationships of power and solidarity.

Clothing codes are another secondary system for signifying distance and managing space. Dress rules in traditional societies that require women to hide their mouths, heads, and other parts of the body in public serve to reinforce the set of rules controlling other signifiers of intimacy, such as touching or appearing in public. There is usually a general equivalence between amount of clothing between people and amount of social distance signified. Thus, formal occasions, where the relationships that are constructed involve mutual deference, are normally characterized by elaborate clothing, which either project outside the body space (e.g., women's ball gowns in nineteenth-century Europe) or are so complex and elaborate that they construct a distinct position for their intended viewer. Carefully coordinated clothing styles are another signifier of distance and hence formality or power because the spectator needs to be far enough away to take in the spectacle at a glance.

Clothing codes are commentaries on meanings that are encoded on bodies, assigning specific meanings to specific parts of men's and women's bodies (e.g., breasts, genitals). Spatial codes can refer to a multiplicity of such reference points (so that the distance from genitalia, for instance, is coded in proxemic terms). In this way, the movement of women's hemlines up or down in relation to ankles or knees can have a transferred erotic meaning, which in turn signals intimacy or nonintimacy for a woman in relation to a presumed male gaze. These meanings are often specific to a particular time and place, but they are built up out of a common stock of signifying elements.

Speech codes are organized on similar principles, and politeness codes typically specify a match between dress style and speech style. "Formal speech" is characterized by elaboration of forms, with transformations and circumlocutions establishing distance between thought and speech. This can be achieved by a variety of means, such as the use of rare or archaic vocabulary, obedience to a set of severe constraints on what can be said and how it can be said, proliferation of number of syllables per word, words per utterance, and utterances per occasion. In general, verbosity signifies distance.

The form of the rules that govern these uses of signifiers of distance, both primary and secondary, follows the pattern described by Brown and Gilman (1960) for pronouns of address in European languages. They noted that the rules for correct use of the intimate pronoun of address (*tu, thou,* and similar forms) were complex and contradictory because they signified either close intimacy or hostility and contempt. As we have seen, this problem arises with all signifiers of proximity and for the same reason: the extreme ambiguity of the meanings of the close-distant continuum. Pronouns of address are just one of many reflections in verbal language of the set of spatial signifiers that plays such a crucial role in the organization of social life.

[See also Cultureme; Face; Habitus; Nonverbal Bodily Sign Categories; and Space.]

BIBLIOGRAPHY

Brown, R., and A. Gilman. "The Pronouns of Power and Solidarity." In Style in Language, edited by T. A. Sebeok, pp. 253–276. Cambridge, Mass.: MIT Press, 1960.

Hall, E. T. "Proxemics." Current Anthropology 9 (1968): 83–108.

Hall, E. T. Handbook of Proxemic Research. Washington, D.C.: Society for the Anthropology of Visual Communication, 1975.

Lurie, A. The Language of Clothes. New York: Random House, 1981.

—ROBERT HODGE

DISTINCTIVE FEATURES. Jan Baudouin de Courtenay (1845–1929), the first linguist to formulate the idea of the phoneme, saw the phoneme as essentially a mentalistic phenomenon, an ideal sound that the speaker aims at but only approximates in actual speech, thwarted by interference from performance constraints, the influence of neighboring sounds, and so on. But while this might just explain "automatic" alternations such as [k]/[q], it could not account for more idiosyncratic oppositions like the Castilian [d]/[ð] or the pre- and postvocalic variants of /l/ in some varieties of English. Linguists such as Daniel Jones (1881–1967), committed to the tradition of British empiricism, saw the matter in more physical terms, assuming that what was important about allophones (i.e., variants of a phoneme) was their phonetic similarity, and described them as belonging to a "family" of phonetically similar sounds in complementary distribution. Thus, we would say that the English phoneme /t/ has an aspirated allophone [tʰ] word-initially (as in tale), a deaspirated one after initial /s/ (as in stale), a nonexploded one word-finally, a partially flapped or devoiced or fricatized one between vowels (depending on the dialect), and so on. The problem with this positivist approach, however, is that each phoneme turns into a rather

arbitrary and open-ended listing of all its possible phonetic variations: given that no two utterances are identical, it is not clear where such a listing should stop. The criterion of similarity is, in any case, not only vague but question begging (since different languages apportion similar sounds to different "families") and is sometimes impossible to determine objectively even for a given language: is the ⟨p⟩ of spin phonetically more like the /p/ of pin, for example, or the /b/ of bin?

What both approaches overlook is one of Ferdinand de Saussure's most fundamental insights: it is difference and opposition within a linguistic system that permit it to function. If you hear the word I utter as pan rather than ban or man or fan, it is not because I have succeeded in reproducing or approximating some ideal /p/ sound, since my articulation can vary in all sorts of ways without disturbing communication: I can utter it with rounded lips, extra breathiness, creaky voice, and so on, provided that I distinguish it from its closest neighbors. Unlike /f/, for example, it must be interrupted or noncontinuant (i.e., it must have the feature [−continuant]); unlike /m/ it must be [−nasal]; unlike /b/ and /m/ it must be [−voiced]; unlike /t/ it must be [−coronal] ([+coronal] sounds are made with the tip of the tongue raised); and unlike /k/ it must be [+anterior] (i.e., involving obstruction or constriction somewhere between the hard palate and the lips). In terms of the system devised by Noam Chomsky and Morris Halle (1968) to replace Roman Jakobson's original formulation (1962), about thirty distinctive features are sufficient to define all the meaningful contrasts employed in all human languages (any given language will only use a subset of these, of course). In both systems, the features are binary (+ or −, present or absent) rather than multivalent or n-ary; arguments in support of this invoke psychology (infants seem to extend their repertoire of sounds by splitting those already mastered according to distinctive features), cerebral physiology, and consistency of description, though such arguments do create what appear to be rather arbitrary problems in the description of vowels in particular (Creider, 1986).

Thus, each phoneme may be described as a "bundle" of distinctive features (DFs) or as a hierarchy (Clements, 1985), though there will be a degree of redundancy in such descriptions, since some features are bound to either exclude or require certain others: [+anterior] entails [−vocalic], for example, since no vowels require restriction or obstruction of the air supply; similarly, in English [+nasal] excludes [−continuant] and [−voiced]. Instead of specifying each feature independently, therefore, it is possible to simplify the underlying representation of sounds by "underspecifying" them and supplying the gaps later in the phonological derivation through "fill-in" rules such as "all vowels are voiced" (i.e., [+vocalic] → [+voiced], where → means "entails") and context-sensitive rules such as "nonlow vowels are round if (and only if) they are back" ([α round] → [α back]/[−low], where α F means "a given value of feature F" and / means "in the following environment"). Underspecification might, indeed, be necessary in order to ensure the correct operation of certain phonological rules. For example, while there seems to be an output filter in English that prohibits structures within morphemes of the kind sC_1VC_2 where $C_1 = C_2$, such as *spop or *skak, and inhibits them where C_1 and C_2 are homorganic (made with the same speech organs), it does not seem to apply to [+coronal] consonants, since we find many forms like *stoat* and *state* with identical [+coronal] Cs and many more with homorganic ones (e.g., *stud, snout, stand*) (Davis, 1990). One way of accounting for this is to claim that in English [±coronal] is not specified in the underlying phonological representation but supplied later in the derivation (after the filter) by a default rule that makes [+coronal] every sound not otherwise specified for place of articulation. Underspecification is a currently much-debated topic in linguistics; for arguments against it, see Mester and Itō (1989).

One great advantage of DF description is that it treats the sounds of the language not as an arbitrary list of items but as a set of natural classes (in general, a class is more natural as fewer DFs are required to specify it: the class of vowels ({[+vocalic], [−consonantal]}) is thus more natural than the class of low vowels ({[+vocalic], [−consonantal], [−high], [+low]}). DF analysis equally facilitates the formulation of synchronic phonological rules, such as that governing the choice of the "regular" or productive plural formative for English nouns (one of /-s/, /-z/, or /-iz/): instead of listing the word-final phonemes that trigger each variant (which would be tedious and nonintuitive), we can say that words with [+strident] (hissy) final sounds take /-iz/ (*horses, watches*), those with {[−strident], [+voiced]} final sounds take /-z/ (*bees, dogs*), and those with {[−strident], [−voiced]} final sounds take /-s/ (*cats, cliffs*). Indeed, according to Chomsky and Halle, we can do away with the concept "phoneme" altogether as not merely otiose but misleading. Take the question of nasal assimilation, for example: though in English /n/ is "normally" (e.g., before a vowel) articulated against the teethridge, in phrases like *in Greece* and *in Paris* the phonemic shape of the word changes: /iŋgris/, /im pæris/. But the same phonological process of assimilation in *in France* or *in Thessaly* leaves the phonemic shape of the word unchanged, since the positional variants of /n/ (dentolabial and dental, respectively) do not constitute separate phonemes of English. But it would be strange to devise two different rules for what is clearly one process: with DF analysis, the problem disappears, since a simple rule that assimilates a [+coronal] nasal to the place of articulation of the following consonant (provided no phonological-word boundary intervenes) will cover both kinds of case. Or take the problem of whether the ⟨p⟩, ⟨t⟩, and ⟨c⟩ in *spin, stun, scan* represent allophones of /p, t, k/ or /b, d, g/: DF analysis reveals this as a pseudoproblem, since all that is required is a rule neutralizing the opposition [±voiced] in that environment. However, phonological processes such as metathesis (the swapping of adjacent sounds—*aks* for *ask*, for example) or spoonerisms do make more sense when viewed in terms of whole phonemes: we never find swapping of single features (e.g., *watf* for *wasp*, with the exchange of [±continuant] in the last two segments).

DF analysis has occasionally been applied to other linguistic areas, usefully in syntax (for marking combinatory categories of words, for example) and with perhaps less success in semantics. Componential analysis (as the semantic version is called) has some value as a way of characterizing classes of nouns in determining conditions of semantic well-formedness: instead of listing all the possible subjects of *admire* or objects of *frighten*, for example, we need only specify that they be [+animate], as subjects of *transpire* must be [+abstract], and so on (cf. the unacceptable *Henry transpired; *The doorknob admired Stella*). Componential analysis is also of some use in representing semantic relations such as antonymy and hyponymy; the standard example is that *man* is [+human], [+male], [+adult], *woman* is [+human], [−male], [+adult], *girl* is [+human], [−male], [−adult], and *boy* is [+human], [+male], [−adult]. But even this example has problems (*girl* and *woman* overlap in reference, for example), and the assignment of semantic DFs becomes much more problematic and arbitrary once we move away from the well-worn examples. See Anna Wierzbicka (1980, 1984) for a discussion of this important problem.

[*See also* Articulation; Binarism; Phoneme; Semiotic Terminology; *and* Structuralism.]

BIBLIOGRAPHY

Chomsky, N., and M. Halle. *The Sound Pattern of English*. New York: Harper and Row, 1968.
Clements, G. N. "The Geometry of Phonological Features." In *Phonology Yearbook 2*, edited by C. J. Ewen and J. M. Anderson. Cambridge: Cambridge University Press, 1985.
Creider, C. A. "Binary vs. N-Ary Features." *Lingua: International Review of General Linguistics* 70 (1986): 1–14.
Davis, S. "An Argument for the Underspecification of (Coronal) in English." *Linguistic Inquiry* 21 (1990): 301–306.
Jakobson, R. *Selected Writings*, vol. 1, *Phonological Studies*. The Hague: Mouton, 1962.
Mester, R., and J. Itō. "Feature Predictability and Underspecification: Palatal Prosody in Japanese Mimetics." *Language* 65 (1989): 258–293.
Wierzbicka, A. *Lingua Mentalis: The Semantics of Natural Language*. New York: Academic Press, 1980.
Wierzbicka, A. "Cups and Mugs: Lexicography and Conceptual Analysis." *Australian Journal of Linguistics* 4 (1984): 205–225.

—Peter Groves

DOUBLE BIND. A notion constituted jointly in the mid-fifties by a research team at the Veterans Administration Hospital, Palo Alto, California, under the leadership of Gregory Bateson, the double bind has come to mean colloquially "darned if you do, darned if you don't." But double bind in its original expression refers to a much more complex set of circumstances, and its colloquial interpretation depicts the circumstances of single rather than a double bind.

Initially, the concept was associated with schizophrenic behavior. Characteristically, members of "schizophrenic" families display extraordinary inconsistencies in their communications with each other, the truly schizophrenic member being noncommunicative and showing almost complete inertia with respect to social relations. The Palo Alto researchers investigated what sequences of interpersonal relationships could induce these unconventional communicative habits. Their answer involves analysis of the circumstances in which a member of

a family or other tight-knit social unit comes to believe that any choice they make in interpersonal relations is untenable. Conditions within a social unit in which a member or members feel bankrupt in the making of any choice give rise to the features of paralysis commonly demonstrated among members of a schizophrenic family. Thus, noncommunication between the schizophrenic and others is, in some sense, appropriate for these circumstances.

Such situations arise only where long-lasting patterns of communication create habitual expectations that the schizophrenic then transposes to the world at large. The origins of this situation appear to lie in the communicative phenomena of paradoxical injunctions. If the latter are inserted repeatedly into interpersonal situations over a period of time, a stream of paradoxical injunctions generates a self-perpetuating oscillation between meaning and nonmeaning that could never be resolved satisfactorily through interpersonal communication. A very simple example of paradoxical injunction is an attempt to obey the command, "Be spontaneous." However, the unresolvable oscillation here cannot explain those situations where self-other communication gives rise to the feeling that no outcome is possible and all alternatives lead to bankrupt choice.

At first, Bateson's research team gave limited examples of paradoxical communication, such as those occurring in a family dyad, mother and son. The following example of an assertion by a mother to her son at one level of meaning also contains its negation at another level. The child thus becomes caught up in rules about approved and disapproved behavior that are mutually negating; finally, as an important addition to the overall situation creating a double bind, the child is forbidden to comment on the situation. Thus, mother might say, "Do not do so-and-so or I will punish you" (message content), while at the same time saying, "Do not see this as punishment," or, "Do not question my love of you when I tell you not to do so-and-so and I punish you" (second-level interpersonal message negating the first), and also at the same time saying, "Don't talk back to me" (child is unable to comment on the paradox in the messages being expressed).

Obviously, these communications could occur in normal as much as in pathogenic situations, and the research team was careful to note that use of paradoxical injunctions in communication does not "cause" schizophrenia and neither did the double binds to which they gave rise. The shift from normal to pathogenic occurs as a result of a failure to learn how to resolve patterns of double binding. In Bateson's terminology, problems arise from an inability to deal with the initiating conditions—that is, failing to adopt patterns of learning how to learn, or deutero-learning. In a pathogenic situation, this could lead to failure in recognizing the pattern of a double bind; for example, it might account for schizophrenics' feeling as if they are on the spot at all times.

Later research depicted double binds that occur as a result of family members forming coalitions or triads in their communicative interactions with each other. Here, double binds arise through sequences in which A and B punish one another for how each sees and acts upon the contingencies of their interchange. In both dyadic and triadic interchanges, the premise behind double binds is that primary messages in communication, which are verbal, are always presented together with classifying messages, which can be but are not necessarily verbal. Classifying messages arise from ongoing relationships between communicators. These are of a different logical type from the former and are "meta" to the verbal content; the logic of the metalevel refers to the condition of trust or validity that a message receiver can impute to the content of the message.

To summarize, the pattern of a double bind is always an encounter with contexts of deutero-learning—that is, habituated patterns of "learning to learn." Double binds concern contexts of behavior between self and other, self and environment, or self and self at another time. These contexts are learned and are altered by learning experiences, but at the time of the double bind the very survival of the self appears to be at stake. Yet a victim of repeated double binding is faced with a situation where other communicators seem to find the context of communication logical, plausible, and consistent; only "the victim" finds the situation untenable or absurd. Double-binding patterns of communication thus have effects upon a victim's understanding of communication contexts and, hence, of the mode of classification of those contexts. Schizophrenics in particular tend to distort signals about the ongoing context of relationship or omit that classification entirely. Typically, schizophrenics will eliminate from their messages everything that refers explicitly or implicitly to the relationship between themselves and the people they are addressing, and therefore their means for understanding and classifying contexts of behavior is diminished considerably.

Bateson was always uneasy with the specific association of the double bind with the phenomenon of schizophrenia, for he believed that the concept referred to a more general set of circumstances. Double-bind sequences precipitate circumstances for a variety of psychic changes. The sequences are painful or traumatic but sometimes funny. They might promote psychotic or psychopathic symptomology, or they might promote humor or invention. It is never evident whether any change initiated through double binds would be pathogenic or therapeutic, creative or mystical. Other aggregates of phenomena to which double binds could be associated include humor, poetry and art, religion, hypnosis, altered consciousness, and dream.

Generally, people have difficulty in speaking about how the pattern of relationships of communicators enters into the meaning of messages. Double binds occur where there is communicative closure, as in family systems or in therapeutic situations in hospitals, or culturally, where there can be no stepping out from the bonds of relatedness between communicators. The reciprocal relations of the communicators not only bind patterns of communication, but these, together with the concomitant relationships among the aggregate members of the communicative system, form a self-maintaining system. In addition, the closure of the system creates contexts and constraints that eliminate or neutralize possibilities of communicating about the double bind. The contexts in which double binds occur either prohibit metacommunication about the pattern of the bind or, in another formulation, invalidate a metastandpoint that would otherwise permit members of the communicative system to stand back and look reflexively at the whole of their interrelations.

A double bind can, therefore, be considered an example of false dialectics, blocked reflexivity, or both. The first case stresses the logic in a falsified dialectics and in so doing explains causal results of contradiction in situations in which the victim is repeatedly required to support both sides of a paradox. The second case focuses on the psychological errors in perspective where the systemic contradiction refers to perceptions of self vis-à-vis perceptions of self and other in the communicative system as a whole. Contexts of communication in a double bind create contradictory interpretations of the value or significance of a given message, at two levels of significance. A victim finds that if the message means A, this invalidates what the victim has learned about the contexts of relationship in which that particular message is valid; or, if the victim chooses B as the significance of the message, then the victim must deny the truth value of the message itself, a "truth" that the victim has also learned at some prior stage. The metaconditions, which satisfy both A and B are absent (and cannot be discussed), leaving the victim to oscillate between either choice A or choice B. Since each choice facing the victim proposes but does not satisfy the other, any choice, as the victim oscillates between alternative levels of significance, eventually results in invalidating the process of choosing alternatives.

In the second perspective, that of blocked reflexivity, the concern is with reflexive hierarchy—the relation between a perspective and another perspective looking back at itself from an outside or more holistic vantage point. The fallacies of perspective that yield double binds are not errors in the logical sense, nor do they refer to the truth value of statements among communicators. Rather, reflexiveness involves gestalt configurations among a collection of communicators. The perceptual errors emerge in a temporal hierarchy (more accurately, "heterarchy") of reflexive loops involving all members. That recursive configuration containing a more holistic pattern or metastandpoint is perceived at the same level or as a narrower configuration of images of self and other within the collection. A double bind emerges when communicators collapse broader configurations, and collapsed reflexivity is followed by a twist in recursive-feedback loops from whole to part. At that point, communicators are somehow prohibited from visualizing a "higher standpoint"; the metaconditions defining the meaning of messages are absent, and the recursive relation between whole and part cannot be discussed. The collapsed reflexiveness of the vertical bind inhibits a change in the context of learning and seals in, as it were, horizontal errors of framed perspectives. Because they are prohibited from visualizing their relations at metalevel, communicators are unable to change patterns of their existing order by involving themselves in a new pattern.

Bateson argues that double-bind sequences are recognizable as one of a definable aggregate of formal characteristics of interaction that are found in all communicative systems. He carefully revised his own definitions of double bind and took strong exception to the term's misuse because he recognized that any logical form is always associated within political and socioeconomic relations to processes of rationalization. The virtue of the concept of double bind lies in its epistemology. Western society had become organized on the basis of competitive exchange, a mode of organization that covers not only values of goods and services arising in economic exchange but also interpersonal activity within such exchanges. Causal efficacy of interpersonal relations is, in the dominant view, adjoined to competitive relations of social power. By contrast, a double bind generates sequences of contradiction and resolution that occur in the absence of competition, social power, or any causal efficiencies derived therefrom.

The causal sequences of double bind have effect because they derive from systemic constraints in informational order. Among the most important constraints are the existence of time—that is, patterns of information always exist in temporally bounded circuits—and information patterns that become learned and habituated. A third pattern of constraint is the organization of the several levels of the senses—speech, sight, hearing, paralinguistic body language, and patterns of communication among members of the communicative system—which must be integrated in order for information to have any meaning. Thus, constraints of an informational order generate coherence and permit understanding despite the enormous array of features in a heterarchical, noncompetitive matrix of relations that communicators are required to take into account.

[See also Bateson; Communication; Dialogue; and Metalanguage.]

BIBLIOGRAPHY

Bateson, G. *Steps to an Ecology of Mind.* New York: Ballantine Books, 1972.

Bateson, G. "Double-Bind." In *Cybernetics of Cybernetics,* edited by H. von Foerster, pp. 419–420. The Biological Computer Laboratory Report, no. 73.38. Urbana: 1974.

Bateson, G., et al. "Toward a Theory of Schizophrenia." *Behavioral Science* 1.4 (1956): 251–264.

Berger, M. M., ed. *Beyond the Double Bind: Communication and Family Systems, Theories, and Techniques with Schizophrenics.* New York: Brunner/Mazel, 1978.

Hoffman, L. *Foundations of Family Therapy: A Conceptual Framework for Systems Change.* New York: Basic Books, 1981.

Keeney, B. P. *Aesthetics of Change*. London: Guilford Press, 1983.

Watzlawick, P., J. Beavin, and D. Jackson. *Pragmatics of Human Communication*. New York: W. W. Norton, 1967.

Weakland, J. H. "One Thing Leads to Another." In *Rigor and Imagination: Essays from the Legacy of Gregory Bateson*, edited by C. Wilder-Mott and J. Weakland, pp. 43–64. New York: Praeger Scientific, 1981.

Wilden, A., and T. Wilson. "The Double Bind: Logic, Mathematics, and Economics." In *Double Bind: The Communicational Approach to the Family*, edited by C. Sluzki and D. C. Ransom, pp. 263–286. New York: Grune and Stratton, 1976.

—PETER HARRIES-JONES

DOUGLAS, MARY TEW (b. 1921), British cultural anthropologist whose diverse writings on religion, economics, organizational behavior, food, and comparative social organization focus on classification and communication. Douglas's work is along the lines of that of Emile Durkheim (1858–1917) and Marcel Mauss (1872–1950), who were similarly concerned with the relations between the symbolic and social orders. For Douglas, the social order is represented symbolically in all communicative acts. Douglas's fieldwork was with the Lele of Congo, but her writings have more often been on European culture or on some transcultural, comparative problem.

Douglas's interest in taxonomy would seem to ally her with ethnoscience, but she is more concerned with the way in which taxa are rooted in social categories and operationalized in social action. She believes that society, much more than language, channels and constrains thought. Indeed, Douglas is interested primarily in nonlinguistic modes of communication. She speaks of the exchange of food and goods as systems of communication, by which she means that these objects have symbolic features derived from their categorical positions in culture, and their exchange is regimented by clearly defined rules. Both the value of the objects and the rules of exchange vary among cultures and classes but within definite parameters, thus allowing comparative study.

This comparative interest is epitomized in a classification of societies in terms of group and grid. The grid dimension measures how strictly a culture imposes its social categories upon its population and how rigorously it controls social patterns of interaction among these categories; the group dimension assesses the relative weights granted individual and collective values. This is close to Durkheim's notions of mechanical and organic solidarity, although rather than opposing them, Douglas's schema places group and grid along x and y axes, as a given society might be strong or weak in terms of both grid and group. Moreover, the relative weighting of the two dimensions varies within society and even among individuals and is at least partly the product of choice. Douglas's basic problematic in the analysis of a culture's "communication systems," especially ritual, is how they reflect the relative emphasis of group or grid. Communication in contexts where group is strong will tend to be ritualized and the symbols condensed; where group is weak, communication is personal and the symbols referential. Her concept of semiosis is drawn from Edward Sapir, whose views on the primacy of society in the semiotic process Douglas found sympathetic.

A further dimension measures discourse as related to social complexity; for this, she borrows the notions of restricted and elaborated speech codes from the sociologist Basil Bernstein. Restricted speech codes are found in societies and groups where division of labor is low and group allegiance is high; elaborated speech codes appear in groups where division of labor is high and group allegiance is low. Speech and other communicative acts do not merely reflect the underlying context of social structure but reinforce it as well. Thus, restricted speech acts in strong group societies fortify the group and generate social solidarity. Elaborated codes emphasize specialization and individualization as well as occupational and social status. It is important to note that restricted and elaborated codes coexist in all complex societies, and their use is thus a prime sociolinguistic fact. A single speaker might use restricted codes in certain contexts, elaborated codes in others. Each utterance makes statements about the speaker and his or her place in society.

Douglas considers virtually all social action a form of communication and thus greatly extends Durkheim's idea of society as a self-creating and re-creating entity. That is, she maintains that at every moment of utterance, a certain image of society is invoked and affirmed by the speaker and interlocutors, endowing that image of society with an objectivity it would otherwise not have. Like totemic rites among Durkheim's Australians, communicative events take on a ritual function. The object of ritual for Douglas is very much what it was for Durkheim: the representation, in the strong sense of making present and real, of the social order.

Ritual employs a restricted code, and it is easy to see how such utterances reinforce the group by generating solidarity. However, it seems to be equally the case (although this feature is less developed) that elaborated codes represent the social order as a complex structure of statuses (i.e., grid). The university lecture, which Douglas cites as a prime example of a speech act that employs an elaborated code, very clearly represents this social order in at least two ways. In semantic content, it represents the division of labor in a branch of learning—a microcosm of the division of labor in society. In pragmatic terms, the lecture organizes the participants by status (professor, graduate students, undergraduates), and these divisions are reflected in seating, rules of speaking, and even codes of dress.

This social self-representation is seen nowhere more clearly than in images of the body. European political philosophy of the seventeenth and eighteenth centuries made explicit the connection between bodies—especially those of sovereigns—and society. For Douglas, this is a universal phenomenon: the body is always the social body. Here we see Douglas's sociological phenomenology most clearly revealed. Unlike Alfred Schutz and his followers, Douglas claims that the natural world is always already socially constructed. There is then no problem of false consciousness, no distinction between a socially constructed consciousness and one that is true. Our discourse is always constrained by the social-symbolic order; Douglas approvingly cites Foucault on this point.

The way in which bodies are presented and represented in social action is functionally related to other dimensions of society, which can be described in terms of grid and group. In strong group and strong grid contexts, the margins of the body will be strongly emphasized in ritual and everyday life. Purity, pollution, food taboos, and bodily discipline will be highly stressed. In weak group and grid contexts, by contrast, internal organs and states will be emphasized. Supernatural intrusions into the body will be viewed positively. A contrast in religious practice between Brahman Hindus and Pentecostal Christians, for example, can be seen in these terms. In the sort of society anthropologists typically study, one with low grid and high group values, witchcraft is the main explanation for bodily affliction. The witch presents a negative image of the social person, an inversion of all "natural" human intentions and proclivities. Witches attack the boundaries of the body, removing or corrupting internal organs. Contrariwise, rites to prevent or counteract witchcraft emphasize prophylaxis and the fortification of bodily and social boundaries. In this kind of social milieu, a dualistic worldview is likely to emerge in which evil is associated with all external forces. If we compare similar societies (those that vary only along the group axis), we will not surprisingly find stronger ideas of sin and evil and more vigorous attempts at their expulsion among the stronger group societies. These variations are not seen as related to demographic or ecological factors but rather to underlying social ideologies.

[See also Code; Communication; Cultural Knowledge; Culture, Semiotics of; Durkheim; Leach; and Lévi-Strauss.]

BIBLIOGRAPHY

Douglas, M. T. *The Lele of Kasai.* London: Oxford University Press, 1963.

Douglas, M. T. *Purity and Danger: An Analysis of the Concepts of Pollution and Taboo.* London: Routledge and Kegan Paul, 1966.

Douglas, M. T. *Implicit Meanings: Essays in Anthropology.* London: Routledge and Kegan Paul, 1975.

Douglas, M. T. *In the Active Voice.* London: Routledge and Kegan Paul, 1982a.

Doulas, M. T. *Natural Symbols: Explorations in Cosmology.* New York: Pantheon, 1982b.

Douglas, M. T., and B. Isherwood. *The World of Goods: An Anthropological Theory of Consumption.* London: Allen Lane, 1979.

—MICHAEL HARKIN

DURKHEIM, ÉMILE (1858–1917), French scholar who, along with Max Weber (1864–1920), is best known as the founder of modern sociology. His theoretical and methodological contributions to the study of large-scale processes in state-level societies are certainly his most important legacy. However, toward the end of his life, his attention turned to problems of meaning and classification. At the same time, he began to draw his data from tribal societies, especially those of Australia. Particularly significant is his shift to the study of symbolism in "primitive" cultures, which can be seen as the founding moment of symbolic and cognitive anthropology.

Durkheim was trained in Paris at the École Normale Supérieure under Numa Denis Fustel de Coulanges (1830–1889), the great classical historian. His early career consisted of teaching philosophy in provincial schools and developing his new science of society. His monograph *Suicide* (1897) was a paragon of the new sociology, combining a sophisticated and testable theory of the relation between the individual and society with a fine-grained analysis of empirical data drawn from census reports. The success of Durkheimian sociology attracted a circle of bright and eager young scholars who founded and published in *L'Année sociologique* (1898–1913). These scholars included Henri Berr, Marcel Granet, François Simiand, Maurice Halbwachs, and Marcel Mauss, among others. The latter two, particularly Mauss, who was Durkheim's nephew and closest collaborator, were especially important in the shift of sociology to the study of meaning and symbolism.

Durkheim's semiotic turn was the logical extension of his concern with the relation of the individual to society. He had always been interested in cultural norms and values and in how they were internalized. His famous antipsychologism is more accurately a rejection of methodological individualism, since he was very much concerned with the functioning of the mind. What he wished to explore was the way in which socially constructed symbol systems provide a basic mental framework that orients individuals toward the world. Moreover, this framework has a pragmatic component, providing motivation for actions not explainable in terms of the utilitarianism that strongly influenced Durkheim's earlier work.

The first working out of these problems is seen in the long article Durkheim wrote with Mauss, translated as *Primitive Classification* (1903). Here the question of the basic philosophical categories of "time, space, class, number, cause, substance, personality, etc." is opened. Though clearly influenced by Immanuel Kant (1724–1804), the authors do reject both a priori and universal models seeking instead to locate the genesis of these categories in the workings of society itself. At this point, they develop the concept of collective representations, which was a way of thinking about the semiotic production of society. Collective representations are vehicles of communication, with special reference to society itself and its states and permutations. The realm of collective representations is *"la conscience collective"* (both collective conscience and consciousness, prefiguring the modern anthropological concept of culture). *La conscience collective* is a realm of symbolic thought isomorphic to the realm of social institutions. It is not merely isomorphic to society but also a direct product of the latter. Thus, people perceive the world as classified into categories because humans are classified into clans. All symbols refer back to the lived experience of society itself, making the semiotic systems of primitive peoples extraordinarily closed and recursive. Collective representations derive their authority from society and in turn exercise that authority in the regimentation of thought, which is the most important form of social discipline.

This line of inquiry reaches its fullest development in Durkheim's last book, *The Elementary Forms of the Religious Life* (1912). As in the earlier work, the emphasis is upon what Durkheim considers the simplest societies. In one sense, these societies offered the perfect testing grounds for a theory of society in general, since the basic forms would presumably be most clearly laid bare in these cultures that lack the accretions of many layers of cultural evolution. However, as a class Durkheim saw them as sui generis, since they lacked science, especially a science of society, that operated outside conventional thought and made modern society much more complex. Durkheim was in this sense consistent with the anthropology of his day, which was still inclined to approach questions from an evolutionary and optimistic perspective.

The *Elementary Forms of the Religious Life* is concerned with totemism and its associated rituals. Drawing exclusively on Australian material, Durkheim develops the fundamental opposition between sacred and profane, a sort of ur-classification upon which all further classification, including that of the basic philosophical categories, rests. The *intichiuma* ceremony of central Australia presents a physical emblem of the totemic ancestor, the holy of holies, revealed only during these rites. It is clearly an object of worship; to Durkheim it is equally clear that the totem represents society itself. Thus, all religion and philosophy are founded on a sort of collective self-worship occurring in the midst of a profound reversal, where the normal and mundane is revealed as fundamentally sacred and mysterious.

The strength of Durkheim's semiotics lies not in the formal analysis of signs, which is rather crude, especially when compared to that of Durkheim's contemporary, Ferdinand de Saussure. The strong point of Durkheim's system, rather, is its pragmatic aspect. The revelation of the sacred occasions collective effervescence, a phenomenon that at minimum reinforces group solidarity and might motivate members to undertake collective action. In a real sense, then, the symbol is at the heart of the social group as a self-organizing entity. The symbol itself is not unaltered in this process. The periodic attachment of emotional energy to its manifestation revitalizes the symbol and makes it more powerful, which in turn makes it more effective in the future.

Undeniably, a certain amount of circularity exists in this model, as in all of Durkheim's work. However, he has located the major elements of a central problem in social and semiotic theory. Everyday experience testifies to the general correctness of his views. Key symbols that have political functions in modern society—national flags, regimental colors, party emblems, even college-sports mascots (which, in the United States, are often also state symbols)—are capable of creating group solidarity and motivating people to action; these actions in turn constitute accretions on the connotative associations of the symbol. Durkheim's framing of this problematic is very important, despite the limitations of his handling of it.

Durkheim has been immensely influential on the fields of anthropology and sociology. His greatest impact on semiotics has been via Claude Lévi-Strauss, who is, despite protestations to the contrary, in many ways his successor. Lévi-Strauss's first book, *The Elementary Structures of Kindship* (1949), echoes Durkheim even in its title. Much of Lévi-Strauss's later work in structuralism, while more obviously indebted to linguists such as Saussure and Roman Jakobson, is concerned with the relation between structures of thought and structures of society. British social anthropology in general has been immensely influenced by Durkheim; when it takes a semiotic turn, Durkheim remains. Mary Tew Douglas and Victor Turner are perhaps the best exemplars of Durkheimians concerned with meaning systems. A more indirect legacy can be seen in the work of Michel Foucault and the poststructuralists who, turning Durkheim on his head, examine the discourse of science—which Durkheim had exempted from *la conscience collective*—as the realm in which knowledge and authority are associated most closely.

[*See also* Culture, Semiotics of; Douglas; Lévi-Strauss; Structuralism; *and* Turner.]

BIBLIOGRAPHY

Durkheim, E. *Suicide: A Study in Sociology* (1897). Translated by J. A Spaulding and G. Simpson. New York: Free Press, 1951.

Durkheim, E. *The Elementary Forms of the Religious Life* (1912). Translated by J. W. Swain. New York: Free Press, 1915.

Durkheim, E., and M. Mauss. *Primitive Classification* (1903). Translated by R. Needham. Chicago: University of Chicago Press, 1963.

Halbwachs, M. "Le doctrine d'Emile Durkheim." *Revue philosophique de la France et de l'étranger* 85 (1918): 353–411.

Lévi-Strauss, C. "French Sociology." In *Twentieth Century Sociology,* edited by G. Gurvitch and W. E. Moore, pp. 503–537. New York: Philosophical Library, 1945.

Lévi-Strauss, C. *The Elementary Structures of Kinship* (1949). Translated by J. H. Bell, J. R. von Sturmer, and R. Needham. Boston: Beacon, 1969.

Lukes, S. *Emile Durkheim, His Life and Work: A Historical and Critical Study.* New York: Peregrine, 1975.

Masuzawa, T. *In Search of Dreamtime: The Quest for the Origin of Religion.* Chicago: University of Chicago Press, 1993.

Parsons, T. "Emile Durkheim." In *International Encyclopedia of the Social Sciences,* edited by David L. Sills, vol. 4, pp. 311–320. New York: Crowell, Collier, and Macmillan, 1968.

Pickering, W. S. F., ed. *Durkheim on Religion: A Selection of Readings and Bibliographies.* London: Routledge and Kegan Paul, 1975.

—MICHAEL HARKIN

E

ECO, UMBERTO (b. 1932), Italian semiotician and novelist whose writings bear upon a wide range of topics from medieval philosophy and the constraints of interpretation to cultural criticism and the resistance to postmodernism. In the 1950s and 1960s, Eco wrote extensively on medieval aesthetics and avant-garde practices. He also engaged in cultural criticism in a parodic mode for journals of the Italian avant-garde, examples of which are found in *Misreadings* (1993), and regularly contributed articles on contemporary events to mainstream publications, some of which appear in *Travels in Hyperreality* (1983a).

Eco's first work, *The Aesthetics of Thomas Aquinas* (published in English in 1988) consists of a detailed exposition of the Thomistic aesthetic system and reveals a contradiction in the system concerning the distinction between natural forms, whose beauty is normally grasped only by their divine creator, and artificial forms, whose beauty is perceived by their human makers. Eco interestingly compares Thomistic and structuralist methodologies in terms of their reliance on binary divisions, their adoptions of synchronic perspectives, interdisciplinary spirits, and pretentions to universal logic. He further surveyed the development of theories and problems in medieval aesthetics in *Art and Beauty in the Middle Ages* (1986).

Opera aperta (The Open Work, 1989b) raised issues to which Eco has returned repeatedly. Using examples from avant-garde music, literature, and painting, he theorizes the concept of openness as an intentional element in an artist's production that is delivered to the performer in the manner of a "construction kit." The interpreter or performer participates in completing an unfinished work. At issue for Eco are works and not random components open to indiscriminate, "gratuitously different," actualizations. The openness of the work is presented as a field of relations with specific structural limits and formal tendencies. An open work exploits ambiguity, which arises from formal innovations and contraventions of existing values and conventions; disorder arises in relation to the existing order, which the work rejects, but the disorder of the new work is organized and avoids both a collapse into chaos and incomprehensibility and a relapse into the predictability of classical forms. In this spirit, Eco diagnosed the medieval disposition of James Joyce in *The Middle Ages of James Joyce: The Aesthetics of Chaosmos* (1989a). The Joycean aesthetic is marked by a dialectical tension between nostalgia for the ordered cosmos of Scholasticism and the striving through chaos toward a new "chaosmic" order.

In *The Role of the Reader* (1979) and later in the essays in *Interpretation and Overinterpretation* (1992), Eco revisits the question of openness as an extreme example of how texts produce their model readers. An open text creates a model reader whose interpretive project is directed purposefully by the text's structural strategy, whereas paradoxically closed texts have a poorly defined model reader whose interpretive choices are free from constraints. Superman comics and Ian Fleming's James Bond novels are examples of closed texts. The empirical author is manifested in a text as style or idiolect. Eco displaces the question of the author's intentions into the text, which itself has an intention about which its model reader makes conjectures. The task of an empirical reader is both to make conjectures about the text's model reader and to interpret the model author coinciding with the text's intention. There are three intentions at issue in interpretation: those of the author, the text, and the reader. In *The Limits of Interpretation* (1990), Eco adds that texts produce two model readers: a naive one attuned to semantic content and a second who critically and metalinguistically describes, explicates, and enjoys the clues the text employs to attract such a reader. By means of a semiotic modeling of the hermeneutic circle that essentially repopulates textual interpretation, Eco advances a sober alternative to intentionalist interpretation and the structuralist death of the author while also warding off the radical freedom and ingenuity of the deconstructive reader of texts.

The Open Work, The Role of the Reader, and *The Limits of Interpretation* all address the problem of the reception of artistic works and literary and theoretical texts. They mark an important transition in Eco's writing from presemiotic to structural and semiotic specifications of the dialectic of openness and the various pressures that guide and restrict interpreters. Eco progressively introduces concepts whose purpose is to protect openness against unlimited drift and arbitrary uses of texts. He consistently turns to the Peircean idea of unlimited semiosis to critically reveal the pragmatic limits it places upon free interpretive play and how it transcends the will of any individual in the building up of a transcendental community of researchers who would be, in the long run, in agreement about the meaning of a text. In this light, Eco also puts a frame around comic freedom in this study of carnival as an "authorized transgression" that recalls the law.

A Theory of Semiotics (1976) lays the groundwork for a general semiotic theory embracing all cultural communication processes and a theory of codes governing the signification systems that make these and other potential processes possible. The theory of codes borrows concepts from Louis Hjelmslev (1899–1965) and Charles Sanders Peirce (1839–1914) and reveals their respective general features by converting the correlation of expression and content into the correspondence of a sign vehicle and meaning and enlisting the Peircean interpretant in order to dispense with the metaphysical concept of the referent. Eco establishes the correspondence the code makes between sign vehicles and cultural units and delineates their segmentation in a semantic field consisting of denotative and connotative markers. Cultural units are further generalized into "sememes"—that is, functional units of meaning comparable to phonemes in structuralist phonology. These sememes are embedded in a network of positions and oppositions within semiotic fields to which sign vehicles refer. The full compositional analysis of sememes that emerges enables Eco to model both the syntactic markers possessed by a sign vehicle and to indicate with encyclopedic complexity its sememe's treelike array of denotative and connotative markers, along with the contextual and circumstantial selections that instruct any semantically competent decoder. Faced with the problem of "infinite semantic recursivity" that emerges because the analysis of sememes produces more sememes to be analyzed, Eco does not appeal to Peirce's idea of transcendental community but instead admits the instability and temporality of the compositional tree and acknowledges the vast network of subcodes of which codes consist. Eco's analysis is limited to the "immediate semantic environment" of given sememes, thus making competence more like a local dictionary serving pragmatic purposes rather than an elaborate semantic encyclopedia. The issue of openness is raised through the problem of the addressee's extracoding or undercoding of a message. Eco reworks the standard communication model by expanding the message as a text subject—first on the side of the addresser, to presuppositional influences (private biases, orienting circumstances, ambiguities relating to the encoding of expression and content planes, the influence of subcodes, suppositions of shared knowledge), then, for the addressee, to "aberrant" presuppositions (private biases, deviating circumstances, aleatory connotations and interpretive failures, as well as the appeal to subcodes and the actual depth of the addressee's knowledge), all of which are further subject to uncoded external influences. Eco retains an element of revolutionary semiotic resistance against the intentional bombardment of addressees with messages eliciting their acquiescence in the tactical freedom of decoding borne of a change in the circumstances that permit an addressee to reinvent the message's content without changing its expression form.

The theory of sign production commences with a study of the types of labor presupposed in the processes that shape expression in correlation with content. Eco appeals to Peirce in order to solve the recurring problem of reference arising from mentioning and treats perceived objects as semiotic entities constituted as such as the basis of "previous semiotic processes." But this appeal also necessitates a critique of iconism because of the naive assumptions governing the so-called similitude of iconic signs and their objects. Eco's typology of modes of sign production takes into account four parameters: physical labor of acts of recognition, ostension (the act of showing, displaying), replication, and invention; type-token distinctions at work in each act; the expression continuum shaped according to motivated or arbitrarily selected material; and the coding, overcoding, or undercoding of combinatorial units.

In *Semiotics and the Philosophy of Language* (1984), Eco deepens his investigation of many of the key semiotic concepts dealt with in *A Theory of Semiotics.*

He stresses the inferential nature and interpretability of signs, distinguishing between three types of abduction: overcoded, undercoded, and creative. These three types involve more and more freedom in adopting rules that will explain a given sememe. Eco also elaborates a further triad to explain the image of the labyrinth that informs the semantic encyclopedia of compositional analysis. The three types are classical, maze, and rhizome. The degree of interconnectedness of their parts becomes progressively more complex with each type. The rhizome indicates that structure of semiosis itself and consists of an infinite network of interpretants, the analysis of which remains a regulative hypothesis. In keeping with his trademark hybrid blend of Hjelmslevian and Peircean categories, Eco reduces the two continua of the expression and content planes of Hjelmslev to one continuum: the matter through which semiosis takes place. Semiotic interpretation involves the application of Peircean concepts to define the segmented portions of the continuum serving as sign vehicles for content segments.

Eco's long-standing interest in detective fiction is evident in his analyses of the narrative structure of Fleming's formulaic novels as well as in his treatment of the abductive conjectures of such famous fictional detectives as Sherlock Holmes. Eco's own entry into this genre came with his novel *The Name of the Rose* (1983b), which ingeniously combines his scholarly interests in medieval culture and modern problems of interpretation with murder and mystery and also presents his metaphor of the labyrinth as a library.

[*See also* Abductive Reasoning; Binarism; Code; De Lauretis; Hjelmslev; *and* Peirce.]

BIBLIOGRAPHY

Coletti, T. *Naming the Rose: Eco, Medieval Signs, and Modern Theory.* Ithaca, N.Y.: Cornell University Press, 1988.
Eco, U. *A Theory of Semiotics.* Bloomington: Indiana University Press, 1976.
Eco, U. *The Role of the Reader: Explorations in the Semiotics of Texts.* Bloomington: Indiana University Press, 1979.
Eco, U. *Travels in Hyperreality: Essays.* Translated by W. Weaver. San Diego: Harcourt Brace Jovanovich, 1983a.
Eco, U. *The Name of the Rose.* Translated by W. Weaver. San Diego: Harcourt Brace Jovanovich, 1983b.
Eco, U. *Semiotics and the Philosophy of Language.* Bloomington: Indiana University Press, 1984.
Eco, U. *Art and Beauty in the Middle Ages.* Translated by H. Bredin. New Haven: Yale University Press, 1986.
Eco, U. *The Aesthetics of Thomas Aquinas.* Translated by H. Bredin. Cambridge, Mass.: Harvard University Press, 1988.
Eco, U. *The Middle Ages of James Joyce: The Aesthetics of Chaosmos.* Translated by E. Esrock. London: Hutchison, 1989a.
Eco, U. *The Open Work.* Translated by Anna Cancogni. Cambridge, Mass.: Harvard University Press, 1989b.
Eco, U. *The Limits of Interpretation.* Bloomington: Indiana University Press, 1990.
Eco, U. *Interpretation and Overinterpretation.* Cambridge: Cambridge University Press, 1992.
Eco, U. *Misreadings.* Translated by W. Weaver. San Diego: Harcourt Brace Jovanovich, 1993.

—GARY GENOSKO

EKMAN, PAUL (b. 1934), American psychologist known primarily for his work, much of it done in collaboration with Wallace Friesen, on the properties of facial expressions of emotion. While working on his master's thesis, which dealt with patients' behavior during group therapy, Ekman became interested in the flow of information that occurs with body movement and facial expression and the problems associated with the measurement of these phenomena. He credits a number of predecessors for inspiring his interests in this field and influencing his thinking, including Robert Berryman, Gregory Bateson, Erving Goffman, and Silvan Tomkins.

Ekman and Friesen's first major theoretical article (1969) was an attempt to categorize various types of body movements, including facial expressions, in communication-theory terms and to codify their sources and properties. This article first outlined many of the themes that came to dominate Ekman's subsequent work, including his focus on the face as a primary site of emotional communication, the notion of a neurologically based "affect program" responsible for the generation of affect signals, the idea that primary emotions have a universal signal, and the influence of culture on the display of emotion.

Prior to the work of Ekman and Carroll Izard (1971), most psychologists were of the opinion that facial expressions were idiosyncratic and culturally specific, reflecting primarily the influences of culture and social learning, and sources of inaccurate information. In the late 1960s, Ekman and Friesen undertook cross-cultural studies on nonverbal communication and obtained evidence that members of a variety of literate cultures showed high agreement in assigning labels of emotions to photographs of facial expressions displaying a number of "prototypic" emotions. Later, in studies of members of preliterate cultures in New Guinea, they confirmed these findings and showed that people agreed on what expressions were likely to be shown in specific situations. These data led Ekman and others to adopt a Darwinian perspective, viewing facial expressions as universal evolutionary adaptations on which culture and social learning may exert influence. By his own description, Ekman's findings and conclusions regarding the universality of emotional expressions were greeted with criticism and occasional hostility by many influential social scientists. Gradually, however, the idea has gained general acceptance, although critiques continue to appear (e.g., Russell, 1994; Ekman, 1994; Fridlund, 1994).

Ekman has also been concerned with providing a comprehensive theoretical model of facial expressions and integrating these phenomena within a general model of human emotions. In the course of this work, he and his collaborators have proffered a number of influential concepts such as "display rules"— socially transmitted factors that affect the regulation of emotional expressions. Display rules influence whether an individual will give full vent to the facial expression of an emotion or modulate the expression by inhibiting, masking, or amplifying. This concept provides a mechanism by which culture can exert its influence on expression.

In the early 1970s, Ekman and Friesen developed a measurement technique that would allow a comprehensive and objective means of describing facial expressions by cataloguing the appearance changes that occur when each of the major facial-muscle groups is activated alone or in combination with other groups. The result was *The Facial Action Coding System* (1978), the system of which can be applied to any facial action, not just those involved in emotion. Since this development, Ekman's work has returned to more basic, theoretical issues. Among these are a continuing interest in the boundary and defining conditions of emotion, the detection of deceptive communication, distinguishing between spontaneous and deliberate emotional states, and the question of whether there are specific physiological correlates of discrete emotional states. An autobiography appears in Ekman (1987).

[*See also* Darwin; Face; *and* Facial Action Coding System.]

BIBLIOGRAPHY

Ekman, P. "A Life's Pursuit." In *The Semiotic Web '86: An International Yearbook*, edited by T. A. Sebeok and J. Umiker-Sebeok, pp. 3–45. Berlin: Mouton de Gruyter, 1987.

Ekman, P. "Facial Expression and Emotion." *American Psychologist* 48 (1993): 384–392.

Ekman, P. "Strong Evidence for Universals in Facial Expressions: A Reply to Russel's Mistaken Critique." *Psychological Bulletin* 115 (1994): 268–287.

Ekman, P., and W. V. Friesen. "The Repertoire of Nonverbal Behavior: Categories, Origins, Usage, and Coding." *Semiotica* 1 (1969): 49–97.

Ekman, P., and W. V. Friesen. *The Facial Action Coding System*. Palo Alto: Consulting Psychologists' Press, 1978.

Ekman, P., and H. Oster. "Facial Expressions of Emotion." *Annual Review of Psychology* 30 (1979): 527–554.

Fridlund, A. J. *Human Facial Expression: An Evolutionary Perspective*. San Diego: Academic Press, 1994.

Izard, C. E. *The Face of Emotion*. New York: Appleton-Century-Crofts, 1971.

Russell, J. A. "Is There Universal Recognition of Emotion from Facial Expression? A Review of the Cross-Cultural Studies." *Psychological Bulletin* 115 (1994): 102–141.

—KENNETH PRKACHIN

ELEMENTS OF SEMIOLOGY (1964). Originally published as an essay in the journal *Communications* (1964), Roland Barthes's *Elements of Semiology* describes four pairs of organizing analytical concepts extracted from structural linguistics: language/speech; signified/signifier; syntagm/system; and denotation/connotation. The semiology assembled from these initial extractions is beholden conceptually to linguistics, since for Barthes meaning is confirmed linguistically. This premise led Barthes to invert Saussure's declaration that linguistics forms a part of a general science of signs. Barthesean semiology is a translinguistics in which semiology is a part of linguistics. Semioticians have treated this controversial inversion unkindly by relegating it to a minor glottocentric tradition in the study of signs. Barthes has also been charged with linguistic imperialism for subsuming nonlinguistic substance under linguistic form. Few critics have noted Barthes's moderating claim that his presuppositions do not mean that "semiology will always be forced to follow the linguistic model closely."

The semiological extension of the relationship between language and speech entails a reflection on the "reciprocal comprehensiveness" of the terms in the dialectic of social object and individual act. Barthes rehearses the remarks of linguists on the problems of this binarism. He socializes speech as usage and formalizes language as schema in Hjelmslevian terms: idiolect phenomena are intermediaries between language and speech; and Roman Jakobson's duplex structures of code and message provide special relational variations between the terms. Barthes observes that the language/speech relation has been developed in philosophy, anthropology, and psychoanalysis rather than in sociology despite the debt he postulates the semiology of the system owes to the sociology of Émile Durkheim (1858–1917).

The semiological prospects of the general category of language/speech are brightest in the case of the garment system. Barthes categorizes clothing as written about, photographed and worn. The fashion system is purest in the first, semiformalized in the second owing to the presence of an individual model, and subject in the third to the "anomic fabrications" of speech or individual styling. Barthes's reading is sociosemiological because he claims the language of the fashion system emanates from an influential group. Barthes elaborates the written system of women's clothing depicted in fashion magazines in *The Fashion System* (1967). Barthes's sociosemiological insight is less well developed in the outlines of the food system, where he contends unconvincingly that there is no such group determining the alimentary system. Usage is guided by the fabricated languages or "logo-techniques" of the "deciding groups," regardless of whether these groups are narrow and highly trained or diffuse and anonymous. The restrictions of speech result from sociological determinations at the level of the system. Despite this insight, Barthes did not develop a political sociology of the sign, for which he had earlier laid the groundwork in *Mythologies* (1957).

Barthes defines the sign as a "relation between two relata" (signified and signifier) and distinguishes semiological from linguistic signs along Hjelmslevian lines. But the essence of the substance of expression of a semiological sign is not to signify. This sign function is utilitarian and subject to a dialectic of semanticization and refunctionalization. The signifier is, Barthes maintains, always material, and he proposes a typology of typical signs "borne by one and the same matter," such as gestural signs. Barthes takes advantage of the bidirectional arrows flanking the body of Saussure's sign and places the signifier over the signified. Noting the clumsiness of representing signification, Barthes rejects "excessively spatial" metaphors and instead valorizes Hjelmslev's concept of planes as what he calls ERC (expression-relation-content), believing them to be "without metaphorical falsification." Barthes criticizes Jacques Lacan's spatialized writing of the algorithm of the sign because the bar in the symbol S/s is given its own value by repressing the signified.

Barthes's unfortunate penchant for constitutive redefinitions of linguistic terms produces an awkward vocabulary in which *arbitrary* means signs formed by the unilateral decision of a deciding group and *motivated* refers to the analogical relation between signified and signifier. Thus, a Barthesean semiological system might be at once arbitrary and motivated, a contradiction in standard linguistic usage. His neologism *arthrology*—the science of appointment in the semiology of the future—has not gained currency.

Barthes substitutes the term *systematic plane* for Saussure's associative paradigm and investigates in detail the "structural proximity" of the theoretical elements syntagm and system. He combines diverse linguistic definitions in order to classify the problems and combinative constraints of syntagmatic units in semiological systems and the rich variety of oppositional relations on the systematic plane. Barthes makes three contributions to the study of semiological systems. He appears to contradict Saussure by introducing positive or nondifferential elements common to the terms of a paradigm into the system in the form of the "support" of signification (i.e., in the garment system, *dress* supports *long/short*). Barthes deepens the puzzle of what Saussure meant by the positive facts of signification and the sign in its totality. He also questions the universality of binarism, claiming that the majority but not the totality of oppositions are binary. This is the position of André Martinet, whose works in general linguistics and on Louis Hjelmslev inspired Barthes. Barthes considers transgressive extensions of the systematic into the syntagmatic by means of the removal of the stroke (/) between oppositions. Once this kind of structural censorship is overcome, linguistic creativity can flourish.

The briefest but most influential section of *Elements of Semiology* concerns denotation and connotation. ERC is inserted into a secondary system in two ways: as the plane of expression or signifier of a second system, constituting a connotative semiotic; and as the plane of content or signified of a second system, indicating a metalanguage. Of these "staggered systems," Barthes hedges that "the future probably belongs to a linguistics of connotation." Semiology is itself a metalanguage that will accede to the future language that will speak it. Semiology will take its place in the diachronic unfolding of the general system of metalanguages of the social sciences.

Barthesean semiology is an immanent translinguistics. The semiologist works upon a corpus whose width is sufficient to supply the elements of a system and homogeneous in substance and in time (synchronic). Semiology simulates, Barthes concludes, the objects of a given corpus, and in this lies its scientificity.

[*See also* Barthes; Denotation and Connotation; Hjelmslev; Mythologies; Saussure; Signification; *and* Structuralism.]

BIBLIOGRAPHY

Barthes, R. *Mythologies* (1957). Translated by A. Lavers. London: Jonathan Cape, 1972.

Barthes, R. *Elements of Semiology* (1964). Translated by A. Lavers and C. Smith. New York: Hill and Wang, 1979.

Barthes, R. *The Fashion System* (1967). Translated by M. Arnold and R. Howard. Berkeley: University of California Press, 1990.

Lund, S. N. *L'Aventure du signifiant: Une lecture de Barthes.* Paris: Presses universitaires de France, 1981.

Martinet, A. *Eléments de linguistique générale.* Paris: Armand Colin, 1960.

—GARY GENOSKO

EMBLEM. Though frequently taken as a heraldic badge, crest, device, flag, banner, standard, coat of arms, or other sign of ownership or membership, *emblem* has a more general meaning as a quasi-literary humanist genre characterized by the combination of a mildly enigmatic picture and an accompanying text. The text usually consists of two or more parts in which intellectual tensions created in the reader by the contemplation of the pictorial enigma are resolved through consultation of the text, whose role is to explain and elaborate on the picture in such a way as to persuade the reader of some general moral truth. Many emblems display a characteristic tripartite structure, consisting of a visual image, a motto, and a short text, usually in verse; each of these parts

has been accorded its own name by emblem scholars. The picture in this so-called emblem triplex is often called the *pictura* by emblem scholars, while the motto is usually referred to as the *inscriptio* and the short text as the *subscriptio*. In addition, some emblems display a longer text in the verse or in prose, sometimes called the commentary. Many emblems, however, consist only of a picture and a single part of accompanying text, so a tripartite structure cannot be taken to be a diagnostic feature of the emblem.

While sixteenth- and seventeenth-century emblem theorists frequently attribute great antiquity to the emblem, relating it particularly to the Egyptian hieroglyph, which the publication of Horapollo's work had popularized in contemporary learned circles, modern scholars are more likely to stress its similarity to other illustrated genres common in the Renaissance. The name of the genre and often its actual invention are now usually attributed to the Italian jurist Andrea Alciato (frequently called Alciati), who, while living in France in the 1520s, circulated among his friends a manuscript collection of short Latin verse pieces that he called *emblemata*, apparently from the ancient Greek noun *emblema*, which had such meanings as graft, insertion, insole, mosaic, and inlay.

Alciato's verses quickly escaped from his immediate control, and in 1531 a pirated edition of them was printed in Augsburg by the printer Steyner, with the inclusion of a crude woodcut illustrating each poem. While many scholars have contended that Alciato himself did not originally intend his pieces to be illustrated, the woodcuts—which were no doubt included at first simply because of the enormous popularity of all forms of illustrated book in the sixteenth century—quickly became an integral part of the emblem genre, and Alciato authorized an edition with radically different blocks that was published by the Paris printer Christian Wechel in 1536. This edition was the basis for many reprints over the course of the next century and served to inspire dozens of emblematists in most if not all the countries of western Europe.

In the seventeenth century, the emblem began to lose its prominent place in cultivated consciousness. The fact that in the latter part of the century the Jesuit Claude-François Menestrier could offer a definition of the emblem so general as to permit the inclusion of almost all forms of illustrated moral literature probably indicates that emblematic picture and text, which had at one time been semiotically fused and equally necessary to the reading of an emblem, had increasingly gone their separate ways. As earlier writers had done, Menestrier continued to stress that the emblem, like the fable and other illustrated moralizing genres, depended on the two traditional Horatian dicta concerning the need to mix the useful (*utile*) with the pleasing (*dulce*) and the supposed similarity of poetry and painting (often referred to as *ut pictura poesis*). Increasingly sophisticated tastes had already caused the emblematic text to became more literary, however, and the emblematic picture, whose primary decorative function had been stressed by Gilles Corrozet as early as 1540, was increasingly able to stand alone. As a result, the emblem book as practiced in the sixteenth and seventeenth century passed away, supplanted on the one hand by books of more or less emblematic designs for craftsmen and on the other by the increasingly popular illustrated works of mythological and traditional symbolism such as Cesare Ripa's *Iconologia* (first published 1593 but frequently reprinted and translated well into the latter part of the eighteenth century).

Modern theorists of the emblem see in it one particularly interesting manifestation of the sixteenth-century delight in the illustrated book, which arose at least in part because of the presence, especially in France, of a number of gifted printers and designers who were able to exploit to the full new techniques of printing. The emblem is thus analogous not only to the personal device or impresa but to genres such as the portrait book, the collections of illustrated Bible stories known as *figures de la Bible,* the *danse macabre* or *Totentanz,* and the Aesopic fable books that were so much a part of popular culture. Unlike the Bible stories and fables, however, emblems for the most part fall into a nonnarrative genre, stressing the atemporal nature of a generalized moral truth whose enigmatic representation might be embodied best in a picture, the full sense of which can be grasped only through an understanding of the accompanying text. The emblematic picture thus does not normally illustrate a particular moment of the text, as is usually the case with other illustrated genres. Unlike the *danses macabres,* most collections of emblems deal with a multiplicity of moral themes, though many specialized emblem books dealing with religious or amatory themes exist as well.

In relating the emblem to the Egyptian hieroglyph, Renaissance theorists were not simply being fanciful; rather, they were stressing the enigmatic character of the emblem genre by connecting to a system of writing generally thought to be hermetic and secretive in nature. In presenting the reader with a puzzle to solve, the emblem is clearly related to such genres as the enigma, the impresa, and the rebus. Unlike the emblem, the enigma typically requires the reader to guess a single word on the basis of a list of attributes given in verse and deliberately cast in obscure language, so obscure in fact that the solutions to many Renaissance enigmas remain hidden from modern scholars. The popular rebus typically demands that the reader assemble the homonyms or paronyms of words represented by a series of pictures into a signifying verbal whole. Unlike these genres, the emblem is intended to be mildly enigmatic rather than truly puzzling, and seventeenth-century theorists of the emblem are in general agreement that the emblematic text should be clear and to the point so that the reader is left in no doubt as to the exact nature of the moral truth that he or she is intended to draw from it. The clarifying function of the text is especially crucial since emblematic woodcuts were frequently reused for different emblems with widely divergent meanings. Not only is the emblem picture enigmatic, it is thus in the final analysis semantically determined only by the accompanying text. It is therefore unlike the traditional allegorical representations of the virtues and vices so frequent in the Middle Ages and the Renaissance and unlike the figures of the saints whose identities can always be told from their accompanying attributes.

Questions of particular interest to modern emblem scholars fall into two broad groups. On the one hand are topics connected with the history of the emblem genre; on the other, matters of emblem theory. Scholars concerned with the history of the emblem have been preoccupied largely with establishing reliable dates for emblem editions; discovering both diachronic and synchronic relationships for the emblem considered as a genre; tracing the evolution of various motifs; establishing a firm basis for deciding exactly what the term means to Renaissance and seventeenth-century theorists; delineating the influence of the emblem on European literature; and, through interpretation, discovering in the common motifs data that help to establish the "histories of mentalities" of the Renaissance. Recent years have also seen the first applications of computer technology to emblem study.

Scholars whose primary interest is theoretical, on the other hand, have tended to be more interested in attempting to discover how the emblem functions as a genre, without regard for those definitions of the emblem imposed on it by emblem writers themselves and by Menestrier and other early theorists of the illustrated genres. They have thus been interested in establishing more definite generic boundaries of the emblem and in assessing its diagnostic features, as well as focusing on the processes by which an emblem can be composed and read (and, by extension, on the more general problem of "reading" any fused combination of picture and text) and on the rhetorical and semiotic techniques adopted by emblematists that focus the reader's attention and drive it ever closer to the intended meaning. From its original meanings of decoration (Latin *emblema* = "inlaid work," " raised ornament on a vessel"), the term came to designate a symbolic picture, or even an object that represents an abstract or moral quality or that symbolizes a social group, such as a family, a nation, a religious faith, and the like, hence its descriptive importance in heraldry and its literary derivations. In the wider, modern sense *emblem* is often used as a synonym for *symbol*. However, *emblem* entered the technical vocabulary of semiotics with David Efron's (1941) assigning of this term to a category of communicative gesture, namely those gestures that have a conventional, culture-dependent meaning. Efron uses *emblematic* as a synonym of *symbolic*, thus emphasizing that such gestures are not mimetic, that is, they do not have any morphological analogy with their referent. Paul Ekman and Wallace Friesen (1969) revived this term to designate a complex category in their classification of gestures. Examples of emblems are the gestures that signify "hitchhiking", thumbs up, "money," and the like. For a full discussion of *emblem* in this technical sense, see Barbara Hanna (1996).

[*See also* Blazon; Heraldry; Impresa; Nonverbal Bodily Sign Categories; Pictorial Semiotics; *and* Poetics.]

BIBLIOGRAPHY

Clements, R. J. *Temie testi*, vol. 6, *Picta Poesis: Literary and Humanistic Theory in Renaissance Emblem Books*. Rome: Edizioni di Storia e Letteratura, 1960.

Daly, P. *Literature in the Light of the Emblem: Structural Parallels between the Emblem and Literature in the Sixteenth and Seventeenth Centuries*. Toronto: University of Toronto Press, 1979.

Efron, D. *Gestures and Environment*. New York: King's Crown, 1941.

Ekman, P., and W. Friesen. "The Repertoire of Nonverbal Behavior: Categories, Origins, Usage and Coding." *Semiotica* 1.1 (1969): 49–98.

Freeman, R. *English Emblem Books*. London: Chatto and Windus, 1948.

Hanna, B. "Defining the Emblem." *Semiotica* 112.3/4 (1996): 289–358.

Hoffmann, K. "Alciato and the Historical Situation of Emblematics." In *Andrea Alciato and the Emblem Tradition: Essays in Honor of Virginia Woods Callahan,* edited by P. M. Daly, pp. 1–45. AMS Studies in the Emblem. New York: AMS Press, 1989.

Loach, J. "Menestrier's Emblem Theory." *Emblematica* 2.2 (1987): 317–336.

Mathieu-Castellani, G. *Emblèmes de la mort: Le dialogue de l'image et du texte*. Paris: Nizet, 1988.

Praz, M. *Sussidi eruditi*, vol. 16, *Studies in Seventeenth-Century Imagery*. Rome: Edizioni di Storia e Letteratura, 1975.

Russell, D. *The Emblem and Device in France*. French Forum Monographs, 59. Lexington, Ky.: French Forum, 1985.

—DAVID GRAHAM

ENONCIATION IMPERSONNELLE OU LE SITE DU FILM, L'

(1991). Christian Metz's last work, *L'enonciation impersonnelle ou le site du film* takes Émile Benveniste's notion of *enonciation,* which had been developed during the late 1960s, as its starting point. For Benveniste, *enonciation* designates an autonomous concept within the theory of language that is directed toward the processes of passage between *langue* (a linguistic system) and *parole* (any instance of speech). This act produces discourse and must not be confused with *énoncé* (the produced text). Accordingly, enunciation, as a process of production, mediation, and appropriation, always implies an *énonciateur* (speaker) and an *énonciataire* (addressee or listener) as structural entities of the text. The question of how this enunciative moment can be present in a text is of central relevance. For Benveniste, indications of a speaker can be found primarily in deictic signs that refer to the speaker and the situation of speaking, such as the personal pronouns of the first and second person, temporal forms of the verb, and local and temporal adverbs. All these signs direct our attention toward the act of speaking.

Benveniste's notion of the enunciation has had an important impact on film theory and film semiotics. During the 1970s, the questions of *discours* (where the instance of speaking is clearly marked) and of *histoire* (where the storyline seems to stand by itself independently of the storyteller—a pattern characteristic of Hollywood cinema) became prominent. Francesco Casetti (1990) has reopened the discussion by presenting a classification of the cinematic apparatus in terms of the enunciative concept. This new proposal forms the background and frame of reference for Metz's reflections upon the notion of impersonal enunciation.

Metz makes very clear that the impersonal enunciation must not be confused with the so-called facts or figures of empirical and "real" communication. The concept of enunciation thus does not refer to models of sender and receiver such as those prominent in communication studies. These models imply anthropomorphic denotations and connotations, which are very often falsely connected with ideas of the *énonciateur* and *énonciataire* as empirical human subjects. The categories of impersonal enunciation have nothing in common with the empirical entities of communication studies. Filmic enunciation is, according to Metz, neither deictic (anthropomorphic) nor personal (in the sense of the personal pronouns). Researchers should avoid anthropomorphism, linguistic labeling, and shifting the concept of enunciation in the direction of communication. The figures of the *énonciateur* and the *énonciataire* are filmic and textual entities that are to be reconstructed but that by no means are to be taken for the empirical author and spectator. According to this premise, the enunciation does not inform us about specific factors outside the filmic text but about the text itself, which carries in itself its source and destination.

These reflections form the starting point of Metz's sophisticated analysis of enunciative figures, which can be found in film. He does not aim at the construction of a comprehensive system of the whole field. That project has been undertaken by Casetti with his elaboration of the four main terms of the enunciative apparatus: so-called objective views, interpellations, so-called subjective views, and irreal objective views. Metz, rather, wants to carry through a thorough and detailed study of a greater number of specific enunciative figures. These analyses have to cope with the fact that the enunciation can never be reduced to separate, isolated, and "anthropomorphic" markers

but is coextensively present in every film and has contributed to the composition of every shot.

This theoretical basis, which is developed in the first chapter of *L'enonciation impersonnelle ou le site du film*, is used later as a frame of reference for the analysis of enunciative constructions and enunciative figures in film such as: addressing voices in the picture and looks into the camera; addressing voices outside the picture and related sounds; written addresses and addressing titles; secondary screens or the rectangle in the square; mirrors; the showing of the apparatus; film(s) in film; subjective images and subjective sounds (points of view); I-voices and related sounds; the oriented objective mode (enunciation and style); and "neutral" images and sounds.

In all these figures, Metz finds specific constellations of signs and textual "entities" where the enunciative process has left its marks. As material for analysis of the enunciative geography of film, he makes use of paradigmatic sequences selected from a broad variety of fiction films and documentaries, stretching from early cinema to modern avant-garde works, with an emphasis on the classic Hollywood period (1930–1950). The common denominator of these studies from various genres and epochs, which lead to very different constellations and enunciative figures, is in the fact that they all can be reduced to the construction of a filmic "pleat" that recalls that it is a film we are looking at. The filmicity of the film results from the intratextual processes of impersonal enunciation. Metz's detailed analyses of a number of enunciative figures proved to be a productive approach and stimulated further case studies.

[*See also* Cinema; Deixis; Film Semiotics; and Metz.]

BIBLIOGRAPHY

Benveniste, E. *Problems in General Linguistics*. Translated by M. E. Meek. Coral Gables: University of Miami Press, 1971.

Bettetini, G. *La conversazione audiovisiva:* Problemi dell' enunciazione filmica e televisiva. Milan: Bompiani, 1984.

Branigan, E. *Point of View in the Cinema: A Theory of Narration and Subjectivity in Classical Film*. Berlin and New York: Mouton, 1984.

Casetti, F. *D'un regard l'autre: Le film et son spectateur*. Lyon: Presses Universitaires, 1990.

Gaudreault, A., and F. Jost. *Le récit cinématographique*. Paris: Nathan, 1990.

Metz, C. *L'enonciation impersonnelle ou le site du film*. Paris: Méridiens Klincksieck, 1991.

Vernet, M. *De L'invisible au cinéma: Figures de l'absence*. Paris: Editions de l'Etoile, 1988.

—JÜRGEN E. MÜLLER

ERROR BACK-PROPAGATION. A learning mechanism for connectionist networks, also known as the generalized delta rule (Rumelhart et al., 1986), error back-propagation was developed as a solution to the problem that supervised connectionist learning strategies were not capable of learning the internal representation of networks with more than two layers: it was not possible to train networks with hidden units. "Three-or-more-layer-networks" are quite important, however, because they do not have as limited mapping capacities as two-layer networks have. The "XOR problem" (i.e., the input pattern is a pair of 0 or 1 for true and false, the output is the XOR function of the two inputs), for instance, cannot be solved with a two-layer network; many mapping problems, however, have a structure similar to the XOR function.

This learning strategy can be understood as an extended delta rule. The original delta rule (Widrow and Hoff, 1960), changes a system's weights with respect to the difference between the desired and the actual output so that in the next step of activation the output will be nearer the desired output (i.e., the teaching of target value). The problem is how to make hidden units responsible for their contributions to the errors in the output units. This is done by propagating an error signal backward—that is, the error signal is computed in the output units and spreads toward the input layer. The weights are weighting this signal and are changed due to the sum of the weighted errors. The new error signal is propagated recursively to the next lower layer.

There are three phases in the process of learning: (1) propagation of activations from the input layer to the output layer; (2) computing of output errors; (3) propagation of error backward to the input units. Consequently, the weights of the hidden units can be changed without having direct access to an explicit error.

From a mathematical perspective, this learning algorithm can be interpreted as a gradient descent strategy: the goal is to minimize the error by finding the path through a high-dimensional error space to a local or better global minimum. Local minima could be a problem because the algorithm can get stuck in them;

"shaking" the weights (i.e., adding small random noise to them) might help sometimes. The generalized delta rule has become the standard learning algorithm for connectionist networks and can be applied for any task in which one pattern has to be mapped onto another (output) pattern. One successful application is "NETtalk" (Sejnowski and Rosenberg, 1986), a network that learns to pronounce English from presenting written input and training it to produce the correct phonemes. There are many variations of the generalized delta rule, but they concern only details such as how to speed up or stabilize the process of learning. In many cases, these variations are adapted to particular applications, such as pattern recognition and classification tasks. From a biological or neuroscientific perspective, however, this learning algorithm seems to be quite implausible, as there a mechanism has not been found that explicitly computes an error and propagates its signal back to the input.

[*See also* Connectionism; Feedback and Feedforward; *and* Knowledge Representation.]

BIBLIOGRAPHY

Rumelhart D. E., G. E. Hinton, and R. J. Williams. "Learning Internal Representations by Error Propagation." In *Parallel Distributed Processing*, vol. 1, edited by D. E. Rumelhart, pp. 318–361. Cambridge, Mass.: MIT Press, 1986.

Sejnowski T. J., and C. Rosenberg, *NETtalk: A Parallel Network that Learns to Read Aloud*. Johns Hopkins University Electrical Engineering and Computer Science Technical Report JHU/EECS-86/01. Baltimore: Johns Hopkins University, 1986.

Widrow G., and M. E. Hoff. "Adaptive Switching Circuits." *Institute of Radio Engineers, Western Electronic Show and Convention: Convention Record*, part 4 (1960): 96–104.

—MARKUS PESCHL

ETHNOMETHODOLOGY. A branch of sociology that analyzes the rules and practices that ordinary people use to create meanings and situations (Garfinkel, 1967), ethnomethodology arose in reaction to earlier sociological theories, notably those based on the premises that social structures cause behavior or on the functionalist model. Ethnomethodology also challenges the symbolic-interactionist paradigm in which stimulus causes meaning and meaning causes response: the stimulus of A's behavior is interpreted by B, who then responds to A in accordance with that interpretation. Ethnomethodology assumes that the process by which A and B attach meaning to their surroundings occurs first. Before there is a stimulus to interpret, A and B have a repertoire of background understandings, of potential accounts of what might happen, on which they draw to determine whether anything is happening, and if so what. Reporters, within this perspective, do not respond to events by classifying them and writing articles in terms of these classifications, as Gaye Tuchman proposed in *Making News* (1978); rather, they produce news events from their daily practices and their largely implicit preconceptions of what constitutes a good story (Ericson, Baranek, and Chan, 1987; Smith, 1981).

From an ethnomethodological perspective, seemingly pedestrian everyday tasks become complex accomplishments, involving a sustained effort to create, maintain, and sometimes redefine one's particular understanding of a situation and one's role in it. Britons who visited a doctor's waiting room in the 1950s, for example, shared a powerful conviction that they were part of an orderly queue. No one received priority on the basis of socially superior position or medical emergency; it was taken for granted that such persons would never seek care in this way. Time of arrival was the sole criterion for priority; yet those waiting chose their seats at various points around the room in order to sit close to friends and relatives and not too close to strangers. No one left their chosen seat until the receptionist called, "Next, please." Seating position thus gave no clue to all-important priority in the queue. As a patient, one had to discover and respect those who had priority by remembering which seats were occupied when one arrived or by negotiating with anyone who might misconstrue or threaten one's perceived position in the queue.

The strategy of ethnomethodology is to study such practical reasoning—the ways in which people create accounts of their location and activity and attach meanings to them, drawing on their repertoire of background understandings. For example, Garfinkel (1967) reported on long accounts by a transsexual of the steps she took during adolescence to maintain the popular belief that she was a woman. Similarly, Dorothy Smith (1978) examined a woman's reports of how she gradually reached the conclusion that her roommate was mentally ill; Smith showed that this report came to exclude other possible explanations of her companion's ways. Ethomethodologists of music exam-

ine how performers decide what constitutes good playing and how they interact to produce it (Weeks, 1990). Conversational analysts seek to uncover the rules by which group members decide when and how to jump in, to draw to a close, to cover an awkward silence, or to respond to what is seen as a gaffe or an argument. In the long run, they hope to ascertain how far certain practices are universal and how far they are cultural or even context specific.

Ethnomethodology has close affinities with semantic analysis in seeking to understand the richness and polyvalence of signs. It studies how far a structure of commonsense knowledge and a pattern of practical reasoning underlie signs, enabling members of a community to translate back and forth between long private narratives and brief public summaries or between the rich, privately known, variable detail of (say) a bridge hand and a single, publicly known, highly standardized bid. Both ethnomethodology and semiotics search for general rules of reasoning that link a simple, deep, hidden structure of language rules to a complex surface of observational dialogues and gestures.

Harold Garfinkel initially demonstrated through breaching experiments that interaction was rule governed at the individual level. His strategy was to illuminate the rules that subjects took for granted by showing the effects of deliberately breaking them. His experimenters would suddenly, in mid-conversation, reply, "What do you mean, 'How are you feeling?' Do you mean physical or mental?" or "I really don't know what you mean." Their subjects, especially those who were close friends or family members, were angered by the accusation that their competence in everyday communication could no longer be trusted; the conversations quickly broke down. Garfinkel also conducted experiments in which a putative advice giver responded to the subject's questions with random, stark yeses or noes. Subjects devoted great ingenuity in making sense of these oracular remarks, and Garfinkel deduced a second general rule of conversation: participants strive to find a comprehensible pattern in one another's words and actions. He was able to confirm, in other experiments, his students' ability to reproduce a brief conversation and then to spell out a much fuller account that it indexed.

Garfinkel struggled with the problem of how to talk about these results. Sometimes, he invented elements of a metalanguage, jargon like *indexical* (context dependent) and *bracketing* (holding in abeyance). At others, he preferred a hyphenated string of evocative words, referring for example to "members' methods for making their activities visibly-rational-and-reportable-for-all-practical-purposes." Garfinkel treats meaning as neither objective nor purely subjective but as intersubjective and defined by the boundaries of shared background knowledge. This, in turn, is not a fixed corpus that could be catalogued but one that evolves as situations and, more broadly, everyday life are negotiated among participants; nor is there a fixed vocabulary through which it is expressed. If there is a set of relative constants on which a structuralist semantics can be built, it is in the rules for conversation on which Garfinkel's experiments focused. An evaluation of his ideas should therefore center on these rules.

Let us focus on their object: simply put, they are rules for continued interaction. When trust was removed by breaching behavior, interaction abruptly came to an angry halt. Conversely, while trust endured, participants made sustained efforts to prolong the interaction, even when faced with apparently nonsensical answers. The experimental controls were not, of course, so tight that one could claim with assurance that trust in the other person's communicative competence was a necessary or a sufficient condition of continuing interactions or that one could generalize these results to larger groups. The second rule was not a condition of interaction but a demonstration of bulldoglike human trust in the communicative competence of the other, at least in certain circumstances. In general, subjects' reactions to an incomprehensible experimenter might be much less consistent than Garfinkel found; psychologists are finding increasingly that some students "see through" their experiments. The second rule, then, is not a separate condition for continued interaction. Further, it is difficult to see how this theory and these experiments can generate a fuller set of rules for continued conversations. Similarly, much more work is necessary before we have more than a commonsense understanding of commonsense knowledge.

There are a number of questions that ethnomethology needs to address more fully in order to understand such phenomena as dialogues of the deaf. If we assume that when conversations are continued there must be some rules that are common to the participants, what is the relationship between a continued and a successful conversation? Can a conversation continue when the participants are only partially following the same rules? How does a conversation continue if one person changes the rules—and, indeed, what would constitute a change of rules? Can there be ruleless conversations, or is every snatch of talk necessarily bound by some rules? If one person manipulates the rules, what higher-order rules can be invoked as rules for breaking the rules, for faking conformity, for playing with the rules? Can unconventional rules gain acceptance? Finally, what is the relationship between continuing and successful interaction as perceived by the participants?

Although in some ways Garfinkel rebelled strongly against the systems theory of his mentor Talcott Parsons (1902–1979), conceptions of structure and value consensus still underlie his work. While he stresses that conversations depend on unexplicated assumptions and the willingness of participants to pretend and behave "as if," his work's focus on rules and the attainment of consensus rather than, say, power and the imposition of the interests of the dominant party, keep it within the functionalist tradition. The main theoretical value of his work has been in offering a radical challenge to the notion that overriding social structures are real entities that change extremely slowly and can therefore be taken as social facts when studying face-to-face interaction. His work thus challenges the structuralism of many Marxists and some feminists, who take the structures of class and patriarchy for granted rather than assuming that they are re-created and freshly threatened daily in the little interactions of everyday life.

The theoretical contribution of ethnomethology has thus been largely iconoclastic, though it has been an important influence on efforts to redirect social research in a number of areas, including the work of Dorothy Smith on theorizing women's everyday lives and work in the social construction of science. Smith and her students have followed Garfinkel's approach but not his experimental strategy in exploring how women and men in their daily activities construct versions of social reality: how teachers construct a version of the single parent who is problematic for them (Griffith, 1984), how employment agencies produce immigrant women for employers (Ng, 1986), and how men have constructed a version of sociology from which women's experience was effectively excluded (Smith, 1987).

In the field of science, Garfinkel, Lynch, and Livingstone (1981) studied how scientists organize their work to be able to report, for example, that pulsars existed as things prior to their discovery, with the researchers doing nothing more than following proper procedures. Yet such scientists' notebooks indicate that the conclusion resulted from a long, confusing, and at times agonizing discussion. Lynch (1985, 1988) has continued to explore how patterns and irregularities are found in scientific data and then interpreted. More broadly, English researchers have elaborated this contradiction into a conception of two types of scientific discourse, empiricist and the contingent. The former governs scientists' accounts of their own work, the latter their critiques of shortcomings in the work of their rivals.

[*See also* Conversation; Dialogue; Goffman; *and* Gossip.]

BIBLIOGRAPHY

Ericson, R., P. Baranek, and J. Chan. *Visualizing Deviance.* Toronto: University of Toronto Press, 1987.

Garfinkel, H. *Studies in Ethnomethodology.* Englewood Cliffs, N.J.: Prentice-Hall, 1967.

Garfinkel, H., M. Lynch, and E. Livingstone. "The Work of a Discovering Science." *Philosophy of the Social Sciences* 11 (1981): 131–158.

Green, B. *Literary Methods and Sociological Theory.* Chicago: University of Chicago Press, 1988.

Griffith, A. I. *Ideology, Education, and Single Parents Families.* Toronto: OISE/University of Toronto Press, 1984.

Lynch, M. "Discipline and the Material Form of Images." *Social Studies of Science* 15 (1985): 37–66.

Lynch, M. "Sacrifice and the Transformation of the Animal Body into a Scientific Object." *Social Studies of Science* 18 (1988): 265–289.

Ng, R. "The Social Construction of Immigrant Women in Canada." In *The Politics of Diversity,* edited by R. Hamilton and M. Barrett, pp. 269–286. Montreal: Book Centre, 1986.

Smith, D. E. "K Is Mentally Ill." *Sociology* 12.1 (1978): 22–53.

Smith, D. E. "On Sociological Description: A Method from Marx." *Human Studies* 4 (1981): 313–337.

Smith, D. E. *The Everyday World as Problematic.* Toronto: University of Toronto Press, 1987.

Tuchman, G. *Making News: A Study in the Construction of Reality.* New York: Free Press, 1978.

Weeks, P. A. D. "The Microsociology of Everyday Life." In *Controversies in Sociology,* edited by S. M. Hale, pp. 70–105. Toronto: Copp Clark Pitman, 1990.

—RAY MORRIS

ETHNOSCIENCE. A branch of cognitive anthropology that arose in the 1950s and was absorbed into the wider field of cognitive science in the 1970s, ethnoscience originated in American structural linguistics, linguistic determination, behaviorist psychology, and the "new ethnography" of "controlled elicitation" (Conklin, 1962). Such elicitation was designed to elicit the mental structures resident in the mind of any member of a culture and thus, by extension, to reveal the cognitive architecture of the culture itself. It was believed that these structures could be inferred from verbal behavior. Ethnoscience boiled down to the question of how different cultures divide up the environment. Its informing philosophy was realist and empiricist; there was no question of how the world is socially "constructed," merely one of how objects are classified. These presuppositions led naturally to the study of systems of classification, mainly natural species and kinship.

Ethnoscience was concerned with the ability to name, describe, and classify—within a strictly natural category—individual species rather than native conceptions of the natural world, which fell under the general heading of totems. These elicited taxonomies were expected to diverge, perhaps radically, from the Linnean system of classification. However, it was equally assumed that the manner in which the identification was made and the principles upon which the taxonomy was built would be quite similar to those of Western science. Native systems of classification were assumed to be both rigorous and self-consistent and, to use a popular phrase of the time, "context free." The data of ethnoscience, elicited by questions such as "What do you call this?" and "Is x a type of y?" were intended to reveal higher-order associations such as paradigms and taxonomies—that is, paradigms that exclusively employ a hierarchical logic of inclusion. In order to "discover" paradigms, ethnoscientists subjected data to formal analysis including, increasingly, computerized coding and analysis.

In the field of kinship studies, the lexical-semantic items of a nomenclature were analyzed into logical or morphological components, revealing an underlying structure of the social universe. Ward Goodenough (1965) pioneered this approach, called "componential analysis," in his study of Yankee (New England) kinship terminology. The methodology consists generally in collecting lexical items (kin terms), grouping these terms according to combinatory criteria (e.g., those that might take the modifier *in-law*), and determining the "discriminant variables"—the features that serve to constitute and separate the various groups. At this point, the researcher might be said to have a paradigm of the kinship system. Of course, this paradigm is not necessarily a map of the social territory; in the Yankee case, it clearly is not. Indeed, computational analysis by itself has nothing to say about such experience-based issues as who lives with whom or from which branch of the family tree allies may be recruited. Componential analysis reveals, rather, a cognitive map of the kinship system that might or might not be recognizable as such to the informant. In some sense, the map might be said to be a mapping of formal genealogical criteria, such as generation, which is meaningful to the anthropologist, onto the native's own conception of his or her social world.

The study of "folk classifications" of the natural world is exemplified by the work of Harold Conklin (1962) among the Hanunoo, a tribal group of the northern Philippines. In attaching names to specific plant species, Conklin went beyond a mere cataloging to examine the formal properties of nomenclature. Simple principles, such as the addition of modifiers to basic terms, revealed native categories. In English, for example, white oaks and live oaks are both considered types of oak. Thus, both contrastive units and a higher-level category are revealed. Elicitation revealed not only further categories but principles of categorical exclusion, inclusion, and articulation.

Brent Berlin and Paul Kay (1969) compared color terms from many different cultures and found, not surprisingly, that the number of color terms available to members of different cultures varied greatly. However, they also discovered an "evolutionary" progression in which color contrasts were always added in more or less the same way. That is, at one end of the spectrum, cultures had terms only for dark and light. If a language has three terms, the third will be a term for red; if four or five, the additions will be yellow or green; if six, blue; if seven, brown. This finding certainly undergirds the realism and empiricism of ethnoscience. Most strikingly, it tends to support the idea of cognitive universalism. It appears, in the case of color terms at least, that human thought does indeed take the same basic form in all cultures.

Almost every aspect of ethnoscience was criticized by the subjective and political anthropologies of the postmodern period: its methodology, its lack of political commitment, its objectivist language, and the

sex and race biases of its practitioners. However, renewed interest in ethnobotany (in part due to the ongoing destruction of the rain forests), ethnomedicine, and other forms of ethnobiology has resulted in the steady increase in knowledge about non-Western and folk sciences. Moreover, some of the theoretical facets of ethnoscience have been absorbed into cognitive science, especially cognitive linguistics. In particular, the California School (George Lakoff et al.) has extended and enriched the ethnoscience paradigm. In place of near obsession with hierarchical taxonomies and lexically derived categories, Lakoff, Mark Johnson, and others have become interested in radical schemata and metaphorically constituted categories. These more sophisticated models, which have been employed extensively in artificial intelligence as well as in linguistics and anthropology, hold out the promise of a renewed interdisciplinary cognitive science and semiotic theory of cultural codes.

[See also Code; Cultural Knowledge; Cultureme; Semiography; and Whorf.]

BIBLIOGRAPHY

Atran, S. "L'ethnoscience aujourd'hui." *Information sur les sciences sociale* 30.4 (1991): 595–662.

Berlin, B. *Ethnobiological Classification.* Princeton: Princeton University Press, 1992.

Berlin, B., and P. Kay. *Basic Color Terms: Their Universality and Evolution.* Berkeley: University of California Press, 1969.

Conklin, H. C. "The Lexicographical Treatment of Folk Taxonomies." *International Journal of American Linguistics* 28 (1962): 119–141.

Frake, C. O. "The Ethnographic Study of Cognitive Systems." In *Anthropology and Human Behavior,* edited by T. Gladwin and W. C. Sturtevant, pp. 72–93. Washington, D.C.: Anthropological Society of Washington, 1962.

Goodenough, W. H. "Yankee Kinship Terminology: A Problem in Componential Analysis." *American Anthropologist* 67.5 (1965): 259–287.

Lakoff, G. *Women, Fire, and Dangerous Things.* Chicago: University of Chicago Press, 1987.

Lakoff, G., and M. Johnson. *Metaphores We Live By.* Chicago: University of Chicago Press, 1980.

Lounsbury, F. G. "The Structural Analysis of Kinship Semantics." In *Proceedings of the Ninth International Congress of Linguists,* edited by H. G. Lunt. The Hague: Mouton, 1964.

Tyler, S. A., ed. *Cognitive Anthropology.* Prospect Heights, Ill.: Waveland Press, 1969.

—MICHAEL HARKIN

EVOLUTION is a continuous gradual change in a thing or a system from one state to another, over time, by natural processes. As such, it can in principle apply to anything, from the whole universe to its smallest part, although it is most commonly used for the organic world. Originally, the term referred exclusively to change in the individual; it now applies more commonly to change through time in organisms considered as groups, while *embryological development* or *ontogeny* designate change in the individual.

The idea of evolution is very much a child of the Enlightenment and its ideology of progress. This is perhaps why organic evolution has often been thought of as implying a rise in value, from the simple to the complex, from the homogeneous to the heterogeneous, to use the language of the nineteenth-century evolutionist Herbert Spencer (1820–1903). Most of today's professional evolutionists, while agreeing that the pattern is there, would deny that there is a rise in value as such.

The first systematic evolutionist was the French biologist Jean Baptiste de Lamarck (1744–1829), well known for his supposed mechanism of change, the inheritance of acquired characters. In fact, although this mechanism (today universally denied) is now called Lamarckism, it was not particularly original with him, nor was it a major part of his theory. It was a popular idea, however, and was accepted as a secondary cause by the Englishman Charles Darwin (1809–1882), author of the revolutionary *Origin of Species* (1859), who today is generally (and properly) thought of as the father of evolutionary thought. More significant for Darwin, however, was his own mechanism of change, natural selection, which is based on the idea that through the ongoing struggle for existence only a few in each generation will be the parents of the next and that such differential reproduction will over time lead to permanent and significant change. The concept of evolution through the "survival of the fittest" (a Spencerian term) was used by Darwin to describe and explain biological phenomena from biogeographical distribution through palaeontology to embryology. It was for him, as it is for biologists today, the supreme unifying principle in the life sciences.

Of course, any such theory demands a method of heredity whereby the gains of one generation can be preserved and transmitted to the next and whereby new features—the raw stuff of evolution—can be generated. Although Darwin's contemporary the Moravian monk Gregor Mendel (1822–1884) had the key insights, it was not until this century that a theory of heredity adequate for the evolutionist was developed. Then, thanks to genetics, it could be shown that the units of heredity—genes—generally persist in unchanged form (although in different combinations) down through the ages, subject only to occasional sharp switches (mutations). It is a key part of today's thought that although the switches or changes are certainly part of the normal causal processes of nature, their effects are totally random in the sense that their appearances have no connections with the needs of their carriers.

In recent years, genetics has become part of molecular biology, and the units of heredity are now understood to be complex linear macromolecules, usually deoxyribonucleic acid (DNA). This reductive approach has paid great dividends, and today evolutionists make use of molecular techniques and theories at all levels, from detecting parentage of birds through the genetic "fingerprints" of blood samples, to calculating the time since the ape-human split through the "molecular clock" based on random changes in the genes at the subselective level.

But in the past decades, there have been major advances in other areas of evolutionary thinking also. Well known is the controversy over the fossil record and the question of whether, in the broad scale, change is always gradual or whether it is, as argued by paleontologist Stephen Jay Gould, essentially one of inaction broken by periods of rapid development—what Gould calls punctuated equilibria. In the realm of behavior, also, there has been much new research, particularly following the formulation of a number of powerful causal models showing how organisms might be expected to put extended effort into cooperation rather than into direct competition with others.

From the semiotic viewpoint, evolution offers insights and challenges at two basic levels, corresponding to what biologists traditionally label that of the genotype (the level of the heredity-determining genes) and that of the phenotype (the level of the physical organism itself, understood to include such things as behavior as well as basic morphology). Considered at the genotypic level, evolution through its history can properly be thought of as something that emerges cumulatively from that one grand system for the conduit of information required to make organisms over time. Evolution occurs because the method of transmission is imperfect, "mistakes" occur, and thus there is change and overall passage from the most primitive forms of life (dating from at least three and a half billion years ago) to the wide range of organisms we see today.

Traditional opinion holds that genotypic information is always transmitted in a vertical fashion—that is, from parent to child—and never horizontally, as between contemporaries (especially nonrelated contemporaries) in the way that a good idea might be shared and passed on. Thanks, however, to our ever deeper understanding of the molecules of life, it is now appreciated that there might be exceptions to this rule. Information (in the form of strips of DNA) could be passed from organism to organism through the medium of viruses. But, even if this is so—and it certainly can be achieved artificially through genetic manipulation—it is not yet understood how common it is or what it might mean in the broader scheme of things. Such transmission might be minimal, for there are good reasons why organisms have defenses against the invasion of alien DNA.

Most organisms, being asexual, simply pass on their genetic information directly and in whole to their offspring. In sexual organisms, with some few exceptions, the parents contribute equal amounts of genetic information to their offspring. Therefore, in each generation there is a recombination of the genetic material from the parental group. Precisely why sex and the consequent mixing should be of value is a matter much discussed today. Presumably there is a worth in having ever-new combinations, but the full reason are not yet known. It might be that sex is connected with defense against parasites.

What is known, thanks to the work in 1953 of James Watson and Francis Crick, is the way in which the genetic information is encoded in the DNA molecule through the ordering and combination, along the macromolecular line, of four and only four kinds of submolecules known as bases. With the cracking of the genetic code, molecular biologists were able to show how the bases (taken in triplets) ultimately can direct the production of the basic bodily parts of their carriers, living organisms. Since, given the falsity of Lamarckism, new transmittable information can never be acquired once the organism is on its personal developmental path, such information must always be a matter of changes (mutations) in

the order of the bases passed on to the next generation.

Given that such change never occurs in response to the needs of the individual organism, the way in which the information at the genotypic level is molded into use for the organism must occur at the phenotypic level. It was Darwin's genius to show how natural selection leads to the survival of those and only those organisms that function better than their competitors precisely because their genotypic information enables such functioning. In other words, the genotypic information encoded in the DNA of organisms is built up by a phenotypically based choice between alternatives rather than by tinkering with just one single model. It is here that Darwinism differs crucially from Lamarckism and other putative forms of change, like one-step macromutations (saltations).

Clearly, much, perhaps most, that occurs at the phenotypic level has little to do with information and its transmission as such. One animal is better able to stand the blazing sun than another, and that is an end to matters, but many of the concerns of animals and plants center on the needs to live with, cooperate with, exploit, and avoid other animals and plants. Hence, at the phenotypic level (as at the genotypic level) there is the need to pass on information, sometimes between members of the same species (in the sexual organisms, within the reproductive breeding group) and sometimes between members of different species. This information can range all the way from outright offers of or pleas for help (as when one wolf calls out to another) to deception of the most extreme kind (as when an anglerfish dangles a lure before the eyes of its unsuspecting prey).

Darwin himself was always much interested in such signaling, praising and promoting the work of others on mimicry and theorizing and observing the phenomenon as it related to his own studies (especially in the relations between the sexes in the higher animals, including humans). It seems fair to say, however, that for these topics the century after the publication of *Origin of Species* was mainly a time of neglect. This was partly a function of the rise of the social sciences, with the frequent assumption that biology has little if anything to say to behavior and related phenomena, and partly a function of the difficulty of working with the ephemeral organic features that lead to signaling, not to mention the activity itself. It is far easier to cut up a dead codfish in the laboratory than to observe its mating behavior in the wild.

In the past decades, however, thanks particularly to the efforts of such pioneers as the ethologists Konrad Lorenz (1903–1989) and Nikolaas Tinbergen (1907–1988), evolutionists have turned full scale to the question of communication, describing its nature in some detail, experimenting, and theorizing. Naturally, there has been much speculation as to whether the transmission of information at the phenotypic level bears significant similarities to transmission at the genotypic level. Clearly, there are some similarities, but it is generally thought that there are major dissimilarities, most notably the way in which phenotypic (but not genotypic) information can be transmitted sideways as well as vertically in time; as noted above, however, this particular aspect of phenotypic transmission might in fact not be quite as great a point of difference as was once thought.

As with Darwin, a subject of ongoing interest today is communication within our own species and the extent to which such communication can be seen as rooted in our biology, thus making us at one with the rest of the organic world (or with the higher animals, at least). A nonverbal signal like a maidenly blush, for instance, tells as much to the human observer as does a dog to other canines when it declares territoriality by urinating on a lamppost. But whether animal-human similarities are strong enough overall to be truly meaningful is another matter. The honeybee tells its fellows the location of a valuable food source by means of an elaborate dance, but whether this dance has any connection to a Highland Fling, let alone to a philosophical discourse, is perhaps debatable.

Controversy continues about both genotypic and phenotypic information transmission. The key point is that communication, whatever the form, does matter. At the phenotypic level, no less than at the genotypic level, passing on information is crucial. Hence, both in theory and in fact, in all respects, evolution has a crucial semiotic dimension.

[See also Biosemiotics; Coevolution; Darwin; Dawkins; Koch; Meme; Sebeok; and Zoosemiotics.]

BIBLIOGRAPHY

Bowler, P. "The Changing Meaning of 'Evolution.' " Journal of the History of Ideas 36 (1975): 95–114.

Bowler, P. Evolution: The History of the Idea. Berkeley: University of California Press, 1984.

Bowler, P. The Non-Darwinian Revolution: Reinterpreting a Historical Myth. Baltimore: Johns Hopkins University Press, 1988.

Darwin, C. Origin of Species. London: John Murray, 1859.

Gould, S. J. Ever since Darwin. New York: Norton, 1977.

Maynard Smith, J. The Theory of Evolution. Harmondsworth, England: Penguin, 1958.

Richard, R. J. The Meaning of Evolution: The Morphological Construction and Ideological Reconstruction of Darwin's Theory. Chicago: University of Chicago Press, 1992.

Ruse, M. The Darwinian Revolution: Science Red in Tooth and Claw. Chicago: University of Chicago Press, 1979.

—MICHAEL RUSE

EXAPTATION. Coined by the paleontologists Stephen Jay Gould and Elizabeth Vrba, *exaptation* was introduced to provide a counterpart to the Darwinian (and natural theological) notion of adaptation. However, whereas an adaptation or adaptive characteristic is intended as a feature that has been introduced by natural selection (or the direct design of a good god) as something of immediate adaptive value to its possessor—the hand or the eye, to take the classic examples—an exaptation is something with a function that comes only by chance or indirectly.

Divided into two kinds, exaptations can arise either in a situation in which "a character, previously shaped by natural selection for a particular function (an adaptation), is coopted for a new use" or when "a character whose origin cannot be ascribed to the direct action of natural selection . . . is coopted for a current use" (Gould and Vrba, 1982, p. 5). Gould and Vrba suggest that feathers are a classic example of an exaptation, for there is good evidence that feathers appeared originally for the purposes of insulation and only later were coopted into service for flight.

An example with a more direct semiotic connection is that of the enlarged clitoris of the female hyena, which is so large and so shaped that it is virtually indistinguishable from the male hyena's penis, with which it also shares the ability to become erect. Controversial since the time of Aristotle, it is now generally agreed that the organ serves the function of in-group recognition, for it (like the penis) plays a significant role in the greeting ceremonies of members of the same pack. But did it evolve directly under the influence of selection—in which case, odd though it might be, it is a straightforward adaptation—or indirectly, with selection only coming into play after it had been produced simply as a by-product of hormonal levels raised for other reasons, in which case it is an exaptation? Gould and Vrba suggest the latter.

The idea of an exaptation is one with obvious implications for any biological theory of communication, such as that of Noam Chomsky, which wants to locate language in evolution but has trouble seeing how the Darwinian mechanism of natural selection can do all that is required. However, it should be noted that orthodox Darwinians are less than overly enthused by the neologism. They agree that the idea might be an important one, but they would deny that this is a particularly novel insight. From Darwin on, it has been recognized that selection is opportunistic, frequently turning features evolved for one end to ends altogether different. Does anyone truly think that the female's breasts originated exclusively as sexual signals, for instance? Probably there is truth in the claims of both Darwinians and critics. Hence, since Gould in particular is notorious for his campaign to put a non-Darwinian cast on evolution, it is surely wise to welcome the notion of an exaptation but to consider with care any broader implications that might be drawn from it.

[*See also* Coevolution; Darwin; Evolution; *and* Signal.]

BIBLIOGRAPHY

Chomsky, N. *Syntactic Structures.* The Hague: Mouton, 1957.
Chomsky, N. *Cartesian Linguistics.* New York: Harper and Row, 1966.
Gould, S. J. "Darwinism and the Expansion of Evolutionary Theory." *Science* 216 (1982): 380–387.
Gould, S. J., and E. S. Vrba. "Exaptation—A Missing Term in the Science of Form." *Paleobiology* 8 (1982): 4–15.
Stebbins, G. L., and F. J. Ayala. "Is a New Evolutionary Synthesis Necessary?" *Science* 213 (1981): 967–971.

—MICHAEL RUSE

EXPERT SYSTEMS are a class of programs in the area of artificial intelligence that have "knowledge" about some aspect of the world and can operate on it. In most cases, this knowledge is represented in rules and by facts (symbols).The rules implicitly represent the relationships between the facts, thus enabling the system to operate on the knowledge. That is, when the rules are applied to the facts, they manipulate the knowledge and produce a result that is

either a hypothesis or a kind of prediction. Thus, such a program can deductively provide solutions to problems. The problem domain is in most cases very limited and restricted to areas that can be formalized in some way, which implies that expert systems do not perform as well in commonsense or very general domains.

Expert systems are capable of finding solutions by applying deductive and heuristic methods on the basis of a given set of knowledge and rules; in some sense, the actual input, the already existing facts, and the rules can thus produce "new" facts in a deductive way. From a very strict perspective, this knowledge is, of course, not new, as it is derived deductively from rules. Hence, the space of all possible solutions is already given implicitly in the rules and the "acceptable" facts (which match the rules' premises). The reason why these systems are nevertheless of interest is that the computer can make explicit this knowledge within milliseconds, whereas humans would need hours or days to do so. Such systems also can explain to the user how they reached a certain solution by showing the deductive path taken.

The architecture of expert systems consists of five main components:

1. The dialogue component is a module managing all the interactions between the user and the expert system. In most cases, the dialogue is organized in a question-and-answer scheme: the system asks the user for some data or information in order to define the problem and to specify the search's reasoning process. The user's answers help the system to limit the possible search and reasoning space.

2. The knowledge base includes both stored knowledge and knowledge provided by the user via the dialogue component. The rules manipulating the facts are also stored in the knowledge base. The factual knowledge base is not a static body of knowledge but is changed almost every time a rule is applied.

3. The rule-application module operates on the knowledge base by searching the database for facts that possibly could match one of the premises of a rule: one (or more) rule(s) is (are) finally fired. This means that a certain rule is applied that leads to an action being determined in the rule's conclusion. In most cases, this conclusion means a change in the knowledge base: new facts are added and existing ones are deleted or changed. This process of manipulating facts by applying rules is called symbol manipulation and is the very heart of traditional artificial intelligence as well as of each expert system. The rules not only cause a change in the knowledge base but also can ask the user questions (e.g., to specify some parameter that is needed more precisely for a certain premise of a rule) or display results on the output device.

4. The problem-solving module interacts closely with the rule-application module. It controls the rule-application module by having the "ultimate" goal "in mind." If there are problems (e.g., the system cannot find a rule matching the actual knowledge base), communication to the user is established via the dialogue component, which may request from the user more specific statements on the particular problem. One single fact added by the user might help to solve the entire problem by triggering a chain reaction of rule applications.

5. The explanation module monitors all the processes in the system. Each rule application, each change in the knowledge base, each interaction with the user, and so on is carefully memorized. It is thus possible to comprehend each step made by the system. This is an important tool not only in developing such systems but also for the user, who can exactly follow each step and thus can decide whether or not to accept all the steps leading to a certain conclusion.

There are also reasoning mechanisms that can deal with uncertain knowledge. The concepts of fuzzy logic provide the theoretical framework for such systems, in which knowledge is associated with certain probabilities. If these probabilities match the given range in a rule's premise, the particular rule is applied. Its result is another fact with a certain probability (or a change in an already existing fact's probability), which is added to the knowledge base. The final result is a solution that now has also a certain probability—thus the user can judge how likely the solution is. Probabilistic reasoning has the advantage of higher flexibility compared with the rigid matching of Boolean rules, which are a special case of probabilistic rules allowing only truth values 1 or 0 (i.e., true or false).

The source of the knowledge of an expert system is the knowledge of a human expert formalized and coded by a knowledge engineer who transfers it to the algorithmic structure of a higher programming language, such as LISP or PROLOG. Most of the implicit parts of the expert's knowledge are lost in this process for two reasons: first, language is a rather poor means of knowledge transfer. Most experts cannot articulate their feelings about their domain. They solve most problems intuitively and do not usually apply any formal reasoning. Natural language is in most cases not capable of transferring or expressing these implicit feelings. A second loss of information occurs in the process of formalization: natural language is much richer than any formal language, as the latter is only a syntactical construct that is capable of handling neither the semantic nor the pragmatic aspect of language. In our everyday use of language, however, these two aspects play central roles, as we are always referring to external events, phenomena, objects, and processes. The computer and its formal program, however, does not have any access to its environment other than the user's formal questions and answers.

This explains why expert systems perform well in domains that are already rather formal, such as mathematics, games, problem solving in natural sciences, and so on. That is why most of the applications of expert systems are found in these domains, such as decision making in banks, diagnostic systems in the medical field, and tools for supporting the development of computer chips. The knowledge engineer plays a very important role in the process of transferring knowledge and bears the responsibility of capturing as much knowledge as possible in the rules and facts that are fed to the system.

[*See also* Algorithm; Artificial Intelligence; Cultural Knowledge; Ethnoscience; *and* Knowledge Representation.]

BIBLIOGRAPHY

Jackson, P. *Introduction to Expert Systems*. Reading, Mass.: Addison-Wesley, 1986.

Patterson, D. W. *Introduction to Artificial Intelligence and Expert Systems*. Englewood Cliffs, N.J.: Prentice-Hall, 1990.

Ringland, G. A., and D. A. Duce, eds. *Approaches to Knowledge Representation: An Introduction*. New York: Wiley, 1990.

Waterman, D. A. *A Guide to Expert Systems*. Reading, Mass.: Addison-Wesley, 1986.

In addition to the works cited above, the journals *Expert Systems* (Oxford) and *IEEE Expert* (New York) cover work in the field.

—MARKUS PESCHL

F

◆

FACE. The principal object of social attention in intra- and interspecies interactions, the face is an important source of information in social communication. Interest in the face as a signaling system has been spotty and inconsistent until recent years, although several influential scholars, including Charles Darwin (1872), have devoted attention to the issue.

Darwin's interest in the face was but one component of his general interest in how animals express emotions and how this adaptive behavior developed through evolution. Interest in the face has waxed and waned in parallel with beliefs about how emotions are related to facial expressions. In the early decades of this century, the initial interest sparked by Darwin and others diminished as evidence emerged suggesting that there was little reliable information about emotional states available in facial expressions, that observers largely disagreed about what expressions went with what emotions, and that whatever signal value there is in facial expressions is socially constructed and culturally determined.

Since the mid-1960s, an alternative view has emerged and gained increasing acceptance. This viewpoint, associated primarily with the work of psychologists Paul Ekman (1993) and Carroll Izard (1971), holds that the face is a system capable of providing information about a number of things, one of which is emotion. This more recent view revivifies and extends Darwin's suggestion that the facial expression of emotion is a biological capability, built in as a product of evolutionary history and therefore common to all humans.

This viewpoint has gained ascendancy primarily for two reasons. First, critical examinations of early studies suggesting that facial expressions are an unreliable source of information revealed substantial methodological flaws that called into question those studies' conclusions (Ekman, Friesen, and Ellsworth, 1972). More important, however, were findings from new studies indicating that people from different cultures, including preliterate ones, show substantial agreement when asked to label the emotions that are associated with different facial expressions (Ekman and Oster, 1979). Such findings, coupled with the increased interest in emotion that emerged among social scientists in the 1970s and 1980s, have fueled attempts to understand the role of the face as a signaling system.

This activity has also been made possible by methodological developments that have facilitated the study of the face. It is difficult to analyze the meaning of a particular facial feature or change in the absence of a way to describe those features objectively, systematically, and comprehensively, a way of making a durable record of a face, or a way to present visual representations of the face in a controlled manner. The development of objective systems for codifying facial behavior, such as the facial action coding system (FACS), and advances in photographic technology and computerized-image analysis and manipulation have abetted the growth of this area.

A semiotic analysis focuses on the ways in which the face can serve as a signaling system. The signaling capabilities of the face are based on its structure and function. The face has both static and dynamic features. Static features such as the thickness of eyebrows or fullness of lips, are physical characteristics that do not change, although they can be disguised or enhanced through various means, including surgery, the application of makeup, or the manipulation of facial hair, such as growing a beard. The manipulation of such features likely plays a role in the communication of a variety of characteristics such as a social class, status, and perhaps even elements of sexual receptiveness. Dynamic features are characteristics that might change, such as the raising of the upper lip and wrinkling of the nose that often occur when a person has been exposed to a noxious odor. Somewhere between these extremes lie features that might develop over time, such as permanent wrinkles between the brows.

It is the shorter-term, dynamic features that have been the subject of the most intensive analysis, largely because they have the potential to be associated with changes in psychological and social processes such as emotions or impression management. The richness and complexity of the face as a source of information about these processes can be appreciated by considering how dynamic changes take place. Changes in facial configurations are brought about by muscles acting on the tissue of the face. Although there is disagreement on the number of muscles or muscle groupings in the face, one measure of the complexity of the musculature is the number of independent actions that are visually distinguishable.

It is likely true, however, that only a limited number of such actions—usually combinations of several actions—are truly signals. Current theory suggests that facial features—facial expressions in particular—convey information about a variety of emotional, motivational, and social factors operating on the individual. These ideas are consistent with a more general evolutionary perspective that suggests that facial expressions have evolved to serve a signaling function, conveying information to others about the current state and likely future behavior of the individual.

Cross-cultural labeling studies suggest that humans are capable of distinguishing and recognizing somewhere between six and ten prototypic emotional expressions. The most commonly cited categories include happiness, interest, surprise, sadness, fear, anger, disgust, and contempt. Studies in which measurements have been made of facial changes also suggest that the motivational and emotional state of pain is accompanied by a discrete set of facial changes (Prkachin, 1992).

Socialization establishes when it is appropriate to display a given facial expression in a given society and when it is not, thus causing individuals to actively modulate the display of emotions and other states. Ekman and Friesen coined the term *display rules* to describe such socially engendered forces that alter facial expression. The fact that people have such control over facial expression raises the question of whether it is ever possible to distinguish displays that represent genuine emotional or motivational states from displays that reflect the operation of social mores. Although little is known about this at the present time, there are some reasons to believe that such a differentiation might be possible. Evidence from neuropsychological studies (Rinn, 1984) indicates that partially independent neural systems might be involved in the control of

spontaneously generated and deliberately produced facial expressions. To the extent that such systems produce expressions that differ in appearances in one way or another, it might be possible to identify actions influenced by one system or the other. The best evidence that this might be possible has come from studies of differences between smiles of enjoyment and nonenjoyment. Frank, Ekman, and Friesen (1993), for example, documented that smiles of enjoyment are more often accompanied by action of the orbital muscle surrounding the eye than are nonenjoyment smiles. Moreover, the lip-pulling action of the zygomatic major is briefer and better coordinated during enjoyment than during nonenjoyment smiles.

The distinction between spontaneous and deliberate expressive systems combined with the concept of display rules might also provide a basis for a further hypothesized property of facial expression: the ability to "leak" evidence of suppressed emotion. According to this concept, partial evidence of the existence of suppressed emotions might be revealed when the suppression is incomplete or ineffective. Alternatively, microexpressions—facial actions that occur very rapidly and that might not be detected by the casual observer—might take place. Evidence for the operation of nonverbal leakage is sparse, but some research into the modulation of pain expression has provided support for the concept (Craig, Hyde, and Patrick, 1991).

Research into the semiotics of the face and facial expression continues apace, driven not only by intellectual curiosity but also by the belief that discoveries in this field might find application in a variety of areas including communication processes in general, psychiatry and health-care, and the social psychology of interpersonal relations. There has been considerable progress evident in the systematic accumulation of knowledge, especially since the late 1970s. New technological developments such as digital-image analysis and computerized "morphing" methods might accelerate this progress even further.

[*See also* Darwin; Ekman; Facial Action Coding System; Nonverbal Bodily Sign Categories; *and* Signal.]

BIBLIOGRAPHY

Craig, K. D., S. A. Hyde, and C. J. Patrick. "Genuine, Suppressed and Faked Facial Behavior during Exacerbation of Chronic Low Back Pain." *Pain* 46 (1991): 161–172.

Darwin, C. *The Expression of the Emotions in Man and Animals*. Chicago: University of Chicago Press, 1965.

Eibel-Eibesfeldt, I. *Human Ethology*. New York: Aldine de Gruyter, 1989.

Ekman, P. "Facial Expression and Emotion." *American Psychologist* 48 (1993): 384–392.

Ekman, P., W. V. Friesen, and P. Ellsworth. *Emotion in the Human Face*. Elmsford, N.Y.: Pergamon, 1972.

Frank, M., P. Ekman, and W. V. Friesen. "Behavioral Markers and Recognizability of the Smile of Enjoyment." *Journal of Personality and Social Psychology* 64 (1993): 83–93.

Ekman, P. and H. Oster. "Facial Expressions of Emotion." *Annual Review of Psychology* 30 (1979): 527–554.

Fridlund, A. J. *Human Facial Expression: An Evolutionary Perspective*. San Diego: Academic Press, 1994.

Izard, C. *The Face of Emotion*. New York: Appleton-Century-Crofts, 1971.

Prkachin, K. M. "The Consistency of Facial Expressions of Pain: A Comparison across Modalities." *Pain* 51 (1992): 297–306.

Rinn, W. E. "The Neuropsychology of Facial Expression: A Review of the Neurological and Psychological Mechanisms for Producing Facial Expressions." *Psychological Bulletin* 95 (1984): 52–77.

—KENNETH PRKACHIN

FACIAL ACTION CODING SYSTEM (FACS).

A generic technique for measuring facial action, the FACS was developed in the mid-1970s and published in 1978 by Paul Ekman and Wallace Friesen. The FACS was designed to allow a comprehensive description of any action of which the face is capable. One of a number of techniques that allow investigators to characterize facial movements, the FACS was developed to overcome some of the conceptual and methodological difficulties in previous systems, chiefly the lack of independence between a description of an event observed and the conceptual premises of the observer. Historically, systems for measuring facial action have been inferential, requiring observers to interpret the event seen before describing it. In addition, they have often required the observer to describe facial acts in terms of configurations of actions that represent gestalt judgments. For example, an observer might be required to decide whether a facial action represents a smile, a frown, or some other global action to which a meaning is imputed. Such systems have proved to be problematic for several reasons: different observers hold different criteria for making judgments of the

same event; observers' definitions of the behavior in question change over time; and many instances of facial behavior do not correspond to the categories designated in the system yet still have meaning.

The FACS overcomes some of these problems. It is based on an anatomic-measurement principle and describes a facial action in terms of the underlying muscular action that produces it. An observer making use of the FACS will "dissect" a facial action into its muscular bases. The system contains rules and decision criteria that allow the discrimination of forty-four separate actions, most of which can be present independently on either side of the face.

The FACS contains descriptions of action units (AUs), which are the fundamental actions of individual muscles (e.g., the zygomatic major, which produces the lip-pulling action characteristic of a smile) or groups of muscles that characteristically act in unison (e.g., the depressor glabellae, the depressor supercilii, and the corrugator that together draw the eyebrows in a downward and medial direction), and action descriptors (ADs), which are unitary movements that may involve the actions of several muscle groups (e.g., a forward-thrusting movement of the jaw). Each AU is labeled by a number and a simple description of its action. This approach helps preserve the distinction between actions and their interpretation and discourages observers from imposing meaning upon the actions.

FACS coding is ordinarily performed using a videotaped record of the action at issue, although coding from still photographs is possible. To perform FACS coding, the observer views the action repeatedly in real time and in slow motion, applying the decision rules to come up with an ultimate code. Various measurable parameters of facial actions include time of onset, time of offset, time of apex, rise time, decay time, and, for many of the actions, intensity. Because it requires an observer to make repeated observations and decisions about a large number of codes, it is a more laborious and time-intensive procedure than many other behavior-measurement systems. Just how laborious depends in part on the density of actions that are taking place; however, a ratio of coding time to real time of 100:1 is typical. This ratio can be reduced if the investigator is interested in only a limited set of facial actions. For investigators who are interested in actions that are thought to be involved in emotion, an abbreviated version of the system, EMFACS has been developed. In addition, a computer program (the emotion dictionary) is available that enables deductions about emotional expressions from raw FACS coding.

[*See also* Ekman; *and* Face.]

BIBLIOGRAPHY

Craig, K. D., K. M. Prkachin, and R. V. E. Grunau. "The Facial Expression of Pain." In *Handbook of Pain Assessment*, edited by D. C. Turk and R. Melzack, pp. 255–274. New York: Guilford, 1992.

Duchenne, B. *Mechanisme de la physionomie humaine: Ou, analyse electrophysiologique de l'expression des passions.* Paris: Bailliere, 1862.

Ekman, P., and W. V. Friesen. *The Facial Action Coding System.* Palo Alto: Consulting Psychologists' Press, 1978.

Ekman, P., W. V. Friesen, and M. O'Sullivan. "Smiles When Lying." *Journal of Personality and Social Psychology* 54 (1988): 414–420.

Frank, M. G., P. Ekman, and W. V. Friesen. "Behavioral Markers and Recognizability of the Smile of Enjoyment." *Journal of Personality and Social Psychology* 64 (1993): 89–93.

Hjortsjo, C. H. *Man's Face and Mimic Language.* Lund: Student-Litteratur, 1970.

Levenson, R. W., P. Ekman, and W. V. Friesen. "Voluntary Facial Action Generates Emotion-Specific Autonomic Nervous System Activity." *Psychophysiology* 27 (1990): 363–384.

—KENNETH PRKACHIN

FEEDBACK AND FEEDFORWARD.

Complementary concepts, feedback and feedforward are at the core of cybernetics. Consider, for example, the processes taking place when you are grasping, say, a book. The motor output action is your hand moving toward the book. But there is also information going back in the sensory system: your visual system monitors the hand's distance from its final target. Thus, information about one's own action is fed back into the system (the brain) that is responsible for generating the appropriate motor output for finding the target. The brain itself uses this information to compute the next steps it has to take in order to fulfill the desired action.

In more abstract terms, feedback is the comparison of actual performance with some desired state. It is important to see that there is urgent need for sensory access to the environment in which the action takes place, because otherwise it would be impossible for the organism or the machine to monitor its performance. Thus, a closed feedback loop is established between the agent and its environment: changes taking place in the environment cause changes in the sensory system (input device), which themselves causes changes in the processing agent's unit, leading to changes in the output and environment, and so on.

The processing unit inside the organism or the machine has two inputs: the desired state, which comes from a "higher order" system, and the actual state (i.e., the information that enters from the environment via the sensory system). It computes the difference between the actual and the desired state, and sends a signal that determines the action to be executed by the agent's output system. The larger the error, the more correction is necessary. Over time, a kind of equilibrium will be reached in which the difference between the actual and the desired states will be zero or at least will not exceed a certain threshold. This equilibrium will persist as long as no changes in the environment occur and as long as the desired state is not changed.

A thermostat is a classical example of a feedback system. The processing unit computes the difference between the actual room temperature and the desired temperature. If this difference exceeds a certain threshold, the thermostat will switch on the furnace. The actual room temperature will rise and this data is fed back via the environment to the temperature sensor and to the processing unit. The furnace will remain on as long as the difference between the actual and the desired temperature is too large (and as long as the furnace has fuel), otherwise the furnace will be turned off. If we plot the temperature over time, its dynamics will be seen to follow a cyclic pattern situated around the desired temperature. The system regulates itself to this temperature by getting feedback from the environment.

Feedforward, on the other hand, does not monitor the incoming feedback signals, waiting until an error occurs, but rather tries to compensate the anticipated error in advance. The advantage of this way of processing is speed: instead of reacting to disturbances that have occurred already, disturbances can be avoided by generating the compensation signal in advance. The disadvantage, however, is that the controller mechanism has to be more complex, since it has to have knowledge about the environment.

An example is a floor-heated room: as it has a quite slow thermal response, a simple feedback mechanism would not be sufficient. Thus, a temperature sensor outside the house monitors the outside temperature, and the processing unit can make predictions about the effects it will have on the room temperature. On this basis, the heating can be turned on or off in advance without having to rely only on information about the room temperature. Such a mechanism makes use of a model of the environment and of the assumption that the inside temperature depends on the outside temperature, but it also takes into account the fact that heat is conserved inside the room for some period of time.

The principles of feedback and feedforward are very basic to almost any process in natural and biological organisms, from very simple biological structures up to human brains. Almost any machine makes implicit use of these principles, which seem to be simple but have a quite complex mathematical foundation, especially if such systems are coupled hierarchically to each other. These principles are crucial for the understanding of communication and have been applied to the analysis of a wide range of animal and human semiotic interactions, from the self-monitoring of gibbons' duets (Haimoff, 1988) to the pragmatics of human communication (Watzlawick, Beavin, and Jackson, 1967).

[See also Conversation; and Cybernetics.]

BIBLIOGRAPHY

Arbib, M. A. *Brains, Machines, and Mathematics*. 2d ed. New York: Springer Verlag, 1987.
Arbib, M. A. *The Metaphorical Brain 2: Neural Networks and Beyond*. New York: John Wiley and Sons, 1989.
Haimoff, E. H. "The Organization of Repair in the Songs of Gibbons." *Semiotica* 68.1–2 (1988): 89–120.
Watzlawick, P., J. H. Beavin, and D. D. Jackson. *Pragmatics of Human Communication*. New York: Norton, 1967.
—MARKUS PESCHL

FEMINISM AND FEMINIST THEORIES. The discursive practices that inform semiotics as a field of inquiry have not overlooked the question of gender difference. Feminism as a critical discourse and sociopolitical movement is an important branch of semiotics. The decisive impact of feminist analysis has been to establish the ideological dimensions of semiosis and hence the politics of meaning making that has contributed to the elaboration of sociosemiotics as an important strand of feminist and cultural studies.

Feminism itself is a complex field with no single, comprehensive definition or integrated theory. Diversity is the key trait of feminist studies which are often interdisciplinary in approach and borrow conceptual tools from a variety of fields. At best, one may speak of feminisms, all of which expose the patriarchal presuppositions of society that serve men's interests above all others and the mechanisms by which they are maintained, with the ultimate aim of transforming social relations. Different strands of feminism are categorized by their model of change—liberal (feminists of equality), radical (feminists of difference), materialist (ideological revolution)—by their object of analysis—ecofeminists (environment), lesbian feminists, African-American feminists—or by their geographical location—third world feminism, Anglo-American feminism, or French feminism. These last two have been further differentiated by Elaine Showalter (1981) as "gynocritics," which focuses on women's absence from canonical knowledge and seeks to recover and promote women's differing traditions to establish "accurate" representations of women that would allow for women's "reconstruction" as full subjects, and "feminist critique," which deconstructs representations of women in male-authored texts. This second approach exposes the contradiction of the first: as a humanist discourse proposing the universal aspects of human beings, it uses historically privileged masculine subjectivity as a paradigm against which these are measured. The focus on sexual difference (women's difference from men) establishes woman as another universal in the name of feminist sisterhood. A further deconstruction of the representation of women is necessary to attend to the differences between women, to the relative privilege of first world and third world women, of straight women and lesbians, of white women and women of color. So-called French feminism and feminist critique, whose two key concerns are meaning and subjectivity, might more accurately be termed "poststructuralist" feminism, which draws on the legacy of Ferdinand de Saussure's structuralist linguistics with its critique of representational theories of language to establish gender as a signifying practice. Feminisms as critical projects are implicated in continuously changing political praxis.

Feminism in the singular, however, most accurately describes the shared concern of the various historical and national movements to transform social relations and enable women to participate fully in every aspect of intellectual, economic and political life. Though women writers since Christine de Pisan (1364–1431) have protested against women's subordination, it was the Enlightenment ideals of individual rights and social equality, put into practice by the French Revolution, which spurred feminist political organization. The *Déclaration des droits de la femme* (1791) by militant feminist Olympe de Gouges (1748–1793) that inspired *A Vindication of the Rights of Women* (1792) by Mary Wollstonecraft (1759–1797), which called for educational reform to enable women to function equally as rational subjects, had little immediate impact. However, the promotion of women's economic and political rights was a platform of Charles Fourier's (1772–1837) socialism from the 1820s, the movement that coined the word "feminist" for an advocate of women's equality. With the exclusion of women upon the passage of universal suffrage legislation in 1848, a new phase of political activism began in France through petitions, feminist periodicals, and women's political clubs to obtain for women the right to vote, to full citizenship, and to material improvement of their lives, struggle in which Jeanne Deroin (1805–1894) and Flora Tristan (1803–1844) were particularly influential. The "Woman Question" was debated in England from the 1820s, initiated by such feminist essayists as Harriet Martineau (1802–1876), whose work on political economy made the issue of women's political participation more pressing after the passage of universal male suffrage in the 1830s.

In the United States, Sarah Grimké's (1792–1873) *Letters on the Equality of the Sexes* (1838) was followed by the Woman's Rights Convention held in Seneca Falls, New York (1848), at which Susan B. Anthony (1820–1906), Elizabeth Cady Stanton (1815–1902), and Lucretia Coffin Mott (1793–1880) proposed a declaration of sentiments for women. They demanded that all women, especially married ones, be considered equals before the law, with the same rights and responsibilities as men. As in France and England, the feminist struggle was linked to the abolition of slavery and other progressive causes, a broad range of reforms including temperance. This social "housekeeping" became known as "maternal feminism." The fight for married women's right to own property, the right to divorce, to entry into the universities and professions, continued as political projects throughout the nineteenth century. The International Council of Women, which first met in the United

States in 1888 with representatives from eight countries, encouraged the organization of National Councils of Women giving institutional support to a wide range of women's suffrage and reform groups. This struggle for suffrage constitutes the "first wave" feminist movement, which ended with the granting of the vote to women in many countries about 1920, following World War I, but as early as 1898 in New Zealand and as late as 1944 in France. "Second wave" feminism began in the 1960s following the translation into English of *Le deuxième sexe* (1949; *The Second Sex*, 1952) by Simone de Beauvoir (1908–1986) and the publication of *The Feminine Mystique* (1963) by Betty Friedan (b. 1921), who founded the U.S. National Organization for Women (NOW) to fight for women's control over their reproductive and economic rights. The struggle for women's rights was again connected to the movement for racial equality in the United States. Feminism has been able to raise the concerns of women on an international scale through four United Nations women's conferences, the first held in Nairobi in 1985, which have helped establish international networks on a variety of issues regarding women's reproductive health and intellectual and economic well-being under a general concern for human rights.

Feminisms have historically been sociopolitical fields of inquiry. Indeed, the early essays on the "woman question" are now recognized as pioneer contributions to the social sciences, particularly in the fields of sociology, political theory, and economy. In the fundamental changes taking place in contemporary society, women's movements have played critical roles, as Josephine Donovan notes (1985). Since the 1970s feminisms have entered the university into the classroom and academic debate. Feminist critiques of received knowledge highlight its exclusionary nature. Woman has been defined as not-man, as other to the subject, as Simone de Beauvoir demonstrated in her critique of Jean-Paul Sartre's (1905–1980) Hegelianism. Gathering historical evidence, she asserted that sexual difference is a social construct. As non-subjects, women have been excluded from the disciplines legitimating knowledge (Dorothy Smith, 1990). Consequently, feminist scholarship has engaged in a searching critique of all disciplinary paradigms for their gender bias. This in turn raises important epistemological questions which challenge models of the rationality and objectivity of knowledge to posit a reflexive relation between the knowing subject and the object of knowledge (Code, 1991). Knowledge is determined from a position within a discursive field. Gender is one system of social relations by which power captures subjects as bodies and sexualizes them, making classifications to hierarchize them. This "sex/gender system" (Rubin, 1975) performatively produces through repetition different identity categories as effects of discourses that order attributes into coherent sequences which then appear permanent (Butler, 1990). Gender is thus an important signifying practice determining knowledge. Historically and culturally variable, it is manifest diversely at different times and places. Literature, popular culture, and film are some of the discursive practices in which gendered subjectivity is constructed. So, too, it is produced through institutional practices in families, schools, sports, and religion.

Feminist scholarship has worked with these insights in different ways. A more theoretical strand rooted in poststructuralism has focused on issues of subjectivity, discourse, meaning, subjecting contemporary theories to rigorous examination to assess their implications for feminist studies (Meese and Parker, 1989) and interrogating feminist theories for their position in relation to debates within feminism, particularly the thorny question of which should take precedence; the study of discursive practices? or the transformational social practices of feminist politics? (De Lauretis, 1986). This strand is contested by a parallel line of investigation more textually and historically inclined which attempts to reconstruct women's history and establish a female tradition in a number of fields, examining the conditions of its production and analyzing its texts (Showalter, 1981). It is faulted for naive empiricism in ignoring the problem of subjectivity and of the signifying systems through which representations are mediated.

Historical approaches have built on the pioneering work of Virginia Woolf, whose polemical essay *A Room of One's Own* (1929) exposes the double standard in historiography: knowledge of women in the past is limited to their relations with men as wife or mother and the material conditions of women's lives past and present have constrained their writing practices. Early studies of literature noted the misogyny of the established canon (Millet, 1970) and of the double standard for assessing women's literary productions which analyzed their lives not their texts (Ellman, 1968). Subsequently, critics such as Elaine

Showalter in *A Literature of Their Own* (1977) have established a tradition of recurring motifs in women's writing. Sandra Gilbert and Susan Gubar's study of nineteenth-century women's writing, *The Madwoman in the Attic* (1979), exposed the double bind hindering women's creativity, the prevailing myths of oedipal rivalry reserving artistic creativity to the masculine sphere, which meant that women's taking hold of the pen or "metaphorical penis" challenged prescribed social roles. Many subsequent studies of women's writing in a number of genres have demonstrated how women's texts negotiate such contradictions imposed by social prescription and generic convention. Linda Hutcheon (1989) focuses on how postmodern parody may account for such a feminist perspective in literary and other artistic fields. Her conclusion echoes most feminist criticism in emphasizing the political: while postmodernism offers a vehicle enabling feminisms to challenge while working within conventional patriarchal discourses, it cannot overcome the problematic reality that feminisms are politicized discourses while postmodernism is not. Feminist politics, which demanded more complex versions of power relations, prompted a revisioning of this new women's literary tradition to account for the cultural productions of black and lesbian women. Early feminist criticism was faulted for racism (Barbara Smith, 1977) and heterosexism (Zimmerman, 1981) while lesbian and black histories shed new light on women's past (Faderman, 1981; hooks, 1981).

A more theoretical turn in the 1980s in the United States followed translation of French feminism and the rise of poststructuralism. In England feminists such as Rosalind Coward (1977), Catherine Belsey (1980) and Jacqueline Rose (1986) had already drawn on Marxism and psychoanalysis, particularly on Louis Althusser's (1918–1990) theory of ideology, to analyse gender as an effect of representational practices constituting subjects in different positions in relation to power in various cultural practices. Influenced by the psychoanalytic theory of Jacques Lacan (1901–1981), poststructuralism critiques the rational Enlightenment model of subjectivity in which the speaking subject is the source and guarantee of meaning. Subjectivity is seen as an effect of language and the subject is decentred, ruled by desire whose fulfillment is endlessly deferred. Feminist theorists have challenged the sexism of Lacan's model of meaning and subjectivity, ordered by the Oedipal complex proposed by Sigmund Freud (1856–1939). It constitutes woman as absence because she lacks the phallus, and so fails to undergo the castration complex which must be surmounted in a series of substitutions whereby a subject is constituted within language, the symbolic system of culture (the Lacanian *law/name of the father*). Luce Irigaray (1985) critiques this phallocentrism, showing how it is a social construct produced by a patriarchal culture as symptom of its desire and not a universal law. Against the supremacy of the autonomous, rational subject, she proposes a theory of embodied subjectivity. Julia Kristeva (1980) theorizes a subject-in-process: in the symbolic may be found traces of pre-symbolic which she terms "the semiotic" and relates to the phallic mother. Highlighting negativity, she postulates a number of borderline states with different positions for the subject in relation to the object of desire—abjection, melancholy, and so forth—and analyzes their manifestation in artistic practices—literature, film, visual art. Hélène Cixous (1981), in a deconstructive move, theorizes the feminine subject not as lack but as abundance: women's writing—"écriture dite féminine"—has the revolutionary power of laughter to de-propriate. Her work draws on Jacques Derrida's critique of logocentrism, of interest to feminist theory because his elaboration of deconstruction has undermined traditional ideologies of male domination by identifying them as the privileged element of a binary opposition of which women are the unnamed constituent part. However, Gayatri Chakravorty Spivak (1983) and others have questioned Derrida's criticism of phallocentrism by pointing out that deconstruction implicitly maintains the power of the masculine while proposing the feminine as its model of uncertainty. Spivak's deconstruction of feminism for implicitly asserting the power of white women while positioning women of color as its model of indeterminacy prepared the way for women who feel marginalized even within feminism to claim voices for themselves. It has also stimulated further theorization about postcolonialism and gender.

Feminism is a discourse in which women as a group have been able to situate themselves vis-à-vis society. Not in unison, however. Other psychologists such as Jessica Benjamin (1988), Nancy Chodorow (1989) and Dorothy Dinnerstein (1976) have worked with object relations theory to investigate the importance of motherhood in the constitution of a sub-

ject-in-relation. Feminist scholarship in the fields of law (Smart, 1989) and science (Keller, 1985) uses discourse analysis. Of particular pertinence to semiotics is recent work in cultural studies and media studies which extends the pioneering theorization of Teresa de Lauretis (1984) on gender and narrative, gender and spectatorship, in film studies. Studies such as those undertaken by Susan J. Douglas (1994) and Karal Ann Marling (1994) deal with the construction and deconstruction of the representation of women in the media, specifically in television. They continue feminist politics of challenging social practices that devalue women. Of relevance, too, are studies promoting a reevaluation of traditional educational discourse from new perspectives in feminist critical pedagogy. Among these are inquiries of Linda Briskin (1990) as well as the contributions of the essayists in *Gendered Subjects: The Dynamics of Feminist Teaching* (Culley and Portugues, 1985).

[*See also* Deconstruction; De Lauretis; Feminist Semiotics; Kristeva; Lacan; Poststructuralism; *and* Queer Theory.]

BIBLIOGRAPHY

Belsey, C. *Critical Practice*. London & New York: Methuen, 1980.

Benjamin, J. *The Bonds of Love: Psychoanalysis, Feminism and the Problem of Domination*. New York: Pantheon, 1988.

Briskin, L. *Feminist Pedagogy: Teaching and Learning Liberation*. Ottawa: CRIAW/ICREF, 1990.

Butler, J. *Gender Trouble*. New York: Routledge, 1990.

Chodorow, N. *Feminism and Psychoanalytic Theory*. New Haven: Yale University Press, 1989.

Cixous, H. "The Laugh of the Medusa." In *New French Feminists*, edited by E. Marks and I. de Courtivron, pp. 245–264. New York: Schocken, 1981.

Code, L. *What Can She Know? Feminist Theory and the Construction of Knowledge*. Ithaca: Cornell, 1991.

Coward, R. and J. Ellis. *Language and Materialism: Developments in Semiology and the Theory of the Subject*. London: Routledge & Kegan Paul, 1977.

Culley, M., and C. Portugues, eds. *Gendered Subjects: The Dynamics of Feminist Teaching*. Boston: Routledge & Kegan Paul, 1985.

de Beauvoir, S. *The Second Sex*. Translated by H. M. Parshley. New York: Knopf, 1952.

De Lauretis, T. *Alice Doesn't*. Bloomington: Indiana University Press, 1984.

De Lauretis, T. *Feminist Studies/Critical Studies*. Bloomington: Indiana University Press, 1986.

Dinnerstein, D. *The Mermaid and the Minotaur: Sexual*

Arrangements and Human Malaise. New York: Harper & Row, 1976.

Donovan, J. *Feminist Theory: The Intellectual Traditions of American Feminism*. New York: Ungar, 1985.

Douglas, S. J. *Where the Girls Are: Growing Up Female with the Mass Media*. New York: New York Times Books, 1994.

Ellman, M. *Thinking About Women*. New York: Harcourt Brace Jovanovich, 1968.

Faderman, L. *Surpassing the Love of Men: Romantic Friendship and Love between Women from the Renaissance to the Present*. New York: William Morrow, 1981.

Friedan, B. *The Feminine Mystique*. New York: Norton, 1963.

Gilbert, S., and S. Gubar. *The Madwoman in the Attic: The Woman Writer and the Nineteenth Century Literary Imagination*. New Haven: Yale University Press, 1979.

hooks, bell. *Ain't I a Woman: Black Women and Feminism*. Boston: South End Press, 1981.

Hutcheon, L. *The Politics of Postmodernism*. London & New York: Routledge, 1989.

Irigaray, L. *Speculum of the Other Woman*. Translated by G. Gill. Ithaca: Cornell University Press, 1985.

Keller, H. F. *Reflections on Gender and Science*. New Haven: Yale University Press, 1985.

Kristeva, J. *Desire in Language: A Semiotic Approach to Literature and Art*. Translated and edited by L. Roudiez. New York: Columbia University Press, 1980.

Marling, K. A. *As Seen on TV: The Visual Culture of Everyday Life in the 1950s*. Cambridge, Mass.: Harvard University Press, 1994.

Meese, E., and A. Parker, eds. *The Difference Within: Feminism and Critical Theory*. Amsterdam and Philadelphia: John Benjamins, 1989.

Millet, K. *Sexual Politics*. Garden City, N.Y.: Doubleday, 1970.

Rose, J. *Sexuality in the Field of Vision*. London: Verso, 1986.

Rubin, G. "The Traffic in Women: The 'Political Economy' of Sex," in *Toward an Anthropology of Women*, edited by R. Reiter. New York: Monthly Review, 1975.

Showalter, E. *A Literature of Their Own: Women Novelists from Bronte to Lessing*. Princeton: Princeton University Press, 1977.

Showalter, E. "Feminist Criticism in the Wilderness." *Critical Inquiry* 8. 2 (1981): 179–206.

Smart, C. *Feminism and the Power of Law*. London and New York: Routledge, 1989.

Smith, B. "Toward a Black Feminist Criticism." *Conditions Two* 1 (1977): 25–32. Reprinted in *The New Feminist Criticism*, edited by E. Showalter (New York: Pantheon, 1985).

Smith, D. *The Conceptual Practices of Power: A Feminist Sociology of Knowledge*. Boston: Northeastern, 1990.

Spivak, G. C. "Displacement and the Discourse of Woman." In *Displacement: Derrida and After*, edited by M. Krupnick, pp. 169–190. Bloomington: Indiana University Press, 1983.

Zimmerman, B. "What Has Never Been: An Overview of Lesbian Feminist Literary Criticism." *Feminist Studies* 7 (1981): 451–475.

—ANNE URBANCIC

FEMINIST SEMIOTICS. Feminists' relations to semiotic theory are ambivalent. The theory affords a sophisticated understanding of women's subordinate condition as cultural, not natural. It must be transformed, however, if it is to serve a feminist emancipatory project of constituting women as the subjects who know rather than the invisible objects of knowledge. While feminists have made important contributions to semiotic theory, these are frequently marginalized within mainstream semiotics as feminist theory, not semiotics "proper." The gap is marked explicitly in Umberto Eco's (1979) refusal of Julia Kristeva's (1973) "speaking subject." Teresa de Lauretis (1984) considers this a "cross-roads" in semiotic research, split between a theory of meaning and a ghostly self-divided subject. De Lauretis follows Eco's path to consider the social constraints rather than the pre-symbolic drives in the signifying process, so denaturalizing it as cultural materialist praxis. However, her subsequent extension of Eco's work to theorize a materialist subject of semiosis has similarly been positioned on the opposite side of this disciplinary distinction, which separates analysis of semiotic structures from subjective determinants. The emphasis on textuality partakes of semiotic theory's focus on the sign and universals—"logocentrism"—which feminists have challenged in the name of the signifying network and the embodied subject to advance models of dynamic processes of signification within theories of complexity. The insights of feminism into power, difference, and the signifying process of identification have contributed to the emergence of studies of racialized difference, postcolonial studies, lesbian and gay studies, and queer theory.

The characteristic feminist stance in semiotics has been to assess the limitations of and then creatively rewrite the master theories. Feminist interventions in semiotics have critiqued its structuralist tendencies for the positivism of their logico-mathematical paradigms taken for the real and advocated a critical semiotics that would recognize the discursive aspects of its paradigms as representations structuring the real.

Feminist engagements with semiotics have contributed to, even as they have benefitted from, poststructuralist theories of meaning as both polysemic—deferred in an infinite web of textuality—and ideological—stories told from an interested perspective. As the only "science" explicitly concerned with elaborating a theory of representation, asserts Kristeva (1969), semiotics becomes self-reflexively critical as well as critical of the representational models of other "sciences." To be a critical theory, however, as Mieke Bal (1985) points out, semiotics needs a social theory and a theory of subjectivity with which to account for the dynamic interactions between the individual and social processes that are mediated transformatively in signification. As Terry Threadgold (1997) sums this up, there is no semiosis without subjectivity and no subjectivity without semiosis. In their "dialogic" relation to semiotic theory, to use the term of Mikhail Bakhtin (1895–1975), feminist semioticians rework established concepts so as to transform their implicit misogyny and create the potential for what Luce Irigaray (1985a) terms "becoming woman," a potential position for women as speaking subjects of theory. This entails a project of working within the interstices of semiotic theory to expose the masculine theorists' elision of their own embodiment that they displace onto women as Other in the constitution of a rational, self-sufficient subject. Feminist rewriting has made important contributions to semiotic theory in a number of areas, including subjectivity, intertextuality, the symptom, linguistic value, differential regimes of signification, theories of enunciation, representation, narrative, and nonlinguistic signifying processes.

In the development of feminist approaches to semiotics, there have been two main phases, one emerging in France in the late 1960s that embraced the project of *Tel Quel* to combine the theories of Ferdinand de Saussure (1857–1913) with those of Karl Marx (1818–1883) and Sigmund Freud (1856–1939), and expansions on those theories and/or reworking of the theories of other key semiotic theoreticians that occurred in the English-speaking world in the 1980s. Julia Kristeva, the first major contributor to feminist critical reworkings of semiotic theory, introduced the category of the subject into semiosis. Kristeva diagnoses the current subordinate state of women in the social rather than transforming it, though she highlights the feminine as the sign of change.

Subsequent feminist semiotic theory follows Kristeva in taking as premise that subjectivity is an effect of signification and that theories are value-laden representations enacting gender differences. However, it differs from her in critiquing the Oedipal model of signification as loss and displacement posited by Freud and Claude Lévi-Strauss (1969) as foundation of the distinction between nature and culture. In doing so, it makes important contributions to the theory of representation and narrative, as well as to concepts of meaning-making as action in the social. It argues against the primacy of linguistic signification the need to attend to the significate effects of feeling, action, and cognition in the embodied practices of the everyday (De Lauretis, 1984). The project of feminist semiotics to theorize non-verbal semiosis and heterogeneity is a meta-semiotic critique of a paradigmatic mind/body dichotomy operating in semiotics and other theories to exclude women's differentiated experiences of the social.

Semiotic theory remains influential in feminist poststructuralist approaches, though the specific terminology and conceptual rigor of these pioneering theorists are rare. Perhaps their most significant contribution is to have developed semiotics as a critical theory and semiosis as social action producing change. They have attempted to transform the terms of cultural transmission by making visible the absent masculine body in modernity's theories of the rational subject and the complicitous relations of the subject who knows to the object of knowledge.

[*See also* De Lauretis; Dialogism; Feminism and Feminist Theories; Kristeva; Queer Theory; *and* Semiotic and Symbolic.]

BIBLIOGRAPHY

Bal, M. *Femmes imaginaires: L'Ancien Testament au risque d'une narratologie critique.* Utrecht: HES Uitgevers, and Montreal: HMH, 1985.

Bal, M. *Double Exposures: The Subject of Cultural Analysis.* New York: Routledge, 1996.

Butler, J. *Gender Trouble: Feminism and the Subversion of Identity.* New York: Routledge, 1990.

Cixous, H. "The Laugh of the Medusa," In *New French Feminists*, edited by E. Marks and I. de Courtivron, pp. 245–264. New York: Schocken, 1981.

Cixous, H., and C. Clément. *The Newly Born Woman.* Translated by B. Wing. Minneapolis: University of Minnesota Press, 1986.

De Lauretis, T. *Alice Doesn't: Feminism, Semiotics, Cinema.* Bloomington: Indiana University Press, 1984.

De Lauretis, T. *Technologies of Gender: Essays on Theory, Film and Fiction*. Bloomington: Indiana University Press, 1987.

Eco, U. *The Theory of Semiotics* Bloomington: Indiana University Press, 1979.

Freud, S. "Femininity." In *Standard Edition of the Complete Psychological Works*, edited by J. Strachey, vol. 22, pp. 112–135. London: Hogarth Press, 1953–1974.

Godard, B. "Translating (with) *The Speculum*." *Traduction, Terminologie, Redaction* 4.2 (1991): 85–121.

Grosz, E. *Sexual Subversions: Three French Feminists*. Sydney: Allen & Unwin, 1989.

Halliday, M. A. K. *Language as Social Semiotic: The Social Interpretation of Language and Meaning*. London: Edward Arnold, 1978.

Irigaray, L. *Speculum of the Other Woman*. Translated by G. Gill. Ithaca: Cornell University Press, 1985a.

Irigaray, L. *This Sex Which Is Not One*. Translated by C. Porter. Ithaca: Cornell University Press, 1985b.

Irigaray, L. *Sexes et genres à travers les langues*. Paris: Grasset, 1990.

Kristeva, J. "Le mot, le dialogue et le roman." *Critique* 21.14 (April 1967).

Kristeva, J. *Sēmeiotikē: Recherches pour une sémanalyse*. Paris: Seuil, 1969.

Kristeva, J. "The System and the Speaking Subject." *Times Literary Supplement*, 12 October 1973, p. 1249.

Kristeva, J. *Desire in Language: A Semiotic Approach to Literature and Art*. Edited and translated by L. Roudiez. New York: Columbia University Press, 1980.

Kristeva, J. *Powers of Horror: An Essay on Abjection*. Translated by L. Roudiez. New York: Columbia, 1982.

Kristeva, J. *About Chinese Women*. London: Marion Boyars, 1986.

Lacan, J. "A Love Letter." In *Feminine Sexuality*. Translated by J. Rose. New York: Pantheon, 1982.

Lévi-Strauss, C. *The Elementary Structures of Kinship*. Translated by C. Jacobson and B. G. Schoepf. London: Eyre & Spottiswoode, 1969.

Moi, T. *Sexual/Textual Politics*. London: Methuen, 1985.

Rubin, G. "The Traffic in Women: The 'Political Economy' of Sex." In *Toward an Anthropology of Women*, edited by R. Reiter. New York: Monthly Review, 1975.

Silverman, K. *The Subject of Semiotics*. New York: Oxford University Press, 1983.

Silverman, K. *Male Subjectivity at the Margins*. New York: Routledge, 1992.

Spivak, G. C. "Displacement and the Discourse of Woman." In *Displacement: Derrida and After*, edited by M. Krupnick, pp. 169–190. Bloomington: Indiana University Press, 1983.

Spivak, G. C. "The Rani of Sirmur." In *Europe and Its Others*, edited by F. Barker, pp. 128–151. Colchester: University of Essex, 1985.

Spivak, G. C. "Imperialism and Sexual Difference." *Oxford Literary Review* 8.1–2 (1986): 225–240.

Spivak, G. C. "French Feminism in an International Frame." In *Other Worlds: Essays in Cultural Politics*, pp. 134–153. New York and London: Methuen, 1987.

Spivak, G. C. "The Politics of Translation." In *Outside in the Teaching Machine*, pp. 173–200. New York: Routledge, 1993.

Threadgold, T. *Feminist Poetics: Poeisis, Performance, Histories*. London and New York: Routledge, 1997.

—BARBARA GODARD

FICTION. Fictional discourse puts several fundamental assumptions about language at risk. When dealing with fiction, the semiotician must grapple at the very least with the difficult notions of truth and lies, two moral concepts that the Western tradition has often linked with it. A semiotic view of fiction must also take into account the complex concepts of reference, intentionality, and sentence meaning as opposed to the meaning of individual signs.

Fiction is first and foremost a meaning phenomenon that operates at the level of the whole discursive unit rather than at that of the single sign. There have been, however, serious attempts at explaining fiction by focusing on the status of particular signs. Such an outlook gains important support from the fact that almost all fictional utterances are mixed with everyday truths and are able to say something true, despite their fictional nature, about specific things in the world. Thus, a fictional utterance is not entirely fictional but rather fictional only to a certain degree and in certain and specific places. Real persons and real events can appear within a fictional work of literature. Only specific signs describing make-believe persons and events are accurately termed fiction.

This view entails that in any fictional utterance there are degrees of fictiveness and that there is always the possibility of mixing reality-based signs with fiction-based signs. From this premise, it becomes reasonable to postulate the existence of specific fiction markers—that is, stock phrases or conventionalized utterance situations that inform the reader more or less directly that the utterance is a fictional text. Opening phrases such as "Once upon a time" or "Did you hear the one about the guy who . . . ?" are often adduced as prime candidates for the status of fiction marker. Archaic turns of phrase, extensive use of metaphorical language, implicit allusions to other fictional texts, and reference to entities we know not to exist can also indicate that the utterance containing them is a fictional one. But fiction is not necessarily the sole province of literature, and we find fiction in such diverse utterance types as jokes, parables, counterfactual discourse, metaphoric discourse, children's games, rituals, myths, and juvenile bragging.

There are, however, major drawbacks attached to this view, and even a subtler view that there are specific situations that indicate the presence of a fictional utterance does not entirely solve the problem. Such a view tends to explain fiction in terms of single signs or particular groups of signs, as if beyond those specific fiction markers everything else was just normal speech. However, the implicit distinction between ordinary language use and fictional use is a problematic one. Indeed, when we read a novel whose action is situated in a particular country, we are still able to believe, despite the fiction, that the word *Russia* refers to the actual country Russia. But theorists of fiction have spent much time arguing about whether or not it is correct to say that in fiction words refer to anything at all. The French school of structuralism believed that it was altogether incorrect to speak of fictional signs as referring to extralinguistic entities. These theorists believed that words such as *Russia* in a fictional utterance are in fact merely conventionalized signs of reality that are used to produce the illusion that the fictional text is anchored in reality.

This way of explaining how fiction works has been questioned. An alternative approach is to consider that the fictional utterance functions as a unit and that it is otiose to sift through signs one by one, deciding which ones are fiction markers and which ones are used referentially. Fiction can take the form of an overarching discursive operator that tells us that all that is said within its domain is to be taken as fiction. The operator lets us understand that the meaning of every utterance in its domain is tempered by the idea "It is not really true that . . . ." A conditional mode is thus added to every sentence, suggesting that what it says would be true if things were not as they really are. When Henry James in *An International Episode* writes, "Four years ago—in 1874—two young Englishmen had occasion to go to the United States," we must understand along with the sentence's core meaning that the statement is only fictively true. There is a neat mathematical quality to this way of showing how fiction works. The operator is similar to a number placed outside parentheses in a mathematical sentence where $a(b + c) = ab + ac$. In other

words, we can imagine a in terms of a fiction operator and b and c as signs used in the fictional utterance. Here, then, both b and c must be understood in the fictional mode (ab and ac).

In this view, such a fiction operator is rarely explicitly present, and this position gets us beyond the fiction-marker view. In other words, when processing a fictional utterance, the receiver must always remember that what is being said is really only fiction and an implicit statement of this accompanies each and every part of it. An alternate form of this operator view of fiction is present in all theories that claim that fiction is a form of make-believe games. According to this picture, since fictional statements are only make-believe statements, they do not entail all the implicit commitments that statements usually oblige the utterer to respect. Yet while it might seem intuitively acceptable to imagine that statements made within fictional utterances are really only make-believe statements, they are not make-believe utterances in any productive sense of the term, and therefore it is difficult to understand what make-believe questions, exclamations, and lyric phrases might be.

It is perhaps advisable to view fiction not as a subtype of the make-believe but as a semiotic mode parallel to it. Possible-world semantics are useful for understanding how we can project hypothetical worlds from our own. Fiction per se is not a type of pretending, but both are part of a larger "as-if" view of the world—the way in which humans often convey their wishes to one another. Fiction, then, is one means in which the limited outlooks of our own life situations can be temporarily bypassed. This tendency to go beyond our limitations appears sometimes in the simple form of a sigh or in the complex form of a literary work of fiction. Fiction, then, is no longer a childlike game, as the make-believe position suggests, but an important strategy in the philosophical enterprise of creating utopian spaces. Fiction can also be conceived in a more sociological framework: it provides us with a mechanism for transcending the strictly delimited meaning positions in which social beings are compelled to operate. Fiction is therefore a strategy for entering not only another personal space but also another social space. Utopia as fiction is at once an imaginary space and a critical space in which the present space is reorganized along desirable values. The social view of fiction goes beyond the limitations of the self-encapsulated game that a theory of fiction as make-believe implies. As ancient myths and religious rituals testify, fiction can take up a tremendous space in our lives because it corresponds to repressed desires in the adult world. But more important, fiction is not a purely private space for solitary mind games; there is an inherent social aspect at the very center of all social and meaning activities that involve fiction and utopia. This is perhaps one of the more profound roles that fiction can play. Interestingly, a notion that early in the Western tradition had so often brought to mind the idea of an implicit lie appears now to be a means toward revealing deep social and personal truths.

[See also Poetics; and Reference.]

BIBLIOGRAPHY

Allen, S., ed. *Possible Worlds in Humanities, Arts, and Sciences: Proceedings of Nobel Symposium 65.* Berlin: De Gruyter, 1989.

Bakhtin, M. M. *Problems of Dostoevsky's Poetics.* Translated by C. Emerson. Minneapolis: University of Minnesota Press, 1985.

Dolezel, L. "Extensional and Intensional Narrative Worlds." *Poetics* 8 (1979): 193–211.

Harshaw, B. "Fictionality and Fields of Reference." *Poetics Today* 5 (1984): 227–251.

McCormick, P. J. *Fictions, Philosophies, and the Problems of Poetics.* Ithaca, N.Y.: Cornell University Press, 1988.

Pavel, T. *Fictional Worlds.* Cambridge, Mass.: Harvard University Press, 1986.

Pelc, J. "On Fictitious Entities and Fictional Texts." *Recherches sémiotique/Semiotic Inquiry* 6.1 (1986): 1–35.

Searle, J. R. *Expression and Meaning.* Cambridge: Cambridge University Press, 1979.

—ANTHONY WALL

FILM SEMIOTICS. Many presemiotic discussions of the cinematic medium can be traced back to the early years of film history. Among the precursors of film semiotics, one of the most prominent is the Russian film director and theorist Sergei Eisenstein (1898–1948). His theory of montage, originating in theater studies and linguistics, influenced many European scholars in the 1920s and 1930s. For instance, Eisenstein drew parallels between the processes of reading hieroglyphs or ideograms and looking at different shots in a film. He also showed that montage (i.e., juxtaposition of images or sequences) produces a psychological effect on the spectator and creates certain significations that are not merely the sum of the elements involved. These processes were studied from the point of view of film stylistics rather than filmic language. In this respect, Eisenstein's position differs from that of other Russians such as Dziga Vertov (1896–1954), Lev Kuleshov (1899–1970), and Vsevolod Pudovkin (1893–1953), who were mainly interested in film syntax.

Christian Metz (1931–1994) is generally considered the semiotician who initiated, in 1964, the semiotic discussion of film as language on a linguistic basis. However, the Belgian Jan Marie Lambert Peters addressed this problem in his 1950 doctoral dissertation. For Peters, if film is to be regarded as a language, its basic elements have to be isolated within the discrete units of the picture (shots), which then can be differentiated into several levels. This position differs from Metz's, in which (at least in the early phase) the single shot constitutes the smallest unit of film semiotics. Peters's work has not been translated from Dutch and has been generally ignored.

Metz's provocative statement that the film is *"langage sans langue"* (1964) gave rise immediately to a heated debate about the semiotic status of films. If filmic language cannot be related to *langue* in the Saussurean sense of system because it does not consist of a finite number of elements organized according to the rules of a specific syntax, then we must ask the crucial question of how this language can be described. Several Italian semioticians were stimulated by this problem. In opposition to Metz, Pier Paolo Pasolini (1922–1975) saw film as a natural language of things and situations that is preverbal and in which style transforms itself only gradually into some kind of syntax. For Umberto Eco, this language cannot possess a "double articulation," as natural language does. Instead, because of the complexity of filmic signs, it must be conceived of as a visual articulation, described in terms of three-dimensional coordinates of kinesic figures. These form the basis of iconic signs that are located in the synchronic and diachronic dimensions. In the wake of this discussion, Emilio Garroni (1968) raised the issue of which level of formalization can be obtained in film semiotics. Rather than being grounded on Metzian syntagmas, such a formalization could start from different filmic codes. These codes were later elaborated by Eco in his writings about the semiotics of the audiovisual (e.g., 1980).

In the Soviet Union, Jurij Lotman's *Semiotics of*

Cinema (1973) did not aim at a systematic elaboration of film language or cinematic grammar but at the creation of some further semiotic reflections on this language. Its detailed analyses, which bear upon the filmic illusion of reality, the filmic shot, forms of filmic narration, the question of film as a synthetic art, and the development of modern cinematography, make a foray into the ideological and aesthetic functions of cinema as the dominant mass-media art of the twentieth century. In Lotman's study, the cinematic language is related to other media and other codes, thus setting an agenda for further research on the relationship between different codes or filmic materials.

In Germany in the 1960s, Friedrich Knilli developed the semiotics of the radio play as a form of art achieving a synthesis of all acoustic arts. This "radio language" induces the listener to construct a proper world of sound processes. Building on these earlier works, Knilli's *Semiotik des Films* (1971) contributed to launching film semiotics in Germany. Other centers of research in Germany included the Münsteraner Arbeitskreis für Semiotik, which collectively edited a series about fundamental problems of film semiotics on topics such as semiotic terminology, iconicity, the shot as the basic element of film semiotics, and the syntax of film. Among members of this circle were Karl-Dietmar Möller-Nass, who published a thesis about the historical development of the theory of the filmic language (1986), and Hans Wulff, the editor of *Film Theory* who founded with other scholars *Montage a/v*, a journal with a strong semiotic component. Around the same time, Walter A. Koch (1971) studied the relationship between filmic codes, linguistics, and biology. Other scholars combined film semiotics with their practical experience as filmmakers and directed their attention toward cinematic reality in terms of its conditions of production (e.g., Bitomsky, 1972).

In English, two early publications were of great influence. The first was Sol Worth's article about "The Development of a Semiotic of Film" (1969), in which film is defined as a communicative process that must consequently include a producer and a spectator. Film semiotics is thus conceived as a study of the making of meaning on the basis of filmic signs, a process that takes place between a producer and a receiver and must be linked not only to linguistics but also to psychology, anthropology, and aesthetics. The second influential publication was Peter Wollen's *Signs and Meaning in the Cinema* (1969), which opened a new debate about the sign system of film by suggesting the replacement of the Saussurean concept of language with the Peircean notion of types of signs. Wollen's approach combined theoretical and historical perspectives and brought into focus media relations, media transformations, and intermediality by locating the filmic signs in the context of other media.

If filmic structures must be embedded in a specific context of production and reception, the logical next step is to consider film as a textual process with dynamic elements that can be analyzed. This insight is one of the starting points of the film semiotics of the 1970s and 1980s that not only make use of Metz's remarks about the practices of signification but also draw from Roland Barthes's semiological proposals, Julia Kristeva's theory of intertextuality, and Jacques Derrida's concept of *écriture*. The filmic text is thus considered a site of an indefinite activity. This approach has found its most prominent exponents in the Latinate countries. In Italy, Gianfranco Bettetini (1975) developed a semiotic model of the making of meaning on the basis of the filmic "material," the corresponding significations, and its mise-en-scène. In France, Marie-Claire Ropars abandoned the static concepts of structuralism and conceived the filmic text as an agglomeration of active and open structural conflicts that cannot be resolved into a single synthesis (Ropars and Sorlin, 1976). That is why a textual analysis can never find a definitive solution.

But there is also a second type of textual approaches (Casetti, 1993), which are directed toward the reconstruction of a text theory or grammar. The starting points of these new approaches are the works of Teun A. Van Dijk, János Petöfi, and S. J. Schmidt. Möller-Nass, for example, is interested in the development of a grammatical analysis that aims—without interpreting the texts—at the reconstruction of the rules that come into play with the production and reception of the filmic text. This grammatical analysis aims primarily at macrostructures that constitute the text and that can be of a narrative, argumentative, or aesthetic character. Casetti conceives of the filmic text as a coherent and communicative entity that can be related to other modes of discourses that exist in our social world. His proposal has led—together with those by other scholars, including Jacques Aumont, Roger Odin, and Michel Marie—to a multitude of thorough studies that are not only applications of semiotic principles but also contributions to the further elaboration of the theory of film semiotics. This can be seen in Raymond Bellour's inspiring studies during the late 1970s (e.g., *L'analyse du film*, 1979).

If film is considered as text and thus has to be studied by methods of textual analysis, it is only a small further step to expand these studies to the dynamics of narrative structures. In England, Peter Wollen (1969) presented an analysis of Hitchcock's *North by Northwest* (1959) in which he tried to apply Vladimir Propp's narrative units and functions of the fairy tale to film; in the United States, Seymour Chatman followed and expanded the concept of narrativics, which has been developed by Gérard Genette, and proposed his theoretical and analytical system in *Story and Discourse* (1978), in which he distinguished between story (narrated events) and discourse (modes of narrating a story). This theory implies a new and dynamic view of filmic and literary narrative structures that leaves the old structuralist models behind. In 1982, Nick Browne set forth these studies by differentiating and characterizing "the narrating agency or authority which can be taken to rationalize the presentation of shots."

Since Metz's syntagmatics was based primarily on and directed toward traditional Hollywood cinema, a group of young French scholars soon realized that this model could not be applied to all filmic genres, especially modern and avant-garde films. *Nouveau roman* and *nouveau cinéma* meant a challenge to the Metzian system. Dominique Chateau, André Gardies, and François Jost met that challenge by expanding and transgressing the former static patterns of analysis. Starting from Genette's theory, Jost and André Gaudreault (1990) differentiated the already existing categories of the narrative system to develop a theoretical framework for the analysis of different narrative instances of film that stretches from modes of ocularization (different forms of visual points of view that are in one way or another related to what the figures of the diegesis are likely to see) or focalization (the specific point of view of a narration) to the meganarrator (the *grand imagier*; the last narrating instance of the film).

But there are other narrative models. In the Netherlands, Emile Poppe developed a semiotic narratology of film based on A. J. Greimas's principles of narrativity as organizing factors of all discourses. In Germany, Rolph Kloepfer aimed at the reconstruction of a global narrative macrostructure at the core of all media, from literature to film, advertisements, and video clips. If films and audiovisual texts are to be considered and analyzed as narratives, then one factor seems to be crucial: the function of the point of view for the narrative process. Edward Branigan presented a study of the role of the point of view in the constitution of a filmic narration. He focuses upon "concrete, textual mechanisms which make point of view into a symbolic process, not a site for 'consciousness' and speculations about the human psyche. Point of view is part of the generative capacity of a text and is one aspect of a reader's general competence" (1984, p. 21). In this sense, narrative has to be regarded as a semiotic and symbolic activity or as a dialectical process between narrator and reader. Starting from these premises, Branigan elaborates a differentiated system for the analysis of point of view in film, which tackles among others the question of the subjectivity of point-of-view shots, the issues of character reflection and projection, and the semiotic approaches (primarily based on the works of Charles Sanders Peirce and Roland Barthes) to new developments in cognitive psychology.

The above-mentioned studies of the filmic text and point of view imply the question of how films are understood or how the processes between text and spectator can be analyzed. A pragmatics of film is directed toward these processes and aims at spatiotemporal coordinates within which any (filmic) discourse takes place, the circumstances of production and reception of the text, and the intertextual elements that are present in and work upon any text. With his concept of a communicative pact, Francesco Casetti (in Müller, 1995) offers a general and very lucid instrument for the analysis of different types of communication. If interaction, convergence, and cooperation are the main elements present in several ways, in every communicative situation, and if the communicative situation seems to depend on a common view regarding the type of action being done, then pragmatic research must be directed toward the understanding of the underlying structure and dynamics of this pact or communicative contract. The basic elements and dynamics of this contract are present in every communicative situation and can be described by a diagram or a Greimasian semiotic square of accord, discord, nondiscord, and nonaccord. This procedure establishes a set of rules for the reconstruction of the play of mental recognition, mental guarantees of maneuverability, and mental participation.

Another pragmatic concept has been developed by Roger Odin (1990), who relies on a model of non-communication that emphasizes the gap between a message's space of reception and space of emission. According to Odin's proposal, there is no homology between the text as it is constructed by the sender and the text as it is constructed by the receiver.

Given this a priori state of noncommunication, the aim of Odin's project of a semiopragmatics must be seen as the construction of a theoretical frame for the study of the making of meaning as it occurs within film and audiovisual texts. This concept consciously stays in close contact with the audiovisual text. It constitutes a frame able to cope with modes (i.e., specific procedures of the making of meaning and affects) and institutions (i.e., normative powers that mutually induce individuals to perform certain practices under the penalty of sanctions and that regulate the choice of specific modes by establishing a priority of their use), which interact in the process of the making of meaning. Odin's proposal, which is conceived as neither a cognitive nor a sociological model, enables the researcher to apply a highly differentiated set of categories in order to reconstruct specific patterns of reading certain audiovisual texts. It leads to the construction of generic modalities in the production of meaning and affects and, finally, to a cluster of fundamental questions with regard to the processes that take place if we look at and listen to a film in a certain context. It is the task of a pragmatic approach to the audiovisual to formulate some answers to these questions.

It is evident that there are many links between a semiopragmatics of film and the concept of enunciation. Starting from Émile Benveniste's notion, many scholars (Aumont, Bettetini, Casetti, Jost, Gaudreault, and others) have been involved since the late 1970s in the study of how the filmic text presents itself to a spectator by "saying": "Look at me. I am talking to you as a film." This process is at the core of Metz's last book *L'enonciation impersonnelle ou le site du film* (1991), in which he studies eleven enunciative figures.

Film semioticians also sought inspiration in the models of generative grammar for film analysis. These studies focused on elementary structures and rules of the medium that are the basis of every filmic text.

Michel Colin, Noël Carol, Dominique Chateau, and Karl-Dietmar Möller-Nass worked on the project of a generative and transformation film grammar whose first results can be seen, for example, in Möller-Nass's book on filmic language (1986). Semiotic research has become increasingly aware of the intertextual and intermedial statuses of film, recognizing that the making of meaning depends on, among other factors, processes of multi- and intermediality. Ernst Hess-Lüttich, Jürgen Müller, and others tackle this problem by analyzing multimedia semioses, the function of transfer processes and code changes in the mental activities of the spectator. But the heterogeneity and complexity of multimodal coded texts require new semiotic concepts and methods of research.

[*See also* Cinema; Enonciation Impersonnelle ou le Site du Film, L'; *and* Metz.]

BIBLIOGRAPHY

Bellour, R. *L'analyse du film.* Paris: Albatros, 1979.

Bettetini, G. *Produzione del senso e messa in scena.* Milan: Bompiani, 1975.

Bitomsky, H. *Die Röte des Rots im Technicolor.* Neuwied: Luchterhand, 1972.

Branigan, E. *Point of View in the Cinema.* Berlin and New York: Mouton, 1984.

Browne, N. *The Rhetoric of Filmic Narration.* Ann Arbor: University of Michigan Press, 1982.

Casetti, F. *Teorie del cinema, 1945–1990.* Milan: Bompiani: 1993.

Chatman, S. B. *Story and Discourse: Narrative Structure in Fiction and Film.* Ithaca, N.Y.: Cornell University Press, 1978.

Chatman, S. B. *Coming to Terms: The Rhetoric of Narrative in Fiction and Film.* Ithaca, N.Y.: Cornell University Press, 1990.

Eco, U. "Towards a Semiotic Inquiry into the Television Message." In *Communication Studies,* pp. 131–149 edited by J. Corner and J. Hawthorn. London: Arnold, 1980.

Eisenstein, S. *S. M. Eisenstein: Selected Writings.* Edited and translated by R. Taylor. Bloomington: Indiana University Press, 1996.

Garroni, E. *Semiotica ed estetica: L'eterogeneità del linguaggio e il linguaggio cinematografico.* Bari: Laterza, 1968.

Gaudreault, A., and F. Jost. *Le récit cinématographique.* Paris: Nathan, 1990.

Ivanov, V. V. "Functions and Categories of Film Language." Translated by L. M. O'Toole and A. Shukman. *Russian Poetics in Translation,* (1981):1–35.

Knilli, F., ed. *Semiotik des Films.* Frankfurt: Fischer Athenäum Taschenbücher, 1971.

Koch, W. A. *Varia semiotica.* Hildesheim, Germany: Olms, 1971.

Kuleshov, L. *Kuleshov on Film: Writings*. Edited and translated by R. Levaco. Berkeley: University of California Press, 1974.

Lotman, J. *Semiotics of Cinema* (1973). Translated by M. E. Suino. Ann Arbor: University of Michigan Press, 1976.

Metz, C. "Le cinéma: Langue ou language?" *Communications 4*, edited by R. Barthes, pp. 52–90. Paris: Seuil, 1964.

Metz, C. *L'enonciation impersonnelle ou le site du film*. Paris: Méridiens Klincksieck, 1991.

Möller-Nass, K.-D. *Filmsprache: Eine kritische Theoriegeschichte*. Münster: MAkS, 1986.

Müller, J. E., ed. *Towards a Pragmatics of the Audiovisual*. 2 vols. Münster: NODUS, 1995.

Odin, R. *Cinéma et production de sens*. Paris: Armand Colin, 1990.

Peters, J. M. L. "De taal vaan de film: Een linguistisch psychologisch onderzoek naar de aard en de betekenis van het expressie-middel film" (The Language of Film: A Linguistic and Psychological Study of the Character and the Signification of the Film as a Means of Expression). Ph.D. diss., The Hague, 1950.

Pudovkin, V. I. *Film Technique and Film Acting*. Translated by I. Montagu. New York: Grove Press, 1960.

Ropars, M.-C., and P. Sorlin. *Octobre: Écriture et idéologie*. Paris: Albatros, 1976.

Vertov, D. *Kino-eye: The Writing of Dziga Vertov*. Edited by A. Michelson, translated by K. O'Brien. Berkeley: University of California Press, 1984.

Wollen, P. *Signs and Meaning in the Cinema*. London: Secker and Warburg, 1969.

Worth, S. "The Development of a Semiotic of Film." *Semiotica* 1 (1969): 282–321.

—JÜRGEN E. MÜLLER

FINGERSPELLING. A gestural means of representing an orthography, fingerspelling as used by the deaf community in the United States is a one-handed system in which each letter of the English alphabet is associated with a particular orientation of a particular hand shape and, in some instances, with a particular movement pattern. The sequence of hand shapes in a fingerspelled word stands in a one-to-one relationship with the letters of the orthographic representation of that word, although the hand shapes might be extensively coarticulated. This fingerspelling system is derived from one apparently invented in the sixteenth century by Spanish monks bound by vows of silence. The system was used subsequently in early attempts to educate the deaf (Lane, 1984). The fingerspelling systems used in much of Europe and the Americas are also derived from this monastic system; however, other apparently unrelated fingerspelling systems also exist.

In Britain, for instance, a two-handed fingerspelling system dating from the seventeenth century is used (Kyle and Woll, 1985). In the British fingerspelling system, each of the five vowels is represented by pointing to a particular finger of the nondominant hand; each consonant is represented by particular hand shapes on each of the two hands and by the relation of the hands to each other. In Guatemala, the fingerspelling system comprises some one-handed and some two-handed forms; several letters are articulated at the face and others are articulated with movement patterns more reminiscent of signs in American Sign Language (ASL) than of ASL fingerspelling. Signers in Hong Kong and Taiwan represent Chinese orthography by tracing characters in the air (Padden, 1991).

In the American deaf community, fingerspelling is commonly used to represent specific English words (often technical vocabulary and proper names) for which there is no exact equivalent in the sign vocabulary of ASL and to translate signs for the benefit of less-than-fluent hearing signers. Much as acronyms are a frequent source of new English words (e.g., *AWOL*, *radar*, *scuba*, *snafu*), fingerspellings are a source of new ASL signs (Battison, 1978). And, as with words such as *snafu*, adoptions often obscure the etymology. Because fingerspelling includes hand shapes and sequences of hand shapes not generally found in the native vocabulary of ASL, fingerspelled loan signs are often restructured phonologically to fit the language. Often, the meaning of a fingerspelled loan sign differs somewhat from the English word from which it is derived historically. For instance, the loan sign *G-S* typically refers to natural gas; there is a nonloan sign used to refer to gasoline. Fingerspelled borrowings also occur in other sign languages. In British Sign Language, for example, there is a loan sign *about*, which is rendered as the sequence *A-B-T* (Kyle and Woll, 1985).

Deaf children of deaf parents are typically exposed to fingerspelling well before they are instructed in reading and writing; common fingerspelled loan signs such as the ASL sign *ball* are often used by deaf parents, even with very young infants. However, not until age three do children understand the relationship between print and fingerspelling (Padden, 1991). Deaf children's early fingerspelling attempts typically preserve the overall contour or movement pattern of fingerspelled items, although they frequently err in their choices of hand shapes or hand-shape sequences.

[*See also* Articulation; *and* Sign Languages.]

BIBLIOGRAPHY

Battison, R. *Lexical Borrowing in American Sign Language.* Silver Spring, Md.: Linstok Press, 1978.

Kyle, J., and B. Woll. *Sign Language: The Study of Deaf People and Their Language.* Cambridge: Cambridge University Press, 1985.

Lane, H. *When the Mind Hears.* New York: Random House, 1984.

Padden, C. "The Acquisition of Fingerspelling by Deaf Children." In *Theoretical Issues in Sign Language Research,* edited by P. Siple and S. D. Fisher, vol. 2, pp. 191–210. Chicago: University of Chicago Press, 1991.

Acknowledgment. Preparation of this article was supported in part by a grant (#5 RO1 DC01691-03) to Richard P. Meir from the National Institute on Deafness and Other Communication Disorders, National Institutes of Health.

—AMANDA S. HOLZRICHTER
and RICHARD P. MEIER

FLAMING. A prominent feature of computer-mediated communication, flaming consists of sudden, often extended flare-ups of anger, profanity, and insult. Although the phenomenon might be relatively rare, it is salient enough to have acquired a name for which semantic elaboration of the term includes *flame on,* to warn readers that a message might anger or insult them; *flame off,* to signal that the potentially controversial material has been concluded; *to flame,* as a transitive verb; *flamage,* for flaming verbiage; and *flame wars,* for extended verbal battles. Sequences of flaming occur not only in synchronous modes of communication but in nonsynchronous, private e-mail messages and in public messages posted to electronic discussion groups, news groups, and bulletin boards.

One explanation for the phenomenon invokes the speed and interactivity of the medium, which create the illusion of conversation though correspondents cannot see one another and the text alone must carry the message. The absence of important cues to the intention behind a message—such as intonation, body language, the age, sex, and demeanor of the writer, and physical features of the setting in which the message is composed—is thought to lead recipi-

ents to misinterpret messages. Thus, joking or ironic messages are taken too literally, with negative results. Advocates of this explanation sometimes recommend the use of emoticons, which are icons composed of typographic symbols and intended to indicate emotion, as in :-), read sideways for a smiling face, or ;-) for a wink, to signal that the message is not to be taken seriously.

Another explanation locates the problem in the effect of the medium on the sender rather than on the recipient. The anonymity of the medium disinhibits correspondents, releasing profanity and other aggressive material that would be suppressed in circumstances under more obvious social control. Writers thus dare to include in their messages offensive content that they would never have included or would only have spoken aloud in informal social circumstances.

Yet another explanation focuses on cultural factors: the subculture of hackers, computer hobbyists, and computer professionals in industry and the universities fosters antiestablishment values and behavior with a resultant blurring of conventional lines between public and private domains and between work and play. These trends, in turn, might encourage uninhibited behavior. Thus, persons not belonging to this subculture who are socialized into the practices now crystallizing in computer-mediated communication might be encouraged to behave more aggressively than they would in preelectronic forms of written communication.

All these approaches tend to imply that flaming is bad and that if we succeed in understanding the reasons for it, perhaps it can be controlled. A very different approach takes a more neutral stance and emphasizes the playful, expressive, and even sporting aspects of flaming. In this view, flaming is one aspect of a partial return to oral culture in digital writing, which tends to be dynamic and playful and which encourages interlocutors to pay attention to how messages are packaged. Flaming might therefore have important affinities with a large variety of stylized oral forms of verbal dueling in which performance is central, such as flyting in medieval England or "playing the dozens" among contemporary African Americans.

There is a great need for research to investigate under what circumstances flaming tends to occur and how it is constituted. How do interlocutors know when an instance of flaming is happening? How do newcomers to cyberspace learn about it? Is it more common in public discussion groups than in private e-mail, and if so why? Might the presence of an audience foster it? How do people react to being flamed, and how does this affect their future communication style? The dominant language of cyberspace is English, yet millions of persons whose first language is not English communicate in this medium. Is flaming more common when one or more interlocutors is not a native speaker of English, or is it equally common among native speakers? Are there differences between the types of flaming that occur in the two cases? Is flaming as a result of genuine misunderstanding especially common when there has been no sustained electronic interaction preceding the incident? Under what circumstances do elements of performance or sport become prominent? Does stylized, expressive flaming tend to occur mainly in situations of repeated, playful contact, as in the electronic pubs and cafés of internet relay chat (IRC) or commercial on-line services? What forms does it take? Is there evidence that participants enjoy some forms of flaming rather than condemn them or become upset or offended? Careful ethnographic research is likely to show that flaming is not a monolithic phenomenon and that under different circumstances different explanations apply.

[*See also* Computer-Mediated Communication; *and* Writing, Ethnography of.]

BIBLIOGRAPHY

Bolter, J. D. *Writing Space: The Computer, Hypertext, and the History of Writing.* Hillsdale, N.J.: Lawrence Erlbaum, 1991.

Edwards, V., and T. J. Sienkewicz. *Oral Cultures Past and Present: Rappin' and Homer.* Oxford: Basil Blackwell, 1990.

Hughes, G. *Swearing: A social History of Foul Language, Oaths, and Profanity in English.* Oxford: Basil Blackwell, 1991.

Kiesler, S., J. Siegel, and T. W. McGuire. "Social Psychological Aspects of Computer-Mediated Communications." *American Psychologist* 39 (1984): 1123–1134.

Kirshenblatt-Gimblett, B., ed. *Speech Play: Research and Resources for the Study of Linguistic Creativity.* Philadelphia: University of Pennsylvania Press, 1976.

Lea, M., T. O'Shea, P. Fung, and R. Spears. "'Flaming' in Computer-Mediated Communication." In *Contexts of Computer-Mediated Communications*, edited by M. Lea, pp. 89–112. Hemel Hempstead, Hertfordshire: Harvester Wheatsheaf, 1992.

McDowell, J. H. "Verbal Dueling." In *Handbook of Discourse Analysis*, vol. 3, edited by T. A. Van Dijk, pp. 203–211. London: Academic Press, 1985.

Walther, J. B. "Interpersonal Effects in Computer-Mediated Interaction." *Communication Research* 19 (1992): 52–90.

—BRENDA DANET

FOUCAULT, MICHEL (1926–1984), French philosopher who began his career as a psychopathologist. Foucault taught psychology in the early 1950s at the University of Lille, and, after several years teaching in Sweden, Poland, and Germany, he defended a doctoral thesis in Paris on the history of madness (1961). He emerged in the 1960s as a major critical thinker, acknowledging the influence of Friedrich Nietzsche (1844–1900) and Martin Heidegger (1889–1976) and the impact of the artistic and literary avant-garde of the twentieth century. He published a series of landmark books that included *The Order of Things* (1970), *The Archeology of Knowledge* (1972), *Discipline and Punish* (1977) while holding academic positions in France and the United States. Until his death in 1984, he intensely engaged political issues through interviews and symbolic gestures, congruent with the critical stands taken in this teaching and writings.

Foucault's work insisted on the controlling, positioning, and productive capacities of signifying practices, denying in the process the primacy of signification itself and radically unsettling common theoretical assumptions about the ways in which signifying practices operate. His work also explicitly connected the discipline of the body, the production of knowledge, and the making of subjectivity. In this context, the term *discourse* has come to mean something precisely not limited to nor constrained by the categories of linguistics and semiotics. On the contrary, a discourse is a way of categorizing and limiting but also producing the objects of which it speaks: for example, the discourse of childhood, the discourse of gender, and so on. In this very broad definition of *discourse*, a discourse might be said to consist of all the visual, verbal, and bodily statements that might be made about a topic.

In Foucault's early work, the term *episteme* is used to characterize the discursive regularities, the "rules of formation," of the discourses of biology, economics, and grammar (linguistics). That term was later replaced by the more fluid term *archive*: "The archive is first the law of what can be said, the system that governs the appearance of statements as unique events. . . . It is that which . . . defines at the outset the system of its enunciability" (1972). For Foucault, the power invested in knowledge, in the will to truth, meant that discipline as an institution was a mode of constraining and producing both knowledge and subjects (people) positioned by and within the knowledges of the disciplines.

Foucault maintained an opposition between what he called the discursive and the nondiscursive. His desire to rethink this relationship emerged only indirectly from a desire to question concepts such as the traditional unities of the book and the oeuvre; the speaking subject as defined by psychology and humanism; context as a simple experience-based explanation of what that intending or knowing subject does; the notion that such a subject constructs unified discourses according to laws; and the a priori authority of knowledge. Foucault's ultimate rewriting of the linguistic and semiotic binaries was a consequence of his perception that these binaries participated in the construction of the above concepts.

What Foucault called the discursive (the verbal) is what linguistics and semiotics see as representing or containing the nondiscursive (the nonverbal). He also saw a homology between this and the tendency in traditional social theory to differentiate, to keep separate, the discursive, the languages of institutions, and the "institutional milieu" or context of those languages—the nondiscursive formations of institutions (their architecture; space technologies), political events, economic practices and processes, and so on. This separation allows power to be located in these nondiscursive areas (e.g., the state, the economy, the law), and there is then a tendency to establish a vertical causality whereby events and institutions determine the discursive so that the power is not in discourse itself.

It was to recover the specificity and difference of these two spheres, to dislocate their apparently self-evident opposition, and to break the homologizing tendencies of any easy dialectic between them that Foucault first separated them. In his initial concentration on the discursive and the institutional, he was interested above all in the discontinuities and the transformations that occurred within what he came to call discursive formations—collocations of discourses that he defined as, among other things, spaces "of positions and of differentiated functions for subjects" (1978). This was the beginning of the poststructuralist concept of the discursively produced subject, the subject positioned in discourse. A discourse (here roughly equivalent to a discipline) was for Foucault a "curious entity" and not something to be taken for granted. What could be more enigmatic than speaking of psychiatry, grammar, or medicine?

In trying to answer that question, Foucault sought to define the play of dependencies that effected transformations in discourses and discursive formations. Among these he included intradiscursive dependencies (between the objects, the operations, and the concepts of a single formation), interdiscursive dependencies (between different discursive formations such as history, economics, grammar, and the theory of representation), and extradiscursive dependencies (between discursive formations and others not produced in discourse: e.g., the correlation between medical discourse and economic, political, and social changes [1965, 1973]). Significantly, the discursive comes to include behaviors, events, practices, technologies, and procedures as well as the linguistically or verbally discursive. Discourse is already not only language, nor is the verbal aspect of it homologous with language either as system or as use. Foucault focused on surfaces and intersections. Hence, he was engaged not in exegesis but in archaeology; his concept of archive was not as an accumulation of texts but as the rules that for a given society defined the limits and forms of expressibility (what it is possible to say in what domain), conservation (what statements disappear, what survive and where and why), memory (what are the terms everyone remembers, what are the relations between the present and past systems of statements), reactivation (what is valued, reconstituted, of the discourses of past epochs and how), and appropriation (who has access to what discourse and how that relationship is institutionalized).

Foucault's critical history of modernity is the story of the restructuring of power and knowledge, the making of new kinds of subjects, in the course of the late eighteenth and early nineteenth centuries in the capitalist societies of Western Europe. He argued that the rise of parliamentary institutions and new conceptions of political liberty were accompanied by a profound and pervasive transformation in the functioning of power. The total power of the absolute monarch is replaced by an unprecedented discipline of the body, a "microphysics" of power that fragments and partitions the body's time, space, and movements and is realized but unremarked in the smallest gestures and postures of everyday life. The seat of this capillary effect of power is a new "technology," a mode of making visible the move (*le geste*) of gridding (*quadriller*) a visible space in such a way as to make its occupants observable, which operates through a constellation of institutions, all of which resonate the structure and effects of Jeremy Bentham's panopticon, including the school, the prison, the police force, the army, and the factory. The disciplinary techniques of regulated isolation and surveillance in these institutions train, position, and produce a hierarchy of docile social subjects, subjected and practiced bodies that Foucault calls "docile bodies." The state of permanent and conscious visibility produced by these disciplines assures the automatic functioning of power as each inmate becomes his own jailer, and the heightened self-awareness and perpetual self-surveillance that results produces the "individualism" of modernity.

At the same time, these increasingly invasive apparatuses of power and surveillance require and generate a new kind of knowledge of the very subjects and behaviors that they themselves produce: the disciplines and discourses of modern psychology and sociology and the discourse of the social sciences. These new knowledges then produce new effects of power that operate through new technologies of behavior: the microtechniques of the interview, the medical examination, the social survey, and the questionnaire. Panoptic and instrumental reason becomes flesh, investing and traversing, specifying and differentiating, taking hold of the body—not only the mind—of the social subject.

The concept of the productivity of discourse and discipline and the ubiquity of governmentality has been appropriated in support of the power of bureaucracy and policy in the discursive work of Ian Hunter on schooling (1994). Other researches that have used Foucault's work in different theoretical and disciplinary configurations to develop an interventionist critical-discourse analysis include those on aboriginality in Australia (Muecke, 1992), photography (Tagg, 1988), pedagogy (Luke, 1989), and the constructed nature of social class (Finch, 1993). Charles Goodwin's (1994) work on "professional vision" is a detailed, ethnographic approach to some of the questions raised by Foucault's account of discipline. All this work is profoundly concerned with questions of language, power, and subjectivity, even with questions of knowledge, sexuality, and desire, but the term *discourse* here has the specifically non-

linguistic connotations that have predominated after Foucault.

[*See also* Bourdieu; Discourse Analysis; Habitus; Poststructuralism; *and* Structuralism.]

BIBLIOGRAPHY

Works by Foucault

Madness and Civilization: A History of Insanity in the Age of Reason. Translated by R. Howard. New York: Vintage Books, 1965.

The Order of Things: An Archaeology of the Human Sciences. New York: Pantheon Books, 1970.

The Archaeology of Knowledge. Translated by A. M. Sheridan Smith. New York: Pantheon Books, 1972.

The Birth of the Clinic. Translated by A. M. Sheridan Smith. New York: Vintage Books, 1973.

Discipline and Punish. Translated by A. Sheridan, New York: Pantheon Books, 1977.

"Politics and the Study of Discourse." *Ideology and Consciousness* 3 (1978): 7–26.

Other Works

During, S. *Foucault and Literature: Toward a Genealogy of Writing.* London and New York: Routledge, 1992.

Finch, L. *The Classing Gaze.* Sydney: Allen and Unwin, 1993.

Goodwin, C. "Professional Vision." *American Anthropologist* 96.3 (1994): 606–633.

Hunter, I. *Rethinking the School: Subjectivity, Bureaucracy, Criticism.* Sydney: Allen and Unwin, 1994.

Luke, C. *Pedagogy, Printing, and Protestantism: The Discourse on Childhood.* New York: State University of New York Press, 1989.

Muecke, S. *Textual Spaces: Aboriginality and Cultural Studies.* Kensington, New South Wales: New South Wales University Press, 1992.

Tagg, J. *The Burden of Representation.* London: Macmillan, 1988.

—TERRY THREADGOLD

FREGE, GOTTLOB (1848–1925), German mathematician and philosopher who attempted to show that the foundation of arithmetic could be proved from a small set of general logical assumptions. Frege developed a symbolic language that embodies fundamental principles of reasoning based on an analysis of language. Introducing the modern concept of quantification for the first time, Frege's system is essentially the symbolic logic widely used by philosophers, linguists, and mathematicians today.

Born in Wismar, Germany, Frege received his doctorate from Göttingen University in 1873 and the following year began a forty-four-year career on the mathematics faculty of Jena University. Rudolf Carnap was one of his students during his twenty-two years of teaching (he was promoted to a research position in 1896), and he corresponded with many important scholars, among them David Hilbert (1862–1943), Edmund Husserl (1859–1938), Giuseppe Peano (1858–1932), Bertrand Russell (1872–1970), and Ludwig Wittgenstein (1889–1951). During his career, Frege published forty works including four important books.

The short book *Begriffsschrift* (Conceptual Notation, 1879) is described in its subtitle as "a Formula Language of Pure Thought Modelled upon the Formula Language of Arithmetic." The *Begriffsschrift* is a symbolic system that introduces many elements of modern logic, among them Frege's assertion sign, which foreshadows the distinction between language and metalanguage by distinguishing the assertion of a statement from its expression. Frege maintained that this turnstilelike (⊢) symbol contains two logical parts that correspond with its two physical parts: a vertical (assertion) stroke, which means that what follows it is true; and a horizontal (content) stroke, which stands for the assertible content (thought) expressed by a certain symbol. Frege held that logically there is only one kind of judgment: namely, the assertion that a particular content is true. He analyzed the Kantian distinctions among judgments (e.g., universal, negative, hypothetical) as assertions of different types of contents. A conditional content such as "if A then B" (where A and B are assertible contents) is represented by a two-dimensional graph standing for the truth function that is false when A is true and B is false and true otherwise. This truth-functional analysis of the logical words is an innovation that Frege extends to *not*, *and*, and *or*. He also replaces the traditional subject-predicate analysis of prepositions with the distinction between a function and an argument for a function. Each proposition is constructed from an n-ary function and n arguments. The proposition "the moon orbits the sun" is analyzed as an expression of the form $f(a,b)$ where a is a name for the sun, b is a name for the moon, and $f(x,y)$ is an expression for the concept x orbits y. This structure allows a complex proposition to quantify over more than one variable. The quantifier words *all* and *some* are understood as functions that take functions as arguments. Each quantifier contains a variable and takes a function of that variable as an argument. The existential quantifier may be expressed as a function $(\exists x)[. . .]$ in which the brackets are filled with a function of the variable x. So, for example, to symbolize "some object orbits the sun," one would write $(\exists x)[f(x,a)]$. "Some object orbits some object" could then be analyzed from this as $(\exists y)(\exists x)[f(x,y)]$. Thus, quantified propositions are analyzed as being built up from simpler components.

Frege uses his *Begriffsschrift* to prove many "judgements of pure thought" from a small set of assumptions. This groundbreaking system of proof relies on the syntactical form of premises to derive its conclusions. Frege's *Begriffsschrift* is now acknowledged as probably the greatest work in the development of logic, yet it received little attention during his lifetime.

Frege's more accessible *Die Grundlagen der Arithmetik* (The Foundations of Arithmetic, 1884) develops his realist philosophy of mathematics and presents an outline of his plan to prove the foundations of arithmetic from purely logical assumptions. In his analysis of the nature of number, he introduces the "context principle": a word has meaning only in the context of a sentence. Frege used this principle in his construction of arithmetic, for he held that a number concept could only have meaning in a sentence in which it applies to other concepts.

Frege's rigorous development of his plan for the foundations of arithmetic was published in the two-volume *Grundgesetze der Arithmetik* (Basic Laws of Arithmetic, 1893, 1903). In this work, he modifies the system of the *Begriffsschrift* in an attempt to derive all arithmetic truths from logic. In 1902, Bertrand Russell wrote to Frege that he had discovered an inconsistency among Frege's fundamental assumptions. Frege assumed (as Russell had) that every concept defines a set, in particular the set of all those things that have the property expressed by the concept. Russell noted that on this general assumption the concept "x is not a member of x" defines a set, but this set gives rise to a contradiction. This problem is known as Russell's paradox, and Frege wrote in his reply to Russell that it "rocked the ground" on which he planned to build arithmetic. Frege described the problem in an appendix to the second volume of the *Grundgesetze* but did not find what he considered to be a satisfactory solution. He eventually abandoned the project of proving arithmetic from logic.

Frege's well-known theory of sense and denotation is contained in three papers: "On Function and

Concept" (1891), "On Concept and Object" (1892), and "On Sense and Meaning" (1892). In them, Frege modifies and elaborates the logical foundations of language given in the *Begriffsschrift*, with particular attention to the distinction between the sign and the thing signified. A name is a sign for an object. Functions differ in kind from objects in being unsaturated; their expression leaves a blank space, as in $2x + 1$. Each function has associated with it what Frege calls a "course of values"—that is, a set of ordered sequences of objects that are inputs and outputs of the function. In the case of $2x + 1$, it is the pairs: $\{<0,1>, <1,3>, <2,5>, \ldots\}$. Concepts and relations are simply types of functions, for a concept such as "x is equal to 2" is a function that takes objects as arguments and yields a true or false truth value as output. The extension of a concept is the set of objects that make that concept true. Each name in a language indicates an object, and this object is the meaning (*Bedeutung*, sometimes translated as *reference* or *denotation*) of the name. In addition, every name expresses its sense. The sense of a name is its mode of presentation of its particular object. Frege's well-known example concerns the expressions "the morning star" and "the evening star." Both expressions have the planet Venus as their meaning, but they have different senses that correspond to the way in which the planet is presented. Frege cites the fact that a person might find the fact that the morning star is the evening star to be evidence for the existence of senses. A much-debated feature of this theory in the philosophy of language is that every sentence denotes a meaning; Frege held that all true sentences denote truth and all false sentences denote falsehood. Frege arrives at this view by a rigorous employment of the principle of substitution of logical equivalents; namely, when one sign is substituted (in a sentence) by another sign that refers to the same object, the resulting sentence should stand for the same object. He thinks of the sense of a sentence as what one might call the proposition expressed by that sentence. Like its meaning, the sense of a sentence is also a function of the senses of its components.

Frege maintained that the fundamental elements of language may be analyzed as types of names or functional expressions; his analysis of logical words and quantifiers are examples of this. This thesis initiated the analytic philosophy of language and it also had an impact on the science of linguistics. In mathematics, Frege's work initiated the growth of entire subdisciplines: mathematical logic, set theory, and others. His original thesis that arithmetic is reducible to logic has been shown to be false by the work of Kurt Gödel in 1931.

[*See also* Denotation and Connotation; Meaning; Russell; *and* Wittgenstein.]

BIBLIOGRAPHY

Frege, G. *The Foundations of Arithmetic*. Translated by J. L. Austin. Evanston: Northwestern University Press, 1950.

Frege, G. *Basic Laws of Arithmetic: Exposition of the System*. Edited and translated by M. Furth. Berkeley: University of California Press, 1964.

Frege, G. *Conceptual Notation and Related Articles*. Translated by T. W. Bynum. London: Oxford University Press, 1972.

Frege, G. *Philosophical and Mathematical Correspondence*. Edited by B. McGuinness, translated by H. Kaal. Oxford: Blackwell, 1979.

Frege, G. *Collected Papers on Mathematics, Logic, and Philosophy*. Edited by B. McGuinness. London: Basil Blackwell, 1984.

Gödel, K. *On Formally Undecidable Propositions of Principia Mathematica and Related Systems* (1931). Edited and translated by J. van Heijenoort. Cambridge, Mass.: Harvard University Press, 1967.

Kenny, A. *Frege*. London: Penguin, 1995.

Sluga, H. *Gottlob Frege*. New York: Routledge and Kegan Paul, 1980.

—JUDY PELHAM

FRYE, NORTHROP (1912–1991), Canadian literary critic and theoretician whose intricate elaboration of a global system of meaning, based on learned competence, represents an important contribution to literary semiotics. *Anatomy of Criticism* (1957), a landmark study of structural poetics, made Frye one of the central figures in Anglo-American criticism. In subsequent publications, he developed the ideas introduced or outlined in *Anatomy of Criticism*. In *The Great Code* (1982), and *Words with Power* (1990), he established a framework for the study of the figurative language of the Bible within the larger context of the Western tradition of discourse.

Frye is perhaps best known for what came to be known as archetypal criticism. The archetype is not for Frye, as it is for Carl Jung, a psychic content of "the collective unconscious"; rather, it is an interpretant whose meaning is largely a matter of convention. It is social and cultural, rather than innate and psychic. He defines archetypes as "associative clusters" that comprise a large number of specific learned associations which form a collective property or sociocultural corpus of conventions, a complex set of rules and instructions that make any individual utterance in literature possible in the first place. Archetypal criticism is, accordingly, the study of the set of genres and conventions that govern literary communication and is simply another name for intertextuality in the strongest sense. Archetypes are thus recurring images through which poems are interconnected and integrated into a unified literary experience. An intertextual network underlies literature, since poetry can be made only out of other poems; novels only out of other novels. Archetypal criticism construes literature as a social fact and as a mode of communication.

The sum of archetypes and conventions forms the global system or code behind all acts of literary expression. In Frye's view, the coherence of this great cluster of interpretants is supplied by the mythological framework of Western culture. Inasmuch as literature evolves within the mythological framework of a given culture, it has a structure and a shape and is not simply a loose aggregate of conventions and rules—thus the importance in so many literary works of cosmology, the form that this total mythological structure ultimately takes. The cosmological structure of imagery provides Frye with the framework to understand narrative structure in terms of direction and movement. In *Anatomy of Criticism*, Frye isolates four story shapes, which he ultimately conceives of as episodes in a hypothetically complete narrative structure: romance and irony concern movement within an idealized world or a world of experience; tragedy and comedy concern the direction of that movement. Frye's discussion of *mythoi* in the third essay of *Anatomy of Criticism* outlines in detail these four "generic plots" or "narrative pregeneric elements of literature," which are "narrative categories broader than, or logically prior to, the ordinary literary genres."

Frye's "contextual" approach to structure thus differs from most structural and semiotic approaches to narrative, which have tended to neglect the conventional basis of communication in literature and to favor abstract linguistic models. It has been noted (Culler, 1975; Scholes, 1974) that the dialectical conception of character types that Frye employs throughout the third essay of *Anatomy of Criticism*, organized

around the structure of the quest and the primary opposition between *eiron* (a crucial agent of the action, who is seemingly unobtrusive) and *alazon* (an agent of an action, who is characterized by self-aggrandizing speech and behavior), is comparable in many respects to Algirdas Julien Greimas's actantial model of narrative action, which is inspired by Vladimir Propp's *Morphology of the Folktale*. Able to account for a great diversity of character types while varying significantly in its application from one narrative category to another, Frye's simple structural opposition manages to maintain internal consistency. Based on conventions clearly observable in works of literature, Frye's conception of narrative structure is faithful to the principle that fictional works are the expression or actualization (by readers or viewers) of learned narrative conventions; the imagination, for Frye, must be educated.

[*See also* Anatomy of Criticism; Burke; Narratology; *and* Poetics.]

BIBLIOGRAPHY

Works by Frye

Anatomy of Criticism: Four Essays. Princeton: Princeton University Press, 1957.

The Secular Scripture: A Study of the Structure of Romance. Cambridge, Mass.: Harvard University Press, 1976.

The Great Code: The Bible and Literature. New York: Harcourt, 1982.

Words with Power: Being a Second Study of "The Bible and Literature." Harmondsworth, England: Penguin, 1990.

Other Works

Adamson, J. *Northrop Frye: A Visionary Life.* Montreal: ECW Press, 1993.

Ayre, J. *Northrop Frye: A Biography.* Toronto: Random, 1989.

Balfour, I. *Northrop Frye.* Twayne's World Authors Series, vol. 806. Boston: Twayne, 1988.

Culler, J. *Structuralist Poetics: Structuralism, Linguistics, and the Study of Literature.* London: Routledge, 1975.

Denham, R. *Northrop Frye and Critical Method.* University Park, Pa.: Pennsylvania State University Press, 1978.

Greimas, A. J. *Structural Semantics.* Translated by D. McDowell, R. Schleifer, and A. Velie. Lincoln: University of Nebraska Press, 1983.

Hamilton, A. C. *Northrop Frye: Anatomy of His Criticism.* Toronto: University of Toronto Press, 1990.

Propp, V. *Morphology of the Folktale.* Austin: University of Texas Press, 1968.

Scholes, R. *Structuralism in Literature: An Introduction.* New Haven: Yale University Press, 1974.

—JOSEPH ADAMSON

G

GAIA HYPOTHESIS. An important branch of semiotics that goes back to Charles Sanders Peirce (1839–1914) does not restrict the relevance of semiotics to the language-centered study of human communication but extends it to the whole universe and attempts to describe all transfer of information in terms of the action of signs. For instance, Thomas A. Sebeok, quoting Peirce's claim that this universe is "perfused with signs," contends that "the scope of semiotics encompasses . . . the entirety of our planetary biosphere" (1977, p. 182). In the same vein, the Danish cell biologist and semiotician Jesper Hoffmeyer, building on the ideas of Peirce, Gregory Bateson (1972), and Sebeok, brings both cosmic events and cellular processes within the purview of a semiotic investigation of signs of meaning in the universe (1992). The Gaia hypothesis represents one of the most striking, counterintuitive, contemporary attempts at semioticizing what is considered by modern, rational common sense as mere interactions of physical forces: the variations of the earth's atmosphere.

First introduced in 1972 by the British atmospheric chemist James Lovelock, the Gaia hypothesis was formulated in 1974 by Lovelock in collaboration with the American biologist Lynn Margulis. In the most general terms, the hypothesis states that the earth's biota (the totality of living organisms), atmosphere, oceans, and soils make up a single planetary system that is self-regulating and so in a certain sense "alive." The term *Gaia*, from the name of the Greek earth goddess, refers sometimes to the hypothesis (or theory) and sometimes to the planetary self-regulating system that it postulates.

Perhaps the best way to appreciate the Gaia hypothesis is in relation to the theory of evolution by natural selection proposed by Charles Darwin (1809–1882). In its original Darwinian form, this theory holds that evolution (the modification of organisms by descent) occurs because there is variation among the traits of individuals in a population, the traits are heritable, and natural selection favors individuals that possess the more fitness-enhancing traits. The so-called modern synthetic theory of evolution is based on combining Darwinian evolution with the genetic account of inheritance due to the work of Gregor Mendel (1822–1884) and with the subsequent molecular account of genes as lengths of DNA.

One of the central concepts of modern Darwinian theory is that of adaptation. An adaptation in the most immediate sense is a design or construction that matches some physical situation more or less optimally. For example, while the fins of fishes are said to be an adaptation to an aquatic environment, most evolutionary theorists do not construe adaptation in this way. Instead, they take adaptation to be the process of adapting linked to survival and reproduction. As Darwin himself knew, the environment is not static but changing. Depending on environmental changes, certain variants in the population will be fitter than others in being able to leave more offspring. Hence, rather than organisms adapting to a fixed environment, the adapting process consists in "selective pressures" applied blindly by environmental changes.

The Gaia hypothesis builds on the Darwinian idea of environmental change in evolution but deepens it in a way that implies a reformulation of the relationship between organisms and environment in evolutionary theory. When Lovelock and Margulis first put forward their proposal in 1974, they called it the Gaia hypothesis and stated that the physical and chemical conditions of the earth's surface, atmosphere, and oceans are kept within limits favorable to life and that this homeostasis is accomplished by negative-feedback processes effected automatically by the biota. Since this original formulation, Lovelock and Margulis have expanded the hypothesis into a theory, according to which the biota and their material environment evolve as a single tight-coupled system, with the self-regulation of the planetary climate and chemistry occurring as an emergent property.

This development from hypothesis to theory occurred partly as a result of criticism from biologists

W. Ford Doolittle (1981) and Richard Dawkins (1982) argued independently that the hypothesis that the earth's climate is regulated "by and for the biota" is teleological, implying impossible foresight and planning on the part of the biota. In response, Lovelock and oceanographer Andrew Watson devised the Daisyworld computer model in which the competitive growth of light and dark daisy species alters the albedo (reflectance) of the planet's surface, thus changing the balance between the heat received from the sun and that lost to space and so regulating the temperature of the planet. Daisyworld thus provides, according to Lovelock, a minimal model of how one property of the planetary environment, temperature, can be regulated by an automatic, homeostatic mechanism realized by the biota.

Margulis and her coworkers have also addressed the issue of the genesis of Gaia by trying to show how local processes could generate self-regulating processes on a planetary scale. The processes they point to are at the microbial level. Within microbial mats, metabolic activity is highly interconnected; in addition, there are billions of distinct microbial communities covering the planet. Margulis and her coworkers suggest that planetary-level effects could have been generated by the local interactions of these microbial communities long before the presence of plants and animals on Earth.

In the Gaian view, then, the material environment of life on Earth, which comprises the atmosphere, oceans, and surface geology, is in part a biological construction. It is a nonliving extension of the activity of the biota that contributes to the maintenance of the planetary environment. Thus, the material environment does not simply provide the selective pressures for evolution, as in classical Darwinian theory, for it is also molded and shaped by the biota so that the two form a tightly coupled planetary system. In Lovelock and Margulis's view, this planetary system constitutes the largest known biological individual. The atmospheric boundary of the planet is in effect a membrane that circumscribes a living organism. Lovelock has introduced the term *geophysiology* to cover both the self-regulating processes that make up this planetary biological individual and the interdisciplinary scientific study of planetary dynamics.

The critics of this view argue that Gaia should not be accorded the status of a living system because it is not a replicating individual and so has no heredi-

tary lineage. It is also argued that it is unlikely that the planetary self-maintaining mechanisms that Lovelock and Margulis hypothesize could result from natural selection, and so, if they exist, they can only be accidental. The issues raised by these criticisms cut across evolutionary theory, theoretical biology, and the philosophy of science. For example, the criticisms are based on the Darwinian framework in which replication and reproduction are taken to be the defining characteristics of life. The Gaia theory, on the other hand, regards metabolism rather than replication as the more central feature of living systems. Margulis in her writings portrays the difference as one between a replication-based approach to biological systems, whose leading exponent is Dawkins, and an alternative approach based on the theory of autopoiesis proposed by the biologists Humberto Maturana and Francisco J. Varela (1980).

The theory of autopoiesis was developed mainly with reference to the single bacterial cell, but Margulis argues that Gaia, too, qualifies as autopoietic. Varela, however, does not appear to share this view, for he argues that although Gaia might constitute an autonomous biological individual, it is not strictly speaking autopoietic because it lacks the precise, membrane-bounded, component specification and unity-constitution processes found at the cellular level. In any case, the important point is not whether Gaia satisfies the original technical sense of *autopoiesis* but rather that it provides a theoretical framework in which replication and reproduction are not taken as defining features of living systems. Replication and reproduction both require a preexisting system to be replicated or reproduced, and so they are logically and operationally secondary to the establishment of the unitary system via the processes of self-production. Evolution, too, is operationally derivative, for it requires reproduction and the possibility of variation. Hence, in the autopoietic framework, replication, reproduction, and evolution do not enter into the defining organization of a living system; they are, rather, complications of autopoiesis that must arise in the course of the self-producing process.

Given this framework, then, Gaia's status as a biological individual is not impugned by the fact that it does not replicate. On the other hand, the idea that, as Lovelock puts it, evolution concerns Gaia itself, not organisms and environments taken separately, is problematic. While organisms and their material environment are coupled tightly in evolution and form a planetary biological individual, it does not follow that evolution pertains to the level of that individual per se, in contrast to the components the individual comprises. Evolution pertains not to individuals taken singly but to populations of differentially reproductive individuals (at whatever level of selection). Gaia, however, in contrast to its component biological systems, is a single entity, and so the critics are right to say it has no coherent heredity. Consequently, Gaia does not, strictly speaking, evolve, for like any individual it has only a history of change. It might therefore be preferable to talk about the ontogeny rather than the evolution of Gaia.

If Gaia is a legitimate biological individual with its own ontogeny, then it not only has its own distinctive emergent properties, as do people in relation to the cells that compose them, but also contains and provides the environment for us, as we do for the bacteria in our intestines. One of the most remarkable aspects of this idea, in relation to our familiar anthropocentric habits of thought, is its scale. Indeed, in Lovelock's view, life is a phenomenon that can occur only on a planetary scale: living organisms must coevolve with the planet to the point where they are able to regulate automatically the planetary environment, otherwise the planet would be rendered uninhabitable for life by physical and chemical processes.

Another notable aspect of the Gaia theory is the challenge that it poses to the very conception of the biological individual that has often been presupposed in the modern synthetic theory of evolution: organisms have been conceived of as discrete and unambiguously definable individuals, rather like the atomic agents of classical social theory. The challenge to this conception emerges especially in Margulis's work on symbiotic evolution in a planetary context. Margulis holds that symbiosis is a basic mechanism of evolutionary change; indeed, she is best known for building a case over many years for the theory that nucleated cells originated from symbioses among bacterial cells. In contrast to the classical conception of the biological individual, symbiosis implies that, as Margulis and Dorion Sagan (1986) put it, we are all walking biological communities. One of her favorite examples is a species of desert termite, in hindgut of which live millions of single-celled organisms; attached to the surface of each live thousands of spirochete bacteria. The bacteria are needed for the termite to digest wood, and so without them it would starve. Once the termite has digested the wood, it expels methane gas into the air. Methane regulates the amount of oxygen in the atmosphere, and the methane-producing bacteria found in termites and other animals account for a significant proportion of the earth's atmospheric methane. Among these many layers of activity, which comprise even the tightly coupled atmospheric and biotic levels, there seem to be no discrete individuals but rather only Gaian embedded, symbiotic communities.

Whether the Gaia theory ultimately stands or falls remains to be seen. But it is undeniable that the theory has given support to those who believe that the earth can be studied as a whole system and that to do so requires novel cross-disciplinary research.

[See also Artificial Life; Autopoiesis; Biosemiotics; Darwin; Evolution; Feedback and Feedforward; Koch; and Sebeok.]

BIBLIOGRAPHY

Barlow, C., ed. *From Gaia to Selfish Genes: Selected Writings in the Life Sciences.* Cambridge, Mass.: MIT Press, 1991.

Bateson, G. *Steps to an Ecology of Mind.* New York: Ballantine Books, 1972.

Bouissac, P. "Semiotics and the Gaia Hypothesis: Toward the Restructuring of Western Thought." *Philosophy and the Future of Humanity* 1.2 (1991): 168–184.

Dawkins, R. *The Extended Phenotype.* Oxford: W. H. Freeman, 1982.

Doolittle, W. F. "Is Nature Really Motherly?" *Coevolution Quarterly* 29 (1981): 58–63.

Hoffmeyer, J. *Signs of Meaning in the Universe.* Bloomington: Indiana University Press, 1992.

Lovelock, J. E. "Gaia as Seen through the Atmosphere." *Atmospheric Environment* 6 (1972): 579–580.

Lovelock, J. E. *Gaia: A New Look at Life on Earth.* New York: Oxford University Press, 1979.

Lovelock, J. E. *The Ages of Gaia.* New York: Norton, 1988.

Lovelock, J. E. *Healing Gaia.* New York: Harmony Books, 1991.

Lovelock, J. E., and L. Margulis. "Homeostatic Tendencies of the Earth's Atmosphere." *Origins of Life* 5 (1974): 93–103.

Margulis, L., and D. Sagan. *Microcosmos.* New York: Summit Books, 1986.

Margulis, L., and J. E. Lovelock. "Biological Modulation of the Earth's Atmosphere." *Icarus* 21 (1974): 471–489.

Maturana, H. R., and F. J. Varela. *Autopoiesis and Cognition: The Realization of the Living.* Dordrecht: D. Reidel, 1980.

Sebeok, T. A. "Ecumenicalism in Semiotics." In *A Perfusion of Signs,* edited by T. A. Sebeok, pp. 180–206. Bloomington: Indiana University Press, 1977.

Thompson, W. I., ed. *Gaia 2. Emergence: The New Science of Becoming.* Hudson, N.Y.: Lindisfarne Press, 1991.

Watson, A. J., and J. E. Lovelock. "Biological Homeostasis of the Global Environment: The Parable of Daisyworld." *Tellus* 35B (1983): 284–289.

—EVAN THOMPSON

GIBSON, JAMES J. (1904–1979), American psychologist who devised an "ecological" approach to perception and whose theories are a basis for realism, the belief that the world can be known accurately through perception. Gibson's main works are *The Perception of the Visual World* (1950), *The Senses Considered as Perceptual Systems* (1966), in which he shows how each of the senses fit his approach, and *The Ecological Approach to Visual Perception* (1979), in which he clarifies the relation between vision, the environment available to perception, and the special kind of awareness that goes with representations of many kinds. Gibson's ambition was to provide a coherent basis for psychology by defining the relations between observation and action, information and knowing, public and private knowledge, and direct observation and the use of representation.

Gibson rejects the traditional theory of perception that took perception to be a mixture of sensations and inferences. The sensations that arise in the perceiver's sensory pathways were said to be ambiguous and meaningless until turned by inferences into percepts of objects. Instead, Gibson contends that the optic patterns in the natural world are not ambiguous. He argues that in the natural, highly textured, well-illuminated, three-dimensional world, the patterns in light coming to a point of observation are highly detailed and specify the objects that give rise to the patterns precisely and unambiguously. For him, a pattern of light is information about its source—the object from which it came—if it could arise from that source and no other. It follows that the task of the observer is to be sensitive to informative patterns and their nuances and differences and to appreciate their significance, distinguishing different patterns from different faces or landscapes and realizing what different patterns indicate about the environment around the point of observation.

Gibson believed his theory of information holds across all the senses. For example, he argues at length that touch is action in a three-dimensional world of surfaces richly endowed with tactile textures.

Gibson, in a metaphor, describes the observer as "resonating"—using inference on the information in light, since there is no intermediate influence between the information and ensuing percept. From information in a natural environment, he goes on to define a still picture as a surface so treated as to deliver some of the information present in a "frozen" or unchanging array of light at a point in front of the picture. The observer normally not only uses still pictures but also readily obtains information from changes in the optic array over time. While still pictures can show texture gradients indicating the relative slants of surfaces (denser texture indicating more distant parts of a surface) and the contours of objects, the optic array can change over time to show much more. Depth, for example, can be shown clearly and convincingly by events such as one object passing behind another or by optical expansion or contraction as an object approaches or recedes from the observer's vantage point.

In connection with his analysis of the useful information for depth and the location of surfaces in optic events, Gibson made an important contribution to perception theory: the flow field. The optic array surrounding an observer moving through a densely textured environment is a single pattern of flow, including optic expansion around the heading point, which the observer is gradually approaching, the passing of objects on either side of the observer, and optic contraction of objects behind the observer, which are gradually becoming more distant. Variations in this overall flow field indicate whether the observer is changing heading or accelerating. Changes restricted to a small part of the flow field can indicate that objects in the terrain are moving independently of the observer. Rotations added to every point in the flow field indicate if the observer is yawing or rolling while maintaining the heading. Hence, optic patterns indicate the observer's actions. Further, one kind of flow field indicates that the observer is moving over a flat terrain, another indicates that the terrain is hilly, and a third specifies that the observer is passing through a flock of individual objects in three-dimensional space.

Flow-field patterns simultaneously specify the observer's motion and the terrain. Also, the information they provide is both public and private, since it is available in principle to any observer, though in practice a given point on a path of motion can be occupied by only one observer at a time. The changes across time that make up a flow field can contain information about a fixed terrain, which led Gibson to dismiss the traditional idea that seeing is only a train of temporary sensations while knowing involves permanent concepts that are stored in memory. He stresses that while seeing does indeed involve momentary changes, optic changes contain a consistent pattern, which is the information for a persisting terrain. His formula is that invariant properties of the changing optic array tell us about permanent properties of the environment.

Gibson takes great pains to distinguish pictures from natural sources of optic arrays. For him, pictures are possible only because there exists a prior world, without pictures, that establishes the laws allowing pictures to be devised. He notes that, like many scientific instruments, pictures do not require the observer to make inferences about the objects they show since they merely select and enhance optic information, clarifying and magnifying the kind of optic information vision normally uses. Where inference is necessary, Gibson writes, is in the use of technical images provided by instruments such as spectroscopes and cloud chambers. He distinguishes between displays that convert the information into a different mode such as a language or a coded message and displays such as pictures that use the optic structures present in direct perception, where the object is present and proffers natural information.

In Gibson's ecological theory of perception, perspective plays an important but limited role. Perspective pictures reveal the location of the observer in the world. They show some of the surfaces and edges confronting that location. Pictures can be made without perspective, however. It is possible to abstract some of the information in natural perspective and draw the invariant features of an object without indicating the location of the observer, as a child does when drawing a table with a rectangular top and four legs splaying from the corners. Gibson theorizes that outline drawings use a particular kind of abstraction from the natural optic array. They show the discontinuities in the environment, such as edges and corners, but cannot show the gradual transitions of a penumbra or a gradient of texture. Furthermore, he argues, the information in a line drawing is carried by the connections between the lines—the x, y, and t junctions, for example, where one line meets another.

Gibson's wife, Eleanor, was an equal partner in the development of a theory of perceptual learning that took its theme from the idea that information lies in differences between optical patterns. The two Gibsons propose that perceptual learning proceeds by differentiation—that is, by increasing sensitivity to meaningful variations in perceptible arrays. In addition to detection of minor variations that distinguish one face from another, for example, perception also learns to make out large-scale patterns, such as the structural relations between the parts of spatial objects such as bridges or temporal compositions such as symphonies. Gibson's work, in particular in flow fields, continues to be a source of controversy and inspiration in psychology and philosophy.

[See also Haptics; and Vision.]

BIBLIOGRAPHY

Gibson, J. J. *The Perception of the Visual World*. Boston: Houghton Mifflin, 1950.
Gibson, J. J. *The Senses Considered as Perceptual Systems*. Boston: Houghton Mifflin, 1966.
Gibson, J. J. *The Ecological Approach to Visual Perception*. Boston: Houghton Mifflin, 1979.

—JOHN M. KENNEDY

GOFFMAN, ERVING (1922–1982), Canadian social anthropologist who formulated an extensive critical apparatus for analyzing and classifying "symbolic interaction" in human behavior, particularly regarding social practices of communication. Goffman believed that this realm is the primary locus for organizing experience and correspondingly assessing the numerous configurations into which experience can be organized. His analysis of social interaction employs models derived from contiguous areas of social semiotics such as dramaturgical paradigms and game theory. An overall emphasis on "face work" provides a heterogeneous yet loosely cohesive organizing principle for Goffman's project that illuminates the functions of codes, encoders, and decoders in interpersonal behavior.

Goffman's professional direction is difficult to label narrowly because he worked in several fields in the course of writing eleven books and more than a dozen essays. Educated in sociology and social anthropology, he received his greatest intellectual guidance from a number of social scientists who engaged in close observation of symbolic interaction and used analogous models for explaining the semiotic nature of this activity. Tom Burns (1992) cites Everett Hughes, Alfred Schutz, Gregory Bateson, and G. H. Mead as relevant examples. While ranging far by expanding his interests and methods for gathering illustrative data, Goffman undertook such activities as interaction fieldwork in a Shetland Isle community, serving in the guise of an employee (such as a ward orderly) and a "visiting scientist" at the National Institute of Mental Health in Bethesda, and working as a casino dealer in Las Vegas. When he joined the Department of Sociology at the University of California at Berkeley in the late 1950s, his work in Chicago and the Shetlands became influenced by research undertaken by Gregory Bateson, John Searle, and H. Paul Grice. He moved to the University of Pennsylvania in the late 1960s as a professor of sociology and anthropology and interacted with sociolinguistic scholars until the end of his career.

Goffman's diverse work is nonetheless characterized by an emphasis on the specifically social aspect of interaction. It also provides countless useful terms and taxonomies for grasping the systemic components of this behavior. For example, his concept of "body idiom," as developed in *Behavior in Public Places* (1963), designated the distinct components of physical presentation (clothing, manner, gestures, speech, etc.); the notion of "footing," in a 1979 essay by the same name, defined the stance between an individual and those with whom he is interacting; and, the "identity kit" indicated the ensemble of signifiers of self an individual employs to create a distinct image (1965, pp. 246–247). Even from the beginning of his academic career, in his doctoral dissertation on the Shetland Isle community, Goffman endeavored to "treat face-to-face interaction as a domain in its own right" (1981). Moreover, Goffman stressed the methodology of "microanalysis" (1983), a closely detailed focus on a unique and specific occurrence, as the most fruitful approach to paradigmatic instances of this behavior.

A strong constructivist, relativist strain runs throughout Goffman's work, providing a tentativeness that aligns him with current semiotic analysis grounded upon theories of semiosis that posit ultimate indeterminacy as the condition of sign exchange. Yet, like Charles Sanders Peirce and Umberto Eco, Goffman views this fluidity as a positive condition, for if social structures are indeed merely and always constructed, then the individual sign user can interact significantly and powerfully with them just

as with any other social construction (see John Lofland in Ditton, 1980). In this respect, Goffman aligns himself with a poststructuralist standpoint on semiotics, which on this view reveal not the way a given sign system works as much as the social possibilities in which it might work. Goffman emphasizes repeatedly the multiple nature of any semiotic activity that ultimately has no mystical essence, no "transcendental signified," that might elude and thus impede the activity of the decoder (see Randall Collins in Ditton, 1980).

A suitable demonstration of this can be found in Goffman's commentary in *Behavior in Public Places*, along the lines of that by John L. Austin and Gilbert Ryle, on at least twenty-four ways that the act of running a red light can be decoded: "(1) Where he comes from they have signs, not lights"; "(12) He just plain forgot to look at the light"; "(22) He was drunk, high," and so forth. From this position, Goffman argues that the codes he explores reveal not the underlying determined logic of a semiotic system but the potential logics that given participants might attach to it. While Goffman does allow for a grounding stage for semiosis that exists prior to semiotic agency, this primacy is never viewed as a hegemonic agency that overpowers human agency; to the contrary, Goffman always views it as merely one more frame to consider within any given act of semiosis.

Goffman's intersection with semiotics is also evident in his projection of an arbitrary epistemological position not unlike what Roland Barthes identifies in *S/Z* (1970) as potential interpretive "structuration" as opposed to a single, immanent structure. By not limiting his focus to specific actions and actors but, rather, looking at "syntactical relations" within interpersonal communication, Goffman illuminates the semiotic structures that could be identified within sign-related activity (1967). Of course, this syntax could be framed as the study of syntagmatic structures within a branch of social semiotics that Goffman arguably founded through his studies of symbolic interaction.

Three books in particular effectively illustrate the connection between Goffman's research and semiotics. *The Presentation of Self in Everyday Life* (1959) extensively segments the performative component of the social self. Goffman views the individual not as an essence but as the result of a multifaceted collaboration that changes constantly depending upon circumstances related to one's "sign equipment," such as region of performance, performance roles, group interaction, and adherence to character. "Impression management" involves an individual's control of a specific image (a sign vehicle) while preventing the transmission of undesirable image traits. Thus, "dramaturgical cooperation" needs to be maintained between the encoder and decoder in order for the image to be successfully conveyed as desired.

The semiotics of team participation similarly entails the individual playing a specific role as "teammate" (without posing a "performance risk") while at the same time necessarily adapting to the altering matrices of group interaction as the team performance advances through various stages and into various realms. And, of course, the audience plays a decoder role in this performance as well. Goffman's stress on the constructed component of social interaction is especially significant here, for he portrays all activity of this nature as essentially crafted. It never exists in a presemiotic state, in other words, for there is always some regulation of image involved in interpersonal behavior.

Stigma: Notes on the Management of Spoiled Identity (1963) explores the possibility of semiotic alteration of individual identity primarily from the standpoint of maintaining a desirable self-image or recovering such an image if it has become "spoiled" in some way. Goffman identifies two forms of identity taint: the discredited, in which a stigma has been attributed, and the "discreditable," in which the individual is vulnerable to stigmatization if an undesirable trait was to be made known to others. This study makes an immensely useful contribution to semiotics by identifying and classifying the numerous strategies that individuals can use to manage the interpretations that can be generated about themselves. Again, Goffman assumes a social-constructivist stance by asserting that the self results from a biography that is disseminated both by the individual concerned and potentially by others as well. Demonstrating his partial alignment with Émile Durkheim, Goffman portrays this self-fabulation as a "moral career." Of course, the individual can engage in what Goffman calls "information control" regarding the self, but the information remains prey to encoding by others. Typical of Goffman's deployment of new terms for the practices he analyzes is his concept of "in-deeperism" in which an individual attempting to control a self-image by covering or passing might, in fact, intensify later self-discredit

as a result. In a related fashion, he also develops new connotations for familiar terms, such as his use of *showdown* to describe the confrontation between a stigmatized individual and those who express dismay at previous concealment of discredit. The showdown, in fact, can be used to mitigate the negative effect of in-deeperism through confrontation with those alleging unethical withholding of information.

Frame Analysis: An Essay on the Organization of Experience (1974) is Goffman's most elaborate and extensive study of the practice of semiotic contextualization, built in part upon Gregory Bateson's employment of the concept of *frame*. The frame grounds this practice, while Goffman distinguishes between "primary frameworks" and those that build upon this essential construct. While Goffman views the natural form of the primary frame (e.g., the weather) as beyond semiotic manipulation, the social form offers immense potential for altering behavior that Goffman refers to as "guided doings." Social frames are eminently vulnerable to designation within a given "key," and Goffman analyzes the extent to which variations of this key ("keyings") constantly take place in social interaction. Furthermore, he considers a wide range of frame components, including "designs" and "fabrications" (in which encoders deliberately manufacture specific keys), "out-of-frame activity," and the ways in which frames can be "anchored." By analyzing numerous "strips" of activity that provide sufficient information for recognizing, analyzing, and classifying a frame, Goffman employs a technique for analysis not unlike Barthes's designation of lexias (in *S/Z*), which are designated similarly through arbitrary selection, as opposed to segmentation that is presumably and necessarily significant in itself.

A good example of Goffman's application of frame analysis is seen in his consideration of "play" fighting among animals as a shift in key in which it is understood that biting and so on is not to be engaged in seriously. When one animal goes too far, this play is rekeyed into serious activity that can then be rekeyed back to play or signal a shift into real fighting. Therefore, comprehension of a specific key involves recognizing a "systematic transformation" in which an activity that was either yet to be framed or already framed in a specific key undergoes a shift in meaning. By utilizing pedestrian, even deliberately idiosyncratic examples of social behavior, Goffman provides a vastly influential model for ongoing studies in social semiotics (see Riggins, 1990).

[See also Barthes; Bateson; Code; Durkheim; Douglas; Ekman; Face; and Habitus.]

BIBLIOGRAPHY

Works by Goffman

The Presentation of Self in Everyday Life. Rev. ed. Garden City, N.Y.: Anchor Doubleday, 1959.

Behavior in Public Places. New York: Free Press, 1963.

Stigma: Notes on the Management of Spoiled Identity. Englewood Cliffs, N.J.: Prentice-Hall, 1963.

"Identity Kits," In Dress, Adornment, and the Social Orders, edited by M. Roach and J. Eicher, pp. 246–247. New York: John Wiley and Sons, 1965.

Interaction Ritual: Essays on Face-to-Face Behavior. New York: Anchor Doubleday, 1967.

Frame Analysis: An Essay on the Organization of Experience. Cambridge, Mass.: Harvard University Press, 1974.

"Footing." Semiotica 25 (1979): 1–29.

"A Reply to Denzin and Keller." Contemporary Sociology 10 (1981): 60–68.

"The Interaction Order." American Sociological Review 48 (1983): 1–17.

Other Works

Burns, T. Erving Goffman. London and New York: Routledge, 1992.

Ditton, J., ed. The View from Goffman. New York: St. Martin's Press, 1980.

Drew, P., and A. Wootton, eds. Erving Goffman: Exploring the Interaction Order. Cambridge: Polity Press, 1988.

Manning, P. Erving Goffman and Modern Sociology. Stanford: Stanford University Press, 1992.

Riggins, S. H. Beyond Goffman: Studies on Communication, Institution, and Social Interaction. Berlin: Mouton de Gruyter, 1990.

—SCOTT SIMPKINS

GOMBRICH, ERNST H. (b. 1909), art historian and theoretician whose writings have soundly criticized the loose way in which the concept of resemblance has been used in art history and visual-art theory. Explicitly grounded on theories of information and learning, the processes of production, and perceptual and cognitive psychology, Gombrich's work effectively analyzes the reception of art.

Presuming there is a language of pictorial representation, Gombrich emphasizes the conventionality of imitative codes—that is, the message from the visible world that must be coded by the artist. His analyses of these conventions in image making focus on the representational method or idiom. This "perceptualism" is foregrounded in his research as visual illusion, illusionistic resemblance, caricature, or visual perception and experience. His later works concern meaning, stylistic evolution and progress, realistic ideological mapping and reduplication of the world, and the visual discoveries of the artists of the Renaissance.

Echoing the perspective on the relationships between linguistics and poetics developed in the Prague Linguistic Circle, Gombrich's primary goal is to discover a signification theory where "just as the study of poetry remains incomplete without an awareness of the language of prose so ... the study of art will be increasingly supplemented by inquiry into the linguistics of the visual image" (1960, pp. 8–9). Visual art is thus construed as a set of interlocking meaningful features or configurations that permit recognition according to some principles of equivalent meaning and various acts of choice between given alternatives that allow the human animal to survive, function, and communicate.

In Art and Illusion (1960), subtitled A Study in the Psychology of Pictorial Representation, and in papers collected in Meditations on a Hobby Horse (1963), Gombrich discusses the development and transformation of styles of representation in art history based on the psychology of recognition. Searching for a scientific explanation of the changing styles of art, he addresses the historical advances made toward the third dimension, which grants the eye its share in the perception of modeling, and thus the development of a purely visual mode of rendering objects as they appear from a distance. Gombrich's primary premise is that representational visual language is a coded system of symbols—that is, of conventional meaning-giving devices adapted to the kind of signals that art is expected to transmit. By arguing that the skills of iconic representation are learned, he reinterprets classical notions such as mimesis (the imitation of nature in the artistic image) and reexamines the role of tradition, the limits of likeness and the translation of vision into representation, visual vocabulary, progress in art, and adaptations and corrective modifications of adopted formula.

In his influential essay on a child's hobbyhorse and the origins of artistic form, Gombrich claims that a stick or broom handle used as if it is a horse because it can be straddled exemplifies iconism based primarily on an analogous function, not on a theoretical idea of resemblance, and therefore is an intrinsically coded act. Discussion about iconicity in theoretical and visual semiotics (by Meyer Schapiro, Umberto Eco, Fernande Saint-Martin, Göran Sonesson, and others) has since deferred repeatedly to Gombrich's groundbreaking intuitions and interpretations.

To encompass what is communicated in an image in order to show how it is communicated and to convert the admittedly diverse cultural sources of his approach into a coherent art-historical method, Gombrich—in later books and papers such as *Norm and Form: Studies in the Art of the Renaissance* (1966), "The Variability of Vision" (1969), "The Visual Image" (1972a), "The 'What' and the 'How'" (1972b), and *The Heritage of Apelles* (1976)—explored further this new set of patterns of perception and "programmed" concerns introduced into the analysis of painting via the notion of iconicity as the basis of the visual image. He focused on particular theories of pictorial representation, perspectival norm, motivated content forms, and the phenomenal world. In *The Sense of Order: A Study in the Psychology of Decorative Art* (1979), for example, he attempted to apply his psychology of style to ornament. But two years later, casting a new look at what in the world is part of nature and what is convention in a paper entitled "Image and Code" (1981), Gombrich revised the more extreme conventionalist stance of *Art and Illusion* and changed his emphasis, finally claiming that pictorial illusionism does have a certain naturalistic basis. Taking his inspiration from the psychologist James Gibson and arguing against Nelson Goodman and Eco, he deduced from both human and animal recognition a process of equivalent meaning that is programmed biologically to function and classify by categorization and modeling. Iconicity then becomes humanity's fundamental cognitive mode and art an overwhelming necessity rather than a luxury.

While moving toward a revised theoretical position, Gombrich has found himself confronted with a methodological controversy concerning his working methods, his definition of reality, Western painting's relation to the idea of mastery of illusion, and the notion that constantly threatens this enterprise: the viewer. For, as stated by art theorists such as Hans Belting (1987) and Norman Bryson (1983), reality is always changing for the viewer and must be defined anew before its imitation can be evaluated because the body has within itself the power to overturn its own representations. Through a critical analysis of Gombrich's *Art and Illusion,* which he considers the most influential statement of the realist position, Bryson has called attention to the historical and social nature of painting and the viewing subject and the intrinsic connection between realist propaganda, political authority, and control of images. By focusing primarily on the steady advance toward the "essential copy," Bryson has argued against an art of copying visual experience, seeing this as a misconception and a false assumption of the realist view in art history, which tends to suppress the status of painting as a complex system of social and political signs.

[*See also* Arnheim; Gibson; Iconicity; Pictorial Semiotics; *and* Wölfflin.]

BIBLIOGRAPHY

Belting, H. *The End of the History of Art?* Translated by C. S. Wood. Chicago and London: University of Chicago Press, 1987.

Bryson, N. *Vision and Painting: The Logic of the Gaze.* New Haven: Yale University Press, 1983.

Gombrich, E. H. *Art and Illusion: A Study in the Psychology of Pictorial Representation.* New York: Random House, 1960.

Gombrich, E. H. *Meditations on a Hobby Horse, and Other Essays on the Theory of Art.* London and New York: Phaidon, 1963.

Gombrich, E. H. *Norm and Form: Studies in the Art of the Renaissance.* London: Phaidon, 1966.

Gombrich, E. H. "The Variability of Vision." In *Interpretation, Theory, and Practice,* edited by C. S. Singleton, pp. 35–68. Baltimore: Johns Hopkins University Press, 1969.

Gombrich, E. H. "The Visual Image." *Scientific American* 227 (1972a), 82–96.

Gombrich, E. H. "The 'What' and the 'How': Perspective Representation and the Phenomenal World." In *Logic and Art: Essays in Honor of Nelson Goodman,* edited by R. Rudner and I. Scheffler, pp. 129–149. New York: Bobbs-Merrill, 1972b.

Gombrich, E. H. *Studies in the Art of the Renaissance,* vol. 3, *The Heritage of Apelles.* Oxford: Phaidon, 1976.

Gombrich, E. H. *The Sense of Order: A Study in the Psychology of Decorative Art.* Ithaca, N.Y.: Cornell University Press, 1979.

Gombrich, E. H. "Image and Code: Scope and Limits of Conventionalism in Pictorial Representations." In *Image and Code,* edited by W. Steiner, pp. 11–42. Ann Arbor: University of Michigan Press, 1981.

—MARIE CARANI

GOODMAN, NELSON (b. 1906), American philosopher, author of original and controversial works in epistemology such as *The Structure of Appearance* (1951), *Fact, Fiction, and Forecast* (1954), and numerous articles, most of which are collected in *Problems and Projects* (1972). In the 1960s, Goodman's interests shifted toward the "theory of symbols." *Languages of Art* (1968), *Of Mind and Other Matters* (1984), and *Reconceptions in Philosophy and Other Arts and Sciences* (1988, written with Catherine Elgin) address a wide range of semiotic problems. In his writings, Goodman combines epistemological and ontological relativism with a rigorous methodology. The latter is strengthened by Goodman's adherence to nominalism, which characterizes almost all his writings.

Goodman's nominalism has consequences for his semantics and his semiotics. He conceives it as a way of preventing "the composition of different entities out of the same elements" but not as an obligation to expel certain entities on other grounds, such as their being abstract. Thus, it is not allowed to count all white things and the property *white* as distinct existing entities. This priority of conceptual simplicity leads to refutations of several categories, which are central to most semiotic and philosophical discourses: there is no place for properties (as distinct from their instances), intensions (as distinct from extensions), connotation (as distinct from denotation), or types (as distinct from tokens). This nominalistic program implies for semiotic theory that statements using terms such as *type, intension,* or *meaning* (in distinction to *reference*) must be disposed of or should be restated in a nominalistic terminology. Charles Sanders Peirce's distinction "type-token" is criticized in *The Structure of Appearance;* instead of taking several tokens as belonging to one and the same type, Goodman prefers to talk of inscriptions (occurrences of words, written or spoken) as coextensive replicas of each other and themselves. Thus, homonyms, for instance, are replicas with different extensions.

The analysis of synonymy and meaning in the article "On Likeness of Meaning" (in *Problems and Projects*, 1972) is much more controversial. That two words with the same extension can have different meanings is most clearly illustrated by words with null extension, such as *centaur* and *unicorn*. Goodman claims that the differences in meaning can be demonstrated without any appeal to intensions, connotations, or mental categories if we attend not only to the extensions of the words but also to the extensions of compounds containing the words in question, such as "picture of unicorn" or "description of a centaur." These phrases, which have the look of relational constructions, are, in logical jargon, one-place predicates—that is, property terms. Goodman calls the extensions of the compound terms "secondary extensions" of the contained, original terms. Synonymy is then defined as identity not only between the primary extensions (that is, the extensions of the investigated words) but also between the secondary extensions of both words. As a consequence, no two words that are not replicas of each other are ever absolutely synonymous; different words can only be more or less close in meaning.

Goodman's exclusion of semantic relations other than reference does not mean, however, that the coupling of the symbol and the symbolized is restricted to denotation in the classical philosophical sense. On the one hand, he introduces a wider notion of denotation than what is usual, and, on the other hand, he presents other referential concepts, foremost exemplification and indirect (or mediated) reference. Not only words denote but so do pictures with respect to what they represent. The very wide concept of compliance (1968), which applies to the relation between note and tone, diagram and diagrammed, measuring instrument and what is measured, and so on, is also a denotational term. However, the terms *denotation* and *reference* are nowhere defined in Goodman's text.

In *Languages of Art,* Goodman gives a detailed account of the referential relation *to exemplify.* The movements of the gymnastics instructor exemplify properties of the actions to be performed by his class, and a sample exemplifies its relevant properties. A symbol can only exemplify such properties that it actually possesses. However, Goodman states the relation as holding only provisionally between a symbol and some of its properties. In his final formulation—the exemplifying symbol exemplifies a label (verbal or not), that is, another symbol—the relation between exemplification and denotation is more clearly visible: an exemplifying symbol exemplifies a label, which denotes that symbol. So, exemplification runs in the tracks of denotation but in the opposite direction.

Indirect or mediated reference plays a dominant role both in Goodman's own writings from the 1970s and 1980s and in works by thinkers influenced by him, notably by Catherine Elgin (1983) and Israel Scheffler (1979). A symbol refers indirectly to an object by several connected links of exemplification or denotation. If a sample is interpreted as referring not only to its property or label but also to what is sampled—that is, what in turn is denoted by the label—we have an indirect reference in two steps: a tailor's swatch might exemplify the label *Red*, which in turn denotes the red fabric in stock. Various semiotic phenomena—such as metaphor, allusion, variation in aesthetic contexts, and narrative layers in a story—have been treated by Goodman as cases of indirect reference. A clear presentation of indirect reference is given by Elgin (1983).

In his theory of notation, Goodman identifies five criteria that discriminate notational systems from other sorts of symbolic systems. These criteria can serve as classificatory tools for symbol systems in general, although Goodman does not himself consider his theory a part of semiotics. Others, notably E. H. Gombrich and Richard Wollheim, have attributed to him a semiotic theory of pictures. He is referred to, somewhat obliquely, in several works by Umberto Eco (e.g., 1976) and has been criticized by Josette Rey-Debove (1971), who claims his nominalist metaphysics is of no use in semiotics, and in more detail by Göran Sonesson (1989), who argues that he confuses ordinary language with a logically reconstructed sign system. His conception has, however, been put to empirical use in the semiotic study of the cinema (notably Kjørup, 1977) and of literature (Rossholm, 1987).

[*See also* Denotation and Connotation; Diagrams; Icon; Iconicity; Image and Picture; Languages of Art; Meaning; Realism and Nominalism; *and* Type and Token.]

BIBLIOGRAPHY

Works by Goodman

The Structure of Appearance. Cambridge, Mass., Harvard University Press, 1951.

Fact, Fiction, and Forecast. Cambridge, Mass.: Harvard University Press, 1954.

Languages of Art: An Approach to a Theory of Symbols. Indianapolis: Bobbs-Merrill, 1968.

Problems and Projects. Indianapolis: Bobbs-Merrill, 1972.

Of Mind and Other Matters. Cambridge, Mass.: Harvard University Press, 1984.

Goodman, N., and C. Elgin. *Reconceptions in Philosophy and Other Arts and Sciences*. Indianapolis: Hackett, 1988.

Other Works

Eco, U. *A Theory of Semiotics*. Bloomington: Indiana University Press, 1976.

Elgin, C. *With Reference to Reference*. Indianapolis: Haskell, 1983.

Kjørup, S. "Film as a Meeting Place of Multiple Codes." In *The Arts and Cognition*, edited by D. Perkins and B. Leondar, pp. 20–47. Baltimore and London: Johns Hopkins University Press, 1977.

Kjørup, S. "Pictorial Speech Acts." *Erkenntnis* 12 (1978): 55–71.

Rey-Debove, J. "Review of Nelson Goodman, Languages of Art." *Semiotica* 4 (1971): 162–170.

Rossholm, G. *Ibsen's "Når vi døde vågner," en analys*. Stockholm: Stockholm University Press, 1987.

Scheffler, I. *Beyond the Letters: A Philosophical Inquiry into Ambiguity, Vagueness, and Metaphor in Language*. London: Routledge and Kegan Paul, 1979.

Sonesson, G. *Pictorial Concepts: Inquiries into the Semiotic Heritage and Its Relevance for the Analysis of the Visual World*. Lund: Lund University Press, 1989.

—GÖRAN ROSSHOLM

GOODY, JOHN RANKIN (b. 1919), British cultural anthropologist whose work focuses on the implications of cultural systems of signification, especially those of language and written communication. His early work of the 1950s and 1960s, influenced by the structural anthropology of Claude Lévi-Strauss, analyzed forms of everyday life in West African culture (northern Ghana), showing how social life and symbolic structure interrelate with codes to produce and reproduce culture. These analyses of kinship structures, cuisine, and religious ritual and myth entail description of the customs, languages, symbols, and images of LoDagaa culture. This work was the beginning of Goody's long-standing interest in economic, social, and political changes wrought by cultural technologies in Africa and Eurasia.

An early critic of colonialist anthropology (1966), Goody turned from traditional anthropological studies and methods to sociological and historical anthropology, and the focus of his inquiry shifted from the means and modes of cultural (re)production to those of communication—the oral and written modes of meaning making—and their implications for human thought and action. Goody and literary critic Ian Watt's groundbreaking paper, "The Consequences of Literacy" (1963), offers a comprehensive argument for distinct social, cultural, and cognitive effects of literacy. Their thesis emerged from a critique of Lévi-Strauss's notion of binary oppositions and his innatist accounts of intelligence, cultural complexity, and human achievement. While Goody and Watt acknowledge that differences exist between cultures, they argue that these can be traced systematically to differences in the means of symbolic communication. Their use of the phrase "technology of the intellect" and their substitution of *preliterate* and *literate* for *primitive* and *advanced, savage* and *domesticated,* and *prelogical* and *logical* aim to deflect emphasis from cognition to the semiotic and material tools and artifacts of information storage, retrieval, and transmission. Goody and Watt argue that the written word is responsible for the restructuring of both mental processes and societal organization, and they frame the consequences of this restructuring in terms of progress, modernization, and civilization.

As they see it, writing establishes a relationship between the symbol or word and its referent that is connected less closely with cultural particularities of time and place than is its oral equivalent. They argue that while spoken language occurs in face-to-face contact and meaning is ratified through cumulations of firsthand concrete experience, phonetic writing symbolizes the natural and social worlds already represented symbolically in linguistic signs. Written language is therefore less immediate, and its meaning is less direct and definite. The material word's detachment from grounded experience and its tendency toward decontextualized abstraction generate the "impersonal" and "immutable" discursive mode of thinking called logic. Allegedly, written text enhances the objective, skeptical, and critical sensibilities and enabled the Greeks to distinguish history from myth, science from magic, fact from fiction. Goody and Watt make the case that the durability and portability of text provide the recoverability and consistency of communication and information processing required for bureaucratic organization, democratic politics, capitalist industry, and science.

This early work was criticized for its Eurocentric perspective. Later work, which extends the theory that difference in cultural style and achievement is the outcome of developments in the graphic representation of language, qualifies this ethnocentrism. In *The Domestication of the Savage Mind* (1977), Goody describes how graphic devices such as the list, table, matrix, and other symbolically coded knowledge forms (logic and the syllogism) were developed to record, organize, and manage the expanding corpus of cultural knowledge. He suggests that these provide tools for increasingly complex cognitive processes, as the ability to mediate these decontextualized symbols generates cognitive capacities that users of oral language do not and cannot have. Goody maintains that as different cultural groups became involved with and contributed to the production of recorded knowledge, conventions for their use and signification were gradually standardized. Norms for word meanings, syntax, punctuation, and text structures were established, especially after the advent of movable type.

To illustrate the role played specifically by writing in the development of human societies and the processes of transition that occurred between them, Goody focuses on society's four fundamental institutions: religion, commerce, law, and polity. *The Logic of Writing and the Organization of Society* (1986) describes sites, texts, participants, and practices involved in the production and transmission of culturally significant knowledge by these organizations.

By privileging meaning channeled through verbal and graphic symbols, as distinct from a culture's material goods and practices, Goody claims that the means of communication is the basis of cultural differentiation. This implies a dichotomy of communicative resources and traditions: oral cultures are small-scale, rural, nonindustrial, conformist, and organized through kinship, tradition, and religion, while literate cultures are urban, industrial, and characterized by rationality, individual achievement, and heterogeneity. Even if this is viewed as a continuum of social development, recent work on literacy from cultural and historical perspectives has shown this to be, at best, a partial interpretation of highly complex cultural constructs and behaviors (Street, 1984).

The equation of forms of language and thought has not been confirmed by empirical investigations (Scribner and Cole, 1981). Researchers and theorists now hesitate to attribute societal change primarily to technological or communicative factors. The heuristics of discourse and social practice have displaced those of technology as an explanatory concept for understanding the constitution and complexities of human organization, signification, and communication. Literacy has been reconceptualized as a facilitating rather than a determining agent, one that promotes or hinders particular cognitive capacities through socially, institutionally, and ideologically patterned practices that use different linguistic and graphic sign systems. Goody's work on the uses and implications of literacy provides an important foundation for and stimulus to ongoing theorizations of text, communication, and culture.

[*See also* Bourdieu; Cultural Knowledge; Habitus; Linguistic Relativism; Whorf; *and* Writing, Ethnography of.]

BIBLIOGRAPHY

Goody, J. "The Prospects for Social Anthropology." *New Society* 13 (1966): 574–576.

Goody, J. *Technology, Tradition, and the State in Africa.* Oxford: Oxford University Press, 1971.

Goody, J. *The Domestication of the Savage Mind.* Cambridge: Cambridge University Press, 1977.

Goody, J. *The Logic of Writing and the Organization of Society.* Cambridge: Cambridge University Press, 1986.

Goody, J. *The Interface between the Written and the Oral.* Cambridge: Cambridge University Press, 1987.

Goody, J. *The Culture of Flowers.* Cambridge: Cambridge University Press, 1993.

Goody, J., ed. *Literacy in Traditional Societies.* Cambridge: Cambridge University Press, 1968.

Goody, J., and I. Watt. "The Consequences of Literacy." *Comparative Studies in Society and History* 5.3 (1963): 304–345.

Scribner, S., and M. Cole. *The Psychology of Literacy.* Cambridge, Mass.: Harvard University Press, 1981.

Street, B. V. *Literacy in Theory and Practice.* Cambridge: Cambridge University Press, 1984.

—CUSHLA KAPITZKE

GOSSIP. A form of communication that consists of evaluative talk about absent others, gossip is described by some as connoting warmth, intimacy, and bonding, though most descriptions stress the destructive nature of talking about others' private affairs. Gossip is associated frequently with triviality, betraying secrets, a trifle of fiction, a bit of speculation, artistic explanations of little incidents, overheard remarks, innuendos, eavesdropping, and malice (Spacks, 1986).

Part of the difficulty in arriving at a universal definition of gossip is due to its context dependence. The same information can be defined as gossip or nongossip, depending on who talks to whom under what circumstances. Research on gossip has converged recently around three main approaches: the syntagmatic (gossip as process and sequence), the paradigmatic (gossip as structure), and the contextual (the social and psychological functions of gossip).

The syntagmatic approach focuses on the narrative sequence of an exchange of gossip as a process by which a communicative genre is realized and reproduced. Discourse analysis reveals three stages of progressive development. In the preliminary stage, among peers, the willingness to gossip is negotiated and ratified (Besnier, 1989). The credibility of the narrator is established, and the collaboration of the audience is confirmed. In the second stage, a story about a conspicuous action by an absent person is reported and evaluated. The narrative is situated by exchanges in which participants demonstrate their authoritativeness as gossipers, their familiarity with the personae, and their shared sentiments as the narrator leads up to the climactic incident. In the third stage, the characterization of the central persona is extended to a social type and explicated by general social rules. The intentions of the narrator are treated as outside the scope of the narrative, which the hearers participate in coproducing by their supportive, restraining, encouraging, or incredulous comments.

The paradigmatic approach has concentrated on the structures and forms of gossip. Similar themes are distributed broadly in different cultural systems. The basis for gossip, according to Norbert Elias and Francine Muel-Dreyfus (1985), is that social acceptance depends on the willingness to provide a satisfactory account of oneself and one's past history. Gossip among equals involves willing participants who share common values and acquaintances. The narrator's personal identity and reputation are then (re)constructed through positive or negative commentary on others' actions and character. Statuses and reputations can be manipulated by participants' discussions of the dialectic between their ideal and their everyday behavior. This need not imply, however, that all are under equal pressure to provide such accounts, nor does it clarify what constitutes a credible account.

Tentative answers to these questions have been formulated by discourse analysts who studied scientists' gossip. Scientific reporting and gossip invoke quite different repertoires. The empiricist repertoire formally narrates the impersonal accomplishment of a major celebrity, while the contingent repertoire reveals informally the personal defeats of a minor upstart. Ray Morris (1991) claims that by associating success with fidelity to method and failure with personal shortcomings, scientific writing and gossip alike seek to explain outcomes in terms that do not impugn the deity of science itself. The construction of scientific articles receives extremely close supervision from peers, in part to excise elements that do not fit empiricist conventions. Similarly, secrecy surrounding Nobel Prize deliberations denies the legitimacy of gossip yet cannot contain or control it.

Newspaper gossip columns follow the forms and conventions of other types of newspaper reporting fairly closely, when the context shifts from two-way interpersonal to one-way media communication. Information about celebrities is presented as if the reader was an insider but with very limited opportunity for coproduction. Tabloid gossip is gossip about superiors and involves participants whose status differs from that of the subject. Susan Rasmussen's work (1991) expanded the horizons of paradigmatic gossip research in two respects. First, she introduced Mikhail Bakhtin's conception that experience and action are inherently conflictual and argued that polyvocality and the cross-cutting social ties of participants are important in understanding the complexity of gossip. A member plays various roles simultaneously and in rapid succession. Second, gossip might become "transforming dialogue," altering the situation and not simply influencing the statuses of those subject to it. This shift, away from discussion of individuals' strategies and collective rules, opens up new possibilities for analysis.

The functional contextualist approach examines gossip within its social setting. Since the publication of Max Gluckman's classic work (1963), most research has treated gossip as taking place within peer groups, with other peers as its main subjects, and with social control and boundary maintenance as its principal functions. For example, Brazilian gossip about domestic conflict flourished in religions where human agency is seen as the main cause of domestic conflict and is inhibited where the blame is placed on spiritual entities. Moreover, gossip tends to thrive where small-group action is construed to be an effective agent for weeding out internal evil or checking others' outward nonconformity. Individuals are inclined to resent and, as much as they can, resist the power that they believe gossip exercises over them in their absence.

The functions of gossip in modern society have changed. Levin and Arluke (1987) have underlined the lessening power of small groups due to increasing geographical mobility and the broadening range of socially acceptable behavior. This implies that public gossip is becoming increasingly important as personal networks become less able to modify it. Elias and Muel-Dreyfus emphasize the positive potential of gossip and stress its function in identity construction. Among low-status groups, such as Puerto Rican gang girls, it serves as a means by which members distance themselves from the negative characteristics generally attributed to them.

While the literature on the nature of gossip appears to be mushrooming, there is not enough empirical research focusing on social characteristics of gossipers. The few studies that have been conducted highlight specialized areas or societies that are difficult to generalize from. We need more studies on the traits of the participants as well as on the frequency, intensity, duration, and levels of gossip interactions.

[*See also* Conversation; Dialogism; Dialogue; *and* Goffman.]

BIBLIOGRAPHY

Besnier, N. "Information Withholding as a Manipulative and Collusive Strategy in Nukulaelae Gossip." *Language in Society* 18.3 (1989): 315–341.

Elias, N., and F. Muel-Dreyfus. "Remarks on Gossip." *Actes de la recherche en sciences sociales* 60 (1985): 23–29.

Gluckman, M. "Gossip and Scandal." *Current Anthropology* 4 (1963): 307–316.

Handelman, D. "Gossip in Encounters: The Transmission of Information in a Bounded Social Setting." *Man* 8.2 (1973): 210–227.

Levin, J., and A. Arluke. *Gossip: The Inside Scoop.* New York: Plenum, 1987.

Morris, R. "Les conventions littéraires de l'écriture sociologique an Québec et au Canada anglais." *Society/Société* 15.1 (1991): 10–15.

Rasmussen, S. J. "Modes of Persuasion: Gossip, Song, and Divination in Tuareg Conflict Resolution." *Anthropological Quarterly* 64.1 (1991): 30–46.

Spacks, P. M. *Gossip.* Chicago: University of Chicago Press, 1986.

—RINA COHEN and RAY MORRIS

GRAMMAR OF MOTIVES, A (1945). Kenneth Burke's book *A Grammar of Motives* deals mainly with what the author calls dramatism, a method of linguistic and conceptual analysis that treats language and thought primarily as modes of action rather than means of conveying information. In *A Grammar of Motives*, Burke uses a grammar in the Aristotelian sense of a set of verbal terms or categories by means of which a discourse can be analyzed. His dramatistic grammar centers on observations such as, for there to be an act, there must be an agent. Similarly, there must be a scene in which the agent acts. To act in a scene, the agent must employ some means or agency, and there cannot be an act, in the full sense of term, unless there is a purpose. Burke labels these five terms—act, agent, scene, agency, purpose—the dramatistic pentad. His aim in *A Grammar of Motives* is to show how their designated functions operate in the imputing of motives.

When one imputes motive to action, the statement of motives involves the dramatistic pentad: act (what was done), agent (who did the act and under what subjective conditions), scene (the environment in which the act took place; the extrinsic factors that determined it), agency (how the act was done; what instruments were used), and purpose (why the act was done; its ultimate motive or final cause). The agent, however, need not be a person: even conceptual "terms are *characters* . . . an essay is an *attenuated play*. . . . Names are shorthand designations for certain fields and methods of action" (1937, pp. 311–312). The grammatical blanks offer opportunities for disposition and transposition, and dialectic explores the combinatory, substitutive, and transformational possibilities. Different philosophical systems emphasize different aspects of the pentad: realism emphasizes act, idealism emphasizes agent, materialism emphasizes scene, pragmatism emphasizes agency, and mysticism emphasizes purpose. The combinatory, substitutive, and transformational possibilities, of course, are endless, but Burke's point is that any statement of motives must deal with the five terms he has isolated, even if it foregrounds one and backgrounds the others.

Burke views the subject or agent as a function of a system. As a method of discourse analysis, dramatism seems protostructuralist in its assumption that structure in all kinds of texts can be accounted for by the terms of the pentad, which in their combinations, substitutions, and transformations account for the gamut of possibilities for verbal action. Yet dramatism also adumbrates poststructuralism in its progressive self-dismantlement. Burke's recurrent focus on the antinomies of definition and the paradox of substance infects his dialectical system with the virus of deconstruction from the very beginning.

Endorsing the claim of Baruch Spinoza (1632–1677) that all determination is negation, Burke concludes that the concept of substance is endowed with an unresolvable ambiguity. As he reflects,

> Men are not only *in nature.* The cultural accretions made possibly by language become a "second nature" with them. Here again we confront the ambiguities of substance, since symbolic communication is not merely an external instrument, but also intrinsic to men as agents. Its motivational properties characterized both "the human situation" and what men are "in themselves." Whereas there is an implicit irony in other notions of substance, with dialectic substance the irony is explicit. For it derives its character from the systematic contemplation of the antinomies attendant upon the fact that we necessarily define a thing in terms of something else. (1945, p. 33)

For Burke, this is "an *inevitable* paradox of definition": "To *define*, or *determine* a thing is to mark its boundaries, hence to use terms that possess, implicitly at least, contextual reference" (p. 24). *Substance,* Burke notes, is etymologically a scenic word. "Literally, a person's or thing's sub-stance would be something that stands beneath or supports the person or thing" (p. 22). The point is not to banish substance terms but to be aware of their equivocal nature. Banishing the term *substance,* he maintains, does not banish its functions; it merely conceals them. Moreover, the unresolvable ambiguity built into the very concept of substance is precisely what facilitates linguistic transformations and makes dialectic possible.

For Burke, as for Ferdinand de Saussure (1867–1913), language is a system of differences without any positive terms, and from its "central moltenness, where all elements are fused into one togetherness, there are thrown forth, in separate crusts, such distinctions as those between freedom and necessity, activity and passivity, cooperation and competition, mechanism and teleology" (p. xix). Herein resides the transformability that gives the terms of the dramatistic pentad their resourcefulness and flexibility. Because of the antinomies of definition and the paradox of substance, one must invoke difference to constitute a meaning. In the Burkean system, as in the Derridean, meaning is disseminated. However substantial distinctions appear, they become meaningful insofar as their terms are cast in opposition to others, and they are forever capable of retreating into the moltenness of the alchemic center and reemerging as something else.

A Grammar of Motives, therefore, is avowedly antifoundationalist; it would be difficult for any epistemology to anchor itself in the great central moltenness out of which such liquid distinctions emerge. The major difference between dramatism and deconstruction, however, is that dramatism seeks to provide an ontological perspective: it tells us who we are in a substantial, constitutive sense. We are the symbol-using animal, whether we substantiate the ambiguities of language or they substantiate us. We thus inhabit, embody, and enact the problematics of language, the duplicities of dialectic. Living out the paradox of substance and its attendant ironies, we are what we are not, and we necessarily define ourselves in terms of something else. Action, for Burke, is above all substantive, a way of being, not merely instrumental or a means of doing. As human beings, Burke contends, we are bodies that learn language, and through the vagaries of identification we incorporate various ways of seeing and not seeing our reflections in the social mirror, a semiotically constructed realm of intersubjectivity and intertextuality, a realm of symbolic action that intersects ambiguously with the realm of nonsymbolic motion.

Dialectic substance is at the heart of dramatism. Whereas Burke's grammar of motives no doubt privileges the human actor who is constituted by his or her acts, it does not privilege truth or knowledge. Such privileging is an ontological move only, not an epistemological one. With dialectic substance, the irony is explicit.

[*See also* Burke; Deconstruction; Language as Symbolic Action; Poststructuralism; *and* Saussure.]

BIBLIOGRAPHY

Burke, K. *Attitudes toward History.* Berkeley: University of California Press, 1937.
Burke, K. *A Grammar of Motives.* Berkeley: University of California Press, 1945.

—Greig Henderson

GRANDE SYNTAGMATIQUE, LA (1966–1967).

The most influential articles written by Christian Metz during his earliest years of film theorizing were, arguably, his explanation and application of the phenomenon that he called "la grande syntagmatique." In its most schematic form, this great syntagmatic system is summarized in a one-page chart that presents the eight paradigmatic options for structuring autonomous segments of films of the American classical cinema (1932–1959). In its full form, his study consists of two well-developed articles, the first of which, "Problems of Denotation in the Fiction Film," explains each of the eight options. The second article, "Outline of the Autonomous Segments in Jacques Rozier's Film *Adieu Philippine,*" applies the identified pattern to a segmentation of the 1962 film.

Metz's project began as an attempt to identify one key structural code in the films of his chosen corpus. Thereby, he would at the same time demonstrate to the skeptics the practical value of cinema semiotics. Such an undertaking was very much in keeping with the spirit of the 1960s narratological projects of his literary colleagues such as Roland Barthes, Gérard Genette, Tzvetan Todorov, and Claude Bremond. His method was to screen every American film of the period available in France and to search for all the segments (units of meaning) that could not be cut shorter without betraying their independence or coherence. By grouping together all the segments with similar structures, he established a taxonomy of all the options used by American filmmakers of the period. His taxonomy, he discovered, consisted of a maximum of eight structural options (see Figure 1). This information in turn became a tool for further researchers who studied the techniques and styles of these films.

In his research, Metz discovered that one of the structures for an autonomous segment is a single shot. The term *plan-séquence* (sequence shot) that Metz chose for this structure has subsequently been used untranslated in much theory written in English today. An example of a *plan-séquence* is any complete dialogue scene presented in an uninterrupted shot. A segment of film that contains only one shot does not, strictly speaking, qualify as a syntagma (which is Greek for "union"), as no montage causing a union has occurred within the segment. The other seven multiple-shot autonomous segments are, though, indisputably syntagmas.

Metz discovered that the remaining seven syntagmas could be divided into achronological and chronological groups. The two achronological

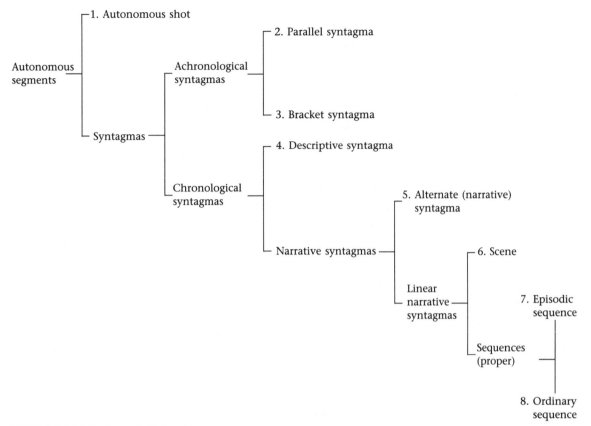

FIGURE 1. *Metz's Syntagmatic Categories*

syntagmas are the parallel syntagma and the bracket syntagma. The parallel syntagma was dear to the heart of Sergei Eisenstein, who, by means of what he called associational or intellectual cuts, compared, for instance, the slaughter of animals to the slaughter of workers in *Strike*. The shots of the slaughtered animals bear no temporal relationship to the strike—hence, the achronological status of the segment. This kind of syntagma is relatively rare in the American classical cinema; however, a truly Eisenteinian example can be found in Fritz Lang's *Fury* (1936), where in a parallel syntagma, gossiping women are replaced on the screen by cackling hens.

The bracket syntagma (*syntagme en accolade*) is also rare. It consists of what appears to be randomly organized shots that either in spite of or because of their disorder form an autonomous unit of meaning. A good example occurs in Rouben Mamoulian's *Applause* (1929), when a young girl's dream reproduces in no particular sequence various images from a confused day that has taken her from a convent to a burlesque hall. Images of singing, praying, or well-wishing nuns alternate randomly with burlesque performers, cheap hotels, vulgar audiences, and even a loving mother. This deceptively "unstructured" technique became a mainstay of rock-music videos in the 1990s.

The five chronological syntagmas can be either descriptive or narrative. In the descriptive syntagma, the camera merely records some diegetic material usually with music but without dialogue; the narrative function of the camera seems to have been suspended temporarily. The shots that form the syntagma are edited, nevertheless, in a normal, fluid chronological order. In *Adieu Philippine,* for instance, one segment consists of a series of lyrical shots from a moving boat. The shots, Metz argues, serve no other readily apparent purpose than to "describe" in a leisurely fashion the surrounding Mediterranean atmosphere. The opening establishing shots of the wealthy neighborhood in Robert Redford's *Ordinary People* (1980) serve the same function and also form a descriptive syntagma.

Of the four kinds of narrative syntagmas, one is referred to as a *syntagme alterné* ("alternate syntagma"), whereas the three others are linear. The alternate syntagma is quite simply a segment structured by cross-cutting, like those found in chase sequences in any number of Western or gangster films. The linear syntagma is the most common structure in the films of this period. Like a scene in a stage play, without ellipses, it consists of a series of shots that reproduce events that occur in a single location over an uninterrupted time period. A segment that presents an uninterrupted dinner conversation is a typical scene.

The remaining two kinds of autonomous segments are called sequences. The ordinary sequence is virtually an interrupted scene. One can imagine, for instance, an elliptical version of a dinner-conversation scene. Drained glasses, new servings, and abrupt changes in conversational tone might indicate that time has passed between two contiguous shots. The episodic sequence (*séquence par épisodes*) consists of shots that might have been, in expanded form, complete autonomous segments themselves. The series of shots in Orson Welles's *Citizen Kane* (1941) of Charles Foster Kane and his first wife at various sequential breakfasts over the course of their marriage is the textbook example of the episodic sequence. The episodic sequence is an efficient means of rapidly communicating an extended, evolving relationship.

There are various virtues to *la grande syntagmatique*. It serves, for instance, to define the nature and function of the *plan-séquence*. It distinguishes clearly between scene and sequence. It provides a blueprint for the segmentation of classical American films, segmentation being the acknowledged first step in the semiotic analysis of films. Certain problems, however, remain. One could still ask if there is indeed such a thing as a descriptive syntagma that cannot also be read as at least minimally narrative as well. Is it always possible to determine the difference between a descriptive syntagma and a bracket syntagma? Can one overcome the ingrained habit of referring to alternate syntagmas as parallel syntagmas, which Metz reserves for his Eisensteinian achronological segments?

Frequently, the division between two segments is not as clear as Metz would have it. For instance, the same shot can be both the last shot of one segment and the first shot of the next. In a single shot, one person leaves a room while another enters. There is no punctuation to indicate the transition to a new autonomous unit of filmic meaning; nevertheless, a new segment is beginning. Metz does not discuss this complication.

Most important, since Metz's study refers to only the image track of the film, it disregards sound bridges, which can be crucial to an accurate segmentation. Continuous music can, for instance, link shots in a way that might not be clear without the sound. A "lightning mix"—such as the one that occurs in *Citizen Kane* when, at the conclusion of one shot, the voice of Thatcher wishes the young Kane "Merry Christmas" before we hear in the next shot (which is set twenty diegetic years later) "and a Happy New Year"—can be problematic. Surely this same portion of film, which without the soundtrack would be considered two autonomous segments, might be deemed one segment once we take the soundtrack into consideration.

Raymond Bellour (1979) saw that the solution to such unresolved challenges might lie in the expansion of terminology to include supersegments, which would be made up of segments, which in turn are made up of subsegments. He found this method especially practical for the segmentation of a musical like *Gigi* (1958). Furthermore, Bellour saw that there are "alternances" in these classical films that are far more subtle and interesting than the alternate syntagma. Bellour's analysis of Hitchcock's *Marnie* (1964) illustrates this thoroughly. Unfortunately, *la grande syntagmatique* does not provide for their identification.

Finally, of course, Metz's scheme does not include the many syntagmatic structures found outside the corpus of classic American cinema. In Godard's *Pierrot le fou* (1965) the hero and heroine flee Paris. Their flight is depicted by a series of brief shots arranged out of chronological order, although one can reconstruct the probable order of events. Some bits of action are shown more than once and in slightly modified versions. Metz calls this a "potential syntagma," since he has no other label for it.

The sheer difficulty in performing a segmentation is illustrated in Metz's own segmentation of *Adieu Philippine,* where his segmentation decisions can often be challenged. Ben Andrews's reconsideration of the segmentation using the soundtrack resolves several of Metz's problems. Problem ridden or not, *la grande syntagmatique* has been and still is one of the most useful tools for film analysis to emerge from the film-semiotics movement. It remains a subject for further refinements.

[*See also* Cinema; Film Semiotics; Imaginary Signifier, The; *and* Metz.]

BIBLIOGRAPHY

Andrews, B. *A Study of the Sound/Image Articulation in "Adieu Philippine".* Toronto: Toronto Semiotic Circle Monographs, Working Papers and Prepublications, 1984.
Bellour, R. *L'analyse du film.* Paris: Albatros, 1979.
Metz, C. *Film Language: A Semiotics of the Cinema.* New York: Oxford University Press, 1974.

—C. D. E. TOLTON

GREIMAS, ALGIRDAS JULIEN (1917–1992), Lithuanian-born French linguist, lexicologist, and semiotician. Algirdas Julien Greimas obtained his doctorate in 1948 at the Sorbonne with a thesis in lexicology, "Fashion in 1830, a Study of the Vocabulary of Clothes according to the Journals of the Times." He left lexicology soon after, acknowledging the limitations of the discipline in its concentration on the word as a unit and in its basic aim of classification. In 1963, he switched to semantics, which was broader in scope, and in 1970 he shifted again to semiotics, an even more encompassing discipline for the study of meaning. But Greimas's early devotion to vocabulary and his love of the word never left him. All throughout his career, whatever his current priorities, Greimas never ceased to maintain his lexicological convictions. He published three dictionaries: one of ancient French (1969), one of middle French (with Teresa M. Keane, 1992), and the dictionary for which he is best known, *Semiotics and Language: An Analytical Dictionary* (with Joseph Courtés, 1979), which is a systematic presentation of the constructed metalanguage and terminology informing his semiotic theory.

Greimas's university career began outside of France. For twelve years, he taught French linguistics on the Faculty of Letters in Alexandria, Egypt, and later at the University of Ankara, Turkey, where he became chair of French language and grammar in 1958. From his first year in Egypt (1949), Greimas made acquaintances whose impact on his intellectual development would be considerable. He met Roland Barthes, and in 1966, they, along with Jacques Dubois, Bernard Pottier, and Bernard Quemada launched the journal *Langages*. At Ankara in 1963, Greimas met Georges Dumézil, who influenced his mythological research. After appointments at the

University of Istanbul, the University of Poitiers, and the Institut Poincaré, Greimas was elected *directeur d'études* (general semantics) in 1965 at the Ecole Pratique des Hautes Études in Paris. The next year, with the support of Claude Lévi-Strauss and the participation of Barthes, he recruited the first research team in semiotics, called the "Groupe de recherches sémio-linguistiques" (Semio-Linguistic Research Group), which would grow and develop into the collective semiotic enterprise known as the Paris School of Semiotics.

Emerging from structural linguistics and the study of folklore and mythology, semiotics began in the 1960s to assert its claim to autonomy, both as a theory of meaning and as a practical methodology for analyzing texts and objects. The relatively rapid development of its theoretical and methodological tools over the following twenty years and the proliferation of its research areas led semioticians to what might be called a crisis of growth, spurring reflections on the epistemological status of the discipline and the history of its concepts. Greimas himself contributed two important essays to these reflections, stressing the implicit logic and continuity of the historical development of the "semiotic project," which he articulated in terms of a progressive conceptualization of the theory. These two articles also serve as the best and clearest introduction to Greimas's own thought.

The first article is the introduction to a book of collected essays, *Du sens 2* (1983), which was translated under the title, "Ten Years Afterward," in Greimas's *The Social Sciences: A Semiotic View* (1990). The second article, "On Meaning" (1989), was published for the first time as an English translation of a conference paper given in 1985. Both of these articles, which are very similar in content, are important as intellectual accounts of the stages of Greimas's thought and as historical surveys of semiotics in Paris since 1956. No other introduction to the works of Greimas achieves quite the same effect within such a brief number of pages, and none is as sweeping, as incisive, and as telling as a self-portrayal of Greimas's mind and his portrayal of a school of thought, both fused on one canvas. One other basic article that complements Greimas's synopses is the annotated bibliography of Greimas's works by Jean-Claude Coquet (1985). (A condensed and updated version of this bibliography appears in Eric Landowski [1993].)

Starting in 1976, Greimas chose to formulate the semiotic theory "as a project with a scientific vocation, that is, more as an ideology than as acquired knowledge" (Coquet, 1985). Its global task is to create "a great anthropology" linking all the humanities and social sciences so that a scientific revolution could finally take place in the human sciences, the way it did in the hard sciences beginning in the seventeenth century. By representing the semiotic project as a constantly evolving process, still incomplete or unfinished, it is possible to interpret it in a historical dimension as a sequence and process of changes. Starting from the end and working back to the beginning, we can try to find the main traces of semiotic practice. Only after the fact can we look back and recognize several stages or distinct states. Greimas briefly traces four major steps in the evolution of his theory.

The first stage, which began in 1956, was influenced by structural linguistics and a linguistically based structuralism borrowed from anthropology and folklore. In 1956, Greimas published an article, "L'actualité du saussurisme" (The Relevance of Saussurism) that his students consider an important starting point. Greimas examined works by Maurice Merleau-Ponty and Lévi-Strauss and concluded that "the Saussurean postulate of a structured world, graspable in its significations" can contribute to the development of a unified methodology in the humanities and social sciences. Greimas became aware that structuralists in various disciplines focused on problems of language from a linguistic perspective and revolutionized their fields by applying Saussure's principles: Lévi-Strauss and Dumézil in anthropology, Barthes in literature, and Jacques Lacan in psychoanalysis. But no structural linguists in France were attempting to do the same, so Greimas moved to bring the work of Saussure and Louis Hjelmslev into linguistics in order to widen the field of semantic research, to leave the strictly linguistic domain, and attempt to relate language theory to that general "semiology" Saussure called for.

The other source of inspiration for Greimas's first stage came from folklore and anthropology. His 1983 historical survey, in fact, begins with folklore and omits structural linguistics entirely, including the above article on the impact of Saussure. Vladimir Propp's *Morphology of the Folktale* became the initial text or object study to serve as a starting point for a new type of narrative analysis and as the basis for more encompassing theories. Propp's model attempts to explain the "surface structure" of narratives—the sequence of actions or syntagmatic dimension—and Greimas thought it could be improved through recourse to Lévi-Strauss's paradigmatic analysis of myth. Greimas then noticed four main segments that could be paired and that two of these pairs made up a Lévi-Straussian schema. The structuration of the functions in Propp's model uncovered a logical and semantic structure behind the linear and canonical succession. Thus, by linking together two complementary narrative models, it became evident that the varied surface structures of stories are generated from a smaller set of deep structures that can be actualized as temporal successions. The structuration of the functions or the projection of paradigmatic categories on the syntagmatic development of stories yielded a new and more complete model; the narrative schema.

The second stage of semiotics began in 1964, when Greimas gave a seminar on Hjelmslev's linguistic and semiotic theories, and culminated with the publication of *Sémantique structurale* (Structural Semantics, 1966), which gave the first elaboration of a linguistic semiotics and the foundation of what became the Parisian school of semiotics. The goal of this kind of study is the semantic and syntactical analysis of texts, which Greimas defines as discourse. *Structural Semantics,* despite its title, is thus more than structural semantics restricted to describing the meaning of words and sentences. It attempts to go beyond the sentence and account for the coherence and totality of meaning of a complete text or set of texts and concludes with a study of the narrative world of the novelist Georges Bernanos. A major component proposed in Greimas's semantic theory is his model of the "elementary structure of signification," later elaborated into the "semiotic square," which attempts to account for the initial articulations of meaning within a semantic microuniverse. The central focus of *Structural Semantics,* however, is the study of narrative texts and the narrative dimension of discourse. The structuration of Propp's functions and the actantial model take up two chapters in the latter half of the book that are recognized for their theoretical genius and as the tour de force of the work; these chapters are the heart of the second stage of semiotics (perceived as the first stage by outsiders) and they make up the early narratological period of Paris School semiotics. Narratology is at the origin of this semiotics and is its very core. In this early stage, however, narratology focused relatively concretely on the relations among events, actants, contracts, and exchanges; later, it moved toward a more complex and abstract modal grammar.

The third stage of semiotics began in the early 1970s and focused on two different aspects of discourse analysis, narratology, and the study of the literary text. One focus was on the modalities and aspectualities of the function as a verb (want, have to or must, and know how or can), leading not only to the exploration of what action is (thus providing a model for the organization of behavior) but also to the construction of a modal grammar, which covers the entire cognitive dimension of discourse. In 1976, having refined Propp's narrative schema, Greimas tested it in an extensive book-length application to a short story by Guy de Maupassant and concluded that the model was valid not only for folktales but also for the more sophisticated literary texts. The literary semiotics of *Maupassant* (1976), however, is more than just an application of earlier theoretical models and the then-current theory of modalities. Greimas's goal is to set up procedures that enable the analyst to bridge the gap between the surface structures of a text and its semantic deep structures and to discover the greatest multiplicity of textual facts and operational concepts while varying methodological parameters. The study is as much a search for methodology as it is an interpretation of a short story. It was at this time that Greimas saw narrativity as the organizing principle of all discourse and "the syntactic form of the organization of the world" (1989).

The other approach pursued in this stage of semiotics was related to narratology and consisted of a progressive formalization of the intuitive components of the Proppian schema to the point that Propp's model was abandoned in favor of an ostensibly more rigorous syntax that functioned as a calculus. "It is not that we completely abandoned heroes and traitors," says Greimas, "but we discovered that Propp's model could be broken down into parts, into important sequences covered over by the model. . . . Without noticing it we began to work on something other than the tale" (1989, p. 543). For example, semionarrative syntax (as the conceptual structure of narrative is called) takes the idea of the confrontation between two subjects from Propp's conceptions of hero and villain and interprets it as a relation founded either on a confrontation, a sort of polemic, or on the contract, postulating therefore that all interaction is polemicocontractual in nature. As the

simplest and most rudimentary model of narrative, the analysis and reevaluation of the Proppian schema led to the blooming of what might be called sociosemiotics: "We discovered a *semiotics of manipulation*—how the sender manipulates the subject; then a *semiotics of action*—how competence is acquired to carry out performance; and finally a *semiotics of sanction*—that is to say, passing judgments on self, on others, and on things" (1989, p. 543). These new semiotics, which are still being worked out, are also modal organizations.

Semiotics was, in a way, freed from the Proppian model, and yet the field's strength and success depended on the fruitfulness as well as the rather unexpected success of that model. Since the 1960s, the Proppian model was considered as the model par excellence of the narrative, and, even when it was abandoned temporarily in the search for more general structures, it was reinstated as an ideological narrative schema, a universal schema to be kept side by side with the modal grammar. To free oneself from the constraints of the Proppian schema and to acquire an autonomous modal syntax was an effort that took on a "revolutionary" aspect, and it gradually changed semiotic practice from top to bottom. The basic theory of the decade was published in Greimas and Cortés's semiotic dictionary (1979). A second volume came out in 1986, edited by the authors of the first volume, thus giving the helm to forty semioticians of the Paris School.

The fourth stage of semiotics, which began in the early 1980s, switched focus from narrative syntax to discursive syntax and set out to construct an aspectual syntax. Unlike the opposing categories of *yes* and *no* or *black* and *white,* aspectualities are tensive, valuative, and gradual. The salient features of temporal aspectualities are duration and becoming, which are continuous and gradual processes. In this stage, semiotics was sufficiently developed to overcome an initial methodological limitation of viewing characters only as vessels of action. Since Propp, structural poetics and semiotics have avoided treating the character in a text as a psychological essence, "person," or even as a well-rounded "being." This self-imposed bias was justified initially when it was necessary to define the actants and differentiate them from psychological issues of characters—their emotions and temperaments. Semiotics began with the theory of actants and initially attributed to subjects only the ability to act. One of the research areas that opened up after 1979 was instigated by the need to grapple with the subject's ability to feel, respond, and evaluate. It became possible at this point to undertake an examination of the traditional theories of passions expounded by René Descartes (1596–1650), Baruch Spinoza (1632–1677), Gottfried W. Leibniz (1646–1716), Freidrich W. Nietzsche (1844–1900), and Sigmund Freud (1856–1939) and give them semiotic interpretations.

It was at this point first noticed that, contrary to the implicit postulations of these classical theories, one rarely encounters solitary passions: they were almost never linked to a single subject, and their description always called for the establishment of an actantial structure. The semiotic interpretation of these passions was undertaken almost exclusively in terms of modalities. Thus, passions can be described in terms of modal syntax and at least two interdependent actants; for example, *avarice = wanting to + conjunction*. Greimas and Jacques Fontanille have explored this passional phase of semiotics in a collaborative work, *Sémiotique des passions* (Semiotics of Passions, 1991). This comprehensive study has extended semiotic analysis and patently integrated a new area of research to the point that Paris School semiotics today has become not only a semiotics of action but also a semiotics of passion—a pathemic semiotics.

In more recent developments, Greimas turned to the more fundamental issue of value, which retrospectively can be seen to underpin the entire theory of semiotics as a basic axiom. The point of interest is to know how an individual selects values relative to truth, the good, or beauty and how that individual evaluates, sanctions, judges, and cherishes these values. In other words, semiotics here focuses on the values that are sought after by individuals and the functioning of value systems in discourse: truth telling, ethics, and aesthetics.

[*See also* Actantial Model; Actants; Narratology; *and* Paris School.]

BIBLIOGRAPHY

Works by Greimas

"L'actualité du Saussurisme." *Le français moderne* 24 (1956): 190–203.

Structural Semantics: An Attempt at a Method (1966). Translated by D. McDowell, R. Schleicher, and A. Velie. Lincoln: University of Nebraska Press, 1983.

"Du discours scientifique en sciences sociales." In *Sémiotique et sciences sociales*, pp. 9–42. Paris: Seuil, 1976. Translated as "On Scientific Discourse in the Social Sciences" in Greimas, 1990, pp. 11–36.

"Introduction." *Du sens 2: Essais sémiotiques*, pp. 7–18. Paris: Seuil, 1983. Translated as "Ten Years Afterward" in Greimas, 1990, pp. 175–184.

Maupassant: The Semiotics of Text. Translated by P. Perron. Amsterdam and Philadelphia: John Benjamins, 1988.

"On Meaning." *New Literary History* 20.3 (1989): 539–550.

The Social Sciences: A Semiotic View. Minneapolis: University of Minnesota Press, 1990.

Greimas, A. J., and J. Courtés. *Semiotics and Language: An Analytical Dictionary.* Translated by L. Crist, D. Patte, et al. Bloomington: Indiana University Press, 1982.

Greimas, A. J., and J. Fontanille. *The Semiotics of Passions.* Translated by P. Perron and F. Collins. Minneapolis: University of Minnesota Press, 1993.

Other Works

Budniakiewicz, T. *Fundamentals of Story Logic: Introduction to Greimassian Semiotics.* Amsterdam and Philadelphia: John Benjamins, 1992.

Coquet, J.-C. "Eléments de bio-bibliographie." In *Exigences et perspectives de la sémiotique / Aims and Prospects of Semiotics*, edited by H. Parret and H.-G. Ruprecht, vol. 1, pp. liii–lxxxv. Philadelphia and Amsterdam: John Benjamins, 1985.

Landowski, E. "In Memoriam Algirdas Julien Greimas." *International Journal for the Semiotics of Law* 5.15 (1993): 227–228.

—THERESE BUDNIAKIEWICZ

H

HABERMAS, JÜRGEN (b. 1929), German philosopher whose theoretical work represents a major synthesis of a number of themes: the reconstruction of historical materialism as a theory of societal evolution; the development of Max Weber's critique of societal rationalization; the theory of communicative action; symbolic interactionism; the construction of a discourse ethics; and the commitment to a critical theory of social emancipation. Unlike recent developments of speech-act theory in linguistic pragmatics, which have tended to favor individualistic, speaker-oriented, and instrumental models, Habermas sees in speech-act theory the possibility of reconstructing an ethics of communicative rationality founded on intersubjective and procedural criteria for reaching understanding. Habermas relocates speech-act theory in the Anglo-Saxon tradition of language-based moral philosophy. Contemporary critical linguistics show evidence of cross-fertilization with Habermas's thought. Habermas assumes that universal metarules for reaching understanding in communication can be established. The notion of maximum transparency (Grice, 1975), founded on universal procedural criteria, is central to Habermas's account.

Habermas proposes both a critical intervention in and a further development of the project of modernity. He attempts to renew the connections with Karl Marx's conception of rationality as grounded in concrete social, historical, and linguistic practices. In *Knowledge and Human Interests* (1968), Habermas shows how a theory of knowledge such as positivism is deeply connected with the communal ways of living that have evolved under cultural modernity. He makes a three-way distinction between practical, technical, and critical interests. Practical interests are based on ways of life that are concerned with reaching a reciprocal understanding between self and other. Technical interests are concerned with the prediction and control of regularities and events in the world of "outer nature." A concern for the emancipation of subjects from nontransparent and distorting constraints of power guides critical interests. These arguments remain central in Habermas's subsequent development of the theory of communicative rationality.

Volume 1 of *The Theory of Communicative Action* (1981) contends that Marx does not make a clear distinction between cognitive-instrumental and communicative forms of rationality. Cognitive-instrumental rationality is foundational for what Habermas calls "subject-centered reason." *The Philosophical Discourse of Modernity* (1985) is a historical reconstruction and critique of the current impasse created by such reason. The essays in that volume provide a wide-ranging critique of G. W. F. Hegel, Friedrich Nietzsche, Georges Bataille, Jacques Derrida, Michel Foucault, and Niklas Luhmann, among others, who failed to go beyond the philosophy of consciousness as the guiding principle of modernity. Instead of the paradigm of the knowing subject who has knowledge of objects, Habermas seeks to develop modernity's counterdiscourse of "communicative action oriented to mutual agreement." His quest for a solution to the impasse of the problematic of modernity has two aspects.

First, the neoconservative acceptance of modernity has led to the increasing colonization of all spheres of social life by cognitive-instrumental rationality. Second, the postmodernists' radical critique of modernity, which takes its inspiration from Nietzsche's totalizing ontology of cognitive-instrumental reason as the "will to power," has tended to equate instrumental rationality with all forms of reason. This view negates the possibility of a rational critique of the processes of societal modernization. Both Habermas and the poststructuralists agree that the philosophy of consciousness is an exhausted paradigm and both center their claims on the same linguistic terrain: discourse. Habermas's solution is to replace this paradigm with one based on intersubjective communicative rationality or communication based on understanding. Cognitive-instrumental reason is then just one form of communicative rationality among others.

The theory of communicative action draws on the same tradition as do the speech-act theorists. *Communication and the Evolution of Society* (1976) sets out an early version of this theory. The aim is a "universal pragmatics," the goal of which is the reconstruction of the "universal validity basis of speech." In the further development of the theory of communicative action (1981), Habermas seeks to restore the emphasis on the illocutionary binding power of speech acts, which have an intersubjective rather than an individualistic basis. Habermas's concern is with the conditions for intersubjective agreement. In a world that has become decentered and divided through the effects of modernization, Habermas wishes to reestablish the possibility of common understanding. *Moral Consciousness and Communicative Action* (1983) explores the universalistic and procedural bases of normative claims to validity. The aim of this project is a discourse ethics based on transcendental and pragmatic principles of argumentation.

Unlike the speech-act theorists, Habermas seeks to reconnect speech acts to their concrete sociohistorical contexts. To do so, he takes up Weber's theory of societal rationalization. The domains of science, morality, and art, Habermas concludes, have become so differentiated through the effects of modernization that different communicative principles apply in each of these domains. The institutions that regulate the different types of social action can be defined in terms of different types of communicative action. In turn, the different types of communicative action operate in terms of different forms of truth or validity claims. Thus, teleological action is founded on the principle of success and on an instrumental rationality of means and ends. Conversation is founded on criteria of truth: Does the speech act truthfully represent states of affairs in the objective world or not? Norm-conformative action is founded on moral-practical criteria: is the action right or wrong, good or bad, and so on according to socially binding moral norms? Dramaturgical action is founded on the principle of sincerity: is the social actor speaking truthfully about his or her "inner" states and feelings or not?

The various types of speech act are linked to specific social institutions. Teleological action characterizes the domain of science and technology but also and increasingly those of politics, social administration, marketing, and so on. Knowledge comprises technologies and strategies for the calculation and accomplishment of goals and effects in an objectified "outer world." Conversation is concerned with theoretical knowledge, which is ordered systematically and constructed. Norm-conformative action is founded on institutional norms of moral behavior with which social actors must comply. Dramaturgical action places the subjective world of the self at the center, especially the self's desires and feelings. Habermas shows that each of these types of action has its own rationality—its own notion of truth—and its own inner logic.

Habermas's "ideal speech situation," oriented to rationally motivated critique and understanding, treats agreement as the telos of speech and as something that speaker and listener arrive at through uncoerced consensus. The cognitive-instrumental conception of the subject is, in contrast, dominated by the production paradigm of cognitive-instrumental reason. Language is characterized as the medium through which speakers get others to fulfill their egocentrically calculated aims and purposes.

Habermas seeks to develop a comprehensive social theory of the kind that has eluded semiotics. But a number of problems need clarification. Habermas bases his theory of discourse ethics in part on the work of Lawrence Kohlberg (e.g., 1973), who, following Jean Piaget (1896–1980), assumes a number of stages in the individual's development of moral reasoning. But there is no convincing evidence to suggest that these stages have a universal basis. Instead, they derive from middle-class Anglo-American norms of moral behavior. Nancy Fraser (1989) has shown that these same norms occult the question of gender in Habermas's critical theory. A second problem concerns the increasing separation of labor from communicative action to the extent that it is not clear how Habermas would theorize the complex and multilevel links between the social means of production and the forms of communicative action in a given society. Habermas has moved in the direction of a contractualism like that in John Rawls's *A Theory of Justice* (1971) or Richard Rorty's *Consequences of Pragmatism* (1982), in which the material economic and conflictual basis of social meaning making is minimized. A third problem is that Habermas's classification of types of social action tends to reconstitute them in folk-linguistic terms. He provides no criteria for showing how his metalinguistic glossing practices might provide a labeling of types of social action that naturalizes its own practices. A semiotically informed account will avoid the problem of constituting classes of social action on the basis of, say, the explicit performative verbs. Instead, it will show how the patterns of the use of grammar and other semiotic resource systems mesh with forms of social life. Nevertheless, Habermas's own call for an empirical pragmatics, informed by a formal-pragmatic theory, points in this direction. No doubt, solutions can be found to these problems. Habermas has much to offer the kind of sophisticated sociocultural theory that semiotics requires.

[*See also* Communication; Discourse Analysis; Implicature; *and* Speech Act Theory.]

BIBLIOGRAPHY

Works by Habermas

On the Logic of the Social Sciences (1967). Translated by S. Weber Nicholsen and J. A. Stark. Cambridge: Polity Press, 1988.

Knowledge and Human Interests (1968). 2d ed. Translated by J. J. Shapiro. London: Heinemann, 1978.

Communication and the Evolution of Society (1976). Translated by T. McCarthy. London: Heinemann, 1979.

The Theory of Communicative Action, volume 1, *Reason and the Rationalization of Society* (1981). Translated by T. McCarthy. London: Heinemann, 1984.

The Theory of Communicative Action, volume 2, *The Critique of Functionalist Reason* (1981). Translated by T. McCarthy. Cambridge: Polity Press, 1987.

The Philosophical Discourse of Modernity (1985). Translated by F. Lawrence. Cambridge, Mass.: MIT Press, 1987.

The New Conservatism: Cultural Criticism and the Historians' Debate. Translated by S. Weber Nicholsen. Cambridge: Polity Press, 1989.

Moral Consciousness and Communicative Action (1983). Translated by C. Lenhardt and S. Weber Nicholsen. Cambridge: Polity Press, 1990.

Other Works

Bernstein, R. J., ed. *Habermas and Modernity.* Cambridge: Polity Press, 1985.

Fraser, N. *Unruly Practices: Power, Discourse, and Gender in Contemporary Social Theory.* Minneapolis: University of Minnesota Press, 1989.

Grice, H. P. "Logic and Conversation." In *Syntax and Semantics: Speech Acts*, edited by P. Cole and J. L. Morgan, pp. 41–58. New York: Academic Press, 1975.

Kohlberg, L. *Collected Papers on Moral Development and Moral Education.* Cambridge, Mass.: Harvard University Laboratory for Human Development, 1973.

Rawls, J. *A Theory of Justice.* Cambridge, Mass.: Harvard University Press, 1971.

Rorty, R. *Consequences of Pragmatism: Essays, 1972–1980.* Minneapolis: University of Minnesota Press, 1982.

—PAUL J. THIBAULT

HABITUS. Cultural sociologist Pierre Bourdieu's most significant contribution to semiotics, sociology, and cultural and feminist studies is the concept of the habitus (a Latin word meaning deportment). Predating contemporary feminist theoretical concerns with the body and embodied difference as both material and symbolic ground for experience and subjectivity, Bourdieu has long argued that the body is the very basis of social differentiation and cultural production. It is in the body that personal predispositions combine with the social and cultural world; the body is the mediating force between subjectivity and the "objective" cultural world. In *Outline of a Theory of Practice* (1972), Bourdieu explains that each individual is born into particular cultural and class meaning systems that code the body in permanent disposition through ways of "standing, speaking and thereby of *feeling* and *thinking* (1972, p. 32). The habitus is acquired and developed in social (home) and pedagogical (school) contexts. Yet the school and family do not set out to teach explicit sets of rules for bodily conduct. Rather, it is the habituation, the repetitive and affirmed performances of certain attitudinal, cognitive, affective, and bodily repertoires, that form the durable, largely unconscious, dispositions of the habitus.

Cultural capital and habitus are related closely in terms of the semiotics of representation. The social goods (e.g., dress, speech patterns, deportment, behaviors) a person brings to the marketplace of social exchange is carried on and in the body in terms of the style of material and physical self-representation, cognition, affect, and attitudes. The embodiment of the habitus Bourdieu calls *hexis* (the Greek correlative of habitus), which refers to the signification of how social actors carry themselves. This includes gestures, stance, ways of walking, looking, sitting, sneezing or coughing, and so forth. Of the North African Kabyle, for instance, Bourdieu notes that women orient their bodies away from men and downward whereas men move forward and upward. In *Distinction* (1979), Bourdieu elaborates the class differences in *hexis* found in people's eating styles: working-class men develop manual and oral repertoires for eating large and simple foods that require plain utensils, "whole hearted male gulps and mouthfuls" (1984, p. 190). By contrast, upper-class males and women generally display restraint through eating habits that require more complicated utensils and oral maneuvers (such as in eating fish or peeling pears). Whereas the working class is characterized by the semiotics of plain speaking, plain eating, and an ethos of plenty, the upper bourgeoisie displays a cultivated discourse of conversation, of "dining," and an ethos of restraint and rarity. For Bourdieu, gendered and classed bodies are constructed and perceived by social actors through social systems of classification that correspond to the distribution of cultural value among the social classes. The signifying body, then, becomes the primary ground upon which culture, social difference, and class location are mapped. The body, for Bourdieu, is a mnemonic device, a "memory jogger" in which a group's most fundamental beliefs and values are embedded. The body incorporates history and (re)produces history in ways that are largely unconscious to individual social actors.

The habitus is both durable and flexible. That is, dispositions appropriate to one social field can be transferred and adjusted according to the contextual demands of another. However, broadly shared lifestyle factors of a given social class generate "stylistic affinity" among members of the same class, which "makes each of them a metaphor of any of the others." Bourdieu's conceptual aim is to retain some measure of human agency by claiming that a person can adjust her or his habitus across social contexts and requirements. However, he believes strongly that the collective habitus of a given social class or group seriously limits the possibilities of subjective reinventions of the self. He explains that the "properties—and property—with which individuals and groups surround themselves, houses, furniture, paintings, books, cars, spirits, cigarettes, perfume, clothes, and in their practices in which they manifest their distinction, sport, games, entertainments" all signify individuals as part of the collective "synthetic unity of the habitus" (1984, p. 173). Individuals share certain class-specific lifestyles and cultural tastes, which are linked to class-based material conditions enabled by income and objectified in signifying systems of commodities, social relations, and practices. For instance, Bourdieu documents class distinctions between the working-class tastes for beer, cheap and fatty foods, team sports, caravan holidays, and informal and plentiful meals and, by contrast, the upper-class tastes

for wines, light and lean foods, the refined sports of tennis, sailing, or polo, holidays to exotic or culturally significant places, and formal meals with polite conversation. Such class-differentiated lifestyles, taste, and social practices inscribe on bodies a repertoire of behaviors, ways of thinking and feeling, that signify class-specific culture. The body, for Bourdieu, "is a social product which is the only tangible manifestation of the 'person,'" and the signs constituting that body (speech, hairstyle, clothing, handwriting, deportment) serve to draw distinctions among groups in terms of their degrees of acquired and semiotically manifest "culture." Thus, semiotic representations of the self function as a class and moral index.

[See also Bourdieu; Cultural Knowledge; Cultureme; Halliday; and Nonverbal Bodily Sign Categories.]

BIBLIOGRAPHY

Bourdieu, P. Outline of a Theory of Practice (1972). Translated by R. Nice. Cambridge: Cambridge University Press, 1977.

Bourdieu, P. Distinction: A Social Critique of the Judgement of Taste (1979). Translated by R. Nice. London: Routledge and Kegan Paul, 1984.

—CARMEN LUKE

HALLIDAY, MICHAEL A. K. (b. 1925), Australian linguist who developed an original theory of language as an inclusive sociosemiotic system whose foundations differ in many important respects from those of the structuralist theory of semiotics. Registers—a key concept in Halliday's theory—are varieties of language associated not with particular regions, as are dialects, but with particular social contexts in which language is used in specific ways. While regional language varieties are characterized primarily by their phonology and syntax, registers are characterized primarily by their semantics—that is, by the kinds of meaning and modes of interaction that typify them. Registers, in turn, cluster into codes: class-based varieties of language that can be described in terms of broad semantic orientations along the lines of Basil Bernstein's work. This concept, which has affinities with Pierre Bourdieu's concept of habitus, has been applied especially to the social institution of the family, where different codes underlie the ways in which middle-class and working-class parents regulate the behavior of their children (Halliday, 1973).

Descriptions of registers must therefore be linked to descriptions of the social contexts with which they are associated. This involves three variables: field, tenor, and mode. A description of the field of a social context is a description of the activity that is realized in whole or in part by means of language, together with the kinds of subject matter associated with the activity. The activity "regulating a child's behavior," for instance, is associated in some countries with such subjects as "talking to strangers," "watching television," and so on. A description of the tenor of a social context is a description of the participants of the activity—for instance, mothers and children—and specifies the roles they play in the activity and their relation to each other in terms of such issues as power and status. A description of the mode of a social context is a description of the way in which language takes part in the activity—for instance, in written or spoken form, as monologue or dialogue, or embedded in nonlinguistic activity or not. All three of the variables have direct bearings on the way language is used in any given context.

Halliday sees language as simultaneously fulfilling three broad functions or metafunctions: the ideational metafunction of representing what is going on in the world; the interpersonal metafunction of constituting social interaction; and the textual metafunction of enabling the ideational and interpersonal meanings to come together in coherent texts. It is by virtue of this multifunctionality that language can realize the three variables of the social context: ideational meanings realize the field of discourse, interpersonal meanings the tenor, and textual meanings the mode.

Each metafunction is associated with specific linguistic systems. Halliday emphasizes the paradigmatic structure of language and views linguistic systems as resources for making ideational, interpersonal, and textual meanings, each register constituting a particular set of choices from among the meanings that can be realized in the language as a whole. The system of mood, for instance, seen from this point of view, makes it possible to choose between such interpersonal meanings as "making statements," "asking questions," and "issuing commands." At a more "delicate" level, further choices are possible—for instance, between different kinds of command (such as requests, instructions, pleas, etc.)—and each of these, too, will have a specific linguistic realization. Which kind of command will be chosen will depend on the tenor of the social context, on the precise relation between those who issue the commands and those who are enjoined to obey them. If the command is issued by someone higher in status, for instance, a direct command (imperative) might be chosen; if it is issued by someone lower in status, a plea might be chosen. And whether such a choice is indeed a choice or should more aptly be called a law, rule, convention, or habit also depends on the social context: different social contexts regulate linguistic behavior in different ways.

It follows that linguistic descriptions—that is, maps of possible meanings—can either be "register specific," charting which choices are regarded as acceptable (or prescribed or habitually used) in a specific social context (for instance, the kinds of command that characterize military contexts or the way in which working-class mothers regulate the behavior of their children) or describe the language as a whole, combining in one paradigm the choices possible in all the social contexts that use the language. The latter is, in a sense, an artificial construct. There is not one social context in which all these meanings can be realized, but it is a useful and necessary artifice for describing and comparing registers.

Coupled with such descriptions of linguistic systems as meaning potentials are descriptions of the ways in which the various possible meanings are realized linguistically, such as the way in which word order realizes such speech functions as "statement," "question," and "command." In his linguistic descriptions Halliday has made the lexicogrammar of the clause the central issue. The term *lexicogrammar* implies that no categorical distinction is made between grammar and lexis: the broadest meanings are realized syntactically, the more delicate meanings lexically. But Halliday has also published systemic-functional accounts of intonation and of the systems, such as conjunction and reference, that are "above the clause" and that ensure textual cohesion. In *Learning How to Mean* (1975), Halliday has provided an original account of language acquisition in which learning language is seen as an active endeavor by the child, with each child developing, for a time, his or her own protogrammar as he or she discovers what he or she can do with language. And although paradigmatic descriptions are by nature synchronic, Halliday has also published diachronic studies, such as a study of the development of the register of scientific English, starting with Chaucer's 1391 *Treatise on the Astrolabe* (1988).

Halliday views his approach to language as essentially ethnographic, inspired more by the work of Bronislaw Malinowski (1884–1942) on language than by that of Ferdinand de Saussure (1857–1913), and focused on social interaction while keeping the idealization of linguistic data as minimal as possible. Halliday's method has been applied extensively to educational research (Lemke, 1995). It also plays a role in critical linguistics (e.g., Kress and Hodge, 1979) and in the developing field of critical-discourse analysis (e.g., Dijk, 1993), forms of text analysis that seek to analyze texts in order to uncover the ideological structures they reproduce and that often have explicit political purposes. It has also inspired research into nonlinguistic semiotic systems, such as visual communication (O'Toole, 1994; Kress and van Leeuwen, 1995).

[*See also* Bourdieu; Code; Habitus; *and* Speech Act Theory.]

BIBLIOGRAPHY

Works by Halliday
Explorations in the Functions of Language. London: Edward Arnold, 1973.
Learning How to Mean. London: Edward Arnold, 1975.
Language as Social Semiotic. London: Edward Arnold, 1978.
An Introduction to Functional Grammar. London: Edward Arnold, 1985.
"On the Language of Physical Science." In *Registers of Written English*, edited by M. Ghadessy, pp. 162–178. London: Pinter, 1988.
Other Works
Bernstein, B. *Class, Codes, and Control.* Vol. 4. London: Routledge, 1971.
Dijk, T. A. van, ed. *Critical Discourse Analysis.* Special issue of *Discourse and Society* (4.2). London: Sage, 1993.
Kress, G., and R. Hodge. *Language as Ideology.* London: Routledge, 1979.
Kress, G., and T. van Leeuwen. *Reading Images: The Grammar of Visual Design.* London: Routledge, 1995.
Lemke, J. L. *Textual Politics: Discourse and Social Dynamics.* Washington, D.C.: Taylor and Francis, 1995.
O'Toole, M. *The Language of Displayed Art.* Leicester: Leicester University Press, 1994.

—THEO VAN LEEUWEN

HAMILTON, WILLIAM D. (b. 1936), British biologist, author of a landmark theory of kin selection, which can be used to solve the problem of hymenopteran sociality. Starting with the assumption that natural selection works in the first instance for the individual and not for the group and reasoning that it values the transmission of copies of units of heredity (genes), Hamilton argued that inasmuch as relatives (that is, possessors of copies of one's own genes) reproduce, one succeeds in the struggle for existence—that is, one is improving one's "inclusive fitness."

Since, identical twins apart, a person is normally more related to him- or herself than to anyone else (one has more copies of one's own genes than does anyone else), it is normally in one's biological interests to do one's own reproducing. But there might be cases when evolution promotes adaptations directed toward the aid of close relatives. This is kin selection, and Hamilton—at one stroke solving a problem that had puzzled evolutionists since Charles Darwin—showed how this mechanism explains the existence in the hymenoptera (ants, bees, and wasps) of sterile workers that apparently devote their lifetimes to the well-being of their fertile sisters and offspring. The hymenoptera have a notable reproductive system in which females have both mothers and fathers but males, born of unfertilized eggs, have only mothers. This means that sisters are more closely related (sharing 75 percent of their genes) to each other than mothers and daughters (50 percent). Hence, from a hymenopteran perspective, it makes more sense to breed vicariously, raising fertile sisters, than it does to breed oneself, raising fertile daughters. Note that this ratio holds only for the females, and it is a striking fact that the workers in the hymenoptera are always female. In humans, as in other vertebrates, siblings are 50 percent related, the same as parents and offspring; kin selection does not, therefore, operate—at least, not for the hymenopteran reason.

Emboldened by his success with this individualist argument, Hamilton has since turned to other problems in evolutionary theory. Most pertinent for semiotics is his recent work on the major outstanding theoretical problem for Darwinian evolutionary theory—namely that of sex. Why in so many organisms are there males as well as females, given that reproduction would be so much more efficient if there were only females? An asexual female can get right on with the problem of reproducing, whereas a sexual female has to find a mate and, moreover, decide that the mate is worthwhile—particularly in the sense of complementing her genes with genes that will aid her offspring to survive and reproduce.

Clearly, there must be some adaptive advantage to the female of having sex in those species that do—most organisms do not. It cannot be that this is a way in which the group can best channel new mutations into the same organism, for this ignores the individualist nature of selection. Hamilton therefore hypothesizes that sex, which leads to a shuffling of the gene complement, is a protection against parasites, which tend to affect higher organisms. Since we have here an arms race between exploiter and exploited and since hosts can rarely if ever respond through their own evolution to the speed of evolution of the parasites, sex is an invaluable tool in making hosts into moving biological targets. No sooner has the parasite evolved to a new, more efficient form than through sexual recombination of the genes the host has been changed, and there is no guarantee that the parasite is still efficient at breaking down the barriers of the host.

If there is truth in this hypothesis, then males must signal to their potential mates that they are just the kinds of organisms that will provide protection to the shared offspring. Most important, they must themselves be fit and show it or, if not fit, deceive the females into thinking that they are. Hamilton argues that many male displays are designed—that is, fashioned by natural selection—to show this fact. Good red blood is a sign of fitness, and many males display, as birds do, through blushing or like phenomena, displaying the direct effects of the blood.

Particularly significant, argues Hamilton, using ideas first developed by Ronald Aylmer Fisher (1890–1962) in his *Genetical Theory of Natural Selection* (1930), is the fact that these displays can lead to a kind of runaway sexual selection. Initially, the displays convey direct, semantic information about their possessor's health. But shortly they become ends in themselves and evolve in enhanced fashions, simply because those males that possess these fashions, including the female's sons, do better than those males that do not have them. This is not to deny that such exaggerated features, although not directly connected to fitness, now fail to signal fitness—perhaps they do it through something like Amotz Zahavi's principle of deliberately demonstrating the ability to survive with a handicap—but it does mean that one has reached a new level of information transmission, even if one ignores all of the qualifications about the

use and detection of deception. In semiotic terms, these signs have evolved from indexical to iconic and symbolic. Hamilton's theory of the evolution of sex is still very much on the hypothetical level, but whether accepted in whole or in part it is clearly advancing our understanding of the evolution of signaling and information transfer.

[*See also* Darwin; Dawkins; Evolution; Manipulation; Trivers; *and* Zahavi.]

BIBLIOGRAPHY

Dawkins, R. *The Selfish Gene.* Oxford: Oxford University Press, 1976.

Fisher, R. A. *Genetical Theory of Natural Selection.* Oxford: Clarendon Press, 1930.

Hamilton, W., R. Axelrod, and R. Tanese. "Sexual Reproduction as an Adaptation to Resist Parasites." *Proceedings of the National Academy of Science, USA* 87.9 (1990): 3566–3573.

Hamilton, W. D. "The Genetical Evolution of Social Behaviour 1." *Journal of Theoretical Biology* 7 (1964a): 1–16.

Hamilton, W. D. "The Genetical Evolution of Social Behaviour 2." *Journal of Theoretical Biology* 7 (1964b): 17–32.

Maynard Smith, J. *The Evolution of Sex.* Cambridge: Cambridge University Press, 1978.

Maynard Smith, J. *Evolution and the Theory of Games.* Cambridge: Cambridge University Press, 1982.

Ruse, M. *Sociobiology: Sense or Nonsense?* Dordrecht: Reidel, 1979.

Ruse, M. *Monad to Man: The Concept of Progress in Evolutionary Biology.* Cambridge, Mass.: Harvard University Press, 1996.

Wilson, E. O. *Sociobiology: The New Synthesis.* Cambridge, Mass.: Harvard University Press, 1975.

—MICHAEL RUSE

HAPTICS. The science of touch in relation to the positions and actions of the body (as optics and acoustics are the technical terms for light and sound), haptics was conceptualized by Gregor Revesz (1934). It refers to touch as a perceptual system, detecting the shapes and sizes of objects during motions that take place across stretches of time.

While the sense of touch has long been studied by philosophers, physicians, and other scholars, the first extensive treatment was in 1749 by the French philosopher and encyclopedist Denis Diderot (1713–1784), who concluded that even if touch uses a two-dimensional surface like the skin, it yields an idea or impression of three-dimensional objects, just as vision does. Touch can use a steady rise and fall of temperature to get an impression of approaching a fire and then receding from it, just as vision uses an increase and decrease in angle to see an object come close and then move away. Touch can judge the proximity of bodies by the action of air on the skin, the wind created by a passing vehicle, for example. Tactile sensations, Diderot contended, can be combined and recombined, can be changed in scale, and can be a good basis for conceiving of objects as point sized, as large as the earth, or, indeed, as filling an infinite space. They allow the blind to have a conception of space that can include points, lines, planes, and solids, with the observer's place in space clear and distinct enough to give an accurate estimate of the direction of objects from the observer.

Ernst Heinrich Weber (1795–1878) founded the thorough and systematic scientific study of skin sensitivity. David Katz (1884–1953), too, theorized about touch as operated by coordinating motion and effects of the object on the skin (1925). Revesz (1950) studied sculptures made by blind people and theorized about touch. Revesz's investigations of the parallels to vision probably did not go far enough.

James J. Gibson (1962, 1966) made striking advances over previous theorists of touch. He defined space as an "amodal" perception—that is, information for spatial arrangements is obtained through each of the senses, albeit vision relies on photic energy and touch uses the resistance of surfaces. The senses each can give distinctive sensations, which the observer in active motion hardly notices except by accident, but the senses offer an equivalent awareness of how surfaces are laid out in the three-dimensional environment surrounding the observer. Gibson listed the tangible properties of the environment as geometrical variables (such as slopes and edges), surface variables (such as texture or slipperiness), and material variables (such as heaviness or rigidity). To discover solid tangible shapes, Gibson found, observers typically do the following: curve the fingers so as to fit the object, including pushing into concavities; explore with the fingers in a nonstereotyped fashion, with the pattern of motion not repeated on the next examination; oppose the thumb and some fingers; and rub or trace with one or more fingers. Gibson hypothesized that the motions serving touch were means to an end, the crucial information being given by "tactile postures," notably finger spans on

which the observer's impression of the shape of the object is based.

As a result of Katz's observation that vibration plays an important role in touch, tactile aids to speech perception are now available, such as microphones that pick up speech signals and vibrators on the skin that relay the vibrations of speech in a tangible form (Kirman, 1973). The skin can distinguish vibrations up to about 600 hertz (cycles per second). Speech ranges from about 200 to 8,000 hertz, but the vowels *oo* and *ah* and nasals such as *m, n,* and *ng* lie within the frequency range of touch. Suitable speech signals are immediately intelligible with virtually no training when transposed to the skin of the ordinary perceiver.

Since touch detects arrangements of surfaces, and edges and corners of surfaces are shown in visual outline drawing, it might be anticipated that raised-line drawings of common objects could be effective stimuli for touch. Recent investigations of simple raised-line drawings of common objects have employed congenitally blind volunteers. The pictures are found to be meaningful to the blind without training in any conventions of depiction (Kennedy, 1993, 1997). Recent studies on skilled blind adults have investigated their abilities to point to targets in a familiar location, to take novel shortcuts after walking an unfamiliar route, and to image three-dimensional layouts.

The centuries since Diderot have been full of debate on the origins of human understanding of space and the role of haptics in the awareness of three-dimensional spatial arrangements. The skills that have been revealed support Diderot's tentative theory: congenitally blind adults have developed a coherent sense of space, with the directions from the observer of objects in the three-dimensional environment well discerned. In contemporary psychology, the weight of the evidence also favors the conception that haptics is a basis for spatial apprehension.

[*See also* Gibson; Nonverbal Bodily Sign Categories; Receptors; Space; *and* Umwelt.]

BIBLIOGRAPHY

Gibson, J. J. "Observations on Active Touch." *Psychological Review* 69 (1962): 477–491.

Gibson, J. J. *The Senses Considered as Perceptual Systems.* Boston: Houghton Mifflin, 1966.

Gordon, G., ed. *Active Touch: The Mechanism of Recognition of Objects by Manipulation.* Oxford: Pergamon Press, 1978.

Katz, D. *The World of Touch* (1975). Edited and translated by L. E. Krueger. Hillsdale, N.J.: Erlbaum, 1989.

Kennedy, J. M. *Drawing and the Blind: Pictures to Touch.* New Haven: Yale University Press, 1993.

Kennedy, J. M. "How the Blind Draw." *Scientific American* 276 (1997): 76–81.

Kirman, J. H. "Tactile Communication of Speech." *Psychological Bulletin* 80 (1973): 54–74.

Magee, L. E., and J. M. Kennedy. "Exploring Pictures Tactually." *Nature* 283 (1980): 287–288.

Revesz, G. "System der optischen und haptischen Ramausschungen." *Zeitschrift für Psychologie* 131 (1934): 296–375.

Revesz, G. *Psychology and Art of the Blind.* Translated by H. A. Wolff. London: Longmans, Green, 1950.

Weber, E. H. *The Sense of Touch.* Edited by J. D. Mollon. New York: Academic Press, 1978.

—JOHN M. KENNEDY

HERALDRY. Strictly speaking, the term *heraldry* simply designates the activity of heralds, but it most often refers in contemporary speech to what might perhaps be more properly called *armory*—in other words to that specific part of the herald's activity that deals with the design, description, attribution, and study of achievements of arms, usually referred to as coats of arms. The description of arms, which is an important heraldic activity in its own right, with its own rules and vocabulary, is called *blazon*. The word *heraldry*, which derives from the Old French *herault*, has itself been in use for a period of time much briefer than that of the set of activities it describes, which was first attested to in English during the middle years of the sixteenth century, by which time the rules governing the attribution and design of arms had been firmly codified.

The first heralds themselves had duties similar to those of town criers, though they quickly became privileged messengers for kings and nobles, normally with immunity from persecution at the hands of their lord's enemies, to whom they could thus be sent to present and discuss terms. The popularity of tournaments from the thirteenth century onward provided new opportunities for heralds to exercise the special knowledge of arms that they had acquired in their travels and in meeting knights from many places, since each knight's arms had to be verified prior to the tournament and announced by the heralds before entering the lists. To assist themselves in this activity, heralds devised rolls of arms containing blazons of coats of arms, which have provided us with detailed knowledge of the arms borne by hundreds of medieval knights.

While heralds later ascribed to heraldry origins as ancient as the standards of the tribes of Israel and the eagles identifying the Roman legions, it seems clear that the earliest truly heraldic arms were those that began to be painted in middle years of the twelfth century on the shields of nobles leading their men into battle. The earliest attested occurrence of a depiction of heraldic arms is frequently asserted to be that on the tomb of Geoffroy le Bel, comte d'Anjou, called Plantagenet (1113–1151), located in the cathedral of Le Mans, France; the actual shield depicted is thought to have been given to Geoffroy by King Henry I in May 1127. The practice of taking arms thus coincides with the development of plate armor in Europe. Previously, soldiers had worn metal helmets with simple nose guards, which did not prevent their features from being recognized (see the depictions of English and Norman soldiers and nobles in the Bayeux Tapestry, in which such helmets can be seen clearly, as can the fact that all the Norman knights are bearing shields that contain no heraldic devices). The "pot helmets" that began to be worn in the first half of the twelfth century covered the entire head, including the face, and thus made recognition of the wearer impossible. As both friend and foe needed to be able to recognize one another on the field of battle, distinctive signs were very soon painted on nobles' shields, and these evolved, over approximately the next four hundred years, into what has become the highly codified art of modern heraldry.

A number of other influences contributed to the rapid spread of the practice of painting arms on shields. Following Pope Urban II's appeal to their kings at the council of Clermont in 1095, many Crusaders had already adopted the cross as the symbol that best differentiated them from the Saracens; soldiers of different nationalities bore crosses of different colors so as to be able to know on sight what language their comrades spoke. Returning Crusaders, particularly those who had achieved some renown through their heroism while in the Holy Land, were perhaps more likely than other men to encourage their sons to adopt arms similar or identical to their own. As the practice of painting arms on the shield spread, it quickly became necessary to insure that insofar as possible a knight's arms should be unique to him; as arms proliferated and became ever more differentiated, it also became crucial to insure that one's arms were designed for easy recognition, since the only way to ascertain a given knight's identity in battle was often from his shield.

With the passage of time, it became important for the holder of a given coat of arms to be able to differentiate them not only from those of the holders of other arms but from those borne by members of other branches of his own family. This segmentation is usually achieved through the use of special marks to distinguish otherwise identical sets of arms (in Britain, for example, each son from the first to the tenth has a special mark that must be placed on his father's arms, though the eldest son assumes those arms in his own right on his father's death) by means of coloring parts of the shield differently or by adding, subtracting, or altering one or more charge on the shield. As families intermarry, their arms are frequently combined, or "marshaled" into "quarters," with that part of the arms that gives the family its name being placed in the upper righthand corner of the shield, as seen from the perspective of the bearer. The medieval achievement of arms might thus betoken a knight's own accomplishments and will in any case reveal to the knowledgeable onlooker the history of the knight's origins, parentage, and descent. It is thus doubly a symbol of the knight's status in feudal society, for his relations of kinship as well as his own attainments stand revealed to all who know how to decipher his arms.

The actual markings used on heraldic shields are in large measure derived from the decorative signs commonly used by medieval craftsmen: the bezants or Romanesque coins, the chevrons or stylized rafters, the various forms of cross, star, sun, and wavy or zigzag lines and bars are all found in other use at the time. It seems logical to assume for this reason that as arms became more common, craftsmen simply adapted to shield painting the decorative forms already in use, altering them as necessary to fit the particular shape of the heraldic shield, which itself varied widely from country to country and century to century. The animals in common heraldic use are those also found in medieval bestiaries. In a great many cases, the charges placed on the shield reflect a pun of some kind on the family name; arms so designed are referred to as "canting" arms and are doubtless related to the punning shop signs and rebuses so popular in the late medieval period.

To ensure that arms would be as instantly recognizable as possible, heralds early on adopted certain conventions that came to govern the placement of the various colors in use. Normal heraldic color schemes are restricted to two "metals" (gold and silver, known in heraldry as *or* and *argent*, respectively, and painted as yellow and white), a small number of colors or *tinctures* (among them red or *gules*, green or *vert*, blue or *azure*, purple or *pourpre*, and black or *sable*, with objects depicted in their natural colors being referred to as *proper*), and a few conventional patterns reproducing furs such as ermine and *vair*, the fur of the Siberian squirrel. Since early times, it has been common practice, in order to ensure maximum legibility, not to place one metal, tincture, or fur on another but rather to juxtapose patterns of different categories.

Current practices in heraldry vary widely. In some countries, such as Scotland and England, where there are colleges of arms, the granting of arms, while not restricted to those of noble birth, is matter of some legal import, and in Scotland legal action might be taken against those who unlawfully display arms to which they are not entitled. In other countries, such as France, much greater freedom prevails, and anyone may lawfully design and display his or her own coat of arms, provided the general rules of uniqueness and recognizability are adhered to. This has resulted in the creation of many modern coats of arms that violate the traditional rules of heraldic composition and that are for this reason despised by those who esteem the traditions of heraldry.

While heraldry, properly speaking, is strictly a European invention and code of practice, similar customs exist elsewhere. While aboriginal peoples in many parts of the world have borne decorated shields reminiscent of heraldic arms, two of the most frequently cited analogous phenomena are the totem poles erected by some North American aboriginal peoples and Japanese family signs or *mon*. Neither of these systems is truly heraldic in nature, however Totem poles are indicative of a clan's mythological provenance, rather than its human line of descent, and are more similar in this respect to the heraldic badge than to the coat of arms, which always belongs to an individual rather than to a family. The *mon*, which display some compositional features analogous to those adhered to by heralds, are nonetheless vastly more stylized in their representations of animals and plants than are most coats of arms; Japanese artists were doubtless more constrained in this regard by the fact that the most frequent geometric basis for *mon* design is the circle. Like the earliest heraldic signs, however, *mon* were often used as rallying points for soldiers in battle, where their placement on banners ensured their ready visibility.

[*See also* Aniconic Visual Signs; Blazon; Code; Face; Logo; *and* Trademark.]

BIBLIOGRAPHY

Brooke-Little, J. P. *An Heraldic Alphabet*. London: MacDonald, 1973.

Fox-Davies, A. C. *A Complete Guide to Heraldry*. London: Thomas Nelson and Sons, 1954.

Franklyn, J. *Heraldry*. South Brunswick, N.Y.: A. S. Barnes and Company, 1968.

Franklyn, J., and J. Tanner. *An Encyclopaedic Dictionary of Heraldry*. Oxford: Pergamon Press, 1969.

Neubecker, O., and J. P. Brooke-Little. *Heraldry: Sources, Symbols, and Meaning*. London: MacDonald and Co., 1988.

von Volborth, C.-A. *Heraldry: Customs, Rules, and Styles*. Poole, Dorset: Blandford Press, 1981.

—DAVID GRAHAM

HISTORY. A survey of contemporary and classic semiotic literature finds very few references to history, even to the history of semiotics. The analytic method employed by most semioticians is itself either atemporal or relies on some abstract dynamism. Since semiotics mostly performs reversible operations on relatively closed systems, it would seem, at first glance, to be at the opposite pole from history. However, since Claude Lévi-Strauss's attempts to open up a theoretical space for a category of history in his semiotic model, history and semiotics have become increasingly open to one another. Although there does not exist yet a fully developed semiotics of history, a range of scholars working with historical material have come under the influence of structuralism and semiotics.

The paradigm of structuralism is associated with Lévi-Strauss, who, like Ferdinand de Saussure, employed a radical dualism that effectively marginalized history. In addition to the Saussurean oppositional categories of synchrony and diachrony, Lévi-Strauss proposed a distinction based on ethnological criteria: "hot" versus "cold" societies. The former, essentially those of the West and to a lesser degree the civilizations of Asia, include change as an integral part of their material and cognitive universe; cold societies, on the other hand, are those characteristically (and, at the time, exclusively) studied by anthropologists. Small-scale "primitive" cultures are essentially well-integrated synchronic structures for which the least exogenous change is threatening. They are closed universes: to the degree that they deal with the outside world at all, such contacts are mediated by the formal principle of structural transformation. Cold societies are, nevertheless, shaped by historical forces. For Lévi-Strauss, these forces can be identified with statistical demographic shifts, which are engaged in a dialectic with structure. "Primitives" are natural *bricoleurs* (tinkerers), fashioning and refashioning structures from materials at hand.

Myth is the central discourse of change in cold societies. In myth, the past is literally re-presented. That is, past events are translated onto the plane of synchrony and thereby impinge upon the present. In his four-volume work on myth, Lévi-Strauss treats especially a class of events that transcends mere history, involving the transition from nature to culture. This transformation is viewed in part as an irreversible Promethean act but also as a reversible synchronic structure that mediates between humans and natural species, as well as between cultured and uncultured humans. Raw versus cooked, improper versus proper social distance in marriage, and other oppositions expressed in myth lay down the framework for the social order. In a sense, cold societies are "frozen" not because of ignorance of their past but because of the extremely powerful ways in which its representation constrains, at the unconscious level, the possibilities for action.

The stability of cold societies belies their extreme fragility when faced with actual exogenous historical change. The appearance of the simplest object, such as a steel axe, has potentially devastating effects by introducing new categories of conceptual and social relations. The ability of structure to mediate this change is strained severely, although attempts are made in the form of bricolage: organizing the flotsam and jetsam of history into a semicoherent structure somewhat resembling the original. From the perspective of cold societies, history, in the sense of contact with the West, thus appears as little more than entropy against which structure, successfully or unsuccessfully, battles.

In *The Story of Lynx* (1991), Lévi-Strauss concerns himself more specifically with the historical implications of mythic structures, seeing the motif of twins in Amerindian myths as a model of asymmetrical dualism in which both halves of the whole define the social world and cosmos. This dualism implies the existence of a fundamental other—a category that is filled by the European upon arrival in the New World. Lévi-Strauss demonstrates how myths involving twins are transformed to include the white man without altering the basic mythic structure. While this is an interesting problem—how mythic and other structures condition cultures to respond to contact and invasion—Lévi-Strauss does little more than raise the issue.

The foremost implementer of structuralism in historical analysis is the anthropologist Marshall Sahlins, who refines the structuralist paradigm while retaining its fundamental problematic: the opposition of structure and history. For him, history is structured by cosmological, mythic, and sociological forms (which are seen as essentially homologous). Cultures are predisposed to certain types of transformation, such as the Fijian axiom that a chief is a conqueror who comes from afar. The overthrow of an established polity by a foreigner can thus be seen as a reproduction of a structure of the long run.

In an encounter between cultures, each culture brings its own structures and structuring acts. On some points, these might be congruent. Thus, both the Maori and the British read the raising of a flagpole with the Union Jack as a symbolic act. In 1845, the Maori hero Hone Heke ferociously attacked the British outpost as Kororareka in New Zealand, not to destroy the settlement but to cut down the flagpole, which he succeeded in doing four times. For the British, the flagpole (or, rather, the flag itself) was indeed an important symbol of British rights and hopes for sovereignty in New Zealand. For the Maori, it was more than that: a claim of ownership over the entire land. This view was based upon the Maori creation myth, in which the earth and sky are separated by a pole; the erection of any pole was thus a commemoration, a re-presentation of the initial constituting act. Hone Heke's revolt is an instance of mythopraxis—the acting out of mythic structures in historical practice.

In the colonial history of the Maori, and even more in that of the Hawaiians, it is clear that structural disjunction, not reproduction, characterizes the process. To explain the radical break with the past in structural terms requires a model of historical praxis.

The dialectic of history and praxis offers a more sophisticated account of structural change than does Lévi-Strauss's dualism. Sahlins considers the extraordinary events on the island of Hawaii in the period 1778–1819. This forty-year period began with the arrival of Captain James Cook and ended with King Kamehameha II's revolutionary and self-destructive overturning of the taboo system, in effect capitulating to the ascendant colonial forces. This is not a history of battles but rather one of signs.

Returning to Saussure's analysis of the sign, Sahlins examines cultural symbols such as the taboo system in terms of the relationships between the sign and referent and between the sign and other signs. The function of reference is essentially dialectical: a sign might refer to "objects" (which are themselves mediated symbolically), but the objects in turn have an effect on the meaning of the sign. The very act of reference not only imposes semiotic structure on experience but introduces potentially new relations of denotation and connotation. As a sign, *taboo* stands for a range of categorical oppositions: between sacred and profane, nobleman and commoner, male and female, reserved and communal property. As the Europeans arrived on the scene, the noble class attempted to use the taboo category to monopolize relations with these powerful outsiders, seen at first as themselves taboo, in the sense of *sacred*. The new referential domain of taboo including Europeans was thus vulnerable to actions by the Europeans themselves, especially in violating other aspects of the taboo system. All that was salvageable in the end was the application of taboo to property, which was exploited by the noblemen to dominate trade. Sahlins thus provides an account that views semiosis, not demography or technology, as history's primary field of battle.

Louis Althusser posits a structuralist historical dynamic grounded on his reading of Karl Marx. As with the Annales school, the human subject is effectively removed, leaving the transformation of impersonal and normally invisible structures to determine historical change. Maurice Godelier, a student of Lévi-Strauss, attempted to create an anthropological application of structural Marxism, which rather than analyzing history has focused on synchrony against the background of evolutionary models of change. The concern with the textuality of history has characterized the work of a number of scholars working in overlapping fields influenced by structuralism.

Paul Ricoeur, whose hermeneutics borrows from Lévi-Strauss and structural linguistics, is concerned with the mimetic properties of narrative—the ability of historical texts to represent authentically the human experience of time. Poststructuralists, on the other hand, practice what Ricoeur calls "the hermeneutics of suspicion"; they wish to show the means by which historical discourse establishes its authority.

This attention to authorial strategies is identified most closely with the work of the American historian Hayden White, who examines representational strategies in terms of master tropes such as irony and metonymy, correlating them with literary genres (romance, tragedy, etc.) and with political philosophies. He thus strongly connects the discourse of history with contemporary political interests through his thorough analysis of narrative strategies. Roland Barthes explores similar themes in his studies of historian Jules Michelet and historical discourse. His concept of the "reality effect" of historical discourse approaches the Ricoeurean problem of the mimetic relationship between text and referent. He demonstrates semiotic "slippage" within the sign relationship so that the signified replaces the referent—that is, discourse becomes reality, much as in Sahlins's analysis of slippage between sign and referent.

The "archaeological" approach of Michel Foucault to intellectual and social history represents a sea change in the fields of semiotics and history. His main interest has been the official discourse of the human sciences in Western Europe in the eighteenth and nineteenth centuries. In particular, he examines medical, anthropological, and penological discourses and, most important, correlates them with the exercise and techniques of power. Like the philosopher of science Thomas Kuhn, Foucault sees communities of discourse established around organizing concepts, which he calls epistemes. Scientific discourse does not progress gradually and progressively but rather is subject to paradigm shifts. For this reason, one must employ an archaeological approach to excavate prior discourses upon which contemporary discourses are built. For Foucault, discourse is inseparable from the institutionalization of power, and the entire post-Enlightenment history of the West is a bleak story of the invention, perfection, and deployment of technologies of power. One possible criticism of Foucault is this very essentialism of power, which as a concept is never itself questioned or placed in ethnographic context, essentially ignoring the fact that different cultures employ different concepts and practices of power.

In perhaps the most direct application of semiotic analysis to historical data, Tzvetan Todorov addressed the historical paradox of Hernán Cortes's conquest of Mexico. How a small band of Spaniards militarily conquered and occupied an empire larger than Spain itself has long been an intriguing problem. Technological and tactical explanations have been popular, as has been the idea that Cortes was mistaken for the god Quetzalcoatl. Working within this latter tradition, Todorov sees the issue as one of semiosis, of the flexibility and creativity of the respective sign systems. He sees a direct correlation between the sophistication of the writing systems of the three great American civilizations—Inca, Aztec, and Maya—and their ability to incorporate the appearance of the white man within their discourse. Moctezuma's inability to act pragmatically with respect to Cortes, although he demonstrated practical logic in other matters, is attributed to the "overdetermined and overinterpreted" discursive world of the Aztecs.

Soviet semiotics has shown a marked concern for history; both Valentin N. Voloshinov and Mikhail Bakhtin are associated with a more historical semiotics. Rejecting Saussurean assumptions of a monolithic, anonymous, synchronic *langue*, they have focused on historically, socially, and politically situated discourse. The universe of communication is inherently much more open and indeterminate. Bakhtin's notion of heteroglossia—a state of the world in which different languages, dialects, and speech registers are present simultaneously—is especially productive in this connection: it challenges many of the assumptions of Saussure-inspired linguistics and cultural anthropology and provides a basis for understanding intercultural events in both language and history.

Primarily a literary scholar, Bakhtin developed core concepts that have wide-ranging applications to history and anthropology. In his study of François Rabelais, Bakhtin develops the concept of carnival as a counterdiscourse that challenges and undermines the dominant, monologic discourse. Stasis, closure, and control are abandoned in favor of process, openness to the outside (exotopy), and freedom. The dangerous margins of the body that are the foci of Rabelaisian grotesque implicate the tabooed margins of society. This concept takes on a poignancy when seen in the light of Bakhtin's difficult life under Stalinism. Antistructural institutions, such as medieval carnival, riots, and rites of passage have become increasingly important in both history and anthropology. Building on Bakhtin as well as the work of historians Emmanuel LeRoy Ladurie, Natalie Zemon Davis, Edward P. Thompson, and anthropologist Victor Turner, a younger generation of scholars has subverted the synchronic assumptions of orthodox structuralism. Structure is historicized by virtue of its dialogical relationship to antistructure.

"Practice theorists" in France, primarily Pierre Bourdieu and Michel de Certeau, have constructed a framework that makes possible a historical semiotics. Bourdieu's habitus is a meaningful structure but fundamentally "looser" and more open to individual action and to history than are Saussurean structures. In practice theory, the acts of everyday life are shown to be culturally constructed but not determined. Strategies, negotiations, and creative acts are all fully possible within this world. As in the Annales School, the minutiae of life are examined as indexes and determinants of historical processes. The utility of practice theory in historical anthropology has been demonstrated in the United States by Sherry Ortner, among others.

The Annales School of historiography was founded in Strasbourg by Marc Bloch and Lucien Febvre in 1929. In contrast to the Rankean "grand school," Annales historiography focused on the humble, the provincial, the obscure. New methods, especially archival research and statistical analysis, brought historiography fully into the social sciences. In part an attempt to discover, Annales historiography focused on entire societies in all their complexity. Rather than the master trope of great men as metaphors for their ages, Annales historians pursued a metonymic strategy in which a minute examination of a part might throw light on the whole.

The second generation of Annales historians is personified by Fernand Braudel. Strongly influenced by Lévi-Strauss, Braudel seizes upon the notion of structure as an unconscious, elementary, and formal pattern of oppositions that determines events at the surface level (la parole). He suggests an analogy between the deep structures of kinship and language and the structures of the longue durée, the time frame that pertains to geological and ecological processes. Other time frames to be considered are the conjuncture, the more human time frame of cultural structures, and the événementielle, which is "a history of short, sharp, nervous vibrations."

The goal of Annales School historiography, best exemplified by Braudel's work, is total history. In his two monumental works on the Mediterranean and on the rise of capitalism, Braudel leaves few stones unturned. In the former, he begins with a history written, as it were, from the perspective of the Mediterranean Sea itself—radically challenging the subjectivity of humanistic history—before moving on in the second volume to a more familiar social and political history. Ultimately, his three historical levels are intertwined, and each can only be understood with reference to the others. Braudel and the other Annalistes, however, privilege material determinants. Economics, demographics, and ecology represent the heart of the annaliste analysis.

Lucien Febvre's work, unlike other Annaliste historiography, emphasizes mental structures. Later generations of Annales-trained historians turned increasingly to reconstructing the mental worlds of societies and groups, thus coming into close proximity to cultural anthropology. Semiotically oriented cultural anthropologists such as Edmund Leach, Claude Lévi-Strauss, and Clifford Geertz are cited increasingly. By the time of the publication of Robert Darnton's *The Great Cat Massacre* (1984), we see an active blurring of genres. Darnton is influenced at least as much by Geertz, in both his theory and rhetorical strategy, as by the Annales School. Darnton and other *mentalistes* such as Emmanuel LeRoy Ladurie do not employ a strictly semiotic approach but rather a loose interpretivism that, in Darnton's words, "work[s] back and forth between text and context." The abandonment of the structuralism of Braudel has placed later historians of France squarely in a humanistic framework, albeit one influenced by anthropology, hermeneutics, and semiotics.

A renewed interest in history among cultural anthropologists has resulted in a number of interesting and theoretically subtle studies. Drawing on a symbolic anthropology, a loose amalgam of semiotic and hermeneutic theories taken from such diverse sources as Lévi-Strauss, Max Weber, Marx, Emile Durkheim, and Edward Sapir, cultural anthropologists began to focus their attention on history, forsaking the rhetorical trope of the "ethnographic present." As long maintained by Marxists and political economists, history was shown to be fully culturally mediated rather than an a priori structure.

Perhaps the most theoretically rigorous of these studies is by Richard Parmentier (1987), who employs a Peircean semiotic model. He transcends the inherent limitations of Saussurean semiotics, especially its lack of a pragmatic dimension. This pragmatic focus is the study's strong point, as it demonstrates how historical representations—signs of history—may be deployed as signs *in* history, affecting actual historical processes. His concern for discourse—that is, the construction of historical meaning—is characteristic of recent anthropological studies.

The work of Jean and John Comaroff (1991) on the Tswana of southern Africa has employed an eclectic semiotic model to examine processes of cultural domination and resistance. Their analysis of the body as a field of semiotic contestation has been particularly compelling. Renato Rosaldo's (1980) work on Ilongot history explores the intersection of narrative, transformation of social structure, and world-historical forces in a small, isolated society. James Boon's (1982) dense postmodernist work on Bali attempts to bring together diverse cultural and historical data within postmodern interpretive rhetoric. Recent Oceanian work brings together many of these concerns along with the traditional Polynesianist interest in myth.

Within fields such as cultural anthropology and literary studies, long influenced by semiotics, historical questions have become central. Conversely, in historical disciplines, semiotic models, usually mediated by anthropology, have given impetus to new types of exploration. Intellectual boundaries between fields have become increasingly porous; remaining differences are primarily in disciplinary praxis. It is worthwhile to historicize this very development within the human sciences. Why have disciplines that were founded in a rejection of nineteenth-century historicism, cultural anthropology (especially of the American school), linguistics, and semantic philosophy taken a historical turn? Is it the effect of the "disappearing savage" or perhaps of the limitations of a rigorously formal theory of meaning? Does Clio's turn to the social sciences and away from the humanities signify, as Jean Baudrillard and other postmodernists have argued, the millennial disappear- ance of the human subject? All of these seem at best partial explanations.

Whatever the source and direction of this paradigm shift, it has proved productive. On the epistemological level, meaning is increasingly seen as a process, an emergent phenomenon located at the middle levels of structure, whether these structures

are linguistic, sociological, or historical. While methods more rigorous than the working back and forth between text and context of Geertz or Darnton are called for, the rapprochement between historical and semiotic disciplines provides fertile ground for the development of new insights, methods, and questions.

[*See also* Althusser; Bakhtin; Bourdieu; Foucault; Lévi-Strauss; Myths; Poststructuralism; Structuralism; *and* Synchronic and Diachronic.]

BIBLIOGRAPHY

Biersack, A., ed. *Clio in Oceania: Toward A Historical Anthropology.* Washington, D.C.: Smithsonian Institution Press, 1991.

Boon, J. *Other Tribes, Other Scribes: Symbolic Anthropology in the Comparative Study of Cultures, Histories, Religions, and Texts.* New York: Cambridge University Press, 1982.

Braudel, F. *The Structures of Everyday Life.* New York: Harper and Row, 1981.

Comaroff, J., and J. Comaroff. *Revelation and Revolution: Christianity, Colonialism, and Consciousness in South Africa.* Chicago: University of Chicago Press, 1991.

Darnton, R. *The Great Cat Massacre and Other Episodes in French Cultural History.* New York: Basic Books, 1984.

Febvre, L. *The Problem of Unbelief in the Sixteenth Century: The Religion of Rabelais.* Translated by B. Gottlieb. Cambridge, Mass.: Harvard University Press, 1982.

Foucault, M. *The Archaeology of Knowledge and the Discourse on Language.* Translated by A. M. Sheridan Smith. New York: Pantheon, 1972.

Haidu, P. "Semiotics and History." *Semiotica* 40 (1982): 187–228.

Lévi-Strauss, C. *The Story of Lynx* (1991). Translated by C. Tihanyi. Chicago: University of Chicago Press, 1995.

Parmentier, R. *The Sacred Remains.* Chicago: University of Chicago Press, 1987.

Ricoeur, P. "Structure, Word, Event." Translated by R. Sweeney. In *The Conflict of Interpretations: Essays in Hermeneutics,* edited by D. Ihde, pp. 79–96. Evanston: Northwestern University Press, 1974.

Rosaldo, R. *Ilongot Headhunting, 1883–1974: A Study of Society and History.* Stanford: Stanford University Press, 1980.

Sahlins, M. *Historical Metaphors and Mythical Realities.* Ann Arbor: University of Michigan Press, 1981.

Sahlins, M. *Islands of History.* Chicago: University of Chicago Press, 1985.

Todorov, T. *The Conquest of America.* Translated by R. Howard. New York: Harper and Row, 1984.

—MICHAEL HARKIN

HJELMSLEV, LOUIS (1899–1965), Danish linguist and semiotician, author of an original theory of

verbal and other sign systems called glossematics, which attempts to radicalize Ferdinand de Saussure's claim that language is form rather than substance. According to glossematics, any scientific study of language must analyze language as a hierarchy of interrelated formal functions. The analysis of any concrete linguistic element is carried out as a calculus of combinations of such functions. Due to their general character, the theoretical foundations and methodological principles of glossematics have had a greater impact in semiotics than in linguistics. This theoretical approach is identified with the Copenhagen School of linguistics.

Hjelmslev was educated in comparative philology but took an early interest in logical and theoretical problems, influenced by among others his father, who was a well-known mathematician. After studying in Lithuania, Hjelmslev visited two important centers of structural linguistics, Prague in 1923–1924 and Paris in 1926–1927. His first major works, *Principes de grammaire générale* (1928) and *La catégorie des cas* (1935–1937) appeared in French.

In his general grammar, Hjelmslev tries to articulate the basic principles for a description of language as form. The grammar itself is a system of forms from which the specific forms of any natural language can be generated. These forms are obtained inductively from an analysis of the syntactical chain. Although his book on case foregrounds morphology and semantics, Hjelmslev still attempts to isolate a few formal features from which all possible manifestations of case can be constructed through calculated combinations. The center of a given case system, called an intensive case, is established inductively, but it acquires its status as a true linguistic element only through the system to which it belongs. Such systems of interrelated elements function according to two general language-specific structural principles: (1) the differences between the elements are more fundamental than the elements themselves; and (2) the elements enter into the system through participation—that is, certain cases, called extensive cases, can absorb or take over the role of the intensive cases, or they might occupy a neutral position, being alternatively extensive and intensive. Hjelmslev justifies his ideas through a vast array of linguistic material.

These two early works are examples of a structural but preglossematic linguistics: they try to develop a description of language as an immanent system of forms, though it is based on elements that are identified through induction—that is, on a nonformal basis. Gradually, Hjelmslev moves from philology and toward a linguistics of pure forms, discarding all inductive knowledge as nonscientific and all nonformal foundation as metaphysical or psychological, thus marking his explicit opposition to both Viggo Brøndal's linguistics and to the Prague School, respectively.

The culmination of his work is the creation of glossematics. The essentials of the theory are contained in *Prolegomena to a Theory of Language* (1943) and *Résumé of a Theory of Language* (1975). Only the first was published during his lifetime, but both were prepared as an inseparable pair during the 1930s: *Prolegomena* was intended to be the popular version of the theory, *Résumé* the strictly scientific presentation. Instead of linguistic definitions based on distinctive features (i.e., element-bound formal properties), glossematics attempts to establish definitions based on functions (i.e., element-independent relations). Although Hjelmslev states repeatedly that he is working on a linguistic theory with general perspectives, the general system of relations takes priority over the specific elements of the system. The semiotic success and the linguistic failure of Hjelmslev's theory can be attributed to the glossematic turn.

In this system, all linguistic elements are defined exclusively by their mutual relations, called their functions. The aim of linguistic analysis is to transform features (such as case, syntactical position, word class, past tense, glottal stop, etc.) into functions, rather than to generalize from the features. Therefore, the linguistic object will be constituted by the method through which the analysis is carried out.

For a text, the method is a procedure of dichotomous partitions of the text. The units isolated at each step of the analysis are defined by their relations to other units through one of three possible relations: mutual interrelation (interdependence), unilateral dependence (determination), and simple coocurence (constellation). The units do not have any properties beyond this functional definition. As the possible functions are given, the analysis is a calculus of the specific distribution of possible functions in a text. The ultimate goal is to turn all linguistically relevant aspects of a text into constants, which are the two units in an interdependent relation or one of the units under unilateral dependence. The structure of a given language phenomenon is the system of relations between the constants. The other unit of a unilateral dependence and the simply cooccurent units are the variables. When the partition has established relations of constants, the analysis is completed and is considered exhaustive. If more than one analysis is possible, the simplest (i.e., the one with the fewest analytical steps) must be preferred. Furthermore, the analysis has to be noncontradictory—no unit must receive more than one definition. These three criteria constitute Hjelmslev's so-called empirical principle.

The basic linguistic units here are called *figurae*. As they have no content except their function, no units are predetermined as expression units or content units. What we call expression and what we call content is an arbitrary choice. This consequence, shocking as it might sound, is the basis of the semiotic influence of Hjelmslev's theory because it points to a radically formal definition of the sign.

The sign is defined as a mutual interdependence between two formally defined planes, the expression plane and the content plane. The two interrelated forms—the expression form and the content form—are the constants of the two planes. However, they also contain variables—namely, the expression substance and the content substance (the last characterized only very vaguely by Hjelmslev). These two substances are articulated by the respective forms so as to bring about a manifested sign in a specific expression substance (for example, a natural language) and in a specific content substance (for example, the psychological content of a text). The variables of substance have to be studied by other sciences in order to acquire formal status as constants.

The consequence of this formal definition of the sign is twofold. First, it allows for an analysis of the content plane of the sign following the same basic principles as the analysis of the expression plane. This is the basis of structural semantics as indicated by Hjelmslev in "Pour une sémantique structurale" (1957, in *Essais linguistiques*, 1959): semantics as adapted phonology. This project was carried out in most detail by Algirdas J. Greimas (1917–1992). The emphasis on pure form also implies that the expression substance is irrelevant for the principles of the analysis: glossematics is applicable to any sign system. A sign system in general is called a semiotic.

Second, since the sign is a formal unit, the sign as a whole can be a content form or an expression form.

As a result, natural language as such is no longer the basic sign system. Natural language is the basic system only when regarded as a denotative semiotic—that is, only when it is considered embedded in a hierarchy of semiotics. Thus, the signs of a given sign system might have the signs of another sign system as their content plane, in which case it is a metasemiotic. If the signs of another sign system are its expression plane, then it is a connotative semiotic. The hierarchy may continue with metametasemiotics and so on. The ultimate goal of this progressive hierarchical stratification is to make a metasemiotic on a higher level transform the variables of the semiotics on the lower levels into constants.

Although the rigid immanence of glossematic structuralism is the main reason for its widespread influence in semiotics, Hjelmslev himself had some doubts about its merits in his later years. In "La stratification du langage" (1954, in *Essais linguistiques*, 1959), he tries to look also upon the two substances of the sign as stratified hierarchies, although not strictly formal ones. This late essay can be read as Hjelmslev's attempt to integrate the variables that are otherwise discarded from the theory in an acute awareness of its limits. One of the three content-substance levels in particular, described as the culturally shared set of collective opinions, shows that it will be necessary to integrate the external-communication situation in the definition of the content plane. The content form alone will not suffice for a scientific linguistic analysis. In one of his last works, "Some Reflexions on Practice and Theory in Structural Semantics" (1961), Hjelmslev even admits that the entire analysis might end up with indefinables of simple behavior situations such as, "I am here, you are there"—elements that constitute language as a process of enunciation and not as an immanent structure.

Hjelmslev's importance in semiotics is a result of his rigorous attempt to turn Saussure's heterogenous and somewhat flexible structuralism into a theory of maximal explicitness and conceptual homogeneity on all levels. Moreover, his willingness to reconsider, albeit somewhat reluctantly, the formal limits of his theory sets the standard for any serious semiotic research.

[*See also* Brøndal; Copenhagen School; Denotation and Connotation; Recent Theories on the Nature of the Language Sign; *and* Recherches Structurales 1949.]

BIBLIOGRAPHY

Hjelmslev, L. *Prolegomena to a Theory of Language* (1943). Translated by F. J. Whitfield. Madison: University of Wisconsin Press, 1961.

Hjelmslev, L. *Essais linguistiques*. Travaux du Cercle Linguistique de Copenhague, vol. 12. Copenhagen: Nordisk Sprog- og Kulturforlag, 1959.

Hjelmslev, L. *Language: An Introduction*. Translated by F. J. Whitfield. Madison: University of Wisconsin Press, 1970.

Hjelmslev, L. *Résumé of a Theory of Language*. Edited and translated by F. J. Whitfield. Madison: University of Wisconsin Press, 1975.

Rasmussen, M. *Hjelmslevs sprogteori*. Copenhagen, 1992. This volume includes a summary in French and a complete bibliography.

Rasmussen, M., ed. *Louis Hjelmslev et la sémiotique contemporaine*. Travaux du Cercle Linguistique de Copenhague, vol. 24. Copenhagen, 1993. This volume includes contributions in both English and French.

Siertsema, B. *A Study of Glossematics: Critical Survey of Its Fundamental Concepts*. The Hague: M. Nijhoff, 1955.

—SVEND ERIK LARSEN

I

I CHING. *See* Yi jing.

ICON. A technical term derived from ancient Greek *eikōn* (image, representation), in its most common religious sense and in art history *icon* refers to a pictorial representation of persons or events derived from the tradition of Christianity. (For a semiotic treatment of this pictorial genre, see Uspenskij, 1976). In the jargon of computer programming or in cognitive psychology (e.g., Kolers, 1977) the term *icon* is used to designate all visual things or whatever is laid out graphically. In semiotic terminology, *icon* has a special meaning that is derived from the work of Charles Sanders Peirce: an icon is a sign in which the "thing" serving as expression is, in one or another respect, similar to or shares properties with another "thing," which serves as its content. In fact, if we follow Peirce, there are two further requirements: not only should the relation connecting the two things exist independently of the sign relation, just as is the case with an index, but in addition the properties of the two things should inhere in them independently.

Thus, icons in the religious sense are not particularly good instances of icons in the semiotic sense, for they are, as Uspenskij has shown, subject to several conventions determining the kind of perspective that may be employed and the kind of things and persons that may be represented in different parts of the picture. Contrary to the icons of computer programs and those of cognitive psychology, iconic signs may occur in any sense modality; for example, in audition, notably in verbal language; as onomatopoetic words, and in the form of morphological regularities and syntactical symmetries (Jakobson, 1965) and in music (Osmond-Smith, 1972). Not all visual signs are iconic in the semiotic sense; indeed, many icons found in computer programs are actually aniconic visual signs.

In most cases, when reference is made to icons in semiotics, what is actually meant is what Peirce termed *hypo-icons*—that is, signs that involve iconic-ity but also to a great extent indexical or symbolic (conventional or, perhaps more generally, rulelike) properties. Peirce outlined three kinds of hypo-icons: images, in which the similarity between expression and content is one of "simple qualities"; diagrams, in which the similarity is one of "analogous relations in their parts"; and metaphors, in which the relations of similarity are brought to an even further degree of mediation. Diagrams in the sense of ordinary language are also diagrams in the Peircean sense, though the Peircean concept is much broader, as is the notion of metaphor, which would, for instance, also include a thermometer. Moreover, no matter how we choose to understand the simplicity of "simple qualities" in the Peircean category of images, this will not include ordinary pictures (which would be metaphors of metaphors). In this sense, a Peircean image might be a color sample used to select paint.

Contrary to the ways in which icons have been conceived in later semiotic schools, diagrams, rather than pictures, are at the core of Peircean iconicity: indeed, mathematical formulas and deductive schemes, which are based on conventional signs, are the most often discussed instances of iconicity in his work. There is still another sense in which pictures are far from being central instances of icons: the fact that an object serving as the expression of an icon and another object serving as its content possess some of the same properties should not be a result of one of them having an influence on the other. In the case of an icon (unlike an index), "it simply happens that its qualities resemble those of that object, and excite analogous sensations in the mind for which it is a likeness" (Peirce, 1931–1958, vol. 2, p. 299). Since both Franklin and Rumford are Americans, Peirce claims, one of them may serve as a sign of the other; but the fact that Franklin is an American is quite unrelated to Rumford being one. There is, however, at least one sense in which this is not true not only of a photograph (which Peirce often pronounces to be an index) but also in the case of a painting or an image on a computer screen: in each case, the thing serving as the expression is constructed expressly in order to resemble the thing serving as the content, although a direct physical connection exists only in the first instance. Leonardo da Vinci painted the canvas known as *Mona Lisa* in order to create a resemblance of the wife of Francesco del Giocondo, and, although the resemblance is of a much more abstract kind, the same is true of Pablo Picasso portraying Gertrude Stein. And it is as true of a synthetic computer picture showing a lamp as of a photograph with the same subject.

When used to stand for themselves, objects are clearly iconical: they are signs consisting of an expression that stands for a content because of properties that each of them possess intrinsically. And yet, without having access to a set of conventions or an array of stock situations, we have no possibility of knowing neither *that* something is a sign nor what it is a sign of, whether of itself as an individual object, of a particular category of which it is a member, or of one or another of its properties. A car, which is not a sign on the street, becomes one at a car exhibition. We have to know the showcase convention to understand that the tin can in the shop window stands for many other objects of the same category; we need to be familiar with the art-exhibition convention to realize that each object merely signifies itself; and we are able to understand that the tailor's swatch is a sign of its pattern and color but not of its shape only if we learned the convention associated with tailoring.

Convention is thus needed to establish not only the sign character but also the very iconicity of these icons. Since iconicity can be perceived only once a particular variety of the sign function is known to obtain, the resulting icons are termed *secondary* (Sonesson, 1994). This also applies to "droodles," a kind of limiting case of a picture exemplified by Annibale Caracci's (1560–1609) trick drawings such as the "key," in which a triangle above a horizontal line is discovered to represent a mason behind a stone wall, once we are told so, as well as by the manual signs of the North American Indians, which, according to Mallery (1881), seem reasonable when we are informed about their meanings.

In these cases, knowledge about the sign function already obtaining between the two things involved is clearly a prerequisite to the discovery of their iconicity. The opposite case, in which the perception of iconicity functions as one of the reasons for pos-

tulating a sign relation, seems more germane to Peirce's conception of the icon. Such a primary icon is actually realized by the picture sign. Indeed, we know from child psychology and anthropology that no particular training is needed for a human being to perceive a surface as a picture. The possibility of this feat remains a mystery: the properties possessed in common by the picture and what it represents are extremely abstract. It has been suggested that picture perception is only possible because there is a taken-for-granted hierarchy of things in the world of everyday life that makes certain objects and materials more probable sign vehicles than others.

[*See also* Aniconic Visual Signs; Diagram; Iconicity; Image and Picture; Index; Indexicality; Peirce; *and* Picture Perception.]

BIBLIOGRAPHY

Jakobson, R. "A la recherche de l'essence du language." *Diogène* 51 (1965): 22–38.

Jakobson, R. *Selected Writings 3: Poetry of Grammar and Grammar of Poetry.* The Hague: Mouton, 1981.

Johansen, J. D. *Dialogic Semiosis.* Bloomington: Indiana University Press, 1993.

Kolers, P. "Reading Pictures and Reading Text." In *The Arts and Cognition*, edited by D. Perkins and B. Leondar, pp. 136–164. London and Baltimore: Johns Hopkins University Press, 1977.

Mallery, G. *Sign Language among North American Indians* (1881). The Hague: Mouton, 1972.

Morris, C. *Signs, Language, and Behavior* (1946). Reprinted in C. Morris, *Writings on the General Theory of Signs*, pp. 73–398. The Hague: Mouton, 1971.

Osmond-Smith, D. "The Iconic Process in Musical Communication." *Versus* 3 (1972): 31–42.

Peirce, C. S. *Collected Papers*, 8 vols. Edited by C. Hartshorne, P. Weiss, and A. Burks. Cambridge, Mass.: Harvard University Press, 1931–1958.

Sonesson, G. "Sémiotique visuelle et écologie sémiotique." *Recherches Sémiotiques/Semiotic Inquiry* 14.1–2 (1994): 31–48.

Uspenskij, B. *Semiotics of the Russian Icon.* Lisse: Peter de Ridder Press, 1976.

—GÖRAN SONESSON

ICONICITY. Conceived in strictly Peircean terms, iconicity is one of the three relationships in which a representamen (expression) may stand to its object (content or referent) and that may be taken as the ground for their forming a sign; more precisely, it is the first kind of these relationships, termed *firstness*, "the idea of that which is such at it is regardless of anything else" (Peirce, 1931–1958, vol. 5, p. 66), as it applies to the relation in question. More loosely, iconicity refers to the similarity or identity that might exist between the expression and the content of a sign.

The study of iconicity sometimes consists of a mere exegesis of the texts of Charles Sanders Peirce (1839–1914) on the matter. The understanding of Peircean iconicity must start with the notion of iconic ground. The ground's function is to pick out the relevant elements of expression and content. For Peirce, two items share an iconic ground if there are some identical or similar properties that these items possess independently of each other. Properties may be perceived or, more broadly, experienced as being identical or similar from a particular point of view. Similarity is taken to be an identity perceived on the background of fundamental difference.

Signs based on similarity were distinguished before Peirce by Joseph-Marie Degérando (1772–1842), for instance, in terms of analogy (1800). Indeed, Peirce also says that an icon (more exactly, a hypoicon) is "a sign which stands for something merely because it resembles it" (1931–1958, vol. 3, p. 362) or "partakes in the characters of the object" (vol. 4, p. 531). This point of view was pursued by Charles Morris (1946), who considered that a sign was iconic to the extent that it had some properties of its referent. According to this conception, iconicity becomes a question of degree: a film is more iconic of a person than is a painted portrait because it includes movement. Abraham Moles (1981) constructed a scale comprising thirteen degrees of iconicity from the object itself (100 percent) to its verbal description (0 percent). Such a conception of iconicity is problematic not only because distinctions of different natures appear to be involved but also because it takes for granted that identity is the highest degree of iconicity and that the illusion of perceptual resemblance typically produced, in different ways, by the scale model and the picture sign are as close as we can come to iconicity besides identity itself. Although Peirce does mention paintings and photographs as instances of iconic signs, he much more often refers to abstract properties.

The same problem exists in other semiotic theories. Umberto Eco's critique of iconicity (1976, pp. 190–216) is concerned almost exclusively with pictures. In pictorial semiotics (e.g., the Belgian semiotic Groupe μ), iconicity is supposed to account for the semiotic function of the picture sign that gives the illusion of seeing something depicted in the sign—as opposed to the plastic function, which is concerned with the abstract properties of the pictorial surface. However, if a circle is taken to stand on the iconic level for the sun and on the plastic level for roundness, which in turn, as psychological tests suggest, might signify softness and other qualities, then what is called here the plastic language is at least as iconic, in Peirce's sense, as the iconic language. Roundness is certainly a property possessed both by the circle representing the sun in this hypothetical drawing and by the circle prototype; beyond that, there must be some abstract, synesthetically experienced property that is common to the visual mode of roundness and the tactile mode of softness.

When conceiving iconicity as engendering a "referential illusion" and as forming a stage in the generation of "figurative" meaning out of the abstract base structure, Greimas and Courtés (1979) similarly identify iconicity with perceptual appearance. In fact, however, not only is iconicity not particularly concerned with "optical illusion" or "realistic rendering," but it does not necessarily involve perceptual predicates: many of Peirce's examples, like those of Degérando before him, concern mathematical formulas.

During the renewal of semiotic theory in the 1960s and 1970s, many semioticians questioned the very notion of iconicity, taking pictures as their favorite example while claiming that pictures were in some curious way as conventional as linguistic signs. Arthur Bierman (1963), Nelson Goodman (1970), and Umberto Eco (1976) all argue against using similarity as a criterion in the definition of iconical signs. Some, such as Bierman and Goodman, were inspired mainly by logical considerations, illustrated with ethnological anecdotes according to which so-called primitive tribes were incapable of interpreting pictures. Further, Eco considered that pictures, conforming to the ideal of the Saussurean sign, were as arbitrary or conventional as the sign studied by the most advanced of the semiotic sciences, general linguistics. Saussure himself never went to such extremes: in his unpublished notes, he recognizes the motivated character of both pictures and miming, but at least in the latter case he argues that the rudiment of convention found in it is sufficient to make it an issue for semiotics.

The most interesting arguments against iconicity were adduced by Bierman (1963), and were later repeated in another form by Goodman (1970). The argument of regression states that all things in the world can be classified into a number of very general categories such as things, animals, human beings, and so on; therefore, everything in the universe can refer to and be referred to by everything else. Thus, if iconicity is at the origin of signs, everything in the world is a sign. This might not be so far from what Peirce thought. It is certainly a conception of the world common in the Renaissance and among the Romantics and the Symbolists. In the case of more common iconic signs, however, such as pictures and models, either a conventional sign function might be superimposed on the iconic ground or the iconic ground itself must be characterized by further properties. Even in the former case, however, the notion of iconicity is still needed, not to define the sign but to characterize iconic signs.

If Peirce meant that there are three properties—iconicity, indexicality, and symbolicity—that by themselves and without any further requirement trigger off the recognition of something as a sign, then the argument of regression undermines this conception. On the other hand, if he wanted merely to suggest that something that was already recognized as a sign could be discovered to be an iconical sign rather than an indexical or symbolic one by tracing it back to the iconic ground, then the argument of regression has no bearing on it.

According to the symmetry argument (Sebeok, 1976), iconicity cannot motivate a sign, for while similarity is symmetrical and reflexive, the sign is not. Pigments on paper or carvings in a rock could stand for a human, but not the reverse; nor will they, in their picture function, stand for themselves. This argument is based on an identification of the commonsense notion of similarity with the equivalence relation of logic. No doubt, the equivalence relation is symmetric and reflexive and thus cannot define any type of sign, since the sign by definition must be asymmetric and irreflexive. But identifying similarity with the equivalence relation ignores the constraints of the particular sociocultural environment of human life. Similarity, as it is experienced in everyday life is actually asymmetric and irreflexive, as has been demonstrated experimentally (e.g., Rosch, 1975; Tversky, 1977). Contrary to the argument of regression, the symmetry argument can thus be warded off

without introducing a supplementary sign function and without amending the definition of the iconic ground.

Goodman (1968) also argues that a painting is actually more similar to another painting than to that which it depicts. However, similarity should not be confused with identity: indeed, between two pictures (two canvases, etc.) there is identity, according to a principle of pertinence, and on the basis of this property a picture, just as any other object, may be used as an identity sign or an exemplification (as, for instance, in an art exhibition or in front of the artist's workshop). There is similarity, on the other hand, only on the basis of a fundamental dissimilarity. It is certainly not in their "important" properties—the attributes defining them as "selves"—that the picture and its referent (or content) are similar. In fact, the hierarchically dominant categories of the picture and its referent must be different, for a picture that is just a picture of the picture-of-x is indistinguishable from a picture of x.

Thus, although the sign relation is not needed in order to render similarity asymmetric and irreflexive, it is required in order to distinguish similarities that are signs from those that are not. At this stage, then, it seems that the picture can be defined by the sign relation together with similarity; but Eco observes rightly that, on closer inspection, there is really no similarity between the painted nose and the nose of a real person. The same observation is even more obviously valid in the case of a stick figure, whether it is drawn on paper or carved in the rock. However, it has no bearing whatsoever on iconic signs that are not picture signs, and the argument really shows the confusion between pictures and iconic signs in general. In the case of the picture sign, it might really be necessary to construe similarity as a result of, rather than a condition for, the emergence of iconicity, but that is an issue that concerns the analysis of a specific variety of iconic signs—the picture—not iconicity generally.

The alternative analysis in terms of convention suggested by Goodman, Eco, and others is conceived to take care of the case of pictures, but, paradoxically, it seems that this would really be needed not for pictures but for some other iconical signs, which rely on identity. The contention shared by Goodman and Greenlee (1973) that the referent of each picture is appointed individually and Eco's proposal that the relations of the picture are so correlated with those of the referent are incompatible with what psychology tells us about a child's capacity for interpreting pictures when first confronted with them at nineteen months of age, as demonstrated in a famous experiment by Julian Hochberg (1978). On the other hand, we do have to learn that in certain situations and according to particular conventions, objects that are normally used for what they are become signs of themselves, of some of their properties, or of the class of which they form part: a car at a car exhibition, the stone ax in the museum showcase or the tin can in the shop window, the emperor's impersonator when the emperor is away, and a urinal (if it happens to be Marcel Duchamp's *Fountain*) at an art exhibition. There is never any doubt about their pure iconicity or about their capacity for entering into an iconic ground, but a convention is needed for them to be construed as signs.

[*See also* Aniconic Visual Signs; Gibson; Goodman; Icon; Image and Picture; Peirce; Picture Perception; *and* Vision.]

BIBLIOGRAPHY

Bierman, A. K. "That There Are No Iconic Signs." *Philosophy and Phenomenological Research* 23.2 (1963): 243–249.

Degérando, J. M. *Des signes et de l'art de penser considérés dans leurs rapports mutuels.* Paris: Goujon fils, 1800.

Eco, U. *A Theory of Semiotics.* Bloomington: Indiana University Press, 1976.

Goodman, N. *Languages of Art.* London: Oxford University Press, 1968.

Goodman, N. "Seven Strictures on Similarity." In *Experience and Theory*, edited by L. Foster and J. W. Swanson, pp. 19–29. Amherst, Mass.: University of Massachusetts Press, 1970.

Greenlee, D. *Peirce's Concept of Sign.* The Hague: Mouton, 1973.

Greimas, A. J., and J. Courtés. *Semiotics and Language: An Analytical Dictionary.* Translated by L. Crist and D. Patte. Bloomington: Indiana University Press, 1979.

Hochberg, J. *Perception.* 2d rev. ed. Englewood Cliffs, N.J.: Prentice-Hall, 1978.

Moles, A. *L'image: Communication fonctionelle.* Brussels: Casterman, 1981.

Morris, C. *Signs, Language, and Behavior* (1946): Reprinted in C. Morris, *Writings on the General Theory of Signs*, pp. 73–398. The Hague: Mouton, 1971.

Peirce, C. S. *Collected Papers*, 8 vols. Edited by C. Hartshorne, P. Weiss, and A. Burks. Cambridge, Mass.: Harvard University Press, 1931–1958.

Rosch, E. "Cognitive Reference Points." *Cognitive Psychology* 7.4 (1975): 532–547.

Sebeok, T. A. *Contributions to the Doctrine of Signs.* Bloomington and Lisse: Indiana University Press and Peter de Ridder Press, 1976.

Sonesson, G. *Pictorial Concepts: Inquiries into the Semiotic Heritage and Its Relevance for the Analysis of the Visual World.* Lund: Lund University Press, 1989.

Tversky, A. "Features of Similarity." *Psychological Review* 84.4 (1977): 327–352.

—GÖRAN SONESSON

IDEOGRAMS. Visual signs consisting of arrangements of lines on a surface, ideograms stand for ideas or concepts rather than represent sources of the perceptual world. Most letters, which represent single sounds and do not carry any meanings except when combined into words, do not count as ideograms proper. However, the position of a letter is a potential ground for use as an ideogram. For instance, the letter *A*, which comes first in the alphabet, does not only encode the corresponding sound but also carries a spectrum of other values, such as something being first, best, of highest quality, and so on.

Ideograms may be grounded on a pictorial representation or can employ nonpictorial iconic grounds; however, they can also be entirely aniconic. A letter may be seen as iconic, though of course not pictorial, of its position in the alphabet. A horizontal line placed higher than other signs may be iconic, but not pictorial, for the sky, as in the Egyptian hieroglyph for the sky, or, more abstractly, for being above, as in blissymbolics. Some hobo signs may be entirely aniconic: ▽ in the United States and England means "ruined—too many have been here."

Approximately one thousand ideograms are used in the Western world today, two hundred of them very commonly. Another one thousand have been used in other eras, some even as early as in prehistoric times. Examples include petroglyphs, alchemists' signs, astrological and astronomical signs, hobo signs, some signs in musical notation, road signs, religious symbols, political graffiti, and commercial logos. Five basic elements may be distinguished in Western ideography: the straight line, —; the circle segment, ⌒; the spirals or exponential curves, ℗ and ℈; and the dot, or small, filled circle, ●. Some ideograms, however, are perhaps more usually seen as unanalyzable gestalts (Liungman, 1991).

There are several ideograms with very different graphic structures for entities such as water, fire, sunshine, salt, and glass, reflecting their importance to human life in the everyday life world. These ideograms, then, may be said to be synonymous. On the other hand, some ideograms are homographs, where one shape carries more than one meaning. A special case in this respect are the five graphically most simple structures found in Western ideography (†, ○, △, □, ☆) since they, and only they, have double meanings that oppose each other. Thus, the Latin cross means *death* and *sorrow*, as well as *eternal life* and *heavenly happiness*. The triangle means both *danger* and *safety*, as can be seen in many road signs. The five-pointed star in some instances means *war, danger, emergency* and in others means *fun, good times, favorable opportunity* (parties, sales). Contrary to what has often been suggested (Greene, 1983), this is not true of all elementary ideograms (the heart, for instance, does not mean both love and hate), let alone all ideograms.

Since the meanings of the most common ideograms are learned by all people during early childhood, regardless of their very different spoken and written languages, everyone understands their meanings. And since their meanings are apprehended much faster than the meanings of written words, as they do not demand much decoding, ideograms are very good for conveying messages in situations where fast reactions are imperative, such as in traffic, warfare, and emergency situations.

Ideograms are often used as logo symbols (logotypes) by commercial enterprises. The word *logotype* now most commonly denotes such identificatory symbols, often used together with the name of the company written in some particular typographic font and style, as they appear on letterheads, signboards, and rubber stamps as well as in television commercials.

Many systems of classification for Western ideograms have been devised, such as that of Walter Shepherd (1971), who uses three categories of seven, sixty-one, and twelve graphic properties and divides ideograms into 434 groups. Liungman (1991) divides ideograms into fifty-four groups by characterizing a sign as being open, closed, or both; drawn with straight lines, curves, or both; being symmetrical around one axis, multisymmetrical, or asymmetrical; and lastly having lines crossing each other or not. Variations of meaning can thus be correlated with graphical combinations. This system also yields the interesting result that signs forming the ideographic systems of different (sub)cultures often belong to one or just a few of the graphic groups resulting from tabulating the graphic dimensions mentioned. Fascist ideograms, for instance, are mostly asymmetrical, straight-lined, open structures; Cherokee Indian signs are symmetrical, open, curved, with crossing lines.

[*See also* Aniconic Visual Signs; Blissymbolics; Icon; Iconicity; Logo *and* Trademark.]

BIBLIOGRAPHY

Aicher, O., and M. Krampen. *Zeichensysteme der visuellen Kommunikation.* Stuttgart: Verlagsanstalt Alexander Koch, 1977.

Chevalier, J., and A. Gheerbrant. *Dictionnaire des symboles 1–4.* 6th ed. Paris: Seghers, 1973.

Cirlot, J.-E. *Diccionario de símbolos.* 2d ed. Barcelona: Editorial Labor, 1969. This book contains a comprehensive bibliography.

Dreyfuss, H. *Symbol Sourcebook.* New York: McGraw-Hill, 1972.

Greene, L. *Relating: An Astrological Guide to Living with Others on a Small Planet.* New York: Samuel Weiser, 1983.

Liungman, C. G. *Dictionary of Symbols.* Santa Barbara: ABC-Clio, 1991.

Shepherd, W. *Shepherd's Glossary of Graphic Signs and Symbols.* London: J. M. Dent and Sons, 1971.

—CARL G. LIUNGMAN

IMAGE AND PICTURE. Often used as synonyms in semiotics, *image* and *picture* refer to signs pertaining to visual perception, which are iconic in the sense that they produce an impression of partial similarity between the signifier and the intended signified or referent. *Image* in this sense must be distinguished from mirror image, memory image, afterimage, camera image, sculpture, and holograms. Images or pictures consist of markings on a two-dimensional surface that are, as a matter of course, taken to represent scenes or objects of the ordinary perceptual world. Although this definition is inadequate to characterize numerous artistic paintings produced since the advent of modernism, it certainly accounts for the commonsense notion of picture and thus may be used as a prototype for the picture category, from which there may be approximations and deviations.

However, not all signs that are visual and iconic are ordinarily described as pictures. Something more is needed in order to characterize pictureness. A semiotic definition of *picture* remains problematic. The peculiarities of the picture sign have been addressed, albeit obliquely, by Charles Sanders Peirce (1839–

1914) in terms of qualities and "exhibitive import" (Greenlee, 1973) and by Ferdinand de Saussure (1857–1913) with reference to spatial dimensions. In philosophy, pictures have been problematized by Edmund Husserl (1980), who describes pictorial consciousness as something that is "perceptually imagined," and by Nelson Goodman (1968), who radically rejects the ordinary sense of *picture* and redefines it in his own prescriptive rather than descriptive terms.

The image is one of the three subtypes of iconical signs (or hypo-icons) mentioned by Peirce and is the one whose iconical relation is assured not by relations, as in the diagram, nor by relations between relations, as in the metaphor, but by "simple qualities." The opposition between image and diagram in this sense echoes that made by the *idéologue* Joseph-Marie Degérando (1772–1842), who in his treatise on signs (1800) proposed a distinction between sensuous and logical analogy. The image so defined is not necessarily a picture in the ordinary sense of the word: it might be addressed to other perceptual domains than the visual one. For instance, onomatopoetic words may be defined as "acoustic images." Degérando claimed that pictures that combined sensuous and logical analogy would be the most effective ones. Pictures, however, unlike diagrams, convey an illusion of similarity of qualities. Therefore, the difference between qualities and relations might have less to do with the difference of iconic ground joining expression and content together than with the effect produced by the two types of iconic signs.

In the *Course in General Linguistics*, Saussure observes simply that whereas language is unidimensional, pictures depend on a semiotic system deployed in multiple dimensions. But this is not peculiar to pictures: clothing certainly supposed at least two combinatory dimensions defined by body parts and degrees of closeness to the body; moreover, if suprasegmental features are taken into account, even verbal language will have to be considered multidimensional, as Roman Jakobson claimed.

Little has been done so far to derive operational criteria for characterizing the peculiarities of the picture sign. These might be phrased, however, in terms of a specifically pictorial exhibitive content. First, exhibitive import permits us to "see" in a drawing of a human face, for instance, those facial traits (such as the forehead, the cheeks, etc.), which are typically rendered by blank spaces between the lines and surfaces. Second, those traits that have no expression

proper may be at least roughly located in relation to the rest of the facial traits: for instance, ears that are not drawn can be shown to be missing from a particular place.

Such properties depend on the way pictures are constructed. In the 1960s, some semioticians tried to demonstrate the existence of minimal units of pictorial meaning, sometimes termed iconemes, which have no meaning of their own but contribute to the meaning of larger wholes, just as phonemes do in relation to words or morphemes. Umberto Eco claims in *La struttura assente* (1968) that pictures have a double articulation, with *figurae*—equivalent to phonemes—combining to form signs, which then were clustered to produce pictures or iconic statements. Although Eco later rejected this conception and argued against the existence of distinctive pictorial features, the approach is still presupposed in his theory of the triple articulation of the cinematic language (1976).

A semiotics of pictures based on the psychology of perception rather than on structural linguistics would consider that the lines and surfaces making up a picture are indeed deprived of meaning, just as phonemes are; but whereas the phonemes, once they have been put together to form a word, continue to lack separate meaning, pictorial traits take on and distribute among themselves the global meaning of the whole configuration. Thus, in the word *face*, the first letter is not the carrier of the meaning "hair," the second of the meaning "forehead," and so on, but that is precisely the case with the lines making up the drawing of a face.

Yet little is known about the peculiarities of the picture sign, in part because the description of picturehood has too often been confused with the broader issues pertaining to iconicity, and we still do not appear to possess the theoretical knowledge that would explain the little we know. Not only must we investigate more deeply the peculiarities of the picture sign but we will also have to understand more precisely the sign types from which pictures differ to various degrees. If we admit that what has been discussed so far is a kind of prototype picture, a core meaning of present-day pictureness, then our first task is to characterize those increasingly deviant notions of picture that have evolved historically within the particular semiotic domains of modern art and those created in the variegated workings of contemporary society—such as pictograms, blissymbolics, computer icons, and other quasi-pictures—or discovered among the traces of earlier civilizations, such as petroglyphs and other prehistoric visual images.

[See also Icon; Iconicity; and Pictorial Semiotics.]

BIBLIOGRAPHY

Degérando, J. M. *Des signes et de l'art de penser considérés dans leurs rapports mutuels.* Paris: Goujon fils, 1800.

Eco, U. *La struttura assente.* Milan, Bompiani, 1968.

Eco, U. *A Theory of Semiotics.* Bloomington: Indiana University Press, 1976.

Goodman, N. *Languages of Art.* Indianapolis: Bobbs-Merrill, 1968.

Greenlee, D. *Peirce's Concept of Sign.* The Hague: Mouton, 1973.

Husserl, E. *Phantasie, Bildbewusstsein, Erinnerung.* The Hague: Nijhoff, 1980.

Sonesson, G. *Pictorial Concepts: Inquiries into the Semiotic Heritage and Its Relevance for the Analysis of the Visual World.* Lund: Lund University Press, 1989.

Wollheim, R. *Art and Its Objects.* 2d. rev. ed. Cambridge: Cambridge University Press, 1980.

—GÖRAN SONESSON

IMAGINARY SIGNIFIER, THE (1977), is an influencial book by the French cinema semiotician Christian Metz. *Le signifiant imaginaire* (the imaginary signifier) is an expression that instantly calls to mind a host of issues connected with the second, psychoanalytic phase in the development of a semiotics of the cinema. The term was first used as the title of an essay by Metz in the 1975 issue of *Communications* devoted entirely to the subject of psychoanalysis and the cinema. That year, the article was translated into English for *Screen* magazine. In 1977, Metz grouped it and three other essays under the collective title *Le signifiant imaginaire* as a book that became the touchstone for most further critical inquiry into the psychoanalytical function of cinema. The principal inspirational sources for the essays were the writings of Sigmund Freud and Jacques Lacan. Some semioticians insist on the inevitability of the coming together of psychoanalysis and cinema, pointing out that both phenomena were born simultaneously in the 1890s as a common answer to the human needs of the times.

Metz's use of the word *imaginaire* can be explained in three ways. It first of all underlines the principal means of communication utilized by the cinema: the filmed image. Second, it calls to mind the over-whelmingly dominant kind of film, the fiction film (*film de diégèse*), which springs from the imagination of the filmmaker at the same time as it communicates with the imagination of the spectator (or, in psychoanalytical terms, with the subject). Last, the word links film with the imaginary register of Lacan's psychoanalytical schema in which identifications are sustained. This register stands in opposition to the symbolic register. In terms of Freud's work, *imaginary* recalls his First Topic and the mother/desire/impulse/pleasure issues, whereas *symbolic* is characteristic of his Second Topic and the notions of the father/restriction/law/reality.

Prior to *Le signifiant imaginaire*, the question of the spectator in the cinema had been consciously ignored. Metz confessed that film semioticians during the structural-linguistics phase had wanted to affirm the specificity of the semiotic approach by placing it in a purely polemical setting. They wished to avoid any confusion with a sociological approach, which might have been evoked by marked attention to the spectator. Indeed, when Metz turned to the question of the spectator, he neatly skirted any sociologically construable issues such as the nature of the viewing publics and their differentiation by education, by occupations, or by nationalities. His method in *Le signifiant imaginaire* is instead entirely committed to discussing the effect of a filmic text on an undesignated subject in an ideal solitary spectatorial setting.

Of the four chapters that constitute the book, the first and third are the most closely linked, having been conceived at roughly the same moment and published in the same issue of *Communications*. Both chapters are best studied in conjunction with two companion essays by Metz's fellow semiotician, Jean-Louis Baudry: "Ideological Effects of the Basic Apparatus" (first published in French in 1970) and "The Apparatus" (which first appeared in the same 1975 issue of *Communications* as Metz's two articles). Metz's first chapter, "The Imaginary Signifier," is clearly indebted to Baudry's 1970 passages on "the mirror phase" in relation to the film spectator's experience. In psychoanalysis, the mirror phase designates the pleasurable moment in an infant's existence when it recognizes in a mirror reflection its own presence in its mother's arms. This is a moment when the child is exceptionally alert visually, especially in comparison with its limited motor skills. The analogy between the perceptive child helpless in its mother's arms and the intently perceiving movie spectator, immobile in the cinema seat, is clear, as is the analogy between the shining surface of the mirror and the surface of the silver screen. The pleasure of the infant and that of the spectator are also parallel. There are some glaring differences as well, such as the presence of the baby in its mirror image and the absence of the film spectator on the screen image.

The process of identification, however, functions similarly in both cases; some semioticians have even insisted that the lingering reflection of the spectator's face on a television screen (used most symbolically in Douglas Sirk's *All That Heaven Allows*, 1955) summarizes the identification process that occurs while watching a film: the viewer sutures himself or herself into the narrative. Codes of film editing involving the gaze contribute to the seduction of the spectator. For example, the *champ/contre-champ* (shot/reverse shot), convention plays an especially privileged role in defining the relationship between the filmic space on the screen and the spectator's perception. For the moviegoer, in effect, the eye doubles for the projector, which already doubles for the camera; the spectator's mental image doubles for the screen image, which is a projected version of the celluloid frames of film. Moreover, the innate voyeurism that semioticians often refer to as scopophilia motivates, as its name suggests, the desire to see. It is only logical to carry the spectator's fascination with the image to an analogy with the psychoanalytical notion of the fetish. In addition, it is natural to link the whole question of the viewer's obsession to the *clivage* of Melanie Klein and Octave Mannoni, that mental state shared by automobile drivers and filmgoers alike: they know that they are driving a car or watching a film; nevertheless, they at the same time lose their awareness of the fact. "I know very well . . . but just the same," quotes Metz from Mannoni. Freud's famous example deals with the male child observing the naked female child and thinking, "I know very well that she never had a penis . . . but just the same." This is the source of the psychoanalytical fear of castration. The fetish (a substitute for the missing penis) thus becomes associated clearly with the spectator's unwavering focus on the screen and desire for the text.

Metz's second chapter, a short, earlier article, is titled "Story/Discourse: Notes on Two Voyeurisms." By linking the question of voyeurism to essentially narratological notions of diegetic material and narrative shifters, Metz adds a psychoanalytical emphasis to his argument. In fact, the inspiration for this article

stems more explicitly from the linguistic theories of Roman Jakobson and Émile Benveniste than it does from the work of Freud and Lacan. Essentially, Metz demonstrates that cinema, which often appears to be narrating itself (Benveniste's *histoire*), discreetly contains as many indicators of a narrating instance as most prose fiction does. In other words, films that appear to be solely stories are in fact discourses (*discours*) disguised as stories. The concealment of the narrative markers eliminates at least one level of narrating intervention and allows the spectator greater identification with the whole narrative fabrication.

The third chapter, "The Fiction Film and Its Spectator: A Metapsychological Study," studies more deeply the mechanism of the unconscious in relation to the film-screening experience. Metz's fundamental idea here is that the passing of the images of the fiction film on the movie-theater screen can be compared to the passing of a dream across the subject's mind screen. There are, however, three major differences: (1) the dreamer does not realize that he or she is dreaming, whereas the filmgoer can (sometimes only with the utmost effort) regain a sense of watching a film; (2) the film spectator is watching the projection of permanently recorded images, whereas the dreamer is experiencing fleeting internal images; and (3) the filmic text results from a conscious structuring of a narrative by a filmmaker, whereas a dream is spontaneous and even uncontrollable. Nevertheless, the two seem similar enough that one can speak of a dream as a text and of the metamorphosis of the projected images of the film into internalized images on the mind screen as dreamlike. Metz concludes, though, that the semiconscious state of the spectator is more like that of a daydreamer than that of a dreamer; thus, he opts for a closer analogy between film and *rêverie* (daydream) than film and *rêve* (dream). A daydream is, after all, more filmlike inasmuch as it is more controlled and structured than a dream is. Nevertheless, the film experience, which at its most successful seems to be a real experience, can still be profitably compared to either a dream or a daydream.

The longest chapter in *Le signifiant imaginaire* is "Metaphor/Metonymy, or the Imaginary Referent," the thrust of which is to reconsider traditional figures of rhetoric in psychoanalytical terms. Deriving his point of view from the distinctions made by Lacan (through Jakobson), Metz is able to discuss filmic metaphor and metonymy from the perspective of dreams and psychoanalysis. After all, in dreams and in film, both the condensation (of metaphor) and the displacement (of metonymy) play a role. Both narrative "structures" can be described and analyzed in terms of their common figuration. As Metz demonstrates, close study of the problems of metaphor and metonymy can reveal that distinctions between the two figures are less clear than are generally assumed. In Sergei Eisenstein's *Potemkin* (1925), for instance, the famous shot of the doctor's glasses caught in the rope of the ship—often selected as a textbook example of filmic synecdoche (a traditional form of metonymy)—can also be read metaphorically. Other issues and examples abound.

It is impossible to overemphasize the importance of Metz's *Le signifiant imaginaire* to the evolution of psychoanalytical consideration of the cinema. It is his work, for example, that opened the doors to the study of hypnosis and the filmic spectator. Further manifestations of his influence occur in the writings of feminist film theorists such as Laura Mulvey and her successors.

[*See also* Cinema; Film Semiotics; Jakobson; Lacan; *and* Metz.]

BIBLIOGRAPHY

Baudry, J.-L. "Ideological Effects of the Basic Apparatus." Translated by Alan Williams. *Film Quarterly* 28.2 (1973–1974): 39–47.
Baudry, J.-L. "The Apparatus." Translated by J. Andrews and B. Augst. *Camera Obscura* 1 (1976): 104–128.
Metz, C. *The Imaginary Signifier.* Translated by A. Guzzetti et al. Bloomington: Indiana University Press, 1981.
Mulvey, L. *Visual and Other Pleasures.* Bloomington: Indiana University Press, 1990.

—C. D. E. TOLTON

IMPLICATURE. A concept developed by the philosopher H. Paul Grice to account for the apparent gap between the literal meaning of an utterance and the way it functions in a context of use, an implicature is an inference of the sort people make routinely in order to interpret each other's discourse as coherent, relevant, and cooperative. Grice's theory suggests why and how interlocutors are able to make sense of a variety of instances that appear to violate these basic requirements on a superficial level. For example, he offers an explanation for apparent tautologies ("a rose is a rose is a rose"), sarcasm (saying

"you're a fine friend" to a person who has betrayed you), and sequences such as:

A: Where's Jason?
B: The bus left two minutes ago.

Grice first outlined his theory in his 1967 William James lectures entitled "Logic and Conversation" (published in part in Grice, 1975, 1978) and put forward conversational implicature as a potential resolution of two issues. One of these was a contemporary philosophical debate concerning the value of "ordinary language," thought by some to be logically imprecise compared to formal logic, the language of science. However, the search for a purely "objective" language has since been extensively critiqued by poststructuralism. Grice's work also engaged with some of the problems speech-act theory was encountering. Grice hoped that by employing a general principle, it would not be necessary to specify unwieldy "appropriateness conditions" for each speech-act type. Despite initial work by John Searle (1975), it is still not clear how implicature fits into a theory of speech acts.

The concept of implicature relies on participants in discourse observing what Grice calls the cooperative principle (CP). Conversation—and, more generally, discourse—he argues, is a cooperative venture, and its participants observe the CP in order to achieve this. Furthermore, talking is seen as a rational and purposeful activity, analogous to other forms of rational behavior. In support of this assumption, Grice argues that the CP and maxims could be applied equally to other such behavior.

Attached to the CP are a set of related maxims, the maxims of quantity, quality, relation, and manner, which set out more specifically how the CP is to be observed. The maxim of quantity deals with the amount of information to be provided and requires participants to be as informative as the exchange requires and not more so. The maxim of quality is concerned with truthfulness and demands that participants not say anything they believe to be false or for which they do not have sufficient evidence. The maxim of relation simply asks speakers to be relevant. Finally, the maxim of manner states that talk should be clear, brief, orderly, and unambiguous.

Conversational implicatures are generated when these maxims are broken, or rather flouted, in apparently deliberate ways. Grice shows how this operates for each of the maxims. For example, the maxim of quantity is violated if, in writing a testimonial about a graduate student applying for an academic position, a professor wrote simply: "X's command of English is excellent, and his attendance at tutorials has been regular." Since this is insufficient information for the purpose and there is no reason to think the professor is ignorant of the student's academic abilities, Grice suggests that the implied information is that the professor is unwilling to say more on the grounds that nothing positive could be said of the candidate's academic abilities.

Hearers and readers thus calculate implicatures on the assumption that although the speaker or writer has apparently violated a maxim, he or she is still observing the CP. Implicatures are thus inferences calculated by hearers or readers in order to reconcile the gap between the flouting of a maxim and the continuing operation of the CP.

Grice's account of this mechanism has generated much interest, although other researchers have disputed the maxims on which the implicatures depend and have also questioned the postulation of the universal CP. Dan Sperber and Deirdre Wilson argue that much of Grice's theory can be subsumed under a principle of relevance and also deny that it is necessary to assume that a principle of cooperation is in force (1986, p. 174–175). E. O. Keenan (1976) demonstrates that the maxims as formulated by Grice are both culturally specific and context dependent rather than generalized language universals.

Grice's models depend on a rationalist approach, which takes communication as the maximally informative exchange of information. This is a problematic definition for a number of reasons. Grice himself notes that it does not allow for purposes such as influencing or directing others, nor does it account for other "types of exchange, like quarreling and letter writing" (1975, pp. 47, 48–49). This limited definition operates to privilege a narrow range of "objective" genres, ignores the way language functions to negotiate and maintain social relations, and treats phatic, playful, and conflictual uses of language as aberrant.

Implicature has been taken up by semanticists and pragmaticists, who have explored its possibilities in solving problems that they regard as relatively intractable, at least within the models of truth-conditional or logical semantics that dominate these fields. These problems include defining meanings for words whose meanings appear to fluctuate in discourse: particles such as *well*, scalar adjectives such as *warm* and *hot*, address forms such as *tu* and *vous*, deictic items, and so on (Levinson, 1983; chap. 3). Implicatures here are a context-sensitive semantic overlay upon these stable "core" meanings. This approach depends on a split between semantics and pragmatics, though alternative models of language meaning, such as the functional social semiotics of Michael Halliday, avoid a distinction between meaning and use and are able to explain many of the above cases within a functional semantics.

The theory of implicature has also been applied by discourse analysts and stylisticians to the study of extended sequences of discourse. Werth (1981) explores implicature as a mechanism that allows the listener to assume discourse is relevant or coherent. However, a theory of implicature is problematic in that it assumes coherence is a cognitive, rule-based procedure that can be standardized for all readers or listeners and depends on a notion of a rational, cooperative subject. The inferential work required to make a text coherent will differ from person to person and context to context. That is, text coherence is achieved in part through textual "triggers" and is in part a function of the way participants construe the situation. Implicature can thus only offer a partial account of textual coherence.

Other issues for the study of implicature in stretches of discourse or conversation are the roles of intonation, stress, and paralinguistic features and the problem of how topic change is achieved without violating the maxim of relation (raised by Grice, 1975, p. 46). Another application is to the theory of metaphor and figurative language. Grice suggests that rhetorical features such a metaphor, irony, rhetorical questions, hyperbole, and understatement work in terms of meanings implicated through the flouting of the maxim of quality (Grice, 1975, pp. 53–54). However, a pragmatic theory of metaphor has not been fully developed and is just one of many competing theories of metaphor.

Applications by literary stylisticians suggest that implicature has some value as a suggestive tool for identifying texts in which a lot of inferential work appears to be required (e.g., Pratt, 1977). By working with fictive texts, stylisticians have moved away from a dependence on truth-conditional and communication-intention theories of meaning. They have also demonstrated that implicatures are motivated largely by interpersonal factors such as attitude, power, tension, and conflict.

A general problem for the study of implicature concerns the epistemological status to which its proponents implicitly or explicitly lay claim. Implicature, along with the general field of pragmatics, partakes in a debate between those who believe formalization, rigor, and rule-based descriptions are necessary and desirable (Gazdar, 1979) and those who believe that this is untenable or undesirable (Sadock, 1978). While formalism allows a new discipline area to make strong claims, it also tends to inhibit the interdisciplinary work that has characterized contemporary semiotics and to close off alternative interpretations and approaches.

As it has been formulated and debated, the concept of implicature raises significant issues for a socially situated or contextualized theory of semiotics. While it does not claim to be such a model, the theory of implicature continually draws attention to the context-dependent nature of all discourse. Problematic for Grice's theory are the questions of cooperativeness as a universal characteristic of discourse, the notion of conversation as an unmarked genre that can stand for all communicative situations, a dependence on an intentional model of communication and a truth-conditional semantics, and the assumption of rational subjects of discourse for whom the context is stable and pregiven. Implicature has played a useful part in the development of a theory of discourse, but further research needs to explore the phenomenon of inferential work in discourse in relation to a much broader range of genres and to consider meaning making not only as information exchange but as conflictual, as play, and as a means of negotiating social relations.

[See also Conversation; Halliday; Pertinence; and Speech Act Theory.]

BIBLIOGRAPHY

Gazdar, G. Pragmatics: Implicature, Presupposition, and Logical Form. New York: Academic Press, 1979.

Grice, H. P. "Logic and Conversation." In Syntax and Semantics, volume 3, Speech Acts, edited by P. Cole and J. L. Morgan, pp. 41–58. New York: Academic Press, 1975.

Grice, H. P. "Further Notes on Logic and Conversation." In Syntax and Semantics, volume 9, Pragmatics, edited by P. Cole, pp. 113–127. New York: Academic Press, 1978.

Keenan, E. O. "The Universality of Conversational Postulates." Language in Society 5 (1976): 67–80.

Levinson, S. C. Pragmatics. Cambridge: Cambridge University Press, 1983.

Pratt, M. L. Toward a Speech Act Theory of Literary Discourse. Bloomington: Indiana University Press, 1977.

Sadock, J. M. "On Testing for Conversational Implicature." In Syntax and Semantics, vol. 9, Pragmatics, edited by P. Cole, pp. 281–298. New York: Academic Press, 1978.

Searle, J. R. "Indirect Speech Acts." In Syntax and Semantics, vol. 3, Speech Acts, edited by P. Cole and J. L. Morgan, pp. 59–82. New York: Academic Press, 1975.

Sperber, D., and D. Wilson. Relevance: Communication and Cognition. Cambridge, Mass.: Harvard University Press, 1986.

Werth, P., ed. Conversation and Discourse: Structure and Interpretation. London: Croom Helm, 1981.

—SUSAN YELL

IMPRESA. A metaphorical combination of quasi-heraldic picture and text that is characteristic of the European Renaissance, the impresa or personal device is intended to convey a coded message concerning its bearer's situation, personal philosophy, current state of mind, or aspirations, whether social or sentimental. Widespread in Europe during the sixteenth and seventeenth centuries, the impresa is closely related both to the heraldic coat of arms and to the emblem. It typically combines a pictorial sign (which, as in heraldry, can be an animal, a plant, an atmospheric phenomenon, and so forth) with a motto similar to the family mottoes often associated with heraldic arms.

Though the impresa, like the coat of arms, contrives to express a coded message about its bearer, it is not normally transmissable from generation to generation, and it usually expresses nothing connected intrinsically to the bearer's family, line of descent, or social standing. Like the emblem, the device fuses picture and text (respectively considered the "body" and "soul" of the impresa) to create an enigmatic whole whose degree of perfection is usually measured in terms of the fusion of the verbal and nonverbal parts, which in the perfect device ought to be equally necessary to its comprehension. Unlike the emblem, however, the impresa does not aim to present a general truth, and it is not normally composed with a view to its didactic or moralizing effect. Rather, it is intended to make a personal statement about its bearer; unlike a grant of arms, it can thus be readily altered or cast off as its owner's circumstances evolve.

Many scholars have pointed out that the appearance of the impresa is more or less contemporaneous with the strict codification of the rules of heraldry in the fifteenth century. As the circumstances in which arms might be granted and transmitted came to be defined more and more rigidly, and as arms became, in most European countries, more and more the prerogative of established nobility (to the point where many knights were refused admittance to tournaments on the grounds that they were unable to prove noble blood in all four grandparents), the practice of taking a personal device gained in popularity. Such devices, insofar as they were frequently worn as emblematic of a love interest, were in some sense equally a continuation of the courtly practice of wearing an *emprise* or token of an enterprise undertaken on behalf of a lady. Such an *emprise* might be a scarf, for example, which the knight could attach to his armor and which would serve as a visible sign of his devotion to his lover's interests.

The advantages of the impresa, when compared to the achievements of arms, were several: it was available to anyone who troubled to compose one; it could be altered to fit personal circumstances; it allowed the display of wit, learning, and taste. Its uses were manifold: in France, Louis XII's porcupine at Blois (with its motto *De près et de loin*, "from near and far") and Francis I's salamander at Chambord (with the accompanying words *Nutrisco et extinguo*, "I feed and extinguish [fire]") are but two of the best-known and most widely admired examples.

The impresa normally seeks to achieve a metaphorical transfer to the bearer of certain qualities thought to be those of the object or being that is represented in the picture; the function of the motto is thus to specify the exact nature of the qualities to be transferred. Thus, in the case of the porcupine, "From near and far" makes it explicit to the reader that the owner of the impresa can, like the porcupine, protect himself either by curling into a spiky ball in defense or by hurling his quills, a trait commonly associated with the porcupine in medieval and Renaissance texts such as the translation of the *Physiologus*, from which so much animal imagery is derived. The enigmatic or ambiguous character of the impresa could, however, involve its owner in difficulties, as in the case of the personal device of Erasmus, which showed the Roman god Terminus with the motto *Cedo nulli* ("I yield to none"). While Erasmus contended that the device was meant as a memento mori, his enemies argued with some justification that the motto of an impresa was normally meant to be taken as being spoken both by the rep-

resented being and by the owner and that his impresa was therefore nothing more than a symbol of his own arrogant defiance of legitimate authority. Especially because of the ambiguity of their visual signs, impresas often lent themselves as well to outright parody and to satirical deformation for political purposes.

The impresa came to find a myriad of uses in Renaissance Europe: on royal devices that appeared on the arches erected to celebrate royal entrances to cities; in cavalcades and carousels enacted in honor of royalty, in which each participant displayed a device intended simultaneously to commemorate the occasion and to celebrate himself and his monarch (thus a device borne by the marquis de Soyecourt, which showed an eagle—himself—gazing on a sun that symbolized his king, Louis XIV); on the reverse of commemorative medals (with the notable exception of Germany, where true heraldic motifs remained more common than impresas); on title pages of books; as printer's devices; and especially in tournaments. The sixteenth-century vogue for the tournament impresa, composed and borne especially to celebrate a combination of the circumstances of the tournament itself and the personal aspirations of the bearer, was particularly evident in Elizabethan England, from which several hundred such devices have been catalogued, though the actual shields on which they were painted have long been lost. Like the coat of arms, the tournament impresa was displayed wherever it might be most evident to onlookers at the tournament: not only on the shield but on the surcoat, the cloak, as part of the helmet crest, and on the horse's bards.

Early theoretical discussions of the impresa, which become more and more frequent after about 1580, owe a great deal to Paolo Giovio, whose *Dialogo dell'imprese militari e amorose*, first published in Rome in 1555, was soon translated into several other European languages and furnished the essential matter for theoretical debate for over a century. Giovio not only laid claim to a heraldic basis for the impresa but set out clear standards by which the merits of a given device could be judged, though not all his rules were followed closely in actual practice. For Giovio, the impresa must give appropriate weight to both picture and text; its interpretation must not be too mysterious while not being perfectly obvious; it must be pleasing in appearance; it should avoid the use of human figures; it should always contain a motto, preferably in a foreign language. It will be apparent that these criteria are formulated so as to spur designers of impresas to attain balance and harmony between visual and verbal codes and to strive to create a visually attractive enigma that will intrigue the reader and whose solution will give pleasure.

Later theoreticians, in assessing the relative importance of picture and text in the perfect impresa, frequently assigned the picture alone the function of attracting the reader's attention. This shifting of aesthetic weight to the pictorial element of the device ensured that over time the picture came to have an almost purely decorative role, while the essence of the device's meaning came to be expressed more and more by the motto. This development is essentially similar to that of the emblem, whose text tends to be assimilated to written literature, while the picture tends to become the province of the visual designer and graphic artist by the late seventeenth or early eighteenth century. Both genres were frequently collected in book form, and seventeenth-century theoretical writers often seemed to experience considerable difficulty in distinguishing clearly between the genres, though they usually emphasized certain formal features that, taken together, were considered diagnostic: the bipartite structure of the device, which lacks the extended text often found in the emblem; the lack of human figures in the device (though this rule seems to have been more honored in theory than in practice); and the fact that the motto of the device cannot, by convention, name the content of the picture. The lack of general moral or didactic intention in the device is also cited frequently as a differentiating feature.

Scholarly interest in the personal device has experienced a revival in parallel with that in the emblem, and to a large degree the historical and theoretical concerns of scholars working on both genres are identical. On the one hand, establishing the provenance and dissemination of many visual and textual motifs used in impresas remains of interest, as does investigating the use of personal devices in Renaissance society and literature. On the other hand, the impresa calls on scholars to examine the mechanisms by which text and picture can be fused to create a semiotic composite of which neither part in isolation furnishes a complete reading. Lastly, even deciding on a valid interpretation for many impresas remains problematic, as their meaning so frequently depends on a knowledge of the personal circum-

stances of their owner at the time of their composition and of the meanings commonly assigned at the time to the pictorial elements, as well as on an ability to recognize and interpret puns whose significance will very often not be readily apparent to a modern reader. Modern scholars can take heart, however, from the fact that Sir Henry Wootton, who in commenting on impresas displayed in a tournament he witnessed in March 1613, wrote that "some were so dark, that their meaning is not yet understood; unless perchance that were their meaning, not to be understood" (quoted in Young, 1987b, p. 134).

[*See also* Blazon; Code; Emblem; Heraldry; Logo; Metaphor; Multimodality; *and* Poetics.]

BIBLIOGRAPHY

Gombrich, E. H. "Icones Symbolicae: The Visual Image in Neo-Platonic Thought." *Journal of the Warburg and Courtault Institutes* 11 (1948): 163–192.

Hill, Sir G. *Medals of the Renaissance.* Revised and enlarged by Graham Pollard. London: British Museum Publications, 1978.

Klein, R. "La théorie de l'expression figurée dans les traités italiens sur les imprese (1555–1612)." *Bibliothèque d'humanisme et Renaissance* 19 (1957): 320–342.

Russell, D. *The Emblem and Device in France.* French Forum Monographs: vol. 59. Lexington, Ky.: French Forum, 1985.

Vanuxem, J. "Emblèmes et devises vers 1660–1680." *Bulletin de la société de l'histoire de l'art français* (1954): 60–70.

Young, A. *Studies in the Emblem*, vol. 3, *The English Tournament Imprese.* New York: AMS Press, 1987a.

Young, A. *Tudor and Jacobean Tournaments.* London: George Philip, 1987b.

—DAVID GRAHAM

INDEX. Variously defined, *index* is an important term for linguists, philosophers, and psychologists. Luis Prieto (1966) attempts to retrace the emergence of evolution of the semiotic function by contrasting "significative indication" and "notificative indication." For the purpose of illustration, he imagines a simple situation in which a set of hoofprints made by a horse are observed. This significative indication informs an observer that there is a horse in the vicinity, but this sign does not carry any notificative indication, which would convey to the observer the supplementary information, "Attention! This is intended to contain a message," as a linguistic sign would do.

Jean Piaget (1967) uses the term *index* differently

when he introduces his idea of the semiotic function (called the symbolic function in his earlier writings), which is the capacity acquired by the child at eighteen to twenty-four months to imitate something outside the direct presence of the model: to use language, make drawings, play "symbolically," and have access to mental imagery and memory. The common factor underlying all these phenomena, according to Piaget, is the ability to represent reality by means of a signifier that is distinct or differentiated from the signified. Even before that age, however, Piaget believes that the child is able to "connect significations" by means of "indices" and "signals" that do not suppose any such differentiation between expression and content. The signifier of the index is, Piaget says, "an objective aspect of the signified"; thus, for instance, the visible portion of an almost entirely hidden object is the signifier of the object for the infant, just as tracks in the snow stand for prey to a hunter and, more generally, as any effect stands for its cause. But the child who uses a pebble to signify candy is well aware of the difference between the two categories of object. This implies for Piaget "a differentiation, from the subject's own point of view, between the signifier and the signified."

In Charles Sanders Peirce's triadic philosophy of signs, *index* is defined in relation to the other two kinds of sign: icon or symbol. It is a sign in which the thing that serves as the expression is, in one way or another independent of the sign relation, connected with another thing, which serves as its content. The term chosen by Peirce certainly suggests that all indexes, such as a pointing finger or the drawing of an arrow, serve to pinpoint particular objects to isolate them and bring them out of the (typically spatial) context in which it is ordinarily enmeshed; and this is, indeed, what Peirce affirms (1931–1958, 3.361; 4.56). However, if we introduce the term *indicator* to describe signs that are employed to single out an object or a portion of space for our particular attention, it may be argued that they are not necessarily indexes in Peirce's sense and that they are not, in any event, sufficiently characterized by being so classified. Thus, certain indicators, such as pointing fingers and arrows, do suppose a relation of contiguity with that which they point to; but this is not necessary or even possible in the case of many verbal indicators, most maps, and the photographic images depending on film, lighting, and frame that are described as indexical in the semiotics of photography. In these cases, the indicative gesture is merely re-created at the level of content. At least some of these examples would not qualify as Peircean "genuine" indexes.

On the other hand, real indicators, such as pointing fingers and arrows, are equally contiguous to a number of objects that they do not indicate, such as things at the opposite side of the arrowhead, in the direction to which it does not point. Therefore, something beyond mere indexicality is required; in the case of the arrow, the forward thrust of the arrowhead as imagined in water, or the sentiment of its slipping from our hands, as René Thom (1983) has suggested. To term certain signs *indicators* is, obviously, to make a categorization of signs on the basis of their functions. We should not expect this categorization to coincide with the one stemming from Peirce's classification, which depends on the nature of the relationship between the expression and the referent or content of the sign.

Apart from being a sign, an index, in the Peircean sense, must contain an indexical ground. The fact that such a ground could exist independently of the sign relation should not be taken to mean that the indexical relation necessarily has to precede the sign relation in real time. Indeed, some indexical relations must come into being at the same time as the sign is produced, as is the case, for instance, of verbal "shifters": the person indexically related to the sign *I* is the one who at a particular moment pronounces the sound /ai/, which is to say that the indexical ground is produced at the very same moment in which the sign is put to use. Similarly, there is no class of "pointed-out objects" known to exist, but a member of such a class is created each time an act of pointing takes place.

Many of Peirce's own examples of indexical signs are of the kind that acquires meaning thanks to a regularity known to obtain between different facts. Since Peirce calls the kind of reasoning that connects two facts by means of supposed regularity an abduction, we might perhaps call this group of signs abductive indexes. They can involve contiguity—as is the case of footprints, fingerprints, the cross as a sign of the crucified, the weathercock contiguous to the direction of the wind—or factorality, when, for instance, an anchor is used to stand for navigation.

Some of Peirce's examples and many of those suggested later are, however, of another kind; instead of presupposing a regularity known to obtain between the thing that serves as expression of the sign and another thing that is taken to be its contents, something that is contiguous or in a relation of factorality to the expression is transformed into its content. These signs may therefore be termed performative indexes. With contiguity, they give rise to such phenomena as the pronoun *you*, the finger pointing to an object, the weathercock (as marking the here and now of the wind), the clock of the watchmaker's (as marking the emplacement of the shop); with factorality, they produce the pronouns and adverbs *I, you, here, now*, the finger pointing out a direction, and so on.

Finally, many secondary signs—signs standing for other signs—are often said to be indexical. Secondary indexical signs are signs, the dominant sign relation of which is pictorial or otherwise iconical, conventional, or whatever, that involve a secondary sign function, which is a relation between several signs or parts of several signs, which is indexical. The most obvious case of such signs are the rhetorical figures of metonymy and synecdoche, in which the entire primary sign is related to another sign by means of the respective contents. Another variety, which is often parasitic on pictorial signs, occurs when the entire primary sign, which is related to another sign via their respective expressions, forms an actual perceptual context. This type is often found in advertising and in surrealist painting.

Peirce himself introduces one distinction between different kinds of indexical signs but in terms that are not easy to interpret: thus, there are designations, which stand for "things or quasi-things with which the interpreting mind is already acquainted," and reagents, which serve "to ascertain certain facts" based on our knowledge of the "connection with the phenomena it indicates" (1938–1951, 8.368n.). Examples of the first kind are personal, demonstrative, and relative pronouns, as well as proper names; an instance of the second kind, however, is when "water placed in a vessel with a shaving of camphor thrown upon it will show whether the vessel is clean or not." Thomas Goudge (1965) and Douglas Greenlee (1973) interpret this as a distinction between genuine, causal indexes and degenerate cases, but there could also be a suggestion of the distinction, formulated above, between abductive and performative indexes.

[*See also* Abductive Reasoning; Indexicality; Peirce; *and* Sign.]

BIBLIOGRAPHY

Goudge, T. A. "Peirce's Index." *Transactions of the Charles S. Peirce Society* 1 (1965): 52–70.

Greenlee, D. *Peirce's Concept of Sign*. The Hague: Mouton, 1973.

Peirce, C. S. *Collected Papers*, 8 vols. Edited by C. Hartshorne, P. Weiss, and A. Burks. Cambridge, Mass.: Harvard University Press, 1931–1958.

Piaget, J. *The Origins of Intelligence in Children*. Translated by M. Cook. New York: W. W. Norton, 1963.

Piaget, J. *La psychologie de l'intelligence*. Paris: Gallimard, 1967.

Prieto, L. *Messages et signaux*. Paris: Presses universitaires de France, 1966.

Sonesson, G. *Pictorial Complex: Inquiries into the Semiotic Heritage and Its Relevance for the Analysis of the Visual World*. Lund: Lund University Press, 1989. See pp. 30–65.

Thom, R. *Mathematical Models of Morphogenesis*. Translated by W. M. Brookes and D. Rand. New York: John Wiley and Sons, 1983. See chapter 14, "Semiotics," pp. 261–273.

—GÖRAN SONESSON

INDEXICALITY is, simply, the property that characterizes a sign as an index according to Charles Sanders Peirce's definitions and examples. However, by a slight shift of emphasis, based at least somewhat on Peirce's work, indexicality can be conceived as the property that, when added to the sign function, creates an index but that in addition might have other parts to play in the constitution of meaning. This qualification might account for the ambiguities of this Peircean notion, as well as for some of the uses to which it has been put subsequently in semiotics.

In spite of the confusion created by the successive definitions and problematic examples given by Peirce over a long period of time (Goudge, 1965), a few defining criteria can be identified. Indexicality pertains to the general category of Secondness—that is, it concerns two items and the relation between them. The sign is a Thirdness, so there is every reason to think that it cannot be constituted by indexicality alone. More likely, when he discusses indexicality, Peirce is considering potential sign vehicles in order to investigate their "capacity to serve as signs" (Bruss, 1978). Substantial arguments for this may be derived from a consideration of the Peircean concept of ground, which helps clarify the notion of indexicality.

In one of his well-known definitions of the sign vehicle, Peirce (1931–1958, 2.228) describes it as something that "stands for that object not in all respects, but in reference to a sort of idea which [he] sometimes called the *ground* of the representation." For Douglas Greenlee (1973), the ground is that aspect of the referent that is referred to by the expression; for instance, the direction of the wind is the only property of the referential object *the wind* about which the weathercock informs us. For David Savan (1976), the ground consists of the features selected from the thing serving as expression, which would include those properties of the weathercock permitting it to react to the wind—not, for instance, its having the characteristic shape of a rooster made out of iron and being placed on a church steeple. In one passage, however, Peirce himself identifies *ground* with abstraction, exemplifying it with the blackness of two black things (1.293). That, of course, would be an iconic ground; an indexical ground, in a parallel fashion, would then be whatever it is that connects the properties of the weathercock as a physical thing to the direction in which the wind is blowing. If so, the ground is a principle of relevance or, in Hjelmslevian terms, the form connecting expression and content. An indexical ground or indexicality would then involve two things that are apt to enter into a semiotic relation, forming an indexical sign, due to a set of properties that are intrinsic to the relationship between them, independent of the sign relation. This kind of ground, which is a relation, is best conceived in opposition to an iconic ground, which consists of a set of two classes of properties ascribed to two different things, which are taken to possess the properties in question independently, not only of the sign relation but of each other, although, when considered from a particular point of view, these two sets of properties will appear to be identical or similar to each other. This is the sense in which indexicality is Secondness and iconicity is Firstness.

Such a view of indexicality seems to conform to the most general formulations given by Peirce, according to which indexicality depends on there being a "real connection," an "existential relation," a "dynamical (including spatial) connection," and even, in one of its many conceivable senses, a "physical connection" between the items involved (1.196; 1.558; 2.305; 3.361; 8.335). It thus seems natural to go on to argue that indexicality is involved with "spatio-temporal location" (Burks, 1949), which underlies the "indices" of such logicians as Yehoshua Bar-Hillel and

Richard Montague, the "egocentric particulars" of Bertrand A. Russell, and the "shifters" of Otto Jespersen and Roman Jakobson. In fact, however, as Savan (1976) observes, location in time and space will result only to the extent that some system of coordinates has been conveyed by other types of signs—or as can be presupposed by the ongoing practice of the ordinary world of our experience.

More generally, many of the examples adduced by Peirce appear to justify Jakobson's claim that indexicality is based on "real contiguity" and is connected with the syntagmatic axis of language and the rhetorical figures of metonymy (1979). To Jakobson, however, metonymy actually involves not only the relation of contiguity of traditional rhetoric but also that of part to whole, known in rhetoric as synecdoche. This distinction may be reestablished inside the category of indexicality (Nöth, 1975) and could be described more generally in terms of contiguity and factorality (Sonesson, 1989).

However, another series of definitions suggests that indexicality is in some way dependent on a relation of causality between the expression and content of the potential sign: that is, the index supposedly "denotes by virtue of being really affected by that object" (2.248). Peirce also makes a number of other claims about indexes, that they refer to unique, singular objects (2.283); that they testify to the existence of their object (2.316); that they show up the object without asserting anything about it (3.361); and that they point by "blind compulsion" to the object of reference (2.306).

Although the definition by causality is probably the most commonly quoted of all the definitions Peirce offers of indexicality, it has come under serious criticism. Some commentators reject the relation between causality and indexicality altogether, while others see it as merely coincidental. Arthur Burks (1949) takes Peirce to task for confusing the semiotic relation with mere causality when treating, for instance, the weathercock, which is causally affected by the wind, as an instance of an indexical sign: it is not clear, however, why causality should preclude indexicality, since the fact of the wind causing the weathercock to turn must be seen by the observer to be a contiguity in order for it to receive an interpretation. More to the point, Thomas Goudge (1965) claims that not all examples of indexical signs given by Peirce are susceptible to receiving a causal explanation: the polestar, for instance, can be an index of the north celestial pole, but it is no way caused by that astronomical location. Nor is a personal pronoun or even a pointing finger actually caused by the person or thing for which it stands; and if they may be said to motivate indexicality, then this is also true of all other signs.

According to Peirce (2.306), all indexes refer to a singular instance, not to some general category. There are objections to this generalization, however. From the size of an imprint left on the ground, it might be possible for an interpreter to determine that the animal that has passed by is a horse rather than a donkey, but normally there is nothing in the expression of this index itself that makes it possible to determine the identity of the horse, although if it is known that there is only one horse and one donkey inside the fence, a plausible conclusion can be drawn as to which individual animal is involved. It might be argued, of course, that in any case, only one particular animal left the imprint; but the case is quite similar to the knock at the door, where, although a particular person must be doing the knocking, the knock itself merely means "there is someone at the door," unless we possess some additional information. The same argument applies to the photograph, in particular to the photogram, in which the referent is not normally recognizable.

Goudge (1965) also argues this generalization, quoting the case in which a demonstrative pronoun (*that*) refers to Newton's first law, which as such is not a singularity. Outside the linguistic domain, other interesting examples can be found. According to Peirce, the rolling gait of a man is an index of his being a sailor, but being a sailor is a social role, not a singularity. More important, however, the gait is part of a social habitus defining this role, which makes it into a part of a whole (a factorality). But if the relationship of a property to that of which it is a part is indexical, then it is reasonable to think that indexicality will also account for the relation between an item and the class of which it is a member. Such examples are apparently not among those mentioned by Peirce, but they are often cited by later semioticians: thus, for instance, if a pretzel is an index of a bakery, then that must be in virtue of its being a member of the class of products sold in the bakery. A class is, of course, not a singular object, but it may be considered a collection of objects. Often, however, such a class is itself determined by abstract properties. A tailor's swatch, for instance, is a sign of a class of cloth having the same quality and pattern but not the same shape or size. Some samples, such as color samples, are even indexes of abstract properties themselves.

In order to consider whether indexes demonstrate the existence of their objects, it might be necessary first to discuss the meaning of existence (Goudge, 1965). However, if existence is taken to imply the physical occurrence in the ordinary world of our experience, it does not seem to apply to all indexes—not, for instance, to the cases considered above in connection with singularity. A person having the rolling gait of a sailor might, in fact, not be a sailor; and the pretzel hanging out above the bakery (admittedly an icon of an index) is still visible when the bakery is closed and no bakery products are for sale. Plausible indexes of a unicorn may be produced using a set of horseshoes and a narwhal's horn, but they do not testify to the existence of unicorns. A faked photograph of a unicorn, or whatever, may be assembled, using pieces of real photographs, processing them in a computer, or even creating them entirely by means of a computer program. Of course, the latter pictures are not photographs and therefore not indexes, but it is not possible to discover that from looking at them. For all practical purposes, then, indexes cannot testify to the existence of their objects.

From the debate triggered by this ongoing exegesis, indexicality emerges as a particular kind of ground characterizing indexical signs but one that may also be found outside signs. Perception would seem to be profuse with indexicality. Indeed, proximity is a basic factor of perception according to Gestalt psychology and is also one of the relationships included in topological-space perception. The relation of part to whole is fundamental to Gestalt relations themselves. All indexical relations involve either contiguity or factorality. Indexicalities that are not as yet signs, being based on items that are not situated on different levels of directness or thematization or are not clearly differentiated, may be described as contexts (or "pairings" in Edmund Husserl's sense). Any experience of two elements being related by proximity, conceived as a primordial perceptual fact, may be considered an actual perceptual context involving contiguity. An actual perceptual context involving factorality is any experience of something as being a part of a whole or as being a whole having parts (Sonesson, 1989).

When only one of the items is given directly and the other precedes or follows it in time, we may speak of an abductive context (protention and retention, respectively). The term *abduction* is employed here in Peirce's sense to signify a general rule or regularity that is taken for granted and that links one singular fact with another. All experience taking place in time is of this kind, such as our expectancy, when seeing a woodcutter with an ax raised over his head, that in the following moment he is going to hit the piece of wood (contiguity protention), and that in the moment just preceding he lifted the ax to its present position (contiguity retention). Abductive contexts involving factorality include, using some Peircean examples, the gait of the sailor, the symptom as part of the disease, part and whole in a picture, a partly destroyed Minoan fresco, a jigsaw puzzle, a piece of torn paper. (Note that the last three examples combine factorality and contiguity). We may use the term *protoindex* for an indexicality that is only momentarily a sign, as would be the *tableau vivant* of the woodcutter, the photographic pose (which is limited in time), that what is seen in the viewfinder (with spatial limits), and indeed many of the examples given above, to the extent that the flow of indexicalities is halted momentarily. The archaeologist's art, from this point of view, would consist in transforming indexicalities of decayed cultures into protoindexes accessible to us.

[*See also* Abductive Reasoning; Icon; Iconicity; Index; Metonymy; Peirce; *and* Photography.]

BIBLIOGRAPHY

Bruss, E. "Peirce and Jakobson on the Nature of the Sign." In *The Sign: Semiotics around the World*, edited by R. W. Bailey, L. Matejka, and P. Steiner, pp. 81–98. Michigan Slavic Contributions. Ann Arbor: University of Michigan, 1978.

Burks, A. "Icon, Index, Symbol." *Philosophy and Phenomenological Research* 9.4 (1949): 673–689.

Goudge, T. A. "Peirce's Index." *Transactions of the Charles S. Peirce Society* 1 (1965): 52–70.

Greenlee, D. *Peirce's Concept of Sign*. The Hague: Mouton, 1973.

Husserl, E. *Zur Phänomenologie des inneren Zeitbewusstseins*. The Hague: Nijhoff, 1966.

Jakobson, R. "Coup d'oeil sur le développment de la sémiotique." In *A Semiotic Landscape/Panorama Sémiotique: Actes du premier congrés de l'association internationale de sémiotique, Milan, juin 1974*, edited by S. Chatman, U. Eco, and J. M. Klinkenberg, pp. 3–18. The Hague: Mouton, 1979.

Nöth, W. *Semiotik*. Tübingen: Niemeyer Verlag, 1975.

Peirce, C. S. *Collected Papers*. 8 vols. Edited by C. Hartshorne, P. Weiss, and A. Burks. Cambridge, Mass.: Harvard University Press, 1931–1958.

Savan, D. *An Introduction to C. S. Peirce's Semiotics*. Toronto: Toronto Semiotic Circle, Victoria University, 1976.

Sonesson, G. *Pictorial Concepts: Inquiries into the Semiotic Heritage and Its Relevance for the Analysis of the Visual World*. Lund: Lund University Press, 1989.

—GÖRAN SONESSON

INFORMATION. A theory of information was first formulated in 1948 by Claude Shannon and Warren Weaver as a theory of communication to study the receiving, conserving, processing, and transmitting of signals. The notion of information, however, goes back to Ludwig Boltzmann (1896), who stated that the increase in information about a certain system is related to a reduction in the number of states of the system and therefore to an entropy decrease. This concept was later generalized by Léon Brillouin (1956), who defined information as negative entropy or negentropy.

If an event results in some outcome, then the definition of information becomes the additional information one can get from the experiment from knowledge of the statistical-outcome probabilities. This is the result of a choice and can be regarded as the amount of uncertainty that exists before an event takes place. It is important to note that the mathematical notion of information says nothing about its quality or value.

The entropy of a system can also be defined statistically by considering the number of possible microstates, N, in which the system can be found such that $S = kln(N)$, where k is the Boltzmann constant. This definition of entropy is the negative equivalent of the definition of information, in which the equally probable outcomes can be thought of as the system's complexions or "solutions." Entropy decreases when information is obtained, thus reducing the number of complexions; therefore, entropy reduction implies information gain. The information is actually furnished by some external agent whose entropy must increase.

Information is generated when an unpredictable outcome results from an experiment and the uncertainty about a system is reduced. In chemical recognition, it is (ideally) certain that a given receptor will selectively bind with one type of molecule and that only information about the occurrence of the binding event is generated (i.e., bound or not bound). This provides no structural information about the ligand. The mathematical concept of information implies the generation of a sequence, as when information is encoded by a sequence of binary digits. A better chemical example of generation of new structural information is found in random mutation of the genetic code, because in this case a new DNA molecule is produced with different informational content. However, "transferring information in bimolecular recognition" is usually implied as communication between the molecular partners, through which the receptor sees the ligand and recognizes that it is right for binding. Mathematically, it is erroneous to speak of information in this case because no sequenced message is either generated or duplicated, and it becomes apparent that the word *information* applied to molecular recognition is simply a substitute for the physicochemical forces that govern binding. From the view of chemoreception, therefore, the focus of attention must be on development of an analytical signal that is derived directly from changes of these physicochemical forces and interpretation of the signal as a quantity that does not by itself provide structural information.

[*See also* Biosemiotics; Chemical Communication; Communication; Receptors; *and* Umwelt.]

BIBLIOGRAPHY

Boltzmann, L. *Lectures on Gas Theory.* Berkeley: University of California Press, 1964.
Brillouin, L. *Science and Information Theory.* New York: Academic Press, 1956.
Shannon, C., and W. Weaver. *Mathematical Theory of Communication.* Urbana: University of Illinois Press, 1949. The first paper is reprinted from the Bell System technical journal, July and October 1948.
—ULRICH J. KRULL

INNER SPEECH. Scientific interest in internal language processes or inner speech goes back at least to the work of Carl Wernicke (1848–1905) on acquired aphasic disorders. Wernicke viewed linguistic events as the association of acoustic images with their corresponding concepts in the brain. Language acquisition for Wernicke coincides clearly with the emergence of consciousness and is its "measuring gauge." Both the nineteenth-century psychological theory of association and the available neuroanatomical evidence allowed Wernicke to postulate the existence of fiber tracts in the brain whereby the auditory images of words are associated with their motor images. The resulting stimulus is then transmitted along the fiber tract "within the foot of the cerebral peduncle . . . until it reaches the speech musculature" (1977, p. 100). In learning to speak, a child associates the sounds he or she hears with acoustic imagery stored in the brain. Importantly, acoustic and auditory images are conceptual rather than physical in status. The phenomenon of inner speech or silent verbal thought depends on this most important fact. In silent verbal thought, acoustic images are associated with their linguistic concepts even in the absence of any externally produced speech sounds. Language exists in the brain as a psychoperceptual phenomenon rather than as a physical one. The psychoperceptual representation of language in the inner realm depends on stored acoustic images and their corresponding concepts rather than on physical sound waves.

Ronald Langacker is one modern linguist who recognizes the psychoperceptual nature of internal language processes. From the perspectives of both articulation and audition, there are cognitive routines that direct both the production and reception of speech sounds. These cognitive routines are directed by stored acoustic images, which serve to categorize speech sounds as being instances of phonological types. Langacker points out that the acoustic or auditory image rather than the physical sound is primary. In this way, listeners have two possible ways of perceiving speech sounds. The listener might actually hear the speech sound as an acoustic event, or he or she might imagine hearing it through the activation of an acoustic image of the sound in silent verbal thought. Analogously, the speaker might actually implement an articulatory routine and utter a given speech sound or imagine doing so. In the latter case, this means that the speaker "can mentally run through the motor routine without this mental activity being translated into muscular gestures" (Langacker, 1987, p. 79). Acoustic images direct and control auditory and articulatory routines in both inner and outer speech.

The postulating of the existence of "imaginary" auditory and articulatory routines does not, however, presuppose the existence of a "ghost in the machine" that mentally causes either inner or outer linguistic activity. This point has been critiqued most eloquently by Gilbert Ryle (1970) in his discussion of imagined language activity "in the head" of the individual. Language activity still goes on, though this is neither heard nor seen by others. Nevertheless, this is merely one semiotic modality whereby the individual engages in language activity. It is not a causal explanation of that activity.

In his book *Freudianism: A Marxist Critique* (1976), the Soviet semiotician Valentin Voloshinov discusses the notion of inner speech. Inner speech is speech turned inward in the sense that it constitutes a specific appropriation by the individual of the social meaning-making resources and practices that individuals draw on and deploy in their interactions with others. An individual psyche is constructed by selectively appropriating, foregrounding, and projecting some meanings and their associated axiological orientations from the social milieu. In turn, inner speech is contrasted with outer speech so as to define the boundary between them. Voloshinov recognizes that inner speech no less than outer speech is always oriented to an addressee. It is shaped by precisely the same social factors that shape outer speech. What really matters is the context—that of psychical experience, the physical body, or social phenomena—in which speech, whether inner or outer, is construed in relation to the wider social dynamics and practices of the social milieu. Further, these may differ from culture to culture as well as between different social groups within the same culture.

The role of inner speech is particularly important in the sociogenetic theory of Lev Vygotsky (1896–1934) concerning the emergence of higher mental functions. Vygotsky's account of inner speech, which was influenced by that of Voloshinov, is perhaps the most influential. This is evidenced by the important recent attempts to elaborate his theory of the sociogenesis of higher mental functions in relation to modern linguistic and semiotic thought (Emerson 1983; Wertsch, 1985, 1991; Hasan, 1992). Like Voloshinov, Vygotsky sees inner speech and thought as motivated by affective and volitional tendencies. In *Thought and Language* (1988), he traces the emergence of verbal thought "from the motive that engenders a thought to the shaping of the thought, first in inner speech, then in meanings of words, and finally in words" (1988, p. 253).

Vygotsky carefully distinguishes between thought and language. There is no simple equation of inner speech with thought. Vygotsky does not claim that language "expresses" or "represents" thought. Thought does not have the status of a "mental representation," which in many modern theories of cognition is then recoded in language. "Thought," Vygotsky argues, "is still more inward than inner speech. . . . Every thought creates a connection, fulfills a function, solves a problem" (1988, p. 249).

Vygotsky makes an important distinction between *sense* and *meaning*. *Sense* is Vygotsky's term for the fully contextualized meanings a word has in discourse; *meaning* refers to the more or less stable core "meaning potential" of the word. That is, meaning designates the decontextualized perspective of language as system, abstracted from actual use. Thus, the external meaning of a word is its typical meanings in the discourse genres of the public realm. The everchanging senses of the word in inner speech reflect the dynamic and shifting nature of its contexts. The fact that inner speech is a specialized internal deployment of language does not mean that it is decontextualized. On the contrary, it is a specialized mode of language use. The specific dynamics of inner speech are a direct consequence of this fact. Vygotsky identified a number of lexicogrammatical features that are foregrounded in inner speech, including omission of the subject, the foregrounding of predication, and a highly elliptical relationship between these forms and the speech situation. In a later refinement, James Wertsch has pointed out that these features refer in actual fact to the distinction between given and new information that has been made in modern functional and discourse-based grammars. Wertsch argues that Vygotsky's term *subject* really refers to given information and *predicate* to new information (Wertsch, 1991).

The lexicogrammatical tendencies that Vygotsky identifies as characteristic of inner speech reflect the specialized uses to which inner speech is put and in relation to which it has both evolved in the species and developed in the individual. As a specialized deployment of the lexicogrammatical and semantic resources of a given language system, inner speech can be seen as a specific semantic register. However, this should not detract from the considerable social and individual variation that inner speech seems likely to display. Such variation is a consequence of the diversity of language practices (heteroglossia) in which the individuals in a given language community participate. The specific ways in which inner speech is deployed by individuals, connected to outer experience as well as to bodily processes and related to historically prior events in the life of the individual, might contribute to the formation of personal psychology. These internalized "idiolects" might provide information about the processes of psychological individuation and the ways in which the psychological is seen as continuous with the biological and the social, rather than as separate ontological domain.

Vygotsky focuses on the ways in which a child learns to transfer "social, collaborative forms of behavior to the sphere of inner-personal psychic functions (1988, p. 35). He contrasts his approach to Jean Piaget's more individual-centered one. To explain this transition, Vygotsky postulates three linguistic stages in child development—social speech, egocentric speech, and inner speech—and proposes a developmental framework for explaining the transition a child makes from one to the next. In social speech, language functions are less differentiated. Around the age of three years, egocentric speech emerges. Vygotsky relates the emergence of this stage to the child's developing capacity for self-regulation. If in social speech the boundaries between self and nonself are not yet clearly differentiated, then the self-regulatory function of egocentric speech marks an important moment in the child's organization of the self-nonself distinction. Vygotsky recognized that egocentric speech semiotically mediates the child's adaptive modification of his or her environment toward the satisfaction and organization of personal needs and desires. Egocentric speech is especially interesting to Vygotsky because it represents in audible form an intermediate stage between social speech and inner speech. Egocentric speech has the same psychological function as silent inner speech, though the former is not fully internalized until around the age of seven.

A number of problems remain in Vygotsky's account. If Vygotsky grants the word an active shaping role in the formation of consciousness, his theory of word meaning is, nevertheless, linguistically unsophisticated. He lacks an explicit and detailed account of language form and function. A second major problem is the lack of any detailed framework for explaining how variant forms of social organization shape consciousness in different ways. This requires a more detailed account of the relations between variant forms of social interactions, their internalization in individual psyche, the implications these have for

different modes of social organization, and the differential ways in which consciousness may be shaped and organized both in different cultures as well as by different social groups in the same culture. A number of scholars are actively accepting this challenge (e.g., Wertsch, 1985, 1991; Hasan, 1992).

[See also Bakhtin; Dialogism; Dialogue; Discourse Analysis; and Meaning.]

BIBLIOGRAPHY

Edelman, G. M. *The Remembered Present: A Biological Theory of Consciousness*. New York: Basic Books, 1989.

Emerson, C. "The Outer Word and Inner Speech: Bakhtin, Vygtosky, and the Internalization of Language." *Critical Inquiry* 10.2 (1983): 245–264.

Hasan, R. "Speech Genre, Semiotic Mediation, and the Development of Higher Mental Functions." *Language Sciences* 14.4 (1992): 489–528.

Langacker, R. W. *Foundations of Cognitive Grammar*, volume 1, *Theoretical Prerequisites*. Stanford: Stanford University Press, 1987.

Ryle, G. *The Concept of Mind*. Harmondsworth: Penguin, 1970.

Voloshinov, V. N. *Freudianism: A Marxist Critique*. Translated and edited by I. R. Titunik and N. H. Bruss, New York and London: Academic Press, 1976.

Vygotsky, L. *Thought and Language*. Translated and edited by A. Kozulin. Cambridge, Mass., and London: MIT Press, 1988.

Wernicke, C. "The Aphasia Symptom Complex: A Psychological Theory on an Anatomic Basis" (1874). In *Wernicke's Works on Aphasia: A Sourcebook and Review*, edited by G. H. Eggert, pp. 91–145. The Hague and New York: Mouton, 1977.

Wertsch, J. V., ed. *Culture Communication and Cognition: Vygotskian Perspectives*. Cambridge and Sydney: Cambridge University Press, 1985.

Wertsch, J. V. *Voices of the Mind: A Sociocultural Approach to Mediated Action*. London and Singapore: Harvester Wheatsheaf, 1991.

—PAUL J. THIBAULT

INTENTIONALITY is a notion associated intimately with phenomenology and particularly with Edmund Husserl (1859–1938). For Husserl, objects in the world and the world itself are "intended" by human consciousness. Everything that is beyond conscious experience is "put in brackets": the only "reality" is that which appears as phenomena in the human mind. Meanings are not transferred from "outside" into consciousness; rather, consciousness, through what Husserl calls its "intentional content," brings those meanings into being by "intending" them. Intentionality in this sense describes the condition in which consciousness is always directed toward something, and it is this directedness that brings the world into being. However, what is brought into being are not "random" phenomena; phenomenological knowledge presents us with the types or universal essences of things. The crux of Husserl's theory of transcendental intentionality is that there is no distinction to be made between universal types on the one hand and the intending consciousness or the intentional content on the other.

How are these universal essences, which are intended by consciousness, communicated? Husserl's work does not place much emphasis on language because intentionality always precedes and in fact constitutes the possibility of communication language. Language, for Husserl, operates at a secondary level as a site for the identification of that which is already present in intentionality. He distinguishes between two types of signs: expressive and indicative. Expressive signs are produced through and informed by intentionality, while indicative signs, lacking this intentional aspect, are more or less empty.

However, as Jacques Derrida, among others, has shown, this kind of distinction, which could be understood as fetishizing signifieds at the expense of the notion of the signifier, is readily deconstructed. Husserl's expressive signs—that is to say, signifieds—are "born," in a sense, without recourse to indicative signs (signifiers). But in order for the process of communication to take place and in order for universal essences to be identified, Husserl's signifieds have to become "something else"—signifiers. Intentionality might precede language, but it can only remain "itself" by "keeping to itself," by refusing to be caught up in and "infected" by indicative language.

In a sense, then, Husserl's notion of intentionality falls prey to its own logic. This notion was designed and employed to great effect as a critique of the way in which any structure of signification (say, positivism) is always "exceeded" by it. Intentionality produces what Derrida has called *différance*, something beyond itself that any structure can never completely intend, take into account, or control. Husserl's theories of intentionality can be read, then, against themselves, as sites where signifieds elude the control of and exceed the signifiers of those same theories.

Phenomenological notions of intentionality, which can be read as positioning the subject as the origin of meaning, have been taken up by a variety of theorists interested in questions of authorship and the "ownership" of meaning. The American literary critic Eric Donald Hirsch (1967, 1976), for example, argues that the movement from the intending of meaning to its identification within language is a process that is fixed for all time. Meanings, for Hirsch, cannot necessarily be reclaimed by subsequent readers; we cannot know exactly what was in an author's mind. However, Hirsch claims, in any text there is always an intentional meaning that belongs to an author and that may be recovered, though only in a "general" way. Further, subsequent readings of a work do not alter its meaning. Different significances may be read into a text, but these in no way alter or challenge what was originally intended by the author.

The notion that intentionality produces a meaning that is fixed and owned by the author has been particularly challenged by five theoretical perspectives: structuralism, deconstruction, Foucaldian notions of subjectivity, psychoanalysis, and neo-Marxism. The seeds of structuralism's challenge to the notion of intentionality can be found in the work of Ferdinand de Saussure. If all meaning is produced through systems of signification rather than being "in the world," then there can be no intention that is not in some way caught up in and dispersed by language. Roland Barthes produced a number of celebrated structuralist "attacks" on authorial intentionality by exploiting this Saussurean insight, and subsequent work has been done by theorists such as Roman Jakobson, Edward Sapir, Benjamin Lee Whorf, and Claude Lévi-Strauss. In *S/Z*, for instance, Barthes takes Honoré de Balzac's *Sarrasine* "to pieces" and then, through the use of various, almost arbitrary, codes, puts it back together in ways that render the "original" text unrecognizable and the notion of an "intentional" text almost unthinkable.

Derrida's most crucial challenge to intentionality is in his critique of the notion of presence. If, following Saussure, we accept that language works in a relational manner—and that therefore, in a sense, language is always "different" to itself—it follows that intentional meaning, being caught up in and produced through language, can never be fully present to itself. Husserl's admission that intentionality must be mediated at some stage by language means that intentionality can never achieve self-identification.

Michel Foucault's work on the relationship between discourse, knowledge, and power, heavily influenced by Nietzschean philosophy, is unwilling to accept the presuppositions underlying Husserlian intentionality; on the other hand, however, Foucault is strongly suspicious of the notion of the death of the author, which he associates with Barthes and Derrida. For Foucault, the idea that writing works to "efface" authorial intention only transposes "the empirical characteristics of an author to a transcendental anonymity" (Foucault, 1977) and leaves out the necessity of interrogating the discursive and political functions of notions such as originality, intentionality, and authorship. For Foucault, these notions, which could be collected under the rubric of subjectivity, are produced by discourses and at the same time "characterize the existence, circulation and operation of certain discourses within a society." Foucault's point is that intentionality and other notions associated with subjectivity are valuable sites of political analysis.

The Freudian intervention against the self-aware and intending subject is well known: for Sigmund Freud, a subject was split because it was always inhabited by desires that could not be articulated openly in consciousness. The Freudian subject is always in a sense removed from and denied full knowledge of itself; that is so say, it is denied a full understanding of the "intentions" of the signs it produces. This insight was developed productively by Jacques Lacan through his appropriation of Saussurean linguistics. The contents of the unconscious, for Lacan, are signifiers that never fix signifieds to produce the Saussurean sign. For Husserl, intentionality is marked, in a sense, through its animation of, control of, and identification through a signifier. But Lacan's appropriation of Saussurean linguistics reads the notion of the primacy of the signifier—what Lacan refers to as the "the illusion that the signifier answers to the function of representing the signified" (Lacan, 1977)—in terms of a demonstration of the impossibility of intentionality: "I think where I am not, therefore I am where I do not think" (1977). For Lacan, a subject and that subject's intentionality are always "lost" in what Husserl referred to as "indicative" language.

The gap between the way individuals understand themselves as freely intending and self-knowing subjects and Lacan's theorizing of the impossibility of "presence" and self-knowledge is addressed and developed by the neo-Marxist Louis Althusser through his notion of interpellation. For Althusser, a belief in individual intentionality is an ideological tool that allows hegemonic groups to dominate other groups in a society. This particular bourgeois notion of subjectivity is produced ideologically in order to "hail" or call up identities—much in the manner that the Lacanian mirror stage allow identities to be "artificially" generated. For Althusser, individuals, through their interpellation as free and intending subjects, come under the domination not just of language but of specific ideologies.

All of these theories of intentionality, from Husserlian phenomenology to Althusserian interpellation, tend to posit the subject as either wholly and freely intentional or completely produced and dominated by language or ideology. An interesting attempt has been made by Pierre Bourdieu to negotiate between these two positions through reference to the notions of habitus and practice. In a sense, Bourdieu's theory of habitus completely deforms and relocates notions of intentionality and agency. For Bourdieu, intentionality does not exist in the way Husserl understands it. Instead, Bourdieu posits a notion of practice that is always between and can never be reduced to reproduction or self-mastery. An agent is aware of the rules of the game that constitute and constrain his or her practices, but only—and here is the most difficult paradox—in an "unconscious" way.

Bourdieu's theory of habitus is the most recent in a long line of attempts to build on phenomenological intentionality without necessarily taking on board the more transcendental and idealist notions associated with Husserl's theories. Structuralist attempts to suspend or eliminate the intending subject altogether have been shown, by Derrida among others, to be predicated on the sleight of hand of the elimination or covering over of their own intentions. Derrida consistently draws attention to this structuralist anomaly, even though his work is perhaps better known for deconstructing phenomenological claims of self-presence and self-identity. Foucault and Althusser, while taking up a poststructuralist position that is oppositional to one of transcendental intentionality, insist on keeping the questions of authorship and intentionality alive because of their importance as organizational and categorizing factors to the functioning of discourse and ideology.

[See also Althusser; Barthes; Bourdieu; Foucault; Habitus; and Lacan.]

BIBLIOGRAPHY

Althusser, L. *Lenin and Philosophy and Other Essays*. Translated by B. Brester. London: New Left Books, 1977.

Barthes, R. *S/Z*. Translated by R. Miller. New York: Hill and Wang, 1974.

Bourdieu, P. *Outline of a Theory of Practice*. Translated by R. Nice. Cambridge: Cambridge University Press, 1977.

Derrida, J. *Margins of Philosophy*. Translated by A. Bass. Chicago: University of Chicago Press, 1982.

Foucault, M. "What Is an Author?" In *Language, Counter-Memory, Practice*, translated by D. F. Bouchard and S. Simon, pp. 113–138. Ithaca, N.Y.: Cornell University Press, 1977.

Freud, S. *On Metapsychology: The Theory of Psychoanalysis*. Translated by J. Strachey. Harmondsworth, England: Penguin, 1984.

Hirsch, E. D. *Validity in Interpretation*. New Haven: Yale University Press, 1967.

Hirsch, E. D. *The Aims of Interpretation*. Chicago: University of Chicago Press, 1976.

Husserl, E. *The Crisis of the European Sciences and Transcendental Phenomenology*. Translated by D. Carr. Evanston: Northwestern University Press, 1970.

Lacan, J. *Ecrits*. Translated by A. Sheridan. London: Tavistock, 1977.

Merleau-Ponty, M. *Phenomenology of Perception*. Translated by C. Smith. London: Routledge and Kegan Paul, 1962.

—TONY SCHIRATO

INTERACTIONIST ANALYSIS. A discourse of questions and intended solutions to problems, interactionist analysis was developed by American social theorist Alan Blum (b. 1935), who paved the way for the translation of dialogical method, personified by Socrates, into contemporary sociological theory. This mode of analysis grew out of a collaboration with Peter McHugh (b. 1929) at the universities of New York, London, and York. The project was augmented by the phenomenological methodologies typical of sociology in the 1970s and the reformulation of the work of Emile Durkheim, Georg Simmel, and Max Weber through a rigorous dialectical interrogation of everyday life.

In Blum's particular work, Durkheim's formulation of concepts as "communicative" is used to suggest that a concept always disguises its function as a central locus that collectivizes an aggregate. The signified is neither an extralinguistic referent nor an intertexual object, but in a special sense it makes reference to the ambiguous but resolute self-understanding of society that animates any repre-

sentation. Blum's work continuously approaches the fundamental ambiguity that is disguised in any content as its problematic elementary social situation and seeks to represent this situation as a paradoxical instance of collective problem solving. The content always masks a problem whose ambiguity demands clarification. What is always concealed is the image of a communality embodied in collective problem solving.

In the development of this work, Blum explored concepts such as positivism as these disguised sites of discursive problem solving (1974a). In this way, positivism became an opportunity for exploring the conditions of adequate conversation and so symptomized the need and desire for ethical discrimination between the quality and the technique of speaking together. Consequently, content and its representation signify an elementary conversation situation animated by the need to solve the problem of their ambiguity.

For Blum, the unspoken ground of any representation is always treated as intimating an elementary socially oriented focus on the question of difference between what is essential and what is inessential, what is internal and what is external, and what is partial and what is comprehensive. These distinctions are imagined as a central locus of collectivization for a social relationship. The ground of any content is the fundamental social relationship mobilized and centered by the problematic nature of the ambiguity of the content itself and the lure of an image of its adequate clarification and representation. Blum's various writings study commonplace contents as discursive sites that conceal elementary social situations in which fundamental ambiguity is addressed as a decisive problem with ethical implications (1991, 1993, 1995, 1996).

Positivism and science originally served Blum as occasions on which to question the work of speaking together, the thinking of difference, and the grounds of criticalnesss, because as contents they accentuated a specific image of conversation in the desire for total explication, productivism, silencing of history, and disputatiousness. Such an interrogation permitted him to pose the question of the ethical commitment to conversation and the way in which this commitment takes different historical shape under modern conditions.

Blum sets his task as restoring genuine ignorance through the vehicle of Socrates (1978). Plato's uses of

Socrates stimulate Blum's thought, but he does not simply transpose to another discipline an already accomplished Socratic method. Like Socratic thought, science's criticalness, as well as sociology's, lies in its thinking of its difference from common sense; yet science's criticalness is its concern with justification and proof. Despite its commitment to the interaction and revisability of opinions and unending consideration of opposition to itself, science sets itself up, Blum thinks, as the limit of conversation. Ultimately, science tries to domesticate the enigmatic through the comprehensive demand for interpretability. Science's ignorance is simulated rather than genuine or Socratic because, instead of acting "as if it does not know what it knows," it presupposes closure and finality. Sociology, too, is unfair to ignorance since, like science, ignorance is just the state of not being sociology or of failing to be scientific. Blum and McHugh (1978) also developed their sense of committed conversation through the analysis of different opinions in debates concerning Canadian nationalism.

From the dialogues of Plato, Blum inherited a conception of social theory as a discourse in which inquiry orchestrates the conversation of views addressed to a particular problem as if the voices involved were guises or images of a fundamental ethical dilemma of collective life. The figure of Socratic irony was developed in several directions around the metaphors of disguise, hunting, sacrifice, and the relation of image to original. On this model, writing itself is conceived as a social process in time that narrates the trajectory of collective self-understanding as if it was a series of face-to-face encounters with common views. The formulative movement of writing is personified in an ideal speaker as a hunter who progressively makes transparent the contents of everyday life as disguises of a quarry imagined as if it was an occasion of collective problem solving. The end of the analysis is conceived of in the unraveling of the disguises in a way that is resolute but always open to revision.

The figure of Socrates is used to emphasize the fate of inquiry that represents the collective in two ways: by holding up to the collective a mirror of its self-understanding, the theorist seeks to represent what the collective understands of itself; in such an endeavor, theorizing offers itself as a sacrifice to the collective insofar as its hubris resides in its presumption to be the voice that stands apart from the collective while simultaneously speaking for it. This sacrifice

becomes intelligible in the execution of Socrates, which Blum reads metaphorically as the fate of theorizing.

Socrates (1978) gathered Blum's reflections on maieutic analysis and its ideal of dialectical conversation. Socrates is the model theorist whose life coexists with theory. He practices nonpossessive speech and renounces both simple and complete explication, engaging and inviting participation in incomplete and continuous explication. Blum's Socratic theorist suffers ambiguity in the work of analysis, and this is especially manifest in recognizing that such analysis cannot totally explicate itself, for to do so would be to end the conversation and make impossible a commitment to the good of unresolved questions.

Blum made available to sociologists the ontological version of classicism in *Theorizing* (1974b). He distinguishes Aristotelian from Platonic dialectic by thinking through Martin Heidegger's ontological difference, giving greater phenomenological expression to the critical concepts deployed in his critique of positivism. These concepts are the inventory (the positions into which Aristotle transforms preceding thought), the externalization of internal relations (in which Aristotelian science treats the part of the whole as two entities, thereby limiting the question of how things come to presence to one of causal interpretation), and the reduction of difference to sameness, in which authority is exercised and limits set to force agreement about agreement.

Blum's version of classicism attempts to reintroduce sociology to the philosophical tradition from which it has wandered and make theorizing intelligible for it. In this effort, he enlists Karl Marx's conception of social production as a metaphor for the genuine and corrupted relationships generated by speaking and theorizing; on the one hand, listening to its ground and wondering why it speaks and, on the other, making a constitutive feature of being alienated from itself.

Blum and McHugh founded the short-lived journal *Maieutics* (1981–1985), whose title employed the metaphor of midwifery attributed to Socrates by Plato in the *Theaetetus* to describe the art of assisting his interlocutors' in giving birth to knowledge. The Centre for Theory in the Humanities and Social Sciences was cofounded by Blum and McHugh in 1979. An annual international, interdisciplinary summer institute was the interactional embodiment of the center, whose activities ended in 1984.

In *Self-Reflection in the Arts and Sciences* (1984), Blum and McHugh present a theorization of self-reflection irreducible to a descriptive inventory of this practice's historic conventions in the human sciences. Since self-reflection is the very condition of the existence and development of the human sciences, Blum and McHugh lay bare the ground of their inquiry by constructing an ideal speaker. Their idealized version of self-reflection as rational, social action is the limit toward which their inquiry is oriented. Self-reflection is for them a social action undertaken by an ideal speaker or theorist in Socratic garb whose problem solving constitutes the topic for the sort of rational conversation the authors valorize as the exemplary image of sociality. The strong theoretic speaker (Blum and McHugh, 1979, 1984) is a device the authors employ not to typify an actual speaker but to personify the exemplary voice of collective life that is imagined as responding to the demand to listen to the logos and engage in the continuing process of disclosing what it withdraws from view as necessary and desirable for its community.

Recently, Blum (1993, 1995, 1996) has analyzed key modes of postmodernism such as travesty, hyperbole, and panic in order to loosen them from their technical, abstract, and textual usages, instead considering them as social phenomena through the ethical rather than semiotic forms of enjoyment these ways of luxuriating in language reveal. In such cases, he seeks to counteract the temptation to identify ambiguity with linguistic indeterminacy by showing the unresolved but accessible question of ethicality that is presupposed in the collective action of language. In this way, every content and its representation is treated as a veil of collectivization that haunts all work as traces of communality absorbed and suffered by theorizing itself.

[*See also* Dialogism; Discourse Analysis; Durkheim; *and* Ethnomethodology.]

BIBLIOGRAPHY

Blum, A. "Positive Thinking." *Theory and Society* 1 (1974a): 245–269.
Blum, A. *Theorizing*. London: Heinemann, 1974b.
Blum, A. "Criticalness and 'Traditional Prejudice': Science as the Perfect Art for Our Times." *Canadian Journal of Sociology* 2.1 (Fall 1977): 97–124.
Blum, A. *Socrates: The Original and Its Images*. London: Routledge and Kegan Paul, 1978.
Blum, A. "The Melancholy Life-World of the University." *Dianoia* 2.1 (Spring 1991): 16–41.
Blum, A. "Travesty." *Studies in Symbolic Interaction* 15 (1993): 83–101.
Blum, A. "Hyperbole, Deceit, and the Lie." *Studies in Symbolic Interaction* 18 (1995): 3–21.
Blum, A. "Panic and Fear: On the Phenomenology of Desperation." *Sociological Quarterly* 37.4 (1996): 673–698.
Blum, A., and P. McHugh. "The Risk of Theorizing and the Problem of the Good of Place: A Reformulation of Canadian Nationalism." *Canadian Journal of Sociology* 3.3 (1978): 321–347.
Blum, A., and P. McHugh. *Self-Reflection in the Arts and Sciences*. Atlantic Highlands, N.J.: Humanities Press, 1984.
Blum, A. and P. McHugh, eds. *Friends, Enemies, and Strangers: Theorizing in Art, Science, and Everyday Life*. Norwood: Ablex, 1979.

—GARY GENOSKO

INTERFACE. Usually defined as a surface forming the boundary between adjacent spaces, an interface technically belongs equally to the two contiguous domains and has some of the properties characterizing each. The concept of interface can be further abstracted and recast in semiotic terms as the plane of contact between two systems modifying each other through some form of sign-mediated interaction.

The computer age brought to expression concern for human-machine interaction. Within this concern, interfacings evolved as the means through which computer users attempt to accomplish their computational needs. Progress in digital technology soon made hardware considerations less critical than considerations of the many ways through which the performance of a machine is affected by the ability to address it in ways as close to natural language as possible. Strictly speaking, one can distinguish between a user interface—describing how a user should "address" a machine—and a process interface, which describes the exchange of messages among a machine's various components. While the two should be understood as constituting a unity, it is clear that user interface is ultimately the decisive factor (accordingly influencing process interface). As the place where two different entities—the user and the machine (computer or not)—meet, an interface is supposed to "know" the user's language and that of the machine. At the meeting point, transactions are represented by a series of accepted commands or formats for the input of information to be processed.

By extension of the definition of communication as an act of bringing together, computer interface is seen as a communication instance between a living entity performing in language and other sign systems (images, sounds) and an artifact controlled by logical operations (best described through Boolean logic) and able to process data, including data presented in symbolic forms. As a framework for communication, interfaces can be designed around a limited subset of natural language, as a pictorial repertory to which admissible operations upon members of the repertory are assigned, or as any other closed language, homogeneous or heterogeneous. From a computational viewpoint, it is significant whether commands are followed by identifiers of entities upon which they are exercised or whether entities are selected first and operations then chosen from a menu of acceptable actions. Contaminated by a tendency to anthropomorphize machines—that is, to describe them in terms pertinent to humans—the entire interface discussion sometimes succumbs to an animistic vocabulary: machines do, machines understand, machines have a language. If we agree that machines are endowed by their designers and makers with knowledge in the form of stored information—data as well as logical operations—then the animistic conversation about machines and interfaces is less offensive and the epistemological consequences less important. Semiotically, this means that a certain artifact was prepared to accept a certain sequence of signs and, if they conform with the agreed code—which can be a format in a database or a specific command—execute what those signs represent or act upon the data within the paradigm of information processing.

The advent of computers as generalized semiotic machines attracted attention to the semiotics of interfacing. But interfacing was implicitly part of human culture since its inception. Herbert Simon (1982) saw fit to view the artifact in its generality as interface and the environment of the human experience involving the artifact and making it necessary as mold. In the context in which human activity becomes increasingly mediated by all kinds of artifacts, conceptual or material, the need for improved interpreters with adequate understanding of human and nonhuman components becomes critical. In many social instances—such as the practice of law, medicine, or financial consulting—mediation is based on human-to-human communication. Nevertheless, the human expert uses an interface language—that is, a

way to convey contents of extreme specialization in professional languages striving toward precision to the detriment of expressivity. Some of these interface functions have in recent times been taken over by artificial systems designed to address patterned activities. In such cases, the difficulty lies in defining appropriate interfaces to connect those formulating questions and the systems designed to answer them. Defining the sign as a mediating entity and semiotics as the theory and practice of mediation, we can actually elaborate a comprehensive solution to interface problems. The contingency of each interface mediation—its likelihood, relative unpredictability, and intrinsic dependence on and conditioning by other factors—is reflected in the intrinsic contingency of the act of conceiving and designing the interface.

With this in mind, we could even introduce a generalized notion of design as interface: an interface, regardless of its type, specifies the optimal set of semiotic devices for the interaction between two entities, animate or not. We see then that everything constituting our culture—all the artifacts and all our values—require an interface in order to be used optimally. The sequence of actions leading to the desired pragmatics becomes, by extension of language definition, a language. The challenge of devising programs capable of generating interfaces—an area of artificial intelligence—is actually one of defining what languages are and how they function in certain contexts characteristic of specific human transactions.

Interface, in its traditional sense, is part of the designed object, and as such has only very limited potential for change. In recent years, interface considerations stimulated yet another area of artificial-intelligence investigation that addresses the possibility that machines "learn" in the process of their use, thus opening the possibility of evolving interfaces. Using neural networks and the training methods for these networks, scientists proposed intelligent interfaces that can recognize the user (by voice or patterns of commands) or even previously solved problems and thus take an optimized path when a new problem resembles an old one. The cognitive effort in this direction and the implications of evolving interfaces are yet to be matched by a better semiotic understanding of the sign processes involved. What is known today is that an interface is a semiotic trade-off between precision and expressiveness. Machine learning might sharpen both or find the optimal compromise, the threshold at which an interface becomes an expression of computational knowledge as it is applied to the domain for which it mediates.

[*See also* Artificial Intelligence; Computer; Computer-Mediated Communication; Cybernetics; Expert Systems; *and* Knowledge Representation.]

BIBLIOGRAPHY

Andersen, P. B. *A Theory of Computer Semiotics*. Cambridge: Cambridge University Press, 1990.

Andersen, P. B., B. Holmquist, and J. F. Jensen, eds. *The Computer as Medium*. Cambridge: Cambridge University Press, 1993.

Marcus, A. "Designing Iconic Interfaces." *Nicograph* 83 (1983): 103–122.

Nadin, M. "Interface Design: A Semiotic Paradigm." *Semiotica* 69.3–4 (1988): 269–302.

Norman, D. "Cognitive Engineering." In *User-Centered System Design*, edited by D. A. Norman and S. W. Draper. Hillsdale, N.J.: Erlbaum Associates, 1986.

Simon, H. *The Sciences of the Artificial*. Cambridge, Mass.: MIT Press, 1982.

—MIHAI NADIN

INTERSPECIFIC COMMUNICATION. The problem of interspecific communication concerns the possibility of transference of information, for adaptive ends, between one species and another. A species is defined as a group of organisms that breed among themselves but that are isolated reproductively from all other organisms. *Homo sapiens* is a species, as is *Drosophila melanogaster*, the vinegar fruit fly.

In the light of modern Darwinism, addressing the problem of interspecific communication involves finding the adaptive advantage accruing either to the communicator (signaler) or the recipient (or both), always with the proviso that the advantage can never be one resulting from a purely altruistic act by one organism for another. Since selection works within a species as well as without, interspecific communication is continuous with all communication and not essentially different, or at least not different because it involves crossing a species border.

The most obvious cases of interspecific communication occur when one organism is signaling to another purely for its own benefit. A classic example is mimicry: a potential predator reads the message, falsely given in this case, and moves on to seek other prey. It is, of course, quite possible that a deceived or exploited predator will itself develop counteradapta-

tions, in which case the information might start to serve the ends of members of both species. Manipulation and "mind reading" would be cases in which one animal sends out information to another but the second anticipates and uses the information to its own purposes.

Less obvious but perhaps more significant is interspecific communication that occurs when members of two species benefit and such benefit is intentional either consciously or in the sense that the performer's actions have evolved by natural selection and confer adaptive benefit on the recipient. The major mechanism by which such communication is supposed to occur is so-called reciprocal altruism, articulated first by sociobiologist Robert Trivers as a mutual exploitation for mutual gain, with potential communication by members on both sides of the species boundary. The classic case of reciprocal altruism, with communication obviously playing a major part, is that of the symbiotic relationship seen when certain predatory species of fish allow other fish (of potential prey species) very considerable liberties. The reason for this is simply that the potential prey perform services of greater value than their value as food. In particular, the prey fish act as cleaners of the predators, eating the growths (fungus and so forth) that the predators acquire around their bodies, especially their jaws, as a result of their lives of predation.

Cleaners get a meal, and the cleaned get improved hygiene. But for this to occur, the potential for significant communication must be in place. The cleaning fish must have signals to inform the predators that they belong to a species that will benefit the predators. The predators conversely must have signals to inform the cleaners that they will shut off their usual aggressive patterns and practices. At the least, there must be appropriate triggers, for one assumes that this far down the chain of being not a great deal of intentional semantic information is being transferred.

What is especially interesting about this is the way that yet other species take advantage of such interspecific communication for their own ends. Certain species of fish mimic the cleaners and get into close range of the potentially cleaned, at which point predators become prey. The mimics bite large chunks out of the pacified predators then escape before retribution descends. This is probably best thought of as the manipulation of already existing information rather than the addition of fresh information.

Although William D. Hamilton's theory of kin selection is clearly ruled out, there might be other motives for social interspecific communication than reciprocal altruism. All we can say at this point is that such communication is a major phenomenon and a key aspect of organic, especially animal, evolution. For this reason, it is, today, a subject of intense investigation.

[*See also* Evolution; Hamilton; Manipulation; Signal; Trivers; *and* Zoosemiotics.]

BIBLIOGRAPHY

Darwin, C. *The Descent of Man.* London: John Murray, 1871.
Dawkins, R. *The Blind Watchmaker.* New York: W. W. Norton, 1986.
Hamilton, W. D. "The Genetical Evolution of Social Behavior." *Journal of Theoretical Biology* 7 (1964): 1–52.
Krebs, J., and N. Davies, eds. *Behavioural Ecology: An Evolutionary Approach.* Oxford: Blackwell Scientific Publications, 1978.
Trivers, R. "The Evolution of Reciprocal Altruism." *Quarterly Review of Biology* 46 (1971): 35–57.
Wilson, E. O. *The Insect Societies.* Cambridge, Mass.: Harvard University Press, 1971.

—MICHAEL RUSE

INTRODUCTION TO THE STRUCTURAL ANALYSIS OF NARRATIVES (1966).

Roland Barthes's influential essay on narratology was originally published in an issue of the journal *Communications* devoted specially to the state of narratological research in the mid-1960s among his fellow members of the Centre d'Études des Communications de Masse in Paris. Barthes both announced programmatically his creative departures from his colleagues and their mentors in linguistics and acknowledged his debts to them on the way to a science of literature.

Narrative analysis is a deductive procedure that moves from a hypothetical model to particular narrative species. The model is based upon structural linguistics, although this foundation is not imperative, Barthes admits. The structural analysis of narrative is a new linguistics of discourse positing a secondary homological relation between sentence and discourse, thus implying the formal identity of language and literature. Taking his general orientation from Émile Benveniste and borrowing specific concepts from Vladimir Propp, Algirdas Julien Greimas, and

Tzvetan Todorov, Barthes cobbles together a "provisional profile" of three levels of discourse (functions, actions, narration) related by their progressive integration and modeled on the relations between phoneme, word, and sentence.

The smallest narrative unit is a function. Alongside integrational indexes, distributional functions constitute one of the two main classes of units. A function is related metonymically to its correlate along the syntagmatic plane, while an index metaphorically signifies its correlate, whose location is higher up in the paradigm. The predominance of either class, notwithstanding intermediary forms and mixed units, provides a crude descriptive classification of narratives (folktales are mostly functional, psychological novels are heavily indexical). Nuclei form a subclass of functions: they are the "real hinge points" of narrative and have direct consequences. Nuclei are complemented by "attenuated" functions called catalyzers, which color consequential narrative moments. Proper indexes have implicit signifieds and thus require acts of deciphering across levels. Informants signify immediately and authenticate their referents.

Syntactically, catalyzers imply the existence of nuclei but not vice versa; indexes and informants combine relatively freely. Barthes claims that the reciprocal bonding of nuclei constitute the "very framework of the narrative." A sequence of nuclei opens and closes respectively in the absence of antecedent and consequent solidarities. In Lévi-Straussian terms, Barthes suggests the "structure of narrative is fugued," alluding to a maximal self-sufficiency, a balance between vertical and horizontal and between prospective and retrospective movement.

Characters are units of the actional level, and they participate in finite, typical, and classifiable spheres of action, understood as the "major articulations of *praxis.*" Besides Barthes's confirmation of this fact and his brief overview of the weaknesses and strengths of Greimas's actantial model, the substantial content of this level is minimal. Barthes later, in the first of several essays on the "novels" of Philippe Sollers, employed the actantial model to render the structural subject's search for the object of the story itself against the enemy of literature and with the ally of a language concerned with its own codes.

The units of the second level are more dependent upon those of the third for their meanings than those of the first were on those of the second. Progressive integration is accomplished unevenly. The third level caps the trilevel hierarchy by reintegrating the units of the lower levels into the narrational code. At this level, structural analysis must describe the systems of narration and overcome the traditional "literary myth" of identifying the narrator with the author. The personal and impersonal systems are immanent to the narrative and therefore do not presuppose referents such as psychological persons. For not only is the author dead or, rather, coded, but the characters, too, for Barthes are "paper beings."

The narrational code transcends its content and forms (functions and actions), and for this reason it is the "final level attainable by [the] analysis." But this "cap" leaks, Barthes indicates, since narrative is dependent upon a situation beyond discourse. The level of narration closes the hierarchy but also requires a semiotics of the situation in which narratives are "consumed," although the signs of this situation are conjured away by mass bourgeois culture. The two powers of narrative form are distortion and expansion. Parts of signs are spread over the length of a story; signifieds are shared among signifiers, themselves remote from one another and interspersed with other signs, whose meaning depends upon their distant relations. Barthes treats suspense as an exacerbated form of distortion because it plays with the structure of sequences; this form is privileged in the novels of Ian Fleming, to whose character, secret agent James Bond, Barthes refers repeatedly. The polyphonic composition of narrative is evidenced further by the intercalation of unforseeable expansions, filled out with catalysts, into such distortions. There are limits, Barthes insists, to the freedom to catalyze around nuclei, just as the derivations in a fugue are guided by its theme. The language of narrative further involves the process of integration. Despite its irregularity, integration prevents meaning from "dangling" at lower levels by rejoining or unifying previously disjoined or heterogeneous elements.

Situated outside the mimetic order, narrative limps along a succession of interconnected elements, restricting and relaxing potentialities along its way. Barthes thinks narrative takes place in the logic of the succession of elements and the variations therein, rather than through the representation of real sequences of actions.

[See also Barthes; Narratology; and Structure]

BIBLIOGRAPHY

Barthes, R. "Introduction to the Structural Analysis of Narratives." In *Image/Music/Text*, translated by S. Heath, pp. 79–124. New York: Hill and Wang, 1977.
Barthes, R. "The Struggle with the Angel: Textual Analysis of Genesis 32: 22–32." In *Image/Music/Text*, translated by S. Heath, pp. 125–141. New York: Hill and Wang, 1977.
Barthes, R. *Sollers Writer*. Translated by P. Thody. Minneapolis: University of Minnesota Press, 1987.

—GARY GENOSKO

ISOTOPY. A technical term first introduced by Algirdas Julien Greimas (1966) to account for the semantic consistency of a text, *isotopy* has been often redefined and discussed in the works of Greimas, the Paris School, Umberto Eco, and Group μ. Coined from the Greek *isos* ("equal," "same") and *topos* ("space," "place"), *isotopy* can be translated literally as "single level" or "same plane." Greimas provides the following definitions with respect to the reading of narratives: "A redundant set of semantic categories which make possible the consistent interpretation [literally, "uniform reading"] of a story, as it results from the reading of the successive segments of the text and the resolution of their ambiguities in view of the quest for a coherent global understanding" (1970, p. 188).

A more technical definition is found in Greimas and J. Courtés' *Analytical Dictionary*: "As an operational concept, isotopy at first designated iterativity along a syntagmatic chain of classemes which assure the homogeneity of the utterance-discourse" (1982, p. 163). (Classemes are semes that recur in a discourse and enable the reader to establish semantic coherence.) Ambiguous and polysemic texts of lesser or greater complexity can be described semiotically in the metalanguage generated by the notion of isotopy. For example, two contrary terms, such as *boys* and *girls* or *boys* and *men*, form the minimal context for establishing the isotopy of gender or the isotopy of age, respectively. From this point of view, the four terms of a semiotic square are isotopes since they hold mutual relationships of contradiction and contrariness with respect to a particular semantic category.

The notion of recurring categories can apply to syntax (grammatical isotopy), content (semantic isotopy), and narrative (actorial isotopy). The coherence of a discourse on its figurative level is described in terms of figurative isotopy and on a deeper level in terms of thematic isotopy. In the same vein, bi-isotopy, pluri-isotopy, and complex isotopy are found in the metalanguage used by the Paris School to account for the semiotic functioning of metaphors, jokes, ambiguous and symbolic texts, and, more generally, all interpretive strategies in any modality. Eco points to the etymologic and conceptual congruence of *isotopy* and *topic*. However, he notes that, technically, topics are means to produce isotopies, since "the topic as question is an abductive schema that helps the reader to decide which semantic properties [semes] have to be actualized, whereas isotopies are the actual textual verification of that tentative hypothesis" (1979, p. 27). For a discussion of the various uses of the notion of isotopy, see Catherine Kerbrat-Orecchioni (1976), Eco (1979, pp. 24–27) and François Rastier (1981, 1987, 1997). Group μ coined the term *allotopy*, from the Greek *allos* ("other," "different"), as an antonym of *isotopy* in order to designate semiotic heterogeneity or lack of semantic redundancy in a verbal or visual text (1977, 1992).

The notions of iso- and allotopy attempt to describe and explain the "natural" process through which a global text is perceived intuitively as making sense or not. This process is formalized as a series of operations (identification of classemes, selection, and cumulation of relevant semes) whose mental or psychological status is uncertain. This raises the same theoretical difficulty as the hermeneutic circle, since the selection of semes depends on the identification of classemes, themselves produced by the iteration of selected semes. Another criticism is formulated by Eco (1976), who denounces the infinite semantic recursivity of this kind of model since "every semantic unit used in order to analyze a sememe is in its turn a sememe to be analyzed" (p. 121). However, as an explicit method for construing meaning out of highly informative or enigmatic texts (i.e., those that lack sufficient redundancy), these operations have a definite pragmatic value.

Take, for instance, the often-quoted "meaningless" utterance, "Colorless green ideas sleep furiously (Chomsky, 1965, p. 15). It is actually relatively easy to build an isotopy out of such an apparently self-contradictory string of words. The most abstract term of the set (and the focus of the sentence) is *ideas*, which denotes a vague notion rather commonly defined as the products of mind or the fruit of thought. If ideas can be categorized metaphorically as fruit, they can be either ripe or not. Ripeness or maturity is prototypically associated with redness; immaturity is similarly linked with greenness. The quality green applied to a fruit might not only be chromatically descriptive but also have the privative value "not yet ripe, not yet colored, colorless." From this point of view, *green* and *colorless* are not contradictory but redundant. Furthermore, vegetal metaphors imply growth, and ideas are indeed conceived of as developing, maturing over time, and sometimes even being unseasonably in advance to the point of being not understood or appreciated because they are out of cultural synchrony; in spite of their potential, they are kept unexploited, dormant, as if they were asleep. Sleep itself is a state that can be qualified as light or deep with various degrees of intensity. *Furiously* is often used as an intensive rather than with the denotative value of extreme anger, furor, and madness. The construction of a textual isotopy thus makes possible the production of a paraphrase or translation. In the present case, a semantically equivalent sentence could be, "Absolutely nothing can activate an idea that has not come of age."

The notion of isotopy and the metalanguage associated with it (including the ideas of seme, classeme, sememe, semic categories, subsumation, presupposition, hypotactic construction, reading grid, level, semiotic square, and others) provide analytic tools that can be applied more generally than componential analysis can. Some researchers have even extended their application from the semantic to the phonological and grammatical domains by defining isotopy as the iterativeness (recurrence) of linguistic units (e.g., Rastier, 1991, pp. 220–223). The question remains whether this approach opens up an explanation of the processes of textual production and understanding and their simulation in artificial-intelligence research or whether it merely offers an interesting interpretive strategy that is particularly useful for the hermeneutics of poetry and the accurate translation of complex discourse.

[*See also* Abductive Reasoning; Actantial Model; Greimas; Meaning; Opposition; *and* Semiotic Square.]

BIBLIOGRAPHY

Chomsky, N. *Syntactic Structures.* The Hague: Mouton, 1965.
Eco, U. *A Theory of Semiotics.* Bloomington: Indiana University Press, 1976.
Eco, U. *The Role of the Reader: Explorations in the Semiotics of Texts.* Bloomington: Indiana University Press, 1979.
Greimas, A. J. *Structural Semantics: An Attempt at a Method*

(1966). Translated by D. McDowell, R. Schleifer, and A. Velie. Lincoln: University of Nebraska Press, 1983.

Greimas, A. J. *Du sens.* Paris: Seuil, 1970.

Greimas, A. J., and J. Courtés. *Semiotics and Language: An Analytical Dictionary.* Translated by L. Crist et al. Bloomington: Indiana University Press, 1982.

Group μ. *Rhétorique de la poésie.* Brussels: Editions complexe, 1977.

Group μ. *Traité du signe visuel: Pour une rhétorique de l'image.* Paris: Seuil, 1992.

Kerbrat-Orecchioni, C. "Problématique de l'isotopie." *Linguistique et Semiologie* 1 (1976): 11–33.

Rastier, F. *Le développement du concept d'isotopie.* Documents de Recherche du Groupe de Recherches Sémio-linguistiques, vol. 3, no. 29. Paris: Institut de la Langue Française, 1981.

Rastier, F. *Semantique interpretative.* Paris: Presses Universitaires de France, 1987.

Rastier, F. *Semantique et recherches cognitives.* Paris: Presses Universitaires de France, 1991.

Rastier, F. *Meaning and Textuality.* Translated by F. Collins and P. Perron. Toronto: University of Toronto Press, 1997.

Schleifer, R. *A. J. Greimas and the Nature of Meaning: Linguistics, Semiotics, and Discourse Theory.* London: Croom Helm, 1987.

—PAUL BOUISSAC

J

JAKOBSON, ROMAN (1896–1982), Russian-born linguist, one of the most influential semioticians of the twentieth century. Jakobson's contribution to semiotics developed from his diverse studies of language, phonetics, dialectology, folkloristics, and poetics. When he was a student in philology at Moscow University in 1917, Jakobson turned to linguistics after being introduced to the work of Ferdinand de Saussure by Sergej I. Karcevskij, who had been a student of Saussure in Geneva. From 1915 to 1920, Jakobson was a leading member of the Moscow Linguistic Circle and of the Society for the Study of Poetic Language (*OPOJAZ*) based in Saint Petersburg. His early interest in poetics and the language of poetry led him to move to Prague in 1920 to pursue studies at Charles University. In 1926, Jakobson was one of the founders of the Prague Linguistic Circle, and it was there, in 1929, that Jakobson coined the word *structuralism*.

The specific meaning of *structuralism*, in its original context, was phonological. Where diachronic linguistics takes words to be differentiated according to philological rules, synchronists argue that words are to be distinguished phonetically within the phonological system of a given language. Differences between phonemes arise from the presence or absence of minimal sound units, named "distinctive features." Thus, phonological systems are to be understood in terms of binary oppositions.

Binarism, shown by Jakobson to operate at the irreducibly minimal level of linguistic structure, was taken by researchers in other fields as a paradigm for analysis at higher levels. Jakobson developed a binary model of language, the two poles of which are the metaphoric and the metonymic. Such a model had been anticipated in Sigmund Freud's pairing of condensation and displacement and in James George Frazer's distinction between homeopathic (metaphoric) and contagious (metonymic) magic. The structuralist model was enormously influential: Claude Lévi-Strauss in anthropology, Jean Piaget and Jacques Lacan in psychology, and Roland Barthes in poetics applied the binary paradigm in transforming their respective disciplines and bringing about a methodological shift in all the human and social sciences.

Jakobson's binarism found empirical and clinical support in the studies of aphasia conducted by American psychologist John Hughlings Jackson (1835–1911). In this research, Jakobson detected two types of aphasia, which corresponded neatly to the two poles of language. Each type results from an inability to operate linguistically, one lacking a sense of similarity, on the metaphoric axis, and the other lacking a sense of contiguity, on the metonymic. The positing of order in disorder, of the structural in the dysfunctional, might explain the attraction of Jakobson's model among psychiatrists.

One month after Hitler's invasion of Czechoslovakia in 1939, Jakobson (who was Jewish by birth; in 1975, he converted to Orthodox Christianity) left Prague for Scandinavia; in 1941, he reached New York City. From 1943, he taught at Columbia University, and in 1949 he was appointed to a chair at Harvard University. It was only in North America that Jakobson came across the work of Charles Sanders Peirce (1839–1914); though not discovered by Jakobson, Peirce owes much of his contemporary prestige within semiotics to Jakobson's advocacy of his work.

The development of modern semiotics is unimaginable without Peirce; it is therefore worth asking what in Jakobson's background prepared him to recognize Peirce's importance. Saussure's ideas had been introduced to Russian students by Sergej Karcevskij in 1917; by 1922, S. I. Bernstejn had provided a detailed and systematic account in Russian of Saussure's *Cours de linguistique générale*. Yet it was apparently only in 1947—in an article by Rulon Wells, "De Saussure's System of Linguistics" in *Word*—that Saussure was introduced to North American linguistics. The parallels between Peirce and Saussure are now evident and virtually constitutive for structuralist semiotics. It was Jakobson who first connected and juxtaposed Saussure and Peirce; he subsequently made much rhetorical and heuristic use of an opposition between them. Peirce became an authority and rhetorical ally in Jakobson's struggle against and with Saussure.

Since the 1920s, Jakobson had contested three of Saussure's axioms. Instead of the Saussurean dichotomy between synchrony and diachrony, Jakobson (who remained devoted to philological research, notably of medieval Slavic texts) preferred to speak of "permanently dynamic synchrony." Jakobson also rejected Saussure's insistence on the linearity and sequentiality of the semiotic chain. The force of Jakobson's theory of the poetic function—that the axis of selection (parataxis, metaphor) is projected onto the axis of combination (syntaxis, metonymy)—is that the linguistic chain must admit the simultaneity of equivalent terms: the one term present invokes absent terms, those unchosen on the parataxis. It is precisely the poetic function that challenges the claim of strict linearity, and Jakobson argued that this function, while dominant in poetry, is present in all forms of discourse. This develops and confirms the structuralist, binary theory of phonology, according to which it is simultaneity rather than linearity that is constitutive of discourse.

This leads to the best known of Saussure's axioms: that the relation between the signifier and the signified is arbitrary. Jakobson (not quite fairly) treated Saussure's bipartite sign as a reformulation of the Stoic and medieval distinction between *signans* (message) and *signatum* (acoustic pattern), the sensible and the intelligible, the acoustic and the mental. Saussure's argument, though it has sometimes been received with controversy, should be as obvious and as irrefutable as Hermogenes' arguments against Cratylus in Plato's dialogue. Jakobson's objections are on the side of Cratylus. If the *syntaxis* of a sentence is determined partially by its rhythm or by alliteration or by other poetic features (present in such alliterative archaisms as "kith and kin," "time and tide," or in trochaic phrases such as "bread and butter," "cup and saucer"), how can we be certain that such examples are exceptions? It might be that, unknown to speakers, the semantic is linked to or even dependent on the acoustic in every utterance. Saussure's axiom assumes an entirely nonaesthetic use of language; Jakobson is one of the very few linguists to place poetics at the center of inquiry. By insisting that to some degree the poetic function is present in all messages, Jakobson suggests that any word or phoneme may be selected not exclusively for its place in the semantic or intelligible chain of signification

but also for its place in an acoustic chain, the order of sounds. Such a Cratylic argument is a provocative response to Saussure's abrupt dismissal of the problem of onomatopoeia.

Peirce classified all signs into three types: symbol, index, and icon. For Peirce, as for Saussure, words operate within a conventional and arbitrary code and are therefore symbols. Indexes and icons are usually taken to be pictorial rather than verbal or alphabetical signs, such as, respectively, an arrow that points, signifying by contiguity, and a photograph that represents by resemblance. The correspondences between index and metonymy and between icon and metaphor led Jakobson beyond Peirce's view that language was the dominant semiotic code because symbols alone were arbitrary; from the late 1940s, Jakobson investigated linguistic instances of index and icon. Some words do operate indexically, notably "shifters," which are words that cannot be understood without reference to both the message and the speaker. A shifter refers to the message, as any symbol must; it also, in the nature of things that point, stands "in existential relation with the object it represents." Peirce had already made an exception, according to Arthur W. Burks's early account (1949) of Peircean semiotics, by speaking of "indexical symbols." The word *shifter* was not Peirce's but was coined by Otto Jespersen in 1922. Jakobson used that concept together with the schematic analysis of "reported speech" outlined in Valentin Voloshinov's *Marxism and the Philosophy of Language* (1929)—evidence of Jakobson's continuing acquaintance with the work of theorists in the Soviet Union, in this instance the circle around Mikhail M. Bakhtin. The double nature of the shifter, both symbolic and indexical, yet again illuminates the importance of the poetic function: every word in a poem refers to the poem as *signans* while simultaneously standing in existential relation to the poem as *signatum*.

Jakobson's argument for the indexical function of the linguistic sign was formulated clearly by 1957. The next step, the last phase of Jakobson's development, completed the recuperation of Peirce and the defiance of Saussure by arguing that linguistic signs might also be iconic. Jakobson referred to not only Peirce but other American linguists, including Benjamin Lee Whorf, William Dwight Whitney, Leonard Bloomfield, and Edward Sapir. In "Quest for the Essence of Language" (1971), Jakobson cites Peirce: "Every algebraic equation is an icon, insofar as it exhibits by means of the algebraic signs (which are not themselves icons) the relations of the quantities concerned." Any algebraic formula appears to be an icon, "rendered such by the rules of commutation, association, and distribution of the symbols." Thus, "algebra is but a sort of diagram," and "language is but a kind of algebra." Peirce thus "vividly conceives" the iconicity of syntax, that "the arrangement of the words in the sentence . . . must serve as *icons*, in order that the sentence may be understood."

Words are always symbolic, and as shifters they may also be indexical. Jakobson cites Peirce again: "It would be difficult, if not impossible, to instance an absolutely pure index, or to find any sign absolutely devoid of the indexical quality" (1971). And, through syntax, Jakobson tries to argue that the arrangement of words, if not each word, is iconic: syntax itself does not conform to the law of pure linearity. Jakobson goes on to cite Whorf, who, with his emphasis on "the algebraic nature of language" knew how to abstract from individual sentences the "designs of sentence structure" and argued that "the *patternment* aspect of language [i.e., syntax] always overrides and controls the *lexation* or name-giving aspect." Saussure's insistence on the linearity of the semiotic chain had obscured precisely this: just as an algebraic formula specifies relations, distributions, and commutations without any referential function whatsoever, so the arrangement of words specifies proportion and disposition prior to reference. This, we might hazard, is obviously so in the case of a sonnet or an epitaph; and as the poetic function is present, however minimally, in all messages, so every utterance must be analyzable in terms of its "sound-shape" (1971).

This is the argument of Jakobson's final monograph, written with Linda Waugh (1979). In this venture, Jakobson and Waugh find a most surprising ally in Saussure, whose "only finished writing during his professorship in Geneva . . . would have innovated the world-wide science of poetics, but . . . was unduly hidden," because it was regarded as merely "futile digressions," until it was published in summary form by J. Starobinski (1971). Saussure detected anagrams or "hypograms" concealed by dispersion through lines of Latin verse. Yet, far from being a crazed obsession, this work was a specific challenge to Saussure's own postulate of linearity. The disposition of proper names as hypograms is virtually algebraic: in linear sequence, the name is hidden, and it is disclosed in spatial terms as iconic. The regrettable

delay in the publication of Saussure's anagrammatic studies meant that Jakobson's sixty-year struggle against Saussure was in part upstaged by Saussure himself, as Jakobson generously recognized.

Jakobson's theory of the iconicity of language—perhaps his single greatest contribution to semiotics, poetics, and linguistics—has itself been disdained within linguistics and treated with insufficient respect in semiotics. Its implications concern the uniqueness of language among sign systems: is language special because, unlike all other sign systems, it is exclusively symbolic? Or does its power lie in the fact that it is the only sign system that operates in all the Peircean modes, symbolic, indexical, and iconic? Positivists and most linguists prefer the former explanation; students of poetry and poetics have yet to explore the consequences of the latter claim.

[*See also* Binarism; Distinctive Features; Iconicity; Indexicality; Phoneme; Poetics; Saussure; Structuralism; *and* Synchronic and Diachronic.]

BIBLIOGRAPHY

Armstrong, D., and C. H. van Schooneveld, eds. *Roman Jakobson: Echoes of His Scholarship*. Lisse: De Ridder, 1977.

Burks, A. W. "Icon, Index, and Symbol." *Philosophy and Phenomenological Research* 9.4 (1949): 673–689.

Grzybek, P. "Some Remarks on the Notion of Sign in Jakobson's Semiotics and in Czech Structuralism." *Znakolog: An International Yearbook of Slavic Semiotics* 1 (1988): 113–128.

Holenstein, E. *Roman Jakobson's Approach to Language: Phenomenological Structuralism*. Translated by C. and T. Schelbert. Bloomington: Indiana University Press, 1976.

Jackson, J. H. "Hughlings Jackson on Aphasia and Kindred Effect in the Production of Speech, Together with a Complete Bibliography of His Publications on Speech." *Brain* 38.1 (1915): 1–190.

Jakobson, R. "Quest for the Essence of Language." In *Selected Writings*, vol. 2, *Word and Language*, edited by R. Jakobson, pp. 345–359. The Hague: Mouton, 1971.

Jakobson, R. *Language in Literature*. Edited by K. Pomorska and S. Rudy. Cambridge, Mass.: Harvard University Press, 1987.

Jakobson, R. *On Language*. Edited by L. Waugh and M. Monville-Burston. Cambridge, Mass.: Harvard University Press, 1990.

Jakobson, R., and L. Waugh. *The Sound Shape of Language*. Bloomington: Indiana University Press, 1979.

Jespersen, O. *Language: Its Nature, Development and Origin*. London: Allen and Unwin, 1922.

Plato. *The Collected Dialogues*. Edited by E. Hamilton and H. Cairns. Princeton: Princeton University Press, 1961.

Rudy, S. *Roman Jakobson 1896–1982: A Complete Bibliography of His Writings*. Berlin: Mouton de Gruyter, 1990.

Starobinski, J. *Words upon Words: The Anagrams of Ferdinand de Saussure* (1971). Translated by O. Emmet. New Haven: Yale University Press, 1979.

Striedter, J. *Literary Structure, Evolution, and Value: Russian Formalism and Czech Structuralism Reconsidered*. Cambridge, Mass.: Harvard University Press, 1989.

Toman, J. *The Magic of a Common Language: Jakobson, Mathesius, Trubetskoy, and the Prague Linguistic Circle*. Cambridge, Mass.: MIT Press, 1995.

A Tribute to Roman Jakobson, 1896–1982. Berlin and New York: Mouton de Gruyter, 1983.

Voloshinov, V. *Marxism and the Philosophy of Language*. Translated by L. Matejka and I. R. Titunik. New York and London: Seminar Press, 1973.

—Charles Lock

JAKOBSON'S MODEL OF LINGUISTIC COMMUNICATION.

The model of communication that has been the most often quoted in the semiotic literature since the 1960s is undoubtedly Roman Jakobson's schema listing the "factors inalienably involved in verbal communication" (1960, p. 353). This model, which merges notions coming from Prague School linguistics, psycholinguistics, and information theory, has been widely used for the analysis of both verbal and nonverbal communication. Its primary source, however, is the functional model of the linguistic sign, developed by German psycholinguist Karl Bühler (1879–1963). Bühler, who elaborated an extensive philosophy of the linguistic sign, participated in and influenced the work of the Prague Linguistic Circle in the 1930s. His critique of Ferdinand de Saussure, which emphasized that the union of signifier and signified must be placed in a larger domain, initiated semiotic functionalism. For Bühler, the sign effects a three-way relation encompassing the sign producer or addresser, the sign itself, and the sign receiver or addressee. He identified three functions associated with these factors: the expressive function is associated with the addresser, the referential function with the sign itself, and the appellative function with the receiver (Innis, 1982).

Prague School semiotics evolved in a situation that demanded engagement. Radical upheaval and experimenting within European art then and in the immediately preceding decades were indicative of a society in the midst of a cataclysm. Some members of the circle who had emigrated to Prague in the shadow of the Stalinist purges had been deeply involved in the intellectual flowering of the immediate postrevolutionary period in Russia, where they participated in the formalist movement in literary criticism. On one side, then, was Stalin; on the other, the ominous burgeoning of Hitler's nationalism, which would eventually decimate the group. Prague theory brought considerable discipline and power to the stance of cultural relativism through which these displaced scholars gave voice to just those principles of tolerance that the societies around them were threatening politically.

Prague functionalism was a direct descendant of Russian formalism. In the 1920s, the formalists had rejected the Romantic psychological theory that literature was determined by the spiritual states of its creators and its public in favor of a formal analysis of the material artwork itself. Yet in the same years that saw the formalist's assertion of autonomous aesthetic structures, the autonomy of art was challenged from a new direction by the aesthetics of dialectical materialism, with its insistence upon the social context and economic function of art. Caught between opposed and irreconcilable theories, both attractive for their novelty, consistency, and explanatory depth, Prague theorists are remarkable for their refusal to simplify their views for the purpose of a clearer intellectual dogma. The concept of sign that served as a sort of home base did not lead quickly to a consistent system, but the notion that the sign served various functions harmonized their several interests: each sign has several functions, but one of these is the *dominant*.

Exploiting relativism, the Prague theorists' work reaches out appreciatively and imaginatively to folk arts, ethnic arts, and discarded periods of art history and welcomes and analyzes new styles and new media. Saussure's unified notion of language is divided up to allow equal priority to poetic language, scientific language, and other socially organized dialects that differ in their communicative functions. We might think of relativism negatively as a refusal to take sides and make judgments, but it allows a constructive aspect. Jan Mukařovský's doctrine of the aesthetic norm is exemplary in this regard. Mukařovský's norm is not statistical; rather, he proposes that cultural behavior, including artistic work, is always understood in relation to a norm that is established by its culture. However, movements of art that conform to social norms are relatively short and rare compared to movements that make their marks by violating them in some respect. The norm is known but not necessarily known explicitly. It is communicated among members of a culture by the ways values are assigned to works. Historically, the norm changes continually, and the interaction between the norm and the works that violate or confirm it are factors in its evolution. Mukařovský provides a full, formal account of this doctrine in *Aesthetic Function, Norm, and Value as Social Facts* (1970). A work of art is one in which aesthetic function dominates, but aesthetic function is not limited to art. Any sign takes on an aesthetic function to the extent that it is regarded as an end in itself. Whether this happens or not is again a question of social norms.

With the "aesthetic function," our repertoire of functions is increased to four. Roman Jakobson incorporated these in a synthesis intended to draw together European functionalism and Claude Shannon and Warren Weaver's mathematical model of communication. Mathematical communication theory is concerned with quite different issues, but it lent to Jakobson the idea of the "channel" and suggested a broader understanding of code. Consequently, the model posits six factors in any linguistic act. There must be an *addresser*, the one who utters or writes or otherwise sends the sign; a *receiver*; a *channel* between the addresser and the addressee, such as live voice, phone, or writing; a *message*—what we have so far called the signifier; a *context*, which includes the signified; and a *code*—the set of rules that determine the relation between the message and some part of the context and that must be at least partially common to the encoder and decoder of the message.

As with Bühler, each factor is associated with a function. All or any subset of functions may be evident in a sign. Following an idea that the Prague Circle had retained from Russian formalism, the one that predominates is the dominant function. A sign in which the *expressive function* is dominant indicates the state of the speaker, as in an exclamation or interjection. The function associated with the receiver is the *conative function*. When dominant, the sign determines the state of the receiver. This means, often, as with a command, a future state. We might say that music, when used to organize and impel marching or dancing, is conative. The function associated with the channel is the *phatic function*, which ensures that the contact is established and maintained. "Do you read me?" Or the parent's, "There, there, it isn't so bad."

The function associated with the message—the vehicle—is the *poetic* or *aesthetic function*: the sign taken as an end in itself. All art understood as art is taken to embody this function, and any object valued for its beauty rather than for its ideological value or usefulness—whether a gorgeous car, an elegant teapot, or some acreage of untouched real estate—takes on this function. Although Jakobson, perhaps more precisely than anyone who preceded him, showed how the aesthetic function could hinge on structure, he argues that cultural norms ultimately determine the dominance of this function. As a striking demonstration, he notes that the aesthetic status that one generation accorded only to the poems of Karel Mácha, a subsequent generation accords only to his diaries (1933).

The function associated with the context is the *referential function*. The interesting idea in this scheme is that reference is just one function among equally important others. The function associated with the code is the *metalingual function*. When we pause to clarify a term, our discourse is metalinguistic.

Jakobson's systematic description of these six functions (1960), has been one of the most enduring models in semiotics. Yet its exposition by Jakobson draws examples only from language, and its application in other spheres is difficult to delineate. Although the specific functions can be attributed to expressions in other media, it is frequently problematic to disengage them and say which is the dominant. When a fugue draws attention to its own system by ingenious arrangements, it might be called metalinguistic or, because the very same structure then turns it back on itself, aesthetic. The phatic function seems always to involve expressive and conative functions: the lullaby is a contact between mother and child (phatic), which has the latter's sleep as its purpose (conative), but which works because it conveys love (expressive). The analysis serves better to inventory the richness of a sign situation than to classify signs or explicate their operations.

Jakobson does not take up the obvious complications that accrue with changing the level of observation: When Hamlet speaks a soliloquy, who is addressing whom? Is Shakespeare addressing the audience? Is Hamlet addressing Hamlet? Is it the English Renaissance expressing itself?

[*See also* Jakobson; Prague School; *and* Russian Formalism.]

BIBLIOGRAPHY

Bühler, K. "Die Axiomatik der Sprachwissenschaft." *Kant Studien* 38 (1933): 19–90.

Bühler, K. *Theory of Language: The Representational Function of Language.* Translated by D. F. Goodwin. Amsterdam and Philadelphia: J. Benjamins, 1990.

Innis, R. *Karl Bühler: Semiotic Foundations of Language Theory.* New York: Plenum, 1982.

Jakobson, R. "What Is Poetry?" (1933). In *Semiotics of Art: Prague School Contributions*, edited by L. Matejka and I. R. Titunik. Cambridge, Mass.: MIT Press, 1976.

Jakobson, R. "Closing Statement: Linguistics and Poetics." In *Style in Language*, edited by T. A. Sebeok. New York: Wiley, 1960.

Mukařovský, J. *Aesthetic Function, Norm, and Value as Social Facts.* Translated by M. E. Suino. Ann Arbor: University of Michigan Press, 1970.

—DAVID LIDOV

JAMESON, FREDRIC (b. 1934), American literary critic and cultural theorist. Jameson's contributions to contemporary cultural studies can be divided into four areas: Marxist theories of culture and ideology; synthesis of Marxism and poststructuralism; critical analysis of poststructuralists such as Michel Foucault and Jacques Derrida; and Postmodernism.

Marxism and Form (1971) contains thorough critical accounts of key twentieth-century Marxist theorists. Three aspects of this text adumbrate Jameson's later and more influential work: (1) his treatment and privileging of a specific area of culture (in this case literature) as a microcosm offering important insights into the workings of capitalist ideology; (2) his taking up of the Frankfurt School's (and particularly Theodor Adorno's) emphasis on cultural mass production and commodification as central to any understanding of contemporary culture; (3) his development of Adorno's thesis that cultural mass production is creating a more complex world that is no longer explicable purely in terms of traditional Marxist notions of class ideology.

The Prison House of Language (1972) constitutes Jameson's first major Marxist engagement with poststructuralist theory, although only by way of descriptions and critiques of some of poststructuralism's antecedents—formalism, structuralism, and, particularly, Saussurean linguistics. His first goal is to contextualize and historicize the development of formalism and structuralism by identifying strong similarities and lines of connection between those

theories and diverse movements, including late romanticism and symbolism. His second aim is to demonstrate, partly via Émile Benveniste's critique of Saussure, that Saussurean linguistics, and consequently structuralism, are flawed theoretically because of their "bracketing off" of extrinsic conditions. Jameson's point is that by emphasizing and hierarchizing the distinction between the synchronic and the diachronic, Saussure locks himself into a kind of linguistic idealism. Jameson identifies other Saussurean distinctions—*langue* and *parole*, paradigm and syntagm—as evidence of Saussure's and structuralism's omissions at the levels of both "historical consciousness" and technical analysis.

The Political Unconscious (1981b) attempts to synthesize various aspects of poststructuralist and postmodernist theory with Marxism. Jameson's method is simultaneously dialectical and polemical as he seeks to demonstrate the superiority of Marxist theory through its ability to incorporate, synthesize, and finally transcend other bodies of theory. Its central arguments (the theoretical reconciliation of Jean-Paul Sartre and Louis Althusser, the accommodation of Althusser within a Hegelian perspective) are complex. One of its more obvious concerns, however, is the use of Althusser and Althusser's appropriation of Jacques Lacan as an antidote to what Jameson understands as Derrida's and Foucault's critiques of the "reality" of history. Whereas Derrida and Foucault, in their different ways, read history as a discursive production predicated on a Nietzschean will to power, Jameson wants to insist, first, that history is both text and narrative and more than text or narrative and, second, that only Marxism can provide an adequate account of the workings of history.

While Jameson accepts the uncertainty of textual mediation, he locates history beyond representation or knowledge as the repressed, the political unconscious. History is a lack (that which cannot be represented) that guarantees the fullness of a Marxist grand narrative. By taking up, somewhat loosely, Althusser's appropriation of Lacan and the Lacanian notion of the "Real" as something that can be discerned through its "prior textualization, its narrativization in the political unconscious," Jameson both accepts and posits a move beyond the poststructuralist notion of history as textuality.

In his 1984 *New Left Review* article, "Postmodernism, or the Cultural Logic of Late Capitalism," Jameson argues that postmodernist culture and theory are products of late capitalism. Then, he specifically identifies what he takes to be the five main characteristics of postmodernist culture, describes and anlayzes the disintegration of the bouregois subject and the loss of aesthetic "distance", and relates these points to questions of epistemology, the workings of ideology, and the possibilities for political activity. Jameson makes use of postmodernist theories and evaluations of contemporary life and culture (particularly Jean Baudrillard's) but then argues that Marxist theory offers the only possibility for any kind of useful explication of postmodernism and its politics.

Jameson reads postmodernism as simultaneously refuting and confirming Marxist theories of history and politics. Developments in postmodern art, architecture, literature, music, cinema, and the mass media, not to mention the crisis with regard to notions of class, ideology, history, social democracy, and the welfare state, all denote "a radical break . . . generally traced back to the end of the 1950s or the early 1960s" (Jameson, 1991). Postmodern theories are useful for identifying and sketching these changes, but for Jameson their denunciation of grand narratives, their celebration of heterogeneity, and their supposed ahistoricism must be understood as symptoms and products of late multinational capitalism.

Jameson identifies five main characteristics of postmodernist culture: the loss of a useful distinction between high and low culture; the domestication of once-subversive modernist and postmodernist works of art; the complete commodification of culture; the fragmentation of the bourgeois subject; and the loss of any sense of temporal distinction and historicity. Depth models based on pairings such as inside and outside, latent and manifest, authentic and inauthentic, essence and appearance, and signifier and signified now give way, according to Jameson, to notions of practice, play, and surface.

How does a Marxist hermeneutics or historical materialism address an age supposedly characterized by the disappearance of any notion of depth and the inability to think historically? And how does an individual or a group respond to a hegemonic late capitalism that has effaced not only itself but subjects and groups as well? Jameson's response is to put forward the notion of cognitive mapping. Jameson takes his cue from Kevin Lynch's *The Image of the City* (1960), which argues that when city residents are "unable to map (in their minds) either their own positions or the urban totality in which they find

themselves," they "construct . . . an articulated ensemble which can be retained in memory and which the individual subject can map and remap along the moments of mobile, alternative trajectories" (Jameson, 1991, p. 51).

Jameson justifies this turn to the notion of cognitive mapping in the same manner that he argues for the importance of the political unconscious in mediating history: via appeals to Althusser and Lacan. He posits an analogy between Lynch's alienated and dislocated urban dwellers and the Althusserian subject, who attempts to negotiate ideological representations of "their Imaginary relationship to his or her Real conditions of existence." Cognitive mapping, for Jameson, is the one way a subject can negotiate the self-effacing and hegemonic totality that is late capitalism. The concept bears some resemblance to Michel de Certeau's notion of practice and to Pierre Bourdieu's notion of habitus. Most of Jameson's subsequent work is largely concerned, however, with specifying and theorizing the workings of cognitive mapping.

Since 1990, Jameson has published *Late Marxism* (1990), *Signatures of the Visible* (1990), an enlarged version of *Postmodernism, or the Cultural Logic of Late Capitalism* (1991), and *The Geopolitical Aesthetic* (1992). *Signatures of the Visible* argues that visual texts and culture occupy preeminent positions in postmodernist culture and attempts to historicize this development so as to "get a handle on increasing, tendential, all-pervasive visuality." *The Geopolitical Aesthetic*'s main concern is to connect Jameson's notion of cognitive mapping with his theories of visual culture. Jameson reads certain contemporary films as instances of a tendency toward cognitive mapping and divides his examples into two groups. The first section of the text seeks to "document the figuration of conspiracy as an attempt . . . to think a system so vast that it cannot be encompassed by the natural and historically developed categories of perception with which human beings normally orient themselves." The second section analyzes film narratives that collapse ontology and geography and that "endlessly process images of the unmappable system." Both instances can be understood, for Jameson, as symptoms of an attempt or desire to once again read and explicate spaces and terrains; therein, for Jameson, "lies the beginning of wisdom."

[*See also* Althusser; Bourdieu; Foucault; Postmodernism; *and* Poststructuralism.]

BIBLIOGRAPHY

Jameson, F. *Marxism and Form*. Princeton: Princeton University Press, 1971.

Jameson, F. *The Prison House of Language: A Critical Account of Structuralism and Russian Formalism*. Princeton: Princeton University Press, 1972.

Jameson, F. *Fables of Aggression: Wyndham Lewis, the Modernist as Fascist*. Berkeley: University of California Press, 1981a.

Jameson, F. *The Political Unconscious: Narrative as a Socially Symbolic Act*. Ithaca, N.Y.: Cornell University Press, 1981b.

Jameson, F. *Late Marxism: Adorno, or the Persistence of the Dialectic*. London: Verso, 1990.

Jameson, F. *Signatures of the Visible*. London: Routledge, 1990.

Jameson, F. *Postmodernism: Or, the Cultural Logic of Late Capitalism*. Durham, N.C.: Duke University Press, 1991.

Jameson, F. *The Geopolitical Aesthetic: Cinema and Space in the World System*. Bloomington: Indiana University Press, 1992.

Jameson, F. *The Seeds of Time*. New York: Columbia University Press, 1994.

Lynch, K. *The Image of the City*. Cambridge, Mass.: Technology Press, 1960.

—TONY SCHIRATO

K

KARCEVSKIJ, SERGEJ IOSIFOVIC (1884–1955), Russian linguist who, with Charles Bally and Albert Sechehaye, belonged to the first generation of Saussure's disciples in Geneva and played an important role in the development of structural linguistics. Born in Tobolsk, Siberia, Karcevskij emigrated as a political refugee to Geneva in 1907. In 1917, after the fall of the Czarist regime, Karcevskij returned to Moscow, where he stayed until 1919, lecturing on Saussurean linguistics at the Russian Academy of Sciences. Roman Jakobson repeatedly pointed out Karcevskij's important role in conveying basic Saussurean ideas to the youngest generation of Russian linguists during this time (e.g., Jakobson 1962, p. 631), a role that was all the more important since the first Russian translation of Saussure's *Cours de linguistique générale* appeared only in 1933 and then in an intellectual context that was critical of his ideas.

In 1920, Karcevskij became a lecturer on Russian language at the University of Strasbourg, where he was exposed to Antoine Meillet's linguistics. In 1922, he moved to Prague, where he taught in the Russian high school and became one of the founding members of the Prague Linguistic Circle; jointly with Jakobson and Nikolaj Trubetzkoy, he signed the phonological theses circulated at the First International Linguistic Congress at The Hague in 1928. In 1927, he returned to Switzerland to receive his doctorate from the University of Geneva, where he taught until 1954.

One of his best-known semiotic studies is "The Asymmetric Dualism of the Linguistic Sign" (1929). His starting point is the well-known fact that the two components of the linguistic sign (the signifier and the signified) do not stand in a one-to-one, reversible relationship: on the one hand, one and the same sign can have various functions (i.e., meanings), and, on the other hand, one and the same meaning can be conveyed by two different signs. A sign, according to Karcevskij, therefore is virtually homonymous and synonymous at the same time, and it is constituted by a "crossing of two series of mental facts." If a sign was simply static and served only a single function, then language would be a mere repertory of labels; if, on the contrary, the signs of a given language were only mobile, one could not signify anything in actual situations. Consequently, a linguistic sign is both stable and unstable (static and dynamic). Karcevskij's conclusion is that the two components of a linguistic sign are asymmetric in nature and in a constant state of unstable equilibrium: whereas the signifier tends toward homonomy or homophony, the signified is characterized by a tendency toward synonymy; homonymy and synonymy thus represent two coordinated correlatives. Still, each time we apply a sign to reality, its identity is maintained because a sign user "tends toward integration and refuses to note any modifications in the set of representations" and because she or he introduces a third term of comparison that guarantees that, in a process of denomination or designation, a given element of reality is categorized and attributed to a particular class. Thus, the meaning of a given sign is modified each time the sign is applied to reality.

Karcevkij's thesis was influential. Jakobson accepted it as an important explanation for language change, and Jan Mukařovský transferred it to processes of poetic denomination. More recently, Karcevskij's ideas have been compared to Jakobson's theory of the two axes of language, and they have been interpreted in terms of a process-oriented language theory.

[*See also* Jakobson; Saussure; *and* Sign.]

BIBLIOGRAPHY

Jakobson, R. O. "Serge Karcevski (August 28, 1884–November 7, 1955)." *Cahiers Ferdinand de Saussure* 14 (1956): 9–13.

Jakobson, R. O. "Retrospect." In *Selected Writings*, vol. 1, *Phonological Studies*, pp. 631–658. The Hague: Mouton, 1962.

Jakobson, R. O., ed. "Publications de S. Karcevski sur la langue et le style." *Cahiers Ferdinand de Saussure* 14 (1956): 14–16.

Karcevskij, S. "The Asymmetric Dualism of the Linguistic Sign" (1929). In *The Prague School: Selected Writings*,

1929–1946, edited by P. Steiner, translated by J. Burbank, pp. 47–54. Austin: University of Texas Press, 1982.

Steiner, P. "In Defense of Semiotics: The Dual Asymmetry of Cultural Signs." *New Literary History* 12 (1981): 415–435.

Steiner, P., and W. Steiner. "The Relational Axes of Poetic Language." In *Jan Mukařovský, On Poetic Language*, translated and edited by J. Burbank and P. Steiner, pp. 71–86. Lisse: Peter Ridder Press, 1976.

Steiner, W. L. "Language as Process: Sergej Karcevskij's Semiotics of Language." In *Sound, Sign, and Meaning: Quinquagenary of the Prague Linguistic Circle*, edited by L. Matejka, pp. 291–300. Michigan Slavic Contributions, 6. Ann Arbor: University of Michigan, 1976.

—PETER GRZYBEK

KNOWLEDGE REPRESENTATION refers to the manner in which an organism stores information about its environment in anticipation of situations in which it needs this information for survival. Cognitive systems live in environments to which they are connected by sensory and motor interfaces. To survive, they must have some kind of representation of this environment in order to operate and behave adequately. This raises many questions: which mechanisms must be provided in order to realize such a representation? What is the relationship between the structure of the environment and its representation? Does representation map the environment's objects, processes, and phenomena more or less iso- or homomorphically onto the representational structure? How is knowledge mediated by signs and symbols?

These questions have been long discussed by philosophers, epistemologists, and semioticians. Twentieth-century philosophy of language and logic have brought about a new understanding of the representational function and central role of language in it. Logical empiricism and formal logic had strong influences on the development of knowledge-representation techniques in the fields of cognitive science, artificial intelligence (AI), and cognitive psychology. However, alternative approaches such as connectionism have developed in recent decades.

The basic idea of the representational paradigm, called "symbolic representation" in AI, is that environmental structures are mapped onto propositional or linguistic structures. These structures and semantic categories (i.e., natural-language words, sentences, etc.) are formalized, and their syntactic structures are mapped onto formal symbols, which are manipulated according to rules that are themselves the result of a similar mapping process. The knowledge-representation system, thus, consists of symbols (and sometimes of relationships between these symbols) and a set of rules or inference mechanisms that operate on these symbols. One or more sentences (in the form of symbol strings) are the input to the system, and they are processed by applying rules. The output again is a string of symbols. Thus, knowledge is represented by formal symbols and rules. This approach to symbolic knowledge representation has been formulated by Newell and Simon (1976) and Newell (1980) in its most extreme form as the physical symbol–systems hypothesis, which claims that symbol systems have the necessary and sufficient means for generating intelligent behavior. Another exponent of this approach is Jerry Fodor (1981).

This hypothesis seems plausible, if it is assumed that all human cognitive processes are constrained by language. Critics of this approach point out that symbol systems are engaged in simulating and manipulating only on the syntactic level and that the semantic and pragmatic aspects of language are ignored. Although AI and cognitive science also claim to represent semantic features in symbol systems, these features are in fact nothing but more complex syntactic structures. From a semiotic perspective, formal and syntactic structures alone cannot account for the performance and representational power of natural language.

Moreover, a more or less isomorphic relationship between the structure of the symbolic knowledge–representation system and the outside world is assumed implicitly. The mostly successful use of language indeed suggests that the world can be described and categorized by linguistic categories. But scientific research on perception has shown that natural human cognitive systems are capable of representing a far richer view of the world that is much more fine-grained than language. Language itself results from a long and complex neural representational process aiming at reducing and categorizing this variety.

For the symbol-systems hypothesis, knowledge representation and processing are restricted to manipulating symbols in the form of, for instance, bit patterns. It is the external human user who ascribes semantic values to these symbols by interpreting them through interactions with the environment. The semantics of each symbol is thus established either directly or indirectly (via other symbols) by interactions with the environment. It follows that pragmatics shape semantics and that the syntactic level is only the very last level of expression of multilayered processes. Thus, symbol systems themselves lack the property of getting or changing their meaning by interacting directly with their environment, since there is always a user mediating between the semantic and the syntactic aspects. In other words, the semantics of symbols can be found only in the brains of the participating cognitive systems, whose experiences are projected or interpreted in the perceived syntactic structure. The crucial questions are how semantics evolves and changes and how a symbol establishes its meaning. Symbol systems are not able to explain or simulate the processes of the development of new symbols and the continuous change of meaning. This dynamics is determined by the current and practical use of symbols, a feature that cannot be achieved by the (syntactically driven) symbol manipulation alone, since it requires a human user to adjust the current meanings to the computer's syntax and vice versa.

Symbolic knowledge representation implicitly assumes a stable dynamics of semantics (meanings of symbols do not change in the course of time) and a common semantics; that is, it presupposes some given, externally defined semantics that is universally valid for everyone using the language. Everyday experiences with misunderstandings of all kinds in communication suggest that this is not the case.

Symbolic systems perform well in the context of rather formal domains (expert systems) but fail in commonsense-related domains. It is relatively easy to perform formal manipulations on syntactic structures and generate well-formed answers to very specific questions in a very restricted, formal domain. But how meaning emerges or changes over time remains a problem that the symbol-system hypothesis does not seem to be able to solve.

The alternative paradigm assumes that human cognition is based on neural activities and that human cognitive abilities, including language, are embedded in neural structures. As an alternative medium for knowledge representation these neural structures are more general than those of language. The connectionist approach contends that artificial neural networks can contribute to a better understanding of knowledge representation: (1) for epistemological reasons, we cannot talk about "the" structure of the environment, because we assume implicitly that our experience of the environment is

"the" environment, which is determined by the structure of our perceptual systems and our brains; (2) we can only talk about the environment with respect to a certain cognitive system having a phylogenetic and ontogenetic history—representation of the environment is always system-relative; (3) already in the sensory systems, a first reorganization and restructuring of the environment takes place, and we cannot expect to find an isomorphic mapping of the environment in the neural system.

However, the unreflexive use of language suggests that such an isomorphic relation does exist between the environment and linguistic structures. As linguistic categories dominate the structure and dynamics of human thinking, these categories appear to be isomorphic with the environment, since each item in the environment has its lexical label. This naive understanding of language has led to many difficulties and problems in the symbolic approach to knowledge representation. Instead of an isomorphic relationship, the connectionist approach considers knowledge the result of an active process of construction embedded in a cyclic structure of trial and error; that is, the knowledge (theory) that is continuously changed by our experiences is tested in the environment for further improvement and, if necessary, changed or even replaced. Such knowledge is responsible for the actions and behavior of the cognitive system in the same sense that a scientific theory determines the hypotheses, methods, and actions (experiments) applied to the environment. Knowledge always remains hypothetical, even in scientific theories.

A closed (external) feedback loop is established between the organism and its environment, as they are coupled to each other via sensors and effectors. Unlike the symbolic knowledge–representation approach, the cognitive system is not embedded in a linguistic environment with an externally given meaning, semantics, and so on (i.e., it is not part of a purely "syntactico-semantic" coupling); rather, it is physically coupled to the environment. The only interaction that takes place is the exchange of energy (mechanical, photo, thermal, chemical, etc.). In any case, the system is confronted with a more or less structured flow of energy that it transforms into neural signals—that is, the sensors are the interface between the environment and the internal representation structure. However, these neural signals do not entirely determine the internal state of the neural system since the organism itself is an active dynamic system with a recurrent neural architecture. Thus, external stimuli can only perturb and modulate the inner dynamics of the system. The activations spreading through the natural or artificial neural structure cause action in the effectors—that is, neural activity is transformed into physical energy (in most cases, the movement of muscles) which causes either a change in the environment or a change of the organism's position in the environment. These changes themselves cause changes in the sensory systems, which again perturb the organism's dynamics. Such a closed loop enables control over the environment as well as direct feedback about the results produced by the actions executed by the organism.

Therefore, the goal of connectionism is *not* to map the environment onto neural structures as accurately as possible but to see the structures of knowledge representation as responsible for generating adequate behavior. If the natural or artificial neural network is seen as a device for generating adequate behavioral responses, rather than representing certain structures of the environment, it fits functionally into its environment by ensuring the organism's survival; this includes all kinds of knowledge, ranging from simple reactive responses to more complex behavioral patterns and language and even to the production of scientific knowledge. Naturally, "survival" has to be understood also in a sociocultural sense. This "generative character" of knowledge representation is one reason why we cannot expect to find explicit linguistic structures or visual categories (pictures, patterns, etc.) in natural or artificial neural networks: (1) the physical neural structures are responsible for generating precisely these (behavioral) structures and referential (representational) categories, such as language or images—there is no reason to assume that the mechanism that generates a certain pattern or category must have exactly the same structure as those it produces; (2) since the architectures that are studied in artificial neural networks as well as their environments and structures of input are completely different from the neural structures in the brain, it is not plausible that similar categories can be found in so completely different dynamic structures.

Such an understanding of knowledge representation implies a more neurobiologically plausible model of cognition and enables the modeling of the evolution of meaning, since its representation is not confined to the linguistic system. Learning strategies are adaptive and inductive processes that establish relations on a pre- or subsymbolic level. Thus, language is understood as a very complex form of behavior, rather than as a mere compendium of syntactic structures. Meaning is established within each system through experiences, which are embodied in the cognitive system's neural architecture. This architecture is determined in its basic form by evolution and is in continuous flow as the system adapts its dynamics to the environment. Knowledge is embodied in the neural substratum, which is responsible for the system's semantics. Communication between two agents can be achieved by each adapting their private use of symbols (i.e., their semantics) to the others. Recent developments in cognitive science and artificial-life research have shown that this concept of knowledge representation seems to be promising and will prompt further research toward the understanding of knowledge representation.

[*See also* Artificial Intelligence; Connectionism; Expert Systems; Gibson; Receptors; *and* Umwelt.]

BIBLIOGRAPHY

Churchland, P. M. *Matter and Consciousness: A Contemporary Introduction to the Philosophy of Mind.* Rev. ed. Cambridge, Mass.: MIT Press, 1988.

Churchland, P. M. *A Neurocomputational Perspective: The Nature of Mind and the Structure of Science.* Cambridge, Mass.: MIT Press, 1989.

Fodor, J. A. *Representations: Philosophical Essays on the Foundations of Cognitive Science.* Cambridge, Mass.: MIT Press, 1981.

Newell, A. "Physical Symbol Systems." *Cognitive Science* 4 (1980): 135–183.

Newell, A., and H. A. Simon. "Computer Science as Empirical Inquiry: Symbols and Search" (1976). In *Mind Design: Philosophy, Psychology, Artificial Intelligence*, edited by J. Haugeland, pp. 35–66. Cambridge, Mass.: MIT Press, 1982.

Rumelhart, D. E., and J. L. McClelland. *Parallel Distributed Processing, Explorations in the Microstructure of Cognition*, vol. 1, *Foundations.* Cambridge, Mass.: MIT Press, 1986.

Smolensky, P. "On the Proper Treatment of Connectionism." *Behavioral and Brain Sciences* 11 (1988): 1–74.

—MARKUS PESCHL

KOCH, WALTER A. (b. 1934), German linguist and semiotician. His first monograph, *Theory of the Sound Change* (1962), approached the foundations of language from a diachronic and explanatory perspective at a time when synchronic and merely descriptive approaches were the predominant paradigm. From the level of the phoneme, Koch's research program expanded progressively to higher levels of analysis via the morpheme, word, and sentence to the level of the texteme, culminating in three programmatic works, *From Morpheme to Texteme* (1969), *Taxologie des Englischen* (1971), and *Das Textem* (1973). Never contented with the restrictions on the scope of research set by the predominating schools of contemporary linguistics, Koch sought to extend his analytic horizon from static to dynamic, from linguistics to text linguistics, from grammar to poetry, from linguistics to semiotics, and from the semiotics of contemporary art and culture to the evolution of culture and semiosis since its very origins.

The step from grammar to poetry began with *Recurrence and a Three-Modal Approach to Poetry* (1966), in which Koch first set forth the idea of poetry as the manifestation of three independent modes of poeticalness, only one of which is due to patterns of phonetic recurrence, the other two being recurrence of elements of content and deviation from conventional structures of expectation. Koch then extended these text-linguistic models of poetry to the more general dimensions of a semiotic aesthetics and soon to the still-larger framework of an evolutionary theory of the arts. *Poetry and Science* (1983), *The Well of Tears* (1989), *The Biology of Literature* (1993), and *The Roots of Literature* (1993) were the milestones on this path exploring the wider evolutionary semiotic horizons of aesthetics.

Koch's first decisive move from linguistics and text linguistics to semiotics proper came with the sociosemiotic theory of culture he developed in 1971 under the title *Varia semiotica*. The concepts of sign, structure, and system were guideposts of his research program at that time, as was the idea of applying the model of language by analogy to the most diverse nonverbal phenomena of culture, such as advertising, ballet, music, paintings, happenings, or everyday gestures and body language. Some of the theoretical foundations of this most ambitious interdisciplinary program of a semiotics of culture received a more rigorous and philosophical elaboration in *Philosophie der Philologie und Semiotik* (1986).

In the 1980s, Koch began exploring the paradigm of evolutionary cultural semiotics, which is both a step beyond semiotics in its synchronic and anthropocentric tradition and a step back to the origins of Koch's own research in diachronic linguistics, the field that links up with the prehistory of modern semiotics in the history of modern linguistics. With *Semiogenesis* (1982), *Evolutionary Cultural Semiotics* (1986a), *Genes vs. Memes* (1986b), *Hodos and Kosmos* (1987), and *Evolution of Culture* (1989), Koch laid the foundations of this general semiotic theory of cultural evolution. The programmatic return to language with the ambitious goal to reveal its evolutionary roots culminated in *Language in the Upper Pleistocene* (1991).

According to Koch (1982), semiogenesis, the evolution and development of semiosis since its origins, "covers the interrelated geneses of such phenomena as animal communication, computer systems, oral language, written language, theater, film, gestural systems, philosophy or religion as languages, the language of the drums and flags, pheromones or logic as sign systems, DNA as genetic 'code,' painting etc. . . . as an array of apparently heterogeneous and yet somehow isomorphic systems" (1982, p. 18). The evolution of semiosis can be studied only in the framework of a semiotics that transcends its anthropocentric limitations. Koch (1986a) hence opts for a broad and even pansemiotic view of the universe according to which there are traces of semiosis as early as the origins of cosmos. Semiotics is hence a metadiscipline that "enables us to discover traces of semiosis . . . in everything: from original atoms through extravagant thoughts."

In contrast to semioticians who have set up various dividing lines between the realm of the semiotic and the nonsemiotic world, Koch has emphasized the continuity between the two, such as when he proposed evolutionary cultural semiotics (1986a, pp. 231–282) as a project to "embark upon the reconstruction of an objective, ultimately indivisible, flow of reality, of which the evolution of matter, of life, of consciousness, of culture, and of signs are but special points of emergence." In his outline of a holistic account for the emergence and evolution of culture from nature, Koch (1986a) distinguishes the following eleven evolutionary stages since the emergence of our cosmic universe: (1) *cosmogenesis* of physicogenesis, beginning 15 billion years ago with the physical expansion of the universe at the moment of the big bang; (2) *galactogenesis*, galactic evolution, beginning 12.5 billion years ago; (3) *geogenesis*, the origin of earth, 4.5 billion years ago; (4) *biogenesis*, the appearance of life on earth (from bacteria to protozoa), from 4 to 1.7 billion years ago; (5) *sociogenesis*, the origins of social organization, beginning 500 million years ago; (6) *semiogenesis* (in the narrower sense), the origins of human culture, beginning with *Homo habilis* 2 million years ago; (7) *glottogenesis*, origins of language, 50,000 years ago; (8) *eikonogenesis*, origins of pictorial representation, 30,000 years ago; (9) *graphogenesis*, the invention of writing, 5,000 years ago; (10) *typographogenesis*, the invention of printing, 1400 CE; (11) *mediogenesis*, the diffusion of television, beginning in 1950 CE.

As the sixth evolutionary level of this model, semiogenesis does not refer to the semiotic threshold at which semiosis begins but to a higher prototype of semiosis in which artifacts begin to be used as sign vehicles in anthroposemiotics. In fact, the earliest beginnings of semiosis are at the lower levels of biogenesis and sociogenesis, where they emerge in the form of biosemiosis, zoosemiosis, and sociosemiosis. The genetically preceding levels, from cosmo- to geogenesis, provide the material basis of semiosis, but the sphere of the material world also evinces structural isomorphies with the world of semiosis. These isomorphisms in the evolution from matter to semiosis are indicators of evolutionary continuity and coherence and justify the assumption of an indivisible evolutionary whole with traces of semiosis since the very origin of cosmos.

Besides its chronological dimension, evolution has a variety of aspects for the study of which Koch provides an elaborate conceptual framework. In contrast to scholars who emphasize the differences between evolution and individual development, Koch emphasizes the similarities between genesis in phylogeny, the evolution of the species, and genesis in ontogeny, the process of individual maturation. Following Ernst Haeckel's biogenetic rule, Koch formulates a general principle of echogenesis according to which phylogenetic processes tend to be recapitulated (echoed) in the processes of ontogeneses and other geneses.

Genesis, evolution at large, is furthermore distinguished from metagenesis, the discovery and reexperiencing of genesis in human consciousness, such as in religious mythogenesis, philosophical theories of cosmogenesis, or epistemogenesis—the "epistemic reconstruction of the entire objective-subjective world." The relation between both is typically one of chronological reversal: metagenesis tends to mirror genesis by ascribing historical primacy to phenomena that evolved later in the course of evolutionary history. For example, whereas *Homo sapiens* comes last in genetic evolution, the human I is imagined to be first in mythogenesis and epistemogenesis.

Besides ontogenesis, Koch distinguishes several other variants of development evolution, including actogenesis, the process of production and reception of signs in actual semiosis, and eugenesis, the processes of regressive simplification as well as progressive complexification of semiotic systems in their historical development. The latter mode of genesis is related to two more general evolutionary principles: anagenesis, the complexification of matter, and catagenesis, the decomplexification of matter.

[*See also* Biosemiotics; Evolution; Meme; Memetics; Sebeok; Semiosis; *and* Semiotic Terminology.]

BIBLIOGRAPHY

Koch, W. A. *Recurrence and a Three-Modal Approach to Poetry.* The Hague: Mouton, 1966.

Koch, W. A. *Varia semiotica.* Hildesheim: Olms, 1971.

Koch, W. A. "Semiogenesis: Some Perspectives for Its Analysis." In *Semiogenesis: Essays on the Genesis of Language, Art and Literature*, edited by W. A. Koch, pp. 15–104. Bern: Peter Lang, 1982.

Koch, W. A. *Poetry and Science.* Tübingen: Narr, 1983.

Koch, W. A. *Evolutionary Cultural Semiotics.* Bochum: Brockmeyer, 1986a.

Koch, W. A. *Genes vs. Memes.* Bochum: Brockmeyer, 1986b.

Koch, W. A. *Hodos and Kosmos*, Bochum: Brockmeyer, 1987.

Koch, W. A. *Language in the Upper Pleistocene.* Bochum: Brockmeyer, 1991.

Koch, W. A. *The Biology of Literature.* Bochum: Brockmeyer, 1993.

Koch, W. A., ed. *Evolution of Culture.* Bochum: Brockmeyer, 1989.

Nöth, W., ed. *Origins of Semiosis.* Berlin: Mouton de Gruyter, 1994.

—WINFRIED NÖTH

KRISTEVA, JULIA

KRISTEVA, JULIA (b. 1941), French linguist, semiotician, and psychoanalyst. Born in Bulgaria, Julia Kristeva went to Paris in 1966, where she studied with Émile Benveniste and Roland Barthes and soon became a member of the influential *Tel Quel* group. Educated in a Marxist system, her early absorption of the works of G. W. F. Hegel contributed to her intellectual topography, which can be difficult to negotiate for those reared in other traditions. The complexity of her work intensified as she was increasingly influenced by the psychoanalytic theories of Sigmund Freud and Jacques Lacan and as she became a practicing psychoanalyst. The overall development of her work is usually considered to have increasing though controversial importance for feminist semiotics.

Her work challenges mind-body dualism and the notion of teleology. Her seminal concepts of the speaking subject, signifying practice, and the semiotic all demand that the so-called discipline of semiotics reconstitute itself as semanalysis, an activity aware of the delusory nature of "discipline" itself. The Kristevan semanalyst cannot conceive of herself as a transcendental ego detached from and capable of completely describing language as an object because she herself can only speak a discourse that is always vulnerable to the operations of psychic energies derived from early bodily experience (that is, she bears the mark of her body in the discourse she speaks). Language must be reconceptualized as "signifying practice," a discourse in which logic itself, which as a concept rests upon a prior concept of pure mental processes detached from the body, is shown to be vulnerable to the operations of its other: the semiotic—a repressed but never forgotten "body-memory." Kristeva's work in the 1970s and 1980s made increasingly clear that body memories are far from agreeable reflections of inner harmony. Revolutionary from its inception in her theory, carved out of Hegel's concept of negativity and Freud's concept of narcissism, the semiotic as she theorized it reveals the human subject's violently and necessarily split origins in an abject (that which is expelled) maternal body. The semiotic is the force that keeps the subject forever "in process" or "on trial"; it keeps the subject in touch with its fascinating but fearful origins in a way that destroys the possibility of a teleological progression to the ultimate harmony of being. Healing, however, is possible through love, a secular notion that replaces the religious comfort of earlier periods and can be realized in the transference of the psychoanalytic exchange between analyst and analysand.

The project of accounting for the semiotic—a prolonged and intense struggle to describe, in psychoanalytic terms, the workings of the unconscious in language—characterizes Kristeva's work in the 1960s and early 1970s, the period of her most explicit contribution to the discipline of semiotics. The endeavor to figure forth the Lacanian other of language took her into the fields of literature and the visual arts. In both, she sought ways of describing in language the manifestations of the prelinguistic, understood in Freudian psychoanalytic terms as the "economy" of the individual human subject composed of instinctual drives. Such manifestations were identified as rhythm (in language) and color (in painting). The paradox of using language to describe the manifestations of the prelinguistic is fully recognized by Kristeva and partly explains how the self-questioning of her enterprise can be built into the theoretical base of that very enterprise. Her introduction of the term *semanalysis* is intended in part to recognize this necessary internal paradox and is meant to make semiotics aware of its own entanglement in the sign system it seeks to define and describe.

Kristeva contributed to the formalist move "beyond the sentence" by insisting that the nonlogical element of language requires analysis to go beyond the site of the interpretation of the individual text to a consideration of the role of the "artist," understood as a dialogic position that subverts the traditional dichotomy of producer and consumer in social revolution. Her concepts of the speaking subject and textuality, through which she insistently addresses the question of how poetic language can be revolutionary, are produced by an original synthesis of formalism, psychoanalysis, and Marxism. She draws crucial concepts from Hegel (negativity); Roman Jakobson (materiality of language); Freud and Lacan (narcissism; the unconscious structured like a language; dreams as "work" or productivity; intersubjectivity); Benveniste (implications of pronoun usage for intersubjectivity); Mikhail Bakhtin (dialogism; intertextuality; the carnival as transgressive utterance); Georges Bataille (expenditure and sacrifice); Louis Althusser (materialist conception of the subject); and Barthes (distinction between conservative or "readerly" and radical or "writerly" texts). While it could be said that she elicited and emphasized the latent materialist implications of psychoanalysis and the latent materialist and psychoanalytic implications of formalism, some of this work had already been done by the thinkers who most influenced her. While psychoanalysis and formalism as theories have often been criticized for ahistoricism, Lacan himself reached back to the formalist most engaged with language as a material entity (signifiers as sounds or graphics that cannot be reduced to signifieds or concepts), Roman Jakobson. Kristeva picks this up (see "The Ethics of Linguistics" in *Desire in Language*) and adds to the field of concern Bakhtin's preoccupation with actual periods of textual production.

In "Word, Dialogue, and Novel" (in *Desire in Language* and *The Kristeva Reader*), Kristeva charted her exploration of Bakhtin. His concept of dialogism is central to her work on the "Revolution in Poetic Language," the title of her doctoral thesis, published in 1974 and the most comprehensive articulation of her psychosemiotic theory. Following Bakhtin's lead, she educed specific textual situations as evidence that dialogic textual practice is neither self-destructive nor destructive of the sociolinguistic order in which it is situated. Dialogism is a revolutionary practice that works in and through existing textual-linguistic formations to transform them. While Bakhtin cites Fyodor Dostoyevsky, Kristeva finds her evidence of "revolutionary" language in the avant-garde writers of late nineteenth-century France, particularly Stéphane Mallarmé and Lautréamont (Isidore Ducasse), and, among English-language author, James Joyce. Her focus on poetry is original within Marxist semiotics, which traditionally has more to say about prose.

Revolutionary language is distinguished from psychotic discourse, which cannot be revolutionary because it does not maintain sufficient points of contact with the symbolic order to be comprehensible. Yet psychotic discourse also falls within the purview of semanalysis, which must not in the end refuse to engage with the "Real." Kristeva's increasing concern with psychoanalytic practice and the pain of actual patients is reflected in "The True-Real," in which she returns to Freud in order to develop the Lacanian concepts of the true and the real beyond where Lacan left them. She posits psychosis as "the crisis of the truth in language" and suggests that the "psychotic text" should be examined using the resources of both semiology and psychoanalysis "in order to isolate certain characteristics relevant to any speaking subject." Her writings from the mid-1970s suggest that semiology and psychoanalysis are jointly in the service of the understanding of the speaking subject as a linguistic-political construct.

The most important concepts to emerge from her encounter with psychoanalysis are those of the semiotic and signifying practice. Through these, she gives a grounding in early infant development to Bakhtin's dialogism and emphasizes—in a conscious disagreement with Freud and Lacan that is crucial for her assessment by feminists—the function of the maternal rather than the paternal in the constitution of the

economy of the individual human subject. Her concept of practice as something that introduces "material contradictions into the process of the subject" and that is not susceptible to dialectical resolution is also a deliberate criticism of Hegel and Marx. It is by means of the concept of the semiotic that Kristeva challenges the tendency of structuralism to focus exclusively on the communicational (logical) aspect of language and proposes instead that signifying practice should be the object of study, as it is the product of the human speaking subject who acquires a certain impetus to signification even before he or she acquires language. Although the subject is then forced by the acquisition of language (understood in Freudian and Lacanian terms as socialization through acceptance of the symbolic law with its incest taboo directed primarily at the infant's relationship with the mother) to repress this impetus in the interests of participating in the communicational aspect of language, he or she never loses the capacity for signification bestowed upon it by its prelinguistic experience. Kristeva schematizes this as a negotiation of the symbolic order (Lacan's term for language as intersubjective communication) by the semiotic, her reworking of Lacan's "imaginary order."

It is through this reworking and through her challenge to the temporal and spatial metaphors implicit in Lacan's theory of the acquisition of language that Kristeva disputes Lacan's contention that while the unconscious is "structured like a language," it is not a rival to logical language. Certainly, Lacan's unconscious, which manifests itself in jokes, puns, and slips of the tongue, disrupts ordinary language, but such is the power of socialization that the unconscious is homogenized and made habitual within ordinary language. In short, Lacan's other of language is not a potential revolutionary. Kristeva thinks this reveals the ahistoricism of Lacan's theory and challenges it by focusing on a particular historical period and finding in its writings evidence that the semiotic is not made habitual by communicational language but rather transgresses it. The semiotic is not superseded by the symbolic but remains a perpetual reservoir of psychic energies that can spill over onto the dominant signifying system in the form of, particularly, rhythm in language and color in painting.

The key to Kristeva's challenge to Lacan (and, incidentally, to the temporal and hierarchical metaphors informing the Marxist variations of the base/superstructure model) is her persistent use of spatial metaphors. She adds to the semiotic the concept of the *chora* (receptacle; drawn from Plato), which, although she denies it is a space, resists being conceptualized in anything other than spatial terms, by either herself or her principal commentators. The metaphors are spatial in part because Kristeva will not allow them to be temporal, and thus in themselves they bear witness to the persistence of binary oppositions in Western thought. Though the semiotic *chora* is, according to John Lechte (1990), a kind of material base for the symbolic, it is not for that reason of a lower order: it is not superseded by the symbolic as a higher (more rational) order of signification. On the contrary, it is the fertility and richness of voice and body that transform the symbolic into "poetic" language.

The preheterosexual nature of the semiotic is crucial to Kristeva's contention that the semiotic as revolutionary signifying practice is available equally to women and men. Her own focus on male writers has been criticized by feminists, but this criticism might have obscured an important issue. Literary texts are a fertile ground for manifestations of a semiotic "bodyspeak" that challenges binary linguistic structures such as that of affirmation and negation or that of male and female by creating a space that is always already preheterosexual and thus free of its restrictions. Kristeva gives the lead in this in her examination of Molly Bloom's monologue with its repeated *yes* in Joyce's *Ulysses*. A deconstruction of *women saying "yes"* via the concept of the semiotic seems a fully feminist activity. More creative work on this aspect of Kristeva's semiotics needs to be done by literature specialists.

Kristeva's writings (in particular *In the Beginning Was Love* and *Tales of Love* [both 1987]) have been major contributions to the understandings of the semiotic and symbolic aspects of Western religion. Even her earlier writings have not been exhausted, particularly in the implications for ethics of her work on embodiment and on the subject in process or on trial, both of which are central to her notion of signifying practice. David Fisher argues that "Julia Kristeva's rethinking of ethics as a signifying practice rather than as a foundational basis for morality makes a substantial contribution to the development of a postmodern ethic" (Crownfield, 1992). He points to her use of fictive models for the healing of the violently split subject. Art as well as religion, philosophy, and psychoanalysis can provide these models,

but the question is whether the discourse of art is capable of sustaining the ethical burden.

There is still much to de done on assessing the significance of later developments in Kristeva's thought for the "discipline." In Lechte's interpretation, even her most recent book, *Strangers to Ourselves* (1991), about the place of the foreigner in France, extends her project of semanalysis in that *foreignness* (*étranger* means both "stranger" and "foreigner") is another term that leads into the nature of the unconscious and of the drive activity that forms the basis of the Kristevan elaboration of the semiotic. This suggests that Kristeva continues to perform the function Barthes attributed to her from her earliest work: expounding upon the boundaries of the discipline of semiotics and forcing it to redefine itself.

[*See also* De Lauretis; Feminism and Feminist Theories; Feminist Semiotics; Lacan; *and* Semiotic and Symbolic.]

BIBLIOGRAPHY

Works by Kristeva

Desire in Language: A Semiotic Approach to Literature and Art. Edited by L. S. Roudiez. Oxford: Basil Blackwell, 1981.

The Kristeva Reader. Edited by T. Moi. Oxford: Basil Blackwell, 1986.

In the Beginning Was Love: Psychoanalysis and Faith. Translated by A. Goldhammer. New York: Columbia University Press, 1987.

Tales of Love. Translated by L. Roudiez. New York: Columbia University Press, 1987.

Strangers to Ourselves. Translated by L. Roudiez. New York: Columbia University Press, 1991.

Other Works

Bowlby, R. *Still Crazy after All These Years: Women, Writing, and Psychoanalysis.* London: Routledge, 1992.

Crownfield, D., ed. *Body/Text in Julia Kristeva: Religion, Women, and Psychoanalysis.* Albany: State University of New York Press, 1992.

Doane, J., and D. Hodges. *From Klein to Kristeva: Psychoanalytic Feminism and the Search for the "Good Enough" Mother.* Ann Arbor: University of Michigan Press, 1992.

Grosz, E. *Sexual Subversions: Three French Feminists.* Sydney: Allen and Unwin, 1989.

Lechte, J. *Julia Kristeva.* London: Routledge, 1990.

Moi, T. *Sexual/Textual Politics: Feminist Literary Theory.* London and New York: Routledge, 1988.

Stanton, D. C. "Difference on Trial: A Critique of the Maternal Metaphor in Cixous, Irigaray, and Kristeva." In *The Poetics of Gender*, edited by N. K. Miller, pp. 157–182. New York: Columbia University Press, 1986.

—JOY WALLACE

L

LACAN, JACQUES (1901–1981), French psychiatrist who became a practicing and training psychoanalyst. Among Lacan's vast output, his writings and seminars of the 1950s are regarded as most immediately relevant to the discipline of semiotics. Before then, his concerns were less with the nature of language and the unconscious than with a stage of infant development and its implications for the constitution of the human subject. Nevertheless, certain aspects of his pre-1950s work help to elucidate elements in the work of his semiotic period. After the 1950s, "the linguistic aspect of his teaching ventured more and more into a formal mathematical idiom" as he tried to "specify the formal characteristics of psychoanalytic discourse" (Forrester, 1990).

A recurrent preoccupation of Lacan's work is with the retrieval of elements of Sigmund Freud's thought that have been either obscured or misrepresented by certain of his followers. Lacan's project is most comprehensibly approached through its attack on the notion of a unified human subject and upon the analysts who persisted in not recognizing the Freudian revelation of a subject irremediably split between conscious and unconscious realms. He objected to American ego psychology because it was based on a non-Freudian notion of a potentially "whole" human subject ("The Signification of the Phallus," 1958). To reform psychoanalysis, under the influences of Claude Lévi-Strauss and Roman Jakobson, Lacan synthesized the works of Freud and Ferdinand de Saussure.

In "The Agency of the Letter in the Unconscious or Reason since Freud" (1957), Lacan theorizes the unconscious by rewriting Saussure in Freudian terms. Lacan approvingly cites Saussure's perceptions that the two parts of the sign are arbitrarily related; that signs are related by a system of differences from each other without positive terms; and that language is a closed, not referential, system. Lacan modifies, however, Saussure's theory of the relative importance of the two parts of the sign to the process of signification. His "algorithm" S/s, in which S represents the

signifier and s the signified, is meant to indicate the incomparably greater power of the signifier. Most of the time, one signifier merely begets another, rather than effacing itself before a secure signified. To theorize this signifying chain, Lacan maps Jakobson's linguistic concepts of metaphor and metonymy upon Freud's psychoanalytic concepts of condensation and displacement. Both sets of terms indicate forms of disturbance to logical speech; both reveal another kind of system at work. Lacan starts with Freud on dreams and notes that the presence of "logical articulations" argues that a dream uses language not mime. But Lacan insists that the unconscious can also be seen at work outside dreams, in jokes, slips of the tongue, and puns. These disruptions take two main forms: condensation/metaphor and displacement/metonymy. The disruptions, when mapped upon the Freudian model of the acquisition of logical language as acceptance of the name of the father, work to avoid the censorship that the incest taboo imposes on the human subject. Condensation/metaphor gets around the censorship barrier by selecting elements and making a new "whole" that is a disguise, while displacement/metonymy avoids censorship by new associations and combinations. The parts of metaphor and metonymy have the relation of one signifier to another, not of a signifier to a signified. For example, in the metonymic "thirty sails," *sail* does not equal *ship* but rather "stands for" or displaces it. Likewise, a metaphorical term abolishes the literal meaning but is itself only another signifier. The word murders the thing.

Moreover, not only does the signifier insist on its materiality (on being taken literally, "to the letter"), but it actually invades the signified. Saussure's diagram of communication as wavy lines implies an incessant sliding of the signified under the signifier, but this is contrary to our experience. In fact, there are *points de capiton* ("upholstery buttons" or "quilting stitches") where the horizontal sliding movement of the signifying chain is punctuated by a vertical movement through which the signifier pins down the signified. Lacan suggests his analogy of the buttons or stitches of the upholstery trade as an approximate schema "for taking into account the dominance of the letter in the dramatic transformation that dialogue can effect in the subject" (Lacan, 1977). That is, what happens in the analytic session remains speech and only speech and is not analogous to the drawing up from the well of the unconscious a bucket of pure signified, purged of all mediation through the signifier. What analysands can access, through the circulation of certain signifiers between themselves and the analyst, is a sense of an earlier attachment of a signifier to a signified. These attachments are for Lacan a kind of bare minimum for psychic survival. They are points where the flux of meaning is held in place so that human beings can preserve their sanity. Thus, while Lacan's concept of the signifying chain appeared to promise a psycholinguistic theory of infinite semiosis, the idea of the *points de capiton* means that something rather different is theorized.

What is theorized instead is "an eroticized science of meaning" (Bowie, 1991), in which the founding *point de capiton* is a powerful signifier—the phallus—and in which Saussure's two-part model of communication is ruptured by the presence of a third term, a version of Hegel's concept of the other: "The Unconscious is the discourse of the Other." But even before Lacan began sustained work on the unconscious, he had employed the Hegelian other to explain how human beings come to form a sense of identity and why this sense of identity is a split and delusory, rather than unified and trustworthy, phenomenon. Lacan's use of the other and "alienation" is grasped most easily in his earlier work on what he calls the "mirror stage" of human development ("The Mirror Stage as Formative of the Function of the I," 1949). Lacan's theory of how the human infant forms a sense of identity introduces the idea of otherness into the very concept of self. He says that an infant first gains a sense of identity by seeing something that both is and is not it: an image in a mirror. This gives us an image of wholeness before we actually feel ourselves to be whole—that is, before we gain full motor control. The mirror indicates the literal nature of Lacan's pronouncement that the human being is faced continually with one outside the self.

The other appears in Lacan's theory of the unconscious to explain how it is made to speak not in its own voice but through a form of mediation. This is best illustrated by the concept of the psychoanalytic transference. While the unconscious is structured like a language, it does not speak in the words of any one person: the unconscious is not "related to an individual reality" (Lacan, 1977). Because speech does not happen in a vacuum but is an act of communication, what the patient says to the analyst passes through and is affected by the analyst before it returns to the patient. The analyst cannot just give the patient words because what the patient says in analysis has already been determined by the very structure of language itself: language speaks us. The analyst cannot "hear" the patient's unconscious any more than the patient can speak it. Each depends on a kind of channel or conduit: the symbolic order.

Lacan's ambitious schema of imaginary, symbolic, and real is at once a reworking of Freud's triadic theory of the mind (ego, superego, id), a criticism of Hegel's dialectic of resolution, and an attack on the dyadic mother-child relation theorized by object-relations psychoanalysts. While the imaginary is a development of Lacan's notion of the mirror stage, Lacan abandons the idea that the imaginary is merely a superseded stage in human development. Instead, like Freud's narcissistic ego, the imaginary is always capable of making its presence felt because it is the tendency in the human mind to reduce others to itself, to cope with the confusing experience of change and instability in the world by becoming rigid. The symbolic is the realm of Lacan's subject, which, rather than reduce others to itself, knows itself through others: it situates itself on the circuit of intersubjectivity and knows that no man or woman is an island. It comprises those flickering and transient moments when conscious and unconscious "languages" are held together through an apprehension of otherness as the condition of being. Achieving the symbolic mode is integrally linked to language in that the symbol, the word, is the "murder of the thing"; by using language, the subject has accepted that his or her relationship to the world is not a direct apprehension of reality but is already mediated linguistically. Lacan's real is not reality in Freud's sense of the "reality principle" (a sort of police officer who prevents the pleasure principle from having full sway) but something less social and more metaphysical in conception, founded on the idea that there is something outside language but that we can never access it directly. A trauma, as an unassimilated event, is a mark of the "outside" that is the real. To alleviate the trauma, the analyst helps the analysand to use language to confront its outside.

What that trauma consists in returns us to Lacan's return to Freud and Freud's theory of human sexuality. The material of semiosis in the analytic session is not sexuality as such but desire-laden speech, for Lacan's emphasis is on how we make meanings out of our sexuality. To emphasize this, he transmutes Freud's "drive" into "desire" and gives it two companions, "need" and "demand" ("The Signification of the Phallus"; "The Direction of the Treatment and the Principles of Its Power," both 1958). For Lacan, desire is what is still unsatisfied when what we actually need as animals (food, shelter, and so on) is subtracted from what we actually demand as human beings: love. Even when our physical hunger is appeased, we are haunted by a sense that there is "something more" that we want, something that cannot be articulated yet really motivates us. This desire, according to Lacan, is endless (if it could be satisfied it would no longer be desire) and systematic because it is locked into language through its connection with demand. The linking of demand, desire, and need is a crucial maneuver in Lacan's transformation of Freud's concept of drive into a quasi-linguistic concept, and it explains Lacan's insistence that analysts need to pay more attention to how speech works. Need is tied to the period before the human infant develops a sense of self and other; it is felt strongly but not in relation to another person. Demand is born with speech but before socialization and the acceptance that some things cannot be said. From a linguistic point of view, it is thus powerfully generative. Its grounding in the realization that there is a split between the self and other other—often the mother—means that demand is not a straightforward translation of desire into words. Instead, to cope with its sense of loss at being split from the (m)other, the force of demand may become, in layperson's terms, "attention seeking"—that is, focusing on some need in particular, such as hunger, while really being a more general plea for love. Thus, demand can function metonymically or metaphorically; it can find as many signifiers as it likes to translate its wishes. The new signifier displaces or abolishes what is really being asked for, as *thirty sails* abolishes *ship*. Bodily needs can be deferred endlessly as demand keeps translating them into noncorporeal signifiers. But the particularity of need stages a return by borrowing the structure contained in the unconditional demand for love, and the result is desire. Chronologically, this happens when the subject becomes socialized or regulated and accepts as the price of sociality that some things cannot be said. What cannot be said does not disappear but is repressed as the unconscious. Its bodily nature (derived from need) stops it from being articulated, but it cannot escape what has been put in place by the operations of demand upon signifiers: Lacan refers to the way desire inhabits the "metonymic remainder" underlying demand (Lacan, 1979).

Sexuality is brought into this formulation through Lacan's identification of socialization and the unsayable with versions of Freud's Oedipus and castration complexes, which Lacan tends to conflate. Freud's mature theories of Oedipus and castration identified male socialization with the acceptance of the prohibition against incest: the son, under fear of being castrated by the father, must defer his desire for his mother until, in later life, he can attach it to a woman outside his family. Lacan reworks this to explain how the human being comes to have a place in language from which he or she can say "I"—that is, attain subjectivity ("On a Question Preliminary to Any Possible Treatment of Psychosis," 1955–1956). The condition of the male being able to establish subjectivity is his acceptance of what Lacan calls the paternal metaphor or name of the father. This acceptance hinges on recognition of patriarchal authority beyond the specific familial situation; the law is embodied in the person one names as father. Within Lacan's patriarchal scheme, human beings cannot situate themselves on the communicative circuit and enter culture unless they can break out of a one-to-one relationship, such as that of mother to child, which patriarchy constitutes as symbiotic and narcissistic. What enables the human being to define and claim subjectivity is the intervention of a father figure—not necessarily the biological father—in the mother-child relationship. This father is the bearer of the law and decrees that certain things (the boy's desire for the mother) cannot be said. In accepting this law, the boy represses the desire for the mother, and this repression simultaneously founds the unconscious and enables the boy to say "I."

The difficulty of transferring this scheme of the attainment of subjectivity to the situation of girls is the cornerstone of feminist criticism of Lacan. The problem lies in how Lacan alters Freud's theory that the actual presence or absence of a penis determines the programmed way for the child of either sex to attain sexual identity (the "penis envy" attributed to women). For Lacan, it is not whether the penis is physically there or not that matters: it is the meaning with which the child invests it that counts. He thus makes much use of Freud's term *phallus*, with its mythic and cultic dimensions. The little girl has as her model a mother who reveals her own subordination in the way that she asserts authority not for herself but on behalf of the authority invested in her by her own internalization of the name of the father (Lacan, 1977). This is a more linguistic orientation of Freud's theory of female passivity and subordination. Freud argued that women's castrated status meant that their actions were only mimicry or masquerade of masculine ones. Lacan allows this notion of a second-order, imitative mode of being to infiltrate language itself, so that the little girl's attainment of subjectivity becomes a kind of echo of the little boy's.

This in itself is problematic for feminists, but becomes more so, as Lacan denies repeatedly that the phallus is the penis: he asserts that it is a signifier that may equally stand for the penis or the clitoris. However, he glosses over the difficulty of using a symbol, traditionally associated with male potency and dominance, for a universal theory of representation. Luce Irigaray provides the most comprehensive critique of Lacan's theory of the phallus as signifier by distinguishing anatomy and morphology (the way bodies are represented or signified), which Lacan conflates, in order to argue that a patriarchal morphology such as that offered by Lacan not merely describes but prescribes the representation of women (1985; see Grosz, 1990). Malcolm Bowie suggests that it is the post-Lacanian feminists who hold the key to a more satisfactory eroticized theory of signification (1991).

Like several feminists, Jacques Derrida criticized Lacan for freezing the infinite regression of the signifier (dissemination) around the hinge of the phallus. In his seminar on "The Purloined Letter" (1966), Lacan presented Edgar Allan Poe's tale as an allegory of what happens in analysis. Derrida argued that Lacan's discussion of Poe's story is no advance on the applied psychoanalysis brought to bear on it in 1933 by Marie Bonaparte, who found evidence in the tale of the classical Freudian Oedipal triangle ("The Purveyor of Truth" in Muller and Richardson, 1988). Derrida argues that the disturbing upshot of this is that Lacan believes that psychoanalysis can place itself outside the play of the signifier and that the analyst alone can reveal the truth about a patient's discourse. This issue emerges again in Michel Foucault's response to Lacan. Foucault's earlier alignment with Lacan disappears in the second volume of his *History of Sexuality* in favor of a more critical analysis of the complicity of Lacanian psychoanalysis in the modern definition of subjectivity (Cotton, 1992). In this context, Jane Gallop helpfully distinguishes between an absolute notion of neutrality and a technique of neutralization that is developed by the analyst for the specific purposes of the session and is closely connected to the notion of the transference (Gallop, 1985). The neutralized position of the analyst in Lacan's terms is no mere easy belief in his or her own privileged access to truth—to an ultimate signified—but a carefully crafted stance based upon the economies of speech in a professional situation. Analyst no less than analysand is dependent upon the signifier, as Lacan's interpretation of "The Purloined Letter" reveals: the signifier—the letter—is empty, as we never discover what the mysterious letter to the queen, the object of everyone's search in Poe's story, contains. But the signifier is also powerful, because it determines people's actions, which is illustrated through the analysis of the repetition of the basic intersubjective situation in the search for the letter. The structure of intersubjectivity (the path of the signifier) stays the same; it is only the people who occupy it who change position. The fact that Dupin and, through him, the queen, end up "winning" can be read as an allegory of Lacan's assertion that analysis can yield "full speech." This is a structuralist idea of fullness. It is not the free speech of the unified liberal-humanist subject but the transindividual speech of the analytic session, in which the analyst helps the analysand to realize as completely as possible his or her place in the structure of language as intersubjective communication—what Fredric Jameson (1972) calls the "prison house of language."

Allegory aside, though, Lacan very seldom gives examples or applications of his theory of the semiosis of the analytic session—at best, we can extrapolate. What the semiosis of analysis can offer is an education in how to live with the idea that there are two systems driving us that will only sometimes connect and "make sense," and then only in ways which we cannot necessarily retap nor repeat. After the 1950s, Lacan turns to mathematical models to try to map the operations of necessity and chance in this science of meaning, but these have generally been found to be inconclusive.

[*See also* De Lauretis; Feminism and Feminist Theories; Kristeva; *and* Semiotic and Symbolic].

BIBLIOGRAPHY

Bowie, M. *Lacan*. London: Fontana Press, 1991.

Brennan, T. *History after Lacan*. London and New York: Routledge, 1993.

Cotton, P. "The Cultural Significance of Lacanian Psychoanalysis." In *The Judgement of Paris: Recent French Theory in a Local Context*, edited by K. D. S. Murray, pp. 77–95. Sydney: Allen and Unwin, 1992.

Forrester, J. *The Seductions of Psychoanalysis: Freud, Lacan, and Derrida*. Cambridge: Cambridge University Press, 1990.

Gallop, J. *Reading Lacan*. Ithaca, N.Y.: Cornell University Press, 1985.

Grosz, E. *Jacques Lacan: A Feminist Introduction*. Sydney: Allen and Unwin, 1990.

Irigaray, L. *This Sex which Is Not One*. Translated by C. Porter and C. Burke. Ithaca, N.Y.: Cornell University Press, 1985.

Jameson, F. *The Prison-House of Language: A Critical Account of Structuralism and Russian Formalism*. Princeton, N.J.: Princeton University Press, 1972.

Lacan, J. *Ecrits: A Selection*. Translated by A. Sheridan. London: Tavistock and Routledge, 1977.

Lacan, J. *The Four Fundamental Concepts of Psycho-analysis*. Edited by J.-A. Miller. Translated by A. Sheridan. Harmondsworth, England: Penguin, 1979.

Macey, D. *Lacan in Contexts*. London and New York: Verso, 1988.

Muller, J. P., and W. J. Richardson, eds. *The Purloined Poe: Lacan, Derrida, and Psychoanalytic Reading*. Baltimore: Johns Hopkins University Press, 1988.

—JOY WALLACE

LANGUAGE AS SYMBOLIC ACTION (1966).

In the first five chapters of *Language as Symbolic Action: Essays on Life, Literature, and Method* and in the essays on symbolism in general that constitute the final seven chapters, Kenneth Burke offers a résumé of some forty years of pondering the vagaries of symbolic action. The middle chapters examine particular works and authors.

In the first essay, Burke defines mankind as "the symbol-using animal." For in spite of our everyday adoption of an attitude of naive verbal realism, "much of what we mean by reality has been built up for us through nothing but our symbol systems" (p. 5). But the ability to use symbols is also the ability to abuse and misuse symbols, which is why Burke advocates an attitude of linguistic skepticism. While we are using language, it is using us. According to Burke, then, mankind is both the symbol-making and "symbol-made animal" (p. 63).

Mankind is also "the inventor of the negative" and is "moralized by the negative." To a nature that is positively what it is, human language adds the negative and all its proscriptions regarding property, law, behavior, morality, and so forth. As a consequence, mankind alienates itself more and more from its own animality, creates a counternature, and becomes the instrument of its instruments. What Burke calls hypertechnologism leads toward hell on earth, and his well-founded fear is that human entelechy might very well be expressed in the perfection of technology itself, which, paradoxically, would be the ultimate form of antihumanism. Finally, mankind is "goaded by the spirit of hierarchy," "moved by a sense of order," and "rotten with perfection." The magic and mystery of social role, status, and hierarchy along with the terminological drive toward perfection in any verbal system are intrinsic to language and symbol using.

Value-ridden from the outset, language, for Burke, is intrinsically rhetorical. Because he feels that language is primarily a species of action or attitudinizing, rather than an instrument of definition, he espouses dramatism as an alternative to scientism. Whereas a scientistic approach to the nature of language "begins with questions of *naming* or *definition*," a dramatistic approach views "the power of language to define and describe . . . as derivative" (p. 44). According to dramatism, the essential function of language "may be treated as attitudinal or hortatory: attitudinal as with expressions of complaint, fear, gratitude, and such; hortatory as with commands or requests, or, in general, an instrument developed through its use in the social processes of cooperation and competition" (p. 44). Whereas a scientistic approach "builds the edifice of language with primary stress upon a proposition such as 'it *is*, or it is *not*,'" a dramatistic approach, in accordance with clause two of Burke's definition of mankind, "puts primary stress upon such hortatory expressions as 'thou *shalt*, or thou shalt *not*'" (p. 44). For Burke, the hortatory negative takes precedence over the propositional negative, for language is a form of life, and the negative is at the center of our linguistic and moral activity. Although the negative is purely a linguistic convenience, it is instrumental in the inculcating of guilt and is an integral part of morality and religion in their dual roles as systems of solace and control. Moreover, symbol using itself "demands a feeling for the negative. . . . The word is not the thing. A specifically symbol-using animal will necessarily introduce a symbolic ingredient into every experience. Hence every experience will be imbued with negativity. Sheer 'animality' is not possible to the sensory experiences of a symbol-using animal" (p. 469).

Terministic screens "direct the *attention*." Burke writes, "Even if any given terminology is a *reflection* of reality, by its very nature as a terminology it must be a *selection* of reality; and to this extent it must also function as a *deflection* of reality." Further, "not only does the nature of our terms affect the nature of our observations, in the sense that the terms direct the *attention* to one field rather than to another. Also *many of the 'observations' are but implications of the particular terminology in terms of which the observations are made*. In brief, much that we take as observations about reality may be but the spinning out of the possibilities implicit in our particular choice of terms" (p. 46). The lurking danger, as Burke sees it, is relativism, for if empirical observations are reduced to terminological implications, then everything is relative to the terminology of the observer, whose own situatedness makes objectivity impossible. In one sense, Burke admits, we must "resign ourselves to an endless catalogue of terministic screens, each of which can be valued for the light it throws upon the human animal, yet none of which can be considered central" (p. 52). But whatever the differences are between these screens, "they are all classifiable together in one critical respect: They all operate by the use of symbol systems" (p. 57).

In an obvious sense, then, Burke's own dramatism can be only a terministic screen, but Burke also wants to believe that the dramatic model is ontological rather than heuristic, literal rather than metaphorical, and that his perspectivism offers more than just another perspective. Such salient inconsistency underscores the problem. If language, as it were, thinks for us (a saying of Samuel Taylor Coleridge that Burke is fond of quoting), then within the cultural scene language may be the agent that acts through agency of human beings for its own inscrutable purposes. The next step is to recognize that what we are as humans is identified uniquely with this semiotically constructed world, and at times, Burke does come close to embracing structuralism's view of mankind as a construct of linguistic and social codes.

[*See also* Burke; Cultural Knowledge; Knowledge Representation; Linguistic Relativism; *and* Whorf.]

BIBLIOGRAPHY

Burke, K. *Language as Symbolic Action: Essays on Life, Literature, and Method.* Berkeley: University of California Press, 1966.

—GREIG HENDERSON

LANGUAGE CHANGE. The arbitrariness of the link between signified and signifier makes language change possible: if a signifier is unmotivated, it has no necessary (and thus stable) form, and if its association with a given signified is merely conventional, then such associations are open to change. The flexible social role of a language as an interrelated diversity of conventions and practices, and its Lamarckian rather than genetic transmission from one generation to the next, renders such change inevitable.

Though speculation about it goes back at least to Dante Alighieri (1265–1321), the systematic study of language change and derivational affinity (now known as comparative philology) is traditionally held to have begun with the remark of the orientalist Sir William Jones (1746–1794), that "no philologer could examine the Sanscrit, Greek, and Latin, without believing them to have sprung from some common source, which, perhaps, no longer exists." That common source, shared by most of the language groups of Europe, Persia, and North India, came to be known as Proto-Indo-European, and the resultant family of descendant languages as Indo-European. Since the pioneering work on Indo-European philology, many other such families have been identified, including, for example, the Hamito-Semitic of North Africa and the Middle East, the Sino-Tibetan of norther Asia, and the Malayo-Polynesian, stretching from Madagascar to the eastern Pacific.

Despite the assiduous amassing of data by early comparativists such as the Danish linguist Rasmus Rask (1787–1832) and August Schleicher (1821–1868), philology lacked a clearly articulated methodology before the advent in the 1870s of the largely German school whose nickname, Junggrammatiker (Young Turk philologists), is represented in English by the well-established mistranslation "neogrammarians." The neogrammarians brought to philology that fundamental principle of nineteenth-century science, uniformitarianism: the belief that the past is explicable in terms of steady, uniform, and predictable processes of change, with no need to invoke catastrophes, discontinuities, or supernatural interventions. Uniformitarianism, though always masked as a statement about the data in question (Natura non facit saltum [Nature does not make jumps]), represents a methodological program for analysis of the data and an assertion of faith in the possibility of reconstructing the past. Through Charles Lyell (1797–1875) and Charles Darwin (1809–1882), uniformitarianism transformed the historical sciences of geology and biology; for the neogrammarians, who naturally rejected organicist metaphors about the "growth" and "decay" of languages, it took the form of faith in the principle of *ausnahmslosige Lautgesetze* ("exceptionless sound laws"), operating by blind necessity, like the laws of physics. Karl Verner (1846–1896), for example, showed in his famous law that a large number of what had appeared to be random exceptions to Grimm's law (which had established relations among Indo-European languages) could be explained by differences in the placement of word stresses in Proto-Indo-European.

The axiom that sound laws operate with blind necessity proved to be a powerful explanatory tool in other areas of linguistic inquiry: since sound change is conditioned only and absolutely by the phonological environment, it can explain the existence of morphological irregularities. Apparent exceptions to the operation of sound laws were explained by the neogrammarians' second restructuring principle, analogy, which works to regularize the morphological paradigms made asymmetric by historical sound change, by remodeling them toward the productive norm. In the neogrammarian model, the incessant interaction of these two forces, disruptive sound change and leveling analogy, ceaselessly reshapes the language system.

The next major development in the study of language change was the publication of Ferdinand de Saussure's *Cours de linguistique générale* (1916), which clearly established the distinction, merely implicit in the work of the neogrammarians, between the diachronic study of historical changes and the synchronic study of a language as a functioning system at a given moment in time, with its own autonomous structure. The realization that any given state of a language must represent a system in which every part

is defined in relation to other parts made it no longer possible to think of linguistic change as merely an autonomous historical process acting on individual sounds over the centuries. A system of phonological contrasts or distinctive features is best served by maintaining a maximal distance in articulatory and perceptual terms between pairs of phonemes, and language change will tend to maximize rather than diminish this because speech is a social activity: if a sound drifts too close to its neighbor, the constant need for speakers to clarify the difference between resultant near homophones will tend to cause them to restore a perceptible difference, perhaps by shifting the place of articulation of the second sound (though phonemes do sometimes coalesce, as did /ɛ:/ and /e:/ in early-modern English, turning previously distinct pairs such as *meat* and *meet* or *quean* and *queen* into homophones). This principle of phonological equilibrium explains why there are no vowel systems with only front or only back vowels and why five-vowel systems (as in Spanish or Japanese) so commonly consist of the maximally spaced /a, e, i, o, u/.

André Martinet (1955) has suggested that the mechanism of sound change might be governed partly by the interplay of two constant factors: the desire to save effort and the need to communicate. Humans, always seeking the quickest and easiest articulation through such processes as the assimilation and elision of awkward consonants and the elimination or reduction of unstressed vowels, tend to reduce, for example, *handbag* to /hæmbæg/, *cupboard* to /kʌbəd/, *boatswain* to /bəusn/, *secretary* to /sɛkrətri/ (British English), and so on; the need for clarity, on the other hand, arrests such processes when they erase too many distinctions and thus interfere with communication. A further brake on erosion has arisen in English since the rise of widespread literacy, in the form of "spelling pronunciations" or the restoration of eroded sounds by referring to the orthography (which is always much more conservative than pronunciation): thus, *grindstone* and *waistcoat*, formerly eroded to /grɪnstn/ and /wɛskɪt/, are now almost universally pronounced /grain(d)stəun/ and /weis(t)kəut/, presumably because the words are now in less common use. (The more familiar *cupboard* has preserved its eroded pronunciation.)

The advent of generative linguistics in the 1960s brought with it a revision of the structuralist dichotomy between the synchronic and diachronic. For the descriptive linguist, it was sufficient merely to record and classify anomalous paradigms such as *keep* and *kept*; for the generativist, however, interested in language not as static product but as dynamic productive system, it became necessary to explain such paradigms, and these explanations could be found only in the history of the language. The "productive" rule that derives *beeped* from *beep* can be stated in terms of the surface phonetic forms; the one that derives *kept* from *keep* can be described, however, only in terms of "morphophonemic" rules operating upon underlying forms. Such rules represent incorporations of historical changes into the synchronic language system. Thus, the underlying form of the verb stored in a contemporary speaker's mental lexicon, according to Noam Chomsky and Morris Halle (1968), would be something like KE:P; a realization rule that raises underlying long vowels converts this to the phonetic output /ki:p/. If, however, the preterite formative -T is added to this underlying form, a realization rule that shortens long vowels before a consonant cluster produces KEPT; vowel raising is irrelevant to this form, and so it is realized as /kept/. Some evidence for the synchronic existence of such rules can be seen in the alternation of pairs like *grAve:grAvity, suprEme:suprEmacy, divIne:divInity*, in which underlying A:, E:, and I: are raised in the first of each pair and shortened in the second. The shortening of the vowel in the antepenultimate syllable replicates a historical sound change of early Middle English that had long ceased to operate before the earliest of these words appeared.

In revealing something of the disconcerting complexity of linguistic rule systems that previous theories of language had obscured, Chomsky and Halle's work problematized the issue of childhood language acquisition; the child must somehow learn not merely a set of words and a few simple patterns but a vastly complex system of productive rules that is never made fully explicit and is for the most part unsuspected by even educated adult users, for whom language remains (like their car or their computer) what engineers call a black box: they know how to use it, but have only the vaguest idea how it works. So although children of eight know more about English, at least in a practical sense, than linguists can adequately formulate, they must somehow have deduced its rule systems by observation of the flawed data of others' speech. Each generation, that is, must reinvent the language of its parents: this explains the possibility of radical discontinuities in the history of

a language. If children acquired language merely by imitating the practices of their parents, there is no reason why, for example, the Middle English inflection of monosyllabic adjectives, as in Chaucer's *a yong man* versus *a yongë man* or *yongë men*, should not have survived in vestigial form as an anomaly to the present day. But it is clear that there must have come a time in the late fourteenth or early fifteenth century when London children failed to notice the by-then rather attenuated difference in their parents' pronunciation between the inflected and uninflected forms, largely restricted in any case to monosyllabic native words, and reconstructed a simplified grammar in which adjectival inflection had no place. This desire to construct the simplest possible grammar consistent with communication might also cause a new generation to reorder the sequence of rules in order to simplify their output.

Some scholars have suggested that language change might show more long-term internally motivated kinds of drift in moving toward a greater typological consistency. In word-order typology, a concept introduced by Joseph H. Greenberg, there is a fundamental distinction between VO languages (which typically place the verb before its object, and, more generally, heads before arguments) and OV languages, which place objects before verbs or arguments before heads. The head of a phrase is the constituent that determines the form class of the whole phrase. VO languages will have prepositions rather than postpositions and modifiers following nouns; in a typically OV language, such as Turkish, the reverse will be true. The emergences of modern English and French have seen distinct movements toward relatively fixed head-argument word orders, and yet both languages show typological inconsistency in that modifiers both precede and follow head nouns (*le petit* HOMME *aveugle; the little* GIRL *in the green dress*). The theory of syntactic drift suggests, implausible as it might seem, that both languages will eventually move toward a single noun-modifier order, producing sequences such as **girl-the little in dress-the green*, as in modern Norwegian or Romanian. Nonetheless, the idea that language change will tend to be guided by consistent long-term tendencies—particularly that related languages will "inherit" such tendencies and thus develop in similar ways even after they have split—has been criticized by Roger Wright (1983) as an artifact of archaic teleological thought habits (but see Michael Shapiro, 1991, for a more sympathetic discussion).

Perhaps the most important mechanism of language change is one that remains largely invisible to the theoretical schools for whom language is conceived of as steady diachronic process, as synchronic stasis—there can be little dynamic for change in a pure Saussurean system—or as the tacit knowledge of what Chomsky calls "an ideal speaker-listener, in a completely homogeneous speech community." What these approaches overlook is the fact that language is a social activity, subject to the same sorts of pressures of emulation as other such activities, and that speech communities of any size are typically not homogeneous but composed of many varieties—regional, social, and situational—with different perceived statuses. The appropriate level at which to consider change is not that of *language* (system) but that of *parole* (utterance)—or, rather, that of the various *paroles* commanded by a speaker: in any given culture, selection pressures will tend to favor certain variations in certain social contexts.

Take the example of rhoticity (the pronunciation of the written character *r* when no sounded vowel immediately follows it, as in *bird* or *for me*), a feature of general American that since World War II has infiltrated the previously nonrhotic dialects of New York: many New Yorkers now use rhotic pronunciations on occasion (though few use them exclusively). The sociolinguist William Labov (1966) has shown that this change is the result not merely of migration to the city from rhotic-dialect areas but of a transformation within the speech habits of New Yorkers due to the selection pressure exerted by the social prestige of rhoticity. New Yorkers of all classes (whatever their dialect) evaluate a speaker who uses rhotic forms as more likely to get a well-paid job, even where they cannot identify the prestige-enhancing feature; informants also tend to identify rhotic pronunciations as those they would normally use, whether or not they do in fact use them. This perceived prestige presumably explains why frequency of use of rhotic forms correlates systematically not only with socioeconomic status but also with formality of register, so that working-class informants in casual speech use the fewest and middle-class informants in careful speech use the most. Those under forty of all classes more consistently saw rhoticity as a prestigious feature than did older people, which suggests that rhoticity is gradually replacing nonrhoticity as a norm in New Yorkers' speech. There is some evidence that the uvular /R/ of standard French arose in the seventeenth century as an aristocratic Parisian affec-

tation and eventually replaced the apical variety that survives only in nonstandard French through a similar process of emulation. Of course, pressures of emulation are various in origin and do not operate uniformly or deterministically; many studies have suggested, for example, that working-class men tend to modulate their speech away from, rather than toward, the prestige norm, and Labov's work on the dialect of Martha's Vineyard shows a community reverting to obsolescent dialectal forms as a way of establishing solidarity against a perceived invasion of mainlanders.

This "emulatory" model of change suggests that innovations do not instantaneously transform a language but originate in a given locality, and, if successful, spread outward in waves. (This is one reason why the isoglosses separating High and Low German do not neatly coincide: different waves of High German have spread northward to different extents.) Such waves of emulation may even spread across language boundaries: the French uvular /R/ seems to have entered standard German (where it remains an option) in some such way. More generally, situations of language contact function as catalysts for change, particularly when there is a marked disparity in prestige and speakers of the less-prestigious language are bilingual. The variety of Finnish spoken by migrants to the United States, for example, has acquired from English a passive construction in which the agent of the verb appears in a prepositional phrase (as in "The door was opened BY MARY"); in standard Finnish, there is only the "impersonal" form, rather like the French reflexive ("La porte s'ouvrit"). In areas where many languages are in frequent contact, formal similarities will tend to arise among genetically diverse languages, as in the case of the retroflex consonants of India or the postposited definite article of the Balkans. It is clear that for this reason the neogrammarians' "evolutionary" tree diagram of linguistic affinity is something of a simplification. Biological species once separated cease to modify each other, but languages do not: in many ways (word order, vocabulary, etc.), English more resembles its neighbor French, for example, than it does its closer relative German.

The insufficiency of exclusively linguistic theories, with their static and uniformitarian models of language structure, to explain the process of language change and the relative success of more open-ended approaches that take into account complex social, cultural, political, historical, and geographical factors has led many recent linguists to abandon the contention (itself a product of academic politics) that linguistics is an autonomous discipline. These linguists now embrace under the banner of "developmentalism," a program of research into the dynamics of language change that sees change itself as something essential to the semiotic description of language (Bailey and Harris, 1985).

[*See also* Articulation; Binarism; Distinctive Features; Langue and Parole; *and* Saussure.]

BIBLIOGRAPHY

Bailey, C.-J. N., and R. Harris. *Developmental Mechanisms of Language.* Oxford: Pergamon Press, 1985.

Binyon, T. *Historical Linguistics.* Cambridge: Cambridge University Press, 1977.

Chomsky, N., and M. Halle. *The Sound Pattern of English.* New York: Harper and Row, 1968.

Fasold, R. W., and D. Schiffrin. *Language Change and Variation.* Amsterdam and Philadelphia: John Benjamins, 1989.

Labov, W. *The Social Stratification of English in New York City.* Washington, D.C.: Center for Applied Linguistics, 1966.

Martinet, A. *Économie des changements phonétiques.* Berne: Francke, 1955.

Shapiro, M. *The Sense of Change: Language as History.* Bloomington: Indiana University Press, 1991.

Wright, R. "Unity and Diversity among the Romance Languages." *Transactions of the Philological Society* (1983): 1–22.

—Peter Groves

LANGUAGES OF ART

LANGUAGES OF ART (1968). A work by Nelson Goodman that has had a growing influence on semiotic thinking, *Languages of Art: An Approach to a Theory of Symbols* incited controversy with its refutation of iconism in its first chapter. Goodman argues by way of counterexamples against the thesis that the concept of resemblance has an essential role to play in definitions of representation and depiction. He concludes that resemblance cannot be equated with representation, being neither a sufficient condition for representation nor a characteristic that separates representation from other kinds of reference.

A second line of argument attacks other formulations of the iconic thesis that holds that pictorial representation is a faithful copying of the object as it really is. A representation, Goodman argues, always represents its object as something in a certain aspect,

and there is not one mandatory way—such as the object as it appears to the unprejudiced, innocent eye under normal conditions—of representing anything. On the contrary, the ways an object is represented are ways of constructing or conceiving of the object. Therefore, what we judge as resemblance between picture and object is not a given correspondence passively reported but something achieved by the symbol. This second line of thought is rooted in Goodman's "irrealistic" view of the relation between symbol and symbolized, stated most explicitly in *Ways of Worldmaking* (1978), according to which we produce worlds by producing versions of the world; there is neither need nor reason to postulate a world separate from any correct version.

Goodman concludes that pictures, like descriptions, denote their objects. There are, however, at least two uses of depiction and representation that cannot be taken as species of denotation: one is the referential aspect: any picture represents something as something; the other is fictive representation. Neither case concerns what is classified and denoted by the picture; it states instead how the picture itself is classified and by what it is denoted. A picture of Winston Churchill as a statesman is a statesman picture, a representation of him as a dog is a dog picture, and a picture of a centaur is a centaur picture. Representation in this sense is not a relation but a property.

The second chapter of *Languages of Art* deals with "expression" in aesthetic contexts (such as when we say that a picture expresses sadness). In this analysis, Goodman introduces his second referential concept after denotation: exemplification. A swatch, for example, is used to exemplify some of its properties—namely, color and texture. A nominalist, Goodman chooses to talk of labels instead of properties. Exemplification runs thus in the opposite direction of denotation: whereas the label *red* denotes the swatch, the swatch exemplifies the same label. But while *red* denotes all red objects (or the whole class of red things), among them the swatch, exemplification is selective. Only some of the labels that denote the swatch are exemplified (for instance, not those concerning the size or the weight of the swatch). Consequently, expression is a special case of exemplification. That a picture expresses sadness means that the picture is sad in a metaphorical sense and that it exemplifies the label *sad* metaphorically.

The third chapter of Goodman's book deals with the question of whether it is in principle possible to produce a perfect forgery of a work of pictorial art; more generally, which arts are possible to fake and which are not? These rather narrow topics are mainly the prelude to the theory of notation in the following chapters. Goodman draws a distinction between autographic arts—which are possible to forge but not to copy—and allographic arts, which are possible to copy but not to forge. A painting is autographic: that is, a fake of it might be successfully produced, but it will never be a perfect duplicate. A poem is allographic: it may be correctly copied, but the result will not be a fake but another instance of the same work.

The theoretically most complex and subtle part of *Languages of Art*, the fourth chapter, starts with a question motivated by the ideas on forgeries and copies: what demands must a symbol system fulfill in order to be allographic (i.e., having same-spelled [in a wide sense] instances of one and the same work)? Goodman's answer is made up of his five claims for a notational system (a subclass of symbol system); differentiation or articulation among characters (that is, sign-types conceived as classes of inscriptions) and compliants (that is, the denotata of the system); disjointedness between characters and compliance classes; and semantic unambiguity.

Violations of the requirements of differentiation among characters and compliants characterize syntactically and semantically dense systems. A system that is syntactically dense throughout affords for characters between any two characters in an infinity of places; in a system that is semantically dense throughout, the places of compliants are likewise ordered continuously. On an ungraded thermometer, for example, between any two indications on the mercury column there is a third; if the thermometer is read in such a way that every position of the column refers to a certain temperature, we will have an infinity of undifferentiated compliants. The question concerning the difference between word and image, which was left without answer in the first chapter, is in this perspective treated as a difference between symbol systems (not singular symbols): the pictorial symbol system is syntactically and semantically dense, while the verbal symbol system is at least syntactically articulate.

In his final chapter, Goodman argues for a cognitive approach toward aesthetic phenomena. He also presents a final criterion for the picture, separating it from other dense systems. A picture is "replete," as distinct from, for example, the dense diagram system:

no features can be dismissed as semiotically irrelevant to the pictorial system as such.

[*See also* Artificial Language; Goodman; Icon; Iconicity; Image and Picture; Realism and Nominalism; *and* Type and Token.]

BIBLIOGRAPHY

Goodman, N. *Languages of Art: An Approach to a Theory of Symbols.* Indianapolis: Bobbs-Merrill, 1968.
Goodman, N. *Ways of Worldmaking.* Indianapolis: Hackett, 1978.

—GÖRAN ROSSHOLM

LANGUE AND PAROLE. A conceptual pairing introduced by Ferdinand de Saussure, *langue* and *parole* are the two parts of a *langage* (e.g., Japanese). *Langue,* or "the language system," is the abstract system of values that make speech possible; *parole,* or "speech," is defined by Saussure as "the sum total of what people say, and comprises (a) individual combinations, depending on the will of who speaks, and (b) equally voluntary acts of phonation, which are necessary for these combinations" (1971, p. 38). Saussure claims that the language system is "social in essence and independent of the individual, it is the product which the individual registers passively," whereas speech is purely individual, subjective, and voluntaristic.

These distinctions appear to derive from the sociological theory of Emile Durkheim, who in *The Rules of Sociological Method* (1902) proposes a morphological definition of the "social fact" that anticipates the concept of *langue* as an anonymous and coercive social phenomenon external to the individual. Nevertheless, Saussure also asserts something that might seem contradictory at first: "*Langue* and *parole* are then interdependent; the former is at the same time the instrument and the product of the latter. But all that does not prevent them from being two absolutely distinct things" (1971, pp. 37–38). In so doing, Saussure avoids hypostatizing *langue* as something independent of the social collectivity itself; instead, it is *parole,* seen as an "individual act of will and of intelligence," that is so independent.

However, Saussure makes it clear that this distinction is a conceptual separation of language into "two parts" and does not refer to two independently existing realities. It is a methodological step in the descriptive approach to a language. From this observation, it follows that (1) a linguistic system is the necessary condition of possibility of any signifying act; (2) the system—itself an analytical abstraction—is, "established" or analytically reconstructed only on the basis of concrete uses of *parole*; (3) the speakers of the language learn to construe meaningful relations between "ideas" and "verbal images" not on the basis of an abstract language system as such but through historically and socially specific acts of communication; (4) the individual child's construction and internalization of the linguistic system occurs in and through his or her participation in concrete uses of language, on the basis of "innumerable experiences," as Saussure puts it; (5) it is the social uses of *parole* that bring about evolutionary changes in the linguistic system and not the other way round; (6) linguistic contacts with others can change one's linguistic practices. It is obvious that there is a tension between the distinction that Saussure wishes to maintain between *langue* and *parole* for strictly methodological and descriptive aims, and the dynamic reality described in the above points.

Saussure did not attempt to develop his thinking about this interdependence, for his privileging of "internal" linguistics pushed him in the direction of an independent and pure science of *langue*. However, the fact that he acknowledged this interdependence indicates that he was aware of the arbitrary nature of this conceptual distinction. There is ample evidence in the *Cours de linguistique générale* that Saussure was a subtler and more flexible thinker than the dominant interpretation of this dichotomy would suggest.

[*See also* Durkheim; Language Change: Lévi-Strauss; *and* Saussure.]

BIBLIOGRAPHY

Durkheim, E. "The Rules of Sociological Method" (1902). In *The Rules of Sociological Method and Selected Texts on Sociology and Its Method*, edited by S. Lukes, translated by W. D. Halls. London: Macmillan, 1982.

Saussure, F. de. *Cours de linguistique générale* (1916). Edited by C. Bally and A. Sechehaye. Paris: Payot, 1971.

—Paul J. Thibault

LAW, SEMIOTICS OF. One can trace an implicit concern with the semiotics of laws back to the British jurist and philosopher Jeremy Bentham (1748–1832), for whom the will of the legislature was communicated to the public through signs with denotative meanings. Bentham called his theory of judicial language "the doctrine of paraphrasis," since lawyers draw meanings from texts by restating them in words that are relevant to particular cases while preserving the intended signified of the legislature. A different approach was developed by Hans Kelsen (1881–1973), who claimed that through acts of will a judge brings intentional meanings into a text. These meanings are subjective except that the judge's norms can be traced to higher and prior norms up to an inarticulated presupposition that Kelsen calls a fundamental norm (*Grundnorm*). For him, the *Grundnorm* was a presupposition of thought rather than an explicit statement ascribable to a historical author. The trace of norms transformed subjective meanings into authoritative, objective norms.

Influenced by the earlier works of Ludwig Wittgenstein (1889–1951) and John L. Austin (1911–1960), H. L. A. Hart (1907–1992) analyzed the concept of law in terms of signs that possess a core meaning and a penumbra of meanings at the core's circumference. Hart even analyzed natural rights in terms of the core denotative, objective meaning of the phrase "natural rights." Legal positivism achieved popularity with the publication of Ronald Dworkin's *Law's Empire* (1986). The successor to Hart's chair of jurisprudence at Oxford University, Dworkin perpetuates the belief in the objectivity of law by insisting that judges interpret texts hermeneutically, as if there is one possible right answer to every legal problem. Dworkin added the notion of the narrative to his theory of "rights as trumps"—a theory he had earlier expounded in *Taking Rights Seriously* (1978). For Dworkin, each judge writes a chapter in a never-ending narrative called "the law." However, objectivity inbues law in that this narrative unfolds against the background of a principled, coherent political theory. The latter grounds each chapter in the grand narrative.

In his *Doing What Comes Naturally* (1989), the American literary critic and legal theorist Stanley Fish exposed the positivism of Hart and Dworkin, who posit an external vantage point from which to camouflage the naked violence upon which each juridical decision rests. Similarly, Continental legal scholars have elaborated a more explicitly semiotic theory of law. Georges Kalinowski (1965) emphasizes that before lawyers try to conceptualize concrete social relations, they must familiarize themselves with the nomenclature of legal language since its signs purport to designate all objects, factual or intentional.

Thus, contrary to Bentham's view, the historical author, such as the legislature, does not represent legal concepts through a statute; rather, the legislature itself is immersed in a web of signs. A legislature's words are dependent upon their semiotic context. The legislature associates certain conceptions with the words of a statute, and those associations precede other scientific and everyday languages.

Influenced by Claude Lévi-Strauss, André-Jean Arnaud undertook to show in *Essai d'analyse structurale du code civil français* (An Essay on the Structural Analysis of the French Civil Code, 1973) how the textual relations in the French civil code ideologically mask the social assumptions of experts who authoritatively interpret the code. Networks of signifiers have progressively saturated the terminology of the civil code to the point that the law has become an autonomous system. The world constructed by this autonomous signifying system creates an impression that peace results from the enforcement of its conceptual objects. Arnaud calls this a "bourgeois peace." While the voluntary actions of an individual are projected as the motor of social events, according to Arnaud this voluntariness is an idealized illusion. The psychological intentionality of the historical authors of the code, the social, economic, political, and historical context of the interpreters, and their nontextual philosophical assumptions constitute indexes for the unconscious structure lying "behind" the signifying system that surfaces in a text. The most important assumption is the legal expert's cult of a legality that exalts the bourgeois peace of an autonomous legal structure. In his later works, Arnaud distinguishes a bourgeois "juridicity" from the social. Although jurists enthusiastically and automatically take sides when the term *juridicity* is invoked, Arnaud cannot trace the term to a first author. However, by tracing it from contemporary legal philosophers back to German, Italian, Spanish, and English texts, Arnaud concludes that *juridicity* is a jargonist synonym for legality that, when expressed, functions to distinguish law from nonlaw. A priori argument cannot explain how the social becomes a part of the formal juridical system; Juridicity allows critics to observe law "from the outside" and to assess the gap between social practice and the legal order. Raw facts do not flood law; rather, a living legal system, informed with a reason of its own, assimilates facts into the system.

The structuralist approach to legal discourse was developed further by Algirdas Julien Greimas (1917–

1992) and Bernard Jackson. In his *Semiotics and Legal Theory* (1985), for example, Jackson examines closely the theories of the sign that he believes lie embedded in the works of such leading exponents of legal positivism as Kelsen, Hart, and Dworkin. Jackson simply cannot understand how Kelsen, for example, can claim to rationally "ground" a valid judgment on a presupposition, claim the judgment to be objective and true, and differentiate such a judgment from that of, say, a gunman who presumably also acts on the basis of a presupposition. For the legal positivist, according to Jackson, the error of a judicial decision may be verified only after a later decision authorizes it, pursuant to a legally recognizable procedure. Whereas the tradition of legal positivism has been preoccupied with understanding why judicial decisions are authoritative, Jackson argues that legal semiotics does not attempt to rehabilitate the problematic of authority. Issues such as the hierarchical character of norms, the objectivity of meaning, and the subsumption of the judicial function vis-à-vis the legislature are not on the agenda of the legal semiotician. Following Arnaud and Greimas and in contradistinction to the Peircean school in the United States, Jackson distinguishes his semiotics by excising the referent from legal analysis: legal language and discourse themselves construct a reality. Further, any psychological or even Husserlian view of a meaning-constituting act is absent from Jackson's semiotics. Even the legislature and the judge are semiotic objects. Without a referent, other than one constructed through language, and without an author whose intentions are believed to control the future, the legal system loses the unity that legal positivism has hitherto assumed it had. Various semiotic systems work separately in constructing what experts take as the law. Even the text, so valued among lawyers and legal positivists, is displaced as the site of analysis in favor of the discursive relations among lawyers.

A different strain of legal semiotics, led by Roberta Kevelson (1990), draws heavily from the work of Charles Sanders Peirce (1839–1914). Kevelson contends that the manner in which laws operate can best be understood in terms of Peirce's semiotics. Like Arnaud, Kevelson emphasizes that legal discourse often departs from the original direction intended by a legal script's author. The speaker and listener in a legal discourse—both experts—apply their consensually held values when they interpret a text, and this consensus encourages the interpreters to believe that their statements are true. As such, the judge's discovery of relevant and authoritative signs becomes as important as the syllogistic reasoning process about the signs. Such a discovery of shared representations constitutes what the judge takes as the true and the real—that is, the judge constructs representations that stand for what she or he takes as the true and real. The real changes because the judge is continually representing and one cannot represent the same object twice. (Kevelson takes such an object to be outside the signifying dynamic.) The referent might be the "facts" of a case, or it might be a legal doctrine. If the posited referent constitutes sociocultural practices, all signifying representations of it approximate and, therefore, idealize social events. The signs of legal discourse are thereby believed to cause real and observable consequences in social life. Legal signs are speech acts, and law reform involves the legislated modification of the nomenclature and grammar of the representations of the true and the real.

In this respect, Kevelson distinguishes her own and Peirce's phenomenology of representation from Continental phenomenology and hermeneutics. Edmund Husserl (1859–1938) and Hans-Georg Gadamer, in his *Truth and Method* (1975), were preoccupied with the interpreter's embodied meanings as the interpreter read a text or heard an utterance. The object was meant rather than posited. A utterer or interpreter presented her or his meanings in the direction of a meant object. Indeterminacy characterizes such presented meanings because both the reading and the fulfillment of the meant object in a posited referent possess multiple possibilities. In contrast, Kevelson does not allow for the embodied presentation of meanings; for her, the lawyer or judge represents all experience through the second representative moment of interpretation.

The Peircean influence can also be observed in the pages of American law reviews that have published special issues on legal semiotics, including the *Indiana Law Journal* (1985–1986), the *Syracuse Law Review* (1992), and *Texas Law Review* (1991). The latter essays reflect an interstitial social pragmatism that arguably characterizes the common law and Peirce's theory of signs. Some essays reiterate how signification arises from arbitrary relations rather than from some fixed denotative meaning believed to be situated in an objective realm. Peirce's explanation of the circulatory and indeterminate configurations of signs is often accepted in these law-review essays without

tracing the explanation to Peirce. In addition, the essays tend to focus on the judicial process and, more particularly, the justifactory process of a judge's "reasons for judgment" at the culmination of the judicial process. Intentionality is expunged from the meaning-constituting act. Instead, meaning is understood in terms of the configuration of signs vis-à-vis a presupposed social referent "out there," a referent that is believed to form the objective standard with which to evaluate the justice and access to justice of any particular configuration. The dichotomy between *is* and *ought*, along with the search for a transcendental signified so prominent in the traditions of analytic philosophy and analytical legal positivism, is absorbed into the law-review analyses of the "deep structures" of legal doctrines. Jeremy Paul's "The Politics of Legal Semiotics" and J. M. Balkin's "The Promise of Legal Semiotics" (1991) reflect this point. Little effort is made to appreciate how legal semiotics, as a discourse, undermines the metaphysics of authority and the is/ought distinction. Working within the is/ought paradigm, the indeterminacy thesis is believed to leave nihilism as the only ramification for the indeterminacy of the configuration of signs, yet there is nevertheless an interesting facet to the use of "legal semiotics" to critique American law.

[*See also* Discourse Analysis; Intentionality; Legal Discourse; *and* Peirce.]

BIBLIOGRAPHY

Arnaud, A.-J. *Essai d'analyse structurale du code civil français: La règle du jeu dans la paix bourgeoise.* Paris: Librarie Générale de Droit et de Jurisprudence, 1973.

Balkin, J. M. "The Promise of Legal Semiotics." *Texas Law Review* 69 (1991): 1831–1852.

Conklin, W. E. " 'Access to Justice' as Access to a Lawyer's Language." *Windsor Yearbook of Access to Justice* 10 (1990): 454–467.

Conklin, W. E. "Teaching Critically within the Modern Legal Genre." *Canadian Journal of Law and Society* 8.2 (1993): 33–57.

Derrida, J. "Force of Law: The 'Mystical Foundation of Authority.' " Translated by M. Quaintance. *Cardozo Law Review* 11 (1990): 919–1045.

Dworkin, R. M. *Taking Rights Seriously.* Cambridge, Mass.: Harvard University Press, 1978.

Dworkin, R. M. *Law's Empire.* Cambridge, Mass.: Harvard University Press, Belknap Press, 1986.

Fish, S. *Doing What Comes Naturally: Change, Rhetoric, and the Practice of Theory in Literary and Legal Studies.* Durham, N.C.: Duke University Press, 1989.

Gadamer, H. G. *Truth and Method*. Translated by G. Barden and J. Cumming. New York: Seabury Press, 1975.

Greimas, A. J. "The Semiotic Analysis of Legal Discourse: Commercial Laws That Govern Companies and Groups of Companies." In *The Social Sciences: A Semiotic View*, translated by P. Perron and F. H. Collins, pp. 102–138. Minneapolis: University of Minnesota Press, 1990.

Jackson, B. S. *Semiotics and Legal Theory*. London: Routledge and Kegan Paul, 1985.

Kalinowski, G. *Introduction à la logique juridique: Eléments de sémiotique juridique, logique des normes, et logique juridique.* Paris: L. G. D. J., 1965.

Kevelson, R. *Peirce, Paradox, Praxis: The Image, the Conflict, and the Law.* Berlin and New York: Mouton de Gruyter, 1990.

Paul, J. "The Politics of Legal Semiotics." *Texas Law Review* 69 (1991): 1779–1829.

—WILLIAM E. CONKLIN

LEACH, EDMUND (1910–1989), British anthropologist concerned mostly with questions of meaning in culture. Leach rebelled against the social realism of Émile Durkheim and Alfred R. Radcliffe-Brown that held sway in British social anthropology through the 1950s. Leach disavowed the idea, central to Radcliffe-Brown's project of a "natural science of society," that "social facts" were of the same order as the data of the natural sciences. Proposing instead a sort of social nominalism that is very familiar to modern anthropologists, Leach argues that raw social data are always mediated by thought, especially by verbal categories. When an anthropologist studies systems, or structures, she or he must always be aware that there is a distinction between structure—even when it is part of a subject's cognitive apparatus—and empirical reality.

The transformation of the concept of structure is one of Leach's most important contributions. Under the influence of Radcliffe-Brown and the inspiration of Durkheim, structure in British social anthropology was seen as an explicit set of rules, paradigmatically kinship and marriage rules, that maintained a discrete culture in a state of equilibrium. Contrary evidence signified a "deviant" individual or group or was explained by an elaboration of the model, such as the adoptive use of epicycles in Ptolemaic astronomy. Leach's idea of structure, to the contrary, is implicit and at least partly unconscious, does not necessarily produce equilibrium, and is constituted dialectically. Not only does structure operate in opposition to lived

reality, but it may consist of two radically opposed sets of ideas (Leach, 1954).

Leach's concept of structure converges with Claude Lévi-Strauss's. Leach was influenced by Lévi-Strauss and was his first and foremost champion in the English-speaking world. However, Leach's advocacy was based initially only on *The Elementary Structures of Kinship* (1949), as Lévi-Strauss's fuller presentations of structuralist theory had not yet been published. Leach's idea of structure is a transformation, but a recognizable one, of English social structure; he is concerned primarily with rules of social interaction, as was Lévi-Strauss at the time. The possibility that the rules of a given culture might conform to some underlying logical pattern of which the members of that culture—or, indeed, the social anthropologist—are unaware, is an important step away from the natural-science model of Radcliffe-Brown.

In light of Leach's reformulation, the problem of ethnic boundaries, which had greatly bothered social anthropologists, was seen in a new light. Neighboring groups, such as those studied in West Africa by Jack Goody, might possess systems that are recognizable transformations of each other. Far from signifying that they are different "cultures," such a circumstance suggests that they should be considered one. Leach proposes the topological concept of mathematical function as a ratio of two terms, themselves relational (e.g., maternal versus paternal filiation) as the basis for the comparative analysis of social structure.

This new conception of comparative analysis rescues kinship studies not only from the fallacy of misplaced concreteness but also from the enthnocentrism of using English verbal categories with their built-in folk models. Categories of consanguinity and affinity must be seen as part of the symbolic systems of cultures. They are primarily verbal categories that are related to actual behavior as structures of constraint and interpretation. As such, it is not surprising that they vary across cultures to a much greater degree than Radcliffe-Brown thought possible.

While cultures do vary greatly—and Leach was always interested in extreme cases, such as cultures where the relationship of mother to child was viewed as "affinal"—their variation is itself systematic and might be seen as the permutating of an underlying transcultural logical structure. Although disagreeing with Lévi-Strauss on points, Leach was in this period occupied largely with translating Lévi-Strauss's ideas into the empiricist milieu of British social anthropology.

Leach applied his method in the 1950s to kinship and other realms of culture. An exemplary case is his analysis, via Greek myth and the structure of ritual, of the construction of time. Leach believes that human experience is bounded by two distinct and opposed concepts of time, reversible and irreversible, which are gounded in the universal experiences of repetition (seasonal and otherwise) and biological entropy. For this reason, the most common conception of time is neither linear nor cyclical (both of which Leach believes to be metaphors drawn from Western culture) but rather one of oscillation or "discontinuity of repeated contrasts." For Leach, time is not measured, it is constructed. Ritual constructs time by creating intervals of sacred "time out of time," against which ephemeral time is perceived. Time is essentially the product of opposition; this is why in classical Greek mythology, time (*chronos*) is associated with Cronos, the king of the Titans and originator of basic cosmological oppositions. This notion of time is characteristic of Leach's thought. Rather than viewing human ideas of time as falling into two opposed camps, he views human time as inherently paradoxical and its construction as dialectical, oscillating between repetition and change.

In the late 1950s, Leach's attention shifted to language, myth, and ritual. He shared these interests with his influential colleagues Mary Douglas and Victor Turner, who came to constitute the core of the symbolic-anthropology school. In addition to following Lévi-Strauss, whose own work underwent a similar shift several years earlier, Leach studied Prague School linguistics, semiotics, and the protostructuralism of Durkheim and Marcel Mauss, which were Lévi-Strauss's own sources of inspiration.

Leach attempted to create a unified model of culture based on semiosis. In an introductory textbook, *Culture and Communication*, he set forth a paradigm in which all actions, representations, and utterances in culture are communication. Binary coding operates throughout, producing digital "messages." This model has been criticized as mechanistic. Of more interest are Leach's specific interpretations of cultural phenomena, such as his analysis of the incest taboo, musical performance, costume, cooking, colors, and the notion of exchange as communication.

[*See also* Cultural Knowledge; Culture, Semiotics of; Douglas; Lévi-Strauss; *and* Structuralism.]

BIBLIOGRAPHY

Leach, E. *Political Systems of Highland Burma*. London: G. Bell and Sons, 1954.

Leach, E. "Magical Hair." *Journal of the Royal Anthropological Institute* 88 (1958): 147–164.

Leach, E. *Rethinking Anthropology*. London: Athlone, 1961.

Leach, E. *Genesis as Myth and Other Essays*. London: Cape, 1969.

Leach, E. *Claude Lévi-Strauss*. New York: Viking, 1970.

Leach, E. *Culture and Communication: The Logic by Which Symbols Are Connected*. Cambridge: Cambridge University Press, 1976.

Leach, E., ed. *The Structural Study of Myth and Totemism*. London: Tavistock, 1967.

—MICHAEL HARKIN

LEGAL DISCOURSE. Written codes and the textual records of the judicial process form an extensive legal discourse, which has come under the scrutiny of semioticians, who approach this specific discourse from the points of view of their respective theories of signs and meaning. Roberta Kevelson has undertaken a wide-ranging semiotic interpretation of legal discourse through the conceptual apparatus established by Charles Sanders Peirce (1839–1914). As lawyers and judges interpret a sign, they give a new signification to the first sign in a text. Peirce calls the interpreter's signification "secondness" and the author's original intent "firstness." That is, the legal sign represents or stands for some concept or doctrine. Even a fact is a physical and chemical fact until it is evaluated and judged through a legal sign or what Peirce calls an interpretant. So, too, social conduct becomes an act and therefore authoritative when the interpreter encloses the conduct with the interpretant. The interpretant, for Peirce, is a mental effect of firstness and secondness. The interpretant might well become another sign that in turn produces a new interpretant in an infinite regress. The sign of secondness is formulated into a thirdness or language. At that moment, the fact is given a name that in turn becomes a sign to be reinterpreted by future lawyers. When the social conduct acquires nomenclature, it then functions as an exchangeable unit of meaning, and thus the sign is capable of growth or free play as new doctrines or clusters of concepts are associated with it. A judicial decision is based upon degrees of possibility through the representation of further representations. This creative combination of signs is indeterminate, according to Kevelson, although she uses the term *indeterminacy* in a very different sense than Edmund Husserl, who used it to indicate failure to fulfill an intentional constitution of meaning.

Algirdas Julien Greimas (1917–1992), in his essay "The Semiotic Analysis of Legal Discourse" (1990), departs from the Peircean strain by dropping the externality of the referent from the configuration of signs. Juridical officials live entirely through a signifying world of signifier and signified, he argues. Signifying relations construct both human subjects as well as their institutional organizations, such as courts and legislatures. Indeed, signs even endow institutions with personality and social functions so that they take on the appearances of living organisms. Semiolinguistic structures pass themselves off as the elements of an objective social and natural world. The lawyer's challenge is to correctly name a thing and inscribe predictable signifying events to the name. This nomenclature and grammar set the stage to evaluate the legality of any illegal behavior. In a sense, existence arises from a legal action named through signifying relations. The signifying relations even create a space and time within which all social action is classified. Such classification constitutes the truth for the discussants of the nomenclature. Accordingly, one must abandon induction as a method of understanding law, whether one is a lawyer within the system or a scholar situated without. One must also abandon the idea that law is reified, because there is no given external social reality from which legal norms can become estranged.

Second, Greimas distinguishes between the deep structure and the surface grammar of a text. The deep structure sets out the minimum conditions for a script to bear meaning. This deep structure has no outside; it is self-referring. A lawyer is an actor at the surface level and an actant at the deep level. The actant plays a role in a grander narrative syntagm that exists autonomously vis-à-vis all other signifying systems. In a sense, the deep structure of a semiotic system possesses a life of its own in which small units combined into a system that is greater than the sum of its parts. This is so even though a legislature in a democratic state is said to promulgate a given statute. Such a claim suggests that a legislature transforms a posited social or natural reality into names. And yet, the deep structure of the signifying relations mediates the script of the legislature. Indeed, the legislature promulgates names that lawyers already recognize as authoritative signs in the structure of signifying relations. Within the law, there are many semiotic agencies that communicate messages to each other through signs that possess meanings only for experts. In this manner, the signifying systems of law function secondarily to natural or everyday languages, although not secondarily to a prior posited natural or social realm, as the American tradition of legal semiotics presupposes for the most part. This is not to say that the legal semiotic structures are isolated from the sociocultural realm, according to Greimas; the structures possess signifying effects upon other signifying systems.

Bernard Jackson (1985) takes up Greimas's structuralist theory and applies it to the subdiscourses of the legal discourse. In particular, Jackson privileges Greimas's claim that one may study the underlying code of a text independent of the pragmatics of its legislature's intent. The legislature merely introduces some nomenclature, organizes the signs, and privileges some messages over others. But the structure of a legal language preexists the legislative nomenclature. A judge may insert her or his own meaning into the legal lexicon even if the meaning departs from natural or everyday language. And yet, legal language reads as if it is natural and self-evident, though such a discourse excludes as well as posits names. The process through which such signification takes place is more important than the concepts or doctrines with which traditional legal education has been concerned beause the signification makes the norms effective in action. So too, such a study of the signifying process is more important than the traditional concern of analytic philosophers with the issue of what makes a sign authoritative.

Where is truth in such a referentless and authorless world? In *Law, Fact, and Narrative Coherence* (1988), Jackson argues that narrative structures reorder facts and law on the same signifying level. Narrative structures inform both the content of stories and the way stories are told. For Greimas's deep structure, Jackson offers a metadiscourse that transcends the particularities of judge and scholar. Jackson continues his probe of the nature of legal signification in the most exhaustive study of legal discourse to date, *Making Sense in Law* (1995). Similarly, Bert van Roermund's "Narrative Coherence and the Guises of Legalism" (1990) argues that the legal narrative even produces the events that Peirce and Kevelson take as externally posited.

For his part, Jackson fills his work with a breadth of examples from lawyer's experiences in the daily practice of law and in the courtroom. Jackson refers continually to the construction of narratives as lawyers represent their evidence during common-law trials. He shows how several narratives with different audiences can crystallize during one trial. Each act in the trial might be understood in terms of the coherence of a particular narrative. The witness's story is only a part of that overall narrative, which constitutes the whole of the social and cultural world. Again, Jackson's analysis of legal discourse does not link the signified events in a witness's story with some posited external social or cultural referent. Truth in a legal discourse surrounds the internal coherence, first, of the witness's story vis-à-vis the stories of the other witnesses; and second, of all stories vis-à-vis an overall coherent narrative that lawyers and the judge can take as authoritative. Jackson claims that the coherence theory of the truthfulness of a legal narrative has displaced the traditional correspondence theory of truth. To make his point, Jackson draws from the speech-act theory of analytic philosophy as well as from the semiotic structuralism of Greimas.

Jackson, like William Twining and his insightful studies of evidence discourse, identifies how different types of narrativization occur during a trial (1988). One narrative goes to the content of a witness's story. Another goes to the rhetoric of persuading the jury or judge through the lawyer's representation of the witness's story. The judge's summary of the evidence and reasons for judgment offer an adjudicatory narrative. After a judgment has been rendered, other lawyers, judges, and scholars elaborate underlying grand narratives represented by networks of doctrines and rules. Such background narratives explain legal doctrines in terms of theoretical and historical reconstructions. Indeed, a judge might participate in several different stories that eventually fuse into the adjudicative narrative. These stories involve "fact discovery," "law discovery," and the application of rules to the "facts." The informal interaction among lawyers outside the courtroom reinforces the adjudicatory narrative, as such interaction does not follow the communicative model of a sender and an addressee but of a semiotic group that uses and constrains the semiotic messages. Each narrative constructs its own referents, although each might refer overtly to a principle or rule of law as the surface ground of a decision.

There are two further strains of the semiotic tradition in the discourse of legal theory. The first, fully explicated by Peter Goodrich (1990) and Dragan Milovanovic (1992), attempts to break from the reliance upon a posited referent, as in the case of the Peircean tradition, and the self-referentiality of a legal system, in the case of Greimasian semiotics. Both traditions possess positivist characteristics, and both privilege the text. And yet, the identification of a deep structure embedded within a system of signifying relations encourages the expert and nonexpert alike to believe in the autonomy of legal discourse. The legal language taught in professional law schools induces a further belief that legal discourse is natural, universally shared, and just. By reinforcing a belief in objectivity and scientism, professional education reproduces the economic elite and excludes public understanding of what the experts take as authoritative signifiers.

Milovanovic adds that since the eleventh and twelfth centuries, professional law schools have placed a premium upon the dissection of cases into smaller components, which experts can then systematize into a logical, rational structure. The retroactive act of interpretation provisionally provides signification with a definite meaning. Higher courts anchor specific signifieds (concepts) with signifiers. The configurations of signs become decontextualized from the context-specific meanings again and again. What becomes important, then, is not the Greimasian and Jacksonian deep structure, which is believed to prefigure the significations of the surface nomenclature of a statute; rather, configurations of signs pose effects that privilege the interpreter as well as the persons who benefit from the configuration. A configuration might even affect other discourses by "authorizing" their actions or excluding their signs as unworthy of protection. The discourses of business, medicine, labor relations, the arts, and gender gain their authority to act through the signifying relations of legal discourse. The biological subject is transformed from the autonomous author of legislated ends into a docile juridical person constructed from signifying relations. Force thus accompanies any particular configuration of signs. (Although he relies heavily upon analytic philosophy in his earlier works, Peter Goodrich attempts to redirect semiotics into a communicative dynamic.)

Rhetoric contextualizes particular signifying practices, and rhetorical tropes work against a background of institutional history. Legal rhetoric, as a discourse about tropes, was the subject of the medieval study of religious tracts. Indeed, beginning with the fifth-century rise of the city-state, rhetoric was juxtaposed with divine law and then with Plato. Plato maintains that rhetoric (along with poetry and the arts) appeals to the whims of the audience rather than to the invisible concepts of truth and justice. However, instead of representing some inaccessible transcendental signified, rhetoric (re)simulates signs. Whereas structuralist theories of meaning oversimplify a particular social context, rhetoric advances the concrete and discrete social circumstance. Even structuralist semiotics overlooks the rhetorical struggle among social groups for mastery over signs. Each privileging of some magic names over others determines who speaks and in which concrete social circumstances.

Beginning in 1988, the *International Journal for the Semiotics of Law*, edited by Bernard Jackson, became the main forum for legal semiotics on the Continent. Roberta Kevelson's roundtables," published as *Law and Semiotics* (1987) and *Law and the Human Sciences* (1992), have become a forum of American legal semioticians influenced by Peirce's pragmatism. By the mid-1980s, important essays, reviewed in William E. Conklin's "Human Rights, Language, and Law" (1995), had argued that the nomenclature and grammar of legal discourse excludes the signifying relations through which women are acculturated. In the vein of Peirce, Drucilla Cornell's *The Philosophy of the Limit* (1992), for example, examines the binary logic endemic to analytic positivism. That binary logic, she argues, privileges the manner in which the male gender has been acculturated to think. Legal analysis has foreclosed the voice of feminine negativity because such a negativity emanates from the voiceless "interspace" between the juridical official and the addressee of texts. Such a space exceeds a genderized discourse that limits legal analysis to the binary of masculine and feminine. As with other efforts to examine legal semiotics in American law reviews more generally, Cornell slips from time to time into the nomenclature of analytical positivism, particularly its preoccupation with signifieds such as rights and principles, and its corresponding presupposed transparency of language. Although she believes that "new worlds" of ethical alterity exist in the multiplicity of possible significations in the "inter-space" before signs are ever configured, Cornell admits that legal discourse inevitably constrains the possibility of recognizing such an alterity. The lawyer cannot escape from the categorization, identification, and analysis of posited referents, she claims.

Patricia Williams's *The Alchemy of Race and Rights* (1991) continues the feminist critique of the semiotics of racism. Williams describes how judges, legal scholars, and lawyers produce new configurations of signifying relations. She also demonstrates how the signifying configurations exclude subjects outside the legal discourse by displacing the nomenclature of semiotics with terms that her audience will better appreciate: namely, *phantom words* displace *signifiers*, and *categories*, displace *signifieds*. The phantom words of judges, lawyers, legal scholars, and law deans categorize and assimilate everyday experiences, she argues. "Interpretive artifice alone" and "rhetorical devices" generalize about "a backdrop of richly textured facts and proof on both local and national scales." The abstractions of the lawyer exclude and omit the pain of others. The sweep of the lawyer's language is total. The phantom words "label" in a machine that (re)produces the same magic names in different combinations without ever touching the lived meanings of particular people, especially those of color. Legal discourse devours the languages of those who speak from outside the discourse, filters out differences, and thereby defaces, disembodies, and conceals the experiencing subject. The term *white skinned*, for example, represents Ludwig von Beethoven in a manner that redefines Western culture generally and German culture in particular. The conceptual boundaries of the term fragment and dehumanize non-"white-skinned" persons. Those excluded from the boundaries are excluded violently. So, too, the master narratives of legal discourse assimilate and neutralize the everyday languages of aboriginal peoples in many Western countries. Also, feminist legal semiotics suggests that lawyers must identify how the dominant configuration of signifiers (re)produces women's everyday languages so as to leave the latter unrecognizable by all but the expert claimants of legal knowledge. Once one appreciates the semiotic character of law, one can also appreciate that multivalent configurations of signifiers flow back and forth across the authoritative and frozen boundaries of the master discourse.

[*See also* Actantial Model; Discourse Analysis; Greimas; Law, Semiotics of; *and* Peirce.]

BIBLIOGRAPHY

Carzo, D., and B. S. Jackson, eds. *Semiotics, Law, and Social Science.* Rome: Gangemil and Liverpool Law Review, 1985.

Conklin, W. E. "Human Rights, Language, and Law: A Survey of Semiotics and Phenomenology." *Ottawa Law Review* 27.1 (1995): 129–173.

Cornell, D. *The Philosophy of the Limit.* New York and London: Routledge, 1992.

Goodrich, P. *Languages of Law: From Logics of Memory to Nomadic Masks.* London: Weidenfeld and Nicolson, 1990.

Greimas, A. J. "The Semiotic Analysis of Legal Discourse: Commercial Laws That Govern Companies and Groups of Companies." In *The Social Sciences: A Semiotic View,* translated by P. Perron and F. H. Collins, pp. 102–138. Minneapolis: University of Minnesota Press, 1990.

Jackson, B. S. *Semiotics and Legal Theory.* London: Routledge and Kegan Paul, 1985.

Jackson, B. S. *Law, Fact, and Narrative Coherence.* Merseyside: Deborah Charles, 1988.

Jackson, B. S. *Making Sense in Law.* Liverpool: Deborah Charles, 1995.

Kevelson, R. *Law and Semiotics.* New York: Plenum Press, 1987.

Kevelson, R., ed. *Law and the Human Sciences: Fifth Roundtable on Law and Semiotics.* New York: Peter Lang, 1992.

Milovanovic, D. *Postmodern Law and Disorder: Psychoanalytic Semiotics, Chaos, and Juridic Exegesis.* Liverpool: Deborah Charles, 1992.

Van Roermund, B. "Narrative Coherence and the Guises of Legalism." In *Law, Interpretation, and Reality: Essays in Epistemology, Hermeneutics, and Jurisprudence,* edited by P. Nerhot, pp. 310–345. Dordrecht and Boston: Kluwer, 1990.

Williams, P. *The Alchemy of Race and Rights.* Cambridge, Mass.: Harvard University Press, 1991.

—WILLIAM E. CONKLIN

LÉVI-STRAUSS, CLAUDE (b. 1908), French anthropologist generally considered to be the principal figure of structuralism. Lévi-Strauss initially conceived of structuralism as the generalization of communication to all aspects of culture: "communication of women, communication of goods and services, communication of messages" (Lévi-Strauss, 1963). Under the influence of Roman Jakobson, whom he met in New York in the 1940s, Lévi-Strauss extrapolated the principles of the Prague School structural linguistics, more specifically its phonology, and applied them to the study of other cultural communication processes, ultimately relying on Saussure's models and methods. He considered these principles to operate universally in language, myth, and social structure and to reside in an unconscious faculty of the human mind. By his own account, his ideas were stimulated originally by a childhood interest in geology. Like geology, structuralism posits universal principles for uncovering hidden levels of reality.

Lévi-Strauss's early theoretical work presented a critique of and an alternative to the kinship studies of British structural functionalism, of which Alfred R. Radcliffe-Brown was the main proponent. Rather than focus on questions such as nomenclature and descent, Lévi-Strauss saw the principle of alliance among groups based on marriage exchange as the key to understanding society, the "glue" holding it together. Dedicated to Lewis Henry Morgan, Lévi-Strauss's *The Elementary Structures of Kinship* (1949) reaches back to the Victorian tradition of universal synthesis based on secondary sources. Indeed, Lévi-Strauss claims in this work to have discovered a universal feature of humanity: the incest taboo and its correlative injunction to seek wives elsewhere. In particular, Lévi-Strauss was interested in complex systems wherein elaborate marriage rules give rise to permanent conditions of exchange. For example, among the Kachin, group A always stands as "wife giver" to group B, which plays this role for group C, and so on, until the system achieves closure. Economic goods such as cattle and social prestige might circulate in the opposite direction, although Lévi-Strauss adamantly denies that his model implies that women are exchanged for goods. Rather, "women are exchanged for women."

Like Émile Durkheim before him, Lévi-Strauss was drawn to the aboriginal Australians, whose marriage customs were as complex as their material culture was considered to be primitive and who had long played the role of evolutionary antediluvian. For Lévi-Strauss, all aboriginal cultures can be explained in terms of a basic moiety system, supplemented by various divisions and subdivisions, upon which permutations of reciprocity were enacted. The sheer complexity of the Kariera system, for example, requires a formal, quasi-mathematical model to describe it. The resulting description resembles an Enlightenment representation of optics or mechanics. This formalism naturally appealed to Lévi-Strauss, whose foray into social organization might be seen, at base, as an attempt to establish human society on the basis of a recognition of difference rather than identity. His arguments on totemism similarly devalue the alleged identification between humans and animals, and replace this with a proportional logic (raven:eagle::group A:group B). Totemic animals, are, in his famous words, not good to eat but "good to think."

It is not until *The Savage Mind* that Lévi-Strauss engages the basic issue raised by Lucien Lévy-Bruhl (1857–1939) (the great "absent presence" of this work) and fundamental to social thought of the twentieth century: cognitive relativism. E. E. Evans-Pritchard had earlier tried to discredit Lévy-Bruhl's idea that "savages" think differently than "moderns", and in this work Lévi-Strauss adopts such cognitive universality as the keystone to his entire system. Lévi-Strauss describes "savage" thought as "the science of the concrete." By this he means that in primitive cultures material objects, including plant and animal species, function as signs. This differs from our thought in two ways, both of which are, in Aristotle's terms, "accidental." First, lacking dedicated semiotic systems apart from spoken language (writing, mathematics, symbolic logic, theology), the savage has no choice but to use real things to symbolize abstract concepts (as we saw in totemism). But these real objects retain their corporeality and instrumental qualities; the two dimensions are in a sense mediated by language. Second, all cultures classify the world in distinctive ways. (Here, Lévi-Strauss is merely repeating the argument of his teacher, Marcel Mauss.) These two features of "savage" thought give it a quality that is at once opaque and understandable. Like geology, we can fathom primitive thought if we examine it at a sufficiently deep stratum.

Like Evans-Pritchard, Lévi-Strauss stresses the astonishing empirical knowledge and practical reason of the "savage." This was thought to belie the argument that their mentalities are fundamentally different from ours. We might each elaborate different spheres of knowledge, but there is no need to resort to quasi-mystical concepts to explain this. Instead, this proves that "savages" are capable of fully realizing the physical component of objects, meaning they fully know when a object is "only" an object and when it is used as a symbol. This tension between the symbolic and corporeal dimensions of objects seems a productive one, upon which much of ritual is based.

One of Lévi-Strauss's most famous essays involves his reading of the myth of Oedipus, in which he uses the Saussurean oppositions of langue and parole; signifier and signified; and syntagmatic and paradig-

matic. While Sigmund Freud also used a depth model of meaning, his exegesis involved a simple transformation of a preexisting narrative. That is, the myth refers somewhat obliquely to a parallel story that occurs outside the myth and is repeated latently in every boy's life. For Lévi-Strauss, the deeper levels of meaning are already inside the myth and can be accessed only by examining the logical structures of the myth itself.

A myth can be read in two ways, either syntagmatically, moving through the text from beginning to end, or paradigmatically, as the mind might reorder it upon reflection. Thus, we might note the parallel structures of two events that occur at widely different points in the text. These parallel events will have both similarities and differences; the differences, naturally, constitute the meaning of the relationship, which in turn is an element of the meaning system of the myth. Thus, in the Oedipus story, we might contrast incest with parricide as the overvaluation against the undervaluation of blood relations. Other transformations and oppositions are not as obvious, such as that between autochthony and impaired mobility. As a reading of Oedipus or of the Tsimshian myth of Asdiwal, Lévi-Strauss's interpretations are at least plausible and, in the latter case, resonate with what we know about other aspects of culture. It seems incontrovertible that Lévi-Strauss discovered something fundamental about the way at least some myths are constructed.

His larger project was to explore another opposition, that between nature and culture, which he believed was the underlying meaning of myth. Again, there are obvious symbols of this opposition, such as raw versus cooked food. It is, moreover, quite clear that many Native American myths are on some level about culture versus nature or, perhaps more interestingly, about culture as constituted versus other possibilities. But if Lévi-Strauss can be faulted for overreaching, it is nowhere more true than here. Mythic and artistic themes diffused widely among cultures in North and South America. However, in general terms, they were not transferred intact. The structural principles of opposition and transformation applied to diffusion across cultural boundaries. Not unlike marriage exchange, the transfer of myths both unites and opposes, and thus in a formal sense constitutes, groups. In his study of Pacific Northwest masks, Lévi-Strauss operationalizes this principle by attempting to prove the hypothesis that when plastic forms are borrowed intact, their meaning and function are inverted, while masks with similar meanings from neighboring groups will be formally opposed, often as mirror images of each other. The key concept here is transformation, which can be taken in the linguistic sense as a repeatable, reversible, structurally established operation. The transformation of a mytheme thus no more threatens the system than the transformation of a declarative sentence into an interrogative one threatens the language.

The late twentieth century has not been kind to grand theories in the human sciences, and although Lévi-Strauss's structuralism is no exception, its legacy remains alive. The various figures associated with poststructuralism, such as Jacques Derrida and Michel Foucault, at the very least assume structuralism as a point of departure. The fruitfulness of the structural study of myth has been clearly demonstrated by the work of Dell Hymes (1981), among others. Lévi-Strauss's corpus stands as a remarkably coherent, consistent body of theory that makes the strongest possible argument for a rationalist, universalist view of humanity.

[See also Durkheim; Jakobson; Poststructuralism; Prague School; Saussure; and Structuralism.]

BIBLIOGRAPHY

Hymes, D. In Vain I Tried to Tell You: Essays in Native American Ethnopoetics. Philadelphia: University of Pennsylvania Press, 1981.
Lévi-Strauss, C. Structural Anthropology, vol. 1. Translated by C. Jacobson and B. Schoepf. New York: Basic Books, 1963.
Lévi-Strauss, C. The Savage Mind. Chicago: University of Chicago Press, 1966.
Lévi-Strauss, C. The Elementary Structures of Kinship. Edited by R. Needham, translated by J. Harle Bell and J. R. von Sturmer. Boston: Beacon Press, 1969.
Lévi-Strauss, C. The Raw and the Cooked. Translated by J. Weightman and D. Weightman. New York: Octagon Books, 1970.
Lévi-Strauss, C. The Way of the Masks. Translated by S. Modelski. Seattle: University of Washington Press, 1982.
Lévi-Strauss, C. Histoire de lynx. Paris: Plon, 1991.
Levy-Bruhl, L. Primitive Mentality. Translated by L. A. Clare. Boston: Beacon Press, 1966.

—MICHAEL HARKIN

LINEARITY. One way in which articulate speech differs from visual modes of symbolic representation is that its component parts cannot be presented to the attention simultaneously; they must unfold in some particular linear sequence, creating a chain of signifiers or "syntagmatic string." For Ferdinand de Saussure, this property of linearity constitutes the most crucial characteristic (after its essential arbitrariness) of the (vocal) signifier. In writing, spatial extension along the line of text substitutes for temporal extension, and so linearity in the sense of a sequential presentation of signifiers is preserved in the visual medium.

That the sounds and thus the words of a univocal utterance must be articulated and perceived successively is certainly true, but in itself it constitutes a relatively uninteresting claim: linearity in this weakest sense is a property that language necessarily shares with any auditory system of signification, such as the calling system of vervet monkeys or the burrs and beeps through which a telephone system communicates the status of a channel. What distinguishes language from such systems is that language has enrolled linearity as a mode of signification in its own right. In language, most arrangements of any given selection of words are meaningless (e.g., *John the bit dog*), and in those that do carry meaning, the order of words is itself a signifier, distinguishing (for example) syntactic categories such as subject and object (*John bit the dog* versus *The dog bit John*) or pragmatic ones such as topic and comment (*I cannot allow French songs* versus Lady Bracknell's *French songs I cannot allow!*; *Johannes canem momordit* versus *canem momordit Johannes*). On the level of discourse, moreover, the sequence of main clauses in a narrative are read as indicating temporal sequence (and, by implication, causality) unless otherwise signaled: *He burst into tears, and she reprimanded him* tells a different story than *She reprimanded him, and he burst into tears*. It is this signifying power of sequence that establishes the syntagmatic string as an autonomous entity, a whole greater than the sum of its parts. To some extent, language shares this property of meaningful linearity with other culturally bound semiotic systems, such as myth and ritual.

But there is a stronger sense of linearity when predicated of language that entails the claim that the syntagmatic string is constructed and decoded in a purely linear or incremental fashion, sound by sound and word by word. That language is linear in this strong sense was a guiding principle of early American structuralists, who were influenced by the typical structure of the Amerindian languages on which they did much of their descriptive work. Many such languages are incorporative—that is, they form utterances by incorporating formative elements sequentially into larger units, like beads on a string. The classic "item-and-arrangement" structuralists of the middle decades of the twentieth century applied this model to English, seeing the syntagmatic string as segmented into phonemes (minimum analyzable units of sound), even at the level of prosody (G. L. Trager and H. L. Smith's classic *An Outline of English Structure* [1951] postulated four discrete phonemes of pitch, stress, and juncture). The string of phonemes was then divided into consecutive morphemes, or minimal units of significant form. Thus, *The dogs walked* was analyzed as a sequence of five morphemes (*the* + [*dog* + /z/] + [*walk* + /t/]), with the /z/ of the plural morpheme and the /t/ of the past-tense morpheme described as positional variants or allomorphs, phonologically conditioned (cp. *The* + [*cat* + /s/] + [*stroll* + /d/]). Anomalous structures such as *The wolves leapt* were explained in terms of morphologically conditioned allomorphs, so that *wolf* was specified as taking the form *wolv-* before the plural morpheme, and *leap* (/li:p/) the form /lep/ before the preterite morpheme. This approach faced insuperable obstacles, however, in dealing with ablaut forms such as *men* and *ran*: there is something clearly fudged about an analysis that claims that in *The men ran*, plurality and past tense are signified in each case by zero allomorphs (*The* + [*men* + Ø] + [*ran* + Ø]) rather than by the "irrelevant" allomorphic variation between *man* and *men* or *run* and *ran*. So procrustean a solution constitutes a desertion of one of the most central tenets of structuralism: its empiricist insistence on the observable rather than on theoretical preconceptions. It was on such principles, after all, that structuralists rejected the traditional humanist grammarians' claim that in a sentence such as *The man bit the dog*, the object status of *the dog* was marked not by the observable circumstance of word order but rather by its being in some theoretical accusative case that happened to be not formally marked. Later structuralists found themselves forced to abandon the notion that English could be described adequately as simply an additive string of morphemic segments and suggested that when the morpheme *man* met the morpheme *Plural* it triggered off a sort of chemical reaction that resulted in a new, unanalyzable compound *men*. This development, known as "item and process," represented a tacit abandonment of strong linearity: the belief that English (or any language) could be described adequately as a static, linear arrangement of discrete items.

A similar problem attended the syntactic side of structuralist theory, in which each morph was identified with its syntactically closest neighbor as a pair of "immediate constituents," that pair was then identified with its own immediate constituent, and so on, producing linear analyzes such as [[*A man*] [*bit* [*the dog*]]], where *the* goes with *dog*, *the dog* with *bit*, and *bit the dog* with *a man*. Such an analysis is easily floored by a sentence with nonlinear constituents: we can slice up a sentence such as [[*You* [[*did do*] *that*]] [*for what*]], but what are we to do with the clearly related "*What did you do that for?*"

It was dissatisfaction with strong linearity as an explanatory principle that (among other things) finally brought about the paradigm shift initiated by Noam Chomsky in the 1950s. For Chomsky (1965), the linear sequence of words in the sentence—the "surface structure"—was merely the end product of a nonlinear combinatory process that was itself concealed. To take a well-known example: no surface-structure analysis of (1) *Jane promised Bill to come* and (2) *Jane persuaded Bill to come* will account for the puzzling discrepancy that the subject of *come* is *Jane* in (1) but *Bill* in (2); only analysis of the combinatory processes that embed one sentence in another will explain the difference. Just as different "deep" structures might produce similar surface structures, so the same deep structure might have different surface representations, as in the case of active and passive versions (*A dog bit Bill, Bill was bitten by a dog*). That such pairs are in some psychological sense similar can be confirmed experimentally by the tendency of people who are asked to memorize a passive sentence to recall it in active form: clearly, the subjects do not memorize mere linear strings of words but store the sentence in some abstract or deep-structure format that is then reconstituted in its simplest form as an active sentence (presumably, the passive requires a further transformation).

There has been a great deal of debate about the notion of classical deep structure in recent years, and alternative models of depth structure have been proposed—in case grammar and generative semantics, for example—but there has been no suggestion of a return to strong linearity as an explanatory model of language. It is clear, in any case, that the processing of language must be nonlinear. This is not to say, however, that simplified signifying systems that are parasitic upon language, such as those of metrics, cannot function in a linear fashion: the primary error of generative metrical theories, for example, was to assume that metrical systems of signification are nonlinear in the way that language itself is nonlinear.

[*See also* Jakobson; Langue and Parole; Saussure.]

BIBLIOGRAPHY

Anderson, J. "The Limits of Linearity." In *Explorations in Dependency Phonology*, edited by J. Anderson and J. Durand, pp. 199–220. Dordrecht: Foris, 1987.

Bierwisch, M. "Poetics and Linguistics." In *Linguistics and Literary Style*, edited by D. C. Freeman, translated by P. H. Salus, pp. 98–115. New York: Holt, Rinehart and Winston, 1970.

Chomsky, N. *Aspects of the Theory of Syntax*. Cambridge, Mass.: MIT Press, 1965.

Malmberg, B. "La linéarité comme élément de forme." In *Logos semantikos: Studia linguistica in honorem Eugenio Coseriu 1921–1981*, vol. 2, *Sprachtheorie und Sprachphilosophie*, edited by H. Weydt, pp. 141–147. Berlin: Mouton de Gruyter, 1981.

Star, Z. "On So-Called Linearity." *Philologica Pragensia* 23 (1980): 185–197.

Trager, G. L., and H. L. Smith. *An Outline of English Structure*. Norman, Okla: Batterburg Press, 1951.

—PETER GROVES

LINGUISTIC MOTIVATION. In the context of Sausserean linguistics, the notion of linguistic motivation usually opposes the notion of arbitrariness that is deemed to characterize linguistic signs. Saussure, however, certainly allowed for the fact that not all signs are arbitrary by making a distinction between absolute and relative arbitrariness. Some signs are said to be "motivated": in the case of onomatopoeia, the "acoustic image" is motivated by a likeness to some natural sound in the domain of substance.

But Saussure was most concerned about developing a systematic conception of language in which signs are defined by the value they have in a system of contrasting relations. For Saussure, the notion of "relative motivation" implies the analysis of the given term, hence a syntagmatic relation, as well as the appeal to one or several other terms, hence an associative relation.

This is none other than the mechanism in virtue of which any term whatsoever lends itself to the expression of an idea. Up to this point, [linguistic] units have appeared to us as values, that is, as elements of a system, and we have considered them above all in terms of their oppositions; now we recognise the solidarities which link them; these are of the associative and syntagmatic kind, and it is these which limit arbitrariness. *Dix-neuf* [nineteen] is solidary associatively with *dix-huit* [eighteen], *soixante-dix* [seventy], etc., and syntagmatically with its elements *dix* [ten] and *neuf* [nine]. This dual relationship confers on it a part of its value." (Saussure, 1983, p. 182)

The implications of this passage for the continuing acceptance of the doctrine of the arbitrariness of the sign appear to have been largely overlooked. Saussure, in his description of the sign as seen as from the token or instance perspective, states very clearly that the two strata of concept and acoustic image are "intimately united." The principle of arbitrariness, contrary to the widespread belief, does not operate on this internal relationship but refers instead to the general conditions of the system of differential oppositions (*langue*) that constitute the conditions of possibility of any particular sign relation in that system. Arbitrariness, then, is a general condition of the overall system of types and is for that reason external to any given sign relation in the overall system of sign types. The apparent paradox of the dually arbitrary and indissoluble link of the internal unity of the sign relation is resolved once this is clear. Relative motivation means that both syntagmatic and associative solidarities, insofar as the linguistic units concerned are no longer defined as pure values in a system of oppositions per se, no longer refer to purely internal relationships. Why, then, does Saussure say that it is this dual relationship of syntagmatic and associative solidarities that "confers a part" of the given unit's value? The point is that Saussure is here describing the way the sign, no longer defined in purely systemic terms, takes some of its value from its relations to the world. At the same time, this relationship confers value on the sign relation itself, as well as vice versa.

These solidarities that limit arbitrariness refer to potential uses of signs in context—that is, to the ways in which a given sign type might construe a meaningful relationship with some entity in the real world or to the complex and multiple ways in which language forms are functionally motivated in relation to the meanings of the various kinds that they realize. In other words, the issue of motivated signs pushes Saussure's principle of arbitrariness—and, by extension, the concept of *langue*—to its theoretical limit. Once it is admitted that motivation occurs, then we are in the realm of the functional relations between meanings, forms, and contexts.

In this view, signs are made through their syntagmatic and associative solidarities. They do not exist ready-made, waiting to be used. The "units as values" or "elements of a system" to which Saussure refers are not fully made signs. They are the systemic resources in and through which meanings are made according to formal, discursive, and social constraints and practices. Once it is understood that the relationship of meanings to forms is a solidary rather than an arbitrary one, then it should be clear that the functionally motivated nature of this relation involves multiple functional solidarities between the syntagmatic and associative axes in the making of signs. This means that different kinds of functional solidarities act upon each other in context so as to produce signs.

A second problem is Saussure's apparently restrictive focus on the word as the basic sign unit. Most commentators have focused on this aspect of Saussure's discussion and overlooked what Saussure said about grammar and lexis, and the relations between them. Thus, Saussure makes a distinction between "*lexicological* languages . . . in which lack of motivation [*l'immotivité*] reaches its maximum," and "more *grammatical* languages . . . in which it falls to a minimum" (1983, p. 183). On this basis, he suggests that *lexicological* tends to equate with *unmotivated* and *grammatical* with *motivated*. But these, Saussure cautions, are "two poles between which the whole system moves" rather than fixed characteristics of particular languages. Further, grammar, Saussure argues, is a means for making meanings; it is not an abstract and formal device for encoding already given nonlinguistic concepts and the like. Saussure notes: "Grammar studies the language system as a system of means of expression; grammatical means synchronic and meaningful [*significatif*]." In other words, the grammar itself makes and construes meaningful distinctions through its systems of value. The latter are the "means of expression" (*moyens d'expression*) or the value-making forms themselves. Saussure explicitly recognizes the motivated relation between grammatical form and meaning when in the same

section on grammar he observes that "forms and functions are solidary [*solidaires*]." However, the restrictive focus on the word did not allow him to build this observation into his definition of the sign in a systematic way.

Saussure does not appear, then, to have a dogmatic view of arbitrariness. Instead, he suggests that it is a product of the particular limitations presupposed by his criterion of a strictly "internal" linguistics. He acknowledges that the arbitrariness principle cannot be contained beyond this point, but the limitations of his theory do not allow him to work through these implications. This would require a theory fully cognizant of the functionally motivated character of linguistic form and its relations to context.

[*See also* Arbitrariness, Principle of; Cours de Linguistique Générale; Saussure; *and* Type and Token.]

BIBLIOGRAPHY

Saussure, F. de. *Course in General Linguistics*. Translated by R. Harris. London: Duckworth, 1983.

—PAUL J. THIBAULT

LINGUISTIC RELATIVISM. A controversial theory, linguistic relativism in its most extreme form claims that cognition is determined by language and is therefore relative to the particular language that one speaks. Although this theory is usually associated with the work of Benjamin Lee Whorf and the so-called Sapir-Whorf hypothesis, it has a longer history, which includes the nineteenth- and early twentieth-century linguistic research of German scholars such as Wilhelm von Humboldt (1767–1835) and Wilhelm Wundt (1832–1920) (Rossi-Landi, 1973). It is now standard practice in psychological and linguistic textbooks to characterize Whorf's theory of language as a version of linguistic determinism. However, this radical formulation does not reflect the actual complexity and subtlety of the works from which it has been derived.

The American linguist Michael Silverstein (1979) has developed a sophisticated rereading of Whorf's linguistic theory against those who have dismissed it as vague, unsystematic, and tautologous. Further developments in this same tradition include the work of John A. Lucy (1992) and Alan Rumsey (1990). Silverstein points out that the real importance of Whorf's "relativity" principle, which Silverstein renames the "linguistic uncertainty principle," concerns the way in which those who think they "can directly penetrate to the linguistic coding of referential 'reality out there' by examining their own propositional system—no matter how 'deeply'— or by examining others' with crude approximation-translations of propositional content, unrecognizably distort the object of investigation in the process" (1979, p. 194). The problematic that Whorf faced was strikingly similar to the metamathematical paradoxes that occupied Kurt Gödel in the 1930s. Gödel showed that a formal theory is unable to include itself recursively in its own domain. In order to remain internally consistent, formal theories must exclude themselves from their own domains. Whorf realized that a positivist linguistic science would thus be unable to free itself from this paradox.

Yet Whorf goes much further than merely asserting that a given interpretive framework perturbs a given observed reality. He raises fundamental questions concerning the nature of the analyst's framework, what is analyzed, and the analytical process. Undoubtedly influenced by the quantum mechanics of Niels Bohr and Werner Heisenberg, Whorf makes scattered references in his writings to "field physics." He understood that while reality may be dissected into discrete entities on analogy with the formally segmentable lexical dimension of language, there exists a complementary principle of "ordered pattern-ment" that has a more unconscious "background character." These two principles are not mutually exclusive but constitute complementary theoretical perspectives whereby language construes physical reality. Thus, Whorf argues, "the physical world may be an aggregate of quasidiscrete entities (atoms, crystals, living organisms, planets, stars, etc.) not fully understandable as such, but rather emergent from a field of causes that is itself a manifold of pattern and order" (1956, p. 269). In the second perspective, there are no discrete, already given entities that correspond to the available terms (cf. lexemes) in the theory and language of the analyst. Instead, the theoretical language, in perturbing the relevant field of relations, allows for the emergence of the given reality as a consequence of the interaction between the two.

Whorf explores the question concerning how what is observed is produced by the interaction with the theoretical-analytical framework of the observer. He argues that the "kind of linguistic analysis employed" and "various behavioral reactions and also the shapes taken by various cultural developments"

(1956) all affect each other in a complex dialectic. The choice of analytical-theoretical framework itself predisposes what is analyzed toward particular types of behavioral reactions. There is no absolute, universal, or objective standard of measurement. Likewise, there is no question of a unilinear and determinist cause-effect relation between the analytical framework and its object of analysis.

Whorf raises foundational questions concerning the techniques and procedures of linguistic analysis itself. Contrary to the positivist assumption that particular analytical categories can be brought into exact correspondence with specific entities in some external and objective realm, Whorf points out that the meaning of a given category is linked to the global state of the entire system of relations; it is not localized in any single element. Whorf's relativity hypothesis is, in fact, a principle of "complementarity" after the fashion of the quantum physics of Bohr and Heisenberg. The issue is not, however, that the object of the analysis and the analytical framework simply render the one indistinguishable from the other. Rather, Whorf realizes the fundamental difficulty raised by the attempt to interpret "a dissimilar language" through our own analytical procedures and categories.

Thus, what Whorf poses with his relativity principle is no simple relativist affirmation of the differences between "dissimilar" languages and cultures. Given that no linguist has at his or her disposal "very many widely different linguistic systems," it "holds that all observers are not led by the same physical evidence to the same picture of the universe, unless their linguistic backgrounds are similar, or can in some way be calibrated" (1956, p. 214). That they can be so calibrated is not in question, but Whorf addresses a more far-reaching problematic: how the tendency "to think in our own language in order to understand the exotic language" renders the exotic language—the object of the analysis—incommensurate with the linguist's theories and analytical procedures. What, for example, would a Hopi or a Pitjantjatjara grammar of, say, English look like?

Whorf fully understood, in ways that still elude most linguists, that the language in and through which a given theory is organized and articulated plays a fundamental role in the construction of the observed object and the meanings imputed to it. Yet he also understood that no theoretical metalanguage can exhaust the meaning of its object, the "undecidability" or "ineffability" of which can never be rendered wholly determinate by a given theoretical framework. The issues raised here have also been explored by the various contributors to a special issue of the journal *Cultural Dynamics* (Halliday, 1993).

Whorf was also interested in the ways in which the linguistic praxis of a community systematically and ideologically constrains members' metalinguistic awareness of language form and function. Such awareness is always skewed in relation to the largely unconscious patterns of the language system. Whorf's deconstruction of the folk ideology of reference in Western "secondary rationalizations" of language bears this out. While Whorf talks about "language habits" and the "cultural norms" as being constraining, he provides no systematic account of the ways in which grammar is deployed in regular, systematic ways in the making of (text-specific) meanings in discourse. Thus, he has no account of the patterned nature of language in relation to its social uses. Whorf left the crucial issue of the links between a grammatical system and social action only very weakly articulated, but a new generation of social semioticians is tackling this task with considerable energy.

[*See also* Arbitrariness, Principle of; Linguistic Motivation; *and* Whorf.]

BIBLIOGRAPHY

Benson, J. D., M. J. Cummings, and W. S. Greaves, eds. *Linguistics in a Systemic Perspective*. Amsterdam and Philadelphia: John Benjamins, 1988.

Halliday, M. A. K., ed. *Cultural Dynamics* 6.1–2 (1993).

Lucy, J. A. *Language Diversity and Thought: A Reformulation of the Linguistic Relativity Hypothesis*. New York: Cambridge University Press, 1992.

Mathiot, M., ed. *Ethnolinguistics: Boas, Sapir, and Whorf Revisited*. The Hague: Mouton, 1979.

Mertz, E., and R. J. Parmentier, eds. *Semiotic Mediation: Sociocultural and Psychological Perspectives*. New York: Academic Press, 1985.

Rossi-Landi, F. *Ideologies of Linguistic Relativity*. The Hague: Mouton, 1973.

Rumsey, A. "Wording, Meaning, and Linguistic Ideology." *American Anthropologist* 92.2 (1990): 346–361.

Silverstein, M. "Language Structure and Linguistic Ideology." In *The Elements: A Parasession on Linguistic Units and Levels*, edited by P. R. Clyne, W. F. Hanks, and C. L. Hofbauer, pp. 193–241. Chicago: Chicago Linguistic Society, 1979.

Whorf, B. L. *Language Thought and Reality*. Edited by J. B. Carroll. Cambridge, Mass.: MIT Press, 1956.

—PAUL J. THIBAULT

LITERARY ANTHROPOLOGY. An area of research developed by Fernando Poyatos (1981), literary anthropology is designed to bridge the disciplinary gap between anthropology and literary studies. It is based on an interdisciplinary, anthropologically oriented approach to the narrative literature of different cultures, from their early epics to the contemporary novel, construed as a rich database of signs that documents peoples' cultural achievements, ideas, and behaviors.

Literary texts provide a wealth of data regarding the sign systems of each culture, comprising the social interactions and material culture described by the writer (paralanguage, gestures, manners, postures, clothes, furniture, architecture, tools, food and drink, etc.) and the social organization and intitutions that form the context of the narratives (rituals, social relationships and role expectations, methods of child rearing, culture-bound diseases, celebrations, games, people-animal relationships, etc.). A systematic semiotic-communicative approach to literary texts thus makes it possible to infer sign systems—for example, "They made me take the bangs off my arms, and the silver wristlets . . . and I had to rub the vermillion marks off my forehead and go and bathe in the river. I knew then I was a widow" (Bibhutibhushan Banerji, *Pather Panchali*, 1968)—subsystems, such as the various kinds of pots (clay or brass) observed in *Pather Panchali* categories (e.g., the various uses of those pots); subcategories (e.g., the distinct ways in which the formerly identified uses are carried out); forms (e.g., how each use of a pot is performed); and types (e.g., the culture-bound or subcultural ways of using a particular utensil).

Nonverbal signs that are used for identifying characters and specifying the nonverbal components of the interactions between them constitute a vast repertoire of culture-bound gestures, manners, and postures. The literary anthropologist can combine the analysis of sensible and intelligible sign systems or culturemes and thus gain a number of insights into various aspects of the culture concerned. For instance, national and regional narratives prove to be invaluable in elaborating a kinesic atlas of a culture, showing, among other things, the distribution and adaptation of postural habits according to terrain, domestic architecture, furniture, moral values, and so on. Naturally, the analysis of a culture through its literature can be applied crossculturally. The cultural domains and areas that literary-anthropological research can cover include paralanguage, which offers a wealth of clues to culture-specific as well as pan-cultural features: "She tapped softly with the key at one of the cell-doors . . . no sound within; so she coughed and listened again" (Charles Dickens, *Oliver Twist*, 1838); "He cleared his throat, and coughed once or twice. He had not the courage to call out" (Banerji, *Pather Panchali*); "Mahatma Gandhi ki jai! and now the police . . . spit on them and bind them with ropes . . . and beat them, and spat into their mouths" (Raja Rao, *Kanthapura*, 1963). Kinesics, of course, might constitute the bulk of an analysis, distinguishing between gestures, manners, and postures in their morphological and functional differences and similarities, which can be classified into five categories:

1. *Interactive and conversational activities.* "Mr. Waterbrook, pursing up his mouth, and playing with his watch-chain, in a comfortable, prosperous sort of way" (Dickens, *David Copperfield*, 1850); "He made the expressive Egyptian gesture of finality: a sudden wiping of the palm of one hand across the palm of the other (Henry V. Morton, *Through the Lands of the Bible*, 1948).

2. *Ritualized activities*, including etiquette norms, games, toy playing, and so on. "A military-looking child who was trundling a hoop" (Dickens, *David Copperfield*); "Having accomplished this preliminary European handshake, he kissed him three times, Russian fashion; in other words, he touched his nephew's cheek three times" (Ivan Turgenev, *Fathers and Sons*, 1862); "He bent respectfully to touch his mother in law's feet" (Banerji, *Pather Panchali*).

3. *Task-performing activities*, including good and bad eating and drinking manners, smoking, and chewing: "Big Bill grasped his cup around the top so that the spoon stuck up between his first and second fingers" (John Steinbeck, *The Grapes of Wrath*, 1939); "The little man gave a double knock on the lid of his snuff-box, opened it, took a great pinch, shut it up again" (Dickens, *Pickwick Papers*, 1836–1837).

4. *Occupational activities*, which reveal different or similar artifacts and associated behaviors with sociocultural implications. "The bearer put the cocks under his left arm . . . and walked off with the swagger characteristic of the white man's servant" (Mulk Raj Anand, *The Coolie*, 1936).

5. *Somatic, random, and emotional acts*, too often neglected as mere curiosities: "The man blew his nose into the palm of his hand and wiped his hand in his trousers" (Steinbeck, *The Grapes of Wrath*); "He . . . blew his nose by catching it between the thumb and forefinger of his right hand" (Anand, *Coolie*).

Objectual or artifactual systems are intimately related to the body and may act as veritable extensions of it, particularly within two of the nonverbal categories. The first of these, body adaptors, includes nutritionals and pseudonutritionals, clothes, food and drink, and cosmetics: "He opened his betel-bag and carefully taking a tobacco leaf, he seated himself and wiping the tobacco leaf against his dhoti, he put it into his mouth, then put an areca nut with it and began to munch" (Rao, *Kanthapura*). The second category, object adaptors, includes eating and drinking utensils, tools, anatomical furniture, conditioning manners, and postures: "We put the water jugs on our hips, and we rushed back home" (Rao, *Kanthapura*).

Objectual, built, and natural environments comprise culture, class, and person-identifying sign systems that afford any kind of semiotic-communicative study. This brings in many interdisciplinary perspectives concerning, for example, decorative objects and other domestic artifacts, architectural forms and spaces that condition socialization and person-environment interaction, residential landscaping and lawn ornaments, terrain and flora, and, very importantly, people-animal interactions (with significant paralinguistic and gesture repertoires): "The animals [bullocks], refreshed, began stepping jauntly again, tossing their heads and jangling the bells that hung from their red-painted horns" (Kamala Markandaya, *Nectar in a Sieve*, 1990).

Literary texts are also rich sources of documentation on cognitive systems such as religion, myths, and beliefs: "I must have lived a very sinful life in my previous birth for all this sorrow to come upon me now" (Rao, *Kanthapura*); festivals, such as in India, Rama, Ganapati, Dasara; religious rituals: "People [in the temple] . . . banged the bell and touched the bull" (Rao, *Kanthapura*); socioreligious ceremonies: "The mourners used always to be given a pair of black gloves and a piece of black silk for their hats" (W. Somerset Maugham, *Of Human Bondage*, 1915); social structure: in India, brahmans, pariahs, swamis; relations, role expectations, and their evolution: "The wife of the family is supposed to look after the rice and the housework" (Banerji, *Pather Panchali*); social ritual and etiquette: "[Shaking her hand] dio aquel tirón enérgico que él siempre daba, siguiendo la moda que en Madrid empezaba entonces" ("[Shaking her hand] energetically as he always did, following the style that was then coming into fashion in Madrid"; Leopoldo Alas, *La Regenta*, 1884–1885); domestic chores: "how to milk the goat, how to plant seed, how to churn butter from milk, and how to mull rice" (Markandaya, *Nectar in a Sieve*); child-rearing and culture-bound illnesses (cholera in *Fathers and Sons*; smallpox and dysentheria in *Kanthapura*); leisure and games: dice in *Pather Panchali*; chronemic (time) patterns: the Hindu calendar in *Kanthapura*; affect displays: "Quando vio Mio Çid asomar a Minaya el cavallo corriendo, valo abraçar sin falla besóle la boca e los ojos de la cara" ("When El Cid saw Minaya appear, riding on his horse, he went to embrace him as always, kissing him on the mouth and eyes" *Poema del Cid*, twelfth century); popular language and sayings, popular literature, popular beliefs, folk celebrations, and music: "Don Quijote . . . afinándola [the "vihuela"] lo mejor que pudo, escupió y remondóse el pecho [carraspeó], y luego . . . cantó" ("Don Quijote tuned the guitar as well as he could, spat and scratched his chest, and then sang" Cervantes, *Don Quixote*).

[*See also* Cultureme; Habitus; Nonverbal Bodily Sign Categories; *and* Nonverbal Communication in the Novel.]

BIBLIOGRAPHY

Poyatos, F. "Literary Anthropology: A New Interdisciplinary Perspective of Man Through His Narrative Literature." *Versus: Quaderni di studi semiotici* 28 (1981): 3–28.
Poyatos, F., ed. *Literary Anthropology: New Approaches to People, Signs, and Literature*. Amsterdam and Philadelphia: John Benjamins, 1988.

—FERNANDO POYATOS

LOGO. The official visual identification of an organization or a brand name, a logo purports to express values and intentions by graphic means. It is displayed through various buildings, signs, advertising, vehicles, uniforms, and other means. Companies and associations invest considerable resources in promoting visual-identity programs. It is estimated that an urban dweller is exposed to more than one thousand logos a day on average. This phenomenon, sometimes labeled "semiological pollution," challenges the natural limit of information processing and retention of the human mind. Hence the necessity for organizations to establish signs that are distinctive, easily recognizable, memorable, and associated with the intended values.

There are three types of logos: the logotype, the icotype, and the mixed logo. The alphanumeric logo or logotype (e.g., IBM, Coca Cola, YSL, 3M) is composed exclusively of alphabetic and numeric signs. The choice of typography and colors gives the logo its identity features and tends to iconize these alphanumeric signs to the extent that the logo eventually becomes an image. The acronym is transformed into an icon through the systematic and repeated use of the same typeface. The iconic logo or icotype is constituted by an image chosen either for the symbolism of the object represented or by virtue of a pure convention. Such logos, which are symbolic by nature because they are not based on similarity or contiguity, can through intensive repetition become indexical and even iconic signs of the organization because the organization's audience has learned to associate such signs with the company. The mixed logo, a combination of images and words, is the most common type of logo. Usually based on the association of a name (logotype) and an image (icotype), these logos metaphorically borrow the elementary signs of human identity (i.e., a name and a photograph).

Mixed logos illustrate three types of relationships between linguistic and iconographic signs. Text and image can be either juxtaposed (the linguistic discourse essentially anchors the image) or mixed (the iconic discourse relays the image and vice versa), or the image can be added to the text to iconize all or part of the text, as in the case of a decorated letter. The linguistic and iconographic discourses must coexist and convey a consistent meaning. There must be a logic in the way signs are organized so that the recipient gets a coherent notion of what is represented (a brand, a company). The continuous use of such mixed associations often provides the iconic discourse with legitimacy. When the company's name becomes redundant, the logo can shed its linguistic component because the company is associated only with the symbol. When the link between the image and the company's name is not obvious or in some ways appears illegitimate, the company often discards the image and retains only the name.

Pictorial logos fulfill both a representative function—that is, they act simultaneously as an icon and an index—and a pragmatic function, in which they act as signals that trigger some reaction in a receiver.

The indexical and iconic functions, which in Peircean terminology govern the relationship between the analogous representamen and the object, are related to both contiguity and analogy. For example, the familiar logo of Shell Oil consists of a red and yellow stylized seashell, which acts as the representamen. This representamen is related to two different objects: first, it is related by an indexical relation of contiguity to the company Shell in the sense that the company is indexically referred to as the sender of the message in every manifestation of this logo. As the logo exists only through its application on media supports, it acts as an index of the company but also of the products and services the company provides. There exists also an iconic relation between the representamen and its pictorial object, which is the object "shell." This representamen can be called an icon because there is a topological similarity between its signifier and its denotatum. The representamen is a stylized representation of a shell according to features that define the visual-identity system of Shell—that is, essentially, the color code (yellow as a primary identity color, red as a secondary identity color). This iconic relation grounds the representative function of the representamen in its figurative dimension. This iconic relation between the representamen and its object is grounded on common pictorial codes of representation and symbolization shared by the sender (the company) and the receiver (its public). That is the reason why, for example, American companies such as Coca Cola usually have to adapt their logo when they sell their products in cultures that employ different pictorial codes.

Second, the representative power of the logo is based on an indexical relation of contiguity between the representamen and its object. The validity of this representative power depends on the acceptance by the interpreter of such a relation. In other words, the question is whether this representation (the choice of a shell to represent the company) is legitimate or not. Thus, the indexical function of the logo is based essentially on its legitimacy. This question raises the important issue of the ability of the logo to act effectively as an identity sign of the organization. The indexical function of the logo is more legitimate and solid if the representamen is contiguous with the organization's identity. Identity is a set of identifying features that the organization tries to convey by their transfer in a figurative and symbolic mode. An organization's identity is its sense of self, formed by its history, beliefs and philosophy, ethical and cultural values, strategies, mission, and the nature of its business. These elements, which contribute to the organization's existence, can be communicated and projected through corporate-identity programs and therefore summarized and condensed in a logo.

In this sense, a logo can be said to be the ultimate identity sign of an organization. The Shell logo is an iconic and indexical representation of the company's identity such as its origin (the company's activities originated in maritime regions), its name (there is a topological similarity between the icotype and the company's name), and its business (oil derives from the process of fossilization). Although identity evolves over time, it is an a priori concept. A legitimate logo is thus one that is the contiguous figurative transcription of the organization's identity features. The logo usually represents an organization's identity insofar as it is a denotative sign that analogically and iconically refers to the identity features of the company. This means that the logo shares a relation of resemblance with what it stands for, based on a referential function of the logo, which is supposed to represent closely the organization analogically and iconically. A denotative logo is legitimate and represents an "identity sign" because there exists both an iconic and indexical relation between the representamen and its objects. These signs act as identity signs because their mode of representation is legitimized by the organization's identity.

Other types of logo include those that are not based on a relation of resemblance with the organization they stand for. These logos are based on a constructive and connotative approach to the pictorial language, such as either when the chosen icotype has no legitimate reference to the organization's identity or when the icotype constitutes an ambiguous icon of its object. Such logos are essentially constructive or connotative and fulfill their representative role through repetition over time so that the conventional association between the organization and its publics becomes contractual. Such logos cannot really be considered identity signs and must therefore be viewed as "image signs" to the extent that they are designed to arouse certain feelings and images in receivers. They are designed to associate an organization with a given image, despite its identity features. This is usually the case when a company decides to change its logo. A connotative sign that is therefore initially a mere symbol can become an index only through repetition on different media supports and also by a strategy of legitimization by the company. In other words, these logos are not self-explanatory and must be justified and legitimized by the use of paratexts (such as advertising campaigns) designed to explain and justify the relationship between the representamen and its objects.

The logo signifies first as a system of discrete elements but also through the interactions and modifications of these elements. The logo is thus a moving and evolving structure of identifying elements. The visual-identity system of an organization, condensed in and assumed by the logo, has the same characteristics as the narrative identity of a human being. Narrative identity, as defined by Paul Ricoeur, articulates acquired identificatory elements into the composition of which otherness can enter and by which alterity can be assumed by the subject. It also articulates a style—that is, the constitution of identifying characteristics by which the sign is recognized. Hence, the structure of the logo might be "consistently" altered and thus identified afterward by reference to the original structure of the sign.

The IBM logo and its alteration operated by Paul Rand (the original designer of the logo), which is a metalinguistic transformation of an iconized logo into a symbolic and indexical pseudologo, is a good illustration of the concept of narrative identity. This logo transformed into a rebus (an eye, a bee, and the letter M) is still recognized and identified as the IBM logo because it keeps the "plastic invariants" and identity features of the original logo: a ternary structure, a stripe pattern, a specific typography of the letterhead (the "Egyptian" typography), and the specific blue color. Even though a principle of alterity has been introduced into the original sign, the recognition of the logo and its attribution to the IBM company is still valid because the deformation integrated new elements into a preexisting structure with easily recognizable and identifiable elements. In other words, it respected the visual style of IBM.

Like any other communication sign, the logo assumes all of the functions defined by Roman Jakobson as related to any verbal communication act: first, a phatic function, the aim of which is to maintain the contact and the control of the communicative channel. A logo's function is always in essence phatic because its first function is to establish contact between the sender (usually an organization) and a receiver (its actual and potential customers). Second,

the logo plays a poetic function that focuses on the aesthetic qualities of the message itself. Third, in its emotive or expressive function, the logo conveys information about its sender because it delivers a message about the identity and qualities of its sender as by proxy. Fourth, the logo's impressive or conative function is determined in part by information about the intended receiver. This is especially the case for brand logos, which usually represent either a consumer using the product or the ideal consumer so that the actual consumer can identify herself or himself with the image projected in the logo. Fifth, the logo plays a metalinguistic function that focuses on the code in which the message is expressed, as in the transformation of a famous logo. Sixth, through a referential function, the logo points to the context of communication and to the goods and services provided by the company or association.

Finally, a logo must differentiate one organization or brand from another. Hence, the logo represents the identity of an organization, and identity exists mainly through difference. Therefore, the logo can be viewed as a totem, as it can represent people from the same group. In this sense, the logo defines a group of central beliefs in pictorial form.

[See also Advertising; Aniconic Visual Signs; Iconicity; Ideograms; Indexicality; Jakobson's Model of Linguistic Communication; Peirce; and Pictorial Semiotics.]

BIBLIOGRAPHY

Floch, J.-M. "La voie des logos: Le face à face des logos IBM et Apple." In *Identités visuelles*, pp. 43–78. Paris: Presses Universitaires de France, 1995.

Green, D., and V. Loveluck. "Understanding a Corporate Symbol." *Applied Cognitive Psychology* 8 (1994): 37–44.

Lévi-Strauss, C. "The Effectiveness of Symbols." In his *Structural Anthropology*, pp. 186–205. London: Penguin, 1969.

Lhote, A. *Les invariants plastiques*. Paris: Hermann, 1967.

Ricoeur, P. *Oneself as Another*. Chicago: University of Chicago Press, 1992.

Schechter, A. "Measuring the Value of Corporate and Brand Logos." *Design Management Journal* 4.1 (1993).

Scott, D. "Air France's Hippocampe and BOAC's Speedbird: The Semiotics Status of the Logos." *French Cultural Studies* 4 (1993): 107–127.

—BENOÎT HEILBRUNN

LOTMAN, JURIJ MIKHAJLOVIČ (1922–1993),

Russian literary scholar and semiotician whose works

have shaped the structural-semiotic approach to art and culture. Lotman studied literary scholarship at the University of Leningrad; among his teachers were former representatives of Russian formalism such as B. M. Ejchenbaum, B. V. Tomaševskij, and V. M. Zirmunskij. In 1952, he defended a thesis on A. N. Radiščev, a leading figure of Russian Enlightenment at the end of the eighteenth century. In 1954, Lotman started teaching at Tartu University in Estonia, where in 1961 he received his degree with a work on prerevolutionary Russian literature. From 1963 onward, Lotman held the chair of Russian literature at Tartu University.

Lotman began his academic career as a specialist in eighteenth- and nineteenth-century Russian literature. But in the late 1950s and early 1960s, he progressively developed a structural theory of literature based on information theory and semiotics. These structuralist studies, which he subsequently applied to art in general and to the semiotics of culture, proved to be influential in non-Slavic countries, where they became available in translation.

Lotman's *Lectures on a Structural Poetics* (*Lektsii po struktural'noi poetike, vvedenie, teorija stiha*) was published in 1964 as the first volume of the series Studies in Sign Systems (*Trudy po znakovym sistemam*), founded by Lotman, which was to become the main outlet of the Moscow-Tartu School. These lectures, given between 1958 and 1962 at Tartu University, marked an important turning point in his research, which had focused up until then on the history of Russian literature and Russia's cultural history (Lotman, 1968). The first printed testimony to Lotman's new interest is his 1963 article "On the Delimination of the Notion of Structure in Linguistics and Literature," which, along with the other lectures, adumbrates Lotman's overall methodology. Following the writings of the late Russian formalists (mainly Jurij Tynjanov), Lotman defined literary works and literature as a whole, as well as the whole process of literary history, as a system of elements that form a hierarchically organized structure. Since this formal approach was a potential challenge to the official Soviet ideology, Lotman's handling of the notion of "model" can be seen as a masterpiece of ideological and methodological brinkmanship that bridged the ideological gap between Soviet Marxism and structuralist semiotics, since the official philosophical-gnoseological discussion of the late 1950s had reached the conclusion that any cognition is model based. Therefore, it was possible for Lotman to redefine art semiotically on the basis of ideas sanctioned by materialist aesthetics. Assuming that a work of art is a model of reality and that it should be understood as a system of signs, art can be defined as an intersection of cognition and communication.

The publication of Lotman's *Lectures* in 1964 coincided with the first summer school held in Kääriku, near Tartu. These summer schools, held from 1964 to 1970, shaped the intellectual profile of the Moscow-Tartu School. In fact, the school as a whole owed its existence mainly to Lotman's organizational activity in the early 1960s: after the Moscow Symposium on the Structural Study of Sign Systems in December 1962, Lotman contacted the organizers, V. V. Ivanov and V. N. Toporov, and initiated a long-term cooperative relationship. The broad horizons and spheres of interest of the involved scholars soon converged around the common denominator of culture, under which their diversity could be encompassed and methodologically integrated.

Beginning in the early 1960s, Lotman himself tried to study the regularities of human culture. Based on categories such as "language," "text," and "model," he tried to understand the process of cultural development and to conceive a cultural typology. Concrete analyses of various "secondary modeling" systems such as puppetry, film, theater, card games, painting, and the like formed the background for his theoretical models. However, his literary analyses remained the source from which he derived his general ideas about text and culture. Lotman's influential work on the semiotics of cultural space in literature and art is best represented by *The Structure of the Artistic Text* (1970), a theoretical work that originated in his analysis of Nikolai Gogol's prose.

Lotman's growing interest in the semiotics of culture is first documented in his "Problems in the Typology of Culture" (1977), followed by "Theses on the Semiotic Study of Cultures (1975), written with other members of the Moscow-Tartu School. In these works, culture is understood generally as information; it is tentatively defined as some kind of "collective memory" and as the "totality of nonhereditary information acquired, preserved, and transmitted by the various groups of human society." Later, Lotman redefined culture as a dynamic "generator of meaning." Based on the concepts of biosphere and noosphere (referring to the Russian scientist Vernadskij), Lotman developed the holistic concept of "semiosphere," which covers the totality of sign users, texts, and codes of a given culture. These ideas were later integrated into Lotman's *Universe of the Mind* (1990). Unlike most of his earlier theoretical articles, more recent works such as his monograph *Culture and Explosion* (1992) or his *Talks on Russian Culture* (1994) have not yet been translated into a Western language.

[*See also* Cultural Knowledge; Culture, Semiotics of; *and* Moscow-Tartu School.]

BIBLIOGRAPHY

Works by Lotman

Lektsii po struktural'noi poetike, vvedenie, teorija stiha. Brown University Reprints 5, edited by T. G. Winner. Providence, R.I.: Brown University Press, 1968.

"Problems in the Typology of Culture" (1967). In *Soviet Semiotics*, edited and translated by D. P. Lucid, pp. 213–221. Baltimore: Johns Hopkins University Press, 1977.

The Structure of the Artistic Text (1970). Translated by R. Vroon. Ann Arbor: University of Michigan Press, 1977.

Analysis of the Poetic Text (1972). Ann Arbor: ARDIS, 1976.

"Theses on the Semiotic Study of Cultures (as Applied to Slavic Texts)" (1973). In *The Tell-Tale Sign: A Survey of Semiotics*, edited by T. A. Sebeok, pp. 57–83. Lisse, Netherlands: Peter de Ridder Press, 1975.

"The Semiosphere." *Soviet Psychology* 27 (1989): 40–61.

Universe of the Mind. A Semiotic Theory of Culture. Translated by A. Shukman. London: Tauris, 1990.

Lotman, J. M., and B. A. Uspenskij. *Semiotics of Russian Culture*. Edited by A. Shukman. Ann Arbor: University of Michigan Press, 1984.

Other Works

"Bibliographie der Arbeiten von Jurij M. Lotman (1949–1992)." *Znakolog: An International Yearbook of Slavic Semiotics* 5 (1993): 201–275.

Jonaid-Sharif, L. "Text—Sign—Structure: The Poetics of Jurij Lotman." Ph.D. diss., University of Southwestern Louisiana, 1984.

Shukman, A. *Literature and Semiotics: A Study of the Writings of Y. M. Lotman*. Amsterdam: North Holland, 1977.

—PETER GRZYBEK

LYOTARD, JEAN-FRANÇOIS (1924–1998),
French philosopher and art theorist, author of a number of books outlining central characteristics and concerns of "the postmodern condition," and a critic of the rigidity of some manifestations of semiotic studies. Lyotard taught philosophy at several universities in France, retiring as professor emeritus at the University of Paris VIII. He also was a professor of French at the University of California, Irvine, before moving to Emory University. While pursuing myriad interests in his research and political activities, Lyotard wrote influential studies such as *Discours, figure* (1971), *Des dispositifs pulsionnels* (1973), *La condition postmoderne: Rapport sur le savoir* (1979), *Le différend* (1983), *L'enthousiasme: La critique kantienne de l'histoire* (1986), *Heidegger et "les juifs"* (1988), *Peregrinations: Law, Form, Event* (1988), and *Le postmoderne expliqué aux enfants* (1988). He also explored the intersections of theory and praxis by working with and writing for the group that published the Marxist organs *Socialisme ou barbarie* and *Pouvoir ouvrier*.

Lyotard's *Économie libidinale* (1974, translated into English as *Libidinal Economy* in 1993) is the work of his that is of most interest to semioticians, although ironically it is a biting, ferocious attack on what he saw as a smugly acquiescent if not quietist semiotics of the time. In the course of surveying related but contiguous facets of semiotics, Lyotard engages in a frenetically cadenced struggle that he articulated in another work as "an agonistics of language" involving "language 'moves'" (1979). While developing this general agonistics, Lyotard's book focuses on the potential intensity of semiosis as the primary site for analysis of signs and sign systems, rather than as a discipline that seeks a comfortable security in taxonomy and structure, monosemy and closure. While this position has been denigrated as merely a "violent affirmation of purely ephemeral desire" (Readings, 1991), it nevertheless outlines a distinctly vital position for semiotics by focusing on the intangible component of sign interaction that is arguably its most engaging, if most intangible, aspect. Lyotard posits the ever-shifting arena for this activity as "the great ephemeral skin," an economy in which opposing forces interact without negating their differences.

Économie libidinale is in particular an attack on structuralism and Marxism, although it also provided an important catalyst to semiotics in the mid-1970s by goading semioticians into intense self-scrutiny about their practices and, more important, the ideological assumptions that subtend them. Semiotics, Lyotard argues, has attempted to enact a move of legerdemain in which the sign is granted the status of a concrete, material entity instead of existing as a perpetual, energetic ebb and flow of deferral and slippery referentiality. It has succumbed to a type of "informational" imperialism motivated by the desire to not only posit but genuinely believe in a stable model of sign function. To Lyotard, semioticians have become "men of the concept," and their analyses are hopelessly myopic undertakings akin to a "voyage of conquest" or, even more vulgarly, a "business trip." Using two famous Edgar Allan Poe short stories as examples, Lyotard contends that contemporary semiotics (circa early 1970s) is concerned only with exercising power and control to the extent that it could be said to parallel the sign system of the reductive and mechanical story, "The Gold Bug," rather than the system of the "irrational" and open-ended story, "The Purloined Letter."

While *Économie libidinale* might appear to offer little constructive input for refining a future semiotics, the combative style that Lyotard actually thematizes offers the greatest potential benefit of his critique. In fact, the book received as much attention for its style as it did for its virulent attack on contemporary theory in general. Moreover, its ceaseless self-scrutiny and denial of its own epistemological capital radically dramatizes the very program Lyotard implicitly offers in the place of a staid and complacent semiotics that tends to favor the comfort of, for instance, a structuralistic paradigm. Years later, Lyotard described his agenda in *Économie libidinale* as an attempt to create a style of effects that would mirror the theoretical orientation that he was subverting at the same time (1988). Perhaps the closest parallels to this replication of content through form are Jacques Derrida's *Glas* (1974) and Roland Barthes's *S/Z* (1970).

For Lyotard, the zest with which structuralist methodologies level the atomistic movement of semiosis can unfortunately result in "the simple reduction of sensuous forms to conceptual structures" (1988). Marc Eli Blanchard (1979) notes that Lyotard attempts to utilize studies of sign systems as stepping-stones to a higher-level endeavor emphasizing intense sensation over the naive projection of rigid formalism.

In opposition to the "intelligent sign" of a more conservative (in several senses) mainstream semiotics, Lyotard proposes the "tensor sign" as a means of embodying a ceaselessly differentiated "incandescent vertigo" (1993, p. 60) that he considers a less nihilist but not necessarily positivist study of signs and sign systems. Lyotard views the pursuit of a rational semiosis as akin to the pedestrian desire to accumulate capital, an undertaking he views as hopelessly mired in a cynical false consciousness. Such a project seeks the essential and referential "information" un-

derlying the exchange of signs, which depends upon a static ground for semiosis and an acceptance of encoder "intention," as Alphonso Lingis notes (1980, p. 91). While semiotics pursues "intention rather than intensity," Lyotard proposes an orientation toward "intensity . . . dissimulated in signs and instances" (1993, p. 63).

In keeping with his abhorrence of the "terrorism" of contemporary theory, Lyotard refrains from presenting his alternative to a more pragmatic semiotics as itself in some way a viably utilitarian enterprise. He proposes a semiotics between radical subjectivism and an equally radical objectivism, one that seeks the thrilling instability that accompanies semiosis within the abyss of tension. In effect, Lyotard asserts, once this nonproject is undertaken, "we quit signs" and "we enter the extra-semiotic order of tensors." Lyotard rejects the notion of a methodology in and of itself through this gesture, preferring in its stead a procedure that constantly projects the sign in its dissimulation. This does not produce merely another kind of sign because such a program remains positioned beyond the easy dynamics of conventional semiotics. Semiosis thus becomes for Lyotard an "emotional event" inextricably bound up in the concept of "libidinal intensity."

But Lyotard does not yield to the "absentification" associated with endless nonreferentiality, "the zero of book-keeping" in which "there is nothing but signs" either. Like Umberto Eco, Lyotard refuses to accept an empty connotation of "infinite semiosis" and considers it instead as a process replete with limitless potential stimuli. And it is this intensity that offers the greatest future prospects for enlivening what Lyotard repeatedly portrays as an otherwise moribund semiotics.

Later in his career, Lyotard became increasingly apologetic about *Économie libidinale*, primarily because of its rhetorical excesses and its emphasis on a Nietzschean "nonmoral" semiotics. But it nonetheless stands as an important contribution to the later critique of semiotics insofar as it identifies substantial weak points in the theoretical investments that had not been troubled sufficiently up to that point and that are still being worked out in ongoing studies.

[*See also* Postmodernism; Semiosis; *and* Sign.]

BIBLIOGRAPHY

Blanchard, M. E. "Never Say Why?" Review of *Économie libidinale*. *Diacritics* 9.2 (1979): 17–29.

Lingis, A. "A New Philosophical Interpretation of the Libido." Review of *Économie libidinale*. *Sub-Stance* 25 (1980): 87–97.

Lyotard, J.-F. *The Postmodern Condition: A Report on Knowedge* (1979). Translated by G. Bennington and B. Massumi. Minneapolis: University of Minnesota Press, 1984.

Lyotard, J.-F. *Peregrinations: Law, Form, Event*. New York: Columbia University Press, 1988.

Lyotard, J.-F. *Libidinal Economy*. Translated by I. H. Grant. Bloomington: Indiana University Press, 1993.

Readings, B. *Introducing Lyotard: Art and Politics*. London: Routledge, 1991.

—SCOTT SIMPKINS

M

MANDALA. A circular design (Sanskrit, *maṇḍala* means "circle"), a mandala represents a symbolic matrix of the universe, often depicted as a complicated icon with many deities. Among the many definitions of *mandala* perhaps the most suggestive has been proposed by Giuseppe Tucci (1961), who called it a "psychocosmogram"—a graphic representation of the cosmos and the individual spirit of the ascetics. According to Yamasaki Taikō, "the esoteric *mandala* illustrates enlightenment, and so the true self. . . . [It] symbolically represents the 'universal form' of all things and beings" (1988). These definitions raise interesting problems: which are the codes of this representation? What is its underlying semiotic system? Usual psychoanalytic and iconographic approaches ignore these questions and fail to explain the epistemic nature of the relations connecting the esoteric cosmos with the mandala.

A mandala is basically a Buddhist sacred space where rituals and religious practices are performed. The model of this sacred space is the area surrounding the tree under which Śākyamuni (Siddhārta Gautama), the historical Buddha, attained Enlightenment. Pictorial and sculptural mandalas developed as representations of ritual platforms and spaces. Later, the ascetic's body and the everyday world purified through meditation also came to be recognized as mandalic spaces. The practice of mandala consists in manipulating signs in order to affect reality and to produce in the ascetic altered states of consciousness with a different perception of reality.

A mandala can take the form of an amulet or a talisman, protecting its owner from illness and misfortune; but it is used also as a summary of doctrines and practices for the memorization and the transmission of esoteric knowledge. As a systematic model of the cosmos, a mandala is a powerful device for absorbing heterogeneous elements, providing them with well-defined statuses within the Buddhist esoteric tradition. In the course of time, mandalic practices were projected onto geographical space, thus giving new meanings to pilgrimage and changing the use of space (Grapard, 1982). Furthermore, as an epitome of a certain knowledge, a mandala presupposes and represents multileveled political conceptions and structures of power.

Iconography in itself, even with its peculiar cultural references, is not sufficient to fully understand a mandala and its usages. In fact, every mandalic object is rooted in texts concerning cosmology and soteriology, in the knowledge of religious and ritual practices, and in social and political ideologies and systems of domination. As a structured set of various semiotic systems, a mandala is a device whose aim is to represent completely the doctrine of esoteric Buddhism and can be defined as a sort of semiotic encyclopedia. Since one of the most striking characteristics of a mandala is that it is designed to be all-encompassing, self-sufficient, and recursive, a mandala presupposes peculiar laws of organization, semiotic concepts, and semiotic practices yet to be studied in depth in order to understand esoteric Buddhism.

Externally, a mandala seems to be an abstract scheme made of arbitrary signs, although the exegetic tradition stresses their esoteric and ineffable meanings. But a historical (etymological) analysis shows that this is not the case (Edeline, ed., 1984). It is clear that all elements of a mandala are chosen in order to express a certain content. The form of the content determines the form of the expression. But it is the structure of reality itself that determines the expression, since the ascetic's meditative journey and its goal influence the choice of the signs with which they are represented (Rambelli, 1991).

The essential identity between expression and meaning in mandalic signs is a consequence of their both being considered as different epiphenomena of a single, nondual reality. In order to assure their efficacy, rituals and soteriologic practices are connected to their supports, to the spaces in which they take place, to the processes in which they are articulated. As a consequence, in the religious practice there is no clear-cut distinction between the "meaning" and the "power" of a mandala. The signs of Tantric Buddhism do not simply stand for a meaning or a possibility of action: they *are* that meaning or that action. Accordingly, expressions are not real signs: they become receptacles of knowledge or power spots where that knowledge is supposed to change into operational force.

Thus, on a certain level of consciousness, a mandala is not just a representation; the unconditioned reality is itself a mandala and the mandala is also the general shape of phenomena. Everything is meaningful, a figure in the picture of the universe. True reality is accessible not through a "reading" of phenomena—this metaphor never appears in esoteric texts—but through the visualization of a mandala, a microcosmic inscription of the soteriological process.

Within a mandala, ordinary language is subordinate to a plurality of systems of representation. In the Tantric tradition, in fact, written texts also tend to be mandalized and transformed into a salvational journey. While a long Western tradition compares the world with a book, Tantric Buddhism understands the universe as an immense mandala.

In the Tantric Buddhist episteme, the mandala seems thus to constitute the principal model and metaphor for interpreting reality, a primary modelling system of the cosmos and human experience. This hypothesis has been suggested by Giorgio Raimondo Cardona regarding the Tibetan mandala, an "expressive form" that "is not immediately translatable in the forms of language" (Cardona, 1988). The modeling nature of the mandala and its cultural impact need further analysis.

[*See also* Buddhism; Cultural Landscape; Mantra; Mindscape; *and* Space.]

BIBLIOGRAPHY

Cardona, G. R. *I sei lati del mondo*. Rome: Laterza, 1988.
Edeline, F., ed. "Herméneutique du mandala." *Cahiers internationaux de symbolisme* 48–50 (1984). Special issue devoted to the hermeneutics of the mandala.
Grapard, A. G. "Flying Mountains and Walkers of Emptiness: Toward a Definition of Sacred Space in Japanese Religions." *History of Religions* 21.3, (1982): 195–221.
Rambach, P. *The Secret Message of Tantric Buddhism*. Geneva and New York: Skira and Rizzoli International, 1979.
Rambelli, F. "Re-inscribing Mandala: Semiotic Operations on a Word and Its Object." *Studies in Central and East Asian Religions* 4 (1991): 1–24.
Tajima, R. *Les deux grands mandalas et la doctrine de l'ésotérisme shingon*. Tokyo and Paris: Maison Franco-Japonaise and Presses universitaires de France, 1959.
Tucci, G. *Theory and Practice of Mandala*. London: Rider, 1961.
Yamasaki T. *Shingon: Japanese Esoteric Buddhism*. Boston and London: Shambala, 1988.

—FABIO RAMBELLI

MANIPULATION. One of the two ways in which an organism might use or exploit the signaling system of another organism to its own ends, manipulation allows one animal to control through semiotic means the behavior of another animal to its own benefit. In "mind reading," the exploiter deciphers the mood or intentions of the targeted victim in order to anticipate its behavior and opportunistically take advantage of it. For example, a lion can guess that its potential prey will go down a certain gully. By contrast, if an anglerfish lures another fish into its mouth by wagging the wormlike flap of shiny skin that has evolved at the tip of its elongated dorsal fin, that is manipulation.

In manipulation, the exploiter sends out ambiguous information that deceives the victim and controls the victim's behavior in ways advantageous to the exploiter. "The most striking and best studied examples of this involve interspecific communication. Bee orchids, for example, present male bees with a supernormal stimulus of the female, and the male collects or transmits pollen while trying to copulate with the flower. . . . So effective is the flower's stimulus that bees of the genus *Andrena* presented with a choice of real females and flowers of *Ophrys litea* prefer to copulate with the latter!" (Hamilton and Zuk, 1982, p. 385).

Assuming that manipulation, like all forms of animal communication, is brought about by natural selection and that it must be of adaptive value to the exploiter (and never or only contingently of value to the victim), how might have it evolved? The key seems to lie in the other side of exploitation: mind reading. The ability of an animal to anticipate the behavior of another is an obvious advantage. However, in many circumstances having one's mind read can be of value to the victim also. If a predator can see that a potential victim is in a high state of alertness, it might then decide to seek other prey that is not so readied. Thus, bluffing can evolve as a powerful semiotic strategy in response to mind reading. If the victim can indeed give the impression of always being in a state of alertness, whether it is or not, then the potential victim is one step ahead of the potential exploiter and has become an exploiter itself. Here we have manipulation, for the former is now controlling the behavior of the latter to its own benefit. More generally, manipulation evolves when one animal or organism relies on the information-gathering adaptation of another and turns it to its own account.

There is much speculation about both manipulation and mind reading (e.g., Whiten and Byrne, 1988, 1997). That such sorts of things can occur and that the one can be built up out of the other was proved by the classic experiments of ethology, as for instance when gulls or sticklebacks were shown to be susceptible to certain specific stimuli, even overreacting when the stimuli were increased artificially. How precisely such things occur is another question, although since we have here a form of coevolution and since often the relationship between manipulator and mind reader is one of rival attempts at exploitation, our new understanding of the nature and importance of biological arms races is probably highly pertinent.

[*See also* Dawkins; Hamilton; Interspecific Communication; Zahavi; *and* Zoosemiotics.]

BIBLIOGRAPHY

Dawkins, R. *The Extended Phenotype: The Gene as the Unit of Selection.* Oxford: W. H. Freeman, 1982.

Dawkins, R. *The Blind Watchmaker.* London: Longman, 1986.

Hamilton, W. "Mate Choice Near or Far." *American Zoologist* 30.2 (1990): 341–352.

Hamilton, W. D., and M. Zuk. "Heritable True Fitness and Bright Birds: A Role for Parasites." *Science* 218 (1982): 384–387.

Krebs, J. R., and N. B. Davies, eds. *Behavioral Ecology: An Evolutionary Approach.* Sunderland, Mass.: Sinauer, 1978.

Krebs, J. R., and N. B. Davies, eds. *An Introduction to Behavioral Ecology.* Sunderland, Mass.: Sinauer, 1981.

Maynard Smith, J. *Evolution and the Theory of Games.* Cambridge: Cambridge University Press, 1982.

Maynard Smith, J. *Games, Sex and Evolution.* New York: Harvester Wheatsheaf, 1988.

Whiten, A., and R. W. Byrne. *Machiavellian Intelligence.* Cambridge: Cambridge University Press, 1988.

Whiten, A., and R. W. Byrne. *Machiavellian Intelligence II.* Cambridge: Cambridge University Press, 1997.

—MICHAEL RUSE

MANTRA. It is virtually impossible to give a simple and exhaustive definition of *mantra*: this Sanskrit term, loosely translated as "prayer" or "hymn," refers to an amazingly wide ambit of linguistic entities used in very different contexts, apparently sharing only an Indian matrix and the fact that they amount to a nonordinary usage of language. A mantra is essentially a sound or a sequence of sounds functioning as an evocator of energy. According to Indian Tantric doctrines, the vibrations constituting the universe manifest themselves as linguistic sounds, as "seed syllables" (*bīja*) that combine to form mantras. The most comprehensive definition remains the one proposed by Harvey Alper (1989): "a mantra is whatever anyone in a position to know calls a mantra."

The concept of mantra is attached closely to Indian culture, where it developed originally and in which it takes an exceptional importance. Such strong cultural characterization did not prevent mantras from spreading throughout Asia with Hinduism and Buddhism. Original Indian mantric doctrines interacted on many levels with the different cultures that they penetrated, also contributing to changes in their linguistic ideas. Mantras themselves, however, remained almost unchanged: their power rests in their sounds, and their pronunciations have been transliterated into numerous writing systems.

Scholarly debates concern mainly mantras' linguisticity—that is, whether mantras are language or not. Some scholars deny such a possibility; others explain mantras as speech acts, language games, or even as instruments of magic. In any case, all agree on the importance of the context—the actual situation in which mantras are used.

In Indian treatises, mantras never seem to take on the traits of a real independent language. The Tantric tradition, on the contrary, especially in East Asia, explicitly attributes to mantras the status of absolute language. Nevertheless, it is not easy to consider mantras as a form or a particular usage of language, conforming to linguistic rules. According to Frits Staal (1989), who thinks that meaning is an exclusive property of ordinary language used denotatively, mantras are pieces of texts that are basically devoid of meaning but that take on the function of ritual objects. Endowed with phonological and pragmatic properties but devoid of syntax and semantics, they do not conform to Western and (nonesoteric) Indian theories of language; therefore, they cannot be considered either linguistic entities or speech acts. For Staal, mantras are ritual elements, and mantric practice as a rite is a behavior defined by rules but lacking meaning and finalities, determined as it is by obscure biological constraints.

There is, however, an authoritative approach that is diametrically opposed to Staal's, according to which everything that is part of a culture must have a sense and be explicable and interpretable. An easy objection to such a position is that the listeners (including many officiants) of mantric expressions almost never understand their meaning. But one might consider, as, for instance, Ludwig Wittgenstein did, that the meaning of linguistic expressions is their use, and therefore it is not necessary to understand the meaning of an expression in order to use it correctly. In this regard, it is important to underline the fact that many esoteric mantric texts presuppose a model reader who is able to understand the meaning of mantras (see also Tambiah, 1968).

Considered from a phonic point of view, mantras are governed by a whole range of norms, transmitted from master to disciple, determining for each entity not only pronunciation, intonation, intensity of voice, rhythm, and melodic structure but also breathing, bodily posture, and appropriate ritual. These rules are such that Staal proposes to take into account "the importance of musical categories for explaining some of the characteristics that distinguish mantras from language." It appears, though, that music explains only one aspect of mantras.

It is not clear if there is a syntax of mantras. Staal denies such a possibility, while Donald Lopez and Stanley Tambiah are inclined to admit it. Certainly, Buddhist mantras constitute a repertoire of fixed expressions that has not changed for centuries. Perhaps a taxonomic, distributive, and componential study of mantric formulas could ascertain if structural and distributive permanencies correspond also to functional and semantic ones.

Mantric linguistic space in Tantric Buddhism is generally marked by formulas such as *om* at the beginning and *hūm* or *svāhā* at the end, between which are inserted linguistic "seeds" (*bīja*) of deities, invocations, and concepts more or less connected by a single theme. Mantras thus form a sort of "scrapbook language": a series of concepts juxtaposed or superimposed. Mantric syntax could then consist of a set of rules establishing a sacred linguistic space through the use of peculiar expressions, as well as an unspecified code associating by analogy a sequence of sounds to a meditative or salvational process, identifying them through the mediation of content. In this manner, it is possible to create new mantras on the basis of a set of doctrines, deities, and aims. In the case of East Asian mantric expressions, at least, each expression is endowed with a definite if complex meaning. But this does not necessarily establish their linguisticity. The denial of linguisticity does not affect their interpretability and therefore their functioning as a semiotic system.

Mantric expressions are not used in everyday communicational interaction; their ambit is one of ritual, meditation, and magic. Mantras are implements, on the one hand, for production, conservation, and transmission of a certain type of knowledge; on the other hand, they are created for the transformation of such knowledge into power over reality through illocutionary and perfomative acts. Tambiah (1968) has underlined this important fact in his studies on power formulas used in Thai Buddhism. The use of mantras is believed to determine precise effects, such as healing, worldly benefits, rebirth, and becoming Buddha. Accordingly, repetition (vocal or just mental) of mantras is not only a saying or a thinking but an actual activity aimed at transforming reality.

Some scholars have attempted to apply speech-act theory to mantric phenomena, but speech-act theory describes usages of ordinary language that have almost nothing in common with the recitation of mantras. However, an integral application of speech-act theory to the ritual usage of language in Buddhism must take into account phenomena not considered by John Austin's original theory: the existence of "transitive" speech acts whose effects are transferred to another person, as well as "graphological" acts or language acts that consist in the transcription of written formulas in order to "illocutionarily" change reality. Thus, it is possible and heuristically profitable to consider mantras as illocutionary expressions endowed with a particular perlocutionary function by a value investment (faith) by the utterer and, above all, by the structure of mantric expressions themselves, motivated signs in which signifier and signified, language and reality are closely related. According to Wade Wheelock's definition, mantric speech acts are "ritual" speech acts, presupposing a different idea of language that allows nonordinary linguistic practices (1982).

It is also necessary to take into account the writing of mantras. Initially, writing, in accordance with mainstream Buddhist ideas of language, was considered a mere device for conveying the meaning of Buddha's words. This attitude changed around the seventh or eighth century CE with the development of a systematic form of Tantric Buddhism for which the sound of esoteric expressions was no longer sufficient: rituals also needed the original graphemes. In China and especially in Japan, the characters of the Indian script called *siddham* were used in various ways. *Siddham* refers to a Gupta type of the Brāhmī writing system, used in India between the fourth and the eighth century CE and now extant only in Japan. In this manner, *siddham* became an important subject of study and practice for Buddhist monks. The East Asian esoteric tradition created practices integrating mantra recitation and *siddham* visualization. It is important to note that *siddham* characters, interpreted as iconic signs, were used as the "body" of the absolute language and therefore of the absolute reality of esoteric Buddhism.

The Chinese graphic system, in particular its most ancient characters, was considered not just a transcription of oral language but a system for the representation of reality, constituted by expressive forms in which sounds and scripts are in perfect harmony. In this way, *siddham* characters acquired the status of microcosms, of absolute entities, in accordance with their myths of origin. Esoteric sources, in fact, consider *siddham* as absolute, unconditioned, noncreated entities. Other sources describe them as spontaneous forms that originally manifested themselves in the sky. In such an absolutist conception of writing, the influence of Daoist elements are also discernible—for instance, the "heavenly talismans" (*tianfu*) and the "cloud seals" (*yunzhuan*). Perhaps in relation to such myths of the origin of mantric language, Staal suggests that mantras might be sorts of fossil vestiges of the process that led to the formation of ordinary language, fragments of the most ancient protolinguistic expressions, the "remnants of something that preceded language" (1989).

[*See also* Buddhism; Daoism; *and* Mandala.]

BIBLIOGRAPHY

Alper, H. P., ed. *Mantra.* Albany: State University of New York Press, 1989.

Bharati, A. *The Tantric Tradition.* London: Rider, 1965.

Gulik, R. H. van. *Siddham: An Essay on the History of Sanskrit Studies in China and Japan.* Sarasvati Vihara Series, vol. 36. Nagpur: International Academy of Indian Culture, 1956. This volume was reprinted as Sata-pitaka Series, vol. 247 (New Delhi: Mrs. Sharada Rani, 1980).

Lopez, D. S., Jr. "Inscribing the Bodhisattva's Speech: On the *Heart Sutra*'s Mantra." *History of Religions* 29.4 (1990): 359.

Padoux, A. *Vāc: The Concept of the Word in Selected Hindu Tantras.* Albany: State University of New York Press, 1990.

Rambelli, F. "Il gioco linguistico esoterico: Per una teoria del linguaggio del buddhismo giapponese 'shingon.' " *Versus: Quaderni di studi semiotici* 54 (1989): 69–96.

Staal, F. *Rules without Meaning: Ritual, Mantras, and the Human Science.* New York: Peter Lang, 1989.

Tambiah, S. J. "The Magical Power of Words" (1968). In his *Culture, Thought, and Social Action: An Anthropological Perspective*, pp. 17–59. Cambridge, Mass.: Harvard University Press, 1985.

Wheelock, W. "The Problem of Ritual Language: From Information to Situation." *Journal of the American Academy of Religion* 50 (1982): 49–71.

—FABIO RAMBELLI

MARKEDNESS. A mark is a distinguishing sign: to be marked is to be differentiated from a class of otherwise similar items by means of some token. The presence of a mark creates a binary opposition between the marked and the unmarked, establishing the unmarked as primary, original, and genuine, and the marked as secondary, derived, and deviant. The mark thus signifies aberration, anomaly, or exception: since the expectation is that trees will remain standing, for example, and that roads may be entered by traffic, the forester marks only those trees that are to be felled, and the traffic authorities mark only those road junctions where entry is forbidden, with a consequent saving both in signs and in strain upon the interpreters' attention.

Thus, markedness both constitutes and represents deviance: the marked signifier is formally deviant in terms of its unmarked counterpart, just as the marked signified includes deviance within its very signification. Markedness is manifested in the relation between signifiers as a supplement, deficiency, or differentiation in form, and in that between signifieds as a narrowing or specializing of application. But there are no rules where signifiers are concerned to distinguish the original from the derived: markedness is for this reason primarily a relation between signifieds that can be reflected a posteriori in the corresponding signifiers.

One of Ferdinand de Saussure's most fundamental premises was that linguistic structure at all levels is based upon binary oppositions, and since inflection and derivation (whether by affix, ablaut, or particle) are basic tools of all languages, markedness seems to be built into the very fabric of speech.

Unhappy is both morphologically and semantically a marked version of *happy*, as *authoress* is of *author*. In such pairs, the unmarked (nonderived) term tends to have a broader and more general signification than the marked one, in that it serves to denote not only one end of the scale or opposition but also the polarized quality itself. Thus, *How unhappy is she?* presupposes that she is unhappy, while *How happy is she?* presupposes only that she is alive; similarly, we may describe both Charles Dickens and Jane Austen as authors, but we can call only one of them an authoress. Since markedness is a relation between signifieds, it is determined by the functional rather than the merely formal association. *Youngster*, for example, is not semantically a marked version of *young*, yet *young* is a marked form of *old* when the terms refer to biological age: we ask (without presupposition) *How old are you, little boy?* just as we say (without incongruity) *The shortest jockey is only one meter tall*, or *The water's very shallow here, just twenty centimeters deep*. The formal marking in such cases consists in a replacement rather than a differentiation of the signifier, a process characterized by the grammatical term *suppletion*.

Because the semantic opposition of unmarkedness and markedness influences our perceptions of naturalness and deviance, it forms part of the tacit system through which ideology is inscribed in language. The marking of one gender in a pair of terms like *author* and *authoress*, for example, constitutes a silent privileging of the unmarked gender: part of the meaning of the unmarked term is therefore "this is the natural gender for this category of beings." Thus, most speakers of English, if asked to picture an author without further information or context, will visualize a man rather than a woman. There are, it is true, some three-gendered series in English—such as *horse* (*stallion*, *gelding*, and *mare*), *pig* (*boar*, *hog*, and *sow*), and *sheep* (*ram*, *wether*, and *ewe*)—in which no gender is privileged. Also, in the case of certain farmyard animals such as ducks (*drake* and *duck*), geese, (*gander* and *goose*), and cows (*bull* and *cow*) the feminine term is unmarked and thus focal, presumably because it is the productive capacities of the female (eggs and milk) that are of central interest to humans; something similar is true of occupations in which women have traditionally preponderated, as evidenced by the terms *nurse* and *prostitute*. In most gendered series, however, such as *dog* (*dog* and *bitch*), *lion* (*lion* and *lioness*), or, notoriously, *man* (*man* and *woman*) and *he* (*he* and *she*), the masculine is unmarked, reflecting a

deeper cultural marking of the feminine; to put it another way, there is a long-standing ideological commitment in Western culture to the centrality and primacy of the masculine, as seen in the history of the pair *man* and *woman* itself: *man* was in Old English equivalent to "human being" (cognate with *mind*, it originally meant something like "the creature that thinks"), and the sexes were distinguished as male *werman* (*wer* meaning "man," cognate with Latin *vir[ile]*) and female *wifman*. Clearly, it is the deeper cultural unmarkedness of the masculine that has caused the retention of marked *wifman* (as *woman*) but replaced *werman* with *man* as the specifically masculine term. Thus, the argument of linguistic conservatives that words such as *man* and *he* "include the feminine" and thus avoid gender bias misses the point: to identify the masculine with the natural or primary category must associate the feminine with deviance, deficiency, or excess. Given a class such as *poet*, for example, it is clear that a *poetess* (like a *poetaster*) cannot be quite the real thing, a suspicion confirmed by the fact that people associate the term more readily with Ella Wheeler Wilcox or Patience Strong than with Sappho or Sylvia Plath. Markedness might, of course, be a feature of the truly natural system of oppositions as well as of the merely naturalized: it is an amusing irony that in nature it is the genetically female, chromosomally XX, that is unmarked and the male, XY, that is marked.

The concept of markedness originated with the Prague School linguists, in particular Roman Jakobson (Andrews, 1990), but was lost sight of for much of this century in Anglo-American circles because the reigning school of empiricists (led by Leonard Bloomfield) had no conception that any feature of any language could be "natural." In reaction as they were against humanist attempts to shoehorn the grammar of English into the paradigms of Latin and faced professionally with the urgent task of describing the diverse and (for Europeans) exotic linguistic fauna of the Americas, for them all languages were arbitrary constructions, like board games. But since the work of Noam Chomsky began to focus attention on language as a unique human attribute rooted in the common psyche, it has become clear that some linguistic traits are indeed more natural than others, if only because they predominate around the globe. Take, for example, the case of nasal vowels (vowels that resonate in both oral and nasal cavities): while phonetic nasalization occurs incidentally in most speech (compare the nasalized variety of /i/ in *me* and *knee*—phonetically, [mĩ][nĩ]—to the nonnasalized /i/ of *pea* and *bee*), only a few languages, such as French and Polish, employ a phonological contrast between nasal and oral vowels, distinguishing pairs of words like *botté* (in boots) and *bonté* (goodness). Thus, although every known language has oral vowels, only some have nasal ones, and those that have both always have fewer nasal than oral ones: French has nine oral to only four nasal (and is losing one of those), Portuguese has eight to five, and Burmese seven to five. Nasal consonants are more widespread (perhaps universal), but they are always fewer than the nonnasal variety; one way of capturing these various facts is to say that the feature [+ nasal] is marked in all languages and the feature [− nasal] unmarked. Such universal features of language construction are not confined to phonology: although there are six logical combinations, for example, only three standard sequences for subject, verb, and object prevail throughout the world's languages: VSO (e.g., Amharic), SVO (English), and SOV (Turkish), which means that subject followed by object is the unmarked sequence for those categories in human language. Of course, linguistic universals of this kind are not observable from within a given language: to the native speaker of English, it is just as "natural" that the verb follows the subject as that the object does: *Then came still evening on* is thus no less a marked word order than *And the darkness He called night*. It is evident, incidentally, that there is a connection worth exploring between markedness theory and stylistics. Style is, in some sense, marked language use.

For post-Chomskyan linguists, concerned not merely to describe linguistic facts but to explain them in terms of the underlying system that produces them, markedness theory provides an important tool for assessing the descriptive economy and generality of linguistic descriptions. Given, for example, that in the rules of phonotactics or phonological word construction consonants are unmarked after vowels, vowels unmarked after consonants, affricates unmarked before front vowels, and so on, it is possible to show that rules of language change such as assimilation and palatalization are in fact more natural than their theoretically possible but rarely observed counterparts.

[*See also* Articulation; Distinctive Features; Language Change; *and* Pertinence.]

BIBLIOGRAPHY

Andrews, E. *Markedness Theory: The Union of Assymetry and Semiosis in Language*. Durham, N.C., and London: Duke University Press, 1990.

Battistella, E. *Markedness: The Evaluative Superstructure of Language*. Albany: State University of New York Press, 1990.

Chomsky, N., and M. Halle. *The Sound Pattern of English*. New York: Harper and Row, 1968.

Tobin, Y. *Semiotics and Linguistics*. London and New York: Longman, 1990.

—PETER GROVES

MARX, KARL (1818–1883), Prussian-born philosopher, journalist, editor, historian, and revolutionary. Marx lived in Prussia, France, Belgium, and England, spending most of his life as a political exile. In London, Marx earned a living as a foreign correspondent for newspapers in the United States and South Africa. Although largely ignored by intellectuals during his own lifetime, Marx's ideas gained rapid currency once they were adopted in 1889 by the Second International, the main institutional forum of the world socialist movement.

Under the early influence of the romantic idealist rationalism of G. W. F. Hegel, Marx believed in a progressive dialectic that would lead society via apocalyptic historical shifts toward a better, more rational world order. However, Marx developed a materialist interpretation of Hegel's dialectic. Whereas Hegel saw dialectical progress as being driven by a subjective "spirit," Marx sought to despiritualize the dialectic. Marx, in effect, developed Marxism as a consequence of his critique of Hegelian philosophy. Marx claimed to have put Hegel "back on his feet" by replacing Hegel's subjective spirit with the notion of objective "relations of production." For Marx, it was the dialectics of material conditions that drove history forward. Marx's materialist conception of history was spelled out in *The German Ideology* (1846).

The Marxist explanation of society shows the influence of the positivist spirit of his times as well as an enthusiasm for empirical "scientific" structuralist explanations of natural and social phenomena. The particular structuralism he developed was that of historical materialism, most clearly expounded in *Capital* (1867). At one level, both Marxism and semiotics share common epistemological roots insofar as both seek to understand human beings via a structuralist mode of thinking. But whereas semiotics searches for subjective structures of meaning, Marx was concerned with the impact that objective economic structures had on social interaction. Class—as the preeminent economic structure—is the primary conceptual building block upon which the Marxist structural view of the world rests.

A central facet of historical materialism is that social change is explained in terms of the way in which different socioeconomic arrangements or modes of production either impede or further "progress." Like other positivist explanations, Marx's theory is a teleological one; human progress is assumed. When a mode of production becomes an impediment to further growth, it will generate a revolution and be overthrown. This occurs because human behavior is determined or structured by the economic relations of production prevailing within the epoch. This materialist determinism is expressed in the notion that the superstructures (the subjective; knowledge; modes of thought) are determined by the base (objective conditions or economic relations of production). This reductionist view considers consciousness and communication derivative of class position. However, during the twentieth century, many Western Marxists (e.g., Valentin Voloshinov, Louis Althusser, Jürgen Habermas) have tried to distance Marxism from this simplistic view.

The methodology that Marx developed has significance for communication theory because of the centrality of the notion of ideology. The key assumption underpinning Marx's methodology is that "reality" exists. At any point in time, Marx maintains, a given constituted world of material phenomena exists "out there." Historical eras are thus marked one from another by the way in which these material phenomena are structured within a particular reality. Human beings live within this material world. However, if human beings are constituted or structured by their material world, they in turn play a role in constituting it. In other words, Marx, especially in earlier work such as the *Economic and Philosophical Manuscripts* (1844), does not discount the role that active human beings and human subjectivity play in structuring the human world.

And yet, for Marx, reality is also masked. Marx's entire theory of ideology is premised upon an understanding of a hidden or disguised reality. The reality of the world as Marx saw it is that capitalists materially exploit the proletariate or workers. Furthermore, capital is unable to solve its internal contradiction. Thus, to keep the socioeconomic system operating in their favor, the capitalist ruling elite has to disguise what they do: the social contradictions of capitalism have to be concealed. When the elite is successful, the exploited live in a state of "false consciousness" in which they do not recognize their own exploitation. For Marx, ideology is not illusion; rather, it reflects material contradictions in the real world. The Marxist method is a "scientific" approach for exposing the "truth" or "reality" by getting "beneath" what is apparent. Marxism is therefore seen as a science of discovering truth or for deideologizing the world. Marxists see their task as explaining this truth to the workers. Marx thought that such "scientific" knowledge would lead the workers to rise up and overthrow the exploitative relations of production through revolution. Ideology cannot therefore be ended by criticism or discussion or the Hegelian spirit; rather, ideology only disappears when the material contradictions of capital are resolved. The ends of ideology and alienation are, in consequence, bound up with a Marxist revolutionary program for changing society.

The Marxist method has undergone considerable developments, refinements, and mutations since Marx's original formulation through the work of Antonio Gramsci, György Lukács, the Frankfurt School, and Louis Althusser and was a factor in the development of communication studies. Since Althusser's intervention in the 1970s, Marxist views on ideology have, for example, become entangled with structuralism and semiotics. Althusser's attempts to rethink Marxism can ultimately be seen to have contributed significantly to the growth of poststructuralism.

By the middle of the twentieth century, Marxism was one of the central "grand narratives," to use Jean-François Lyotard's terminology, that was used to both explain and order human life. However, many of Marx's explanations and predictions about the course of human history failed to materialize. Hence, from the 1970s onward a "collapse of the Marxist dream" set in—a collapse that first manifested itself in western European communist parties and then spread to eastern Europe during the 1980s. But despite this political collapse of Marxism, the value of Marx's ideas as a theoretical tool cannot be discounted. His stress on the economic factors in society has proved enormously useful as an analytic tool across the humanities and social sciences. The usefulness of Marx's method is far from spent, especially in its mutated forms. Significantly, the most creative contemporary adaptions to the Marxist method have been formulated by theorists concerned with the phenomenon of communication. Both Jürgen Habermas and Stuart Hall have, for example, undertaken a "reconstruction" of historical materialism because of their "Marxist" concern with communication and culture. The result is that Marx's ideas have reemerged in the mutated form of critical theory and cultural studies to influence late-twentieth-century communication studies.

[*See also* Althusser; Habermas; Materialist Semiotics; *and* Rossi-Landi.]

BIBLIOGRAPHY

Gouldner, A. *The Two Marxisms*. London: Macmillan, 1980.
Hall, S. "Rethinking the 'Base and Superstructure' Metaphore." In *Papers on Class, Hegemony, and Party: The Communist University of London*, edited by J. Bloomfield. London: Lawrence and Wishart, 1977.
Kolakowski, L. *Main Currents of Marxism*. Oxford and New York: Oxford University Press, 1981.
Korsch, K. *Marxism and Philosophy*. New York: Monthly Review Press, 1970.
Larrain, J. *The Concept of Ideology*. London: Hutchinson, 1979.
McLellan, D. *Karl Marx: His Life and Thought*. London: Paladin, 1976.
Sayer, D. *Marx's Method*. Sussex: Harvester Press, 1979.
Williams, R. *Marxism and Literature*. Oxford and New York: Oxford University Press, 1977.

—ERIC LOUW

MASS COMMUNICATION. Produced and distributed by the mass media for the explicit purposes of entertainment and information, mass communication can be technologically reproduced in quantities that are limited only by economic expediency. The mass media are channels of communication located at the institutional and corporate levels of society that use large-scale high-technology methods to supply standardized communication products to widespread heterogeneous audiences. Material usually considered to be mass communication includes newspapers, magazines, radio, television, cinema; popular fiction, and music. The aim of mass-communication theory and analysis is to examine the interactions of the various elements of the communication process—sender, receiver, message, medium, and context—in the production and consumption of mass communication.

The invention of the printing press in the fifteenth century, of photography, audio recording, and motion pictures in the nineteenth century, and of radio and television broadcasting in the twentieth century provided the basic technology of mass communication. Until the introduction of television in the 1930s (in America) and 1940s (in Britain), the print media were the dominant channels of large-scale communication, with the first newspapers in English appearing in the late seventeenth century followed by mass-circulation papers produced by steam-driven presses in the early nineteenth century.

Developments in technology during the twentieth century have lowered the cost of communication hardware and products, which has facilitated the growth of the mass media and their audiences. New inventions have also widened the scope of mass communication and encouraged the growth of global markets and international audiences. Technology is a major prerequisite for the development of the mass media and its products, but there are two other factors that media theorists regard as important: industrialization and a capitalist economic system. Industrialization has created a large urban workforce, skilled and unskilled, with sufficient leisure time and disposable income to become the consumers of mass communication. Capitalism has provided an economic context for the growth of large, privately owned communication organizations, with the facilities to produce and distribute standardized products to a wide, heterogeneous, and often multinational audience. Capitalism has also facilitated the growth of advertising as a crucial form of revenue to support the mass media.

Since mass communication is materially related to the social structure that produces it, the main concern of mass-communication theory and analysis is the relationship between society and mass-media "texts"—newspapers, television programs, films, and so on—and between the institutions and products of the mass media and the economic and social conditions that give them meaning. This concern with the interface between communication and society developed in relation to other theories of society, texts, and culture. From their beginnings in the 1930s, mass-communication studies have been shaped by two major political and philosophical perspectives: liberal empiricism and Marxism, both grounded in theories of social and economic organization. The first generation of mass-communication theorists, who held sway from the 1930s to the 1960s, interpreted the relationship between mass communication and society as a potentially negative and harmful one for the consumer. This position was based on the sociological theory of mass society prevalent in the 1920s and 1930s that understood *mass* in terms of an uneducated and oppressed proletariat or underclass of workers in industrialized capitalist societies. Both liberal empiricists and Marxists saw the mass media as a significant factor contributing to the oppression of the masses.

The liberal-empiricist approach is primarily media centered in that it begins with studies of the nature and function of the mass media and emphasizes the role of mass communication in bringing about social change. The liberal-empiricist position rested on the philosophical principles of individualism expounded by John Stuart Mill, Matthew Arnold, and others and treated mass communication as part of a modern industrial culture built on the desire for wealth and power. Such a society betrays the needs and aspirations of the individual, whose only hope is to turn to the "great tradition" of literature.

Early British critics such as Frank Raymond Leavis and Denys Thompson (1933) and Queenie Dorothy Leavis (*Fiction and the Reading Public*, 1932) privileged the language and content of "literary" texts over those of mass-communication forms such as advertisements and popular novels in order to argue that the latter deprived consumers of access to "real" experience and creative insights. Literature was anticommercial and offered meaningful and important experiences, while mass communication was driven by commercialism and the desire to sell shallow fantasies and emotions.

In America, empirical studies came to dominate media theory, especially after the spread of television, and they are still an important aspect of American communication research. Extensive statistical studies, based on quantitative sources of social-science research such as audience-survey data, were used to assess the impact—mainly negative—of mass communication on cultural standards and values, notably in the area of violence on television. Paul Lazarsfeld (1948; see also Lazarsfeld et al., 1944) and Wilbur Schramm (1964) in particular documented the social

effects of the mass media through numerical studies while emphasizing the ultimate power of individuals to resist the manipulative strategies of the media. Detailed empirical analyses of the strength of the media in imposing change and determining social structures were also carried out by Harold Innis (1951) and Marshall McLuhan (*The Gutenberg Galaxy*, 1962; *Understanding Media*, 1964).

The Marxist approach to mass society is less concerned with the need to protect or retrieve individualism and more concerned with social and political oppression. Marxist communication theorists see mass communication as a powerful weapon wielded by the dominant class and argue that the mass media work on behalf of this dominant capitalist class to keep the masses docile and uncritical. The proletariat accept their role in society because it is endorsed for them by the mass media.

This view of mass communication was disseminated in particular by the Frankfurt School of theorists, originally located at the Frankfurt Institute for Social Research in the 1920s and subsequently in America on account of World War II. Its major theorists were Theodor Adorno and Max Horkheimer (1986), Herbert Marcuse (*One Dimensional Man*, 1964), and Walter Benjamin (1968). The Frankfurt School interpreted commercialized mass culture as the means by which capitalism is sold to the very classes that fail to gain from a capitalist economy. Mass communication, as part of a mass culture, is one of the key methods by which ruling-class ideology dominates the working class and inhibits social change. The Marxist approach is therefore society centered in that it views the mass media as part of a social and economic construct in which the function of the media is to disseminate a view of the world, or an ideological perspective that serves the interests of the ruling class. Raymond Williams (1958, 1962) was among the first critics to establish a Marxist approach to mass communication in Great Britain.

The era of growth in mass-communication products and technology—the last quarter of the twentieth century—has coincided with the development of new theoretical approaches to the concept of signification. The work of the French structuralists and their successors during the late 1960s and early 1970s challenged the liberal-empiricist concept of meaning as direct and unmediated and emphasized the working of ideology and the social construction of meaning in all areas of communication. In this line, the most influential theorists for communication studies have been Roland Barthes (*Elements of Semiology*, 1967; *Mythologies*, 1972) and Umberto Eco (*A Theory of Semiotics*, 1976), who explore and foreground the interface between message and society in mass communication. Their work has led to the development of more message-centered studies that draw on linguistic and semiotic theory to account for the cultural construction and mediation of media texts.

Message-centered and society-centered research form the basis of a "cultural" approach to mass-communication studies that developed during the later 1970s and 1980s. This approach embraces all forms of popular culture, including the output of the mass media, and examines and explains the function and significance of popular culture in relation to specific social groups, such as those defined by age, class, and ethnic origin. Cultural-studies theory draws on both liberal-empiricist and Marxist concepts of social and economic organization and uses feminist, linguistic, and semiotic theory to describe the production and consumption of popular culture.

The early impetus for a cultural approach to mass communication came from the work of Richard Hoggart, who was the founding director of the Centre for Contemporary Cultural Studies at the University of Birmingham from 1964 to 1968. His book, *The Uses of Literacy* (1957), analyzes the effect of popular culture in reshaping "traditional" working-class culture in Britain and affirms the power of the individual to resist manipulation by the mass media. Hoggart's work is a valuable study of a cultural group and its practices, based on an essentially liberal-empiricist theoretical position that saw the media acting as a "trigger" that directly influenced behavior. This position has become associated with the contemporary schools of behavioral psychology and linguistics, which look for direct causal connections between external stimuli and individual behavior.

After 1968, the Birmingham School of cultural theorists began to establish itself as an influential group of both liberal empiricists and Marxists under the leadership of Stuart Hall (1976). In the wake of structuralist and semiotic theory, the school broke away from the "direct-influence" and stimulus-response models of earlier media theory and moved toward a concern with the ideological role of the media and the relationship between the "encoded" media text and the audience's "decoding" of its message.

Research into the nature and function of televi-sion has been influenced strongly by the Birmingham School. The first British studies of television emanated mainly from that school in the 1970s and took up the American concern with media violence from the point of view of signification and the ideological role of televised violence. The main focus of television research, however, has been on the construction of news and current-affairs broadcasting, work pioneered by the Glasgow University Media Group (*Bad News*, 1976; and subsequent volumes). This group collected extensive empirical data in order to argue that the selection of news items, like any form of cultural selection, has ideological significance and that news programs, far from being neutral or objective, work to disseminate a consensual and mainstream ideology.

News reporting through the medium of print has also been a focus for both society-centered and message-centered cultural studies. An early collection of articles edited by Stanley Cohen and Jock Young (1973) drew attention to the social processes underlying the selection and creation of news in the British press. More recent studies of news reports as socially produced means of communication have been carried out by John Hartley (1982), Teun van Dijk (1988), and Roger Fowler (1991), all of whom draw on Michael Halliday's linguistics, discourse analysis, and semiotics to describe the language of news in terms of discourse and ideology.

Advertising has attracted a range of studies, both economic and interpretive. Economics and marketing textbooks in Britain and North America have promoted advertising as a marketing strategy that makes use of the mass media and can be targeted toward particular media outlets. At the same time, liberal-empiricist research in America has examined advertising itself as a powerful and highly manipulative form of mass communication, a view first put forward by Vance Packard in a famous study (1957) and later by Eric Clark (*The Wantmakers*, 1988). As with other types of mass communication, recent research has taken a cultural approach to advertising. The society-centered method of using empirical data to describe ideological function has been adopted by Fred Inglis (1990), while a message-centered approach to advertising as a social and semiotic process has been taken by Judith Williamson (1978) and Gillian Dyer (1982).

The study of film, more than that of any other kind of mass communication, has tended to emphasize the aesthetic quality of the medium itself as the most significant part of the communication process. Early film theory of the 1960s located itself between literary criticism and fine arts and regarded film as a type of drama. The auteur theory developed at that time privileges the work of a small number of individual directors, just as individual authors are similarly privileged within the liberal tradition of literary criticism.

The new theoretical perspectives opened up by the work of Claude Lévi-Strauss, Roland Barthes, and Umberto Eco have enabled the study of film as a type of sign system. Like those of television, film studies have moved from a basically liberal-empiricist approach to a message-centered cultural-studies approach. Film theorists became concerned with the processes of signification encoded in film, the concept of a "mediated transfer" of meaning from sender to receiver, and the independence of filmic signs from their "real" referents. Seen as a sign system, the cinema can provide a model of reality but can never reveal actual experience, a theoretical position that undermines claims by earlier theorists that the cinema occupies a uniquely intimate relationship with the real world of experience and is therefore a superior form of art.

The dominant film theory of the 1970s drew strongly on the psychoanalytic writings of Jacques Lacan in order to account for the ways in which individuals become social subjects. Since film texts literally "show" a version of reality to audiences, film theory tries to describe how the viewer is located in relation to filmic reality, a process that depends on the Lacanian concept of the subject and its interpellation in specific discourses. Language, representation, and ideology all operate at the level of the subject, which is therefore the main focus of inquiry, and film texts are analyzed in terms of their capacities to construct subject positions for viewers. Psychoanalytic theory of film has been influenced extensively by the French school of cultural theorists, particularly Julia Kristeva, Michel Foucault, the *Tel Quel* group, Louis Althusser, and Lacan. It also draws on feminist theory, which suggests ways in which the constructed subject is "gendered" within the text. The later work of the French cinema theorist Christian Metz (*Psychoanalysis and Cinema*, 1977) has been influential, and the French journals *Cahiers du cinéma* and *Cinétique* have provided forums for the development and debate of various theoretical positions.

Psychoanalytic theory has been both promoted and challenged by a number of British critics, mainly through the journals *Screen* and *Screen Education*. Stuart Hall and others (*Culture, Media, Language*, 1980) have offered a more society-centered film theory that argues for the importance of the social and economic context in determining ideology and subject position. There is also a growing interest in analyzing the narrative of film as *écriture* (the work of writing), a project that uses structuralist and semiotic analysis of film texts to show how meanings are constructed by the codes operating in film discourse. Such work is influenced strongly by Barthes, Mikhail Bakhtin, and the *Tel Quel* group and is represented by critics such as Stephen Heath, Raymond Bellour, and others.

Popular fiction as a form of mass communication has received increased attention during the last two decades. Historical studies have charted the growth of popular fiction during the nineteenth century and located it as part of the novel tradition. Studies of modern popular fiction, especially the genres of romance, crime novel, and science fiction generally take a cultural-studies approach in exploring the mediations between text and society, while more text-based studies analyze narrative structures by drawing on linguistic and semiotic theory. Feminist theory has been particularly influential in the area of popular romance, where recent studies have focused on the function of this literature in perpetuating social constructs of femininity.

Because of the dominance of the cultural approach, there has been a tendency in the late 1980s and early 1990s to replace the term *mass communication* with the term *popular culture*, indicating the shift from empirical studies to studies of cultural forms and meanings. Areas of research have moved to reception and audience theory and to new kinds of mass communication, including rock-music videos, soap operas, satellite broadcasting, computer games, and the Internet. While some research, particularly in North America, continues to focus on media-centered issues, especially the links between mass communication and social behavior, the dominant trend in mass-communication research is toward a general theory of popular culture that includes media studies. The most recent work explores the interface between message and society through message-centered or society-centered studies that draw on the cultural theories of a number of disciplines, including sociology, economics, history, feminism, linguistics, and semiotics.

[*See also* Barthes, Baudrillard; Cinema; Communication; Cultural Difference; Film Semiotics; Lacan; Materialist Semiotics; Metz; *and* Text.]

BIBLIOGRAPHY

Adorno, T., and M. Horkheimer. *Dialectic of Enlightment.* Translated by J. Cumming. London: Verso, 1986.

Andrew, D. *Concepts in Film Theory.* Oxford: Oxford University Press, 1984.

Benjamin, W. *Illuminations: Essays and Reflections.* Edited by H. Arendt, translated by H. Zohn. New York: Schocken Books, 1968.

Cohen, S., and J. Young, eds. *The Manufacture of News: Deviance, Social Problems, and the Mass Media.* 2d rev. ed. London: Constable, 1981.

Dyer, G. *Advertizing as Communications.* New York: Methuen, 1982.

Fiske, J. *Introduction to Communication Studies.* London: Methuen, 1982.

Fowler, R. *Language in the News.* London: Routledge, 1991.

Hall, S. *Resistance through Rituals: Youth Sub-cultures in Postwar Britain.* London: Hutchinson, 1976.

Hartley, J. *Understanding News.* London: Methuen, 1982.

Hoggart, R. *The Uses of Literacy.* London: Chatto and Windus, 1957.

Inglis, F. *Media Theory: An Introduction.* Oxford: Basil Blackwell, 1990.

Innis, H. *The Bias of Communication.* Toronto: University of Toronto Press, 1951.

Lazarsfeld, P. *Communications Research.* New York: Harper, 1948.

Lazarsfeld, P., B. Berelson, and H. Gaudet. *The People's Choice: How the Voter Makes up His Mind in a Presidential Campaign.* New York: Duell, Sloan, and Pearce, 1944.

Leavis, F. R., and D. Thompson. *Culture and Environment: The Training of Critical Awareness.* London: Chatto and Windus, 1933.

McQuail, D. *Mass Communication Theory.* London: Sage Publications, 1983, 1994.

Morley, D. *Television, Audience, and Cultural Studies.* London: Routledge, 1992.

Packard, V. *The Hidden Persuaders.* New York: D. McKay, 1957.

Schramm, W. *Mass Media and National Development: The Role of Information in Developing Countries.* Stanford: Stanford University Press, 1964.

Van Dijk, T. *News as Discourse.* Hillsdale, N.J.: Lawrence Erlbaum, 1988.

Williams, R. *Culture and Society 1780–1950.* London: Chatto and Windus, 1958.

Williams, R. *Communications* (1962). London: Chatto and Windus, 1966.

Williamson, J. *Decoding Advertisements.* London: Boyars, 1978.
—HELEN FULTON

MATERIALIST SEMIOTICS. Inspired mainly by Karl Marx's philosophy, materialist semiotics comprises a set of theoretical approaches to signs production and communication. The Marxist emphasis on material conditions stands in contrast to those semiotic approaches concerned with "apparently" intangible structures that cannot be observed directly such as language and consciousness, and tend to construct formalistic abstractions for which historical contexts are irrelevant. Orthodox Marxists criticize such work as idealist, ahistorical, and subjectivist. By contrast, materialist semiotics insists on putting socioeconomic contexts back into the picture. Signs and codes are not seen as standing outside of time, place, and socioeconomic relationships. Rather, materialist semioticians explicitly examine the ways in which sign systems and socioeconomic systems interpenetrate and influence each other.

Marxist studies of communication, and by extension materialist semiotics, make the relationship between text and context explicit. Within the American pragmatic tradition, the Peircean model of semiosis implies that the historical context of a community is instrumental in molding the milieu within which social discourse takes place, although exponents of materialist semiotics seem to have paid little explicit attention to Charles Sanders Peirce's work. But Valentin Voloshinov appears to have been aware of Peircean pragmatism, and Ferruccio Rossi-Landi showed an early interest in the work of Charles Morris, a disciple of Peirce.

Voloshinov was part of the Leningrad School of Soviet semioticians, which formed around Mikhail Bakhtin during the late 1920s and early 1930s. There is some disagreement over whether Voloshinov was in fact a mask used by Bakhtin in publicizing work he believed would be unacceptable to the Stalinists. At any rate, Voloshinov disappeared during the purges of the 1930s, and his work was consigned to oblivion in Soviet academic circles. Voloshinov attempted to merge the semiotic concern with subjective structures and the Marxist concern with historical materialism's objective structures. He developed an approach to semiosis premised upon a subject-object totality. Although Voloshinov's concern was with language and subjectivity, he managed to stay clear of subjectivism, in which the "material" is forgotten. Voloshinov's approach shares with the wider materialist tradition a rejection of methodologies that claim the existence of purely autonomous subjectivities. His study of language sees signs as the sites where subjects and objects meet or interpenetrate each other. So the sign is where the social world and the psyche (consciousness and the subjective) intersect, but the sign is also objective. Hence, for Voloshinov, semiotics becomes a site from which to study the subjective from a materialist perspective. Through studying the sign, it becomes possible to initiate a materialist study of ideology. Voloshinov's semiotics does not locate ideology purely in consciousness, nor does he define ideology as the mere subjective reflection of the economic base. Rather, ideology is interpreted as the way in which society enters the mind through signs within a particular context. Voloshinov's understanding of "ideology as semiosis" is historically and materially grounded. It is a neo-Marxist semiotics: consequently, it is not a semiotics that seeks universals but one that investigates the context-bound nature of semiosis.

This is a significant modification of the traditional Marxist understanding of ideology because, for Voloshinov, language communities do not coincide with class categories. There is no Marxist reductionism in terms of which language and sign systems in general are comprehended in only one-on-one relationships with class. Rather, different classes use the same language or sign system. Hence, language and signs become sites of struggle. In this sense, signs and meaning are dynamic and may even be contradictory. Voloshinov builds the notion of dialectic into his understanding of sign systems, but it is not a materially driven dialectic in the strictly Marxist sense. For Voloshinov, class struggle does not determine language use, as it does in the orthodox Marxist concept of ideology; instead, class struggle takes place within a shared sign system used by a single community of users. In fact, the sign itself becomes a site of class struggle. Social contradictions can manifest themselves in sign systems as surely as they can in the economic system.

Voloshinov's semiotics, then, unlike Saussurean semiology, is a dialectical structuralism that is concerned with both material and subjective structures: there can be no generalized "given" sign. Rather, each sign is historically and materially conditioned and actively "struggled over" within the totality of its social context. The sign dialectically "connects" the "interface" of the subject-object totality—the individual psyche and the social context—within class struggle. Ideology is seen to emerge within this dialectical totality of subject and object. Voloshinov, however, recognizes that the "dominant ideology" as a sign system in a given context will try to stabilize itself, though he allows space for active human minds and praxis within his nondeterministic subject-object structuralism. Human beings are seen as active cocreators of meaning as they use, make, modify, and struggle over signs.

There is an alternative, more orthodox, Marxist conception of language and semiosis to the one formulated by Voloshinov. In this rival approach, a direct relationship is drawn between language and other sign systems and class-based ideology, and language becomes a means of class rule in which reality is disguised. This approach is derived ultimately from György Lukács's notions of reification and alienation as developed in *History and Class Consciousness* (1971). For Lukács, capitalism has destroyed the subject-object "totality" of a humanized world. Under capitalism, people (subjects) can be treated as things or commodities—that is, they are "objectified." The result is alienation. Thus, Marxist semiotics derived from the Lukácian view of ideology is concerned with subjective "linguistic alienation."

A key exponent of this form of Marxist semiotics has been Ferruccio Rossi-Landi, for whom humans are social beings and hence need to exchange ideas and actions via signs within code systems. The control of sign systems translates into the control of people. For Rossi-Landi, capitalists control economic relations of production and thus control linguistic exchange and sign systems. Capitalism therefore affects how and what humans are able to communicate. The result of capitalism is a curtailed linguistic exchange that results in linguistic alienation. In developing his theory of exchange within sign systems, Rossi-Landi developed numerous concepts that have enriched materialist semiotics, such as "linguistic work," "linguistic tools," and "linguistic capital."

Both Rossi-Landi's and Lukács's concepts of communication, however, ultimately face the limitations of the orthodox Marxist conception of ideology in which the economic base is seen to determine the subjective superstructure. Both assume that a direct correlation can be drawn between economic exchange and the exchange of signs within language structures. It is a somewhat problematic assumption that Marx's methodology can be shifted in this way, but this idea that Marx's method of analyzing material structures can simply be transferred into a means for analyzing language structures also bears some resemblance to the premises underpinning Louis Althusser's work.

The key break that Althusser initiated within Marxism came in his effective destruction of the traditional historical-materialist model of base and superstructure (object and subject). As with Voloshinov's construct, there is no one-on-one relationship between class and language in the Althusserian model. For Marx, the economic structure was the center; it determined other structures. Similarly, in his structuralism, Althusser specifically detaches ideological state apparatuses (ISAs) from the economic base. ISAs become "autonomous" within a complex reality. Within this model, human thought or consciousness can be formed independent of given economic conditions, purely as a result of the interpellation of people into subjective structures. The Althusserian structural model argues that at any historical conjuncture there will be multiple and complex interrelationships and causations. Althusser used the term *overdetermined* to describe this complex structural reality. Althusser's structuralism is premised upon a decentered hierarchy of practices within which one of the structures is dominant at any particular point in time. Theoretically, a subjective structure could even be dominant at some point. This possibility represents a radical departure from the original Marxist model.

The Althusserian approach to materialist semiosis differs significantly from the Voloshinovian approach precisely because of the implications of the notion of "decenteredness" and because of the granting of autonomy to subjective structures. In fact, the Althusserian approach can be seen as no longer strictly materialist. By detaching subjective structures (ISAs, language) from material structures, Althusser effectively moved into the realm of free-floating subjectivities and thereby opened the door to what Marx had objected to about philosophy—namely, its subjectivism and idealism. Ironically Althusser's philosophy is a subjectivism without an active human subject. By ignoring the humanist strand and the subject-object dialectic within Marxism, Althusser merely succeeded in transforming the most reductionist aspects of Marxism's materialist determinism into a subjectivist determinism. He collapsed ideology as false consciousness into determining subjective structures.

In this respect, there is a parallel between Althusser's work and Roland Barthes's Marxist phase.

Barthes fused a Maoist interpretation of Marxism with a Saussurean semiology to produce a social critique that rested upon the decoding of meanings. Barthes and the *Tel Quel* group sought to strip away the myths of bourgeois life by applying a structuralist methodology to the texts and intertextuality of their society. Ultimately, however, Barthes and the *Tel Quel* group drifted into the production of subjectivist semantic games or metalanguages that were divorced from considerations of the historical material context.

Althusser's work, on the other hand, attempted to deal with the methodological crisis of Marxism. But Althusser's "solution" to this crisis proved to be no solution at all. In fact, his work seems to have accelerated the collapse of the Marxist dream. However, even if Althusser failed to save Marxism, he unintentionally enriched the debate about structuralism, as Althusserian structuralism melted into post-Althusserianism, poststructuralism, and deconstruction. Materialist semiotics has, however, resurfaced in the expanding field of cultural studies, which includes among its models Althusser's and Voloshinov's reformulations of structuralism, Antonio Gramsci's notion of hegemony, and Raymond Williams's culturalism. The resultant concern with an active human subjectivity within a material context has meant that cultural studies has developed a specific interpretation of materialist semiosis in which to undertake a humanist rereading of structuralism.

[*See also* Althusser; Marx; Mass Communication; *and* Rossi-Landi.]

BIBLIOGRAPHY

Benton, T. *The Rise and Fall of Structural Marxism.* London: Macmillan, 1984.

Coward, R., and J. Ellis. *Language and Materialism: Developments in Semiology and the Theory of the Subject.* London: Routledge and Kegan Paul, 1977.

Fiske, J. "British Cultural Studies and Television." In *Channels of Discourse*, edited by R. Allen, pp. 254–289. Chapel Hill: University of North Carolina Press, 1987.

Gramsci, A. *Selections from Prison Notebooks.* London: Lawrence and Wishart, 1971.

Lukács, G. *History and Class Consciousness.* London: Merlin, 1971.

Rossi-Landi, F. "Ideas for the Study of Linguistic Alienation." *Social Praxis* 3.1–2 (1976): 77–92.

Rossi-Landi, F. "Introduction to Semiosis and Social Reproduction." *Working Papers of Centro Internazionale di Semiotica e Linguistica* 63, series C. Urbino: University of Urbino, 1977.

Voloshinov, V. *Marxism and the Philosophy of Language*. New York: Seminar Press, 1973.

Williams, R. *Culture and Society*. Harmondsworth, England: Penguin, 1961.

Williams, R. *The Long Revolution*. Harmondsworth, England: Penguin, 1965.

—ERIC LOUW

MEANING. A problematic concept that stands at the center of semiotic inquiry, up to the nineteenth century meaning was considered mostly the proper domain of semantics and philology. Two types of criticisms have rendered this position largely untenable today: first, semantics and philology are now seen as extracting meanings from their particular contexts, usages, and functionings in order to "objectify" them; second, the production of the "true" meaning of a word fails to take into account the varying influences of ongoing cultural and ideological conflicts.

The turn of the century was marked by the "suspicion of meaning" engendered by the works of Karl Marx, Friedrich Nietzsche, and Sigmund Freud. The Marxist version of ideology contends that meanings are, by and large, the meanings of a dominant class. For Nietzsche, meanings are signs of the domination of one group by another. And for Freud, conscious meanings are always liable to be haunted by "something else" in the form of desires that have been repressed. Equally important for this development was the theorizing of language and meaning carried out by Ludwig Wittgenstein, whose theory of language games denies that there is any one-to-one relationship between words and their meanings and holds that language consists of series of games, each with its own particular rules, that are used to "do things." Wittgenstein's insights have been crucial for recent theories, of meaning making understood as "practice" (e.g., Bourdieu, 1990).

However, in twentieth-century semiotics, Ferdinand de Saussure's work overshadowed all these contributions to the theorizing of meaning, mainly through his insistence that language is essentially relational and that all meaning is produced through a linguistic system based on differences rather than on identities. A particular sound or mark "means" something only because of an arbitary relation between itself and a signified or referent. Rather than being in the world, meaning is conceived of as being produced by semiotic systems.

Two main problems have been identified in Saussure's theories of language and meaning. The first concerns Saussure's failure to distinguish clearly between the notions of signifier and signified. If there is no meaning outside semiotic systems, what status can we give to, say, the concept "sheep"? Is the notion of sheepness part of a semiotic system, or is it somehow bound up, in a presemiotic manner, with its referent? The latter point, however, makes no sense in terms of Saussure's strongly implied theory of the systemic production of meaning. The second problem is that meaning is conceptualized only in terms of "artificially" produced sign systems: Saussure contextualizes meaning in terms of someone producing a sign for someone else. There is no place, then, for talking about what a landscape might "mean" unless some divine architect is introduced as the agent of that meaning.

Charles Sanders Peirce's treatment of meaning does not raise the same problems. For Peirce, every signifier is and can only be mediated by another signifier, which he refers to as the interpretant; this means that it is impossible to produce meaning outside of or prior to a semiotic system. The logical extension of this point is that there is no possibility of any "natural" or unmediated meaning. Peirce is equally useful with regard to the question of whether signs need to be emitted. One of the more important points of his definition of a sign is that it "stands to somebody." This allows us to read unintentional signs in terms of their potential meanings within various cultural codes—that is, without naturalizing or objectifying that meaning.

The semiotic theories advanced by Saussure and Peirce are important for the notion of meaning not only because they identify the objectivist and idealist blind spots associated with semantics and philology but also because they simultaneously anticipate and problematize the phenomenological theories of meaning associated with Edmund Husserl, Martin Heidegger, and Maurice Merleau-Ponty. Meaning, for Husserl, predates language since meaning is found in a subject's perception of the universal essence of an object or thing. This essence could be produced and mediated in different ways through language, but "true" meaning exists outside language. For Husserl, before the word there was the world as word—a word and a meaning retrievable only in the interaction between perceiving, self-conscious subject and object. Heidegger's contribution to phenomenology and meaning is closer to the "productivist" positions of Saussure and Peirce in that he sees language as pre-dating both the subject and meaning. Heideggerian phenomenology is still tied to the idealist and pre-semiotic theories of Husserl, however, in that while meaning is posited as historical and language is put forward as the place where meaning is "uncon-cealed," these meanings are always subject, in a sense, to another, primary meaning—being—that comes "from the earth." The notion that things mean out-side of language is also found in the theories of less-idealizing phenomenologists such as Merleau-Ponty. This degree of idealization constitutes the main dif-ference separating semiotic and phenomenological theories of culture, language, and meaning.

Early semiotic and linguistic theories of meaning were not only important for critiquing theories of meaning produced by phenomenologists; in a more positive way, the notion that language systems and codes produce meaning provided the groundwork for the disparate structuralist versions of meaning asso-ciated with theorists such as Roman Jakobson, Jan Mukařovský, Edward Sapir and Benjamin Lee Whorf, Claude Lévi-Strauss, Noam Chomsky, and Roland Barthes. Despite their many differences, most struc-turalist theories of meaning share two assumptions: first, that, contra phenomenology, the individual subject is not the center and origin of meaning; and second, that there is no meaning outside structures. This second point effectively does away with the quasi-ontotheological explanations of meaning within the Kantian tradition and in the works of post-metaphysicians such as Heidegger. Meaning, for structuralism, is not the property of individual agents, nor is it to be divined through exegesis; rather, it is, more prosaically, the product of different codes or systems of signification.

Structuralist theories of meaning develop Saus-sure's initial insights that meanings are relational rather than substantive and that the relationship be-tween the signifier and the signified is arbitrary. The development of such theories owes a great deal to the linguists Jakobson, Sapir, and Whorf, who were par-ticularly interested in the communication of mean-ing and in the application of structuralist linguistics to wider issues of cultural codes and structures. For Jakobson, meanings were unstable relations that changed depending on the specific contexts, codes, and means of communication in operation at any one time, rather than commodities that move, un-

problematically, from a sender to a receiver. Sapir and Whorf take Jakobson's interest in this "total act" of communication further. Starting from Sapir's point that phonemic structures reproduce themselves in the utterances of speakers of a language (that is, it is difficult for speakers to hear and speak sounds that are not distinguished within their own phonemic sys-tem), Whorf extended this insight so as to explain the relationship between language codes and cultural "realities" and meanings. For Whorf, the distinctive-ness of a culture is determined by that culture's lan-guage.

Semiotic, formalist, and structuralist theories ex-plain how meaning is produced but not how mean-ing changes or why one meaning is produced rather than another. These issues, however, have received considerable attention from Marxist critics. For in-stance, Voloshinov's theories, expanding upon the insights of structuralist linguistics, criticizes its fail-ure to theorize the motivated relationship between signifier and signified. For Voloshinov, all signs are both saturated with meanings and the sites where struggles over the control and naturalization of meanings are fought out. In other words, for Voloshi-nov, the production of a meaning has to be under-stood as the forgetting of "meanings"—that is to say, all meaning is ideological.

Saussure's theories of the production of meaning and Voloshinov's insistence on the politicization of that process constitute perhaps the two most impor-tant moves in the relocation of questions of mean-ing from the domains of semantics and philology. The question of meaning has been taken up in post-modernist contexts through Derridean deconstruc-tion, Lacanian psychoanalysis, feminism and gender theory, and Jean Baudrillard's notion of simulation.

Derridean deconstruction is predicated on Saus-sure's point that all meaning is in some way produced out of and therefore partly defined by what it is not: its other. For Jacques Derrida, the binary logic that underpins structuralism and allows meanings to be identified and fixed can be made to work in exactly the opposite way. If meaning is predicated to some extent on its other—the word *up*, for instance, is un-derstood as *not down*—then signifiers and their mean-ings are forever sliding across each other without the possibility of being stabilized. Meaning, then, is al-ways different to itself. Deconstruction has been crit-icized as being an academic or abstruse philosophical game that flies in the face of the fact that meanings are always being made and controlled. A more constructive reading sees it as an adjunct to Voloshinov's politicization of the sign; that is to say, deconstruction is a means of taking apart texts and discourses that normalize meaning, as well as a means for disputing the rationales that accompany such normalizations.

Lacanian psychoanalysis and its theorizing of meaning owes as much to Saussure as does deconstruction, to which it is closely related. For Jacques Lacan, the unconscious is structured like a language, but instead of producing stabilized and fixed meanings—which are "performed" in conscious practices, texts, and discourses—the unconscious is the site of an evacuation of meaning. In the Lacanian unconscious, the linkage between signifier and signified that produces the Saussurean sign never occurs: instead, unconscious "texts"—dreams, for instance—are characterized by interruptions in this process of signification and identification. For Lacan, the production of meaning is always a failed performance that reveals meaning as the site of a *lack* of meaning. Unconscious texts are privileged in Lacanian theory precisely because they demonstrate most clearly the failure of the desire to mean, which is generally repressed in conscious texts.

This Lacanian insight has been taken up by feminists and other theorists of gender in order to critique the processes whereby bodies are "sexed"—that is, produced as sexual identities. Following Lacan, feminists point out that the meanings ascribed to bodies, for instance, are always the sites of a failed performance—a text in which the play of signifiers produces not stable identities but evidence of an interrupted patriarchal repression and domination of women.

Although Michel Foucault would have eschewed any Lacanian or feminist comparisons or analogies, there are considerable similarities between Lacanian theories of meaning, feminist appropriations of them, and Foucault's own theories. Most particularly, there is a shared awareness that the body is a site where the supposedly "true" meanings and explanations of subjectivity can be sought and identified. Foucault differs from Lacan, however, in that he specifically historicizes this tendency, tracing its "development" from Greek and Roman times to its more rigorous and scientific manifestations in the nineteenth and twentieth centuries. More generally, Foucault is interested in the fetishizing of meaning as

knowledge and its relation to the workings of power. In this, he displays a close affinity with Nietzschean theories, in which meaning is strongly informed by the notion of a will to power. Because of the attention he gives to the relation between institutions, discourses, and the production of meaning on the one hand and the regulation of groups and practices on the other, Foucault's work has been taken up by theorists of race, colonialism, government, and the politics of culture, much as Lacan's work has been taken up by feminists.

Following Lacan, Derrida, and Foucault, postmodernist and poststructuralist theorists tend to characterize the present age in terms of the disappearance of meaning. The most extreme and persistent advocate of this position is probably Baudrillard, whose notion of the simulacrum banishes meaning precisely because simulations, which he says characterize our own time, do not represent and therefore do not mean anything. What Baudrillard's notion of simulation neglects, however, is that while meanings might now be performing only their own absences, meanings are still negotiated and exchanged within cultures as if they were real—which makes them real enough. In other words, the production of meanings, which continues apace, continues to have pragmatic effects.

[*See also* Baudrillard; Bourdieu; Foucault; Intentionality; Lacan; Markedness; *and* Wittgenstein.]

BIBLIOGRAPHY

Baudrillard, J. *Simulations.* Translated by P. Foss, P. Patton, and P. Beitchman. New York: Semiotext(e), 1983.

Bourdieu, P. *In Other Words: Essays Towards a Reflexive Sociology.* Translated by M. Adamson. Cambridge: Polity Press, 1990.

Derrida, J. *Of Grammatology.* Translated by G. C. Spivak. Baltimore: Johns Hopkins University Press, 1976.

Foucault, M. *The History of Sexuality*, vol. 1, *An Introduction.* New York, Random House, 1980.

Freud, S. *Metapsychology: The Theory of Psychoanalysis.* Harmondsworth, England: Penguin, 1984.

Greimas, A. J. *On Meaning: Selected Writings in Semiotic Theory.* Translated by P. Perron and F. Collins. Minneapolis: University of Minnesota Press, 1987.

Lacan, J. *Ecrits: A Selection.* New York: Tavistock, 1977.

Merleau-Ponty, M. *Phenomenology of Perception.* Translated by C. Smith. London, Routledge, 1992.

Morris, C. "Signs and the Act." In *Semiotics: An Introductory Anthology*, edited by R. Innes, pp. 178–189. Bloomington: Indiana University Press, 1985.

Voloshinov, V. N. *Marxism and the Philosophy of Language.* Cambridge, Mass.: Harvard University Press, 1986.

—TONY SCHIRATO

MEDIEVAL SEMIOTICS. The association of the words *medieval* and *semiotics* is an anachronism of sorts. *Semiotics* in its contemporary sense is the study of signs in all their extent and variety; its foundational sense, however, as established by Charles Sanders Peirce (1839–1914), is based on the program proposed by John Locke (1632–1704) in the conclusion to his *Essay Concerning Human Understanding* (1690). There, semiotics was first outlined as an investigation of the essential nature and fundamental varieties of signs. In this understanding of semiotics, therefore, the term *sign* is not only the focal notion but also applies to signification within as well as outside of human culture. The medieval expression equivalent to the contemporary sense of *semiotics* is *doctrina signorum* ("doctrine of signs"). This expression is used in Locke's early statement and also by Peirce, as well as in some contemporary discussions. Thus, in speaking of medieval semiotics, we are looking back upon the Latin age from a contemporary perspective that is congenial to medieval thought.

In medieval times, (c.400–1650 CE), the notion of sign is understood precisely as embracing the universe as a whole—the world of nature as well as the world of culture—precisely as the two come together in human experience understood semiotically. We can, of course, speak of an ancient as well as of a modern semiotics, but in order to do so we have to introduce restrictions on the term that do not apply either to contemporary or to medieval semiotics. Strictly speaking, the ancient period is more properly termed presemiotic, while the modern period is better termed semiological, if we are to speak of it in terms of that anthropomorphically restricted part of the doctrine of signs to which it has properly contributed. The *doctrina signorum*, by contrast, first introduced and developed in Latin times, has been taken up anew in contemporary thought and developed beyond the point where the Latins left it before their subtle achievements were obliterated by the mainstream modern development of philosophy in the wake of René Descartes (1596–1650). Here, we will trace the notion of sign in the contemporary sense from its first appearance in the work of Au-

gustine of Hippo (c.354–430 CE) up to its establishment in the *Tractatus de signis* of John Poinsot (1632).

Augustine formally initiates the development of semiotic consciousness with the definition of sign he proposes in his *On Christian Doctrine*, in which he presents the sign as superior to the division of being into the natural and the cultural: any material structure, whether from nature or art, that on being perceived conveys thought to something besides itself functions as a sign. The context in which this definition is proposed helps in understanding both its originality and its shortcomings. Augustine's own use of this general notion of sign begs the question of how to overcome the ancient dichotomy between the causal relations linking natural phenomena to the things of which they are signs and the imaginary relations linking cultural phenomena to the things of which they are signs. Thus, unwittingly, Augustine presages the famous medieval dispute over nominalism: is it sufficient to propose a common term for diverse phenomena in order to establish or reveal a nature truly common within the diversity? Without facing the question, Augustine leaves to his posterity the concern over whether any general doctrine of signs is not, after all, a mere nominalism.

Augustine's authority as the "last of the Church Fathers," together with the inclusion of his definition of sign in Peter Lombard's compilation of patristic views, the *Sentences* (c.1150), was enough to ensure that Augustine's general notion of *signum* became a permanent component of medieval intellectual life. From the point of view of philosophical discourse, however, and especially in terms of the perspective implicit in and presupposed by the new general notion, the religious concerns met by Augustine's definition are far less interesting than the questions his definition raises but leaves unresolved. First among these is the question of how is it possible for there to be parity in any sense between the inferences based on the causal relations of "natural" signification and the equivalence relations stipulated or imagined between cultural symbols and their objects? Gradually but inevitably, the Latins became uncomfortable with the parameters of Augustine's proposed definition for the sign as such. In this definition, two elements appear essential: the genus of sign as a material structure accessible to the senses; and the differentiating manner of making something other than itself come into awareness. Both these elements came under the scrutiny of later medieval analysis, and both were found wanting.

Already in the work of Thomas Aquinas (1225–1274), we find reservations expressed about the first element. Aquinas explains that Augustine is speaking only from the point of view of what is true for intelligence precisely considered as dependent on the senses for its material object, rather than from the point of view of intelligence as such, which in the cases of God and the angels as pure spirits does not depend on sense impression. After Aquinas, against the background of the powerful clarification and amplification of the semiotic status and role of psychological states in the activity of human understanding provided in the work of John Duns Scotus (1265–1308), professors of logic took up Aquinas's line of criticism more pungently by pointing out that on purely experiential grounds the essential function of the sign seems to be fulfilled by the bringing into awareness of an object other than the sign vehicle, regardless of whether the vehicle of that awareness is itself sensed or even sensible. The essential function of the sign in question is realized transparently by the "passions of the soul," whether conceptual or emotional—this phenomena came to be designated near the end of modern times as "intentional" by Franz Brentano (1838–1917) (Beuchot, 1994). Thoughts in the mind and feelings in the heart, the post-Aquinas medieval Parisians argued, make present objects other than themselves without having first to make impressions on external sense. Therefore, the criteria of being an external, sense-accessible structure in the definition of the sign is mistaken.

The conclusion of this argument was incorporated into a discussion that formed the basis of a revision of Augustine's definition. A sign, the Parisians said, is anything known that serves to make present in the awareness something other than itself, regardless of whether that "precognized" thing is itself an object of sense or not. Signs, accordingly, they concluded, may be divided into two fundamental classes: if the sign has for its vehicle a sensible object—that is, a material structure accessed as such by sensation, then it should be called an instrumental sign. But if the sign has for its vehicle a psychological structure that is not sensed outwardly but merely felt or experienced inwardly and, by being so felt or experienced, serves to make present some object, then it should be called a formal sign.

According to this argument, which Domingo de Soto (1494–1560) carried from Paris to the schools of Iberia in the early 1500s, what is essential to the sign is not how it is experienced—whether by sensation or feeling or purely by intellect—but that it makes present something more than itself, something other. In Augustine's definition, the first part is not generic but extraneous, while the second part contains the whole essence, which, in medieval thought, of course, could not be expressed simply but only through a genus and a difference. The genus of sign, the Latins argued by about 1400, is not "something sensible" but merely "something cognized," while the differentiating factor is simply "making present in cognition another."

The main thrust of this distinction, whatever its specific textual origin, is that signs may be either material or psychological in their vehicle but are equally signs in either case. With this distinction, semiotic consciousness is brought to a new level: the sign transcends not only nature and culture (as for Augustine) but also the distinction between inward and outward experience. The truly differentiative element constituting the sign—namely, that it is relative to something other than its vehicle—remains to be explained. This part of the foundational problem of semiotics came only gradually to the foreground of the Latin discussions. Just as Augustine's original definition of *signum* accommodated the "commonsense" tendency to identify signs with sense-perceptible objects, so it accommodated the notion that, among the objects of our experience, some are signs, others are merely objects. Even the expansion of the notion of sign to include interior or psychological states did not definitively rule on the question of whether signs are, as it were, a permanent class to which only certain things belong.

A decisive moment for medieval semiotics arrived when Latin authors began to face directly the problems raised by the second part of Augustine's original definition, according to which a sign is distinguished by always bringing into awareness something other. The sign vehicle requires always the conveyance of a content distinct from itself as the object signified. This distinctive feature constituting any sign as such is the one point of common agreement that emerges across all the discussions of signs, ancient as well as medieval or modern. Whatever else it might be, a sign is in every instance something relative. Medieval Latins found themselves in an especially privileged position to discuss this part of the notion of sign for not only were they the heirs of the ancient Greek discussions of relation, but this ancient discussion had been given a decisive new twist in the Boethian translations of Aristotle's work on the categories according to which we speak of being as thought to exist in its own right.

For the Latins, what Aristotle essayed in his categorical list had little or nothing to do with linguistics and everything to do with the variety of ways in which physical being is found to exist in our experience independent of human society. Whatever truly exists in nature as an individual Aristotle classed as a substance, while whatever exists in nature as some modification or characteristic of an individual, however important, Aristotle classed as an accident. Among the accidents (some but by no means all of which can come and go without destroying the individual they modify and characterize at a given time), Aristotle counted relations. In order to include relation in his list as a distinct category, Aristotle had to formulate a definition that covers all and only relations. In this effort, he encountered a major difficulty: just as the accidents of substance ultimately have to be explained in terms of the ability of substance to sustain them, so substance itself has to be explained ultimately in terms of the ability of the environment to sustain individuals ("principles and causes and sustaining conditions of existence," in medieval terms). In other words, in actual existence, every substance and every accident is maintained by realities of circumstance and being other than themselves; so it appears that "relation" is not a distinct category of physical being but rather a condition that applies to physical being in every category. How, then, is relation to be conceived of as a distinct category?

To resolve this problem, Aristotle proposed a distinction: "the fact that a thing is *explained* with reference to something else does not make it *essentially relative*" (*Categories*, chap. 7). Relation as a distinct category, then, comprises all and only those features of being whose very conception involves being toward another. We can conceive of an individual apart from knowing the parents; we can conceive of a size apart from conceiving of what sort of thing might be that size; and so on. But a relationship in the categorical sense cannot be conceived of except in terms of something other than itself: an *individual* son might be thought of without giving any consideration to the parents, but an individual *son* cannot be

conceived of apart from consideration of parents as well, for they mark the offspring as a son, even though the son as an individual exists independently from them.

Thus, the classical medieval definition of relation as "that whose whole being consists in a reference or being toward another," intended to convey Aristotle's idea of relation as verifiable under a distinct category of physical being. The medievals circulated a distinct name to memorialize Aristotle's unwelcome realization that even those types of being that are not relations in this sense (namely, individuals and whatever characteristics of individuals there are besides relations, such as quantity, quality, and the rest) are relative in their existence and in their potential for being explained. This profound sense of relativity reaching to the very foundation of finite being they called *relatio secundum dici* or relation according to the requirements of bringing being to expression in discourse. This terminology was introduced by Boethius (c.510 CE) in *Categorias libri quattuor*, his translation of and commentary upon Aristotle's *Categories*. The medievals also called this sense of relation the *relatio transcendentalis*, *transcendental* being the accepted medieval term for any notion that applies to more than one category.

Boethius termed the sense of relation that applies to only the single category of relation (i.e., that designates only what is relative in its very definition as well as in its possibilities for explanation and conditions for existence) the *relatio praedicamentalis*—the "predicamental" or "categorial" relation (*praedicamentalis* is a Latin qualification for both category and predicate). This terminology reflected the medieval understanding that Aristotle's scheme of categories identified those senses in which being could be said (hence, "predicated") in a single sense ("univocally").

A further complicating dimension arose from the medievals' development of logic as a science of relations obtaining among things as they are thought of, as distinct from things (and relations among things) as they are in themselves. Categorial relations are supposed to be relations among things existing independently of our thought. Logical relations exist only in and as a result of our thought and hence obtain even among imaginary or mistaken beings. The medievals called these relations *relationes rationis* ("relations of reason") not because only rational animals formed them but because only rational animals could become aware of them and study them in their own rights. Inasmuch as they could not exist apart from thought, such relations were neither transcendental nor predicamental (i.e., categorial). The question arose in medieval debate of whether the whole idea of relation as a category had not been an objective confusion, mistaking a referral made by thought for a mode of being existing in nature independently of thought. In other words, in the medieval debate over the notion of relative being, the dispute centered on whether in the physical world there were only transcendental relations, with categorial relations being only comparisons made by the mind, *relationes rationis*, in the consideration of objects.

This last was a view that came to be held widely among the medievals, especially among those Latins who later came to be known as "nominalists," a school associated especially but not exclusively with the work of the fourteenth-century Scholastic William of Ockham (1285–1349). The Thomists and the Scotists who made up the two other main schools of late medieval thought (the Latin Age from the fourteenth to the seventeenth century) held on the contrary that so-called relations of reason or mind-dependent relations, while indeed essentially relative, are distinct from any being essentially relative in a categorial sense, inasmuch as "only things independent of the soul pertain to the categories" (Aquinas, *Quaestiones disputatae de potentia*, q. 7, art. 9). The categories in mainstream medieval thought are only those univocal ontological rationales according to which physical being must be thought in order to be understood. Categorial relation, even though relative in its very definition (as is also any relation formed in and by thought), cannot be reduced to any relation of reason because we find in our experience of objects relative aspects that are not invented by us— that is, essential relativities that are discovered, not created.

The fact that categorial and rational relations share a common "essence" or definition as something the whole being of which consists in a reference to another was not a point of central interest in the original medieval debates over relation, focused as they were on the differences between physical being (*ens reale*) and logical being (*ens rationis*). Nonetheless, the point did not escape notice entirely, and the medievals even had an expression to designate relation in its indifference to the distinction between mind-independent and mind-dependent being—namely, *relatio secundum esse*.

In the medieval discussion of sign, the semiotic importance of the theory of relation did not appear until rather late. Not until attention focused on the differentiative part of Augustine's definition as revised to include psychological as well as physical vehicles of signification did Latin authors begin to address the import of the sign as a relative being: since a sign in every case imports something relative to something else—*aliquid stans pro alio* (something standing for another thing) in a classical formula— what precise meaning does "relative to" (the *stans pro*) have in the semiotic case? Given the terms of the development of the notion of relative being, the medieval discussion at this turn could be given a very precise sense: is the sign to be identified with a being relative in the transcendental sense (*secundum dici*) or in the ontological sense (*secundum esse*)? Once it is understood that the whole of the physical universe is relative at least transcendentally (i.e., in its explainability) and sometimes ontologically as well (i.e., in its very definition), then it is also clear that anything relative must be relative in at least one of these two senses. Which is the case, then, for the sign? Eventually, the medieval discussion of sign came to be stated in just these terms (Poinsot, 1632; pp. 117–123). But as a matter of historical fact, this level of clarity in principle was reached only slowly and with much preliminary groping.

The Latin author who initiated the turn of the discussion in this direction might have been Pedro da Fonseca (1528–1599), for the Hispanic Aristotelian school he inspired, the Conimbricenses, is the first to begin framing the discussion of sign in these terms (*De Signo*, 1606, 1607). Compared to the writings after the Conimbricenses, earlier discussions of sign that speak mainly in terms of categorial relation (such as the famous 1267 *De signis* of Roger Bacon) appear hopelessly naive. How far the Conimbricenses had advanced in realizing the perspective of semiotics can be seen in the following remark: "There is nothing which leads to the cognition of anything else which cannot be reduced to some sort of sign" (Conimbricenses, 1607; q. 2, art. 3, p. 27).

Unfortunately, two points confused the developing discussion as Fonseca and the Conimbricenses influenced it. Natural signs, such as clouds or smoke, seem to belong to the order of physical being, whereas conventional signs, such as words or monuments, seem rather to be *entia rationis* (mind-dependent beings). Transcendental relatives pertain to the physical order, while rational relatives pertain to the logical or cultural order. Hence, we find Fonseca opining that "formal" signs are perhaps not signs in the same sense as "instrumental" signs (1564; lib. 1, cap. 8). We also find the Conimbricenses, citing as their principal predecessors in this view Alexander of Hales (1185–1245) and Peter of Ledesma (d. 1616), identifying signs as being or resembling transcendental relatives in all cases—that is to say, they identify a sign as consisting mainly and essentially in the foundation for a given sign relation, which is a physical structure in the case of natural signs and a cultural construction in the case of conventional signs (Doyle, 1985).

Not until the synthesis of John Poinsot (1589–1644), a student of the Conimbricenses, do we find the definitive establishment of a unified object for semiotic inquiry. Poinsot's argument follows an entirely novel line: since rational and categorial relations have the same essence or definable structure of essential relatives that as such exist both dependently upon some subjective foundation but also superordinately to that foundation, it matters not whether the foundation is a material structure or a psychological structure. In either case, the foundation as such does not constitute the sign formally. Whether the foundation gives rise to a categorial relation or a rational relation makes no difference to the fact that the relation to which it gives rise is what constitutes the sign formally as a sign. In either case, this relation is an ontological relation, in contrast to a transcendental one. Moreover, whether the relation in which the sign consists is rational or categorial is a matter of indifference to the sign as such, inasmuch as this normally depends on circumstances extrinsic to the signification. Thus, a dinosaur bone recognized as such functions as a natural sign vehicle, even though the relation to which it gives rise, which would be categorial if the dinosaur was alive, is purely rational in the circumstance of the dinosaur's not existing. Thus, like the division of signs into formal and instrumental, the division of signs into natural and conventional is made not from the point of view of that which constitutes every sign as such—namely, an ontological relation (which may be either rational or categorial depending on circumstances, and even sometimes one and sometimes the other)—but from the point of view of that subjective or "absolute" characteristic of some individual that makes of that individual the foundation for a relation in the essential sense of existing over and above its subjective ground.

With this identification of signs with pure relations as such, medieval semiotics reaches its highest point of development. The question of whether signs can be identified with any definite class of things able to exist subjectively, whether as physical or psychological realities, is answered definitely in the negative. In every case, the sign as such, consisting in the relation between sign vehicle and object signified, is something suprasubjective and invisible to sense. Those "things" or perceived objects that we call signs—such as traffic lights, flags, and words—are not technically speaking signs but vehicles of signification. The actual signification itself consists in the relation between the vehicles and the knowability of their objective content. Similarly, those psychological states, such as images or concepts, that the later medievals called "formal signs" are also not technically speaking signs but vehicles of signification.

At this stage, a new definition of signs may be said to be implicit: a sign is that which any object presupposes. Any subjective structure, whether physical or psychological, is never a sign strictly speaking but merely something that can enter into a sign relation, either as its foundation (as sign vehicle) or as its terminus (as an object signified), or as now one, now the other, in an unending process of developing and changing significations. The being in which the sign consists, properly and formally speaking, is never some object as such nor any subjectivity as such but is rather the network of real and unreal relations as a function of which objects appear to exist objectively.

The medieval distinction between "things" as what exists whether known or not and "objects" as whatever exists as known appears in Poinsot's synthesis as mediated by signs, used as a third term of the distinction, for things cannot become objects except through psychological states and conditions. Psychological states and conditions themselves cannot exist as such save through how they give rise to relations indifferently categorial and imaginary ("rational" in the broadest sense of mind dependent) that have as their termini objects also indifferently physical (such as the planets and stars and whatever of the physical universe happens to be known at any given time) or merely objective (as in the case of leprechauns, dragons, and Dracula), among the many objective features constituting the world of culture.

The objects known, in their turn, become signs of one another as new relations among them are imagined or discovered. And so, in the end, the universe as a whole, in terms of medieval semiotic theory, comes to be "perfused with signs, if it is not composed exclusively of signs," exactly as Peirce later projected.

At this point, the medieval development of a semiotic consciousness is definitively disrupted. The rich stirrings among the Latins of semiotic thought, particularly in its last Hispanic phase, disappears into oblivion with the seizure of philosophy's center stage in the mid-1650s by the classical modern authors. Beginning with Descartes and culminating with Immanuel Kant, modern epistemological theory develops in a direction antithetical to semiotic thought by suppressing the carefully developed Hispanic Latin distinction between representation, in which an object may present itself, and signification, in which an object or a concept can only present something other than itself. In equating ideas with objects represented, modern thought obviated the medieval notion of concepts as formal signs. And by discarding questions about the quality of ontological relations, modern epistemologists precluded the medieval notion of signified objects that might or might not also be things of nature. Thus, modern idealism developed as the notion of the universe of thought closed unto itself and ignorant in principle of nature.

Not until the work of Peirce in the late 1800s were the threads of medieval semiotic development taken up again. Peirce drew not upon the synthesis of Poinsot, of which he knew nothing, but upon the very Latin sources from which Poinsot made his creative synthesis (Beuchot and Deely, 1995). From the study of these sources, Peirce drew Poinsot's main conclusion: that the sign as such consists not in any physical or psychical structure but in an irreducibly triadic relation sustained by some physical or psychological structure as its vehicle. Arguments for this triadic character are stated clearly in medieval thought by Francisco de Araújo's time (*Dubitatur*, vol. 2, 1617), with some thematization of pertinent points already stated by the Conimbricenses. But Peirce brought medieval discussion of this point onto a new plane by introducing a distinct name for the third term of the relationship: the interpretant. With this notion, contemporary semiotic development begins with what is truly original and indigenous to it. Medieval semiotics is present in this development not just as a previous stage but as a living achievement of many of the most important discoveries on which contemporary semiotics rests and from which it continues to develop.

[*See also* Abélard; Augustine of Hippo; Poinsot; *and* Realism and Nominalism.]

BIBLIOGRAPHY

Aristotle. *Categories*. In *The Basic Works of Aristotle*, edited by R. McKeon; translated by E. M. Edghill, pp. 3–37. New York: Random House, 1941.

Augustine of Hippo. *De doctrina christiana libri quattuor* ("On Christian Doctrine"). In *Patrologiae cursus completus*, edited by J. P. Migne. Series Latina (P. L.), vol. 34. cols. 15–122. Paris: Desclée, 1949.

Bacon, R. *De signis*. In *Traditio*, vol. 34, edited by K. M. Fredborg, L. Nielsen, and J. Pinborg, pp. 81–136. New York: Fordham University Press, 1978.

Beuchot, M. "Intentionality in John Poinsot." *American Catholic Philosophical Quarterly* 68.3 (1994): 279–296.

Beuchot, M., and J. Deely. "Common Sources for the Semiotic of Charles Peirce and John Poinsot." *The Review of Metaphysics* 48.3 (1995): 539–566.

Conimbricenses. "De signis." [Chapter 1 of their commentary on Aristotle's *De interpretatione*.] In *Commentarii Collegii Conimbricensis et Societatis Jesu. In universam dialecticam Aristotelis stagiritae*. Secunda pars. 4–67. Lyon: Symptibus Horatii Cardon, 1607.

Deely, J. *New Beginnings: Early Modern Philosophy and Postmodern Thought*. Toronto: University of Toronto Press, 1994.

Doyle, J.P. "The Conimbricenses on the Relations Involved in Signs." In *Semiotics 1984*, edited by J. Deely, pp. 567–576. Lanham, Md.: University Press of America, 1985.

Eco, U., R. Lambertini, C. Marmo, and A. Tabarroni. "Latratus Canis or: The Dog's Barking." In *Frontiers in Semiotics*, edited by J. Deely, B. Williams, and F. Kruse, pp. 63–79. Bloomington: Indiana University Press, 1986.

Fonseca, P. *Instituiçoes dialecticas (Institutionum dialecticarum libri octo)*, (1564). Edited by J. F. Gomes. 2 vols. Coimbra: Instituto de Estudos Filosoficos da Universidad de Coimbra, 1964.

Locke, J. *An Essay Concerning Human Understanding*. London: Thomas Bassett, 1690.

Poinsot, J. *Tractatus de signis: The Semiotic of John Poinsot* (1632). Edited and translated by J. Deely with R. A. Powell. Berkeley: University of California Press, 1985.

—JOHN DEELY

MEME. Coined by the British evolutionist Richard Dawkins in his book *The Selfish Gene* (1976), a meme is a unit of culture—such as "tunes, ideas, catch-phrases, clothes fashions, ways of making pots or building arches." In humans, memes have supposedly taken over much of the evolutionary burden of the traditional units of heredity, the genes. Dawkins introduces them because in his opinion the rate of human cultural evolution is far too rapid to be simply a function of gene-centered evolution.

Memes arise quite possibly by chance, but once they exist, they propagate themselves by copying or imitation, jumping from one meme user (generally a conscious human but possibly also another vertebrate such as a bird) to another. There, they settle in, as it were. This process should be understood fairly literally; quoting the psychologist Nicholas Humphrey, Dawkins writes that "memes should be regarded as living structures, not just metaphorically but technically. When you plant a fertile meme in my mind you literally parasitize my brain, turning it into a vehicle for the meme's propagation in just the way that a virus may parasitize the genetic mechanism of a host cell. And this isn't just a way of talking—the meme for, say, 'belief in life after death' is actually realized physically, millions of times over, as a structure in the nervous systems of individual men the world over" (1976, p. 207).

Dawkins's does not regard meme evolution as exactly analogous to gene evolution, nor does he claim that the two always work together harmoniously. A belief, for instance, might be of physical reproductive benefit to the believer, but in Dawkins's opinion it could as easily be of no benefit whatsoever or even be counterproductive reproductively. A meme is transmitted because of its own "selfish" properties rather than because its human possessors consciously will its future success.

Dawkins's thinking about memes resonates strongly with the claims of "evolutionary epistemologists," a group of naturalist thinkers who have tried to model their thinking about human knowledge and culture on evolutionary—more specifically, Darwinian—lines. There are two main branches of this kind of thought: those who see units of culture as analogous to units of biology, (where, for instance, rival theories struggle for supremacy in scientists' minds); and those who argue that the human brain is shaped by selection and that culture must be seen as an adaptation designed to help its possessors in life's struggles. Obviously, Dawkins falls most naturally into the former branch, which raises the traditional problem about intentionality—namely, that cultural evolution

must be necessarily different from biological evolution because the raw units of culture are introduced with a purpose in a way quite different from the random appearance through mutation of genes. However, in some respects Dawkins inclines to the latter branch, if only because he insists (following Humphrey) that his is a literal theory rather than an analogical one. But he then runs afoul of the literalist insistence that in some sense these units of culture must be tied to biological adaptive advantage.

Obviously, Dawkins can retort that these are problems for evolutionary epistemology and not for him. He can pick and choose as he pleases, as does Karl Popper (1972) (to whose work Dawkins makes passing reference). However, even the sympathetic reader might point out that, stimulating though Dawkins's ideas might be, they are no substitute for an articulated body of theory, like the one we have for the genes in population genetics. Nor does it provide the great amount of empirical work that has been performed to support such theory as population genetics. At the moment, even twenty years after it was first proposed, what Dawkins offers us is a prolegomenon to a theory of culture rather than one that is, in the language of Thomas Kuhn, a functioning mature paradigm. We must therefore await further developments.

[See also Cultureme; Culturgen; Darwin; Dawkins; Evolution; and Memetics.]

BIBLIOGRAPHY

Dawkins, R. The Selfish Gene. Oxford: Oxford University Press, 1976.
Dawkins, R. The Extended Phenotype: The Gene as the Unit of Selection. Oxford: W. H. Freeman, 1982.
Dawkins, R. The Blind Watchmaker. New York: Norton, 1986.
Dennett, D. Darwin's Dangerous Idea. New York: Simon and Schuster, 1995.
Hull, D. "The Naked Meme." In Learning, Development, and Culture: Essays in Evolutionary Epistemology, edited by H. C. Plotkin, pp. 273–327. Chichester: Wiley, 1982.
Popper, K. R. Objective Knowledge: An Evolutionary Approach. Oxford: Oxford University Press, 1972.
Richards, R. J. Darwin and the Emergence of Evolutionary Theories of Mind and Behavior. Chicago: University of Chicago Press, 1987.
Ruse, M. Taking Darwin Seriously. Oxford: Blackwell, 1986.
—MICHAEL RUSE

MEMETICS. A fledgling discipline, memetics studies how culture evolves through the creation, selection, and replication or transmission of information patterns or memes: ideas, beliefs, theories, and other sorts of mental constructs, often expressed through action or vocalization. Much as a population geneticist studies the distributions of various alleles (possible forms of a gene), a memeticist studies why some memes fade into obscurity while others rise to prominence, becoming progressively refined and embellished as they spread horizontally across society and vertically from one generation to the next.

The evolutionary perspective gives memeticists a place to begin the ambitious project of analyzing systematically the complex assemblage of gestures, stories, scientific theories, rituals, and artifacts that human culture comprises. Whether the meme in question is a recipe, catchy melody, or attitude of racial prejudice, it is prone to multiply through social interaction and exhibit adaptive responses to the constraints and affordances of the environment it inhabits. For example, cars—artifacts resulting from memetically driven manipulation of the external world—have evolved to meet our desires for improved safety, maneuverability, and speed, capitalizing on new materials and technological breakthroughs.

Progenitors of memetics have been developing in diverse academic arenas for some time, particularly over the last quarter century. Philosophers have described epistemology as an evolutionary process (e.g., Popper, 1962, 1973; Hull, 1982; Campbell, 1987). Sociologists have spoken of social diffusion (e.g., Rogers, 1962) and social epidemics (e.g., Mackintosh and Stewart, 1979). Evolutionary accounts of the development of technology (Nelson, 1987) and institutional change (Hodgson, 1993) arose in economics.

These works were primarily descriptive. A more rigorous approach was taken by anthropologists and biologists who drew on mathematical models of population genetics and epidemiology to model the spread of ideas (e.g., Cavalli-Sforza and Feldman, 1981; Lumsden and Wilson, 1981). These models were a necessary first step toward a formal understanding of social phenomena. However, they did not address how ideas are grounded in experience or how they are stored, retrieved, and implemented. Moreover, since novelty generation is limited in these models to trial and error or inaccurate transmission, they cannot cope with the open-ended diversity of culturally derived information.

Meanwhile these sorts of issues have also been addressed by psychologists and cognitive scientists. However, their models of problem solving, strategic planning, and creativity focus on the individual, though creativity is a collective affair. Thus, they suffer from the opposite problem: knowing how knowledge is stored in the mind of an individual does not take us far toward understanding why people interpret and respond to the world as they do or why their worldviews differ from those of their ancestors. Each individual's model of the world, though experienced in private, is a collaborative effort, an amalgam of social learning and creative construction that has arisen in a particular cultural context.

In sum, although at a sufficiently abstract level the notion that culture evolves is obvious, what has been lacking is a theoretical framework that connects studies of meme transmission to studies of creativity and spells out explicitly how the concept of evolution maps onto the case of culture. In order for evolution to take place, there must be (1) a pattern of information (a state within a space of possible states); (2) a way to generate variations of the pattern (that is, to explore or transform the space); (3) a rationale for selecting variations that are adaptive and thus tend to give better performance than their predecessors in the context of some problem or set of constraints (a fitness landscape applied to the space); and (4) a way of replicating and transmitting (or amplifying, as molecular biologists refer to it) the selected variations.

In biological evolution, the evolving patterns of information are genes encoded as sequences of nucleotides. Variations arise through mutation and recombination, and natural selection weeds out those that are maladaptive. Replication takes place at the level of the genotype. In cultural evolution, the evolving patterns of information are memes, perhaps encoded as patterns of neuron activation. Variation arises when memes are transformed, reorganized, or combined. The generation of variation is less random than in biology because culture uses "shortcuts" (internalized models of the world, strategic planning, counterfactual thinking, etc.) to bias the production of variants. Therefore, the differential survival of variants after they have been produced is not as pivotal a concept. In the jargon of computer science, biology takes a relatively "breadth-first" approach to searching through a space of possibilities, while culture is "depth-first."

Since humans preferentially implement memes that satisfy their needs, useful memes tend to be selected over useless ones. However, a meme need not be beneficial to humans in order to proliferate. Much like runaway selection in biology, once a meme can replicate with variation on the basis of some selection criterion, it can evolve out of the orbit of the need that originated it. Spurious basins of attraction sometimes arise in recurrent neural networks through the compositional interaction of explicitly trained attractors, and the proliferation of neutral or even detrimental memes might result from the same phenomenon. This might become more commonplace as an individual or "meme host" progresses from infanthood to maturity and simple needs give way to needs that are increasingly complex and hard to predict.

Cultural replication is phenotypically mediated; it occurs when memes are transmitted through processes such as imitation and reproduced, more or less, in another brain. Incorporation of these new information patterns into a society alters the selective pressures and constraints exerted by the social environment, which in turn leads to the generation of yet more patterns. For example, much as the evolution of rabbits created ecological niches for species that eat them and parasitize them, the invention of cars created cultural niches for items such as gas stations, seat belts, and garage-door openers.

Thus, at an abstract level of analysis, biological and cultural evolution amount to the same process: self-perpetuated exploration and transformation of a space of possible patterns through variation, selection, and replication. The possibility that the two have enough in common that the former can pave the way for the latter therefore seems at least worth pursuing.

Although the meme concept was met with enthusiasm when it was introduced by Richard Dawkins in 1976, it has yet to generate much research. Skeptics ask how we can hope to develop a theory of cultural evolution before we understand fully how memes are instantiated in the brain. The situation has a precedent: Charles Darwin came up with the theory of biological evolution through natural selection before genes were discovered. Genes, however, are laid out in a fairly straightforward way in physical space, which does not appear to be the case with memes. This does not mean that memes cannot evolve, so long as the components of any one meme can be retrieved at once whenever necessary so they can function together as a unit. Neural networks and related models show that the storage and retrieval of distributed patterns is computationally feasible, though it is uncertain to what extent these models portray what goes on in the brain.

Very recently, memetics has become a focus of much attention, largely due to the publication of popular books (Lynch, 1996; Brodie, 1996) and an academic journal devoted to the subject (*The Journal of Memetics*, http://www.cpm.mmu.ac.uk/jom-emit/). Some of this work assumes that to understand the dynamics of meme evolution, all we need is a quick and dirty list of what makes a meme catchy. This approach is probably too simplistic to be of serious theoretical or predictive value. We need to consider how experience in the world turns into new memes in our brains and why a meme resonates with and enriches the complex web of assumptions, beliefs, motives, and attitudes of its host. We must also look at how memetic novelty is expanded further through creative processes and how the ideas and inventions of one individual build on the ideas and inventions of others (a phenomenon known as the ratchet effect).

Theories about memetic processes can be tested and refined using computer models (e.g., Gabora, 1995; Spector and Luke, 1996). With the advent of fast massively parallel computers, it is increasingly feasible to place even complex models of individual creativity and problem solving in a cultural context. Many interesting questions can be addressed by creating a society of artificial agents that use both strategy and imitation to explore an open-ended space of possible memes and learn for themselves which memes best satisfy each of their needs. This work will ideally be conducted alongside empirical studies similar to Durham's work on coevolution (1991) or Rodgers and Rowe's work on social contagion (1993).

In this work, we might find cultural analogues to biological phenomena such as epistasis or drift (random statistical bias due to sampling error) or reciprocal altruistic interactions between like-minded individuals, analogous to biological altruism. Out of such interactions, a memetically derived social structure might emerge wherein individuals who regularly generate pleasurable or powerful memes come to be observed carefully and imitated frequently, while other individuals are ignored. These outcasts might be consequently excluded from memetic exchange and come to exhibit a cultural version of the founder effect: reduced variation due to drift. Our knowledge of biological speciation could be applied to the study of individuation and division of labor in a family or society—for example, questions of why siblings are often so different from one another. This work could provide insight into not only problems pertaining to culture but evolution in general through comparison with biology. For example, the question of why there is so much redundancy in the genetic code has generated much discussion that might also apply to the question of why there are redundant mental maps in the brain; both might reflect constraints on the nature of an information-evolving code. Applications to other areas, such as the prediction of economic trends or the development of social policy, might also be possible.

[*See also* Artificial Life; Coevolution; Cultureme; Culturgen; Darwin; Dawkins; Evolution; Language Change; *and* Meme.]

BIBLIOGRAPHY

Brodie, R. *Virus of the Mind: The New Science of the Meme.* Seattle: Integral Press, 1996.

Campbell, D. T. "Evolutionary Epistemology." In *Evolutionary Epistemology, Rationality, and the Sociology of Knowledge,* edited by G. Radnitzky and W. W. Bartley, pp. 47–89. La Salle, Ill.: Open Court, 1987.

Cavalli-Sforza, L. L., and M. W. Feldman. *Cultural Transmission and Evolution: A Quantitative Approach.* Princeton: Princeton University Press, 1981.

Dawkins, R. *The Selfish Gene.* Oxford: Oxford University Press, 1976.

Durham, W. H. *Coevolution: Genes, Culture, and Human Diversity.* Stanford, Calif.: Stanford University Press, 1991.

Gabora, L. M. "Meme and Variations: A Computational Model of Cultural Evolution." In 1993 *Lectures in Complex Systems,* edited by L. Nadel and D. Stein, pp. 471–486. Redwood City, Calif.: Addison-Wesley, 1995.

Gabora, L. M. "A Day in the Life of a Meme." *Philosophica* 57 (1996): 901–938.

Hodgson, G. *Economics and Evolution: Bringing Life Back into Economics.* Cambridge: Polity Press, 1993.

Hull, D. L. "The Naked Meme." In *Learning, Development, and Culture: Essays in Evolutionary Epistemology,* edited by H. C. Plotkin, pp. 273–327. New York: John Wiley and Sons, 1982.

Lumsden, C., and E. O. Wilson. *Genes, Mind, and Culture.* Cambridge, Mass.: Harvard University Press, 1981.

Lynch, A. *Thought Contagion: How Belief Spreads through Society.* New York: Basic Books, 1996.

Mackintosh, D. R., and G. T. Stewart. "A Mathematical Model of a Heroin Epidemic: Implications for Control Policies." *Journal of Epidemiology and Community Health* 33 (1979): 299–301.

Nelson, R. R. *Understanding Technical Change as an Evolutionary Process.* Amsterdam: North-Holland, 1987.

Popper, K. R. *Conjectures and Refutations.* New York: Basic Books, 1962.

Popper, K. R. *Objective Knowledge: An Evolutionary Approach.* Oxford: Oxford University Press, 1973.

Rodgers, J. L., and D. C. Rowe. "Social Contagion and Adolescent Sexual Behavior: A Developmental EMOSA Model." *Psychological Review* 100.3 (1993): 479–510.

Rogers, E. M. *Diffusion of Innovations.* London: Macmillan, 1962.

Spector, L., and S. Luke. "Culture Enhances the Evolvability of Cognition." In *Proceedings of the Eighteenth Annual Conference of the Cognitive Science Society,* edited by G. Cottrell, pp. 672–677. Mahwah, N.J.: Lawrence Erlbaum Associates, 1996.

—LIANE GABORA

METALANGUAGE. A technical language devised to describe and discuss the categories and rules of a natural language or any other system of signs, a metalanguage raises both technical and philosophical issues. Hence the link between metalanguage and scientific knowledge.

The distinction that Plato (c.429–347 BCE) made between the sensible or perceptible world and the world of ideas is generally taken to be the first Western attempt to distinguish between knowledge of the true or authentic reality—the realm of the idea or pure form—and knowledge of its mere reflection, the material world. According to Plato, only the former can correctly represent truth. That is, true scientific thinking can only take place in the world of ideas, where the mind is not required to refer to the sensible world. In *The Republic* and especially in his discussion of the divided line and the cave (Plato, 1973, pp. 274–286), Plato goes to some lengths to refine this line of thinking. He postulates a hierarchy of knowledge as follows (from lowest to highest): (1) illusion, concerning the apprehension of the mere shadows and images of things; (2) commonsense opinion and belief concerning both the physical things themselves and the practical morality of ordinary people; (3) mathematical reason, based on assumptions and deductions derived from the images of things; and (4) philosophy, or dialectic, based on universal first principles that are entirely free of the sensible world. Whereas (1) and (2) refer to the world of perceptible phenomena and physical things, (3) and (4) refer to the intelligible world of the idea or pure form.

Plato's student Aristotle (384–322 BCE) both critiqued and extended Plato's dualistic conception of the physical world and the world of forms. Aristotle rejected Plato's view that the world of forms is transcendent with respect to things and images. Rather, according to Aristotle, the former is immanent in the latter. Thus, scientific inquiry is not confined to just one side of Plato's dualistic conception. Instead, Aristotle was interested in investigating the nature of the relationships that link the material world and the world of pure forms. Aristotle agreed with Plato that philosophy was the highest form of scientific knowledge. Aristotle, however, in investigating the connections between the two realms, divided philosophy into a number of subdisciplines: physics, mathematics, and metaphysics. In introducing the notion of a metaphysics, Aristotle did more than simply produce an overarching basis for the organization of knowledge into separate areas of inquiry, which had already been achieved by Plato. With his metaphysics, Aristotle proposed a common basis both for talking about the foundational principles on which all of the various domains of inquiry are based and for specifying their respective positions in the overall hierarchy of knowledge.

Thus, Aristotle distinguishes physics from metaphysics on the following grounds: physics is based on direct observation and a posteriori demonstration by means of syllogistic reasoning; metaphysics, by contrast, is a speculative mode of inquiry that goes beyond the direct observation of physical phenomena so as to investigate the essences of things. That is, metaphysics is a contemplative rather than practical or experimental form of scientific inquiry. In his metaphysical inquiry into the essences or the ultimate realities of the universe, Aristotle proposed in a series of linguistic treatises (e.g., *Topics, Categories*) a subtle account of the relationship between the categories of Greek grammar and this speculative metaphysical enterprise. According to the classical scholar R. G. Tanner, Aristotle's linguistic analyses showed how the patterns of Greek grammar are projected by analogy onto the world of substance, thereby constituting its further articulation as a complex system of causes (Tanner, 1969, p. 143).

In the modern era, practitioners of scientific discourse have, on the whole, turned away from Aristotle's insights and embraced a neo-Platonic conception of scientific theory and practice. Rather than concern itself with the essences of things, as originally conceived by Plato, modern science, as conceived of by its epigones such as Galileo, Francis Bacon, and Isaac Newton, has sought, on the basis of systematic observation and experiment, to discover the lawlike regularities that regulate the behavior of the natural world. Modern science, so defined, has sought to explain observable phenomena on the basis of abstract mathematical principles that have universal applicability, independent of human perception and experience. This has led to the widespread belief in the scientific community that there are two distinct ways of knowing: by "direct perception" and by the "application of rational reasoning and higher intellectual functions" (Davies, 1993).

In taking up a modern form of Plato's transcendental realism, Western scientific discourse has, until recently, lost sight of Aristotle's subtle insights into the ways in which language is not simply a formal calculus for discovering eternal truths about a superior external reality. Rather, language is immanent in the practices of those scientists and philosophers who use the patterns of natural language to discover and understand what the universe is like and how we relate to it. The two questions turn out to be not so separate or separable. Thus, Aristotle's highly original linguistic analyses of essences may be seen as an attempt to understand how the language of observation and demonstration helps to constitute what is observed or demonstrated, as well as the observer's or demonstrator's relationship to it. In this sense, Aristotle's system of syllogistic reasoning might be considered the first expert system for manipulating observable reality and our knowledge of it.

Rather than shying away from the big questions of how, for example, the world we perceive with our senses relates to "reality," Aristotle's linguistic analyses of the relationship between the categories of Greek grammar and the world of substances center on the normative character of our metalinguistic resources for understanding and acting on the world. Aristotle shows that the agent who uses language for the purposes of scientific observation and demonstration is also engaged in an act of self-observation. That is, both observer and observed are embedded in a language system, and this gives meaning to the act of observation.

In a number of important respects, the views of Immanuel Kant (1724–1804) concerning the systematization of knowledge represent an important bridge linking Aristotle to twentieth-century notions of metalanguage. Kant was probably the first philosopher of the modern era to propose a unified or architectonic system "of all knowledge arising from *pure reason*" (1781; p. 655). In Kant's view, this system permits "the unity of the manifold modes of knowledge under one idea" (p. 653):

Kant uses a range of biological metaphors to show that the systematic, unified organization of the "diverse modes of knowledge" cannot be talked about on the same level as the various modes themselves. That is, he recognizes that the higher-order idea imposes constraints on the lower-order relations of the parts to each other. Such constraints are informational rather than physical. Further, they exhibit properties of self-organization such that the higher-order idea provides the systemic environment in which knowledge, on the biological analogy, individuates along a specific developmental trajectory. (In the more familiar terminology of twentieth-century philosophy, linguistics, and semiotics, Kant's architectonic ordering is a second-order metalanguage that takes the various modes of knowledge as its first-order object language. The metalanguage is the source of both integration and further development of the object language.) It is important to emphasize the importance of Kant's use of biological metaphors in this connection. Systems of knowledge, like biological organisms, individuate under informational constraints and undergo developmental processes that are only implicit in their early stages. Kant's phrase, the "sheer self-development of reason" (1970, p. 655), refers to the growth and development of uniquely individual systems of knowledge. As "members of one whole," they exhibit properties of self-determination on the basis of principles of top-down conceptual integration rather than on the basis of a mechanistic or bottom-up assemblage of parts.

Kant showed more clearly than any previous philosopher had that scientific knowledge is limited by higher-order or metalevel informational constraints. In the process of their self-organization relative to some cultural environment, both the unity of scientific knowledge and the importance of inquiring into its principles of organization come to the fore. That is, the moment that scientific knowledge begins to take seriously the question of how to describe and model itself, the familiar epistemological problems of self-reference and recursiveness become central.

Our experience of the phenomenal or material world through our various senses is not the same as our linguistic and other semiotic constructions of it.

Language and other semiotic systems are systems of interpretation. For this reason, they constitute a theory or a complementary plurality of theories of the world that they interpret (Halliday, 1988). As Gregory Bateson has observed, "language bears to the objects which it denotes a relationship comparable to that which a map bears to a territory" (1973). Like map and territory, language and the objects it denotes exist at two distinct levels of abstraction or two orders of logical typing. There is not, then, a simple relation of correspondence between the map (language) and the territory (phenomena) that the map is used to interpret. Rather, systems of interpretation such as natural language incorporate into their own internal designs the very principles of organization whereby the relationship between object and system of interpretation is constituted. They incorporate usually implicit metalinguistic rules that must be learned at the same time that language itself is learned and that specify how and when particular words are related to particular objects. This means that the systems of interpretation that we use to model the infinitely richer and more complex phenomena of the world are self-referential to their users. In other words, such metalinguistic principles provide local criteria of meaning that enable language users to contextualize the relationship between a given object and a system of interpretation.

This can be modeled in a number of ways: (1) object a and language form b are related to each other in the context c; (2) the relation of a to b is of the type c; or (3) the relation of a to b is enacted or constituted by c. This simple formalism tells us that the relation $(a/b//c)$ is a contextualization of the relation (a/b) by the higher-order context c (Lemke, 1984). (Following Bateson and Lemke, the single slash denotes a first-order relationship, and the double-slash a second-order relationship in the overall hierarchy represented by the formalism.) The basic assumption underlying the formalism, irrespective of the specific mechanisms involved, is that the first-order relationship (a/b) is completed or given a local meaning only when it is in turn contextualized by context c. That is, c is a context recognizable in the culture in question. If a is some real-world object, then b might be the word used to denote that object. In such a case, c is the metalinguistic rule that, as Bateson puts it, "governs" the relation between word and object.

A further reading shows more clearly the implications of higher levels of contextualization. If we say that *c* comments on (*a*/*b*) in that it classifies this relation as being of a certain type or as being formed according to a certain normative (metalinguistic) rule, such a rule might tell us how and when *a* is related to *b*. In all of these possible readings, the higher-order or metalevel context *c*, in construing the lower-order (*a*/*b*) relation, imposes a form of closure on it and does so in ways that integrate it into the given system of interpretation whereby social agents make sense of it. This basic principle is also the foundation upon which the stratified view of semiosis proposed by Ferdinand de Saussure and Louis Hjelmslev in the early decades of the twentieth century is built.

In this view, the semantic or conceptual stratum constitutes a higher-order or metalevel context for construing the lower-order relation between a particular phonological or graphological pattern and the lexicogrammatical form it signifies. The way that metalanguage talks about itself means that it is always at least two removes from the phenomena of experience. If language is used to construe the phenomena of experience—Bateson's "territory"—then metalanguage is used to construe the metaphenomena of language itself (Bateson's map). As Halliday (1988) points out, the metaphenomenon itself comprises two levels or strata of explanation: one grammatical, the other semantic. This means that metalanguage is required to interpret at least two levels of linguistic reality: the lexicogrammatical form and its meaning.

Metalinguistic discourse is not simply a calculus of axioms that defines all and only all the objects of a given metalanguage (Droste, 1983). Typically, metalanguage is seen as a taxonomic hierarchy of terms, either folk or scientific, when what is needed is an account of the ways in which metalinguistic discourses are themselves operative in particular context types. There is a need for a more dynamic, praxis-oriented approach rather than a static, taxonomy-oriented one. That is, we need to investigate the relations among the local interactional context, the metasemiotic consciousness of the interactants, their always partial viewpoints, and the ways in which the interaction of all of these perspectives serves to bring into or out of focus particular metalinguistic forces of a given utterance, as construed from some social viewpoint. A metadiscourse is a discourse through which participants can construe higher-order relations across local occasions. The construal of such relations is a means of reconstructing the global system—the metasystem—of possible contextualizations of a given utterance, relative to some social viewpoint. There is no viewpoint that stands outside the relevent system of relations, and the notion of metadiscourse should not be taken to refer to a neutral or objective point of view.

[*See also* Multimodality.]

BIBLIOGRAPHY

Aristotle, "On Interpretation." Translated by H. P. Cooke. In *Aristotle in Twenty-Three Volumes*, vol. 1, pp. 111–179. Loeb Classical Library. London: Heinemann, 1983.

Bateson, G. "A Theory of Play and Fantasy." In his *Steps to an Ecology of Mind*, pp. 150–166. London and New York: Paladin, 1973.

Davies, P. *The Mind of God: Science and the Search for Ultimate Meaning*. Harmondsworth, England: Penguin, 1993.

Droste, F. G. "Reflections on Metalanguage and Object-Language." *Linguistics* 21 (1983): 675–699.

Halliday, M. A. K. "On the Ineffability of Grammatical Categories." In *Linguistics in a Systemic Perspective*, edited by J. D. Benson, M. J. Cummings, and W. S. Greaves, pp. 27–51. Amsterdam and Philadelphia: John Benjamins, 1988.

Hjelmslev, L. *Prolegomena to a Theory of Language*. Translated by F. J. Whitfield. Madison, Wisc., and London: University of Wisconsin Press, 1969.

Kant, I. *Critique of Pure Reason* (1781). Translated by N. Kemp Smith. London: Macmillan, 1970.

Lemke, J. L. "Action, Context and Meaning." In *Semiotics and Education*, edited by P. Perron, pp. 63–93. Toronto: Victoria University, 1984.

Matthiessen, C. "Language on Language—The Grammar of Semiosis." *Social Semiotics* 2.1 (1992): 69–111.

Plato. *The Republic*. Translated by H. D. P. Lee. Harmondsworth, England: Penguin, 1973.

Rumsey, A. "Wording, Meaning, and Linguistic Ideology." *American Anthropologist* 92.2 (1990): 346–361.

Tanner, R. G. "Aristotle as a Structural Linguist." *Transactions of the Philological Society* (1969): 99–164.

Thibault, P. J. *Social Semiotics as Praxis: Text, Social Meaning Making, and Nabokov's "Ada."* Theory and History of Literature series, vol. 74. Minneapolis and Oxford: University of Minnesota Press, 1991.

—PAUL J. THIBAULT

METAPHOR. In the most general sense, metaphor is a figure of speech that foregrounds some similarity between two markedly different objects. In his *Poetics*, Aristotle counseled tragic poets on the significance of metaphor, pointing out that "the ability to use metaphor well implies a perception of resemblances" (1979 p. 65). In our own age, Aristotle's advice has been heeded above all by those concerned with drama and literature. The past few decades, however, have witnessed a remarkable broadening of interest in metaphor.

A key development in recent interest in metaphor was Max Black's rejection of the idea that in the metaphor "*a* is *b*" the *b*-term (the vehicle in Ivor A. Richards's nomenclature) is "substituted" for the *a*-term (what Richards calls tenor) (Black, 1962; Richards, 1936). Rather, a number of relevant features of the vehicle are projected upon and integrated with the tenor. These features, moreover, are not necessarily "objectively" present in the vehicle, as older theories had suggested. Instead, projectable features might include facts, connotations, emotions, or any combination of these as long as they are associated somehow with the vehicle. The range of associations, moreover, is to a considerable extent determined by the (sub)culture in which the vehicle is used. That is, in the phrase "she is a cow," the feature projected from *cow* onto *she* is stupidity or holiness, depending on whether the metaphor is used in a Western or a Hindu context.

The modern view of metaphor, in addition, emphasizes the tensive character of the relation between tenor and vehicle: clearly, only some of the features (which defy exhaustive enumeration anyway) of the vehicle domain are used in the metaphorical transfer to the tenor. As Paul Ricoeur puts it, "the metaphorical 'is' at once signifies both 'is not' and 'is like' " (1977, p. 7). Black's interaction theory, which forms the basis of most contemporary views of metaphor, also entails that a metaphor should be understood at the level of the sentence rather than of the word. But understanding often requires taking extrasentential and situational contexts into account as well. This means that metaphor theorists are increasingly aware that examples of the *a*-is-*b* type might fail to do justice to the ways in which metaphors are embedded in a text. They might also realize that the study of metaphor inevitably involves pragmatics.

One of the reasons why metaphor had long been neglected by philosophy and the sciences is that metaphors are literally false. Under the influence of logical positivism, often only true statements were seen as contributing anything to human knowledge, and metaphor was hence regarded by many as irrelevant to epistemology. Indeed, novel metaphors are false ("Man is a wolf") or trivially true ("No man is an island"), but the issue of truth or falsity is simply not pertinent. What matters is to what extent metaphors provide new, exciting, unexpected, fruitful, or even dangerous perspectives on their respective tenors. Black's insight that the similarity between tenor and vehicle is often not preexistent but created by the metaphor itself is one reason for metaphor's remarkable rehabilitation outside literary studies; another is his suggestion that metaphor is a mode of thinking rather than of language.

This last notion is captured by the title of the influential collection *Metaphor and Thought* (Ortony, ed., 1993), in the first edition of which (1979) Black's modified-interaction theory appeared as the opening article. Some twenty contributions from scholars in the humanities, the social sciences, and the natural sciences testify to the invigorating impulses the study of metaphor has given to a wide range of disciplines. Inasmuch as a metaphor uses that which is better known (embodied in a well-structured vehicle domain) to propose something about that which is less known (embodied in the tenor domain), metaphors are excellent instruments for teaching. Similarly, the use of metaphors might stimulate and aid scientific discovery processes: a puzzling or unfamiliar phenomenon can be construed as the tenor domain in a metaphor that takes certain structured vehicle domains as candidates for imposing (more) coherence on that phenomenon—alternatively, a vehicle domain can radically restructure the understanding of a phenomenon.

The most influential book-length study on metaphor is undoubtedly George Lakoff and Mark Johnson's *Metaphors We Live By* (1980). Where Black had focused on isolated literary and philosophical metaphors, Lakoff and Johnson argue that metaphors are a far more pervasive occurrence in everyday speech and writing than has been acknowledged hitherto. According to their view that "the essence of metaphor is understanding and experiencing one kind of thing in terms of another" (p. 5), such utterances as "she *attacked* my proposal"; "your claims are *indefensible*"; and "if you use that *strategy*, he'll *wipe you out*" exemplify manifestations of a single conceptual metaphor—namely, ARGUMENT IS WAR (capital letters are used conventionally to denote the cognitive level). Such expressions as "what is the *foundation* of your argument?" and "the claim requires further *support*," by contrast, reveal another pervasive metaphor in Western society—namely, ARGUMENT IS BUILDING.

One consequence of Lakoff and Johnson's views, anticipated in various contributions to *Metaphor and Thought*, is that metaphor is no longer seen as an exclusively verbal phenomenon. Indeed, "Metaphor is primarily a matter of thought and action and only derivatively a matter of language" (1980, p. 153). That is, a certain conceptual metaphor gives rise to many different verbalizations, each, of course, with their own communicative emphases. Since Lakoff and Johnson's book, the old terminology of tenor (or topic) and vehicle, while still used in literary studies, has been generally replaced by the terms *target domain* and *source domain* (sometimes *donor domain*). Further, features are now "mapped" rather than "projected," but the basic principles of the interaction theory still apply. A minor problem solved by this emphasis on the importance of cognition at the expense of verbal manifestation is the often-debated difference between metaphor ("*a* is *b*") and simile ("*a* is like *b*"). The old argument in favor of making a fundamental distinction was that while a metaphor is usually untrue, a simile is always trivially true inasmuch as any two things in the world are alike in some (albeit usually irrelevant) respect. Considered from a cognitive viewpoint, however, the difference disappears; simile and metaphor are thus now regarded as variants of basically the same phenomenon.

Far more momentous in Lakoff and Johnson's work is their amply demonstrated tenet that people continually describe and communicate about the world they inhabit in a manner that, while technically metaphorical, allows for no "literal" alternative—or else is at least fully conventional. Whereas isolated metaphors of the kind Black discussed, however worn they may be, resist the criterion of truth or falsity, the situation is different for the structural and orientational metaphors that are the staple of Lakoff and Johnson's work. "Shakespeare passed away" is both a metaphor (here, a manifestation of the structural metaphor DYING IS DEPARTING TO ANOTHER LOCATION) and a fully acceptable manner—"truthful" if you like—to convey the fact. The same holds for "my spirits *rose*" and "she was on *cloud nine*" versus "he was *depressed*" and "I'm feeling *down*" (manifestations of the orientational metaphors HAPPY IS UP and SAD IS DOWN, respectively). As Lakoff and Johnson's later research shows, metaphor is a central building block for a more inclusive theory of human

representations of reality. The study of metaphor thus helps reveal which basic schemas (such as UP-DOWN, CENTER-PERIPHERY, CONTAINMENT, SOURCE-PATH-GOAL) underlie, in various forms, human conceptualizing.

Lakoff (1987), building on the work of Eleanor Rosch, extends the framework of metaphor in the direction of categorization, while Johnson (1987) shows how the specificities of the human body affect the ways we make sense of the world. Many scholars are currently pursuing this line of research. The constructivist notion of "world making" that this growing body of work presupposes and elaborates should be of interest to theorists discussing the "crisis of representation" of postmodernist society. That is, metaphors openly embody the paradox that we know reality mainly by its representations; yet no representation transparently describes reality.

A critical consequence of the shift of focus from the verbal to the cognitive level is the appreciation that conceptual metaphors can be concretized in other than verbal forms. In recent years, various studies have sought to demonstrate the validity of postulating visual or pictorial metaphors (see, for example, Hausman, 1989; Whittock, 1990; and Forceville, 1996). Since pictorial metaphors, like images in general, seldom occur without accompanying text, the analysis of pictorial metaphors often requires an awareness of verbal information as well. In principle, the two terms of a metaphor might even be represented in different media: a metaphor can, for instance, be verbo-pictorial. The realm of nonverbal and cross-media metaphors, however, remains largely unexplored.

The use of metaphors in artificial intelligence studies and on the Internet deserves special attention, too. Here, metaphors are often structurally "wired into" the setup of programs, at once shaping and "freezing" perceptions of barely understood phenomena. Thus, INTERNET AS INFORMATION HIGHWAY or INTERNET AS WORLD WIDE WEB provide structure for what to the layman is a largely mysterious concept, but the metaphors also have ideological implications, not all of them attractive. Webs and nets, for instance, are tools meant to capture prey, and their use as metaphors may underlie the predatory and exploitative motivations that are at the root of the development of the electronic media.

The three sizable bibliographies on metaphor that have appeared since the early 1970s as well as the steady flow of articles in *Metaphor and Symbolic*

Activity, Poetics Today, Poetics, Cognitive Linguistics, and many other journals prove that the topic is by no means exhausted. Various problems remain to be solved, and there is still much uncharted territory. Thus, since most theorists have tended to focus on examples of the paradigmatic "*a* is *b*" type, the identification of target and source has seldom been problematized. However, the existence of metaphors with different grammatical forms (cf. George A. Miller's 1979 example, "rusty joints") and nonverbal metaphors should make it obvious that the principles guiding identification of target and source are themselves worthy of further investigation. Another challenge is the formulation of rules to guide the selection of features that can be mapped from source to target. This is a vital issue since it concerns the possible and acceptable interpretations of a metaphor. One candidate here is the invariance hypothesis, first formulated by Lakoff and Turner (1989) but hotly debated and fine-tuned since. In one version, the invariance hypothesis has been formulated as the following exhortation: "In metaphoric mapping, for those components of the source and target domains determined to be involved in the mapping, preserve the image-schematic structure of the target, and import as much image-schematic structure from the source as is consistent with that preservation" (Turner, 1990, p. 254), in which "image-schematic structure" is described in terms of what are to be regarded as crucial features in the source. Whereas a version of the invariance hypothesis might ultimately prove tenable for structural and orientational metaphors, it is doubtful that it will be capable of covering the innovative metaphors often encountered in literary texts. More generally, the issue of similarities and differences between structural and novel metaphors merits more attention.

The renewed interest in metaphor has in turn stimulated research into neighboring tropes. After all, metonymy, symbolism, irony, hyperbole, and many other nonliteral forms of language (and thought) share with metaphor a more or less explicit tension between sign and reference. In this respect, there is ample room for a revaluation of the study of classical and medieval rhetoric, both as elements of the study of literary and nonliterary texts and of the craftsmanship involved in either (see Turner, 1991). Such a study of rhetoric should not be restricted to purely verbal texts alone.

[*See also* Cultural Knowledge; Mandala; Mindscape; Parallelism; Pertinence; Pictorial Semiotics; *and* Poetics.]

BIBLIOGRAPHY

Aristotle. "On the Art of Poetry." Translated by T. S. Dorsch. *Classical Literary Criticism* (1979): 31–75.

Black, M. *Models and Metaphors: Studies in Language and Philosophy.* Ithaca, N.Y.: Cornell University Press, 1962.

Forceville, C. *Pictorial Metaphor in Advertising.* London and New York: Routledge, 1996.

Hausman, C. R. *Metaphor and Art.* Cambridge: Cambridge University Press, 1989.

Indurkhya, B. *Metaphor and Cognition: An Interactionist Approach.* Dordrecht: Kluwer, 1992.

Johnson, M. *The Body in the Mind: The Bodily Basis of Meaning, Imagination, and Reason.* Chicago: University of Chicago Press, 1987.

Johnson, M. *Moral Imagination: Implications of Cognitive Science for Ethics.* Chicago: University of Chicago Press, 1993.

Lakoff, G. *Women, Fire, and Dangerous Things: What Categories Reveal about the Mind.* Chicago: University of Chicago Press, 1987.

Lakoff, G., and M. Johnson. *Metaphors We Live By.* Chicago: University of Chicago Press, 1980.

Lakoff, G., and M. Turner. *More Than Cool Reason: A Field Guide to Poetic Metaphor.* Chicago: University of Chicago Press, 1989.

Miller, G. A. "Images and Models, Similes and Metaphors." In *Metaphor and Thought*, edited by A. Ortony, pp. 202–250. Cambridge: Cambridge University Press, 1979.

Noppen, J. -P. van, and E. Hols, eds. *Metaphor 2: A Classified Bibliography of Publications from 1985–1990.* Amsterdam: John Benjamins, 1990.

Noppen, J. -P. van, S. de Knop, and R. Jongen, eds. *Metaphor: A Bibliography of Post-1970 Publications.* Amsterdam: John Benjamins, 1985.

Ortony, A., ed. *Metaphor and Thought.* Rev. and expanded ed. Cambridge: Cambridge University Press, 1993. Other relevant collections of essays are S. Sacks, ed., *On Metaphor* (Chicago: University of Chicago Press, 1979); R. P. Honeck and R. R. Hoffman, eds., *Cognition and Figurative Language* (Hillsdale, N.J.: Lawrence Erlbaum, 1980); and W. Paprotté and R. Dirven, eds., *The Ubiquity of Metaphor: Metaphor in Language and Thought* (Amsterdam: John Benjamins, 1985).

Richards, I. A. *The Philosophy of Rhetoric.* New York: Oxford University Press, 1936.

Ricoeur, P. *The Rule of Metaphor: Multi-disciplinary Studies of the Creation of Meaning in Language.* Translated by R. Czerny et al. Toronto: University of Toronto Press, 1977.

Shibles, W. A. *Metaphor: An Annotated Bibliography and History.* Whitewater, Wisc.: Language Press, 1971.

Turner, M. "Aspects of the Invariance Hypothesis." *Cognitive Linguistics* 1–2 (1990): 247–255.

Turner, M. *Reading Minds: The Study of English in the Age of Cognitive Science.* Princeton: Princeton University Press, 1991.

Whittock, T. *Metaphor and Film.* Cambridge: Cambridge University Press, 1990.

—CHARLES FORCEVILLE

METONYMY. Like metaphor and synecdoche, metonymy is one of the figures of speech in ancient Greek rhetoric. It was later included in the more comprehensive taxonomies elaborated in French treatises of rhetoric in the seventeenth and eighteenth centuries. In the latter works, metonymy, like the two other figures, is a trope (a turn, a change of meaning) that applies to words rather than sentences and involves the exchange of one element for another rather than the suppression or addition of an element or the permutation of the order of several elements. What differentiates metonymy from metaphor and synecdoche is the nature of the relationship between the two elements entering into such substitutions. Whereas in metaphors the tenor and its vehicle are joined by similarity, and in synecdoches they are related as part to whole, metonymies connect them by means of contiguity. In semiotics, these figures of speech are interesting for the relationship they entertain with more basic theoretical concepts, such as the distinction between syntagm and paradigm or the notion of indexicality, as well as for the part they have played in the renewal of modern rhetoric.

The two most basic relationships of verbal language identified by Ferdinand de Saussure, the paradigmatic (or "associative") relations and the syntagmatic relations (also known as the axes of substitution and selection), were equated by Roman Jakobson (1971) with metaphor and with metonymy and synecdoche. Jakobson applied these terms to nonverbal discourses, claiming that metaphor characterized lyrical poetry, Romanticism, Charlie Chaplin's films, and the Freudian dream symbols, while metonymy and synecdoche were embodied in epic poetry, realistic novels, D. W. Griffith's films, and Freudian dream projections. Further, he distinguished two kinds of aphasia depending on whether a language impairment resulted from some dysfunction of the metaphoric or metonymic aspects of linguistic competence. Jakobson's identification of substitution, paradigm, and metaphor on the one hand and of combination, syntagm, and metonymy on the other has inspired many followers, the most famous of whom is the psychoanalyst Jacques Lacan.

The idea that narrative prose and film are essentially metonymic has influenced many literary scholars and film semioticians. Classic Hollywood clichés are often described as metonymic, such as falling calendar pages, the driving wheels of a railroad engine, or synecdochic, such as close shots of marching feet that represent an army. Ever since Roland Barthes described the tomato as a metonymy for Italy in his celebrated essay on the rhetoric of the image, students of advertisements have claimed to discover numerous visual instantiations of this figure.

Jakobson's analogy has been questioned on several counts. First, it collapses metonymy and synecdoche into a single category. This amalgamation has sometimes been justified by saying that it can be difficult to tell the two figures apart: for example, a crown is considered a metonymy for a king if the latter is considered as a physical person with whom the crown is in spatial contiguity, but it is a synecdoche for a king if royalty is seen to be primarily an office of which the crown is a significant part. But this really shows that in these two cases the functions are distinct: it is the object that is defined ambiguously.

By identifying the two figures, however, Jakobson interestingly highlights what they have in common: they are both founded on what we can call, following Charles Sanders Peirce, indexical grounds. There are, however, two principles of relevance that define indexicality: contiguity and the relation between a whole and its parts, which could be called factorality. According to Groupe μ (1970), objects may be decomposed in two ways: materially (a tree can be divided into stem, branches, leaves, etc.) and conceptually (the same tree can be replaced in the conceptual hierarchy from living things to cork oaks). This distinction relates to the one made in logic between extension and intension. However, this approach overlooks the real perceptual decomposition, which depends on the position of the subject and is fundamental in all visual semiosis—that is, the division into perspectives. Factorality must therefore be of three kinds: proper parts, properties, and perspectives.

The second problem raised by Jakobson's theory is that by equating syntagm and paradigm with metonymy and metaphor, respectively, it confuses relationships within sign systems with relationships between particular sign tokens or secondary relationships between signs. Indeed, metonymies, like metaphors, either are created in a particular given text or are stock images that relate signs, or at least sign contents, in stable relations. The similarity present in a paradigm is often simply the position in the syntagm, whereas some more pregnant similarity relation is required in the case of metaphors. At least, both types of similarity are relations *in absentia*. However, the contiguity of syntagms is a relation *in praesentia*, whereas that of metonymies, like all true figures, is a relation *in absentia*.

True metonymies (as well as true synecdoches) are actually secondary indexical signs: they relate two preexisting signs by means of their respective contents, which means that a sign present in the syntagmatic chain serves to invoke another sign absent from it. A more common case, however, is when no particular absent expression plane is brought to mind, but only a secondary content is implied by the content plane of the sign that is present: here we have what we could call, by analogy with "dead metaphors," "dead metonymies," like the cross for Christ and the sword for the army, or "dead synecdoches," like the sail for the ship and the clock for the watchmaker's (both as words and as visual signs). Barthes's tomato standing for Italy to a Frenchman (but not, for instance, to a Mexican) is probably a metonymy, or perhaps better a synecdoche.

In the original design for the project of a general rhetoric by the Belgian Groupe μ (1970), metonymy plays an important part. Synecdoche may lead from the whole to the part—that is, from the general to the particular—or the reverse: thus, we obtain generalizing and particularizing synecdoches. According to this scheme, combinations of synecdoches give rise to two kinds of metaphors and two kinds of metonymies, the other combinations being impossible: a generalizing conceptual synecdoche followed by a particularizing one is a metaphor (e.g., flexibility connecting girl and birch), as is a particularizing material synecdoche followed by a generalizing one (the French word *voile* ("sail" and "veil") connecting a boat and a widow). However, a generalizing material synecdoche followed by a particularizing one (Caesar standing for his book *De bello gallico* as a part of Caesar's life) is a metonymy, and so is the combination of conceptual particularizing and generalizing synecdoches. But in the theory of conjuncts as the foundation of general rhetoric, structure is not taken into account. The theory cannot explain, for instance, why *Caesar* but not any odd part of the life of Caesar may serve as a secondary sign for *De bello gallico*. Salience of features is no doubt fundamental in the explanation of metonymies.

It is not surprising that, turning to visual rhetoric, Groupe μ (1992) abandoned this system of explanation. Instead, figures were cross-classified as being *in absentia* or *in praesentia* and conjuncted or disjuncted. The figure is *in absentia* conjuncted if the two units occupy the same place in the statement, one being totally substituted for the other. It is conjucted *in praesentia*, to the extent that the units appear in the same place, with only partial substitution of one for the other. In addition, there will be a figure that is *in praesentia* disjuncted if the two entities occupy different places, without any substitution taking place. Finally, a figure will be disjuncted *in absentia* when only one unit is manifested, while the other is exterior to the statement but is projected onto it. In fact, the first two cases involve factorality and the second two contiguity.

It is easy to see that there are more cases than the system of classification allows for: different degrees of integration of the part into the whole (features or proper parts of an object, coalescence of different objects, objects in a set, objects in their proper environment, etc.) and different degrees of unexpectedness of the combination (pure alterity, contrariness, cultural and anthropological universals, and logical contradictions). The rhetoric of what is often confounded in the single term *metonymy* might turn out to be even more complex than suggested by Groupe μ's latest contribution.

[*See also* Denotation and Connotation; Indexicality; Jakobson; Metaphor; Opposition; Paradigm; *and* Rhetoric of the Image.]

BIBLIOGRAPHY

Groupe μ (J. Dubois, et al.). *Rhétorique générale*. Paris: Larousse, 1970.

Groupe μ. *Traité du signe visuel: Pour une rhétorique de l'image*. Paris: Seuil, 1992.

Jakobson, R. "Two Aspects of Language and Two Types of Aphasic Disturbances." In *Selected Writings*, vol. 2, pp. 239–259. The Hague: Mouton, 1971.

Sonesson, G. *Pictorial Concepts: Inquiries into the Semiotic Heritage and Its Relevance for the Analysis of the Visual World*. Lund: Aris and Lund University Press, 1989.

—GÖRAN SONESSON

METZ, CHRISTIAN (1931–1994), French linguist of the Hjelmslevian school whose writings on film semiotics have, more than any others, both launched new approaches and created disciples and dissenters. Among his academic colleagues in the university world of Paris in the early 1960s, Metz was an acknowledged film fan. Inspired in general by the structuralist discourse of the day and in particular by attention that both Roland Barthes and Claude Lévi-Strauss paid briefly to aspects of cinema, he turned his own scholarly attention to film in 1964.

Metz's generally laudatory review of Jean Mitry's *Esthétique et psychologie du cinéma* (1963) signaled the conclusion of personalized humanistic, thematic, or formalist film theory at the same time as it opened the doors for rigorous, scientifically oriented theory and analysis of film (1964, p. 61). His own first step was to remove film discussion from repetitive comparisons with the other arts and with language and place it, with an acknowledgment of film's own specificity, under the aegis of semiotic methodology. Some of his earliest writing reflects as well the phenomenological preoccupations of the time as he engaged in the then-lively debate on the creation of the impression of reality in the cinema. Metz held that the representation of movement on the screen is the key to filmic *vraisemblance* or realistic believability.

Metz's work led to articles by both himself and others on the question of cinematic codes. The principal code that is associated with him particularly is that of *la grande syntagmatique*. His explanation of this paradigm of autonomous filmic segments and his application of his schema to an analysis of *Adieu Philippine* (1962) appears in the first volume of his collected articles, *Essais sur la signification au cinéma* (1968). His second volume of *Essais* (including the Mitry review) appeared in 1972. In the meantime, Metz published his extended scholarly study, *Langage et cinéma* (1971), which was densely written so as to demonstrate the degree of complexity that film theory could achieve. Clearly, Metz was in competition with the literary theorists of the era. As a result, *Langage et cinéma* introduces a whole new lexicon for filmic discussion and for many pages indulges in pure theory devoid of filmic examples.

In the mid-1970s Metz accompanied another film theorist, Jean-Louis Baudry, into the second, psychoanalytical phase of film semiotics. Metz had undergone psychoanalysis himself and had read closely Sig-mund Freud and Jacques Lacan. In *Le signifiant imaginaire* (1977), his thoughts on the subject begin with something as banal as "spectator positioning" (*le dispositif*) and its relationship to the mechanics of film projection, but these thoughts lead him quickly into considerations of the spectator's hypnosis by the projected images and to thoughts on the psychoanalytical experiences of identification in several senses of the term. The notion of the projection hardware soon became so associated with these topics that it seemed natural for a collection of essays on the film spectator to carry the title *The Cinematic Apparatus* (De Lauretis and Heath, 1980).

During the 1980s and early 1990s, Metz published little on the subject of film semiotics, but his importance remained undimished as film scholars debated his theories and applied them to film analysis. In the intervening years, Metz contemplated the importance of the classic film theorist Rudolph Arnheim (decidedly *not* a semiotician). He also analyzed some essays of Freud unrelated to cinematic considerations. A return to cinematic interests in the late 1980s was colored by his colleagues' ongoing work in literary and filmic narratology. His ensuing papers have been on the filmic *énonciation*, climaxed by the publication of his *L'énonciation impersonnelle ou le site du film* in 1991.

Characteristic of Metz's books and articles is his frankly acknowledged indebtedness to his predecessors, whether they are linguists, philosophers, literary theorists, psychoanalysts, or film writers. It has been Metz's habit to share essays as works in progress and to solicit opinions and expanded ideas from his advanced seminars in Paris. His greatest challenge seems to have been how to conceal the pleasure he personally took in the medium he was discussing and in the theories he was explaining.

[*See also* Arnheim; Cinema; Enonciation Impersonnelle ou le Site du Film, L'; Film Semiotics; Grande Syntagmatique, La; *and* Imaginary Signifier, The.]

BIBLIOGRAPHY

Works by Metz

"Le cinéma: Langue ou langage?" *Communications* 4, edited by R. Barthes, pp. 52–90. Paris: Seuil, 1964.

Essais sur la signification au cinéma. 2 vols. Paris: Klincksieck, 1968, 1972. The first volume has been translated into English by M. Taylor as *Film Language: A Semiotics of the Cinema* (New York: Oxford University Press, 1974).

Langage et cinéma. Paris: Larousse, 1971. This book was translated into English by D. J. Umiker-Sebeok as *Language and Cinema* (The Hague: Mouton, 1974).

Le signifiant imaginaire. Collection 10/18. Paris: UGE, 1977. This book was translated into English by A. Guzzetti et al. as *The Imaginary Signifier: Psychoanalysis and the Cinema*. (Bloomington: Indiana University Press, 1981).

L'énonciation impersonnelle ou le site du film. Paris: Méridiens Klincksieck, 1991.

Other Works

Block de Behar, L., ed. *Semiotica* 112.1–2 (1996). Special issue on Christian Metz.

De Lauretis, T., and S. Heath, eds. *The Cinematic Apparatus*. London: Macmillan, 1980.

Marie, M., and M. Vernet, eds. *Christian Metz et la théorie du cinéma*. Paris: Editions Méridiens Klincksieck, 1990. Special issue of *Iris*, vol. 10.

Mitry, J. *Esthétique et psychologie du cinéma*, vol. 1. Paris: Editions Universitaires, 1963.

—C. D. E. TOLTON

MILITARY. All military systems are more or less rigid status hierarchies. Because people are not born into them but must learn as adults their places in the hierarchy, most military groups devote a tremendous amount of energy to symbolizing and signifying their social orders to their members. Membership in different miliary subgroups is signified by the wearing of various uniforms and accoutrements. Individuals' statuses in the hierarchy are symbolized by a wide range of badges and insignia that signify rank and placement. Armed forces vary in the complexity and formality of their systems of communicating rank and unit membership, and this variety of responses to a universal military problem is the site of study using semiotic methods and theory.

Military ranks are also communicated through many different modalities at the same time. Along with the variations in dress and insignia, for instance, are differences in saluting practices, as noted by Alexandra Jaffe (1988). On the larger scale, all military forces practice saluting, but there is a great range in the formality and importance attached to saluting by armed forces of different countries.

Another way in which the military social order is symbolized for its members is through the use of ritual. Military parades and ceremonials can be read as texts that make statements and send messages about the legitimacy of the military system and about changes in the status of members of the group. Most military groups mark changes of command, graduations, promotions, and funerals with formal military parades. In these parades, the social order and the status hierarchy are reified and thereby forcefully internalized in the psyches of the members of the military group. It is also significant that totemic symbols of military groups such as regimental flags, standards, and ritual complexes surround these important signs.

Communication and the cooperation involved in it are critical to success in battle, and consequently all military groups devote many resources to attempts at developing efficient systems of internal communications. All these systems share competing imperatives: they must be able to convey information effectively and accurately within the military force while simultaneously masking the information's meaning from the enemy. Included in this type of communication are highly technological systems such as VHF radios as well as the very "primitive" hand signals used, for instance, by infantry patrols. Within this subtopic of military semiotics fall the study of codes and cryptographic measures. Besides the use of complex coding, military personnel also use "veiled speech" over the radio, for example, to try to hide the size of the military operation and the level of command involved. Camouflage is also used extensively to conceal the presence of vehicles, trenches, and personnel. Soldiers become very adept at masking signs of their presence and show a great deal of personal style and individuality in their camouflage. A study of these types of military activities would be an important contribution to the semiotics of deception and dissembling.

Communication systems are used not only to pass information at various levels of the hierarchy but also to pass orders and commands from higher to lower command levels in the organization. While military forces differ in the level of initiative and decision-making ability expected of those in the lower ranks, all groups at certain times require instant, unquestioning obedience on the part of some members. Some commands, then, are meant to be obeyed blindly and instantly. To this end, a large part of military training is devoted to turning signs into signals that evoke an automatic response from the recipient. Some required responses can be quite complex series of activities, but the goal is still automatic response. A study of how this is accomplished through the practice of routine drills under all sorts of conditions might be quite fruitful for semiotics in general.

Another topic of interest to semioticians is the interaction between members of the military and their physical environment. Soldiers and sailors learn to read the environment like a text, interpreting signs in the land and on the sea to predict the weather and to establish the presence and intentions of the enemy. Visual cues are not the only signs that are interpreted for these purposes. Infantrymen on patrol and on sentry duty, for example, learn to identify various sounds as signs of enemy presence, such as the sound of a rifle being cocked. They also become very sensitive to smells and even to the movement of the air, both of which might provide them with important information.

Also important are representations of the environment, the enemy, and friendly activity. Both soldiers and sailors depend to a large degree on maps and charts to represent the land and the sea. They both also have complex and comprehensive coding systems for recording the presence and movements of friendly and enemy forces, vehicles, weapons, ships, and installations. Included in the system of coding is an evaluation of the reliability of the information represented on these maps, and a great deal of effort is expended to ensure that the information is accurate and up-to-date. Because of the importance of these representations, members of the military play with the concepts of mapping and reality. Many of their jokes involve confusing features of the map with those of the reality it represents.

The interplay between reality and its representations leads to another potential area for semiotic study. All military groups are contingent organizations that spend much of their time training for events that most of their members hope will never occur. Much of this training must be made as realistic as possible while recognizing the constraints of safety and economics. Soldiers, sailors, and members of air forces spend much time training in mock battles of differing levels of realism. There is frequently a mock enemy and supposed enemy weapons and equipment to be notionally destroyed. At the same time, there are real medical emergencies and logistical requirements to be met. The subject of how the notional enemy and its equipment are signified and communicated is a potentially interesting one for semiotics. How are real events such as vehicle accidents distinguished from "exercise" or "pretend" events? How do umpires assess the outcome of mock battles and decide who are the casualties and who are the winners? Are the distinctions between reality and the imaginary ever confused in the minds of those taking part in military training? All these are questions a semiotician interested in the military should ask her- or himself.

It is surprising that semioticians have not as yet discovered the military as a society rich in signs. Some of the problems of communication facing members of the military are universal, but some are specific to the military itself, and these specific problems can provide semioticians with a rich field of inquiry.

[See also Cartography; Code; Communication; Manipulation; and Nonverbal Bodily Sign Categories.]

BIBLIOGRAPHY

Ben-Ari, E. "Masks and Soldiering: The Israeli Army and the Palestinian Uprising." Cultural Anthropology 4 (1989): 372–389.
Elkin, F. "The Soldier's Language." American Journal of Sociology 51 (1946): 414–422.
Jaffe, A. "Saluting in Social Context." Journal of Applied Behavioral Science 24 (1988): 263–275.
Lakoff, G. "War and Metaphor: The Metaphor System Used to Justify War in the Gulf." In Cultural Semiotics, edited by P. Grzybek, pp. 73–92. Bochum: Brockmeyer, 1991.
Linton, R. "Totemism and the A.E.F." American Anthropologist 26 (1924): 296–300.
Zurcher, L. A. "The War Games: Organizational Scripting and the Expression of Emotion." Symbolic Interaction 8 (1985): 191–206.

—ANNE IRWIN

MINDSCAPE. A conflation of *mind*, intended to refer to the act of contemplation, and *scape*, defined as a representation or formation; a mindscape is a space that is both conceptual and has a definable, physical locus. It is thus an internal space of contemplation that has reference to an external reality that is equivalent to the world.

The concept of a mindscape is useful for grasping the idea that realities perceived as external to a Cartesian unitary self or ego—such as people, events, and the "landscape"—are not value-free, neutral givens that exist independently of human cognition. The presence and spatial dimension of an object of the mindscape, such as a landscape, is largely arbitrary so long as it fits the mind's conceptual model of external realities. Thus, both the mind and the physical landscape affect each other in recursive fashions. The very act of labeling a landscape or a wilderness as such imbues that space with a cultural bias and is an attempt at cognitive control of a physical reality. A good example of such attempted cognitive and consequent ideological control is the etchings and paintings American colonists made of their new domains. The often hostile and alien landscape was domesticated and made familiar by, for example, placing trees native to the colonists' homeland in the etching or painting and by depicting the indigenous inhabitants in nonthreatening pastoral scenes. These images developed within a colonial paradigm that stressed the natural dominance of Europeans over the other and over their landscapes (Fabian, 1983). The mindscape of the indigenous inhabitants, on the other hand, usually found expression verbally in complex oral accounts and songs that often selected the most negative qualities of the colonists.

Each person is capable of constructing innumerable mindscapes and adding nuance to them by expressing them in a variety of forms; such as visual, verbal, and tactile manifestations, as well as less easily definable expressions such as emotional tones and intent. These mindscapes change constantly as a person's knowledge is altered, challenged, or added to, though there are almost always certain fixed points of reference, such as a personal identity or certain relationships such as mother and son. A mindscape that challenges such fixed points is considered a traumatic one. Alternatively, most mindscapes serve to legitimate personal and group identities.

Certain symbolically and visually literate people are able to translate elements of a mindscape into appealing or provocative idiom that becomes integrated into a society or, more broadly, into a system of signification that then functions as a concept-forming, world-ordering cognitive resource (see De Certeau, 1984). These symbolic literates have long been recognized by all societies and are often placed in unique categories. For example, many non-Western, nonindustrialized societies have shamans or ritual specialists. The shaman is most often a person who practices institutionalized altered states of consciousness and who is believed to be in contact with and to journey between multiple worlds or scapes. The shaman is aware of which icons, signs, symbols, and indexes most fundamentally move people, and he or she deliberately manipulate these terms to produce ever-changing scapes. In many Western societies up until the late eighteenth century, "mad" people were not kept in institutions but were seen as "touched by the

hand of God," and their presence in a community was seen as a mark of especial favor. The voices "mad" people heard and visions they saw were considered real but part of another mindscape.

Though difficult to quantify or even describe clearly, the mindscape operates in a pervasive, synergistic fashion on the most deeply held and most change-resistant elements of a cognitive matrix. Not all mindscapes will be accepted because, in an as yet poorly understood process, people immediately know if a mindscape is "not right," even if they cannot articulate and adumbrate why.

The mindscape operates on at least two levels. First, the internal space of contemplation, like the colonists and indigenous people's perceptions of each other, is unavoidably the product of the articulation or misarticulation of specific social and historical factors that are difficult for people not privy to that system of signification to comprehend. Second, mindscapes also have universal validity and, at times, assume the character of a common human heritage. For example, all anatomically modern humans of the last one hundred thousand years share an identical central nervous system comprising the brain, sense organs, and spinal column. This biological given is, of course, subject to specific cultural experiences, yet certain images and concepts appear to move all humans in similar ways. This type of insight is what concerns developmental psychologists such as Jean Piaget and what informs Carl Jung's idea of a collective unconscious. It seems that almost all human societies, in whatever cognitive, economic, political, or religious modality they operate, have a concept of a stratified universe, almost always with upper, middle, and lower realms that might be further subdivided. Sometimes this concept of a stratified universe is only an abstract deictic device devoid of much emotional force. This was not always the case, however: it appears that at some point in antiquity, possibly with the emergence of conscious representation or "art" about forty thousand years ago, the mind underwent a fundamental shift or embedding, and a largely binary, oppositional mode of thinking replaced a mode in which multiple levels of phenomena such as dreams, hallucinations, and the products of mental disorders were all considered "real" (Jaynes, 1976).

This internal space of contemplation has an external but equally conceptual referent—namely, the landscape or those observable objects perceived as external to the self or a group. The landscape consists not only of hills, trees, and people but also of innumerable relationships involving people and/or things. Unlike the mindscape, which is reasonably unfettered, the landscape is usually tightly bounded by either natural features such as rivers and oceans or arbitrary, surveyed boundaries. This observable landscape might further conceal an equally real but unobservable landscape underneath the observable one. This underworld is a pervasive feature of almost all cosmologies yet is not often explicitly acknowledged by theory. Possibly this is a case of one obvious feature blinding us to another.

Archaeologists are sensitized to the concept of landscape and understand that landscapes have had many "lives" and may have numerous lives simultaneously. These lives are represented partly by the very fragmentary material-culture remains of human communities past and present. Such observable material culture consists of day-to-day domestic refuse, dwellings, household items, religious structures, tools, and broader cultural modifications to a physical locus by individual people and communities. By studying a specific locus or site, we can understand how the people who lived there perceived the landscape. In other words, their mindscape is encoded in their physical remains. Put differently, landscapes are made up of both "places" and "spaces" (Tilley, 1994) in which a place is a definable physical locus at which human action or thought is manifest, whereas a space is a fairly undifferentiated area that nevertheless provides the general character, texture, and context of a place.

Mindscapes often find visual expression at certain places, though they can be suppressed. For example, many rock-art sites appear to have been places at which ordinary reality was suspended and reordered. This reordering is ambiguous as it was often specific to a certain place and even a certain event, beyond which the ordinary world order held sway. Yet after coming into contact with a new mindscape, people are unable to return wholly to the mindscape they had previously. For this reason, the landscape is an essential component of a personal and corporate identity. Though culturally and cognitively structured, the landscape does represent a fixed point in all people's lives. Nomadic people are not attached to any one place and are more inhabitants of spaces than places and thus have a decentered perspective of landscape. Sedentary communities tend to have a more centered perspective in which one moves from definable place to definable place with each representing a different set of activities and values such as work, worship, relaxation, and so on. This attachment to places and spaces is known as topophilia (Tuan, 1974) and might explain why the transformation of landscapes from agrarian to industrialized, for example, causes such profound social dislocation and radical reordering of mindscapes.

The study of mindscape and landscape is thus an important sociological endeavor, though such studies are not unproblematic. One of the problems in the study of either mindscape or landscape is that neither forms a specific, bounded body of inquiry. Landscapes, like mindscapes, are thus incapable of closure and perhaps even certainty; there might always be an element of the unknown hidden or ignored in a landscape that is threatening. It is thus impossible to trust a mindscape entirely as its vision of the world might be dysfunctional or in opposition to another mindscape. Our existence is based largely on the premise that we will persist because we have always done so, and there is thus no escape from the mindscape.

[See also Cultural Landscape; Gibson; Morphology; Rock Art; and Space.]

BIBLIOGRAPHY

De Certeau, M. *The Practice of Everyday Life.* Berkeley: University of California Press, 1984.

Fabian, J. *Time and the Other: How Anthropology Makes Its Subject.* New York: Columbia University Press, 1983.

Jaynes, J. *The Origin of Consciousness in the Breakdown of the Bicameral Mind.* London: Windus, 1976.

Orians, G. H., and J. H. Heerwagen. "Evolved Responses to Landscapes." In *The Adapted Mind: Evolutionary Psychology and the Generation of Culture*; edited by J. H. Barkow, L. Cosmides, and J. Tooby, pp. 555–579. Oxford: Oxford University Press, 1992.

Tilley, C. *A Phenomenology of Landscape: Places, Paths, and Monuments.* Oxford: Berg, 1994.

Tuan, Y-F. *Topophilia: A Study of Environmental Perception, Attitudes, and Values.* Englewood Cliffs, N.J.: Prentice-Hall, 1974.

Wilson, R. O. *Biophilia.* Cambridge, Mass.: Harvard University Press, 1984.

—SVEN OUZMAN

MORPHOLOGY. The study and description of form or structure, especially in biology and linguistics, morphology addresses the developmental and transformational features of systems rather than their static characteristics. Hence, what comes under the rubric of the morphological are irregular, inexact, or changing shapes rather than ideal, geometrical forms. While *morphology* occasionally designates a topology or broad system of classification, more often it implies an attention to individual variation—objects as they appear in the real world—over and above general categories. When the term is used in humanist disciplines, it has therefore tended to be used with varying degrees of rigor and precision to impose order on not readily formalizable entities such as history and language.

Goethe coined the word *morphology* in his botanical writings ("Zur Morphologie," 1817–1824; see Goethe, 1988) as he sought, through comparative anatomical methods, to discover a primal plant form that would contain all others—the celebrated *Urpflanze*. Ultimately, for Goethe, morphology is a descriptive enterprise that would unify the sciences by merging experience and theory, holding out the hope of a *mathesis matheseos*, a science of science. Goethe expressed this morphological vision not only in his scientific projects but also in his poetic explorations of the world.

In the 1920s, the term achieved an unprecedented popularity due to the dissemination of biological theories in works such as D'Arcy Thompson's *On Growth and Form* (1917), as well as to Oswald Spengler's influential account of "Morphology of History" in *The Decline of the West* (1918–1922), which attempted to conceive of the totality of world history in terms of recurrent organic patterns. Carol O. Sauer's "Morphology of Landscape" (1926) founded the study of geography in America by applying Spengler's method to the study of landforms. Vladimir Propp, in *Morphology of the Folktale* (1928), a key text of the Russian formalist movement and precursor of Lévi-Straussian structural anthropology, paid homage to Goethe's holistic vision in developing a complex classificatory scheme of literary motifs. Alfred North Whitehead, in his major philosophical treatise, *Process and Reality* (1929), extended the concept of the morphological to encompass a metaphysical dimension of the cosmos. Louis Hjelmslev (1899–1965) and others also underscored its importance as a linguistic category.

In recent years, new mathematical paradigms have furthered the investigation of transformational phenomena, including those of morphogenetic or self-organizing formal systems. Alan Turing, the inventor of the concept of the computer, pioneered research in chemical morphogenesis in 1952, and this work has led to a growing field of biological studies of embryology, as well as to new understandings of the nature and variety of formal complexity (see Turing, 1992). Scientific thinkers such as Ilya Prigogine, René Thom, and Benoit Mandelbrot have used the morphological as a springboard for articulating original and comprehensive philosophies of becoming and mathematical theories of morphogenesis.

[*See also* Catastrophe Theory; Hjelmslev; Spengler; Thom; *and* Turing.]

BIBLIOGRAPHY

Boutot, A. *L'invention des formes.* Paris: Odile Jacob, 1993.

D'Arcy Thompson, W. *On Growth and Form: An Abridged Edition.* Edited by J. T. Bonner. Cambridge: Cambridge University Press, 1961.

Goethe, J. W. von. *Scientific Studies.* Edited and translated by D. Miller. New York: Suhrkamp, 1988.

Mandelbrot, B. *The Fractal Geometry of Nature.* New York: W. H. Freeman, 1983.

Petitot-Cocorda, J. *Morphogénèse du sens.* Paris: Presses Universitaires de France, 1985.

Prigogine, I., and I. Stengers. *Order out of Chaos: Man's New Dialogue with Nature.* Toronto: Bartam Books, 1984.

Propp, V. *Morphology of the Folktale,* (1928). Austin: University of Texas Press, 1968.

Sauer, C. O. *Land and Life: A Selection from the Writings of Carl Ortwin Sauer.* Edited by John Leighly. Berkeley: University of California Press, 1963.

Thom, R. *Structural Stability and Morphogenesis.* Translated by D. H. Fowler. Reading, Mass: Benjamin, 1975.

Turing, A. M. *Morphogenesis.* Edited by P. T. Saunders. Amsterdam and New York: North Holland, 1992.

Virilio, P. *Lost Dimension.* New York: Semiotext(e), 1990.

Whitehead, A. N. *Process and Reality: An Essay in Cosmology.* Cambridge: Cambridge University Press, 1929.

—ALBERT LIU

MOSCOW-TARTU SCHOOL.

A group of Russian scholars who dominated the Soviet semiotic scene from the early 1960s until the end of the 1980s and made fundamental contributions to the semiotics of culture, the Moscow-Tartu School had two intellectual and organizational centers: the Estonian city of Tartu and Moscow, where, historically speaking, the linguistic and structuralist roots of the school can be found. It is important to remember that the development of structuralism in the Soviet Union was constrained by the cultural and political context. The very first discussions of structural phonology (S. K. Šaumjan) took place in the early 1950s, and only after the Twentieth Party Congress in 1956 did the process of de-Stalinization lead to a "thaw" in politics and culture. Young scholars, mainly in the social sciences, started questioning the monolithic ideology and its official methodology and tried other approaches. Although there were no public discussions on this topic, it became clear that language was the dominant means of conveying ideological contents and, thus, was an ideological instrument. Consequently, contributions from ideologically less-sensitive domains such as cybernetics, information theory, machine translation, and structural and mathematical linguistics shaped the early structuralist discussions.

The year 1956 turned out to be crucial for the development of structuralism. One important event was the discussion on structuralism that arose in *Voprosy jazykoznanija*, the official publication organ for the study of linguistics. In the same year, a seminar on the application of mathematical methods in linguistics was initiated by A. A. Kolmogorov at Moscow State University. This seminar, guided by Vjačeslav V. Ivanov, was attended by many young scholars who later became important members of the Moscow-Tartu School (among them I. I. Revzin, B. A. Uspenskij, and T. M. Nikolaeva). Also in 1956, Ivanov, Revzin, and others founded the Association for Machine Translation in Moscow, an event that paved the way for the First All-Union Conference on Machine Translation in Moscow in 1958 and its follow-up conference in Leningrad in 1959. These initiatives were closely related to the activities of V. J. Rozenvejg, who in 1958 organized a meeting between the young Moscow linguists and Roman Jakobson. Jakobson was on his first visit to Moscow, for the International Congress of Slavistics, after his emigration from the Soviet Union.

All these initiatives were characterized by a close cooperation between linguists and mathematicians and by the additional integration of specialists in aphasiology (A. R. Lurija), psychology (N. V. Žimkin), surdopedagogy (Sokoljanskij), analysis of writing systems (J. V. Knorozov), and many others. They all were members of a separate linguistic section at the Academy of Sciences, initiated by A. I. Berg and headed by Ivanov. The orientation of this group's work was clear: multidisciplinary approaches to language, which necessarily led to questions beyond pure linguistics. Crucial figures in initiating and organizing the activities were Ivanov and V. N. Toporov, both of whom became the main exponents and promoters of semiotics as a broadly conceived discipline in its own right. Toporov had shocked his audience at a 1957 conference on the relationship between synchrony and diachrony in linguistics, during which he declared that the topic of the conference could as well have been brought up some thirty years earlier and that also the proposed solutions to obsolete questions were far from new; he explicitly criticized the lack of acquaintance with modern methods of scholarly research, and he called the discussion deeply provincial.

In 1960, the Section of Structural Typology of Slavic Languages was founded as an integral part of the Academy of Sciences, first headed by Toporov (until 1963), then by Ivanov. Many of Ivanov's and Toporov's former students (e.g., T. V. Civ'jan, M. I. Lekomceva, D. Segal) became attached to this institute as researchers, which soon was to be considered the leading organizational center for semiotic studies. The institute was the main organizer of the seminal Symposium on the Structural Study of Sign Systems in Moscow in December 1962 that was the official breakthrough of semiotics as an autonomous discipline. These activities raised controversial discussions on the status and ideological foundations of semiotics in the Soviet Union. Still, a commission on the improvement of the status of semiotics was founded at the Academy of Sciences in 1963, again on the initiative of A. I. Berg. Soon after the symposium, close cooperation began with J. M. Lotman and his colleagues (I. Černov, Z. G. Minc, A. G. Egorov, and others) from Tartu University. This cooperation resulted in unrestricted discussions on almost any potentially semiotic theme and, as a result, an enormous number of papers, frequently with varying coauthorships. Many of these contributions were formulated as tentative hypotheses.

Organizationally, the Moscow-Tartu cooperation had two important results: first, the Tartu Summer Schools which took place every alternate year, from 1964 to 1970; here, Moscow and Tartu scholars met on the (geographic and academic but also political) periphery of the Soviet Union and discussed freely semiotic issues. Second, Lotman began to edit the journal *Trudy po znakovym sistemam* (Studies on sign systems). His twenty-five issues (1964–1992) contributed to the establishment of the Moscow-Tartu

School's international reputation, and many articles from it have been translated into many languages. Still, many other papers were published in peripheral publications not always easily accessible to outsiders.

The 1962 Moscow symposium was concerned with the whole spectrum of semiotic systems, starting from natural language, including artificial languages and nonverbal communication, and extending to topics such as traffic signs, card games, art, and many others. The introduction to the symposium, which was written anonymously by Ivanov, contained a blueprint for Soviet semiotics in the decades to come. Hence, methodological insights gained from the analysis of natural language were applied, at least tentatively, to other sign systems. In this sense, Moscow-Tartu semiotics was oriented from the onset toward application rather than theory. The claim of semiotics to the leading role in the analysis of human communication (implying that semiotics is both one discipline among others and an integrative metadiscipline) necessarily implied competing with the official ideology in explaining social behavior. Consequently, *semiotics* was not a term welcome by official ideology; therefore, semioticians avoided it and called sign systems other than natural language "modeling systems." After the 1964 summer school, the notion of secondary modeling systems was generally accepted, and the term became a key concept of the Moscow-Tartu School. Defining sign systems such as literature, myth, theater, painting, and puppetry as secondary modeling systems implied natural language as a primary modeling system on the basis of or corresponding to which all secondary systems are constructed. In this sense, Moscow-Tartu semiotics continued Ferdinand de Saussure's and Louis Hjelmslev's ideas, understanding sign systems as structures consisting of elements in a particular (functional) relationship.

The semiotic analyses of the 1960s were characterized by an extension and reformulation of many terms originating in linguistics. The central term *text*, for example, was applied not only to linguistic texts, but in its broader semiotic understanding to any meaningful sequence of signifying elements (thus, paintings or films could be regarded as texts, too) organized by a particular underlying "language." Thus, the conceptual extension was oriented toward the convergences of various sign systems. This extension was paralleled by crucial restrictions, however: only those structures analogous to those of natural lan-

guage (or to the categories of metalanguage) were likely to be considered semiotic. Further, semiotic systems were likely to be analyzed selectively, since only those elements that could be assimilated to linguistic structures were taken into consideration. The specificity of other sign systems was likely to be reduced to the structures of natural language.

The previously more or less exactly defined terms became increasingly metaphoric, which in turn allowed for a greater freedom in their semiotic application. Since the Moscow-Tartu School was at that time a rather closed circle, there was a tacit understanding of both orientation and usage of the basic terms and concepts, although not all scholars used one and the same term identically. Only later did external criticisms of the Moscow-Tartu School's concepts point to their terminological problems.

In 1970, Lotman presented his seminal "Propositions" for the Fourth Tartu Summer School, which was attended by both Roman Jakobson and Claude Lévi-Strauss. From then on, the notion of "culture" guided the school's activities. Based on the assumption that the human production, exchange, and storage of information by way of signs form a particular unity, culture was understood as the functional correlation of the various sign systems used by individuals as members of groups and societies. The semiotics of culture thus studies these sign systems in their correlation and hierarchical organization.

The "Theses on the Semiotic Study of Culture" (Lotman et al., 1973) guided the semiotic research of subsequent years. Partly in the form of programmatic hypotheses, it included issues such as the relevance of natural language for the definition and functioning of culture; the minimal preconditions of culture; the relation of culture to its obligatory counterpart, nonculture; the relevance of internal and external points of view in the analysis of culture; the temporal status of culture as experience, as collective memory, as nonhereditary information, and as a program for the future; the topological organization of culture; the typological diversification of cultures; the relation of "utterance" (in a semiotic sense) and culturally relevant texts; the relation of texts and their functions; and the evolution of culture. It was mainly Lotman who proposed these research perspectives. On the basis of his structural studies of literature and art, he developed topological descriptions of literary artifacts. Applying concepts such as "external/internal," "we/they," "own/alien," "sacred/profane," "chaos/cosmos," and others, Lotman strived for the spatial description of relations and values in general. The application of semantic oppositions in order to describe cultural texts was not uncommon to the Moscow linguists. As early as 1965, Ivanov and Toporov had established a list of sixteen semantic oppositions such as "life/death," "fortunate/unfortunate," "even/odd," and others to describe Old Slavic cultural texts; they claimed this list was one concrete realization of a universally valid repertory, consisting of about eighty semiotic classifications.

Thus, heterogeneous tendencies converged in the term *culture*, and the 1970s were characterized by the intensive study of cultural texts. Semiotic studies confirmed the orientation toward applied semiotics, although various attempts were made to relate the results to semiotic roots and foundations of semiosis, whether linguistic-etymological reconstructions in their cultural relevance, the reconstruction of protomyths, or functional brain asymmetry as the biological basis of semiosis. Ultimately, these attempts led to a diversification of interests.

Contemporary Soviet culture was usually not the object of semiotic analyses, and there was no overt discussion of its semiotic organization; rather, by denying Soviet culture the status of a semiotic topic in its own right, it was implicitly treated as a nonculture. On the other hand, Moscow-Tartu scholars were aware of the fact that scientific texts are not only ways to study a given culture but also part of that culture, since they contribute to their culture by modeling its character. In this sense, the Moscow-Tartu School can be regarded as a particular subculture in its own right, and the semiotic texts produced by it can be considered as an alternative cultural model.

[*See also* Cybernetics; Jakobson; Jakobson's Model of Linguistic Communication; Lotman; Multimodality; *and* Text.]

BIBLIOGRAPHY

Baran, H., ed. *Semiotics and Structuralism: Readings from the Soveit Union.* White Plains, N.Y.: International Arts and Sciences Press, 1976.

Broms, H., and R. Kaufmann, eds. *Semiotics of Culture: Proceedings of the Twenty-fifth Symposium of the Tartu-Moscow School of Semiotics, Imatra, Finland, 27–29 July 1987.* Helsinki: Arator, 1988.

Eimermacher, K., and S. Shishkoff. *Subject Bibliography of Soviet Semiotics: The Moscow-Tartu School.* Ann Arbor: University of Michigan Press, 1977.

Grzybek, P. "The Concept of 'Model' in Soviet Semiotics." *Russian Literature* 36.3 (1994): 285–300.

Lotman, J. M., et al., "Theses on the Semiotic Study of Culture (as Applied to Slavic Texts)." In *Structure of Texts and Semiotics of Culture,* edited by J. van der Eng and M. Grygar, pp. 1–28. The Hague: Mouton, 1973.

Lucid, D. P., ed. *Soviet Semiotics: An Anthology.* Baltimore and London: Johns Hopkins University Press, 1977.

Rudy, S. "Semiotics in the U.S.S.R." In *The Semiotic Sphere,* edited by T. A. Sebeok and J. Sebeok-Umiker, pp. 555–582. New York and London: Plenum, 1986.

Seyffert, P. *Soviet Literary Structuralism: Background, Debate, Issues.* Columbus, Ohio: Slavica Publishers 1983.

Uspenskij, B. A. *A Poetics of Composition: The Structure of the Artistic Text and Typology of a Compositional Form.* Translated by V. Zavarin and S. Vitting. Berkeley: University of California Press, 1973.

—PETER GRZYBEK

MOTIVATION. *See* Linguistic Motivation.

MUKAŘOVSKÝ, JAN (1891–1975), Czechoslovakian structuralist, known mainly for his contributions to aesthetics and the semiotics of art. Mukařovský studied linguistics and aesthetics at the philological faculty of Charles University in Prague until 1915; in 1923, he received his doctoral degree for his dissertation, "Contribution to the Aesthetics of the Czech Verse." He became a founding member of the Prague Linguistic Circle in 1926. After teaching at the University of Bratislava from 1931 to 1937, he returned to Prague to become director of the Institute of Aesthetics and professor at Charles University. From 1948 to 1953, Mukařovský was rector of the university.

Mukařovský's works can be divided into several periods. The "formalistic" period (1923–1928) is characterized predominantly by stylistical analyses; not yet acquainted with Russian formalism, Mukařovský understands the works he studies as a continuation of the formalist tradition going back to scholars such as J. F. Herbart (1776–1841), Joseph Durdík (1837–1902), Otakar Hostinský (1847–1910), and Otakar Zich (1879–1934). In his study *Máchův Máj: Estetická studie* (Mácha's "May": A Study in Aesthetics, 1928), Mukařovský claims that the work of art must be understood as a phenomenon sui generis, regardless of any external relations, including those to its creator and to reality.

Mukařovský's second period (1929–1934) is characterized by the rise of reflections on general aesthetic problems; it can be seen as the preparation of what was to become structural aesthetics. During this time, Mukařovský became increasingly influential in the Prague Linguistic Circle. He prepared an article, "O jazyce básnickém" (On Poetic Language), for the theses presented at the First International Congress of Slavicists in Prague in 1929. During the early 1930s, he wrote studies on a broad spectrum of questions, such as the artist's personality, the poetic work of art as a totality of values, language culture, film, and drama.

His third period (1934–1941) deals with aesthetics in terms of functional structuralism. In his 1934 review on the Czech translation of Šklovskij's *Theory of Prose*, Mukařovský rejects the tendencies of Russian formalism because of their exclusive focus on formal devices. In his study *Polákova Vznešenost přírody* (Polák's "Nature's Sublimity," 1934), Mukařovský defines a work of art as a "structure, i.e., as a totality whose character is defined by its elements and their interrelations, and which, in turn, defines the character and the relations of its elements." One of these elements (the structural dominant) rules over the others and provides the unity of the work of art. Unlike in his earlier works, Mukařovský here rejects immanent analyses in favor of complex structural studies comprising both internal and external (social, political, ideological, etc.) elements and relations. The character of the "structure of structures" cannot be predicted on the basis of the work of art and its structure alone: different structures (with different dominants and different hierarchies of elements) of one and the same work of art may be perceived in changing historical contexts. Thus, the work of art is understood as a particular means of social communication, and it is consequently conceived of as a sign mediating between the sending and the receiving subjects, both being part of a given society. This new semiotic perspective is developed most clearly in Mukařovský's presentation at the 1934 International Philosophical Congress in Paris, "Art as a Semiotic Fact." In it, Mukařovský refers to the Saussurean concept of sign and modifies it for aesthetic purposes by way of introducing the juxtaposition of "material artifact" and "aesthetic object." He also integrates Karl Bühler's tripartite concept of language functions with the Russian-formalist opposition of the practical and poetic functions of language by charactizing

Bühler's three functions as practical and adding a fourth, autonomous, "aesthetic" function to them. Mukařovský's works in the late 1930s are characterized by studies of specific aesthetic concepts such as the aesthetic norm, value and function, and the semantic gesture.

In his works from 1941 to 1948 (most of which were not published at that time), Mukařovský repeatedly deals with questions of individuality in art as a predominantly social phenomenon; this leads him to anthropological theories on the one hand and to Marxism on the other. In this context, he discusses possible connections between structuralist aesthetics and the principles of dialectical materialism as in his 1949 essay "Kam směřuje dnešni teorie uměni?" (The Direction of Contemporary Theory of Art). Later, after the Communist takeover of Czechoslovakia and the subsequent establishment of Marxism as the official doctrine, Mukařovský reached the opposite conclusion in his essay "Ke kritice strukturalismu v nasí literární vědě" (On the Critique of Structuralism in Our Literary Studies, 1951), in which he praises the "great example and brotherly support of Soviet literary studies" and calls structuralism a "masked form of idealism in bourgeois scholarship." In the late 1960s, Mukařovský returned to his former theoretical positions when he published his articles from the 1940s in his *Studie z estetiky* (1966; 2d ed., 1971), followed by the publication of his *Cestami poetiky a estetiky* (1971). These editions paved the way for the international reception of his contributions to structuralism.

[*See also* Aesthetics; Art; Marx; Materialist Semiotics; Poetics; Prague School; *and* Russian Formalism.]

BIBLIOGRAPHY

Mukařovský, J. "The Esthetics of Language." In *A Prague School Reader on Esthetics, Literary Structure, and Style*, edited by P. L. Garvin, pp. 31–69. Washington, D.C.: Georgetown University Press, 1964a.

Mukařovský, J. "Standard Language and Poetic Language." In *A Prague School Reader on Esthetics, Literary Structure, and Style*, edited by P. L. Garvin, pp. 17–30. Washington, D.C.: Georgetown University Press, 1964b.

Mukařovský, J. *Aesthetic Function, Norm, and Value as Social Facts*. Translated by M. E. Suino. Ann Arbor: University of Michigan Press, 1970.

Mukařovský, J. *Cestami poetiky a estetiky*. Prague: Ceskoslvenský Spisovatel, 1971.

Mukařovský, J. "Art as a Semiotic Fact." In *Structure,*

Sign, and Function, edited by J. Burbank and P. Steiner, pp. 82–88. New Haven: Yale University Press, 1977.

Mukařovský, J. *The Word and Verbal Art: Selected Essays.* Edited by J. Burbank, P. Steiner, and W. Steiner. New Haven: Yale University Press, 1977.

Mukařovský, J. *Structure, Sign, and Function: Selected Essays by Jan Mukařovský.* Translated and edited by J. Burbank and P. Steiner. New Haven: Yale University Press, 1978.

Mukařovský, J. "Structuralism in Esthetics and Literary Studies." In *The Prague School: Selected Writings, 1929–1946,* edited by P. Steiner, pp. 65–82. Austin: University of Texas Press, 1982.

Sedmidubsk, M. "Bibliographie zur Rezeption J. Mukařovský's im westlichen Kontext." In *Zeichen und Funktion: Beiträge zur ästhetischen Konzeption Jan Mukařovský's,* edited by H. Günther, pp. 180–207. Munich: O. Sagner, 1986.

—PETER GRZYBEK

MULTIMODALITY.

Semioticians are increasingly paying attention to the fact that human social meaning making rarely if ever deploys the resources of a single semiotic system such as language. Generally speaking, the participants in a given occasion of discourse orchestrate the resources of two or more semiotic systems into a single semiotic action. Linguistics has concentrated on the analysis of language in isolation from its codeployment and coevolution with other semiotic modalities, and this is reflected in the kinds of scientific metalanguages that have evolved in the Western tradition since the time of Plato and Aristotle. With the flow of speech sounds, for example, linguistics deploys the specialized metalanguages of phonetics and phonology to analyze distinctive phonetic features and phonological units such as the phoneme and the syllable. The analytical procedures of phonetics and phonology allow the practitioners of these disciplines to determine that any given number of speakers can utter a sound that belongs to a single general class or phonological category. However, this essentially categorical mode of analysis puts to one side many other linguistically nonsalient features that might be relevant to the context of a speech event, such as the affective states of the speaker, individual differences in voice, and so on.

But what of our metasemiotic resources for talking about language and other social semiotic-resource systems and practices? Is verbal metalanguage alone adequate or even desirable for describing the theoretical abstractions that linguists use to model language? How can a purely verbal metalanguage fully or adequately describe graded or continuous phenomena, varying scalar levels and their interrelations, dynamically emergent phenomena, and complex hierarchical levels of organization in both language and other semiotic modalities? Take the notion of stratification in linguistic theory: for those linguists who view language as a stratified system, the following properties hold:

1. the system consists of an unbounded hierarchy of scalar levels, going in both directions with reference to some focal level;
2. the units and structures at any given level in the hierarchy entertain principles of organization that are specific to that level;
3. there is no direct or causal relation linking the units and structures on any given level and those on some other level—instead, each stratum mutually constrains the other strata and contributes its own specific dynamics to the whole;
4. the further apart two strata are, the weaker the constraints they impose on each other. Thus, lexicogrammar and semantics are strongly cross-coupled in this sense; semantics and phonology or graphology much more weakly so;
5. no level is reducible to some more essential reality at the level below it.

Many of these characteristics involve both topological and multidimensional criteria that might not be described adequately by the primarily digital and categorical criteria of a purely verbal metalanguage.

The diagram presented in figure 1 attempts to communicate all of the features referred to in (1) to (5) that use the combined resources of at least three semiotic systems: the visual grammar of the abstract diagram, the graphological resources of print, and the lexicogrammatical and semantic resources of language. In so doing, this diagram is an instance of a specific multimodal genre of text for describing abstract scientific concepts—in this case, the metatheoretical concept of stratification in language.

Circles contrast paradigmatically in visual grammar with angular forms such as squares and rectangles. The curved form of the circle is associated with organic wholeness and harmony. The center of the circle constitutes the focal point for the concentric rings that "emanate" from this. In figure 1, however, the three innermost circles do not emanate concentrically from a shared center of focus owing to the asymmetric disposition of the circles in relation to

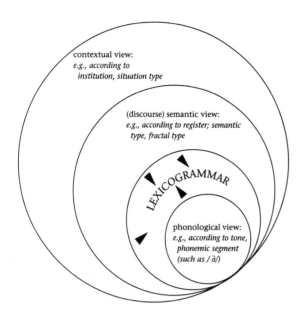

internal views on lexicogrammar

FIGURE 1. *Multimodal metasemiosis; stratification and lexicogrammar* (from Matthiessen, 1996).

each other. Note, too, how all four circles intersect at a common point on their circumferences. These two features suggest that the hierarchical nature of the relations at each level does not entail that any given level is necessarily more important than the others and that the four stratal perspectives on language that are represented in the diagram intersect with each other in the creation of the whole.

The naturalness and holism of circular forms also suggest here the unbounded and continuous nature of the stratal relations represented. It also plays down conflict; no level is inherently more important that the others. However, a given level can be selected as the reference point for a given theoretical purpose. This is the focal level. In figure 1, the lexicogrammatical stratum is focal in this sense. The use of larger and bolder type, along with the curved shape of the word *lexicogrammar* are instances of specific visual-graphic conventions that the makers of such diagrams use in order to signal the relative prominence of some features rather than others. At the same time, the curvature of the word *lexicogrammar* reminds us that the lexicogrammatical stratum of language is not a reified order, separate from the whole of the language phenomenon, as presented in this diagram.

The focal status of this stratum is also suggested by the vectorial nature of the three arrows that are internal to the diagram. Each of these originates from a given stratum other than the lexicogrammatical, and they converge on a focal point that coincides both with the center of the overall figure and the lexicogrammatical stratum. The convergence of these three vectors thus coincides with the selection of the lexicogrammatical stratum as the focal point of the diagram and the linguistic discussion that accompanies it.

The codeployment of the resources of a number of different semiotic systems produces a complex meaning that could not have resulted if each semiotic modality remained isolated from the others. Thus, the copatterning of the visual regions enclosed by any given circle with the nominalized labels associated with it—"contextual view," "(discourse) semantic view," "phonological view"—represents some of the theoretical objects in this particular scientific metalanguage. The converging vectors and the foregrounded graphological status of the word *lexicogrammar* construct a specific viewpoint for the reader of the diagram. Further, the embedding of the four circles suggests the scalar nature of the units and relations at any given level with respect to those on the other levels. The outwardly expanding effect of the circles additionally suggests the open-ended and potentially infinite nature of the orders of scalar relations that are presented. The schematic character of the diagram interacts with the absence of specific deixis in the nominalized labels to suggest the normative status of the theoretical statement to which the diagram gives voice. The diagram, as a metatheoretical statement, claims that the property of stratification holds generally for any instance of natural language constituted as its theoretical object.

Through the codeployment of diverse semiotic resources, the diagram reconstrues natural-language phenomena as a metaphenomenon in terms of the theoretical concepts of the object language—e.g., theoretical concepts such as strata, context, discourse semantics, lexicogrammar, and so on—in order that these and the theoretical relations that hold between them become subject to metatheoretical reflection. The object language is not, then, natural language per se (Droste, 1983); rather, it is the theoretical categories that the metasemiotic constitutes as the objects of its own theoretical activities. The diagram does not refer directly to natural language as such.

Its function is to selectively reconstitute the objects of the theory in specifiable relations to each other. The multimodal nature of this metasemiotic shows how the scalar relations involved in stratification are more flexibly enhanced than they would be in a monomodal metasemiotic.

[*See also* Conversation; Diagrams; Metalanguage; *and* Nonverbal Bodily Sign Categories.]

BIBLIOGRAPHY

Droste, F. G. "Reflections on Metalanguage and Object-Language." *Linguistics* 21 (1983): 875–899.

Halliday, M. A. K. "On the Ineffability of Grammatical Categories." In *Lingustics in a Systemic Perspective*, edited by D. Benson, M. J. Cummings, and W. S. Greaves, pp. 27–51. Amsterdam and Philadelphia: John Benjamins, 1988.

Matthiessen, C. "Language on Language: The Grammar of Semiosis." *Social Semiotics* 2.2 (1992): 69–111.

Matthiessen, C. "Systemic Functional Lexicogrammar for All Seasons." Plenary lecture handout, p. 9. Twenty-third International Systemic Functional Congress, University of Technology. Sydney, July 1996.

Reddy, M. J. "The Conduit Metaphor: A Case of Frame Conflict in Our Language about Language." In *Metaphor and Thought*, edited by A. Ortony, pp. 284–324. Cambridge and Melbourne: Cambridge University Press, 1979.

Thibault, P. J. *Social Semiotics as Praxis: Text, Social Meaning Making, and Nabakov's "Ada."* Theory and History of Literature Series, vol. 74. Minneapolis and Oxford: University of Minnesota Press, 1991.

—PAUL J. THIBAULT

MUSIC. Although there have been systematic descriptions of music since the Pythagoreans, the semiotics of music established itself as a discipline in its own right only in the 1960s, within the context of French structuralism. Structuralist approaches assume that music cannot be said to have meaning in the same way that language can. Music is a language that "only signifies itself" (Jakobson, 1970). The denotation of a musical sign, such as a note, lies not in its relation to extramusical content but in its position within the musical system, its relation to other notes. If music appears to convey extramusical content, this derives not from syntactic structures but from the connotations of, for instance, musical genres and musical instruments, from nonmusical codes such as the lyrics of a song, or from the social context with which the music is associated. Iconic signs, such as the musical imitation of birdsong, form a marginal phenomenon and cannot be used to construct a semantics of music.

The harmonic system that developed in European tonal-functional music from approximately 1600 onward is generally thought to constitute the *langue*—the system that underlies musical structure—of Western music. In studying it, structuralist music semioticians have turned to phonology for inspiration, in particular to the "commutation test" phonologists use to establish the identities of phonemes. This method is used to establish, for instance, that the interval C–E does not "mean" the same thing as the interval C–E-flat, so the E and E-flat have "emic"—that is, functionally relevant—status in the system, forming minimal units of musical distinctions. Playing the same interval an octave higher or lower, on the other hand, or singing it with a different vocal timbre, does not affect the harmonic relationship and therefore is considered a nonpertinent variant with respect to harmonic syntax.

The assumption that music has no meaning, however, makes it difficult to formulate exactly how two intervals like C–E and C–E-flat might differ in significance. One solution is to state the difference in intramusical terms as a difference in harmonic function: the interval C–E, for instance, sets up major tonality; the interval C–E-flat sets up minor tonality. Another solution, favored by Jean-Jacques Nattiez (1990), is to look for equivalence rather than difference and to base the identification of the minimal units of the musical system on an "emic sentiment of identity."

Nicolas Ruwet's approach (1987) requires even less reference to signification. His method consists of segmenting the musical text into significant units on the basis of repetition and transformation at various levels of magnitude, from the musical phrase down to the simple interval. The boundaries between such units are established on the basis of repetition when an interval (or motif or phrase) is repeated (for instance C–E-flat/C–E-flat), transposed (for instance C–E-flat/D–F), inverted (C–E-flat/E-flat–C), or otherwise varied. This results in a reliable method of constituent analysis but one that remains entirely syntagmatic, even though the method has, paradoxically, been called the "paradigmatic approach."

Another structural semiotics for music pursues generative analysis, adapted from Noam Chomsky's transformational-generative grammar. Here the emphasis lies not on establishing a hierarchy of musical units and segmenting the musical text into its constituents but on describing the musical knowledge—the "competence"—that allows composers and musical improvisers to generate a seemingly inexhaustible variety of musical phrases. This competence is described in terms of a limited set of basic patterns (deep structures) that are transformed into actual musical phrases (surface structures) via an ordered set of transformations. The deep structures tend, again, to be conceived of as basic intervals or motifs that, in the process of generating the musical phrase, undergo such transformations as metrification, expansion, and substitution. This approach has been applied to jazz improvisation (Steedman, 1984), where simple harmonic schemata, such as the I-IV-I-V-IV-I blues schema, can generate a seemingly infinite number of different performances. It has also been applied to rhythm to show how complex durational patterns can be derived from basic meters such as 2/4 and 3/4.

In contrast to these formal schemes, Derryck Cooke (1959) provides a broad semantic gloss for a range of basic intervals and motifs. A motif such as 5-3-1 (e.g., G-E-C), for instance, expresses "incoming" rather than "outgoing" emotions because it descends in pitch, "positive" rather than "negative" emotions because it establishes the major triad, and a sense of "coming home" or "finality" because it returns to the tonic, the note in the key of which the piece is set. Combining these factors results in "a sense of experiencing joy passively, i.e. accepting of welcome blessings, relief, consolation, reassurance, fulfilment" (Cooke, 1959). Cooke believes that such meanings derived originally from the associations of these motifs with certain kinds of song texts and that they have remained remarkably stable during the whole period of Western tonal-functional music.

These approaches to music semiotics have all concentrated on the level of the musical phrase or on levels below it, just as linguists have, in the main, concentrated on the syntax of the clause and on levels below it: the phrase, the word, the morpheme, the phoneme. To describe the structure of larger units ("movements," whole works), concepts and methods have often been borrowed from structuralist narratology. In the same way as narrative structure is driven by the binary oppositions between characters (e.g., male and female; upper class and middle class) that provide the sources for possible dramatic conflict, musical narration is driven by sets of binary oppositions between "themes." Susan McClary has

shown how ever since the beginning of Italian opera around 1600, when the *stile rappresentativo* (the "representative style") began to be developed, composers have elaborated musical codes for the delineation of characters and actions—including, very prominently, signifiers of gender. The most telling example is that of the sonata form, the schema used in the first movement of most late eighteenth- and nineteenth-century symphonies. A "masculine" theme opens the movement so that the sounds of masculinity act as the protagonist in the musically realized drama. A second, "feminine" theme follows, less martial, less "thrusting," and in a different key. These two themes then engage in interaction, traveling during the "development" of the movement through different tonal territories until, in the "resolution," the feminine theme is subjugated, transposed into the key of the masculine theme. With this schema, many stories can be told: the violent stories of Beethoven, which "often exhibit considerable anxiety with respect to feminine moments and respond to them with extraordinary violence," or the gentler stories of Mozart and Schubert, who "tend to invest their second themes with extraordinary sympathy" so that "one regrets the inevitable return to the tonic and the original materials" as the feminine theme is "brutally, tragically quashed in accordance with the destiny predetermined by the 'disinterested' conventions of the form" (McClary, 1991).

With this approach to musical narration, McClary, though using structuralist methods, has moved beyond formal description and restored the semantic dimension to musical semiotics, just as Cooke attempted to do on the level of the interval and the basic motif. In mainstream musicology, such approaches remain fairly marginal. Music is still widely regarded as absolute and autonomous, an abstract tonal mathematics, the proper understanding of which lies in comprehending the formal relations it sets up, in what Theodor Adorno called "structural hearing" and regarded as the highest form of music listening. Semiotic approaches to contemporary popular music (e.g., Shepherd, 1991) and to ethnomusicology (e.g., Lomax, 1968) have been less reticent in dealing with musical meaning and have also dethroned harmony from the central position that it has in Western tonal-functional music but does not necessarily have in the music of other cultures or in certain forms of modern popular music. Richard Middleton (1990), for instance, writes that in punk rock "the hoarse, manic, shouted timbre is the primary emic category": therefore, "almost any pitches would serve, all being variants of each other."

In this context, the meanings conveyed by the principal musical systems—melody, harmony, rhythm, timbre, and so on—are seen as social meanings. Musical structures represent and, because of music's emotionally affective nature, celebrate social structures. Alan Lomax describes, for instance, how in many societies men and women sing together in two-voiced polyphony and how such societies tend to have a distinctive division of labor between men and women without, however, valuing men's work higher than women's work or vice versa. This is precisely what polyphony enacts ritually: two melodies of equal musical interest and value, intertwining to form a cohesive piece of music. This line of reasoning can be applied also to Western tonal-functional music, such as symphonic music. Symphonic music is "homophonic"—based on a division of labor in which a soloist or group of instruments carries the melody, the dominant part that would also have musical interest and value by itself, while the other voices accompany or support the melody with parts that have little or no musical interest in themselves and acquire meaning only in the context of the whole. Similarly, the activities of factory workers are meaningful not in themselves but only in relation to the factory as a whole. Homophonic music, then, celebrates relations of inequality and domination, although these relations can, of course, be inflected or even subverted in individual works, for instance by making the accompanying voices clash with the dominant voice. Other musical systems, such as the system of musical time, can also be said to represent structures of social interaction: some forms of music require strict adherence to a regular, metronomic beat, just as some social institutions require strict adherence to the mechanical time of the clock, while other forms of music are polyrhythmic, allowing each player to keep his or her own time without endangering the cohesion of the whole. Musical choices of this kind may either form a general characteristic of a particular kind of music—for instance the regular beat of the military march or of disco music—or be used narratively within a work, for instance to set up gender contrasts in relation to concrete characters, as in an opera, or in relation to the themes of abstract, instrumental music. Social approaches to musical semiotics have, in the main, been less methodologically

rigorous than structuralist and generative approaches, but there is no reason why they could not be developed in greater detail in the form of exhaustive paradigms of the sociosemantic choices that the language of music allows, together with descriptions of the musical forms that realize them.

Music semiotics has also felt the influence of poststructuralism, with its greater emphasis on subjectivity and the body. In "The Grain of the Voice" (1977), Roland Barthes distinguishes between musical signification, the social and communicative meanings of music, and musical *signifiance*, a kind of musical meaning that is individual and constitutes an experience of pleasure (*jouissance*) that derives from the materiality, the "voluptuousness," of the signifier—that is, to a large extent, from what escapes the music as a system. These are aspects of the signifier that, from the point of view of music as a system, are "nonsignificant variants," such as the very "grain" of the voice of singers or the way they roll their *r*s. This approach has been taken up to validate the pleasures derived, for instance, from different kinds of popular music but not to take critical distance from these pleasures, as has happened in comparable approaches to the semiotics of the cinema. One of the challenges for future research in music semiotics might be to reintegrate the poststructuralist emphasis on the psychological effect of music with the study of musical structure, an approach that has already led to significant results in the semiotics of the cinema.

[*See also* Aesthetics; Articulation; Clynes; *and* Nattiez.]

BIBLIOGRAPHY

Barthes, R. *Image-Music-Text*. Edited and translated by S. Heath. London: Fontana, 1977.

Cooke, D. *The Language of Music*. Oxford: Oxford University Press, 1959.

Jakobson, R. "Language in Relation to Other Communication Systems." In *Linguaggi nella societa e nella technica*. Milan: Edizione di communita, 1970.

Lomax, A. *Folk Song Style and Culture*. New York: Transaction Books, 1968.

McClary, S. *Feminine Endings: Music, Gender, and Sexuality*. Minneapolis: University of Minnesota Press, 1991.

Middleton, R. *Studying Popular Music*. London: Open University Press, 1990.

Nattiez, J.-J. *Music and Discourse: Toward a Semiology of Music*. Translated by C. Abbate. Princeton: Princeton University Press, 1990.

Ruwet, N. "Methods of Analysis in Musicology." In *Music Analysis* 6 (1987): 11–36.

Shepherd, J. *Music as Social Text.* Cambridge: Polity Press, 1991.

Steedman, M. "A Generative Grammar for Jazz Chord Sequences." In *Music Perception* 1.2 (1984): 52–77.

Tagg, P. *Kojak: 50 Seconds of Television Music.* Goteborg: Skrifter fran musikvetenskapliga institutionen vol. 2, 1979.

—THEO VAN LEEUWEN

MYTHOLOGIES (1957). A collection of short essays by Roland Barthes, *Mythologies* comprises works that appeared originally, for the most part, as regular monthly installments in the French journal *Les lettres nouvelles* between 1954 and 1956. Barthes subsequently provided a theoretical foundation in "Myth Today" (1972). Mixing structural-linguistic, phenomenological, Freudian, and Marxian conceptions, Barthes considered mythology a kind of political semiology.

Since myth is imperative, signification is a kind of notification. Myth is also motivated and for this reason duplicitous. The Barthesean mythologist deciphers the transformation of history into nature and unveils the pretense of how myth passes itself off by means of signs treated as a factual system. Armed with Marx's image of "inversion," Barthes reads the myths of French society in the 1950s in terms of the processes of bourgeois ideology that falsely impart universal standing to their particular historical status. This ideology "ex-nominates" itself while spreading over everything, for the bourgeoisie is *the social class which does not want to be named.* Hiding its intention, bourgeois myth naturalizes and eternalizes itself, better enabling it to depoliticize itself. Although myth presents itself as depoliticized speech, the prefix *de-* indicates that this appropriation of normative status is an active political process. Accordingly, Barthes considers the work of the mythologist in laying bare this process and describing its dominant rhetorical forms to be fundamentally political as well. Barthes stipulates that the production of mythologies, understood as ideological criticism, is not a revolutionary act since, while revolution abolishes myth, the mythologist is condemned to metalanguage. Barthes chides "the Left" for too often "exnominating" and naturalizing revolution, therefore producing inessential and artificial myths. Statistically, myth is a right-wing bourgeois phenomenon.

Bourgeois myths contain seven principal rhetorical figures. Barthes defines the first, inoculation, as the injection of a contingent evil into the public domain in order to build homeopathically society's immune system for use against an essential evil. This "new vaccine" is evident for Barthes in the myths of striptease, in which eroticism is absorbed into a reassuring ritual afforded the status of a sport and a career, and of margarine, in which doubts about this product's inferiority relative to butter are voiced in advertisements for it in order to clear the way for its acceptability.

The privation of history refers to the way that myth dehistoricizes the objects of which it speaks. This is most evident for Barthes in the French travelbook series "The Blue Guide," whose book on Spain treats the country as a series of tourist sites, reducing ethnic and political realities to exotic flavoring and history to monuments. Relatedly, the figure of identification concerns the limitations of the petit bourgeois's consciousness of others. This consciousness consists of "small simulacra" of roles and types to which others must be reduced before they are granted a social existence. Barthes draws upon the media coverage of several French trials to illustrate this figure.

The figure of tautology creates a motionless world into which one takes refuge when language is thought to fail in the face of an object's resistance. All the mythologies touching upon the petit bourgeois attitudes of the right-wing populist politician Pierre Poujade, as well as those Barthes entitles "Racine Is Racine" and "Billy Graham at Vel' d'Hiv'," demonstrate that tautologies equal nothingness and have as their mortal enemy dialectical reasoning. The figure Barthes calls neither-norism is a variant of liberalism in which realities are reduced to two opposites, choices are weighed, and, owing to the embarassing poverty of options, both are rejected. In "Neither-Nor Criticism," Barthes describes the immobilization of choice by double exclusion as a system based upon the refusal of a priori judgments in the name of freedom despite its adherence to bourgeois myths.

The quantification of quality is latent in all the preceding figures of bourgeois myth. Intelligence is managed economically so that reality may be understood more cheaply. The conspicuous quantification of effects is one of the myths of the bourgeois theater Barthes describes in "Two Myths of the New Theatre." A quantitative equality is established between the spectator's costs and the calculable yield of the expressiveness of the performers and the luxuriousness of the set.

Unlike popular, ancestral proverbs involving an active engagement with the world about which they speak, Barthes reasons that bourgeois maxims are metalinguistic statements of fact. These maxims concern proverbs, the character of which they mask with nothing less than the recapitulation of bourgeois common sense. This is the case in "The Man in the Street on Strike," since strikes are an affront to bourgeois good sense because such events typically affect those whom they do not concern.

Mass-produced objects such as cars and toys, including certain materials (plastic), as well as performances, exhibitions, films, food and drink, and sporting events, all yield mythological significations to Barthes. The objects of his mythologies are often the representations of events and objects found in the popular French print media. Women's magazines such as *Elle*, newspapers such as *Le Figaro*, and glossy news magazines along the lines of *Paris Match* are for Barthes treasure troves of myths. The Barthesean mythologist may study anything since myth touches and corrupts everything; even those objects that resist myth are "ideal prey." By the time Barthes published his reflections on his early work as a mythologist whose task was to "upend the mythical message," he considered semiology itself to be a myth that required unmasking.

[*See also* Barthes; *and* Myths.]

BIBLIOGRAPHY

Barthes, R. *Mythologies*. Translated by A. Lavers. London: Jonathan Cape, 1972.
Barthes, R. *The Eiffel Tower and Other Mythologies*. Translated by R. Howard. New York: Hill and Wang, 1979.
Eco, U., and I. Pezzini. "La sémiologie des mythologies." *Communications* 36 (1982): 19–42.

—GARY GENOSKO

MYTHS. Authoritative and culture-specific discourses that gravitate around key symbols and basic metaphors, myths display and develop signs that ground a culture's foundations. Many myths arise from a root metaphor that they develop into scripts to draw social dynamics in their orbits. Such generative metaphors provide "frames" within which plots take shape. Myths usually serve to relate historical time to a primeval era so that they ground current behavior in archetypal patterns.

For example, in Mato Grosso in central Brazil, the fiery eyes of the jaguar that glow in the dark are read as a metaphor for fire, and scripts develop this conception by depicting the jaguar as the original master of fire. A cultural hero will then undertake a dangerous trip into the jungle to steal the fire from the jaguar and bring it to humankind. Young men of this culture accordingly have to duplicate that event in an initiation rite through which they attain adult status. The powerful mythic discourse that exploits that metaphor endows it with the capacity of ritual implementation, making it metamorphic—that is, it effectuates what it symbolizes and acts as an actual transformation.

In Malaita in the Solomon Islands, the visual resemblance between the scales of a large fish and the cuttings into which yams are chopped to be planted serves as the generative metaphor for the myth of the origin of yam. In it, tuber and fish undergo symmetrical metamorphoses that draw into their orbits relationships between sea and land and between men and women and that charter the complex exchange system in markets where hill people trade vegetables for the fish brought there by the lagoon people. Here again, we see a myth working to implement a metaphor in such a way that it becomes metamorphic and charters economic as well as social life as a whole.

Each generative metaphor is a syntagm (e.g., jaguar's eyes = fire; fish = yam). Myths develop and connect such syntagms, thus networking a number of social facts "attracted" by the signs that ground them. This occurs through episodes. Often, however, the interlocking of episodes according to an Aristotelian narrative model turns out to be an ethnographer's artifact, since many ethnographers record myths as structured linearly, with clear beginnings, middles, and ends, as recounted in formal recording sessions. On the other hand, myths told spontaneously in everyday circumstances do not follow the Aristotelian pattern. In those real-life contexts, linear episodes are told in seemingly haphazard order or at least with great narrative freedom. The knowledge of myths pervades a culture's cognitive universe to the point that linear processing appears pointless. Even in formal recording sessions, some narrators follow parallel-processing patterns instead of linear ones. Thus, in Malaita, many complex myths include metanarrative statements such as "Now the narrative strikes back to," "Here the narrative returns to," or "The narrative now hits." Sophisticated narrators structure their scripts so that they unfold on several planes at the same time.

Myths are usually related orally, but they may also be conveyed through other codes such as dance, acrobatics, cuisine, music, pantomime, plastic art, architecture, and even, some would argue, philosophy and science. When cast in static visual forms, myths obviously cannot be linear. For instance, to those who know how to read them, Australian bark paintings tell myths as explicitly as any oral performance would. As for architecture, cathedrals as well as Melanesian temples or ceremonial shell–inlaid and feather-decorated plank canoes in the Solomon Islands are infused with mythical knowledge and often summarize whole cosmologies as well as rules of behavior.

Myths usually provide answers that anticipate and preempt the fundamental questions humans ask of their societies: "Who are we?" "Where do we come from?" "Where are we going?" "What is the road to get there?" "Who can lead us where we should be going?" "Where does real power rest?" and so on. Answers take the form of messages of which the relative coherence and power depend on specific cultural parameters but also on human universals and on the limited scope of our minds (Lévi-Strauss, 1964–1971).

> The treatment of similar myths from different regions, by arranging them in large compared groups, makes it possible to trace in mythology the operation of imaginative processes recurring with the evident regularity of mental law; and thus stories of which a single instance would have been a mere isolated curiosity, take their place among well-marked and consistent structures of the human mind. Evidence like this will again and again drive us to admit that even as "truth is stranger than fiction", so myth may be more uniform than history. (Tylor, 1871, p. 282)

Contrary to common prejudice, myths do not wander haphazardly. They address basic questions within a culture's idiom and semiotic space. Their pedagogic discourses belabor stereotypes, explore boundaries, gloss and develop metaphors, and investigate possible or thinkable scripts. Myths must offer rationales for some shared allegiances so that their carriers can evoke, be attuned to, and feed cognitively

on the same semiotic foundation charters and also reenact them in rituals.

For myths to work, however, their culture-specific messages must also contain ambiguities and offer polysemic statements without which cultures could not survive. Myths structure the semiotic connotative spaces in which members of a society are born, in which they mature, and that provide them with a measure of cognitive harmony. But since cognitive dissonance is unavoidable—no imperial education has yet succeeded in producing absolute mental cloning—semiotic consonance can occur only through relative polysemy of myths. To relate to others, we need to share at least partially common universes and tolerate divergent views in myth polysemy. Indeed, how could we communicate with others—which involves taking them for granted to a degree—outside the fuzzy orbit around myth nodes? Even so-called monist cultures tolerate pseudosystematicity and variations despite their totalitarian ambitions of complete coverage.

Myths order the society that support them, and they steer it through history (Clastres, 1990; Heusch, 1988). As basic encodings of ideologies, mythic discourses sacralize or at least consolidate the cultural axioms that made a society governable by some of its members. Endowed with cognitive supremacy, these individuals can exert control over those through which they and the myths they stand for prosper. But myths also permeate and structure the personalities of their creators, who constitute live implementations to which their subjects must react, either submissively or deviantly.

How to produce and validate interpretations that would be "true"? Myths analysts are confronted by the polysemy that myths derive from their root metaphors (Lévi-Strauss, 1964; Dundes et al., 1971; Liszka, 1989). Variations exist even in the smallest and simplest societies. No sociolect, however tyrannical, can overpower all the idiolects within its constituency. Substantive models have been developed to help myth analysts to cope with this challenging task, especially since Vladimir Propp proposed an "algebraic syntax" of the folktale that was developed subsequently by Elizar Meletinsky (1970) and his associates. (Thirteen such models are presented in Maranda, 1972.)

Whatever the degree of sophistication of available models, analysts of myth must still allow for a margin of indeterminancy in their interpretations. They should adopt a probabilistic approach. What myths say to an individual—whether analyst or native—does vary according to social and individual parameters. What myths talk about also varies over time. These are two types of variations that, given adequate knowledge of a culture and of its members, one might be able to predict with a fair degree of probability. If myth analysis is to become somewhat more scientific, it should rely on such experimentation whenever possible.

[*See also* Culture; Discourse Analysis; Douglas; Leach; Lévi-Strauss; Metaphor; Narratology; Paroemiology; Russian Formalism; *and* Semiography.]

BIBLIOGRAPHY

Cassirer, E. "The Power of Metaphor." In *Mythology*, edited by P. Maranda, pp. 23–31. Harmondsworth, England: Penguin, 1972.

Clastres, H. "Comment vivent les mythes: Réflexions sur la mythologie guarani." *Amerindia* 15 (1990): 75–83.

Dundes, A. et al. "An Experiment: Suggestions and Queries from the Desk, with a Reply from the Ethnographer." In *Structural Analysis of Oral Tradition*, edited by P. Maranda and E. K. Maranda, pp. 292–324. Philadelphia: University of Pennsylvania Press, 1971.

Heusch, L. de "Myth as Reality." *Journal of Religion in Africa* 18 (1988): 200–215.

Lévi-Strauss, C. *Mythologiques*. 4 vols. Paris: Plon, 1964–1971.

Liszka, J. J. *The Semiotic of Myth: A Critical Study of the Symbol*. Bloomington: Indiana University Press, 1989.

Maranda, P., ed. *Mythology*. Harmondsworth: Penguin, 1972.

Meletinsky, E. "L'étude structurale et typologique du conte." In V. Propp, *Morphologie du conte*, pp. 201–254. Paris: Seuil, 1970.

Tylor, E. B. *Primitive Culture*. London: Murray, 1871.

—PIERRE MARANDA

N

NARRATIVE STRUCTURES. As an ordered sequence of events that "unfolds" in the course of a reading, a narrative has temporal and chronological dimensions. Yet these events must be held together in a single image if one is to be aware of temporal progression at all. The unity established through the organization of "temporal wholes" derives from the organization of successive events in such a way that they form a unified sequence of change in which there is a beginning, middle, and end. Structuralist definitions of this unity have been advanced from the angle of an elementary actional sequence that also governs the simple macrostructure of the narrative in its temporal synthesis. A composite of these structuralist models yields a five-part sequence that corresponds to the temporal phases of any event, be it an action, a process, a motion, or a communication:

1. Before—Initial state—Equilibrium (before the event)
2. Perturbation—Provocation—Trigger (beginning of event)
3. Event itself—Taking action (the event)
4. Consequence—Outcome of action—Sanction (end of event)
5. After—Final state—Equilibrium (after the event)

This definition of an event-sequence distinguishes static from dynamic situations. A state in itself is by definition a static moment that can remain indefinitely immovable. In order to get the story going, a perturbation must be introduced that destroys the equilibrium of the initial situation and initiates action. This is where V. A. Propp's archetypal folktale begins, in disequilibrium, and it ends with marriage, a sanction. Hence, the before and after of the tale are theoretical and implicit stages that anchor two static situations of equilibrium as fixed points between which something happens: the *event* itself. In the folktale the event encompasses the three major episodes of the "tests."

Propp's first seven functions out of a sequence of thirty-one are said to make up "the preparatory part of the tale" whereas the actual movement of the tale is initiated by an act of villainy. These seven functions constitute the perturbation and alienation. For instance, the villain inquires about the location of a precious object and receives information about his victim in order to take possession of him or his belongings. The hero-victim submits to the deception and unwittingly helps his enemy. Finally, the villain does his act of villainy and causes harm to a member of the family. If villainy is absent, the tale proceeds from a situation of insufficiency or lack which Propp considered as an equivalent of seizure.

The first pair of functions, inquiry versus information, is a negative communication where the villain fraudulently and misleadingly swindles information. The second pair of functions, trickery versus complicity, robs the hero of his powers and his potential to be a hero. The third pair, villainy versus lack, an object-value is appropriated by the villain, depriving the hero or his family or people. A crescendo can be easily observed in the progression of negative exchanges. The three pairs of functions appear as an increasing redundancy of privations undergone by the hero, and as acquisitions, equally redundant, by the villain. The extortion of information is followed by the act of deception that is crowned by the villainy. In the final sequence of the tale, the succession of the concluding functions restores to the hero everything of which he was deprived and deprives the traitor of everything he had extorted. The recognition of the hero is followed by the unmasking of the traitor. The hidden nature of the nonrevealed hero turns into his transfiguration at the end. The hero appears in all his splendor, dressed in royal clothes. The trickery of the villain is exposed and the villain is punished. The lack is liquidated first by the restoration of the stolen object-value to the community—the paradigm being the princess—and, second, by sanctioning the hero's victory positively and rewarding him with marriage.

For Algirdas Julien Greimas (1917–1992), a narrative has two complementary dimensions: (1) the narrative model, which accounts for the cohesion of the tale and makes its plot summary possible, and (2) the global semantic structure, which accounts for the meaning of the story.

Narrative Units. From its very beginning, Greimassian narratology aimed to develop a model that would go beyond the specificities of Vladimir Propp's archetypal folktale and account for the organizing principles of all narrative discourses. Some of the tasks in this development involved identifying elementary narrative units and how they combine into intermediate and recurrent units called "tests."

Through a critical examination of Propp's *Morphology of the Folktale* (1928), Greimas set out to reinterpret and formalize both the notion of function and the definition of the tale as a sequence of thirty-one functions. The Proppian function corresponds referentially to an event and linguistically to a proposition. The sentence explanations and variants of the function are formulated by Propp in descriptive, nontechnical language that Greimas compares to a documentary style. Some examples are given by Greimas (1971), but they are not direct quotations from Propp: "The traitor makes off with the king's daughter"; "The king sends the hero off on a mission"; "The hero finds the traitor."

Propp's descriptions can be generalized and presumably made more rigorous by using linguistic procedures and defining the narrative as a sequence of narrative propositions. Since there are several possible ways of conceiving the nature of the elementary proposition, the selection and commitment to one view has important theoretical ramifications. Rejecting traditional and transformational grammars because they give the subject a privileged focus and subordinate all other terms in its sphere, Greimas turns to the relational grammar of Lucien Tesnière. This grammar, like the grammar of propositions in predicate calculus, starts with the verb as the ultimate nucleus of the proposition and gathers the nouns into its orbit all at the same and equal level, emphasizing "action in concert"—that is, interconnecting the various terms into a semantic and relational network. Looking at Greimas's first Proppian sentence above, we see that *traitor* and *the king's daughter* are on an equal syntactical footing relative to the verb, *makes off*. At a more abstract and textual level of analysis, they are considered the *actants*, which are related by a function and are represented formally in the following notational frame: Function (Actant) or F(A) or

$F(A_1, A_2, \ldots, A_6)$. Function and actant are postulated as the two immediate constituents of the elementary narrative unit, defined as the simplest narrative proposition. The verb, action, or event is the function, and the participant(s) in the event is (are) designated as the actant(s).

The paradigmatic analysis and structuration of the Proppian chain of functions brings out the existence of recurrent episodic units that punctuate the dynamics of narrative progress from beginning to end. These intermediate units are the contract and the test that link together to form a larger test, a recurrent macro sequence in the quantitative organization of plot. The larger test may be viewed as an episode in the conventional sense, as a distinctive story or scene that is integral to but separable from a continuous narrative.

The recognition of the recurrent unit of the contract in Propp's simple folktale makes it possible to extend the range of applications to more complex narratives and to other texts. It is a significant achievement toward reconceiving plot structure in a more palpable and less figurative way than the conventional four-part pattern of the plot with its exposition, rising action or complication, climax, and resolution. The notion of the contract introduces semantic content and rigor into a vague diagram. With this tool, it is possible to interpret the structure of any narrative plot from the perspective of the establishment and breaking of a contract. Indeed, all the units that articulate the contract or the agreement freely made govern narrative development: the establishment of the contract, the suspension, the reestablishment, the execution, the completion, or the breaking of the contract. Polar changes in the status of the contract, from negative to positive or the reverse, describe the movement of most stories. Moreover, they provide the closure to most stories, and this involves a resolution of some kind. The denouement would not take place were it not for the underlying change in the status of the contract, however subtle the manifestation might be.

Propp's archetypal folktale begins with a breach of contract and ends with the establishment of a contract in the form of marriage. The two limits of the story are marked by a contractual event. At the very origin of the tale, a serious conflict is set into motion between the subject's desire and the sender's law or social norms when he or she violates a prohibition, thereby defying the reigning social order and precipitating chaos. The initial breach of contract indicates an inherent normative or legal conflict between the first sender and subject-hero, and it activates an extended sequence of privations and trouble for the hero, figuring forth a society on the brink of dissolution. In this initial sequence, named "breakup of the order and alienation," the villain tricks the hero into giving him information, deceives him about his possessions, and finally causes the trouble—the act of villainy—that creates the actual movement of the tale, the mainspring of the quest.

Narrative starts when the world is thrown out of kilter and chaos ensues. It ends with marriage, the perfect union and harmony between the individual and the community. From the syntagmatic point of view, the archetypal folktale is framed by a legal system (presupposed by the contract), and the main change that takes place between the two poles is in the social-political order and consists of the agreements that the subject reaches or fails to reach with the senders or powers that be. The subject rejects the legal system at the start and becomes part of a new social order and clinches a contract with the sender at the end.

The tale not only starts and ends with a contract but the passage from one end to the other takes place through three other contracts or three positive exchanges with a different sender on a graduating scale of mutual trust, cooperation, and integration. The archetypal folktale, therefore, manifests five contractual episodes. The macro sequence of the test is a syntagmatic chaining of the contract, the struggle, and the consequence. The discovery of this major recurrent sequence that Propp himself did not recognize is a decisive accomplishment in narratology. The test may be represented summarily as shown below, by the five functions that make it up, and by listing those that pair off into higher units:

CONTRACT   injunction, acceptance
STRUGGLE   confrontation, success
CONSEQUENCE   acquisition

Propp's archetypal folktale manifests the recurrence of three such tests that form the three major episodes of the story as a whole. These are the qualifying test, the decisive or main test, and the glorifying test. All three tests are variations of the generalized-invariant schema given above. After the hero accepts his or her mission, he or she must undergo a rite of initiation or a rite of passage that will enable him or her to undertake the quest prepared. This rite of passage is the qualifying test, which ends with the hero receiving a magical agent from the donor. The overall process, in general, is the acquisition of competence, know-how, and power needed to qualify the hero as such. The main test and the quest deal with the acquisition of the object of desire and performance of the heroic deed. The struggle between two equal competitors, the hero and the villain, and the hero's victory enact and make real the heroic self, which is also the idealized and masterful self. Following these high deeds, the new self-image and heroic identity of the hero are tested in a social environment and acknowledged. The hero is recognized and glorified as a hero.

By and large, the three tests are the qualification of the subject, his or her achievements, and the recognition of those achievements by society. In the main, these three major episodes also articulate the major stages of an individual's history and growth. If the structures underlying the folktale are identical to those that organize history, biography, and our sense of pattern in our own lives, the question of how they are constituted takes on renewed interest. Identification of universal narrative patterns seems to tell us not just about folktales or literature but about the nature of the mind or universal features of culture.

Even though the test has a syntagmatic character, it maintains a parallel with the actantial structure. Not only are all six actants implied in the test, but the three axes that make up the actantial model also have equivalents in the test. Thus, the axis of communication that is bounded by the sender and receiver corresponds to the contract, subsuming the injunction and acceptance. The struggle, consisting of a fight, expresses the opposition of forces that manifest themselves as helper (external or internal to the hero) and opponent. The consequence shows the various forms of object value that the hero acquires following his or her victory. Since the recurrence of the tests shows semantic redundancy, a single test is sufficient to define the minimal narrative. Thus, the minimal narrative can be defined as a syntagmatic sequence made up of the following propositions:

CONTRACT   (Sender, Receiver)
STRUGGLE   (Helper, Opponent)
CONSEQUENCE   (Object, Subject)

Here, the sequence of the contract and the struggle entail the consequence of getting the desired object.

This sequential chaining is necessary since both the contract and the struggle can occur by themselves, outside of the schema of the test.

The test is the irreducible nucleus or kernel that accounts for the definition of the narrative as diachrony. It also operates the transformation of axiological contents that fix the limits of the "reversal of the situation" by marking the end of the narrative before and the beginning of the narrative after.

The test that represents a central point of transformation in the narrative, a locus of decision and denouement, is the main or decisive test. It marks the high point of the action in which the conflict between the subject-hero and the opponent is brought out to the fullest extent as they join in direct combat. The situation is characterized by a polemical antagonism, a genuine contest, and total engagement of forces that are equal and contradictory. At the zenith of this duel, we come to the breaking point, the moment when the stakes will be won by only one party; the victory of the one will be the defeat of the other. The acquisition of the object by the protagonist is at the expense of the antagonist. The conjunction of the subject with the object simultaneously and necessarily corresponds with the disjunction of the opponent from the object.

The other two tests, the qualifying test that precedes the main test and the glorifying test that follows it, are simulated, symbolic tests within the context of an agreement or contract with the sender—hence, their meanings are determined completely by cooperative exchange with the sender. The interaction of subject and sender is mutually beneficial rather than antagonistic, and the victory of the subject will not result in a domination over the sender.

The sender takes on the role of a symbolic, make-believe opponent who tests the hero on his or her competence or identity and rewards him or her with an object value if the hero passes the test. The consequence consists of the sender's sanction, the fulfillment of his or her contractual obligation to the hero and honoring the promise made earlier. We have here an exchange with two objects, and the transaction can be compared loosely to an economic trade. The subject-hero earned an object value from the sender by executing his or her share of the initial agreement.

Narrative Schema. As noted above, for Greimas the basic and general structure of narrative has two complementary dimensions: (1) the narrative model that summarizes the cohesion of events in a narrative, comparable to a plot summary or a story's schematic structure, and (2) the global semantic dimension or macrostructure, which is manifested by events and through the plot model. The narrative model is comprised of the narrative schema, which is a paradigmatic projection on the syntagmatic development of stories, and the corresponding actantial model, which focuses not on events but on the actants or the invariant roles that perform them. We might refer to the narrative schema, sometimes also designated the "canonical tale," as the Greimassian plot model. The schema is depicted in figure 1, together with the traditional plot structure for comparison and contrast. One of the most striking differences between these plot models is that, unlike the traditional plot pattern that isolates a single climax

FIGURE 1. *Comparitive Formal Frameworks of Narrative Models.*

Narrative schema or the Greimassian plot model				
INITIAL SEQUENCE *Breach of contract* Breakup of the order and alienation	QUALIFYING TEST *Competence* Acquisition of means	MAIN OR DECISIVE TEST *Performance* Acquisition of object of desire or object value	GLORIFYING TEST *Sanction* Recognition granted	FINAL SEQUENCE *New contract* Reintegration and restoration of order
Traditional plot model				
Perturbation Complication	Rising action	Climax Reversal of situation	Falling action	Resolution Conclusion

or turning point, the narrative schema highlights two peaks in the tale. The second climax, even though less marked than the first, is a request or second quest that is a demand of recognition due to the hero. Where there is falling action in the traditional model, we have the height of social acknowledgment, sanction, and reward of the hero's deeds in the semiotic model. Linearly, the plot model is represented as an organization of four sequences: Manipulation (establishment of contract), Competence, Performance, and Sanction (of contract). This reduced plotline, however, is not in agreement with the table of the narrative schema: in the table, the tale starts with a *breach* of contract. Ten years after Vladimir Propp established the classical structuration of the chain of functions, Greimas reinterpreted the final contract, through a reverse order of logical presupposition, as the global, main contract established implicitly from the start. Since the three tests also exhibit a retrogressive logic but are not reversed in the narrative schema, objections to this model arise in the issues of why the retrogression was not carried consistently throughout and why the whole plot model turned backward. As it stands, the linear and reduced version of the narrative schema has two different temporal frameworks superimposed on it, both retrogressive and sequential.

The narrative schema, like the traditional plot model, is a formal framework that takes place in a straightforward, chronological order. Both models offer a general and ideal pattern, whereas actual stories will be variations of it. The narrative schema is said to be canonic because it serves as an ideological reference model relative to which deviations can be noted and evaluated. Unlike the traditional plot model, however, the narrative schema is more than just an ideal pattern or a formal framework. It records the "meaning and form of life" in a complete individual history and presents it as a schema of action—more specifically, as the quest, with episodes of qualification, realization, and recognition. "The Proppian organization," says Greimas, "suggests to us the possibility of reading every narrative as a quest for meaning, for the meaning to attribute to human action" (1976, p. 10). The actantial structure makes up the second aspect of the narrative model, regrouping the events according to the actants who accomplish them.

Narrative Semantics. According to Greimas, narrative semantics and fundamental semantics are com-

plementary. Their units are the elementary structures of signification, which can be articulated on the semiotic square, a diagram through which semantic selections are correlated. Greimas differentiates between signification and meaning by defining the first term as "articulated meaning" and the second as "that which is anterior to semiotic production" and about which nothing can be said (1982). The totality of significations forms the semantic universe. Thus, the key and operational concept in semiotics is articulated meaning, which is signaled by the relation between two terms and the perception of their differences and similarities.

Greimas forms conjectures about the conditions that allow meaning to be grasped. He argues that in constructing cultural objects (literary, mythical, pictorial, etc.) the mind is subject to various constraints that define "the conditions for the existence of semiotic objects." The most important of these is the "elementary structure of signification," which is of semantic and logical nature and underlies surface narrative structures. Hence, it is located at the level of deep and abstract structures in the narrative grammar, forming a fundamental semantics and morphology in addition to a fundamental syntax.

Meaning depends on oppositions. The elementary structure of signification is, in its simplest form, a binary opposition such as those between white and black, life and death, and nature and culture. In its more complex form, it is the correlation of two oppositions, represented as a homology $(X:Y::-X:-Y)$ or as the semiotic square. Even in its complex form, the semiotic square has a simple logicosemantic structure. It lays out all the combinational relationships possible among types of oppositions, some of which include: contraries, such as life and death; contradictions, such as life and nonlife; implications or presuppositions, as in nonlife and death; and double presuppositions, or homologies, as those between pairs of oppositions like life and nonlife and death and nondeath. The interrelationships of all these types of oppositions (which are vizualized through a diagram called the semiotic square) is what enables meaning to signify. Dynamically (some would say "syntagmatically"), the semiotic square also indicates the semantic movement of text by punctuating passages from one situation to another, each situation leading to another by being either negated or inverted, thus leading to its contrary or contradictory.

To have meaning, the narrative must form one

signifying whole and thus must be organized as a simple semantic structure. The basic configuration of the semiotic square also holds for the semantic macrostructure of the narrative in which a temporal opposition is correlated with a thematic opposition; for example, *before:after::inverse content:posited content*. In other words, the relation between the situation preceding the "reversal of the situation" or climax and the situation following it is correlated with the opposition between an initial thematic problem and a thematic resolution. Thus, the narrative can be grasped as a whole only by relating its semantic and thematic development to the development of plot. The posited and inversed contents refer to the retrogressive determination of the narrative, which is settled beforehand by its closure, the end determining what precedes it. Hence, the starting point is from the end, with final contents that are posited or resolved. Before the reversal of the situation, the contents are, therefore, inverted.

Another type of articulation allows a distribution of the contents according to the body of the narrative, as opposed to the framing sequences. The body contains two topical contents, whereas the initial and final sequences form two correlated contents that in principle manifest the same type of transformation as the topical contents. With further analytic refinements, the narrative is segmented into six sequences. Figure 2 summarizes both the event-related and semantic structures of the narrative and sets up the correspondences between them (Greimas, 1966a).

This global, unifying model of the abstracted narrative illustrates only formal and invariant properties. By segmenting the text into sequences, the model provides the formal parameters into which the contents can be poured and then analyzed. It allows the analyst to identify the important themes or contents manifested as consequences of tests as object values. Since the main test is the peak of the tale and the manifestation of the transformation of contents, its consequence will indicate the dominant theme or message of the narrative. It is the pivotal area from which the semantic analysis starts by means of the semiotic square. The contents projected upon the square may be articulated in foreseeable positions and constituted in semantic categories. In the analysis and interpretation of a Bororo myth that also served as material for Claude Lévi-Strauss's *The Raw and the Cooked* (1964), Greimas presents the five stages in the application of the semiotic square and the gradual, elaborate construction of the semantic code underlying and governing the myth (1966a). In the first stage, which starts at the topical content of the main test, the consequences consist of: (1) negating the term *raw* (nonlife); (2) affirming the term *cooked* (life); (3) affirming the term *fresh* (nondeath); and (4) negating the term *rotten* (death). Without Greimas's three pages of comment and explanation of how these results were obtained, the semantic categories affirmed or denied in the myth would not be obvious or open to being duplicated by another interpreter. Thus, Greimas's explanation is essential to enable the reader to follow each move on the square and in the semantics of the myth.

The semiotic square plays the role of description procedure and, to some extent, the role of discovery procedure with its basic operations of assertion and negation to obtain a particular microsystem of oppositions in one text or another. But, ultimately, in texts longer than a paragraph that have any

FIGURE 2. *Relations between Narrative and Semantic Structures.*

Contents and thematics (semiotic square)	Inversed content			Posited (resolved) content		
	Correlated content	Topical content		Topical content		Correlated content
Narrative schema	Initial sequence	Qualifying test	Main test	End of main test/ Return	Glorifying test	Final sequence

complexity whatsoever, the analytic results obtained by the square presuppose a prior interpretation and evaluation that need to be made explicit in order to be comprehensible and for the square to be "readable." A demonstration is required that in addition to filling the four slots in the square, matches the thought processes of the analyst. Many applications of the square fail in this regard, pressing home a neglect that Greimas (1979) characterized in a different context as courting "the real danger of confusing operational techniques (rewriting rules, trees, graphs, etc.) with scientific doing itself" and confusing taxonomic analysis with a complete as well as textualized analysis, interpretation, and evaluation.

[*See also* Actantial Model; Actants; Greimas; Narratology; *and* Semiotic Square.]

BIBLIOGRAPHY

Budniakiewicz, T. *Fundamentals of Story Logic: Introduction to Greimassian Semiotics*. Amsterdam and Philadelphia: John Benjamins, 1992.

Greimas, A. J. "The Interpretation of Myth: Theory and Practice" (1966a). In *Structural Analysis of Oral Tradition*, edited by P. Maranda and E. K. Maranda, pp. 81–121. Philadelphia: University of Pennsylvania Press, 1971.

Greimas, A. J. "Searching for Models of Transformation" (1966b). In Lévi-Strauss, 1983, chap. 11.

Greimas, A. J. "Elements of a Narrative Grammar" (1970). In Greimas, 1987, pp. 63–83.

Greimas, A. J. "Narrative Grammar: Units and Levels." *Modern Language Notes* 86 (1971): 793–806.

Greimas, A. J. "Les acquis et les projets." In *Introduction à la sémiotique narrative et discursive*, edited by J. Courtés, pp. 5–25. Paris: Hachette, 1976.

Greimas, A. J. *On Meaning: Selected Writings in Semiotic Theory*, translated by P. Perron and F. Collins. Minneapolis: University of Minnesota Press, 1987.

Greimas, A. J., and J. Courtés. *Semiotics and Language: An Analytical Dictionary* (1979). Translated by L. Crist and D. Patte. Bloomington: Indiana University Press, 1982.

Greimas, A. J., and F. Rastier. "The Interaction of Semiotic Constraints." *Yale French Studies* 41 (1968): 85–105.

Hénault, A. *Les enjeux de la sémiotique*. Paris: Presses universitaires de France, 1979.

Lévi-Strauss, C. *The Raw and the Cooked* (1964). Translated by J. and D. Weightman. New York: Harper and Row, 1969.

Lévi-Strauss, C. *Structural Semantics*. Translated by D. McDowell, R. Schleifer, and A. Velie. Lincoln: University of Nebraska Press, 1983.

Propp, V. *Morphology of the Folktale*. (1928). Translated by L. Scott. Austin: University of Texas Press, 1968.

—THERESE BUDNIAKIEWICZ

NARRATOLOGY. As the study of the invariant properties and the underlying compositional principles common to all narratives that characterize the storyness of stories and the narrativity of narratives, narratology was conceived of by Tzvetan Todorov to refer to structuralist studies of the 1960s and 1970s, mainly in France. Narratology is inspired largely by the approaches to folk narratives taken by Vladimir Propp, the Russian formalist, and Claude Lévi-Strauss, the structural anthropologist. Propp's work exemplifies the syntagmatic type of narrative analysis with its focus on the plotline, and Lévi-Strauss's work exemplifies the paradigmatic type of analysis with its emphasis on underlying semantic structures. Later, Greimassian narratology developed an original and seminal fusion of the two approaches. Algirdas Julien Greimas assessed his own contribution to the first stage of semiotics, devoted to narratology, thus: "My theoretical genius, if I can so call it, was a form of 'bricolage.' I took a little of Lévi-Strauss and added some Propp" (1989). The impact that Propp and Lévi-Strauss had on later studies of folklore and narrative is due to the nature of the materials they chose to investigate, folktales and myths, the ancestors of later fictional forms and the prototype of all narrative, and also to the insight and scientific passion they brought to bear on them. Structuralist linguistics, chiefly in the work of Ferdinand de Saussure, Louis Hjelmslev, and Roman Jakobson, makes up the third source of narratology, in which it played the role of pilot science and gave principles of methodology and research.

Narratology may be said to begin with Propp's seminal study, *Morphology of the Folktale* (1928), which became the point of departure for a number of later theorists, notably Greimas and the Parisian school of semiotics that included Roland Barthes, Claude Bremond, Paul Larivaille, and Tzvetan Todorov. Propp's work pioneered the search for isolating the minimal units of a narrative and specifying the ways and principles in which these units combine. The "morphology" he constructed for a certain kind of narrative was later called a grammar of the story or plot. From a corpus of one hundred Russian folktales, Propp worked on deriving the invariant structure of a master tale or an archetypal folktale. With ingenious simplicity, he deduced that the actions of the characters, which he called functions, provide stable and constant units and constitute a tale's fundamental structure. Furthermore, this structure is the same for all tales and can be represented by a sequence of thirty-one functions that always occur in the same, relatively fixed, linear order.

A single article, "The Structural Study of Myth" (1958), made Lévi-Strauss's paradigmatic analysis famous and influential. In its procedure, Lévi-Strauss's method is similar to Propp's in its attempt to isolate minimal units, which he calls mythemes, and their laws of combination. But the differences are more salient. Lévi-Strauss, for example, focuses on only one myth, the myth of Oedipus. In a two-dimensional notational system that Lévi-Strauss compares to an orchestra score, the syntagmatic sequence of the mythemes is blown up spatially and arranged paradigmatically into four vertical columns to reveal semantic and thematic commonalities among the units of each column. The striking result is a semantic network that interrelates these columns. The first two columns form a pair of opposites, and so do the next two. Moreover, a correlation or homology links the two pairs. Thus, generalizing, every myth contains a kernel of four mythemes related by opposition and correlation. A logical and semantic deep structure exists, yielding something akin to a "deep meaning," and can be uncovered behind the linear, surface sequence of the myth.

Structuralist narratology moved in two directions, following the distinction between two levels of narrative representation and analysis, story and discourse, corresponding respectively to the content plane and the expression plane or the signified and the signifier. Both the syntagmatic and paradigmatic structural analyses obtain their basic units from the story level, abstracted from the concrete textual manifestation. Greimassian narratology, in fusing the two types, also works primarily on the story. The area of discourse is represented mainly by the systematic and erudite work of Gérard Genette, who refines and builds upon concepts evolved in Continental and Anglo-American theoretical traditions.

The nonreferential approach has dominated both types of narratological framework. The moratorium on referential issues is apparent in the view of the narrative as a complex sign system as it is in the attempts to define minimal units together with the rules for their combination and functioning. For the traditional interpretation, which asserts that the narrative is a realistic or mimetic representation of life, the narratological view substitutes the semiotic thesis that all stories are shaped by conventions and generic structures. Within the older, prestructuralist perspective, narrative is just a decorative vehicle through which content is transmitted. The narrative is assumed to have a maximum claim to realism and to emphasize the transparency of its referential function in providing information about that simulated world. From the newer perch, the narratologists assert that real events do not take the form of a ready-made "untold story," and hence both the narrative world (the story) and the discourse through which that world is presented are constructed or made-up. The alleged realism of narrative is seen to be greatly compromised or even entirely undermined by the narrativity of representation—that is, by the constructed, fabricated nature inherent in narrativity itself. In light of these narratological premises, the prototype of narrative has ceased to be a self-effacing, plain account of real life, held to be an imitation or representation of an extratextual, storylike reality. Fictional or historical narratives always involve a narrator in the act of mediation, responsible for selecting, organizing, and verbalizing information about events and people. The focus on the narrative thus shifts to calling attention to the narrative material and the means of its making. Since the prototype of the narrative is deemed to be self-referential rather than oriented to a worldly context, the construction is studied in terms of textual and formal features, the conditions of meaning, and intrinsic principles of organization.

Greimas has done more, perhaps, than anyone else within the French-speaking and Continental world to stimulate the narrativist recognition that narrative or semionarrative structures account for the appearance and development of all, not merely verbal, meaning. Semionarrative structures are, in his view, reservoirs of fundamental signifying forms. He has gone so far as to say that narrativity has "gradually appeared as the very principle of organization of all discourse, narrative and non-narrative (1982, p. 209). This amounts to saying that any text (narrative, philosophical, legal, etc.) or any manifestation of meaning (painting, dreams, comics, etc.) can be analyzed as a story.

Given the expansion of narratology as a transdisciplinary pursuit in the 1990s, the movement outward from its earlier center in folklore and literary study, and the increasing recognition of the ubiquity of narrative, Greimas's statement appears prophetic. Greimas's concept of narrativity, however, has become so highly abstract and enlarged as to risk losing its effectiveness as an operational tool. The distinction between narrative and nonnarrative that characterized the earlier notion of narrativity has become totally vacuous under the later, all-embracing version. Thus, as the scope of narrativity widened, the precise meaning of narrativity has tended proportionately to become blurred. This fluctuating meaning of narrativity in Greimassian narratology, together with the transdisciplinary proliferation of the term in the 1990s and the lack of agreement among narratologists on a precise definition of the term, all effectively suggest returning to the initial privileged object of study, *Morphology of the Folktale*. It was inside this distinctly narrative domain, the domain of the archetypal folktale, that the primacy of narrativity was first staged in a sharply focused way.

[*See also* Greimas; Lévi-Strauss; Narrative Structures; Paradigm; Russian Formalism; *and* Structuralism.]

BIBLIOGRAPHY

Budniakiewicz, T. "Conceptual Survey of Narrative Semiotics." *Dispositio* 3:7–8 (1978); 189–217.

Budniakiewicz, T. *Fundamentals of Story Logic: Introduction to Greimassian Semiotics*. Amsterdam and Philadelphia: John Benjamins, 1992.

Greimas, A. J. *Maupassant: The Semiotics of Text: Practical Exercises*. Translated by P. Perron. Amsterdam and Philadelphia: John Benjamins, 1988.

Greimas, A. J. "On Meaning." *New Literary History* 20.3 (1989): 539–550.

Greimas, A. J., and J. Courtés. *Semiotics and Language: an Analytical Dictionary*. Translated by L. Crist and D. Patte. Bloomington: Indiana University Press, 1982.

Lévi-Strauss, C. "The Structural Study of Myth." In his *Structural Anthropology*, vol. 1, chap. 11. New York: Basic Books, 1958.

Lévi Strauss, C. "Structure and Form: Reflections on a Work by Vladimir Propp." In his *Structural Anthropology*, vol. 2, pp. 115–145. New York: Basic Books, 1976.

Propp, V. *Morphology of the Folktale* (1928). Translated by L. Scott. 2d ed. Austin: University of Texas Press, (1968).

—THERESE BUDNIAKIEWICZ

NATTIEZ, JEAN-JACQUES (b. 1945), French-born Canadian musicologist, semiologist, and a prominent exponent of musical semiotics as a distinct discipline. He was awarded the world's first doctorate in the semiology of music by the University of Paris VIII in 1972. In addition to his own thorough and characteristic development of semiotic theory, Nattiez has given the field substance through his influential teaching, organizational, editorial, and bibliographic endeavors. It is due largely to his intellectual leadership that the semiotics of music is now sustained by a very diverse and productive community of scholars, whose range arguably exceeds that of any other concerned with semiosis in a special, nonverbal field. For several years, while he directed the Research Group in Musical Semiotics at the University of Montreal, he edited numerous special issues of *Musique en jeu*, *Semiotica*, *Langages*, and other journals, produced records documenting folk and popular musics, organized symposia, and, as collaborator or producer, facilitated the publication of diverse research.

Nattiez's own theory is strongly empirical, rejecting any kind of immanent signification for the sign vehicle. Drawing on the ontological premises of Jean Molino, he regards the sign as a transmission rather than a communication. The sign is understood as tripartite (but in a sense entirely different than in the works of Charles Sanders Peirce or Gottlob Frege), comprising three planes: the aesthesic (what is received), the poietic (what is produced), and the trace or neutral level, in which the sign structure is physically embodied and which supports but does not fully correspond to either of the other two. Both the aesthesic and poietic object are patently constructions. The neutral trace is not intrinsically a construction in the same sense (though it is a manufactured object), but it is unknowable except insofar as it is modeled by some other construction.

This foundation, which by its denial of communicated representation seems to fly in the face of the very motivations of semiotic inquiry, proves very illuminating for music and might help to resolve the paradox of music's status as a sign. A composer might understand what he or she writes in terms of the constructive devices that produce the music—whether these are the elaborations of fugue or the manipulations of an electronic linear synthesizer or whatever. The auditor, who might know nothing of this technical wizardry, perceives the result in a framework conditioned by other factors. Of course, the composer could be sensitive to perception and the audience could be well informed about production, but ab initio no assumption of concurrence is invoked. In much of contemporary art-music and in many of the world's musical cultures, activities of musical production carry values quite different from those constructed through listening.

But producer and hearer are connected, possibly by culture but minimally by the sound itself, which retains an identity of some sort. Structural analysis attempts to capture this identity as the neutral level, the physical trace (we might say the vehicle) that can never be known in itself but that is approximated with more and more refinement. Analysis at the neutral level subjects schemas imported from the sign's aesthetic and poietic images to an empirical dialectic of explication and verification that explores the roots of musical logic. To this end, Nattiez adopted and extended the analysis of repetition in music proposed by Nicolas Ruwet and inspired by Zellig Harris's linguistics. Such segmental analysis provides a minute accounting of sonic variants and invariants with strict attention to explicit categorization (paradigmatic groupings) and serial order (syntagmatic hierarchy).

In keeping with the model that underlies all his work, Nattiez attends to all facets of the discourses that surround and interpret music as primary elements of the semiotic universe of music. He does not place any a priori limitations on the concept of music itself yet recognizes the efforts of each culture to constitute fields of music as fundamental to musical semiosis. The touchstone of this viewpoint is found in his extensive research on Inuit musics.

Nattiez's elaboration of a musical semiotic in which communication holds a secondary place has drawn strong reactions from several scholars who have felt challenged to exhibit equally systematic work supportive of shared understandings or intrinsic meanings in music. Eero Tarasti (1994) presumes that we can only approach music within cultural presuppositions and has developed a rich adaptation of Greimassian theory to this end. Robert Hatten (1994) synthesizes Leonard Ratner's concept of musical topics (a musical semiotics that does not carry that label) and Michael Shapiro's Peircean elaboration of markedness theory to produce a detailed, highly disciplined description of emotional reference in Beethoven's late style. David Lidov constructs musical semiotics within a comparative framework. Raymond Monelle (1992) has contributed a wide ranging overview of musical semiotics that includes aspects of his own very distinctive work in musical semantics.

In the English-speaking world, Nattiez's best-known works are his *Fondements d'une sémiologie de la musique* (1975), *Proust as Musician* (1989), *Wagner Androgyne* (1993) and *Music and Discourse*, (1990). He is known as a speaker throughout the world of musicology and has won numerous prizes.

[*See also* Aesthetics; Art; Clynes; *and* Music.]

BIBLIOGRAPHY

Works by Nattiez
Fondements d'une sémiologie de la musique. Paris: Union générale d'éditions 10/18, 1975.
Proust as Musician. Translated by D. Puffet. Cambridge and New York: Cambridge University Press, 1989.
Music and Discourse: Toward a Semiology of Music. Translated by C. Abbate. Princeton: Princeton University Press, 1990.
Wagner Androgyne: A Study in Interpretation. Translated by S. Spencer. Princeton: Princeton University Press, 1993.

Other Works
Hatten, R. S. *Musical Meaning in Beethoven: Markedness, Correlation, and Interpretation.* Bloomington: Indiana University Press, 1994.
Monelle, R. *Linguistics and Semiotics in Music.* New York: Harwood Academic Publishers, 1992.
Ratner, L. *Classic Music.* New York: Schirmer, 1980.
Shapiro, M. *The Sense of Grammar: Language as Semiotic.* Bloomington: Indiana University Press, 1983.
Tarasti, E. *A Theory of Musical Semiotics.* Bloomington: Indiana University Press, 1994.

—DAVID LIDOV

NEUROSEMIOTICS. Coined by Vjačeslav V. Ivanov (1979) to refer to the study of signs from the point of view of the neurological processes involved in the production and reception of messages and initially used in the context of language dysfunctions and brain-lateratization research, neurosemiotics has come to designate a wider subdomain of biosemiotics, including most of the field of inquiry covered by the cognitive neurosciences (Gazzaniga, ed., (1995). In this sense, neurosemiotics can be defined as the branch of the neurosciences that investigates the neurophysiological basis of semiotic behavior—namely, the production (encoding) and understanding (decoding) of signs, the perception of the environment as meaningful, and the general capacity to engage in symbolic interactions. Neurosemiotics attempts to correlate neurophysiological processes with well-defined aspects of semiotic behavior in order to better understand the information-processing systems that sustain them and to devise appropriate remedial strategies when these capacities become impaired because of disease or injury. However, neurosemiotics today designates a rather virtual domain within the neurosciences, which are still compartmentalized along traditional lines such as the study of aphasias, apraxias, memory disorders, cognitive deficits, asymbolism, and so on. Relevant research in these specialties has been brought together by Justine Sergent (1985).

A great deal of research has been conducted for well over a century on the role played by various brain subsystems in the production and understanding of language. André Roch Lecours and his coauthors (1983) have traced the history of aphasiology, the medical discipline that focuses upon one of the most important semiotic competences of *Homo sapiens*: language. In their chapter devoted to neurolinguistic terminology, the authors provide a carefully worded definition of language that clearly sets forth its semiotic status: "Language is the result of complex nervous activity which permits inter-individual communication of psychological states through the actualization of multimodal signs which symbolize these states in accordance with the established conventions of a linguistic community" (1983, p. 31).

Systematic investigations of the neurological basis of language bring into focus other important aspects of semiotic behavior. For instance, gestures, both as supplementary and complementary systems of communication, became, in the late 1970s and 1980s, legitimate objects of investigation by neuroscientists, notably but not exclusively in relation to sign languages, developmental kinesics, and apraxia (Nespoulous, Perron, and Lecours, eds., 1986). Moreover, an increasing concern for the context of communicative instances called for a broadening of the theoretical and methodological scope of neurolinguistics, as well as the establishment of subspecialties that are clearly semiotic without being linguistic, such as, for instance, research dealing with the decoding of the human face and its rich repertory of signs. As knowledge of the architectures and functions of the brain progresses, the correlation of behavior in general with neurological processes becomes a realistic goal of science. The emergence of the concept of neuroethology bears witness to this (e.g., Camhi, 1984). But the higher cognitive functions that semiotic behavior presupposes—such as symbolic thinking, short-term and long-term memory, or the control of logical consistency in social interactions and text production—have also attracted the attention of researchers confronted with dramatic disturbances of these functions in conditions that were traditionally labelled agnosia, dementia, and asymbolia but remained necessarily vague as long as the "normal" condition was not formally described. It seems obvious, in view of this new situation, that neurolinguistics can be only a part, albeit an essential one, of a more inclusive program of research. The term *neurosemiotics* designates an epistemological domain that includes the empirical and theoretical investigation of the neurological processes underlying communicative behavior in all its forms as well as the cognitive prerequisites for such behavior—namely, the capacity of categorizing, structuring, combining, encoding and decoding, and so on, that is to say, the capacity of making sense out of the environment, both physical and social, and of acting vicariously upon it.

[*See also* Biosemiotics; Chemical Communication; Receptors; *and* Umwelt.]

BIBLIOGRAPHY

Camhi, J. M. *Neuroethology: Nerve Cells and the Natural Behavior of Animals.* Sunderland, Mass: Sinauer Associates, 1984.

Gazzaniga, M. S., ed. *The Cognitive Neurosciences.* Cambridge, Mass.: MIT Press, 1995.

Ivanov, V. V. "Nejrosemiotika ustnoj reči i funkcional'naja asimetrija muzga." *Učenye Zapiski Tartuskogo Gosudarstvennogo* 481 (1979): 121–142.

Lecours, A. R., F. Lhermitte, and B. Bryans. *Aphasiology.* London: Baillère Tindall, 1983.

Nespoulous, J. L., P. Perron, and A. R. Lecours, eds. *The Biological Foundations of Gestures: Motor and Semiotic Aspects.* Hillsdale, N.J.: Lawrence Erlbaum, 1986.

Sergent, J., ed. "Neurosemiotics." Special issue of *Recherches sémiotiques/Semiotic Inquiry* 3 (1985): 223–322.

—PAUL BOUISSAC

NOMINALISM. *See* Realism and Nominalism.

NONVERBAL BODILY SIGN CATEGORIES.
Seeking a way of classifying bodily communicative activities, both interactive and noninteractive, determining their forms and functions, and giving them specific labels, David Efron (1941), Ray Birdwhistell (1952), and Paul Ekman and Wallace Friesen (1969)

established certain nonverbal bodily sign categories. These categories were further elaborated and supplemented by Fernando Poyatos (1986) without limiting the scheme to face and body movement and positions but recognizing the semiotic values of all external somatic behaviors. These categories—emblems, language markers, space and time markers, identifiers, externalizers, regulators, and emotional displays—can be used for any type of observational analysis.

Emblems are mostly nonambiguous gestures but they are also certain paralinguistic utterances that have their equivalences in words or a phrase (e.g. /Okay/, /Stop/, "ss!" for "hush!" "uh-uh" for "no"). Besides those that become quite universal (e.g., the hitchhiking gesture), each culture possesses a rich repertoire of specific emblems, quite often sharing homomorphic emblems that are actually antonyms (in the case of cognates, for example, the raised finger-ring gesture that signifys "okay" in North America, "money" in Japan, a sexual insult in Venezuela, and an emphatic conversational-language marker or attention getter in Spain). They are necessarily used in reduced-interaction situations, whether imposed (e.g., due to deafness or distance or when used as remedial communication between speakers of different languages) or mutually agreed upon (e.g., in the operating room, in a game of charades). Much needed research includes the child's acquisition of emblems and the elaboration of systematic inventories containing the more universal emblems as well as inventories of problematic forms and deceptive cognates in intercultural interaction and the introduction of graded emblem repertoires in foreign-language teaching.

Language markers are conscious or unconscious behaviors that punctuate and emphasize the acoustic and grammatical succession of words and phrases according to their location and relevance in the speech stream. They may coincide with written punctuation symbols, which are grammatical and attitudinal themselves, and even reveal verbal and nonverbal cultural peculiarities. The kinesic markers, always present in discourse more or less conspicuously, include various forms of pronoun markers (e.g., personal, pointing at present and even absent persons with nods and gazes, head tilts, hand palm, etc.); possessive markers (e.g., "Let's take our things," said with a sweeping, inclusive finger movement); reciprocal markers (e.g., "We always write to each other," said whether or not the other one is present and indicating both with a hand gesture); prepositional markers (e.g., brief face and hand gestures for *until*, *in order to*, or *without*; conjunctional markers (e.g., brief gestures for *and*, *so*, and *which* and longer ones for *however* and *therefore*; verbal markers, indicating both temporal and modal differences (e.g., phrases like "there was," "there has been," there will be," and "if there were any," symbolizing with varying emphasis something past and real, immediately preceding, expected with certainty, or only possible); stress markers (e.g., emphasizing with head movements, eyebrow raises, or the hands); punctuation markers, perfectly equivalent to punctuation symbols, indicating kinesically and paralinguistically the various breaks represented by [,], [:], [( )], etc., silences like [. . .], and voice qualities like those punctuated by ["—"], [!], and [?]. Other markers include kinesic-paralanguage markers—that is, using movements with voice features such as drawling ("Weeell," with wide-open eyes and raised brows), high pitch ("Whaaat?!"), or huskiness matched with rather stiff movements; proxemic language markers, such as leaning toward or away from someone to coincide with key words and stresses and to express peak syntactical and semantic elements while standing in a group; and even chemical markers since tears may act as true semantic markers of softly uttered or tensely loud words, and dermal ones since blushing or sudden gooseflesh can play similar functions. But even purely kinesic language markers deserve psychological and linguistic attention within studies of development, both as socioeducational identifiers and as displayed pathological states, emotional situations, and reduced-interaction situations.

Space markers and time markers are mainly kinesic behaviors that represent direct reference to the two basic dimensions of human life. While space markers illustrate size, distance, and location (e.g., "over there" indicated with a head-and-gaze nod among North Americans and a chin-and-gaze motion among Latins), time markers refer to the past, present, and future as well as to the duration of events. Besides many interesting cross-cultural differences based on the exact characteristics of the gesture and on its complementary paralinguistic behaviors, the hand gesture varies typically in distance from the body, proportionally to the indicated point in space or time and accompanied in many instances by emphatic quickening and drawling of syllables, respectively.

Deictics are movements, sometimes utterances,

that truly point to the location of a person, object, or place in space, even if the referent is not present (e.g., "I just came from there," said with a vague thumb-pointing gesture). These movements can also refer to an event in time (e.g., "This graduation is the best ever!" as if saying in incorrect English, "This graduation here"). There are cultural differences in the acceptability of pointing, and in some cultures finger-pointing is tabooed. In North America, "polite" pointing gestures during social introductions, wagging an accusing finger at someone, using even direct touch in a situation of superiority can be within the range of acceptable gestures.

Pictographs, apart from emblems, are the purest iconic (imitative) language-illustrating behaviors in social interaction. Pictographs are gestures that draw in the air or on a surface a picture of the shape or contour of something or someone. They are used out of economy of expression, mental laziness, and verbal limitation, often accompanied by qualifying paralinguistic voice modifications.

Echoics—of which comic books are spreading a large worldwide repertoire of English linguistic and paralinguistic origin—are imitations of sounds, done either paralinguistically (e.g., the clicking of a typewriter, the roaring of a lion, a gun going off), kinesically (e.g., a horse's galloping simulated by rapping our fingers on a surface), or kinetic-paralinguistically (e.g., if we add the vocal "tuk-ku-tuk, tuk-ku-tuk" to the rapping but without truly imitating the galloping). Similarly, kinetographs depict, perhaps accompanied by nonimitative sounds, any type of action (e.g., the way someone runs, the looping of an airplane). In the same way, kinephonographs combine imitations of movement and sound done kinesically and paralinguistically (e.g., the galloping and the sound of the hoofs simultaneously or a child's imitation of a car's steering-wheel handling and engine).

Ideographs and event tracers are movements, sometimes accompanied by paralinguistic utterances, that trace the direction of a thought or an event being described, respectively. We use ideographs when recollecting a pleasant experience, a great deed, a beautiful person, and so on. Sometimes, the manipulation of an object can be iconic, as when clutching a hat or a table while remembering an embrace. Event tracers, which accompany kinesically and paralinguistically the descriptive words, follow the development of an event (e.g., the comings and goings of a person and his or her actions).

Language markers, identifiers, and externalizers are responsible for the specific expressive style of a person (usually vaguely referred to as "assertive," "cool," "shy," "very articulate," "vulgar," and the like, betraying sex, age, socioeconomic and educational status, and culture) as well as of a whole culture (which we often identify without even hearing the accompanying words). They are more or less conspicuous kinesic behaviors or paralinguistic utterances (in reality-forming kineparalinguistic constructs, slight as the movement might be) displayed mostly in interaction, simultaneously to or immediately alternating with verbal language to refer or, literally, give bodily form to and identify certain abstract concepts (e.g., the impossible or the absurd), moral and physical qualities of people, animals, and things and qualities of objectual and environmental referents.

Externalizers are behaviors that constitute the most complex of all categories and do not illustrate words but at most react to them. They are reactions to other people's past, present, anticipated, or imagined realities, to what has been said, is being said, or will be said, silenced, done, or not done by us or others, to past, present, anticipated, or imagined events, to our own somatic phenomena, to animal and environmental agents, and to aesthetic or spiritual experiences. This definition could be paraphrased by referring, for instance, to facial expressions elicited by a present, remembered, or imagined other person, to what someone told us, is telling, or we think will tell us, and to what remains untold or undone (but felt nevertheless) or to an embrace or its absence, verbal or nonverbal expressions of affection toward animals, expressions of grief and bereavement, patients' pained expressions, audible exhalations elicited by real or imagined romantic involvements, ecstatic expressions of music listeners or players, or the open-arms gesture of awe before a breathtaking view. Only their definition will suggest once more why speakers can be said to communicate and identify themselves, both personally and culturally, mostly through language markers, identifiers, and externalizers. Each externalizer has an origin or first referent that triggers an elicitation (sensory, psychological, emotional, mental, random, or unconscious), which is displayed through an encoding somatic channel (kinesic, proxemic, chemical, etc.), which in turn constitutes the externalizer proper, finally perceived in the receiver's decoding channel (auditory, visual, olfactory, dermal, or kinesthetic). There are nine kinds of externalizers: self-generated, human, animal, objectual, environmental, events, literary reading (including the aesthetic appreciation of the stylistic composition and the multichannel metamorphoses whereby the reader reimagines all the imagined and equally multichannel experiences of the writer that were reduced to the visible printed text), musical experience, and spiritual referents. Of special cross-cultural importance are those random social behaviors displayed daily by all of us in personal and culture-defining ways as reactions to hidden states or past, present, or anticipated motives—although it is difficult to ascertain whether a lint-flicking gesture, desk tapping, or throat clearing, for instance, are unconscious and random, conscious and random, unconscious and habitual, or conscious and habitual. These are channeled mainly through paralanguage (e.g., clicks, sniffs, throat clearings), and kinesics (e.g., preening hair and clothes, fidgeting).

Adaptors are a group of nonverbal categories that includes activities or positions in which parts of the body come in contact with other parts, another body, objects and substances closely associated with the body, and objects of the environment (which itself comprises those objects and substances). Self-adaptors, which depend on the articulatory possibilities of the human body to touch itself, serve to adopt different postures (e.g., standing or walking with hands clasped in front or behind), to facilitate or conceal certain somatic needs (e.g., scratching, wiping tears, coughing), to groom and cleanse the body, to preen oneself, to display or conceal emotional states and reactions, to engage in mental activities (e.g., pinching brows or lips during memory searching), and are differentiated cross-culturally and by age, sex, and status. Alter-adaptors can be voluntary or involuntary—as in forced crowding—and are experienced differently if they are mutual (e.g., an embrace). They serve to initiate and terminate social encounters (i.e., greetings and good-byes), as bond-seeking and intimacy attitudes, in mother-infant interaction, for aggression and self-defense, to soothe, to groom, to express sexual and nonsexual love, to participate in games, as part of the mechanism of conversation, and so on. Their cross-cultural differences, their positive and negative aspects (e.g., in deception), the ontogeny of tactile and kinesthetic experiences and memories and their absence in the physically impaired among other aspects, are still in need of much research. Body

adaptors can be defined both as the objects and substances most immediately attached to the body because they are aimed at protecting it, nurturing it, and satisfying it, modifying its appearance, assisting it in various ways. The behaviors they condition serve to facilitate the oral ingestion of nutritional and pseudonutritional products or surrogates (e.g., the many culture-specific and personal behaviors conditioned by eating, drinking, chewing, and smoking), to display, conceal, enhance, or modify the natural visual and olfactory qualities of the body (e.g., through clothes, cosmetics, jewels), to perform unconscious random acts (e.g., fidgeting with crumbs, creases, buttons, jewelry), and so on. Object adaptors can be defined as cultural artifacts and organic or inorganic objects of the natural, modified, and built environments (that is, farther removed from the body than body adaptors and closer to it than the rest of the environment), as well as the resulting movements and positions. They serve to rest the body on body-oriented furniture and other structures (widely differentiated among many cultures), to perform household and occupational instrumental tasks (e.g., utensils, tools, water-carrying containers), to produce music, to perform animal-oriented tasks (e.g., training, branding, riding), and some, as with furniture, have determined historical changes in postural habits.

Regulators of conversational or nonconversational interaction and emotional displays are two categories that have practical applications, although they must be recognized as ubiquitous in the sense that they can be displayed through some of the other categories and can be channeled through verbal language, para-language, kinesics, proxemic positions and shifts, chemical, dermal, and thermal reactions and adaptors. Also, while regulators are subject to self-regulatory and interactional functions as well as to their costructuration with preceding, simultaneous, and succeeding activities and their location, intensity, and duration, different emotional displays can be combined into so-called emotional blends, which words alone cannot convey.

The scientific micro study of face-to-face interaction constitutes a challenging domain for further semiotic investigation. Advances in the understanding of the production and perception of co-occuring visual and auditory patterns and their cognitive correlates provide new insights into the subtle and complex ways in which the flow of information shapes human semiotic transactions (Massaro, 1998).

[*See also* Ekman; Face; *and* Nonverbal Communication in the Novel.]

BIBLIOGRAPHY

Birdwhistell, R. *Kinesics and Context: Essays on Body Motion Communication* (1952). Philadelphia: University of Pennsylvania Press, 1970.

Efron, D. *Gesture, Race, and Culture* (1941). The Hague: Mouton, 1972.

Ekman, P., and W. Friesen. "The Repertoire of Nonverbal Behavior Categories: Origins, Usage, and Coding." *Semiotica* 1 (1969): 49–98.

Massaro, D. W. *Perceiving Talking Faces*. Cambridge, Mass.: MIT Press, 1998.

Poyatos, F. "Nonverbal Categories as Personal and Cultural Identifiers: A Model for Social Interaction Research." In *Iconicity: Essays on the Nature of Culture: Festschrift for Thomas A. Sebeok on His Sixty-fifth Birthday*, edited by P. Bouissac, M. Herzfeld, and R. Posner, pp. 469–525. Tübingen: Stauffenburg Verlag, 1986.

—FERNANDO POYATOS

NONVERBAL COMMUNICATION IN THE NOVEL. The application of the results of nonverbal-communication research to the analysis of literary texts began to receive systematic treatment in the 1970s. Various aspects of the nonverbal elements in the narrative texts can be classified according to the writer-to-reader semiotic-communicative itinerary, the role of vision in reading, the implicit and explicit paralanguage in the text, explicit and implicit kinesics in the text, extrasomatic personal and environmental sounds, communicative functions of nonverbal elements, and technical functions of nonverbal elements. Each of these parameters will be treated in turn.

The transmission of nonverbal elements between writer and reader offers rich perspectives not only for research but for the lay appreciation of a literary work, particularly the novel. The whole real-life sensorial world of the writer is transmitted through writing and printing by the power of the word, which in turn elicits all manner of sensory experiences (acoustic, visual, tactile, kinesthetic, olfactory, and gustatory) in readers' imaginations.

The intimate relationship between the functioning of macular vision (covering twelve to fifteen degrees horizontally and 7.5 centimeters vertically) and peripheral vision (ninety degrees on each side horizontally) puts constraints on the reader's perception of the text. The re-creation of the text's nonverbal elements, particularly when the latter qualify other verbal or nonverbal actions or silences, is a neglected domain of inquiry. In "'You're a liar!', he yelled, banging the table with his fist. 'You're a liar, you're a liar!'" (D. H. Lawrence, *Sons and Lovers*, 1913), the banging is perceived immediately after the first "You're a liar!" and therefore the words already read and those that follow are "heard" together with the banging. This is not so with the actions described in "Mr. Pyser took his pipe from his mouth, and looked at Hetty in mild surprise for some moments. . . . 'Why, what's put that idea into your head, my wench?' he said at last, after he had given one conservative puff" (George Eliot, *Adam Bede*, 1859).

Paralanguage is found explicitly in narrative texts through the writer's verbal descriptions or—much less frequently because of the representational problems—transcriptions: "Halloa! . . . earnestly but whisperingly urging his crew" (Herman Melville, *Moby-Dick*, 1851). However, writers might not be able or wish to transcribe, for instance, their characters groaning, when they write "he groaned," this graphically visual signifier that depicts the four phonemes of the spoken label truly becomes for readers not just an audible signifier but in fact its very signified, for readers actually hear it in the imagination by virtue of its echoic nature. This is a marvelous literary tool that suffuses the otherwise silent, visual text with true life but also suggests the uncertain fate of written signifiers in translation: "Victoria . . . giving tight little cackles of swallowed laughter and murmuring, 'Bless his heart!'" (James Agee, *A Death in the Family*, 1957).

Explicit and implicit kinesics can be only described in the text, but they constitute the other most important repertoire of the characters' personal, situational, and cultural behaviors and the most fruitful research area in literary diachronic and synchronic analyses: "said the elder Mr. Weller, shaking up the ale, by describing small circles with the pot, preparatory to drinking" (Charles Dickens, *Pickwick Papers*, 1836–1837). In this brief survey, however, it is more relevant to mention that the more sensitive reader usually perceives kinesics' implicit presence by a character's words or paralanguage, transcribed or described: "'Are you crazy?' he hissed frantically. 'Put it away and keep your idiot voice down.'" (Joseph Heller, *Catch-22*, 1961). It can also be visualized in conjunction with another, described kinesic behavior: "'This very good, Mrs. Burden'—she clasped her hands as if she could not express how good—. . . oh, so good!" (Willa Cather, *My Antonia*, 1918). Kinesics can be described by chemical reactions such as tears; by the known correlation between dermal reactions such as blushing and kinesics: "he muttered and blushed still more deeply . . . as he realized the imbecility of what he had said" (Aldous Huxley, *Point Counter Point*, 1928); and by the character's personality, as we become familiar with it. One important caveat, however, in this respect concerns the reality of cross-cultural differences, which can create critical interpretive challenges for the foreign reader.

The communicative significance of sounds generated by our bodies and through objects can be found in narrative literature as intentional or unintentional components of interactions: "The two combatants leaped forward and crashed together like bullocks . . . the cushioned sounds of blows" (Stephen Crane, "The Blue Hotel," 1898). They are also qualifiers of actions similar to paralinguistic voice qualifiers: "she rapped imperatively at the window" (Lawrence, *Sons and Lovers*). Environmental sounds can also acquire, as in real-life interaction, an impressive speechlike quality related to characters' behaviors, interwoven with the other verbal and nonverbal elements in the experience of reading; here, synesthesia operates powerfully at the visual level of the printed page, although it is based only on the written verbal evocation of the secondary sources— and thus is in fact tertiary—rather than on the secondary sources themselves. Naturally, some sounds may not be part of a given reader's audible world, due to differences in time or culture: "'Squish squash!' echoed the milk in the great cylinder. . . . The milk in the revolving churn at that moment changed its squashing for a decided flick-flack" (Thomas Hardy, *Tess of the D'Urbervilles*, 1891).

From a communicative point of view, there are four ways in which writers can convey information through descriptions or transcriptions of paralanguage and kinesics: (1) by describing the behavior and explaining its meaning, too (signifier and signified), the traditional method of realism: "He emitted a laboured breath, as if the scene were getting rather oppressive to his heart, or to his conscience, or to his gentility" (Hardy, *Tess of the D'Urbervilles*); (2) by describing the behavior without explaining its meaning (signifier but not signified), not always allowing the reader to interpret the meaning, especially true when the reader is of a different culture or historical period: "[When El Cid returns from exile and meets

the king] los inojos e las manos en tierra los fincó, / las yerbas del campo a dientes las tomó, / llorando de los ojos, tanto avíe el gozo mayor" ("[When El Cid returns from exile and meets the king] he fell to the ground on his hands and knees, / he took the grass of the fields with his teeth, / his eyes welled up from the great happiness"; *Poema del Cid*, v. 2021); (3) by explaining the meaning without describing the behavior (signified but not signifier), which might or might not be understood by the reader as meant by the writer, let alone by a foreign reader: "'No,' returned Carrie with a touch of pride" (Theodore Dreiser, *Sister Carrie*, 1900); (4) by using a verbal expression always concurrent with a paralinguistic one, more obvious and easier to evoke in the case of gestures, as some verbal, verbal-paralinguistic, or paralinguistic expressions are always combined with kinesics. As with the previous technique, this might be totally missed by a foreign reader, as in "—Por aquí me entra y por aquí me sale" ("It goes in this way and out this way"; Rafael Sánchez Ferlosio, *El Jarama*, 1956, p. 214), the Spanish equivalent of "it goes in one ear and out the other," but with the added gesture of pointing at one's ears as one says *aquí*.

From a technical and sign-location point of view, central to the craft of fiction, nonverbal elements can perform four functions: (1) initial definition of the character by means of one or more idosyncratic verbal or nonverbal features: "His speaking voice, a gruff husky tenor, added to the impression of fractiousness he conveyed: (F. Scott Fitzgerald, *The Great Gatsby*, 1925); (2) progressive definition by means of new additional features, as when, after the first image of Daisy Fay in *The Great Gatsby*, we hear "her voice glowing and singing" and, much later, "that voice held him [Gatsby] most, with its fluctuating, feverish warmth . . . that voice was a deathless song"; (3) subsequent identification by means of a feature or features repeated for the first time (particularly useful in densely populated large novels), a way of preserving those defining nonverbal behaviors that will ensure the reader's experience of the characters, as with Charles Dickens's Mr. Micawber in *David Copperfield* and "the condescending roll in his voice," six chapters after being introduced as having "a certain condescending roll in his voice, and a certain indescribable air of doing something genteel"; (4) recurrent identification by means of an already familiar feature repeated as many times as necessary, as with Thomas Hardy's Arabella in *Jude the Obscure* (1896), who three times is said to form "a perfect dimple" in each cheek.

[*See also* Conversation; Ekman; Face; *and* Nonverbal Bodily Sign Categories.]

BIBLIOGRAPHY

Birdwhistell, R. *Kinesics and Context: Essays on Body Motion Communication.* Philadelphia: University of Pennsylvania Press, 1970.

Efron, D. *Gesture, Race, and Culture.* The Hague: Mouton, 1972.

Ekman, P., and W. Friesen. "The Repertoire of Nonverbal Behavior Categories: Origins, Usage, and Coding." *Semiotica* 1 (1969): 49–98.

Korte, B. *Body Language in Literature.* Translated by E. Ens. Toronto: University of Toronto Press, 1997.

Portch, S. R. *Literature's Silent Language.* New York and Frankfurt: Peter Lang, 1985.

Poyatos, F. "Forms and Functions of Nonverbal Communication in the Novel: A New Perspective of the Author-Character-Reader Relationship." *Semiotica* 21. 3–4, (1977): 295–337.

Poyatos, F. *La comunicación no verbale,* vol. 3, *Nuevas perspectivas en novela y teatro y en su traducción.* Madrid: Istmo, 1994.

Poyatos F. "Aspects, Problems, and Challenges of Nonverbal Communication in Literary Translation." In *Nonverbal Communication in Translation,* edited by F. Poyatos, pp. 17–47. Amsterdam and Philadelphia: John Benjamins, 1997.

Poyatos F., ed. *Advances in Nonverbal Communication: Sociocultural, Clinical, Esthetic, and Literary Perspectives.* Amsterdam and Philadelphia: John Benjamins, 1992.

—FERNANDO POYATOS

NUMBER REPRESENTATION. Probably no system of number representation can quite function without some arbitrary elementary signs. Western words, for numbers under ten and Indo-Arabic numerals do not show either how the numbers designated by them are related to each other. Nothing in the form of the words or in the shape of the figures reveals that, say, five is greater than four, or that 4 is the doubling of 2. We must first memorize these words and figures by establishing a fixed series of words or figures that corresponds to the rising sequence of the numbers designated by them.

Fortunately, the part of this procedure that most burdens our memory ends at *twelve,* as the word *thirteen* can be analyzed into *thir* and *teen,* which remind us of words we encountered in the preceding series: *three* and *ten.* With the figures, this occurs even ear-

lier, at *10,* which consists of the elementary figures *1* and *0.* By composing numeral expressions out of other numeral expressions, we are spared having to learn continually new expressions, and our memories are not needlessly burdened because we can keep the lexicon of our sign system small.

Simplicity in the lexicon is, however, not available without extra cost. Whoever understands the meaning of words such as *thirteen* does so by following certain rules, and rules must be learned along with the elementary signs. We are dealing here with rules of two different types: a syntactic rule, which determines the pattern according to which the elementary signs are combined into complex signs, and a semantic one, which determines how the value of each complex sign is derived from the values of its constituents. In the above case, we need the syntactic rule that the numeral words between *three* and *nine* may form new words by attaching *teen* to them. And we need the semantic rule that the value of a word composed in this way is derivable from the value of its parts by addition (and not by, say, multiplication, since $4 + 10 = 14$, whereas $4 \times 10 = 40$).

These examples show that a system of number representation, like every sign system, consists of a lexicon, a set of syntactic rules, and a set of semantic rules. Our desire to fulfill our needs with the least possible effort plays an important role in the development of sign systems. But how does the mental effort necessary for the learning of a rule compare with the effort necessary for learning new elementary signs? These are questions concerning the economy of signs. Naturally, they cannot be answered independently of the solutions that a given culture has found for related problems in other areas. For example, the learning of a sign system can be facilitated considerably by the facts that its elementary signs are already used by its learners in other contexts and that their meanings are characterized by relationships that are analogous to those in the other contexts.

Such was the case with the ancient Egyptians, who were already using numeral signs more than five thousand years ago and were able to represent nearly a million numbers with only six hieroglyphs. Not without reason did the Egyptians consider their country a gift of the river Nile, which in an annually recurring pattern burst its banks and flooded the desert with fertile mud. These circumstances determined the economy (tillage and husbandry), trade (farming produce), science (computation of a calendar by observation of the stars), administration (annual land surveys), art, and religion. Therefore, it is not surprising—and explicable on the basis of a culture-embracing sign economy—that the Egyptian numeral signs also came from these areas. The number 1 was designated by one notch on a tally; it had the same form as that found on Stone Age bones. The number 10 was represented by the shape of a yoke, similar to that used by the Egyptians to harness oxen. The design of a rolled-up measuring tape, as was used in land surveying, served as the figure for 100. The figure for 1,000 had the form of the lotus plant, which grew in large numbers in the Nile valley and thus had come to symbolize abundance in the cults of Isis and Osiris. The number 10,000 was represented by the reed spadix which was even more plentiful than the lotus. The silhouette of a frog stood for 100,000, since frogs appeared in upper Egypt regularly and in such proliferation that they had become a plague. Although the quantities of the objects portrayed by the figures did not always increase tenfold, there was nevertheless a clear relationship between the rise of the quantities and the increase in the numerical values.

The Egyptians employed a syntactic rule that required juxtaposing the elementary signs in groups of up to nine each and ordering according to decreasing numerical values. For *7*, the sign for *1* was written seven times; for *400*, the hundred-sign was written four times; and *2,407* was represented on the papyrus by two thousand-signs, four hundred-signs and seven one-signs, written one after the other. The overall direction of writing varied according to the circumstances. The semantic rule was equally simple. In general, it required that two juxtaposed signs be interpreted by addition. The first part of figure 1 shows the application of both of these rules to the number 2,407.

Additive number codes are typical of the earliest civilizations: they were used with slight variation by the Sumerians, the Greeks (Attic figures), and the Romans. But after a millennium and a half of such use, another early civilization developed a number code that followed a different semantic principle. Ancient Chinese logograms, which were in use from about 2000 BCE and written from top to bottom, systematically required the interpretation of concatenation by multiplication. Instead of writing the hundred sign four times in a row and adding the values of these signs step-by-step to get four hundred, the Chinese

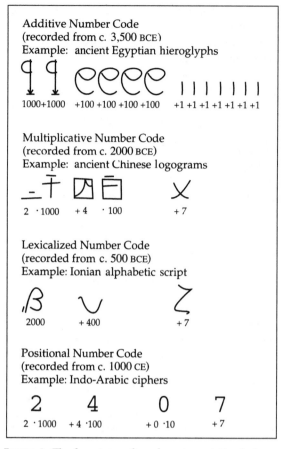

FIGURE 1. *The four stages of number representation in human history, illustrated by the notation for the number 2,407; writing direction from left to right.*

simply wrote the sign for *4* on top of the sign for *100* and multiplied their values.

This procedure introduced greater sign economy, since in this case only two signs were needed instead of four. Generally speaking, in a numerical expression of the additive code, all groups of up to nine signs of identical shape were replaced by pairs of signs, where the first designated a number less than 10 and the second a number equal to or a power of 10. The advantage of this solution becomes manifest in the second illustration in figure 1: while a representation of the number 2,407 in the Egyptian way necessitates thirteen signs (2 + 4 + 7), the Chinese system requires only five (2 + 2 + 1). A comparison of the expressions for 99,999, the largest number representable in ancient Chinese logograms, makes the difference even clearer: the Egyptians needed forty-five individual signs, whereas the Chinese managed with nine.

The Chinese innovation improved the economy of sign performance. But this was not achieved without a price since it constituted a sizable increase in the mental effort needed for learning the Chinese number code: The lexicon has more than doubled, growing from six to thirteen elementary signs, since for the introduction of pairs of signs each number from 1 to 9 must have its own sign. The syntactic system is more complex; instead of the succession of elementary signs of various shapes, it must now regulate the composition and succession of sign pairs, each of which is made up of an elementary sign below 10 and an elementary sign equal to or a power of 10. The semantics is more complex; it demands two different rules of interpretation instead of one, since the operation of concatenation can no longer be interpreted in a uniform way. According to the first rule, which covers concatenation within sign pairs, the values of the concatenated signs must be multiplied to yield the value of the sign pair. According to the second rule, which covers concatenation outside sign pairs, the values of the concatenated sign pairs must be added to yield the value of the total expression.

Thus, an advantage in performance economy is accompanied by a disadvantage in system economy. Chinese scribes reduced the mental effort required in their daily work by raising the mental effort required in their professional training. The question whether such a redistribution of work is beneficial or not cannot be answered independently of the context, since there exists no absolute rate of exchange for different types of effort. The biological constitution of the sign user, his or her personality structure, and the structure of his or her society must be taken into account. A society with an elaborate division of labor, one that could afford a highly specialized scribe caste, might gladly have accepted a longer period of professional training if the result was higher efficiency in everyday business. An egalitarian society, however, which strives for the broadest possible education for the greatest number, might put up with less efficiency in particular areas of everyday life if this sets free learning capacity for other areas.

The tendency toward an improvement of performance economy at the cost of system economy is, in any case, established in history. After the first appearance of the multiplicative code, it was a further millennium and a half until the invention of the written alphabet, which led to the introduction of the alphabetical representation of numbers by the Greeks of Asia Minor (the Ionians). The Ionians simply took twenty-four letters of the Greek alphabet (α, β, γ, . . . ω), including three defunct archaic signs (ς,$\text{\text?}$,π) and two auxiliary signs ($,\alpha,\ddot{\alpha}$), and assigned to each one a numerical value as its meaning. For greater effect, they structured their lexicon in a way similar to that of the Chinese; that is, they projected the first ten letters of the alphabet (α, . . . , ι) onto the first ten natural numbers (1, . . . , 10), then increased the semantic distance between two adjacent letters tenfold and repeated this step after each ten further signs. While one unit is to be added to $\alpha = 1$ to get the value of the next sign $\beta = 2$, ten units must be added to $\iota = 10$ to reach the value of the following sign $\kappa = 20$. By analogy, the transition from $\rho = 100$ to $\sigma = 200$ no longer requires the addition of ten but one hundred units, and comparable changes occur at the transition from $,\alpha = 1,000$ to $,\beta = 2,000$ and from $\ddot{\alpha} = 10,000$ to $\ddot{\beta} = 20,000$. Thus, the syntactic space of the Ionian sign repertory does not have the same structure as the semantic space of the number arrow but, rather, absorb it telescopically.

How were the numbers that fell in the resulting gaps (10–20, 100–200, 1,000–2,000, etc.) to be designated? The Ionians solved this problem in the same way as the Egyptians, simply by adjoining one or more of the preceding signs and adding the values. Thus, the number 407, which lies between $\upsilon = 400$ and $\varphi = 500$, was represented by $\upsilon\zeta$, which designates 400 + 7; and the number 2,407 was represented by $,\beta\upsilon\zeta$, which designates 2,000 + 400 + 7.

In this way, the Ionian Greeks were able to manage with syntactic and semantic rules that were just as simple as those of the Egyptians and to decrease the performance effort for a number such as 2,407 from thirteen to four individual signs and for 99,999 from forty-five to seven signs. The price they paid for this was a near quintupling of the lexicon from six elementary signs in the Egyptian number code to twenty-nine.

The Egyptian additive code, the Chinese multiplicative code, and the lexicalized number code of the Greeks did not emerge from each other in continuous historical development, as is evident from the distribution of their geographical areas of use. They are, rather, examples of particularly early and concise applications of semiotic principles that have been tried out independently in many different cultures in this same historical order. In accordance with the historical development of the basic number operations, most ancient cultures have experimented successfully with additive, subtractive (e.g., the Roman numeral IV indicates 5 − 1), multiplicative, and divisional (fractional) systems of number representation. Examples are found not only in the later development of hieroglyphs toward the so-called demotic script in Egypt but also in the history of the Sumerian, ancient Indian, and ancient American number codes.

In order to encode the number 4, Egyptians wrote the sign for 1 four times in a row; IIII. The structure of this complex sign reflects the structure of its signified. The Chinese, using a single elementary sign, instead located the generation of meaning in the lexicon; there is nothing in the Chinese sign for *4* that reflects the quadruplicity of this number. Accordingly, the Chinese did not represent the number 400 by writing the hundred sign four times; but at least they used a complex sign that referred to the factor 4. The Greeks removed even this last piece of perspicuity. They did not construct the number in their code by forming a sum or a product but designated it with an unanalyzable elementary sign: *v*.

Even if elementary signs are distributed along the number arrow as cleverly as they were by the Greeks, there are still limits to this development, since the set of natural numbers is infinitely large. If one wants to use an elementary sign for every multiple of 10 as the Greeks did or for every power of 10 as the Egyptians and the Chinese did, one needs an infinitely large repertory of elementary signs. Nevertheless, the method adopted by the Greeks helped clear the way for a solution to this problem. If the signs are not tied by their form to a structural characteristic of the signified, they can even have different values in different contexts. The Sumerians were the first to come upon this idea, and it was also developed independently by the Maya. In the first millennium CE, the Indians constructed a complete system of number representation on the basis of this idea. At the beginning of the second millennium, this system was introduced in Europe through the mediation of Arabs.

The Indo-Arabic number code has elementary signs that in isolation designate something different from what they designate in complex numeral expressions: the *1* has the value 1 only when found on the outside right of an expression (without comma or decimal point). For every positional shift to the left, its value is multiplied by ten (compare the values of the expressions *1, 10, 100, 1,000*, etc.). But in order to reach this effect, the Indians had to introduce a new elementary sign with a seemingly paradoxical task: it did not designate anything itself, but when placed to the right of another sign it increased the latter's value ten times. This was the task of the sign *0*. Western Europeans were still in the additive stage with their Roman numerals when confronted by the Indo-Arabic figures. "How can something which itself designates nothing multiply by ten the value of the figure to which it is attached?" they argued, not distinguishing between sign and signified and between isolated value and positional value. This semiotic confusion had repercussions in the business world, and some city governments, like that of Florence in 1299, forbade the use of the Indo-Arabic numerals altogether.

If the positional number code established itself nevertheless, that was due first to its greater system economy: it does not require elementary signs in addition to those that designate the numbers below ten and the zero sign. This allowed for a drastic reduction of the lexicon. In exchange, the semantics became more complex. Although two rules are not necessary, as in the Chinese system, the interpretation of the concatenation is comparably complicated: instead of adding the values of two concatenated signs immediately, one has to multiply the value of the sign on the left by ten before adding it to the value of the sign on the right. But unlike any previous system, the positional number code does not require the introduction of ad hoc elementary signs for the representation of high numbers; thus, it is the first number code that covers the infinite set of numbers in its entirety. This progress opened undreamed-of possibilities to the sciences (e.g., astronomy) as well as to administration and business (e.g., banking).

Even more important was how the new method of number representation revolutionized computing. In all ancient civilizations, the principles used for the representation of number were different from those used for doing calculations with it. The Greeks and Romans employed an abacus with stones made of chalk (*calculi*), and the Chinese had a sort of slide rule with balls on a string (*suanpan*). To compute a problem in writing, a double recoding of the numeral expressions was required: from the writing surface to the computing instrument and, after the computing process was completed, from the instrument back onto the writing surface. The Indo-Arabic code permitted calculations in writing for all essential purposes in business and trade and thereby saved two-thirds of the coding effort.

Is the Indo-Arabic system of number representation still up-to-date? Or are there useful alternatives? Its way of composing complex signs through linear concatenation of single signs is optimal, and the interpretation of the single signs according to their position in the complex expression is an efficient basis for the representation of numbers of any size. Therefore, we will certainly continue to require a code based on positional value. There is, however, room for experiment in the choice of the lexicon and thus in the design of performance. Instead of using ten elementary signs (digits) and semantically interpreting a shift of digit one place to the left as a tenfold increase, other scales can be used. For technical reasons, instead of a system based on ten (decimal code), a system based on two (binary code) was chosen for use in the first electric computing machines. The computer only has two possibilities for each position of a complex sign, realized by the presence (1) or absence (0) of an electric current in the corresponding part. With appropriate programming based on positional value, it is nevertheless capable of forming and processing expressions for numbers of any size.

[*See also* Abacus; Alphabet; Pragmatics; Sign; *and* Writing, Ethnography of.]

BIBLIOGRAPHY

Benacerraf, P., and H. Putnam, eds. *Philosophy of Mathematics: Selected Readings.* Englewood Cliffs, N.J.: Prentice-Hall, 1964.

Brainerd, C. J. *The Originals of the Number Concept.* New York: Praeger, 1979.

Cajori, F. *A History of Mathematical Notations*, vol. 1, *Notations in Elementary Mathematics.* La Salle, Ill: Open Court, 1928.

Gullberg, J. *Mathematics from the Birth of Numbers.* New York: Norton, 1997.

Hurford, J. R. *The Linguistic Study of Numerals.* Cambridge: Cambridge University Press, 1975.

Hurford, J. R. *Language and Number.* Oxford: Blackwell, 1987.

Ifrah, G. *Histoire universelle des chiffres.* Paris: Seghers, 1981.

Menninger, K. *Number Words and Number Symbols.* Cambridge, Mass.: MIT Press, 1969.

Posner, R. "Balance of Complexity and Hierarchy of Precision: Two Principles of Economy in the Notation of Language and Music." In *Semiotic Theory and Practice*, edited by M. Herzfeld and L. Melazzo, pp. 909–920. Berlin and New York: de Gruyter, 1988.

Posner, R. "Denkmittel als Kommunikationsmittel." *Zeitschrift für Semiotik* 17 (1995): 247–256.

Pullan, J. M. *The History of the Abacus.* London: Hutchinson, 1968.

Sondheimer, E., and A. Rogerson. *Numbers and Infinity: A Historical Account of Mathematical Concepts.* Cambridge: Cambridge University Press, 1981.

—ROLAND POSNER

O–P

OPPOSITION. The logic of opposition, which goes back at least to Aristotle (384–322 BCE), makes an important distinction between contradictories (two propositions that cannot be both true or both false) and contraries (two propositions that cannot both be true but might both be false). This relation was soon extended to relations between concepts. For instance, contradictory terms include *white* and *not white*; contrary terms include *white* and *black*. The latter pair allows for the conceptual introduction of all the intermediaries of gray, whereas the former is of the all-or-nothing type. The logical tradition has influenced the semiotic organization of concepts based on the notion of opposition.

In Ferdinand de Saussure's linguistics, the notion of opposition is associated closely with the notion of structure. Saussure argued that in language systems there are only differences without positive terms; every element derives its identity from its opposition to other elements in the same system. Phonemes are considered to be purely oppositive, relative, and negative. This conception was radicalized by the Copenhagen School with Louis Hjelmslev's claim that any language can be analyzed independently of its "substance"—that is, whether conveyed by speech, writing, or some kind of flags or manual signs—and purely with respect to its "form."

The Prague School took a less radical approach. However, in his pioneering study of phonology, Nikolaj S. Trubetzkoy (1939) foregrounded the notion of opposition, distinguishing different types. These distinctions are based on his insight, often overlooked in later semiotics, that any opposition between two terms presupposes some kind of similarity, which provides a base for comparison as well as some properties that are different. Thus, an opposition is one-dimensional if the base of comparison is found only in two items, but otherwise it is multidimensional (e.g., the common factor in the letters *E* and *F* is not found in any other letters of the alphabet, but the one present in *P* and *R* also appears in *B*). On the other hand, an opposition is proportional if the difference between two terms is found in other pairs of elements (e.g., some irregular plurals in English, such as *geese* and *teeth*); otherwise, the opposition is isolated.

In privative opposition, one of the terms consists simply in the absence of the trait found in the other term (e.g., in phonetics, unvoiced sounds as opposed to voiced ones; in semantics, the plural *s* opposed to its absence). In an equipollent opposition, both terms are complete in themselves (e.g., irregular plural modification in which the singular form is not indicated by the mere absence of plurality marking, such as with *foot* and *feet*). In gradual opposition, finally, some properties are present in various degrees in several terms (e.g., the traditional phonetic description of the degree of aperture in expressing vowels).

Jean Cantineau (1952) and, in particular, Roland Barthes (1964) have transferred these phonological distinctions to the domain of semantics and general semiotics. However, there is no place in such a scheme for purely quantitative opposition of the kind found, for instance, in the theory of semantic differentials, where the distance between two extreme instances is ascribed some numeral value. Even gradual oppositions are construed as categorical rather than continuous.

Roman Jakobson (1942) was the first to show that, at least in phonology, all opposition can be reduced to the binary, privative kind. This requires the reduction of nonbinary, equipollent opposition based on a redefinition of the constitutive categories. In the case of phonological features, Jakobson, Gunnar Fant, and Morris Halle (1952) identified these categories from an acoustic point of view; whether they are also perceptually relevant is an open question (see Petitot-Cocorda, 1985). In any case, it does not follow that the reduction to binary, privative oppositions remains valid outside the domain of linguistic expression.

Jakobson himself, in his 1942 lectures at the New School of Social Research in New York, questioned Saussure's belief that semantic oppositions are purely negative on the ground that the meanings of *night* and *day* are not derived entirely from their opposition. Yet Claude Lévi-Strauss, who attended these lectures, later championed the idea of semantic opposition being purely negative, binary, and privative in the domain of myths and visual semiotics. This approach influenced French structuralism, which conceived all opposition as being purely privative, an idea taken for granted in the work of Algirdas Julien Greimas and his disciples. Critics of this theory contend that the kinds of opposition that structuralists elucidate in myths, literary works, pictures, and cultures are markedly different from those that govern the phonological system of natural languages and that even Trubetzkoy's abstract classifications appear to be of limited applicability.

For this alternative approach, oppositions may be constitutive of the identity of signs, as in the case of phonology, or they may be merely regulative of already constituted identities, such as two pictures or two objects represented in a single picture. This kind of opposition is secondary with respect to the recognition of the represented objects themselves—hence the necessity to distinguish opposition *in absentia,* or true opposition, from opposition *in praesentia*, or contrasts. Rather than deriving from a system, the latter are construed in a given text, such as poetry, visual art, advertisements, or myths. Moreover, even oppositions *in absentia* are not necessarily conceived as being systemic. An advertisement or a postmodern artwork, for instance, might allude to another text from the large stock of pictures which the culture of reference comprises and with respect to which it positions itself. In this case, most nonphonological opposition is abductive rather than structural. Far from resulting from a set of systemic opposition, meanings derive from the contrasting regularities obtaining in the commonsense knowledge of the culture of reference.

One argument that seeks to invalidate the extrapolation of phonological opposition beyond linguistic systems of sounds holds that these systems do not admit neutral and complex terms between their constitutive oppositions, whereas semantic oppositions admit such intermediary terms. Intermediary terms are not functional relative to the distinction between the marked and unmarked members of an opposition. What is normally meant by an intermediary term is that some properties that we are accustomed to ascribing to one superordinate term (e.g.,

nature) are ascribed to an object that also contains properties normally associated with the opposite superordinate term (e.g., culture). Here we find the "deviant animals," "taboos," and "monsters" recognized by many anthropologists. Thus, the intermediary terms are best seen as inversions of what are known in cognitive psychology as prototypes—that is, as the least rather than the most probable conjunction of attributes (Rosch and Mervis, 1975). The fundamental issue remains whether relevant semiotic oppositions can ever be construed compellingly as logical contradictions. The relative deviance of intermediary terms obviously depends on the exact nature of the relation between the terms and whether they are conceived of as mere differences or as actual contraries more or less loaded with semantic values.

[*See also* Abductive Reasoning; Barthes; Copenhagen School; Greimas; Jakobson; Lévi-Strauss; Prague School; *and* Structuralism.]

BIBLIOGRAPHY

Barthes, R. *Elements of Semiology* (1964). Translated by A. Lavers and C. Smith. New York: Hill and Wang, 1967.

Blanché, R. *Structures intellectuelles.* Paris: Vrin, 1966.

Cantineau, J. "Les oppositions significatives." *Cahiers Ferdinand de Saussure* 10 (1952): 11–40.

Cantineau, J. "Le classement logique des oppositions." *Word* 11 (1955): 1–9.

Jakobson, R. *Six leçons sur le son et le sens* (1942). Paris: Minuit, 1976.

Jakobson, R., G. Fant, and M. Halle. *Preliminaries to Speech Analysis.* Cambridge, Mass.: MIT Press, 1952.

Lévi-Strauss, C. *The Way of the Masks.* Translated by S. Modelski. Seattle: University of Washington Press, 1982.

Petitot-Cocorda, J. *Les catastrophes de la parole: De Roman Jakobson à René Thom.* Paris: Maloine, 1985.

Rosch, E., and C. B. Mervis. "Family Resemblances: Studies in the Structure of Categories." *Cognitive Psychology* 7.4 (1975): 382–439.

Sonesson, G. *Pictorial Concepts: Inquiries into the Semiotic Heritage and Its Relevance for the Analysis of the Visual World.* Lund: Aris and Lund University Press, 1989.

Trubetzkoy, N. S. *Principles of Phonology* (1939). Translated by C. A. M. Baltaxe. Berkeley: University of California Press, 1969.

—GÖRAN SONESSON

PARADIGM. In Western traditional grammar, *paradigm* (derived from the Latin *paradigma* and the Greek *paradeigma*) refers to the pattern of inflections of nouns and verbs or to typical samples of such systems of inflection. Hence, the meaning of the adjective *paradigmatic*: serving as a pattern, or an example.

During the twentieth century, the meaning of this word has evolved in two directions, becoming epistemologically active in two different contexts. First, in European structural linguistics derived from Ferdinand de Saussure, it has the broad sense of "a class of linguistic elements" that can be associated because of certain similarities. Saussure speaks of associative relations between linguistic elements that may occupy the same structural position and can be substituted for one another depending on the context. This is a clear generalization of the traditional grammatical sense, but this sense has been transformed considerably by its complementary association with the notion of syntagm. From the opposition set by Saussure between relating what is *in absentia* (paradigm) and what is *in praesentia* (syntagm), a general model of language has developed and has been extended by analogy to other domains of human activities inasmuch as they imply choices made among classes of elements and functional combinations of the chosen elements. These complementary notions are usually represented in a diagrammatic form as two axes of selection and combination (Jakobson, 1960) intersecting at right angles. They have been further generalized as the twin concepts of system and process. The program of French structuralist semiology consisted mostly of "uncovering" the systems presupposed by given domains of processes such as dreams, myths, discourses, and so on.

The second context in which *paradigm* is epistemologically alive is the domain of inquiry formed by the philosophy, history, and sociology of sciences. Here, the word was introduced and used abundantly in Thomas Kuhn's *The Structure of Scientific Revolutions* (1962), the provocative theses of which triggered a fundamental controversy over the nature of scientific theories. Although Kuhn's use of *paradigm* was rooted in the current sense of "typical pattern" or "model," it received privileged treatment in his work and became the focus of an intense definitional debate. Kuhn himself acknowledged that his own use of the term lacks conceptual clarity. One critic found no less than twenty-two different meanings of the word, ranging from "a concrete scientific achievement" to "a characteristic set of beliefs and preconceptions." In his subsequent publications (notably in Frederick Suppe, 1977), Kuhn comes to grips with this definitional problem: "one sense of 'paradigm' is global, embracing all the shared commitments of a scientific group; the other isolates a particularly important sort of commitment and is thus a subset of the first" (Suppe, 1977, p. 460).

Both the linguistic and sociological meanings of *paradigm* are found in semiotic literature. The context is usually helpful in clarifying the potential ambiguity.

[*See also* Saussure; *and* Semiotic Terminology.]

BIBLIOGRAPHY

Jakobson, R. "Linguistics and Poetics." In *Style in Language*, edited by T. A. Sebeok, pp. 350–377. Cambridge, Mass.: MIT Press, 1960.

Kuhn, T. S. *The Structure of Scientific Revolutions*. Chicago: University of Chicago Press, 1962.

Suppe, E., ed. *The Structure of Scientific Theories*. 2d ed. Urbana: University of Illinois Press, 1977.

—PAUL BOUISSAC

PARALANGUAGE comprises the nonlinguistic voice qualities, voice modifiers, and independent utterances, as well as the intervening momentary silences, that humans use consciously or unconsciously to support or contradict verbal, kinesic, chemical, dermal, thermal, and proxemic messages, either simultaneously or alternating with them, in both interaction and noninteraction. They are all described profusedly in the literature of the various cultures. Paralanguage began to receive scientific attention in linguistics and psychiatry in the 1950s and 1960s (Trager, 1958; Pittenger and Smith, 1957; Pittenger, Hockett, and Danehy, 1960), was formally recognized in phonetics in the 1960s (Abercrombie, 1968; Catford, 1964, 1968), developed mainly in studies of personality and of emotion within psychology (Scherer, 1982), received serious consideration from David Crystal (1974), reached phonetic maturity mainly with John Laver (1980), and has developed linguistically and interdisciplinarily in the work of Fernando Poyatos (1993). Four categories of paralinguistic phenomena can be distinguished: primary qualities, qualifiers, differentiators, and alternants.

Primary qualities are voice characteristics that are always present in speech and individuate speakers. Their conditioning factors are biological (e.g., lower and higher timbre in males and females, respectively), physiological (e.g., pitch disorders due to abnormal vocal-fold growth or hormonal therapy), psychological (e.g., the higher volume of extroversion), social (e.g., the slow tempo of superiority), cultural (e.g., the higher volume of Latins and Arabs), and occupational (e.g., the use of higher pitch by many nurses when talking to patients). The key features include timbre, which is a person's permanent voice register and has positive or negative connotations, as evidenced by the frequently assumed correlation between a person's size and physique and timbre. Resonance in this context can be oral (e.g., "orotundity," sometimes associated erroneously with large body size and in general with positive personal characteristics in men), pharyngeal ("throatiness," which sometimes suggests positive traits in men but negative ones in women), or nasal (associated mostly with negative attitudes). Loudness of biological, pathological, cultural, personal, and attitudinal characteristics, as well as grammatical ones correlates personally and culturally with "loud" or subdued gestural behavior (e.g., in Kenya and Ghana, shouting in the street and talking too loudly indoors is considered unacceptable; social situational norms forbid loud voice as a form of invasion of privacy; higher volume is used in direct quotations but lower is often used for interpolations). Tempo also functions as a grammatical, attitudinal, and even cultural feature (e.g., parenthetical comments are usually made with accelerated speed; slow speech is seen as threatening; fast speech often warns about impending danger; culturally, United States Southerners often speak relatively slowly). Also important are pitch level (high in the Japanese female, very high in the North American English speaker's surprised "What?!" and even higher when requesting information over the telephone), pitch range, which can be narrow or wide, correlating with lively or slow gestural features (e.g., narrow in postsleep voice), pitch registers (e.g., an Anglo North American typically applies to Spanish [usually with three pitches] four and even five registers in the expression "¡¿De verdad que viene?! ¡Qué bien!" ["Is he really coming? Oh, good!"]), and pitch intervals between them—spread in "Wonn—derful!" or squeezed with weariness). Intonation range can be monotonous (toneless, dull, singsong, droning) or melodious. Syllabic length is also relevant, whether in attitudinal drawling, as in "Mmmyes, I believe so" (James Joyce, *Dubliners*, 1914), or clipping, as in a quick "I'm sorry!" superimposed to words but also as in paralinguistic utterances such as a laugh or "uh-uh." Last, rhythm ranges from very smooth to very jerky.

Qualifiers are a large number of voice types, modifying short or long (even as primary qualities) speech segments, mainly through how air is controlled in the speech organs, by muscular tension and articulation, by anatomical configuration and speech movements of the lips, tongue, teeth, and mandible, and even by interferences such as food or a pipe in the mouth. Qualifiers are conditioned biologically (e.g., laryngeal configuration), physiologically (e.g., the articulation mechanism in the mouth), psychologically, and socioculturally. They are grouped by production areas: breathing control is relevant as we use mostly exhaled air to speak, but ingressive air is used in short, emotional utterances and as a second affirmation or negation in the typical "yeah!" and "no!" of the Atlantic Provinces of Canada ("Winters aren't as cold as they used to be. ¡No!"). Laryngeal control makes the voice whispery, breathy, creaky, harsh, falsetto, shrill, metallic, strident, screechy, squeaky, squealy, husky, hoarse, gruff, growling, tremulous, tense, or lax, for example, along with various combinations. This is the richest paralinguistic expressive repertoire to choose from and the one that characterizes literary descriptions of characters' voices: "The woman's voice shrilled in Harkand's ears like the screech of chalk on a blackboard" (John Dos Passos, *Manhattan Transfer*, 1925); "he was not only red in the face, but hoarse as a crow, and his voice shook too, like a taut rope (Robert L. Stevenson, *Treasure Island,* 1885). Esophageal control is used mainly in the hoarse, "belched" voice of laryngectomized persons. Through pharyngeal control, which is separate from proper pharyngealization (in which the root of the tongue approximates the back wall of the pharynx), the voice can be hollow or sepulchral, muffled, and so on. Velopharyngeal control produces all nasalized voice types, such as whining (e.g., children coaxing adults), bleating (high or low pitched, nasalized, or with a quavery, laryngealized quality), whimpering (lower and intermittently creaky), twangy (stereotyped in films to portray the American hillbilly but produced also voluntarily by pinching the nostrils), moaning (e.g., in grief or distress or out of physical or psychological pain), groaning (deeper, nasopharyngeal, harsh, creaky), and grunting (qualifying the whole delivery and typically correlating with a sour facial expression, as when expressing strong disapproval or contempt). Lingual control can involve not only making the voice, according to tongue position, velarized (a *gya-gya* effect), palatalized (e.g., in babylike speech), or alveolarized (a little lispy) but, abnormally, tongue thrusting (showing through the teeth). Labial control involves all postures of the lips as part of the "speaking face," but some are distinguishable as basic forms with different communicative functions: close lip rounding, or lip protrusion, as when using baby talk with children, lovers, or pets; horizontal lip expansion, as when expressing irritation; horizontal lip constriction, including so-called lip rounding, which typically produces a harsh or slightly pharyngeal quality, as in "Oh, no, you are just too proud to do it!"; vertical lip constriction, as when speaking with contempt or repressed anger; diagonally upward lip expansion, as in a typical bashful type of country folk in many cultures; diagonally downward lip expansion, as in the stereotyped speech of villains and thugs in films; and trembling lips, as from cold or emotion. Mandibular control—that is, the visual changes of the mandible during speech—affect internal sound movements, resonance, and our perception of a speaker, such as through the wide-open-jaw voice, used often for comicality and especial effects; the half-closed-jaw or clenched-teeth voice, used for muttering and mumbling: "Her chin shot out. She jumped to her feet. 'You git away from me'" (John Steinbeck, *The Grapes of Wrath*, 1939). Mandibular control can also produce the rotating-jaw voice of the stereotyped growling or muttering villain, the trembling jaw that modifies also labial articulations (as from cold or emotional tension), and abnormalities such as the protracted-jaw voice (thrusting the lower jaw forward and causing the voice to resonate more nasally than orally, as in mock threatening or in the portrayal of villains) and the retracted-jaw voice (caused by jaw recession, used also to portray the mentally retarded, the somber, or the abnormally shy).

Differentiators, paralinguistic-kinesic constructs, and sometimes qualifiers of language characterize physiological (many of a reflex nature) as well as psychological states and emotional reactions, whether produced naturally (mostly uncontrollably) or voluntarily. Their semiotic-communicative relevance and their revealing socioeducational, personal, cultural, and cross-cultural subtleties merit extensive study, as there are a number of functions, subsumed under each of the categories shown here in parentheses for each differentiator: laughter (affiliation, aggression, fear, social anxiety, joy, sadness, comicality and ludicrousness, self-directed amusement); cry-

ing (affiliation, empathy, joy, social anxiety, psychological pain, deception, self-directed crying, aesthetic enjoyment, god-directed crying); shouting (overcoming obstacles, calling, summoning, commanding, warning, aggression, psychological and physical pain, startling, fear and alarm, encouragement, triumph and praise, joy, merrymaking and comicality, controlled and uncontrolled excitement, ritualized and folk cries, and yells); sighing and gasping (prespeech, pleasurable feelings, displeasure and pain, love, longing, nostalgia and reverie, happiness, wonder, admiration and awe, boredom, weariness and confusion, annoyance and uneasiness, sadness and unhappiness, psychological pain, fear and relief, surprise, bewilderment, alarm, and starting); panting (medical, physical, and psychological strain); yawning (boredom, fatigue, and sleepiness); coughing and throat clearing (interaction regulation, satisfaction, uncertainty, embarrassment, social anxiety, disinterest and rejection, impatience, reproach, and anger); spitting (physiological, social, random, and task-performing rejection, aggression, ritual, healing, and play); belching (physiological and social); hiccuping (culturally and socioeducationally conditioned reactions to it); and sneezing (social and associated behaviors). As with qualifiers, differentiators constitute an important part of the literary writer's arsenal of personal, attitudinal, and cultural behaviors for characters.

Alternants comprise clicks, nasal frictions, language-free sighs, hisses, moans, groans, sniffs, snorts, smacks, blows, slurps, gasps, pants, "u-huh," "uh-uh," "Mm," hesitation vowels, momentary silences, and so on. They have been traditionally shunned as nonspeech and marginal, although they occur all the time, either isolated or alternating with words and gesture, and are consistently encoded and decoded in each language and culture—often as semantic blends—as unambiguously as words found in dictionaries. Their sign-meaning relationship can be (1) arbitrary—that is, if their sound, like that of most words, bears no resemblance to the signifier, as with "tz," "h'm," a snort of disgust, a hesitating "uh—," and so on. It can be (2) iconic or imitative when the signifier resembles its signified, as with those that imitate or evoke alter-adaptor behaviors (e.g., "whack!" for slapping), object adaptors (e.g., "bang!" for door slamming), artifactual sounds (e.g., "rrrmm-rrrmm!" for a motor), natural sounds (e.g., "whissss!" for the whistling wind), or animal sounds (e.g., "eeeeeh!" for a mouse). Some can be part of a double iconicity, as with "kinephonographs" (which combine iconic movement and iconic sound, as when imitating the whirring of an airplane engine paralinguistically and its flying with the hand. The sign-meaning relationship can also be (3) intrinsic when the sign actually is its significant, such as not only trying to reproduce the blowing sound of a fan but actually blowing and humming or using closely resembling "phonetic" qualities to roar like a lion. This is not doing something like something else but being, so to speak, the model and not its replica.

People also strive to evoke by means of sound abstract qualities and physical properties that actually do not sound—for instance speed (e.g., "And he, *ffss!*, came out like a shot"), activity (e.g., "He's always *rrn-rrn-rrn*"), intensity (e.g., "She's a very *hmm!* intense person"), blandness (e.g., "I don't know, he's too *uu-uuhn*, you know, not like his brother, so *uhn! uhn!*")—but often resorting to paralinguistic identifiers when their verbal equivalent is not used might simply be due to actual verbal deficiency. In addition, many alternants seem to have the kind of iconicity that develops through use, becoming the replica of a model, if we agree with Sebeok (1976). That iconicity is possible along all channels of bodily sensorial communication; for instance, because of previous experience, a sound like "umph!" perceived as the result of physical exertion, evokes immediately a visually perceivable image, even though we may not see it; a groan, grunt, or growl will appear as a replica of the model of angry attitude, a double "*tz-tz!*" will "resemble" anger—that is, will contain angriness in its sound, much as a snort may contain contempt. The snort, however, might need some sort of context in order to "resemble" contempt beyond doubt, for it could be amusement, which prompts considerations of single and multiple iconicity (still more obvious in the case of "*H'm!*" which has so many meanings), which weakens the entire distinction. In the end, however, iconicity in the purest semiotic sense is truly a characteristic of alternants and is most prevalent and effective in the expressive power of the innovative comic-book use of written alternants.

There are four problems posed by alternants that still hinder the development of their deserved status (although we find more and more in the dictionary). First, we have both a label and a written form, as with "a click," "several clicks," "to click," "tut-tut"; "a growl," "their growls," "to growl," "grrr!"; "a hiss,"

"several hisses," "to hiss," "ssss!"; "he fretted, pished and pshawed" (Charlotte Brontë, *Jane Eyre*, 1847). Second, we have a label but not a written form, as with "a blow," "his blows," "to blow"; or the sounds of kissing, clapping, gurgling, hawking, sneezing, swishing, and so on. Third, we have a written form but no label, as with "humph!" "umph!" (exerting oneself), "psst!" (for which *hissing* is much too ambiguous), "whew!" "uh-uh!" "er—" "tsch!" "phew!" "ho!" "oho!" "yum" and so forth: "'Whooee' yelled Dean. 'Here we go!'" (Jack Kerouac, *On the Road*, 1957). Fourth, we have neither label nor written form, as with "He made a noise of pain" (Stephen Crane, *The Red Badge of Courage*, 1895). What is clear is that alternants are very far from being merely interjective or vehicles only for the expression of emotions, a very limited but widely expressed view of them. Rather, they constitute the richest nonverbal lexicon that so often blends with the kinesic one: "'Whew!' said the housebreaker wiping the perspiration from his face [after exerting himself]" (Charles Dickens, *Oliver Twist*, 1838).

[*See also* Conversation; Nonverbal Bodily Sign Categories; *and* Nonverbal Communication in the Novel.]

BIBLIOGRAPHY

Abercrombie, D. "Paralanguage." *British Journal of Disorders of Communication* 3 (1968): 55–59.

Catford, J. C. "Phonation Types: The Classification of Some Laryngeal Components of Speech Production." In *In Honour of Daniel Jones*, edited by D. Abercrombie, D. B. Fry, and P. A. D. MacCarthy, pp. 26–37. London: Longmans, 1964.

Catford, J. C. "The Articulatory Possibilities of Man." In *Manual of Phonetics*, edited by B. Malmberg, pp. 309–333. Amsterdam: North Holland, 1968.

Crystal, D. "Paralinguistics." In *Current Trends in Linguistics and Adjacent Arts and Sciences*, vol. 12, edited by T. A. Sebeok, pp. 121–129. The Hague: Mouton, 1974.

Laver, J. *The Phonetic Description of Voice Quality*. Cambridge: Cambridge University Press, 1980.

Pittenger, R., C. F. Hockett, and J. Danehy. *The First Five Minutes: A Sample of Microscopic Interview Analysis*. Ithaca, N.Y.: Paul Martineau, 1960.

Pittenger, R. E., and H. L. Smith. "A Basis for Some Contributions of Linguistics to Psychiatry." *Psychiatry* 20 (1957): 61–78.

Poyatos, F. *Paralanguage: Interdisciplinary Approach to Interactive Speech and Sound*. Amsterdam and Philadelphia: John Benjamins, 1993.

Scherer, K. M. "Methods of Research on Vocal Communication: Paradigms and Parameters." In *Handbook of Methods in Nonverbal Behavior Research*, edited by K. R. Scherer and P. Ekman, pp. 136–198. Cambridge: Cambridge University Press, 1982.

Sebeok, T. A. "Iconicity." *Modern Language Notes* 91.6 (1976): 1427–1456.

Trager, G. "Paralanguage: A First Approximation." *Studies in Linguistics* 13.1 (1958): 1–12.

—FERNANDO POYATOS

PARALLELISM. As a figure of style, of interest to rhetoric and literature, parallelism provides means to emphasize and suggest relations by using repetitive patterns, mirrored sentences, or paraphrases. Its aim is often to balance one literary element with others of equal significance. Literary semiotics has identified such examples in the oral poetry of almost all known cultures and in the entire history of literature. During rhetoric-dominated forms of literary expression, parallelism flourishes.

In somewhat related terms, an entire aesthetics is built around a variation of parallelism within the symbolic movement in the arts. This aesthetic holds that the inner nature of humanity can be expressed most effectively by repetitive patterns, including parallel lines, that symbolize the order—which some see as mystical—that underlies nature. The Swiss artist Ferdinand Hodler (1853–1918), influenced by symbolist poetry, painted under the guidance of this aesthetics of parallelism. Many other artists followed his example, if not necessarily the concept.

By no surprise, parallelism strategies of emphasis are used widely in the fields that have become the mass media, especially advertising. The types that emerged are synonymic (using words or images or sounds in subtle repetitive patterns), antithetical (choosing one thing against another presented in a parallel manner), and synthetic (synthesizing a selection from the parallelism of presentation). Some advertisements combine parallel synonymic expression, antithetical figures, and synthetic strategies.

Also seduced by the metaphor of parallelism, philosophers for the longest time entertained the notion that material and spiritual phenomena take place in parallel, though separate, sequences. While along each sequence there are causal connections, one can at best state correlations between the two streams of occurrences. In the attempt to understand the relation between the body and the mind, this view focused on the relation between physiological processes and what would eventually be called cognitive or mental processes. Parallelism holds that mental changes correlate with neural modifications—the firing of a neuron is the most recent expression, inspired by the experience of electronic circuitry. No apparent determinist connection can be further assumed between cognitive or conscious processes and what takes place in the nervous system. This view offers an alternative to theories of interaction in an effort to avoid difficulties arising from explanations based on assuming that correlations are actually interrelationships. In none of the parallelism-based body-mind theories is a spiritual substance, a substantial soul, or a homunculus either implied or accepted, but a variety of theories evolve around an assumed though not evident underlying entity through which unity is reached. Therefore, mind and body can be seen as fundamentally identical, while the parallel mental and physical processes embody aspects of unified real processes.

The psychophysical conception, at least as varied as the philosophy of parallelism, rests more radically on the assumption of a one-to-one correlation between events in nature (the physical world) and mental states. Gottfried Wilhelm Leibniz (1646–1716) is the originator of this idea. A more nuanced view refers to the parallelism and the refined correlation between psychoses, affecting individual minds, and neuroses. Suggested within this view is that processes such as physicochemical changes or neural activity might not have cognitive correlates.

Credited to Gustav Theodor Fechner (1801–1887) (*Zendavesta*, 1851, book 3, chapter 19), the term *parallelism* came into use after the thought it labels had literally propagated from the philosophy of ancient Greece to the religious concepts of the Middle Ages and to Baruch Spinoza's (1632–1677) *Ethics*, in which the doctrine seems to have been first articulated explicitly. The notion of correlation adopted by the Scholastics and occasionalists was reactivated in debates—triggered by the psychological experiments of Wilhelm Wundt (1832–1920)—over the nineteenth-century idealist philosophy of Friedrich Schleiermacher (1768–1834), Friedrich Adolph Trendelenburg (1802–1872), Friedrich Beneke (1797–1854), and Eugen K. Dühring (1833–1921). The solution advanced reflected the obsession in the humanities for a scientific foundation, similar to that of the sciences but not so crude as to reduce the complexity of psychic phenomena to a mechanistic explanation of the relation between such phenomena and the brain's activity. The neo-Kantians and the empiricists of the nineteenth century were quite critical of the doctrine of parallelism, but there were also arguments in its favor, especially from within the emerging hermeneutic philosophy. Wilhelm Dilthey (1833–1911), extending the work of Franz Brentano (1838– 1917), and William James (1842–1910) both ascertained that a localization and explanation of conscious connections could not be accomplished from physiological laws. Each time new objections against parallelism were raised—and there were plenty of these—its proponents ended up refining the initial thought.

The basic explanatory model is attractive on account of its clean answers to exceptionally complex problems. That some aspects of human psychology or psychic activity are describable in terms of parallelism seems clear now, as does the understanding that there is more to human psychic processes than parallelism can explain. "In short, from our perspective, conscience is a system of implications (among concepts, affective values, etc.) and the nervous system is a causal system, while psychophysic parallelism is a special case of isomorphy between implications and causal systems," wrote Jean Piaget (1896–1980) in 1950. When conclusions are drawn through conscious processes from precise premises, the result is based on the logical content of the premises, not on the basis of some causality that leads from the premises to the inference. This makes psychophysical parallelism the place where the circle of science from deductive mathematics to realistic inductive biology closes and in which psychology and sociology take intermediate positions.

More recently, this discussion was refined further through the implication of emergent properties or characteristics. William C. Wimsatt (1976), taking a cybernetic viewpoint, has drawn attention to the tripartite construct "hardware-software–program performance." The psychophysical problem can be seen at the levels of neuronal processes, the functional performance of a brain in the sense of a program, and behavior. It remains unclear to what extent the architecture of a computer program is comparable to an organism's cognitive performance and to what extent the brain's physiological organization imposes conditions upon the design of the program. In the terminology of the older controversy around parallelism, this can be restated as the question of to what extent physiological sequences, mental processes, and artificial-intelligence modeling are isomorphic or whether they are bound to create conditions for their reciprocal emergence. The new critics of parallelism (Roger W. Sperry, Karl Popper, John Eccles, John R. Searle) tend to accept the emergence view. This bird's-eye view of the subject as it unfolded over time and in various theoretical approaches obviously omits some of the successive views (probably parallel themselves) that eventually crystallized in the Gestalt theory, in post-Piaget cognitive projects, and in some of the more recent attempts within the neurosciences, especially chaos-theory models of brain activity.

From a semiotic perspective, parallelism is of extreme interest in view of the difficulties encountered in defining the sign (standing in parallel to what it designates), sign typologies (resulting from the type of representation), and sign processes. While we assume an operational view of sign processes, we really do not know where and how they take place. Semioticians might indeed face the challenge of choosing between the "Scylla of parallelism and the Charybdis of interaction," as J. B. Watson expressively defines these two positions. Or, adopting a logical-positivist perspective of semiotics, similar to work by Rudolf Carnap (1891–1970), semioticians might, in sync with the new cognitive theories, discard parallelism altogether, since there are many parallel occurrences that offer little if anything to either our understanding of complex sign systems (such as language) or of their actual functioning in various pragmatic contexts.

Nevertheless, here the challenge of parallel computation emerges. The so-called Von Neumann paradigm of computation states that the human mind does not operate sequentially but in parallel processes. The element of simultaneity is essential in both understanding and implementing parallelism. The two major types of parallel computation are defined by the data processed. Either all parallel processors operate in the same way upon homogeneous data—a new type of brute-force processing—or they execute truly parallel different operations upon a variety of data. In some cases, this leads to very sophisticated connections among different simultaneous or successive processors. Another distinction refers to the granularity of the process: macroparallelism (of a limited number of processors) is quite different from microparallelism (of a vast number of processors).

New concepts of distributed computation overlap with parallel processing. On the one hand, there is the need to decompose problems into smaller parts, each to be operated upon in parallel in a distributed environment. On the other hand, there is the need to address synchronization and communication among these distributed tasks. While computer science met the challenge of designing powerful systems based on the expectation and requirement of parallelism, semioticians are still shy about taking advantage of technological progress in order to address questions pertinent to their own field of inquiry. The basic known semiotic theories imply that human beings operate in parallel upon various simultaneous signs and that semioses are parallel and distributed processes. Elements of semiotic correlation could be understood if, using the knowledge gained in designing both parallel processors and algorithms for parallel processing, semioticians would revisit sign theories. In many ways, these new cognitive engines are semiotic machines on which some of the hypotheses advanced to date could be effectively evaluated or through which new theories could be formulated.

[See also Algorithm; Computer; Connectionism; and Sign.]

BIBLIOGRAPHY

Brentano, F. C. *Psychology from an Empirical Standpoint*. Edited by L. L. McAlister. London: Routledge and Kegan Paul, 1973.

Frechner, G. T. *Zendavesta, oder über die Dinge des Himmels und des Jensetis*. Leipzig: Voss, 1851.

Hockney, R. W., and C. R. Lesshope. *Parallel Computers: Architecture, Programming, and Algorithms*. Bristol: Adam Hilger, 1981.

James, W. *The Principles of Psychology*. 2 vols. New York: Holt, 1890.

Kohler, W. *Gestalt Psychology*. New York: Liveright, 1929.

McDougall, W. *Body and Mind: A History and a Defense of Animism*. London: Methuen, 1911.

Nadin, M. *Mind—Anticipation and Chaos*. Stuttgart: Belser Verlag, 1991.

Piaget, J. *Genetic Epistemology*. New York: Columbia University Press, 1970.

Wimsatt, W. C. "Reductionism, Levels of Organization, and the Mind-Body Problem." In *Consciousness and the Brain: A Scientific and Philosophical Inquiry*, edited by G. G. Globus, G. Maxwell, and I. Sabovnik, pp. 205–267. New York: Plenum, 1976.

Wundt, W. "Über psychische Causalität und das Prinzip des psychophysischer Parallelismus." *Philosophische Studien* 10 (1984).

—MIHAI NADIN

PARIS SCHOOL. The structuralist movement in French semiotics that developed in Paris in the early 1960s around Algirdas Julien Greimas (1917–1992) and Roland Barthes (1915–1980). Barthes, however, definitively distanced himself from Greimas and his followers with the publication of *S/Z* (1970). The designation "Paris School," which replaced the earlier "Groupe de Recherches Semiolinguistiques," first appeared in print in 1982 in a book edited by Jean-Claude Coquet. In his detailed, programmatic first chapter, Coquet both retraces the history of the movement—which began in 1956 with two articles published by Greimas—and outlines an agenda for the future. What distinguishes the Paris School from other Saussurean, Hjelmslevian, or Peircean movements that consider semiotics the theory of signs or the study of signs and symbols in various fields is that the Paris School's proponents define semiotics as a theory of system of signification. Rather than as an observable phenomenon or a given, the sign is considered first of all as a construct. This point of departure has crucial theoretical and practical consequences.

From the early 1960s, Greimas's position among other European linguists who were working mainly within the theoretical framework of generative and transformational grammar was somewhat unique insofar as he adopted a semantic point of view and extended the syntactic "generative" perspective to the semantic domain. The elementary structures of signification form the basis of this model. As Coquet (1982) notes, the discursive or transphrastic (beyond the sentence) model develops the principle of narrativity that constitutes a fundamental level for the organization of discourse. Within the framework of such a narrative semiotics, transformations are both intratextual and syntagmatic. This is illustrated most clearly in Greimas and Courtés's *Semiotics and Language* (1982), a dictionary of the theory in which semionarrative transformations are defined as complementing the intratextual and paradigmatic Lévi-Straussian transformations without contradicting them. Transformations are thought of as logical operations when they are located at the level of deep semiotic structures. They are described as shifting from "one term of the semiotic square to another, carried out through the operations of negation and assertion" on the logicosemantic plane and are interpreted as operations of conjunction and disjunction between subjects and objects of value at the narrative level. Since narrative discourse is conceived of as "'something that happens' *i.e.*, as a trajectory leading from an initial state to a final state, then a *transformation algorithm* should be able to account for this trajectory: discourse then appears as a string of transformation" (1982, p. 350).

Both *Semiotics and Language* and Greimas's study of a short story by Guy de Maupassant (1988) show the theoretical importance of elementary forms of narrativity. In the latter work, Greimas explored syntactic and semantic regularities, such as a series of tests on the syntactic level or the inversion of contents on the paradigmatic level, which led him to study fundamental relations such as the lack (e.g., a missing object) and its liquidation (e.g., the recovery of the missing object). Within the framework of narrativity, members of the Paris School worked out a narrative grammar and a syntax of narrative programs in which subjects were joined up with or separated from objects of value and thereby transformed. The subject's changes of state were accounted for by simple operations such as conjunctions, disjunctions, and transformations. The principle of confrontation between subject and antisubject was interpreted as an elementary polemicocontractual relation. Whether engaged in conversation or argumentation or actually fighting, the subjects were considered to be involved in relations of trust or conflict. A series of modalizations was then postulated: two virtualizing modalities (wanting and having to) and two actualizing ones (being able to and knowing how to) that could account for the subject's competence, existence, and performance. Although narrativity theory remained the cornerstone of Paris School research, the early 1980s were marked both by a greater diversification in the domains investigated and by a number of moves that opened up the theory from an "objectal" to a more "subjectal" orientation.

The term *Paris School* refers to a specific localization, but semioticians who identify with this label are spread far and wide in many countries of Europe as well as of North and South America. A number of notable volumes published in French (Parret and Ruprecht, eds., 1985; Greimas and Courtés, eds., 1986; and Arrivé and Coquet, eds., 1987) and two volumes of collected papers translated into English (Perron and Collins, eds., 1989) compile works by the most active researchers in the group. Important works have been published in literary semiotics, the semiotics of religious discourse, the semiotics of legal discourse, eth-

nosemiotics, the semiotics of scientific discourse, psychosemiotics, the semiotics of didactic discourse, the semiotics of space, visual semiotics, and the semiotics of music. Some philosophers and semioticians are exploring how the model relates to studies in the cognitive sciences, mathematics, and philosophy.

While engaged in the pursuit of a common semiotic project, the members of the Paris School are involved in the study of extremely diverse objects by means of an ever-developing core of theoretical concepts. The second volume of Greimas and Courtés's *Sémiotique: Dictionnaire raisonné de la théorie du langage* (1986), which includes contributions by forty members of the group, gives a clear idea of this evolution. Far from being a hierarchized and interdefined set of concepts, the entries in this dictionary form a polyphony of complementary and sometimes discordant utterances, so much so that the concept of "sufficient scientific consensus" is severely tested, leaving to the distant future a possible synthesis. Greimas and Courtés limited their role to classifying the entries in relation to the corpus of accepted definitions as C (complement, continuation, conformity), P (proposition, prolongation, project), or D (debate, discussion, divergence, digression).

Jean-Claude Coquet, one of the major exponents of the Paris School, has questioned a number of fundamental positions of Greimassian semiotics that consider discourse as a syntagmatic organization of constructed utterances (1984–1985). For Coquet, Greimas condenses discourse into a series of utterances of state and utterances of doing that inexorably follow one another. Each act is carried out by a subject or antisubject within the context of polemicocontractual relations. The subject is defined either as an operator of transformations in an utterance of doing or a locus of conjunction in an utterance of state, and signification depends on a preestablished schema, not on the position occupied, defended, or sought by the subject. In short, the subject is considered a nonperson (what Emile Benveniste termed *s/he*) and not a subject or I. This nonperson constitutes a locus of functioning and not a preestablished position in a predetermined structure. Coquet stresses the importance of elaborating a "subjectal" semiotics founded on discourse linguistics, in contradistinction to standard Greimassian semiotics founded on the structural linguistics of the 1960s that he qualifies as "objectal."

In recent years, members of the Paris School have turned their attention from a semiotics of action and cognition to a semiotics of passion (emotion), which culminated in the publication of *The Semiotics of Passions* (Greimas and Fontanille, 1993). This study lays out the theoretical issues that are still under investigation by the members of the Paris School. In the first part, Greimas and Fontanille establish their critical practice within the general epistemology of any theory that attempts to attain "scientific" status. For them, there exist two possible extreme attitudes that enable the situating of various sciences in relation to one another: either the world is considered discontinuous (this is the position of the physical sciences, mathematics, and linguistics) or continuous (as in the organicist or biological sciences that affirm the world's "tensive" nature).

The authors of the Paris School acknowledge the influence of Edmund Husserl and Maurice Merleau-Ponty, who provided the philosophical tools that allow them to reconceptualize semiotic theory in terms of perception and hence to introduce the crucial element of continuity in the relation of subject to world. Three types of properties are thus distinguished: exteroceptive, stemming from the external world; interoceptive, universals conditioning the possibility of perception; and proprioceptive, corresponding to the perception of the body by itself. The introduction of these concepts was necessary to explain what happens at the linguistic level between the natural world and natural languages. As far as perception is concerned, the external world is seen as composed of figures or, in Saussurean terms, signifiers of the world. At the moment of perception, exteroceptive semes (minimal units of signification) are transformed into interoceptive semes and integrated into the activity of the mind. Such an operation, whereby figures of the world become figures of thought through the body, enables the Paris School to develop the concept of figurativity. The mediating role of the body becomes fundamental to understanding how the external world is transformed into a signifying whole, and such a proprioceptive component added a "pathemic" dimension in which the cognitive forms of the imagination include a passional or "thymic" component (from the Greek *tumós*, meaning "heart," "mood," "emotion"). The thymic component is articulated into three categories: euphoria (positive), dysphoria (negative), and aphoria (neutral).

Moreover, at another theoretical level, the world is considered constituted by states of affairs that are transformed into states of feeling, again through the intervention of the body. This shift makes it possible to introduce the notion of continuity by means of the body, thereby avoiding the rational sentimental duality that comes from the separation of body and soul, world and mind. This same problem of continuity occurs at the discursive level, where aspectualities and tensions extend beyond rationally and cognitively established categories and where the modulations of sentences and emphases placed on words (the idea that certain verbs express things intensely in order to represent them) constitute phenomena that cannot be accounted for by the rational procedures of a semiotics of action. Such modulations of discourse demand a reexamination of the deep structures of theory in light of the horizon of tensions that occur at the discursive level.

In addition to the semiotic theory represented by Greimas and Courtés's 1979 dictionary, a new theoretical component was proposed at the epistemological level, one which, in addition to the conditions for the manifestation of signification, now included its preconditions. Tensivity and phoria were the two fundamental concepts chosen to simulate a representation of the ontic horizon of the preconditions: tensivity translates the notion of universal attraction, whereas phoria directs tension. What led to this reconfiguration of the theory is that when passions or human behaviors were defined as passional, economical, or social roles, it was discovered, for example, that the roles of a miser and a thrifty person were semiotically identical and that only a phenomenon such as sensitization could account for the miser's not being thrifty. However, when passions such as anger and despair were studied, the unfolding of passional discourse or normal pathemic discourse was perturbed at a given moment. It was as though a different subject began to speak, one that could be accounted for only by the intervention of the body at the moment of the integration of the natural world as interiority. Hence, in their theory, tensivity, an attempt to represent the world according to physics, and phoria, corresponding to vitalistic organicist concepts of the biological sciences, come together as phoric tensivity on the ontic horizon. On this horizon appears the veil that makes it possible to represent the way in which, from such an energetic and vitalistic minimum, the subject and the world begin to emerge. In short, a sort of phoric or semic mass rises to the surface and can be articulated into two types of discrete units: modalizations—that is, the organization of the thymic into modalities—and passional modulations or undulations in the unfurling of discourse. Thus, an attempt was made to present a more or less coherent foundation to complete the semiotic theory begun over thirty years ago.

In their study, elaborated in collaboration with members of the Paris School during their annual collective seminar, Greimas and Fontanille started from an intuition and imagined positions that enabled the polarization of the universe. This permitted, on the one hand, the positing of a sort of prototype of an actant, linked by G. W. F. Hegel to intentionality and rearticulated by Husserl in the form of the protensivity of the subject, a sort of minimal state of the subject who is not yet a subject but simply a subject striving for something. On the other hand was envisioned a sort of potentiality of the object, which made it possible to consider the world as value. What now appears to be the thorniest issue in the theory is the problematics of the object, not of the subject. To understand subjects as being, as meaning, they must be defined by the values they acquire. From this viewpoint, the semiotics of passions becomes a semiotics of the values acquired, lost, or suspended by the subject. In brief, theorists are now dealing with a subject defined by its protensivity, faced with an object of value that is unformed, a shadow of the value that can be semanticized. In a later phase, the shadow of value becomes the valence, which then leads to the question of the value of value. Thus, whether it is examining the semiotics of passions or the semiotics of aesthetics, the two main domains of current investigation, Paris School semiotics has as one of its fundamental preoccupations the problematics of value.

[See also Greimas; and Narratology.]

BIBLIOGRAPHY

Arrivé, M., and J.-C. Coquet, eds. *Sémiotique en jeu à partir et autour de l'oeuvre d'A. J. Greimas.* Amsterdam and Philadelphia: John Benjamins, 1987.

Barthes, R. *S/Z.* Paris: Seuil, 1970.

Coquet, J.-C., ed. *Sémiotique: L'école de Paris.* Paris: Hachette, 1982.

Coquet, J.-C., ed. *Le discours et son sujet*, vols. 1, 2. Paris: Klincksieck, 1984–1985.

Greimas, A. J. *Maupassant: The Semiotics of Text: Practical Exercises.* Translated by P. Perron. Amsterdam and Philadelphia: John Benjamins, 1988.

Greimas A. J., and J. Courtés. *Semiotics and Language: An Analytical Dictionary.* Translated by D. Patte and L. Crist. Bloomington: Indiana University Press, 1982.

Greimas, A. J., and J. Courtés, eds. *Sémiotique: Dictionnaire raisonné de la théorie du langage*, vol. 2. Paris: Hachette, 1986.

Greimas, A. J., and J. Fontanille. *The Semiotics of Passions: From States of Affairs to States of Feelings.* Translated by P. Perron and F. Collins. Minneapolis: University of Minnesota Press, 1993.

Parret, H. "Introduction." In Perron and Collins, 1989, vol. l, pp. vii–xxvi.

Parret, H., and H.-G. Ruprecht, eds. *Exigences et perspectives de la sémiotique.* Amsterdam and Philadelphia: John Benjamins, 1985.

Perron, P., and F. Collins, eds. *Paris School Semiotics*, vol. 1, *Theory*; vol. 2, *Practice.* Amsterdam and Philadelphia: John Benjamins, 1989.

—PAUL PERRON and PATRICK DEBBÈCHE

PAROEMIOLOGY. The scholarly study of proverbs (in Greek, *paroimia*), one of the "primary" or "simple" communicative forms of oral cultures, paroemiology is not institutionalized as an autonomous discipline. It seems, however, to be as old as the collection and codification of proverbs (paroemiography), which has to deal with three interrelated paroemiological tasks: a definition of genre, the selection of the material, and the classification of it.

Explicitly semiotic approaches to the proverb are fairly recent; Pëtr Bogatyrëv (1893–1971) in the mid 1930s was one of the first to propose such an approach. In his studies on Moravian folklore, Bogatyrëv developed the concept of polyfunctionality: one and the same sign or text may serve different functions, just as one and the same function may be fulfilled by different signs or texts. The functions of a particular text are organized hierarchically but the dominant function may be replaced over time by another, previously secondary function. Bogatyrëv's awareness of the close interrelationship between function and meaning in general coincided with his concrete observation that the meaning of a single same proverb may change completely in a particular period of time.

Proverb scholarship focusing on the relation between pragmatics and semantics is also found in early pragmatically oriented studies such as those by Raymond Firth (b. 1901), a functional cultural anthropologist. In 1926, Firth claimed that the meaning of a proverb is made clear only when a full account of the accompanying social situation—the reason for the proverb's use, its effect, and its significance—is given side by side with the translation. Still, one might consider the study of a proverb's function(s) and the pragmatic conditions of its use merely pre-semiotic or partially semiotic, since it lacks a comprehensive semiotic framework. This qualification also concerns the "ethnography of speaking" approach used by Ojo Arewa and Alan Dundes (1964) and the pragmatic approach of Barbara Kirshenblatt-Gimblett (1973), who argues that the meaning of a proverb emerges from its use in a specific context and that the researcher should focus on "the meaning of proverb performances."

These pragmatic-semantic approaches have succeeded in establishing the various functions a proverb may fulfill: they have either identified meaning with usage or, in a more moderate way, shown that the meaning of a proverb cannot be described adequately without reference to usage. Estonian scholar Arvo Krikmann (1984) has concluded from his observations on the semantic indefiniteness of the proverb that various modal, functional, pragmatic, or situational aspects and the chosen metalanguage are crucial factors influencing proverb meaning and usage; these factors are responsible for the proverb's semantic indefiniteness. Thus, it is impossible to define a proverb's meaning exactly; for him, it is a "mere semantic potential."

According to Krikmann, the analysis of a proverb may be oriented either toward the "absolute sum" of all possible meanings, which represent its potential of interpretability, or toward the sum of all real (actual) meanings manifested in all its previous realizations. Since we do not usually know all the actual realizations, the proverb's semantic potential must be explicated in such a way that it corresponds to its actual meanings. In doing so, we face the proverb's semantic indefiniteness. One of the most important sources of this indefiniteness is the multiple possible interpretations of the proverbial tropes (i.e., metaphors, metonymies, synecdoches, etc.) that are parts of the proverb text. In this context, Krikmann distinguishes two methodological approaches in attempting to explain a proverb's meaning. The first considers the proverb internally heterogeneous and tries to separate "content elements" (*c*-elements) from "formal elements" (*f*-elements). Formal elements are, among others, any kind of relational words or quantifiers, syntactic formulas, and others such as *every* and *all* and constructions such as *if . . . then* and *bet-*

ter . . . than. All other words belong to the *c*-elements, which can in turn be divided into semantically "literal" (c_1) and "transferred" (c_2) elements. The exact distinction between *c*-elements and *f*-elements may vary, of course, but all approaches along these lines share the assumption that poeticalness (or metaphoricalness) is not assigned to the proverb text as a whole but is restricted to its individual elements (or even to the c_2- elements alone).

The second approach considers the proverb text as internally homogeneous—that is, totally poetical. All of its elements belong to a specific, secondary ("poetic") language; they must be distinguished strictly from all (particularly the homonymous) elements of the primary ("ordinary," "nonpoetic") language, as well as from all elements of metalanguage used for describing the content of the proverb text. This constitutes an important step in paroemiology, since a proverb can then be construed as a secondary modeling system, in the terms of the Moscow-Tartu School—that is, the first, denotative level of signification serves as expression for the second level of signification (the connotative meaning).

Russian scholar M. A. Čerkasskij (1984) first applied this analytical method to proverbs; independent of him, Pierre Crépeau (1975) developed this idea with reference to Roland Barthes and Algirdas Julien Greimas. Čerkasskij's view that a proverb is, in fact, the "minimal unit of the supralinguistic semiotic level" provides arguments for considering proverbs as paradigms for cultural studies in general. For Čerkasskij, an utterance such as "The apple does not fall far from the tree" is the complex sign of a particular, individual situation, on the denotative level of signification; on the connotative level, it is the sign of a class of situations, and only in this case can the text serve as a proverb. Actually, the proverb itself is seen as a sign of a class of situations.

A heuristic model of proverb use proposed by Peter Seitel (1969) is based on the central assumption that the situation in which a proverb is used (the interaction situation) is not identical to the situation verbally inherent in the proverb text (the proverb situation) and that both of them are not necessarily identical to the situation to which the proverb refers or in which it is intended to be applied (the reference situation). According to Seitel, proverb usage is thus related to two distinct though closely related processes—namely, first, the process of relating proverb situation to reference situation and, second, the speech act of applying the proverb in an interaction situation. This differentiation yields the results shown in figure 1. According to Seitel's model, proverb usage can be expressed by the analogy *A:B::C:D*, since we are concerned with an analogy between the relationship of entities of the proverb situation and entities of the reference situation (e.g., apple:tree::drunken son:drunken father).

However, the matter is even more complex than assumed in this basic schema, in which the proverb situation is restricted to the proverb's literal meaning; no attention is paid to the fact that in most proverbs, the secondary (connotative) level of signification is more important than the primary (denotative) level of signification. Therefore, when speaking of an analogy between proverb and reference situation, we are concerned with the proverb's abstract idea on the connotative level of signification rather than the proverb situation in its literal, denotative meaning. Furthermore, similar to any referential act in general, the individual and unique reference situation has to be interpreted as belonging to an adequate class or type of situation to which it corresponds as a situational token.

If a proverb thus conveys a situation on its denotative level of signification, we can term the abstract general idea on the connotative level the corresponding "situation model" (since it is an abstract model based on the concrete proverb situation); similarly, we can call the class of situation related to the individual reference situation the model situation. A proverb can thus be considered to be applied appropriately when, in a given interaction, that model situation is derived from the proverb situation, which is, as situation model, assumed to underlie the reference situation. This latter view implies that proverbs are not "eternal truths" but possible models that are true only under certain circumstances; this view also explains why there may be antonymous proverbs within one and the same culture, such as "out of sight, out of mind" and "absence makes the heart grow fond."

Proverb usage thus involves a process of double analogy. If we call the abstract idea representing the situation model (or the model situation, respectively), *p:q*, we obtain the overall formula *A:B::p:q::C:D* (or, in the concrete example, apple:tree::begetted:begetter::drunken son:drunken father). This modification yields the results shown in figure 2. Ultimately, the relationship *p:q* obtains the status of an invariant: both the concrete verbal form (or even the language in which the proverb's idea is expressed) and the concrete situation to which the proverb is applied may vary, but the modeled situation remains invariant.

In trying to establish which invariant situations are modeled in proverbs, Grigorii L'vovich Permjakov's studies (1979) are highly relevant. For Permjakov, proverbs are "signs and at the same time models of various typical situations." Consequently, he postulates that "a classification of the situations themselves" has to be worked out if one wants to categorize proverbs on the basis of their meanings. Although Permjakov did not specify his notion of situation according to the above-mentioned schema, it seems clear that he had in mind the situation model, which he called the logicosemiotic analysis of the invariant types of situations.

Permjakov distinguished four different "higher logicosemiotic invariants." Two of them model the relationship between objects or that between objects and their properties; the other two are more complex in that they model the dependence between the relationships of things and the relationships of their properties. In detail, we obtain the following four invariants (the ultimate logicosemiotic classification was developed later in a more complex way than can be demonstrated here):

FIGURE 1. *Reference Versus Interaction Situation in Proverb Use.*

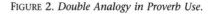

FIGURE 2. *Double Analogy in Proverb Use.*

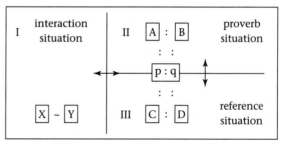

1A. Every object has a particular quality or property. (Example: Water always flows down, not up.)

1B. If there is one object, there is or will be another object. (Example: No smoke without fire.)

2A. The relationships between the properties of objects depend on the relationships between the objects themselves. (Example: Like father, like son.)

2B. The interrelationships of objects depend on the existence of particular properties of these objects. (Example: Four eyes see more than two.)

Permjakov's classification displays a clear parallel to Zoltán Kanyó's approach: both consider the logical operation of implication central to the proverb's logical structure. For Kanyó (1981), the most general and simple logical formulation of the proverb is: A_x $(P_x ?? Q_x)$. Despite such convergences, there is a crucial difference between Kanyó's and Permjakov's approaches: whereas Kanyó logically classifies the proverb's linguistic surface structure, Permjakov ultimately strives for a logical classification of its semantic deep structure.

Additionally and, perhaps more important, a thematic classification complements the logicosemiotic classification in Permjakov's approach. He would classify three proverbs such as "No smoke without fire," "No rose without thorns," and "No river without bank," as belonging to invariant 1A: each of them maintains that one of the two objects mentioned cannot exist without the second object. Still, the meanings of these three proverbs differ completely: the first maintains that there can be no indication of an object unless the object itself exists; the second claims that there can be no good things without faults; the third says that no whole can exist without one of its obligatory parts. As a consequence, Permjakov added a thematic classification to the logicosemiotic one. He thus describes a proverb's meaning by a twofold reference to one of the logicosemiotic invariants and one or more thematic pairs such as *near* and *far*, *cause* and *consequence*, *hot* and *cold*, and so on. These semantic oppositions are very similar to those found in the semiotic analysis of culture.

Quite logically, a description cannot cover all semantic, functional, situational, and modal aspects in the concrete use of a proverb and, consequently, in its meaning. This indefiniteness might even give rise to contradictory meanings out of one proverb; for example, whereas the Scottish interpretation of "Rolling stones gather no moss" seems to be "Keep abreast of modern ideas, keep your brain active," the English reading rather alludes to the desirable qualities of the moss found draped over stones in a peaceful brook. We seem to be concerned, then, with a question of cultural, not linguistic, differences; it seems clear that a proverb's meaning cannot be deduced simply from its verbal surface. It turns out that attention has to be paid to the important interdependence of three basic categories; polyfunctionality, polysemanticity, and heterosituativity. Since none of these three categories, which condition each other in one way or another, can be interpreted in isolation, no ultimate meaning can ever be ascribed to a particular proverb text.

[*See also* Cultural Knowledge; Implicature; *and* Speech Act Theory.]

BIBLIOGRAPHY

Arewa, E. O., and A. Dundes. "Proverbs and the Ethnography of Speaking Folklore." *American Anthropologist* 66 (1964): 70–85.

Čerkasskij, M. A. "Versuch der Konstruktion eines funktionalen Modells eines speziellen semiotischen Systems." In *Semiotische Studien zum Sprichwort: Simple Forms Reconsidered* I, edited by P. Grzybek. Special issue of *Kodikas Code—Ars Semeiotica* 7. 3–4 (1984): 363–377.

Crépeau, P. "La définition du proverbe." *Fabula* 16 (1975): 285–304.

Grzybek, P. "Foundations of Semiotic Proverb Study." In *Wise Words: Essays on the Proverb,* edited by W. Mieder, pp. 31–71. New York: Garland, 1994.

Grzybek, P. "Proverb." In *Simple Forms,* edited by W. A. Koch, pp. 227–241. Bochum: Brockmeyer, 1994.

Kanyó, Z. *Sprichwörter: Analyse einter einfachen form.* The Hague: Mouton, 1981.

Kirshenblatt-Gimblett, B. "Toward a Theory of Proverb Meaning." *Proverbium* 22 (1973): 821–827.

Krikmann, A. A. "On Denotative Indefiniteness of Proverbs: Remarks on Proverb Semantics 1." In *Proverbium: Yearbook of International Proverb Scholarship,* vol. 1, pp. 47–91. Columbus, Ohio: Ohio State University Press, 1984.

Mieder, W. *International Proverb Scholarship: An Annotated Bibligrahy.* New York: Garland, 1982.

Mieder, W. *International Proverb Scholarship: An Annotated Bibliography, Supplement 1 (1800–1981).* New York: Garland, 1990.

Mieder, W. *International Proverb Scholarship: An Annotated Bibliography, Supplement 2 (1982–1991).* New York: Garland, 1993.

Mieder, W., ed. *A Dictionary of American Proverbs*. New York: Oxford University Press, 1992.

Permjakov, G. L. *From Proverb to Folktale: Notes on the General Theory of Cliché*. Moscow: USSR Academy of Sciences, Nauka, 1979.

Seitel, P. I. "Proverbs: A Social Use of Metaphor." *Genre* 2 (1969): 143–161.

—PETER GRZYBEK

PAROLE. *See* Langue and Parole.

PARSING. While its literal meaning involves analyzing a sentence into its grammatical parts (or, more generally, examining something minutely), in computer science *parsing* refers to an operation that takes place in the process of compiling. When a computer program is translated into machine language, the computer cannot directly interpret a higher programming language, so this language has to be translated into a "machine assembler code" that the computer can "understand." This code can then be executed by the computer's central-processing unit (CPU). We have to differentiate between at least two phases in the process of translating. First, lexical analysis (lexical parsing), in which the primary code (i.e., the original program) is "cleaned up." This means that blanks, the programmer's comments, and other miscellany are removed. The text of the primary program is structured in elementary strings of symbols (i.e., tokens), which can be translated by the syntactic analyzer. The second phase of translation, syntactical analysis, is often called parsing. In this process, the formal structure of the code provided by lexical analysis is extracted and forms the basis for the final machine code. The process of parsing extracts, for instance, variable names, types, functions, and procedures. Using these results, memory can be allocated, structural and formal relations between various parts of the programs and variables can be detected, and so on. If the program contains syntactical errors, such as undefined variables, inconsistent type assignments, or unclosed loops, the process of parsing will detect it.

The program is then transformed into a parsing tree that abstractly represents the structure of the program and allows the analysis to proceed. There are two methods of working through the tree: bottom-up, which means that complex program instructions are built out of elementary parts of the tree, and top-down, in which one starts at the root of the parsing tree and works through to the leaves. Complex instructions are split up into simpler ones that represent the program. Both methods lead to a well defined machine program, unless there are errors in the original program.

The final machine code is generated in the process of parsing. This code is ready to be executed by the CPU. In case of an error in the original program, an inconsistency appears in the course of parsing. The parsing algorithm stops and, in most cases, can tell the programmer the cause of the error, which has to be corrected. The procedure of lexical analysis and parsing has to be repeated until no error is found. A positive parsing result (e.g., in the form of an executable program), however, does not guarantee the semantic correctness of the program; it entails only that the program is syntactically correct and does not make any statements about whether the program's executions lead to the desired results.

[*See also* Algorithm; Artificial Intelligence; Expert Systems; *and* Knowledge Representation.]

BIBLIOGRAPHY

Aho, A. V., and J. D. Ullman. *The Theory of Parsing, Translation, and Compiling*. Englewood Cliffs, N.J.: Prentice-Hall, 1972.

Backhouse, R. L. *The Syntax of Programming Languages: Theory and Practice*. Englewood Cliffs, N.J.: Prentice-Hall, 1979.

—MARKUS PESCHL

PEIRCE, CHARLES SANDERS (1839–1914), American philosopher, scientist, polymath, and pioneer in the modern study of semiotics. Although raised in an intellectual environment with strong currents of Anglo-American empiricism such as that of David Hume, Thomas Reid, and Sir William Hamilton, Peirce never accepted the notion that knowledge was a natural outcome of the result of a knowing faculty or that truth is what is knowably evident. Rather, Peirce studied the history of epistemology as an ethnologist studies a foreign culture, as an outsider trying to understand and make sense of an activity that appears at first blush to be uncomplicated, natural, spontaneous, and yet on reflection largely unintelligible. Peirce had to develop a new vocabulary for this new general science of knowing—the study of signs, or semiotics—a task that took a lifetime to even clarify.

As a freshman at Harvard in 1855, Peirce was strongly influenced by Friedrich Schiller's *Letters on the Aesthetic Education of Man* (1795) and Immanuel Kant's *Critique of Pure Reason* (1781). In 1857, he developed his first of many versions of a triadic system of categories: this one consisted of the I, which he identified with reason, goodness, and permanence; the thou, reflected in love, beauty, and causality; and the it, manifested in sensation, truth, and community. During the 1860s, Peirce struggled with various Kantian problems: how can the mind have a concept of infinity if it knows only what is particular? If knowledge is particular, how is metaphysics possible? If reasoning follows the structure of the syllogism, how is hypothetic inference possible? As he reflected on these questions, he moved from materialism and empiricism to transcendentalism and idealism and then back again. He never fully adopted either traditional theory because he rejected foundationalism and the possibility of metaphysics based on ultimate, unchanging primal truths.

Out of his reflections on the history of epistemology, one truth seemed to emerge: the structure of the knower's relation with the known, as well as both the structure of the process of knowing and the content of whatever is known in particular, is governed by the invariable form of triadic relations. To be is to be in relation to something else; to exist is to exist as a sign of something for something. If God holds the blueprint of creation, it is a short list of relational categories that operate iteratively, creating quality out of quantity and complexity out of simplicity. This notion gives rise to the view that there are two lists of categories, a short list for formal relations, which Peirce calls firstness, secondness, and thirdness, and a long list of categories that are the iterated instantiations of the formal categories. Examples of the latter include, on the level of computation, Unity, Plurality, and Totality; on the level of cognition, Thinking, Thought of, and Abstraction; on the level of the form of language, Subject, Predicate, and Meaning; on the level of communication, Language, Expression, and Meaning; on the level of philosophical reflection of cognition, Sensation, Existence, and Reality. Abstraction, Meaning, and Reality are examples of thirdness: they are the result of a synthesis of opposites, as well as a condition for the synthesis. For example, language, as a First, consists of distinguish-able marks and noises; as a Second, it is modified by the style in which the marks are inscribed or inflected; as a Third, it becomes the vehicle to carry meaning to express the energy that originates from the need for articulation.

Peirce's metaphysical speculations test the limits of language. Since he uses language outside of its generally utilitarian context, he devised new terms to capture his insights. This struggle itself heightened awareness of the need to study language and systems of notation extensively. Peirce calls the ability of a language to express meaning its plasticity, which exists when the symbols are physically capable of expressing meaning and when that meaning can be understood. Plasticity, in turn, produces "regulation"—that is, the ability of language to govern personal and social conduct in the form of commands and commandments, scientific formulas, statutes and laws, and so forth. "Influx" was the name Peirce coined for the cosmic process that continually joins Firsts and Seconds to make Thirds. Taking Kant's lead, Peirce abandoned the commonsense notions of linear time and physical causality. In Peirce's view of creation, everything happens at once, and time and space are merely perspectival. This view at first appears ironic—in 1858, Peirce had begun a thirty-year association with the United States Coast Survey—but upon deeper reflection reveals the surveyor's acceptance that fixed points are mere conventions and that all measurements are estimates. By the mid-1860s, Peirce had turned from the arduous tasks of metaphysics to logic and scientific explanation. In 1863, he wrote an article for the *American Journal of Science and Arts* entitled "The Chemical Theory of Interpenetration." The theory of chemical combination must have seemed a small, attainable goal for him after his early efforts to explain the general workings of creation at large. He proposed that chemical combination could not be explained in terms of the physical shapes of molecules because the shapes themselves were combinations of atoms, and that furthermore the hypothesis of atoms ultimately explains nothing. Instead, Peirce proposed a general theory of chemical combination based on dynamic concepts of energy and equilibrium.

In 1865, Peirce gave a series of Harvard lectures on the logic of science. His first lecture concerned logic in general, which he defined as the science of the conditions that enable symbols to refer to objects, while he defined "symbolistic" or semiotics as the science of the formal conditions of intelligibility of symbols. Subsequent lectures were concerned with deductive and inductive inference, providing Peirce with the opportunity to tell his audience that inferences may be made that are neither inductive nor deductive but are hypothetic insofar as the particular inference may suggest a theory about itself, as in scientific invention and creativity.

Peirce also introduced his Harvard audience to the most recent variants of his metaphysical vocabulary of triadic forms: Thing, Representation, and Form; and Signs, Copies, and Symbols. By *Form*, he referred to the way in which a thing can be represented, while a thing was the bare "it" of the representation, and "representations" were unities of Thing and Form insofar as they have singular identities, as do Things, but also refer beyond themselves to Things themselves. Representations are always known directly because there is nothing to know about them except as they represent, even if intersubjective agreement about what they represent is not possible. Peirce called the ability to distinguish representations from the represented and from the manner of representation "precission." Thus, the color blue may be thought of (prescinded) apart from the color red, and space may be prescinded from color, but color may not be prescinded from space, nor red from color. The triadic categories are prescindable, but that does not mean that each has a discrete existence as an entity apart from the others.

The second triad follows the logic of the first. Signs are representations that are connected to their objects by a simple, direct, and particular connection; they are fixed by convention. Representations that are copies, on the other hand, share a form with what they represent through similarity or congruence. Symbols, however, stand in relation to the represented by their power to suggest other symbols, which Peirce called semiosis—the energetic process of symbolizing activity we commonly know as thought or intelligence.

In a later lecture that year, Peirce elaborated on the manner or Form of representation, again in its prescinded triadic manifestation: Reference to Subject, Reference to Object, and Reference to Ground. Ground itself contains three marks of determination: reference to subject, reference to object, and reference to representation. The last is immediate, the others intermediate. Representation cannot take place unless there is a Ground that "thinks" the triadic

forms together. There can be no representation by instinct or constant conjunction. What is separate remains separate. Peirce calls this ground "reason."

The following year, 1866, Peirce delivered another series of public lectures at the Lowell Institute in Boston, this time describing his two sets of triadic categories as quality, relation, and representation and as ground, correlate, and interpretant. Here, the ground is a pure form or abstraction of which a concrete thing is only an incarnation. A correlate is the thing related to, and the interpretant is the mediating representation between ground and correlate.

In 1867, Peirce's associations with the Coast Survey deepened; he became assistant to the superintendent and later took a position with the Harvard Observatory, making spectroscopic measurements and publishing the results in scientific journals. He also plunged into the study of medieval logic and the works of John Duns Scotus. His library at the time on this subject surpassed Harvard's. Meanwhile, the first philosophical journal in English, *The Journal of Speculative Philosophy*, was inaugurated by the Saint Louis Hegelians and edited by William Torrey Harris. Peirce began subscribing and submitted several papers.

During this period, Peirce never lost interest in the question of the referential capacity of terms. As a youth, he wondered how the term infinity could refer to what could not be known or comprehended in any empirical way and yet still be a term about which mathematical reasoning could be possible. He also wondered how we could speak of God and not obviously believe that we were speaking nonsense. In his quest to understand and resolve this problem of the reference of certain symbols, he studied the works of the post-Kantian logicians Ernst Reinhold, Heinrich Ritter, Johann Herbart, Jakob Fries, Moritz Drobisch, Friedrich Adolph Trendelenburg, and Friedrich Uberweg, as well as the logical works of George Boole, Augustus De Morgan, and William Thomson. Peirce was probably one of the most knowledgeable American scholars of the European philosophical tradition. From his investigation, he concluded that nothing could be thought that did not impart to the thinker some quality of the thing thought of. Without this notion as the first condition of thought, thinking would be nothing but an empty series of meaningless relations. But Peirce did not mean that whatever could be thought is true; rather, he meant that whatever could be thought contains a referent that may be prescinded from the thought itself and that is in some way separate from our thought of it. The implications of this view are sweeping: accepting it means accepting the notion that the sheer activity of thought reflecting continually upon itself will lead to a greater comprehension of what reality is truly all about. Knowledge starts to perfect itself as soon as it becomes systematic—that is, as soon as it begins to study itself in disciplines such as psychology and logic. At that point, it becomes clear that knowing cannot be reduced to deduction or induction or a combination of both. It also becomes clear that knowing is never immediate but always requires the act of making an inference, even when it has the character of being immediately evident. Being evident is merely being able to make the inference naturally and without effort.

For Peirce at this time, positivism was entirely false because it required concepts that would be impossible to comprehend if the tenets of positivism were true. Positivism fails to understand, Peirce argues in "Questions on Reality," the implications of the view that every thought is a sign: that knowledge requires abstraction before it may know the particular. These notions inspired the three papers Peirce published in *The Journal of Speculative Philosophy* in 1868: "Questions Concerning Certain Faculties Claimed for Man," "Some Consequences of Four Incapacities," and "Grounds of Validity of the Laws of Logic: Further Consequences of Four Incapacities."

During the late 1860s and early 1870s, Peirce primarily studied and wrote on logic, contrasting the realism of Duns Scotus with the nominalism of William of Ockham, and used some of his work in this area as the basis of another series of lectures at Harvard University. Peirce appreciated the simple, lucid approach of Ockham but knew that Duns Scotus was closer to the truth. Peirce also worked extensively on a "logic of relatives" as an elaboration of the work of DeMorgan, Boole, and W. Stanley Jevons. At this time, he also began to synthesize his views on science, logic, and metaphysics into an evolutionary whole, viewing the process of knowing as a communal rather than personal activity. Truth is not the conformity of thought and the thought of in the mind of a given knower, which his theory of signs reveals as a synthesis that can never be fully achieved; rather, the development of truth is an asymptotic process that a community of interacting knowers might achieve as long as the community continues to develop and refine the languages through which it communicates and as long as artificial barriers such as force or dogma do not impede thought.

During the 1870s, Peirce had an opportunity to witness the importance of this idea in practice: he did pendulum studies in Europe for the Coast Survey, consulted with European scientists such as James Clerk Maxwell at Cambridge, and researched medieval and Renaissance manuscripts of Ptolemy's calculations, which later gave rise to a book of his on photometry. He also participated in the activity of a philosophical society called the Metaphysical Club, which included Chauncey Wright, William James, Oliver Wendell Holmes, and John Fiske, among others.

In 1877, Peirce published a series of papers in *Popular Science Monthly* that was intended to impress upon the readers the need to embrace the scientific method as the best way of knowing reality. Two papers, "The Fixation of Belief" and "How to Make Our Ideas Clear," expressed the ideas of early pragmatism with which Peirce later became associated. But these were popular essays designed for easy comprehension, and they do not make explicit all of Peirce's assumptions. His description of belief as merely a resting point to "appease doubt" and create habit was not a turn to subjectivity. Rather, it was a recognition that when thinking is allowed to proceed, the forces of nature govern the thinker and allow him or her to think more and more about what is true, just as the weathercock is guided by the wind, the direction of which it subsequently becomes a sign. But for it to serve as a sign, the weathercock must be free to turn. When thought is controlled by a priori dogmas or religious and political oppression, beliefs become fixed without the opportunity for the natural flow of inferential thought to take full effect. In "The Order of Nature," Peirce makes clear that the view of mind as a purely adaptive response to experience, as described in the hypothesis of natural selection and British epistemology, is inadequate and that a grander hypothesis is required.

The *Popular Science Monthly* series illustrates Peirce's view that the universe and human experience result from an interplay of order and disorder. Knowledge is born when a lack of equilibrium is able to be recognized; it is achieved when order is recognized. However, the resting point of mind in a sense of order is not an objective feature of the world but a function of the capacity of the mind that knows. To a polyp, for example, that represents to Peirce the vanishing point of intelligence, all events in the universe are unrelated and appear to be the result of pure chance. On the other hand, to the most advanced human minds, such as that of Maxwell, even the random activity of the particles of a gas may be conceived so as to reveal (mathematically—i.e., semiotically) an orderly process, provided that the knower is capable of adopting and using a sufficiently complex system of signs.

In 1879, Peirce received an offer to become a lecturer in logic at Johns Hopkins University, which had opened in 1876. Among his students were John Dewey and Thorstein Veblen. By 1881, Peirce had become an established international figure in the field of logic, winning the praise of W. Stanley Jevons and John Venn in Britain. In 1883, *Studies in Logic* was published, consisting of essays by Peirce and his students. In spite of his intellectual successes, Peirce did not receive tenure, left the university after some controversy, and returned to full-time duties with the Coast Survey in May 1884 as head of the Office of Weights and Measures. However, the Coast Survey at the time was also at the center of political controversies involving conflicting views of its mission, and in 1887 Peirce and his wife moved to Milford, Pennsylvania, where he spent the rest of his life.

Distracted only by his increasing poverty, Peirce spent the next decade writing on "philosophic architectonic," a vast project to create a system of notation that would not only clarify the process of scientific discovery but accelerate it as well. He published five articles in *The Monist*, beginning with "The Architecture of Theories" and followed by "The Doctrine of Necessity Examined" and "The Law of the Mind." These papers attack atomism and particularism in epistemology by arguing that knowing implies a continuum and cannot take place without it. But a continuum implies ordered relations, while every relationship contains an element, more or less complex, of representability. Therefore, the theory of signs is the foundation of all science and knowledge. Peirce called the philosophy that embraces the implications of the logical and epistemological conception of continuity "synechism."

In his final two *Monist* papers, "Man's Glassy Essence" and "Evolutionary Love," Peirce describes the process of knowing as an example of the working of a universe that favors certain kinds of relationships over others. Evolution increases not only the numbers of relations but also their quality, level of complexity, and interactive capacity. Once certain patterns of relations or "personalities" arise, they are difficult to extinguish. They become semiotic engines that are themselves complex signs to even more complex personalities.

In his later years, Peirce repeatedly refined the language of his metaphysical ideas, always needing new terms through which to express his novel conceptions. In 1896 and 1897, he developed a "logic of mathematics" that replaced firstness, secondness, and thirdness, with monad, dyad, and triad and further perfected his recursive logic of relations, the systematic iterations of relations to themselves. He also perfected his theory of signs, applying the recursive relations to his earlier trichotomy of signs. Signs seen qualitatively or monadically were qualisigns (pure qualities that represent), sinsigns (unique things or events that represent), and legisigns (pure conventions that represent). Signs that are dyads are icons (signs that represent by virtue of shared qualities), indexes (signs that represent by being affected by their objects), and symbols (signs that are related to their objects by an abstraction). Signs as triads are rhemes (signs that refer to objects that are possible), dicent signs (signs that represent actualities or facts), and arguments (signs that represent by reference to a law of logical form). From these triads, more signs may be classified. For example, a diagram of a unique thing, such as a drawing showing the way to a particular house, is an iconic sinsign because it contains the form of the spatial relation of the house to the surrounding streets but is also the sign that only stands in relation to a particular object and location. On the other hand, a schematic diagram of a mechanical device, like a lawn mower, is an iconic legisign because although its form is congruent with the form of the actual object, it does not represent any particular lawn mower. A weathercock is a dicent sinsign because it is the sign of the particular wind that affects it, and it represents that wind by being affected in a particular way.

In the remaining years of his life, Peirce tirelessly reworked his ideas but no longer with an audience. He had become convinced that the logic of triadic relations was the logic that governed the world, evolution, and the emergence of spirituality. He was also convinced that pragmatism—or, as he preferred, pragmaticism, to distinguish it from its more mechanistic cousin—was really just the realization that thinking does not take place unless something called mind is under the influence of a living fact. At the bottom of Peirce's deepest thoughts is the anthropic view that the universe exists in order to become known. Abstract unity (firstness) and concrete plurality (secondness) are but manifestations of a concrete unity (thirdness) that operates throughout nature. Establishing this hypothesis upon logical grounds would prove that pragmaticism and the scientific method are the road to truth and would make traveling on that road progressively easier and more rewarding. Peirce never accomplished his dreams for a complete philosophic architectonic, a logic of discovery, but he has inspired many generations, and his work has spread far and wide as a result.

[*See also* Abductive Reasoning; Iconicity; Indexicality; Jakobson; Postage Stamps; *and* Type and Token.]

BIBLIOGRAPHY

Brent, J. *Charles Sanders Peirce: A Life.* Bloomington: Indiana University Press, 1993.

Esposito, J. L. *Evolutionary Metaphysics: The Development of Peirce's Theory of Categories.* Athens, Ohio: Ohio University Press, 1980.

Fisch, M. H. *Peirce, Semeiotic, and Pragmatism: Essays by Max H. Fisch.* Edited by K. L. Ketner and C. J. W. Kloesel. Bloomington: Indiana University Press, 1986.

Kent, B. *Charles S. Peirce: Logic and the Classification of the Sciences.* Montreal: McGill-Queen's University Press, 1987.

Ketner, K. L., et al., eds. *A Comprehensive Bibliography and Index of the Published Works of Charles Sanders Peirce with a Bibliography of Secondary Studies.* Greenwich, Conn.: Johnson Associates, 1977.

Murphey, M. G. *The Development of Peirce's Philosophy.* Cambridge, Mass.: Harvard University Press, 1961.

Peirce, C. S. *The Collected Papers of Charles Sanders Peirce*, vols. 1–6, edited by C. Hartshorne and P. Weiss; vols. 7–8, edited by A. Burks. Cambridge, Mass.: Harvard University Press, 1931–1935, 1958.

Peirce, C. S. *Semiotic and Significs: The Correspondence between Charles S. Peirce and Victoria Lady Welby.* Edited by C. S. Hardwick. Bloomington: Indiana University Press, 1977.

Peirce, C. S. *Writings of Charles S. Peirce: A Chronological Edition*, vol. 1, *1857–1866*; vol. 2, *1867–1871*; vol. 3, *1872–1878.* Bloomington: Indiana University Press, 1982–1984.

Peirce, C. S. *Reasoning and the Logic of Things.* Edited by K. L. Ketner. Cambridge, Mass.: Harvard University Press, 1992.

—JOSEPH L. ESPOSITO

PERTINENCE. Since in order to decode the pertinent content of a message we need to know something both of its code and of its context, any message that is interpretable will be at least partly predictable and, to that extent, redundant. If we meet a "q" in an English text, for example, we can be fairly certain that the next letter will be a "u"; if a word begins with a "t," the next letter is highly unlikely to be a "g." Thus, if we listen to a speech in English on a subject we know nothing about, we will still be able to predict a fair amount about it, simply because it will obey the rules of English phonology, syntax, lexical collocation, and so on; if we understand the context of discourse, we will be able to predict far more—indeed, if we are listening to a friend on a familiar topic, we might even be able to finish his or her sentences. A message that is completely predictable, however, in both its form and its context of occurrence—an "OPEN" sign that is never taken down from outside a shop, for example, even when the shop is closed for business—conveys no information in the linguistic code in which it claims to operate; equally, a message that is almost completely unpredictable in form, such as a speech in an unknown language, conveys no information.

Redundancy in a message, therefore, is in practical terms unavoidable, and for this reason it is not to be identified as excess or superfluity: it is, paradoxically, essential in the process of communication. To understand a message, we must be able to recognize what is and is not pertinent to it: that is, before we can attach signifieds to signifiers, we must discriminate those signifiers from the irrelevant information or noise that inevitably accompanies them. The task here is analogous to that of someone listening on a bad telephone line or radio link to faint speech punctuated by interference: a high degree of predictability in the message allows us to substantiate gaps, errors, ambiguities, and mishearings with well-informed guesses. Such redundancy-rich discourse—such as a casual, repetitive chat about well-known matters (for context can itself be a source of redundancy—is much more likely to be communicated successfully than, say, a set of technical instructions on a new topic. But redundancy is necessary for successful communication even in less noisy channels of communication. Imagine the strain on the reader's attention and the endlessly burgeoning possibilities of error if there were no redundancy in written language: suppose, for example, that all sequences of letters in an English text were equally likely and that any change in any six-letter sequence produced a new word, such that *ksnfbr lsmduf bcjhge* constituted a different message than *ksnbfr lsmduf bcjhge, ksnfbr lmsduf bcjhge*, and so on.

The task of decoding is not made simpler by the fact that actual signifiers are variable tokens of a type; we need to be able to recognize the identity of each signifier in all the possible embodiments it may take on. Think, for example, of the variety of fonts, typefaces, scripts, and physical methods of inscription that are used in written language. Certainly, such features may carry information as indexes, as symptoms (handwriting might reveal a writer's exhaustion, paranoia, and so on), or as participants in other kinds of codes: the German word *Heimat* (homeland), for example, has a special historical resonance when printed in Gothic type. Except in one or two cases, however (such as the use of italics to signify contrastive accent), this information is not part of any linguistic code: a sentence of English remains the same sentence whether chiseled in ornate capitals on a monument, printed in Times Roman, or scrawled hastily on a notepad.

The process of tracing the type in its various tokens is by no means a merely mechanical task, even in the optimal case of black letters on a white page. For example, devices such as computer-driven text scanners or optical character readers work by attempting on probabilistic grounds to relate each black mark on the page to one of a repertoire of ideal shapes and then assess which of a finite number of typographical symbols the marks are most likely to represent. For human decoders, however, it is not—or not merely—the resemblance of the signifier token to some type that permits us to identify it but rather its difference from other signifier types: pertinence is more a matter of paradigmatic difference than it is of syntagmatic similarity. To put it another way, I recognize a given signifier at a given point in the syntagmatic chain not because it conforms to some ideal pattern but because its form succeeds in excluding the others that might have occupied that particular position. Speech provides a useful illustration of this, since every speech sound ever uttered is unique in acoustic and articulatory terms, and yet each token of, say, /p/ uttered in English is accepted as representing the same type. In order, for example, that you should hear the word I utter as *pat* (rather than *bat* or *cat*), it is not necessary nor possible that

I should reproduce perfectly some ideal acoustic template of an ideal /p/ sound; it is merely necessary that the sound I make is sufficiently unlike any of the other possible occupants of that position in English speech. In other words, my sound should display a unique set of distinctive features. In features that are nondistinctive for English /p/—degree of aspiration, for example—the final and postfricative versions of /p/ heard in *top* and *spot* resemble more closely the [b] of *bog* than the initial [p] of *pot*; we recognize them as instances of /p/ rather than /b/, however, because phonologically they share the distinctive feature [−voiced], even though in phonetic terms that feature is represented differently in each.

In the same way, we distinguish a crucifix from a Maltese cross or a Saint Andrew's cross in that while all are [+cruciform], only the crucifix is [+extended descender]. Clearly, an actual token of this type may vary a good deal in such matters as relative length, thickness, and straightness of upright and bar, angle of incidence between them, orientation of whole, and so on, before we decline or fail to recognize it as a crucifix. But unlike a computer, a human being reads signs in a context that recognizes that they are produced: the most unmistakable cruciform will not be read as a signifier in circumstances that establish it (for atheists, at any rate) as natural or accidental—a formation of clouds or sand dunes, for example. On the other hand, a Catholic priest looking for a sign of remorse in a dying sinner might accept the vaguest of gestures as constituting a crucifix. In the same way, we do not register passively but rather read the utterances of others in terms of the intention we assume lies behind them; this process enables the operation of Gricean implicature, in which apparent irrelevance in conversational exchanges is construed as the tacit insinuation of pertinent information, on the assumption that out interlocutor intends to be informative and cooperative. If student A asks "Is X a good teacher?" and B responds "Well, he's got nice eyes" A will not dismiss B's answer as "merely" irrelevant but will take it to be an evasion of the question and will further construe that presumed evasion as compliance (feigned or otherwise) with the code of politeness that forbids backbiting—in brief, as "No."

Because we attempt to interpret messages as evidence both of the sender's intention and of their compliance with existing linguistic codes and conventions, the acoustic features of another's speech are in the end only a set of clues. The question of which of those clues will be taken to be pertinent and which dismissed as noise will depend finally upon the evaluation of probabilities based upon immediate and general context. Thus, while a computer (due to the presence of noise or performance error) might simply fail to construe an utterance, human beings actively misconstrue, usually in the direction of greater predictability and redundancy. To take an observed example: a visiting academic borrowing an office was abruptly asked, on entering a room, "How's your off spin?"; nothing being further from her mind at that moment than cricket, she heard the question (with no consciousness of mishearing it or guessing at it) as "How's your office been?"

[See also Articulation; Distinctive Features; Markedness; Phoneme; and Type and Token.]

BIBLIOGRAPHY

Armengaud, F. "Pertinence et communication: Les bonnes questions et celles qui le sont moins." Degrès: Revue de synthese à orientation semiologique 33 (1983): d1–d18.
Bouissac, P. "Iconicity and Pertinence." In Iconicity: Essays on the Nature of Culture, edited by P. Bouissac et al., pp. 193–213. Tübingen: Stauffenberg, 1986.
Forget, D. "La: Un marqueur de pertinence discursive." Revue québecoise de linguistique 18 (1989): 57–83.
Grice, H. P. "Logic and Conversation." In Syntax and Semantics, vol. 3, Speech Acts, edited by P. Cole and J. Morgan, pp. 41–58. New York: Academic Press, 1979.
Prieto, L. Pertinence et pratique: Essais de sémiologie. Paris: Minuit, 1975.

—PETER GROVES

PHONEME. The word phoneme is a transcription of the Greek phōnēma, meaning "a sound uttered" or "a thing spoken," which is a nominal derivation from phōnē meaning "sound" or "voice." Early twentieth-century dictionaries define a phoneme as "a sound of language," but by that time the word had already acquired a more technical meaning in some linguistic circles. Mikolas Kruszewski (1851–1888), a disciple of the Polish linguist Jan Baudouin de Courtenay (1845–1929), is credited for defining the term as distinct from phone in 1879 (Firth, 1934). But as Daniel Jones notes, "through an . . . oversight, it has come about that many American linguisticians [sic] have unfortunately given to the term 'phoneme' a signification differing greatly from that used previously in England and by the great Eastern European scholars

who first gave us the theory" (1962, p. v). Jones also advocates the introduction of the term signeme to denote "any speech feature whatever (segmental or otherwise) which can be made use of for distinguishing meanings." A useful account of the term is found in The History and Meaning of the Term "Phoneme" (Jones, 1957).

In modern linguistics, phoneme is commonly defined as the smallest meaningless unit that can be delimited in spoken language—as opposed to morpheme, which indicates the smallest meaningful unit that can be delimited in spoken language. Louis Hjelmslev (1938) proposed instead the neologisms cénème ("empty unit," "devoid of meaning," from the Greek kenos, "empty") and plérème (from plērēs, "full") to denote the opposition between meaningless and meaningful elementary units.

Among the terminological resources that modern semiotics derived from structural linguistics, phoneme provided one of the most prolific prototypes. Very soon, the idea of functionality or pertinence in a system became attached to the ending -eme rather than to the less frequently used phone, which came to refer to the concrete sounds of language as they are realized in each individual utterance. In this particular context, phonetics pertains to the study of the vocal sounds of a language, as opposed to phonemics, which studies the relatively small number of mutually defined abstract entities whose combinations account for the meaningful forms of a given language. From the relationship perceived between phone and phoneme and between phonetics and phonemics, a matrix has been derived through which, on the one hand, -etic and -emic can be applied to any communicative field other than natural language (Pike, 1967), and, on the other hand, any cultural entity can be construed, because of the valuation of the systematic approach, as a pertinent element of a system by the suffixation of -eme.

Most of the subsequent enterprises that can be described as "semiotics of . . . " are characterized by the search for functional units equivalent to phonemes in language. Within linguistics itself, terms such as chroneme and toneme have appeared (e.g., Jones, 1944). The study of body movements and gestures has led to the series: kine (from the ancient Greek kinein, "to move"), kinesics, kineme, kinemics, kinemorph, kinemorphic, and so on (Birdwhistell, 1970). Terms such as proxemics, chronemics, tacsesics, and their derived forms have proliferated. In French, one can find *mythème* and *gustème* (Lévi-Strauss), *vestème* from the Latin *vestis*, meaning "cloth" (Barthes), *chorème* from the Greek *chōra*, meaning "space", "spot" (Eco), and *gestème* and *graphème* (Mole). The case of *sème*, usually rendered in English as *seme*, is particularly interesting because of the confusion generated by its ending and the many definitions it has been assigned and because of a theoretical difficulty in the hypothesis that "meaning" is structured somewhat like phonological systems. Thus, *sème* enters first in the series of other assumed constitutive elements such as *phone* and *phème*. However, as it becomes obvious that it is impossible to conceive of or even describe a meaning anterior to a structured meaning—as is allegedly possible with sounds—*sème* has to be defined as the counterpart of the distinctive features used in Prague School phonology. As a result, the word *sémème* was coined as the semantic counterpart of *phonème*.

In stratificational grammar, the following layers of language structure are distinguished: phonemic, morphemic, lexemic, and sememic (Lamb, 1966). In other branches of the Saussurean tradition, the term *sémie* has been used with specific meaning (Buyssens, 1967), as has an alternative series derived from the Greek noun *noos* (*nous*) whose general meaning is "mind" but can also refer to the "sense of a word": *noologie, noème, noétique, noëmatique* (Prieto, 1964). Gregory Nagy (1983) has also elaborated on the ancient value of *noos*. An informative overview of the most successful neologisms can be found in the article on "Linguistics and Semantics" by Eugenio Coseriu and Horst Geckeler (Sebeok, ed., 1974). The numerous terms coined or redefined by the Paris School are explained in the dictionary by Algirdas Julien Greimas and Joseph Courtés (1982).

[*See also* Articulation; Distinctive Features; Pertinence; Saussure; *and* Semiotic Terminology.]

BIBLIOGRAPHY

Birdwhistell, R. *Kinesics and Context.* Philadelphia: University of Pennsylvania Press, 1970.

Buyssens, E. *La communication et l'articulation linguistique.* Brussels: Presses universitaries de Bruxells, 1967.

Firth, J. R. *The Word "Phoneme."* Paris: Le maître phonétique, 1934.

Greimas, A. J., and J. Courtés. *Semiotics and Language.* Translated by L. Crist, D. Patte, and others. Bloomington: Indiana University Press, 1982.

Hjelmslev, L. "Essai d'une théorie des morphèmes" (1938). In *Travaux du cercle linguistique de Copenhague,* vol. 12, pp. 152–164. Copenhagen: Nordisk sprog- og kulturforlag, 1959.

Jones, D. "*Chronemes and Tonemes.*" Acta Linguistica 4.1 (1944).

Jones, D. *The History and Meaning of the Term "Phoneme."* London: Association phonétique internationale, 1957.

Jones, D. *The Phoneme: Its Nature and Use.* 2d ed. Cambridge: W. Heffer and Sons, 1962.

Lamb, S. *Outline of Stratificational Grammar.* Washington, D.C.: Georgetown University Press, 1966.

Nagy, G. "Sēma and Nóēsis: Some Illustrations." *Arethusa* 16. 1–2 (1983): 35–55.

Pike, K. *Language in Relation to a Unified Theory of the Structure of Human Behavior.* The Hague: Mouton, 1967.

Prieto, L. *Principes de noologie: Fondements de la théorie fonctionnelle du signifié.* The Hague: Mouton, 1964.

Sebeok, T. A., ed. *Current Trends in Linquistics*, vol. 12. The Hague: Mouton, 1974.

Stankiewicz, E. *Baudoin de Courtenay and the Foundation of Structural Linguistics.* Lisse, the Netherlands: Peter de Ridder, 1976.

—PAUL BOUISSAC

PHOTOGRAPHY. The semiotic status of photographs has been one of the most disputed topics since Charles Sanders Peirce diversely characterized them as icons, indexes, and symbols. According to Philippe Dubois (1983), the first semiotic theories of photography tended to consider photographs as mirrors of reality or, following Peirce's more elaborated conception, as icons. Later iconoclasts who tried to demonstrate the conventionality of all signs contended that photographs present "coded" versions of reality and as such stand closer to the Peircean notion of symbol. Finally, photographs have been assessed as indexes—that is, as traces impressed on a surface by the referent itself. Notwithstanding Dubois's simplifications of the debate as a linear evolution, his distinctions effectively present the relevant epistemological attitudes.

The sources for the first period are mostly literary and presemiotical ones such as Charles Baudelaire (1821–1867), Hippolyte Taine (1828–1893), Walter Benjamin (1892–1940), and André Bazin (1918–1958). The early semiotic writings of Roland Barthes, which point to the "quasi-tautological" nature of photographic expression in relation to its content, are also significant. However, Barthes adumbrates the conventionalist approach by analyzing the connotative potential of photography and the role of captions as verbal "anchorage," which restricts the range of meanings that photographic images can evoke. Some consider Barthes also a pioneer of the index theory since he notes that each photograph implies that "this has taken place." The strongest exponent of the conventionalist view is René Lindekens (1971), who argues for the structuring of photographs in binary features because nuance diminishes as contrast is increased and vice versa, so that one of these factors must always be untrue to reality. This certainly shows that photographs are, to some extent, conventional, but Lindeken's claim that they have double articulation or duality of patterning is not thus substantiated.

Lindekens further demonstrated that the interpretation of a photograph is influenced by how it is more or less contrasted or shaded off in the process of development. Quite independent from Lindekens, Hartmut Espe (1983) shows experimentally that differently contrasted prints of a single photograph might carry very different affective imports. As a consequence, evaluation is often projected onto the subject matter, so that a person depicted appears more or less beautiful, a landscape more or less melancholic, and so on.

Those who disagree with this view point out that—barring chirographic or chemical local interventions during the developing process—photography is merely able to pick up or restrict features on the global level. This also applies to all other terms of photographic transposition: abolition of the third dimension, delimitation of space through the frame, exclusion of movement, monofocal and static vision, granular and discontinuous structure of the expression plane, abolition or distortion of color, limitation to scenes having a certain range of luminosity, and absence of nonvisual stimuli.

Since the 1980s, several theoreticians have insistently foregrounded the indexical status of photographs. Henri Vanlier (1983) and Philippe Dubois (1983) derive their views from Peirce's ruminations on the index, while Jean-Marie Schaeffer (1987) takes indexes in the most literal sense of mere traces in order to argue eventually that photographs can be either indexical icons or iconic indexes. When photographs are said to be indexical, they are treated as contiguous, particularly in terms of abrasion: that is, the referent has at some prior moment in time contacted and then detached itself from the expression plane of the sign, leaving on its surface some visible trace, however inconspicuous, of the event. However, as Vanlier notes, the photograph must be taken as a direct and certain imprint of the photons and only as an indirect and abstract one of the objects depicted.

Certain limitations are imposed on the photographic trace by the support on which it is inscribed. Some of these are mentioned by Vanlier: the typically quadrangular shape of the photograph, its digital nature, the information it leaves out, its inability to record the temporal aspects of the process giving rise to the trace, and so on. The photograph is thus not only an index of objects or even of photons but also of the properties of the film, of the lenses, of the photographic device generally, of the space traveled through by the photons, and so on. This observation is quite parallel to the one made in the study of animal traces, according to which the same animal will leave different traces on different areas of ground.

The trouble with a purely indexical account of photography is that it cannot explain what the photograph is a picture of. There is no intrinsic reason for considering the cause producing a trace (and even so, we have seen many other causes can be held responsible for it) to be a more important type of cause than the others. Indeed, we can only explain the importance of the motif when we realize that a trace, in the most central sense of the term, contains not only indexical but also iconical aspects, and when we admit that a photograph is a kind of pictorial sign and that all such signs are first and foremost grounded in the illusion of similarity.

However, the photograph, contrary to a hoofprint, for example, can be said to be always primarily an icon. While both the photograph and the hoofprint stand for a referent that has vanished from the scene, the latter signifier continues to occupy the place held by the referent and it remains dated, whereas the photographic signifier, like that of the verbal sign, is omnitemporal and omnispatial. Tokens of this type are apt to be instantiated at any time and place (although only after the referential event of and the time needed for its development). In sum, in the case of a footstep or a hoofprint, both the expression and the content are located at a particular time and place; in verbal language, neither are; in the case of photography, it is only the content (or, strictly speaking, the referent) that is bound up spatiotemporally. Thus, hoofprints, present where the horse was present, tell us something like "horse here before"; the photograph of a horse, which most likely does not occupy the scene where the horse was before, only tells us "horse" and we must otherwise reconstruct the time and the place of the sign.

[*See also* Chirography; Denotation and Connotation; Iconicity; Index; *and* Indexicality].

BIBLIOGRAPHY

Barthes, R. *Camera Lucida: Reflections on Photography*. Translated by R. Howard. New York: Hill and Wang, 1981.

Burgin, V., ed. *Thinking Photography*. London: Macmillan, 1982.

Dubois, P. *L'acte photographique*. Paris: Nathan/Labor, 1983.

Espe, H. "Realism and Some Semiotic Functions of Photographs." In *Semiotics Unfolding: Proceedings of the Second Congress of the International Association for Semiotic Studies, Vienna 1979*, vol. 3, edited by T. Borbé, pp. 1435–1447. Berlin and New York: Mouton, 1983.

Floch, J.-M. *Les formes de l'empreinte*. Périgueux: Pierre Fanlac, 1986.

Lindekens, R. *Eléments pour une sémiotique de la photographie*. Paris: Didier/Aimav, 1971.

Schaeffer, J.-M. *L'image précaire*. Paris: Seuil, 1987.

Sonesson, G. *Semiotics of Photography: On tracing the Index*. Semiotik Projektet, report 4. Lund: Institute of Art History, 1989.

Tomas, D. "The Ritual of Photography." *Semiotica* 40.1–2 (1982): 1–25.

Vanlier, H. *Philosophie de la photographie*. Laplume: Les Cahiers de la Photographie, 1983.

—GÖRAN SONESSON

PICTORIAL SEMIOTICS. To many of its pioneers, the study of pictures as particular vehicles of signification has consisted merely of mapping individual pictures onto verbal descriptions, while retaining a minimum of confidence in the objectivity of the procedure. Only recently have practitioners of pictorial semiotics come to realize the importance of developing a critical approach to this method.

French structuralism fostered the beginnings of pictorial semiotics. Roland Barthes's 1977 article on the rhetoric of the image is usually considered to be the starting point of the semiotics of advertisement and of the visual arts in general. Barthes and his followers attempt to describe all meanings in terms of a model inspired by structural linguistics. Their approach combines a pretheoretical notion of the picture with the concept of language as reconstructed in linguistic theory. It is characterized by its exclusive attention to the contents of the pictorial sign or, more exactly, to the referent and its ideological implications in the social world.

Another influential figure in early pictorial semiotics is Umberto Eco, who raises two basic questions in the context of structuralism: does pictorial "language" exhibit double articulation (or duality of patterning)? Are pictorial signs conventional (that is arbitrary) like linguistic signs? His answers remained mostly undisputed for about two decades. Since for Ferdinand de Saussure only conventional signs were of interest to semiotics, Eco set out to show that pictures are as conventional as linguistic signs. Pursuing even further the analogy with linguistic signs, Eco went on to suggest that pictures could be analyzed into elementary signs, which in turn could be dissolved into features with no meanings of their own. Although Eco himself qualified the latter view, the thrust of his approach continues to be accepted by many scholars in the field.

Equally important to the development of pictorial semiotics is René Lindekens (1927–1980), who, like Eco, addresses the basic structure of the pictorial sign as exemplified by photographs. His eclectic reliance on Hjelmslevian semiotics, phenomenology, Greimasian semiolinguistics, and Gestalt psychology provides him with a more complex theoretical background than Eco uses. In order to demonstrate the conventionality of pictures and to show how they are structured into binary features, Lindekens (1976) suggests, on the basis of experimental data and common sense, the existence of a primary photographic opposition between the shaded off and the contrasted; at the same time, he calls upon experiments with geometric drawings such as brand marks in order to discover the different plastic meanings of elementary shapes, which he calls "infra-iconic." In fact, Lindekens seems to argue for the same conventionalist and structuralist thesis as Eco (1968) did at first, but while Eco tends to ignore the photograph as a potentially embarrassing counterexample, Lindekens confronts it.

In the 1980s, pictorial semiotics evolved into several schools, some based on other premises than structuralist principles. These divisions included the Greimasian or Paris School, the Group μ School, the Quebec School, and the Australian School.

The Greimas or Paris School used the conceptual tools provided by A. J. Greimas's systematic redefinition of notions borrowed from the linguistic theories of Ferdinand de Saussure, Louis Hjelmslev, and Noam Chomsky. This approach deliberately remains within the boundary of its conceptual universe and uses theoretical consistency as sole criterion of scientificity. Consequently, all other knowledge about an object of study is taken to be irrelevant to semiotics (e.g., perceptual psychology).

The productivity of this approach results from its application of a model that uses well-defined terms and has the capacity to account for at least some of the peculiarities of pictorial discourse. Thus, for example, Jean-Marie Floch (1984) and Felix Thürlemann (1982) distinguish two levels of signification in the picture: the iconic and the plastic. On the iconic level, the picture is supposed to stand for some recognizable object (which is, of course, a much more restricted notion of iconicity than that found in Peirce); on the plastic level, simple qualities of pictorial expression serve to convey abstract concepts. Floch tries to generalize these notions to other domains, most notably to literature.

Another, more controversial, aspect of this approach holds that pictorial meaning is organized into contrasts that are based upon abstract binary oppositions—such as continuity and discontinuity or dark colors and light colors—both elements of which are present in different parts of the same picture. Indeed, each analysis starts out from an intuitive division of the picture into two parts that might then be repeated inside one or both of the division blocks. The task of the analyst is to justify this segmentation, setting up long series of oppositional pairs, the members of which are located in the different division blocks resulting from the segmentation. Although Floch shows considerable ingenuity in discovering binary divisions in all pictures studied, such an analysis might not be equally productive in all cases and might not remain consistently on the same level of abstraction. Two main criticisms have been addressed to the Paris School's approach: the method distorts pictures and other nonlinguistic objects by treating them a priori on par with natural language; the school's redefinition of linguistic terminology introduces biases that undermine comparisons between linguistic and nonlinguistic meanings.

The Groupe μ or Liège School, a group of Belgian multidisciplinary scholars, in the late 1960s collectively produced a book of "general" rhetoric in which they analyzed in a novel way the "tropes" that appear in the elaborate taxonomies of classical rhetoric, using linguistic feature analysis and mathematics. As in classical rhetoric, a figure of speech is defined as a deviation from a norm, which is understood as redundancy and thus identified with the Greimasian concept of isotopy, which became one of the essential tenets of the theory.

While at the beginning Groupe μ was concerned mostly with figures of rhetoric as they appear in verbal language (1976), it has subsequently given almost exclusive attention to the pictorial domain. Over the years, the theory has evolved under the pressure of the peculiarities of pictorial meaning while somewhat emancipating itself from Hjelmslev's theory and integrating, albeit timidly, some aspects of cognitivism and the psychology of perception.

Like the Greimas school, Groupe μ distinguishes iconic and plastic levels in the picture sign. Groupe μ holds that iconic figures can be interpreted because of the redundancy of the iconic level and that plastic figures acquire their sense thanks to a corresponding redundancy of the plastic level. More recently, Groupe μ (1992) also recognizes iconicoplastic figures, which are produced on the plastic level while the redundancy occurs on the iconic one or vice versa. (A comic-strip character that is like a human being but has blue skin is of this kind, in that the bodily shape permits recognition while the blue color creates deviation.) Norms may be either general and valid for all pictures or local, if they are created in a particular picture in order to be overturned: thus, the repetition of identical geometrical shapes in Victor Vasarely's paintings forms the backdrop on which another geometrical shape stands out as a deviation. It has been argued, however, that the grid permitting the classification of the rhetorical figures fails to distinguish functionally dissimilar cases and lacks a clear relation to general semiotic concepts such as indexicality and opposition. The norm concept as used here also lacks a social dimension (Sonesson, 1996).

The Quebec School is formed around Fernande Saint-Martin and her collaborators. Saint-Martin elaborates a theory of visual semiotics based on the idea that a picture is primarily an object of meaningful visual perception. Visual meaning can be analyzed into six variables, equivalent to a set of dimensions on which every surface point must evince a value: (1) color or tonality, (2) texture, (3) dimension or quantity, (4) implantation into the plane, (5) orientation or vectorality, and (6) frontiers or contours that generate shapes. The surface points, specified for all these values, combine with each other, according to principles of topology and of Gestalt theory (Saint-Martin, 1990). This approach integrates some analytical concepts from earlier art history and Gestalt psychology.

The Quebec School took a critical stand toward the Greimasian approach. Marie Carani, whose research bears upon pictorial abstraction and perspective, clearly articulates these criticisms (1987). Rather than the binary opposition, which is the regulatory principle of the Greimas school approach, or the idea of a norm and its deviations, which determines the conceptual economy of Groupe μ rhetoric, the Quebec School emphasizes the analysis of visual-perception phenomena. The extent to which it provides sufficiently specific tools for the semiotic analysis of pictorial signs remains open to debate.

The Australian School, focused on the work of Michael O'Toole (1994), derives its principles from the linguistic theory of M. A. K. Halliday, in which every work realizes some alternative from among the ideational, interpersonal, and textual "macro-functions" that O'Toole, borrowing from traditional art criticism, renames the representational, modal, and compositional functions. The first function relates to the participants and processes in the real world, the second concerns the way in which this world is presented by the creator of the sign, and the third deals with rules of internal patterning and focuses on the work as such.

In the work of the pioneers, pictorial semiotics, even when it concerned itself with pictures in advertisements, tended to adopt the traditional views of art and literary history, according to which the object of study is the purportedly unique individual work of art. Although some scholars have developed models of analysis that embody hypotheses about wide-ranging regularities found in pictorial semiosis, there has been little awareness until recently that pictorial semiotics, if it is to be a part of general semiotics, must be concerned with all kinds of pictures and formulate principles applicable to all empirically occurring kinds of picture, as well as objects potentially recognizable as pictures. Such a conception, although extended to the wider domain of visual semiosis, is implied by Saint-Martin (1990) but is applied only to artistic pictures. Arguments that pictorial semiotics should be a general science of depiction or of visual images were developed mostly in the 1990s by Groupe μ, Sonesson (1989), and O'Toole (1994).

The challenge remains to discover in what respects pictures are like other signs, most notably other visual signs and iconic signs, and how they differ from them. Do photography and painting pertain to institutional or sociocultural, rather than visual, categories of semiosis? Or are they primarily varieties of picture signs, embodying a specific principle of pertinence that serves to relay expression and content and as such should be of interest to semiotic theory rather than sociology? Further research could bear upon aspects specific to pictures such as rules of construction, intentional effects, channels of circulation, and configurational categories.

[*See also* Advertising; Articulation; Barthes; Gombrich; Icon; Iconicity; Image and Picture; Isotopy; Rhetoric of the Image; Riegl; *and* Wölfflin.]

BIBLIOGRAPHY

Barthes, R. "Rhetoric of the Image." In *Image—Music—Text*, translated by Stephen Heath, pp. 32–51. Glasgow: Fontana/Collins, 1977.

Carani, M. "Sémiotique de l'abstraction picturale." *Semiotica* 67.1-2 (1987): 1–38.

Eco, U. *La struttura asiente*. Milan: Bompiani, 1968.

Floch, J.-M. *Petites mythologies de l'oeil et l'esprit*. Paris: Hadès, 1984.

Groupe μ (J. Dubois, P. Duvois, F. Edeline, J. M. Klinkenberg, and P. Minguet). "La chafetière est sur la table." *Communication et langage* 29 (1976): 36–44.

Groupe μ (F. Edeline, J.-M. Klinkenberg, and P. Minguet). *Traité du signe visuel: Pour une rhétorique de l'image*. Paris: Seuil, 1992.

Lindekens, R. *Eléments de sémiotique visuelle*. Paris: Klincksieck, 1976.

Marin, L. *To Destroy Painting*. Translated by M. Hjort. Chicago: University of Chicago Press, 1995.

O'Toole, M. *The Language of Displayed Art*. London: Leicester University Press, 1994.

Saint-Martin, F. *Semiotic of Visual Language*. Bloomington: Indiana University Press, 1990.

Sonesson, G. *Pictorial Concepts: Inquiries into the Semiotic Heritage and Its Relevance for the Analysis of the Visual World*. Lund: Lund University Press, 1989.

Sonesson, G. "An Essay concerning Images." *Semiotica* 109. 1-2 (1996): 41–140.

Thürlemann, F. *Paul Klee: Analyse sémiotique de trois peintures*. Lausanne: L'Age d'Hommes, 1982.

—GÖRAN SONESSON

PICTURE. See Image and Picture.

PICTURE PERCEPTION. A picture can be defined as a surface treated so as to allow the perception of objects or scenes not actually present. There is a lively debate in perception psychology and philosophy about the material properties of displays that enable them to function as pictures.

Graphic art in the form of designs and intricate patterns that do not appear to have pictorial functions has been made for about fifty thousand years and can be found on every continent. Prehistoric pictures that show recognizable objects, including the flora and fauna of various regions and eras, indicate that the ability to perceive portrayed scenes is common to all peoples. In modern times, it has been shown that children and adults unfamiliar with pictures can recognize depicted objects in outline drawings and photographs without training in any pictorial convention (Hochberg and Brooks, 1962; Kennedy and Ross, 1975).

Loosely speaking, pictures look similar to what they are said to portray. A theory of depiction must account for this kind of similarity and must explain how the elements and patterns on the picture surface generate perceptible properties, such as light, and how those properties relate to the portrayed layout. While pictures are used to convey messages of many kinds, as in political cartoons, the fundamental theory of picture perception needs to describe the basis on which perception conveys information. The rhetorical functions of pictures rely on pictures representing some kind of scene in the first place.

Pictures consist physically of marks or elements on the actual picture surface. The marks denote or represent features in the depicted environment. The marks consist materially of patches of color or brightness. Each patch has a border, called a contour if the border is an abrupt one and a gradient if the border is fuzzy or gradual. Borders enclose the patches, creating "closed" contours or Jordan curves. The enclosed region has a shape—such as an ellipse or a circle or a square—and one of the chief tasks of a theory of depiction is to explain why a shape in a picture, such as an ellipse, can suggest a different object in the pictured world, such as a tilted circle. Another problem is to show how a contour, which is physically a flat boundary on a level surface, can show an edge in relief, such as the profile of a foregrounded mountain seemingly standing out against a background sky. Another key problem is to show how two contours can be elongated, close together, parallel, or form a line in an outline picture—a kind of feature that acts more abstractly than either of its contours. We will focus here on abrupt borders and outlines, though a similar account can be given for gradients.

The layout of the world consists of arrangements of flat and curved surfaces. When two surfaces meet, they form a corner, which can be concave or convex. A convex corner such as the roof of a house can be the profile or occluding edge of a foreground surface, set against a background surface such as a hill. The hill, in turn, can also provide a feature of occlusion, providing a profile against a mountain as a backdrop, if the tangent to the hill's rounded surface passes through the observer's vantage point. Two convex corners close together and parallel form a bar or rail or ridge protruding up from the background. Two rounded, occluding boundaries, close together and parallel, form a cylindrical wire or column. The converse of a bar or cylinder is a crack or fissure between two surfaces.

Surface patches reflect light to varying degrees, some reflecting one set of wavelengths more than others (and hence appearing colored). Additionally, surfaces are not all uniformly illuminated. They might, for instance, be dappled with shadows. Differences in reflectance and shadowing have two functions, iconic and plastic: they allow real scenes to be perceived (iconic function), and they also make up the physical constituents of pictures (plastic function). To describe these dual roles, it is helpful to list some distinctions. While the margin of a surface patch is a contour, an attached shadow's border is a terminator, and a cast shadow's border can be said to be a margin. A stain has a contour. The edge of the sun's illumination on the moon is a terminator. A person's long shadow on a beach in the evening has a margin. All of these different kinds of edges have one crucial optic property in common: they provide optic contrasts in the optic array they project to the observer's vantage point. These contrasts are divisions between light and dark (high- and low-intensity light, properly speaking) or between one set of wavelengths and another (red and white, for instance).

Contrasts can be projected by pictures and by real scenes. A real, three-dimensional concave corner might have only one of its two surfaces highly illuminated by a given light source. The result is an optic contrast. An occluding edge of a flat foreground surface also provides an optic contrast if the background projects light of a different type. A picture's patches—or, in the case of a projected slide, its shadows and illuminated regions—also project contrasts. Indeed, the contrasts projected by a still picture and by a static, real scene can be essentially the same.

Hence, any visual system that can appreciate the contrasts projected by the real scene can do the same when confronted by the picture. However, pictures cannot always be explained simply by showing how their contrasts match the array of contrasts in the real world. More needs to be said, for there are several kinds of influences on the perception of surface edges and important kinds of abstraction that occur in picture perception.

The inputs to perception that produce impressions of corners and occlusions include contrasts and relationships based on contrasts. The relationships are of two kinds: binocular and motion. The visual system can use factors present only in movement or binocular observation to discern surface layout. A well-known example is a red-and-green stereogram, a flat display that is viewed simultaneously with one eye through a red filter and the other eye through a green filter. Binocular vision finds something not visible through either eye alone, such as a square floating in front of a wall. Similarly, a random-dot kinetogram can engender the square in front of the wall even though any single frame of it may be simply a flat, random-dot texture. The square is seen as a result of relationships between two frames, inspected binocularly or across time. In viewing real scenes, binocular and kinetic relationships are very helpful in discerning individual trees standing out in front of a copse of similar trees, or the edge of a grassy hill seen against a similar backdrop.

Vision readily uses abstract binocular and motion relationships. Equally, it uses abstract relationships at times in reacting to the contrasts projected by pictures. While it is true that an optic contrast from a flat picture can support the same percept as, for example, an optic contrast of a foreground silhouetted object seen against a background sky, a much more abstract account has to be given for many outline pictures. The lines in an outline drawing have two contours, one on either side, of course. They provide two material contours and two optic contrasts. But often the two support a percept of just one corner, not two, one feature of surface layout rather than two.

Why do the two physical contours of a line engender only one depicted feature? The answer is that the two contours can be used by perception to provide just one axis in between the contours. An axis is a feature like a diagonal of a black square. It is ultimately a location defined by the physical borders, such as contours. Just as there is no physical mark to

correspond with a diagonal of the square, so, too, there is no physical edge to correspond with the axis of the line. The axis lies in the space between the contours of the outline. It is not itself a difference in brightness or reflectance, unlike the contour. The outline abstracts from brightness contours, and while it loses many connections with shadow- and brightness-difference vision, it gains immeasurably at the same time. The axis is able to stimulate the same kind of processing as binocular and motion relationships. It triggers perception of surface edges, such as convex and concave corners and profiles formed by occlusion.

In sum, picture perception includes impressions of surface layout, including boundaries of surfaces. In part, this is due to brightness borders in flat pictures providing optic contrasts that function just like contrasts from an illuminated three-dimensional surface layout. In part, picture perception succeeds because vision abstracts axes from sets of contrasts, such as pairs forming outlines. This kind of abstraction creates the same result as vision's use of binocular or motion relationships, which are also an abstraction from the contrasts present in monocular, still displays.

The link between the physical marks on the picture surface and the surface arrangements depicted by the marks is the medium of light and contrasts thereof. Marks, however, can be tangible. Surface arrangements are also tangible, for corners, columns, and cracks, for example, are all easily detected by touch. Touch can also abstract form in making out circles, squares, straightness, and curvature. Therefore, the medium for pictures can be tangible pressure, not just optic intensity or wavelength. Indeed, blind people can recognize raised-line drawings of common objects and make such drawings (Kennedy, 1993, 1997). In the case of tactile pictures, as with visible pictures, the key defining principle is that pictures allow perception of surface arrangements that are not actually present.

Once an arrangement of surfaces can be depicted, the form of the surfaces can be subject to laws of shape and projection. Perception is readily able to use perspective principles, including convergent or polar perspective and parallel perspective. Divergent perspective appears less realistic to most observers. Convergent perspective is constrained by the angle subtended by the pictorial display. That is, a polar-perspective picture looks correct when viewed from the correct vantage point, where all the parts of the picture subtend the correct angle. The pictured world looks distorted if the picture is viewed at too large or too small an angle to be correct.

Parallel perspective is an approximation of the shapes projected by objects at a small angular subtense. Hence, given an outline picture of a cube drawn in parallel perspective, the picture looks realistic if it subtends only a few degrees. Also, the receding sides of the cube should be shown with foreshortening (about 65 percent of the length of the lines in a square showing the front face of the cube). The longer the object depicted, the less foreshortening is used by vision in examining parallel perspective drawings. That is, receding sides of a city block or parallelepiped with a square front face and sides three times as long as the front face shown in an outline drawing are portrayed aptly by lines almost three times the length of the lines for the square front face. Chinese and Japanese paintings frequently employ parallel perspective to show landscapes. Long walls or fences in these pictures might have no foreshortening and can show 1:1 proportions in the object by 1:1 proportions on the picture surface.

Besides showing arrangements of surfaces, subject to laws of form, pictures can serve rhetorical functions. Political cartoons are an obvious case in point. A politician can be shown metaphorically as leaving the ship of state adrift, with the pictured ship a symbol for the country. The juxtaposition of a ship with the politician is not to be taken literally. In hendiadys (one by means of two), the doubling of an image of a person might mean they are drunk, not literally twinned. In prolepsis, time is anticipated. A bride's mirror reflection could show how the young woman will be as a marriage partner ten years hence. In a cliché, a person with a bright idea is shown with a lightbulb over her head. In hyperbole, a large nose and chin of a well-known personality can be shown as enlarged to the point of meeting each other. In catachresis, a metaphoric item is used to fill a gap in the lexicon. Still pictures cannot literally repeat motion, and since the mid- to late nineteenth century, a host of graphic devices including "speed lines," resembling flowing ribbons behind a rushing figure, have been added catechrestically to pictures to fill the gap. Synecdoche is the representation of an item by a key part. In pictures, a solid wall is often shown by explicitly drawing a few of its bricks; a drawing of a skyscraper might only fill in some of the windows,

perhaps drawn incompletely—a kind of "et cetera" principle. Personification is common in pictures, showing a lawyer as a shark, for example, a policeman as a guard dog, and a semiotician perhaps as a bloodhound on a trail.

In sum, pictures can be literal or metaphoric. Literal pictures involve surface arrangements shown following laws of the normal three-dimensional world, and metaphoric pictures present juxtapositions that fit different types of trope to convey a message.

[*See also* Cartoons; Comics; Cultural Landscape; Gibson; Mindscape; Pictorial Semiotics; *and* Vision.]

BIBLIOGRAPHY

Hochberg, J. E., and V. Brooks. "Pictorial Recognition as an Unlearned Ability." *Ameican Journal of Psychology* 75 (1962): 624–628.

Kennedy, J. M. *Drawing and the Blind: Pictures to Touch*. New Haven: Yale University Press, 1993.

Kennedy, J. M. "How the Blind Draw." *Scientific American* 276 (1997): 76–81.

Kennedy, J. M., and A. S. Ross. "Outline Picture Perception by the Songe of Papua." *Perception* 4 (1975): 391–406.

—JOHN M. KENNEDY

PICTURES AND COMPUTERS. Computer technology can be used to store and transport, create and display, analyze and interpret, search and categorize, and enhance and transform pictures. Pictures can be a means for communicating and interacting with computers. Pictures can also be used by computers to represent a problem domain.

Three general roles for pictures can thus be distinguished: external pictures, where the pictorial format is a purpose or condition for computer support; pictures used to interact with computer applications; pictures used internally in computer applications to support problem solving in the depicted domain. More than one mode of use may be in operation at the same time. For instance, solving a picture-processing task might encourage the use of pictorial interaction technique, and it might also involve calculations concerning the things depicted, conveniently made in terms of some internal pictorial representation of the domain.

External Pictures as Purpose or Condition. Situations in which an external picture is of central interest lies closest to traditional forms and uses of pictures. The involvement of computers, however, does make a considerable difference: accentuating certain aspects and tendencies, raising new problems, and creating new possibilities.

Earlier thinkers on pictorial semiotics have tended to take continuity as essential: in distinction to linguistic tokens, pictorial tokens pass into each other without breaks or gaps (e.g., Goodman, 1968). In contrast, the digital representation that is basic to current computer technology is restricted to tokens that are unambiguously distinguishable by the computer. Electronic pictures on computer screens, laser printouts, and other forms inherit this digitality, and when conventional pictures are scanned and used as input, they are also digitized. The underlying rationale for digital representation is its imperviousness to corruption, enabling perfect transmission and copying and perfect, consistent retrieval of stored information over time, without which programs of any complexity could not be made to work.

There certainly was a time when graphic digitality was emblematic of computer technology (e.g., punch cards, arrays of blinking diodes, digitized characters in displays and for optical scanning). Yet with sufficiently high resolution, the viewer will perceive and experience a digital image no differently than he or she will an analog one. The consequences of digitality are less direct. For instance, when perfect copying is possible, the conceptual distinction between original and copy is undermined. A related tendency is to detach the signifying stratum of an image from its material substratum, making the image a more abstract entity. This is supported further by a very fundamental principle of current theory of computation—namely, the medium independence of representation and computation.

At the same time as digitality gives unprecedented guarantees of incorruptibility, it gives unprecedented possibilities of manipulating and fabricating images, disrupting traditional links to reality, with consequences for all kinds of pictures. An image can no longer be its own guarantor of authenticity; skepticism toward images is becoming imperative. This development has taken a range of different forms, from simple noise elimination and retouching to removing or adding objects in a given picture and pure image synthesis: the generation of pictures, which can be completely photorealistic, from entirely nonpictorial descriptions (Foley et al., 1990). The boundary between fact and fiction is dissolving (partly in parallel with the boundary between utility and pleasure), and the increasing flow of purported information is not accompanied by a corresponding flow of confidence. At the same time, some types of computer-supported images are becoming so vivid and engrossing that they approach the experience of reality, and the real world becomes just one among an infinite number of possibilities, thus challenging the supremacy of reality. By calling in question the credibility of an image, the image is emancipated from reality; in the process, the existence and independence of that reality is reaffirmed at first, but as the images become more engrossing in themselves and loom ever larger in our awareness, they make us doubt the importance and ultimately the existence of a reality beyond the image.

Computer-generated pictures tend to flout the ordinary pragmatics of images; they give misleading cues as to the amount of work, intent, or commitment invested in the image. A first sketch might look as definitive and finished as a final drawing. Word processing is going through a similar development to which people are now trying to adjust; for instance, we tend to judge a text's seriousness by the straightness of its right margin. Still, different styles and qualities of rendering continue to have an impact, and it is possible to play on existing expectations and connotations. The situation is complicated further by the emergence of pictures generated more or less automatically, with little or very complex and obscure connection to human intentions. Paralleling the evaporation (or multiplication, depending on point of view) of reality, the process of image production also seems to be dissolving: the existence of a purpose, an import, or even an origin seems in doubt.

Computers can produce active, dynamically changing pictures. Unlike film, these images need not be prerecorded and edited; like television images, they can be generated on the fly as a reflection of some concurrent process. Unlike television, this process need not exist in the real world. Also, the changes an image goes through are not limited to the basically movement-induced changes of film and television.

A current trend in information systems and computer-supported education involves the use of multimedia. The idea is to integrate images with text, sound, voice, and other elements in order to engage several senses at once in a carefully orchestrated manner. One ambition is to approach the richness and redundancy of a real situation: when a presented object is seen as well as heard and may be commented on in writing at the same time, perception and understanding will benefit. Another, somewhat different direction of development is hypermedia, which aims, rather, to create an extended collage of bits and pieces out of several different media, interconnected by links.

A general tendency today is to transform information into experience, to turn numbers into images. Through visualization, very large numbers of data, difficult to grasp and hard to resolve into interesting patterns or irregularities, are rendered into pictures that are cognitively more manageable. A common source of such masses of data is computer simulation. Depending on the domain, the visualization can present an image of some spatiotemporal thing or process or of some invented visual model of something more abstract. Efforts are made to pack more, but still easily interpreted, information into a basic three-dimensional image by augmenting it with various qualities (e.g., color coding, transparency, textures, vectors). Some of these techniques are borrowed from cartography, but computer technology offers many more possibilities, and much experimentation is going on.

Pictures Shared by Computer and User in Interaction. Human-computer interaction has developed from a purely linguistic exchange of messages to an increasing use of graphical-interaction techniques. So-called icons are used to symbolize objects and activities. Computer screens, or parts of them, are conceived as windows opening into spaces containing objects. So-called pointing devices, such as the mouse and the data glove, are used to indicate, position, orient, draw, trace, and simulate grabbing, feeling, molding, and so on.

It is instructive to compare three general forms of interaction, here illustrated by the operation of discarding an unwanted object. First, it can be done linguistically by issuing a command in a command language, which usually requires explicit names for the target object and the operation ("delete my file"). Second, given that we have an image of an object in a containing space, it can be done with a gesture, such as making a cross sign over the object. Third, it can be done with direct manipulation by "grabbing" the object, moving it, and dropping it into a trash can. Similarly, states of affairs, objects, and events can be presented to the user in writing (or speech), by using nonlinguistic signs such as highlighting or short tunes, or by presenting an image—a scene reflecting a visual model of the situation. In the first two instances, interaction can be viewed as an exchange of message tokens, while in the third case interaction can be viewed as physical, working by causes and effects.

With direct manipulation, an extension of the user's hand enters the picture. The actions of the user are modeled on actions in the real world (such as grabbing or moving) and cause changes in the world of the picture directly, as when an object is moved to the trash can, or indirectly—when destroying an object that is a container, any contained object is destroyed as well. A spatial world of data is created that the user can access through the interface, the most important part of which is the image.

From this, it is but a step to virtual reality: the image is made fuller and richer and is coordinated with other sense impressions (preferably including tactile and force feedback), and the user enters the picture, ideally with the whole body (using devices such as headsets and data costumes). In the picture, there is a world to move around in and explore and to affect by body movements and other means of interaction. These images—if, indeed, they are still images—are not something to observe calmly from a safe distance. Rather, they submit the viewer to an engaging and bewildering experience. Where is the picture when you are fighting for your life in a virtual-world interactive version of, say, *Jurassic Park*?

Augmented reality is a variant of virtual reality in which the image is superimposed on the real world, very deliberately blurring the edge between reality and image. The added image might make visible certain properties that are present but otherwise invisible; it might enrich reality by conventional information and annotations, and it might also introduce objects and properties that are absent or fictional (representing, for instance, a planned state of the world).

Terms such as *virtual reality* and *artificial reality* seem to reflect a wish to produce perfectly "transparent" images—that is, "images" that have ceased to be images to the viewer. But it might well turn out to be not technically feasible to produce virtual worlds as richly interactive as the real world. In a longer perspective, paintings in a medieval church that depict life in hell might have been as much "virtual reality" in their time as technologically more sophisticated attempts are now. (Compare also the reception of the first moving pictures.) If nothing else, every new technique attempting to push illusion into delusion has helped to sharpen our perceptions, our abilities to discriminate, and our conceptual tools for analyzing, comparing, and describing.

An interesting constituent of a virtual world, present already in simpler interactive images, is what might be called the virtual point of view of the user, produced partly from the perspective imposed on the viewer and, partly from the user's "self-image." The user extrapolates a place in virtual space ("where am I in order to perceive this?") and identifies with particular features of the image such as a cursor or a hand image (coupled to a data glove). This virtuality of the user might extend to user properties and abilities ("how tall are my legs, how flexible my neck, in order to have these impressions as I move about?") and perhaps even character (as in role-playing games). In a virtual world, the user might enact a bat, having a bat's view, flapping its wings by moving her arms, and so on. It is an open question how far our ability to integrate and identify extends, making up a coherent virtual self along with a coherent virtual world, in view of a prima facie distorted and incoherent image. How and how far can experiences be translated or transmuted?

Sometimes the "virtual world" is equated with cyberspace. The original notion of cyberspace implies, however, that the user remains aware of residing in a world of information, which is not intended to be true of virtual worlds. Also, whereas a virtual world might be the wholly idiosyncratic experience of a single user, the very idea of cyberspace is to present a shared world image to a community of users, in which people perceive and interact with each other as well as with the symbolic world (Benedikt, 1991).

A few more down-to-earth examples of applications of pictorial interaction should be mentioned. A geographic-information system (GIS) is a database containing geographically related information, which has an interface combining linguistic and pictorial access based on a map. Queries may be put by combining written query language with indications on the map; answers may be presented as text or by modifying the map image; the semantics of questions and answers includes geographic concepts and spatial relations. Also, visual programming is an area of computer science exploring the possibilities of programming languages based on nonlinguistic, visual notations (Shu, 1988). Visual-programming languages range from simple data-flow charts to languages that use a more complex syntax of image tokens and those that make more serious attempts to exploit spatial relations. Large and complex computer applications can be difficult to handle—with a common spatial metaphor, users are said to have problems in keeping their orientations and being able to navigate to various points in the system. It is natural to develop the spatial metaphor into a visual model, presenting the user with a very large image in which the user moves about (again approaching the idea of a virtual world). The crucial problem is how to build visual models and present images in which each point is enclosed in a context supporting interpretation and understanding that at the same time provides cues and indications useful for navigation.

Internal Pictures Supporting Problem Solving. Internally, the computer has remained a world of linguistic, nonpictorial signs. With few exceptions, pictures do not serve primarily as internal representations: they are there only when a task calls explicitly for a pictorial interface. Yet there is some research and experimentation in artificial intelligence on the situation. One source of inspiration is the study of mental imagery in cognitive psychology; another source is the use of models in science and the use of diagrams to support reasoning by analogy.

Typically, these experiments use pictures as complements and supports to linguistic (logical) representation and inference techniques. The scene in the problem domain is depicted as well as described, and the picture helps to determine which further descriptions apply. If the picture can be set in motion, it can also be used to make predictions. Some examples of such techniques are hypothesis selection, in which the picture is used to exclude hypothetical descriptions that do not apply to it; hypothesis generation, in which some observed condition in the picture is used to suggest a description that might hold more generally; coreference check, using the picture to find out if two descriptions might have the same reference; amalgamation, consolidating a number of descriptions by producing a common picture and then observing emergent features; and change of perspective, which starts with a description, produces a picture complying with it, and then generates a new description, possibly using a different vocabulary (Janlert, 1985). From the point of view of pictorial semiotics, this research makes possible the exploration of various hypothesized mechanisms of image use and the development of more articulated theories of the cognitive functions of pictures in contradistinction to linguistic representations.

[*See also* Computer-Mediated Communication; Denotation and Connotation; Iconicity; Knowledge Representation; Pictorial Semiotics; Type and Token.]

BIBLIOGRAPHY

Benedikt, M., ed. *Cyberspace*. Cambridge, Mass.: MIT Press, 1991.

Foley, J. D., et al. *Computer Graphics*. Reading, Mass.: Addison-Wesley, 1990.

Goodman, N. *Languages of Art*. Indianapolis: Bobbs-Merrill, 1968.

Janlert, L.-E. *Studies in Knowledge Representation*. Report UMINF-127.85 Umeå, Sweden: Umeå University, 1985.

Shu, N. C. *Visual Programming*. New York: Van Nostrand Reinhold, 1988.

—LARS-ERIK JANLERT

PLAY. The notion of play encompasses a great variety of phenomena—behavioral, psychological, cultural. Ethologists have studied the functional and evolutionary biology of play in animals (Fagen, 1981). Johan Huizinga's depiction helps to frame the common premises play entails as an

> activity which proceeds within certain limits of time and space, in a visible order, according to rules freely accepted, and outside the sphere of necessity or material utility. The play-mood is one of rapture and enthusiasm, and is sacred or festive in accordance with the occasion. A feeling of exaltation and tension accompanies the action, mirth and relaxation that follow. (1955, p. 132)

Like any other sign system, play contains many elements of concern to semiotics in terms of social engagements with encoders, decoders, codes, contexts, media, chronology, domains, and so on.

The issue of play rules, for instance, parallels many constraints on sign use proposed in semiotic theory. Rules formally designate play, and Roger Caillois argues that every form of play has concomitant rules. "They determine what 'holds' in the temporary world circumscribed by play." "The rules of a game are absolutely binding and allow no doubt" (1961, p. 11). In semiotics, this distinction determines whether communication takes place. Both play and communication, in this respect, share "certainty": there is almost no doubt when one is playing or communicating. At the same time, play theorists and semioticians recognize the inherent problems of such designations, since this certainty is always questionable. Adhering to rules, in both cases, corrals these practices. In semiotics, the rules of a sign field establish "context" of communication that, by definition, exists only because rules predetermine it.

Like social-semiotic conventions that bind sign users, rules produce communicable continuity in play, unlike everyday life, which lacks readily verifiable meaning. "The confused and intricate laws of ordinary life are replaced, in this fixed space" of the game, "and for this given time, by precise, arbitrary, unexceptionable rules that must be accepted as such and that govern the correct playing of the game" (Caillois, 1961, p. 7). In semiotics and play theory, however, the reliance on rule containment can formally rigidify, counter to the very elements that make semiosis and play so engaging.

Yet, in play as well as in semiosis, rules do have a place, and even authoritative agency. As Caillois notes, adopting a "play attitude" could suffice to create rule binding. Arguably, in semiotics and play theory, the institutionalization of rules creates illusory reification. This is not wholly an illusion, as preexisting social recognition is needed to constitute "play." In fact, "progress" in play and semiosis is often identified as their sole productive capacity. When semiosis is "unlimited," like play that is dangerously unfettered by rules, both are then less "useful" than activities demanding consensual rule adherence.

Vertiginous play illustrates this lesser activity. Caillois characterizes it as "the taste for gratuitous difficulty" in contrast with rule-bound play, "to which, without exaggeration, a civilizing quality can be attributed" (1961, p. 33). To Caillois, this "give[s] the fundamental categories of play their purity and excellence" consistent with Huizinga's belief in play's aesthetic potential (1955, pp. 8, 45). Like complexly organized semiosis, games of this nature (and their "play") "reflect the moral and intellectual values of a culture, as well as contribute to their refinement and development" (Caillois, 1961, p. 27). This accounts for the diminished status of some play in play theory.

Adhering to rule-constrained play provides the order that many semioticians also prefer. If vertigo affects either field, this order is potentially lost. Significantly, Caillois depicts vertigo negatively because it removes desirable restraints while the individual "gratifies the desire to temporarily destroy his bodily equilibrium, escape the tyranny of his ordinary perception, and provoke the abdication of conscience" (1961, p. 44). Mihaly Csikszentmihalyi, similarly, though less negatively, characterizes play as "a moratorium from reality" (1981, p. 16). To socially justify play, one has to avoid the pitfalls of vertigo and aspire for the progress play can yield.

James Carse's finite and infinite play distinction usefully recalibrates play often derided as unproductive. In finite play, a game is won by triumph over an opponent and "rules of play" impose "a range of limitations on the players" (1986, p. 8). Rules are pivotal for identifying and specifically prescribing the finite play facets involved (duration, play perimeters, etc.). But, the type of play invoked dictates the impact of rules. Rules, in this sense, have varied influence depending on the player's approach. "Finite players play within boundaries; infinite players play with boundaries" (p. 10). Infinite players do not act contrary to rules; rather, they act freely in relation to them. In effect, finite rules "are like the rules of debate" while infinite rules are "like the grammar of a living language" (p. 9).

While the finite orientation toward rules is motivated by "victory", the infinite play goal is to continue playing in an exuberant, transformational manner. A good illustration of this approach to semiotics is Roland Barthes's proposed open-ended methodology which seeks "the generation of the perpetual signifier . . . in the field of the text" (1977, p. 158). Barthes's object under scrutiny is conceived as a Text (as opposed to a Work, which is limited by its encoder origin). One does not ultimately "win" in an encounter with the Text by discovering the codes and system that reveal its immanent significations. One simply plays the Text, winning only if this play carries on effervescently. The Text, in this sense, "practises the infinite deferment of the signified, is dilatory; its field is that of the signifier and the signifier must not be conceived of as 'the first stage of meaning', its material vestibule, but, in complete opposition to this, as its *deferred action*."

Clearly, Barthes's stance toward the Text is related to the infinite player's approach to rules. In this enterprise of "signifiosis" the analyst "dismisses all meaning of the support text" (1977, p. 207). The Text would "lend itself only to a signifying efflorescence" in which "one associates, one does not decipher." While this position toward specifically literary semiotics seems to cultivate "lesser" play (i.e., purposelessness), Barthes's proposed semiotics actually engages encoding-decoding to generate infinite significations. As a result, this enterprise has no more of a specfic goal than does infinite play.

A substantial hesitation remains for many play theorists regarding its ostensible lack of seriousness, and Barthes's perorations about semiosic play have prompted similar responses. Nonetheless, as Huizinga comments on the accomplished player taking play seriously, some theorists have endeavored to rescue play from this complaint. Carse, however, identifies this desire as a preference for finite play. "From the outset of finite play," he argues, "each part or position must be taken up with a certain seriousness" (1986, p. 12). Yet, this attitude diminishes potential player growth by needless limitation. "Seriousness always has to do with an established script, an ordering of affairs completed somewhere outside the range of our influence" (p. 15). The finite player, accordingly, only engages a modest form of play which exists solely to begin and end in a cheerlessly circumscribed fashion.

The infinite player, on the other hand, plays *with* seriousness without limitation. Carse maintains that infinite players "continue their play in the expectation of being surprised" (1986, p. 18). Surprise is the mainspring behind infinite play, for it potentially leads—as Barthes intimates—to semiosic developments that perpetually (and "usefully") remake the sign user's relation to the universe of signs.

Ultimately, play theory offers semiotics an emphasis on cognitive constructivity and perspectival affect of each agent involved—and perhaps especially that of the decoder, as Barthes maintains. Indeed, Csikszentmihalyi contends that "any given activity can be utterly earnest or entirely playful at the same time, depending on the perspective held by the viewer" (1981, p. 19). As a result, significance is always brought to the "play" of a given semiosic event, rather than immanent to it.

[*See also* Barthes; Baseball; Semiosis; *and* Sport.]

BIBLIOGRAPHY

Barthes, R. "From Work to Text." In *Image—Music—Text*, translated by S. Heath, pp. 155–164. New York: Hill and Wang, 1977.

Barthes, R. "Writers, Intellectuals, Teachers. In *Image—Music—Text* (see above), pp. 190–215.

Bruner, J. S., A. Jolly, and K. Sylva. *Play: Its Role in Development and Evolution*. Harmondsworth: Penguin Books, 1976.

Caillois, R. *Man, Play, and Games*. Translated by M. Barash. New York: The Free Press, 1961.

Carse, J. P. *Finite and Infinite Games*. New York: The Free Press, 1986.

Csikszentmihalyi, M. "Some Paradoxes in the Definition of Play." In *Play as Context*, edited by Alyce Taylor Cheska, pp. 14–26. West Point, N.Y.: Leisure Press, 1981.

Fagen, R. *Animal Play Behavior*. New York: Oxford University Press, 1981.

Huizinga, J. *Homo Ludens: A Study of the Play-Element in Culture*. Boston: The Beacon Press, 1955.

Stewart, L., and C. Stewart. Play, Games and Affects: A Contribution Toward a Comprehensive Theory of Play." In *Play as Context,* edited by Alyce Taylor Cheska. pp. 42–51. West Point, N.Y.: Leisure Press, 1981.

—SCOTT SIMPKINS

POETICS. The first systematic discussion of the art of poetry, understood in the broad sense of literature, was Aristotle's treatise *Poetics*, which served as a model for discussions of literary works for hundreds of years in terms of both its organizing assumptions and the issues it raises. The Aristotelian model of poetics deals not so much with specific individual texts but with their general categories or underlying principles and therefore with virtual productions as well as already existing ones. Aristotle exemplifies the principles or categories with specific tragedies, but this is the sole purpose specific works serve. This method lays the groundwork for a distinction between a poetics—a general study of the principles of literature—and interpretation, the explanation or elucidation of single works.

The governing principle in such a model is its rational, systematic approach to its subject, whether poetry, tragedy, or epic. An important underlying assumption in such a poetics is that the object under discussion can be described by a language that is distinct from it—that is, a metalanguage that is cognitive in that it yields knowledge about its object. In this respect, poetics may be considered scientific, as it is based on the idea that each genre is defined by specific characteristics that distinguish it from others. Thus, poetry or tragedy can be described in a logical, systematic manner. The Aristotelian model of poetics is generally concerned with a relation between parts and wholes, such as tragedy and its six parts: plot, character, thought, diction, song, and spectacle. Each part is discussed in relation to other parts and to the whole. These parts are arranged hierarchically in order of decreasing importance: plot (*mythos*) dominates, while spectacle (*opsis*) is the lowest; character (*ethos*) occupies a lower position than plot. This model is also teleological, since it considers the parts-whole complex as serving the specific purpose of catharsis.

Aristotle's model has been influential not only in outlining and exemplifying a method of constructing a poetics but also in the problems it poses. The question of mimesis (imitation), which attempts to explain the relation of the created object such as (the literary work) to reality, has vexed all discussions of literature and art in general as it attempts to define the natures of imitation, artifact, and reality. Another question is the relation of poetry (literature) to history and the degree of truth imparted by each, which anticipates modern discussions of fictionality.

The Aristotelian model does not set down explicitly prescriptive rules, but in the very fact, for example, that Aristotle prefers one type of tragedy—the complex—a normative element is introduced. The normative attitude is evident, for example, in neoclassical poetics, which emphasized the prescriptive aspects (the insistence on the unity of action, time, and place; the rejection of the mixture of genres). In some modern poetics, the normative aspect appears implicitly (e.g., the rather long-lived normative poetics of post-Jamesian critics of narrative fiction and their insistent preference for "showing" over "telling").

The most important flourishing of poetics—understood as the science or scientific study of literature—occurs in the twentieth century under the impetus of developments in modern, especially Saussurean, linguistics. Philosophy in general and philosophy of language in particular have also influenced modern developments in poetics. Until the early 1970s, poetics established itself as the dominant research avenue in literary studies through different schools, particularly Russian formalism, the Prague Linguistic Circle, French structuralism, Northrop Frye's work, and, to a limited extent, New Criticism (Wellek and Warren, 1966; Beardsley, 1958; Wimsatt, 1970). From the 1970s onward, doubts were raised concerning the very possibility or necessity of a science of literature, and a new set of problems emerged.

The first stage in modern poetics is associated explicitly with a theory of literature understood as a field or discipline with its own methods, definitions, and taxonomies. It aims at a systematic, rational account, constituting a body of knowledge and aspiring to methods and results that are verifiable, improvable, subject to debate, and, if necessary, replaceable. Despite the differences among them, all the above-mentioned schools believe that literature or the language of literature or literariness constitutes a distinct object of study, to be described systematically in order to distinguish it from adjacent fields. The purpose of the science of literature is to yield knowledge that is generalized and systematized about the "rules," "principles," and "laws" underlying the phenomenon called literature. These schools develop distinct metalanguages with which to describe the object, with their focus always on its distinctive features or qualities. All these schools adopt an "intrinsic" approach, using or constructing a metalanguage that describes the text not by means of history, psychology, philosophy, or other "extrinsic" fields but by means of categories belonging to literature. The literary text is considered to be self-reflexive—that is, directed at itself, serving no outside purpose; its language is dominated by the poetic function rather than the referential; the text is autonomous, divorced both from its author and from its audience. The point is always to highlight the fact that literature or the language of literature is distinct from both ordinary and scientific language.

Within modern poetics, the genre that comes into prominence is narrative. A new metalanguage about fictional narrative describes them by means of distinctions between story and discourse (or equivalent terms such as *fabula* and *suzhet*). The first term in each pair designates the narrated events reconstructed chronologically together with their participants but abstracted from their disposition in the text. The second term in each pair designates the events as actually disposed in the text. Modern poetics develops different typologies of narrators and draws important distinctions between narration, which deals with the aspect of telling in narrative, and focalization, which deals with the perspective from which events are seen. It attempts to study narrative and its underlying rules or generating principles.

The different schools emphasize the distinction between poetics and interpretation, of which poetics is or should be free. This idea originated in the assumption that poetic taxonomies, descriptions, and theories are semantically neutral. While interpretation is concerned with the meaning of the single text, poetics is meant to be a meaning-neutral study of principles, rules, and laws.

In the tradition of poetics derived from Aristotle, mimesis or representation occupies a central position in discussions of literary works and art in general; in modern poetics, fictionality—which has to do with the question of the relation, if any, between the words in the text and their referent objects in nonlinguistic reality—has become central. Questions about the truth value of fictional statements become of central concern in light of developments in philosophy, linguistics, and philosophy of language.

Because poetics is understood as a theory of literature, it is to some degree affected by the late 1970s' and early 1980s' debates over theory in literary circles; however, *theory* in this context has a different meaning. Since the 1970s, the term *poetics* has been broadened to mean "theory of" in general. For example, in titles such as "The Idea of Authorship in America: Democratic Poetics from Franklin to Melville" and "The Poetics of Primitive Accumulation: English Renaissance Culture and the Genealogy of Capital" the use of *poetics* is so generalized and expanded that it has little to do with poetics as the science of literature.

This kind of theory develops in North America but under strong Continental influence. Perhaps its coming into prominence is due to the untenableness in poetics, especially of the structuralist kind, of the claim that poetics is meaning neutral and can be totally divorced from interpretation. This new theory, by contrast, is concerned with the question of interpretation—its validity, norms, and authority. The debates within this school of theory are conducted on a philosophical rather than a literary level. The debate centered originally on the questions of whether there is a way to validate one interpretation over another (the author's meaning, the text's meaning, communities of interpretation) and how it would be determined, but in its latest stage it has taken a strong philosophical turn with its most extreme exponents (e.g., Fish, 1980) claiming that interpretation is always the first step, that no description of a text can precede interpretation, that there are no facts to be described since interpretation is always there. Ultimately, such a position denies any possibility of grounding any theory altogether.

The concern with theory in general is part of the poststructuralist stage in literary studies, a stage influenced by developments in philosophical discussions of language, particularly Derridean ones, and their dissemination through the school known as deconstruction. The discussion over theory and its place in literary study has brought about a significant change in emphasis in theoretical discussions of literature.

Poststructuralist schools (a label that covers diverse groups such as psychoanalytic, semiotic, feminist, Marxist, and new historicist criticism) focus on language in texts of all kinds, not just literary ones, in order to expose or demystify its workings. This takes various forms according to the particular school: a Marxist looks at the workings of ideology; a feminist at those of patriarchy and gender; a new historicist at those of culture; and a psychoanalytic critic at those of the unconscious. In this respect, the "linguistic turn" initiated by Saussurean linguistics is still in effect. However, this stage of theory overturns the underlying assumptions that held true for both the Aristotelian and modern models of poetics. The belief in the specificity of "literature" or "literariness" is denied. Literary language is not different from ordinary language or scientific language; in fact, it has nothing to distinguish it, except that it best exemplifies, through its tropological (figurative) elements, how language serves to undermine its own workings, to work against itself. In fact, according to this view, poetics (which Aristotle distinguishes from rhetoric, the art of persuasion) seems subsumed under rhetoric and its tropological figures of speech.

Since in this view all language is basically similar to literary language, all language is "creative," and the distinction between an object language and a metalanguage is undermined as well. "Literature" and "criticism," traditionally distinguished from each other, are considered to be equally creative. The idea of a scientific, systematic study of literature is put in doubt by the notion that "objective," universalizing, categorizing language is a fallacy, since all language is situated in specific cultural and temporal spaces. Language must be analyzed for its ideological underpinnings (whether of class, gender, or race), those mystifying practices that generate the perceived inevitability or "natural" status of universalizing terms (e.g., the use of *man* to include both men and women). The literary text is considered just another cultural text among many, and the methods of analysis shift away from a scientific inquiry into the literary system and toward an interpretation of texts using what under scientific poetics are extrinsic or extraliterary methods. (The distinction between extrinsic and intrinsic is also undermined, since literature is no longer considered a distinct object.)

If both the Aristotelian and the modern model of poetics see the text or system as a coherent whole—a separate, distinct object—poststructuralist theory turns everything (even whole cultures) into texts and uses methods borrowed from different fields of study in its discussions. While the older poetics insisted on a boundary between disciplines, poststructuralist theory is interdisciplinary, with no specific methods, categories, or descriptions that distinguish literary study. Literature is thus considered part of cultural studies. The relation of literature to history (first introduced by Aristotle with regard to the question of truth) is reexamined relative to the ways in which history is seen as only another fictionalized, tropological narrative, not very different from literature, or as a means of showing how historical accounts contain the ideological mystifications found in literary texts of the same period.

Modern poetics assumes that there is such an object as literature and accepts, usually without much debate, the works that constitute literature—the canon. The current stage of poststructuralist theory is preoccupied by the whole question of the canon, along with a general questioning and reevaluation of all aspects of literary studies. Questions of canon formation, attempts to account for inclusions and exclusions, and to broaden the canon through historical research, and the question of values in regard to canonical texts are facets of a renewed preoccupation with literary values and values in general. This area is one more area of dispute between those who believe values have an objective status and reside in the text and those who believe values are contingent on historical, cultural, gendered, racial, or class circumstances and on the power of institutions.

A long tradition of poetics as a science of literature, which Aristotle's theoretical, generalized approach gave impetus to and which continued through the 1970s, has perhaps come to an end. Poetics in the scientific sense seems, for the time being, to have been pushed to the background. Its successor, poststructuralist theory, is concerned with issues, methods, interpretations, and analyses that are interdisciplinary and that see literature and literary studies not as a distinct bounded discipline but as part of a broad cultural and historical text.

[*See also* Deconstruction; Frye; Metaphor; Metonymy; Polysystem Theory; Poststructuralism; *and* Text.]

BIBLIOGRAPHY

Beardsley, M. C. *Aesthetics: Problems in the Philosophy of Criticism.* New York: Harcourt, Brace, and World, 1958.

Brinker, M. *Is Literary Theory Possible?* Tel Aviv: Sifriat Poalim, 1989.

Doležel, L. *Occidental Poetics: Tradition and Progress.* Lincoln and London: University of Nebraska Press, 1990.

Ducrot, O., and T. Todorov. *Encyclopedic Dictionary of the Sciences of Man.* Translated by C. Porter. Baltimore and London: Johns Hopkins University Press, 1979.

Else, G. F. *Aristotle's Poetics: The Argument.* Leiden: E. J. Brill, 1957.

Fish, S. *Is There a Text in This Class? The Authority of Interpretive Communities.* Cambridge, Mass.: Harvard University Press, 1980.

Hrushovski, B. "Poetics, Criticism, Science: Remarks on the Fields and Responsibilities of the Study of Literature." *Poetics and Theory of Language* 1 (1976): iii–xxxv.

Preminger, A., et al. eds. *Princeton Encyclopedia of Poetry and Poetics.* Princeton: Princeton University Press, 1965. See especially the entries on poetics, conceptions of; medieval poetics; neoclassical poetics; and modern poetics. See also the *Dictionary of the History of Ideas: Studies of Selected Pivotal Ideas*, vol. 3 (New York: Charles Scribner's Sons, 1973).

Seamon, R. "Poetics against Itself: On the Self-Destruction of Modern Scientific Criticism." *PMLA* 104 (1989): 294–305.

Wellek, R., and A. Warren. *Theory of Literature.* 3d ed. London: Jonathan Cape, 1966.

Wimsatt, W. K., Jr., ed. *The Verbal Icon: Studies in the Meaning of Poetry.* London: Methuen, 1970.

—NILLI DIENGOTT

POINSOT, JOANNES

POINSOT, JOANNES (1589–1644), Iberian theologian and philosopher who published an introductory logic text under the rubric of *Summulae* in 1631. This text was followed the year after by the *Tractatus de signis* (Treatise on Signs), in which all the traditional basic issues concerning signs are clarified and systematized.

Poinsot begins his *Treatise* with exactly the point that Augustine's famous and first attempt at a general definition of sign had presupposed. Instead of simply stating what a sign is, Poinsot asks rather what a sign must be in order to function in the way that we all experience it—namely, as indifferent to the distinction between real and imaginary being, or as conveying indifferently cultural and natural objects.

Poinsot distinguishes sharply between representation and signification. This becomes his basis for differentiating between signs and objects: an object may represent itself, but a sign must represent something other than itself. Thus, representation is involved in the being proper to a sign as the foundation for the relation of signification, but signification itself always and necessarily consists in the relation as such, which is over and above that characteristic of a material being upon which it is founded.

Thus, in Poinsot's semiotics, things are fundamentally distinct from objects in that things do not involve a relation to a knower, while objects do so necessarily. Things may or may not also be objects, and objects may or may not also be things, but every object signified exists as such as the terminus of a sign relation. Whatever exists as a thing has a subjective structure—that is, a structure indifferent to being or not being known. But whatever exists as signified has an objective structure as terminus of a relation founded upon some subjective structure of being, such as the psychological reality of a concept in the mind or the physical reality of a spoken, written, or gestured word. Signs mediate between objects and things by giving rise to objects as significates and by objectifying things in sensation. Thus, objects participate in the indifference of sign relations to being based in cultural or natural constructions, and sign vehicles are distinct from signs much as the foundations of relations are distinct from the relations they found. The foundation as such belongs to subjective being; the relation as such is always suprasubjective, as is the object that terminates the relation, even though nothing prevents this object from coinciding with some actual natural or cultural structure of subjective being.

Previous medieval criticisms of Augustine's original attempt to define *sign* in general, brought from the University of Paris to the Iberian university world notably by Domingo de Soto in the early sixteenth century, had gone no further than to distinguish between signs whose relation to the object signified is founded on physical structures of subjectivity accessible to outer sense (the case of so-called instrumental signs, to which alone Augustine's definition applies) and signs whose relation to the object signified is founded on psychological structures accessible to inner sense and understanding (the case of so-called formal signs). Despite the novelty of the terminology, the reasoning itself of Soto and his Paris masters amounted to nothing that could not already be found explicitly in the works of Thomas Aquinas (1225–1274).

Poinsot, on the other hand, advanced the discussion dramatically. He showed that this distinction was in fact secondary to the primary consideration of the being proper to the sign as such consisting in a pure relation according to the way relation has being; signs are called "formal" or "instrumental" not according to what is proper to them as signs but only according to the representative aspect that in the sign belongs to the foundation of the sign relation, rather than to the relation itself, in which the sign as such exists in its actual signification. In achieving this watershed advance, Poinsot brought new clarity to a number of points in the doctrine of signs that the late Latins had debated concerning the nature or being proper to signs. The root insight into the possibility of semiosis—namely, that sign relations share with all relations, whether physical or cognitive and purely objective, the property of being intersubjective in principle or superordinate to their foundations—Poinsot indeed found in Aquinas, even though Poinsot's own application of the insight was unprecedented (Deely, 1988). At the same time, the relation in which a sign consists also exhibits an irreducible and unique feature: namely, triadicity or "thirdness"—the involvement always of three terms. This conclusion, however, though widely shared among the late Latin authors, remained much in need of clarification even after Poinsot's unequivocal treatment of the point. Indeed, the third term of the sign relation did not receive a name of its own prior to Charles Sanders Peirce's introduction of the term *interpretant*.

Poinsot's *Treatise on Signs* came at the very end of medieval Latin development (Beuchot, 1980). Its novelty and decisive clarification of previously discussed insights was largely hidden from view by the conservative design of his philosophical and theological volumes, of which his semiotics was a part. Poinsot, retaining the fundamental cast of the medieval thinker, wrote with an eye to ordering new insights relative to past achievements in the dominating Latin context, particularly as expressed in the writings of Thomas Aquinas. This is an attitude of mind at least as difficult for postmodernity to relate to as it was for modernity (see Poinsot, 1985, pp.

417–420, esp. p. 418 n. 27). The novelty of a discovery taken on its own terms held almost no fascination for the truly medieval writer. That he found in Aquinas the fundamental account of why relations are indifferent to their subjective ground was everything for Poinsot. The originality of his ingenious application of this previously obscure insight as a means of clarifying the foundations of the general notion of sign, something neither Aquinas nor anyone else before him had accomplished, was to Poinsot a mere detail in a vast philosophical synthesis worked out before him, even though it implied a reworking of that entire synthesis from its foundations in human experience as the source and measure of discursive rationality.

Poinsot's *Treatise on Signs* went all but unnoticed until it was discovered by Jacques Maritain in the early 1900s, and it did not receive an independent edition until 1985, when it was published in the context of contemporary semiotic developments. Nonetheless, it is clear that Peirce launched his semiotic theory by resuming the Latin discussion at almost the very point where the work of Poinsot had left it off. This is not entirely surprising in that Poinsot and Peirce substantively shared many of the same Latin sources (Beuchot and Deely, 1995). Certain of Poinsot's ideas also prove to be essential to the successful realization of Peirce's "grand vision" of the action of signs at play throughout the whole of nature.

Given the fundamental role of semiosis in human knowledge and the consequent centrality of semiotics to epistemology, the increased study of Poinsot's semiotics has led to the realization of other philosophical insights in his work that are germane to contemporary interests. For example, Poinsot addresses the very problem Bertrand Russell (1872–1970) tackles with his "Theory of Descriptions" and that Franz Brentano (1838–1917) addresses with his idea for "intentionality," but Poinsot has considerably more success than either and in terms not otherwise found in philosophical literature. Given Poinsot's historical position as a contemporary of René Descartes (1596–1650) and a precursor of Peirce's fundamental notion of semiosis, his work in semiotics serves as the missing link between contemporary semiotics and the early modern development of philosophy, at least in those areas still of contemporary relevance (Deely, 1994).

Over and above the semiotic material in Poinsot's philosophical volumes whence his *Treatise on Signs* derives, there is a mine of further, unexplored material in the huge Latin volumes of his theological writings. Poinsot provides us with one of the most striking examples of how dramatically the development of semiotics sometimes imposes drastic revision of our conventional picture of intellectual history.

[*See also* Augustine of Hippo; Medieval Semiotics; Peirce; Semiosis; *and* Sign.]

BIBLIOGRAPHY

Beuchot, M. "La doctrina tomista clásica sobre el signo: Domingo de Soto, Francisco de Araújo, y Juan de Santo Tomás." *Critica* 12. 36 (1980): 39–60.

Beuchot, M., and J. Deely. "Common Sources for the Semiotic of Charles Peirce and John Poinsot." *The Review of Metaphysics* 48.3 (1995): 539–566.

Deely, J. "Reference to the Non-Existent." *The Thomist* 39.2 (1975): 253–308.

Deely, J. "Semiotic in the Thought of Jacques Maritain." *Recherche sémiotique/Semiotic Inquiry* 6.2 (1986): 1–30.

Deely, J. "The Semiotic of John Poinsot: Yesterday and Tomorrow." *Semiotica* 69.1–2 (1988): 31–128.

Deely, J. "Philosophy and Experience." *American Catholic Philosophical Quarterly* 66.4 (1992): 299–319.

Deely, J. *New Beginnings: Early Modern Philosophy and Postmodern Thought.* Toronto: University of Toronto Press, 1994.

Guagliardo, V. "Hermeneutics: Deconstruction or Semiotics? A Comparison and Contrast of Poinsot and Derrida." In *Symposium on Hermeneutics*, edited by E. F. Bales, pp. 63–74. Conception, Mo.: Conception College, 1992.

Poinsot, J. *Tractatus de Signis [of 1632]: The Semiotic of John Poinsot.* Edited and translated by J. Deely with R. A. Powell. Berkeley: University of California Press, 1985. This volume is also available in an electronic-database version on CD-ROM or floppy disk (Charlottesville: Intelex, 1992).

Raposa, M. "Poinsot on the Semiotics of Awareness." *American Catholic Philosophical Quarterly* 68.3 (1994): 395–408.
—JOHN DEELY

POLYSYSTEM THEORY. A theory that seeks to establish scientifically the cultural laws and conditions governing literary production, polysystem theory is also a theory of culture. Developed by Itamar Even-Zohar (1990) of the Porter Institute for Poetics and Semiotics at Tel Aviv University in response to problems concerning translation, polysystem theory is grounded in Russian formalism, especially in the work of Victor Shklovsky (1893–1984), Jurij Tynjanov (1894–1943), and Roman Jakobson (1896–1982).

Even-Zohar regards such work as instances of what he calls dynamic functionalism or dynamic structuralism, as opposed to the static functionalism of Saussurean structuralism. The theory starts out from the semiotic premise that a culture is less a unified, monolithic entity than a system composed of various internal systems—hence, "polysystem." Literature belongs to and indeed forms one such system, but because of the interrelatedness of the cultural polysystem, literature cannot be considered in isolation from other systems, as they function both synchronically and diachronically within the culture and in relation to the literary system. Polysystem theory is concerned less with investigating what constitutes literature than with how and why certain kinds of literary work come into or go out of favor; it also explores the relationships between various kinds of literary products and between these and other aspects of the polysystem. It is thus as concerned to explore questions of transfer, translation, and cultural or literary interference as it is to identify the nature and extent of the literary system itself.

The individual system can be seen as a replica in miniature of the entire polysystem. (In fact, polysystem theory allows for divergences in structure between system and polysystem, depending on historical factors.) As in conventional Marxist theory, a primary postulate is that this system—which we will assume to be the literary system, though it might indeed be any of a culture's multiple systems—is stratified rather than homogeneous. However, while Marxist theory connects the distinctions between "high" and "low" culture with the social means of production and the consequent division of people into classes defined by their relations to the means of production (as owners, workers, sellers, buyers, and so on), polysystem theory considers culture to have a center dominated by a group that establishes an official ideology. This ideology in turn influences the various systems within the polysystem by affecting their respective centers. Stratification in polysystem theory is thus like that of rings in a cross section of a tree trunk, rather than vertical stratification as seen in conventional Marxist theories of culture.

Systems within the polysystem may be imagined as distributed between the center of the polysystem and its periphery. Those at the center dominate and control the polysystem and thus both provide and govern its official ideologies and practices, while those toward the periphery represent alternative or marginal systems. The whole structure of the poly-system, however, is dynamic in that noncentral sys-tems will tend to attempt to take over the center, whereas more central ones will tend to defend their positions, either by excluding or marginalizing the others or by appropriating them and converting them into agencies for central ideology and practice. Thus, for instance, whereas fifty years ago "green" issues in the political system or issues concerning health foods, organic farming, and so on in the culture's pro-visioning system were largely perceived and treated as the preoccupations of eccentrics or extremists and hence peripheral, today those same issues have moved toward the center. Politically, "green" issues in many countries have become an identifiable threat to conventional (that is, central or official) politics concerned with industry, science, technology, and the exploitation of the land and its resources, so that representatives of conventional politics have often found it expedient to adopt "green" stances (that is, they appropriate a particular ideology already present within the political system). Culturally, the notions of health food and organic farming have been adopted by major food companies as a sort of slogan to help sell their products. The possibility of alterna-tive methods of food production and processing has been adopted by and adapted to the central system of mass production and marketing of foodstuffs.

It is through the struggle of systems within the polysystem to attain and hold the center that the cul-ture survives and evolves: a totally static polysystem is an extinct one. The same struggle is evidenced within individual systems, where different models representing the system are engaged in competition for the center. The model is not identical with an ac-tual object or procedure but is rather an abstract bun-dle of possible features or codes that contributes to a system's repertoire. The repertoire, in turn, allows people in the culture to actualize these models as "real" (that is, tangible) products—in the literary polysystem, as actual texts.

Models come into existence and may be located at the center or toward the periphery of the appro-priate system, depending on their consonance with the models dominant at the center and, beyond that, with the systems dominant at the center of the poly-system itself. They may be generative or nongenera-tive, depending on whether people in the culture adopt them to produce actual texts—if they do, they may in fact add features to or change the config-

uration of the model. Moreover, models or certain of their features may become canonized—that is, deemed as legitimate and worthy of preservation. Noncanonized norms and works are often forgotten, though *canonization* and *noncanonization* are descrip-tions, not valorizations.

Once a model (or its features) enters the system's repertoire and becomes stabilized through canoniza-tion and imitation, it ceases to be a primary type and becomes a secondary one. This is a distinction be-tween innovation and conservation, the latter lead-ing to the establishment of normative features for texts so that deviations are regarded as shocking or as tending to produce inferior texts. Traditional mod-els of genre provide a useful instance of how models become secondary: the model for dramatic tragedy established by Aristotle in the *Poetics*, for instance, became canonized and later secondary in many Eu-ropean cultures, so that it was still possible in the eighteenth century to condemn a tragedy because it did not observe the Aristotelian model, which in-cluded the so-called unities of time, place, and ac-tion.

Canonical status is usually conferred by the group that controls the center of the polysystem and that therefore often determines the relative prestige of possible repertoires. Should that group fail to preserve its government of both polysystem and canonized repertoire, it will be replaced by another group, which will then usually introduce a different repertoire, with other canons. Epigonism, or inferior imitation, oc-curs when the older, displaced repertoire and canon continue to function as workable models for groups at the periphery. Canonized but no longer generative texts may reenter the repertoire at a later point in a culture's history, whereupon they serve rather as models for the generation of new texts.

Models may migrate from one system within the polysystem to another or even from one polysystem to another, depending on geographical contiguity or cultural contact. An interesting case is that of the epic narrative, whose canonized model, represented by Homer's *Iliad* and *Odyssey*, contains such major fea-tures as the narrating of significant events in a cul-ture's history, its formulation as a story in verse, its vast spatial and temporal scope, and minor features such as accounts of the mustering of armies and de-scriptions of weapons. This model proved generative for many centuries, so that epic narrative poems con-tinued to be written in a number of cultures during the Renaissance, often with revisions or renovations of various features that helped the form to regain primary status. Thereafter, however, with a few exceptions, the epic narrative poem became secondary, and by the nineteenth century such works as Victor Hugo's *La légende des siècles* are clearly epigonic imitations. By this time, though, prose had become foregrounded as a feature of epic narrative, enabling the production of prose fiction epics (for instance, Leo Tolstoy's *War and Peace*, Hugo's *Les misérables*). Subsequently, the model was transferred to the theater system (for example, J. W. von Goethe's two-part play, *Faust*), from which it was launched into the music system, especially in opera (Richard Wagner's operatic cycle, *Der Ring des Nibelungen*) and, in the early decades of the twentieth century, into film (D. W. Griffiths's *Intolerance*, for instance, Cecil B. De Mille's various biblical extravaganzas, or, later, George Lucas's *Star Wars* trilogy). The prose model underwent a revival in the twentieth century, not only in national(ist) narratives such as Margaret Mitchell's *Gone with the Wind* (probably better known as a film epic) but also in fantasy narratives, of which the primary instance is J. R. R. Tolkien's *The Lord of the Rings*. The epic narrative model thus provides an illuminating exemplification of the migration of a model within the literary system and the transfer of a model both to other systems within a cultural polysystem and to other polysystems.

[*See also* Cultural Knowledge; Metaphor; Metonymy; Poetics; *and* Russian Formalism.]

BIBLIOGRAPHY

Poetics Today 11.1 (1990). This special issue of Itamar Even-Zohar's work in polysystem studies includes an extensive bibliography.

—DAVID BUCHBINDER

POSTAGE STAMP. The semiotic structure of the postage stamp involves multiple sign functions. Although the stamp is primarily an indexical sign, it is more usually conceived of as iconic. Its indexical role, most clearly fulfilled in the regular definitive stamp, is to identify the country that issued it, indicating whence the mail to which it is attached comes, and to signify that the postage has been paid. As an icon, the stamp represents its country with some national emblem that, in addition to the country's name

(spelled out in all cases except Britain and using the conventional symbols of language), facilitates rapid recognition of the issuing state. The stamp may also employ additional icons that represent more specific events, anniversaries, persons, or places associated with the country of issue. This is the commemorative function of the stamp. But, just as Charles Sanders Peirce indicates in adumbrating his "Ten Classes of Signs" (1955) that some image-based signs are not "mere icons," so the postage stamp, even when presenting an iconic or commemorative image, is still at bottom an indexical sign.

The basic semiotic form of the stamp is created by the meeting in a small format of two qualisigns: an oblong of color (usually surrounded by a white border) and perforation (the latter sign sometimes absent in some of today's self-adhesive stamps). Color as a qualisign takes on an indexical function as soon as it becomes associated with the format of the stamp, since the primary function of a definitive stamp's color is to mark its face value and in some cases the standard postage rates. In French stamps, the standard letter rate is marked by red, and the indexical function of this color means that the price of postage, usually marked clearly on a stamp, can be omitted: the color red itself indicates, for instance, that 2.8 francs have been paid. The protostamp, therefore, uniting two qualisigns to form a rhematic iconic sinsign, is already more than a mere icon; its latent indexical function becomes explicit, however, only with the addition of the issuing country's name.

The protostamp is converted from a rhematic iconic sinsign (the sign of a stamp, second in Peirce's ten classes of sign) to a rhematic indexical sinsign (the sign of a stamp indicating something beyond itself, the third class of signs) by the addition of one or two sets of symbols: the name of the country of origin and the price of the postage. In this way, the icon is converted into a sign indicating a specific place and a specific face value; by the same token, a piece of colored paper becomes an official stamp whose semiotic integrity is guarded closely both by the post offices who issue them and by the Universal Postal Union, which was set up in 1874 to fix the conventions of postal practice as observed internationally. The official nature of the stamp and its function as conveyor of conventional practices and values make it, as a general phenomenon produced in vast quantities and used by millions of people, a legisign ("a law that is a sign") and therefore categorizable as a rhematic iconic legisign (the fifth in Peirce's classes).

Between Peirce's third and fifth classes is the dicent indexical sinsign, that is, "any object of direct experience, in so far as it is a sign, and, as such, affords information concerning its Object" (Peirce, 1955, p. 115). It is necessarily an index since, according to Peirce, it must be affected by its Object. This class of signs perhaps best characterizes the individual postage stamp, as it fulfills both its indexical and iconic (its definitive and commemorative) functions. Here we have a sign actually existing, indicating a place and a value (also a time if the stamp is franked and thus includes a postmark) and articulating some proposition (the dicent dimension). In the stamps classed as commemorative, the proposition can concern a specific event, person, place, organization, or propaganda campaign. Although the basic semiotic constituents of the stamp are those of a rhematic indexical sinsign, in fact very few stamps restrict themselves to such a bare and functional approach. Although there have been successful stamps of this kind (such as the classic sets designed for the Dutch Post Office by Jan van Krimpen in 1946 and by Wim Crouwel in 1976), most countries, even from the stamp's inception 150 years ago, prefer to include an iconic element, whether monarch, head of state, or national symbol. The function of this element is not only to offer a supplementary index to the issuing country but also to represent it in one of its essential political, historical, or cultural aspects.

The classic type was established by Sir Rowland Hill in 1839 with his famous "Penny Black" stamp; this popular appellation is semiotically significant in its stress on the indexical functions of the stamp. The semiotic status of the head of Queen Victoria is, of course, ambiguous in the "Penny Black"; since Britain invented the postage stamp in its modern form, it did not need to inscribe its name on its stamps. The indexical function was taken over by the icon of the royal head. This dual iconic and indexical function of the head results in an exceptionally economical and efficient use of signs. The royal head also serves another indexical function, since it reminds us that the British postal system is within the purview of the monarch. Given the economical way this formula fulfills a number of semiotic functions, it is not surprising that it has been retained without change in British stamps (see figure 1) and copied widely by other countries, albeit with the addition of the issuing country's name.

The semiotic status of the stamp, already ambiguous in its definitive form, with its tendency to shift from rhematic to dicent indexical sinsign, is exacerbated in the commemorative stamp. In the British stamp commemorating the sesquicentenary in 1990 of the issue of the "Penny Black," a commemorative image articulating a proposition is created merely by joining two icons: the heads of Queen Victoria and Queen Elizabeth II. These icons are normally definitive or indexical in their function, but become commemorative by their juxtaposition within the one frame. In the small, standard, definitive format, it is thus possible to propose a fully commemorative message without supplying a single supplementary sign (no dates, no text).

FIGURE 1. *Royal Heads in British Postage Stamps*. Left to right: Victoria: Penny Brown, 1854; Elizabeth II Definitive Stamp, 1967; 150th Anniversary of the Postage Stamp, 1990.

Similarly, a French stamp marking the bicentenary of the French Republic in 1992 creates a commemorative message using purely definitive signs by reproducing within the standard definitive format against a red background the standard devices: *République française 2,50* and *La Poste*. This stamp appears to be the rhematic indexical sinsign of the basic definitive stamp, lacking even the Marianne icon that appears on current French definitive stamps. It is possible to read it as commemorative, however, and discover in it a proposition that converts a rhematic indexical sinsign to a dicent one by noticing the iconization of the symbolic elements through their increase in size and their idiosyncratic typography: this signals that the message is to be read in a more than usual way—that is, both as an indexical sign and as a commemorative sign.

In this way, a sign classified as symbolic in Peircean terminology can become iconic merely by virtue of becoming disproportionately prominent or isolated from its conventional context. So, even within the relatively fixed framework of a given sign class, shifts of status among the constituent semiotic elements can result in a destabilizing or even reformulating of the overall reading of the stamp message. The recent standard first-class letter-rate stamp issued by Switzerland, for example, consists merely of an *A* set against an orange background, surmounted by the word *Helvetia* and the number *80*. For the Swiss post office, *A* means "priority" and, as an indexical sign, it will be read primarily as that. The letter *A* on this stamp, however, owing to its disproportionate size and elegance, also takes on an iconic dimension; this is enhanced by the context created by the word *Helvetia*, since this tall and pointed sign, edged in brilliant white, is like the snowcapped mountains (such as the Matterhorn) that have long been a standard iconic motif on Swiss stamps.

Similar attempts to transform a symbolic sign indicating a geographical phenomenon or region into an icon can be seen in commemorative stamps that, while using the larger format normally associated with special stamps, nonetheless make use of no other pictorial or iconic resources. In a recent French stamp, the symbols constituted by the letters that make up the word *aquitaine* are transformed into an icon, a visual representation of the Aquitaine region in which modern planned urbanization (the pale pink surface of the letters) has developed against a rich agricultural and forest background (the green re-

lief extension of the letters) beneath a blue sky (the background color of the text). The indexical messages of the stamp are in small letters, squeezed in almost imperceptibly at the bottom margin of the stamp.

A tactic employed by typographical stamp designers to promote iconic expressivity at the expense of symbolic legibility is to shift the stamp back toward what Peirce calls an iconic sinsign. In a Dutch typographical stamp of 1969, commemorating the fiftieth anniversary of the International Labour Organization (IAO in Dutch), the acronym *IAO* appears as a concrete poem in which the interpreter seems at first to be confronted merely with a blur of typography and color within the stamp frame, a superimposition of qualisigns that invites the postponement as long as possible of any literal reading of the sign and thus its conversion to an indexical or symbolic entity.

It is important, however, that such further reading is possible and that the iconic sign first proposed should be perceived subsequently as legible in indexical and symbolic terms. If this were not the case, stamps would revert to being "mere icons"—colored bits of paper with no official value—affording, as Peirce would say, no real "information about [their] Object." Some countries, in fact, produce vast quantities of commemorative stamps proposing images that have no real connection with the post offices that issue them. Thus, San Marino, Monaco, Andorra, and small British colonies in the West Indies have built their economies around issuing stamps (usually for schoolboy collectors) that incorporate colorful icons—World War II aircraft, vintage cars, famous sportsmen, pop stars—that have no real connections with their historical, geographical, or cultural realities. A further severing of the authenticating indexical link is the fact that these stamps (often not even printed in the country issuing them) never appear on mail but are purchased unused in packets from stamp shops. No longer in any sense communicators of messages, such images become merely the philatelic equivalent of staged media events.

The use of commemorative icons need not necessarily lead, however, to such indexical vacuity. Indeed, the closer the commemorative icon comes to the object it is deemed to represent, the more authentic the image becomes. The Dutch and the British, for example, have been very successful in taking an image of an object more or less as it is, reducing it in scale, enclosing it in the commemorative format, and merely adding the necessary symbolic message (name or sign of country and face value) to confirm the sign's postal status. In 1968, for example, the stamp commemorating the fiftieth anniversary of the Dutch postal giro adds only the indexical sign *Nederland*, the value *20c*, and the message *Postcheque en Girodienst* to a reduced image of a giro. Similarly, in 1991, a set of British stamps marks the bicentenary of the Ordnance Survey merely by cutting a square from four chronologically successive maps of the same geographical location and adding the queen's head, the face value, and the commemorative message *Ordnance Survey*.

[*See also* Iconicity; Indexicality; *and* Peirce.]

BIBLIOGRAPHY

Peirce, C. S. "Ten Classes of Signs." In *Philosophical Writings of Peirce*, edited by J. Buchler, pp. 115–119. New York: Dover, 1955.

Scott, D. *European Stamp Design: A Semiotic Approach to Designing Messages*. London: Academy Editions, 1995.

—DAVID SCOTT

POSTCOLONIALISM is defined by the interdisciplinary, transnational study of the legacy of European imperialism in Europe's former colonies and in Europe itself. In *Culture and Imperialism* (1993), Edward Said defines imperialism as the theory and practice of a dominant metropolitan center ruling a distant territory, while colonialism is the implanting of settlements on such a territory. The European empires began forming in the fifteenth century and by 1914 covered roughly 85 percent of the earth. After World War II, nations such as India, Algeria, and Vietnam won independence from colonial rule, and as the old empires receded—particularly those of Britain and France—they left behind a global network of exchange and interconnection linking Europe to the decolonized world. For Said, realist fiction of the nineteenth and twentieth centuries cannot be fully understood unless it is read in counterpoint with the histories of colonization, resistance, and native nationalism.

One of the enduring residues of imperialism is the stereotyping and villainization of formerly colonized peoples. Frantz Fanon (1925–1961) assesses the psychological consequences of colonial racism in *Black Skin, White Masks* (1952). Fanon argues that to legitimate its domination of the Third World, Europe de-ployed an imperialist semiotics that made whiteness the signifier of reason, virtue, and beauty and blackness the signifier of irrational intuition and raw sensuality. According to Fanon, racial value coding imposes a sense of inferiority on colonial subjects, alienating them from themselves and sometimes making them want to become white. But since the codes of blackness and whiteness are arbitrary fictions imposed by imperialism, it remains possible to claim a subject position outside them. Often writing in the first person, Fanon affirms that he can escape his colonial alienation by introducing invention into his existence. To assume his freedom, he has only to look for the foundation of an unalienated identity within himself. By breaking with the colonial past, Fanon concludes, he ceases to be bound by the slavery that dehumanized his ancestors. In rejecting a symbolic structure that defines him as the European's inferior, Fanon outlines a theory of the decolonized mind and, in *The Wretched of the Earth* (1961), he theorizes the decolonized nation.

Said's *Orientalism* (1978) testifies to the size and complexity of the Western intellectual apparatus that for centuries justified the West's domination of Asia. Said defines Orientalism as an institutionally supported discourse that does not represent the Orient but rather invents it. The Orient invented by Orientalism is therefore not a place. It is a text without a referent. This phantasm informs the work of countless Western essayists, philosophers, and travel writers and provides an exoticized subject matter for some of the West's most celebrated poets and novelists—including Lord Byron, J. W. von Goethe, Victor Hugo, and Gustave Flaubert.

Until the mid-eighteenth century, Orientalism limited itself to the study of the Bible, Semitic languages, Islam, and China. Research into the Sanskrit and Avestan languages exposed middle Asia to Orientalist inquiry at the end of the century. By the mid-nineteenth century, a secularized Orientalism scanned virtually the whole of the Orient. Said argues that this secular Orientalism is a reconstructed religion that makes man, not God, into the creator of new worlds and aims not to redeem humanity from sin but to save Asia from itself. Paradoxically, Orientalism constructs the Orient both as a dead relic of antiquity and as a dynamic participant in contemporary history.

Orientalism operates as a mode of knowledge that opens up avenues for the deployment of imperial power. Known today as "Area Studies" or "Oriental Studies," it is an academic inquiry pursued in Western universities. It is also a rule-bound system of writing that at once produces and presupposes the distinction between the Orient and the Occident. And it is a government-sponsored institution for giving the West authority over Asia. Said's study focuses on material dealing with the Islamic Orient.

Homi Bhabha exposes the ironic, self-defeating structure of colonial discourse in "Of Mimicry and Man" (1994, pp. 85–92. He notes that when English administrators dreamed of converting India to Christianity at the end of the eighteenth century, they did not want their colonial subjects to become too Christian or too English. Their discourse foresaw a colonized mimic who would be almost the same as the colonist but not quite. However, since India's mimicry of the English blurred the boundary between ruler and ruled, the dream of anglicizing Indians threatened to indianize Englishness—a reversal the colonists found intolerable. Mimicry is therefore a state of ambivalence that undermines the claims of imperial discourse and makes it impossible to isolate the racialized essence of either the colonized or the colonizer.

In *The Location of Culture* (1994, pp. 19–39), Bhabha cites repetition as a mode of resistance to today's neocolonialism, particularly the recolonization of migrants within the contemporary Western metropolis. For Bhabha, the human subject is not grounded in a fixed identity but rather is a discursive effect generated in the act of enunciation. When migrants, refugees, and the decolonized take up positions in Western discourse, they divide it from itself by repeating it and clear space within it for new, hybrid subjectivities. The hybrid postcolonial subject negotiates the interstices of Western discursive systems, operating in between the dichotomies of colonizer and colonized, self and other, East and West. Once a mode of Western discourse is altered through repetition, moreover, it loses its "westness" and exposes itself to difference. Iteration is therefore a way of translating between cultures. It opens the possibility of an international culture of hybridity generated through discursive activity.

Gayatri Chakravorty Spivak advocates deconstruction as a strategy for negotiating the postcolonial condition. In *Outside in the Teaching Machine* (1993), Spivak defines deconstruction as the act of critiquing a conceptual structure that one cannot not inhabit. Postcoloniality is such a structure, for there is no way to get beyond its global reach. The deconstruction of the postcolonial condition follows a pattern of catachresis, which Spivak defines as a concept or metaphor without an adequate referent (for Spivak, all concepts are also metaphors). Catachresis cuts words from their proper contexts and grafts them into situations to which they do not usually refer. When deployed in postcolonial criticism, catachresis maps the exchange of concepts between the Western metropolis and its former territories. Concepts such as nationhood, constitutionality, and democracy, for example, have a catachrestic place in the decolonized world because they were developed in the social formations of western Europe.

Since it shuttles between Europe and decolonized space, postcolonial deconstruction involves an incessant recoding of fields of value. Drawing on Karl Marx's analysis of the value form in chapter 1 of *Capital* (1867), Spivak defines value as the possibility of mediation. Value coding marks commodities, concepts, and even emotions with a minimal trace of difference that distinguishes them from one another and allows them to be exchanged one for another. By making exchange possible, value coding provides a ground for communication, sociality, and a postcolonial mode of political agency.

For Spivak, the deconstruction of postcoloniality bears not only on the status of migrants in the Western metropolis but also on conditions in the decolonized world, especially among the rural poor. She notes that decolonized nations include disenfranchised, subaltern populations that were exploited by the old colonialism yet do not share in the energy of decolonization. Spivak is concerned particularly with the "gendered subaltern"—for example, the woman forced, through a system of bonded labor, into prostitution. The subaltern woman actually lives the logic of catachresis because the concept of national liberation does not refer adequately to her but rather leaves her suspended between colonization and decolonization. The international division of labor also exploits the gendered subaltern by putting her (more often than men) to work for multinational and neocolonial capitalism.

[*See also* Cultural Difference; Deconstruction; De Lauretis; Feminism and Feminist Theories; Postmodernism; *and* Poststructuralism.]

BIBLIOGRAPHY

Ashcroft, B., and G. Griffins, eds. *The Post-Colonial Studies Reader*. London and New York: Routledge, 1995.

Barker, F., P. Hulme, and M. Iversen, eds. *Colonial Discourse, Postcolonial Theory*. Manchester and New York: Manchester University Press and St. Martin's Press, 1994.

Bhabha, H. K. *The Location of Culture*. London and New York: Routledge, 1994.

Bhabha, H. K., ed. *Nation and Narration*. London and New York: Routledge, 1990.

Fanon, F. *Black Skin, White Masks* (1952). Translated by C. L. Markmann. New York: Grove Press, 1967.

Fanon, F. *The Wretched of the Earth*. Translated by C. Farrington. New York: Grove Press, 1968.

Gates, H. L., ed. *"Race," Writing, and Difference*. Chicago: University of Chicago Press, 1986.

Goldberg, D. T., ed. *Anatomy of Racism*. Minneapolis and London: University of Minnesota Press, 1990.

Guha, R., and G. C. Spivak, eds. *Selected Subaltern Studies*. New York: Oxford University Press, 1988.

Said E. *Orientalism*. New York: Pantheon Books, 1978.

Said, E. *Culture and Imperialism*. New York: Knopf, 1993.

Spivak, G. C. *Outside in the Teaching Machine*. New York: Routledge, 1993.

—CHRISTOPHER BRACKEN

POSTMODERNISM. The much-debated attempt within the contemporary West to think the history of the present, postmodernism has its roots in American literary criticism of the 1950s, notably in the essays of Charles Olson, where the term first surfaced. In the 1960s and 1970s, critics such as Ihab Hassan, Susan Sontag, Leslie Fiedler, and Robert Venturi opened discussions of new trends in film, photography, the visual arts, music, architecture, and popular culture that directly or indirectly came to bear on questions of postmodernism. Today, postmodernist theory measures innovations in such areas as representation, technology, global economics, and the legitimation of knowledge.

Perhaps the most prominent theorist of the sign in postmodernity is Jean Baudrillard. In "The Precession of Simulacra" (1983), Baudrillard argues that no matter where signs are deployed today—whether in speech or writing, television or ethnology—they do not refer to the real. The sign is neither a substitute for a referent nor an imitation of one. Rather, the sign precedes its referent: representation is logically and temporally prior to reality. The precession of the sign before the real ushers the West into a state that Baudrillard calls the hyperreal. The citizens of hyperreality inhabit a simulated world composed of models without origin. Although capitalism otherwise maintains a strict law of equivalence between commodities, it works to undo the equivalence of sign and real because it cannot function outside of reality. Power in today's industrialized societies is a simulation that reinjects referentiality into everyday life to convince people of the gravity of the economy and the necessity of work. Reestablishing the difference between sign and real is the task of fantasy worlds such as Disneyland: they are simulacra that mask the fact that the everyday world is itself a simulacrum.

Baudrillard's "hyperreal" finds an echo in Fredric K. Jameson's argument (1991) that the definitive signifying practice of postmodernism is pastiche. Like parody, pastiche is the imitation of one style by another. Yet pastiche is a neutral form lacking parody's satiric irony. Pastiche thrives in a postmodern culture in which the idosyncracies of personal style have faded along with the individual human subject. Pastiche finds expression in nostalgia films such as *American Graffiti* (1973) and in the eclecticism of postmodern buildings, which randomly cite older architectural styles.

Besides pastiche, the key markers of postmodernism for Jameson are a depthlessness that situates meaning on the surfaces of texts, a weakened sense of historical time, a conflation of high and mass culture, a commodification of art, and a self-referentiality that makes each detail of the present into a symptom of all of postmodernity. Yet postmodernism's moment of truth is a new form of space: the decentered network of a global, neocolonial economy grounded in technological advances and dominated by the United States. To define this transnational space, Jameson distinguishes today's multinational capitalism first from the market capitalism that lasted from the 1840s to the 1890s and second from the monopoly or imperialist capitalism that ended in the 1940s. Postmodernism is the dominant cultural form of the multinational phase of capitalism.

Jameson also associates postmodernism with a euphoric loss of emotion: a "waning of affect" that he compares to schizophrenia. In contrast, Arthur Kroker, Marilouise Kroker, and David Cook (1989), find a heightening of emotion in postmodernism. For them, the postmodern is a state of panic that wavers between ecstasy and dread. The new mood follows the disappearance of external measures of human conduct and the dissolution of the internal foundations of human identity. Jürgen Habermas insists, however, that there is nothing postmodern in the panic about the norms that ground Western culture, for a sense of crisis has always defined the modern age. Since its origins in the European Enlightenment, modernity has anxiously sought to forge its standards of normativity out of itself, through the use of reason alone. Reason is modernity's capacity for self-grounding. Modernity's unfinished project of rational self-legitimation constantly produces claims that the present age has broken conclusively with the past. Habermas elaborates this analysis in "Modernity versus Postmodernity" (1980) and *The Philosophical Discourse of Modernity* (1987).

For Habermas, Georg Wilhelm Friedrich Hegel (1770–1831) was the first Western philosopher to gain a clear concept of modernity. As modernity sought to legitimate itself on its own terms, without reference to past norms, so does Hegel's philosophical system posit a self-unifying subjectivity that produces itself out of its own substance. Hegelianism put the rational pursuit of subjective freedom at the center of the modern age. After Hegel, Western philosophy split into three branches: Marxism, neoconservatism, and Nietzscheanism which marks the entry into postmodernism. Friedrich Nietzsche's exposure of subject-centered reason as sheer will to power generated two further critiques of rational subjectivity: Martin Heidegger's destruction of Western philosophy and Georges Bataille's theory of sovereignty.

Yet Habermas recalls that the modern age contains its own critique of the philosophy of the subject. This self-critique is a theory of communicative action based on an intersubjective paradigm of mutual understanding. When people engage in communicative action, their goal is not to agree on a course of action determined by preexisting standards; rather, as each participant represents states of affairs, establishes interpersonal relationships, and expresses private experiences, he or she comes to recognize that other perspectives have legitimate claims to validity. Eventually, the noncoercively unifying and consensus-building power of discourse leads the participants to overcome their personal biases and arrive at a rationally motivated agreement. Communicative action occurs within the context of a "life world" that

supplies participants with fallible background knowledge, patterns of social relations, and norms deriving from shared socialization. The theory of communicative action transfers the self-grounding of modernity from subject-centered reason to a communicative reason working between speaking subjects.

Despite Habermas's argument for philosophical continuity, Jean-François Lyotard sees the postmodern age as marked by a renewed crisis in the status of Western knowledge. Lyotard (1979) argues that postwar innovations in the sciences and technologies of language—notably linguistics, cybernetics, algebra, and computing—have made knowledge into an informational commodity. Consequently, the worldwide expansion of capitalism has become a struggle for control of information stored in computer databases.

Computerization has, moreover, transformed the standards that decide what counts as knowledge in the arts and sciences. The defining feature of postmodernity is that the "grand narratives" of enlightenment and emancipation, which validated Western knowledge since the eighteenth century, have lost their credibility. The narrative of enlightenment affirmed that knowledge was its own justification and gave it the task of deciding what society and the state should be. The narrative of emancipation validated forms of knowledge that served humanity's struggle for self-determination. The decline of grand narratives signals a general erosion of narrative knowledge amassed in stories, myths, and legends.

Borrowing from Ludwig Wittgenstein, Lyotard describes both narrative and nonnarrative knowledges as "language games," not because they are frivolous but because they are bound by rules that players agree to follow. (Otherwise there is no game.) Language games are also agonistic: to speak is to fight. Examples of language moves include prescriptive utterances, such as rules and recommendations, and denotative utterances, such as truth claims. In postmodernity, knowledge springs from the linguistic and communicative practices of researchers engaged in language games that generate "little narratives." Knowledge is considered valid when it obeys the rules of its game. Innovations occur and are valid when a game's players agree to follow new rules capable of generating new statements. In the postmodern condition, then, what decides whether knowledge is legitimate or not are the prescriptive utterances that govern the formation of valid denotations.

Each branch of learning is a distinct language game. Hence, no system of rules is binding for all games. Since it is impossible to transcribe the diversity of games into a single master game, Lyotard rejects Habermas's argument that speaking subjects can reach a universal consensus through discussion. The scientific game of "paralogy"—the search for contradictions—exemplifies the irreducible heterogeneity of the postmodern condition. Since paralogy foregrounds the inconsistencies in existing scientific knowledges, it leads not to agreement but to dissent. Lyotard advances paralogy as a model for an agonistic and antitotalitarian society that nurtures differences instead of imposing consensus.

[*See also* Baudrillard; Deconstruction; Habermas; Jameson; Lyotard; Play; *and* Postcolonialism.]

BIBLIOGRAPHY

Baudrillard, J. "The Precession of Simulacra," translated by P. Foss and P. Patton. *Art and Text* 11 (1983): 3–47.

Bertens, H. *The Idea of Postmodernism: A History*. London and New York: Routledge, 1995.

Bhabha, H. "How Newness Enters the World: Postmodern Space, Postcolonial Times, and the Trials of Cultural Transition." In his *The Location of Culture*, pp. 212–235. London and New York: Routledge, 1994.

Butler, J. "Contingent Foundations: Feminism and the Question of 'Postmodernism.'" In *Feminists Theorize the Political*, edited by J. Butler and J. W. Scott, pp. 3–21. London and New York: Routledge, 1992.

Gottdiener, M. *Postmodern Semiotics: Material Culture and the Forms of Postmodern Life*. Oxford: Blackwell, 1995.

Habermas, J. *The Philosophical Discourse of Modernity*. Translated by F. G. Lawrence. Cambridge, Mass.: MIT Press, 1987.

Habermas, J. "Modernity versus Postmodernity." *New German Critique* 22 (1980): 3–14.

Huyssen, A. "Mapping the Postmodern." *New German Critique* 33 (1984): 5–52.

Jameson, F. K. *Postmodernism, or the Cultural Logic of Late Capitalism*. Durham, N.C.: Duke University Press, 1991.

Jencks, C. *What Is Postmodernism?* New York: St. Martin's Press, 1986.

Kroker, A., and D. Cook. *The Postmodern Scene: Excremental Culture and Hyper-Aesthetics*. New York: St. Martin's Press, 1986.

Kroker, A., M. L. Kroker, and D. Cook. *Panic Encyclopedia*. Montreal: New World Perspective, 1989.

Lyotard, J. F. *The Postmodern Condition: A Report on Knowledge* (1979). Translated by G. Bennington and B. Massumi. Minneapolis: University of Minnesota Press, 1984.

—CHRISTOPHER BRACKEN

POSTSEMIOTICS. A number of theorists have extensively scrutinized modern semiotics. This endeavor can be labeled "postsemiotics," following John Stewart (see below) or "critical semiotics," following loosely the "critical linguistics" undertaking that Robert Hodge and Gunther Kress outlined in *Language as Ideology* (1979). Their critique of linguistics involves granting priority to ideology in a blend of history and linguistics that emphasizes the social components of language. Hodge and Kress suggest in a later work that semiotics is "more comprehensible for being offered as provisional, a stage in a continuing debate, a continuing struggle for clarification" (1988, p. 36). Several examples of this undertaking can be identified.

John Stewart's *Language As Articulate Contact* (1995) is a detailed version of a history of semiotics that he pits against an "improved" future discipline identified as postsemiotics, a "postmodern critique of representationalism" undertaken to "develop a postsemiotic account of the nature of language as dialogic." Instead of accepting a falsely totalized conception of semiotics, Stewart merely highlights provisionally characteristic "features."

Semiotics is doomed, in Stewart's opinion, by its symbol model basis, which assumes language is "fundamentally a system of signs or symbols." As a result, semiotic explanations of language as a social phenomenon are hampered by "serious problems of plausibility, coherence, and applicability." For Stewart, the "theoretical commitments" of semiotics render it incapable of explaining how language works as a communicative medium. The most prominent stumbling block is a two-world orientation that posits "a fundamental distinction between two realms or worlds, the world of the sign and the signifier, symbol and symbolized, name and named, word and thought" (1995, pp. 6–7). This is not a "coherent" position, Stewart insists, because the two-world perspective runs contrary, from a historical standpoint, to "*world* as the *single* coherent sphere that humans inhabit" (p. 105). This model of communication is not demonstrable and it cannot support the existence of one world consisting of concepts and another of "reality."

Moreover, Stewart asserts that only samples of actual conversations practically illustrate language usage in a single world. Stewart touts a one-world view of interpersonal "conversation" consisting of "two-person dialogue in real time." This is "articulate contact" in which "naturally-occurring interchanges" reveal "language as it is lived." Focusing on this "living language" incorporates the dialogic instabilities that structural/systemic accounts deny in order to create stable subjects for analysis. "Little purpose is served by focusing one's explicative energy exclusively on reducing language to its atoms," he suggests. "The anchor for understanding languaging should be the contact event as its participants live it" (p. 125).

In a vein similar to Stewart's postsemiotics, Hodge and Kress's *Social Semiotics* (1988) expands the range of semiotics to "texts and contexts, agents and objects of meaning, social structures and forces, and their complex interrelationships" (p. viii). They take into account "all sign systems" while depicting semiotics as "a general theory of the social processes through which meaning is constituted and has its effects."

Hodge and Kress orient semiotics away from system and toward dynamic social interaction. "A practical semiotics should have some account of the relationship of semiosis and 'reality,' that is, the material world that provides the objects of semiosis and semiotic activity," they observe. As long as semiotics does not account for this interaction, "it can have no relevance to the world of practical affairs with its confident assumptions about 'reality', and it cannot account for the role of semiotic systems in that world" (1988, p. 23). One way to incorporate this social effect is to consider instances of semiosis over time. "A diachronic account of a tradition," they note, "frees the reader from the oppressive sense that it is monolithic, unchanging, without inconsistencies" (p. 36).

Hodge and Kress challenge the essentialistic view of semiosis that denies ideology. In this respect, they emphasize the ubiquity of power relations in social signification and assert, as a consequence, that semiosis is necessarily ideological. For example, they maintain that semiotic structures operate according to a "logonomic system" consisting of "a set of rules prescribing the conditions for production and reception of meanings" (p. 4). Such a system is political, they contend, structured by way of "ideological complexes" that serve the interests of power. This maintenance is established through characteristic structures of domination that partially determine the agency of individual sign users. Within this conception, semiotics is affected by both "production

regimes (rules constraining production)" and "reception regimes (rules constraining reception)." Ultimately, this emphasis on semiosic politics offers substantial revisionary potential for a modern semiotics that prefers to deemphasize extrastructural components of sign systems. Like Stewart in this respect, Hodge and Kress try to avoid the emphasis on system and product characteristic of mainstream semiotics and focus, instead, on "speakers and writers or other participants in semiotic activity as connected and inter*acting* in a variety of ways in concrete social contexts" (p. 1).

Jean-François Lyotard (1974) had issued a similar call, for a semiotics that displaces *product* with semiosic *production*. To Lyotard, semiotics has adopted a solely "informational" paradigm in which a "thing is posited as a message, that is, as a medium enriched with a sequence of coded elements" (p. 43). Furthermore, from this standpoint, the "addressee, himself in possession of this code, is capable, through decoding the message, of retrieving the *information* that the sender meant him to receive." The investigators of this semiotics function as spiritless "men of the concept" (p. 211) on a pedestrian "business trip," or more heroically, engage in a "voyage of conquest." Moreover, Lyotard criticizes those who, in the thrall of remaking semiotics with a social dynamics emphasis (like Hodge and Kress), end up myopically insisting that "there is no sign or thought of the sign which is not about power and for power" (1974, p. 45). Lyotard laments the "structuralist enthusiasm" in semiotics which leads to "the simple reduction of sensuous forms to conceptual structures, as if understanding were the unique faculty qualified to approach forms" (1988; p. 10). At the same time, Lyotard nevertheless acknowledges the benefits of aligning semiotics with real-life correlatives consistent with Stewart as well as Hodge and Kress in this regard. Accordingly, for Lyotard, the sterile, systemic rendition of semiosis presumes falsely that "signification itself is constituted by signs alone, that it carries on endlessly, that we never have anything but references, that signification is always deferred, meaning is never present in flesh and blood" (1974, p. 43).

This neat conception of semiosis neglects the considerable flux and uncertainty within signification. The hermetic—and systemically ruled—view of semiotics leads to a celebration of "the zero of bookkeeping" (1974, p. 164), Lyotard charges. "To continue to remain in semiotic thought is to languish in religious melancholy and subordinate every intense emotion to a lack and every force to a finitude" (p. 49). Furthermore, he argues, the dichotomous sign within semiotics is "hollowed out into a two-faced thing, meaningful/meaningless, intelligible/sensible, manifest/hidden, in front/behind" (p. 50).

Lyotard's alternative (like Stewart's) envisions signs as "living," generative entities moving vitally and assuming figurative embodiments unhampered by an "intelligent" ground. The semiosis that this generates is patterned after the psychological effect of vertigo. In order to reach this condition, "we quit signs," Lyotard declares; "we enter the extra-semiotic order of tensors" (1974, p. 50), a field that offers "the chance of new intensities" (p. 210). For semiotics to transcend its inadequacies without resorting to postsemiotics, Lyotard allows that its existing conceptual framework is sufficient. In other words, "another kind of sign" (p. 50) is not needed to effect this theorization. Signs do not have to stand as "only terms, stages set in relation and made explicit in a trail of conquest." "They *can also* be, indissociably, singular and vain intensities in exodus." Lyotard's vision of the future potential for semiotics is motivated by the cultivation of these intensities. "To understand, to be intelligent, is not our overriding passion," he says (p. 51). "We hope rather to be set in motion."

Floyd Merrell's "trilogy of sorts" (1991, 1995, and 1996) proposes a related remodeling of semiotics that rigorously assesses its contested issues. For instance, he suggests that the problematic flux of semiosis provides "a fruitful vision of ongoing sign generativity" (1995, p. 44). Like Lyotard, Merrell hazards the possible reconfiguration of semiotics as "a new form of order" that is nevertheless "not schematic, determinable, or rigid" (1995; p. 22). Merrell aligns his project with systemically loose models of "dynamic interconnectedness and nonlinearity." These models would, effectively, reflect semiosis as a "process, not static product" (1995, p. 180). Merrell situates generativity as an energizing force behind sign use and views signification as similar to life processes in general. For Merrell, structural arrangements unguided by what Lyotard calls "intelligence" (1974) would, as a result, be patterned after what Félix Guattari calls "chaosmosis" (1995). "Semiosis is ordered," Merrell maintains, "according to its own style of ordering" (1995, p. 221). From this perspective, Merrell offers comfort for a semiotics willing to entertain the belief

that "mere happenstance generation may be the dominant fact in the process of evolution" (p. 220).

Gilles Deleuze and Félix Guattari (1987) propose a contiguous model of an *organic* semiotics based on structure *per se*, but one that is "rhizomorphous." In other words, they imagine a sign network that possesses systemicity only in the most undetermined sense. This reflects their insistence that the only way to produce a nuanced, responsive rendition of semiosis is to actually engage in a semiosic experience in the process. This paradigm (what they call a "multiple") would replicate the fluid web of interactions constituting signification in an indeterminate and generative fashion by building upon already existing semiotic concepts. "The multiple *must be made*," they argue, and "not always by adding a higher dimension, but rather in the simplest of ways, by dint of sobriety, with the number of dimensions one already has available" (p. 6).

The rhizome is ideal for this venture as an entity on which "any point . . . can be connected to anything, and must be" (p. 7). While "possessing no points or positions" (p. 8) itself, it allows for the highest degree of openness since "it always has multiple entryways" (p. 12). In effect, the rhizome is an "acentered, nonhierarchical, nonsignifying system without a General and without an organizing memory or central automaton, defined solely by a circulation of states" (p. 21).

This unstructured structure allows for a new theorization of semiotics arguably resistant to reduction. A rhizomorphous semiotics, as envisioned by Deleuze and Guattari, might thus follow James Bunn's "polydimensional semiotics" (cited in Merrell, 1995, p. 108), which, in the end, may also be the collective agenda of critical semiotics. M. A. K. Halliday contended in 1985 that "dynamic models of semiotic systems are not yet very well developed" (p. 10), but clearly critical semiotics is working to rectify this shortcoming.

[*See also* Dialogism; Halliday; Lyotard; Play; Postmodernism; Poststructuralism; Semiosis; *and* Sign.]

BIBLIOGRAPHY

Bunn, J. H. *The Dimensionality of Signs, Tools, and Models: An Introduction.* Bloomington: Indiana University Press, 1981.
Deleuze, G., and F. Guattari. *A Thousand Plateaus.* Translated by Massumi. Minneapolis: University of Minnesota Press, 1987.

Guattari, F. *Chaosmosis: An Ethico-Aesthetic Paradigm*. Translated by P. Bains and J. Pefanis. Bloomington: Indiana University Press, 1995.

Halliday, M. A. K. "Systemic Background." In *Systemic Perspectives on Discourse*, vol. 1, *Selected Theoretical Papers from the Ninth International Systemic Workshop*, edited by J. D. Benson and W. S. Greaves, pp. 1–15. Norwood, N.J.: Ablex Publishing Corp., 1985.

Hodge, R., and G. Kress. *Language as Ideology* (1979). 2d ed. London: Routledge, 1993.

Hodge, R., and G. Kress. *Social Semiotics*. Ithaca, N.Y.: Cornell University Press, 1988.

Lyotard, J.-F. *Libidinal Economy* (1974). Translated by I. H. Grant. Bloomington: Indiana University Press, 1993.

Lyotard, J.-F. *Peregrinations: Law, Form, Event*. New York: Columbia University Press, 1988.

Merrell, F. *Signs Becoming Signs: Our Perfusive, Pervasive Universe*. Bloomington: Indiana University Press, 1991.

Merrell, F. *Semiosis in the Postmodern Age*. West Lafayette, Ind.: Purdue University Press, 1995.

Merrell, F. *Signs Grow: Semiosis and Life Processes*. Toronto: University of Toronto Press, 1996.

Stewart, J. *Language as Articulate Contact: Toward A Post-Semiotic Philosophy of Communication* Albany: State University Press of New York, 1995.

—SCOTT SIMPKINS

POSTSTRUCTURALISM. Some of the conceptual, practical, and ideological problems raised by structuralism (conceived of as the description of closed and self-regulating systems) have provoked a set of reactive movements known collectively as poststructuralism. Recent developments have proposed more dynamic models of the notion of structure and have renewed interest in the stratified nature of systems of relations, which is brought into clearer focus by the dialectical nature of the contextualizing relations. Stratification is central to the process-oriented view of semiosis that Ferdinand de Saussure and Louis Hjelmslev began to propose, though these scholars are more traditionally accredited with a static and purely formal view of the sign. Recent developments of a more dynamical structuralism do not encourage this view (Petitot-Cocorda, 1985; Lemke, 1991; Halliday, 1992).

Michael Halliday (1992) has proposed a dynamic model of stratification that arises from asking what the relationship is between the meaning-making potential of the code of language and what lies "outside" of it. In Hjelmslevian terms, the content plane appears as an "interface"—one "face" of which, Halliday notes, being the phenomena of experience that the content plane construes. But, Halliday goes on, our "experience is at once both material and conscious; and it is the contradiction *between* the material and the conscious that gives these phenomena their semogenic potential. The other 'face' is the meaning—the signified, if you prefer the terminology of the sign" (1992, p. 22). The process does not end here, however, for the notion of stratification means that the content plane connects with the expression plane of the phonology (expression form) and its phonetics (expression substance). Halliday remarks, "there has to be a second interface, a transformation back into the material, or (again, rather) into the phenomenal—this time in its manifestation in the meaning subject's own body: as physiological processes of articulation or gesture" (1992, p. 22). Halliday designates this the "phonetic/kinetic interface." There is no meaning without expression. Halliday's point is that the "interface" of expression substance, just like that of the content substance, embodies "both the material and the conscious modes of being." The central concept here is the stratified nature of the whole system of relations that is involved.

How is this possible? Halliday refers to Jay Lemke's principle of "metaredundancy" (1991). This is a formalism for representing the hierarchical (stratified) nature of contextualizing relations. In a minimal semiotic system, the principle of metaredundancy may be expressed as follows: contents p, q, r are "realized" by expressions a, b, c. There is a redundancy relation between the two levels (strata) in that, given p, we can predict, say, sound a; and given a, we can predict meaning p. Because the relationship is a symmetrical one, we can say either a "realizes" p or p "is realized by" a or both. More simply, the two-way nature of this relation is rendered by the expression "p redounds with a." In a slightly more complex case, comprising not two but three strata, the basic point is the same. Thus, expressions a, b, c redound with contents p, q, r, while contents p, q, r redound with contextual relations x, y, z. Now, there is no simple linear correlation between terms on each of the different levels. In other words, we do not say, for instance, that x is realized by p, which is, in turn, realized by a. Instead, there is a metaredundancy relation such that x, y, z redounds not with p, q, r but with the redundancy of p, q, r with a, b, c. Thus,

$$x, y, z \text{ REDOUNDS WITH}$$
$$(p, q, r \text{ REDOUNDS WITH } a, b, c).$$

The relations between levels are hierarchical and symmetrical at all levels. There is no causality here: we do not say that x is caused by p and p is caused by a. The redundancy relation means that x construes and is construed by the redundancy of p with a.

The symmetrical nature of these relations means we can look at them from the point of view of either the content substance or the expression substance. The above description construes these relations from the perspective of the content plane. The reverse point of view, as seen from the expression plane, may be formulated as follows:

a, b, c REDOUNDS WITH
(p, q, r REDOUNDS WITH x, y, z)

Semiotically speaking, both points of view apply simultaneously; better, they are two different perspectives on the same phenomenon.

The relations between strata are permeable. The units and relations on any given stratum are not fixed: their values change through their exchanges with those on other strata. This is the essence of the metaredundancy relation, which is a contextualizing one. If classical structuralism remains hampered by closed and self-regulating system models, dynamic structuralism operates with open and dynamic system models. The system both maintains itself and changes though its transaction with its environment(s). In other words, structures are metastable.

The intersection of the phenomenal and the conscious, which Halliday speaks of, implies a "catastrophic" impact of the one on the other. In this way, consciousness construes order in the phenomena of experience. This can occur only in and through a topologically organized system of categorical distinctions that model such phenomena.

Halliday's argument recognizes that an adequate structuralist analysis must be a dynamic one. Metaredundancy formalism is not specific to the code of language. Rather, it is a way of talking about the structure and the transformations of any dynamic, open system of relations, including both biological and social semiotic systems. Structuralism insists on the patterned nature of relationships. Recent developments are now attempting to model the dynamics of structures through the central concept of contextualization: how relationships are made meaningful through their implicit and increasingly higher-order connections with their contexts. The recursive nature of metaredundancy formalism expresses this concern by focusing on the regression of contexts: not just patterns, but patterns of patterns, and so on, which are the second- and increasingly higher-order relations that express what the context of something is. Each level in the contextualization hierarchy is defined by the dialectical duality of contextualization's syntagmatic and the paradigmatic dimensions. In other words, these two dimensions operate at all levels.

The recursive and stratified nature of the levels of relations involved is not something that refers uniquely to the internal structural organization of the linguistic code, or any other semiotic code. This brings us back to the relationship between this and what lies "outside" it. The linguistic system is a multistratal and self-organizing system on account of its exchanges with its environment(s). The stratified nature of the internal organization of the code ensures that it is meaning making. The internal stratification of the code is the very basis for the system's potential to construe what lies outside it in meaningful ways—that is, as phenomena of experience. Hjelmslev's constant invocation of criteria of immanence in his *Prolegomena* (1969) embodies this understanding. The "interface" between what is internal to the code and what lies "outside" it is a permeable one, in terms of both content substance and expression substance. Matter, energy, and information exchanges occur at both interfaces. In this way, differences that are in some way criterial "redound with" meaning-making (value-producing) differences that are intrinsic to the internal organization. Other differences will be noncriterial and therefore nondistinctive. There is, however, always the potential for slippage along both interfaces. In this way, material distinctions that did not previously make a difference may enter into the hierarchy of contextualizing relations.

The further implication of this is that the topological categorizations that are internal to the meaning-making potential of the code and the phenomena of experience that this construes categorically do not, in the final analysis, constitute two separate realities or ontological realms. "Reality" is, to be sure, ontologically stratified, but it is not split into two components. The recursive nature of the contextualizing relations allows "inside" and "outside" to be incorporated in a single system of relations; it is this system that is ontologically stratified. In this way, the phenomena of our experience emerge out of what can, in the final analysis, only be called "nonmeaning." These phenomena emerge by virtue of the recursive nature of the contextualizing relations involved.

The above suggests new directions for structuralism that might free it from the context-free reductionisms that Anthony Wilden (1980) has identified as a major problem in Claude Lévi-Strauss's myth analysis. Wilden identifies the "error" of this type of analysis as both epistemological and methodological: myth is treated as if it is like the "context-free system of oppositions" whereby Nikolaj Trubetzkoy and Roman Jakobson characterize the phonological system. Wilden is right to point to the error of "treating myth as if it were a language representable by a context-free grammar, or treating mythemes as 'information' in the technical sense of the quantitative and closed systems of information transmission studied by Shannon and Weaver" (1980, p. 9). Such an error arises out of assumptions concerning the scientificity of the binary character of phonemic oppositions, and these assumptions are then coupled with others concerning the closed nature of these relations. In many ways, this reflects the concerns of classical structuralism, models of which were coarticulated with those of first-generation cybernetics, homeostatic models of self-regulating systems, and the formalisms of the mathematical theory of information.

The ontological stratification of the entire system of relations suggests another story. Recent developments have proposed more dynamical and contextual models that show that structuralism need not be imprisoned by closed, self-regulating system models. For instance, the phonological-phonetic interface can be seen as anything but context free and closed. For example, Jacques Derrida has drawn attention to the "spatial metaphor" that informs the structuralist enterprise and that occurs to the detriment of the "play" that is going on. Derrida appeals to the process, to use Hjelmslev's term, of meaning making, with its indeterminacies, lacunae, variations, and ambiguities that are never reducible to a single, determinate, or fixed "meaning" because of the dynamic interplay of the two dimensions of contextualization.

Much of structuralism, especially in its "classical" phase, was implicated in a largely unconscious social project of regimentation and control of social phenomena. This has had a number of consequences. First, structuralists have invested in a totalizing and objectivist belief in the possibility of culture-free universals. They have in turn reified these alleged universals in their analytical and theoretical practices as universal structures of "mind." Wilden (1980) has given voice to a profound and insightful critique of many of the ethnocentric and phallocentric impulses that inform the structuralist enterprise. Second, structuralists all too often have failed to account for the relationship between their own theoretical practices and the phenomena they investigate. Third, structuralists have understood rightly the patterned and relational character of structures. Yet the predominance of closed-system models has vitiated any possibility of moving much beyond second-order relations. Thus, structuralists have failed to understand the contextualizing, nontotalizing dynamics involved, which are partial hierarchies that are always constructed through culturally specific practices. Overall, there has been a tendency to impose order too early, which has resulted in an emphasis on homogeneity and integrable, relatively closed systems. Much of this theoretical impetus derives from a decidedly restricted and partial reading of Saussure. The result has been the ontologization of Saussure's explicitly methodological distinction between *langue* and *parole*. In actual fact, as Umberto Eco's study (1983) demonstrates, much of structuralism "oscillates" between views of structure as "ontology" and as "model."

The poststructuralist critique of structuralism has drawn attention to structuralism's technocratic impulses and to the rigidities of its metalanguage. Where this metalanguage is seen as too rigid, determinate, or totalizing, the poststructuralists have emphasized play, indeterminacy, discontinuity, flux, chaos, and individual variation. In terms of the Saussurean distinction, this indicates a renewed engagement with *parole*. In terms of more contemporary preoccupations, they have restored an emphasis on chaos and chance rather than order and necessity. But modern theories of the relation between order and chaos in the physical and life sciences do not see these qualities as opposed (for an overview, see Prigogine and Stengers, 1985).

A *parole*-based ontology of the instance is self-contradictory, as system and instance are not opposed but are alternative and complementary semiotic perspectives on the same phenomenon. Saussure and Hjelmslev already understood this in the first decades of this century, and the implications of their teachings are far from exhausted. There are signs that a more dynamic structuralism of metastable states, structures, and systems is up to the task of inventing the new metalanguage that is called for to continue these investigations. Such a structuralism is fully informed by the new epistemology of complex, dynamic, adaptive, and evolving open systems.

The prefix *post-* in this context is not without a certain historical irony. In his essay "On the Potentiality of the Phenomena of Language" (1911), Vilém Mathesius (1882–1946), who was a linguist of the Prague School, examined the dialectic between what he called the "static" or "synchronic oscillation" of the individual's use of language and the systemic potentiality of the code. The progenitors of structuralism did not overlook what became the lessons of poststructuralism.

[*See also* Binarism; Catastrophe Theory; Halliday; Hjelmslev; Lévi-Strauss; Metalanguage; Opposition; Structuralism; *and* Thom.]

BIBLIOGRAPHY

Derrida, J. *Writing and Difference.* Translated by A. Bass. London: Routledge and Kegan Paul, 1978.

Halliday, M. A. K. "How Do You Mean?" In *Advances in Systemic Linguistics: Recent Theory and Practice*, edited by L. Ravelli and M. Davies, pp. 20–35. London and Dover, N.H.: Frances Pinter, 1992.

Hjelmslev, L. *Prolegomena to a Theory of Language.* Translated by F. J. Whitfield. Madison: University of Wisconsin Press, 1969.

Lemke, J. L. "Text Production and Dynamic Text Semantics." In *Functional and Systemic Linguistics: Approaches and Uses*, edited by E. Ventola, pp. 23–38. Berlin and New York: Mouton de Gruyter, 1991.

Mathesius, V. "On the Potentiality of the Phenomena of Language" (1911). In *Praguiana: Some Basic and Less Known Aspects of the Prague Linguistic School*, edited by J. Vachek and L. Dusková, pp. 3–43. Amsterdam and Philadelphia: John Benjamins, 1983.

Petitot-Cocorda, J. *Morphogenèse du sens.* Paris: Presses Universitaires de France, 1985.

Prigogine, I., and I. Stengers. *Order out of Chaos: Man's New Dialogue with Nature.* London: Fontana, 1985.

Prodi, G. *Le basi materiali della significazione.* Milan: Bompiani, 1977.

Salthe, S. *Evolving Hierarchical Systems.* New York: Columbia University Press, 1985.

Waddimgton, C. H. *Principles of Embryology.* London: Allen and Unwin, 1956.

Wilden, A. *System and Structure: Essays in Communication and Exchange.* 2d ed. London: Tavistock, 1980.

—PAUL J. THIBAULT

PRAGMATICS. American philosopher Charles Morris (1901–1979) defined pragmatics as the study of the relations of sign vehicles to interpreters. This definition has been given various explications in the semiotic research of the last half century. Morris himself used to paraphrase this formula as "the relations of signs to their users" (1938), which implies that signs are produced for a purpose and therefore seems inapplicable to signals and indicators that are not so produced. Rudolf Carnap (1891–1970) further restricted the scope of pragmatics to "the action, state and environment of a man who speaks or hears" a verbal sign (1939). Such approaches make pragmatics part of the theory of human action and focus on speech acts and other ways of intentional signing that rely on the use of codes. It was only later (1955) that Carnap explicitly included nonlinguistic signs and noncommunicative semiosis.

Bearing Morris's very special kind of semiosis in mind, analytic philosophers, linguists, anthropologists, sociologists, and psychologists have tended to characterize the task of pragmatics negatively as "the study of meaning insofar as it is not treated by semantics." Semantics describes the meaning signified by signs without reference to actual interpreters, and pragmatics studies what actual interpreters do in order to make sense of this meaning in actual situations.

But there are also those who want to replace this negative delimitation of the subject matter of pragmatics with a positive characterization. Assuming that the relation between sign vehicles and interpreters becomes manifest in the processes that interpreters perform in order to interpret a sign vehicle, these processes can become the central object of investigation. In contrast to abstract relations, processes cannot be assumed to be the same for sign producers as for sign recipients, or for addressers as for addressees. In a communication process, a sender, intending to convey a message to an addressee, makes sure that he or she is connected to the addressee by a medium, chooses an appropriate code, and selects from it a signified that approximates the intended message. Since the signified is correlated through the code with a corresponding signifier, the sender then produces a sign vehicle that is a token of this signifier. The addressee, on the other side, perceives the sign vehicle through the medium and takes it as a token of the signifier, which refers him or her to the signified on the basis of the code. He or she then reconstructs the message from the signified with the help of indications given by the shared situation.

Such a characterization, although oversimplifying, shows that there are two types of process involved and that they occur in inverse order, even if they cannot be separated from each other in real time: code-related sign processing and situation-dependent inferencing. While the first process takes the form of encoding in the sender and decoding in the addressee, the second process can be described only as a complex of inferences, some of which occur in sequence, others of which take place simultaneously within a single interpreter. Strictly speaking, all processes involved in sign interpretation must be called "pragmatic" according to Morris's formula. It has become customary, however, to call situation-dependent inferencing "pragmatic" in a narrow sense in order to contrast it with the processes of syntactic and semantic encoding and decoding.

Pragmatic investigations that focus on the situation-dependent inferencing of the sign producer and the recipient usually concentrate on the principles that govern such inferences. These principles include: (1) the felicity conditions of speech acts assumed by John L. Austin (1962) and John Searle (1969); (2) the conversational postulates introduced by David Gordon and George Lakoff (1975); (3) the principle of charity discussed by Donald Davidson (1973, 1980); (4) the cooperative principle and the conversational maxims formulated by H. Paul Grice (1975); (5) the principle of rationality discussed by Asa Kasher (1976); (6) the strategy of interactional pessimism described by William Labov and David Fanshel (1977) and Stephen C. Levinson (1983); (7) the principle of transparency discussed by Marcelo Dascal (1983); (8) the politeness principle explored by Geoffrey N. Leech (1983) and Penelope Brown and Stephen C. Levinson (1987); and (9) the principle of relevance taken as basic by Dan Sperber and Deirdre Wilson (1986).

A field in which the analysis of the complex relations between sign vehicles, senders, and addressees has become especially fruitful in the last decades is the study of literature. Literature can be analyzed in terms of the interaction between institutions such as a writer (possibly with a secretary and a team of assistants), a publishing house (including a reading department and production and public-relations sections), a distribution system (including bookstores in collaboration with wholesale firms and libraries with

acquisition, catalogue, and users' sections, as well as book clubs), a network of literary critics (including in some cases state censors, as well as private literary critics who publicize their views in periodicals, broadcasts, and discussion meetings), and, last but not least, ordinary readers (who communicate about books with one another privately or in the context of readings, literary cafés, etc.). Further, the real writer of a literary text has to be distinguished from the special role of author that he or she assumes in the text, and the real reader has to be distinguished from the special role of addressee that the text imposes on her or him. Such text-determined roles have been investigated thoroughly in terms of the "implied," "internal," or "fictional" author and reader.

In ordinary communication, the sender usually has some personal knowledge of the addressee, and at least in speech, he or she can rely on the jointly experienced communication situation to supply indications that will help the addressee infer the intended message from the coded meanings signified by the words. Literary communication, however, tends to separate senders from their addressees and has done so increasingly in the last centuries. The visual medium enables the sender to produce signs in a situation different from that of their reception, and while authors formerly wrote for a closed set of addressees—among them the person who commissioned the work and to whom it was explicitly dedicated—they now write for an indefinite number of possible readers. The members of this open set are recipients intended by the author and thus qualify as "addressees," but since the author does not know them personally and in most cases will never even know who they are, she or he is forced to compensate for the lack of contextual indications by developing a system of textual indicators that show readers how to interpret what is written. This is achieved by deliberately choosing specific verbal registers, inserting reflections and commentaries about the narrative techniques, alluding to other literary texts that require similar background knowledge and communicative attitudes, and thus making the text itself indicate to the reader what kind of sender is to be imagined and what kind of addressee the reader is supposed to be. When this strategy is successful, the real readers behave as if they were the author's preferred addressees, and they assume the writer to be like the author presented to them in the text. Real communication with literary texts thus becomes guided by the fictional communication implicated in the text (Moeschler and Reboul, 1994). There is also a formal correspondence between the fictional author and the fictional addressee. When the writer explicitly introduces herself or himself as author, as in first-person narrative, she or he can also address the reader explicitly and thereby specify a preferred role. The reader's communicative attitudes required for optimal literary communication are usually kept constant in a given text. This is why specific effects can be produced when a writer changes them from one paragraph to the next.

In the study of literature, there have been many attempts to define what characterizes literary discourse in general. The introjection of the roles of sender and addressees into the text seems to be one of the few invariants among them. This introjection enables the interpreter to set up fictional referents in the reading process and enables the addressee to convert any given text into a means of literary reception. Such an approach to the pragmatics of literature is currently also influencing musicology and art history. Charles Morris himself did not study fully these intricacies of aesthetic discourse, but they can be analyzed adequately within a suitably extended framework based on his work.

[*See also* Conversation; Meaning; Reception and Reader-Response Theories; Signal; *and* Speech Act Theory.]

BIBLIOGRAPHY

Austin, J. *How to Do Things with Words.* Oxford: Clarendon Press, 1962.
Brown, P., and S. C. Levinson. *Politeness: Some Universals in Language Usage.* New York: Cambridge University Press, 1987.
Carnap, R. *Foundations of Logic and Mathematics.* Chicago: University of Chicago Press, 1939.
Carnap, R. "On Some Concepts of Pragmatics." *Philosophical Studies* 6 (1955): 89–91.
Dascal, M. *Pragmatics and the Philosophy of Mind.* Amsterdam: John Benjamins, 1983.
Davidson, D. "Radical Interpretation." *Dialectica* 27 (1973): 313–328.
Davidson, D. *Essays on Actions and Events.* New York: Oxford University Press, 1980.
Dijk, T. van, ed. *Pragmatics of Language and Literature.* Amsterdam: North Holland, 1976.
Gordon, D., and G. Lakoff. "Conversation Postulates." In *Syntax and Semantics: Speech Acts*, edited by P. Cole and J. L. Morgan, pp. 83–106. New York: Academic Press, 1975.
Grice, H. P. "Logic and Conversation." In *Syntax and Semantics: Speech Acts*, edited by P. Cole and J. L. Morgan, pp. 41–58. New York: Academic Press, 1975.
Jakobson, R. "Linguistics and Poetics." In *Style in Language*, edited by T. A. Sebeok, pp. 350–377. Cambridge, Mass.: MIT Press, 1960.
Kasher, A. "Conversational Maxims and Rationality." In *Language in Focus: Foundations, Methods, and Systems*, edited by A. Kasher, pp. 197–216. Dordrecht: Reidel, 1976.
Labov, W., and D. Fanshel. *Therapeutic Discourse: Psychotherapy as Conversation.* New York: Academic Press, 1977.
Leech, G. N. *Principles of Pragmatics.* London and New York: Longman, 1983.
Levinson, S. C. *Pragmatics.* Cambridge: Cambridge University Press, 1983.
Mey, J. L. *Pragmatics: An Introduction.* Oxford: Blackwell, 1993.
Moeschler, J., and A. Reboul. *Dictionnaire encyclopédique de pragmatique.* Paris: Seuil, 1994.
Morris, C. W. *Foundations of the Theory of Signs.* Chicago: University of Chicago Press, 1938.
Posner, R. *Rational Discourse and Poetic Communication: Methods of Linguistic, Literary, and Philosophical Analysis.* Berlin and New York: Mouton, 1982.
Searle, J. *Speech Acts.* Cambridge: Cambridge University Press, 1969.
Sperber, D., and D. Wilson. *Relevance: Communication and Cognition.* Oxford: Blackwell, 1986.
Stachnowiak, H. *Pragmatics: A Handbook of Pragmatic Thought.* Hamburg: Meiner, 1986.
Verschueren, J., J.-O. Östman, J. Blommaert, eds. *Handbook of Pragmatics.* Philadelphia: John Benjamins, 1996.

—ROLAND POSNER

PRAGUE SCHOOL. A group of linguists and literary scholars who between the mid-1920s and the mid-1940s developed some of the most influential concepts in functional structuralism and modern semiotics, the Prague School originated in the Prague Linguistic Circle (Cercle linguistique de Prague). The Circle was founded on 6 October 1926, when two anglicists (Bohumil Trnka and Vilém Mathesius), two slavicists (Roman Jakobson and Bohuslav Havránek), one orientalist (Jan Rypka), and one general linguist (Henrik Becker, a visiting scholar from Leipzig) met in Mathesius's faculty office to discuss a paper delivered earlier that day by Becker. This paper was critical of contemporary linguistic theory, more particularly the neogrammarian approach. In addition to this general dissatisfaction, all participants shared an interest in language as a functional system, shaped not only by intrinsic laws but also by external, social factors. This meeting ended with the decision to meet regularly.

Nine meetings were held the following year including ones led by Jakobson on the concept of phonological laws and the teleological principle, Sergej Karcevskij on the relationship between language and thought, and Jan Mukařovský on motor processes in poetry. In 1928, more than half of the papers were given by Russian formalists. Nikolaj Trubetzkoy spoke twice: once on the relationship between alphabet and sound system, then on a comparison of vowel systems. Boris Tomaševskij spoke on literary history; Pëtr G. Bogatyrëv on ethnological ethnography; Grigorij Vinokur on linguistics and philology; and Jurij Tynjanov on literary evolution. This range of papers underlines the conceptual interface between late formalism and early structuralism.

Only a week after Trubetzkoy's visit to Prague, Jakobson presented to the Circle a draft of the "Phonological Theses for the First International Congress of Linguists" to be held in The Hague. The final version, which was signed by Jakobson, Mathesius, and Trubetzkoy, was distributed at the congress in April 1928 and was published in the *Proceedings* together with a "Program of Linguistic Analysis," jointly formulated and signed by Charles Bally and Albert Sechehaye as members of the Geneva School and by Jakobson, Mathesius, and Trubetzkoy as members of the Prague School.

Trubetzkoy's impact on Jakobson is symptomatic of the general influence late Russian formalism had on the Prague School. In his paper on literary evolution, Tynjanov defined literature as a system interrelated with other cultural and social systems, and he emphasized the evolutionary interplay between particular forms and functions. In his and Jakobson's seminal program on "Problems in the Study of Literature and Language" (1928), they claimed Saussure's radical antinomy between diachrony and synchrony was an illusion, since "every synchronic system necessarily exists as an evolution, whereas, on the other hand, evolution is inescapably of a systematic nature."

The "Theses Presented to the First Congress of Slavic Philologists in Prague 1929" represent the switching point from late formalism to early structuralism. These theses, published as the introduction to the first volume of the *Travaux du cercle Linguis-*tique, marked the beginning of what might be called the classical period of the Prague School (1929–1939).

Particular emphasis was laid on the fact that languages are systems performing communicative functions, to the point that the notion of "function" became the trademark of the Prague School. This term was not used in its mathematical sense (denoting the dependence of the changes of *x* upon the changes of *y*); rather, it was used in order to refer to the idea that any item of language serves some purpose, fulfills some communicative need: language was not considered as a self-contained whole, and it was not separated from extralinguistic factors.

The most significant achievements were made in the field of phonology, which they defined explicitly as "that part of linguistics which deals with phonic phenomena from the viewpoint of their function in language." This definition was first presented to the 1930 International Phonological Conference in Prague. In 1932, when the First International Congress of Phonetic Sciences was held in Amsterdam, the term *L'école de Prague* (Prague School) was used officially for the first time to refer to the Prague linguists.

For Prague School linguists, mainly Trubetzkoy and Jakobson, the delimitation of phonology as a linguistic discipline distinct from phonetics (understood as a natural science and, thus, as an auxiliary discipline) was most important. The concept of the phoneme was central, of course, and the history of its definition is interesting. In the very first attempts of the late 1920s, psychological approaches (such as those by Russian scholars Jan Baudouin de Courtenay and L. V. Ščerba) to the phoneme still dominated. The theses presented to the International Phonological Conference in 1930 defined the phoneme more linguistically as "a phonological unit not dissociable into smaller and simpler units." Based on the concept of "phonological opposition" (understood as "a phonic difference able to serve, in a given language, for the differentiation of intellectual meanings"), a "phonological unit" was defined as the member of such a phonological opposition. Later, the assumption of the phoneme's indivisibility into smaller units was corrected: In his seminal *Grundzüge der Phonologie* (Foundations of Phonology 1939), Trubetzkoy first defined a phoneme as "the smallest phonological unit of a given language" then defined it as "the sum of the phonologically relevant properties of a sound." This latter definition clearly implies the division of the phoneme into even smaller units, which were later termed *distinctive features*, a notion that became a precious methodological commodity in modern semiotics.

Mathesius concentrated on what he called "functional onomatology," "functional syntax," and "functional analysis of the utterance." Instead of analyzing language only into its formal elements, he emphasized its functional elements and communicative function(s). In this context, the distinction between "theme" and "rheme" (later termed "topic" and "comment"), received central importance: whereas the theme is the informative basis of a statement, derived from the accompanying or preceding situational or verbal context, the rheme is the actual new information communicated about the theme. According to Mathesius, in the normal sequence the theme precedes the rheme (T-R). Expectedly, the concrete realization of this principle differs in various languages. In Russian (which employs a relatively free word order), for example, the sentence "Papa prinës ëlku)" (Daddy brought the Christmas tree) may be transformed easily into "Ëlku prinës papa" or "Ëlku papa prinës" in order to arrive at different semantic functions. Whereas in the first sentence, *papa* clearly is the theme and the rest of the sentence is the rheme, the new information (and thus emphasis) is contained either in the fact that it was papa who brought the Christmas tree or in the fact that he brought the tree (and did not send it, for example). The functional differences expressed here by means of word order can be conveyed in other languages by other means, such as periphrasis ("It was *Daddy* who brought the Christmas tree"), sentence stress ("Daddy has *brought* the Christmas tree"), or passive voice ("The *tree* was brought by Daddy").

The distinction between practical language and poetic language, which was crucial for Russian formalism, was expressed in a corresponding definition: language has either a predominant communicative function (when it is directed toward the signified) or predominant poetic function (when it is directed toward the sign itself). The functions are seen as a hierarchically organized system, and the dominance of one function does not exclude the cooccurrence of other functions. This principle was applied later by Bogatyrëv to ethnological studies through his concept of polyfunctionality.

This explicitly semiotic orientation requires a clear departure from formalist approaches, both in lan-

guage and art. In the mid-1930s, many formerly structuralist tenets were reformulated in semiotic terms and concepts. This can be clearly seen in the introduction to the newly founded periodical *Slovo a slovesnost* (Word and verbal art, 1935), in which Havránek, Jakobson, Mathesius, Mukařovský, and Trnka say explicitly that "the problem of the sign is one of the most urgent philosophical problems in the cultural rebirth of our time."

The structural-semiotic shift in orientation and the overcoming of both formalism and functional structuralism is best documented in Jan Mukařovský's review of the Czech translation of Viktor Šklovskij's *Theory of Prose* in 1934. For Mukařovský, the main significance of the Russian formalists' work in general and of Šklovskij's writings in particular was their polemical negation of preceding theories. Mukařovský interprets the formalist concentration on form as the antithesis of the unqualified emphasis on content, forming a polemic that, according to him, paved the way for structuralism as a synthesis of the two. Mukařovský's rejection of Šklovskij's "weaving metaphor" clearly shows his new orientation. According to Šklovskij, literary scholarship should concentrate on the internal laws of literature, much as in the analysis of weaving techniques (cf. the metaphor of the "textual" and the "textile"), in which solely the count of yarn and the weaving techniques are important, not the condition of the world market and the politics of the trusts. Mukařovský objects that it is impossible to separate the problem of weaving techniques from the economic situation on the world market, since the market mechanism of supply and demand has a direct impact on the development of weaving techniques. Based on these ruminations, Mukařovský draws two important conclusions: first, he polemically replaces Šklovskij's formula that "everything in the work of art is form" with the equivalent formula that "everything in the work of art is content"; second, he claims that external factors must also be considered in the analysis of art, although, of course, the internal laws still represent a major interest of structuralism. As a result, structuralism emerges as a method synthesizing intrinsic (formalist) and extrinsic (sociological) approaches.

The semiotic shift is best documented in two of Mukařovský's papers: "Art as a Semiological Fact" (1934) and "Poetic Denomination and the Esthetic Function of Language" (1936). The former was presented at the Eighth International Congress of

Philosophy in Paris in 1934, in which Charles Morris, whose "Esthetics and the Theory of Signs" appeared in 1939, took part. In the 1934 paper, Mukařovský defined a work of art, explicitly referring to Ferdinand de Saussure and the Viennese linguist and psychologist Karl Bühler and implicitly relating their concepts to Edmund Husserl's phenomenological ideas, as an autonomous sign consisting of three components: (1) the "material artifact," the work-thing (*dílo-věč*), conceived as an external (sensory) symbol; (2) the correlated "esthetic object" (a term taken from German philosopher of art Broder Christiansen), defined as a meaning represented in the collective consciousness; and (3) a relation to the thing signified. The term *collective consciousness* is here an obvious reference to Émile Durkheim's sociology; according to Mukařovský, it should not be understood as a psychological reality or as a summarizing concept of individual states of consciousness but as the "social fact" of the realm of the individual systems of cultural phenomenon, such as language, religion, science, politics, and so on. And it is to this "total context of social phenomena" (later explicitly called "culture"), that art as an autonomous sign refers, unlike communicative signs, which refer directly to a specific reality.

Mukařovský's 1936 paper is a systematic elaboration of Bühler's concept of language functions. (Bühler, who cooperated closely with Trubetzkoy, repeatedly visited the Pargue Linguistic Circle.) Mukařovský summarizes Bühler's three basic functions of language—the expressive function with respect to the sender, the appealing function with respect to the receiver, and the informational function with regard to the objects and states of affairs—as its three practical functions. He then added a fourth, aesthetic function that tears language out of its direct practical context and directs the sign user's attention toward the sign itself. Mukařovský thus arrives at a description of language function that integrates the early formalist dichotomy of practical language and poetic language in a systematic way; this typology was complemented only much later by Jakobson. Mukařovský himself later interpreted the aesthetic function as a basic type of human relation to reality. He also interpreted the aesthetic function in its interrelation to the aesthetic value (as a social and dynamic phenomenon) and the aesthetic norm (a historical fact regulating the aesthetic function).

Mukařovský's concept of the collective representation of the aesthetic object was later modified, mainly by Felix Vodička (1909–1974) and by Miroslav Červenka. Vodička particularly emphasized the individual recipient's role in the process of "concretization" (*konkretizáce*)—in constituting the aesthetic object on the basis of the material artifact. The term *concretization* was taken from the Polish phenomenologist Roman Ingarden, but it was reframed within a structuralist concept in order to concern not only the internal structure of the artifact but the artifact's structure as compared to the structure of the contemporary tradition. In this sense, concretization not only replaced the earlier (formalist) juxtaposition of automatization (*automatizáce*) and actualization (*aktualizáce*; often termed "foregrounding" in English) but also paved the way for a structuralist theory of literary history and literary evolution.

After the Nazi occupation of Czechoslovakia and the outbreak of World War II, the activities of the Prague School became sporadic. In 1939, Trubetzkoy, one of the most active members, died; Jakobson and René Wellek emigrated; Bogatyrëv returned to the Soviet Union; and all universities were closed by the Nazis. *Slovo a slovesnost* was suspended in 1943 and reappeared in 1947, only to disappear again with volume 10 in 1948); Mathesius died in 1945. Immediately after the war, the Circle resumed its activities in its former manner, presenting, among others, a number of foreign guest lecturers, such as Louis Hjelmslev from Copenhagen, Maria Renata Mayenowa from Warsaw, and A. Belič from Belgrade. Still, 1948 saw the end of the Prague School, when I. I. Meščaninov imported Marxist doctrine from the Soviet Union, followed two years later by Stalinist linguistics. Only after de-Stalinization in the USSR was the tradition of the Prague School revived, when a number of scholars (among them Trnka and Havránek) took active parts in a discussion of structuralism, mainly in linguistics. This development resulted in the rise of the so-called Prague School of the 1960s. One indication of this renewed activity was the publication of the *Travaux linguistiques de Prague* (1964–1971). This "new" Prague School became active in various fields, such as linguistic stylistics, information theory, verse theory, literary scholarship, literary evolution, philosophy, and aesthetics. After the demise of the Prague Spring in 1968, many of these scholars emigrated and continued their work abroad. Within the country itself, the heritage of both the early ("classical") and the renewed structuralist movements were officially continued until the very end of the 1980s.

[*See also* Art; Articulation; Distinctive Features; Jakobson; Mukařovský; Phoneme; *and* Trubetzkoy.]

BIBLIOGRAPHY

Galan, F. W. *Historic Structures: The Prague School Project, 1928–1946.* Austin: University of Texas Press, 1984.

Garvin, P. L., ed. *A Prague School Reader on Esthetics, Literary Structure, and Style.* Washington, D.C.: Georgetown University Press, 1964.

Luelsdorff, P. A., ed. *The Prague School of Structural and Functional Linguistics: A Short Introduction.* Amsterdam: John Benjamins, 1994.

Luelsdorff, P. A., J. Panevova, and P. Sgall, eds. *Praguina 1945–1995.* Amsterdam: John Benjamins, 1994.

Matejka, L., ed. *Sound, Sign, and Meaning: Quinquagenary of the Prague Linguistic Circle.* Michigan Slavic Contributions, Ann Arbor: University of Michigan, 1978.

Steiner, P., ed. *The Prague School: Selected Writings, 1929–1946.* Austin: University of Texas Press, 1982.

Titunik, I. R., and L. Matejka, eds. *Semiotics of Art: Prague School Contributions.* Cambridge, Mass.: MIT Press, 1976.

Tobin, Y. *The Prague School and Its Legacy in Linguistics, Literature, Semiotics, Folklore, and the Arts.* Amsterdam and Philadelphia: John Benjamins, 1988.

Vachek, J., ed. *A Prague School Reader in Linguistics.* Bloomington: Indiana University Press, 1964.

Wellek, R. *The Literary Theory and Aesthetics of the Prague School.* Ann Arbor: University of Michigan, 1969.

—Peter Grzybek

PUNCTUATION. Conventional graphic signs designed to supplement writing systems by providing visual cues concerning the vocal organization of language productions, punctuation uses encoded intonation and pauses to clarify the syntactic patterning of a text and prompts the reader to conform to the intended form of its verbal delivery. Through the centuries, a variety of graphic devices have been invented in order to create visual equivalents of the complex temporal patterning conveyed by the triple structure of speech: what is said (linguistic information), how it is said (paralinguistic information), and how it is gestured (kinesic information). Punctuation can also evoke silence and stillness and convey indirectly some purely visible features, mainly facial expressions. In computer-mediated script, abstract facial icons are used to express the moods of the writer or his or her attitudes toward a statement.

Written language has always been alienated in some degree from the living, psychosomatic, organized reality of speech; written language, in any script system, is reductive relative to the live, organized reality of speech. Despite the profusion of written communications, a totally arbitrary and very limited system of punctuation symbols has been developed to encode graphically the nonliteral parameters of speech and enunciation. Early Greek and Roman texts used only capital letters; Greek inscriptions do not separate words or sentences, but in some [:] or [:] separate clauses. Greek literary texts indicated a change of topic with a dash (*paragraphos*) under the beginning of a line. In the third century BCE, Greek used [·] (*komma*) after a short clause, [.] (*kolon*) after a longer clause, and [˙] (*periodos*) after the longest sentence. In reading, [,] separates words, ['] indicates elision, and [‿] under two letters marks the separation of compound words. In Roman texts, words are separated by points, and new topics are signaled by projecting the first letters into the margin, but Latin scripts are mostly written continuously, at most with spaces between sentences or an occasional period. Around 600 or 700 CE, there is a transition from majuscule to minuscule handwriting; words, sentences, and paragraphs are then separated, with high or low points still used for sentences. In the following century, Gregorian chants prompt the inflectional *punctus elevatus* [✓] and the *punctus interrogativus* slanted to the right [?]. In the ninth century, word separation is more common, particularly in Latin; in Greek, [,] replaces [·], and [;] symbolizes interrogation in Latin manuscripts. In the following centuries, a variety of signs appear with new values: for instance, [-] divides words at end of line, *punctus circumflexus* [.>] raises inflection at end of subordinate clause, a virgule [/], later replaced by [:], marks a light pause (before *punctus elevatus*)—sunk to the bottom of the line, it became a comma [,] (reading aloud in churches and refectories contributed much to establishing a consistent system in the thirteenth and fourteenth centuries. In 1455, the Vulgate printed by Gutenberg has [.], [:], and [·] as commas; words are separated, and phrases begin with capital letters. At the end of the fourteenth century, William Caxton of Westminster uses punctuation irregularly ([:], a lozenge-shaped period, and sometimes [‖] instead of virgule). Around 1490, Aldus Manutius (Venice's Aldine Press) uses italic and Roman types in the reverse of our present practice and replaces the Greek system with a new one that includes [,], [;], [:], [.], and [?] with syntactical functions. In 1500, [( )] appears. In the fifteenth and sixteenth centuries, French [« »] and [- -] are introduced for quotations. In the seventeenth century, paragraphs are indented. In the seventeenth and eighteenth centuries, [,], [" "], [-], and ['] take on their modern names. Since the mid-eigthteenth century, Castilian has adopted opening [¡], [¿], and [« »], [" "] for quotations; German uses [» «] and [,,"] for quotations; and Cyrillic script adopts European punctuation, particularly German. Also in the seventeenth and eighteenth centuries, Japanese uses [○] as closing period and an inverted virgule [،] as comma; beginning in 1868, it adopts [.], [—], [!], and [?]. In the nineteenth and twentieth centuries, Chinese starts using [○] at end of phrase or for emphasis, then also [,], [?], [!], as well as [○] as closing period.

The following listing of established punctuation symbols includes in round brackets ( ) those that have been suggested (Poyatos, 1981) as feasible and logical additions, all distributed according to the three types of functions punctuation can play: syntactical, quantitative, and qualitative. Syntactical ones include those for pause: [,], [;], [:]; stop: [.]; and interpolation: [,,], [( )], [- -], [— —]. Quantitative functions comprise shortening: letter deletion with or without [']; lengthening: letter reepetiitioon hy-phen-a-tion, [- -], [...]; acceleration: (>) or (→); ending with (<), (←), or nothing; slowness: letter reepeetiitioon, hy-phen-a-tion; brokenness: reepeetiitioon, hy-phen-a-tion; silence: [-], [—], [——], [...], [.....]. Qualitative functions cover emphasis: ['], [" "], *italics*, hy-phen-a-tion, CAP-I-TALS; shouting: [¡ !], (¡), [!], [¡¡ !!], (¡¡), (!!), [¡¡¡ !!!], [¿¡ !?], (¿¡), (!?); vehemence: (¡ !), (¡), (!), *italics*; susurro: (++), (¡++!), (¡+), (+!), (¿++?), (¿+), (+?); interrogation: [¿ ?], (?), (¡¿ ?!); risa: (˄ ˄), (î î), (î), (î), (ê ê), (ê): (ê); crying: (˅ ˅), (ï ï), (ï), (ï), (ë ë); and inhaled speech: (><), (¡><!), (¡>), (<!), (¿><?).

Apart from the omissions of apocopated speech (e.g., English *mos* for *most*, Spanish *pa* for *para*) and syncopated speech (e.g., English *catt'l* for *cattle*, Spanish *veá* for *verdad*), the present ambiguity in the representation of silences could be avoided by consistently differentiating voluntary or controlled silences (e.g., prequestion, between repetitions, understood ellipsis, withholding a word), symbolized with a variable [...], [......], and internally or externally imposed silences (e.g., interruption, word or thought searching, stuttering, fatigue, hesitation), represented with

[-] and variable continuous lines [—], [——] but not dots, as is usually done in Spanish and French, much less in English.

The length of words can be modified in three ways, not always represented visually: first, by acceleration of speech, possibly symbolized by [>] or [→] under the starting syllable and at the end with [<] or [←] ("'Oh, no, no, no!' said Father Keon quickly" [James Joyce, *Dubliners*, 1914]; "¡Ven corriendo!" ["Come running!"]). Second, there is lengthening of phonemes, perhaps brief but followed by a brief silence (two different ones usually undifferentiated in punctuation: "Es decir, si tiene vergüenza . . . / —¿Y si no la tiene?/ —Pues si no la tiene . . . ¡dependerá de tí!" ["This is to say, if he is ashamed . . . / —And if he is not? / —Then if he is not . . . it will depend on you!"; Miguel de Unamuno, *Niebla*, 1914]), in French and Spanish usually written [. . .] ("—Moi, qui aime tant madame . . . , balbutiait Zoé" ["But I love madame so much . . . , stammered Zoé"; Emile Zola, *Nana*, 1880]; "Mamá . . . —empezó la hija" ["Mama . . . started the daughter"; Unamuno, *Niebla*]) and a varying solid bar [——] in English ("'Oh—George— George—George—" [Stephen Crane, *Maggie*, 1893]), but it would be clearer to use [letter duplication] for lengthening and [——] for silence. Third is broken lengthening ("HIGGINS . . . Now say cup./ LIZA. C-c-c—I cant. C-cup," [G. B., Shaw, *Pygmalion*, 1913]).

For intensity and emphasis; ['] could represent main stress, even in English (e.g., "Excuse me!" versus "Excuse mé!" which is so attitudinally different) better than the ubiquitous italics (" 'Feel my forehead . . . /'Why?'/ '*Feel* it. Just feel it once'" [J. D. Salinger, *Catcher in the Rye*, 1951]). As for the emphasis given to words and phrases in various degrees, it is symbolized with [*italics*], [hy-phen-a-tion], and [CAPITALS], but hypertense emphasis could be indicated with [ÁCCÉNTÉD CÁPÍTÁLS] or hyphenated [MÁYÚS-CÚ-LÁS], adding [¡¡ !!] to capitals if shouted. Both [!] and Spanish [¡ !] can be very ambiguous, as they indistinctly represent intense loudness, vehemence, attitudinal use of low ("No!") or high ("What!") register, and even stage whispers ("'Are you crazy?' he hissed frantically. . . . 'keep your idiot voice down'" [Joseph Heller, *Catch-22*, 1961]). Besides, shouted speech is a continuous voice feature that (except in Spanish, as profusedly illustrated in literature) the longer the sentence, the less the reader can detect in time the final [!] and thus cannot attach it mentally to the text read through macular vision; on the other hand, both [!] and [¡ !] can be also unrealistic because loud voice can cover only the first or the last part of what is said, even only its middle past.

Thus, what [!] or [¡ !] attempts to symbolize at times is not loudness but vehemence of thought, reflected in tensely articulated voice (perhaps with breathiness and even whisperiness), often actually soft, not loud, even full of tenderness ("'Oh, to-day, to-day!' . . . speaking very low. 'But they used to be magnificent!'" [Henry James, *The Aspern Papers*, 1888]); thus, vehemence constitutes a unique feature that deserves its own consistent symbol, [¡ !], leaving [¡¡ !!] for actual loud voice.

Since there is no punctuation mark for such a common and eloquent voice feature as whispering, there is no reason (given the arbitrary development of punctuation) for not using the one proposed, [+ +], enclosing the whispered-speech segment, susceptible to combinations such as [¡+ +!] for vehement whispering, [¡¡+ +!!] for stage whispering, and [¿+ +?] for whispered interrogation.

As with the exclamation mark, the function of the interrogation mark is not as visually clear with [?] as it is with the Spanish [¿ ?], as word order is not sufficient: "'You remember a certain famous occasion when I was more drunk than—than usual?'" (Charles Dickens, *A Tale of Two Cities*, 1859), just as if we deleted [¿] in "—Tú te quedas con lo mío después del favor que te hice?" ("—You keep what's mine after the favor I did you?"; Luis Berenguer, *El mundo de Juan Lobón*, 1967). As with exclamation, the interrogation mark can be placed only where its phonetic features actually occur: "—Je suppose que le compagnon auquel vous faites allusion n'est pas Alfred Meurant?" ("I suppose that the companion to whom you allude is not Alfred Meurant?"; Georges Simenon, *Maigret aux assises*, 1960), and then combined with other symbols as required to reflect speech ([¡¿ ?!], [¿+ +?], etc.).

Very often we do not verbalize our thought after a conditional main clause but sort of leave it in the air with a rising pitch, which writers symbolize ambiguously with [—] or [. . .]: "—¿Y cómo no me lo dijo?/ —Como usted no me lo preguntó . . ." ("And how come you didn't tell me?/ —Since you didn't ask

me . . . "; Unamuno, *Niebla*). It would seem quite justified to use a meaningful mark, such as ['] after the last letter.

If punctuation strives to convey a basic emotional reaction such as shouting, which in turn warrants the visual representation of whispering, perhaps we should be able to qualify our written words with such equally basic features as laughing and crying. For instance, we could use [ˆ ˆ] for laughing speech and [_ _] for crying speech. And if we can significantly utter a few words with ingressive or inhaled air (not only out of surprise, fear, etc., but as in the typical "Yeah" and "No" of the Canadian province of New Brunswick or the Danish feminine "Ja!"), it could be marked with [> <] (eg.,">¡Oh, no!<,"">Yeah!"). The present-day occasional efforts to symbolize certain speech features not yet included in punctuation systems suggest, therefore, that the punctuation repertoire could easily be enriched by both professional and occasional writers, as has become usual in computer-mediated script.

[*See also* Computer-Mediated Communication; Flaming; Nonverbal Bodily Sign Categories; Paralanguage; *and* Writing, Ethnography of.]

BIBLIOGRAPHY

Drillon, J. *Traité de ponctuation française*. Paris: Gallimard, 1991.

Husband, T. F., and M. F. A. Husband. *Punctuation: Its Principle and Practice*. London: George Routledge and Sons, 1905.

Levenston, E. A. *The Stuff of Literature: Physical Aspects of Texts and Their Relation to Literary Meaning*. Albany, N.Y.: State University of New York Press, 1992.

Parkes, M. B. *Pause and Effect: An Introduction to the History of Punctuation in the West*. Berkeley: University of California Press, 1993.

Partridge, E. *You Have a Point There*. Londres: Hamish Hamilton, 1953.

Poyatos, F. "Punctuation as Nonverbal Communication: Toward an Interdisciplinary Approach to Writing." *Semiotica* 34.1–2 (1981): 91–112.

Skelton, R. *Modern English Punctuation*. London: Sir Isaac Pitman and Sons, 1933.

—FERNANDO POYATOS

Q–R

QUEER THEORY. Though written in the singular, "queer theory" is not a totalizing discourse on sex and sexuality. It is a political coalition of theories of oppression. And one of its basic premises is that the construction and regulation of sexuality has to be studied alongside the regulatory constructions of race, class, ethnicity, nationality, language, religion, and ability. As Judith Butler (1990) notes in "Against Proper Objects," if queer theory is to account for the persecution of all "sexual minorities," it cannot, and must not, have a "proper" object of study. It must also maintain a progressive yet provocative relationship to feminism.

Early formulations of this critical approach include Gayle Rubin (1984) and Eve Kosofsky Sedgewick (1985). Rubin called for a radical theory of sexuality that would also be a radical politics. Such a theory would use "refined conceptual tools" to build "rich descriptions of sexuality" while respecting the historical diversity and cultural specificity of erotic practices. As political action, it would fight the systematic oppression of dissident sexual communities in western European societies. As political theory, it would map the relations of power that simultaneously produce and constrain the identities of lesbians, gay men, bisexual women and men, transgendered people, sex workers, fetishists, sadomasochists, onanists, and people involved in cross-generational relationships. The radical theory of sex would overturn the doctrine of "essentialism"—"the idea that sex is a natural force that exists prior to social life and shapes institutions"—and advocate instead the "constructivist" axiom that "sexuality is constituted in society and history, not biologically ordained." The work that Rubin sketched in 1984 has blossomed today into the discipline of queer theory.

Sedgewick's work is an early effort to ally feminism with gay scholarship in a study of patriarchal social relations. She puts sexuality at the foundation of the social ties that knit together the male-dominated and heterosexist cultures of England and the United States. Patriarchy is a social system that creates solidarity and interdependence among men in order to allow them to dominate women. What binds men in patriarchal relations is "male homosocial desire." Homosocial bonding occurs when men exchange women with other men—as if the social order were a network of erotic triangles drained of their eroticism. Homosociality, though, forms a broken continuum: it ranges from the love shared by gay men to the hatred that joins heterosexual men in the practice of homophobia.

The most "emblematic" example of an anti-essentialist theory of sex is *The History of Sexuality, Volume One* (1976) by Michel Foucault. Sexuality, for Foucault, is not a force to be liberated. It is instead the product of the powers that constrain it. "Pleasure and power do not cancel or turn back against one another," he says, "they seek out, overlap and reinforce one another." Sexuality is a social rather than a biological fact: a "historical construct" deployed around the body in order to imprison it. The nineteenth century built up a vast *scientia sexualis* aimed at producing true discourses on sexuality. The sexual science performed what Foucault calls a "perverse implantation": it took certain acts performed by and upon the body—such as the everyday act of sodomy—and made them into signs of an underlying personality. Classifying sexual acts became a means of categorizing, and rendering intelligible, the sexual subject. Foucault argues, for example, that the "medical category of homosexuality" came into being in the 1870s, for where formerly there had been the act of sodomy, the new science found the sodomite, a person thought to be utterly determined by a perversion lingering just under the surface of his skin: "The nineteenth-century homosexual became a personage, a past, a case history, and a childhood, in addition to being a type of life, a life form, and a morphology, with an indiscreet anatomy and possibly a mysterious physiology" (1976, p. 43). But if discourses on sex open up avenues by which power takes hold of the body, they simultaneously offer ways to resist power's designs. Every discourse gives rise to an opposing counter-discourse. Hence in the late twentieth century the assertion of a "homosexual" identity becomes the ground of gay liberation.

Monique Wittig (1992) explores the significance for queer communities of the claim that discursive regimes produce the material oppression of individuals. Since it is the "discourses of heterosexuality" that organize social relations under patriarchy, Wittig says it is impossible for queer "societies" to be thought of or spoken of *as queer* "even though they have always existed" (1992, p. 28). To underline the exclusion of lesbian life from the sign systems of compulsory heterosexuality, Wittig closes her essay by declaring that "lesbians are not women."

"Homographesis" (1994) is Lee Edelman's strategy for opening up queer ways of signifying within the hetero-normative empire of signs. A queer deconstruction, homographesis liberates gay communities from the closet by inscribing them with the mark of "homosexual difference." Paradoxically, though, making "homosexuality" visible mimics the work of sexual classification which regulates gay communities by observing them. Indeed, as Jeff Nunokawa argues in " 'All the sad young men': AIDS and the Work of Mourning" (in Fuss, 1991, pp. 311–323), the "homosexualization of AIDS" is based on the stereotype that gay males are "marked men": marked since the 1980s for an AIDS-related death that the homophobic mainstream anticipates with neither concern nor grief. Yet Edelman's gay graphesis takes the body made legible by regulatory coding and interprets it as a homograph: "a word of the same written form as another but of a different origin and meaning" (1994, p. 12). Homographesis reads gay bodies otherwise. It inhabits regulatory sign-systems without submitting to their terms.

Sue-Ellen Case argues in "Tracking the Vampire" (in De Lauretis, 1991, pp. 1–20) that it is possible to recast "the ground of being itself" by testing the borders of nature with a desire that borders on the unnatural. Case defines "queer desire" as a signifying transgression "at the site of ontology." By desiring to transgress the "natural" limits of being, queer theory initiates a shift in the meaning of being-sexed.

In her classic critique of sexual ontology Butler (1990) rejects the premise that sex determines gender, while gender gives rise to desire, for such a theory gives compulsory heterosexuality its conceptual and political justification. For if we were to agree that it is nature that divides the universe of bodies into two sexes, male and female, and that sex is in turn the basis of two genders, men and women, then we would be trapped into conceding that the heterosexual desire of one gender for the other is the necessary consequence of sexual biology. This logic would reduce sexual minorities to the status of rebels against nature's laws. To undermine the sex-gender-desire triangle, Butler argues that the body gains its contours not from a pre-given biological substance but from the repetition of signifying practices. Just as in John L. Austin's (1962) theory of speech acts a performative is an utterance that does something, while a constative is one that states something, so in Butler's theory of "subversive bodily acts" the body is a performative elaboration rather than a constative fact. It is not innately male or female, heterosexual or queer, white or of color; instead it enacts its identity daily in a social field of signifying practices that can be shifted by being repeated. What matters is not the sexual substance that the body contains, but the identifications and object choices it actively excludes. Butler finds instances of performativity in "the cultural practices of drag, cross-dressing, and the sexual stylization of butch/femme identities" (1990, p. 137). By imitating gender, drag shows that gender itself is a structure of imitation rather than an extension of sexual anatomy.

While the bisexual movement has claimed its place in the field since at least the late 1980s, for example in Marjorie Garber's *Vice Versa*, current debates emphasize that queer theory has not paid sufficient attention to the most oppressed sexual dissidents. In "Black (W)holes and the Geometry of Black Female Sexuality" (in Schor and Weed, 1997, pp. 136–156), Evelyn Hammonds asks whether lesbian and gay studies has excluded people of color—for example by failing to examine how black women's sexuality is constructed as "an empty space that is simultaneously ever visible (exposed) and invisible and where black women's bodies are always already colonized." Hammonds situates the practice of black lesbian sexualities within a larger "politics of articulation" that not only makes black women's sexuality visible but interrogates "what makes it possible for black women to speak and act." Kobena Mercer, in *Welcome to the Jungle* (1994), underlines the "competing psychic and social forces" deployed around the bodies of gay men of color; the act of "coming out," for example, strains family relationships that provide "a necessary source of support against racism." Richard Fung underlines the complexity of the intersections between race, nationality, and sexuality in "The Trouble with 'Asians'" (in Dorenkamp and Henke, 1995, pp. 123–130); Fung points to the "burden of representation" that requires him to be authentically "Asian" for non-Asian audiences, and accurately Asian for Asian audiences, though he is also a gay "fourth generation Trinidadian Chinese" man who lives in Canada and whose "claim to Asian authenticity" is at best "tenuous." Ki Namaste insists in "'Tragic Misreadings': Queer Theory's Erasure of Transgender Subjectivity" (in Beemyn and Eliason, 1996, pp. 183–203) that queer theory has ignored how transgendered people tend to be classified either as "performers" or as "anomalies" in both heterosexual *and* queer communities. Such technique of control, adds Namaste, are elided when drag queens, transsexuals, and transvestites are cited as models of anti-essentialism. The current tendency of queer theory, then, is to build a radically inclusive and agonistic democracy that defends the rights and dignity of all sexual dissidents by foregrounding their differences.

[*See also* De Lauretis; Discourse Analysis; Feminism and Feminist Theories; Foucault; Postcolonialism; *and* Speech Act Theory.]

BIBLIOGRAPHY

Abelove, H., M. A. Barale, and D. M. Halperin, eds. *The Lesbian and Gay Studies Reader*. New York and London: Routledge, 1993.

Austin, J.L. *How to Do Things with Words*. New York: Oxford University Press, 1962.

Beemyn, B., and M. Eliason, eds. *Queer Studies: A Lesbian, Gay, Bisexual, and Transgender Anthology*. New York and London: New York University Press, 1996.

Bell, D., and G. Valentine, eds. *Mapping Desire: Geographies of Sexualities*. London and New York: Routledge, 1995.

Butler, J. *Gender Trouble*. New York and London: Routledge, 1990.

Chauncey, G. *Gay New York: Gender, Urban Culture, and the Making of the Gay Male World, 1890–1940*. New York: Basic Books/HarperCollins, 1994.

Crimp, D., ed. *AIDS: Cultural Analysis/Cultural Activism*. Cambridge, Mass.: MIT Press, 1988.

De Lauretis, T., ed. "Queer Theory: Lesbian and Gay Sexualities." *differences* 3.2 (1991).

Dorenkamp, M., and R. Henke, eds. *Negotiating Lesbian and Gay Subjects*. New York and London: Routledge, 1995.

Edelman, L. *Homographesis: Essays in Gay Literary and Cultural Theory*. New York and London: Routledge, 1994.

Foucault, M. *The History of Sexuality: An Introduction*. Volume One (1976). Translated by R. Hurley, New York: Vintage/Random House, 1978.

Fuss, D., ed. *Inside/Out: Lesbian Theories, Gay Theories*. New York and London: Routledge, 1991.

GLQ: A Journal of Gay and Lesbian Studies.

Kennedy, E. L., and M. D. Davis. *Boots of Leather, Slippers of Gold: The History of a Lesbian Community*. New York: Routledge, 1993.

Mercer, K. *Welcome to the Jungle: New Positions in Black Cultural Studies*. New York and London: Routledge, 1994.

Rubin, G. "Thinking Sex: Notes for a Radical Theory of the Politics of Sexuality" (1984). In Abelove, Barale, and Halperin, eds. (1993), pp. 3–44.

Schor, N., and E. Weed, eds. *Feminism Meets Queer Theory*. Indianapolis: Indiana University Press, 1997.

Sedgewick, E. K. *Between Men: English Literature and Male Homosocial Desire*. New York: Columbia University Press, 1985.

Warner, M., ed. *Fear of a Queer Planet: Queer Politics and Social Theory*. Minneapolis and London: University of Minnesota Press, 1993.

Wittig, M. "The Straight Mind." In *The Straight Mind and Other Essays*, pp. 21–32. Boston: Beacon Press, 1992.

—CHRISTOPHER BRACKEN

RABELAIS AND HIS WORLD (1965) is an influential work by Mikhail Bakhtin (1895–1975) through which François Rabelais (1494–1553) became a standard bearer in Bakhtinian semiotics by means of his association with the *carnivalesque*. This phenomenon is seen less as a weak derivative of the medieval institution of the carnival than as a particularly potent cultural mechanism whereby a culture is able to renew and revive itself from within. While the carnival as a cultural event occurs within a specific time frame, the *carnivalesque* is a critical and analytic construct that can help to identify and explain a great diversity of cultural forms from various historical times and places. Thus, according to Bakhtin, the *carnivalesque* plays an important role for a given social structure as a whole. Just as dreams clear the nervous system of excess energy and allow it to regenerate itself with out-of-the-ordinary synaptic charges, so, too, does the carnivalesque encompass for any social environment all those mechanisms whereby excess tensions can be released and through which regeneration of the social body can be achieved.

The title of the English-language translation, *Rabelais and His World*, does not convey the same information as the original Russian, which can be translated more literally as "The Work of François Rabelais and Popular Culture during the Middle Ages and the Renaissance." The latter phrasing stresses the intricate connections Bakhtin sought to establish between, on the one hand, Rabelais as a cultural figure and, on the other, popular culture as it evolved in the Middle Ages and during the Renaissance. Bakhtin sees Rabelais's creative writing as an important crossroads of a number of historical and cultural developments that have to do largely with the significant transition in Western Europe from Latin to the vernacular languages. The *carnivalesque* is first and foremost for Bakhtin a chronotope (a theoretical and critical construct used to gauge specific forms of time and space within a culture) through which various and often rival languages can come together with all the different social stigmata attached to them and with all their cultural power and influence. As a manifestation of the *carnivalesque*, Rabelais's fascinating creativity is, then, the offshoot of a cultural situation in which the high languages of official authority intermingle freely with the languages of the most intimate and corporeal realms of everyday experience.

Several divergent readings have been proposed for explaining Bakhtin's use of Rabelais as a cultural figure. Some Renaissance specialists have seen his reading of Rabelais's work and of Renaissance culture in general as grossly inaccurate. Other readings have tended to accept such judgments about Bakhtin's "misreading" but go on to state that it is more important to understand the allegorical presence of Stalinist Russia in what Bakhtin writes. A number of critics have pointed out that Bakhtin's view of medieval popular culture is ultimately reductive and even ethically dangerous because it is based on a binarism that opposes high and low (official and popular), precisely the type of cultural framework the *carnivalesque* is supposed to challenge. This latter view suggests that Bakhtin's carnival places too much emphasis on bodily excesses and utopian values at the expense of rationalism and a more controlled view of humanism.

Bakhtin was intensely optimistic about culture's capacity to uphold the individual's possibilities of subverting even the most oppressive of cultural systems. This optimism is linked to a belief that the most pervasive of cultural instruments—language—is itself constituted out of a multiplicity of alterities. Even when language is itself used as a tool of repression (as was the case of official Stalinist circles),

there remain within this very language the seeds of subversion, which can ultimately engender its downfall.

This might constitute an overly utopian bias in many of Bakhtin's essays. Authors such as Rabelais, Fyodor Dostoyevsky, or J. W. von Goethe are seen as exemplary figures in a generalized historical process that leads to the inevitable dismantling of repressive regimes and repressive discourse everywhere. Thus, *Rabelais and His World* is both an antidote to repressive thinking on culture and a teleological view of history. Bakhtin's views on history and culture are interwoven with a down-to-earth reflection on how occidental culture has consistently sought to repress bodily contact, laughter, and promiscuousness in general because, on the whole, such modes of social behavior are not codifiable. Bakhtin's semiotics thus proceeds without reliance on the notions of either moral or signifying codes; instead, it takes a long view of history and searches for a means of studying how cultures are capable of renewing themselves by developing interfaces with what is unknown to them. In this respect, the *carnivalesque*, the social and artistic mechanisms by which a chronotope can be constituted for this coming together of otherness, must be linked with both an individual's and a society's memory. Otherness can be encountered creatively only from within a strong sense of the self, which cannot exist without memory. The *carnivalesque* is not a synonym for revolution or subversion; rather, it is one possible cultural space where, because no outside is conceivable (since there is no difference between participant and spectator) and because renewal is undertaken from within, cultural stagnation can be avoided without reliance on unpredictable assistance from another realm.

[*See also* Bakhtin; Binarism; Code; *and* Postmodernism.]

BIBLIOGRAPHY

Bakhtin, M.M. *Rabelais and His World.* 2d ed. Bloomington: Indiana University Press, 1968.

Bakhtin, M.M. "Forms of Time and of the Chronotope in the Novel." In *The Dialogic Imagination: Four Essays by M. M. Bakhtin,* edited by M. Holquist, translated by C. Emerson and M. Holquist. Austin: University of Texas Press, 1981.

Belleau, A. *Notre Rabelais.* Montreal: Boréal, 1990.

Berrong, R. *Rabelais and Bakhtin: Popular Culture in "Gargantua and Pantagruel."* Lincoln: University of Nebraska Press, 1986.

Kinser, S. *Rabelais's Carnival: Text, Context, Metatext.* Berkeley: University of California Press, 1990.

Lachmann, R. *Gedächtnis und Literatur: Intertextualität in der russischen Moderne.* Frankfurt: Suhrkamp, 1990.
—ANTHONY WALL and CLIVE THOMSON

READER-RESPONSE THEORIES. *See* Reception and Reader-Response Theories.

REALISM AND NOMINALISM. One of the main intellectual preoccupations of medieval theologians and philosophers was the distinction between realism and nominalism, also known in the history of ideas as the "quarrel of universals." The writings of Porphyry (c.232–305 CE) and Boethius (480–c.526), based on the ten categories of Aristotle and some excerpts from Plato, were the primary references for all these discussions.

At the beginning of the twelfth century, this debate was represented primarily by Roscelin (1045–1120), the nominalist, and Guillaume de Champeaux (1070–1121), the realist. The Aristotelian nominalists believed only in the substantial existence of individuals; universal ideas were considered to be only the results of mental processes. For the Platonist realists, universal ideas had intrinsic, substantial reality, and individuals were only accidents. Pierre Abélard (1079–1142) intervened in this debate and proposed a theoretical compromise, known as conceptualism, that was considered a variety of realism or nominalism depending upon the beliefs of his adversary. Abélard claimed that the whole question of universals pertained to the relationship between words and things through the intellections that words generate. He extended the dispute about the distinction between species and genres to the domain of signification and thus became one of the precursors of modern semiotics. Abélard's argument was presented in the *Logica ingredientibus* (Logic for Beginners, 1973).

There are three main questions concerning species and genres. First, do the species and genres have an authentic existence, or do they exist only in our opinion? Second, are they corporeal or incorporeal? Third, are they separated from sensible realities, or are they situated within the realities? Abélard argues that in fact there are two types of the incorporeal: the ones capable of subsisting in their incorporeality outside what is perceptible by the senses—such as God and soul—and those that are inseparable from the sensible, such as a line, which cannot be separated from the body that holds it.

As species and genres are universals, let us first define universals and see if their characteristics apply to words (*vocibus*) alone or also the things (*rebus*). While it seems that they apply to both, we have to understand how a universal definition can be applied to individual things. In fact, there exists neither a thing nor a collection of things that can be attributed individually to a plurality. Expressions such as *the people, the house,* and *Socrates* refer to all the parts taken together of the people, the house, and Socrates, yet they cannot be called universals. Hence, if a collection cannot serve as a predicate to a plurality of beings, a single thing can do even less.

The realists argue that a universal is an essential substance within a number of realities with different forms. For example, the substance "human" is identical in all people considered individually; the same substance is Plato in one case and Aristotle in another. If we can separate forms from their substances, these realities will all become identical with each other, as their matter is essentially the same, form being the only differentiating element. For Porphyry, all people are identical on account of their participation in the species. Similarly, an individual is what each one of them has as a set of characteristics that is not found in any other individual. The same is true of animals that possess a unique and essential substance—"animal"—but are divided into several species due to their accidental forms in the same way as a single piece of wax can form at times a statue of a man and at others a statue of an animal. Boethius, in fact, defines a universal as something that is totally and simultaneously identical across different realities and that even outside these forms subsists in itself in nature without existing in a certain manner. By nature it will be universal, but in act it will be singular, and as incorporeal and nonsensible it will constitute in its simplicity and universality an object of intellection.

If in fact, argues Abélard, it is the same essence, which in different forms constitutes various singular things, it would then imply that the one that acquires one form is confused with the one that has another form. An animal that acquires the form of rationality will remain the same animal that acquires the form of irrationality even though that animal as a singular object will be deprived of all rationality. Hence, we will have a coexistence of contrary determinations. There will be no more contradiction when two contraries meet in the same essence. It can follow from this that rationality and irrationality are not less contradictory even when they coexist in the same species or in the same genre. It is also true that rationality and irrationality coexist in the same individual, as we find in Socrates. That both these contraries meet in Socrates is evident from the fact that they meet in Socrates and Bruneau (a horse), for Socrates and Bruneau are Socrates, and, also, Socrates is Socrates and Bruneau; Socrates is, in fact, Socrates, and Socrates is Bruneau. That Socrates is Bruneau is a necessary consequence of this doctrine. In fact, all that exists within Socrates outside the individual of Socrates is identical with what exists within Bruneau outside the individual form of Bruneau.

Some realists try to escape this dilemma by criticizing only the form of the proposition, "the rational animal is an irrational animal," for this formulation implies that the same and identical reality will get from two opposing forms two opposing determinations; rationality and irrationality. However, they do not object that different but compatible forms are applied simultaneously to the same reality, and this is why these authors do not object to formulations such as "a rational animal is a mortal animal," for it is not as a rational animal that it is mortal. The same animal can be indicated simultaneously by these two determinations, for otherwise they will not be able to accept that an animal is also a man, for inasmuch as he is animal, he is not human.

The realists also believe that the totality of real things have only ten essences or ten supreme genres, for within each category there is only one essence that is diversified due to subordinated forms, without which there would be no variety. Following this, all substances are the same substance; all quantities are the same quantity; all qualities are the same quality. As Plato and Socrates possess the reality of each of these categories, and as these realities are fundamentally identical, all the forms of the one belong equally to the other, for they are not distinguished any more by their essence than by their substance, and they cannot be qualitatively different.

Can we then accept that distinctions between individuals are due only to accidents? It cannot be, for if individuals receive their beings from accidents, these accidents should be prior to them. If this specific difference distinguishes man from animal, Socrates will be defined by his accidents. Outside these accidents, there is no Socrates, as outside these accidents there is no person. It is not Socrates who is the basis of these accidents any more than a person is the basis of the accidents that constitute him or her as a person. If the accidents do not belong to individual substances, they do not belong to universals either. Abélard concludes that it is obviously not reasonable to think that diverse beings possess the same unique essence.

Confronted with this argument, the extreme realist Guillaume de Champeaux changed his position to that of an indifferentist, contending that individual realities differ from each other not only due to form but in their essences and that it is wrong to believe that what belongs to one in form or matter belongs also to another. Furthermore, he argued that even when the forms are revoked, they still remain distinct due to their essences, for their distinction is not based on the difference of forms, but they constitute an essential diversity analogous to that of forms. The contrary hypothesis requires multiplying the diversity of forms to infinity. Porphyry, according to Abélard, seems to hold this opinion when he states that their difference is due to the fact that the essence of one is never the essence of another. All realities are so different from each other that none participates in the domain of another, neither in form nor in matter. Similarly, it is argued that the universals exist: there is no identity of essence, but there is an identity due to indifferentiation. Individually, people are distinct from each other, but they are all people due to their similar nature of humanity.

Universals have raised so many problems because their signification is not very certain, for they do not seem to possess any substantial reality, nor do they present authentic intellections of real things. Universal nouns do not seem to designate anything real, for all that exists subsists in itself; separated from others, universals do not meet in any real thing. Universals signify diverse realities that they designate. These intellections, of course, are not due to the realities themselves but are still applied to each of them. The word *person* that designates each person derived from the common cause that they are people, produces a certain common intellection that is applied to each of those in which our understanding conceives a similitude.

For Abélard, the intellections of the universals are necessarily derived through abstraction. When we hear words such as *person*, *whiteness*, or *white*, these nouns do not remind us of all the natural properties of the corresponding real substances. The word *person* evokes for us only the rational and mortal animal, and we conceive other secondary accidents in quite a confused manner. This is why it is said that the intellection of the universals is "isolated, naked and pure": isolated, for it does not perceive the thing as sensible; naked, for it makes abstractions of forms, totally or partially; pure, for it does not certify any reality of matter or form.

Abélard raises three main questions in this context. First, do the genres and species have a real subsistence—that is, do they signify veritable, existing realities, or do they exist only in intellection? His response is that genres and species really signify the things that exist when we refer to singular nouns, but in another sense they represent isolated, naked, and pure intellection. It also depends upon how the enunciator and the auditor understand these terms.

Second, are these subsisting realities corporeal or incorporeal? Do they signify separate or nonseparate realities? This can be answered by stating that in a sense they are corporeal realities, distinct in their essence but incorporeal in the context of universal terms, for the universals do not denominate things that are separated and determined. Thus, universal terms are corporeal with reference to the nature of things and incorporeal with reference to their mode of signification, for if the realities that they signify are separated, they do not denominate them as separated and determined.

Third, do the genres and species belong to sensible realities? Some philosophers believe that the universal subsists in the sensible—that is, that it signifies an intrinsic existing substance in the sensible reality due to external form; in so signifying, the universal manifests this substance as naturally separated from this reality.

The intellection of the universals is claimed to be isolated from the sensible. Some of the genres and species are sensible with reference to the nature of things but nonsensible with reference to the mode of signification, for these sensible realities that they denominate are designated in terms of the mode in which they are the objects of sensation—that is, in which they are separated—but one cannot perceive them as sensible in the process of their revelation.

All these problems are posed with reference to universal words alone, for singulars do not pose any problem. The mode of signification of singulars corresponds perfectly with the real state of things. Even when things are separated, singular words signify them separately, and the intellection that is applied to these words corresponds well to the related objects. The case of universals is quite different, as universals signify neither things separated nor correspondence of things because there is nothing real within which they can meet.

Even though the definition of universals, whether genre or species, is based on words, often their domains are extended to real things that correspond to these words. This happens when a species is said to be composed of genre and difference—that is, the specific reality is constituted from the generic reality. The natural significance of words refers at times to words alone, at others to things, and this confusion is quite common.

Abélard argues that Boethius, whose *Commentaries* all philosophers of the Middle Ages referred to, created this confusion by giving an incorrect definition of genres and species. Boethius stated that one never finds a real thing, singular or multiple, that can be universal or attributed to a plurality. All that is unique and numerically one is separated from its proper essence; genres and species are necessarily common to a plurality, and so they cannot be numerically singular or unique. Boethius rejected the argument that genres and species are numerically singular in the sense that they are common by asserting that all that is numerically singular can be common in three ways: by possessing common parts, by remaining totally common in the succession of time, or by remaining totally common within a given time. Abélard, in contrast, argues that species and genres do not respond to any of these hypotheses, for they are simultaneously and totally present in each of the singulars and constitute their substance. The universal nouns are not derived partially from the diverse realities but are constituted of each of these realities simultaneously and entirely. They constitute the very substance of the realities they are common to, and, by transfer, they may signify realities that by themselves constitute other realities, much as *animal* denominates in man or in horse what is their matter and, at the same time, denominates the beings that are inferior to humanity. Further, they constitute the substance of things in the sense that they define it. This is why they are called substantial with reference to things, as *man* for example, denotes to Abélard all that is animal, rational, and mortal.

Boethius stated that the intellection of these universals is empty because they have a mode of subsistence other than that of the real things—namely, abstractive operation. Abélard argues that Boethius took the word *thing* in the sense of "real thing," not "word," for a common word, even though it constitutes in itself an essence or unique reality, is common only insofar as it denotes several realities; it is only as such, not following its proper essence, that it can be attributed to a plurality. It is the plurality of real things that is the basis of the universal character of the noun, for there is no universal that does not contain a plurality. However, the thing does not possess the very universality that it confers on the word. It is not the thing that gives the word its signification. A noun is considered appellative according to the plurality of things it designates, even though these things themselves do not have this signification and are not appellative.

Jean Jolivet (1982) believes that in resolving the questions of ontology by defining the universal as a word, Abélard has generated two movements in Western philosophy. On the one hand, by questioning the reality of genres and species and reducing them to the signs of natural states, he inaugurates a new analysis dealing with signification and abstraction. On the other hand, in the domain of logic, he poses the questions of language within the problems of metalanguage. Indeed, what began as a quarrel of universals in the context of species and genres is transformed by Abélard into a field of inquiry in the domain of signification. However, the question of whether there are abstract objects has continued to divide philosophers.

[*See also* Abélard; Medieval Semiotics; *and* Poinsot.]

BIBLIOGRAPHY

Armstrong, D. M. *Nominalism and Realism*. Cambridge: Cambridge University Press, 1978.

Bakar, O. *Classification of Knowledge in Islam: A Study in Islamic Philosophy of Science*. Kuala Lumpur: Institute for Policy Research, 1992.

Geyer, B., ed. *Peter Abaelards Philosophische Schriften*. Münster: Aschendorff, 1973.

Gill, H. S. *Mental Images and Pure Forms: The Semiotics of Abelardian Discourse*. Delhi: Bahri, 1991.

Goodman, N. *Problems and Projects*. Indianapolis: Bobbs-Merrill, 1972.

Jolivet, J. *Arts du langage et théologie chez Abélard*. Paris: Vrin, 1982.

Kneale, W., and M. Kneale. *The Development of Logic*. Oxford: Clarendon Press, 1962.

Quine, W. V. O. *Word and Object*. Cambridge, Mass.: MIT Press, 1960.

Strawson, P. F. *Individuals: An Essay in Descriptive Metaphysics*. London: Methuen, 1959.

—HARJEET SINGH GILL

RECENT THEORIES ON THE NATURE OF THE LANGUAGE SIGN (1954).

One of the few works of the Copenhagen School that explicitly and entirely centers on the sign, Henning Spang-Hanssen's book *Recent Theories on the Nature of the Language Sign* addresses fundamental problems in semiotics. Published in 1954, it was written in 1948, in the heyday of Louis Hjelmslev's glossematics. The book does not focus on the historical development of sign theories, nor does it give a bibliographical survey from the point of view of one specific linguistic theory. Spang-Hanssen explicitly uses the theoretical foundation provided by glossematics to investigate the nature of the language sign. Like Ferdinand de Saussure, he wants to place the sign as the basic constituent of the theory of language in a way that is generally relevant to the understanding of sign systems.

Spang-Hanssen considers the sign as a set of theoretical fundamentals that allows for a hypothesis that can be tested empirically. He defines his approach in terms of four typical theories of the sign: a philosophical-epistemological theory (such as those of Ernst Cassirer and Wilbur Urban), a logical-positivist theory (Rudolf Carnap), a psychological theory (Charles Kay Ogden, Ivor Armstrong Richards, and others), and a linguistic theory (Saussure and his followers). He rejects the philosophical approach because of its lack of interest in arbitrary forms, although he appreciates its focus on the general aspects of the language sign. An epistemology related to language, however, does not take into account the language-specific aspects of language. There is no empirical object on which to test the validity of such a notion of the sign.

The sign concept of logical positivism has two important features of linguistic relevance: it is defined as form, independent of its material manifestation and its reference. Only its position in a network of relations is of interest. But logical positivism tends to underestimate the independent role of the "expression plane." The second important feature of this sign concept is a corollary of the first: the sign is generalized through a hierarchy of metalevels, the bases of which are monoplane systems. Although language and linguistics stand out as specific and clearly distinguishable levels, in linguistics monoplane systems can never be taken as the basic point of departure for definitions, as they can in logic.

In the psychological sign theory, Spang-Hanssen makes a brief introductory reference to the works of Edmund Husserl and Charles Sanders Peirce before going on to more thorough analyses of Ogden and Richards's, Karl Britton's, Bertrand Russell's, and Charles Morris's sign notions. These scholars see signs in a context of reference and communication that constitutes the basis for the identification of language signs from among the totality of signs produced in the context. Here, a presupposed mentally patterned readiness to identify the linguistic signs is at work, whether it is linked to perception, intentional goal-oriented behavior, or emotional motives. Although the positioning of the sign in a structure of linguistic and nonlinguistic elements is acceptable to Spang-Hanssen, he holds that the supremacy of psychology over linguistics leaves both the basic mental pattern and the resulting linguistic-sign structure undefined. He wants to replace the referential and the emotional sign function with the denotation and connotation used in glossematics. In this way, the sign and its context receive a formal definition on linguistic ground, clearly distinguishable from a psychological definition and thus open to a relation of this type of definition on a well-defined basis.

In the linguistic section, Spang-Hanssen relies primarily on Saussure and Hjelmslev, but he also takes into account other linguists such as Karl Bühler, Leo Weissgerber, Alain Gardiner, Leonard Bloomfield, and Eric Buyssens. Some of them participated in the seminal debate on the sign that was launched in the first four issues of *Acta Linguistica* (1939–1944). Both groups assume the arbitrariness of the language sign. Nevertheless, the latter group looks for a nonarbitrary basis for the sign, which turns out to be psychological. Only Saussure and Hjelmslev draw the conclusion that the arbitrariness of the sign implies that language must have specific formal properties manifested in the sign. Only on this condition can the two planes of the sign, expression and content, be subject to a linguistic analysis of general value. And only in glossematics are the constituents of the sign, not the signs themselves, the basis of language. Therefore, the sign is not a given fact but an explic-

itly defined linguistic entity that can therefore be related to other, eventually nonlinguistic entities on an empirical basis.

The teaching of structural semiotics has not changed much since Spang-Hanssen's analysis. His selection of material and combination of authors dealing with the sign, however, shows a nondogmatic openness and willingness to confront a hypothesis from opposing viewpoints. *Recent Theories on the Nature of the Language Sign* can still engage semioticians.

[*See also* Brøndal; Copenhagen School; Hjelmslev; Recherches Structurales 1949; *and* Russell.]

BIBLIOGRAPHY

Spang-Hanssen, H. *Recent Theories on the Nature of the Language Sign.* Travaux du Cercle Linguistique de Copenhague, 9. Copenhagen: Nordisk Sprog- og Kulturforlag, 1954.

—Svend Erik Larsen

RECEPTION AND READER-RESPONSE THEORIES. A critical theory that came to prominence during the 1970s and early 1980s, reception theory encompasses a cohesive and collective critical movement emanating from the University of Constance in Germany. Its chief exponents are Hans Robert Jauss and Wolfgang Iser. The term *reader-response theories* is wider in application and has been assigned retrospectively to diverse theories, including Iser's, circulating mostly in North America over roughly the same period. These theories include Stanley Fish's affective stylistics, Norman Holland's transactive criticism, and Jonathan Culler's structuralist and poststructuralist poetics. While the critics involved in both movements have in common a new emphasis on the role of the reader and the importance of reception processes rather than production processes, they start from and arrive at vastly different positions. Despite Iser's prominence in English-language critical debates, the two areas have not exerted major influences on each other. A third strand, synthesizing insights both from the philosophy of language and from European structuralism, poststructuralism, and semiotics, is developed by Umberto Eco (1979, 1990) and his colleagues, notably Marco De Marinis in the field of theater semiotics (1993).

Reception theory draws on many influences, including: Russian formalism's attention to the process of interpretation; Prague structuralism's notion of art as a semiotic fact mediating between artist and addressee; Roman Ingarden's phenomenology, which views literary works as schematized structures full of indeterminacies to be filled out in the act of reading (1973); and Hans-Georg Gadamer's hermeneutics (1979), which stresses the prestructured and prejudiced nature of understanding. Reception theory constitutes a move away from the positivist assumptions of formalism and New Criticism concerning the objectivity and self-sufficiency of the literary text; instead, it focuses on the construction or deconstruction of a text by its interpreter, "insofar as such a function is implemented, encouraged, prescribed or permitted by the textual linear manifestation" (Eco, 1990).

The contemporaneous rise of such critical enterprises is indicative of a conceptual shift involving a lessening of critical emphasis on the relation between the author and the work (taken traditionally to be an objective reality, an autonomous product). Instead, there is a greater concentration on the effect of the work on the reader—though this has been a concern since Aristotle's *Poetics*, with its notion of catharsis as central to aesthetic experience—and the response of the reader to the work. The "reality" of the text is thus reduced to a hermeneutic construct that comes into being only by and through the act of reading. The privileged position, the priority and authority of the work of art (as manifested in New Criticism, where response is seen to be inscribed in and controlled by the work itself), is thus challenged by placing the reader at the center of investigation. In contrast to traditional interpretation, which seeks to elucidate hidden meanings in texts, Jauss and Iser see the relationship between reader and text not as a unidirectional communication and reception but rather as a dynamic interaction of two linked realities. Meaning is the result of this text-reader interaction—an effect to be experienced rather than an object to be defined—and the work is a never-completed unfolding of its readings.

This approach probes the practical or theoretical consequences of the event of reading by asking what happens—consciously or unconsciously, cognitively or psychologically—during the reading process and examining the ways meanings are made, authenticated, and authorized. In various ways, Jauss, Iser, Culler, Fish, and Eco all stress the extent to which the reader's operations are not merely passive or receptive but are actually constitutive of the text. Jauss's celebrated *Erwartungshorizont* (horizon of expectations), for instance, refers to a structure of expectations developed intersubjectively by reading processes, a mindset or system of references that a hypothetical individual might bring to any text and against which the text will be read (Jauss, 1982).

Such positions have clear implications for the structure of the text: since it is the product of an author who is in turn a reader of texts (and hence equipped with the generic competences produced by reading), the text will be structured for and by the expected "moves" of its potential readers. The nature of such structuring is addressed by theoretical constructs such as the "ideal reader," "model reader," or "super-reader," which refer not to a real reader in the act of reading but to the reading strategies that a work presupposes. The act of felicitous reading is then seen as the process whereby the real reader assimilates himself or herself to the model reader, taking up the interpretive challenges of the text by activating an encyclopedia of knowledge that constitutes reading competence: "A text is a device conceived in order to produce its Model Reader" (Eco, 1990). Eco's theory of the model reader (1979) sees the textual strategy as a system of instructions aimed at producing a possible reader whose profile is designed by the text and can be extrapolated from it. This implied reader is thus both a text condition (a prestructuring of potential meaning by the text) and a process of meaning production (the reader's actualization of this potential through the reading process).

For Iser, the reader's tasks include filling out indeterminacies or bridging gaps in the text; such indeterminacies or blanks chart a course for reading by organizing how the reader responds to their shifting structure. At the same time, they encourage the reader to complete the incomplete structure and thereby produce (rather than just interpret) the aesthetic object. Some of these blanks might also cause the reader to become aware of the norms of his or her social system and so will call into question the reader's socially derived presuppositions (Iser, 1978).

For Eco, the act of reading is extremely complex, active, and dynamic. He sees as one important feature of texts their structured capacity to engage the reader in dialectical processes, such as inferring forward to probable outcomes of narrative sequences ("inferential walks"). Eco considers reading to be an exercise in "consistency-building" through a process of abduction based on incomplete information due to the text's indeterminacies. In confronting the various signs or schemata of a text, readers try to establish connections between them that lend coherence to their activity.

This critical direction is thus clearly one that moves away from objectivity and toward subjectivity, and the prospect of unbridled subjectivity has been a concern of most of these critics, with the exceptions of Fish (1980), who finally opts for a subjective and monistic system, and Norman Holland (1968), whose affective criticism effectively reduces the text to a pretext for reading operations that involve projections onto the text of the reader's archetypal psychic fears. Eco (1990) provides an elegant argument for a mixed position that defends multiple but not infinite readings through a critique of a radical theory of misinterpretation whereby every reading is a misreading—therefore there can be no discrimination between "good" and "bad" readings. He maintains that the internal coherence of a text must be taken as the parameter for its interpretations. Accepting a distinction between interpreting and using a text, Eco maintains that reading involves a process of intuiting the text's structural parameters and hence interpreting it as a coherent whole, but at the same time it involves projections of the reader's own parameters, which Eco terms *use* rather than *interpretation*. Every empirical reading is always a mixture of both interpretation and use, and even the use of texts can mean freeing them from previous interpretations and misinterpretations and discovering new aspects of them.

The gap between theoretical and empirical approaches to the reader is wide. Despite some attempts at experimental validation of theory, in general these critics have been slow to build links to more empirical approaches such as the sociology of literature, which describes social usages, socialized interpretations, and the actual public effect of a text rather than the formal devices or the hermeneutic mechanism that has produced those usages and those interpretations. There have been significant moves in this direction in the field of theater semiotics. This is partly due, perhaps, to the fact that reception in the theater is more public and "standardized," since it involves a group response. One of the overriding strategies of comedy, for instance, is to ensure that the members of an audience all laugh at the same time. Of note is Marco De Marinis's empirical study of the

role of the spectator (1989), which develops from his abstract, Eco-derived notion of the model spectator. Empirically, the work of Henry Schoenmakers, Willmar Sauter, and others of the European Committee for Reception and Audience Research has been important in examining both audience's reactions to particular performances and in analyzing more general attitudes they bring to performance. There has also been some experimental work on audience members' visual attention patterns (Fitzpatrick and Batten, 1991) that attempts to gauge the extent to which production processes clearly aimed at structuring the audience's perceptions of the performance (by directing their attention in certain directions at certain points in the performance) do in fact achieve the desired audience responses and so affect cognition and interpretation.

Reception theory has made a significant contribution to the question of textual interpretation. However, having deconstructed one pole of the text-reader relationship, it has to some extent also been superseded by poststructuralist questioning of the other pole, that of the reader. For instance, Roland Barthes's view in *S/Z* is that the reader is not a unified center from which meaning and interpretation originate but rather is itself a plurality of other texts, of infinite and lost codes. Similarly, reception theory has been overtaken by such developments as postmodernism, where criticism is seen to involve not so much an interpretive act as a creative one.

[*See also* Barthes; Eco; Poetics; Prague School; Riffaterre; *and* Russian Formalism.]

BIBLIOGRAPHY

De Marinis, M. "Cognitive Processes in Performance Comprehension: Frames Theory and Theatrical Competence." In *Performance: From Product to Process*; edited by T. Fitzpatrick, pp. 173–192. Sydney: Frederick May Foundation, University of Sydney, 1989.

De Marinis, M. *The Semiotics of Performance*. Translated by A. O'Healy. Bloomington: Indiana University Press, 1993.

Eco, U. *The Role of the Reader: Explorations in the Semiotics of Texts*. Bloomington: Indiana University Press, 1979.

Eco, U. *The Limits of Interpretation*. Bloomington: Indiana University Press, 1990.

Fish, S. *Is There a Text in This Class? The Authority of Interpretive Communities*. Cambridge, Mass.: Harvard University Press, 1980.

Fitzpatrick, T., and S. Batten. "Watching the Watchers Watch: Some Implications of Audience Attention Patterns." *Gestos* 12 (November 1991): 11–31.

Freund, E. *The Return of the Reader*. London and New York: Methuen, 1987.

Gadamer, H.-G. *Truth and Method*. Translated by W. Glen-Doefel. 2d ed. London: Sheed and Ward, 1979.

Holland, N. *The Dynamics of Literary Response*. New York: Oxford University Press, 1968.

Holub, R. C. *Reception Theory*. London and New York: Methuen, 1984.

Ingarden, R. *The Literary Work of Art*. Translated by G. G. Grabowicz. Evanston: Northwestern University Press, 1973.

Iser, W. *The Act of Reading: A Theory of Aesthetic Response*. Baltimore: Johns Hopkins University Press, 1978.

Jauss, H. R. *Towards an Aesthetic of Reception*. Minneapolis: University of Minnesota Press, 1982.

Schoenmakers, H., ed. *Performance Theory: Advances in Reception and Audience Research*. Utrecht: Instituut voor Theaterwetenschap, 1986.

Suleiman, S. R., and I. Crosman, eds. *The Reader in the Text: Essays on Audience and Interpretation*. Princeton: Princeton University Press, 1980.

Tompkins, J. P., ed. *Reader-Response Criticism: From Formalism to Post-Structuralism*. Baltimore: Johns Hopkins University Press, 1980.

—TIM FITZPATRICK

RECEPTORS. Entities at the surfaces of living systems, receptors are instrumental in picking up and responding to signals from outside, whether they are signals from the organism's surroundings or the surroundings of an individual cell. In both cases, the signal crosses a barrier, whether the skin or the cell membrane. Inside the barrier, the signal is translated into a form that makes sense to the organism or the cell. Originally, the term *receptor* denoted the nerve endings found within the sensory organs, but today it is also applied at the molecular level.

The receptor is the key to understanding biosemiotics, the semiotics of nature. A look at the sense of balance in vertebrates provides an example of how a sensory receptor works. In this case, the receptors are comprised of tiny "hair cells"—cells with a little hair-like tuft (a cilium) at one end and a link to a nerve at the other end. These hair cells are arranged in rows on the inside of the utricle, a chamber of the inner ear that is full of a gelatinous substance. Floating in this substance are a number of pebblelike concretions of calcium carbonate. When these crystals collide with a hair, causing it to bend, the hair cell transmits a nerve impulse. If the animal is at rest, the pattern of the bent hairs reflect the head's position in the field of gravity. If it is in motion, the "sloshing" of the crystals reflect every change in its pace.

In this instance, position and speed are first translated into pressure (on the hair cells) and then into electrical nerve impulses that are transmitted along the nerve fiber until they reach the brain. Inside the brain, these nerve impulses are checked against hosts of other nerve impulses coming, for example, from some of the other organs governing the balance or from sight or hearing. In this way, each impulse is absorbed into the animal's actual actions.

So the receptors are directed at the surrounding world, which they allow to slip through to the animal. Which fragments of the surrounding world manage to slip through is determined by the disposition of the receptors, which thus hold the key to the kind of *umwelt* an animal possesses.

Just as the body has its sensory apparatus, so each and every cell has its "receptors" (i.e., proteins), which have the job of collecting and translating signals from around the cell. These signals are usually chemical in nature, since each receptor recognizes or responds to only one or a very few molecules. Each cell's outer membrane is home to millions of such receptors. Generally speaking, all of these receptors can each do two things: they can recognize and bind themselves to one specific molecule, and they can alter their spatial structure. There is, for example, one kind of receptor that specializes in recognizing a particular signal molecule sent out by its neighboring cell. Another recognizes the protein that conveys iron around the body, a third might latch on to a particular hormone, and so on. Recognition and bond are based on the "hand in glove" principle: the receptor's spatial surface is covered with hollows and projections that form a sort of cast of the corresponding spatial surfaces on the signal molecule. The bonding process also receives help from the electrical charge on the molecule surfaces. In short, the receptor is, both spatially and electrostatically, an analogic code of the signal molecule. This bonding process causes an abrupt change in the spatial structure of the receptor. Usually, the receptor pokes its one end out through the cell membrane in order to make contact with the signal molecules, while the other end stays on the other side of the membrane. It is here, on the end of the receptor molecule inside the cell, that the steric alteration takes place, thus triggering an internal reaction of some kind within the cell.

The complexity of this reaction can be impressive and usually engages the cooperation of many different protein molecules. Some of these proteins might be shared by several receptor pathways in the cell, which allows the cell to regulate the response. Since there might be thousands of receptors for a given molecular signal, the signal will not be a single molecule as such but rather a concentration of signal molecules. The cell measures the degree of saturation for each of its many kinds of receptors and makes an integrated interpretation in the form of the activity it chooses to initiate in response to any changes. This interpretation depends not only on the present situation but also on previous experiences that have left indelible cytoplasmic marks.

[*See also* Biosemiotics; Chemical Communication; Umwelt; *and* Vision.]

BIBLIOGRAPHY

Barlow, H. B., and J. D. Mollon, eds. *The Senses*. Cambridge: Cambridge University Press, 1982.

—JESPER HOFFMEYER

RECHERCHES STRUCTURALES 1949

(1949). A landmark collection of twenty-four articles in English and French, representing different fields of structural linguistics, *Recherches structurales 1949: Interventions dans le débat glossématique* was published in Copenhagen on the occasion of Louis Hjelmslev's fiftieth birthday. It shows the widest possible range of application for glossematics or for structural linguistics in a broader sense, from the whole field of linguistics to aesthetics. Although not all the articles are of equal relevance for semiotics, as a whole they show how the glossematic challenge places the scholar in a delicate balance between theory and practice, a position familiar to many semioticians of different orientations who try to reconcile theoretical ambitions with practical analyses. In this wider perspective, the book still makes a stimulating reading.

Some of the articles deserve special attention. Niels Ege's penetrating analysis of the arbitrariness of the language sign sheds new light on the interpretation of arbitrariness, alternately holding between sign and object or between the expression plane and the content plane. In contrast to Émile Benveniste, who points to an ambiguity that needs clarification in the work of Ferdinand de Saussure, Ege convincingly

claims that Benveniste's interpretation results from a misreading. Ege concludes that Saussure unambiguously defends the idea that arbitrariness is an immanent relation and that only immanent relations are relevant for linguistics.

A common feature of the articles that deal with general problems is that they focus on the difficult borderlines between expression and content and between speech and language. André Martinet, for example, introduces the important notion of double articulation. The semiotic interest of the more linguistically specialized articles by Jerzy Kuryłowicz, Henning Spang-Hanssen, Hans Jørgen Uldall, and C. E. Bazell is, on the one hand, in their challenges to certain glossematic dogmas concerning the clearcut limits and supposedly purely formal interrelations between expression and content, and, on the other hand, in their attempts to give necessary differentiations of the notions of relations to the point of breaking away from the glossematic claim for simplicity. Further, in the section on the analysis of the expression plane, Roman Jakobson and Eli Fischer-Jørgensen point to a necessary presupposed nonlinguistic or nonformal foundation for the glossematic analysis of phonematic structures and also for the identification of linguistic elements through commutation.

The volume ends with the two semiotically most interesting papers. Adolf Stender-Petersen gives the outline of a structural theory of literature to be applied in literary history, as, for example, in his three-volume history of Russian literature (1952). The two planes of the linguistic sign are reworked in literature, where an instrumentalization of expression runs parallel to an emotionalization of content, though they are still related arbitrarily to each other. Hence, they produce a fictitious universe that manifests different rhetorical features. Arbitrariness precedes representation. The system of literary genres is defined through two dichotomies: minimal versus maximal instrumentalization and emotionalization; and direct versus indirect reproduction of language. From this system, the genres of literature and its history can be seen as an immanent development of literature as a verbal art.

Svend Johansen gives a less historically and more theoretically oriented account of aesthetics in a glossematic perspective. First, he relates all four aspects of the glossematic sign: the constitutive interrelation of expression form and content form, each of which presupposes a substance—respectively, expression substance and content substance. This relational complex makes up a denotative sign that functions as the expression substance of the connotative sign. The connotative sign, in turn, is constituted by the interdependently related expression form and content form of the connotative sign. This sign also has a content substance that, according to Johansen, is the interpretation embedded in a physiological reaction to the aesthetic text.

Johansen's decisive point is that there is not only one connotative sign but four so-called simple connotative signs. As the denotative sign as a whole functions as the expression substance of the connotative sign, this sign can relate a connotative content to each of the four aspects of the denotative sign. The effect of rhyme arises from how the connotative content relates to the denotative expression substance, while the effect of rhythm arises from the expression form. The reworking of the denotative content through the artistic use of syntax and morphology is the connotative content as related to the denotative content form. The last possibility, the connotative content linked to the denotative content substance, is seen as the culturally or individually given preferences that determine an author's selection of literary themes.

[*See also* Copenhagen School; Denotation and Connotation; Hjelmslev; *and* Recent Theories on the Nature of the Language Sign.]

BIBLIOGRAPHY

Recherches structurales 1949: Interventions dans le débat glossématique. Travaux du Cercle Linguistique de Copenhague, 5. Copenhagen: Nordisk Sprog- og Kulturforlag, 1949.
—SVEND ERIK LARSEN

REFERENCE. Although interest in the many aspects of reference—the relation between language and reality; the capacity of language to designate or denote objects of the world or possible worlds, as well as to parts of discourse—dates back to the Middle Ages, intensive research on this subject did not begin until the end of the nineteenth century, notably with the works of Gottlob Frege (1848–1925) and Alexius Meinong (1853–1920). Most contemporary critics dealing with reference tend to distinguish between two different types of inquiry: the linguistic (Continental) school of thought and the analyt-

ical (Anglo-Saxon) philosophical tradition. While linguists conceive of reference as a process and an act, philosophers view reference as a relationship between an expression and its referent. The linguistic tradition, initially hampered by its reliance on Ferdinand de Saussure's theory, which accords the extratextual referent no place, has made noteworthy contributions to the study of intratextual reference, focusing on factors such as modalizers, deixis, anaphora, and cataphora that determine and affect reference. The philosophical inquiry, conducted largely within the framework of logic and modal logic (as in the writings of Frege, Bertrand Russell, Gilbert Ryle, Willard V. O. Quine, and the early P. F. Strawson), began with ontological questions concerning the logical status of the referent and the truth value of the referring expression (see Linsky, 1967). In what could be considered a second stage of the analytical debate, theorists such as John Austin, John Searle, and the later Strawson have been less preoccupied with questions of existence and have emphasized instead semantics, speech acts, and other pragmatic issues, especially the role of contextuality and conventions in reference.

In contrast to these well-travelled "routes of reference" (Goodman, 1981) of the philosophical tradition, the question of reference in literary texts has remained, until quite recently, a largely unexplored territory. The reluctance of scholars to tackle the thorny problem of referring in literature has been variously rationalized. In his study of literary reference in terms of reception theory, Brian Fitch (1991) notes both the predominance of textual approaches inspired by Saussure's linguistic model and the consequent refusal to admit any relationship between fictional referentiality and the "real," extratextual context. In addition, philosophical studies of the ontological status of the referent have not seemed overly relevant to literary critics, who have not been particularly interested in the truth value or the "real" existence of referents in literature. Indeed, the path leading from analytical philosophy to the study of referring in literature is by no means a direct route, especially given the lack of interest among these philosophers in literature per se. Whereas certain literary theoreticians (Pratt, 1977; Hewitt, 1987) have attempted to adapt speech-act theories to the analysis of literature, analytical philosophers preoccupied with literature have been more interested in imposing philosophical standards on literary texts than in exploring possible relationships between literature and philosophy.

Despite the lack of attention accorded to reference in literature in the past, the increasing number of publications on this subject in recent years, almost all written by literary theoreticians, attests to the pertinence, relevance, and necessity of this area of inquiry. Not only does our sustained interest in storytelling throughout the ages indicate a connection (however direct or indirect) between literature and life, but the analysis of the meanings of a text inevitably entails the issue of reference, as Anne Whiteside explains: "Though the signs of literary discourse constitute a text's linguistic dimension, its particular ideological significance lies beyond, and is determined by, the referent" (1987, p. 176). Indeed, recent studies demonstrate without doubt that the study of reference forms an essential part of literary interpretation and that literary texts provide a privileged and complex setting for the exploration of the referential functions of language.

[*See also* Deixis; Frege; Meaning; Pragmatics; Reception and Reader-Response Theories; Russell; *and* Speech Act Theory.]

BIBLIOGRAPHY

Avni, O. *The Resistance of Reference: Linguistics, Philosophy, and the Literary Text*. Baltimore: Johns Hopkins University Press, 1990.

Fitch, B. *Reflections in the Mind's Eye: Reference and Its Problematization in Twentieth-Century French Fiction*. Toronto: University of Toronto Press, 1991.

Frege, G. "On Sense and Reference." In *Translations from the Philosphical Writings of Gottlob Frege*, translated by P. T. Geach and M. Black, pp. 56–78. Oxford: Blackwell, 1960.

Goodman, N. "Routes of Reference." *Critical Inquiry* 8.1 (1981): 121–132.

Harshaw (Hrushovski), B. "Fictionality and Fields of Reference: Remarks on a Theoretical Framework." *Poetics Today* 5.2 (1984): 227–251.

Hewitt, L. "Getting into the (Speech) Act: Autobiography as a Theory of Performance." *SubStance* 16.1 (1987): 32–44.

"La référence littéraire." *Tangence* 44 (June 1994).

Linsky, L. *Referring*. London: Routledge and Kegan Paul, 1967.

Meinong, A. "The Theory of Objects" (1904). In *Realism and the Background of Phenomenology*, edited by R. Chisholm, pp. 76–117. Glencoe, Ill.: Free Press, 1960.

Pavel, T. *Univers de la fiction*. Paris: Editions du Seuil, 1988.

Pratt, M. L. *Toward a Speech Act Theory of Literary Discourse*. Bloomington: Indiana University Press, 1977.

Riffaterre, M. *Fictional Truth*. Baltimore: Johns Hopkins University Press, 1990.

Whiteside, A. "Conclusion: Theories of Reference." In *On Referring in Literature*, edited by A. Whiteside and M. Issacharoff, pp. 175–204. Bloomington: Indiana University Press, 1987.

Whiteside–St. Leger Lucas, A. "Framing Fictional Reference." *Recherches sémiotiques/Semiotic Inquiry* 11.1 (1991): 27–46.

—BARBARA HAVERCROFT

RHETORIC OF THE IMAGE (1964). Roland Barthes's landmark article in visual semiotics, "Rhetoric of the Image" ("Rhétorique de l'image," *Communications* 4 [1964]) probably represents the first attempt to use a simple model to identify recurring elements of pictorial signification. In spite of some confusions and inconsistencies in its use of linguistic terms, this essay has been so influential that later theorists who do not take Barthes's model for granted usually feel the need to justify their divergences.

The article analyzes a publicity picture promoting a brand of spaghetti. Not surprisingly, it captured the attention of all those concerned with advertising, both marketing specialists in search of ways of improving their skill and Marxist cultural analysts looking for critical methodologies. But it also influenced semioticians of the fine arts such as Louis Marin (1971), who tried to apply Barthes's approach to seventeenth-century paintings. Those who denied the feasibility of developing a semiotics of pictorial art (e.g., Hubert Damisch) critically identified attempts such as Marin's with Barthes's stand.

The article consists of a text analysis of one color photograph, defined with respect to both its goal (publicity) and, somewhat more loosely, its medium (magazine picture). The photograph shows samples of the advertised products (spaghetti, Italian tomato sauce, and grated cheese), together with a selection of fresh vegetables presented in a string bag, assumed to be held up by a hand outside the picture's frame. The brand name can be read on the packaged products, and there is also a short text below the string bag. Barthes first comments on the importance of the linguistic part of the message and then specifies a series of "connotations" supposedly appearing partly in the verbal text and partly in the picture.

Here Barthes reasserts his famous paradox, first proclaimed in 1961 in "Le message photographique," according to which the picture is a message deprived of a code. He seems to use *image* and *photograph* as if these terms were equivalent, although he distinguishes between them later on. Many followers of Barthes, however, have retained the wider interpretation, using it to analyze paintings and other works of art. Actually, Barthes does not really attempt to analyze the picture but merely comments on the referent—that is, on the depicted scene. René Lindekens (1971) rightly pointed out that a "rhetoric of the referent," rather than of the picture sign, was at stake in this article.

Another influential idea in Barthes's article is that no picture is able to convey information by itself or, alternatively, contains so much contradictory information that a verbal message is needed to fix (or anchor) its meaning. Thus, pictorial meaning is considered to depend on linguistic meaning. In this case, the picture itself contains the reproduction of a written message in addition to the short text printed on the lower part of the page.

In both the verbal and pictorial parts, Barthes distinguishes between the denoted and the connoted messages. The brand name, Panzani, is said to connote "Italianity"; the picture, however, supposedly conveys the same connotation, in addition to "still-life," "abundance" (analyzed into "complete meal" and "identity of commodities in their natural state and the corresponding industrial products"), and "return from the market place" (implying "freshness" and "domestic preparation").

It has often been suggested that in applying the categories of connotation and denotation to pictures, Barthes is simply recasting Erwin Panofsky's iconological model in other terms. A closer comparison, however, shows the differences: since iconographic symbols are composite signs, Panofsky's second, iconographic level remains on Barthes's first, denotational level; and since the history of styles is located by Panofsky on the first, preiconographic level, it must contain Barthes's "rhetoric"—that is, the expression plane of connotational language. Moreover, whereas the relation between the second and the third levels of Barthes's model is intrinsic and semantic, it is causal for Panofsky, relating the sign to outer reality or thought. Yet if we ignore the fact that the subject matter of iconography is formed by stories and allegories and that the sources of interpretation should be literary, we might argue that many of Barthes's examples fit Panofsky's model better than

the concepts that Barthes borrowed from Louis Hjelmslev.

[*See also* Barthes; Iconicity; Photography; Pictorial Semiotics; *and* Reference.]

BIBLIOGRAPHY

Barthes, R. "Rhétorique de l'image." *Communications* 4 (1964): 40–51.

Barthes, R. "Rhetoric of the Image." In his *Image-Music-Text: Essays*. Selected and Translated by Stephen Heath, pp. 32–51. London: Fontana, 1977.

Floch, J.-M. "Roland Barthes: Sémiotique de l'image." *Bulletin du groupe de recherches sémio-linguistiques* 4–5 (1978): 27–32.

Lindekens, R. *Eléments pour une sémiotique de la photographie.* Paris: Didier/Aimav, 1971.

Marin, L. *Essais sémiologiques.* Paris: Klincksieck, 1971.

Panofsky, E. *Studies in Iconology.* New York: Harper, 1962.

Panofsky, E. *Meaning in the Visual Arts.* Harmondsworth: Penguin, 1970.

Sonesson, G. *Pictorial Concepts: Inquiries into the Semiotic Heritage and Its Relevance for the Analysis of the Visual World.* Lund: Lund University Press, 1989.

—GÖRAN SONESSON

RIEGL, ALOIS (1858–1905), one of the founders of modern art historiography. Riegl has long remained the least known, certainly outside the German-speaking countries. Although schooled in the psychological-philosophical tradition of Johann Friedrich Herbart, and a member of Theodor Sickel's famous Austrian Institute for Historical Research for five years, Reigl became known in the first place as the art historian who actually touched and saw art objects during the eleven years he worked as a curator at the Museum of Applied Arts in Vienna. For both *Stilfragen* (1893) and *Spätrömische Kunstindustrie* (1901), he used material from the collection of this museum. Later, he became a professor at the University of Vienna and there founded the Vienna School of art history.

Like Adolf von Hildebrand (1847–1921) and Heinrich Wölfflin (1864–1945), Riegl developed art-historical principles (*Kunstbegriffe*) as instruments to analyze the different historical modes of perception. He distinguished the tactile (haptic) mode of perception from the optical one and used this distinction in his account of the development of the interior space of religious buildings from the tactile Egyptian pyramids, in which there was almost no concern for space, to the longitudinal late Roman and early Christian basilicas, in which objectlike coherence is exchanged for an optical construction of space. He distinguished a similar development in sculptural reliefs on sarcophagi, triumphal arches, and other forms. Riegl found that the optical mode of perception was also important for Dutch painting of the sixteenth and seventeenth century, as he described in his *Holländisches Gruppenporträt* (1902).

Riegl was primarily interested not in a thorough examination of the developments in applied and autonomous art as an object in itself but rather in the explanation of the generative force responsible for the changing of forms, which he found in the intentionality of the object or, as he termed it, the *Kunstwollen*. By introducing this concept, he was criticizing the materialistic aesthetics of his time, for which Gottfried Semper (1803–1879) was to a certain extent responsible. According to this dogma, the work of art is defined as "a mechanical product consisting of a particular purpose, raw material, and technique," offering no opening to artistic volition. While Semper was influenced by the comparative and historical linguistics of Franz Bopp, Riegl's vision was more in accordance with that of the neogrammarians. In more recent literature (Iversen, 1993), Ferdinand de Saussure's conception of the arbitrariness of language has been compared to Riegl's understanding of both art and applied art as transforming themselves from within, only occasionally motivated by nature, as in the case of onomatopeia in language. Riegl's teleological theory of artistic development and his conception of a *Kunstwollen* (the intentionality of the work of art)—and not *Kunstwille* (the author's intention or will)—can easily be misunderstood. Although he considered art to possess intentionality—obviously more in the sense of *intentio operis* (intention of the work) than *intentio auctoris* (intention of the author)—and purposiveness, the direction of artistic development is never predictable: the objective is constantly changing.

During the 1920s, Riegl's *Kunstwollen* concept was widely discussed, not only by art historians such as Erwin Panofsky but also by the literary scholars whom we now classify as early semioticians—namely, the Bakhtin circle. Both Mikhail Bakhtin (1924) and Pavel Nikolaevich Medvedev (1928) agreed with Riegl in their devastating criticisms of material aesthetics that modalities such as ability (*können*) have no formative influence on artistic volition. Even though the

Marxist Medvedev had some difficulties with the concept of artistic volition, it was obviously of crucial importance to his and Bakhtin's semiotic theory. Bakhtin's "The Problem of Content, Material, and Form in Verbal Art" (1924) has the greatest importance in this matter, but themes in Bakhtin's later works might also be connected with Riegl's thought. The greatest admirer of Riegl in the 1920s and 1930s was Walter Benjamin, who mentioned the methodological strength of *Spätrömische Kunstindustrie* in his biographical notes and particularly stressed the way in which Riegl illuminated works of art without relying on external data or factors (Benjamin, 1986, p. 32). All of these authors well comprehended the diverse and complicated implications of Riegl's theory of intentionality and perception; that is to say, they recognized in it basically a theory of the dynamics between the work of art and the beholder.

Benjamin's evaluation considerably influenced the reception of Riegl's work by Italian structuralists and poststructuralists from the late 1940s onward. Long before translations of his most important books appeared in French or English, *Spätrömische Kunstindustrie* had been translated twice into Italian. Since the 1980s, there has been a growing awareness of Riegl's ideas and their affinity with the theories of the Konstanz School, as well as other reception-aesthetic orientated theories. The German art historian Wolfgang Kemp, who wrote about the relation between Benjamin and Riegl in 1973, is to a large extent responsible for this renaissance. Also, through the adaption of his theory by Leo Steinberg, Riegl's influence is evident in the semiotic analyses of Mieke Bal (1991), among others.

A French translation of *Stilfragen* was published with an introduction by Hubert Damisch (1992), who after his critical evaluation of Panofsky's iconography now pays tribute to Riegl. Damisch stresses the strong interlocking of a historical and a systematic approach to visual data in Riegl's writings. Whereas structural linguistics chose the language system as its object, Riegl made style, not art, the focus of attention. Damisch situates Riegl in relation to Saussurean linguistics and Sigmund Freud's theory of drives and in opposition to the evolutionist theory of Charles Darwin. The development of style has no natural cause in a Darwinian sense nor a technical or material ground, as is argued by the followers of Semper; therefore, the evolution of art is not comparable to that of the human race. Damisch considers Riegl the great historian of the *Historische Grammatik der Bildende Künste*—the title of the book based on his lectures (1966)—whose contemporary relevance lies above all in his reflections on the concept of artistic evolution.

[*See also* Bakhtin; Benjamin; Haptics; Pictorial Semiotics; Reception and Reader-Response Theories; *and* Saussure.]

BIBLIOGRAPHY

Bakhtin, M. M. "The Problem of Content, Material, and Form in Verbal Art (1924). In *Art and Answerability: Early Philosophical Essays by M. M. Bakhtin*, edited by M. Holquist and V. Liapunov, pp. 257–325. Austin: University of Texas Press, 1990.

Bakhtin, M. M., and P. N. Medvedev. *The Formal Method in Literary Scholarship: A Critical Introduction to Sociological Poetics*. Cambridge, Mass.: Harvard University Press, 1985. This volume was published originally as P. N. Medvedev, *Formal'nyi metod v literatoerovedenii: Krititsjeskoe vedenie v sotsiologitsjeskoe poètikoe* (Leningrad: Priboi, 1928).

Bal, M. *Reading "Rembrandt."* Cambridge and New York: Cambridge University Press, 1991.

Benjamin, W. *Gesammelte Schriften*, 5 vols. Frankfurt: Suhrkamp Verlag, 1974, 1982.

Benjamin, W. *Reflections*. Translated by E. Jephcott. New York: Schocken Books, 1986.

Damisch, H. "Préface: Le texte mis à nu." In Alois Riegl, *Questions de style: Fondements d'une histoire de l'ornementation*, pp. ix–xxi. Paris: Hazan, 1992.

Iversen, M. *Alois Riegl: Art History and Theory*. Cambridge, Mass.: MIT Press, 1993.

Riegl, A. *Stilfragen: Grundlegungen zu einer Geschichte der Ornamentik*. Berlin: G. Siemens, 1893.

Riegl, A. *Spätrömische Kunstindustrie nach den Funden in Österreich-Ungarn, Part 1*. Vienna: Verlage der K. K. Hof- und Staatsdruckerei, 1901.

Riegl, A. *Holländisches Gruppenporträt* (1902). Vienna: Osterreichische Staatsdruckerei, 1931.

Riegl, A. *Historische Grammatik der Bildende Künste*. Graz: Bohlau, 1966.

—MARGA VAN MECHELEN

RIFFATERRE, MICHAEL

RIFFATERRE, MICHAEL (b. 1924), French-born American literary theorist. A professor of French at Columbia University since 1953, Riffaterre has published influential books and articles in French and in English, formerly on stylistics from a structuralist viewpoint and more recently bearing upon the semiotics of style and text. His *Semiotics of Poetry* (1978) presents a comprehensive theory designed to explain the processes, both heuristic and interpretive, used by a reader in decoding a poetic text. It should be noted that the "obliqueness" of expression according to which a text "says one thing and means another" is characteristic above all of modern poetry, and Riffaterre's approach is most appropriate when applied to poetry written since the time of the French Symbolists, up to the advent of postmodernism.

Riffaterre's theory is founded on the idea that the poetic text is generated by the "expansion" and "conversion" of an invariant matrix into a set of variant images whose underlying propositional structure remains constant. Riffaterre proposes the following rule: "Expansion transforms the constituents of the matrix sentence into more complex forms" (1978, p. 48). Generally, then, expansion develops the lexical form of the image, though the degree of the expansion, as well as its lexical content, varies among individual images.

The development of an invariant "matricial" proposition, through expansion into a system of images extending across the whole text, guarantees its semiotic unity. On this intratextual level, the successive images have the roles of subject and object signs (in Peircean terms) in relation to the matrix as interpretant. It is the surface strangeness—or "ungrammaticality"—of the expressions used in individual images that alerts the reader to the underlying presence of a matrix generating an image system. The vocabulary of the individual image—and by extension, that of the whole system—to some extent reflects a preexisting literary or sociolectic commonplace that functions as what Riffaterre calls a "hypogram."

The propositional structure of the matrix has an intertextual phrase—which the reader must discover—capable of generating one or more other texts. On the level of the whole text, this "intertext" plays the role of the object sign, relative to the subject sign of the matricial phrase of the primary text. The interpretant of these two signs, which completes the triad of the Riffaterrean model of poetic signification, is based in principle on a proposition according to which the reader may relate the two other textual signs. "The other text enlightens the reader through comparison: a structural similarity is perceived between the poem and its textual referent despite their possible differences at the descriptive and narrative levels" (1978; pp. 99–100).

Riffaterre designates the semantic effect of the underlying semiotic structure of a poetic text with the term *significance* or *semiosis*, by way of contrast to the disparate "meanings" furnished by individual images on the level of mimesis—the referential or mimetic language of the sociolect, society's linguistic code. In order to distinguish poetic language from the referential conventions of sociolectic discourse, Riffaterre appeals to the notion of indirect signification ("poetry expresses concepts and things by indirection," 1978, p.1). The individual images of a poem might have a certain meaning on the mimetic level, but on the level of the semiotic system of the text they combine to give it a quite different significance. Riffaterre stresses that the linguistic mechanisms involved in transmitting poetic significance differ qualitatively from those used in sociolectic language to transmit the meaning of a piece of discourse. The basic characteristic of mimesis is that it produces a continuously changing sequence of semantic references. The sociolectic text "multiplies details and continually shifts its focus to achieve an acceptable likeness to reality, since reality is normally complex" (1978, p. 2). Semiosis, by contrast, depends upon the reader's perception that all the variants of the matrix sentence point to the same underlying invariant proposition. These images—"ungrammatical" on the superficial level in that they tend to contravene the norms of the sociolectic code—become perfectly grammatical when they are considered as components of the underlying signifying system. Examples of the linguistic mechanisms available to the poet as a means of indicating indirect signification are (1) "displacement": metaphor and metonymy; (2) "distortion": ambiguity, contradiction, or nonsense; and (3) "creation": formal equivalence, such as rhyme or syntactic parallelism.

The matrix as the invariant core concept that generates a whole system of variant images is that "constant other" to which every poetic constituent of the text points. Riffaterre insists that the matrix never manifests itself on the level of surface structure. It follows that in principle the matrix is accessible only through its "ungrammatical" variants situated on the textual surface. The matrix may be expressed in a single word, but it always has the structure of at least a potential predication; often, it takes the form of a complete phrase. The search for this underlying concept is the principal aim of a Riffaterrean reading of a poem.

In order to further define the internal semantic structure of a matrix, the reader may turn to the au-

thority of an intertextual structure—which Riffaterre usually calls simply "the intertext"—chosen from the stock of textual materials existing in his or her memory. Thus, although the matrix might be a hypothesis put together by the reader, once an intertext is found, the "model," so to speak, of the internal structure of the matrix is legitimized. The matrix is a semantic structure, in the classically structuralist sense. "Like all structures, [it] is an abstract concept never actualized per se" (1978, p. 13).

The hypogram is a group of words already existing in the sociolect that contributes lexical material to a poetic expression or image—for example, a cliché; a descriptive system ("a network of words [metonymically] associated with one another around a kernel word, in accordance with the sememe of that nucleus" (1978, p. 39); or a particularly well-known part of another text. Riffaterre adds that "for the poeticity to be activated in the text [i.e., in order that a literary image may become a poetic sign contributing to the semiotic structure of a poetic text], the sign referring to a hypogram [by virtue of its lexical content] must also be a variant of that text's matrix." In view of this double constraint—both lexical and semantic—on the form of the poetic sign, a given poetic text might include isolated poetic expressions that do not participate in the signifying system of the text. Since the vocabulary of all the images of a textual system may borrow from the same hypogrammatic structure, the matrix might also contain words—or semes—from this hypogram. However, even though a hypogram itself might be an intertextual structure or come from another text, neither its syntax nor its internal semantic structure need have any relation whatsoever with the structure of the matrix in question.

Riffaterre (1978) raises the question of universality: "The theoretical aims of this book make it applicable, I believe, to all Western literature, and in all likelihood some of the rules I propose reflect universals of literary language." A number of essential concepts define the literariness of the individual literary work: (1) catachresis, which includes all kinds of indirection of expression. Since Riffaterre is dealing with literariness in general, one expects to find indirection created by distortion and creation more often in poetry than in narrative; (2) monumentality, which is based on the idea of the generation of a set of images by an underlying common structure but also includes hypogrammatic overdetermination on the lexical level; (3) representation or artificiality, which are concerned with how the essential components of a literary work never refer directly to extratextual reality; (4) textuality, which focuses on how all the essential components of the work participate in a system of images generated by a single matrix, the text as a literary construct being coextensive with this system; and (5) intertextuality, which is concerned above all with the concept of an intertextual model (cf. Riffaterre, 1988).

In 1990, Riffaterre published a book dealing with narrative literature. This work focuses on the way matrixlike structures generate a series of variant situations that recur in the course of novels, such as those of Proust (Riffaterre, 1990, pp. 49–52).

[See also Poetics; and Text.]

BIBLIOGRAPHY

Hopkins, J. A. F. *Présentation et critique de la théorie sémiotique littéraire de Michael Riffaterre*. Special issue of *Sophia Linguistica* 36 (1994).

Riffaterre, M. *Essais de stylistique structurale*. Paris: Flammarion, 1971.

Riffaterre, M. *Semiotics of Poetry*. Bloomington: Indiana University Press, 1978.

Riffaterre, M. *La production du texte*. Paris: Seuil, 1979a.

Riffaterre, M. "Generating Lautréamont's Text." In *Textual Strategies*, edited by J. V. Harari, pp. 404–420. Ithaca, N.Y.: Cornell University Press, 1979b.

Riffaterre, M. "The Interpretant in Literary Semiotics." *American Journal of Semiotics* 3 (1985): 41–55.

Riffaterre, M. "Relevance of Theory/Theory of Relevance." *Yale Journal of Criticism* 1–2 (1988): 163–176.

Riffaterre, M. *Fictional Truth*. Baltimore: Johns Hopkins University Press, 1990.

—JOHN A. F. HOPKINS

ROCK ART. A global phenomenon that has its origins in the nascent cognitive and representational capabilities of foraging communities who lived approximately forty thousand years ago, rock art is physically manifest in the form of engravings, paintings, sculptures, and combinations thereof. These images are most often executed on a rock support such as a boulder, cave, glacial pavement, stone, or even landscape. For example, the Nasca lines found in modern-day Peru are a synthesis that incorporates imagery, rock, and landscape.

Rock art is both an ancient and contemporary practice and is found among many communities. It is most often practiced by forager or hunter-gatherer societies, though certain pastoralists and farmers of the last ten thousand years have also produced such works. It is a visual distillate that both represents and is constitutive of an individual or corporate worldview. However, rock art is not a monolithic category but an ambiguous class of material culture, governed by certain human universals as well as by very specific historical and intellectual factors. For this reason, the dominant intellectual trend in rock-art studies has been anthropological and archaeological, though there is much potential for interdisciplinary work.

Prior to the archaeological investigation of European Upper Paleolithic rock art and associated material culture, the reigning academic authorities either ignored rock art, ascribed it to some mythic golden age or ridiculed it as recent, poorly executed idle scribblings. However, even this archaeological focus was not unproblematic, since, for the late nineteenth century and three quarters of the twentieth, rock-art research was situated in a European cultural milieu influenced by notions of unilinear evolution and a hierarchical distinction between "primitive" (other) and "civilized." This social context often led to a fundamental contradiction in the thinking of rock-art researchers. On the one hand, rock art was seen as art, comparable to the best the Western world had to offer. On the other hand, the material culture of the Upper Paleolithic rock-art producers was, relative to the industrialized age, simple and apparently primitive. How, then, could such "primitive" people produce "art"? Many interpretations have occurred and recurred over the last 150 years to account for the worldwide existence of rock arts of great antiquity. These interpretations may be placed into four broad, yet interconnected categories.

The first interpretation is based on the assumption that rock art is, in fact, art. This interpretation is known as *art pour l'art* (art for art's sake). Simply stated, this approach derives from a distinctly Western understanding that there exist distinct categories of images and image making. Rock-art researchers who subscribe to this interpretation implicitly trust their sensory perceptions—principally sight—and assume that the engravings, paintings, and sculptures are direct, if artistic, two-dimensional representations of observable three-dimensional phenomena such as animals, landscapes, and people. These researchers mostly believe in an external reality or world as defined from their post-Enlightenment intellectual perspective. They assume their sensory perceptions are capable of unproblematically perceiving, assimilating, and understanding rock-art imagery.

The *art pour l'art* approach to rock art was, like all interpretations, a product of its time. The expansion of the European colonial world led to a greater exposure to and interest in the "other" (Clifford, 1988). For example, the primitivist movement pioneered by Pablo Picasso was influenced directly by non-Western arts, including rock art. The others were often considered appropriate examples of Jean-Jacques Rousseau's hypothetical noble savage, and rock art was considered a product less of cultural complexity than of a powerful, primal, human urge to create. The principal flaw of the *art pour l'art* approach is that it assumes that nonrock art–producing researchers can, from an etic position, intuitively understand visual images across time, space, and cultures (Maquet, 1986).

An attempt to understand rock art in emic terms was made through the second principal rock-art interpretation, which is known as "sympathetic magic" or "hunting magic." This approach led researchers such as Salomon Reinach to the ethnographic accounts of the Australian aborigines, who were believed to inhabit relic "Stone Age" communities totally unaffected by agriculture, industrialization, or anything Western. As such, the aboriginal beliefs and practices were substituted directly for the beliefs and practices of European Upper Paleolithic rock artists, for whom no ethnography exists. Researchers have argued that animals were engraved, painted, and sculpted by foragers as an expression of wished-for control over the animal depicted. This control could mean both success for the human hunters in the hunt as well as ensuring the long-term proliferation of the animals depicted. It has even been argued that elaborate ceremonies are held, with certain rock-art images as props, to propitiate vaguely defined deities, forces, and spirits. For example, the sculpted clay cave bear (*Ursus spelaeus*) at Montespan cave in what is today southern France has numerous round holes in its body. These holes are said to be the residue of a ritual in which hunters stabbed and speared the sculpture in a simulacrum of a successful hunt, even though the sculpted cave bear is located in a very low (more than one meter down) part of the cave and the holes appear to be of natural origin. In addition, archaeological excavation of the domestic deposits left behind at this and other sites has demonstrated that the animals most often painted were usually those least often eaten. There are very few unambiguous hunting scenes depicted in most rock arts. The sympathetic-magic approach fails to realize that rock-art imagery is often polysemic and not reducible to a single grand theory.

The third approach to rock-art interpretation is the narrative approach. Certain researchers have assumed that rock art represents a narrative of actual or mythical events that can be reconstituted by a study of the weapons, clothing, dwellings, and postures depicted, as well as by studying the relationships between rock-art images. Like the *art pour l'art* interpretation, researchers once again assume that the imagery is an "art" and sign, signifier, and referent, and even index, are considered equivalent and similar. Rock art is thus construed as a fairly simple representation of forager life, which is also treated as fairly simple. The narrative approach, however, confuses appearance and meaning: that which is depicted (an animal) is what it is (an animal)—an example of circular reasoning. Alternatively, that which is depicted (an animal) is a resource (food, clothing, and such like).

Rock art may, at a certain level, incorporate information relating to day-to-day activities and events. However, rock art is a multilayered phenomenon, and we should not confuse the apparently facile motivation to produce images (for personal aesthetic pleasure) and the meanings of these deeply held and societally cross-referenced signs and signifiers, which are often metaphorical in nature (Fernandez, 1974). For example, what would someone unfamiliar with Christianity make of the faithful's apparently cannibalistic tendency to consume their founder?

Over the last thirty years, a fourth interpretive approach to rock art has been developed by anthropologists and archaeologists who might also be described as episodic semioticians. This is not to say that rock-art imagery necessarily constitutes a language or text, only that rock arts are structured representations that have the potential to communicate information, whether mundane or extraordinary. The current state of rock-art research has a distinctly postmodern character, with people from all manner of research backgrounds converging on rock-art interpretation. The most important theoretical commonality among these researchers is the realization that "rock art" is not a clear-cut category and cannot be studied in isolation but has to be situated in a broader context. This context has at least four components; theoretical position, ethnography, archaeological material culture, and rock art.

First, a theoretical position is essential, for it is no longer true to say that a researcher follows a procedural chain in which data are found, collected, described, and interpreted. Rather, interpretation is an inextricable component of all stages of research (Lewis-Williams, 1983). By adopting an explicit theoretical position, a researcher makes it easier for others to follow and critique their discourse.

Second, the use of ethnography as a bridge between researchers and rock-art producers is an essential though highly problematic practice (Wylie, 1988). Even though the information it gathers passes through linguistic, conceptual, and power-relations filters between informant and ethnographer, ethnography does allow an approximation of an emic understanding of certain parts of a rock-art corpus. Where possible, specific ethnography can retain something of the nuances and subtleties that distinguish rock art–producing communities. If this is not done, rock art and its producers coalesce into an undifferentiated homogeneous whole, which masks the fact that each rock art–producing group, however loosely defined, has a different cognitive construction and understanding of the world, and hence their expression of this world in media such as rock art differs, sometimes substantially, in meaning. For example, certain foragers—such as the Australian Aborigines, European Upper Paleolithic people, and the southern African San—have an understanding of the world in which "real" observable phenomena and "nonreal" hallucinatory phenomena are interdigitated, producing a highly ambiguous, nuanced social reality. Nonforagers, such as the pastoralists of the Fezzan in North Africa and the Anasazi of North America, appear to have a more rigid, even stratified construction of external realities, and their rock art tends to relate to kinship relations, moieties, and initiations.

Third, the use of material culture obtained from archaeological excavation and anthropological fieldwork can add further detail to knowledge of a rock art–producing community. Material-culture studies (Miller, 1994) indicate that all items of material culture have the potential to encode societal information, elements of which can be reconstructed, according to the theoretical position of the researcher. On a practical level, material culture can indicate whether the rock-art producers are foragers, pastoralists, or farmers, whether they exist in nuclear-family groups or larger social groupings, whether they have trade and alliance networks, and so forth. This kind of study includes the dating of material culture, but rock-art dating is a highly contentious activity that is subject to numerous biases and flaws. Researchers do usually agree on broad age estimates, and dating does contribute toward constructing a general social, spatial, and temporal context for each piece of rock art. However, rock art is principally a social phenomena generated out of social contexts that are largely independent of dating and that can become manifest in any place at any time, and sometimes many times.

The fourth component of a rock-art context is the imagery and its interrelationships. It is this component that most fully occupies the domain of semiotics. Rock-art imagery immediately triggers a wealth of ideas and associations in the mind of the person who visually apprehends such art. This might also have been the case among the people who produced the images, but we have no independent referent that allows us to determine whether our etic associations and ideas in any way approximate an emic understanding of the imagery. These associations are not necessarily inherent in the visual appearance of the image or sign, which would then make the image an icon or representation with a necessary visual link to a physical entity; rather, they are dependent on the conceptual and physical context of the rock-art image.

It is therefore necessary to establish a necessary and sufficient relation of relevance between the meanings intended by the rock artist and the meanings constructed by the researcher. This relation of relevance becomes particularly important in instances where there is no ethnography specific to a rock-art corpus. Here, Richard J. Bernstein (1983) argues for the use of multiple strands of evidence, twisted together in a ropelike fashion to support an argument. Though no one strand of evidence is in itself necessary or sufficient nor is, in fact, the "rope" of evidence, there is a cumulative evidential weight that, when combined with a broad, working consensus among the most dominant or influential researchers in a field, allow an argument to hold for a time.

Other strands that have been pursued recently involve neuropsychology, considerations of the entire landscape within which one or more sites are located, and replication studies of how images were made. However, not all researchers agree on which strands and ropes of argumentation are valid. There is robust terminological debate, with words such as *art*, *image*, *representation*, and *meaning* being contested. Certain researchers, especially those from structural linguistics, have considered a textual or linguistic metaphor useful to a study of rock art. These researchers hold that images are structured, analogous to language, as idiographic, with phonemes and sentencelike meanings. Rock art is like language in that the images, like words, have no inherent referent to a meaning. However, rock art is unlike a language in structure as it is ambiguous, polysemic, and incomplete. Most problematically, rock art is often very idiosyncratic, and certain images make little or no reference to a system or set of rules. In addition, rock-art studies suffer from an overwhelming visual bias at the expense of analysis into how touch, sound, and even smell relate to rock art, as studies of the use of engraved and painted caves as huge resonators attest.

Most researchers do agree that rock art represents something extraordinary and is a conscious, structured product that is nonetheless problematic for a search for nomothetic rules. Further complications arise out of numerous ethnographies that indicate that rock art was considered not as a representation of a thing, quality, or concept but as an entity sufficient unto itself. It might thus be useful to consider rock art in terms of metonymy and synecdoche, not necessarily to imply that a whole exists or can be described but to sensitize researchers to what is a partial and differentially preserved visual residue. Archaeological material culture is very partial, and archaeologists thus have developed skills in using the parts of things to make broader inferences about a past social reality. The synthesis the rock-art images represent is considerably more than the sum of their parts.

While the link between rock-art producer and researcher is almost always sundered, rock art does have certain universal resonances. Many forager rock arts derive from hallucinations that are governed by the central nervous system. Also, the attraction to rock art and sometimes the places at which it is depicted often persist across time and cultures, as does the aesthetic appreciation of imagery.

The inputs from disciplines as diverse as archaeology, anthropology, literary theory, physics, semiotics, and others act as sources of independent verification or falsification for archaeological argumentation. This informal association of disciplines has made rock art one of the most theoretically informed classes of archaeological material culture. A further source of verification is the continuing discovery of new rock-art sites, often tens of thousands of years old. These new discoveries can both challenge and support reigning interpretations.

Possible future directions for rock-art research might come from nonvisual and nonverbal approaches that, though logically difficult to define precisely, do appear to represent a dynamic, creative process that might provide researchers with ways of thinking, if not specific details. Possibly, we need to step ever so slightly outside of our current intellectual tradition and subtly realign our understanding of rock art to include information that is novel and that exists somewhat uneasily beside received and accepted knowledge. In short, we might have to learn to live with some ambiguity in our interpretations of rock-art imagery. It is somewhere in that creative tension between the known and unknown that our most profound insights might emerge, from which we might appreciate even more what remarkable realities rock art represents.

[*See also* Mindscape; Phoneme; Pictorial Semiotics; Postcolonialism; Semiotic Terminology; *and* Vision.]

BIBLIOGRAPHY

Bernstein, R. J. *Beyond Objectivism and Relativism: Science, Hermeneutics, and Praxis.* Oxford: Blackwell, 1983.

Clifford, J. *The Predicament of Culture: Twentieth-Century Ethnography, Literature, and Art.* Cambridge, Mass.: Harvard University Press, 1988.

Fernandez, J. "The Mission of Metaphor in Expressive Culture." *Current Anthropology* 15 (1974): 119–133.

Lewis-Williams, J. D. "Introductory Essay: Science and Rock Art." *South African Archaeological Society Goodwin Series* 4 (1983): 3–13.

Maquet, J. *The Aesthetic Experience: An Anthropologist Looks at the Visual Arts.* New Haven: Yale University Press, 1986.

Miller, D. *Material Culture and Mass Consumption.* Oxford: Blackwell, 1994.

Wylie, A. "Simple Analogy and the Role of Relevance Assumptions: Implications for Archaeological Practice." *International Studies in Philosophy* 2 (1988): 134–150.
—SVEN OUZMAN

ROSSI-LANDI, FERRUCCIO (1921–1985), Italian philosopher whose work was dedicated to the elaboration of an original dialectic and materialist sign theory. Rossi-Landi's sociosemiotics conceptualizes sign production, including language production, as work embedded in a system of the production, reproduction, distribution, and exchange of social tools. He thus tries to circumvent the mentalist tendencies of Saussureanism and structuralism, the formalism of Peircean semiotics, and the pansemioticism of bioevolutionary approaches.

Rossi-Landi's first contribution to European semiotics was to introduce and discuss Charles W. Morris's work (1953, 1975). Morris's work is central to Rossi-Landi's own theoretical approach, from behaviorism to the thematization of societal behavior. After his study of Morris, Rossi-Landi's next work of theoretical interest (1961) featured his conception of "common speech," a notion he developed subsequently into that of linguistic work and sign work at large and that of social reproduction (Ponzio, 1988). Rossi-Landi then addressed the problem of the constitution of meaning in everyday language ("common speech"), and with *Ideologies of Linguistic Relativity* (1973) he reckoned with the modern "innativist" theories of language. *Linguistics and Economics* (2d ed., 1977) presented most of the essential elements of his theory in elaborate form. His main philosophical work, *L'ideologia*, translated under the somewhat misleading title *Marxism and Ideology* (1990), is concerned with the interdependencies of (partly "false") consciousness, Weltanschauung, and social practice.

Rossi-Landi's important editorial activity concerned works by Charles Morris, Giovanni Vailati, Gilbert Ryle, and several journals and serials, the most important of which was *Ideologie* (1967–1971), where parts of his work first appeared in article form. At his death, Rossi-Landi left several unpublished manuscripts (Ponzio, 1988). *Between Signs and Non-Signs*, edited by Susan Petrilli, appeared in 1992.

"Ideas for a Manifesto of Materialistic Semiotics" (1979) presents his theory in a nutshell. Resting on the fundamentals of Hegelian dialectics and Marxist anthropology, Rossi-Landi developed an original system of thought bearing on language and signs in general. Besides the influence of Marxist philosophies, Rossi-Landi was also well acquainted with Peirce's work and was led from there to Morris, whose tendency toward semiotic-philosophical synthesis fascinated him. According to Rossi-Landi, Morris emphasizes the importance of the unification of a radical empiricism, a rationalist method, and a critical pragmatism. These are the three components that correspond to the three dimensions of semiotics. The unity of science results from the unity of its language structure, the semantic relations it is capable of establishing, and the practical effects it evokes. Later on, Rossi-Landi focused on not only the unification of sciences but also the dialectical unity of theory and practice when he examined the sign-guided and sign-mediated integration of the modes of production and the ideological institutions in the framework of social reproduction as a whole. Apart from the broad knowledge of the Peirce and Morris line of modern semiotics, Rossi-Landi had a comprehensive, encyclopedic familiarity with the history and the present of semiotics, analytic philosophy, theory of language, and related fields. For example, he recast Ludwig Wittgenstein's concept of "language use" in a Marxist perspective.

A further important model that Rossi-Landi used within the framework of his approach is the classical Marxist model of structure and superstructure. In his version, however, this model is complemented by a third essential component: the semiotic. Augusto Ponzio summarizes his theoretical approach as follows: "Rossi-Landi's theoretical pivot [. . .] is the working hypothesis that recurrent difficulties in the study of the relations between structure and superstructure come from the lack of a mediating element. According to Rossi-Landi, the mediating element consists in the totality of the sign system, verbal as well as nonverbal, operating in every human community." Ponzio contends that this approach led him toward a semiotics of social reproduction, a topic later to become central in his final book, *Metodica filosofica e scienza dei segni* (1985), and concludes that "according to Rossi-Landi, somewhere must lie the end of a skein of social reproduction the pulling of which may allow us to propose a typology of signs" and, eventually, "from the methodics of common speech Rossi-Landi arrives at a methodics of common semiosis" (1986, p. 219).

BIBLIOGRAPHY

Works by Rossi-Landi

Charles Morris. Milan: Bocca, 1953.

Significato, comunicazione e parlare comune. Padua: Marsilio Editori, 1961.

Ideologies of Linguistic Relativity. The Hague: Mouton, 1973.

"Signs on a Master of Signs." *Semiotica* 13.2 (1975): 155–197.

Linguistics and Economics. 2d ed. Janua Linguarum Series Major, 81. The Hague: Mouton, 1977. This work was first published in *Current Trends in Linguistics,* vol. 12, *Linguistics and Adjacent Arts and Sciences,* part 8, pp. 1787–2017 (The Hague: Mouton, 1974).

"Ideas for a Manifesto of Materialistic Semiotics." *Kodikas/Code* 2 (1979): 121–123.

"Towards a Theory of Sign Residues." *Versus* 23 (1979): 15–32.

Language as Work and Trade: A Semiotic Homology for Linguistics and Economics. Translated by M. Adams et at. South Hadley, Mass.: Bergin and Carvey, 1983.

Metodica filosofica e scienza dei segni. Milan: Bompiani, 1985.

Marxism and Ideology. Oxford: Clarendon Press, 1990.

Between Signs and Non-Signs. Edited by S. Petrilli. Critical Theory, 10. Amsterdam: John Benjamins, 1992.

Other Works

Bernard, J. "The Social Philosophy and Socio-Semiotics of Ferruccio Rossi-Landi." In *Readings su Ferruccio Rossi-Landi: Semiosi come pratica sociale,* edited by J. Bernard et al., pp. 69–94. Naples: Edizioni Scientifiche Italiane, 1994.

Ponzio, A. "On the Signs of Rossi-Landi's Work." *Semiotica* 62.3–4 (1986): 207–221.

Ponzio, A. *Rossi-Landi e la filosofia del linguaggio.* Bari: Adriatica Editrice, 1988.

—JEFF BERNARD

RUSSELL, BERTRAND (1872–1970), British philosopher, founder of analytic philosophy, a movement preoccupied with language and logic that has a complex and sometimes controversial relation to semiotics. Russell's early work concerns both mathematics and philosophy. He is credited with demonstrating that formal logic supplies sufficient foundations for arithmetic, geometry, and the calculus. After 1910, he published extensively on the philosophical foundations of psychological and physical knowledge, including aspects of commonsense knowledge as well as more specialized scientific knowledge, which he held ultimately depended on the former. In his later years, Russell claimed that learning how science and perception are related had been his chief interest throughout his career. As a point of method, Russell characteristically studied this problem by analyzing the conditions under which verbal propositions could be logically interpretable, referred to perception, and warranted. While he did not regard propositions as the only forms of thought relevant to the problems that motivated his inquiry, he regarded them as a sufficiently important and difficult test case

to merit the greatest parts of his efforts outside of mathematics.

Russell's early work in logic parallels that of Gottlob Frege, whom he reviewed in an appendix to his *Principles of Mathematics* (1903), noting the similarity of their results and regretting not having been aware of them earlier. Russell understands Frege's concepts of *Sinn* and *Bedeutung* to correspond with his own of "concept" and "that which a concept designates," but he believes Frege errs in attributing *Sinn* to proper names. Frege and Russell also developed comparable distinctions between mentioning and asserting and between bound and variable propositions, but they had differing ideas about truth functions.

Russell understood linguistic propositions as signs of an external reality. In consequence, studies of language that did not take acount of its representational vocation were of little interest to him. He dismisses the later work of Ludwig Wittgenstein on this basis. The same insistence on representational function marks Russell's attitudes toward mathematical foundations: he rejects logically adequate axioms that produce only an abstract arithmetic, not guaranteed to serve for counting objects. His general method in analyzing language is to center his attention on descriptive statements. Consequently, he largely overlooks the use of language for emotional expression, fiction, or persuasion, though he does not entirely ignore it. Descriptive language is then interpreted by logical paraphrase. In this latter task, Russell adumbrated the "logical form" of Noam Chomsky's later theory. Russell's elaborate analysis of the word *the* (two chapers of the introduction to *Introduction to Mathematical Philosophy,* 1919) provides a striking example.

Russell's analysis of language is linked strongly to the construction of logic that appears in his mathematical work. Both share the total segregation of syntactic study from the analysis of substantive terms that characterizes the whole of modern formal logic since George Boole (1815–1864). Both also share recourse to the theory of types, his own invention, which assigns propositions to different levels on the principle that a proposition at one level can refer only to propositions of lower levels. The theory of types reappears as the "linguistic level" in the work of Louis Hjelmslev. This device expunges paradoxes from logical language at the cost of self-reference. For example, by this method, the liar's paradox ("I never tell the truth") must be analyzed as either not referring to itself or else—in advance of any regard to its confusing consequences—as logically inadmissible simply on the basis that it violates the rule.

The theory of types entails the view that language has atomic propositions that refer to facts but not to other propositions, as well as basic terms that refer to items of experience but lack any implication of structure. Russell takes "proper name" as a category for these basic terms that refer to distinct individuals rather than classes, but his specific applications of the idea evolved over his career. His analyses of syntax, quantifiers, and deictic words and structures are more convincing than his analyses of basic terms; despite his insistence on their representational function, Russell did not determine the nature of representation per se. In *An Inquiry into Meaning and Truth* (1940), he acknowledges the difficulty: "'Signs' depend, as a rule, upon habits learnt by experience. . . . We may say that A is a 'sign' of B if it promotes a behaviour that B would promote, but that has no appropriateness to A alone. It must be admitted, however, that some signs are not dependent upon experience . . . The precise definition of 'sign' is difficult. . . . there is no satisfactory definition of 'appropriate' behaviour" (1940, p. 13). *An Inquiry into Meaning and Truth* deals with such issues as the interpretations of sentences, psychological aspects of language apart from literal meaning, the relation of language to knowledge, and the conditions under which statements are warranted. In the same work, Russell develops a semantic theory of basic words, based on association by habit that does not clearly distinguish meaning from the acquisition of it.

Russell appears to have acknowledged Charles Sanders Peirce's work very rarely, despite the close parallel of their motivations, but he did so most notably with regard to the foundation of the algebra of relations. The shortcoming of Peirce's algebra, for Russell, was its reliance on the extensional definition of classes, which resulted in a notation too cumbersome to permit progress because it requires all operations on classes to be shown in terms of summations. Otherwise, Peirce appears in many respects to have anticipated Russell's interests and methods, as in his analysis of the concept of force in "How to Make Our Ideas Clear" (1878), his atomistic characterizations of perception, and his lifetime immersion in the practice and philosophical theory of science.

A major difference between them lies in Peirce's adherence to a phenomenology of consciousness.

Lacking any probing consideration of consciousness, Russell's notion of mind is very constrained. His *The Analysis of Mind* (1921) is concerned with the questions of whether physics and psychology deal ultimately with the same objects and, if they do, what constitutes the difference between their viewpoints. Russell finds very few grounds on which psychology and physics might differ. In order to identify the concerns of physics and psychology, however, Russell abandons any functional distinction between consciousness and unconsciousness so that unconscious memory can provide a physical explanation of conscious association. Neither Russell nor many theorists of semiotics seem fully aware that a theory of signs becomes gratuitous when the unconscious is regarded as part of the mind rather than part of the conjectural physical world.

[*See also* Frege; Meaning; Peirce; Sign; *and* Wittgenstein.]

BIBLIOGRAPHY

Russell, B. *The Principles of Mathematics*. London: Allen and Unwin, 1903.
Russell, B. *Introduction to Mathematical Philosophy*. London: Allen and Unwin, 1919.
Russell, B. *The Analysis of Mind*. London: Allen and Unwin, 1921.
Russell, B. *An Inquiry into Meaning and Truth*. London: Allen and Unwin, 1940.

—DAVID LIDOV

RUSSIAN FORMALISM. In the 1920s and 1930s, a group of Russian scholars, collectively known as formalists, developed the basic concepts of a theory of literature and art that laid the foundations for modern structuralist and semiotic concepts of art and culture. The rise of a radically new theory of art and culture is best understood against the background of the contemporary historical and cultural events. Literature, in particular realistic prose, had lost its dominant ideological function at the turn of the century. The first Russian Revolution in 1905, the beginning of World War I in 1914, and the October Revolution in 1917 meant significant changes in whole of society. In academia, the younger generation began to question traditional concepts. Within linguistics, the neogrammarian theory as represented by Jan Baudouin de Courtenay was criticized by younger linguists for the exclusive emphasis it put on historical linguistics at the expense of the study of functions.

In 1915 and 1916, two groups of young scholars formed the organizational centers of Russian formalism: in Moscow, the Moscow Linguistic Circle (Moskovskij Lingvističeskij Kružok, MLK) and in Saint Petersburg, the Society for the Study of Poetic Language (Obščestvo po Izučeniju Poètičeskogo Jazyka, OPOJAZ). In the beginning, they were small circles of young scholars or students who discussed questions of literary and linguistic theory.

The MLK existed from 1915 to 1924; its founders were Pëtr Bogatyrëv, Roman Jakobson, and Grigorij O. Vinokur, with Jakobson serving as its first president from 1915 to 1920. The circle's main interests were language and linguistic approaches to literature and folklore; in addition to dialectological studies (including fieldwork), the basic activities of the circle were methodological discussions, on topics such as the distinction between practical and poetic language. The group was in close contact with contemporary poets, and many theoretical insights were derived from the futurist writings by Velimir Khlebnikov, Vladimir Majakovskij, and Aleksej Kručënych. A few, like Osip Brik, were both poets and theoreticians.

The Petersburg OPOJAZ was founded in 1916 by linguists including Lev P. Jakubinskij and Evgenij D. Polivanov, both disciples of Jan Baudouin de Courtenay. This group was later joined by literary scholars such as Viktor B. Šklovskij, Sergej I. Bernštejn, Boris M. Ejchenbaum, Jurij N. Tynjanov, and Boris V. Tomaševskij. At least at the beginning, there was no formal organization or institution, although Šklovskij has repeatedly been called the first president of this circle; his essay "The Resurrection of the Word" (1914) is one of the first documents of Russian formalism, and his "Art as a Device" (1917) has been called its manifest. In 1916 and 1917, OPOJAZ published two volumes called the *Theory of Poetic Language* (*Sborniki po teorii poètičeskogo jazyka*), followed by a third volume in 1919 (*Poetika: Sborniki po teorii poètičeskogo jazyka*). In 1920, OPOJAZ received a formal structure when the Section for Verbal Arts was founded at the State Institute for the History of Arts (GIII), headed by Viktor Žirmunskij, who later distanced himself from formalism; Ejchenbaum, Šklovskij, Tomaševskij, Tynjanov, V. V. Vinogradov, and others joined this section, which started to play an increasing role in the academic sphere.

Both OPOJAZ and the MLK supported the close interaction of linguistic and literary scholarship. Despite this common basis, they developed different approaches: whereas the MLK was more linguistically oriented, for OPOJAZ, linguistics was merely a related and helpful discipline from which methodological innovations in the study of literature could be gained. OPOJAZ more than the MLK sought to establish literary scholarship as an autonomous discipline; for the MLK, poetics was only one particular branch of a broadly conceived linguistics. Jakobson's statement that "poetry is nothing but language in its poetic function" is quite characteristic of the MLK's orientation. Regardless of these differences, both groups shared a broad spectrum of common interests and concepts, and there were close personal and professional contacts between their members, thus justifying the umbrella terms "Russian formalism," "Russian formalist school," and "formalist method." In addition, scholars who were not associated directly with either of these two groups identified with the movement and contributed important works in its overall endeavor, such as A. P. Skaftymov's analyses on the Russian folk epic (the *bylina*), Bogatyrëv's prestructuralist works, Vladimir Propp's *Morphology of the Folktale* (1928), psychologist Lev S. Vygotskij's *Psychology of Art* (1925), and many others.

In the formalists' own view, the notion of "form" was not opposed to "content," and it was not a correlative term to it; rather, form was treated as an independent notion, as something essential for art. The concrete "material" and the specific techniques of the material's "formation" were at the center of their interest. Consequently, some formalists refused this very name and preferred to be called "specifiers," since their primary aim was to specify the properties of literariness (*literaturnost'*) and the techniques by which artificiality is achieved.

One of their basic and generally shared assumptions was that, as the expression of an author's individuality, as a social phenomenon, or as a historic document, a literary artifact might well be the object of psychological, sociological, historiographical, and other studies. But none of these disciplines deals with literature as a phenomenon in its own right. The object of literary scholarship is literariness: that is what makes a verbal text a poetic text or a literary artifact. Consequently, the formalists declared the literary device (*priëm*), not "literature" in general, the true object (the "hero") of literary scholarship. However, the notion of "device" and the formalists' understanding of its role evolved with time.

In view of such conceptual developments and individual divergences among the formalists, it is difficult to establish a clear-cut chronology of Russian formalism. Three successive stages of methodological relevance are usually identified: reductionism; intrinsic systemic functionalism; and extrinsic systemic functionalism.

The reductionist stage focused on specific devices, starting from the basic assumption that art liberates perception from automatization. Poetic language was defined as the deformation of everyday practical language, which is characterized by economy—that is, a maximum of automatization and a minimum of effort in perception. Thus, from a productive perspective, art was characterized by a process of "making strange" (*ostranenie*) in order to render perception more difficult; from a receptive perspective, artistic perception was understood as "seeing anew" (*videnie*) as opposed to "re-cognizing" (*uznavanie*). Consequently, art is characterized by deautomatization or defamiliarization, a process that is achieved by way of specific literary devices. The reception process itself becomes an end in itself: the process of making strange causes the recipient to detect or to "lay bare" the devices (*obnaženie priëma*), and it thus directs the recipient's attention toward the literary artifact's "differential qualities" or its "markedness."

At this stage, these literary devices were considered in isolation rather than interacting within a literary artifact. This overall view culminated in Šklovskij's 1921 definition of an artifact as "the sum of the stylistic devices applied in it." The emphasis on the individual devices, however, should not be understood as the isolation of the artifact from the communication process; although Russian formalism is strictly text oriented in its analyses, it conceptualizes the artifact's location within a communication process. For Šklovskij, indeed, artistic artifacts are exclusively those that are created by specific devices that make highly probable their reception as artistic objects. Thus, the focus on text aesthetic is framed by an aesthetics of intentional production and an aesthetics of competence-dependent reception.

In the second stage, the focus shifted from the device per se to the function of the individual device(s) in the artifact's overall structure. A work of art became understood as a system with an underlying structure in which the various elements are closely interrelated and interdependent; they are organized hierarchically by a "constructive principle."

Tynjanov's *Problem of Verse Language* (1924) is a major theoretical work typical of this period. Tynjanov rejects the notion of the artifact as a closed, symmetrical whole; instead, he defines it as a dynamic unity whose elements are not related by the static sign of equality or by addition but by the dynamic sign of correlation and integration. A literary work must be understood as dynamic. Tynjanov's later distinction between the autofunction and synfunction of the individual elements is helpful in this respect: autofunction is directed at one and the same function in different works of art (whether in synchrony or diachrony); synfunction, by contrast, alludes to one particular function that interacts with all other functions within a given work of art. Obviously, this concept of functionality also refers to elements external to a given text by situating it either in a synchronical or a diachronical relation to other texts; consequently, this concept was soon expanded to the whole area of art and culture, as expressed explicitly in the third stage.

In the third stage, both single works of art and literature as a whole are defined as systems and are also perceived in correlation with other social or cultural phenomena. The text, understood as a system, is part of a larger system (the genre), which in turn is part of the whole cultural-environment system. In analyzing art, immanent structures of the artifact are thus related to external structures. Although this sounds very close to the basic tenets of Czechoslovakian structuralism and a full-fledged semiotics of culture, the formalists themselves restricted their theoretical applications to two areas: literature and art's socioeconomic and institutional environment and its evolution.

Their views on literary evolution were rather mechanical, derived from the early writings of the movement: if art mainly consists of "making strange" automatized forms, these new forms had to be made strange in turn as art evolves while maintaining an innovative character. In the second and third stages, the concept of artistic evolution was elaborated further. A given device is not simply eliminated or replaced by another device; literary evolution does not consist of sudden and complete innovations or mere transfers of formal elements but of a shifting process from center to periphery. Thus, a device and its function do not disappear but acquire a new function: all devices remain virtual in a given culture's memory and can always be reactualized in a focal position at a later time. This process was assumed to be relevant with regard not only to single devices and functions but also to particular genres. Finally, the history of a system is itself endowed with systematic properties, and only the analysis of the correlation between intrinsic and extrinsic structures can yield insights into questions of literary or artistic evolution.

However, the Russian formalists did not go as far as Marxist theoreticians in their socioeconomic analyses. Marxist critique of formalism began to appear in the early 1920s; although many formalists had initially seen themselves as revolutionaries in the realm of literature and as participants in the total transformation of society, their early, provocative neutralization of the social aspects of art was a challenge to Marxism. From a Marxist perspective, art is an expression of particular social relations and a means of cognition that primarily reflects social relations and, consequently, conveys a particular content. Therefore, the official ideology could not accept the formalists' insistence on the autonomy of art. The first Soviet commissar of education, Anatolij V. Lunačarskij, called both formalist art and theory "the last phalanx of bourgeois intelligence."

In the mid-1920s, there were also competent and fair critical remarks from other politicians, such as Lev D. Trockij and Nikolaj I. Bukharin. The most intriguing contemporary critique of formalism came from a philosophical group around Mikhail M. Bakhtin, Pavel N. Medvedev, and Valentin N. Vološinov. Analyzing the formalist approach, Medvedev's book *The Formal Method in Literary Scholarship* (1928) attempted to establish a sociological poetics. But the fate of Medvedev's book is quite telling: whereas the first edition appreciated the role of formalism in asking the right questions about literary theory, the preface to the second edition (1934) placed the book into an ideologically militant context and endeavored to unmask anti-Marxist concepts. In 1930, Šklovskij's autocritical article "A Memorial to a Scholarly Mistake" officially ended the formalist movement in the Soviet Union. Many of its ideas were continued and further elaborated in Czechoslovakian structuralism (the Prague School) and Soviet semiotics (the Moscow-Tartu School).

[*See also* Bogatyrëv; Jakobson; Moscow-Tartu School; *and* Prague School.]

BIBLIOGRAPHY

Bann, S., and J. E. Bowlt. *Russian Formalism: A Collection of Articles and Texts in Translation*. Edinburgh: Scottish Academic Press, 1973.

Bennett, T. *Formalism and Marxism*. London: Methuen, 1979.

Erlich, V. *Russian Formalism: History—Doctrine*. The Hague: Mouton, 1955.

Lemon, L. T., and M. J. Reis, eds. and trans. *Russian Formalist Criticism: Four Essays*. Lincoln: University of Nebraska Press, 1965.

Matejka, L., and K. Pomorska, eds. *Readings in Russian Poetics: Formalist and Structuralist Views*. Michigan Slavic Contributions, 8. Ann Arbor: University of Michigan, 1978.

O'Toole, L. M., and A. Shukman. *Formalism: History, Comparison, Genre*. Oxford: Holdan Books, 1978.

Pomorska, K. *Russian Formalist Theory and Its Poetic Ambiance*. The Hague: Mouton, 1968.

Steiner, P. *Russian Formalism: A Metapoetics*. Ithaca, N.Y., and London: Cornell University Press, 1984.

Striedter, J., and W. Kosny, eds. *Texte der russischen Formalisten*. Munich: W. Fink, 1969–1972.

Šklovskij, V. *Theory of Prose*. Translated by B. Sher. Elmwood Park, Ill.: Dalkey Archive Press, 1990.

Thompson, E. M. *Russian Formalism and Anglo-American New Criticism: A Comparative Study*. The Hague: Mouton, 1971.

Tynjanov, J. N. *The Problem of Verse Language* (1924). Ann Arbor: Ardis, 1981.

—PETER GRZYBEK

S

SAUSSURE, FERDINAND DE (1857–1913), Swiss linguist and comparative philologist best known to semioticians for the posthumously published *Cours de linguistique générale* (*CLG*; *Course in General Linguistics*, 1916). The cycle of lectures on which this text is based occupied a relatively brief period in Saussure's scholarly life, which was mostly spent working within the tradition of comparative and historical linguistics with which *CLG* is generally presented as a decisive break. Saussure draws on his comprehensive knowledge of the historical processes of linguistic change, a theme ever present in *CLG*, as it is throughout Saussure's career. There is considerable continuity in both theory and methodology between Saussure's first published study, *Mémoire sur le système primitif des voyelles dans les langues indo-européennes* (Essay on the Early System of Vowels in Indo-European Languages, 1879), and the discussion in part 3 of *CLG* of sound change. In the earlier work, Saussure already demonstrates an explicit awareness of the systemic imperatives that are assumed to drive sound change.

Saussure makes a basic distinction between an "internal" linguistics of the language system (*langue*) and an "external" linguistics of the "individual part of language" (*parole*). Saussure privileges *langue* as a way of delimiting the object of study, which he sees as an internal system of terms regulated by the differences, or oppositions, among them. "External" linguistics, which Saussure conceives of as secondary to the more "essential" internal linguistics, is concerned with the individual's use of language. This includes the study of language in relation to its historical development, social institutions such as church and school, its literary development, and its political history.

This dichotomous way of thinking about the study of language remained the dominant reading of Saussure throughout mainstream European twentieth-century linguistics. Some linguists and semioticians take it for granted that this is a description of what language is, though these dichotomies are merely constructed by a theory of linguistics. This fallacy continues to cause confusion between description or methodology, on the one hand, and ontology, on the other. A careful reading of *CLG* shows that the separating of *langue* and *parole* does not pertain to the "reality" of language but is a methodological tool for gaining a useful perspective on language. Saussure is not talking about language itself but about the theoretical and descriptive activities that the linguist performs in the process of transforming—"demarcating," "approximating," "demonstrating," and "simplifying"—the data into terms compatible with his science of a "static linguistics."

This emergent linguistics is based in part on the concept of the linguistic sign, which requires Saussure to define this new approach to language in ways fundamentally different from the then-prevailing historical and comparativist perspectives. Philologists had to that point been unable to offer any analysis of language as a coherently organized system of relations at any given point in time and as seen by the current users of the language. Saussure uses the term *synchronic linguistics* to describe this perspective on the study of the abstract linguistic system. He conceives of the synchronic study of *langue* in terms of two analytical dimensions: relations based on the linear combinations of words, phrases, and other components into sequences, or syntagmatic relations; and relations of association that words have in common with other words in memory (i.e., those "outside of discourse"), or paradigmatic relations. Saussure's starting point is that linguistic signs are the products of, and are not independent of, a complex system of differences or contrasts among the various elements that make up the system of language or that occur in some structure. Signs thus have values along both the associative and the syntagmatic dimensions. These differences are, according to Saussure, recognized implicitly by language users on every occasion of language use.

Saussure needs, then, to explain the apparent disjuncture between concrete, individual acts of communication, which are characterized by the irreducible and irrepeatable physical dimensions of communication, involving particular soundings and writings at given times and places with particular individuals, and the fact that language users attribute to these soundings and writings on particular occasions specific meanings that are approximately replicable from one occasion to another, in spite of differences in, say, their physical and material manifestations, or the persons, places, and so on involved. Accordingly, Saussure maintains that the physical and material dimensions of these soundings and writings are merely the material or concrete vehicles through which meanings are expressed: they occur at the level of what Saussure calls substance, and they are not the same as the meanings that they, in some sense, carry. Saussure understands that the variability of sound and writing materials in this physical and material sense contrasts with the fact that individuals who share the same linguistic code succeed more often than not in communicating with each other through the use of the soundings and writings to which meanings are attributed in regular, fairly predictable ways from one occasion to another.

In order to explain the meanings themselves and to avoid equating them with their physical manifestations, Saussure proposes a more abstract level of analysis, which he characterizes as the level of form. At this level, soundings and writings and the meanings attributed to them are interpretable as classes of abstract units, independent of their physical manifestations as phonic substance (sound waves) or graphic substance (written marks on the page). These abstract classes of formal elements or sign types are dependent only on their contrasting relations with the other elements or terms in a given system. Thus, the sign is not the same thing as the phonic or graphic physical medium that embodies it. The sign is a formal and abstract relation derived from the innumerable actual occasions of its use. The emptying of the sign of any consideration of the physical substance that manifests it entails a high level of idealization. This is theoretically consistent with the requirements of a purely "internal" linguistics, which is in principle concerned only with the abstract relations among linguistic forms in a system.

But just as Saussure does not make any specifically ontological claims concerning the system of internal value-producing oppositions or differences, neither does he privilege the system per se. Saussure does not stop at the claim that language is a system of differ-

ences. No less important is his discussion of the formation of "syntagmatic solidarities" through the linguistic "groups" that linguistic units combine to form. Saussure's linearity principle concerns one of the two main ways in which we can speak about meaning as "function in context"—that is, what a given linguistic unit is doing in grammatical structure (some group of linguistic units) rather than simply what it is. The linearity principle thus provides a way of talking about the combinations of linguistic units into structures larger than, say, the single word. Further, Saussure's arbitrariness principle begins to show that a given linguistic form is always functionally related—in various ways that Saussure did not clearly distinguish—to the "higher" level meaning(s) it realizes or expresses. In other words, the meaning of a given linguistic form is a part of the "higher"-level context that the form expresses, and it must always be related to that context. This is so because functional accounts of linguistic meaning additionally seek to understand what linguistic forms are doing in the contexts in which we use them. This is not an explanation in terms of language form sui generis. It is in this sense that Saussure's account of linguistic form needs to be understood.

Saussure does not fully develop the implications of his insights for the theory and analysis of grammar. He mostly restricts his discussions to single, isolated sign units at the level of the morpheme, word, and phrase. Further, Saussure places considerable emphasis on the linear character of the linguistic syntagm, thereby playing down the fact that the functional basis of linguistic meaning does not depend entirely on the linear nature of linguistic structure. Nevertheless, in *CLG* Saussure provides a blueprint and a set of foundational principles for many subsequent developments in twentieth-century linguistics and semiotics.

Latter-day commentators such as Jonathan Culler (1976) and Terence Hawkes (1977) have tended to emphasize the Copernican revolution, as Roy Harris puts it in his introduction to his translation (1983) of *CLG*, that Saussure inaugurated. Saussure's achievement, according to this view, lies in his systematic elaboration of a general science of signs: a semiology. In *CLG*, these principles are elaborated with respect to language, which Saussure envisages as just one component in a more comprehensive "science which studies the life of signs as part of social life." Thus, Saussure stakes out this future science of semiology right from the outset. Further, Saussure does not view this science of semiology as an autonomous science. "It would," Saussure claims, "form a part of social psychology, and consequently of general psychology."

It is doubtful that Saussure used the terms *social psychology* and *psychology* in exactly the contemporary sense of these terms. Saussure does not take this point any further. Instead, he undertakes a quite precise division of labor, leaving it up to the psychologist "to determine the exact place of semiology" in the overall field of human knowledge. The more specific and limited task of the linguist, Saussure continues, "is to define what makes the language system a special type of system within the totality of semiological facts." In making such a claim, Saussure is enacting a strategic move that is both political and theoretical in its implications. Linguistics becomes constituted as an "autonomous" realm of scientific inquiry. Saussure is intent on shifting the study of language from the purely instrumental basis that had prevailed up till then, in which language was a means of studying something else, to one in which it is an object of systematic inquiry in its own right.

In effecting this shift, most commentators have assumed that for Saussure the concrete social and historical production and use of signs is necessarily split off from his envisioned science of semiology. Wlad Godzich (1984) has suggested that Saussure's notion of social psychology might constitute the locus of just such a renovated semiotics. Far from the closed and static system that an oversimplified reading of Saussure reiterates as a form of doctrine, Saussure's conception of the sign is entirely compatible with such a project. In this way, *CLG* gives voice to two distinct models of scientific inquiry.

[*See also* Arbitrariness, Principle of; Binarism; Cours de Linguistique Générale; Langue and Parole; Linearity; Linguistic Motivation; Opposition; *and* Synchronic and Diachronic.]

BIBLIOGRAPHY

Culler, J. *Ferdinand de Saussure*. London: Fontana, 1976.

Godzich, W. "The Semiotics of Semiotics." *Australian Journal of Cultural Studies* 2.2 (1984): 3–22.

Hawkes, T. *Structuralism and Semiotics*. London: Methuen, 1977.

Lévi-Strauss, C. *Structual Anthropology*. Translated by C. Jacobson and B. Grundfest Schoepf. Harmondsworth: Allen Lane and Penguin, 1972.

Saussure, F. de. *Mémoire sur le système primitif des voyelles dans les langues indo-européennes*. Hildesheim, Germany: Georg Olms Verlagsbuchhandlung, 1968.

Saussure, F. de. *Course in General Linguistics*. Translated by R. Harris. London: Duckworth, 1983.

—Paul J. Thibault

SEBEOK, THOMAS A. (b. 1920), American linguist, anthropologist, and semiotician whose multidisciplinary research and editorial activities have contributed to the epistemological development and institutional emergence of modern semiotics worldwide. Born in Hungary, Sebeok did his graduate work in the United States. His early mentors were Roman Jakobson and Charles Morris, whose classes he took at the University of Chicago and from whom he first heard of semiotics (Morris, 1938). Despite his admiration for and friendship with Morris himself, Sebeok was not particularly inspired by this version of semiotics, and he began his intellectual career in traditional scientific linguistics (Sebeok, 1942).

In the intellectual climate of the postwar period, it was almost natural for a linguist to move in the direction of what was then called semiology, the general study of signs as proposed by the Swiss linguist Ferdinand de Saussure as early as 1894. In this context, linguistics was regarded as a pilot science for any general study of signs. This approach to the study of signs, however, was not the route Sebeok followed, and he contributed to the shift in common usage whereby the term *semiotics* has come to be the preferred term for this kind of study, which Sebeok, following Joannes Poinsot, John Locke, and Charles Sanders Peirce, prefers to call the doctrine of signs.

Sebeok's decisive involvement with semiotics can be traced back to 1960–1961, when he was a fellow in residence at the Stanford Center for Advanced Study in the Behavioral Sciences. Here, following up on earlier interests he had entertained in biology, he turned from his background in human languages to the study of animal communication. He was struck by the discontinuity between the various channels of animal communication and the species-specific human one thematized in linguistics and took up the general questions raised by the action of signs in diverse species. This interest eventually resulted in a series of landmark publications (notably Sebeok and Umiker-Sebeok, 1980; Sebeok and Umiker-Sebeok, eds., 1981; and Sebeok and Rosenthal, 1981) that effectively questioned the theoretical soundness and methodological integrity of research investigating the linguistic abilities of apes, chimpanzees, dolphins, and other mammalian species outside the genetic pool of *Homo sapiens sapiens*.

In 1962, Sebeok organized at Indiana University the first conference on semiotics held in the United States (Sebeok, Hayes, and Bates, eds., 1964). This conference launched the term *semiotics* as associated with a comprehensive research program encompassing a vast array of disciplines. Sebeok's first actual publication in semiotics (1963) introduced the term *zoosemiotics* for the general study of animal communication, in contrast to anthroposemiotics, which studies species-specific human communicative modalities. The coinage of this term proved to be emblematic for Sebeok's eventual influence on the entire field of sign studies. He succeded in displacing the linguistic paradigm of semiology, which he dubbed "the minor tradition" (1989), in favor of "the major tradition" (represented by Peirce, the programmatic 1690 statement of Locke, and the earlier Latin semiotics developed between Augustine of Hippo and Poinsot), which sees signs as an intersection of nature and culture through an activity—semiosis—that is confined to neither side of the divide. One of the most important manifestations of Sebeok's influence in this regard appeared in Umberto Eco's discussion of the boundaries of semiotics (1976), which marked Eco's own transition from minortradition semiotics to something more like Sebeok's view. This constant theme of Sebeok was eventually embodied in an anthology bearing a dedication to his work, *Frontiers in Semiotics* (1986; see the discussion of "Pars Pro Toto" in the preface).

In 1976, with his volume titled *Contributions to the Doctrine of Signs* (reprinted 1985), Sebeok launched his trilogy in general semiotics. The second volume was his 1970 collection, *The Sign and Its Masters* (reprinted 1989), and the third, supposedly final, volume was *The Play of Musement* in 1981. However, a fourth volume in general semiotics, *I Think I Am a Verb: More Contributions to the Doctrine of Signs*, appeared in 1986, and fifth and sixth volumes of essays on general semiotics, *A Sign Is Just a Sign* and *American Signatures: Semiotic Inquiry and Method*, appeared in 1991, along with a monograph, *Semiotics in the United States* (ambiguously proclaiming "the view from the center"). Clearly, the original trilogy idea had been discarded. Later on, the publication of the

last of these titles became the occasion for a seminar sponsored by the Centro Internazionale di Semiotica e Linguistica at the Università di Urbino (1992), results of which constitute a special issue of *Semiotica* (1993).

Through his numerous public speeches and publications, Sebeok has propounded a wide-ranging vision of semiotics coextensive with the study of the evolution of life itself, which he sees as a fundamentally semiotic phenomenon. From this vantage point, linguistic ability is but a small, albeit crucial, part of human endowment. Sebeok's concept of communication, rooted in evolutionism and information theory, encompasses all the realms of nature and strives toward a truly pansemiotic understanding of the universe. This comprehensive vision leads him to assert, for instance, that "neither comparative nor diachronic semiotics is feasible any longer without a meticulous inventory and full comprehension of the manifold ways of prokaryotic semiosis" and that "although bacterial communication is radically different from, say, animal communications, we cannot fully grasp semiosis in multicellular organisms, including ourselves, without an appreciation of its ancestral operations two billion years ago, when our planet was still without eukaryotes" (1996, p. 101).

Until his retirement in 1992, Sebeok chaired at Indiana University the Research Center for Language and Semiotic Studies, a position he used to bring together many scholars over the years. Through his numerous editorial enterprises, Sebeok shaped the field through publication of the works of hundreds of other scholars. His long editorship of the official journal of the International Association for Semiotic Studies, *Semiotica*, since its inception in 1969, together with his Approaches to Semiotics and Advances in Semiotics series bear special note in this regard, as does his founding role in establishing the Semiotic Society of America in 1975, with its *American Journal of Semiotics* and volumes of annual proceedings (since 1981). In short, from the standpoint of the sociology of knowledge, Sebeok has been the single most important living figure in the late twentieth-century development of semiotics.

In the history of Western thought, he might compare to Marin Mersenne (1588–1648), who midwifed the birth of modern science and philosophy as Sebeok had midwifed the birthing of contemporary semiotics in the full amplitude of its possibilities as presaged by Poinsot, outlined by Locke, and undertaken in detail by Peirce. Richard Popkin's description of Mersenne (Edwards, 1972, vol 5, p. 282) readily transfers to Sebeok in our time: "a significant figure in his own right and also, through his immense correspondence, publications, and personal acquaintances, a key figure in coordinating and advancing the work of the new philosophers and scientists."

[*See also* Biosemiotics; Chemical Communication; Gaia Hypothesis; Koch; Peirce; Receptors; Umwelt; *and* Zoosemiotics.]

BIBLIOGRAPHY

Bernard, J., et al., *"Symbolicity."* Papers from the International Semioticians' Conference in Honor of Thomas A. Sebeok's Seventieth Birthday, Budapest and Vienna, 30 September–4 October 1990. This work was published as a volume bound together with *Semiotics 1990*, the Proceedings of the fifteenth annual meeting of the Semiotic Society of America, edited by K. Haworth, J. Deely, and T. Prewitt (Lanham, Md.: University Press of America, 1993.) This is the most recent of several Festschriften that have been assembled for occasions in Sebeok's honor.

Deely, J., et al., eds. *Frontiers in Semiotics*. Bloomington: Indiana University Press, 1986.

Deely, J. *The Human Use of Signs, or Elements of Anthroposemiosis*. Lanham, Md.: Rowman and Littlefield, 1994.

Deely, J., ed. *Thomas A. Sebeok: Bibliography, 1942–1995*. Bloomington, Ind.: Eurolingua, 1995.

Eco, U. *A Theory of Semiotics*. Bloomington: Indiana University Press, 1976.

Edwards, P., ed. *Encyclopedia of Philosophy*. New York: Macmillan, 1972.

Morris, C. *Foundations of the Theory of Signs*. Chicago: University of Chicago Press, 1938.

Sebeok, T. A. "Analysis of the Vocalic System of a Given Language Illustrated by Hungarian." *Quarterly Journal of Speech* 28 (1942): 449–452.

Sebeok, T. A. "Communication among Social Bees; Porpoises and Sonar; Man and Dolphin." *Language* 39 (1963): 448–466.

Sebeok, T. A. *The Play of Musement*. Bloomington: Indiana University Press, 1981.

Sebeok, T. A. "'Semiotics' and Its Congeners" (1971). In his *Contributions to the Doctrine of Signs*. Sources in Semiotics, 4. Lanham, Md.: University Press of America, 1985.

Sebeok, T. A. *I Think I Am a Verb: More Contributions to the Doctrine of Signs*. New York: Plenum, 1986.

Sebeok, T. A. *The Sign and Its Masters*. Sources in Semiotics, 8. Lanham, Md.: University Press of America, 1989.

Sebeok, T. A. *American Signatures: Semiotic Inquiry and Method*. Norman, Okla.: University of Oklahoma Press, 1991.

Sebeok, T. A. *Semiotics in the United States*. Bloomington: Indiana University Press, 1991.

Sebeok, T. A. *A Sign Is Just a Sign*. Bloomington: Indiana University Press, 1991.

Sebeok, T. A. "Signs, Bridges, Origins." In *Origins of Language*, edited by J. Trabant. Collegium Budapest Workshop Series, no. 2, pp. 89–115. Budapest: Institute for Advanced Study, 1996.

Sebeok, T. A., A. S. Hayes, and M. C. Bates, eds. *Approaches to Semiotics: Cultural Anthropology, Education, Linguistics, Psychiatry, Psychology*. The Hague: Mouton, 1964.

Sebeok, T. A., and R. Rosenthal, eds. *The Clever Hans Phenomenon: Communication with Horses, Whales, Apes, and People*. New York: New York Academy of Sciences, 1981.

Sebeok, T. A., and D. J. Umiker-Sebeok. "Clever Hans and Smart Simians: The Self-Fulfilling Prophecy and Kindred Methodological Pitfalls." *Anthropos* 76.1–2 (1981): 89–165.

Sebeok, T. A., and D. J. Umiker-Sebeok, eds. *Speaking of Apes: A Critical Anthology of Two-Way Communication with Man*. New York: Plenum, 1980.

—JOHN DEELY

SEMIOGRAPHY. In computer science, *semiography* designates the structure and economy of signs in a computer language, including the designing of user-friendly icons. Specifically, semiography designates a computerized research method developed in the late 1980s with the purpose of investigating the fundamental semiotic structures of a given culture or subculture. More generally, it points to the materiality or artificiality of any representational system (Bertin, 1973). It also refers to a protocol of data collection as well as to a type of calculus and graphic representation of semiosis that can be used on data collected independently of that protocol. In the latter sense, semiography shows some congruence with semantic graphs, semantic nets, conceptual dependency, probabilistic grammars, neoassociationism, connectionism, and especially neural nets (Lisboa, 1992). Pierre Laurette (1993) has developed a computer program along this line for the treatment of literary texts. Most of these approaches belong to the same general paradigm and resort to more or less similar types of methodology and tools. In this respect, the notions of "attractors" (also used in fractal theory) and "attraction basins" appear most useful in semiotic analysis (Kamp and Hasler, 1990). Indeed, one can compute the power of attraction and the attraction range of a culture's nodes (Maranda and Nze-Nguema, 1992).

If semiosis is defined as a constructionist process within a mental space in which symbols, signs, icons, and other carriers of meaning (hereafter called "nodes") interact and interrelate under the impact of pragmatics, then discourses, thoughts, dreams, and other systems of signs transit from one "mental locus" to another and the frequencies of those transitions can be computed, as can the relative importance of each locus in that space. A step further takes us to the calculus of empirical transition probabilities in a semiotic web between the different nodes that make up a mental space.

Thus, semiographic analysis computes the flow of semiosis along its different, culture-specific vectors. It enables analysts to measure semiotic inertia: the well laid-out ways of the mind, the most common paths "meanings" tramp along, the crowded alleys in which they slow down, their semiotic dead ends, the turnpikes on which they cruise, and so on. Concomitantly, analysts can spot exceptional, innovative paths, thus generating new, live metaphors (Maranda, 1974). All in all, semiography computes degrees of stereotypy according to variable social dimensions that are considered to be their determinants. The knowledge of relative association strength and of node power yields testable significant statements on social and individual semiodynamics.

These results can be obtained through the following methodology, which in this case has been applied comparatively to segments of the French, Quebecois, and Melanesian cultures, in which an optional data-collection protocol is followed by semiographic analysis. The optional data-collection protocol consists of four steps; the first of which involves continuous-words association tests (CWATs). The use of such tests has proved fruitful in a number of disciplines, including psychology, semantics, and cultural anthropology (Szalay and Deese, 1978). The usefulness of a CWAT comes from, among other things, the elicitation of paradigmatic sets ("associative series") from informants selected along some specific comparative variables. Most CWAT protocols use triads of stimuli, one triad at a time, which are basic, culturally loaded terms in the context of the culture being investigated, such as *snake, woman, man,* or *Amerindian, Canadian, Quebecois.*

Second, plot-association tests (PATs) add to a CWAT a further probe of informants' semiosis. Informants are asked to invent "stories" whose characters must be the same three stimuli to which they have already responded associatively in the CWAT. The results are syntagmas that cast heavy symbols in

dynamic patterns and echo paradigmatic sets in a measurable way. Such scripts constitute the corpus of a "subliterature" of a sort; that is, they display inertia vectors of "popular subdiscourses" (for somewhat related approaches, see McFeat, 1974, and Vandendorpe, 1989).

In the third step, informants sort the words of their responses into categories of their own, so that emic tags become available for content analysis. Not all informants can perform that task adequately: while some come up with several categories, others use only two or three fuzzy ones. Tagging thus requires the use of a fuzzy-set methodology to weigh its component descriptors. Then, in the last step, informants fill out a questionnaire to allow for correlations of their responses and the variables describing their sociographic profile.

Semiography is not bound to this protocol but can be used on any text. Indeed, semiography took originally the shape of a "semiographic cube" in folkloristics (Maranda and Maranda, 1971); developments followed through digraph theory and probabilistic network analysis (Maranda, 1974), which helped map out semiotic processes and formulate testable semiotic hypotheses of a probabilistic nature using one- to n-step Markov chains. This computerized method draws semiotic maps composed of nodes and vertices with a calculus of directionality—algorithms that compute relative node power and transition probabilities from each node to all the others. This method purports to formalize natural cognitive processes.

Semiography is performed "spontaneously" or "intuitively" when someone can predict with a relatively high probability the network of mental "tracks" on which run the "trains of thoughts" of a person with whom she or he is acquainted. For instance, strings of conversational topics (macro nodes) can be anticipated. To practice intuitive semiography in interpersonal relations means to know the nodes that make up other person's mental spaces and also the types, directionality, and strengths of interconnectedness (transition probabilities) that dynamize differentially the relations between those nodes. Likewise, in classic semiotic analysis, given an adequate knowledge of a culture, one may predict that some metaphors will be flattering to its members (e.g., "You are an angel!" in Christianity-influenced cultures; "you are a son of a bitch!" in Melanesian cultures that worship the dog as a god), while others will be taken as offensive and others will remain completely opaque, such as "he is a bear" in some Amerindian societies that accept "she is a bear" as perfectly meaningful (Maranda, 1974). In such cases, there are positive, negative, and void associations between two nodes. Such relations are represented in diagrams of signed networks by solid lines, broken lines, and dotted ones.

Because of the complexity of such networks, however, a computer program is needed to carry the analysis further. For example, the program DiscAn ("discourse analyzer") produces dynamic semiotic maps in the form of transition-probability networks (Maranda and Nadeau, 1989). It takes as input any data in ASCII and first processes it through a (preferably user-made) thesaurus. It then maps their relationships in terms of relative-node input and output and in terms of transition probabilities. The digraphic calculus it performs takes into account diffraction and condensation indexes for each node: for some, inputs equal outputs, so that they function as mere transmitters or "carriers"; for other nodes, output emissions are more diversified than their reception inputs—that is, they "diffract" semiotic flows; for still others, outputs ("attractors") "contract" or "condense" (lenticular effect) semiotic flows. Finally, for some nodes, outputs arise without inputs, while for others, the reverse is true: the former are called "sources," the latter, "sinks." Once a "text" (conversation, circus act, meal, etc.) has started to flow from its source, it will eventually reach certain points where it will either hit a sink or "absorption barrier" where it will end; or it will default and cycle or loop back; or it will bounce and connect with or rebound on another set of interconnected nodes that acts as a "reflecting barrier." Thus, the differential semiotic power of each node in a text is computed in addition to transition probabilities from each node to every other one, producing a semiography of the whole database.

[See also Artificial Intelligence; Cultural Knowledge; Ethnoscience; Knowledge Representation; Metaphor; and Stereotype.]

BIBLIOGRAPHY

Bertin, J. *Sémiologie graphique*. 2d ed. The Hague: Mouton, 1973.

Kamp, Y., and M. Hasler. *Réseaux de neurones récursifs pour mémoires associatives*. Lausanne: Presses polytechniques et universitaires romandes, 1990.

Laurette, O. *Lettres et technè: Informatique, instrumentations, méthodes, et théories dans le domaine littéraire*. Candiac, Quebec: Editions Balzac, 1993.

Lisboa, P. G. J. *Neural Networks: Current Applications*. London: Chapman and Hall, 1992.

Maranda, P. "Myth as a Cognitive Map: A Sketch of the Okanagan Myth Automaton" (1974). In *Textverarbeitung/Textprocessing*, edited by W. Burghardt and K. Holker, pp. 253–272. Hamburg: De Gruyter, 1979.

Maranda, P. "Mother Culture is Watching Us: Probabilistic Structuralism." In *Reader Response to Literature: The Empirical Dimension*, edited by E. Nardochhio, pp. 173–192. Berlin: De Gruyter, 1992.

Maranda, P., and E. K. Maranda. *Structural Models in Folklore and Transformational Essays*. Paris: Mouton, 1971.

Maranda, P., and S. Nadeau. *DiscAn: A Computer System for Content and Discourse Analysis*. Version 2.0. Quebec: Nadeau Caron Informatique, 1989.

Maranda, P., and F. P. Nze-Nguema. *L'unité dans la diversité culturelle: Une geste Bantu*. Quebec and Paris: Presses de l'Université Laval and A.C.C.T., 1992.

McFeat, T. *Small Group Cultures*. New York: Pergamon, 1974.

Osgood, C. E., G. J. Suci, and P. H. Tannenbaum. *The Measurement of Meaning*. Urbana: University of Illinois Press, 1957.

Szalay, L. B., and J. Deese. *Subjective Meaning and Culture: An Assessment through Word Associations*. Hillsdale, N.J.: Lawrence Erlbaum Associates, 1978.

Vandendorpe, C. *Apprendre à lire des fables: Une approche sémio-cognitive*. Montreal: Editions du préambule, 1989.

—PIERRE MARANDA

SEMIOSIS. Generally understood to refer to signification as a process or to the activity of signs, *semiosis* easily invites suspicion as inflated jargon or obfuscatory: why should we speak of signification as a process rather than a relation? Are signs active or passive? Activity occurs in time and entails an agent. Do signs generally have features that relate to time? If *semiosis* is taken to include interpretation, is that an action *of* signs or an action *on* signs by another agent? Yet if we accept that signs are active agents that at least partly determine the growth of meaning across time, then a radical but coherent semiotics comes into play that takes semiosis as its central concern.

The pedigree of the term *semiosis* is not completely clear, but it plays a major role in the writings of Charles Sanders Peirce and of Charles Morris, as well as in the works of several theorists influenced by them. In some instances, the term does not seem well motivated: a static picture of sign relations has the same descriptive power. The ambiguity can be stated in terms of Peirce's system of categories, in which a philosophical foundation is established for a distinction between dyadic dynamic action and triadic sign action. While the distinction applies sharply to descriptions of actions, it is vague with respect to actions themselves. For example, a seismograph's performance appears dyadic or dynamic if described in terms of its physical input and output but triadic or semiosic if its output is considered a sign of its input.

The notion of cause involved in construing signs as active obviously does not refer to physical force. At the same time, given our present state of knowledge about the physical world, we could not readily accept any notion of sign action that contradicts physics. A partial accommodation of the claims of semiotics and physics in this respect is established in cognitive science. Taking the electronic computer as a model of intelligence, the translation of semantic relations into syntactic relations permits the former to determine the results of calculation. Generalizing this relationship, in appropriate situations (e.g., in organisms, in computers) semiotic structures can be understood as independent constraints on physical structures, within which the "forces of nature" follow their natural paths. As an analogy to semiosis, consider an irrigation ditch that "causes" water to spread over a wide area without contradicting the rule that water flows downhill over the path of least resistance. As an immediate instance of semiosis, consider a person who behaves over several years in a manner that seems at most only very indirectly responsive to his or her biological needs because semiotic structures of religious or political commitment—or even of neurosis—determine a different path. Here signs are efficacious, and semiosis refers to the efficacy of signs.

While it does not require heroic examples to justify the concept of semiosis, situations of some specificity and complexity are required to demonstrate a clear distinction between physical and semiotic action and to show how signs can establish paths of action through time that are not well explicated by any description other than a semiotic one. Some of the phenomena generally taken as especially symptomatic of semiotic relations are ambiguous in this respect. For example, the transmission of information *per se* does not appear in a new light if described as semiosis, as all physical changes transmit informa-

tion, and this information might be fully revealed by a physical description. The state of a lightbulb transmits information about the state of a light switch; a semiotic paraphrase adds nothing to the physical description. Similarly, little in ethology or genetics is explained better in semiotic terms than in biological terms. On the other hand, there are more complex phenomena for which the existence of a physical description is merely hypothetical but for which semiotic explanations are illuminating and can well be taken to deal with primary causes. Such phenomena might be called critical phenomena of semiosis. Plausible candidates are nondeductive inference, the rationale deliberation of alternative plans, contra-instinctual behavior, the production and reception of radically individuated texts, the evolution of style, and the manipulation of models of possibilities and fictions.

The transactions of the physical world are either necessary or random. There is no freedom in its relations, for chance follows rigid statistical rules. Any action analyzed according to its physical concomitants decomposes into only those two factors. But if we ask, "Why did Professor X vote against the motion?" answers in terms of necessary or chance determinations are usually beside the point. Nor are the factors that render the problem irreducible to physical description essentially psychological. The act queried has an intrinsic freedom (possibly reduced by psychological circumstance) that resides in the matrix of the possible alternatives—here voting yes, voting no, or abstaining—and in the networks of arguments for each of the available choices. The alternatives and networks are sign structures that are independent of the individual minds of those who conceive of them in the same way that propositions of mathematics are. Furthermore, the networks of argument in play are necessarily of indefinite extent, and decisions within that network use processes about which we barely know how to speculate. When asked why she voted as she did, Professor X will likely be able to supply a rationale—a sign structure—which will appear as the most plausible cause of her decision.

In this sense, signs do actively determine each other, and the single phenomenon that most dramatically and clearly requires a theory of semiosis for its explanation is the cogent but unpredictable development of ideas. The question about semiosis that this phenomenon poses concerns what there is about

signs that permits them to play this role. While the concept of semiosis emerges in the traditions of semiotics furthest removed from structuralism, structuralism suggests the most concrete answer.

The capacity of signs to determine each other arises to the extent that the universe of signs has some measure of autonomy. A semiotic system or even a single text can exhibit coherence in isolation from the external texts or conditions to which it relates by reference or by other kinds of interaction. Autonomy is relative. It is a function not only of any boundaries observers place on a system but also of the structure of the sign or signs themselves. Structuralism explains the coherence of autonomous texts and systems in terms of the diagrams that can be ascribed to them (e.g., phonological matrices, phrase markers, Greimasian squares, relations of paradigm and syntagm, etc.). The diagrammatic model entails understanding texts or systems as being composed of discrete elements that have relationships of equivalence and opposition. The configurations that emerge in such sign systems have a kaleidoscopic mobility and fecundity.

While structuralism provides the initial insight regarding the kinds of sign configurations that can establish autonomy, it fails to show why these are dynamic rather than static. No single theory has provided a comprehensive response to this question, but many contribute relevant ideas. Peirce noted the discussion of play by Friedrich von Schiller (1759–1805) in the *Aesthetic Letters* (1795–1797) as pertinent to his own idea of semiotic growth (Sebeok, 1981, chap. 1). Throughout semiotics, the motif of dialogue figures as a model of the development of ideas. The semiotic notion of dialogue is not restricted to or even centered on exchanges between actual persons but draws attention instead to the response each sign finds in a subsequent one. These responses can be charted on many different levels. Sentences and mental images form a dialogue, as do artworks and art criticism. Within culture generally, we can trace a dialectical exchange between structures emerging from rule-governed systems such as language and rule-generating texts such as myths. In interacting with these semiotic resources, the individual has access to patterns of thought and action that would otherwise exceed his or her own capacities and that biology could never predict. In this context, the philosophically maligned idea of free will might be understood constructively not as a human psychological faculty but as a description of

the interplay between individuals as autonomous sign systems—a symptom of fully developed semiosis.

The philosophical roots and epistemological entailments of an acceptance of semiosis are outlined in John Deely (1990, 1994). Peirce's idea of semiotic (or semiosic) growth receives an important elaboration in Michael Shapiro (1983), with particular reference to linguistic change. Jurij Lotman (1990) provides a profound analysis of cultural development especially relevant to the arguments discussed here. Mikhail Bakhtin and Valentin Voloshinov (1928) is a forceful exposition of dialogue. Floyd Merrell (1995) considers semiosis from a postmodern perspective.

[*See also* Bakhtin; Biosemiotics; Dialogism; Meme; Peirce; Play; *and* Sign.]

BIBLIOGRAPHY

Bakhtin, M., and V. N. Voloshinov. *Marxism and the Philosophy of Language.* Translated by L. Matejka and I. R. Titunik. New York: Seminar Press, 1973.

Deely, J. *Basics of Semiotics.* Bloomington: Indiana University Press, 1990.

Deely, J. *The Human Use of Signs, or Elements of Anthroposemiosis.* Lanham, Md.: Rowman and Littlefield, 1994.

Lotman, J. *Universe of Mind: A Semiotic Theory of Culture.* Translated by A. Shukman. Bloomington: Indiana University Press, 1990.

Merrell, F. *Semiosis in the Postmodern Age.* West Lafayette, Ind.: Purdue University Press, 1995.

Merrell, F. *Signs Grow: Semiosis and Life Processes.* Toronto: University of Toronto Press, 1996.

Sebeok, T. A. *The Play of Musement.* Bloomington: Indiana University Press, 1981.

Shapiro, M. *The Sense of Grammar: Language as Semeiotic.* Bloomington: Indiana University Press, 1983.

—DAVID LIDOV

SEMIOTIC AND SYMBOLIC. In *Revolution in Poetic Language* (1974) and *Polylogue* (1977), linguist and psychoanalyst Julia Kristeva theorizes the constitution of the subject by distinguishing between the semiotic and symbolic modalities of the signifying process. These modalities are relatively exclusive and necessarily dialectical. This distinction is established through the subtle combination of concepts drawn from the later works of Plato and from psychoanalytic, phenomenological, and linguistic theories. Semiotic processes predate the symbolic ones and are instinctual and maternal. They are unregulated but ordered according to biological and social constraints, as well as by drives organized around the mother's body. Kristeva uses the concept of *chora* to describe the continuous rhythmic and feminine space shared by mother and child prior to the emergence of what she calls the *thetic* phase that prepares the sign for emergence into the symbolic order.

In the thetic phase, the subject is on the threshold of language. Kristeva sets out the phenomenological description of the thesis by positing existence through propositions that are the foundation of signification. Kristeva then subjects descriptions of intentionality, judgment, the constitution of objects, and predicative syntheses derived from studies of the transcendental ego to a genetic psychoanalytic perspective, enlisting both the mirror stage of Jacques Lacan and the castration complex of Sigmund Freud. Thetic consciousness is essentially a two-sided intentional structure of constitutive acts and objects in which the transcendental ego belongs and is revealed in operations of predication and judgment. For Kristeva, the speaking subject is a "split unification" of conscious and unconscious levels, of semiotic and symbolic dispositions. Psychoanalysis functions for Kristeva as a way to dislodge the transcendental ego and the overinvestment in consciousness and reason and as a way to investigate the signifying process at work on both the conscious and, especially, the unconscious sides of the speaking subject. Unlike thetic consciousness, the speaking subject is not sequestered by the phenomenological reduction from the social constraints of family, modes of production, the unconscious, and the body, all of which support signifying practices, beyond the single support of meaning provided by the transcendental ego.

Semiotic processes disrupt the symbolic domain of meaning and significance described as paternal, rational, and transcendental. The semiotic breaks into the symbolic through a transgressive breach, exploding the unity of transcendental consciousness. The symbolic is best taken in terms of the oppositional interdependencies across the field of language and culture, understood in the structural sense developed by Lacan and Claude Lévi-Strauss. Language presupposes both modalities in the engendering of the speaking subject, but Kristeva uses the semiotic to develop an analysis capable of accounting for instinctual drives, which explains her heavy reliance on a variety of psychoanalytic theories. Kristeva's goal is to overcome the debt linguistics has to phenome-

nology, in which the transcendental ego sustains signification by disembodying heterogeneous drives of the unconscious. Still, semiotic phenomena tend to establish quasi-symbolic signifying apparatuses in order to communicate, even if what is communicated is undecidable and indeterminate; without them, however, discourse goes mad. It is for this reason that Kristeva allows that heterogeneous semiotic processes remain near the thetic.

In terms of the functioning of texts, Kristeva defines a text's genotext as a nonlinguistic, semiotic processuality that articulates ephemeral structures and is heterogeneous to meaning. The phenotext, in contrast, denotes language that is in the service of univocity and is obedient to the rules of communication. It is thus homogeneous with meaning and the direct passage of univocal information between subjects and does not wander like the genotext does. The grammatical and syntactical deviations of the genotext may be seen at work in certain experimental literary practices such as James Joyce's *Finnegans Wake* and in revolutionary periods during which the structure of the phenotext is modified.

For Kristeva, semiotics is limited by its subservience to linguistics and the homogenizing reduction of signifying practices to a system. Semiotics cannot, then, identify the heterogeneous operations of the signifying process. The goal of Kristevan "semanalysis," then is to include both the genotext and the phenotext in the study of signifying practices. Toward this goal, the phenomenological reduction must be demystified, leading to the liberation of the speaking subject and its reconnection with socio and biohistorical factors. Semanalysis is materialist, in non-Hegelian and non-Marxist senses, in that it develops a topology rather than an algebra of the signifying practices of a subject in process.

In avant-garde art, Kristeva sees semiotic operations that she identifies with what she calls the polylogical subject. The polylogue is primally musical and material. It is the rhythm of the unconscious before it is repressed and dematerialized in a signifying system. It is also the presyntactic enunciations of the child and the psychotic operating before and outside of the confines of the symbolic network. The polylogue forces language out of the transcendental position by means of multiplication and breaks through the boundaries of the symbolic by means of what Kristeva calls the transfinite element of language, which goes beyond the sentence and naming.

Kristeva privileges the study of the languages of children and psychotics because they reveal in concomitant ways the entrances to and exits from the symbolic order of language and sociality.

Powers of Horror (1982) theorizes the space between the semiotic and the symbolic and between subject and object by using the concept of the abject, which defines the boundaries around the subject in terms of what is cast out and rendered other. The concept essentially concerns the problematic corporeality of the subject, which the symbolic order seeks to transcend. The symbolic subject's abjection of what is improper, unclean, and defiling is a requirement that is never accomplished with any finality. The abject is never fully other, since it was once part of the subject, and so it dwells on the unclear border between subject and object, thus threatening the subject's need to master it and distinguish itself from it. Bodily waste must be excreted so that the subject's body may continue to live, yet eventually the body itself becomes waste, a corpse. But the corpse is ambiguous because it can no longer be maintained as the subject's location, nor is it solely an object. The corpse is the future of every embodied subject. Kristeva's example of the corpse shows how the abject shifts the border between life and death into life, revealing a necessary relation that the symbolic order can tolerate only through repression.

[*See also* Kristeva; *and* Lacan.]

BIBLIOGRAPHY

Grosz, E. *Sexual Subversions: Three French Feminists.* Sydney: Allen and Unwin, 1989.
Kristeva, J. *Polylogue.* Paris: Seuil, 1977.
Kristeva, J. *Desire in Language: A Semiotic Approach to Literature and Art.* Translated by T. Gora, A. Jardine, and L. S. Roudiez. New York: Columbia University Press, 1980.
Kristeva, J. *Powers of Horror.* Translated by L. S. Roudiez. New York: Columbia University Press, 1982.
Kristeva, J. *Revolution in Poetic Language* (1974). Translated by M. Waller. New York: Columbia University Press, 1984.
—GARY GENOSKO and RACHEL ARISS

SEMIOTIC SQUARE. A diagram representing the logical relationships that articulate semantic categories according to Algirdas Julien Greimas's semio-linguistic theory, a semiotic square is meant to visualize the mutual oppositions and reciprocal presuppositions that determine the structures of signifi-

cation. Semiotic squares are based on a conception of meaning as being produced or manifested by determinable sets of complex, multipolar semantic oppositions and implications.

Starting from the notion of phonological binarism proposed by Ferdinand de Saussure and developed further by structural linguists such as Nikolai Trubetzkoy and Roman Jakobson, Greimas postulates that meaning is structured or "articulated" along the same principles, but he considers binary oppositions too simple to account for the complexity of significations. Finding inspiration in the works of the French logician Robert Blanché (1898–1975), whose *Structures intellectuelles* (1966) offers many diagrammatic models of the oppositional organization of concepts based on the tradition of Apuleius's (second century CE) propositional "logical square," Greimas in collaboration with François Rastier (1968) laid the basis for an axiomatic formalization of the elementary structures of signification expressed diagrammatically by the semiotic square. In his earlier *Sémantique structurale* (1966), Greimas had adumbrated this approach with the notion of a "dialectical algorithm," a formula whose purpose was to make explicit a whole semantic structure through assertion and negation of its oppositional terms: two interdefinable terms such as *life* and *death*, for example, are both negated so as to be complemented by the terms *nonlife* and *nondeath*. This operation consists of applying an algorithm to any given term and its contrary and effecting the negation of the two related terms. This enterprise is rooted in and further develops the Aristotelian notion of a logical organization of the conceptual universe, but it also draws from contemporary attempts to formalize the organization of language and thought. Besides Blanché, Viggo Brøndal (1943), for instance, had proposed representing the natural categories that map thought as a diagram comprising six forms of relation: positive, negative, complex positive, complex negative, complex (i.e., both positive and negative), and neutral (i.e., neither positive nor negative). In developmental psychology, Jean Piaget (1896–1980) had made use of a logical structure called the "Klein group V4," named after the German mathematician Felix Klein (1849–1925), in order to describe the operational mental structures that mature in children between ages eleven and fifteen and that make possible the logical transformations of inversion, reciprocity, correlation and identity, and various combinatorial activities manipulating implications, incompatibilities, and disjunctions (Piaget, 1976, pp. 202–207).

While acknowledging a heuristic kinship between the semiotic square and these logical diagrams, Greimas emphasizes that its purport is distinct since the semiotic square is not an empty form, a "pure syntax" but bears upon the very "conditions of existence and production of signification" with respect to "concrete linguistic objects." As a diagram, the semiotic square is a convenient way to memorize the relevant algorithm by representing the configuration of fundamental operations through which meaning—which according to Greimas cannot be accessed in itself—manifests itself by articulating signification through oppositions and transformations. But it should be remembered that the logicosemantic relations that are mapped onto the square are dynamical rather than static, though this characterization is somewhat better rendered by the successive operations of an algorithm than by the visualization of a stable symmetrical pattern like the square. Notwithstanding this qualification, the geometrical properties of the square make it possible to grasp intellectually in a single vision all the relationships through which the categorical terms are articulated. Indeed, by virtue of its four equal sides and its two diagonals, the square relates each one of the four nodes to the other three.

Greimas distinguishes three phases in the generation of the categorical terms that articulate semantic categories. There is first a set of relations between a term and its contrary and between these two terms and their contradictories. Geimas defines contraries as two concepts that presuppose each other (e.g., *life* and *death*, *being* and *seeming*, *assertion* and *negation*). Contradictories are two terms that mutually exclude each other (e.g., *life* and *nonlife*). In the elementary structure of signification, each of the two contrary terms are negated so as to produce their contradictories. The notation used by Greimas for representing the elementary structure of signification is A and non-A for the contraries and $\bar{A}$ and $\overline{\text{non-}A}$ for the contradictories (the bar above the term signifies its negation). The term A is in a relation of implication with the contradictory of its contrary (e.g., *life* implies *nondeath*), just as the term non-A implies the contradictory of the term A (*death* implies *nonlife*). Contraries are identified intuitively, but their relation is verified "if, and only if, the contradictory term of each of them implies the contrary of the other." These somewhat strained definitions are extrapolated from the Aristotelian logic of propositions in which contradictories are statements that cannot both be true and cannot both be false, whereas contraries are statements that cannot both be true but may both be false. However, the borrowing of this logical terminology and its redefinition does not raise any theoretical problem for Greimas because the articulation of the elementary structure of signification is considered axiomatic for his whole semiotic system, and therefore it must ultimately account for the meaning of Aristotle's discourse itself. This elementary structure (figure 1) is implemented in the semiotic square in which the letter S stands for *signification* and the lowercase may represent *seme* (a minimal unit of signification) or *sememe* (a structured set of semes) (figure 2).

In the second diagram, the two contrary terms are the symbols S_1 and S_2, and their respective contradictories are written $\bar{S}_1$ and $\bar{S}_2$. The connecting lines indicate the copresence of all the relations in the generation of any semantic category. There is a relation of contradiction between S_1 and $\bar{S}_1$ and between S_2 and $\bar{S}_2$. There is a relation of contrariety between S_1 and S_2 as well as between $\bar{S}_1$ and $\bar{S}_2$. And, finally, there is a relation of complementarity between S_1 and $\bar{S}_2$ and between S_2 and $\bar{S}_1$.

The first relational model, in which two parallel negations are effected on the two "primitive terms" (the contraries), can generate further operations that result in more complex relations, called "the second generation of categorical terms." Indeed, the relations formed between terms "may serve, in their turn, as terms establishing between themselves hierarchically superior relations." Two relations of contrariety such as, on the one hand, S_1 and S_2 and, on the other hand, $\bar{S}_1$ and $\bar{S}_2$, form a relation of contradictoriness. Similarly, two relations of complementarity form a relation of contrariety. Because these relations are second-order relations, Greimas labels them meta-

FIGURE 1. *Elementary Logical Relations.*

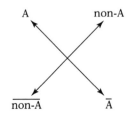

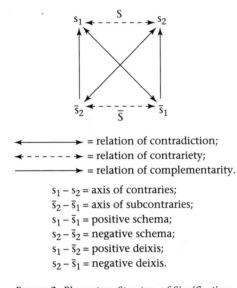

→ = relation of contradiction;
◄------► = relation of contrariety;
──────► = relation of complementarity.

$s_1 - s_2$ = axis of contraries;
$\bar{s}_2 - \bar{s}_1$ = axis of subcontraries;
$s_1 - \bar{s}_1$ = positive schema;
$s_2 - \bar{s}_2$ = negative schema;
$s_1 - \bar{s}_2$ = positive deixis;
$s_2 - \bar{s}_1$ = negative deixis.

FIGURE 2. *Elementary Structure of Signification.*

relations and distinguishes the categories of contradictory metaterms and contrary metaterms. The example provided in the canonical account of the semiolinguistic theory (Greimas and Courtés, 1982) makes these categories and their mutual relations clear (see figure 3).

The two primitive terms that establish the semantic domain encompassing the related notions of reality and appearance are given as *being* and *seeming*. These contraries are negated in order to produce their respective contradictories, *nonbeing* and *nonseeming*. These four terms and their relations constitute the first order of categorical articulation. The re-

FIGURE 3. *Complex Structure of Signification (the notion of truth).*

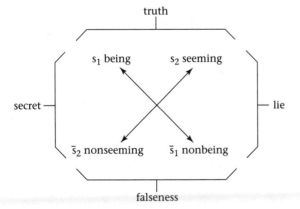

lation between *being* and *seeming* as it relates to the relation between *nonseeming* and *nonbeing* generates the term *truth* (i.e., *being* plus *seeming*), with *falseness* (i.e., *nonseeming* plus *nonbeing*) as its contradictory. *Truth* and *falseness* are thus called contradictory metaterms. Similarly, if the relations between *being* and *nonseeming* and between *seeming* and *nonbeing* are related, they form a relation of contrariety that generates the contrary terms of *secret* and *lie*, which are called contrary metaterms. Thus, *truth* and *falseness* are mutually exclusive, but *secret* and *lie* are not.

The generation of semantic categories starts, according to Greimas, from primitive relations that are governed by axioms which are nondefinable a priori concepts and nondemonstrable propositions that impose themselves as intuitively evident. They form a set of interdefinable concepts from which the theory is derived deductively. There are constraints but no closure imposed upon the generation of categorical terms. Greimas accordingly evokes the possibility of a third generation of categorical terms that would comprise various metametaterms, suggesting that mythic and poetic discourse might be the locus in which such complex categorical terms are manifested. But, obviously, this theoretical horizon cannot be limited in principle to only three categorical generations. In his teaching, Greimas often emphasized the tentative nature of the semiotic square as a rather simplistic didactic and heuristic tool and conjured up the vision of the far more complex geometry that would be needed to represent the full semiotic articulation of meaning. Other theoretical problems raised by the earlier elaboration of the semiotic square as a model for signification have been addressed by Greimas and Courtés in the second volume of their dictionary (1986).

[*See also* Algorithm; Binarism; Brøndal; Diagrams; Greimas, Isotopy; Metalanguage; Narrative Structures; *and* Opposition.]

BIBLIOGRAPHY

Blanché, R. *Structures intellectuelles.* Paris: Vrin, 1966.
Brøndal, V. *Essais de linguistique générale.* Copenhagen: Munksgaard, 1943.
Greimas, A. J. *Structural Semantics: An Attempt at a Method* (1966). Translated by D. McDowell, R. Schleifer, and A. Velie. Lincoln: University of Nebraska Press, 1983.
Greimas, A. J., and J. Courtés. *Semiotics and Language: An Analytical Dictionary.* Translated by L. Crist et al. Bloomington: Indiana University Press, 1982.

Greimas, A. J., and J. Courtés. *Sémiotique: Dictionaire raisonné de la théorie due langage*, vol. 2, *Compléments, débats, propositions*. Paris: Hachette, 1986.

Greimas, A. J., and F. Rastier. "The Interaction of Semiotic Constraints" *Yale French Review* 41 (1968) 86–105.

Nef, F., ed. *Structures élémentaires de la signification*. Brussels: Editions complexe, 1976.

Piaget, J. "Piaget's Theory." Translated by G. Gellerier and J. Langer. In *The Process of Child Development*, edited by P. Neubauer, pp. 164–212. New York: Meridian Books, 1976.

—PAUL BOUISSAC

SEMIOTIC TERMINOLOGY. The term *semiotics* comes from ancient Greek. Modern etymologists believe that the word *sēma*, from which the verb *sēmainein* ("to signify") and the noun *sēmeion* ("sign") are derived, is related to a hypothetical Proto-Indo-European root **dhyā*, which is found in Sanskrit *dhyāti* ("he thinks") and *dhyā-man* (see Chantraine, 1974). The sibilation of *dentals* + *y* is indeed a common feature in phonetic changes. It seems that the basic meaning of this root is "mental activity" and that its nominal derivation by the suffix *-ma* refers to whatever can be construed as a cause or result of this activity, hence the various meanings of *sēma*: signal, sign, funerary monument, and graphic character. For a reassessment of this etymological and conceptual issue, see Nagy (1983).

The first development of a technical terminology based on the word *sēma* appears to have taken place in the fourth century BCE in the context of the medical art. The Hippocratic writings, in which the art of interpreting the symptoms (*symptōma*, "coincidence") and syndromes (*syndromē*, "concurring coincidences") exhibited by patients is perpetuated, were expanded on more than five centuries later by Galen, who used the expressions *ē sēmeiōtikē teknē* or *sēmeiōtikon* ("the art of the signs") to refer to one of the six branches of medicine. A systematic investigation of the medical terminology related to this branch remains to be done. There is no doubt that the remarkable permanence of the Hippocratic tradition in Western cultures has sustained a large portion of its initial terminology. The 1914 edition of *A New English Dictionary* provides much evidence for this phenomenon: all the forms that are sometimes alleged to have been coined since the end of the nineteenth century are in fact attested to much earlier in the English language, most of them in the medical sense but also quite often with a more general value.

Semeiography: 1. symbolic notation (1706); 2. a description of symptoms (1855, 1890).
Semeiologic (semiologic), semeiological: pertaining to semeiology (1839, 1862).
Semeiologist: one skilled in sign language (1848).
Semeiology (semiology): 1. sign language (1641, 1694); 2. the branch of medical science which is concerned with symptoms (1839, 1855, 1876, 1887).
Semeiotic (semiotic, semioticke): 1. relating to symptoms (1625, 1876, 1898); 2. symbolic, serving to convey meaning (1797).
Semeiotics (semiotics): the branch of medical science relating to the interpretation of symptoms (1670, 1793, 1867, 1873).

The meanings that do not pertain to medicines incidentally are noted as obsolete. In Emile Littré's 1883 *Dictionnaire de la langue française*, the French words *séméiologie* or *sémiologie* and *séméiotique* or *sémiotique* are similarly defined as pertaining mainly to the interpretation of pathological symptoms but also as pertaining to the use of signs, as in military commands through gestures. *Sémiographie* is defined as notation by signs, as in music.

The Stoics (third century BCE), considered to be the first philosophical school to have produced a semiotic theory, appear to have been inspired by the medical model. Latin translations of four items of their technical vocabulary derived from *sēma* have enjoyed persistent careers. However, the successive contexts in which *sēmainon* ("signifying"), *sēmainomenon* ("signified"), *sēmeion* ("sign"), and *sēmeiōton* ("to be signified") or their Latin equivalents have appeared are far from forming a homogeneous conceptual continuum. Plato and Aristotle also use terms derived from *sēma* (Canto, 1982).

From Augustine of Hippo, whose writings are directly related to the Stoics' tradition, to Ferdinand de Saussure, Western theologians and philosophers have made intensive use of all the forms that can be derived from the Latin *signum*, which is defined by Cicero as "something that is perceived and signifies something." This abstract and somewhat tautological definition should not obfuscate the more common meanings the word has in Latin, such as "mark," "seal," "signal," "insignia," "picture," and "sculpture." Etymologists hesitate between two possible origins for this word: first, it could be related to the same root as the verb *secare* ("to cut") and would essentially mean "a mark made by incision"; second, it could be derived from the root **sek^w-* ("to follow"), and *sek^w-no-m* (*signum*) would originally be "that which one follows" or "track"; the other meanings would have developed under the influence of the Greek *sēma* and *sēmeion*, while *signare* would have been formed after *sēmainesthai*, "to signify" (Ernout and Meillet, 1967).

This classical terminology has been used and independently redefined in modern times in various fields such as logic, phenomenology, and semiotics, each of which has several schools with their own understandings of these terms. As a result, such basic words as *sign* and *symbol* are currently used with vastly different meanings in semiotic literature, depending on the user's school or the implicit tradition to which she or he relates. The American semiotic tradition since Charles Sanders Peirce usually takes *sign* as a generic word denoting the class of whatever stands for something else in some respect for someone; in this use, *symbols* are a kind of signs—namely, the subclass formed by those signs whose relation to what they stand for is purely conventional. In the Saussurean tradition, *symbole* tends to mean the opposite—a motivated sign—whereas *signe* is used sometimes as a synonym of *signifiant* (signifier), other times as a referent to the conventional association of a perceptual form and a concept, and at still other times in the generic sense, as in Peirce. The terminological situation is made still more complex by the existence of other definitions and usages of these two terms in other disciplines within the social sciences—notably, anthropology, sociology, and psychology. For example, the neuropsychologist Karl Pribram (1971) sets forth two types of mental processes: signs and symbols, the former being defined as context free, the latter as context dependent.

The term *symbol*, from the Latin *symbolus*, a transliteration from Greek *súmbolos* ("sign of identification") is a nominal form related to the verb *sunballein* ("to put together," "to bring together," "to compare"). Other derivations include *sumbolaion* ("mark," "token," "contract") and *sumbolaios* ("based on convention"). In the third century CE, *symbolum* refers, in the context of Christianity, to the baptismal creed that is the mark or sign of a Christian. It came to mean a "formal statement of belief" or a "confession of faith" (e.g., the Nicene creed). The term *sym-bol* is found in sixteenth-century texts with the mere value of "statement," "formula," or "synopsis," but it is also often used in the sense of "something sacred," and it applies to artifacts or actions representing something immaterial or spiritual (e.g., the Catholic Church's sacraments). Thus, giving a symbolic character to objects or actions results in attributing a particular (symbolic) meaning to these objects or actions. Interesting discussions of the notion of symbol can be found in Raymond Firth's *Symbols: Public and Private* (1973), Mary Douglas's *Natural Symbols* (1970), Umberto Eco's "On Symbols" (1982), and Tzvetan Todorov's *Theories of Symbols* (1977).

In computational theory, *symbol* refers generally to a basic unit in cognition and designates the elementary units manipulated by information-processing systems. In much of anthropology, linguistics, psychology, and psychoanalysis, it denotes some element or feature used in communication. It is not completely arbitrary in form but is chosen to be freighted with meaning and significance for the particular culture that incorporates it. Terminological chaos exists also in psychology; Paul Kolers and William Smythe (1979) point out, in an article discussing mental imagery, the confusion coming "from an uncertain, even erroneous, use of the notion of symbol in the psychological literature," a notion that they define as "anything that denotes or refers to anything else."

The technical terminologies used in the various branches of modern semiotics include a large number of neologisms in addition to traditional terms. It is indeed a marked tendency of Western scientists and philosophers to coin new words based on Greek and Latin radicals. The discovery of new objects, new perspectives on already-known objects, and new technologies makes it necessary to create adequate terminologies in order to communicate and manipulate the cognitive categories that keep emerging. This tendency can go unchecked for some time in a given field, mainly at the preparadigmatic stage of a science or in purely speculative enterprises that ape the normal sciences. Semiotic and linguistic neologisms that have appeared since the end of the nineteenth century form a vast field of study. Some neologisms have had relatively short life spans. Such was the destiny of *significs*, *sensifics* (1896), *semasiology*, *sematology*, and a few others listed in Sebeok (1976). Others seem to have gained only limited currency (e.g., *semanalyse* and *grammatology*).

As a large portion of Peirce's manuscripts is still to be published, it is difficult to assess the exact dimensions of his neological contributions. Peirce, one of the main sources of modern semiotics, does, however, exhibit in his semiotic writings published to date a definite proclivity to give new meanings to existing words and to coin as many new words as his speculations require, relying when necessary, on Greek and Latin terms introduced in transliterated form into the English language (e.g., *representamen*, *rheme*) or on new ones constructed from various elements (e.g., *legisign*, *sinsign*, *phaneroscopy*). Peirce's terminology is inseparable from his idiosyncratic views of the realm of signs. In modern semiotic texts, their use often takes for granted a certain familiarity with the whole system. *Icon*, *index*, and *symbol* alone seem to have gained wide acceptance, but at the cost of serious conceptual impoverishments.

Communication theories have also generated a large number of neologisms that have found their way in the current semiotic terminology, such as *binarism*, *cybernetics*, *entropy*, and *information*, as well as common words such as *message*, *noise*, and *code* that are used in this context with the specialized meanings that they are given in the landmark books by Norbert Wiener (1948), Claude Shannon and Warren Weaver (1949), and Ross Ashby (1952). Why such a profusion of neologisms? Why is classical Greek the main purveyor of radicals? The polysemy or semantic fuzziness of most words in a natural language makes redefinition a very frustrating task because, in spite of the efforts of those who propound such precise meaning in their specialized language, words remain loaded with emotive values or traditional meanings that introduce semantic biases whenever they are used (e.g., René Thom's "catastroph" theory). It is therefore necessary to create a new terminology by using the words of a dead language whose definitions have been frozen for ages in dictionaries and are not likely to evolve. At present, semioticians obviously prefer Greek radicals to Latin ones because the latter are usually much too close to existing abstract words both in the Romance languages and in English, for historical reasons, whereas the former offer both a sort of logic and a relative freshness (i.e., they can be combined into really new informative forms). The potential of Latin for providing neologisms seems to have been already almost exhausted, and Greek still offers some unexploited resources while remaining within the Western scientific tradition (e.g., *topeme*, *chroneme*, *isotopy*). In fact, the limited stock of radicals that are variously combined provide relatively transparent neologisms once one is familiar with the device. Two examples illustrate the motivations and logic of word coinage in this context: the first is Ross Ashby's commentaries on cybernetic terminology in *Introduction to Cybernetics* (1956), emphasizing the advantages offered by a new terminology that makes it possible to conceptualize phenomena as apparently diverse as servomechanisms and organs such as the cerebellum as instances of the same type of process. As long as the properties of servomechanisms were expressed in terms of automatic pilot or hydraulic brake, and those of the cerebellum in terms of gross anatomy, surgery, and dissection, any attempt to bring together what was known of these two processes was extremely difficult, if possible at all. Cybernetic terminology brought about a set of concepts that can apply adequately to both systems as special cases of a more general one. Thanks to the principle of isomorphism, it became clear that advances in one domain could be transferred advantageously into another.

The second example comes from Charles Lumsden and Edward Wilson's justification for introducing the neologism *culturgen* (from Latin *cultur[a]*, "culture," and *gen[ere]*, "to produce"). They state: "New terms should be put forward reluctantly, for jargon is the anaesthetic of scholarship. But we recommend an exception in the case of the 'culturgen', for the reason that a neologism can be defined more precisely. 'Culturgen' does not share exactly the same meaning as the other expressions—idene, instruction and meme—that have been used in various ways for approximately the same category, and it can therefore be incorporated without ambiguity into this first comprehensive gene-culture theory" (1981, pp. 26–27). In addition, they claim that the linguistic derivation is proper and "graceful," that its adjectival form (culturgenic) is transparent, since culturgens generate culture, and that its advantage is to enable one to consider as members of the same class artifacts, behaviors, and "mentifacts"—an argument similar to Ashby's. These two examples are representative of the epistemological and stylistic motivation that accounts for the thousand terminological flowers of semiotics.

[*See also* Deixis; Paradigm; Phoneme; *and* Sign.]

BIBLIOGRAPHY

Ashby, R. *Design for a Brain*. New York: Wiley, 1952.

Ashby, R. *An Introduction to Cybernetics*. London: Chapman and Hall, 1956.

Bellert, L., and P. Ohlin. *Selected Concepts in Semiotics and Aesthetics*. Programme in Communications. Montreal: McGill University Press, 1978.

Canto, M. "Le premier nom du signe: le sèmeion dans la pensée platonicienne." *Recherches sémiotiques/Semiotic Inquiry* 2.1 (1982): 1–14.

Chantraine, P. *Dictionnaire étymologique de la lange grecque*. Paris: Klincksieck, 1974.

Deely, J., B. Williams, and F. E. Kruse, eds. *Frontiers in Semiotics*. Bloomington: Indiana University Press, 1986.

Douglas, M. T. *Natural Symbols*. London: Barrie and Rockliff, 1970.

Eco, U. "On Symbols." *Recherches sémiotiques/Semiotic Inquiry* 2.1 (1982): 15–44.

Ernout, A., and A. Meillet. *Dictionnaire étymologique de la langue latine*. Paris: Klincksieck, 1967.

Firth, R. *Symbols: Public and Private*. London: Allen and Unwin, 1973.

Jones, D. *The History and Meaning of the Term "Phoneme."* London: I. P. A. Department of Phonetics, University College, 1957.

Kolers, P. A., and W. E. Smythe. "Images, Symbols, and Skills." *Canadian Journal of Psychology* 33.3 (1979): 158–184.

Lumsden, C., and E. O. Wilson. *Genes, Mind, and Culture*. Cambridge, Mass.: Harvard University Press, 1981.

Moller, W., et al. "Zur Terminologie der Semiotik 1." In *Papmaks*, vol. 10. Münster: Münsteraner Arbeitskreis für Semiotik, 1978.

Nagy, G. "Séma and Noésis: Some Illustrations." *Semiotics and Classical Studies*: Arethusa 15.1–2 (1983): 35–55.

Pike, K. "Etic and Emic Standpoints for the Description of Behavior." In *Communication and Culture*, edited by A. G. Smith, pp. 152–163. New York: Holt, Rinehart, and Winston, 1966.

Pribram, K. H. *Languages of the Brain*. Englewood Cliffs, N.J.: Prentice-Hall, 1971.

Read, A. W. "An Account of the Word Semantics." *Word* 4 (1948): 78–97.

Sebeok, T. A. *Contributions to the Doctrine of Signs*. Lisse, Netherlands: Peter de Ridder Press, 1976.

Shannon, C., and W. Weaver. *The Mathematical Theory of Communication*. Urbana: University of Illinois Press, 1949.

Todorov, T. *Theories of Symbol* (1977). Ithaca, N.Y.: Cornell University Press, 1982.

Wiener, N. *Cybernetics or Control and Communication in the Animal and the Machine*. New York: Wiley, 1948.

—PAUL BOUISSAC

SEMIURGY. A French neologism that came into use in substantive and adjectival forms in the early 1970s, semiurgy designates the logic of mass-mediated environments and is modeled on *demiurgey*, in some usages adding evil to artifice. Literally part "sign" and part "work," the concept appeared at once in Jean Baudrillard's description of the philosophy of design of the Bauhaus school and René Berger's distinction between sciences that take the suffix *-logies* (imposition of a model in a cognitive attitude) and those that take *-urgies* (implementation in a creative attitude).

Baudrillard argued that the Bauhaus's vision of a universal system of functional objects entailed a designed environment in which participation is completely controlled. Hence, semiurgy simulates participation by reducing it to moves in a functional calculus. Human experience is alienated from the signification of objects whose meaning is determined by their interdependent and oppositional relations with other objects in a closed system. The combinatorial possibilities of the system are dictated by the Bauhaus's ultimate signified of functionality. Conversely, Berger cleansed semiurgy of its negative attributes by connecting it with creative involvement through appeals to the ideas of Marshall McLuhan. Accordingly, semiologists must become sign readers and makers, seizing the opportunities of the communications revolution, for signs shift in the directions of those who act upon them and influence their work of signification.

Semiurgy is a key process in the endless self-reflexive play of signs in postmodern theory. In this literature, the origin of semiurgy is located in McLuhan's idea of massage, or how media intensify certain faculties, diminish others, and establish new proportions between them. The stresses and pains of massage are overcome in favor of stimulating social communication. Semiurgy and massage both name powerful forces that shape social experience. Contrary to the conception of McLuhan and his followers, Baudrillardian semiurgy impoverishes social experience and prevents genuine communication between persons.

[*See also* Baudrillard; *and* Semiotic Terminology.]

BIBLIOGRAPHY

Baudrillard, J. *For a Critique of the Political Economy of the Sign*. Translated by C. Levin. Saint Louis: Telos, 1981.

Berger, R. *La mutation des signes*. Paris: Denoël, 1972.

Kroker, A., and D. Cook. *The Postmodern Scene: Excremental Culture and Hyper-Aesthetics*. Montreal: New World Perspectives, 1986.

McLuhan, M. *Understanding Media: The Extensions of Man*. New York: McGraw-Hill, 1964.

McLuhan, M., and Q. Fiore. *The Medium Is the Message*. New York: Bantam, 1967.

—GARY GENOSKO

SIGN. Widely understood as the primary concept of semiotics, the notion of sign is easy to understand informally, building on the word's everyday usage. Looking for a common denominator, we might say, following a medieval formula, that a sign is something that stands for something else. This trivial definition, however, is quickly shown to be circular. One of the main challenges of semiotics is to develop a formal definition of sign that is informative and also intuitively satisfying. Various doctrines of semiotics attempt to meet this challenge differently and are built from fundamentally contrasted and, in some cases, even irreconcilable notions of sign. A survey of approaches to understanding the word *sign* by exemplification or by definition must have as its first priority a display of the problems rather than a synthesis of their solutions.

In ordinary language, a number of nouns and verbs are more or less synonymous with *sign* and, in their effects, with sign functions: for example, the terms *symbol*, *name*, *signal*, and *representation* and the functions "to signify," "to mean," "to refer to," and "to indicate." While particular academic theories specialize their usage of some or all of these terms, there is no common agreement in scholarly discourse that differentiates them systematically. The fundamental problem of the concept of sign does not lie in distinguishing these terms from each other but in specifying what, if anything, they have in common. Therefore, we can take the word *sign* in what follows to represent the class of words with which it is extensively synonymous.

There is certainly no consensus that a single unified idea of sign makes good sense (even among philosophers who do not denigrate general abstract concepts as a matter of course). At one extreme, Charles Ogden and Ivor Richards's study (1923) concludes that the idea encompasses at least sixteen independent notions. On the other hand, much of Charles Sanders Peirce's work aims at elucidating a core of common principles among the most diverse types of sign. The difference represented by these extreme views is fundamental but not a point of very active academic controversy at present, as their proponents align with separate schools (and thus publish in different journals and attend different meetings). An interest in semiotics as a declared affiliation tends to connote a sympathy for a unified concept.

The technical usage of *sign* in semiotics is generally more comprehensive than the popular usage. In scholarly writing, the term *sign* might include, for example, words, sentences, marks on paper that represent words or sentences, computer programs (hardwired, electronically recorded, or written out), pictures, diagrams, graphs, chemical and physical formulas, fingerprints, ideas, concepts, mental images, sensations, money, postures and gestures, manners and customs, costumes, rules and values, the orienting dance of the honeybee, avian display, fishing lures, DNA, objects made of other signs (including poetry and fiction, even if not considered to "stand for something else"), and also nonrepresentational objects (perhaps in music or mathematics) that have types of structure characteristic of other signs. Furthermore, while all these items affiliate with the idea of sign in that their primary functions concern knowledge, information, or communication, nearly any object can possess signification secondarily by context or aesthetic design: architecture, automobiles, and home furnishings, and any gift or souvenir, for example.

By contrast, a general characteristic of common usage is to elide the concept of sign where its circumstances are the most frequent and transparent. Thus, in commonplace, naive usage, we speak of "sign language" for the deaf but do not use that term for routine oral speech, as the semiotician does. In popular parlance, a totem pole is a sign, but the words *totem* or *pole* or *totem pole* (all of which are signs from the technical standpoint of semiotics) are not. One speaks of an addition sign or a square-root sign but not of *2* as a "two sign." Asked to name a half dozen of the most usual traffic signs, an unprompted respondent is unlikely to include in his or her list the yellow lines often painted in the middle of the road. The inconsistencies of common speech in this regard are easy to grasp, and this disposition toward generalization is itself initial evidence of a coherent concept beneath the surface of common usage.

Nevertheless, this coherent concept is not easy to elicit. Usages such as the English *sign* have parallels but certainly not exact homologues in other languages (for example, English uses *sign* and French uses *enseigne*). Standard dictionary definitions are mere compilations, listing several different senses of the word. The technical approach emerges from an attempt to get at the unity.

The scholastic dictum might introduce some recurrent problems in the formal elaboration of the concept of sign. In the definition "aliquid [stat] pro aliquo" ("something [that stands] for something else"), the preposition is evasive. The notion of substitution is frequently invoked, and some signs can be understood this way—for example, the ritual bread and wine of Catholic communion, which take the place of the flesh and blood of Christ. Similarly, the approval of a blueprint partially substitutes for the inspection of a house. But in general, a sign is not automatically permitted to substitute for its object. In most cases, *pro* simply means "means" or "represents" and thus renders the definition circular.

A more elaborate definition that is often attributed to Augustine of Hippo but is likely older, explains the sign as "something which besides manifesting itself to the senses also indicates to the mind something beyond itself." The insufficiencies of this definition illustrate further theoretical watersheds in the conception of sign. One problem here is the status of thoughts, ideas, mental images, and concepts as signs. These entities certainly partake of a representational function but do not manifest themselves to the senses, at least in our usual frame of reference.

The deep circularity of this definition resides in its recourse to a presupposed notion of mind, for the idea of mind seems impossible to establish without referring to signs, if not literally, then by invoking a collection of concepts (images, knowledge, etc.) that presuppose an idea of representation like that of signs. Furthermore, the term *indicates* is ambiguous here. Certainly, physical transportation ("brings to mind") is not proposed. We might interpret *indicates* as "to cause a transfer of attention." The formula then identifies signs by their control of a succession of thoughts or images. However, the thought control envisioned is typically learned, not innate, being embodied in a rule (e.g., a definition) that is itself another sign or sign complex, effective only insofar as it asserts meaning. Analyzed this way, *indicates* is

merely another synonym for *means* or *signifies*, and again the definition is ultimately circular.

In the twentieth century, doctrinal progress in developing the concept of sign has hinged on two points: establishing that a sign is a relation, and taking account of the asymmetry or nonequivalence of the related entities. With regard to the relational conception of the sign, stimulus for work in very different directions emerged in linguistics, mathematical logic, and philosophy.

Ferdinand de Saussure's general linguistics broached the possibility of describing sign systems as autonomous structures. In his scheme and in its further elaborations by others the sign can be understood as a correlation of differences. Saussure's terms *signifié* and *signifiant*, for which the awkward English equivalents *signifier* and *signified* are now consensually employed, indicate two faces of the sign. In the case of a word, for example, the signifier is a sound structure determined not by the immediate sound of a particular pronunciation in a naive material sense but by its identifying features of similarity to and difference from other sound structures in its language. The signified is a comparable meaning complex, determined not by the immediate burden of a particular usage but again by patterns of equivalence and contrast the one word has established with other words in its language. In Louis Hjelmslev's theoretical system, which pursues the direction set by Saussure, the key corresponding terms (though they take a different nuance) are *expression* for the signifier and *content* for the signified. Hjelmslev's *Prolegomena to a Theory of Language* (1943), with its elegant and dramatic axiomatic method, signaled the prospect of a description of signs that makes no reference to an external context or "real world"; the sign is accounted for solely as a relation inside an autonomous system. The mode of thought arising in this vein, which finds sympathy in economics and sociology as well as in linguistics, gave rise to structuralism.

The opposite tack in analyzing the concept of sign is to take its dependence on a real context of use as its central fact. In this perspective, which inspired an elaborate Latin-language philosophical development as well as much contemporary investigation, the point of departure is the nonequivalence of a designated object with the image of it conveyed by its sign. There are many ways to picture this nonequivalence according to the relative roles ascribed to mental and nonmental elements of the total sign situation. The scholastic terms *signum*, *signatum*, and *designatum* form a basic scheme that differentiates a signifier (*signum*), a signified concept (*signatum*), and a particular entity to which the concept is ascribed by the sign (*designatum*).

Gottlob Frege invented a method of investigating the relationships in such a triangle through mathematical modeling. His terms for the three parts of the sign are *Zeichen*, *Sinn*, and *Bedeutung*. His study proceeded through a meticulous and mathematically strict analysis of synonymy and in a novel manner linked the logic of representation to truth relations. His work deeply influenced Rudolf Carnap and Bertrand Russell, among others, and set directions in analytical philosophy. However, the positivist thrust of these researches has tended to deflect effort and attention from a development of a broad conception of sign in favor of a very critical examination of particular mathematical or linguistic cases in which a global sense of sign is not at issue.

With respect to the analysis of sign vis-à-vis a real world rather than systemic (e.g., linguistic) context, Peirce left the richest legacy of ideas, though the degree to which he made his ideas coherent is a matter of controversy. His work was propelled by the at least partially conflicting energies of his genius for practical science, logical abstraction, and the analysis of introspective experience. In evidence of this, his writings include some three dozen different definitions of sign. It is not always clear which of these are the drafts and which are more developed. His prosaic description of the sign as "something which stands for something to somebody in some respect or capacity" seems scarcely related to his definition, "A *Sign* or *Representamen*, is a First which stands in such a genuine triadic relation to a Second, called its *Object*, as to be capable of determining a Third, called its *Interpretant*, to assume the same triadic relation to its Object in which it stands itself to the same Object."

The latter definition presumes an understanding of Peirce's system of phenomenological and ontological categories, for which his theory of semiotics was the linchpin linking them to epistemology. In Peirce's philosophy, the category of sign is implicated in all aspects of the universe that manifest pattern or continuity. An implication of his definition of the sign that proves fundamental to the whole of his system is that the defining characteristic of signs is their capacity to determine additional signs. In this tripartite scheme, the different possible relations among the three components of the sign generate an extensive system of sign taxonomy. The subsequent classification of signs as indexes, icons, and symbols according to the relationship between the representamen and the object has been widely adopted in semiotic literature. Peirce demonstrated to his own satisfaction that four-, five- and higher-part relations could be generated from three-part relations but not from two-part relations. In consequence, he was interested in construing the sign formally only as characterized by three-part relations. The first of his definitions quoted above has four terms, not three, so this alerts us that the second formula is the building block of a complex rather than a full description. His own elaborations, which allow for (as a minimum) two aspects of the object and three of the interpretant, follow suit.

For Peirce, it was of paramount importance to maintain the reality of both the mental and extramental worlds, and he relied on his theory of semiotics to connect them, suggesting that every sign was a bit of mind. The decades following his work witnessed a widespread interest in accounting for the world without reference to mentality and in reducing mind to behavior. Charles Morris developed a semiotic philosophy that, while founded on Peirce's work, transformed it into a behaviorist model. His explanation of the sign process (1964) reveals his commitment to excluding any entailment of mentality in how he formulates a notion of sign in terms of stimulus and response. As he later described it, "semiosis (or sign process) is regarded as a five-term relation—v, w, x, y, z—in which v sets up in w the disposition to react in a certain kind of way, x, to a certain kind of object, y (not then acting as a stimulus), under certain conditions, z" (1971, pp. 401–402). While Morris's intention is to achieve greater precision, the result is the opposite, with a loss of both clarity of principle and motivation. The adjective *certain* hides all the real problems. Russell, who was strongly attracted to this mode of theorizing and formulated a very similar definition, was nevertheless aware of its inadequacy. The idea of sign seems to lose its essential function and its boundaries when its role in establishing the reality of mind is denied.

Aside from the central question of whether or not sign can be construed as a unified, nontrivial category, and aside from major differences of theoretical allegiance to Saussurean, Peircean, behavioral, and other traditions of thought, the literature of semiotics expresses other particular disagreements about the appropriate way to construct the idea of sign. These differences are indicated here by example but not comprehensively. The notion of sign is regarded by some authors as virtually limitless in scope, while other restrict their formal use of the term to signs as used in human thought, and still others to signs that have a distinctly arbitrary or conventional component. The hierarchical range of sign is also an issue: we might speak of a word, a sentence, a paragraph, a book, or a whole culture as a sign, or we might restrict the term to a portion of that series. At one end of the scale, for the smallest components, such as the distinctive features of linguistic phonemes, Hjelmslev proposed the term *figurae*, distinguishing these elements as less than full-fledged signs because they are incapable of independent reference. The opposing view (advanced by Roman Jakobson, among others) is that these least components are still signs and refer to "difference." At the other end of the scale, where large sign complexes are involved, the term *text* is frequently preferred, but recent discourse, especially in literary criticism, has tended to oppose text to sign on the basis of polysemy rather than material size, so that a single word might be viewed as a text when its usage is sufficiently charged with multidimensional reference. The problem of typology, though not a particular focus of current debate, is another for which no consensual resolution has gained sway, and it is complicated by our increasing sensitivity to differences among media and sensory channels. Finally, the place of the concept of sign within the whole doctrinal apparatus of semiotics is not a matter of universal agreement; many see it as a less-central fulcrum than sign function, semiosis, or text.

Does semiotic theory even require a definition of sign? It is a commonplace that sciences require primitive terms that they do not define. Physics does not define *matter*, nor biology *life*, nor psychology *mind*; but two objections arise immediately to offering semiotics this easy way out. First, the philosophies of the other sciences do tackle these issues, and semiotics is a philosophical field with comparable responsibilities. Second, in the experimental sciences there are always explicit principles of interpretation that permit research to determine whether or not its undefined objects are present or absent. The biologist or physicist knows how to tell if life or matter is present. In the case of semiotics, such a test returns us to the problem of definition and the ongoing

dialectic of exemplification and delineation that achieves no axiomatic basis.

[*See also* Augustine of Hippo; Frege; Hjelmslev; Medieval Semiotics; Peirce; Saussure; Semiosis, Semiotic Terminology; *and* Signification.]

BIBLIOGRAPHY

Carnap, R. *Introduction to Semantics*. Cambridge, Mass: Harvard University Press, 1942.
Cassirer, E. *The Philosophy of Symbolic Forms*. 3 vols. New Haven: Yale University Press, 1953–1957.
Clarke, D. S., Jr. *Sources of Semiotic: Readings with Commentaries from Antiquity to the Present*. Carbondale, Ill.: Southern Illinois University Press, 1990.
Deely, J., B. Williams, and F. E. Kruse, eds. *Frontiers in Semiotics*. Bloomington: Indiana University Press, 1986.
Lidov, D. *Elements of Semiotics*. Toronto: University of Toronto Press, 1996.
Manetti, G. *Theories of the Sign in Classical Antiquity*. Translated by C. Richardson. Bloomington: Indiana University Press, 1993.
Morris, C. W. *Signification and Significance: A Study of the Relations of Signs and Values*. Cambridge, Mass.: MIT Press, 1964.
Morris, C. W. *Writings on the General Theory of Signs*. The Hague: Mouton, 1971.
Ogden, C. K., and I. A. Richards. *The Meaning of Meaning* (1923). New York: Harcourt, 1946.
Russell, B. *An Inquiry into Meaning and Truth*. New York: W. W. Norton, 1940.
Sebeok, T. A. *Contributions to the Doctrine of Signs*. Lisse, Netherlands: Peter de Ridder Press, 1976.

—DAVID LIDOV

SIGNAL. While generally conceived of as a sign that conveys information, a signal in the biological sense usually refers to those signs that convey information that incite a recipient to action. A signal can be morphological or physiological and can involve the direct transference of information through, for instance, acoustic or chemical productions; in insects, certain macromolecules known as "pheromones" are highly significant, but many animal signals also involve behavior. The "dance" by which honeybees convey to their nest mates information regarding a source of food is a classic example.

It is thought that many, probably most, signals have evolved for some other reason and have been turned adaptively to information transmission only as a secondary function. This is surely the case of those mating practices of birds that involve preening and the like. The evolutionary production of such derived activities is called ritualization. Sometimes, but not necessarily, the original function is lost entirely.

Assuming, as today's evolutionists do, that signals are produced by natural selection pushing toward various functional optima, ethologists have spent much effort in studying the design aspects of signals and signaling. It seems clear that economic factors are highly significant. Apart from the difficulty with mistakes in complex signals, simpler signals are easier to produce. Hence, frequently used signals tend to be simple and infrequently used signals more complex. Of course, there might be other selective factors involved, and it might then be necessary for an organism to use a complex signal, especially if there is danger of an exploiter trying to use the signal to its own ends.

Other selective factors are also important. If it is crucial that a particular signal is never misunderstood, then there will be strong pressure on it toward clarity, precision, and lack of variation. There is much discussion about the nature of the information transferred by signals. It is an analytic truth that there will be a reduction of uncertainty about an organism's behavior after signaling—for example, after an appropriate male signal, we can more readily predict that a female will do x rather than y.

More interesting than the bare assertion that there will be transference of what is known as "Shannon information" (the measurement of the quantity of novelty conveyed by a message) is the question of whether signals can actually transfer semantic information. Part of the problem here is itself a semantic issue. Clearly, the dance of the honeybee acts as a signal to transfer information in the Shannon sense; after the dance, we can more readily predict the behavior of the bees, but whether one bee actually "tells" the others about the environment becomes a moot point. Certainly, in the higher animals it seems unduly anthropocentric to deny that they ever give and receive meaningful (semantic) information. In less complex organisms, it is probably best to regard signaling in a behavioral or operational fashion.

[See also Communication; Evolution; Information; and Sign.]

BIBLIOGRAPHY

Darwin, C. The Descent of Man. London: John Murray, 1871.
Hamilton, W. D., and M. Zuk. "Heritable True Fitness and Bright Birds: A Role for Parasites." Science 218 (1982): 384–387.

Krebs, J., and N. B. Davies, eds. Behavioral Ecology: An Evolutionary Approach. Sunderland, Mass.: Sinauer, 1978.
Shannon, C. E., and W. Weaver. The Mathematical Theory of Communication. Urbana: University of Illinois Press, 1949.
Wilson, E. O. The Insect Societies. Cambridge, Mass.: Howard University Press, Belknap Press, 1971.
Wilson, E. O. Sociobiology: The New Synthesis. Cambridge, Mass.: Harvard University Press, 1975.

—MICHAEL RUSE

SIGNIFICATION. In common usage, *signification* has come to mean either "the act of signifying" or "the intended meaning" of a message and applies to both verbal and nonverbal sign productions. In semantics and semiotics, signification has been the object of controversies and redefinitions. It has often been defined by contrast with other terms, such as "designating" (e.g., Linsky, 1967), "significance" (e.g., Morris, 1964), and "communication" (e.g., Prieto, 1975, and Eco, 1976), without any terminological consensus emerging in the metalanguage of semiotics. An early conceptual elaboration is found in the work of Ferdinand de Saussure. However, the inherent difficulties encountered in providing a theoretical definition of this term are compounded by the problems of translation.

Saussure used the terms *sense* (*sens*) and *role* (*rôle*) to talk about the semantic value attributed to each separate linguistic unit that the linguist "delimits" in an overall linear phonic sequence. These two terms are translated variously by Wade Baskin (Saussure, 1959) as "meaning" and "function" and by Roy Harris (Saussure, 1983) as "meaning" and "role." The rendering of the French *sens* as "meaning" blurs the distinction Saussure makes between *sens* and *signification*, given that the latter is sometimes translated by Baskin as "meaning" and is consistently so translated by Harris. When Saussure refers to the global process of the construction of meaning in a sequence by an interpreter, then *sens* appears to be restricted to the local functional semantic roles of the individual units. (These roles are known in some later linguistic accounts as the internal sense relations of grammatical units.) Saussure makes it clear that for him *sens* is so restricted: "Considered in itself, the phonic sequence if nothing but a line, a continuous ribbon, in which the ear perceives no clear or precise divisions; in order to segment it, appeal must be made to meanings [*significations*]. . . . But when we know *what sense and what role must be attributed to each part of the chain*, then we see the parts detach themselves from each other, and the shapeless ribbon is cut up into pieces" (1971, p. 145; emphasis added).

Saussure does not explicitly build this set of distinctions into his basic model of the sign, which is given in part 1, chapter 1 of his *Course in General Linguistics*. Saussure also draws attention to the solidary or nonarbitrary nature of the relationship between grammatical forms and their functions. In the basic model of the sign, the relationship between signified and signifier is generally taken to be arbitrary, therefore, the nonarbitrary or solidary nature of the relation between grammatical form and function requires redrawing the basic model. Grammatical form and function belong on the stratum of the signified, not the signifier. The grammatical forms are the delimited grammatical units, and the functions are the "sense" or "role relations" these have in the linear sequence. This distinction means that the stratum of the signified is itself internally stratified in such a way that grammatical form and function are related in a nonarbitrary, motivated, or solidary way.

This brings in a new term: *signification*. If the grammar is said to be significative—that is, "able to mean" or "having the potential to mean"—then the process of noun signification designates the actual process of making or construing meaning in the phonic sequence. Saussure distinguishes this term from the notion of *valeur*, ("value") in his definition of the sign. In the discussion of the stratification of the sign in part 2, chapter 2, Saussure also claims that the "phonic sequence" can be delimited and defined only in terms of relevant linguistic units on the basis of the meaning(s) (*signification*[s]) we attribute to the overall sequence. This process, in turn, takes place on the basis of the sense or functional semantic roles of each of the constituent parts (grammatical forms) that are so delimited.

Instead of saying that expressions have a "semantic nucleus" that would be the basis of signification, Saussure claims that signification is the higher-level contextualization or construal of the instance; it is the process whereby the interpreter or language user construes or "attributes" an overall meaning to the entire sequence. Further, we cannot attribute a necessary or given semantic nucleus to the sense or functional roles of each of the units that have been delimited in a given sequence because these are a product of the role each

part plays in the whole sequence. This semantic role or sense relation cannot be separated from its relations to all the other units. This is a necessary condition if the relations among the various delimited units are to be defined in functional terms. Furthermore, a given unit can have quite a different functional role in some other sequence.

These distinctions are rich in implications. First, it is clear that Saussure has a much more complex view of the sign than the simple biplanar opposition between signifier and signified that is generally attributed to him. Second, Saussure underlines the functional basis of the delimited units that his stratified views of the sign and linear sequences of signs reveal. Third, these units, functionally defined according to their roles in the overall sequence, do not have meaning per se but are defined in relation to three perspectives: (1) the "lower" stratum (the phonic sequence) in relation to which they are delimited; (2) their sense or functional semantic role relations to each other in the overall sequence (i.e., on their own stratum, which is that of the signified); and (3) their relations to the overall or global meaning (*signification*) that is attributed to the whole sequence on the stratum "above."

The process that Saussure calls signification construes or interprets extralinguistic "thought-substance" in and through the value-producing distinctions made by the units delimited in the grammatical stratum at the level "below." Signification, as well as being a stratum in its own right, is the interface between the internal organization of language form and what lies outside it. Saussure, however, does not specify what kind of organization this stratum might have. Louis Hjelmslev's further development of this stratal model provides important insights on this question.

[*See also* Arbitrariness, Principle of; Hjelmslev; Linguistic Motivation; *and* Saussure.]

BIBLIOGRAPHY

Eco, U. *A Theory of Semiotics* (1976). Bloomington: Indiana University Press, 1979.

Linsky, L. *Referring*. London: Routledge and Kegan Paul, 1967.

Morris, C. W. *Signification and Significance: A Study of the Relations of Signs and Values*. Cambridge, Mass.: MIT Press, 1964.

Prieto, L. *Études de linguistique et de sémiologie générale*. Geneva: Droz, 1975.

Saussure, F. de. *Course in General Linguistics*. Translated by W. Baskin. New York and London: McGraw Hill, 1959.

Saussure, F. de. *Course in General Linguistics*. Translated by R. Harris. London: Duckworth, 1983.

—PAUL J. THIBAULT

SIGN LANGUAGES. The naturally evolved visual and gestural languages of the deaf, sign languages such as American Sign Language (ASL) appear to be ubiquitous in deaf communities. In hearing communities, which universally rely on one or more spoken languages as their primary languages, alternate signed languages are also well attested. ASL and other signed languages are not mere representations of the spoken language of the dominant hearing community, although gestural representations of spoken language do exist (e.g., fingerspelling, cued speech, and signed English). Instead, the grammars of signed languages such as ASL are largely independent of whatever spoken languages exist in the surrounding hearing communities. Consistent with this, different sign languages are used in different English-speaking communities: in fact, British Sign Language and ASL are mutually unintelligible languages.

The existence of sign languages with independently evolved grammars demonstrates the plasticity of the human language capacity with regard to the channel or modality in which language is produced and perceived. The fact that human language is not restricted to a particular modality raises a crucial issue: to what extent does the transmission modality determine the structure, acquisition, and processing of language?

The demography of deaf communities raises interesting questions for studies of first-language acquisition and for sociolinguistic studies of language variation. In general, 90 to 95 percent of deaf children have hearing parents. First-generation deaf children (deaf children of hearing parents) often receive no input from a sign language during early childhood; moreover, their ages at first exposure to ASL or any other sign language vary widely. Consequently, studies of linguistic knowledge and processing in signers allow an important test of the hypothesis that there is a critical period for first-language acquisition. Second-generation deaf children receive input from deaf parents who are nonnative signers. Only the very small minority of third-generation deaf children (deaf children who have at least one deaf grandparent) who receive input from parents who are themselves native signers.

Primary Sign Languages. Sign languages such as French Sign Language (FSL) and ASL are not artificial creations; several factors have contributed to their development. Residential schools are wellsprings of the deaf community. The first such school (the National Institution for Deaf-Mutes) was established by Abbé de l'Epée in Paris in 1755. The deaf individuals who joined that community brought to it a vocabulary of signs. In an attempt to create what might now be called Signed French, de l'Epée introduced *signes méthodiques* that encoded the grammatical particles and inflectional morphology of the French. In general, such methodical signs have been rejected by the deaf community. Importantly, Epée's school validated the use of signing in the education of deaf children. The French also sought to spread their methods to other countries, thereby accounting for the introduction of French signs into many signed languages in Europe and the Americas. Other signed languages, notably those used in Asia, appear entirely unrelated to FSL.

The first school for the deaf in the United States was established in 1817 in Hartford, Connecticut, by Thomas Gallaudet, who had recently returned from France after having studied the educational practices of the Paris school. A deaf Frenchman, Laurent Clerc, accompanied Gallaudet on his return to the United States and taught at the Hartford school until 1858. The sign language used in the Hartford deaf community was not simply a variant of FSL but also incorporated signs already in use in the American deaf community. The deaf community from Martha's Vineyard, Massachusetts, may have had a particularly strong influence on the development of ASL, inasmuch as a disproportionate number of the students in Hartford came from that island. As in some other genetically isolated populations, a high incidence of deafness on Martha's Vineyard supported a local signed language in the seventeenth through nineteenth centuries; almost nothing is known about the linguistics of that language. The recessive variety of deafness on Martha's Vineyard came from the county of Kent in England, so there is also a possibility that the sign language on Martha's Vineyard may have been related to a sign language once used in Kent, although no deaf individual is known to have immigrated from Kent to Martha's Vineyard.

Children might be key contributors to the development and maintenance of ASL and other sign languages. Deaf children born to hearing, nonsigning parents innovate gestural systems (so-called home signs) that display many languagelike properties, including statistically reliable word order (gesture order) tendencies (Goldin-Meadow and Mylander, 1990). The gesturing of these deaf children is much more systematized than that of their hearing parents. Particularly dramatic evidence of the role of children in the creation of sign languages comes from recent research on the Idioma de Signos Nicaragüenses (Nicaraguan Sign Language); Judy Kegl, A. Singhas, and M. Coppola (1996) argue that, through a creolization process, this sign language has been created since 1979 by the first generation of young children to enter the newly established public schools for the deaf in Nicaragua. As input, these children used the pidginlike sign system of their older schoolmates.

Iconicity and arbitrariness. Since the work of Ferdinand de Saussure, the arbitrariness of linguistic symbols (*signes*) has been seen as a fundamental design feature of human language. However, on first glance, observers of sign languages are often struck by the iconicity of their signs. For this reason, sign languages have sometimes been dismissed as systems of pantomime. Indeed, many signs in signed languages are quite iconic; for example, the ASL sign *cat* suggests the distinctive whiskers of that animal. Nonetheless, the meanings of signs are not so transparent that they can be guessed by the naive observer. Moreover, the iconic qualities of signs can be suppressed by historical change (Frishberg, 1975) or in colloquial conversation. In addition, morphological processes in ASL often override the iconic qualities of simple signs, although those morphological processes are sometimes themselves nonarbitrary in form.

Even when several sign languages represent a given concept iconically (see Klima and Bellugi, 1979, and their discussion of the sign *tree* in ASL, Danish Sign Language, and Chinese Sign Language), they might display different icons, and consequently different linguistic forms, for that concept. In some instances, several sign languages exhibit the same icon for a given concept: as in ASL, the sign for *cat* in many sign languages suggests that animal's whiskers. Yet even with this motivated relationship between form and meaning as a constant, the resultant signs vary substantially in movement and hand configuration. Thus, iconicity is not sufficient to predict the form of signs. Importantly, the vocabularies of sign languages also include many signs that are fully arbitrary in their form-meaning relationship (e.g., the ASL signs *curious* or *seem*). Whether arbitrary or not, the relationship between the form and meaning of lexical items in signed languages is conventional, just as in spoke languages. The occurrence of iconically and indexically motivated signs and of onomatopoetic words in speech suggests that the pairing between form and meaning in linguistic symbols need not be arbitrary. But all human languages allow arbitrary form-meaning pairs in their lexicons, and this seems to be a fundamental design feature of language.

The iconicity of many signs has little or no effect on adult processing of ASL, as shown by studies of production errors in conversation (slips of the hand) and of short-term memory for lists of signs. The same is true in the acquisition of ASL as a first language by children of deaf, signing parents. Although the gestures in the home sign systems of deaf children of hearing parents are generally highly iconic or indexical (and therefore comprehensible to the parents), deaf children who acquire conventionalized signed languages such as ASL seem remarkably insensitive to the iconicity of signs, even when little or no cultural knowledge is required to detect the imagistic basis for those signs. In general, children acquiring ASL seem to acquire signs as if they were arbitrary (Meier, 1991).

The internal structure of signs. Signs are not holistically organized, as might be expected if they were fundamentally pantomimic. Rather, signed languages exhibit duality of patterning, just as spoken languages do. In "phonological" analyses of ASL and other signed languages, debate has centered on the extent to which the internal organization of signs is fundamentally simultaneous (and thus different in character from the phonological structure of spoken languages) or sequential (i.e., segmental, as in spoken languages). The *Dictionary of American Sign Language* (Stokoe, Casterline, and Croneberg, 1965) characterizes signs in terms of three simultaneous parameters or "aspects." In the notational system that they developed, each sign is specified by its place of articulation, hand configuration, and movement. For each parameter, there is a limited set of possible values. Studies on short-term memory and on slips of the hand have yielded psychological evidence for the existence of such sublexical organization in the mental representations of native signers.

Although Stokoe et al.'s analysis posits three simultaneous parameters, some sequential structure is accommodated by their notational system. For example, certain signs display changes in hand shape (typically either a change from a relatively open hand shape to a relatively closed one or vice versa), some signs (generally compounds) involve a sequence of places of articulation, and still other signs show movement sequences. In contrast, Scott Liddell (1984) argues that there are sequentially ordered constituents within signs. He posits two types of phonological segments: movements and holds. In the articulation of signs, these two segment types appear as static phases (holds) or dynamic ones (movements). Liddell's evidence for this segmentation comes from analyses of the articulatory form of signs, from comparisons of citation-form signs with their more colloquial variants, and from an analysis of compounds.

In linguistic research on sign languages, the phonological structure of signs remains an area of lively debate (e.g., Brentari, 1995). Important issues include the correct segmentation of signs and the nature of a hypothesized sign syllable. It is fair to conclude that all current models of sign-internal structure posit some phonologically significant role for sequential structure.

The use of space in sign languages. In ASL and other signed languages, signs are with a few exceptions produced in the so-called sign space. In *The Signs of Language* (1979), Edward Klima and Ursula Bellugi define that space as follows: "Signs normally do not extend below waist level or above the head, nor beyond the reach of the arms to the sides, with elbows close to the body." Within the sign space, the empty region in front of the signer is often called "neutral space" because signs made within it are not articulated with respect to any landmarks on the body.

Neutral space serves a key function within the pronominal system of ASL. Deictic pronouns are fairly straightforward: the first-person pronoun is a point to the center of the signer's own chest, and reference to the addressee or to a nonaddressed participant is indicated by a point to that person. Reference to nonpresent referents is more interesting: the signer can refer to such referents by establishing "loci" within neutral space. To sign the proposition that Mary looked at John, the signer (who is neither Mary nor John) might arbitrarily establish a spatial locus on the right for Mary and one on the left for John. Through verb agreement, the movement ex-

cursion of the verb *look-at* would then begin at the right locus and end at the left locus, thereby marking that the subject of *look-at* is Mary and that its object is John. As the discourse continues, these spatial loci remain available for anaphoric reference, which can be achieved through indexical signs or eye gaze toward these loci and by verb agreement with these loci. (See Meier as well as Lillo-Martin and Klima in Fischer and Siple, 1990).

Morphology. ASL has extensive inflectional and derivational morphology (Klima and Bellugi, 1979). The derivational morphology of ASL means that new signs can be added to the open-class vocabulary (nouns, verbs, and adjectives), and that the open-class vocabulary is therefore open-ended. ASL has much more extensive inflectional morphology than does English: in particular, ASL has a rich set of inflectional contrasts indicating verb agreement (through the incorporation of spatial loci), reciprocal events, temporal aspect, and distributive aspects. ASL has relatively few affixes (though it does have an intensifier infix and an agentive suffix). In general, inflections for temporal and distributive aspect are repetitive, rhythmically organized movement patterns that extend throughout the production of the inflected sign. In their form and in the semantic contrasts that they mark, these inflections are very much akin to the reduplicative morphology of many spoken languages. Extensive use of such morphology seems typical of sign languages.

ASL verbs of movement and position have particularly complex morphological structures. In such verbs, the hand shape is a classifier that indicates the semantic category to which the moving (or positioned) object belongs; thus, ASL has distinctive classifiers for vehicles, small animals, and bulky objects. The particular type of vehicle (car, motorcycle, ship, etc.) is indicated by a separate noun. This system of classifiers bears many structural similarities to classifier systems in spoken languages, as in Navaho.

Syntactic structure. The markers of grammatical role in ASL are word order and verb agreement. Many but not all ASL verbs agree with spatial locations associated with their subject and object arguments. Agreement is indicated typically by path movements between those locations (usually movement from the location associated with the subject to the one associated with the object). As in Romance languages such as Spanish and Portuguese, rich-agreement morphology sanctions null arguments (so-called pro-drop). If the verb in a clause is noninflecting (e.g., *eat*), sign order in SVO (subject-verb-objects) and null arguments are not permitted, except when licensed—as in Chinese—by the discourse topic (Lillo-Martin, 1991).

Grammaticized facial expressions serve as syntactic markers in ASL, marking distinctions sometimes indicated by prosody and sometimes by function words in spoken languages (Liddell, 1980). Thus, there are facial expressions that are obligatory markers of topic constituents, of wh-questions (i.e., questions with "who," "what," "when," "where," or "why"), and of yes-no questions. These facial expressions overlay the manual signs that are within their scope. There is also a set of adverbials that are signaled solely by distinctive facial expressions.

Comparisons of signed and spoken languages indicate that the key architectural elements of language do not inhere in a particular modality: such design features of language as conventionality, duality of patterning, productivity, and allowance of arbitrary form-meaning pairings are not properties of a particular language modality. Rather these properties of language properly belong to whatever cognitive and linguistic capacities underlie the knowledge and use of language in any modality. If we identified an independently evolved language in a third modality (say, a tactile-gestural language), we should expect to encounter these same properties in that language.

Crucial research remains to be done on sign languages. As yet, we know much too little about the range of cross-linguistic variation that is possible in sign languages. To achieve that understanding, much more research is needed soon on sign languages other than ASL; the survival of smaller signed languages might be threatened by the impact of prestige signed languages and by educational practice that is little informed by research on the linguistics of sign languages.

Alternate Sign Languages. Although every known hearing community uses a spoken language as its primary language, the use of alternate signed languages in hearing communities is well attested. One common use of such sign languages is as a medium of communication where speech is, for ritual reasons, taboo. Such use of sign languages has been reported in many Australian aboriginal tribes, particularly in Australia's North Central Desert (Kendon, 1988). In these tribes, the two most common occasions for use of an alternate sign language

are mourning periods and male initiation rites. Widows in many aboriginal tribes are bound by speech taboos until their husband's deaths are avenged, a period sometimes lasting up to two years. During their time of mourning, these women communicate through the tribe's alternate sign language. In certain tribes, widowers and female relatives other than the widow also observe speech restrictions and use an alternate sign language exclusively. Initiation is seen as the symbolic death of the boy, and young males—and in some tribes, their female relatives—are often forbidden to speak during the period of preparation preceding their initiation or during the period of seclusion following the ceremony. During these periods, both the young males and their female relatives communicate through signs. Although aboriginal alternate signed languages show some degree of independence from the spoken languages of their communities, sign syntax and morphology largely follow that of the tribe's spoken language. Between tribes, there is a considerable degree of variation in sign vocabulary.

Monastic sign languages also arose from prohibitions on speech (Umiker-Sebeok and Sebeok, eds., 1987). Monastic signs have been in existence for several centuries in orders that follow the daily periods of silence set by Saint Benedict in the sixth century. The Benedictines, Cistercians, Cluniacs, and Trappists currently follow these rules of silence. In addition to the lists of official signs maintained by the orders, unofficial signs have been created by the monks, although many such signs are known only within a single monastery. In general, monastic sign languages demonstrate little independence from the spoken language that their users share; many lexical items are compounds derived from sound play, and their syntax follows that of the signers' spoken language. Fingerspelling, not a sign language but rather a way of manually encoding the alphabet, is also a product of the monastic environment. Invented by sixteenth-century Spanish monks, who used it in early attempts to educate the deaf, fingerspelling is now used in American Sign Language (ASL) and other sign languages of the deaf to represent words (for example, technical vocabulary and proper names) for which there exist no exact sign equivalents.

Plains Indian Sign Talk (PST) exemplifies a different use of an alternate sign language (Farnell, 1995). PST was used as a lingua franca between Native American tribes who spoke mutually unintelligible languages and as a medium for storytelling and rituals within each tribe. Although English has now replaced PST as the lingua franca, PST can still be found, for example, among old Nakota speakers, who use signs during storytelling, and in families with deaf members. Among younger generations, a tradition of ritual sign performance has also developed. The syntax of PST appears to be independent of any spoken language: to a greater extent than aboriginal or monastic alternate sign languages, PST incorporates certain grammatical features, such as use of space, that are characteristic of sign languages of the deaf. PST also demonstrates the conventional nature of indexical pointing gestures that serve as deictic pronouns in all sign languages. The ASL sign *me*, for instance, is an indexical point to the chest, whereas in PST, *me* is articulated at the nose. Thus, although the ASL sign *me* at first appears to be completely motivated, the selection of the chest as the place of articulation is at least partially arbitrary.

Although they share some characteristics with primary sign languages, the fact that alternate sign languages are used by speakers whose first language is a spoken one appears to have consequences for the structure, and possibly the learnability, of the signed languages. Adam Kendon, for instance, suggests that deaf individuals do not become fluent in hearing communities' alternate sign languages but, rather, like isolated deaf people elsewhere, rely on locally created home signs. Further research is needed to fully understand the grammatical differences between primary sign languages and alternate sign languages.

[*See also* Articulation; Face; Fingerspelling; Markedness; *and* Nonverbal Bodily Sign Categories.]

BIBLIOGRAPHY

Brentari, D. "Sign Language Phonology: ASL." In *The Handbook of Phonological Theory*, edited by J. A. Goldsmith, pp. 615–639. Cambridge, Mass.: Blackwell, 1995.

Farnell, B. *Do You See What I Mean? Plains Indians Sign Talk and the Embodiment of Action*. Austin: University of Texas Press, 1995.

Fischer, S. D., and P. Siple, eds. *Theoretical Issues in Sign Language Research*, vol 1. *Linguistics*. Chicago: University of Chicago Press, 1990.

Frishberg, N. "Arbitrariness and Iconicity: Historical Change in American Sign Language." *Language* 51 (1975): 696–719.

Goldin-Meadow, S., and C. Mylander. "Beyond the Input Given: The Child's Role in the Acquisition of Language." *Language* 66 (1990): 323–355.

Kegl, J., A. Senghas, and M. Coppola. "Creation through Contact: Sign Language Emergence and Sign Language Change in Nicaragua." In *Comparative Grammatical Change: The Intersection of Language Acquisition, Creole Genesis, and Diachronic Syntax*, edited by M. DeGraff. Cambridge, Mass.: MIT Press, 1996.

Kendon, A. *Sign Languages of Aboriginal Australia*. Cambridge: Cambridge University Press, 1988.

Klima, E. S., and U. Bellugi. *The Signs of Language*. Cambridge, Mass.: Harvard University Press, 1979.

Liddell, S. K. *American Sign Language Syntax*. The Hague: Mouton, 1980.

Liddell, S. K. "THINK and BELIEVE: Sequentiality in American Sign Language." *Language* 60 (1984): 372–399.

Lillo-Martin, D. C. *Universal Grammar and American Sign Language: Setting the Null Argument Parameters*. Dordrecht: Kluwer, 1991.

Meier, R. P. "Language Acquisition by Deaf Children." *American Scientist* 79 (1991): 60–70.

Stokoe, W. C., D. C. Casterline, and C.G. Croneberg. *A Dictionary of American Sign Language on Linguistic Principles*. Washington, D.C.: Gallaudet College Press, 1965.

Umiker-Sebeok, J., and T. A. Sebeok, eds. *Monastic Sign Languages*. Berlin: Mouton de Gruyter, 1987.

—AMANDA S. HOLZRICHTER
and RICHARD P. MEIER

SOCIOBIOLOGY. A subbranch of the Darwinian evolutionary paradigm, sociobiology deals with the origin and nature of social behavior, including human social behavior. Although the name is relatively new, the subject goes back to the *Origin of Species* (1859). In that work, Charles Darwin discusses at some length and in considerable detail the evolution of behavior in social animals, most particularly the social insects (especially the Hymenoptera: the ants, the bees, and the wasps). Darwin argues always that the behavior shown by such animals is a direct function of the action of natural selection, although he has considerable difficulty in seeing how selection can promote features apparently of value to the group rather than directly to the individual organism. In his later work, the *Descent of Man* (1871), Darwin again broaches questions of sociality, particularly issues to do with the evolution and maintenance of morality. Although he had no true understanding of its underlying genetic foundations, Darwin is inclined to think that morality is promoted by what is known now as reciprocal altruism, behavior through which organisms help others and in return can expect help where nonhelpers cannot.

For various reasons, the study of the evolution of social behavior did not mature rapidly. A major factor was the rise of the social sciences and an increasing belief that all behavior is explained better in cultural terms than as functions of the strictly biological. In this century also, the horrendous political philosophies in Europe that directly endorsed genetic interpretations of human differences have been considerable barriers to the forward movement of any science that supposes that biology has a significant input into behavior. Nevertheless, even after World War II, an increasing number of students of animal behavior—the so-called ethologists—started to promote theories and hypotheses that give a significant role to Darwinian factors in the social interactions of organisms, particularly intraspecies interactions.

Major breakthroughs in this work came in the 1960s. Particularly noteworthy are the efforts of William D. Hamilton, who shows how hymenopteran sociality could be given a firm Darwinian underpinning: that is to say, a selective explanation consistent with our understanding of modern genetics. In particular, Hamilton argues—in an example of what is now known as kin-selection explanation—that the sterility of worker ants, bees, and wasps is of direct benefit to the individuals; indeed, paradoxically, the sterility furthers the biological well-being of these individuals because the Hymenoptera have a haploid-diploid method of reproduction. Males are born asexually, whereas females have both mothers and fathers. The effect of this is to make sisters more closely related to each other than mothers to daughters. Therefore, the sterile workers, by raising sisters, are better improving their own reproductive chances than by raising daughters (see Dawkins, 1989, p. 175).

Other mechanisms were added to Hamilton's explanations, including reciprocal altruism and a range of causes based on the idea of a "evolutionary stable strategy." Such a strategy refers to a method of reproduction that in some sense is stable because through it individuals in a group do better than they would under any rival method, assuming the existence of competitors—namely, fellow species members.

Finally, in 1975, the whole area came together and was christened sociobiology thanks to the work of Harvard entomologist Edward O. Wilson. In his magisterial *Sociobiology: The New Synthesis*, Wilson discusses a range of mechanisms that promote animal sociality. At the same time, he gives a detailed survey of such sociality as it exists in the real world, offering a spectrum that ranges from the social insects through the mammals and up to our own species. All forms of behavior, both aggressive and interactive (altruistic), are, he argues, the direct function of natural selection working for the good of individuals.

A year later, in England, the science of sociobiology was given a further boost by the publication of a more popular-directed work: *The Selfish Gene*, by biologist Richard Dawkins. Making his points succinctly through new metaphors, Dawkins backs Wilson's general approach, arguing that social behavior is a direct function of selection. However, Dawkins shows more sympathy for cultural elements than does Wilson. At the end of his work, Dawkins introduces the very notion of a meme as a unit of cultural information that functions analogously to a gene. Whereas Wilson argues that human behavior (including human thought) is very much a product of direct biological factors, Dawkins, although no less a stalwart Darwinian, argues that in the human realm we find near-autonomous processes that stand, as it were, on but above the purely biological.

Sociobiology, particularly applied to humans, has proved highly controversial. Expectedly, social scientists have not been keen on the subject, seeing with reason a threat to their own independence. More surprising, many good biologists, including evolutionists, have written critically about sociobiology, seeing within it the thin end of a very large wedge that leads back to the vile social doctrines prominent in Europe through the end of World War II. They argue that sociobiologists are guilty of facile reasoning and undue dependence on Darwinian mechanisms, stretching far beyond any evidential base. Particularly effective have been the criticisms of Wilson's Harvard colleagues, population geneticist Richard Lewontin and paleontologist Stephen Jay Gould. In a celebrated attack, they argue that sociobiologists frequently mistake organic characteristics (including social behavioral characteristics) for adaptations that are tightly under the control of selection. Rather, argue Gould and Lewontin, much culture has little connection with biology and is as directly nonfunctional as are the points at the tops of pillars in medieval buildings, so-called spandrels. Just as the latter serve no direct end, so likewise much social behavior serves no direct end. Thus, for instance, whereas Wilson and Dawkins argue that human social differences between the sexes are a function of biology, the critics hold that these differences are due simply to culture and tradition. For instance, males tend to be more dominant and pushy in Western societies today than are females; but whereas Wilson argues that this is something ingrained in human nature, explicable by Darwinian factors, critics such as Gould and Lewontin maintain that such differences are removable ephemera of cultural forces.

Today, some twenty years after sociobiology arrived with such fanfare and controversy, much of the dispute seems to have subsided. The critics are less vociferous, but at the same time sociobiologists are more careful in what they claim—and, indeed, they frequently hide their activities under alternative names, such as "human behavioral ecology" or "evolutionary psychology." It is perhaps invidious to pick out particular examples of sociobiological work today, but highly praised by all are studies by the Canadian psychologists Martin Daly and Margo Wilson on the nature and causes of homicide. From a biological point of view, it makes little or no sense for a parent to kill its own offspring. Why, then, is there so much intrafamilial violence? Daly and Wilson argue that the most reasonable answers from a sociobiological perspective are that such violence is either not real or not truly between family members. After careful analysis, they support the latter hypothesis, showing that violence by parents toward children is far more likely to result from abuse by stepparents than from the actions of biological parents. Daly and Wilson thus claim a triumph for Darwinian explanation.

Sociobiology by whatever name is now an established part of Darwinian evolutionary biology and moves forward strongly both in the animal and the human realm. It is as yet still much undeveloped in many areas but already has significant triumphs to its credit. It is a subject of considerable interest to the student of semiotics, both directly and indirectly. There has in recent years been much interest in the evolution of language generally and of the ways in which humans use words to signify different entities and ideas. The traditional biological approach to language launched by Noam Chomsky and his followers, although evolutionist, does not endorse a Darwinian perspective. Now we find that there has been much interest in showing not only that the development in language is evolutionary but that it is indeed truly something tightly under the control of natural selection, as a Darwinian would expect.

Indirectly, throughout the animal world the use of signs is now seen to be of significant importance from a Darwinian perspective. Particularly significant here are adaptations that develop under the control of sexual selection—that secondary mechanism first postulated by Darwin to explain such things as the peacock's tail coming about through the competition for mates rather than simply from a crude struggle for existence. Sociobiologists are much interested in the ways in which such adaptations can directly and indirectly convey information even—especially—in nonverbal contexts.

Of particular interest and importance is one recent hypothesis by Hamilton to the effect that sexuality might in some sense be connected with signaling. He argues that sexuality came about in order to offer protection against parasites. Thanks to sexuality, organisms' genetic makeups are shuffled in each generation, thus offering, in a sense, moving targets to the greatest threat against them: the diseases brought on by parasites. Hamilton argues that many organic characteristics have developed as signals to prospective mates, either to advertise biological fitness or to pretend to do so. Hamilton particularly highlights the way in which organisms frequently display their attributes by using blood vessels, a feature that informs prospective mates of the healthy state of an organism's vascular system. What at first set out to be a purely physiological mechanism can end by being a signal to a mate. This is ongoing and far from established work, but it shows clearly how the Darwinian paradigm in its modern manifestations has much of importance to offer the student of semiotics at all levels.

[See also Darwin; Dawkins; Evolution; Hamilton; Manipulation; Meme; Memetics; Signal; Wilson; and Zahavi.]

BIBLIOGRAPHY

Daly, M., and M. Wilson. *Homicide.* Hawthorne, N.Y.: Aldine de Gruyter, 1988.

Darwin, C. *On the Origin of Species.* London: John Murray, 1859.

Darwin, C. *The Descent of Man.* London: John Murray, 1871.

Dawkins, R. *The Selfish Gene.* new ed. Oxford: Oxford University Press, 1989.

Gould, S. J., and R. C. Lewontin. "The Spandrels of San Marco and the Panglossian Paradigm: A Critique of the Adaptationist Program. *Proceedings of the Royal Society of London,* Series B, biological sciences 205 (1979): 581–598.

Hamilton, W. D. "The Genetical Evolution of Social Behaviour." *Journal of Theoretical Biology* 7 (1964): 1–32.

Ruse, M. *Sociobiology: Sense of Nonsense?* Dordrecht: Reidel, 1979.

Wilson, E. O. *Sociobiology: The New Synthesis*. Cambridge, Mass.: Harvard University Press, 1975.

MICHAEL RUSE

SOUNDS. The human body is provided with a great variety of muscular-skeletal possibilities for visually perceived movements that serve locomotive, interactive, noninteractive, and task-performing functions. Many of these functions produce sound, and they all can be part, though in different degrees, of the verbal, paralinguistic, and kinesic structure of speech and discourse. Movements and sounds can function either by themselves with communicative value or blend with language and paralanguage in complex semiotic processes. Beyond them, even the sounds of the objectual and natural environments can become components of an interactive encounter.

The sounds produced by self-adaptor activities (e.g., fingersnapping, thudding on chest, hitting palm with fist) appear to be the closest, organically and anatomically, to linguistic and paralinguistic sounds, since they are truly bodily "articulations." An energetic slapping of the thigh can qualify a verbal statement as much as an equally intense paralinguistic modifier can, and it is that intensity that we can measure as we gnash our teeth in anger or glower at someone while drumming with our fingers impatiently. Such sounds function as auxiliaries to the basic structure of language, paralanguage, and kinesics, as eloquently as paralinguistic "alternants" do (e.g., a sigh, a meaningful cough, a groan). They thus can play also the same type of functions performed in discourse by kinesic and paralinguistic language markers (i.e., punctuating words). This confirms the mutually inherent nature of sound and movement and demonstrates how the whole body contributes to a finely structured communicative totality: there is a perfect congruence between those kinesic actions and the verbal and paralinguistic actions when both co-occur. The intensity of the movement equals the volume of the voice and the articulatory tension; their range in space corresponds to the lengthening or shortening of syllables (drawling, clipping); and their visually perceived speed correlates with speech tempo. They are perfectly segmental components of interaction for, for instance, self-adaptors: brushing (hand to hair), caressing (to any surface), chattering,

gnashing, grating, grinding or gritting (teeth to teeth), chopping (to any surface), clapping (hand to hand), clicking (teeth to teeth, fingernail to fingernail), cracking (hand to knuckles), drumming (fingers to surface), flapping (hand to ear), knocking (knuckles to skull), and so on.

As for alter-adaptors, they partake of similar communicative qualities. They can also qualify in an additional quasi-paralinguistic fashion what is being expressed verbally and paralinguistically or replace those two modalities altogether (hence their importance in interaction with the blind) as one person contacts another by batting, beating, biffing, biting, brushing, bumping, caressing, clapping, clipping, cuffing, flicking, fondling, hugging, jabbing, kicking, patting, pointing, punching, raking, rubbing, scratching, slapping, snapping, stroking, sweeping, tapping, or thudding, among other actions. As we speak about these actions, we evoke the contactual perception of those actions, as when we hear or read that "he was pounding on his chest defiantly," although we might describe it as the imagined visual perception only. In addition, there is an audible evocation of the audible self-adaptors and alter-adaptors, as in "the two men hugged each other heartily."

The sound-producing movements involving body adaptors (food, drink, clothes, jewelry, etc.) provide two distinctive audible experiences: one is the sound of biting, chewing, crunching, or chomping on solid food and pseudonutritionals such as hard candy, which, depending on intensity and speed, can be interpreted (perhaps intentionally encoded) as betraying certain feelings (e.g., derision, impatience, contempt), social status (e.g., the careless smacking and chomping accompanied by audible nose breathing), childishness, or even pathological regression (e.g., crunching on hard food or candy). The other audible experience occurs, for instance, when the hands slide over a piece of velvet or silk and produce the characteristic swishing sound or rub on corduroy or denim to cause a soft rustling. This can be important in interpersonal encounters, since those tactile and acoustic sensations are associated in various degrees and with different interactive consequences, to certain characteristics of the touched person's body, and to personality qualities such as softness, ruggedness, and sensuality. At a deeper intrapersonal level—which can affect the interpersonal encounter—those actions, which we perform with varying degrees of speed and intensity or friction, are conscious or unconscious contacts with our own bodies, mediated solely by the material, and those sounds are perceived simultaneously by the tactile receptions transmitted to the brain by our skin organs and by the hands' perception of texture and our kinesthetic perception of shape and area size. These perceptions might at times respond unconsciously to certain narcissistic impulses. Much interdisciplinary semiotic research can be done regarding this aspect of clothes: how it has changed over time, how it can affect face-to-face interaction, and even the historical development, including the appearance and disappearance of certain tactile-audible experiences determined, for instance, by tight hose, crinoline, long skirts, jeans, and other materials. As for the same activities in the form of alter-adaptors, both the sounds and the sensations of active touch are still present, but here the articulations are between the two bodies.

Banging on a desk, knocking on a door, scraping feet, or trampling through a room possess communicative qualities that make them integral parts of the verbal, paralinguistic, and kinesic structure (e.g., pounding on a lectern as an emotional language marker) and sometimes stand by themselves as powerful segmental elements (e.g., that same pounding by itself). In addition, they may allow us to infer with varying reliability certain personality traits and, with more accuracy, mood, emotional state, and health state, as when hearing various characteristic footsteps (i.e., dragging, floundering, halting, hobbling, hopping, kicking, plodding, scraping, shuffling, tottering, tramping, etc.) or the gentle or authoritative door knocking that might set the tone of the ensuing interaction. Typical object-adaptor audible actions are banging, beating, brushing, bumping, drumming, flapping, flicking, flopping, knocking, patting, pounding, punching, raking, rapping, rubbing, scratching, scraping, sliding, slapping, splashing, stamping, stomping, striking, sweeping, tapping, thudding, tramping, trampling, wiping, and whisking.

The sounds of object-mediated activities depend on the material of which the objects are made as well as that of what they are in contact with. These sounds function as true extensions of our organism and qualify our movements (intensity, range, and velocity) with meaningful modalities. They can be used intentionally as communicative signs: "He slammed the door angrily" "They clinked their glasses gently while staring at each other" "By the slow, spaced rat-

tle of her dishes I could tell her mind was fixed on that idea." The handling of the door, the tapping with the pencil on the desk, or the jingling of coins in a pocket operate on two levels: one is the kinesic visual one, while the other is its powerful quasi-paralinguistic function. They are more than mere "noises," and they are far from being marginal to interactions. The person who walks into a room and slams the door might have communicated already the central message of the encounter. Peter Ostwald (1973) explains their development vis-à-vis sound effects in theater, radio, and cinema and the various evoking qualities of variations of pitch, volume, tempo, and silence.

Environmental sounds beyond bodily generated ones might acquire human relevance and, consciously or subconsciously, also become true components of interaction. These semioticized sounds might be generated mechanically (e.g., street sounds, the whirring of a motor, the pendulum clock that might enhance the intimacy of a silent place) or part of the natural environment (e.g., the howling of the wind, the gurgling of water in a gutter or a murmuring brook). Those that are variously generated by people are subject to a sort of "sound schedule" throughout the day: "From noon to evening . . . a vast and prolonged murmur arose—the mingled shuffling of feet, the rattle of wheels, the heavy trundling of cable cars . . . the newsboys chanted the evening papers" (Frank Norris, *McTeague*, 1899).

[*See also* Communication; Nonverbal Bodily Sign Categories; Paralanguage; *and* Speech.]

BIBLIOGRAPHY

Ostwald, P. *The Semiotics of Human Sounds*. The Hague: Mouton, 1973.

Poyatos, F. "The Communicative Status of Human Audible Movements: Before and Beyond Paralanguage." *Semiotica* 70.3–4 (1988): 265–300.

Poyatos, F. *La communicación no verbal*, vol. 2, *Paralenguaie, kinésica, et ineracción*. Madrid: Istmo, 1994a.

Poyatos, F. *La communicación no verbal*, vol. 3, *Nuevas perspectivas en novela y teatro y en su traducción*. Madrid: Istmo, 1994b.

—FERNANDO POYATOS

SPACE. Time and space—the fundamental dimensions of the physical universe—provide, separately and together, the material basis for a large number of important semiotic systems. Because these material dimensions are the same for all humans and other animals, codes based on space and time often employ relatively "motivated" signs whose meanings are inherent in their material forms and are constant from one culture to another. However, codes based on spatial signs are never purely motivated but always incorporate, to varying degrees, specific elaborations, transformations, and associations that are conventional or arbitrary—that is, specific to particular groups or codes. As a group, spatial codes are typically more motivated than verbal codes, but different spatial codes are ranged at different points along the continuum of motivated and conventional signs.

Just as bodies are worked over by various semiotic systems, so also the physical environment is normally assigned meanings by various codes, many of which derive from or incorporate proxemic components. The built environment (including houses, public buildings, localities, and cities) is one major site of this kind of semiotic activity. The semiotics of architecture studies buildings in urbanized societies. These built forms typically signify in ways that are similar to how clothing codes work, organizing space in terms of relations of solidarity (who can eat or sleep or converse with whom and who should be excluded) and power (expressing the power of individuals and groups). They use spatial signifiers (e.g., walls, doors, passages, windows, and roofs) that are reinforced or modified by secondary systems of spatial signifiers (e.g., ornamentation, designated pathways, and gardens).

Structuralist analysis in the tradition of Claude Lévi-Strauss has been successfully applied to domestic architecture in traditional societies in ways that have implications for the analysis of all forms of housing. Walls are motivated signifiers of boundaries, reinforced by other sign systems that limit who can go where. Developing the basic opposition between inside and outside, domestic structures are composed of complex nested structures within structures, with access to the innermost places restricted to a privileged few, even within the overall extended family. Other categories that are important in defining domestic spaces involve orientations such as up and down, left and right, and the cardinal points of the compass. These oppositions reflect and organize the basic functions and relations within the extended family group: women's and men's spaces, public versus private, work versus leisure, family versus non-

family. Similar categories and meanings are found in domestic architecture in contemporary industrialized societies. In societies where the dominant social-semiotic system emphasizes differences of wealth and power, the architectural systems normally emphasize boundaries (elaborated doorways, massive walls, etc). In societies or social groups where these differences are minimized, the primary spatial signifiers are typically less prominent, and inequalities are signified and managed through secondary sign systems that are more ambiguous (e.g., well-manicured front lawns, signifying both "I am open to view" and "do not walk on me").

Structuralist methods have also been applied to analyze space in narrative. In his analysis of the Amerindian myth of Asdiwal, for instance, Lévi-Strauss shows that spatial dimensions encode important meanings that act like a kind of commentary on the significance of the narrative. Similarly, the spaces in which rituals are performed are often carefully structured in significant ways (e.g., the site of the ceremony and reception, who is on which side of a church at a wedding, position in relation to the altar, etc.).

Public buildings are more likely than private buildings to be elaborately legible, drawing on spatial and other codes to carry messages about the power and status of owners or communities. The primary spatial signifiers normally provide the basis of the meaning of these public buildings, with height and space signifying power and status. Normally, public buildings are surrounded by and incorporate functionless space—that is, space that is devoted to spectacle and no other purpose. The division between inner and outer, expressing the greater powers and privileges of some over others, is typical of public buildings, both religious and secular.

Michel Foucault (1973) has made an influential analysis of the panopticon, an experimental prison design of the early nineteenth century. This was a circular building, with a central tower from which wardens could watch the prisoners in the peripheries, without themselves being seen. Where public buildings are normally designed as spectacles, to be seen and semiotically consumed by the public, a panopticon reverses the gaze, so that the public is under surveillance.

Poststructuralist forms of semiotics, among which Foucault's work can be included, draw attention to the shifting meanings that arise from different conditions of use. In his *Empire of Signs* (1982), for instance, Roland Barthes notes the phenomenon of the empty center in Japanese cities, something apparent in many other cities. In addition to interpreting signs inscribed on buildings and streets, Barthes looks at the mapping strategies used by Japanese people to negotiate and make sense of their urban spaces. Michel de Certeau in a similar vein examines the ways in which cities are constructed by the act of walking through them in a series of narratives. The kinds of meanings generated by dynamic signs like this are different, more fluid, and more unstable than the fixed signs built into the environment by walls, doors, and other structures. The two kinds of meaning, however, coexist in a complex and dynamic relationship with each other. Streets, for instance, coerce the feet and the gaze to construct one set of meanings rather than another, but eyes and feet have powers of their own.

The dimensions of space and time normally act together to define physical space, and there are many transformations between the two. As a simple instance, speech unfolds in time, but writing translates it into spatial sequence, so that in English writing a space signifies a pause and moving rightward and down signifies "later." In many other ways, graphic systems translate dynamic or auditory signs into static, spatial ones, a tendency that can be seen as characteristic of the cultural forms built and modeled on the preeminence of the written code.

European art of the Renaissance, for instance, effectively signified movement and history by representing the disposition of bodies in space in static but realistic images. Western science, at the same time, translated processes into diagrams, models, and mathematical schemata. Benjamin Lee Whorf (1956) noted the tendency of European languages to transform concepts of time and movement into spatial terms, thus constructing the characteristic forms of Western rationality associated with Newtonian science. But modernism in art and Einsteinian physics in science attempted to reinstate time against space, movement against stasis. Chaos theory in science and postmodernism in art and culture continue this tendency. Foucault notes how for modernism "space was treated as the dead, the fixed, the undialectic, the immobile" while "time, on the contrary, was richness, fecundity, life, dialectic." From the point of view of a semiotics of culture, the dialectic between spatial and nonspatial codes is itself an important phenom-

enon, quite apart from the meanings carried by the specific codes.

[*See also* Architecture; Cultural Landscape; Distance; Mindscape; Nonverbal Bodily Sign Categories; *and* Urban Semiotics.]

BIBLIOGRAPHY

Barthes, R. *The Empire of Signs*. Translated by R. Howard. New York: Hill and Wang, 1982.
Bourdieu, P. "The Berber House." In *Rules and Meanings*, edited by M. T. Douglas, pp. 98–111. Harmondsworth: Penguin, 1973.
De Certeau, M. *Practice of Everyday Life*. Berkeley: University of California Press, 1984.
Foucault, M. *Discipline and Punish*. Translated by A. M. Sheridan Smith. New York: Pantheon Books, 1973.
Lévi Strauss, C. *Structual Anthropology*, vol 2. New York: Basic Books, 1976.
Paul-Lévy, F., and M. Segaud. *Anthropologie de l'espace*. Paris: Centre Georges Pompidou, 1983.
Pinxten, R., et al., eds. *Anthropology of Space*. Philadelphia: University of Pennsylvania Press, 1983.
Riggins, S. H., ed. *The Socialness of Things: Essays on the Sociosemiotics of Objects*. Berlin: Mouton de Gruyter, 1994.
Whorf, B. L. *Language, Thought, and Reality*. Cambridge, Mass.: MIT Press, 1956.

—ROBERT HODGE

SPEECH. An audiovisual communicative process, speech involves linguistic, paralinguistic, and kinesic signs integrated in a single dynamic structure centered mainly on the "speaking face." These signs involve breathing, the larynx, the pharynx, the teeth, the lips, the tongue, the mandible, the nose, and the vowels.

The simple hissing sound of respiration can become quite conspicuous in heavy or deep breathing: audibly through either mouth, nose, or both, with pharyngeal friction or dorsovelar friction—all with true paralinguistic voluntary or involuntary communicative value—and visibly through, for instance, the emotional expansion or contraction of the thorax as the lungs become inflated or deflated. This is susceptible of functioning as a truly eloquent kinesic behavior, which can be but a more complex kinesic cluster involving also general facial expression with tense dilation of the nostril wings.

During normal breathing, the air produces at the most a gentle rustling or hissing sound that might have paralinguistic functions, as during certain silences. This noise increases with muscular tension as the flow of air from the lungs becomes turbulent. In distressed breathing there is not only audible friction but even visible muscular tension in the neck, truly a paralinguistic and kinesic behavior with communicative status. The shape and movements of the larynx produce many voice types, for instance: breathy voice, with its typical sighing quality (e.g., a passionate "I love you" or whispery voice in a confidential but not quite whispered conversation, but often overriding only some unstressed syllables, as in "Why, that's fantastic!"); glottal trill, creaky voice, or laryngealization, if much less air than for normal voice goes in slow periodic bursts, producing a cracking type of voice; falsetto voice, with high pitch and tension; and harsh voice, which produces high laryngeal and usually pharyngeal tension and rather low pitch, causing harshness of the whole verbal, paralinguistic and kinesic cluster.

The various communicative roles of the kinesic behaviors caused by pharyngeal movements are seen, first of all, in the audible-visual act of swallowing, which is either an unconscious muscular movement triggered by, say, social tension or part of a conscious kinesic repertoire (e.g., in mock fear, even more visible in the up-and-down movement of a man's Adam's apple, which is a possible silent clue to tension or emotion). As part of the upper pharyngeal zone, the muscular faucal pillars or arches help in swallowing and in keeping food or drink from returning to the mouth, except when regurgitating or when retching, with the typical accompanying kinesic behaviors.

The teeth, intimately associated with the lips, contribute to perceptions of speakers and evaluations of the speaking face. Their shape, position, and color appear and disappear during the formation of sounds. It is mostly during speech and smiling and laughing that the teeth are perceived, as with the proverbial "string of pearls." Most of the dental articulations engage the teeth as passive articulators with either the tongue or the upper lip, but the lower teeth can actively produce certain paralinguistic articulations without either lips or tongue interfering (e.g., blowing through the teeth). The lip posture required changes the visual kinesic component according to anatomical configuration and to the emphasis given to the articulation.

Besides their various anthropomorphic and anthropophonic possibilities by themselves and in di-

rect coarticulation with the teeth, the tongue, and the hands and fingers, the lips can be much more expressive and communicative than any of them, for they can become in speech an object of visual as much as acoustic perception. As we talk or emit paralinguistic utterances, the lips alternate between two stages. First, they have periods of rest in which they are perceived as static signs of the face and in which they may be evaluated as attractive (sensual, beautiful, innocent), unattractive (repulsive, cold), emotion laden (sad, happy, nervous, angry, anxious, contemptuous, scornful), or simply as neutral and not thought of. Second, due to their great plasticity, they have periods of ever-changing communicative mobility in which they give actual bodily shape to each of those utterances in such a way that we see what we hear: words that denote abstract concepts, moral and physical qualities, the environment, or things of the objectual world. But lips can also give peculiar visual form to such functional utterances as interjections ("Wow!"), conjunctions (an emphatic "BUT be careful!"), prepositions ("That's for you"), or pronouns ("Oh, I love you!"). Interjections can be much more eloquent if we add to the audible expression of fear, hate, repulsion, grief, or disapproval its visible (kinesic) representation as well, qualified, as all kinesic acts are, by muscular tension or intensity, range of the movement, and velocity or temporal length. When those visible signs might blend with, for instance, a smile, we speak through a smile, or "smile our words," adding another dimension to speech. Naturally, the manipulation of the lips (moistening, use of lipstick, etc.) can change their role in interaction according to interpersonal distance: the closer the speaker, the more aware we are of their permanent and dynamic characteristics. Finally, their anatomical configuration acts as a permanent postural conditioner (e.g., permanent opening posture of the interlabial space due either to a lowered mandible or to a raised upper lip, permanent moderate protrusion of both lips as if ready to speak in the open-rounded position, or very fleshy lips, very thin ones, etc.), any of which may have a marked visual effect during conversation and be evaluated consciously or subconsciously by the listener. We should analyze, therefore, their correlation with the rest of the facial gestures of the eyes, brows, nose, and forehead as dynamic components of speech, as well as with the static signs of the face. On the other hand, we must consider certain congenital or pathological configurations, such as a protruded mandible or a retracted one or slightly open jaws that keep the lips parted at all times. The anomalies of the lips can prevent the normal production of sounds but also affect interaction on many different levels, as with underdevelopment, deficiency from disease, trauma or surgery, restricted mobility due to paralysis, asymmetry of muscular contraction, and the like.

The tongue is the most mobile and versatile speech organ, and its function is far more complex than just the articulation of a word. It can become in some persons a much more conspicuous component of their repertoires than in others, such as the tendency to articulate some front sounds with excessive tongue showing along with cobehaviors such as rolling of the eyes or head tilting and hand movements and postures. The tongue's versatility is seen when we identify the possible acoustically or visually meaningful lingual articulations and the so-called secondary articulations (e.g., alveolarization, palatalization, velarization).

A first impression can be influenced by the personality and temperament characteristics we attach to morphological features of the mandible. We refer to a square jaw to suggest the energetic, self-confident, aggressive, or forceful type. At the other extreme is the lantern-jawed person with a droopy mouth posture who makes unpleasant remarks seem more unpleasant because of that visual component. As with the other external speech organs, narrative literature and theater provide countless illustrations of the communicative functions of the mandible and the chin, particularly in the initial presentation of characters as part of their physical portrait: "Abbie . . . , buxom, full of vitality. . . . There is strength and obstinacy in her jaw, a harsh determination in her eyes" (Eugene O'Neill, *Desire under the Elms*, 1924). Its extreme audiovisual characteristics are caused by protrusion, which makes the lower teeth touch the upper lip and affect articulation because of dental malocclusion and lends the speaker's face a stern look, qualifying what he or she says; retraction, a recession of the chin because of abnormally small mandible, causing also dental malocclusion and a visual effect with various negative connotations; attraction, a shortening of the vertical dimension that brings the chin closer to the lip; and abstraction, a lengthening that causes the typical lantern jaw.

In association mainly with the lips and cheeks, the nose can play important communicative functions within our repertoires. Many nasal and some oral sound productions are accompanied by kinesic behaviors visible on the outer sides of the nose through widening and narrowing of the nostril wings, deepening the nasolabial furrows and wrinkling the bridge and sides of the nose near the infraorbital corners. These actions can form inherent parts of various expressions that individually, culturally, or universally signal emotions such as fear or contempt coupled with specific sounds, as in doubt, disgust, rage, happiness, or skepticism. They are all included in our conversational repertoires, exposing our features to the perception of others as "lively," "cute," "nervous," "sour," and so forth (labels that may very well correspond to the linguistic and paralinguistic components of our delivery). The nose can be more or less conspicuous, "ugly" or "beautiful" according to our own aesthetic values, "large," "small," "beaky," or "flat," of smooth complexion, or scaly or warty. A person can be perceived as "snub-nosed" or "hook-nosed." All those visible features share the effect of nasality in speech, of paralinguistic nasal sounds, and even of the words being delivered: "a long well-shaped nose with wide nostrils, a short upper lip, resolute but filled-lipped mouth, and handsome fighting chin" (G. B. Shaw, *Saint Joan*, 1923).

The shape of the lips, the opening between the jaws, the position of the soft palate, and most of all the shape and position of the tongue are the factors that determine differences in the articulation of vowels and, consequently, certain peculiar facial expressions that naturally vary among speakers and according to attitudinal changes. Vocalic gestures have a strong kinesic and communicative potential, accompanied by degrees of eyelid opening and brow raising, lowering, and knitting, as well as by hand gestures and other body movements. Furthermore, as with certain conspicuous consonantal articulations, some vowels can differentiate visually the kinesic repertoires of members of specific language groups, as with the close and round vowels of French and their correlation with facial expression.

It is only when we see sounds and movements as inseparable coactivities that we can truly define them and interpret them in their full signification. This process is complex and ongoing.

[*See also* Nonverbal Bodily Sign Categories; *and* Nonverbal Communication in the Novel.]

BIBLIOGRAPHY

Poyatos, F. *Paralanguage: Linguistic and Interdisciplinary Approach to Speech and Interactive Sounds*. Amsterdam and Philadelphia: John Benjamins, 1993.

—FERNANDO POYATOS

SPEECH ACT THEORY. A branch of linguistic philosophy that proposes a pragmatic theory of meaning, speech-act theory is both distinct from and to some degree competitive with theories of significatory and systemic difference proposed by semioticians. The basic premise of speech-act theory is in John L. Austin's *How to Do Things with Words* (1962). Countering the propositional attitude of the dominant linguistic philosophy of his time, Austin argues that propositions (simple or complex declarative sentences) are in fact only a minor subset of any natural language. Since their primary pragmatic function is to state facts, he calls them constatives. As opposed to the constatives, Austin deliberated on another class of utterances that he calls performatives. These have a rather unique property of uniting utterance and performance. For example, I do not say "I bet you six dollars I can jump this fence" and *then* perform the actual betting; similarly, I do not say "I name this ship 'S. S. Titanic'" and *then* do the actual naming. In saying those things, I actually perform the betting and the naming, respectively.

In addition to this basic premise, Austin goes on to show how speech acts perform three types of act. The first type is the locutionary act, which refers to the rather simple fact of uttering in the first place. In saying "I promise," for example, I am uttering a sequence of words. The second type of act Austin calls the illocutionary act, which is the act performed by the locution. In saying "I promise," I actually do something (promising) that might or might not be valid in the particular social circumstances in which I say it. Third, performatives may contain perlocutionary acts, which are effects or results of the locution. In saying "I promise," I might cause someone to be pleased—or not. It is probably best to think of these three acts (locution, illocution, and perlocution) as subcomponents of a speech act.

Last, Austin argues that while constatives can be analyzed to see whether they are true or false—that is, whether or not they map onto actually existing states of affairs—performatives are not susceptible to such an analysis. That is, it is absurd to ask if "I name this ship" is true or false. Rather, I actually name it, or I do not. If my performative comes off successfully and acceptably, then it is said to be felicitous; if not, it is infelicitous. What decides this has nothing to do with conditions of truth or falsehood. Rather, it is a matter of the felicity conditions surrounding any particular performative. Thus, for "I do take this woman for my lawfully wedded wife" to be felicitous, it must be said in the proper place (say, a church or registry office); it must be said in front of a person (priest or celebrant) duly appointed to perform marriages; both of the parties must be eligible to marry (in terms of age, sex, and lack of encumbrance), and so forth through a very long list of pragmatic conditions. If any of the conditions are not met, the utterance is infelicitous and the "marriage" does not occur.

Following somewhat in Austin's footsteps, the linguistic philosopher John R. Searle attempts in *Speech Acts* (1969) to categorize the broad class of performatives into five distinct types (representatives, directives, commissives, declaratives, and expressives), though it is by no means clear that the categories are as exclusive as Searle claims. Thus, "I swear I will tell the truth, the whole truth and nothing but the truth" might be a representative, since it commits me to the truth of the proposition it contains, but it might also be a commissive, since it commits me to a particular course of action. As with so much of speech-act theory after Austin, this seems like codification purely for the sake of codification.

This is most clear in Searle's attempted analysis of what he calls indirect speech acts (1975). For example, if someone says to me, "Can you pass the salt?" it is more likely that this is not an interrogative that inquires as to my physical abilities. Rather, it is likely to be a type of what Searle calls a directive and, more specifically, a request (though in some circumstances there might be a suspicion of a command). Searle's question is how we tell that it is a request (if that is what it is) when there is no direct mention of requesting. How do we hear that phrase as a transform of "I request you to pass the salt"? In order to answer the question, Searle sets out a long table of ten steps by which the hearing can be made and the conclusion drawn that this is in fact a request.

Taking just the first of these steps, we can see Searle's difficulty: "STEP 1: Y [the speaker] had asked me a question as to whether I have the ability to pass the salt (fact about the conversation)" (1975, p. 73). The step is crucial to Searle's analysis—the remaining nine steps hinge on it. Yet it is false. Y has *not* in fact at any stage asked a question about my abilities. If he or she had, then I could simply answer yes and do nothing at all. This might be a good enough joke, but it is premised on my possibly deliberate misunderstanding of the social and pragmatic upshot of this utterance specifically as a request all along and in the first place. Searle wants to treat the request as if it is a transformed question, when in fact it is not a question at all.

Jeff Coulter (1983) has shown clearly that conversational analysis, with its concepts of sequential implicativeness and adjacency pairs is much more capable than speech-act theory of telling us how, for example, questionlike utterances can act as requests, invitations, and so forth. Since conversation analysis tends to use materials from naturally occurring conversations, it has been able to discover important phenomena about how hearings are made, phenomena that speech-act theory has been unable to construct, let alone analyze. A case in point is another of Searle's (1975) examples:

STUDENT X: Let's go to the movies tonight.

STUDENT Y: I have to study for an exam.

Searle's problem is to determine by what steps X can hear that Y is denying X's request (though it is more like an invitation). But as A. Terasaki (1976) has pointed out, in ordinary conversations invitations are not made in simple pairs (invitation and denial or invitation and acceptance). More routinely, the inviter issues a preinvitation in order to find out what the likely result of any subsequent invitation will be. Thus:

A: What are you doing tonight? [Preinvitation]
B: Not much. [Positive response to projected invitation]
A: How about a movie? [Invitation]
B: Okay. [Acceptance]

Or:

A: What are you doing tonight? [Preinvitation 1]
B: I have to study for an exam. [Negative response to projected invitation]
A: How about Wednesday? [Preinvitation 2]

Demonstrably, we can also tell that utterances are invitations by virtue of what they follow (positive responses to preinvitations) rather than just by virtue of what follows them (acceptances, denials, equivocations). They are invitations rather than transformed questions by virtue of their positioning in a broader sequential grammar of conversation and not by virtue of the steps that speakers and hearers might implicitly perform.

[*See also* Conversation; Discourse Analysis; *and* Implicature.]

BIBLIOGRAPHY

Austin, J. L. *How to Do Things with Words.* New York: Oxford University Press, 1962.

Coulter, J. "Contingent and A Priori Structures in Sequential Analysis." *Human Studies* 6.4 (1983): 361–376.

Searle, J. R. *Speech Acts.* New York: Cambridge University Press, 1969.

Searle, J. R. "Indirect Speech Acts." In *Syntax and Semantics*, vol. 3, *Speech Acts*, edited by P. Cole and J. Morgan, pp. 59–82. New York: Academic Press, 1975.

Terasaki, A. "Pre-announcement Sequences in Conversation." Social Science Working Paper, no. 99, School of Social Sciences. Irvine: University of California at Irvine, 1976.

—ALEC MCHOUL

SPENGLER, OSWALD (1880–1936), German historian and political theorist, author of the two-volume *The Decline of the West* (*Der Untergang des Abendlandes*, 1918, 1922). Though not a semiotician in any strict sense, Spengler is noteworthy for attempting in *The Decline of the West*, which was subtitled "Sketch Toward a Morphology of History," to give a totalizing account of world history based on morphological principles.

Spengler was born in Blankenburg in the Harz Mountains. Trained as a mathematician, he gave up a Realgymnasium teaching position to become a private tutor in 1911. In that year, he claims to have experienced the revelation that morphology held the secret to historiography. From then on, he lived reclusively, with few friends or interlocutors to interrupt his independent scholarship.

Inspired by J. W. von Goethe's idea of organic transformation and Nietzschen concepts of will and destiny, Spengler claims that the growth and decay of cultures can be modeled rigorously on repeating patterns such as those found in the natural sciences. In contrast to both Hegelian notions of an absolute spirit actualizing itself in the dialectical process of history and historicist strategies to grasp the past "as it really was," Spengler's project is an ambitious attempt to semanticize history—that is, to seek the formal principles of its development. The morphological pattern Spengler identifies leads him to conclude that Western culture is currently at the end of its "Faustian" phase and, accordingly, is fated to decline not catastrophically but gradually and slowly before it could renew itself. Spengler's rhetoric often has a markedly primitive cast, yet at other times his views appear quite progressive. While he makes inflammatory claims about national destiny and race, he is also one of the first historians to take a non-Eurocentric view of world history, discussing the cultures of China, America, and the Middle East, among others.

Because of its ambitious synthesis and universal perspective, *The Decline of the West* became the target of numerous attacks by specialists throughout the 1920s. The resulting controversy, known as the *Streit um Spengler*, ended with general academic dismissal of his theories. But Spengler's hold on the popular imagination was great and provides a telling index of the somber mood of the Germany between the two world wars.

Most of Spengler's writings other than the *Decline* focus on contemporary German politics. In "Prussianism and Socialism" (1919), he argues that the two extreme poles of German politics, the conservatives and the socialists, have a similar aim: the establishment of a strong state designed to further the welfare of its people. Every nation within a larger historical culture (e.g., "Faustian," "Magian," etc.), Spengler claims, has a spirit that must be the basis of its government, and this fact ought to unite the two opposing revolutionary parties. *Man and Technics* (1913) was a disappointing account of the origins and political use of technology. In 1933, Spengler published *The Hour of Decision: Germany and World-Historical Evolution*, which was condemned by the Nazis and which led to an official boycott of his work. Spengler is read infrequently today, partly because his rhetoric, like Friedrich Nietzsche's, came to be associated with fascist ideologies, despite explicit provisions in his texts to the contrary.

[*See also* History; *and* Morphology.]

BIBLIOGRAPHY

Works by Spengler
The Decline of the West (1918, 1922). Translated by C. F. Atkinson. London: Allen and Unwin, 1926.

Man and Technics: A Contribution to a Philosophy of Life (1913). Translated by C. F. Atkinson. Westport, Conn.: Greenwood Press, 1976.
The Hour of Decision: Germany and World-Historical Evolution (1933). Translated by C. F. Atkinson. New York: Knopf, 1934.
Other Works
Adorno, T. "Spengler after the Decline." *Prisms*. Translated by S. Weber. Cambridge, Mass.: MIT Press, 1981.
Hughes, H. S. *Oswald Spengler: A Critical Estimate*. New York: Charles Scribner's Sons, 1952.
Huizinga, J. H. "Two Wrestlers with the Angel." In *Dutch Civilization in the Seventeenth Century and Other Essays*. New York: Ungar, 1968.
Ludz, P. C., ed. *Spengler Heute*. Munich: C. H. Beck, 1980.
Neurath, O. "Anti-Spengler." In *Empiricism and Sociology*, edited by M. Neurath and R. S. Cohen, pp. 158–213. Dordrecht: D. Reidel, 1973.
Schroeter, M. *Der Streit um Spengler: Kritik seiner Kritiker*. Munich: Beck, 1922.

—ALBERT LIU

SPORT. After 1860, the English word *sport* ceased to denote pastime or amusement, often of a physical and erotic nature, and came to signify exclusively the serious participation in a set of competitive athletic activities and, eventually, the activities themselves. Throughout the nineteenth century, almost all modern languages began adopting *sport* and have appeared since then to use the word in the same way it is used in English. It has thus been assumed, with a few significant exceptions, that sport is a modern invention and that it is a universally identical phenomenon. Correlatively, it has often been supposed by nostalgics that sport, imagined as a morally edifying physical pursuit, also existed in ancient Greece. Semiotic definitions of *sport* have largely been determined by these assumptions.

What is the denotative extension of *sport*? What is the set of features that connote *sport* and that are common to the activities whose status as sports is unchallenged? Is there some minimum number of signs or features that, if not met, excludes a given praxis from the domain of sport? Writers on the subject customarily state the criteria they consider essential to any definition of *sport*. These criteria are at times very sophisticated (e.g., Guttmann, 1978), but they are most often applied inclusively rather than exclusively (see, however, Jeu, 1972).

Ontologically speaking, sport remains an abstract

concept whose extension seems boundless and whose connotative set appears to be self-defining and all-inclusive. We know from history, however, that certain forms of athletics once considered sports now only connote "play" (e.g., the three-legged race) or "spectacle" (e.g., jousting). Conversely, certain forms of spectacle have become sport (e.g., mat gymnastics and horse vaulting). New sports have been invented (e.g., basketball) and some forgotten sports on occasion revived. The set of sports is thus an evolving one. The fact that some previously nonsporting activities can become sports implies either that they underwent a morphological change or that the denotation of *sport* was altered; on the other hand, the elimination of some activities from the category implies most likely only the latter: changing cultural or moral or technological contexts redefine what is sport. Old signifiers become dissociated from the signified and new ones replace them.

Phylogenetically, *sport* is most often explained as an outgrowth, transformation, or ritualization of some prior activity, usually play, but more recently physical training (Plato's *gymnastik*) or primitive hunting. Modern sport, it is said, arises either because of a catastrophic change in the nature of play or incrementally through the progressive addition of new distinctive features or by introducing morality and competitiveness into promilitary gymnastics or through the desire to preserve and institutionalize in a symbolic way an activity once thought essential but now obsolete. Semiotically speaking, these explanations depend on the existence of a sign system that is shared at least partially by both sport and its antecedents.

This is, of course, easy to demonstrate. Like play, sport is a functionally ludic activity whose performance produces no immediate material benefit, whose content seems culturally determined, and which appears to convey meanings. Like physical training, sport often consists of series of rhythmically executed—which is to say, ideally graceful—purposeful, goal-oriented gestures that demand muscular discipline and coordination. Like hunting, sport can be both a solitary and a collective effort, both competitive and communal, both sensitive to the terrain and (with some exceptions) deliberately indifferent to the weather. Both the hunter and the athlete, though not the player or the trainee, wear special costumes that signify the nature of their activity, and both display the trophies that index their success.

Obviously, no single one of these phylogenetic explanations provides more than a partial semiotic for the complex phenomenon that is sport. Sport can be understood only as an activity sui generis that happens to share certain semiotic features with other activities but that has certain characteristics of its own. On that basis, it seems most straightforward to define sport initially through an analysis of its distinctive features.

First, then, sport is a physical activity that is ludic but also disciplined and competitive. The competition may be immediate, and the sport may therefore involve defensive as well as offensive maneuvers; or the athletes might simply strive to achieve their personal best and have no opportunity or wish to hinder other competitors; or they might be attempting—simultaneously or not—to establish a record and therefore compete against a previous performance more or less removed in time. Sport is therefore serious and teleological (the Greek *athlos* means a "contest for a prize"), and these features have been articulated increasingly through quantification that has extended beyond what is needed to establish records.

Though sport is agonistic and oriented toward victory and therefore requires physical and psychological training, paradoxically it is also ritualistic in that it is performed according to rules, regulations, and conventions; some of these may be practical, but most are arbitrary and consequently ceremonial and arealistic. Within the rules, however, sport is innovative because it encourages imaginative exploitation of the rituals and regulations as well as feats of individual prowess not originally conceived of as possible. As a result, sports evolve, either in terms of their general practice or of the degree to which the rituals are observed. Ultimately, the rules might be changed in order to institutionalize desirable innovation.

Sporting contests represent "ideal" or "possible" worlds in which the rules and rituals are enforced by bureaucracies and applied equally to all. These possible worlds are thus also perfectly moral worlds, and this morality is usually indexed by as precise forms of measurement as are available. The measurements and the moral autonomy that sport expresses are customarily visible as real or symbolic barriers around the place of sport and often subdivide the interior of that space into areas that are hierarchically related to each other. As the icons of possible worlds, sports had in ancient times and have had again since the nineteenth century their own permanent, reserved spaces, which are sometimes shared with other ludic activities but not generally with any practical pursuit. Sports are thus physically isolated from and even counter to the places of the ordinary conduct of life. This isolation is also marked by the costumes and equipment that are peculiar to each sport and often unusable outside sport.

Concomitantly, but with a very few notable exceptions such as medieval tournaments or modern soccer, sports are temporally autonomous. In some cases, their time stops and starts according to the motivated decision of the judge or referee; in others, they are conceived as contests between individual athletes and time. Conversely, they might have no time at all, in that any given contest lasts until a winner can be declared according to the system of rules. In addition, the time of sport may be understood as seasonal, in some cases for obvious practical reasons, but in others, perhaps, to perpetuate in a ludic mode rhythms of life that have been superseded by technology. But often, sport either ignores the weather or makes it part of the competition. It is thus as heedless of meteorological contingencies as it is of physical or even mortal injury, even when physical contact or a hazardous terrain are not officially involved. Sport, since ancient times, has implied pushing the body to or beyond the limits of normal physical capabilities, often using means deleterious to health. Sport is thus excessive and, correlatively, ostentatious in the expenditure of athletes' energy. These two features are obviously linked to what has been called the "quest for records," but they are also compensated by the requirement that prowess be graceful, controlled, almost nonchalant.

But it is also through physical excess and ostentatious indifference to danger that sport displays another essential feature: passion. An athlete's intense individual emotional desire to win might become collective, as it is transmitted to teammates, and finally communal, as it affects spectators and instigates action on their part. An athlete's or a team's victory is interpreted as a victory for the communities that claim the athlete or the team for their own. On the other hand, sports, placed in ideal worlds, are also conciliatory in that passionate competition ceases with the end of the event, and equilibrium, iconicized by the initial disposition of the athletes and the terrain, is reestablished. A sporting event is thus digressive and not permanent because it usually does not fundamentally alter the relations of force among the competitors.

Finally, sport, in sharp contradistinction to play, is primarily economic. From earliest times, athletes have competed for real monetary rewards, and their competition has generated such transactions as purchasing equipment, erecting facilities, paying groundskeepers, charging admission, attracting tourists, and, more recently, selling goods and services whose quality is arbitrarily linked to specific athletes and specific sports events. Given that the most spectacular athlete often generates the most money, sport has become increasingly democratic. If the meaning of play derives out of the relation it bears to work, the meaning of sport, anthropologically speaking, is a function of the kinds of financial dealings that are its end product and its justification.

The nearly thirty features that have been identified as the connotative signs of *sport* are not all present to the same degree in all sports or indeed in any given manifestation of a particular sport. Any attempt to define sport as an activity displaying some minimal number of these features is, however, fraught with perplexity: the long-distance swimmer is as much of an athlete as the professional ice-hockey player, even though their respective sports are not commensurable according to the paradigm. The absence of certain signs might thus be deemed inconsequential. The presence, however, of any of the polar opposites of the features disqualifies an activity as sport. Yet the set of these polar opposites does not in fact constitute the paradigm of any specific human activity, though it might, with all its internal unresolved contradictions, be the paradigm of our ordinary modes of existence. Semiotically, then, sport is the denial of the ordinary and the affirmation of both the extraordinary and of the means of attaining it.

[See also Baseball; Cultural Knowledge; Habitus; and Play.]

BIBLIOGRAPHY

Brohm, J.-M. *Critiques du sport.* Paris: Christian Bourgois, 1976.

Friedrich, G., E. Hildenbrandt, and J. Schwier, eds. *Sport und Semiotik.* Sankt Augustine: Academia Verlag, 1994.

Guttmann, A. *From Ritual to Record.* New York: Columbia University Press, 1978.

Hardy, S. "Entrepreneurs, Structures, and the Sportgeist." In *Essays on Sport History and Sport Mythology,* edited by D. Kyle and G. D. Stark, pp. 45–82. College Station, Tex.: Texas A&M University Press, 1990.

Huizinga, J. *Homo ludens*. Amsterdam: Pantheon, 1939.

Jeu, B. *Le sport, la mort, la violence*. Paris: Vigot, 1972.

Mandell, R. *Sport: A Cultural History*. New York: Columbia University Press, 1984.

Sansone, D. *Greek Athletics and the Genesis of Sport*. Berkeley and London: University of California Press, 1988.

Ulmann, J. *De la gymnastique aux sports modernes*. Paris: Presses universitaires de France, 1967.

—JOHN McCLELLAND

STEREOTYPE. Referring literally to a process in typesetting whereby a mold is made of a page that has been typeset, a stereotype is a page prepared as a single block in this way. From this technical sense has come a common metaphorical use referring to any representation in which the forms are pregiven and fixed. Ideas and attitudes may be stereotyped in this sense, as can choice of words—a word with similar origins and meanings is *cliché* (the French *clicher* means "to cast a stereotype"). Plot and character in narrative can also be described as stereotyped, implying a negative judgment and opposing the rigidity, predictability, and conformity of stereotypes to a kind of writing and thought that is free, unconstrained, individual, and original.

Stereotype does not have a technical meaning in semiotics. However, it carries a specific ideology of the composition process that is very influential in everyday discourse and in certain styles and theories of pedagogy. Different traditions in semiotics retheorize the phenomena referred to by stereotype and associated terms and provide a fuller or alternative account and a more complex evaluation of stereotyping (Perkins, 1979).

The stereotype is similar in many respects to what Roman Jakobson has described as one of the two classic types of aphasia. Jakobson (1971) proposes two basic pathologies, corresponding to the two fundamental planes in semiotics: the planes of selection (the paradigmatic plane) and combination (the syntagmatic plane). A stereotype, in which there is no freedom in choice of elements and absolute bonds between syntagmatic elements, is an exemplary instance of "selection-restriction" pathology. Jakobson describes a number of disabilities associated with selection-restriction disorders, which help to explain why they attract such negative judgments. People with this disability tend to use general words, not specific ones. Their vocabulary range is narrow, and they are not precise. They find it difficult to commence an utterance or exchange. However, once started they find it relatively easy to continue along set paths of language and thought, and they do not have problems with syntax. The moment of starting is fraught with the risk of choice, and they do not cope well with that risk. They fall back readily on the stock of formulaic phrases and actions that languages provide for precisely such moments. Their discourse is tied closely to the immediate context, and they prefer iconic and indexical signs, to use Charles Sanders Peirce's terms, to symbolic signs. They lack a well-developed metalanguage, since this requires the paradigmatic elaboration of higher-order categories. All this means that among semiotic codes verbal language is most affected by this disorder, since it has a larger, more complex paradigmatic dimension and is less context dependent than most other codes.

Basil Bernstein's work provides a framework for the study of stereotypes. Bernstein (1971) proposes a dichotomy to describe the range of kinds of discourse available in contemporary British society. "Elaborated code" is characterized by complexity of organization, independence of context, and freedom of choice and is the code that underpins the dominance of the ruling class. "Restricted code" is characterized by the opposite qualities and explains the continuing subordination of the working classes, who are socialized into restricted codes that limit their access to the language and ideas of power. Bernstein's notion of restricted codes is similar to Jakobson's selection-restriction pathologies in that both of them are marked by stereotypes in language and thought.

It should be stressed, however, that Jakobson was describing severe pathologies, usually associated with organic damage, that incapacitated people in direct ways, whereas use of stereotypes is normal and functional in many everyday situations. Similarly, Bernstein's negative judgment on restricted codes has been criticized for incorporating an elitist middle-class judgment on working-class language and style. Faced with such criticism, Bernstein has modified his argument, acknowledging that restricted codes are functional in working-class culture, contributing to a sense of solidarity and belonging that is not sustained by the elaborated codes of alienated middle-class culture.

The debate over restricted codes enables us to set the issues regarding stereotypes into a broader semiotic framework. Negative judgments on stereotypes, formulas, and other categorizations imply that choice is an absolute good. However, semiotics provides many counterinstances to this proposition. Grammar is just one important example. Grammars contain many selection-restriction rules that are not regarded as pathological but the contrary. It is no accident that people suffering from selection-restriction aphasia find that grammatical knowledge remains when much other vocabulary has gone. Grammatical hypercorrection is similar in function to the use of stereotypes. Both are especially frequent in situations of semiotic risk, when choice is dangerous. That grammatical hypercorrection is normally an upper-class strategy (as part of an elaborated code) whereas stereotypes tend to be labeled as lower class does not conceal the basic similarity in form and function. In British social life, powerful institutions such as Parliament, the courts, and the royal family are sustained by ritualistic repetitions of rigidly prescribed actions and behaviors that have the same qualities as stereotypes but that are not normally seen as symptoms of linguistic or cultural deprivation.

In semiosis, freedom of choice is beneficial only if it increases options. But choice takes time and uses up semiotic resources, which are always finite. Stereotypes displace complexity from outside a given encounter, keeping immediate problems of choice to a minimum, though the full scope of complexity can be enormous. It is a paradox, in light of the etymological association of *stereotype* with print, that the phenomenon finds its fullest expression in oral cultures. Part of the negative value of the term comes from a judgment on the preferred forms of oral culture by an elite culture based on the technologies of literacy.

Folktale structures rely heavily on formulaic plots, recurring episodes, and stock characters, yet narratives with these characteristics have been culturally valued for most of human history. Milman Parry (1971) and Albert B. Lord (1991), analyzing the techniques of oral composition, have shown that bards have to draw on a remembered stock of formulaic phrases, themes, and episodes if they engage in extended extempore oral composition. Parry and Lord also show that many of the distinctive qualities of Homer's poetry derive from these traditions. In practice, the use of formulaic phrases along with other stereotypic features of composition release the artist to be "original" at another level (e.g., the architectonics of a large poem). Since stereotypes can be used

as the basis for creativity, the opposition between creativity and stereotypes does not hold. On the contrary, the majority of artists within all media work with conventions, using taken-for-granted means to achieve their effects.

Because of their mode of construction, myths from pretechnological societies often have the characteristics of what Claude Lévi-Strauss calls bricolage: an assemblage of preformed elements from other structures that in their new place in a new structure create a kind of incoherence. The contributing elements in this kind of text can be highly traditional and formulaic, yet the overall effect is neither predictable nor rational. Again, we see how stereotypes need not be opposed to originality.

However, it is also the case that originality is not always a highly desired quality in works of art. Repetition gives the pleasure of memory, binding readers or spectators to their past, and in so doing binding them to their community. So formulas, stereotypes, and other forms of repetition are found in genres that are socially cohesive, especially genres from popular culture, where the act of rehearsing the familiar is a large part of their appeal. Popular works subscribing to strong generic conventions are easily controlled by commercial institutions and processes, thus confirming the widespread view that popular culture is inferior because it draws strongly on stereotypes.

The term *stereotype* is too loaded ideologically to be a useful addition to the vocabulary of semiotics. It implies no freedom of choice and no semiotic value. In practice, what is described in this way usually involves some choice and always has some semiotic function and value. Moreover, stereotypes are normally associated with a particular ideology and strategy that are effective in their own terms and widespread in social life, too complex to be easily encapsulated in a single description or judgment. Stereotypes reduce choice, but often this is only a strategy to defer and thereby increase choice and control. Stereotypes serve to strengthen solidarity and encourage conformity, and in so doing they often signal and create a conservative community, but they are also characteristic of the language of effective resistance. Paradoxically, they are found equally in the discourse of revolutionaries and conservatives, one trying to construct a community of resistance, the other preserving the community against the threat of change. They are found in the language of the working class, in the antilanguages of subcultures, and in the rituals of élites. So protean a phenomenon ought not to be dismissed lightly through such a dismissive term as *stereotype*. However—a final paradox—the judgment that *x* or *y* is a stereotype is itself normally a stereotypical judgment.

[*See also* Code; Cultural Difference; *and* Cultural Knowledge.]

BIBLIOGRAPHY

Bernstein, B. *Class, Codes, and Control.* London: Routledge and Kegan Paul, 1971.

Jakobson, R. "Toward a Linguistic Classification of Aphasic Impairment." In his *Selected Writings*, vol. 2, pp. 281–307. The Hague: Mouton, 1971.

Lord, A. B. *Epic Singers and Oral Tradition.* Ithaca, N.Y.: Cornell University Press, 1991.

Parry, M. *The Making of Homeric Verse: The Collected Papers of Milman Parry.* Edited by A. Parry. Oxford: Clarendon Press, 1971.

Perkins, T. E. "Rethinking Stereotypes." In *Ideology and Cultural Production,* edited by M. Barrett et al., pp. 135–159. London: Croom Helm, 1979.

—ROBERT HODGE

STRUCTURALISM. The school of thought that developed in France in the 1960s in the wake of Claude Lévi-Strauss's landmark book, *Anthropologie structurale* (1958), structuralism is not reducible to a single movement or trend: in one form or another, it spans the entire twentieth century. Nor does structuralism constitute a single field or discipline in the sense of a specialized and discrete body of knowledge, with its own specialized texts, practices, rules of entry, and so on. Instead, structuralism can best be described, to adapt a term proposed by Basil Bernstein, as a "thematic region" that brings together disciplines and the technologies they make possible, much as cognitive science, management, engineering, and medicine do. Which other disciplines a thematic region selectively recontextualizes depends on the social base and its pedagogical and political practices. The main disciplines so selected in structuralism include structural-functional linguistics, first-generation cybernetic theory, systems theory, and the mathematical theory of information.

While the history of these recontextualizations remains largely unwritten, some of the key currents in the structuralist enterprise include: (1) Karl Marx's protostructuralist theory of capitalist economic relations, which sought to identify the general premises and laws that regulate and govern these relations. At the same time, Marx was careful to emphasize that such models do not explain the observed phenomena but constitute them; (2) the dynamic and morphogenetic structuralism that took its inspiration from early-twentieth-century biology and the philosophy of vitalism. Conrad H. Waddington's notion of the "chreod" is part of the development of this strand (1956); (3) the phenomenological and Gestalt theory, which inspired structuralism, may be traced back to the work of Franz Brentano (1838–1917) at the beginning of the twentieth century; (4) structural-functional linguistics, the foundational principles of which were established in Ferdinand de Saussure's posthumously published *Cours de linguistique générale* (1916). The principles set out in this text were developed subsequently by a number of important schools of thought, including the Moscow Linguistic Circle of Nikolaj Trubetzkoy and Roman Jakobson, the Prague Linguistic School, the London School of Raymond Firth and Michael Halliday, and the work in the United States by Kenneth Pike; (5) American structural linguistics, which was inspired by formalist and behaviorist doctrine, as in the work of Leonard Bloomfield and Zellig Harris. Noam Chomsky's concept of mentalism is a specific reaction to this work, though it is still in the same formalist-structuralist tradition; (6) structural-functional sociology and anthropology, of which there are partly overlapping French and Anglo-American traditions. The first includes Émile Durkheim, Marcel Mauss, and Claude Lévi-Strauss; the second Bronislaw Malinowski, Alfred Radcliffe-Brown, and Talcott Parsons; (7) French structuralism, whose chief exponents include Roland Barthes and his Louis Hjelmslev–inspired semiology, Algirdas Julien Greimas's semiotic theory, and Tzvetan Todorov's narratology; (8) the phenomenological and realist structuralism of Jakobson's linguistics; (9) the "genetic" (i.e., developmental) structuralism of Lucien Goldmann's sociology and Jean Piaget's theory of cognitive development; (10) the morphogenetic and structuralist theory of catastrophes developed by René Thom and Jean Petitot-Cocorda; and (11) the dynamic theory of metastable structures and their contextualization in biology, as in the work of Giorgio Prodi and Stanley Salthe. Here, the emphasis is on self-organizing and evolving hierarchical structures and systems.

There is considerable interaction between these

various trends, which have often reciprocally influenced each other. The basic conceptual features of structuralism comprise seven categories: relations, topology, distribution, generation, dialecticalism, immanence, and difference.

First, one of the fundamental a priori of structuralism is that structures are relational. Structuralist analysis is concerned with second- and higher-order relations, especially in the patterns that are construable among the "entities" in a given phenomenon. For this reason, structuralist analysis does not treat the material substrate of the relations as a "truer" or "superior" reality in which, following positivism, the only significant relations are those between entities observable by our sense perception—what Western culture defines as zero-order realities or observable things. Rather than structure as such, structuralist analysis seeks to represent the relationships that define a structure. These relationships are not those between things or entities, for in the final analysis these are themselves always relationships. The decision to call something an entity, in a given instance is always a result of the theoretical and practical contingencies of that particular analysis. However, a given structuralist analysis always postulates a level of first focus on which entities are taken to be the ground for the analysis of a particular patterned relationship.

Second, structures are not based on logical or typological principles of combination; the central organizing concept is that of topological space. A topology is a mathematical concept that in structuralist terms is used to mean a set of criteria for establishing degrees of closeness among the entities whose relationships constitute the structure. Thus, a structure is a space defined by the relationships among these entities. The entities that enter into some patterned relationship are defined as being closer or nearer to the criteria whereby the structure is defined. Criteria themselves are defined by relations of similarity and difference along some dimension. A given instance of some phenomenon can be represented as more or less alike with respect to these abstract criteria.

Two pioneering examples of structuralist analysis that follow these topological principles are Vladimir Propp's (1928) analysis of a corpus of Russian folktales and Claude Lévi-Strauss's structural study of myth (1958, chap. 11). For example, Lévi-Strauss arranges the Oedipus myth into a series of four vertical columns. Each column includes features, semantically defined, that are in some sense similar. In this way, the features grouped in any given column are seen as different from or contrasting with those in the other columns. Lévi-Strauss points out that such a topological form of analysis overcomes the problem posed by "the quest for the *true* versions, or the earlier one." In topological analysis, all known versions can be defined thus, according to the ways in which each version clusters in the abstract topological space.

Third, Propp pioneered the type of distributional analysis that became so important to structuralist analysis. Lévi-Strauss's later analysis of myth starts with a hypothesis concerning the distribution of semantic features in particular configurations. He then proposes a model of how these distributions are a function of the structure of the topological space, which can be a given corpus of myths or a given linguistic system. The important point for both the analyst of myth and the linguist is to show how these instantiate some more general social, linguistic, or other principles. The kind of analysis that Propp and Lévi-Strauss developed for such large-scale corpora has focused attention on significant regularities of distribution in such texts or other data.

Fourth, structuralism seeks to overcome the opposition between form and content with the notions of surface structure and deep structure. This distinction is formulated most precisely by Chomsky (1965), though there are many terminological variations that approximate this distinction. One of these is Lévi-Strauss's distinction between mechanical models and statistical models. Mechanical models, Lévi-Strauss claims, are "on the same scale" as the social phenomenon under investigation. A statistical model, on the other hand, is used for the formulation of a given social system's "invariants," which are accorded a generative power. Proponents of this type of analysis claim that the deep-structural invariants so identified generate the observed phenomenon.

There is a degree of slippage in the use of these terms. It is not always clear just where the distinction between the "generative" and the "causal-explanatory" lies. In the Chomskyan framework, the deep structure expresses "the semantic content of some well-formed sentence" (1965). The "base" component in Chomsky's account generates deep structures, which is where semantic interpretations are assigned. Chomsky claims that the base "may be universal, and thus not, strictly speaking, part of particular grammars." By the end of the 1960s, these claims had been subjected to some serious challenges. Chomsky himself subsequently abandoned the purest and most classical form of the distinction between deep and surface structure. It has since become clear that the deep structures that Chomsky and other linguists postulated as the underlying mechanisms for surface linguistic forms were simply more abstract versions of the very phenomena that they purported to generate.

Fifth, structure is defined by the dialectical duality of the syntagmatic and the paradigmatic dimensions of contextualization. The relationships that constitute a given structure are always defined by their positioning relative to the other terms whose relations constitute the structure. No term is defined positively as having an intrinsic value outside the system of relations to which it belongs. Instead, it is defined negatively by what it is not, in a system of terms that contrast with each other. This is the essence of Saussure's concept of linguistic value. Value operates along two interdependent dimensions of contextualization that Saussure calls the syntagmatic and the associative axes. (It is more usual now to refer to the latter with Hjelmslev's term *paradigmatic*.)

According to the original Saussurean hypothesis, the paradigmatic dimension of signification determines the organization of the syntagmatic dimension. The former is projected onto the latter. A given analysis always takes as its point of entry some particular level of structure. In the case of language, this might be any one of the levels of phonology, graphology, lexicogrammar, or semantics. Or, in the case of some larger-scale social event, it will be the entire hierarchy of relations that contribute to the event's structural unity and integrity (Pike, 1967). On any of these levels, there are specifiable syntagmatic relations into which the units and structures on that level can enter. Typically, these relations are of the part-whole kind. Structural linguistics has shown how relations of this kind are assignable to a constituent structure hierarchy. There is also a second, paradigmatic type of relation into which these elements enter. Each of the elements plays its part in some larger structural whole to which it belongs. At the same time, each element is related to the others in a system of possible alternatives. These alternatives form a system of differential terms which contrast with one another. Such a set of alternatives is always a structured system of purely positional values, in the Saussurean sense. It is a fundamental postulate of structuralism that paradigmatic organization is purely relational and determined by abstract terms that have no positive identity of their own (Petitot-Cocorda, 1990).

Sixth, the paradigmatic dimension specifies the categorical distinctions that the value-producing forms in the lexicogrammar of a given language distinguish (Petitot-Cocorda, 1985), and it is a fundamental a priori of structuralism that these categorical distinctions in meaning are immanent in the forms which realize them. The forms themselves constitute a topological space of categorical distinctions that do not simply classify an already discrete and given reality but model it. This criterion of immanence has radical implications, which have been recognized by researchers in both the biological and the social sciences.

Seventh, the ontological priority of difference over identity, an axiom that can be traced back to Immanuel Kant's category of reciprocal determinations, is one of the cornerstones of structuralism. The terms in a paradigm are, as Petitot-Cocorda (1985) points out, "structural connections, relations of dependency or of reciprocal determination." It is for this reason that *langue* is, for Saussure, a form rather than a substance.

[*See also* Binarism; Catastrophe Theory; Hjelmslev; Jakobson; Lévi-Strauss; Marx; Opposition; Poststructuralism; Prague School; Structure; *and* Thom.]

BIBLIOGRAPHY

Bloomfield, L. *Language*. Chicago and London: University of Chicago Press, 1984.

Chomsky, N. *Aspects of the Theory of Syntax*. Cambridge, Mass.: MIT Press, 1965.

Harris, Z. *Structural Linguistics*. Chicago and London: University of Chicago Press, 1966.

Hjelmslev, L. *Prolegomena to a Theory of Language*. Translated by F. J. Whitfield. Rev. English ed. Madison and London: University of Wisconsin Press, 1969.

Lévi-Strauss, C. *Structural Anthropology* (1958). Translated by C. Jacobson and B. G. Schoepf. Harmondsworth, England: Penguin, 1972.

Petitot-Cocorda, J. *Morphogenèse du sens*. Paris: Presses Universitaires de France, 1985.

Pike, K. L. *Language in Relation to a Unified Theory of the Structure of Human Behavior*. 2d rev. ed. The Hague: Mouton, 1967.

Propp, V. *Morphology of the Folktale* (1928). Translated by L. Scott. 2d rev. ed. Austin and London: University of Texas Press, 1968.

Saussure, F. de. *Cours de linguistique générale* (1916). Edited by C. Bally and A. Sechehaye. Paris: Payot, 1971.

Thom, R. *Structural Stability and Morphogenesis*. Reading, Mass.: Addison-Wesley, 1975.

Waddington, C. H. *Principles of Embryology*. London: Allen and Unwin, 1956.

—PAUL J. THIBAULT

STRUCTURE. While the initial understanding of structure in terms of a building or its underlying stability has not been discarded, more recent interpretations of it fall within two distinct perspectives: as a stable set of relations among constitutive elements; and as a holistic entity defined by its intrinsic properties. The first perspective is relatively static and close to the original architectural meaning; the second is dynamic, implying an overarching notion of system that includes structure and the elements structured. Nevertheless, both have Platonic overtones since they echo a concern for an immanent form, or at least for some of the ways in which it might be embodied in particular structures. Indeed, structure emerges as what is beyond the physical, different from the material fabric, and free of historic development, function, or purpose. Probably first acknowledged in the terminology of seventeenth-century biology, structure became a powerful concept due to its linguistic and subsequent anthropological foundations. In many ways, the linguistic foundation results in the implicit assumption of an extraordinary role attributed to language, one emphasized further by the psychoanalytical and philosophical appropriation of and reelaboration upon structure. Preoccupation with structure as a given or projected underlying set of relations and preoccupation with particular structures identified or assumed as cognitive devices in well-defined areas of investigation are related phenomena, but they are not reducible to each other. The process of defining structure and questioning its nature—whether objective or subjective or as an interplay of the two—is influenced by a concern with systems. From this perspective, one view holds that structures are structures of systems, which are entities that are supposed to function precisely because they are structured (since structures themselves do not function).

Previous to Wilhelm Dilthey (1833–1911), who introduced the term within the humanities *Geisteswissenschaften*, structural considerations in their episte-mological use were at most sporadic. After the major contributions to the definition of structure in linguistics and anthropology were made, the term entered a phase of loose usage from which gnoseological return could no longer be expected, which is one reason why some researchers of structure (Michel Foucault is the example par excellence) simply opted out of a structuralist school of thought or direction of concern. Other reasons lie in the political appropriation of the term (in particular, in Marxist-inspired philosophical, economic, and social discourse), as well as in the expectation of scientific rigor, which structuralists are generally reluctant to meet. All these reasons make the need for reassessing the definitions of structure even more critical.

Structure as relations among relata—a subject that brings to mind the *signans* and *signatum* of the Stoics and the *signified* and *signifier* of Ferdinand de Saussure—was pursued in the establishment of structural semantics by Algirdas Julien Greimas. In his view, a relation to another element defines the meaning of each individual element. By extension, structuring is then seen as perceiving differences and, moreover, organizing. This brings the issue into the direct proximity of information theory, where indeed Greimas's thought meets that of Max Bense, whose semiotic orientation is influenced more by Charles Sanders Peirce than Saussure.

Claude Lévi-Strauss issued what he calls the requirements of a model for embodying a structure: "First, the structure exhibits the characteristics of a system" (change of one element affects change of all the others). "Second, . . . there should be a possibility of ordering a series of transformations resulting in a group of models of the same type" (a property of homology). "Third, we can predict the behavior of the model when elements are modified." "Fourth: the model should be constituted so as to make immediately intelligible all the observed facts" (1963, pp. 279–280). Somehow, at the opposite end of the spectrum is Saussure's implicit understanding of language as structure, with the two primary relations of difference and opposition as the nucleus. His thesis that "there are no signs, there are only differences among signs" resonates in Louis Hjelmslev's theory, which is concerned not with sounds, letters, or meanings in themselves but with their reciprocal relations. But even deeper, Hjelmslev illustrates the difference between a nominalist understanding of structure—as a means or result of analysis—and the realist understanding: not only is language to be analyzed structurally (as Hjelmslev ascertains), but language is structure.

Noam Chomsky's contribution is in distinguishing surface structures, which traditionally preoccupied grammarians, and deep structures, which are basic entities out of which the variety of surface structures are realized. Language as a potential set of realizations is controlled by its deep structure. The hope that the structure of the mind might be revealed in what is common to languages with different surface structures is echoed in similar hopes expressed in anthropological, psychoanalytic (Jacques Lacan), and philosophical (Jacques Derrida, Louis Althusser) structural research. Other distinctions, such as the conscious and unconscious or the open and closed structure have also captured the attention of cognitive researchers. Claiming to examine the "mind in its natural state," Lévi-Strauss (1962) examines primitive cultures as the result of successive transformations against the background of perceived mental patterns. Through the notion of structure and its implicit system correlations, semiotics and cognitive science come closer together than the critics of psychologism ever anticipated they would.

The ontology of structure and its epistemological and logical understandings are not independent of each other. This is why, in reviewing the historic evolution of the notion, we cannot ignore all other aspects, as they actually constitute the metalevel of structure.

As a premise for the elaboration of a structural semiotics or of a system of semiotics, the notion of structure has been appropriated by various authors, along with all it carries in one or another of its definitions. In its shift from a concern with form (or even Gestalt) and comparative methods to a preoccupation and infatuation with structure, semiotics underwent a reevaluation of its major concept, that of sign. By no accident, aesthetic research was at that time in the forefront, almost in pace with linguistics, frequently surrendering the artistic to the logocratic model. Jan Mukařovský, whose initial area of interest was artistic artifacts and value, implicitly assumed that Gestalt or form and meaning constitute a whole best captured by the notion of artistic structure. What counts is the immediate reality of the work, its concrete existence as matter structured according to aesthetic intentions. The aesthetic effect is to be explained from the aesthetic structure of the work itself,

not by artistic, psychological, or sociological causes. This line of thought extends the approach of the Russian formalists, who were intent upon discovering structural laws governing the relation between literary accomplishments and other historic events. They all interpose between the work of art and the individual the aesthetic structure that acts as a mediating entity between the collective conscience and the individual experience of art. The work is a complex web of signs that carries a complicated structure of interpretations. This semiotic implication triggers the decisive step from the prior understanding that "everything in a work of art is form" to "everything is meaning," as meaning results from a realization of the semiotically constituted aesthetic structure. In the area of aesthetic concern, a distinction needs to be made between structure applied or revealed in literary criticism—evidently in the spirit of the linguistic foundation—and that applied to nonlanguage-based expression, in particular music and the visual.

After quickly establishing a structural context, Roland Barthes pushed his semiological investigations into the territory opened to inquiry by Saussure. The relations of difference and opposition apply to the literary signifier and signified but also to the referent. Barthes extends the understanding of literary structure as the foundation of semiotics in order to capture higher-level structures where the ideological comes to expression and can be revealed. He went beyond the work to the making, which is seen as structure generating and a semiotic endeavor nonetheless. Pursuing his fascination with structure into the visual arts, Barthes effectively reduces them to the word, as fashion or photography, for instance, are for Barthes not the actual clothing or photographs but the discourse about them or, better yet, the process leading to the discourse.

Umberto Eco (1971) reflecting on Jean Piaget's notion of structure—which involves unity of wholeness, transformation, and self-regulation—comes up with a semiotics within which structure is identified as a dynamic system (of culture, in this case). In the so-called absent structure, what was considered determined and perfected opens up to the many realizations of the work through its interpretations. Here it becomes obvious that the complementary concept of function needs to be accounted for if the desired epistemological reward of a structural perspective (even if applied to absent structures) will ever come to fruition. Structures are, after all, defined through their function in a system, text, or communication endeavor. The reciprocal relation between function and structure, which seems of interest from a system perspective, thus becomes critical for the understanding of dynamic semiotic phenomena.

Finally, in extension of Peirce and reflecting his shift between nominalism and realism, an entire semiotic development celebrates the functional triadic relations among the elements constituting the sign (object, representamen, and interpretant). In fact, this definition is as much structural as any other, only the structure here is more complex than in the dyadic (dualistic) tradition. Consequently, structure dominates all Peirce-inspired typologies (followed mainly by Charles Deledalle and Robert Marty, as well as by Max Bense and the school around the journal *Semiosis*).

The dynamic view—focused on the functions, so close to semiotic implications, of design, architecture, and political action and even more on the semiotic considerations of computing (programming, artificial intelligence, man-machine interaction)—has informed the work of many American and Canadian scholars. Beyond the structuralist thought and the heavy baggage it carries from a long history of obsessions with structure, attempts are currently being made to deal with the self-organizing nature of sign processes (a notion inspired by artificial-life research). Other notable attempts are based on Edmund Husserl's definition of the sign (a revival of Plato's theory of ideas), an approach focused on the extramental existence of eidetic essences. It is clear in both cases that, beyond their very dissimilar nature, these attempts try to transcend the thought of structure and proceed toward a better understanding of the underlying motivation for the construct we call structure. Even Jacques Derrida's notions of trace, "the arch-phenomenon of memory," and *différance* are designed to perform this function.

[*See also* Aesthetics; Art; Autopoiesis; Bense; Deconstruction; Marx; Opposition; Prague School; Realism and Nominalism; Russian Formalism; *and* Structuralism.]

BIBLIOGRAPHY

Bastide, R., ed. *Sens et usage du terme structure dans les sciences humaines et sociales.* The Hague: Mouton, 1962.

Berlyne, D. *Structure and Direction in Thinking.* New York: Wiley, 1965.

Broekman, J. M . *Structuralism: Moscow, Prague, Paris.* Trans-lated by J. F. Beekman and B. Helm. Dordrecht: Reidel, 1974.

Burnham, J. *The Structure of Art.* New York: George Braziller, 1971.

Eco, U. "A semiotic Approach to Semantics." *Versus* 1 (1971): 21–60.

Lévi-Strauss, C. *Structural Anthropology.* Translated By C. Jacobson and B. Grundfest Schoepf. New York: Basic Books, 1963.

Lévi-Strauss, C. *The Savage Mind* (1962). Chicago: University of Chicago Press, 1966.

Piaget, J. *Structuralism.* Edited and translated by C. Maschler. New York: Basic Books, 1970.

Robey, D., ed. *Structuralism: An Introduction.* London: Oxford University Press, 1973.

Sturrock, J., ed. *Structuralism and Since.* Oxford: Oxford University Press, 1979.

—MIHAI NADIN

SYMBOLIC. *See* Semiotic and Symbolic.

SYMBOLIC TYPE. In traditional, modern, and postmodern worlds, certain religious figures, cult leaders, political personages, stars of the mass media, and the like have become symbolic types, a term that refers to human beings whose presentations of self are of such extreme self-consistency that they affect and mold the contexts of social order rather than are determined by them. The symbolic type upends conventional relationships between social order and person.

The idea of symbolic type originated with the social phenomenologist Richard Grathoff (1970), who contrasts the symbolic type to the role type—the social role in conventional usage. The concept of role is elemental to understanding human beings who act in concert. Although persons know one another through cultural categorizations and their associated normative prescriptions, the social roles they enact are constructed through interaction with others. Therefore, roles are modified continuously and created anew through interpersonal negotiation and thus constituted through perspectives that join self and other. This follows from George Herbert Mead's (1934) idea of "taking the role of the other" as the interactionist basis of social life.

The role is a locus of dialectical contradictions that are controlled by and elaborated through the higher-order integration of context. As its etymology implies, *context* connotes a thrust or momentum toward the orchestration of disparate characters, themes, and behaviors. Their "weaving together" as context enables the coexistence of normative prescriptions and the practice of give-and-take. Context controls and directs the interaction of roles in social order. Grathoff is concerned with conditions in which context does not hold and in which social roles either lack the capacity or are too conflict ridden to reintegrate social order. These are conditions of social inconsistencies, the most extreme manifestation of which is anomie.

Grathoff argues that symbolic types appear in these conditions, tying together context so that an integrated field of social action can be maintained once more. The symbolic type is a living, performing body of being whose embodiment is itself reflective or refractive of versions of culture and social order. Embodiment here refers to the formation, coalescence, and incorporation of an integrated holism through the model and medium of the body (Handelman, 1991). Thus, the embodied symbolic type operates as the equivalent of context, while the type's premise of internal self-consistency replaces that of give-and-take among social roles that are directed by context. This embodied holism of the symbolic type enables it either to create or to destroy order.

The transformation from social role to symbolic type is profound in its consequence for social order, and yet it depends in principle on a single premise: a symbolic type comes into existence when and only when a person ceases to modify his or her behavior in response to the reactions of others. Then that person becomes wholly self-referential. The person contains not only his or her own self but also himself or herself as other, since others outside no longer partake of nor participate in his or her being.

Symbolic types are characters that first and foremost signify themselves. In the perceptions of others they vary from the inhuman (for example, the madman) to the superhuman (for example, the prophet or savior). These extremes are inherent in the limits set on others by a symbolic type's closure, which radically limits interaction to only two choices: either to reject the vision or design of reality projected by the type or to accept it. If one accepts the type's vision, one is then encompassed by the type, who determines one's own perception of reality in keeping with its own. If one rejects the type, it becomes peripheral to the reality of others and is often controlled severely through normative prescriptions. Charisma becomes

a function of the closing off of alternatives that is embodied in symbolic typing. As such, charisma can be removed from the study of individual depth psychology (whence it was relegated by default by Max Weber) and may be analyzed instead as a response of cultural design to extreme social conditions (Handelman, 1985).

The visions or projections of many symbolic types are more akin to designs of culture than they are to the personal idiosyncrasies of the individuals in question. This is why, in Grathoff's terms, the accepted symbolic type can resynthesize a disintegrated social order. To take the viewpoint of a symbolic type is not to see oneself in the type but rather to perceive and feel the symbolic type in oneself. In extreme religious and political aesthetics alike, this is virtually akin to possession—that is, to the enchanted loss of self in the other and therefore to becoming an object constructed by that other.

These qualities of the symbolic type reify the type above the social order because the type holistically subsumes the totality of its own reality. Thus, the symbolic type is its own context. The symbolic type is an ambulatory and performative body, an embodying organism that, as others take on its perspective, projects its own self-referential, holistic vision of the world. In this regard, the idea of symbolic type differs from those of symbol, sign, and icon. This distinction should be clarified because the latter concepts have long dominated discourse on symbolic action.

Umberto Eco's discussion of the Greek etymology of symbols locates precisely how this concept and that of symbolic type are at odds. Eco (1985) comments that "originally a symbol was a token, the present half of a broken table or coin or medal, that performed its social and semiotic function by recalling the absent half to which it could have been potentially reconnected." A symbol is thus seen as fragmentary, leading to other places and times. The impulse of a symbol is to join with its absent, completing part. In usual discourse, a symbol stands for, evokes, or brings into conjunction something else, something absent. It denotes the kind of relationship in which certain components exist elsewhere but are brought into some sort of connectivity with others that are present. This relationship between presence and absence constitutes social action as a performative symbolic structure. Therefore, an enactment that leads to other times and places should indeed be seen as symbolic.

Sign is similar to symbol in its play on the relationship between presence and absence and in its reproduction of the dualism of the ideal and the real. However, the sign is distanced even further from the symbolic type in that the former is constituted as an arbitrary designation, without any naturalistic linkage to whatever it signifies. On the other hand, the idea of icon is closer to that of symbolic type. An icon is figurative and holistic, conveying significance through the medium of the body. Nonetheless, the icon is only a representation of life; its form is static, its shape a reflection. The icon is performative primarily in miracles.

The symbolic type's antithetical relationship to symbol, sign, and icon is demonstrated most profoundly through its propensity to annihilate metaphor. Both symbol and metaphor exist through analogies. They enable one thing to relate to something different through the found similarities between them. Symbol and metaphor substitute and represent. Multivocal and polysemic, both open numerous possibilities of interpretation and meaning. Through substitution, symbol and metaphor can create relationships in series, hypothetically without end. Such chains of relationship have no necessary "natural" or principled closure. Symbol and metaphor open toward a possible infinity of alternatives and therefore to the fragmentation of holism.

Applications of the concept of symbolic type have focused on the knotty problem of how particular performative characters transform ritual context and thereby enable certain rituals to actualize their programs by moving sequentially from one phase of the ritual to another (Kapferer, 1983; Handelman, 1981). One study has used the concept to discuss the social impact of a liminal rabbi in the Moroccan Atlas Mountains (Bilu, 1993). The idea of symbolic type also is being employed in attempts to further understanding of how the uncertain give-and-take of mundane interaction becomes ritualized (and therefore more certain) without invoking a formal ritual context (Handelman, 1979). Thus, Smadar Lavie (1990) has developed the concept of "allegorical type" to explain how Bedouin personae ritualize the banality of everyday life through the telling of allegories when conversation becomes stuck on problematic issues of identity. The allegorical type transforms and reorganizes the context of discourse through the narration of spontaneous, emergent allegories that enable interaction to proceed.

More generally, the idea of symbolic type extends the thinking of Gregory Bateson on "schismogenesis" (the processes whereby new cognitive structures emerge through social action), of Victor Turner on liminal conditions for the emergence of antistructures, and of Erving Goffman on mundane "interaction ritual" and its social consequences. The development of the concept of symbolic type contributes to an understanding of the genesis of ritualization as an emergent property of social behavior, rather than as a product of normative prescription (Hazan 1994). The symbolic type focuses analysis on the transformations of social life rather than on its reproduction.

[*See also* Bateson; Goffman; Icon; Semiotic Terminology; Stereotype; *and* Turner.]

BIBLIOGRAPHY

Bilu, Y. *Without Bounds: The Life and Death of Rabbi Yaacov Wazana.* Jerusalem: Magnes Press, 1993.

Eco, U. "At the Roots of the Modern Concept of Symbol." *Social Research* 52 (1985): 383–402.

Grathoff, R. H. *The Structure of Social Inconsistencies: A Contribution to a Unified Theory of Play, Game, and Social Action.* The Hague: Martinus Nijhoff, 1970.

Handelman, D. "Is Naven Ludic? Paradox and the Communication of Identity." *Social Analysis* 1 (1979): 177–191.

Handelman, D. "The Ritual Clown: Attributes and Affinities." *Anthropos* 76 (1981): 321–370.

Handelman, D. "Charisma, Liminality, and Symbolic Types." In *Comparative Social Dynamics: Essays in Honor of S. N. Eisenstadt,* edited by E. Cohen, M. Lissak, and U. Almagor, pp. 346–359. Boulder, Colo.: Westview, 1985.

Handelman, D. "Symbolic Types, the Body, and Circus." *Semiotica* 85 (1991): 205–225.

Handelman, D., and B. Kapferer. "Symbolic Types, Mediation, and the Transformation of Ritual Context: Sinhalese Demons and Tewa Clowns." *Semiotica* 26 (1980): 41–71.

Hazan, H. *Old Age: Constructions and Deconstructions.* Cambridge: Cambridge University Press, 1994.

Kapferer, B. *A Celebration of Demons: Exorcism and the Aesthetics of Healing in Sri Lanka.* Bloomington: Indiana University Press, 1983.

Lavie, S. *The Poetics of Military Occupation: Mzeina Allegories of Bedouin Identity under Israeli and Egyptian Rule.* Berkeley: University of California Press, 1990.

Mead, G. H. *Mind, Self, and Society.* Chicago: University of Chicago Press, 1934.

—DON HANDELMAN

SYNCHRONIC AND DIACHRONIC. Ferdinand de Saussure's distinction between synchronic

and diachronic linguistics introduced the problematic of the time-dependent nature of linguistic phenomena. This distinction relates closely to the one he made between *langue* and *parole*. This is a consequence of Saussure's methodological decision to separate the study of *langue*—language as a system of pure differential values—from that of *parole*, which is the individual's use of language.

The speaking subject who uses a particular language system is unaware of the history of that system when he or she uses it. In order to study this system, the linguist must "suppress his own knowledge of the past." However, Saussure does not say that the language system is apart from history. On the contrary, Saussure constantly emphasizes history, change, evolution, and flux as inherent properties of the dynamics of the system.

Saussure was steeped in the very traditions of historical and comparative linguistics—he studied in Leipzig, which was a major center for the Neogrammarian school of linguistics—and spent most of his professional career working on problems that belong to those traditions. Far from attempting to exclude diachrony, Saussure attempted to reformulate the question of linguistic change, albeit in ways that were radically different from the prevailing substance-based and evolutionary models that characterized the approach of the Neogrammarians. The Neogrammarians had an organismic and evolutionary view of linguistic change. They described individual or collective linguistic behavior on the basis of physiological traits. The "facts" that they described were the traits that a given group exhibited at some particular historical moment. The Neogrammarians had no means of showing how the facts at any one moment related to the facts at prior moments or to possible future moments because of the total absence in their description of any conception of the language system. Moreover, their view of language change was a teleological one that outlined a linear succession of synchronic moments oriented to the achievement of some ideal future state.

Saussure rejected both the Neogrammarians' lack of a systemic, *langue*-based, conception and their teleology. He worked out theoretical positions on both of these points. First, he showed that diachronic change "is extraneous to all intentionality": a new sign does not come into being with the express purpose of creating a new value in the system. For Saussure, the system changes because of cultural and func-

tional factors that are specific to that particular "diachronic fact." Second, Saussure, in emphasizing the language system, places a lot of value on the continuity that underlies change. The system is the theoretical constant against which change can be measured. But if change were no more than a temporal succession of discrete moments or diachronic facts then there would be no basis for describing systemic continuity. The concept of the system, however, provides precisely a model for studying how change occurs against a background of systemic stability and continuity.

In the final analysis, it is the system itself that changes, not isolated facts external to it. Only a synchronic model of the system can, seemingly paradoxically, provide the basis for a study of system change. Further, Saussure's use of the concept of system is not totalizing in its implications. It is more accurate to say that he is talking about a given language's particular subsystems, which change against the background of the wider system. Saussure's own examples make this clear. Thus, the phonemic opposition between the German singular and plural forms *Gast* ("guest") and *Gäste* ("guests") is a synchronic fact. It refers to one significant opposition in one subsystem of the language. It is a part of that subsystem of phonemic oppositions that constitute the difference in meaning between the singular and the plural morphemes in modern German. Saussure's point is that the replacement of the historically prior plural form *Gasti* by the modern one *Gäste* is a change that occured against a stable background of systemic oppositions in other parts of the language system. The main limitation of Saussure's account is not the purportedly rigid separation between synchrony and diachrony but his ascription of a "forever *fortuitous* character" to a given linguistic state. This is an expression of the presumed arbitrary nature of the sign as seen from the purely *langue*-based perspective.

Saussure distinguished two perspectives on diachronic analysis. The first is prospective in that it consists of a simple recounting of the events from their starting point in the past, based on the available documentary evidence, and, thence, forward to some future moment. The second is retrospective and requires the linguist to "go back in the flow of time by means of retrospection," involving "a reconstructive method which is based on comparison" (1971, p. 292). Saussure gives priority to the second perspective. The point is that the linguistic forms that the linguist uses to reconstruct some "original" form are themselves subject to change. The critical factor in the retrospective method is continuity of change. Saussure emphasizes the "absolute continuity of development" of a language system. The comparative basis of the retrospective method means that the linguist can see which forms provide a common basis for comparison. In this way, the stages that lead from the precursor system to its successors can be reconstructed.

Saussure does not, however, reify the processes of reconstruction. The linguist's reconstruction can tell us something about the possible histories of the system that are "contained" in a given synchronic state. In actual fact, it is only the linguist's "synchronic projection" that corresponds to such a state. For Saussure, the source of both change and stability has a systemic basis. Any given value-producing term in the system may participate in the processes of either change or stability.

There is a still deeper reason why Saussure preferred the retrospective reconstruction of the flow of time to the prospective one: he realized that each of these new systems has its own internal system time. The prospective viewpoint is a mechanical and external recounting of a linear succession of "facts," while the retrospective point of view grasps the topological nature of the system.

Retrospective reconstruction views probability as internal to the system. This conception anticipates the intrinsically time-oriented and dynamical systems described by thermodynamics (Prigogine and Stengers, 1985). The dynamics of *parole* introduce elements of instability into the system itself. *Parole* perturbs *langue* and in so doing brings new probability features into the description of the system. Such features might take the form of newly relevant or newly salient patterns of difference. The inherent instability of the system has to do with the nondeterministic and irreversible nature of its dynamics. The system does not already contain its possible futures: instead, it irreversibly moves from present to future.

One of Saussure's great merits in developing this perspective was to show that change is not confined to the sound system but extends to the grammatical systems of the language. Saussure acknowledges the role of *parole* in this process. He is aware that the system changes in and through its patterns of use by speakers in specific contexts. It is these patterns of use of the system's potential that act back on the system and, in time, change it. This is the instance perspective. Saussure did not theorize this perspective, from which each signifying act derives its history. It is the very different history of the real-time unfolding of the discourse in the context of its semiotic and material environments.

See also Language Change; Langue and Parole; Saussure; Structuralism; *and* Structure.]

BIBLIOGRAPHY

Culler, J. *Ferdinand de Saussure*. Harmondsworth: Penguin, 1976.

Halliday, M. A. K. "How Do You Mean?" In *Advances in Systemic Linguistics: Recent Theory and Practice*, edited by M. Davies and L. Ravelli, pp. 20–35. London and Dover, N.H.: Frances Pinter, 1992.

Harris, R. "Translator's Introduction." In Ferdinand de Saussure, *Course in General Linguistics*, translated by R. Harris. London: Duckworth, 1983.

Hawkes, T. *Structuralism and Semiotics*. London: Methuen, 1977.

Hodge, R., and G. Kress. *Social Semiotics*. Cambridge: Polity Press, 1988.

Prigogine, I., and I. Stengers. *Order out of Chaos: Man's New Dialogue with Nature*. London: Fontana, 1985.

Saussure, F. de. *Cours de linguistique générale*. Edited by C. Bally and A. Sechehaye. Paris: Payot, 1971.

—PAUL J. THIBAULT

T

TEXT. According to a long-standing distinction, a text in traditional scholarship is what it is by virtue of a separation between it and its immediately surrounding material: commentary, glossary, footnotes, preface, bibliography, colophon, page number, marginalia, publication details, and so on. Thus, we may distinguish the text of the play *Romeo and Juliet* from, say, the editor's explanatory notes.

This idea is connected with the etymology of the word *text*, which is derived from the Latin *textus* (from the verb *texere*, "to weave"), which refers to anything woven. Hence, the traditional definition retains the idea of a piece of writing as being of whole cloth, effectively indivisible. In this sense, a modifier that is used frequently with the word *text* is *original*. Editors are expected to get as close to "the original" as possible—or else it might be said of them that they have not kept to the text. Traditionally, then, the term is used to delimit the range of "authentic" interpretability of a piece of writing. It is a way of attempting to designate "the actual words" (such as those of an author) and to hold them stable through time against what might be called corruptions.

With the advent of structuralism, the term *text* came to be used in a different but related way. Text came to be associated with the distinction between *langue* and *parole*, and particularly with *parole*. A language system (*langue*) generates specific utterances (*paroles*), but these utterances do not appear randomly. If a speaker simply rolled off a series of utterances purely on the basis that each in its own right is a proper or grammatical realization of linguistic rules, then communication would be a very precarious affair indeed. There would be no guarantee that utterances would be connected to one another. Signs, therefore, must not simply be linguistically competent in order to be understood; they must also be pragmatically competent. And the term *text* can be used in combination with the terms *code* and *message* to refer to one possible way in which signs or utterances are grouped pragmatically.

According to this structuralist approach, then, a text is a complex message that is usually more than one utterance in length and in which each of the utterances is connected sequentially to the one before it and the one after it. A text, then, is a coherent chain of utterances that usually has a single material existence: as a book or a poem; as a television program or a film; as a song or even a painting (in which case, the signs are not verbal ones); and so on. Texts, therefore, can sometimes be distinguished from other kinds of signs, such as conversational turns. With a text—as opposed to a fragment of everyday speech—the message becomes disconnected from its sender or author and may be read or decoded by a broad range of receivers or readers. While it is possible to think of spoken utterances as texts, even if they are never written down, it is much more common, under the structuralist definition, to think of texts in terms of written language or, by extension, of coherent multiple utterances that have a public (rather than just a local or private) existence.

The traditional definition seems to attach the idea of text to the idea of an origin or authentic source, usually an author; by contrast, the structuralist definition attaches it to a way of receiving or reading, a point (or set of points) of consumption—usually a reader or readership. But both definitions, so far, are definitions by negation: they only tell us what a text is not. There is a good reason for this. The concept of text is what the linguistic philosopher Willard V. O. Quine calls an "ultimate class"; it contains things (particular texts), but it is not contained by a "higher" concept. There is no class of things that contains the concept of text along with other things. "A class is a set if it is a member of a class. A class is an ultimate class if it is a member of none" (Quine, 1987). By analogy, we can see that the concept of car is a class which is a set because it is contained by the class of all vehicles. In its turn, the set of cars contains Fords, Toyotas, Hondas, Datsuns, and so on. Thus, we can say that a particular thing is a member of the class of texts, but, crucially, we can never name that class of things to which the concept of text itself belongs.

Turning back to the traditional definition that distinguishes "the text" from "the other parts," we can see that there will always be intermediate entities that sometimes seem as if they are part of the text and other times do not. One example is the title of a poem. Is it part of the text of the poem or extraneous to it? Does the text of the poem remain the same if it is reprinted in a different typeface or transposed from handwriting into print? Is the signature at the end of the letter a part of the text of the letter, or is it part of the surrounding material? Is the envelope a part of the letter? And if so, are the address, the stamp, the franking mark, the adhesive, and the preglued fold? Even this simplest definition of text threatens or promises to get out of hand, to spread beyond whatever containing system we establish for it.

If the text does threaten to overflow into its own marginalia, it is tempting to think of text metaphorically instead of literally and materially. Then text becomes anything that can be read or interpreted; it can be a film or a city, my body or yours. More drastically, it can be completely immaterial, merely an idea, or even the whole of the material universe (the "book of nature" interpreted by science or a religion). And what is there that needs absolutely and utterly no interpretation of any kind? Are there nontexts, objects in the world that simply arrive and make their presence known completely to us in one fell swoop; objects beyond any possible interpretation; objects that simply exist in their own fullness and that remain in an identical self-presence "inside" our consciousness? If not, is everything a text? Does a text come into being as soon as we discern an object, differentiate it from its background of other objects (thus creating that background) and make it distinct? If this is true, all forms of conceptualization are texts.

If, against this impulse, we try to keep the definition of *text* narrow in a very strictly structuralist sense, the term becomes simply a collecting point for types of written materials that are formed primarily in alphabetic or quasi-alphabetic scripts or, by a kind of extension and license only, in pictographic scripts or in pictures, perhaps in music or musical notation, perhaps in mathematical or diagrammatic forms, and so on. In the mainstream of such a definition, the term *text* will include books, papers, poems, drama scripts, and shopping lists, as well as, secondarily, art catalogs, paintings, photo albums, records, scores, equations, theorems, and so on.

Because of these definitional problems and others, *text* is often used very loosely. But this does not mean that the term is not productive. On the contrary, by using *text* heuristically—deliberately abstaining from strict definitions in order to see where it might lead—it is possible to derive interesting insights about a whole range of semiotic fields. An example is the work of the film analyst Christian Metz (1971). By thinking of films as texts, Metz was able to speculate on the existence of a filmic language that could then be analyzed into its component codes. This led to useful research questions: to what extent are shots like utterances? What pragmatic rules hold them together so that they can appear coherent (or indeed, incoherent) to viewers? Such questions opened up a new research project around the question of cinematic codification and its relation to more general, "extracinematic" forms of codification.

The intrinsic looseness of the concept of text has also been used in the field of sociological research on ideology. In this area, *text* has been applied to a very broad range of social phenomena (Coward and Ellis, 1977). And if such social phenomena in general (for example, sexuality, race, education, and so on) can be conceived of as texts (or like texts), then they are left open to readings. In this way, they appear less like given social (or even natural) facts. Instead of taking, for example, social class as a fixed or given attribute of a particular society, textualist sociologists have argued that one must read or interpret social class and, moreover, that social class only appears to exist as a "thing" because the dominant mode of its reading has tended to be a realist one. Other readings can be proposed and, in some cases, these will by contrast reveal the ideological positionings of dominant readings. The research question then becomes: if there is a dominant reading, whose interests and purposes does it serve? Why, for example, do we read sexuality today in such a way as to divide it into various categories (including the hetero-, the homo-, the bi-, and the trans-)? Who is served by such a reading, and what are the possible alternatives? And how do we persuade others to read sexuality differently?

Textualist sociology, therefore, might be predicated on a logical fallacy. Because the only class that the concept of text could possibly belong to would be so all-encompassing that it would have to be called something completely nebulous, it is tempting to invoke that class with such names as "the world" or "the social world." Then it appears, wrongly, that "the world" must be composed of texts and only texts. The mistake is then compounded by the argument that holds that to change how we read texts is to change the world.

[*See also* Frye; Langue and Parole; Metz; Pragmatics; *and* Saussure.]

BIBLIOGRAPHY

Beaugrande, R. de. *Text, Discourse, and Process.* Norwood, N.J.: Ablex, 1980.

Coward, R., and J. Ellis. *Language and Materialism.* London: Routledge and Kegan Paul, 1977.

Lotman, J. M. *The Structure of the Artistic Text.* Translated by R. Vroom. Michigan Slavic Contributions. Ann Arbor: University of Michigan, 1977.

Lucid, D. P., ed. and trans. *Soviet Semiotics.* Baltimore: Johns Hopkins University Press, 1977.

Metz, C. *Language and Cinema* (1971). Translated by D. J. Umiker-Sebeok. The Hague: Mouton, 1974.

Quine, W. V. O. *Quiddities: An Intermittently Philosophical Dictionary.* Cambridge, Mass.: Harvard University Press, 1987.

Riffaterre, M. *Text Production.* New York: Columbia University Press, 1983.

—ALEC MCHOUL

THEATER. Semiotics has provided theater specialists with methods of analysis to explore the ways in which meanings are created and communicated in the theater, a terminology for talking about the processes involved, and a theoretical framework to situate these processes in relation to others in other social and cultural areas. Looking back over the last sixty years, it is possible to see three stages in the development of theater semiotics: a first stage associated with the Prague Linguistic Circle in the 1930s and early 1940s (though much of this work was not available in the West until the 1970s); a second stage associated largely with semiotically inclined French and Italian theater specialists in the 1970s; and a third stage, more broadly based on the Continent, beginning in the 1980s and marked by a shift of emphasis from the work of art conceived as product to the processes of its production and reception and to the idea of performance as a social event.

English translations of most of the writing about theater produced by the Prague group can be found in Ladislav Matejka and Irvin Titunik (1976), Jan Mukařovský (1978), and Paul Garvin (1955). Key texts from the later period include Anne Ubersfeld (1977), Patrice Pavis (1976), and Alessandro Serpieri et al. (1978), while Tadeusz Kowzan (1975) forms a connecting link between the two. A good deal of pertinent work was published in the form of articles at the time, and collections such as André Helbo (1975) and a special issue of *Poetics Today* (1981) are still vital sources for theoretical and analytical insights. All these works share a number of features. First, their main thrust is a preoccupation with essentially text–centered dramatic performance. Notwithstanding Karel Brusak's work on Chinese theater and Roman Jakobson's inclusion of cinema (Matejka and Titunik, 1976), the principal focus of theoretical reflection was the culturally dominant form of theatrical performance. These theorists were concerned with the nature of the play text, its function in the elaboration of performance, and the methods of analysis that would best illuminate the particular textual practices involved and the performance practices they were perceived to underpin.

Another common feature in the Prague writings is the attempt to define in theatrical terms and to explore the specifically theatrical operation of semiotic notions such as sign, code, and referent (Pavis, Ubersfeld, Pëtr Bogatyrëv, Jindřich Honzl) as they were being developed by other theorists. This was also the period of grand general theories of theatrical function (Kowzan, Helbo, Mukařovský). The work of all these theorists is language centered, both in terms of the theatrical corpus being explored and in terms of the communication models being applied. Structural linguistics certainly released a fertile stream of new thinking about human communication in all its aspects, but it was also limiting in terms of providing a genuine semiotics of theatrical process. While some commentators have criticized theater semiotics for its reliance on linguistic models, the problem might be more in the nature of the linguistic models in vogue, in both the 1930s and the 1960s. One of the major factors that marks the development of theater semiotics in the 1980s is the use of more flexible models of language, which acknowledge that speech is embodied and gendered, that it is socially and culturally situated, and that in any transaction the receiver is as active a participant as the sender.

In later Western European semiotic theory, theater is either perceived as a problem or ignored completely. Apart from Roland Barthes's essay "Literature and signification" (1972, pp. 261–279), in which he referred to theater as a "cybernetic machine," and Umberto Eco's 1977 article on ostension, little reference to theater appears in the writings of the Paris School theorists. The first book-length study of semiotic theory to include a chapter devoted to theater was Georges Mounin's *Introduction à la sémiologie* (1970), but this was hardly an encouraging start: Mounin's main point was that theater does not function like language and that the attempts being made to explore it in terms derived from linguistics and semiotics were fundamentally wrongheaded. The dominant focus in American semiotics has been even more unsympathetic.

The work of Marco de Marinis (1982) marks an important shift of perspective from discussion of the relationship between text and performance to performance itself viewed as a text. Even if this terminology still betrays the imprint of the logocentric critical tradition, the shift of emphasis is decisive and heralds the second main phase in the development of theater semiotics. In this phase, French and Italian scholars have been joined by others, notably from Germany, Scandinavia, and the Netherlands. Each group has brought with it particular concerns, their knowledges of different performance traditions, and the methods that mark their national traditions of scholarship and inquiry.

The focus on performance itself has led to a new perception of its processual nature. Perhaps the most significant development in theater semiotics in the 1980s was the recognition of the dynamic role of the spectator in the meaning-making process: Eco's theorizing of the role of the reader, German reception theory, and Michael Halliday's functional systemic linguistics have all been important influences. The key texts here include Ubersfeld (1981), Pavis (1982), and Eschbach (1979). Just as important in marking this shift in focus are the empirical studies carried out in the theater by scholars such as Ed Tan and Henry Schoenmakers in Holland, Carlos Tindemans in Belgium, Willmar Sauter in Sweden, and Tim Fitzpatrick in Australia. Another feature of the work in this phase is that theory came to be grounded in detailed analysis of culturally situated performance (e.g., Fischer-Lichte, 1983).

A third generalization that can be made about the semiotics of theater in the 1980s concerns its increasing reliance on empirical studies to validate the claims of theory. One of the most interesting features of the Prague School group is that it contained practicing theater artists as well as scholars and critics; it is disappointing that in subsequent developments the traditional Western gulf between artistic practice and academic theory has widened. Semiotics has played an important part in the movement that is forcing the academy to take the actual practice of performance as the object of study, and not the least of its achievements is that it has provided a set of analytical procedures that makes this a feasible goal. It has also made it possible to bring together text and performance and to show how they work dynamically to constitute each other, and it has illuminated the role of the text in the practitioners' work process.

Theater semiotics in the 1990s is concerned chiefly with theatrical performance conceptualized as a dynamic relationship between performers and spectators. Such performance might or might not have a preexisting written text or texts as part of its genesis, and it might or might not tell a story, but it will necessarily entail a substantial collaborative production process involving a number of artists and technicians working in a range of media. It will exist at a given place for a given period of time, and it will give rise to a variety of physical, emotional, and cognitive experiences on the part of its spectators. Every part of this chain of production, performance, and reception and the sociocultural context in which it occurs and which it helps to construct are of interest to theater semioticians, who are increasingly defining their field of study in terms of interconnected processes of socially situated signification and communication.

Research in the 1990s is building on the analytical and descriptive work of the 1980s, and it is evident that a great deal more exploration of an empirical sort is needed before we can theorize in a satisfactory manner the whole production, performance, and reception chain. We also need to develop and critique our own methodology: there is no commonly accepted means to notate theatrical performance, nor are there institutionalized ways in which to exchange information about performance. There are not generally acceptable methods for recording or documenting performance, and only minimal documentation of audience-reception processes.

The theatrical focus of the 1970s and 1980s appears to be giving way to a more broadly based concept of performance, and the achievements of theater semiotics now make it feasible to attempt to analyze and explore the performance dimension of much extratheatrical social behavior. In this work, as in studies of other modes of cultural performance, the lessons learned from two decades of analysis of and theoretical reflection on theatrical performance will be relevant. Pavis, in a note on theater semiotics written for Michel Corvin's *Dictionnaire encyclopédique du théâtre* (1991) foresees the next phase as the development of "an anthropological socio–semiotics." His phrase indicates both a broad conceptual framework (theater seen as a dynamic part of a culture's mode of action) and the continued breaking down of disciplinary boundaries that has been occurring in recent years. The study of theater is necessarily interdisciplinary, and the sociological and anthropological ground indicated by Pavis will also be marked by the distinctive contribution that feminist critics have made in so many of the associated disciplines over the past decade.

[*See also* Acting; Nonverbal Bodily Sign Categories; *and* Turner.]

BIBLIOGRAPHY

Amossy, R., ed., "Semiotics and Theatre." Special issue of *Poetics Today* 2.3 (1981).

Barthes, R. *Critical Essays* (1964). Translated by R. Howard. Evanston: Northwestern University Press, 1972.

Corvin, M. *Dictionnaire encyclopédique du théâtre*. Paris: Bordas, 1991.

Eco, U. "Semiotics of Theatrical Performance." *The Drama Review* 21.1 (1977): 107–112.

Eschbach, A. *Pragmasemiotik und Theater*. Tübingen: Narr, 1979.

Fischer-Lichte, E. *The Semiotics of Theater* (1983). Translated by J. Gaines and D. L. Jones. Bloomington: Indiana University Press, 1992.

Garvin, P., ed. *A Prague School Reader on Esthetics, Literary Structure, and Style*. Washington, D.C.: Georgetown University Press, 1955.

Helbo, A., ed. *Sémiologie de la représentation*. Brussels: Complexe, 1975.

Helbo, A., et al., eds. *Approaching Theatre*. Bloomington: Indiana University Press, 1991.

Kowzan, T. *Littérature et spectacle*. The Hague: Mouton, 1975.

Kowzan, T. *Sémiologie du théâtre*. Paris: Nathan, 1992.

Marinis, M. de. *The Semiotics of Performance* (1982). Translated by A. O'Healy. Bloomington: Indiana University Press, 1993.

Matejka, L., and I. Titunik, eds. *Semiotics of Art: Prague School Contributions*. Cambridge, Mass.: MIT Press, 1976.

Mounin, G. *Introduction à la sémiologie*. Paris: Minuit, 1970.

Mukařovský, J. *Structure, Sign, Function*. Translated by J. Burbank and P. Steiner. New Haven: Yale University Press, 1978.

Pavis, P. *Problèmes de sémiologie théâtrale*. Montreal: Presses de l'Université du Québec, 1976.

Pavis, P. *Languages of the Stage*. Translated by S. Melrose et. al. New York: PAJ Publications, 1982.

Pavis, P. *Theatre at the Crossroads of Culture*. Translated by L. Kruger. London: Routledge, 1992.

Schmid, H., and A. van Kesteren, eds. *Semiotics of Drama and Performance*. Amsterdam: John Benjamins, 1984.

Serpieri, A., et al. *Come comunica il teatro: Dal testo alla scena*. Milan: Il Formichiere, 1978.

Ubersfeld, A. *Lire le théâtre*. Paris: Editions Sociales, 1977.

Ubersfeld, A. *L'ecole du spectateur*. Paris: Editions Sociales, 1981.

—GAY MCAULEY

THOM, RENÉ B. (b. 1923), French mathematician and founder of catastrophe theory. Catastrophe theory (from the Greek verb *katastrophein*, "to turn backward"), refers to the mathematical definition of a singularity in an otherwise continuous field. When a function exhibits a discontinuity in a point, changing sharply in value, this point is called catastrophic. Thom originated a topological system of basic catastrophes and manipulations by which forms themselves, as well as the ways in which forms change into one another, can be characterized mathematically. The major interest of Thom's distinction between regular (continuous) points and catastrophic (discontinuous) ones is its generality; the opposition between continuity and discontinuity is at work at many levels of our experience, and catastrophe theory provides a way of formally modeling the morphology of extremely diverse phenomena, from shock waves in physics to the syntactical forms of language to sociological occurrences such as riots or animal behavior.

Thom was born in Montbéliard, France, and earned his doctorate at the Ecole Normale Supérieure in 1946. He pursued his mathematical research at the Centre National de la Recherche Scientifique in Paris, and in 1958 was awarded the Fields Medal, the equivalent of the Nobel Prize in mathematics, for his work in topology. After teaching at the University of Strasbourg, Thom became a permanent member of the Institut des Hautes Études Scientifiques, where he has elaborated in numerous publications both the general principles of catastrophe theory and the range of its possible applications.

In 1972, Thom published *Stabilité structurelle et morphogénèse*, which set out the main tenets of his theory. Using the mathematics of Hassler Whitney on the singularities of differentiable application, and those of Henri Poincaré (1854–1912) and Aleksandr A. Andronov (1901–1952) on the theory of bifurcating dynamic systems, Thom addressed the immense problem of understanding the stability, transformation, and succession of forms. In particular, he produced a dynamic model for the process of biological morphogenesis, the emergence of form in living matter. He identified seven elementary catastrophes: fold, cusp, swallowtail, butterfly, elliptic umbilic, hyperbolic umbilic, and parabolic umbilic.

Thom has developed this pioneering work in numerous subsequent books: *Modèles mathématiques de la morphogénèse* (1974), *Paraboles et catastrophes* (1983), *Apologie du logos* (1990), and *Prédire n'est pas expliquer* (1991). In *Esquisse d'une sémiophysique* (1988), he constructs a model of meaning, called "semiophysics," that by addressing the processes and varieties of signifying forms offers a general theory of intelligibility. Thom proposes the following hypothesis: imagine a spectator in a movie theater observing a succession of natural forms evolving over time. Ask him or her to describe the meanings that these forms have. Only certain forms and configurations of elements, Thom contends, will produce meaning for the spectator and can serve as the basis of an intelligible construction, susceptible to linguistic description. This operation of signification can be described by two kinds of objects, which Thom names *salient* and *pregnant*, borrowing terms from Gestalt theory.

Salient forms are defined as forms that are experienced as individuated and detached from a continuous background; they have an impact on the sensorial apparatus that is of short-term duration, leaving no lasting effect on the subject's behavior (e.g., a flash of light). By contrast, pregnant forms are defined as being biologically relevant and, as such, endowed with meaning. They incite large-scale reactions in the human or animal subject: hunger, fear, desire, repulsion. Salient forms are topologically separate, whereas "pregnancies" are nonlocalized entities that are emitted and received by salient forms. When a salient form captures a pregnancy, it becomes charged with it, and thereby undergoes transformations of its internal state that might produce external manifestations in its forms: these are termed figurative effects. While abstract in its definitions, the usefulness of the semiophysical schema is that it permits Thom to translate qualitative, language-based, and psychological phenomena into formal terms that can then be topologically and algebraically represented.

[*See also* Catastrophe Theory; Meaning *and* Morphology.]

BIBLIOGRAPHY

Works by Thom

Structural Stability and Morphogenesis (1972). Translated by D. H. Fowler. Reading, Mass.: Benjamins, 1975.

Modèles mathématiques de la morphogénèse. Paris: Union générale d'édition, 1974.

"Morphologie du sémiotique." *Recherches sémiotiques/Semiotic Inquiry* 1.4 (1981), 301–309.

Paraboles et catastrophes. Paris: Flammarion, 1983.

Esquisse d'une sémiophysique. Paris: InterEditions, 1988.

Apologie du logos. Paris: Hachette, 1990.

Prédire n'est pas expliquer. Paris: Eschel, 1991.

Other Works

Petitot-Cocorda, J. *Morphogénèse du sens.* Paris: Presses Universitaires de France, 1985.

Saunders, P. T. *An Introduction to Catastrophe Theory.* New York: Cambridge University Press, 1980.

Zeeman, C. *Catastrophe Theory: Selected Papers, 1972–1977.* Reading, Mass.: Addison-Wesley, 1980.

—ALBERT LIU

TOKEN. *See* Type and Token.

TRADEMARK. A distinguishing name or logo intended to identify the goods or services of one or a group of sellers, a trademark or brand was designed originally to signal to customers the source of a product and to protect both customers and producer from competitors who might attempt to provide identical-looking goods of lesser quality. The other purpose of branding is to confirm the legal protection afforded by an inventor's patent in order to fight counterfeiters. The first historical role assigned to the trademark was thus to represent the manufacturer by transmitting information about a product's origin, its enunciator, and its sender. A brand was perceived as no more than a sign added to the product for the purpose of identification.

During the twentieth century, the emergence of trademarks became a much more complex phenomenon, comprising not only this original function but also a symbolic discourse that represents a variety of values, ideas, and attributes. Therefore, branding goes beyond the fact of naming and is an indication that a given product or service has received an organization's imprint or mark (Kapferer, 1992). Further, a trademark provides a product or service with an array of meanings, a story, and an imaginary universe, all of which impart significance. This complexity explains the perceived cultural aura surrounding some trademarks. Thus, by creating value and by providing a combination of attributes, both practical and symbolic, tangible and intangible, a trademark enhances the value of a product beyond its functional purpose.

Roland Barthes (1964) postulated the universal semanticization of usage whereby the use of an object is converted into a sign. This approach was developed further by Jean Baudrillard, who contended that in consumer society objects lose their material and functional status by being integrated into sign systems. Consumption is defined by Baudrillard as the organization of material substance into signifying substance: "To become an object of consumption the object must become a sign" (1996). The brand can therefore be considered as a sign—that is, it exists through the association of a signifier and a signified. The brand is the complex association of a set of stimuli expressed through various media (logo, packaging, advertising discourse, etc.), whose functions are to arouse in the minds of actual and potential customers an array of meanings and a set or configuration of imaginary elements. These elements constitute a brand's universe or a brand image; they might include "technical matters," "product characteristics," "financial value," and "sociability" (Levy, 1978). Semiotically, such components constitute the signified of the product, while the material object is the signifier of the commodity as a sign.

Epistemologically, the brand—which was a sort of transparent sign asked to deliver information about the producer—has gained opacity; that is to say, the brand has acquired some characteristics of its own (personality, identity, image, etc.) that contribute to giving it a different mode of existence. The brand as a sign operates within a system of signifying relations. Brands have meaning through paradigmatic and syntagmatic relations to other brands and in relations to consumers. This means that the brand's value is to add value to the various partners in the economic exchange.

A brand's identity, defined as the way the brand gains visibility and is described by various actors, re-

sults from a process of interaction and transformation from three systems: the system of production, the environment, and the system of consumption. Each system is more than a mere sender of messages; each can be viewed as a set of competencies, actors, memories, and relations that are articulated by a common enunciative structure (Semprini, 1992). The production system, which contractually emits constitutive signs of the brand's identity, is made of the company's values, culture, mission, objectives, communication mix, and other such elements. Brand identity in this sense articulates three levels: a surface level that includes the rhetoric principles, the actors, and the vision of time and space used in the brand's discourse. The second, narrative level, conveys how these elements are structured and articulated. The deepest level is the axiologic one, which deals with the main value orientations (on the continuum of instrumental and base values) to which the brand's universe refers. The system of consumption or reception articulates attitudes, motivations, values, and consumption habits that influence the understanding and decoding of the brand's contractual identity as proposed by the production system. Finally, the environment articulates the social, cultural, legislative, and political context as well as competitors' reactions. It interacts with both the production and reception of the brand's identity. It becomes therefore possible to consider the various interactions between these three universes as a text governed by both syntagmatic and paradigmatic relationships. Therefore, the brand can be approached in a narrative perspective, granted that it exists only through a complex system of relationships with other brands, consumers, and the environment. In this respect, a given market can also be read as a text. The narrative approach provides, for instance, a good way of decoding the interaction in relationship between brand and consumer. From the consumer's perspective, brands are value providers endowed with a narrative program that is oriented toward the satisfaction of a need or, more generally, the reduction of a state of tension.

In conformity with basic narrative structures, derived from the work of Vladimir Propp, trademarks must first acquire competency through trials, competitions, and initiation rituals (qualifying test) and finally be recognized for what it has accomplished and thus for what it is (glorifying test). A brand that fails to successfully implement each step might have negative attitudes develop about it, leading to its eventual commercial demise.

[*See also* Advertising: Barthes; Baudrillard; Logo; Narratology; *and* Rhetoric of the Image.]

BIBLIOGRAPHY

Barthes, R. "Rhetoric of the Image" (1964). In *Image-Music-Text: Essays*. Selected and translated by S. Heath, pp. 32–51. London: Fontana, 1977.
Baudrillard, J. *The System of Objects* (1968). Translated by J. Benedict. London: Verso, 1996.
Heilbrunn, B. "My Brand the Hero: A Semiotic Analysis of the Consumer-Brand Relationship." In *European Perspectives in Consumer Behavior*, edited by M. Lambkin et al, pp. 370–401. Hemel Hempstead: Prentice-Hall, 1998.
Hirschman, E., and M. Holbrook. *Postmodern Consumer Research: Consumption as a Text*. Newbury Park, Calif.: Sage Publications, 1992.
Kapferer, J.-N. *Strategic Brand Management*. London: Kegan Paul, 1992.
Kehret-Ward, T. "Using a Semiotic Approach to Study the Consumptions of Functionally Related Products." *International Journal of Research in Marketing* 4 (1988): 187–200.
Levy, S. *Marketplace Behavior*. New York: AMACOM, 1978.
Mick, D. "Consumer Research and Semiotics: Exploring the Morphology of Signs, Symbols, and Significance." *Journal of Consumer Research* 13 (September 1987): 196–213.
Semprini, A. *Le marketing de la marque: Approche sémiotique*. Paris: Editions liaisons, 1992.
Umiker-Sebeok, J., ed. *Semiotics and Marketing*. Berlin: Mouton de Gruyter, 1987.
Wilkins, M. "The Neglected Intangible Asset: The Influence of the Trade Mark on the Rise of the Modern Corporation." *Business History* 34 (1992): 66–95.
—BENOÎT HEILBRUNN

TRIVERS, ROBERT (b. 1943), British zoologist and one of the first sociobiologists. Trivers has proposed some of the most powerful and widely used evolutionary mechanisms for the understanding of social behavior. Starting from the perspective of individual selection—that is, assuming that selection must essentially benefit the individual actor—Trivers is best known for his idea of reciprocal altruism, which argues that there can be cooperation between organisms, including between nonrelatives, for basically selfish ends. ("You scratch my back, and I will scratch yours.") But Trivers has also worked on other important evolutionary topics, such as conflict between parent and offspring. Unlike the traditional views, which sees family units as by nature harmonious wholes supported and preserved by natural selection, Trivers argues that conflict is natural, since parents and children pursue different and even conflicting reproductive aims. Therefore, family strife is not necessarily a sign of dysfunction.

Communication has been a topic of major importance and interest to Trivers, particularly in the context of reciprocal altruism. An example that shows strongly how his individualistic perspective differs from that of others is given by his analysis of avian warning cries. Why, in some species of birds, do members cry out on seeing predators? Does this not put themselves in danger, thus reducing their biological fitness? Trivers dismisses "group-selection" explanations, which interpret the cries as benefiting the group or species as a whole at the expense of the individual. These theories yield unsatisfactory answers, since cheating and remaining silent in order to rely on the risks of others would become a superior, selectively favored, and thus dominant strategy. Trivers dismisses also the suggestion that such cries are just evolutionary junk or garbage or even maladaptive, the linked remains of cries that do still have direct evolutionary value (such as courting songs). Such explanations for the Darwinian are always those of the last resort.

Rather, Trivers argues that the warning cries benefit the individual. Apart from the help that one's cries might give to close relatives, crying out should provoke others to do the same when one needs such warning oneself. Moreover, there are strong selective pressures against cheating. In addition, such cries often bring on a joint response by the threatened species (as when small birds mob a large bird), which again benefits the original vocal individual. In short, reciprocal altruism, explains warning cries. As always in Trivers's work, there is no need to invoke any explanations other than those that benefit the individual first and foremost.

[*See also* Darwin; Dawkins; Evolution; Hamilton; *and* Signal.]

BIBLIOGRAPHY

Ruse, M. *Sociobiology: Sense or Nonsense?* Dordrecht: Reidel, 1979.
Trivers, R. "The Evolution of Reciprocal Altruism." *Quarterly Review of Biology* 46 (1971): 35–57.

Trivers, R. *Social Evolution*. Menlo Park, Calif.: Benjamin/ Cummings, 1985.

Williams, G. C. *Adaptation and Natural Selection*. Princeton: Princeton University Press, 1966.

Wilson, E. O. *Sociobiology: The New Synthesis*. Cambridge, Mass.: Harvard University Press, 1975.

—MICHAEL RUSE

TRUBETZKOY, NIKOLAJ SERGEEVIČ

(1890–1938), Russian linguist who played an important role in the development of structural linguistics and structuralism. Born in Moscow in one of the foremost aristocratic families of Russia, one that included several eminent scholars—his father was professor of philosophy and the first elected rector of Moscow University—Trubetzkoy (also spelled Trubeckoj) was educated privately at home. After studying at Moscow University from 1908 to 1913, Trubetzkoy graduated after writing a work on the expression of the future in Indo–European and was appointed a special research associate, thus becoming a candidate for a professorship. Having spent the academic year 1913–1914 in Leipzig, a leading Neogrammarian center where he attended courses together with Leonard Bloomfield and Lucien Tesnière, he passed his doctoral exams in 1915. Appointed *privat-dozent* at Moscow University, Trubetzkoy began to teach Sanskrit. For reasons of health, he left Moscow for the Caucasus in 1917. The civil war prevented him from returning to Moscow. In 1918, he fled to Tbilisi, then to Baku and Rostov, where he taught at the university. In 1919, Trubetzkoy fled again, this time to the Crimea and from there to Constantinople. In 1920, he was appointed a *docent* at Sofia University, where he stayed for two years. In 1922, Trubetzkoy moved to Vienna, where he held the Slavic chair at the university until his death in 1938.

Although Trubetzkoy was not one of the six founders of the Prague Linguistic Circle, he soon became one of its most active members. He was informed about the Circle's activities as early as the end of 1926; in February 1927, he delivered his first speech there ("The Alphabet and the Sound System"). Together with Roman Jakobson and Sergej Karcevskij, he signed the theses presented at the First International Congress of Linguists at The Hague. As a result of his activities, he was appointed president of the Association phonologique internationale, created at the International Phonological Conference held in Prague and organized by the Circle in 1930.

Although probably best known as a linguist, Trubetzkoy's interests were not restricted to this field: many of his studies are devoted to the history of culture, folklore, ethnology, and literature. Yet even as early as his university studies, he considered linguistics as the only discipline in the humanities with a scientific method, while the other disciplines were still at the stage of "alchemy." And although Trubetzkoy's name is most closely associated with the development of structural phonology, his linguistic interests covered a variety of themes, such as the history of literary language, the typology of language structures, comparative grammar, and the theory of language contact.

In 1915, Trubetzkoy shifted his interest from general Indo-European to Slavic philology after he became acquainted with a recent book by the leading Russian linguist A. A. Šachmtov, the *Outline of the Oldest Period of the Russian Language*, which contains a treatment of sound development in pre-Slavic and its relevance for modern Russian. After his public discussion of the methodological drawbacks of this book, Trubetzkoy endeavored to write a systematic "Prehistory of the Slavic Languages," assuming that they evolved from a pre-Slavic language that in turn derived from Indo-Germanic. During his migratory years between 1917 and 1919, he began this work, which was never published. He left the manuscripts at Rostov University, where they perished during World War II; his later reconstructions and partial elaborations at Vienna have also been lost.

His first book, *Europe and Mankind (Europa i čelovečestvo*, 1920) was published during his stay in Bulgaria; in it, he proclaims the equality and incommensurability of all peoples and cultures, argues against Romano-Germanic–dominated Eurocentrism, and calls upon other European ethnic intellectuals to remember their specific cultural values. In 1921, he coedited *Exodus to the East (Iskhod k vostoku)* and was a cofounder of the Eurasian movement, which held a scientific, ideological, and political position according to which Russia and Asia are seen as an integral ethnogeographical and cultural unity. For Trubetzkoy, linguistic and cultural diversity was a necessary element of mankind; his writings on this topic are a blend of moderate version of nationalism and a rejection of cultural ethnocentrism. In Vienna, Trubetzkoy continued this line of thinking in studies such as *The Legacy of Genghis Khan (Nasledie Cingiskhana*, 1925), and *On the Problem of Russian Self-Awareness (K probleme russkogo samopoznanija*, 1927). In one of these studies, "The Tower of Babel and the Confusion of Tongues" (1923), he formulated the outlines of his theory of language contact and developed the concept of language unions and cultural zones according to which not only genetically related languages but also languages from different language families or branches in permanent contact with each other may develop and display parallel structures (e.g., in Europe, the Balkan languages: Bulgarian, Romanian, Albanian, and Modern Greek). At Vienna University, Trubetzkoy taught Slavic literatures and also published several monographs in this field of research, such as his *Vorlesungen über die altrussische Literatur* (1973), *Die russischen Dichter des 18. und 19. Jahrhunderts* (1956), and *Dostoevskij als Künstler* (1964).

Despite Trubetzkoy's broad spectrum of publications, his *Grundzüge der Phonologie* (1939) remained his magnum opus and was the source of his international fame. In a way, it can be regarded as a counterpart to his unpublished "Prehistory," which was in its original plan diachronically oriented. At that time, synchronous phonological analyses were outside of Trubetzkoy's sphere of interest; only in 1926, when he was confronted with the problem of bridging the gap between a synchronic analysis of the phonological system and historical phonetics did he reach the conclusion that any phonological change can be explained only by recourse to the whole phonological system in question. This confirmed his assumption that comparative-historical grammar can be studied best on the basis of a system derived from living languages.

Based on Ferdinand de Saussure's distinction between *parole* and *langue*, Trubetzkoy introduced the terminological and conceptual opposition of phonetics and phonology (or phonemics): whereas phonetics is the study of the material sounds and their articulation in speech, phonology is concerned with language sounds as functional elements in a system. The theoretically infinite number of phonetic realizations are thus reduced to those differences that play functional roles in the system—namely, phonological oppositions. As opposed to phonetics, phonology is thus related directly to semantics, since phonological functionality is determined by a semantic effect.

Trubetzkoy's concept of phonology has been extremely influential: it was elaborated further by Roman Jakobson in terms of a system of distinctive features; this approach has been successfully transferred to other semiotic systems (e.g., that of Claude Lévi-Strauss). Also, Trubetzkoy's general distinction between phonology and phonetics has been extended methodologically by distinguishing generally between *etic* and *emic* approaches in semiotics: an *etic* approach is nonstructural and studies surface phenomena, whereas an *emic* approach is structural and considers elements of sign systems with regard to their function in the system.

[*See also* Language Change; Langue and Parole; Opposition; Prague School; Saussure; Semiotic Terminology; *and* Structuralism.]

BIBLIOGRAPHY

Works by Trubetzkoy
Principles of Phonology (1939). Translated by C. A. M. Baltaxe. Berkeley: University of California Press, 1969.
Three Philological Studies. Ann Arbor: University of Michigan Press, 1963.
Writings on Literature. Edited and translated A. Liberman. Minneapolis: University of Minnesota Press, 1990.
The Legacy of Genghis Khan and Other Essays on Russia's Identity (1925). Edited and translated by A. Liberman, preface by V. V. Ivanov. Ann Arbor: University of Michigan Press, 1991.
Other Works
"Bibliographie des travaux de N. S. Trubetzkoy." *Travaux du cercle linguistique de Prague* 8 (1939): 335–342.
Jakobson, R. *N. S. Trubetzkoy's Letters and Notes*. The Hague: Mouton, 1975.
Matejka, L. "N. S. Trubetzkoy's Concepts of 'Language Unions' and 'Cultural Zones.'" *Wiener Slawistischer Almanach* 25–26 (1990): 291–298.

—PETER GRZYBEK

TURING, ALAN (1912–1954), British mathematician whose works on computation had a crucial influence on the development of computer science, artificial intelligence, and cognitive science. His abstract machine, known now as the Turing machine, provides a mechanism for using algorithmic structures to perform automated computations. In other words, he provides the mathematical and theoretical framework and foundation for the physical realization of today's computers, most of which are based implicitly on these theoretical considerations.

During World War II, Turing worked in a research

group that was trying to decipher coded German messages. Simple forms of computers and automated computing devices were needed urgently in order to perform the transformations. In the course of developing his abstract machine, Turing realized that it could also perform "intelligent" tasks. He formulated what is called today the Turing test for deciding whether a computer can be considered intelligent or not: person A is sitting in front of two output devices (screens, for example)—one is connected to another human, the other is connected to a computer. A has to find out which of these two screens is connected to the computer by asking questions and receiving answers. This test is, of course, only a very crude method, but it has been the object of serious discussions ever since.

One of the most important concepts "invented" by Turing (1936, 1950) involves his Turing machine, which represents the simplest, very popular, and most widely used theoretical mechanism for the execution of computations. Turing showed that his machine could capture everything that we understand by the notion of computation, including all functions that are computable by any other conceptual scheme, such as recursive functions or the functions that can be computed by a random-access or Von Neumann machine. As a conceptual machine, Turing machine consists of a tape, a read/write device, and an internal table of state transitions. The tape consists of symbols of an alphabet A. The Turing machine computes a mapping from an input string i on the tape (i is an element of $A*$) to an output string o on the tape (o is an element of $A*$). This is done via the read/write device, which is capable of reading a symbol from the current position on the tape, writing a symbol to the current position, and moving the tape to the left or right. The rules for reading, writing, and moving are represented in the machine's state-transition table, which can be compared to the machine's internal program. This table determines the machine's behavioral dynamics. At each time, the Turing machine finds itself in a certain state $s(t)$. When a certain symbol is read by the reading device, this causes a state transition in accordance with the rules and the current internal state. As a result, the writing device writes a certain symbol and moves the tape. There is a designated initial state in which the system finds itself at the beginning of its actions and a halting state that the machine reaches when the program has terminated.

The result of these operations is a string of symbols that has been written to the tape in the course of the state transitions and the computing processes. It has been shown that such a conceptual device is capable of computing any possible function. It represents the theoretical basis for modern computer technology and computer science. Of course, it would be too difficult and much too slow to build such a machine as a real device, but the conceptual scheme of states, state transitions, and the tape as input/output device are concepts found in every computer. The Von Neumann computer architecture, for instance, which is the most common architecture in today's computers, is one possible realization of the Turing machine.

A powerful achievement of abstract reasoning, Turing's work is also interesting from the standpoint of its general consistency and philosophical implications. Turing's fundamental thesis, in its strongest physical form, amounts to this: if one can build a Turing machine that can compute, then this machine coincides with its object: namely, nature itself, which in turn would be nothing more than a Turing machine. And indeed, Turing's later pioneering work on chemical morphogenesis can be seen as extending his mathematical research to the domain of nature. This work, unfortunately, was cut short by the governmental persecution that subjected him to hormone therapy after his arrest and conviction on charges of homosexuality in 1952. Turing committed suicide in 1954.

From his initial hypothesis of a computing machine capable of solving the 1928 *Entscheidungsproblem* (Decision Problem; see Hilbert and Ackermann, 1950, pp. 112–124) by testing every value of a given recursive function to the formulation of the celebrated Turing test and his later experimentation in fluid autotelic systems, Turing's thought seems to be deeply concerned with notions of testing and provisionality instead of proof *more geometrico*. The reunion of testing and technology was perhaps Turing's vision of the essential function of the machine that is his legacy.

[*See also* Artificial Intelligence; Autopoiesis; Computer; *and* Knowledge Representation.]

BIBLIOGRAPHY

Hilbert, D., and W. Akermann. *Principles of Mathematical Logic* (1931). Translated by L. M. Hammond et al. New York: Chelsea Publishing, 1950.

Hodges, A. *Alan Turing: The Enigma.* New York: Simon and Schuster, 1983.

Turing, A. "On Computable Numbers, with an Application to the Entscheidungsproblem." *Proceedings of the London Mathematical Society*, series 2, 42 (1936): 230–265.

Turing, A. "Computing Machinery and Intelligence." *Mind* 69.2236 (October 1950): 433–460. This article is reprinted in M. Boden, *The Philosophy of Artificial Intelligence* (Oxford: Oxford University Press, 1990).

Turing, A. "The Chemical Basis of Morphogenesis." *Philosophical Transactions of the Royal Society* Series B, vol. 237 (1952): 37–72.

—MARKUS PESCHL and ALBERT LIU

TURNER, VICTOR (1920–1983), British anthropologist whose theoretical approach to rituals and symbols influenced social anthropology, religious studies, cultural and performance studies, and challenged structuralism and formalist semiotics. At issue in British social anthropology of the 1950s was the value of conflict in the practice of social order. Functionalist canons had viewed conflict as an aberrance that signaled the breakdown of organic social systems. By contrast, Max Gluckman (under whose supervision Turner did his postgraduate studies) attacked organic analogies, stressing that conflict was integral to the practice of social life. In his first major work, *Schism and Continuity in an African Society* (1957), now regarded as a classic of analytical ethnography, Turner created the concept of "social drama" to analyze crisis and change over time in Ndembu village social relationships. Social drama addresses eruptive disruptions in the social life of communities and constitutes a limited focus of deep transparency into the otherwise opaque, uneventful surface of social life. The social drama has a regularized, processual form of three successive phases: breach, crisis, and redress. But Turner, in contrast to functionalist thinkers, added another possible outcome to the social drama: that of schism, rupture, and the destruction of relationships. Thus, there are no essentialist structural grounds for enduring stability in social order. This profound theme runs through all of Turner's work, brought him close to postmodernist thinking, and has vibrant resonances with chaos theory, and deeply colored his perception of ritual and performance.

In Turner's view, the indeterminacies of social order give to rituals in tribal societies the specialized and privileged mandate of making controlled transformations that reproduce mundane order. His attention shifted from mundane life to the internal logics of ritual as developmental progressions of symbolic formations. His next major work, *Chihamba, the White Spirit: A Ritual Drama of the Ndembu* (1962), is a signpost of conceptual change in the symbolic analysis of ritual forms in two respects. First, this study develops the conception of ritual as processual and performative; second, the work is composed as an interpretive and reflexive enterprise in the seeking of meaning—one in which the anthropologist and the native informants together are included explicitly in the creation of the analysis. Chihamba is discussed as an additive progression of ritual sequencing, and each phase emerges through the observations of the anthropologist together with the exegeses of Ndembu ritual practitioners. Neither the authorship of the Ndembu nor that of Victor Turner is hidden. Theirs is a joint performance in which subject and object, text and context, exchange positions and perspectives as consociates in an ongoing dialogue. This work also marks the outset of Turner's ideas on a universal "comparative symbology."

Turner referred to the symbol as the "molecule" or building block of his theory of ritual. Influenced by Sigmund Freud and Carl Jung, Turner argued that the connection between symbolic behavior in ritual and the practice of mundane life was semiotic. This means that the meaning of symbols is exegetical on the one hand and consequential on the other. In his view, tribal rites often are composed through different combinations of cultural symbols that in concert act with consequence and causality on those who pass through the ritual sequence. Any dominant cultural symbol is characterized by "multivocality" (polysemy), which gives to such a symbol a wide spectrum of referents and a multiplicity of meanings. Depending on how symbols are orchestrated, especially in ritual contexts, they can bring into conjunction quite different, even contradictory meanings. The meanings of symbols cluster around two distinct poles: the "ideological" (or the normative) and the "sensory" (or the orectic). The ideological pole indexes cognitive referents to moral and social order, and the sensory that of referents to the body, emotions, and nature. In the tribal rituals that Turner studied, these two poles coalesce within dominant symbols, enabling the exchange of their meanings within these symbols. Therefore, these symbols are media of transformation. Among the Ndembu, rites of passage, rites of affliction, and rites that treated infertility were all characterized by this transformative interchange between ideological and sensory meanings.

Borrowing from Arnold Van Gennep's 1909 structural division of rites of passage into three phases (separation, or the preliminal; transition, or the liminal; and incorporation, or the postliminal), Turner located the transformative power of tribal ritual in its liminal phase. His thinking on the capacity of ritual to effect radical change in the being of those who passed through it began in Manchester but reached its crescendo after Turner moved to the United States in 1964. In 1966, he gave the Lewis Henry Morgan lectures that were turned into his most widely read book, *The Ritual Process: Structure and Anti-Structure* (1969), in which he developed his theory of liminality.

Turner understood the liminal phase as a locus for the programmed deconstruction of mundane social-structural perceptions and relationships. This controlled, processual dissolution of particular cultural and social structures often focuses on the being of particular categories of person. Thus, the being of an initiate who undergoes a rite of passage is symbolically taken apart, negated, and effaced. Aspects of mundane social structure that are relevant to personhood are replaced by what Turner called antistructures. These are alternative versions of moral and social order that have little or no place in mundane reality and that serve as symbolic templates for reconstituting the being and social relationships of those who are undergoing ritual transformation. So, for example, boy is transformed into man and girl into woman, in keeping with particular cultural premises of personhood.

One of these antistructures Turner called "communitas," which refers to liminal conditions in which human beings not only shed their categorical distinctions and differences but then also relate to one another through the equality and fullness of being, whose mundane actualization is routinely prevented by social structure. More generally, Turner characterized liminality as a subjunctive mood of potential that challenges established orders and that provides a cultural means of generating variability and change in tribal societies. As critiques of social structure, antistructures that arise under liminal conditions are essential to the adaptability and survival capacities of society. Antistructure and structure continuously engage one another in a reflexive dialectic of subversion and modification.

During the 1970s, Turner's thinking turned increasingly toward ritual and religion in complex and modern societies and more generally to performative genres and to their significance for the human condition. He and others applied liminality to an extremely wide range of diverse cultural phenomena, overextending the viability of the concept (Handelman, 1993). In the late 1970s, Turner drew back from this diffusion of the liminal to argue as he had in the early 1960s that the concept's applicability was most relevant to ritual with a rite-of-passage structure. He concluded that a postindustrial social order is characterized by a vast variety of secular forms of performance that are dramatistic, entertaining, and often ludic in their character. Although these forms may be rituallike, participating in them is voluntary rather than normative. Moreover the designs of such occasions—ranging from pilgrimages and carnivals to experimental theater—are shaped to the desires of participants and audiences rather than to the demands of societal reproduction. Turner called these performances genres "liminoid." Unlike the liminal genres, the liminoid ones are tailored more to the needs of modern, autonomous individuals and to a host of newly emerging social and religious groups, many of which are temporary, reflecting the immediacy of swiftly changing social situations. Turner virtually argued that only change can revive human beings and their social orders.

From his perspectives on the liminal and the liminoid, Turner pioneered a theoretical understanding both of the deep indeterminacies upon which all moral and social order teeters and of the uncertainties that pervade social life. His life work opened toward postmodernism, all the while maintaining the deeply rooted conviction that personal, anthropological field research was the best way to learn of the perceptions, emotions, and ways of living of others.

[*See also* Culture, Semiotics of; Structure; *and* Symbolic Type.]

BIBLIOGRAPHY

Works by Turner

Schism and Continuity in an African Society: A Study of Ndembu Village Life. Manchester: Manchester University Press, 1957.

Chihamba, the White Spirit: A Ritual Drama of the Ndembu. Manchester: Manchester University Press, 1962. This material is reprinted in V. W. Turner, *Revelation and Divination in Ndembu Ritual* (Ithaca, N.Y.: Cornell University Press, 1975).

"Betwixt and Between: The Liminal Period in Rites de Passage." In *Symposium on New Approaches to the Study of Religion*, edited by J. Helm, pp. 4–20. Proceedings of the American Ethnological Society. Seattle: University of Washington Press, 1964.

The Forest of Symbols: Aspects of Ndembu Ritual. Ithaca, N.Y.: Cornell University Press, 1967.

The Ritual Process: Structure and Anti-Structure. Chicago: Aldine, 1969.

"Liminal to Liminoid in Play, Flow, and Ritual: An Essay in Comparative Symbology." *Rice University Studies* 60.3 (1974): 53–92.

"Process, System, and Symbol: A New Anthropological Synthesis." *Daedalus* 106.1 (1977): 61–80.

From Ritual to Theater: The Human Seriousness of Play. New York: Performing Arts Journal Publications, 1982.

Turner, V. W., and E. Turner. *Image and Pilgrimage in Christian Culture: Anthropological Perspectives*. New York: Columbia University Press, 1978.

Other Works

Handelman, D. "Is Victor Turner Receiving His Intellectual Due?" *Journal of Ritual Studies* 7.2 (1993): 117–124.

—DON HANDELMAN

TYPE AND TOKEN are terms used to denote a distinction between the general and particular, class and class member, signified and sign. A type is that "which does not exist but governs existents, to which individuals conform" (Peirce, 1958, par. 313). Tokens, on the other hand, always exist in some particularized form.

In nature, types are manifested in the form of natural classes such as the elements, chemical compounds with analogous properties, and organisms. Conventional types, with personal or legislated meanings and uses, abound in art, literature, and law. Peirce regarded the type as the essential component of a token that makes the token what it is. The written terms & and *and* and the sound of the word *and* are tokens of a type reflected in the conventional system of English as a rule of conjunction. Within his system of signs, Peirce referred to types as legisigns and to tokens as sinsigns (as in singular). Using the same example, the word *and* as it appears in its dictionary entry refers to a type only fully understood within the framework of the syntax and semantics (i.e., laws) of English. But that *and* and all others found elsewhere in the dictionary are sinsigns because they are replicas of the legisign.

Type and token both have definite significant characters. In contrast, a sign that has indefinite significant character Peirce called a tone or qualisign. Thus, tone, token, and type regarded as types of signs are icon, index, and symbol; as types of thought process, they are manifested as term, proposition, and argument. Without some sort of distinction between type and token, language, mathematics, and probably all forms of representation would not be possible.

[*See also* Artificial Language; Goodman; *and* Peirce.]

BIBLIOGRAPHY

Peirce, C. S. *The Collected Papers of Charles Sanders Peirce*, vol. 8. Edited by A. Burks. Cambridge, Mass.: Harvard University Press, 1958.

—JOSEPH L. ESPOSITO

U–V

UMWELT. In everyday German, *umwelt* means simply "surroundings" or "environment," but through the work of the German biologist Jakob von Uexküll (1864–1944) the term, at least in scientific literature has acquired more specific semiotic meanings as the ecological niche as an animal perceives it; the experienced world, phenomenal world, or subjective universe; and the cognitive map or mind-set. Work with simple marine animals, especially sea urchins, convinced Uexküll of the subjective nature of signs received by a living organism. He found that environmental cues could only have an effect on the animal if the combination of stimuli was specific to the respective living being. "Beyond that," he observed in 1905, "the objects of the environment" do not exist for the sea urchin. Organisms from different species experience the world differently—that is, they have different *umwelts*. Uexküll uses a meadow flower to illustrate this: for the child who picks the flower, it is an ornamental object; for the ant walking along the stem, it is a path; when the cicada larva pierces the stem, the flower is transformed into a source of building materials; finally, the grazing cow transforms the flower stem into wholesome fodder. "Every action, therefore, that consists of perception and operation imprints its meaning on the meaningless object and thereby makes it into a subject-related meaning-carrier in the respective umwelt" (1982, p. 31).

Uexküll did not believe in Darwinian evolution, which he found absurd. But from the point of view of modern biology, the real scope of the *umwelt* theory becomes apparent only when the theory is interpreted in an evolutionary context. The *umwelt* theory tells us that it is not only genes, individuals, and species that survive but also—and perhaps rather—patterns of interpretation (Hoffmeyer, 1997). A creature's *umwelt* can be seen as the conquest of vital aspects of events and phenomena in the world around it, inasmuch as these aspects are continually turned by way of the senses into an integral part of the creature. The *umwelt* is the representation of the surrounding world within the creature.

The *umwelt* is also the creature's way of opening up to the world around it in that it allows selected aspects of that world to slip through in the form of signs. Even a moth's *umwelt*, otherwise so silent, has kept one chink open to admit the few fatal soundings of bats. The specific character of its *umwelt* allows a creature to become a part of the semiotic web found in that particular ecosystem. It becomes part of a worldwide horizontal semiosis.

The *umwelt* theory necessarily leads us to the epistemological problem of how scientists can study the *umwelts* of other animals when they themselves are bound to a human *umwelt*. "Everyone carries around with him his universe like a gigantic impenetrable bubble," wrote Unexküll in 1935. His son Thure von Uexküll has explained the epistemological position of *umweltsforschung* ("*umwelt* research") thus:

> Since the activity of our mind consists of the receiving and decoding of signs, the mind is, when all is said and done, an organ nature has created in order to perceive itself. So nature can be compared to a composer who listens to his own compositions, which he plays on an instrument he has created himself. There arises here, therefore, a strangely reciprocal relationship between nature, which has created mankind, and man, who creates nature, not only in his art and his science, but also in his subjective universe. . . . The aim of umwelt-research is to create a theory of the composition of nature, in other words, a score for the symphony of meanings that nature performs with the vast multiplicity of numberless Umwelts, as if playing on a gigantic keyboard on which our life and our umwelt constitute but one of the keys. (1982, pp. 3–4)

[*See also* Biosemiotics; Mindscape; *and* Receptors.]

BIBLIOGRAPHY

Hoffmeyer, J. *Signs of Meaning in the Universe*. Bloomington: Indiana University Press, 1997.
Uexküll, J. von. "The Theory of Meaning." *Semiotica* 42 (1982): 25–87.

Uexküll, T. von. "Introduction: Meaning and Science in Jakob von Uexküll's Concept of Biology." *Semiotica* 42 (1982): 1–24.

—JESPER HOFFMEYER

URBAN SEMIOTICS. The study of how significations are produced and communicated in and by the city, urban semiotics is conceived of as a complex semiotic process involving three sign systems: the built environment, the patterns of social interaction, and the means of communication. These interacting patterns change along historical time and from culture to culture. Urban semiotics comes under the purview of cultural and spatial semiotics. It includes subdisciplines such as semiotics of architecture, social behavior, and specific communicative media such as fashion, food, advertisements, design, and language.

The goal of urban semiotics is to investigate the cultural signs produced in the city, as well as specific processes through which the interaction of the three semiotic systems give the city its specific cultural profile. Therefore, urban semiotics also includes the study of self-referential urban sign systems (film, literature, art, videos, advertisements, maps, urban planning, virtual scenarios, architectural imitation, and other sign systems representing the city) inasmuch as they contribute to the processes of producing urban space, social order, and symbolic identity.

Self-representation has evolved over time. Before the emergence of the modern metropolis, in late eighteenth-century Europe, the city was a clearly delimited locality. Its material layout represented the social order, which in turn constituted a microcosmic representation of a larger order. Although the specific signification of such a sign complex varied from one culture to another, its basic semiotic structure persisted until the dawn of the modern urban structures.

In the modern industrial and postindustrial world, the role of the city has changed to become the horizon of modern culture. The modern city is an integral part of the ongoing transformation of the three basic sign systems involved in terms of both their internal structures and their interrelationships. The city as a dynamic signifying process constantly defines and redefines the borderline between the urban and the nonurban and ultimately the one between culture and nature. The contribution of urban semiotics to the understanding of modern culture as a whole thus has become important.

Urban semiotics offers two methodological approaches to this process. The first is the structural analysis of sign systems, emphasizing the immanent sign relations of the specific sign systems of the city and their interrelationships. The outcome is a description of the signs actually in use in a city at any given moment. On a synchronic level, the urban sign complex is seen as the sum of separate but interrelated specific subgroups of the three basic sign systems. The diachronic perspective is realized through a comparative analysis of specific sign systems in different epochs of urban history.

The second methodological approach is the phenomenological analysis of sign processes, which highlights the role of the subjects perceiving and using the urban signs and thereby stabilizing or changing the urban process. From this point of view, urban signs are analyzed according to the appeal or affordance by which they address the experiencing subject. On a synchronic level, urban sign systems are seen as forming a specific human environment (or *umwelt*) constituted by the perceptual and interpretative competencies of humans who are present bodily in the urban space and the material layout of the surroundings. A diachronic analysis focuses on how historical differences in the construction of urban sign systems are related to the changing role of our senses and bodily behavior and to new definitions of individual and social identity.

[*See also* Affordance; Architecture; Cultural Landscape; Cultureme; Distance; Mindscape; Space; *and* Umwelt.]

BIBLIOGRAPHY

Broadbent, G., R. Bunt, and C. Jencks, eds. *Signs, Symbols, and Architecture.* New York: Wiley, 1981.

Goffman, E. *Frame Analysis: An Essay on the Organization of Experience.* Cambridge, Mass.: Harvard University Press, 1974.

Gottdiener, M., and A. P. Lagopoulos, eds. *The City and the Sign: An Introduction to Urban Semiotics.* New York: Columbia University Press, 1986.

Kostof, S. *The City Shaped: Urban Pattern and Meanings through History.* Boston: Bulfinch Press, 1991.

Larsen, S. E. "Et in Arcadia Ego: A Spatial and Visual Analysis of the Urban Middle Space." In *The Semiotic Web 1992–93,* edited by T. A. Sebeok and J. D. Umiker-Sebeok, pp. 537–557. Berlin: Mouton de Gruyter, 1995.

Lynch, K. *The Image of the City*. Cambridge, Mass.: MIT Press, 1960.

Preziosi, D. *The Semiotics of the Built Environment: An Introduction to an Architectonic Analysis*. Bloomington: Indiana University Press, 1979.

Sennett, R. *The Conscience of the Eye: The Design and Social Life of Cities*. New York: Knopf, 1990.

Singer, M. *Semiotics of Cities, Selves, and Cultures: Explorations in Semiotic Anthropology*. Berlin: Mouton de Gruyter, 1991.

Tuan, Yi-Fu. *Space and Place: The Perspective of Experience*. Minneapolis: University of Minnesota Press, 1977.

—SVEND ERIK LARSEN

VALUE. Disciplines as varied as economics, philosophy, aesthetics, logic, linguistics, and via linguistics, semiotics all employ a concept of value, though with varying applications and meanings. In the work of Karl Marx, for example, the notion of value has foundational importance for an understanding of the dynamics of capitalism. Ferdinand de Saussure introduces the concept of linguistic value in his *Course in General Linguistics* (1916), in which it acts as the fulcrum of his general thesis about language. When Saussure attempts to explain linguistic value, he uses several different analogies, one of which invokes an economic resonance by comparing language with money.

Through the metaphor of currency, Saussure observes that money mediates exchange between both similar and dissimilar things. He notes that the worth of a particular coin can be compared with that of other coins in the same system of exchange. For example, a five-cent coin can be compared with a twenty-cent coin and exchanged for four times its value. Or, alternately, the worth of the twenty-cent coin can be measured against a fixed quantity of something dissimilar, such as flour. The amount of flour received in exchange for the coin determines the value of both. Like Marx before him, Saussure observes that concrete value does not inhere within a particular coin. He excludes the actual substance of the coin from this calculation and focuses instead on the functional equivalences and differences that make up a particular system of exchange. Through this economic analogy, Saussure hopes to explain the "paradoxical principle" whereby the value of a word derives from the place it occupies in a system and not from what appears to be the "substance" of the word itself. According to Saussure, "language is a form

and not a substance" (1974). Consequently, the nature of the linguistic sign is arbitrary.

The "sign" is the minimal unit of exchange that can be compared and contrasted within the system of language (*langue*). Saussure argues that the constitutive elements of the sign are mental and not physical. The sign, which Saussure routinely equates with individual words, unites a concept ("the signified") and a sound image ("the signifier"). The two parts of the sign are unified and inseparable, and their interdependence is called signification. The value of the sign, however, is produced through a relationship of interdependence with other signs. What makes a word work as a token of signification is "the concurrence of everything that exists outside it" (Saussure, 1974). Therefore, value makes signification possible.

There is some conceptual overlap between the notion of linguistic value and other concepts such as signification, sign, and system. For Saussure's critics, these terms are impossibly muddled and confused. However, it is in the paradox of their mired relationship that many poststructuralist theorists locate Saussure's most radical achievement. The interpretation of these concepts has consequently engendered considerable disagreement and debate.

One point of contention concerns the curious nature of the sign. On the one hand, value presumes a linguistic entity through which functional use and meaning is expressed, and Saussure devotes half of the *Course* to unraveling this aspect of the sign's identity. If, however, signification is internal to the sign, then the theory of value that involves an external system of relations (upon which signification is also dependent) becomes something of a contradiction. Within this relational interdependence, the identity of the sign becomes both stable and dynamic, circumscribed and open. Saussure is aware of the conflict here and explains that the concept of signification operates only "when we look upon the word as independent and self-contained" (1974). In other words, the self-enclosed unit of the sign is entirely undermined by the notion of value and is therefore more accurately understood as a provisional construct or heuristic entity rather than a linguistic fact. Unfortunately, this clarification addresses one problem by generating others. For example, when Saussure undermines the possibility of the sign's closure and displaces questions about semantics with descriptions of the economy of semiosis, he leaves out of his account any mention of meaning and reference. The heightened abstraction that results from this omission seems to threaten Saussure's whole thesis. Saussure's apparent inattention to semantics is, however, actually a reconceptualization of what meaning is and how it is produced, rather than a mere oversight.

This point is better explained by returning to the sign. Although previous conceptions of the sign also conceded its bipartite structure, Saussure's antecedents actually conjured with three terms; thing, word, and idea. Saussure departs radically from his predecessors when he cuts the sign adrift from the material world of objects and the representational-denominational theory of language. In other words, for Saussure, meaning is constituted not by reference to extralinguistic entities but rather in and through the semiotic process itself.

As language is a form and not a substance, the connection between the sign and the thing is arbitrary. But there is a consistent conflation in Saussure's text of the signified and the thing itself. Amid this confusion, Saussure employs the mimetic logic of nomenclaturism (naming theory) that he argues against elsewhere and inadvertently implies that the relationship between sign and thing is motivated and not arbitrary (see Benveniste, 1971). Comparing the different signifiers *ox* and *boeuf*, Saussure presumes that they share the same signified. Saussure also contrasts *sheep* in the English language system with *mouton* in the French. He argues that although *mouton* has the same signification as *sheep*, it does not have the same value. He attributes this difference to the fact that *sheep* has another word, *mutton*, which sits "beside it" to describe a serving of the cooked meat, a linguistic distinction that is not present in French. Yet if these words have an arbitrary relationship to the thing itself, and if value undermines signification's return to naming theory, then according to Saussure's own argument there can be no equivalence between signifiers from different language systems. By explaining value in terms of an extralinguistic referent, Saussure recuperates the previous conceptual conventions of linguistics and thereby elides what is arguably his most radical contribution to contemporary semiotic and philosophical thought.

It is important to emphasize Saussure's perception that thinking is inseparable from the operations of the language system. Saussure believes that language does not name a world whose meanings exist prior

to language because it is only through language that the world is made meaningful. "Instead of pre-existing ideas then, we find . . . values emanating from the system. When they are said to correspond to concepts, it is understood that the concepts are purely differential and defined not by their positive content but negatively by their relations with the other terms of the system" (Saussure, 1974, p. 117). According to this view, language is not a passive reflection of the world but rather something that actively constitutes it, an economy with productive force. Saussure's thesis can be interpreted as a direct attack on logical positivism and empiricism, which in their different ways both appeal to an extralinguistic real world to verify truth claims. For Saussureans, however, "truth" is a linguistic category produced within language. As the human condition prevents unmediated access to the real world, nature cannot provide the ground for logical, ethical, and political calculations.

The implications of this thesis are considerable, especially those deriving from Saussure's assertion that the source of linguistic value is difference: "In language there are only differences without positive terms" (1974). If the sign is constituted through its relationship with other signs—that is, if it is negatively delimited—then according to Saussure difference is organized through a binary dependence between presence and absence. This belief that linguistic difference is produced through oppositional relationships is foundational for the structuralist movement, which models the analysis of all cultural production on this linguistic insight. For example, Claude Lévi-Strauss argues in *Structural Anthropology* (1958) that the human mind organizes information through binary structures and that evidence of these inherent oppositions is manifest in cross-cultural data, in social organization, marriage rules, the structure of myths and legends, and, indeed, in all human endeavors.

Poststructuralism, however, while acknowledging its structuralist inheritance, critiques the concept of difference as opposition. If the language system is made up of differences (values) that constitute identity and yet is truly absent and separate from the identity it is supposed to produce, then this process of semiosis could have no effect. As the notion of value entirely replaces that of identity or entity for Saussure, his work implies that the identity of the system—its border and integrity—is just as problematic as that of the sign. Indeed, value undermines the very possibility of definition, as there can be no discrete and self-defined existence of any sort. This in turn raises questions about the anchor of all linguistic and cultural analysis—namely, the identity or unity of the interpreter, the thinking and speaking subject.

If the language system already includes whatever it defines itself against, then, as Jacques Derrida argues, there can be no "outside" of language. Clearly, language in this general sense is entirely reconceptualized, a move that is anticipated by Saussure when he muses that linguistics will be subsumed under a general science of signs that he called semiology. Saussure's semiology has since become Derrida's grammatology (1967), with Saussure's "sign" given much greater complexity in Derrida's notion of "the trace." Derrida's argument is also informed by the philosophies of Friedrich Nietzsche and Martin Heidegger because, in their different ways, they each interrogate the essence of valuation itself: the logic that measures the binary structures of good and evil, truth and falsity, and time and eternity.

Through the interconnecting weave of the trace, value as difference becomes a "textile" that exceeds the binary opposition of presence versus absence or signifier versus signified. For example, this play of differences can no longer be confined to linguistics or, indeed, to semiotics because difference also inscribes the cinematic, the choreographic, the painterly, the genetic, and so on. In other words, the divide that separates one category from another, one identity from its binary opposite—even nature from culture—is rendered undecidable. A poststructuralist rereading of Saussurean value recognizes that the opposition of presence and absence is a hierarchical relationship, a logic of *a* and *not-a* rather than *a* and *b*. The politics of this division whereby presence is privileged over absence, such that absence is interpreted as a lack of presence, has been described as a sexualized and sexualizing division by many poststructuralist and feminist writers; *man* is the positive term and *woman* the negative. The logic of this political economy, said to inform all writing and thinking, has been described as both logocentric and phallocentric. The representation of cultural difference is also inscribed within this same logic and, because it again measures difference in binary terms, is described as ethnocentric. In view of these broader issues, the question of value remains at the center of contemporary debate within semiotics.

[*See also* Cultural Difference; Deconstruction; Pertinence; Postcolonialism; Poststructuralism; Saussure; *and* Structuralism.]

BIBLIOGRAPHY

Benveniste, É. *Problems in General Linguistics.* Translated by M. E. Meek. Coral Gables, Fla.: University of Miami Press, 1971.

Culler, J. *Ferdinand de Saussure.* Ithaca, N.Y.: Cornell University Press, 1986.

Derrida, J. *Of Grammatology* (1967). Translated by G. C. Spivak. Baltimore and London: Johns Hopkins University Press, 1984.

Gadet, F. *Saussure and Contemporary Culture.* Translated by G. Elliot. London: Hutchinson Radius, 1989.

Harris, R. *Reading Saussure: A Critical Commentary on the Cours de Linguistique Générale.* London: Duckworth, 1987.

Jay, G. S. "Values and Deconstructions: Derrida, Saussure, Marx." *Cultural Critique* 8 (1987–1988): 153–196.

Lévi-Strauss, C. *Structural Anthropology* (1958). Translated by C. Jacobson and B. G. Schoepf. London: Allen Lane, 1968.

Marx, K. *Capital: A Critique of Political Economy*, vol. 1. Translated by B. Fowkes. New York: Vintage, 1977.

Saussure, F. de. *Course in General Linguistics.* Edited by C. Bally and A. Sechehaye, translated by W. Baskin. London: Fontana Collins, 1974.

Weber, S. "Saussure and the Apparition of Language." *Modern Language Notes* 91 (1976): 913–938.

—VICKI KIRBY

VICO, GIAMBATTISTA (1668–1744), Italian philosopher and professor of rhetoric at the University of Naples. Vico's ideas have long fascinated scholars in a great variety of fields of knowledge. Often considered an inspiration for such contemporary movements as structuralism, pragmatism, new historicism, Marxism, and deconstruction, his writings range across topics such as the cyclical nature of history, the origin of language and mythical thinking, the creative role of the imagination, and the nature of truth. Vico's work lies behind many major figures of contemporary thought: Jules Michelet, Karl Marx, Sir Isaiah Berlin, Benedetto Croce, Erich Auerbach, Kenneth Burke, and Jacques Derrida, as well as James Joyce, who, old and blind, hired an Italian native to read him Vico's most important work, *La scienza nuova* (The New Science, 1725).

Vico's ideas on interpretation and language seem his most revolutionary and the ones most important for semiotic studies. Vico stands in radical opposition to the Enlightenment context that surrounded him.

For the Enlightenment, interpretation is a science of knowing facts, an attempt at grasping ultimate truths. But Vico contests that notion of interpretation with his famous dictum *"verum et factum convertuntur"* ("the true is the made"). The ideal standard for an interpretive work in the Enlightenment was that it should represent reality truthfully, but when Vico challenged that standard, he was quickly aligned with the eighteenth-century derogatory notion of the "mythical" or "the irrational." For Vico, the "irrational" expressions of the past are "truthful narrations," since they were created according to a "poetic" rather than a rational logic. Against the dogma of rationalism, Vico proposes that true knowledge is valid only insofar as it is a creative understanding of a communal past. Moreover, he proposes that what humans can know about the external world is superficial compared with the knowledge of things they themselves create—and humans create not only when they know but when they act, imagine, and desire. Thus, because of the contingent nature of these activities, interpretation is no longer tied to eternal or changeless principles and laws but requires a profound understanding of the cultural work that interpretation performs in a given historical period.

If humans can know only what they themselves have made, the relationship between the knower and the outside world shifts radically, especially in the human sciences. Rather than conceiving of the world as something available for knowledge, Vico envisions it as known only as far as the knower produces it through a faculty of imagination Vico calls *fantasia*. Vico is perhaps at his most radical when he articulates a relationship between interpretation, imagination, and language to create what he calls a poetic logic.

For Vico, poetic logic encapsulates the way in which humans—especially "primitives"—apprehend and signify the world. In *The New Science*, Vico claims that since the first humans were "stupid, insensate, and horrible beasts," they did not rationalize but "felt and imagined" (par. 375). When the first inhabitants of the world, whom Vico calls giants, hear the sound of thunder for the first time, they are unable to understand rationally what it is and so interpret it as God communicating with them. The logic of these primitives differs from those of rational humans in the way they characterize things; interpreting the sound of thunder as a God is an interpretative move

from the known to the unknown, from the familiar to the unfamiliar. The example of the giants is important for Vico because in it lies the key to what he understands by interpretation and knowledge: the attribution of familiar qualities to unfamiliar objects. To put it differently, interpretation and knowledge are intricately related to the process of naming.

Vico understands the naming process as being dependent on his views of myth and metaphor. Whereas the Enlightenment associates myths with useless, untrue stories, Vico suggests that the heroes of mythology should be understood as "poetic characters" (*caratteri poetici*). By the use of the word *character*, meaning both "person" and "written sign," Vico proposes that these heroes express ideas in concrete forms. These heroes, products of popular sources, of common sense, or of the lingustic and ethical beliefs that tie a community together, are the clearest examples available to us of the primitive mode of thought that Vico claims gave rise to human society and culture. Vico is frequently championed as the originator of what is currently known as tropology on account of his statement that the evolution of societies follows the mental operations indicated by metaphor, metonymy, synecdoche, and irony. But this tropological progression always hinges on the centrality Vico places on metaphor, which he describes as "the most luminous and therefore the most necessary." Vico links metaphors and myths together in his statement that "every metaphor is a fable in brief" (1725, par. 404). By *fable*, Vico refers to the naming operation through which something unknown becomes known. Because that naming operation is based on similarities, Vico concludes that every act of interpretation is in fact a metaphor. And since to be known the world has to be interpreted, Vico concludes that the world does not exist until it becomes, in fact, a metaphoric creation.

Vico's reputation and centrality in the humanities has already been well established. But this reputation has flourished primarily in fields such as philosophy, legal studies, and the history of ideas. It is only comparatively recently that scholars have noted the tremendous influence his ideas have on questions of interpretation and literary criticism. When he challenged the reigning mode of interpretation of his times, Vico set the agenda that has produced much of what we understand as interpretation today.

[*See also* Meaning; Metaphor; *and* Poetics.]

BIBLIOGRAPHY

The New Science of Giambattista Vico. Translated by T. G. Bergin and M. H. Fisch. Ithaca, N.Y.: Cornell University Press, 1968.

Danesi, M. *Vico, Metaphor, and the Origin of Language*. Bloomington: Indiana University Press, 1993.

Lilla, M. *G. B. Vico: The Making of an Anti-Modern*. Cambridge, Mass.: Harvard University Press, 1993.

Schaeffer, J. D. *Sensus Communis: Vico, Rhetoric, and the Limits of Relativism*. Durham, N.C., and London: Duke University Press, 1990.

Verene, D. P. *Vico's Science of Imagination*. Ithaca, N.Y., and London: Cornell University Press, 1981.

—GUSTAVO GUERRA

VIENNA CIRCLE. In 1922, philosophically minded physicist Moritz Schlick went from Kiel, Germany, to the University of Vienna to become the fourth occupant of the chair in the philosophy of the inductive sciences, which was founded originally for Ernst Mach in 1895. Building on the generally positivist tradition in Vienna at the time, Schlick gathered around him a group of scientists, logicians, and philosophers that became known as the Vienna Circle. In August 1929, in order to celebrate Schlick's decision to remain in Vienna, the Circle put out a famous pamphlet outlining its conception of science and philosophy, *Wissenschaftliche Weltauffassung: Der Wiener Kreis* (Scientific World Conception: The Vienna Circle). Written by Otto Neurath with the editorial help of Rudolf Carnap and Hans Hahn, the monograph lists the following members of the Circle: Schlick, Neurath, Carnap, Hahn, Gustav Bergmann, Herbert Feigl, Philipp Frank, Kurt Gödel, Victor Kraft, Karl Menger, Marcel Natkin, Olga Hahn-Neurath, Theodor Radakovic, and Friedrich Waismann. The Circle worked closely with other contemporary Viennese intellectuals, including Edgar Zilsel, Karl Popper, and Ludwig Wittgenstein. As a clue to the self-conception of the Circle, the monograph listed Wittgenstein, Albert Einstein, and Bertrand Russell as the leading representatives of the scientific conception of the world.

Along with a related group of thinkers in Berlin that included Hans Reichenbach and Carl Hempel, the Circle was a leading exponent of logical positivism or logical empiricism. Logical empiricism was based in the Circle's interpretation of the logical atomism of Russell's work in the late 1910s and early 1920s and of Wittgenstein's *Tractatus Logico-Philosophicus* (1922). The chief idea of logical empiricism is that truth divides into two distinct types: empirical truths that make claims about the world and logical truths that are true by virtue of linguistic conventions and that make no claims about the world. Any putative truth that could not be placed univocally into one of these two groups is cast aside as meaningless. The casualties of this procedure were supposed to be largely the theses of traditional metaphysics, whether conceived of as synthetic a priori truths in Immanuel Kant's sense or as contentful theses about a world beyond experience in the sense of Leibnizian rationalism or Hegelian absolute idealism.

The Vienna Circle viewed its philosophical task as a consideration of the language systems of science. In large part, they were concerned with elaborating the theses stated above. They made a principled distinction between empirical and logical truth and provided a workable criterion of empirical significance that could accommodate high-level theoretical claims while showing how metaphysics is meaningless. These are related tasks, since failure to distinguish between logical and empirical truth renders it less likely that a criterion of significance could divide all of science, including mathematics and logic, from metaphysics.

The solution to the problem of the criterion of empirical significance that was most attractive to some members of the Circle is verification. A typical expression of this point of view is found in Schlick's paper, "Realismus und Positivismus" ("Realism and Positivism," 1932–1933):

> A statement has a specifiable meaning only if it makes a verifiable [*prüfbaren*] difference whether it is true or false. A sentence which is such that the world looks precisely the same whether it be true or false therefore says utterly nothing about the world; it is empty and communicates nothing; I cannot give it a meaning. We have a *verifiable* difference, however, only when it is a difference in the given. . . .

Of course, the given simply is experience. Thus, the verification criterion requires every sentence to have specifiable experiential verification conditions if it is to be counted as empirically meaningful. In essence, this amounts to a way of translating all empirical science, sentence by sentence, into a language of experience. It is easy to see the point of the verification criterion, since metaphysical claims such as "all truth is one" seem to have no specifiable experiential content and are therefore meaningless. On the other hand, it is hard to see what experiential difference a claim such as "electrons have spin one-half" has when taken out of the context of a quantum theory and considered individually. As many have argued—most notably Willard V. O. Quine in his seminal article "Two Dogmas of Empiricism" (1953)—sentence-by-sentence translation into a language of experience is far too strict a criterion of empirical significance since almost all of science fails that test. This point was registered fairly early by members of the Vienna Circle, and several, including Carnap, tried to weaken the condition while preserving the philosophical work it was intended to do.

Not all of the Circle's rejections of metaphysics relied on verification or, indeed, on any notion of empirical significance. For example, Carnap's famous reflections in his "Überwindung der Metaphysik durch logische Analyse der Sprache" ("Overcoming of Metaphysics through Logical Analysis of Language," 1931) on Heidegger's discussion of Nothing do not ask for the empirical sense of Heidegger's claims but rely only on logic to reject them. Carnap's leading idea is that any discussion of any topic must allow regimentation into a syntactically precise and univocal logical language—hence Carnap's rejection of Heidegger's famous statement "The Nothing itself nothings" as meaningless. In essence, Carnap attempts to regiment Heidegger's language into first-order logic and thus discovers that Heidegger is being ambiguous in his use of the word *nothing*. Sometimes *nothing* simply plays the standard role of a negative existential quantifier, as in "What is to be investigated is Being and nothing else," which is to say, "We must examine exactly one topic, Being." Elsewhere, the word is used as a name of an object, and still elsewhere it is used as a predicate. On Carnap's view, Heideggerian philosophy violates syntactical rules and is an effort to take deeply serious certain surface ambiguities of natural language that are best treated as sources of jokes, as in Lewis Carroll's *Through the Looking Glass* (1872).

Carnap's argument against Heidegger exhibits his view of philosophy as a discipline that offers well-understood formal languages for use in the sciences. Such languages make precise the meanings of scientific claims and render a service in understanding and testing such claims. For Carnap, to recommend a language was to offer a precise account of the logical framework of it. This was done in large measure through an account of those sentences in the language that count as analytic truths in it. Such sentences partially constitute the meanings of the terms in them. Thus, for Carnap, making a sharp distinction between logical truth and empirical truth is crucial. Famously, Quine has also called into question Carnap's distinction between synthetic and analytic truth (1953).

Quine's understanding of Carnap on this point divides the philosophical point of analyticity into two parts. First, Carnap wants to show that empiricism is compatible with the existence of truths that we can know with certainty, including logical truths, mathematical truths, and truths such as "all bachelors are unmarried." Second, empiricism is compatible with the certainty of such truths because the account of analyticity will show that these truths are not contentful claims about the world but are guaranteed by the meanings of the terms contained in them. Thus, these truths, being independent of the vagaries of experience, will be verified come what may. Quine's objection to this again relies on holism. If experiential consequences cannot be specified on a sentence-by-sentence basis, then this way of working out analyticity will not work; verification makes sense only when larger blocks of theory are taken together as corporate bodies.

There is, however, a second way of reading Carnap on the philosophical point of analyticity. Rather than trying to allow room for certainty within empiricism, Carnap can be seen as trying to show the priority of logical notions over epistemological ones. On the second reading, Carnap is not trying to show that analytic truths are independent of the vagaries of verification; rather, as principles constitutive of meaning, truths must be in place before any question of verification has a determinate sense. On this reading, Carnap's view has a more Kantian flavor: analytic sentences are not simply those that do best on the measure of verification by experience; rather, they provide the conditions without which there could be no verification of theoretical sentences by experience at all.

Another theme in the work of the Vienna Circle—and one that has not received much attention—is the unity of science. Given their linguistic leanings, the unit of science was most usually expressed as a commitment to the possibility of and a search for a language for science within which all matters of fact can be stated. The unity of science is frequently associated with verificationism and a strict reductionist tendency of thought. But it is clear that Neurath and Carnap both held nonreductionist versions of this hypothesis from the mid-1930s onward. This nonreductionist version of the thesis guided the most ambitious publication project attempted (but not completed) by the Circle, Neurath's "*Encyclopedia of Unified Science.*" For Neurath, the encyclopedic form was ideally suited to the notion of nonreductive unity he saw in the sciences, since an encyclopedia refers the reader back and forth from topic to topic without imposing any particular order of intellectual priority among the entries.

The discussions of the unity of science in the Circle hark back at least to disputes in Germany and Austria among generally neo-Kantian authors about the unity of method and structure in the sciences. Some thinkers, such as Heinrich Rickert and Wilhelm Dilthey, thought that the social sciences were methodologically distinct from the natural sciences, while others, such as Ernst Cassirer and Paul Natorp, argued for a thoroughgoing unity. The theme of unity is, moreover, an expression of perhaps Neurath's and Carnap's deepest philosophical commitment to the importance of intersubjective communication and reasoned agreement in the sciences and in life generally. For both of these philosophers, this commitment went beyond their academic lives: for Carnap, it was expressed through an interest in international languages such as Esperanto; for Neurath, it informed his development of a system for the visual representation of information, ISOTYPE (an acronym for International System of Typographic Picture Education), which is one ancestor of the international picture codes used today (Neurath, 1973).

The Vienna Circle ceased its official weekly meetings in 1936, the year that Schlick was murdered on the steps of the university. During the roughly fourteen years of its existence, it became an important voice within European philosophy. It provided a forum for many individuals and groups—notably Alfred Tarski and other Polish logicians—with interests in scientific knowledge, logic, and language. It was also a point of contact between European and English language philosophy, enticing A. J. Ayer to visit from Oxford and Quine from Harvard early in their careers. In the early 1930s, the encyclopedia project was joined by University of Chicago semiotician and pragmatist philosopher Charles Morris, who served as a coeditor of the project with Neurath and Carnap. Morris also provided an important contact in North America for Circle members during their flights from Nazism.

The surviving members of the Vienna Circle had an even greater impact on North American intellectual life after World War II. Bergmann, Feigl, and Carnap, along with Reichenbach and Hempel were instrumental in making logical empiricism a dominant theme in postwar American philosophy. Gödel was a leading intellectual light at the Institute for Advanced Study in Princeton, New Jersey, where he solidified his reputation as one of the finest logicians in the world. Many of the particular philosophical proposals of the Vienna Circle members have since been criticized and rejected, but the continuing influence of logic and logical analysis, as well as interest in language and meaning within contemporary analytic philosophy, especially in the realm of scientific theorizing, speaks to a continuing influence of the scientific world conception that guided their work.

[*See also* Cassirer; Russell; *and* Wittgenstein.]

BIBLIOGRAPHY

Carnap, R. "Überwindung der Metaphysik durch logische Analyse der Sprache." *Erkenntnis* 2 (1931): 219–241.

Carnap, R. "The Elimination of Metaphysics through Logical Analysis of Language." In *Logical Positivism*, edited by A. J. Ayer, pp. 60–81. New York: Free Press, 1959.

Neurath, O. "From Vienna Method to Isotype." In *Empiricism and Sociology*, edited by M. Neurath and R. S. Cohen, pp. 214–248. Dordrecht: D. Reidel, 1973.

Neurath, O., R. Carnap, and H. Hahn. "The Scientific Conception of the World: The Vienna Circle." In *Empiricism and Sociology*, edited by M. Neurath and R. S. Cohen. Dordrecht: D. Reidel, 1973.

Quine, W. V. O. "Two Dogmas of Empiricism." In his *From a Logical Point of View*, pp. 20–46. Cambridge, Mass.: Harvard University Press, 1953.

Schlick, M. "Positivism and Realism." In *Moritz Schlick: Philosophical Papers*, vol. 2, edited by H. L. Mulder and B. F. B. van de Velde-Schlick, pp. 259–284. Dordrecht: D. Reidel, 1979.

Wittgenstein, L. *Tractatus Logico-Philosophicus.* London: Routledge, Kegan Paul, 1922.

—ALAN RICHARDSON

VISION. As the sensory system that is stimulated by the energy in light and transduced into nervous impulses by receptors in the eyes, vision's chief function is to extract information in optic patterns and events. The study of vision involves analyses of energy, pattern, information, meaning, and communication via visible displays.

The energy in light consists of individual packets or photons that are capable of modifying the activity of individual receptors in the eye, but most of the information in light depends on the patterns in the optic array that affect banks of receptors in the retina of the eye simultaneously. A single ray of light has an intensity and a wavelength (with longer wavelengths of about 650 nanometers generally appearing red and shorter wavelengths of about 400 nanometers generally appearing violet). A pattern of light contains more information since it can allow a viewer to recognize objects, notice depth and spatial arrangements, detect the useful properties of surfaces, and communicate. The patterns in light have significance that depends on both natural factors, like the changes that indicate a fruit is ripening, and artificial conditions, like the exaggerations in caricatures.

Vision depends in the first instance on sources of light. One or more luminous bodies, like the sun, must provide light. Typically, the light is reflected by the surfaces of nonluminous bodies before forming an optic array that enters the eye. The reflected light can be rereflected time and again before constituting an optic array accessible to vision: for example, the sun's light can be reflected by the moon, and moonlight can be reflected by a lake, and then by a tree, before providing an optic array "for the eye." The arrival of light from the tree does not ensure that the tree can be seen. The environment of the tree and the observer must meet strict conditions if the tree is to be visible: the light from the tree will not provide information about it if it is diffused too much by a fog, or if background light sources provide glare. Also, the pattern of light in the optic array from the tree can be broken up by shadows falling on the tree. Further, the background for the tree might be so similar to the tree's contours, color, and texture that the tree's borders are not distinct visually. Also, at night, if the light from the tree is too similar to light from other objects, such as rocks, then it would be ambiguous. Therefore, while vision depends on light for energy, it also needs an appropriate environment for visual patterns to be distinct.

In the second instance, vision relies on a medium for transmission of light—chiefly, space, air, water,

and glass. The medium is clear or murky in various degrees. The terrestrial daytime sky is blue because blue light cannot penetrate the atmospheric medium as readily as red light can. Blue's short wavelengths are comparatively readily reflected by atmospheric particles. Hence, no matter where the observer looks, blue light will be reflected toward the observer. A sun at sunset will look deep red if its blue light has been severely scattered by a heavy concentration of atmospheric particles and only its red light can penetrate directly to the observer. Water scatters all wavelengths more than air does, with the result that patterned vision in water is restricted to a few feet. Abyssal depths are dark because light from the surface waters has been scattered back to the surface—the deeper the water, the more scattering has occurred.

Attempts to manipulate the medium, controlling the direction of light rays and shadows, have produced various spectacles, microscopes and telescopes, windows, and sensory aids.

For vision to occur, the eye itself must accept optic input from the medium. The curved transparent front of the eye (the cornea), aided by the lens in a chamber behind the cornea, brings the entering optic array to a focus on the light-sensitive retina at the back of the eye, with the bulging cornea having a fixed focusing power and the lens being variable. In the retina, optic energy is transduced into electrochemical action by the sensory receptors, some of which (the "cones") are especially sensitive to light of particular wavelengths, while others (the "rods") are much less selective. The cones are found chiefly in the fovea—the center of the eye—which insures that color vision is present only in the central four or five degrees of vision. The rods are much more sensitive than the cones, and since they are the only receptors that can operate in low-light conditions, such as night vision, which is as a result colorless.

The fourth link in the chain of events underpinning vision is the neuronal functions of transmission to different nervous-system centers, analysis in each of the centers, and then reactions subsequent to the analysis, including feedback to the previous levels of analysis. Some of the feedback is straightforward and easy to observe since it includes adjustments to the eye via muscles attached to the eye, blinking, and changing the focal length of the lens or the radius of the iris. Some of the feedback is less observable, since it occurs entirely within the nervous system, "higher" neuronal centers controlling "lower" ones in order to serve the functions of attention, for example.

The first transmissions between visual neurons occur when the rod and cone receptors synapse with other neurons in the retina. A network of connections, involving three kinds of cells (horizontals, bipolars, and amacrines, in that order), is at work in the retina before connections are ever made with the ganglion cells that carry visual information out of the eye toward the brain. Consequently, considerable visual analysis occurs entirely within the eye itself. Physiological recordings from ganglion cells reveal considerable sophistication in the kind of optic stimulus controlling their responses or "firing rates" of nervous signals. Some ganglion cells accept influences from retinal receptors in a large retinal region or field. The receptive field may be organized so that light in the center of the field increases the ganglion cell's firing rate, while light in a surrounding annulus decreases the firing rate. This is called a center-on/surround-off receptive field. The receptive fields show that pattern analysis begins in the eye itself.

The ganglion cells have a relay station on the way to the brain: the lateral geniculate nucleus (LGN). Feedback systems from two brain areas (the reticular activating system, having to do with general levels of arousal or wakefulness, and the visual cortex, having to do with visual analysis) reach the LGN. This means that higher brain functions have a modifying effect on visual information at their very first opportunity after visual information leaves the eye. The kinds of modifications this can produce are not yet clear, though the LGN's signals seem to be either strengthened or weakened by the feedback input.

Besides feedback, three additional principles are evident in the organization of LGNs. Each LGN has six layers, and each layer is a map of the retina, referred to as the retinotopic principle. Two of the layers—the magnocellular layers—have comparatively large cells, and they accept stimulation from light of any color in their retinal receptive fields. Four—the parvocellular layers—have smaller cells, and each cell is differentially sensitive to the color of light in their retinal receptive fields. This is strong evidence for a "modular" or feature-pathway principle in vision. Indeed, color and intensity features often have quite different pathways in vision. Strikingly, the color-difference parvo cells hardly respond to rapid motion in their retinal receptive fields, while the brightness magno cells are readily stimulated by

rapid motion. Thus, different pathways emerge for moving and static stimuli also. A third principle in the LGN organization is the influence of binocular organization. Adjacent layers in the LGN accept input from different eyes. These layers in turn feed to cells in the occipital cortex in such a way that a cortical cell might respond most strongly when it receives binocular input—that is, input from an LGN cell controlled by the right-eye receptive field and input from another LGN cell controlled by the left eye.

Each synaptic relay station offers an opportunity for successive stages of analysis to become more specialized in vision. The next relay after the LGN is primarily the occipital cortex, which feeds a succession of further relay stations in the brain. Firing cells in the cerebral cortex can require more complex signals in the eye than firing bipolars in the retina or magnocellular layers in the LGN, for example. Brain regions that receive input from the visual cortex can be still more specialized. One such region is the medial temporal region in the temporal lobe, which is highly specialized for the analysis of visual motion. Another is a second temporal region that is specialized for complex familiar patterns such as faces or species such as birds. Another is the parietal region, which is important in visual and likely in tactile space perception, often concerned with egocentric localization in a three-dimensional space. The result of increasing specialization is that a single cell in the cortex can respond to a signal such as binocular inspection of a straight contour with a well-marked terminus, moving swiftly left to right, while another single cell favors a human facial configuration.

Relay stations in the cerebral hemispheres have many feedback systems that serve many functions besides directing and redirecting attention. They might help pattern analysis by changing decisions about whether to apply one character-recognition system or another (to decide, for example, if a character is a B or a 13); they might govern the implications of recognizing an object (e.g., insuring its expression is examined once it is decided that the object is a face); and they might help group features or objects, once a higher center deems that the items are all of one kind with visual differences due merely to their orientations, illumination factors, depth, and, say, age and sex. The existence of many feedback loops and cross-connections between higher visual centers means human vision might be capable of being modified by many influences. The result is an unanswered puzzle: how far can vision be transformed by personal or cultural differences.

In the employment of muscles, the principles of control in the visual system, with higher relay stations altering the work of centers of activity that input to them, operate widely and straightforwardly. The observer can affect the direction and coordination of the two eyes via the six extraocular muscles attached to them. But in addition, vision is served by the whole body platform for vision. The neck muscles contribute by turning the head to see what is on the visual periphery, bringing a peripheral object onto the central fovea or region of highest acuity. The torso does the same to help see what is behind the observer. The entire body is used to locomote to see around an obstacle blocking vision, to see the rear of an object, and to explore an environment. The feet are as much a part of the system controlling vision as are the muscles attached to the actual eyeball.

Vision occurs within an environment as the observer moves, changing his or her vantage point. For vision to be useful, the optic patterns at particular vantage points and the changes in pattern that accompany motion must provide unambiguous information. Evidently, the optic relations between surfaces, texture, opacity, and illumination provide distinctive optic events that indicate matters of depth, vantage points, and motion.

Surfaces define objects, objects in turn fall into different types, myriads of classes and subclasses. However, there is visible order in the many kinds of objects. The principles on which animals and their motions are based are different than the principles on which plants are based, which in turn are different than the principles on which the inanimate terrain is based, and so on. Mountains and coastlines, for example, have particular fractal structures. Plants tend to be based on the principle of a branching stalk. Among mammals, a plan involving head, body, and limbs is followed, with variations more matters of proportion than changes of plan. The classes of objects in the natural world do not admit gradations: there is no continuum between a dog and a tree, with some objects being more tree than dog and some being more dog than tree. The world of artificial objects in practice also contains few gradations: there is no object midway between a dog and a tree. The principles that constrain natural objects are the inexorable laws of continents, erosion, and evolution.

Artificial objects are less constrained because of whimsy and deliberate eschewing of practicality, but in the main, perception of types of object has available to it remarkable, detailed information in light from natural objects and serviceable information, barring deliberate camouflage and staged decor, in the world of artifice.

Perception requires a vantage point. Consequently, perspective is an ever-present influence on perception. Perspective is a clear case of an important aspect of perception: to use perspective, the perceptual system must in some respects have available to it a capacity for computation. It is now thought that vision in some fashion engages in several kinds of computations, such as Fourier analysis and calculus. Perspective is certainly an instance where the raison d'être of vision's mathematical component is clear. When an object is presented to the vantage point, its front facet must subtend a larger angle than its rear. If the front face of a cube subtends fifty-three degrees at the vantage point, the rear face subtends about half of this. However, when the front face subtends one degree, the rear face subtends almost that much. The ratio of front-to-rear subtense changes as the subtenses grow and the cube approaches the vantage point. In order for vision to appreciate that a solid object is not altering its shape as its distance changes, it must be able to calculate the appropriate ratio at each angular subtense. It must also relate this to the proportions of the object, for a long block could have a front face subtend fifty-three degrees when the rear face subtends one degree. Vision is in fact responsive to the ratios of angular subtenses and how these are related to an object's actual angular subtense. Hence, perspective is not just a formal geometry of the environment but one that vision employs.

Vision has strict limits, despite its ability to employ unambiguous environmental information and influences from higher brain centers serving recognition or mathematical calculations. Certain types of objects are entirely conceptual and cannot be perceived. One can define a category of objects that cannot be perceived, but by definition no instance of it can ever be perceived. Other instances are "no object" or "an infinite length." Hence, vision must serve conception by tuning the observer to some geometrical facts of the environment and to many types of objects, but comprehension has to go beyond vision. Vision allows metonymy, but the appreciation of the possible significance of the individual must on some occasions go beyond what a visual pattern can unambiguously specify.

The study of vision at present has limits, too, that are just as imposing as the limits on vision itself. The principles used in the study of vision notably include "retinotopic maps," "modular organization," and "specificity of information." However, if vision succeeds in creating a map or model of the three-dimensional environment inside the brain, that cannot explain vision. A copy is not an understanding. A copy needs some further action, as if by a homunculus, to make its information known. Further, color cannot be copied at all by any neuronal center. That is to say, no neuronal center can turn red or yellow. Hence, the search in physiology for retinotopic organization in higher brain centers cannot be the final goal of theorists of perception.

Modular organization is evident in the fact that complex visual signals are needed to fire single cells in higher brain centers. However, analysis of a perceptual input by a single cell is not possible. No single cell can indicate anything more than its own firing rate or change of firing rate. A population of cells is needed to support a percept of a complex object. The different pathways evident in vision, leading to specialized single-cell detectors, superficially suggest that vision breaks down the input into different features. In some fashion, these individual features, each reflected in different pathways, need to be coordinated into a single percept. Vision needs to know not only that there is something shiny and something furry, something circular and something square, something still and something moving but that there is a circular furry moving thing—a tennis ball—and a square, shiny still thing: a sheet of paper.

Specificity of optical, patterned information is necessary for vision to have something useful available to it, but the visual system cannot wait to decide whether an incoming pattern x is sufficiently distinctive. That is, it cannot gather information about other patterns and compare these with pattern x prior to deciding what pattern x might betoken. Vision must be capable of responding to patterned information without comparisons. In principle, the very existence of optical information requires that pattern x be distinctive in comparison to others, but vision must resonate entirely to pattern x, not to potential comparisons. Hence, distinctive information sets the conditions under which a visual system is usable, but in the actual workings of vision as a computational system, comparisons are not present. In principle, vision must compute, not compare. The distinctions between patterns that make the computations useful are not straightforwardly reflected in those computations.

In short, vision is an information-obtaining system using sophisticated connections borne by relay stations, relying on accurate optical information governed by the laws of an environment including laws of illumination and media. Vision uses transduction, transmission, mapping, modular specialization, and pattern computation to regard surfaces, their texture, relation to a vantage point, and classification by types of surface arrangements.

[See also Picture Perception; Pictorial Semiotics; Receptors; and Umwelt.]

BIBLIOGRAPHY

Blakemore, C., ed. Vision: Coding and Efficiency. Cambridge: Cambridge University Press, 1990.
Kosslyn, S. M. Image and the Brain. Cambridge, Mass.: MIT Press, 1994.

—JOHN M. KENNEDY

WYZ

WHORF, BENJAMIN LEE (1897–1941), American scientist and linguist whose name is usually associated with the Sapir-Whorf hypothesis of linguistic relativity, so named on account of the close links between Whorf and his teacher at Yale University, the linguist Edward Sapir (1884–1939). Whorf did not train as a professional linguist, having studied chemical engineering instead at the Massachusetts Institute of Technology. Later, his professional duties consisted of fire-prevention engineering inspections of commercial companies. Whorf's academic studies in linguistics did not begin until 1931, the year in which Sapir took up the chair in linguistics in the Department of Anthropology at Yale University. Whorf had undertaken studies of Aztec and Maya, though prior to this date, it was his association with Sapir that led to his serious consideration of American Indian languages. Whorf combined the insights and experiences he gained from the two seemingly disparate areas of chemical engineering and linguistics to produce his subtle analyses of language form and function.

Whorf was interested in the complex dialectic between, on the one hand, grammatical processes and the linguistic praxis and, on the other hand, the social institutions of a given community. Toward the end of his 1956 essay on the relation of habitual thought and behavior to language, Whorf discusses the historical implications of his linguistic arguments. Comparing the history of what he called Standard Average European (SAE) languages, their associated technologies, and their cultural institutions to those of the Hopi, Whorf argues that language change occurs through the interaction of all of these factors. Language is not an autonomous system evolving independently of ideologies, technologies, and institutions. With the grammar and semantics of the languages of the Hopi and those of the SAE languages, he adopts a comparative approach to the analysis of grammatical form and meaning. Whorf attempts to show that whereas SAE languages constituted a Newtonian worldview—in which space and time are continuous constants—the language of the Hopi constituted an Einsteinian one—in which time and space are relative variables.

Whorf's principal object of analysis is the grammatical systems of language. In "Linguistic Factors in the Terminology of Hopi Architecture" (1956), he contends that the categorical basis of lexical classifications is continuous with rather than separate from the categorical basis of grammar itself. Grammar, for Whorf, is both a way to understand reality and a way to act on it. A lexis is only the most explicit and, hence, consciously available level of formal grammatical organization; grammar, for the most part, lies below the level of conscious awareness of the speakers of the language. Thus, Whorf is interested in making grammar an object of conscious metalinguistic reflection and awareness. This obliges him to develop some very subtle and powerful modes of grammatical analysis. Furthermore, the ethnosemantic and cultural bases of his approach imply constant awareness of the ways in which grammar is organized on the basis of the culturally specific meanings it realizes. Whorf does not see grammar as arbitrary or autonomous but as cross-coupled with culturally specific models of causation: becoming, personhood, gender, and so on.

In his work as a fire-prevention engineer, Whorf observed and analyzed many fires and explosions. He became aware of the fact that physical factors alone (defective wiring, etc.) were not always the sole or necessary agents of fires. Instead, Whorf observed, "the meaning of that situation to people was sometimes a factor, through the behavior of the people, in the start of a fire" (1956). Whorf's analysis of the case of the supposedly "empty gasoline drums" provides anecdotal evidence in support of a far-reaching hypothesis that Whorf explores in his essay "Language in Relation to Habitual Thought and Behavior" (1956):

> Yet the "empty" drums are perhaps the more dangerous, since they contain explosive vapor.

Physically the situation is hazardous, but the linguistic analysis according to regular analogy must employ the word "empty", which inevitably suggests lack of hazard. The word "empty" is used in two linguistic patterns: (1) as a virtual synonym for "null and void, negative, inert", (2) applied in analysis of physical situations without regard to, e.g., vapor, liquid vestiges, or stray rubbish, in the container. The situation is named in one pattern (2) and the name is then "acted out" or "lived up to" in another (1), this being a general formula for the linguistic conditioning of behavior into hazardous forms. (Whorf, 1956, p. 135)

The American linguist Eric H. Lenneberg (1953) has attacked Whorf's linguistics on the grounds that it is circular or tautologous. According to Lenneberg, this results from Whorf's privileging of linguistic differences at the expense of the nonlinguistic events with which they are supposedly correlated. However, a careful reading shows that Whorf is sensitive to both the nonlinguistic, physical situation and to what he calls "the linguistic conditioning of behavior" as causal factors in fires.

Lenneberg's critique was an important early influence in the largely negative reception of Whorf as a "linguistic determinist." In this reading, it is presumed that language per se is the causal agent of human thought and perception. Thus, Ronald Langacker (1967), before he shifted from formal linguistics to a more recent position that is closer to Whorf's, argued strongly against the view that the grammatical structure of our language holds our thoughts in what he, caricaturing Whorf's position, referred to as "a tyrannical, vice-like grip." Whorf did not subscribe to such a view and was a much more complex and dialectical thinker. First, Whorf notes, with respect to the above example, that "the linguistic analysis according to regular analogy must employ the word 'empty', which inevitably suggests lack of hazard." In other words, the regular, habitual linguistic collocation of empty and gasoline drum entails an analysis or interpretation by the human participants involved. They attribute the quality "empty" to the gasoline drums in the given situation in routine ways, without, however, checking as to whether this word adequately describes the physical situation. The reasons for proceeding in this way are largely implicit in the linguistic behavior of the group. Whorf then comments on the paradigmatic distribution of the word

empty: semantically, it can occur in two different patterns, which he describes. The first of these has a more abstract meaning; the second is more usually applied to physical states and processes.

In the particular situation at hand, Whorf has noted that language users, who tend not to be consciously aware of the two patterns when they use the word empty, nevertheless consciously attribute the second meanings to the physical situation at the same time that the situation is, as Whorf puts it, "acted out" or "lived up to" in terms of the first meaning.

Whorf then describes this as "the linguistic conditioning of behavior into hazardous forms." This is a complex and difficult noun phrase by which Whorf means first that it is the behavior of people involved in the situation that takes on hazardous forms: they behave in ways that are not commensurate with the physical danger posed by the "empty" gasoline drums. Insofar as the gasoline drums were often filled with waste materials that constituted a fire hazard, in failing to attend to these waste materials, the participants had formed selective awarenesses of the situation that did not correspond to the given physical reality. Second, Whorf observes that such behavior is linguistically conditioned. The participants selectively yet routinely attended to the given physical reality by attributing the second meaning of empty to it. At the same time, they also projected the first meaning onto the situation as if this corresponded to the physical reality in a straightforward or analogical way.

Both Whorf and Sapir stood in the tradition of ethnosemantics founded by Franz Boas. Linguists in this tradition are committed to the observation and description of language in relation to the behavior of its users. They are also interested in how grammatical meanings relate to the psychological reality of language users. Boas himself did not restrict his inquiries to the linguistic dimension; he was also interested in primitive art (1955) and in the distribution of North American folktales. Boas made an influential distinction between the "psychological explanation" of a custom and its "historical development." Boas's interest in psychological explanation needs to be understood in a collectivist sense as the psychology of the cultural group. It does not refer to the perceptual and cognitive processes of the individual in the sense intended by modern psychology. Boas owed his use of the term to Wilhelm Wundt's (1832–1920) conception of a Völkerpsychologie ("folk psychology"). The same applies to Whorf's use of the term *thought*, which does not have the meaning intended by modern psychology.

When, in his discussion of the empty gasoline drums, Whorf draws attention to the "LINGUISTIC MEANING residing in the name or the linguistic description commonly applied to the situation," he is applying the theoretical principle that a grammar is itself a theory of reality. Thus, the grammatical systems of a language—its grammar$_1$—are a culture's ways of knowing about and acting on reality. Yet there are two other senses in which Whorf used the term *grammar*. A second sense has to do with the cultural group's own "secondary interpretations," to use the Boasian turn of phrase, of grammatical form and function (Silverstein, 1979). This is evidenced in the way in which participants selectively interpret the meaning of *empty* and then referentially project this meaning out of language as if it did not have its basis in the lexicogrammar to start with. In other words, language users assume that this grammar corresponds in a straightforwardly referential way to the physical situation. Whorf used the term *objectification* (1956) to describe the "language habits" or grammar$_2$ involved in this process. Whorf's grammar$_3$ refers to the ethnolinguist's metatheory of both grammar$_2$ and grammar$_1$. Whorf does not use separate terms or subscripts to distinguish these three senses, but that must be so distinguished in order to do full justice to his linguistic theory and analysis.

Whorf makes a fundamental distinction between phenotypical and cryptotypical categories in grammar. A phenotype is an overt grammatical category that is realized by one local and formally segmentable marker at any given level of grammatical analysis, from the morpheme to the clause. A phenotype is a semantic category that is coded in a single, isolable segment of linguistic form. Morphemic categories such as the plural suffix *-s* or the past-tense marker *-ed* are examples.

Cryptotypes are covert grammatical categories that do not have a single, isolable formal realization in the grammar. Their unifying principle is an underlying semantic category that is not realized by a single, isolable formal marker. Instead, a cryptotypic category "moors" a whole set of systems in various areas of the grammar to a single covert semantic category. Whorf calls the various systems with which a cryptotype interacts its "reactances" (1956), a term he adapted from chemistry. A cryptotypic category is,

then, an abstract semantic principle—"a deep persuasion of a principle behind phenomena" (1956)—that both entails specific selections in some areas of the grammar while excluding others. Some of the covert categories Whorf discusses include causation, gender, force, time, and space. A cryptotype is always realized by what Whorf calls a "configurative rapport" of features that may cut across grammatical systems as diverse as voice, tense, aspect, and participant roles or case markers.

Cryptotypic categories, given their implicit though no less felt character, are unconscious categories. They are not easily lexicalized, and any gloss of them invariably fails to do full justice to the semantic value of the category. Whorf's theory of cryptotypes explains why, for example, different choices of tense "react" with different classes of verb processes. For example, in English the simple present is the unmarked present tense with verb processes of the mental type. (e.g., "She knows the truth") and the present continuous tense is the unmarked present tense with verb processes of the material type (e.g., "She's swimming"). Whorf's theory of cryptotypes shows that this is so because of a covert semantic category that distinguishes between the linguistic coding of situations in the world of external experience and that of the world of internal, nonspatial experience. In his essay, "Gestalt Technique of Stem Composition in Shawnee" (1956), Whorf makes a fundamental distinction between the external and the "egoic" fields of experience in order to explain the deeper rationale behind this categorical semantic distinction. The fact that unmarked present tense "reacts" with material processes in the way it does has to do with the fact that this type of verb process involves change through time. This change always entails some relation of a figure to a ground in the visualizable external world. On the other hand, mental processes, which are ego centered, entail no such time boundedness as they pertain to the internal field of ego-centered experience that cannot be visualized in terms of a figure-ground relation. Some recent examples of the kind of comparative linguistic analysis that Whorf pioneered in his efforts to tease out submerged cryptotypical categories include James R. Martin's comparative study of Tagalog and English (1988) and Alan Rumsey's study of referential and pragmatic folk ideologies in English and some Australian aboriginal languages (1990).

In the North American cultural context in which

Whorf lived and worked, values such as individualism, pragmatism, and positivism dominated. Whorf, to be sure, was thoroughly steeped in the positivist science of linguistics. Nevertheless, he struggled to give voice to very different scientific criteria. In this regard, his intellectual affinities with Eastern thought found expression in works including his essay "Language, Mind, and Reality" (1956). Against the atomism of scientific positivism and the not-unrelated ideology of individualism, he writes of a "higher level of organization" or a "realm of patterns" that the individual conscious mind is not, in normal circumstances, capable of apprehending. Against the pragmatist, commonsense view, which sees language as a tool both for the transmission of prelinguistic thoughts and ideas and for the fulfillment of immediately perceivable social needs, Whorf argues that "the forms of a person's thoughts are controlled by inexorable laws of patterns of which he is unconscious" (1956, p. 252).

Whorf, like Saussure, was a thoroughly modernist thinker in the sense that his theoretical privileging of the grammatical systems of language emphasizes those principles of unity shared by all users of that language. He assumes, implicitly, that there is a common culture and grammar that links all members and that is shaped by the specific nature of the lexicogrammatical level of organization. Further, Whorf also refers to a higher-order nonlinguistic consciousness that transcends specific language systems and unites all humans in a common semiotic "brotherhood." Whether one accepts the mystical turn here or not, Whorf does on such occasions raise a question of fundamental concern to semiotics: is there, at least in part, a transsemiotic basis to the meaning systems of a given culture? He mentions music, art, and language in this connection and speculates as to whether there are higher-order principles of "patternment" that connect them at some more fundamental, unconscious level.

Whorf took language, culture, and behavior to be a single network of relations. He was interested in the underlying, largely unconscious, unity of cultural phenomena. Whorf's thinking about the nature of this unity, while speculative, shares affinities with the modern theory of autopoiesis as developed by Humberto Maturana and Francisco Varela, in which language, seen as a system of Gestalten or higher-order principles of patternment rather than as an assemblage of norms, produces and elaborates the knowledge and the organization it needs. The results of these operations are, recursively, its own operations. The continual production and elaboration of the system by language habits (grammar$_2$) and by the linguist's metatheory (grammar$_3$) are both the results of these operations and the operations themselves. Whorf is thus reluctant to assign a one-way causal relation to either "language patterns" or "cultural norms," as if they were separate issues. Whorf sees that they are not separate to start with and that each is both cause and effect; it is the dialectical unity of the two that constitutes the horizon of possibilities of the given culture. Whorf, in fact, rejects a cognitive-representational model of knowledge whereby an isomorphism between the language system and the external world is presupposed. There is no external environment that constitutes input or data to the system. Instead, the principle of organized closure means that the constant synchronic and diachronic dialectic of language, culture, and behavior acts as stimuli for the system's own self-referential organization. Language does not mirror or reflect an already given external reality, as the Western folk ideologies of reference and individual mind would have it. Rather, the interaction of language, culture, and behavior coproduces reality. In so doing, the overall system of relations maintains, in time, its global principles of self-organization. At the same time, it enacts these from a point of view that is limited and relative yet irreducible. Language as system is not in this view a "vice-like grip" on thought but the conditions of possibility for the autonomy, albeit culturally constrained, of its users. Language users do not simply apply pregiven norms; they elaborate the systemic possibilities in and through which autonomy is created.

[See also Autopoiesis; Cultural Knowledge; Ethnoscience; Linguistic Relativism; and Reference.]

BIBLIOGRAPHY

Boas, F. Primitive Art. New York: Dover, 1955.

Langacker, R. W. Language and Its Structure. New York: Harcourt, Brace, and World, 1967.

Lenneberg, E. H. "Cognition in Ethnolinguistics." Language 29 (1953): 463–471.

Martin, J. R. "Grammatical Conspiracies in Tagalog: Family, Face, and Fate—with regard to Benjamin Lee Whorf." In Linguistics in a Systemic Perspective, edited by J. D. Benson et al., pp. 243–300. Amsterdam and Philadelphia: John Benjamins, 1988.

Mathiot, M., ed. Ethnolinguistics: Boas, Sapir, and Whorf Revisited. The Hague: Mouton, 1979.

Rumsey, A. "Wording, Meaning, and Linguistic Ideology." *American Anthropologist* 92.2 (1990): 346–361.

Silverstein, M. "Language Structure and Linguistic Ideology." In *The Elements: A Parasession on Linguistic Units and Levels*, edited by P. R. Clyne, W. F. Hanks, and C. L. Hofbauer, pp. 193–241. Chicago: Chicago Linguistic Society, 1979.

Wallis, W. D. *An Introduction to Anthropology.* New York: Harper and Row, 1926.

Whorf, B. L. *Language, Thought, and Reality.* Edited J. B. Carroll. Cambridge, Mass.: MIT Press, 1956.

Wundt, W. *Elements of Folk Psychology.* Translated by E. L. Schaub. London: Allen and Unwin, 1921.

—Paul J. Thibault

WILSON, EDWARD O.

WILSON, EDWARD O. (b. 1929), American zoologist and foremost specialist on ants, Wilson is the synthesizer and chief spokesperson for the amalgam of evolutionary subdisciplines—ethology, population genetics, ecology, and others—that studies questions of social behavior. In a series of books and articles, notably *Sociobiology* (1975), Wilson has argued that social behavior is widespread in the animal kingdom, from the insects to our own species, and that the key to understanding it lies in Darwinian evolutionary theory—that is, in the perspective of adaptation brought on by individual-based needs in the struggle for existence and reproduction. Drawing on the models of such theoretical biologists as William Hamilton and Robert Trivers, supplementing this with a broad understanding of a massive number of empirical studies, and cementing everything with his own deep knowledge of sociality among the Hymenoptera (ants, bees, and wasps), Wilson has made sociobiology into a major branch of evolutionary biology.

Communication has a major and privileged position in the Wilsonian worldview. If animals are to work together socially, whether within or across species boundaries, they must be able to communicate. In this area, Wilson's own special field of research has been with pheromones, the chemicals that animals (especially insects) use to transfer information. But his scope extends to all methods of communication, its forms, and its functions. He has made the most important and creative contributions in this last area. It has been Wilson's special aim to survey and categorize the adaptive functions that such communication plays. As a Darwinian, Wilson sees communication as tightly under the control of natural selection: "Biological communication is the action on the part of one organism (or cell) that alters the probability pattern of behavior in another organism (or cell) in a fashion adaptive to either one or both of the participants. By adaptive I mean that the signaling, or the response, or both, have been genetically programmed to some extent by natural selection" (1975, p. 176).

Wilson lists some twenty different functions for animal communication, including facilitation and imitation, as when ants send signals to their nest mates to get them all to perform some tasks jointly, such as nest construction; monitoring, seeing information in the acts of others, as when watching behavior at a water hole; contact, simply sending signals to keep in touch; individual and class recognition, which is particularly important for the social insects, who need to recognize their nest mates and only their nest mates; status signaling, letting others know one's rank in the group; and begging and offering of food, often activities that convey a lot of information, and not just about immediate needs of hunger and thirst.

Next come grooming and grooming invitation, which is clearly very important among the primates and demands much signaling and communication to avoid misinterpretation of desires and intentions, but which occurs in other vertebrates and in the invertebrates also; alarm, as when an individual warns a fellow species member of danger (though this is done from an individualist perspective, not in terms of the group); distress, as when an individual calls out for help (again, individually); assembly and recruitment, which occurs in all groups, although "by far the most dramatic form of assembly in social insects is exercised by the mother queens of colonies. Except in the most primitively social species, any well-nourished, fertilized queen attracts a retinue of workers who tend to press close in with their heads facing her" (1975, p. 212).

Leadership is very important among vertebrates, and often there are elaborate signaling methods between parents and offspring, especially when danger threatens. Incitement to hunt is often connected with leadership, although it is not necessarily the dominant member of the group who incites. Embryonic communication is similar to inciting in that it occurs when chicks make a sound as they are about to hatch, thus inciting their nest mates to hatch also. Initiation of physical transport is also very significant in the Hymenoptera, especially when it is necessary to move the whole nest site.

Other communication functions include play invitation, especially important among young mammals as many learned things needed for adult life are transmitted through play; work initiation, much used by social animals such as ants and beavers to get nest construction started; threat, submission, and appeasement, much studied and discussed by the ethologists, particularly when animals engage in stylized combat and its substitutes; nest-relief ritualizing, occurring in birds when it is necessary to change roles in incubation and feeding of the young; sexual behavior, of which Wilson distinguishes five different acts: "sexual advertisement, courtship, sexual bonding, copulatory behavior, and postcopulatory behavior" (1975, p. 216); and finally, caste inhibition, where queens direct the growth of their offspring into worker roles, again a phenomenon that is only on the verge of communication, although the transferral of information certainly is involved.

As with Wilson's zoosemantical classification of the higher functions of communication and signaling, he would warn that such a list should not be taken as written in stone. But it does cover the obvious cases of animal communication, giving a valuable perspective on the whole. Most important, the evolutionary significance of adaptation for the individual is stressed throughout.

[See also Darwin; Evolution; Hamilton; Sociobiology; and Trivers.]

BIBLIOGRAPHY

Allen, E. "Sociobiology: A New Biological Determinism." In Biology as a Social Weapon, edited by the Sociobiology Study Group of Boston, pp. 133–149. Minneapolis: Burgess, 1977.

Lumsden, C. J., and E. O. Wilson. Genes, Mind, and Culture. Cambridge, Mass.: Harvard University Press, 1981.

Lumsden, C. J., and E. O. Wilson. Promethean Fire: Reflections on the Origin of Mind. Cambridge, Mass.: Harvard University Press, 1983.

Ruse, M. Sociobiology: Sense or Nonsense? Dordrecht: Reidel, 1979.

Ruse, M. Monad to Man: The Concept of Progress in Evolutionary Biology. Cambridge, Mass.: Harvard University Press, 1996.

Ruse, M., and E. O. Wilson. "The Evolution of Morality." New Scientist 1478 (1985): 108–128.

Wilson, E. O. The Insect Societies. Cambridge, Mass.: Harvard University Press, Belknap Press, 1971.

Wilson, E. O. Sociobiology: The New Synthesis. Cambridge, Mass.: Harvard University Press, 1975.

Wilson, E. O. On Human Nature. Cambridge, Mass.: Harvard University Press, 1978.

Wright, R. Three Scientists and Their Gods. New York: Times Books, 1987.

—MICHAEL RUSE

WITTGENSTEIN, LUDWIG

WITTGENSTEIN, LUDWIG (1889–1951), Anglo-Austrian philosopher who was concerned with questions of meaning. In the first period of his work, completed before and during World War I and marked by the Tractatus Logico-Philosophicus (1921), Wittgenstein was interested in the very restricted area of logical propositions. A proposition can be thought of as a simple declarative sentence ("The cat sat on the mat") or, perhaps, as a completed arithmetic expression ("2 + 2 = 4"). The early Wittgenstein believed that such propositions could be said to be meaningful only if they were capable of mapping onto or picturing an actual state of affairs in the world. Hence, his "picture theory of the proposition" was a correspondence theory of meaning.

But the picture theory was slightly more complex than this. Wittgenstein held that the world consists of states of affairs that in turn consist of more basic or atomic facts that themselves consist of simple objects. If we then think of these objects as having simple names, we can imagine the names composing very basic or elementary propositions. Further, we can think of these making up the actual propositions we use (if we do use them). Last, the sum total of propositions can be thought of as constituting the whole of language. There is therefore a fourfold parallel between language and the world, with each reducing in complexity as the parallel proceeds "down" to the point of direct correspondence between names and objects:

Language	World
propositions	states of affairs
elementary propositions	atomic facts
names ⟷	objects

If, according to this analytic scheme, a proposition in language can be shown to correspond directly to a state of affairs in the world, then it is said to be "true." If, on the contrary, while it was capable of corresponding in this way but turned out not to correspond to a genuine state of affairs, then it would be said to be "false." Last, if the proposition can never correspond to any real state of affairs, it is said to be neither true nor false but "senseless." The early Wittgenstein believed he had shown in the *Tractatus* that only the propositions of the natural sciences are capable of being true or false. All other propositions—such as those of ethics, aesthetics, religion, and so on—he believed to be senseless. This is why the *Tractatus* begins with the famous dictum, "The world is all that is the case," and ends by saying that the propositions of the *Tractatus* themselves (because they are not scientific propositions) must be senseless.

The propositions of the *Tractatus* themselves might add nothing to our knowledge, but they appear to be able to show where the boundaries between sense and senselessness lie. They give us a "feeling" of knowing where these lie, even though they can say nothing directly about those boundaries or, still less, help us to know where they occur. This is why Wittgenstein ends by saying that those who have understood him must eventually discard the means of that understanding, just as someone might throw away a ladder once they have climbed up it.

Whatever else it might be, this theory of meaning is almost the antithesis of the traditional semiotic (or at least Saussurean) view of signs having meaning by virtue of their difference from other signs within a signifying system. The theory of meaning in the *Tractatus*, on the contrary, holds that when signs are meaningful (and very few actually are), this meaning derives not from difference but from identity between signs and their referents. And this is precisely the "level" that Saussure sought to avoid with his basic division of the sign into signifier and signified.

During the second period of Wittgenstein's thinking about meaning, as evidenced by his *Philosophical Investigations* (1958), he utterly rejected his earlier correspondence theory. Wittgenstein became much less interested in the rather restricted philosophical or logical domain of propositions and came to think of language in terms of the many uses it has and things it can accomplish in ordinary, everyday life. He calls these activities with language "language-games"—for example, giving orders and obeying them; describing the appearance of an object or giving its measurements; reporting an event; speculating about an event; and forming and testing a hypothesis.

As a consequence of this rethinking, Wittgenstein takes the meaning of an utterance to be closer to its use in a language game, and he closes off all questions of an utterance's possible correspondences with some "realer" world of objects. This also has consequences for philosophical language. When philosophers claim, for example, to know something, they often use rather special sorts of expressions. George E. Moore, for example, claimed access to absolutely certain knowledge by holding up his hand and saying, "I know this is my hand." But the view of language espoused by Wittgenstein in the *Investigations* might lead us to ask of Moore: under what ordinary circumstances would you actually say such a thing? In what language game could it occur and what would be its use there? Does it have a use? And if not, how can it have any meaning? Wittgenstein pursued this line of inquiry in the notes now collected as *On Certainty* (1969). He argues there that, while there might be some special occasions when we could say "I know this is my hand," they are quite rare and, moreover, the utterance of this sentence under such circumstances does not tell us anything "deep" about human knowledge, let alone about certainty. Returning to ordinary use can be a kind of "therapy" for philosophical hang-ups.

Finally, the "theory" of language games has much to say on the question of expressions that appear to be about our internal states, such as expressions of thought. If an expression such as "I am thinking such and such" cannot be meaningful by virtue of its mapping onto or picturing a real state of thought (as it might under the *Tractatus* view of meaning), how then does it actually come to mean? This issue leads Wittgenstein into an investigation of the different circumstances under which we use a number of terms that at first sight seem to refer to ghostly mental processes: *reading, knowing, intending, thinking,* and so on. Importantly, he shows the crucial differences between and within these mental predicates. They are not somehow held together by virtue of all being expressions of "real" mental contents; moreover, each of them alone can be used in quite distinct ways. How we know they have meaning is connected with our recognizing that they are being used correctly. This pragmatic sense of correctness or cultural appropriateness leads Wittgenstein to the theory that certain criteria must be in place before an expression can be used properly. The question is by what criteria do mental predicates (such as "is thinking," "remembers such-and-such," and "decides upon an action") actually come to be used in practical social fields? The rather loose and situation-specific notion of criteria then becomes the new "anchor" for meaning (see Coulter, 1979).

[*See also* Implicature; Meaning; Pragmatics; Speech Act Theory; *and* Vienna Circle.]

BIBLIOGRAPHY

Works by Wittgenstein
Philosophical Investigations. Oxford: Blackwell, 1958.
Tractatus Logico-Philosophicus (1921). London: Routledge and Kegan Paul, 1961.
"Lecture on Ethics." *Philosophical Review* 74 (1965): 3–12.
On Certainty. Oxford: Blackwell, 1969.

Other Works
Coulter, J. *The Social Construction of Mind: Studies in Ethnomethodology and Linguistic Philosophy.* London: Macmillan, 1979.
Winspur, S. "Wittgenstein's Semiotic Investigations," *American Journal of Semiotics* 3.2 (1984): 33–57.

—ALEC MCHOUL

WÖLFFLIN, HEINRICH (1864–1945), German art historian and theorist whose most famous book, *Kunstgeschichtliche Grundbegriffe* (Principles of Art History) appeared in 1915, after years of relative silence. He had published three other important books during the late 1880s: his doctoral dissertation *Prolegomena zu einer Psychologie der Architektur* (1886), *Renaissance und Barock* (1888), and *Die Klassische Kunst* (Classic Art, 1899). After *Kunstgeschichtliche Grundbegriffe*, Wölfflin wrote only one more book but issued quite a few self-corrections in the wake of the reception of the *Kunstgeschichtliche Grundbegriffe*. Erwin Panofsky was the first art historian to respond to Wölfflin's principles shortly after the publication of his lecture "Das Problem das Stils in der bildende Kunst" (1911), in which he announced the appearance of the book. Panofsky's critical reception was diametrically opposed to the influence Wölfflin's book had among archaeologists, ethnologists, psychologists, and theoreticians in literature, music, and elsewhere. The most famous among them was perhaps the literary scholar Oskar Walzel, who wrote *Wechselseitige Erhellung der Künste: Ein Beiträg zur Würdigung kunstgeschichtlicher Begriffe* (1917).

The second international congress of the Vereiniging für Asthetik und Allgemeine Kunstwissenschaft, which was held in 1924, was devoted to Wölfflin's concept of style. In the years following this congress, Russian formalists as well as the postformalist circle around Mikhail M. Bakhtin (1895–

1975) responded to the theoretical concepts of Wölfflin, who was considered as one of the most important representatives of what they called West European formalism. From 1912 onward, translations of his books were published in Russian. The name *Wölfflin* and his topos of "art history without names" were mentioned in Boris Ejchenbaum's "Theory of the Formal Method" (1927/1971) and also in M. M. Bakhtin and P. N. Medvedev's *The Formal Method in Literary Scholarship* (1928/1985). Both authors subscribed to this topos, which puts the works of art and not the artists themselves in the center. As Osip Brik stated in 1923: "There are only poems and literature, and no poets or writers."

Although Wölfflin was admired by the formalists, his ideas were much closer to those of the postformalists, who were particularly interested in both a general but nonidealistic aesthetics and the dynamics of author, work of art, and beholder. Contrary to Walzel, they were focused not so much on application of Wöfflin's art-historical principles as on a synthesis of knowledge concerning the arts within the context of a philosophically oriented aesthetics. Karl Vossler was in this respect an important link between Wölfflin and the Bakhtin circle. The reception of West European formalism in the writings of Bakhtin and Medvedev is remarkable. Their knowledge was profound, not only regarding the sources themselves but also as far as the philosophical background of German psychological aesthetics was concerned.

The Russian authors apparently did not consider Wölfflin's *Kunstgeschichtliche Grundbegriffe* as a rupture in his development but acknowledged the relation between it and his Einfühlungs (sensitivity) psychologically oriented writings. This connection was soon forgotten, not only by literary scholars and semioticians but also by art historians. Meinhold Lurz, the author of a most extensive and profound intellectual biography of Wölfflin (1981), advocated the continuity of his thoughts.

An effort to apply the *Grundbegriffe* within a semiotic analysis has been made by Jean-Marie Floch in his essays on the photography of Alfred Stieglitz and Paul Strand (Floch, 1986). Floch became acquainted with Wölfflin's topoi through Abraham Zemsz, whose "Les optiques cohérentes" (1967) was reprinted in the *Actes sémiotiques-documents* (1985) of the Paris School. Zemsz convinced Floch that Wölfflin, whom Zemsz considers as a structuralist *avant la lettre*, is of much greater importance to visual semiotics than the iconology of Panofsky or the rhetoric of Roland Barthes (Floch, 1984, p. 14). Wölfflin developed these art-historical principles in his studies on Renaissance and Baroque art. His key concept with regard to Baroque art was the idea of the "painterly," as opposed to the "linear" style of the Renaissance and classical art in general. The other pairs he uses in his *Kunstgeschichtliche Grundbegriffe* are plan versus recession; closed versus open form; multiplicity versus unity; and the absolute versus the relative clarity of the subject.

In Zemsz's terms, Renaissance and Baroque art represent two optical schemes. According to him and Floch, these principles can be considered as a model that can serve the purpose of a structural analysis: the principles are independent of the substance of expression; they are structurally defined and have no meaning in themselves. In more classical semiotic terms, Floch recognizes in the Renaissance scheme a paradigmatic principle and in the Baroque a syntagmatic one—that is to say, both are considered as part of an elementary structure. While Wölfflin only suggested that his principles could also function in relation to style periods other than Renaissance or Baroque art, Floch is convinced of the universality of this model, ignoring the criticisms of the *Kunstgeschichtliche Grundbegriffe* in art historiography (see, for example, Schapiro, 1961).

Although it seems that Wölfflin was interested primarily in the expression plane and not in the correlation between an expression and content plane, a more profound study of his thoughts that rely in particular on Johannus Volkelt's (1848–1930) theory of empathy shows that the relation between form and content always was one of his main concerns. However, we will not find in Wölfflin's work the systematic approach to both planes and their correlation that is so characteristic of the Greimas school. But when we compare, for example, the procedures of the semiotic analyses of early abstract art by Floch or Swiss art historian Felix Thürlemann with the ideal procedure of a formal analysis as proposed by archaeologist Heinrich von Brunn, Wölfflin's most important teacher, we come to the conclusion that the first steps of both procedures are quite similar. Their ideal procedure consists in starting with points and lines, advancing through forms, and arriving via a "syntaxis of forms" at the expression of an idea.

[*See also* Bakhtin; Paris School; Pictorial Semiotics; Riegl; *and* Russian Formalism.]

BIBLIOGRAPHY

Bakhtin, M. M., and P. N. Medvedev. *The Formal Method in Literary Scholarship: A Critical Introduction to Sociological Poetics* (1928). Cambridge, Mass.: Harvard University Press, 1985.
Ejchenbaum, B. M. "The Theory of the Formal Method" (1927). In *Readings in Russian Poetics*, edited by L. Matejka and K. Pomorska, pp. 3–37. Cambridge, Mass.: MIT Press, 1971.
Floch, J.-M. *Petites mythologies de l'oeil et de l'esprit: Pour une sémiotique plastique.* Paris: Hadès, 1984.
Floch, J.-M. *Brandt, Cartier-Bresson, Doisneau, Stieglitz, Strand: Les formes de l'empreinte.* Périgueux: Fanlac, 1986.
Hansen-Löwe, A. A. *Der Russische Formalismus: Methodologische Rekonstruktion seiner Entwicklung aus dem Prinzip der Verfremdung.* Vienna: Verlag der Osterreichischen Akademie der Wissenschaften, 1978.
Hart, J. "Heinrich Wölfflin: An Intellectual Biography." Ph.D. diss., University of California, 1981.
Lurz, H. *Heinrich Wölfflin: Biographie einer Kunsttheorie.* Darmstadt: Werner'sche Verlagsgesellschaft, 1981.
Schapiro, M. "Style." In *Aesthetics Today*, edited by M. Philipson, pp. 81–113. Cleveland: World, 1961.
Wölfflin, H. *Principles of Art History: The Problem of the Development of Style in Later Art* (1915). Translated by M. D. Hottinger. London: G. Bell and Sons, 1932.
Zemsz, A. "Les optiques cohérentes (la peinture est-elle un langage?)." *Revue d'esthétique* 20 (1967): 40–73.

—MARGA VAN MECHELEN

WRITING, ETHNOGRAPHY OF. The study of writing as a form of everyday communication, the ethnography of writing focuses on writing practices and their social functions as observed in the situations of their use. The ethnography of speaking studies the speech community, its shared knowledge and competence with respect to the speech code, the norms for its use in a repertoire of oral genres of communication, and the strategic choices speakers make in specific situations. Similarly, the ethnography of writing aspires to study shared knowledge and norms for culture-specific genres of written texts, produced in specific media: who uses writing for what purposes? What genres and subgenres of texts are recognized? How do these genres develop? What media are considered appropriate for which kinds of messages? What are the norms for the various genres? What range of deviation from them is tolerated and under what circumstances? What range of strategic choices are available for personal expression, given these general normative constraints?

In historical accounts of writing practices, one can reconstruct functions of writing and genres of texts only from surviving exemplars. Analyses of texts from the ancient world show that writing was used to indicate ownership, to make contracts, to write letters and wills, to record treaties, to curse someone, to transmit works of literature, to record chronicles, and so on. In modern times, researchers have the additional advantage of using techniques of interviewing and observation to observe at first hand the uses that groups and subgroups make of writing. The emergence of the ethnography of writing as a research agenda has been influenced by developments in the sociology, psychology, and history of literacy. Claims for the social, cultural, and psychological consequences of literacy by early theorists such as Marshall McLuhan, Eric Havelock, and Jack Goody met with criticism for lack of empirical verification or lack of verifiability and for ethnocentric emphasis on the pattern of development of literacy in the West.

Beginning in the 1980s, ethnographic studies of literacy identified uses of writing in non-Western societies that differ from those of mainstream, urban Western culture. In addition, researchers began to study the interrelations between oral and written modes of communication in rural and lower-class groups in modern society. Wherever large groups are illiterate or only marginally literate but writing is central to the business of society, literate brokers play an intermediate role, writing letters on behalf of petitioners to government bureaucracies and the courts, for example. Who uses their services? How do these letter writers acquire their skill and their status? What strategies do they employ to enhance the interests of their clients and with what effect? What features characterize the documents they create?

The ethnographic approach calls for attention to informal, expressive, and controversial or subversive uses of writing, as well as to formal, instrumental, and institutional ones. Thus, rather than focusing only on children's classroom compositions, researchers have studied note passing among students during classes and graffiti on public-toilet walls, outdoor walls, and subway cars. Other expressive, ephemeral forms of writing include skywriting, fire inscriptions set alight during ceremonies, inscriptions on birthday cakes, posters at political demonstrations, and stickers distributed for political causes.

In a deep (non-Derridean) sense, speech always lurks behind or beneath writing. In the tradition of Western essayist literacy, writing has generally been characterized by processes of decontextualization: texts are supposed to "speak for themselves." Thus, prose essays, scientific articles, and legal documents have come to be characterized by prominent use of nominalizations, the passive voice, and other devices that suppress the voice of the author. Texts are supposed to omit information about the circumstances in which the author creates them, such as the location in place and time, mood while creating them, how awake or sleepy the author was, and so on.

Recent critical thinking on self-reflexivity in anthropology and on the rhetoric of objectivity in scientific and journalistic writing has led to a return of linguistic features that resemble speech. Authors more openly use the first-person pronoun, avoid passives, and signal emotional involvement. The plain-language movement of the 1970s, which called for reform of the mystifying language of legal and bureaucratic documents, in effect made documents more speechlike. These developments strongly suggest that the processes of decontextualization thought to be essential to the transition to literacy are not inevitable but are in part culturally constituted. The idea of a great divide between speech and writing is therefore now widely rejected, and researchers recognize that some genres of speech are quite writinglike (e.g., a university lecture) and that some genres of writing are speechlike, such as a personal letter.

Some researchers suggest that there is evidence of a general cultural drift toward increased proximity of speech and writing in our own times. The advent of computer-mediated communication challenges many received notions about writing and might foster dramatic changes in beliefs and practices associated with it. The immediacy, ephemerality, and interactivity of the medium contribute to its dynamic, conversationlike quality. Messages sent by electronic mail (e-mail) contain many speechlike features, along with classically written ones, as well as some new, uniquely digital features. Writers are inventing and reinventing devices known from other genres of communication, such as comics, to enhance the representation of intonation in digital messages.

An ethnographic perspective also calls attention to the material aspects of writing, including both the surfaces on which messages are inscribed and the material appurtenances of their creation. What material means are used to enhance the performative capacity of official documents of all kinds and how does this vary from one culture to another? What conventional meaning is conveyed by color in ribbons and seals, calligraphy, gilt lettering, special lettering or fonts, distinctive size and shape of a document, and so on?

While the West has probably invested less than traditional Chinese, Japanese, or Muslim cultures in the aesthetics of written texts, handwriting has continued to be valued as a trace of the unique personal touch of an individual. Among collectors of autographs, entire documents in handwriting are more valuable financially than documents with only a signature. Traditions of production of fine papermaking and of connoisseur-quality fountain pens also persist to this day in the West. How is digital word processing changing writing practices? To what extent do people who own computers continue to draft their compositions or write personal letters by hand? If they compose letters on a computer, do they try to personalize them? What other situations involving written messages are still considered to require the personal touch? Do some cultures, subgroups, or types of individuals give it up more quickly than others?

With the transition to computerized texts, hard copies become optional. To what extent do they continue to be important to people and why? Under what circumstances are people becoming weaned off of them? As they learn to draft documents on a word processor, do they continue to print out interim hard copies? Or do they print only at the end, when the document is completed? Does printing an interim hard copy really facilitate editing, as many believe, or is it an expression of a magical need to see the text as material object?

Ethnographers of speaking distinguish between two senses of speaking as performance: performance as praxis, the situated use of speech in the conduct of social affairs or any use of a code to convey a message; and performance as the display of skill and artfulness to an audience. The same distinction can be made for writing. The ethnographic perspective leads one to recognize that not only fine calligraphy but also graffiti and other types of playful writing in popular culture are forms of artful performance. Graffiti artists, who call themselves writers, adopt nicknames called "tags" and proudly display their skill in spray painting compositions created in the dead of night in forbidden public places. Audiences are not ordi-

narily present when graffiti artists produce their works; their achievements are observed and appreciated at a later time. Skywriters, on the other hand, perform for an invisible audience in real time. Writing as artful performance flourishes in synchronous modes of computer-mediated communication. In these new forms of interactive writing, individuals perform together and for each other. Using the ostensibly meager resources of the computer keyboard, they demonstrate their skill in playing with typography, language, their own identities, and frames of social interaction.

[See also Computer-mediated Communication; and Flaming.]

BIBLIOGRAPHY

Basso, K. H. "The Ethnography of Writing." In R. Bauman and Sherzer, 1989 (below), pp. 425–432.

Bauman, R., and J. Sherzer, eds. Explorations in the Ethnography of Speaking. 2d ed. Cambridge: Cambridge University Press, 1989.

Biber, D., and E. Finegan. "Drift in Three English Genres from the Eighteenth to the Twentieth Centuries: A Multidimensional Approach." In Corpus Linguistics, Hard and Soft, edited by M. Kyoto and O. Ihalainen, pp. 83–101. Amsterdam: Rodopi, 1988.

Cooper, M., and H. Chalfant. Subway Art. London: Thames and Hudson, 1984.

Danet, B. "Books, Letters, Documents: The Changing Aesthetics of Texts in Late Print Culture." Journal of Material Culture 2.1 (1997): 5–38.

Heath, S. B. Ways with Words: Language, Life, and Work in Communities and Classrooms. Cambridge: Cambridge University Press, 1983.

Lakoff, R. T. "Some of My Favorite Writers Are Literate: The Mingling of Oral and Literate Strategies in Written Communication." In Spoken and Written Language: Exploring Orality and Literacy, edited by D. Tannen, pp. 239–260. Norwood, N.J.: Ablex, 1982.

Morris, I. The World of the Shining Prince: Court Life in Ancient Japan. Harmondsworth: Peregrine, 1985.

Shuman, A. Storytelling Rights: The Uses of Oral and Written Texts by Urban Adolescents. Cambridge: Cambridge University Press, 1986.

Street, B. V. Literacy in Theory and Practice. Cambridge: Cambridge University Press, 1984.

—BRENDA DANET

YI JING. Originally a repository of ancient Chinese divination practices, the *Yi jing (I Ching)* or *Book of Changes*, gradually acquired prestigious status as a book of wisdom. From the ninth century BCE, when it was first shaped into a coherent text, this wisdom consisted in understanding the moves and transfigurations of the cosmos in order to assess what one's own place was and how to act to meet the challenges of time.

The *Book of Changes* consists of two parts: sixty-four hexagrams representing the abstract symbols of all processes in the continuously changing cosmos; and commentaries and explanations concerning these hexagrams. As elucidated by Wang Bi, a prominent third-century CE commentator of the book, the combination of the symbols and the text is crucial, because "symbols are the means to express ideas. Words [i.e., texts] are the means to explain the symbols."

The hexagrams (*gua*) consist of the combination of two trigrams (also *gua*). They are formed by six lines (*yao*) arranged one atop the other in vertical sequence and read from bottom up. Each line is either solid _____ or broken ___ ___. So for instance the hexagram 24, *Fu* ("return") is represented by the following symbol

☷☳

This symbol consists of the bottom trigram *Chen* ☳ and the top trigram *kun* ☷.

The system of hexagrams contains several layers of signification. The first level of signification consists of what can be described as two morphemes, with a continuous straight line _____ representing the male (*yang*) and a broken line ___ ___ representing the female (*yin*). The abstract antithetical principles *yin* and *yang* represent in Chinese cosmology the fundamental movers of the cosmos in their reciprocal relation. Four combinations emerge when these two morphemes are paired in the following ways: ⚌ ⚏ ⚍ ⚎. These characteristic pairs of lines generate the four double-lined figures Old Yin ⚏, Young Yang ⚎, Young Yin ⚍, and Old Yang ⚌. To each of these combinations a third line is then added, which results in the fundamental eight trigrams (*ba gua*): ☰ ☷ ☶ ☵ ☴ ☳ ☲ ☱.

These eight symbols represent the primordial components of nature: heaven, earth, mountain, fresh water (lake), thunder, wind, water (in ditches and holes), and fire. The signification is, however, not confined to the denotative correspondence between symbols and the primordial components of nature.

For each trigram includes a range of associative meanings, including gender, kinship, animal species, natural objects, cardinal points, seasons, times of day and night, social positions, colors, parts of the human body, and spiritual or physical characteristics, as well as secondary abstract concepts. For example, trigram 1, ☰, signifies male, father, dragon (or stallion), heaven, metal, south, late autumn, early night, king, deep red, head, strength, and donator. As the visual symbol and the significations of trigram 2 show, the trigrams are arranged in systematic paired sequences, with each member of the pairs positioned antithetically to the other. Trigram 2, ☷, signifies female, mother, mare, earth, soil, north, early autumn, afternoon, people, black, abdomen, docility, receptor.

Sixty-four hexagrams are formed by combinations of trigrams. Again, they are arranged in antithetical pairs and the sequence of the hexagrams is indicated by a systematic new configuration. Still expandable if necessary, these sixty-four hexagrams encapsulate the cosmos since they were designed to represent all things, phenomena, and processes in continuous change from the past to the present. To reckon the past, one follows the order of their progress, and to know the future, one works backward through them. The combination of the hexagrams are determined by the numerical manipulation of divining sticks, originally yarrow stalks or, later, by the casting of coins.

The *Book of Changes*, as we know it today, is not the product of a single time. According to the traditional four-sage theory of *Yi jing* authorship, the trigrams were invented by the mythical cultural demiurge Emperor Fu Xi (twenty-fourth century BCE). The hexagrams were fashioned by the founder of the Zhou dynasty, King Wen, while he was imprisoned by the Shang (c.1140 BCE). The next venerable sage, the Duke of Zhou (d. 1104 BCE), added the earliest texts, the *Judgments for Hexagrams* and the *Exegesis for Lines*. Finally, Confucius (551–479 BCE) added the commentaries known as *The Ten Wings*. All these authorships are dubious, and there is no consensus on the age and source of the system. The earliest texts might date from the beginning of the Western Zhou; the basic texts assumed their present shape between the eighth and seventh centuries BCE. *The Ten Wings* appears to be more recent than their purported author, Confucius, perhaps written for the most part during the Warring States era (403–221 BCE). The whole of the book is evidently the product of a long period of accretion. The symbolic system behind the book grew out of imagistic, magical, and correlative approaches to the universe. Its practice provides a way to guide people in the world of their particular experience at a particular moment and in a given situation.

The cyclic infinite paradigm of sixty-four hexagrams "ends" with the hexagram characteristically titled "Before Completion" (Wilhelm, 1960) or "Ferrying Incomplete" (Lynn, trans., 1994) or "Not-yet-fording" (Ritsema and Karcher, trans., 1994). And any cast hexagram is open to change because of the transformative quality of so-called old lines so that Old Yin becomes Yang, Old Yang becomes Yin, and thus a new additional hexagram arises.

Yi jing's semiotic functioning and symbolic dynamic system defined Chinese nonimitative, metaphoric, and paradoxical ways of language and diction: "Images are the means to express ideas. Words are the means to explain the images. . . . The images are generated by the ideas, but if one stays fixed on the images themselves, then what he stays fixed on will not be images as we mean them here. Getting the ideas is in fact a matter of forgetting the images, and getting the images is in fact a matter of forgetting the words" (Wang Bi, 226–249 CE, *General Remarks on the Zhou's Changes*). This semiotic paradigm functioned as an archetypal pattern in a variety of domains of interpretation. For art critic Wang Wei (fifth century), "painting should correspond with the *Yi jing* in essence." For literary critic Liu Xie (sixth century), "the origin of human pattern (form, sign, and symbol) began in the primordial. The images of the *Yi jing* were first to bring to light spiritual intelligence that lie concealed. . . . the *Yi jing* says that which stirs the world into movement lie in language." For Dai Rongzhou, "the scene of poets, like the warm sun in the blue fields, and smoke engendered from pearls, is visible but not placeable before the eyes. Form [image] beyond form [image, hexagram], scene beyond scene: it is not speakable." The particular configuration that results when the yarrow stalks or coins fall is indicative of the shape and character of that particular time and supposes that everything that occurs in that given moment is interrelated and shares the same basic character.

Yi jing served as a wellspring of both Daoist and Confucian thought, and it was especially instrumental in defining the metaphysical concept of a dynamic universe in the twelfth-century Neo-Confucian school of thought led by the philosopher Zhu Xi (1130–1200). Since the seventeenth century, the *Book of Changes* has had a direct effect on ideas formulated by several Western philosophers and scientists. For instance, Gottfried Leibniz (1646–1716), who studied the works of the twelfth-century Neo-Confucian school in the Latin translations made by the Jesuits, put forward the idea that the ultimate reality in the universe are "monads," which are indestructible and have no causal relation with each other but contain within themselves the principle of change. This idea echoes the ancient Chinese view of nature as expressed in the *Yi jing*. Leibniz's claim that the present state of a substance must include its future states and vice versa is especially congruent with the fundamental vision of the *Book of Changes*. Leibniz also saw in the *Yi jing* a definite anticipation of his binary arithmetic (1987). In the twentieth century, Carl G. Jung (1875–1961), inspired by the associative thinking of the *Yi jing*, developed a concept of synchronicity to explain occurrences of meaningful coincidences without causal connection. Joseph Needham, the historian of Chinese science, asserts that the *Yi jing* is crucial for a deep understanding of Chinese scientific thought. He maintains that some elements of the structure of the world as modern science sees it are adumbrated in the speculations of the early Chinese philosophers, including those who were the authors of the *Yi jing*. The extent to which the modern development of semiotics was influenced by *Yi jing*, both as an archetypal system of differences and as a model of dynamic processes of signification coextensive with the cosmos, remains to be investigated.

BIBLIOGRAPHY

Translations of the *Yi jing*

I Ching. Translated by C. F. Baynes from the German version by R. Wilhelm. Princeton: Princeton University Press, 1950.

I Ching: The Classic Chinese Oracle of Change. Translated by R. Ritsema and S. Karcher. Rockport, Mass.: Element Books, 1994.

The Classic of Changes: A New Translation of the I Ching as Interpreted by Wang Bi. Translated by R. J. Lynn. New York: Columbia University Press, 1994.

Other Works

Chan, Wing-tsit. *A Source Book in Chinese Philosophy*. Princeton: Princeton University Press, 1963.

Fung, Yu-lan. *A History of Chinese Philosophy*. Translated by D. Bodde. 2 vols. Princeton: Princeton University Press, 1953.

Jung, C. G. *Synchronicity: An Acausal Connecting Principle*. Translated by R. F. C. Hull. Bollingen Series. Princeton: Princeton University Press, 1973.

Kunst, R. *The Original "Yijing": A Text, Phonetic Translation, Translation, and Indexes with Sample Glosses*. Ann Arbor: University Microfilms International, 1985.

Leibniz, G. *Discours sur la théologie naturelle des chinois*. Translated by C. Frémont. Paris: L'Herne, 1987.

Needham, J., with Wang Ling. *Chinese Science*. London: Pilot Press, 1945.

Needham, J., with Wang Ling. *Science and Civilization in China*. Cambridge: Cambridge University Press, 1954.

Ronan, C. A. *The Science and Civilisation in China*, vol. 1. Cambridge: Cambridge University Press, 1980. This volume is an abridgement of Needham and Ling, 1954.

Shchutskii, I. *Researches on the I Ching*. Princeton: Princeton University Press, 1979.

Wilhelm, H. *Change: Eight Lectures on the I Ching*. Translated by C. F. Baynes. New York: Pantheon, 1960.

Wilhelm, H. *Heaven, Earth, and Man in the Book of Changes*. Seattle and London: University of Washington Press, 1980.

—OLDRICH KRÁL

ZAHAVI, AMOTZ (b. 1928), Israeli biologist who has formulated a comprehensive theory of animal display and signaling. The theory asserts that the reliability, hence effectiveness, of signals depends on the cost, or handicap, born by the signaler. Zahavi is known for this so-called handicap principle, by which he intended to supplement and make more secure the Darwinian notion of sexual selection. A major problem with this notion or mechanism, which presupposes intraspecific rivalry for mates, is that it relies unduly upon anthropomorphic assumptions. In particular, especially within studies of the subbranch of selection through female choice, many Darwinians have assumed that animals like the peacock have human standards of taste and beauty, as the peahen chooses the male with the more beautiful tail.

Rather than with human standards of beauty, Zahavi starts with the assumption that the males of a species must show the females that they are healthy and have the qualities needed in the female's offspring. Adornments as handicaps function as signs of excellence, but displays are always open to cheating by inadequate males who try to mimic the healthy and successful males. Hence, Zahavi suggests that such showing or displaying must involve features that are difficult for the inadequate to copy or falsify, such as large antlers, long tails, or other such physical characteristics.

Pushing this idea to the limit, Zahavi has suggested that such features that display health or strength might start to evolve in their own right until they are positively maladaptive, demonstrating to the females that their possessors can survive *despite* the handicaps. "Think of a woman watching two men run a race. If both arrive at the finishing post at the same time, but one has deliberately encumbered himself with a sack of coal on his back, the woman will naturally draw the conclusion that the man with the burden is really the faster runner" (Dawkins, 1978 p. 172).

Claims like this have been singled out by critics as paradigmatic examples of the just-so stories the Darwinians like to spin, with surface plausibility but little ground in reality. However, while it is certainly true that claims about the handicap principle pose problems in testing them, something not entirely dissimilar to the handicap principle is at the heart of William D. Hamilton's more compelling claims about the evolution of sex. Hence, even if not as first formulated, this principle, which applies to a wide range of signaling behavior (Zahavi and Zahavi, 1997), might survive in a modified form.

[*See also* Darwin; Dawkins; Evolution; Hamilton; Sociobiology; Trivers; Wilson; and Zoosemiotics.]

BIBLIOGRAPHY

Dawkins, R. *The Selfish Gene*. Oxford: Oxford University Press, 1976.

Dawkins, R. *The Extended Phenotype: The Gene as the Unit of Selection*. Oxford: W. H. Freeman, 1982.

Hamilton, W. D., and M. Zuk. "Heritable True Fitness and Bright Birds: A Role for Parasites." *Science* 218 (1982): 384–387.

Zahavi, A. "Mate Selection: A Selection for a Handicap." *Journal of Theoretical Biology* 53 (1975): 205–214.

Zahavi, A., and A. Zahavi. *The Handicap Principle: A Missing Piece of Darwin's Puzzle*. Translated by N. Zahavi-Ely. New York: Oxford University Press, 1997.

—MICHAEL RUSE

ZEN GARDENS. Japanese gardens built under the influence of doctrines, religious practices, and aesthetic concepts related more or less directly to the Zen tradition of Buddhism, Zen gardens are relevant to the semiotician for at least two reasons. First, they are the expression of a peculiar episteme (i.e., of a particular way to create and interpret signs). Second, they show the inner dynamics both of a culture—they are a good example of the way in which a culture re-creates its own signs, redescribing itself in the course of history—and of intercultural communication: they can be instances of signs of a certain culture being interpreted and appropriated by a different culture.

It is possible to recognize two main kinds of Zen gardens: landscape gardens and dry landscape gardens (*kare sansui*), the latter of which are commonly considered to be the epitome of Zen art. Dry landscape gardens are very often composed by mere rocks, sand, and pebbles, but these apparently unsophisticated elements are symbols that reveal a complex reality that transcends them. The rocks are often taken from already extant gardens, where they had been placed according to precise aesthetic criteria. Particularly appreciated are rocks recalling mountains and gorges of the Chinese ink landscapes of the Song dynasty (960–1127 CE).

In other words, *kare sansui* gardens are meant to reproduce paintings ("culture") rather than pure "nature." Sometimes the referents, direct or indirect, of a garden are explicit (a certain mountain or landscape, a painting, a literary description); sometimes they are not specified. Such richness of intertextual references at the core of the meaning of the gardens, lay at the base of the "depth of sense" (*yūgen*) typical of Zen art, and this semantic depth is paradoxically identified with the Buddhist concept of emptiness (*kū*).

A striking peculiarity of Zen gardens is that they are not only reproductions of landscapes; on a deeper level, they are the manifestation of more abstract formal relations. Spatial disposition of the elements creates oppositional relations such as vertical and horizontal, big and small, round and oblong, subject and background, dense and rarefied, light and shadow, undifferentiated substratum and articulated objects emerging on it, quiet and dynamism, centrifugal and centripetal, and near and far. Groups of rocks are often organized on the basis of formal arrangements and devices such as mathematical patterns and axes. Depth is suggested by peculiar perspective techniques, and the garden's visibility is regulated by an itinerary. The design creates an asymmetrical abstract space representing various dichotomies. The geometrical center is empty, but since the attention

focuses on the particulars, the global perception of the garden changes accordingly.

In the interpretation of a Zen garden, both figurative and abstract levels are important. The first is rooted in painting and literary intertextuality; the latter is embedded in Buddhist thought and religious practice. Without an understanding of these references to intertextuality, the outside observer is left only with a vague aesthetic impression (connoted with Orientalism) or with a perception of abstract relations (assimilated to Western abstract art). This is a matter requiring further analysis, and an accurate semiotic study of the codes presupposed by Zen gardens as texts is still to be done. In any case, Roland Barthes's interpretation of Zen semiotics as aimed at the "exemption of sense" (1970) needs to be revised.

In general, the interpretive discourse on Zen gardens (and on Zen in general as a cultural phenomenon) is articulated on two contradictory levels. The first explains the objects with reference to a tradition (art, poetry, philosophy, religion). The second level denies the value of tradition and of discursive explanations and stresses spirituality and the substantial ineffability of the object in question. Although this might seem a mystification, this two-layered discourse reproduces in contemporary terms the structure of Chan and Zen argumentation. According to Bernard Faure (1991), in fact, Zen discourse oscillates between "the unwillingness . . . to use the mediation of the available methodologies to understand" Zen and the "tendency to identify with one particular structure or methodology."

The traces left by the rake in the sand of dry-landscape gardens represent, at the level of a figurative landscape homology, the waves of the sea. In the Buddhist universe of discourse, the sea represents consciousness and the waves the discriminating activity of the everyday, unenlightened mind. Zen gardens are thus also representations of the minds of the viewers. The traces of rake may also represent themselves as the result of religious practice; they are the visible traces of everyday practices as a form of Zen meditation and enlightenment.

A garden is thus able to represent both a precise geographical or heavenly space (through the mediation of paintings, literary sources, culturally marked landscapes, and so on) and the mental space of the observer (whether the ordinary mind that is the prey of the passions or the peaceful mind attained through

Zen practice). In this way, the identity of subject and object, the goal of Zen garden art, is realized. Behind its apparent mystical and ineffable character, it is possible to discern general philosophical concepts (epistemology, characteristics of the mind, etc.) and rhetorical strategies to embody them in art objects. As a place in which to contemplate the identity of subject and object, the interrelation of all things, and the relative nature of semantic oppositions, the garden acquires the status of a representation of Buddhist emptiness.

[See also Buddhism; Mandala; Mindscape; and Umwelt.]

BIBLIOGRAPHY

Barthes, R. L'empire des signes. Paris: Skira, 1970.
Casalis, M. "The Semiotics of Visible in Japanese Rock Gardens. Semiotica 44.3–4 (1983): 349–362.
Faure, B. The Rhetoric of Immediacy: A Cultural Critique of Chan/Zen Buddhism. Princeton: Princeton University Press, 1991.
Hayakawa, M. The Garden Art of Japan: The Heibonsha Survey of Japanese Art, vol. 28. New York and Tokyo: Weatherhill and Heibonsha, 1973.
Rambach, P., and S. Rambach. Le livre secret des jardins japonais. Paris: Skira, 1973.
Shinoda, K. "Amitachi no bunka: Tendai hongakuron no shiten kara." In Mujo to bi, edited by Mezaki Tokue, pp. 213–249. Bukkyo to nihonjin, 5. Tokyo: Shunjusha, 1986.
Stein, R. A. Le monde en petit. Paris: Flammarion, 1987.

—FABIO RAMBELLI

ZOOSEMIOTICS. Coined in 1963 by the American semiotician Thomas A. Sebeok, zoosemiotics designates the study of animal communication. The name reflects both the biological component, drawing heavily on the adaptation-oriented approach of ethology, and the analogy with human-directed semiotics or studies of communication. The biologist Edward O. Wilson refers to the "grail" of zoosemiotics as the understanding of the deep structure of animal communication—that is, the basic semantics of information transferral from one animal to another.

Modifying the lists of others, especially these by W. John Smith (1974, 1977), Wilson (1975) suggests that at least for vertebrates the following twelve categories are surely very significant: identification; probability, meaning the likelihood that an animal will follow through on a message; general set, showing that some action of some sort will occur; locomotion; attack; escape; nonagonistic subset, showing that the animal will not attack; association, showing that the animal simply wants to be close to the animal it is signaling; bond-limited subset, keeping up ties, as between mates or between close relatives, such as parent and offspring; social play; copulation; and frustration, which occur when an animal is thwarted in its aims. While the making of such lists can certainly direct research and codify results, even the very best lists are somewhat limited and subjective and do not necessarily hold outside the particular group of animals being considered. In Wilson's words: "We should continue to make and revise such lists, but not to take any one of them very seriously" (1975, p. 218).

[See also Communication; Sebeok; Signal; Trivers; and Zahavi.]

BIBLIOGRAPHY

Hauser, M. D. The Evolution of Communication. Cambridge, Mass.: MIT Press, 1996.
Sebeok, T. A. "Communication among Social Bees; Porpoises and Sonar; Man and Dolphin." Language 39 (1963): 448–466.
Sebeok, T. A. "The Word 'Zoosemiotics.' " Language Sciences 10 (1970): 36–37.
Sebeok, T. A., ed. How Animals Communicate. Bloomington: Indiana University Press, 1977.
Smith, W. J. "Zoosemiotics: Ethology and the Theory of Signs." Current Trends in Linguistics 12 (1974): 561–626.
Smith, W. J. The Behavior of Communicating: An Ethological Approach. Cambridge, Mass.: Harvard University Press, 1977.
Wilson, E. O. Sociobiology. Cambridge, Mass.: Harvard University Press, Belknap Press, 1975.

—MICHAEL RUSE

Directory of Contributors

JOSEPH ADAMSON
Associate Professor of English and Comparative Literature, McMaster University
Anatomy of Criticism; Frye, Northrop

RACHEL ARISS
Doctoral student, Faculty of Law, University of Toronto
Semiotic and Symbolic

JEFF BERNARD
Director, Institute for Socio-Semiotic Studies, Vienna
Rossi-Landi, Ferruccio

PAUL BOUISSAC
Professor of French, University of Toronto
Architecture; Deixis; Isotopy; Neurosemiotics; Paradigm; Phoneme; Semiotic Square; Semiotic Terminology

CHRISTOPHER BRACKEN
Assistant Professor of English, University of Alberta
Benjamin, Walter; Deconstruction; Postcolonialism; Postmodernism; Queer Theory

DAVID BUCHBINDER
Associate Professor of Literature, Curtin University of Technology
Polysystem Theory

THERESE BUDNIAKIEWICZ
Independent scholar, Indianapolis, Indiana
Actantial Model; Actants; Greimas, Algirdas Julien; Narrative Structures; Narratology

MARIE CARANI
Professor of Comparative Art History and Visual Semiotics, Université Laval
Art and Illusion; Gombrich, Ernst H.

HAN-LIANG CHANG
Professor of Comparative Literature, National Taiwan University
Chinese Ideograms

RINA COHEN
Assistant Professor of Sociology, York University
Gossip

WILLIAM E. CONKLIN
Professor of Law, University of Windsor
Law, Semiotics of; Legal Discourse

BRENDA DANET
Professor of Communication, Hebrew University of Jerusalem
Computer-Mediated Communication; Flaming; Writing, Ethnography of

PATRICK DEBBÈCHE
Research Associate, Department of French, University of Toronto
Paris School

JOHN DEELY
Professor of Philosophy, Loras College
Augustine of Hippo; Medieval Semiotics; Poinsot, Joannes; Sebeok, Thomas A.

NILLI DIENGOTT
Senior Lecturer in English and Comparative Literature, The Open University of Israel
Poetics

ERSU DING
Professor of Comparative Literature, Beijing University
Chinese Ontological Realism

JOSEPH L. ESPOSITO
Independent scholar, Tucson, Arizona
Peirce, Charles Sanders; Type and Token

JOHN FIELDER
Lecturer in Communication Studies, Curtin University of Technology
Dialogism

TIM FITZPATRICK
Associate Professor, Centre for Performance Studies, University of Sydney
Reception and Reader-Response Theories

CHARLES FORCEVILLE
Lecturer in English Literature, Universiteit van Amsterdam
Metaphor

HELEN FULTON
Senior Lecturer in English, University of Sydney
Alphabet; Mass Communication

LIANE GABORA
Independent scholar, San Diego
Memetics

GARY GENOSKO
Independent scholar, Winnipeg, Manitoba
Barthes, Roland; Baudrillard, Jean; Critique of the Political Economy of the Sign; Eco, Umberto; Elements of Semiology; Interactionist Analysis; Introduction to the Structural Analysis of Narratives; Mythologies; Semiotic and Symbolic; Semiurgy

HARJEET SINGH GILL
Professor of Linguistics, Jawaharlal Nehru University
Abélard, Pierre; Realism and Nominalism

BARBARA GODARD
Professor of English, York University
Feminist Semiotics

DAVID GRAHAM
Professor of French, Memorial University of Newfoundland
Blason Poétique; Blazon; Emblem; Heraldry; Impresa

PETER GROVES
Lecturer in English, Monash University
Distinctive Features; Language Change; Linearity;
Markedness; Pertinence

PETER GRZYBEK
Assistant Professor, Karl-Franzens Universität Graz
Bogatyrëv, Pëtr Grigor'evic; Karcevskij, Sergej Iosifovic;
Lotman, Jurij M.; Moscow-Tartu School; Mukařovský,
Jan; Paroemiology; Prague School; Russian Formalism;
Trubetzkoy, Nikolaj S.

ROMAN GUBERN
*Professor of Audiovisual Communication, Universidad
Autónoma de Barcelona*
Comics

GUSTAVO GUERRA
*Visiting Assistant Professor of English, Northern Illinois
University*
Vico, Giambattista

DON HANDELMAN
Professor of Anthropology, Hebrew University of Jerusalem
Symbolic Type; Turner, Victor

MICHAEL HARKIN
Associate Professor of Anthropology, University of Wyoming
Douglas, Mary Tew; Ethnoscience; History; Leach,
Edmund; Lévi-Strauss, Claude

PETER HARRIES-JONES
Professor of Anthropology, York University
Bateson, Gregory; Double Bind

BARBARA HAVERCROFT
*Associate Professor of Literary Studies and Semiotics,
Université du Québec à Montréal*
Reference

BENOÎT HEILBRUNN
*Assistant Professor of Marketing, Ecole Supérieure de
Commerce, Lyon*
Logo; Trademark

GREIG HENDERSON
Associate Professor of English, University of Toronto
Burke, Kenneth D.; Grammar of Motives, A; Language as
Symbolic Action

ROBERT HODGE
*Foundation Professor of Humanities, University of Western
Sydney*
Communication; Distance; Space; Stereotype

JESPER HOFFMEYER
Professor of Biochemistry, Københavns Universitet
Biosemiotics; Receptors; Umwelt

AMANDA S. HOLZRICHTER
*Doctoral candidate in linguistics, University of Texas at
Austin*
Fingerspelling; Sign Languages

JOHN A. F. HOPKINS
Professor of Linguistics, Tamagawa University
Riffaterre, Michael

ANNE IRWIN
Doctoral student, University of Manchester
Military

LARS-ERIK JANLERT
*Associate Professor of Computing Science, Umeå Universitet,
Sweden*
Pictures and Computers

CUSHLA KAPITZKE
*Head of Information Services, The Cathedral School of Saint
Anne and Saint James, Townsville, Queensland*
Goody, John Rankin

BRIAN L. KEELEY
Postdoctoral fellow, Washington University
Artificial Life

JOHN M. KENNEDY
Professor of Psychology, University of Toronto
Affordance; Gibson, James J.; Haptics; Picture
Perception; Vision

VICKI KIRBY
*Lecturer in Sociology, Culture, and Communication,
University of New South Wales*
Cultural Difference; Value

OLDRICH KRÁL
*Professor of Chinese and Comparative Literature, Univerzita
Karlova*
Yi Jing

ULRICH J. KRULL
Professor of Analytical Chemistry, University of Toronto
Chemical Communication; Information

SVEND ERIK LARSEN
*Professor of Literature and Cultural Studies, Odense
Universitet*
Brøndal, Viggo; Copenhagen School; Hjelmslev, Louis;
Recent Theories on the Nature of the Language Sign;
Recherches Structurales 1949; Urban Semiotics

THEO VAN LEEUWEN
Professor of Communication Theory, London College of Printing
Halliday, Michael A. K.; Music

DAVID LIDOV
Associate Professor of Music, York University
Aesthetics; Articulation; Artificial Language; Clynes, Manfred; Diagrams; Jakobson's Model of Linguistic Communication; Nattiez, Jean-Jacques; Russell, Bertrand; Semiosis; Sign

AKIRA LIPPIT
Assistant Professor of Film Studies and Critical Theory, San Francisco State University
Animal

ALBERT LIU
Design Consultant, Wave Loch Inc., San Diego, California
Morphology; Spengler, Oswald; Thom, René; Turing, Alan

CARL G. LIUNGMAN
Independent scholar, Kristianstad, Sweden
Aniconic Visual Signs; Ideograms

CHARLES LOCK
Professor of English Literature, Københavns Universitet
Jakobson, Roman

ERIC LOUW
Lecturer in Media and Cultural Studies, Charles Sturt University
Althusser, Louis; Apartheid; Marx, Karl; Materialist Semiotics

CARMEN LUKE
Associate Professor of Education, University of Queensland
Bourdieu, Pierre; Habitus

FRANSON MANJALI
Senior Assistant Professor in Linguistics, Jawaharlal Nehru University
Bhartṛhari; Catastrophe Theory

PIERRE MARANDA
Professor Emeritus of Anthropology, Université Laval
Myths; Semiography

GAY MCAULEY
Associate Professor in French and Director of the Centre for Performance Studies, University of Sydney
Acting; Theater

JOHN MCCLELLAND
Professor of French, Comparative Literature, and Sports History, University of Toronto
Allegory; Sport

ALEC MCHOUL
Associate Professor in Communication Studies, Murdoch University
Speech Act Theory; Text; Wittgenstein, Ludwig

MARGA VAN MECHELEN
Lecturer in Art History, Universiteit van Amsterdam
Riegl, Alois; Wölfflin, Heinrich

RICHARD P. MEIER
Associate Professor of Linguistics and Psychology, University of Texas at Austin
Fingerspelling; Sign Languages

RAY MORRIS
Professor of Sociology, York University
Cartoons; Ethnomethodology; Gossip

JÜRGEN E. MÜLLER
Associate Professor of Theater and Film Studies, Universiteit van Amsterdam
Enonciation Impersonnelle ou Le Site du Film, L'; Film Semiotics

MIHAI NADIN
Professor and Head of Computational Design Program, Bergische Universität-Gesamthochschule Wuppertal
Bense, Max; Cassirer, Ernst; Computer; Coseriu, Eugen; Interface; Parallelism; Structure

WINFRIED NÖTH
Professor of Linguistics and Semiotics, Universität Gesamthochschule Kassel
Advertising; Art; Koch, Walter A.

SVEN OUZMAN
Head of Rock Art Department, National Museum of South Africa, Bloemfontein
Mindscape; Rock Art

JUDY PELHAM
Assistant Professor of Philosophy, York University
Frege, Gottlob

PAUL PERRON
Professor of French, University of Toronto
Paris School

MARKUS PESCHL
Professor of Philosophy of Science and Cognitive Science, Universität Wien
Abacus; Algorithm; Artificial Intelligence; Computational Neuroscience; Connectionism; Cybernetics; Database; Debugging; Error Back-Propagation; Expert Systems; Feedback and Feedforward; Knowledge Representation; Parsing; Turing, Alan

ROLAND POSNER
Chair of Linguistics and Semiotics and Director of the Research Center for Semiotics, Technische Universität Berlin
Number Representation; Pragmatics

FERNANDO POYATOS
Professor of Spanish and Latin American Cultures, University of New Brunswick
Conversation; Cultureme; Literary Anthropology; Nonverbal Bodily Sign Categories; Nonverbal Communication in the Novel; Paralanguage; Punctuation; Sounds; Speech

KENNETH PRKACHIN
Professor and Chair of Psychology, University of Northern British Columbia
Ekman, Paul; Face; Facial Action Coding System

FABIO RAMBELLI
Assistant Professor of Religion, Williams College
Buddhism; Daoism; Mandala; Mantra; Zen Gardens

ALAN RICHARDSON
Assistant Professor of Philosophy, University of British Columbia
Vienna Circle

GÖRAN ROSSHOLM
Associate Professor of Literature, Stockholms Universitet
Goodman, Nelson; Languages of Art

MICHAEL RUSE
Professor of Philosophy and Zoology, University of Guelph
Coevolution; Culturgen; Darwin, Charles; Dawkins, Richard; Evolution; Exaptation; Hamilton, William D.; Interspecific Communication; Manipulation; Meme; Signal; Sociobiology; Trivers, Robert; Wilson, Edward O.; Zahavi, Amotz; Zoosemiotics

FERNANDE SAINT-MARTIN
Professor of Contemporary Art and Visual Semiotics, Université du Québec à Montréal
Arnheim, Rudolph

TONY SCHIRATO
Senior Lecturer, School of Contemporary Communication, Central Queensland University
Intentionality; Jameson, Frederic; Meaning

HANSGEORG SCHLICHTMANN
Professor of Geography, University of Regina
Cartography

DAVID SCOTT
Professor of French, Trinity College, Dublin
Postage Stamps

BRADD SHORE
Professor of Anthropology, Emory University
Baseball; Cultural Knowledge; Culture, Semiotics of

SCOTT SIMPKINS
Associate Professor of English, University of North Texas
Goffman, Erving; Lyotard, Jean-François; Play; Postsemiotics

O. F. G. SITWELL
Professor of Geography, University of Alberta
Cultural Landscape

GÖRAN SONESSON
Associate Professor of Semiotics, Lunds Universitet
Aniconic Visual Signs; Blissymbolics; Chirography; Denotation and Connotation; Icon; Iconicity; Image and Picture; Index; Indexicality; Metonymy; Opposition; Photography; Pictorial Semiotics; Rhetoric of the Image

PAUL J. THIBAULT
Associate Professor, Università di Venezia
Arbitrariness, Principle of; Binarism; Code; Course in General Linguistics; Dialogue; Habermas, Jürgen; Inner Speech; Langue and Parole; Linguistic Motivation; Linguistic Relativism; Metalanguage; Multimodality; Poststructuralism; Saussure, Ferdinand de; Signification; Structuralism; Synchronic and Diachronic; Whorf, Benjamin Lee

EVAN THOMPSON
Assistant Professor of Philosophy, York University
Autopoiesis; Gaia Hypothesis

CLIVE THOMSON
Professor of French Language and Literature, University of Western Ontario
Bakhtin, Mikhail M.; Rabelais and His World

TERRY THREADGOLD
Professor of English, Monash University
De Lauretis, Teresa; Discourse Analysis; Foucault, Michel

C. D. E. TOLTON
Professor of French and Cinema Studies and Director of the Cinema Studies Program, University of Toronto
Cinema; Grande Syntagmatique, La; Imaginary Signifier, The; Metz, Christian

ANNE URBANCIC
Senior Tutor in Italian Studies, University of Toronto
Feminism and Feminist Theories

ANTHONY WALL
Professor of French and Comparative Literature, University of Calgary
Bakhtin, Mikhail M.; Fiction; Rabelais and His World

JOY WALLACE
Lecturer in English and Cultural Studies, Charles Sturt University
Kristeva, Julia; Lacan, Jacques

UWE WIRTH
Professor of Literature, Johann Wolfgang Goethe Universität Frankfurt
Abductive Reasoning

SUSAN YELL
Senior Lecturer, School of Contemporary Communication, Central Queensland University
Implicature

Index

Note: Page numbers in boldface type indicate a major discussion.

A

Abacus, **1**, 136, 456
Abax, 1
Abductive opposition, 460
Abductive reasoning, **1–3**, 211, 311, 324, 460
Abélard, Pierre, **3–5**, 529–532
  on process of intellection, 3–4, 530–531
  study of sacred texts, 4–5
  theory of conceptualism, 3–5
  theory of signification, 3, 4
Aberrant coding, 133
Abhidharma, 93
Abhihitanvayavādins, 75
Abhyāsa, 96
Abolition movement, 234
Aboriginal alternate sign languages, 581
Aboriginal cultures, 249, 284, 364, 545, 546, 639
Abraham and Ishmael, allegory of, 21
Absent structure, 602
Absolute arbitrariness, 368
Absorption barrier, 561
Abstract painting, 26
Academy of Sciences, Section of Structural Typology of Slavic Languages, 423
Acculturation, 168
Achronological syntagma, 268–269
Acoustic image, 119, 299, 312, 368
Acronym, 245, 373
Act, in dramatistic pentad, 267
Acta Linguistica (Acta Linguistica Hafniensia), 92, 148, 533
Actantial Model, **5–8**, 111, 273, 439, 440, 441
Actants, **8–11**, 361, 438, 439
Actes sémiotiques-documents, 644
Acting, **11–13**
Action
  communicative, 275–276
  in dramatism, 267

Action, *cont.*
  dramaturgical, 276
  in Indian grammatical tradition, 75–76
  as level of discourse, 322–323
  norm-conformative, 276
  teleological, 276
Action descriptors (ADs), 231
Action sets, 158, 159
Action units (AUs), 231
Activations, of the connectionist network, 141, 143, 218
Actogenesis, 340
Actorial isotopy, 323
Actors (performing), 11–12
"Actualité du saussurisme, L'" ("The Relevance of Saussurism"; Greimas), 272
Adamson, Joseph, *as contributor,* 25–26, 251–252
Adaptation, 253, 321
Adaptors, 450
Additive number codes, 454, 455, 456
Adept, 174, 175
Adhikaraṇa (location of action), 76
Adieu Philippine (film), 121, 122, 268, 269, 270, 417
Adorno, Theodor, 332, 390, 430
Advertising, 389, 539, 614–616
  parallelism in, 465
  secondary indexical signs in, 308
  semiotics of, **13–16**
  studies of, 391
Aesthetica (Bense), 72
Aesthetic Function, Norm, and Value as Social Facts (Mukařovský), 39, 331
Aesthetic Letters (Schiller), 563
Aesthetic norm, doctrine of, 330–331, 520
Aesthetic overcoding, 39
Aesthetic (poetic) function, of sign, 17, 39, 330–331, 520
Aesthetics, **16–18**
  classical semiotic, 36
  codes, 39–40
  of dialectical materialism, 330
  Eco's semiotics of, 36–37

Aesthetics, *cont.*
  and formalism, 644
  functional structuralist, 426
  generative, 73
  glossematic, 36
  Goodman's symbol theory of, 37, 262–263, 354–355
  information-theoretical, 36, 72–73
  and intentionality, 541
  l'art pour l'art, 38
  materialist, 376, 541
  Morris's theory of iconicity, 36, 37–38
  parallelism, 465
  Peircean semiotic, 17.36, 37, 73, 210
  Prague School, 17, 36
  quantitative, 72–73
  self-referentiality, 37, 38
  semiogenetic theory of, 37
  semiotics of the Moscow-Tartu School, 36
  structuralist semiotics of, 36
"Aesthetics and the Theory of Signs" (Morris), 36
Aesthetics of Thomas Aquinas, The (Eco), 209
Aesthetic value, 520
Affective criticism, 533, 535
Affective stylistics, 533
Affect program, 211
Affordance, **18–19**
Africa, 155, 263
Afrikaner nationalism, 30–31
"Against Proper Objects" (Butler), 525
"Agency of the Letter in the Unconscious or Reason since Freud, The" (Lacan), 345
Agent, 8
  in dramatistic pentad, 267
Agnosia, 447
Agon, 26
Agonist, 112
Agonistics of language, 377
Agons, 100
AIDS, 526
Aiken, Howard, 137
Alas, Leopoldo, 373

ālaya-vijñāna, 96, 97
Alazon, 252
Albedo (reflectance), 254
Alchemist signs, 297
Alchemy of Race and Rights
  (Williams), 363
Alciato, Andrea (Alciati), 214
Alexander of Hales, 403
Algebraic sign, 328
Algebra of relations, 550
Algorithm, **19–20**, 45, 141, 560
  dialectical, 565
  genetic, 49
  learning, 142, 144, 218
  for parallel processing, 467
  parsing, 474
  transformation, 468
Alice Doesn't (De Lauretis), 184
Alienation, linguistic, 394
Allegorical type, 605
Allegories of Reading (De Man), 182
Allegory, **20–22**
Alleles, 406
Alliteration, 159
Allographic art, 355
Allophones, 199
Allotopy, 324
All That Heaven Allows (film), 301
"'All the Sad Young Men': AIDS and
  the Work of Mourning"
  (Nunokawa), 526
Alper, Harvey, 383
Alphabet, **22–24**
  Greek, 23
  letters as nonverbal signs, 23
  modern English, 23, 47
  Phoenician, 23
  phonetic, 47
  Roman, 23
  Semitic, 23
"Alphabet and the Sound System,
  The" (Trubetzkoy), 617
Alter-adaptors, 450, 585
Alternants, 461, 463–464
Alternate syntagma (*syntagme
  alterné*), 269–270
Althusser, Louis, **24–25**, 156, 195,
  332
  influence on film theory, 122, 392
  and Marxism, 24–25, 388, 395
  materialist concept of subject,
    333, 341, 395
  notion of interpellation, 316
  structuralist historical dynamic,
    286
  theory of ideology, 24–25, 186,
    235
Altman, Rick, 122
Altruism
  biological, 407
  reciprocal, 582, 583

Amacrines, 633
Amalgamation, 492
American Graffiti (film), 507
American Indian languages, 637
American Journal of Semiotics, 558
*American Signatures: Semiotic Inquiry
  and Method* (Sebeok), 558
American Sign Language (ASL), 245,
  579, 580, 581–582
Amerindian myth, 286, 365
Amérique (America; Baudrillard), 69
Amharic, 387
Amulet, 173, 381
Anagesis, 340
Anagnorisis, 26
Anagogical interpretation, of
  scripture, 21
Anagram, 116
Analogic codings, 65, 160
Analogy, 295, 299, 351, 374
Analyse du film, L' (Bellour), 121,
  243
Analysis of Mind, The (Russell), 550
Analyte, 112–113
Analytical (Anglo-Saxon)
  philosophical tradition, 538
Anand, Mulk Raj, 372
Anaphora, 116, 538
Anasazi, 546
Anatomy of Criticism (Frye), **25–26**,
  251–252
Ancestor, 50, 51
Andrews, Ben, 122, 270
Andronov, Aleksandr A., 614
*Angels Fear: Toward an Epistemology
  of the Sacred* (Bateson), 67
Aniconic visual signs, **26–27**, 85–87
  heraldry, **283–285**
  logos, **373–375**
Animal, **27–30**, 37
  allegory and, 21
  communication, 382–383,
    557–558, 641–642, 652
  magnetism, 29
  play, 493
  symbolicum, 108
Annales School of historiography,
  286, 288
Année sociologique, L', 206
Annotation, in mapping, 103, 104
Anomie, 604
Anthony, Susan B., 234
Anthropological linguistics, 133
Anthropologie structurale (Lévi-
  Strauss), 598
Anthropology
  cognitive, 221
  cultural, 158, 204–205, 288
  historical, 287–288
  self-reflexivity, 646

Anthropology, *cont.*
  social, 359
  structural-functional, 598
  structural Marxism, 68
  symbolic, 165, 205, 359–360
Anthropomorphism, 217, 650
Anthroposemiotics, 83, 340, 558
Antiperspectivism, 198
Anti-Subject, 10, 11
Antithetical parallelism, 465
Antonymy, 200
Anvitabhidhānavādin, 75
Apadāna (source of action), 76
Apartheid, **30–32**
Aphasia, 86–87, 312, 327, 415, 596,
  597
Aphasiology, 423, 447
Aphoria, 469
Apocopated speech, 522
Apologie du logos (Thom), 614
"Apparatus, The" (Baudry), 300
Appellative (conative) sign of
  function, 330, 331
  in advertising, 15
Applause (film), 269
Applied semiotics, 10
Appropriation, principle of, 116
Apraxia, 447
Apuleius, 565
Aquinas, Thomas, 400, 499
Aragon, Louis, 60
Araújo, Francisco de, 404
Arbitrariness, principle of, **32–33**,
  153–154, 368–369, 537, 556,
  579
Arcades, 71
Archaeology of Knowledge, The
  (Foucault), 247
Archemes, 33
Archetypal criticism, 251–252
Archetypal morphologies, 110–111
Archetype, Frye's concept of,
  251–252
Arche-writing, 182
Architectonic systems, 33–34
Architectura, De (Marcus Vitruvius
  Pollio), 33
Architecture, **33–35**, 434
  as language, 33, 161–164
  recurrent, 142
  semiotics of, 587, 624
  structuralist analysis of, 587
"Architecture of Theories, The"
  (Peirce), 478
Archive, 247–248
Arcs, in graphs, 190
Area studies (Oriental studies), 506
Arewa, Ojo, 471
Arguments, signs as, 478
Ariss, Rachel, *as contributor*, 563–565

Aristotle, 318, 529, 568
  concept of language, 149, 150
  concept of mimesis, 22
  concept of relation, 401
  concept of sign in terms of
    psyche and *physis*, 150
  linguistic universality, 117
  logic of propositions, 565, 566
  narrative model, 433
  philosophical categories, 92
  poetics, 495, 496, 497, 534
  on significance of metaphor,
    411–412
  study of biology, 27–28
  types of oppositions, 43
Arithmetic, Frege's thesis of, 250,
  251
Arluke, A., 266
Armory, 283–284, 305
Arms races, in coevolution, 129, 180
Arnaud, André-Jean, 357
Arnauld, Antoine, 187
Arnheim, Rudolph, **35–36**
Arnold, Matthew, 390
Arrêter le langage, 97
Art, **36–40**
  allographic, 355
  as an autonomous sign, 520
  autographic, 355
  avant-garde, 564
  Bense on, 73
  changing styles of representation
    in, 260
  decorative, 261
  empirical study of, 35–36
  history, 40–41, 540–542
  and illusion, 40–41
  indexicality, 37
  mass-produced, 71
  mathematical approaches to, 36
  as mimesis, 37
  neurosemiotics of, 18
  origins of form in, 260–261
  pragmatics of, 38–39
  reception of, 260
  semantics of, 37–38
  semiogenetic theory of, 37
  as sign, 16
  symbol theory of, 37, 262–263,
    354–355
  theory of interpretive openness
    of, 37
"Art and Answerability" (Bakhtin),
  57
Art and Beauty in the Middle Ages
  (Eco), 209
*Art and Illusion: A Study in the
  Psychology of Pictorial
  Representation* (Gombrich),
  40–41, 260, 261

Art and Visual Perception (Arnheim),
  35
"Art as a Device" (Šklovskij), 551
"Art as a Semiotic Fact"
  (Mukařovský), 426, 519, 520
Artaud, Antonin, 69
Arthrology, 213
Articulation, **41–44**
  distinctive features, 41, 42, 79,
    199–201, 327, 351, 480, 519
  double, 33, 41, 42, 43
  extrasemiotic factors, 42–43
  fingerspelling, 245–246
  hierarchies of, 44
  linguistic and nonlinguistic, 42
  markedness, 41, 42, 385–387
  pertinence, 479–481
  phoneme, 481–482
  structures of, 43–44
  syntactic, 47
Artifactual environment, 168
Artifactual signs, in mapping, 104,
  105
Artificial intelligence (AI), **44–46,**
  65, 97, 109, 135, 222, 466, 618
  and concept of abductive
    reasoning, 3
  and expert systems, 45, 179,
    226–227
  and interface, 319–321
  and internal pictures, 492–493
  methodological and other
    problems, 45–46
  relation to artificial life, 49
  and symbolic representation, 336
Artificiality (representation), of
  literary work, 544
Artificial language, **46–48,** 86–88
Artificial life (AL), **48–51,** 603
  and autopoiesis, 54
  relation to artificial intelligence,
    49
Artificial (virtual) reality, 491
Artistic development, teleological
  theory of, 541
Artography, functional, 103–104
Art pour l'art
  aesthetics, 38
  approach to rock art, 544–545
Asanga, 96
ASCII, 561
Asdiwal, Tsimshian myth of, 365,
  587
Ashby, W. Ross, 171–172, 570
Aspectual syntax, 273–274
Assertion sign, 250
Assimilation, linguistic, 387
Association, theory of, 312
Association for Machine
  Translation, 423

Association phonologique
  internationale, 617
Associative learning, 142
Associative solidarities, 368–369
Astrological signs, 297
Astronomical signs, 297
Asymbolia, 447
"Asymmetric Dualism of the
  Linguistic Sign, The"
  (Karcevskij), 335
Athletics. *See* Play; Sport
Atomic instructions, 19
Attic figures, 454
Attraction basins, 559
Attractors, 559, 561
Audio recording, 389
Audiovisual texts, 243, 244
Auerbach, Erich, 59, 627
"Aufgabe des Übersetzers, Die" (The
  Task of the Translator;
  Benjamin), 71
Augmented reality, 491
Augustine of Hippo, 38, **51–53,**
  498, 568, 573
  definition of sign, 399–400
Aumont, Jacques, 121, 242–243,
  244
Aura, 71
Ausnahmslosige Lautgesetze
  (exceptionless sound laws), 351
Austin, John L., 196, 258, 356, 384,
  516, 526, 538, 591
Australian Aborigines, 249, 545,
  546
  languages, 639
  sign languages, 581
Australian School, 484, 486
Austrian Institute for Historical
  Research, 540
Auteur theory, 392
"Author als Produzent, Der" (The
  Author as Producer; Benjamin),
  71
"Author and Hero in Aesthetic
  Activity" (Bakhtin), 57–58
Authoritative discourses, 191–192
Authors and heroes, relation
  between, 58
Autofunction, 552
Autographic art, 355
Automaton, 171
Autonomy, and autopoiesis, 55
Autopoiesis, **53–55,** 98, 254, 640
Auxiliants, in Greimas's actantial
  model, 10
Axes of substitution and selection,
  415
Axis, 488
Ayer, A. J., 631
Aztecs, 287, 637

B

Babbage, Charles, 137
Bacon, Roger, 402
Baiblé, Claude, 121
Bakhtin, Mikhail M., **57–59,** 107, 167
  centripetal and centrifugal forces, in language, 58, 191, 192
  concept of carnivalesque, 59, 192, 287–288, 341
  concept of language, 528
  construction of subjectivity, 59, 192
  critique of formalism, 553
  critique of material aesthetics, 541
  deconstruction of myths, 192
  dialogism, 156, 191–193, 341, 342, 563
  double-voiced discourses, 58
  on the formal method, 644
  heteroglossia, 192, 195, 287
  notion of social multiaccentuality, 192
  study of Rabelais as cultural figure, 527–528
Bakhtin Circle, 57
Bal, Mieke, 238, 541
Bali, 289
Balibar, Etienne, 24
Balkin, J. M., 358
Ballet, 47
Bally, Charles, 58, 150, 335, 518
Balzac, Honoré de, 60, 315
Banerji, Bibhutibhushan, 371
Baptismal creed, 569
Bar-Hillel, Yehoshua, 309
Bark paintings, 434
Baroque painterly style, 645
Barthes, Roland, **59–61,** 195, 258, 392, 598, 602
  and actantial model, 322
  arthrology, 213
  attack on authorial intentionality, 315
  on binarism, 213
  on cinema, 417
  concept of lexias, 60, 259
  concept of zero degree, 60, 97
  on denotation and connotation, 213–214, 540
  and development of French structuralism, 467
  expression-relation-content (ERC), 213–214
  food system, 213
  foundations of semiotic advertising research, 13–14
  garment system, 213

Barthes, Roland, *cont.*
  on historical discourse, 287
  interpretation of Zen semiotics, 651
  introduction of Buddhist concepts into semiotics, 97
  on Japanese mapping strategies, 588
  and *Langages* (journal), 271
  on language/speech relation, 212–213
  levels of discourse, 322
  Marxist phase, 395
  on musical significance, 431
  on myth, 59–60, 108, 432
  narratology, 268, 322–323, 443
  neither-norism, 432
  on photography, 482–483
  on pictorial signification, 539–540
  on readerly vs. writerly texts, 341
  on the rhetoric of the image, 415, 484, 539–540, 615
  scientist period, 60
  on semantic opposition, 459
  semiology, 151, 212–214, 242
  on signified/signifier relation, 213
  staggered systems, 60, 214
  on syntagm and system, 213
  on systematic plane, 213
  textual analysis period, 60–61, 494
Baseball, **61–64**
Bases, 224
BASIC, 19, 47
Baskin, Wade, 150, 576
Bataille, Georges, 68, 275, 341, 508
Bates, Henry Walter, 177
Bateson, Gregory, **64–67,** 211, 605
  biosemiotics, 66–67, 82, 83
  concept of frame, 259
  distinction between types of codes, 65, 126, 160
  on double bind, 64, 201–203
  ethnographic film, 64
  focus on rituals, 166
  on logical typing, 64, 410, 411
  redundancy principle, 128
  on report and demand dimension of communication, 127, 166
  schismogenesis, 605
  and semiotic nature of social interaction, 258
Bateson, Mary Catherine, 67
Bateson, William, 64
Baudelaire, Charles, 71, 482
Baudrillard, Jean, **67–70,** 289, 333
  concept of hyperreal, 68, 69, 507
  concept of semiurgy, 571
  on consumption, 615

Baudrillard, Jean, *cont.*
  logics of value, 152
  notion of the simulacrum, 68–69, 398
  structural analysis of the system of object-signs, 68, 152–153
Baudry, Jean-Louis, 121, 300, 417
Bauhaus school, 571
Baumgarten, Alexander G., 16, 36, 72
Bayeux Tapestry, 283
Bazell, C. E., 537
Bazin, André, 482
Beaugrande, Robert de, 196
Beauty, phenomenon of, 16, 17
Becker, Henrik, 517
Becker, Oskar, 72
Bedeutung (reference or denotation), 251, 549
"Before Completion" ("Ferrying Incomplete" or "Not-yet-fording"), 649
"Begriff der Geschichte, Uber den" (Theses on the Philosophy of History; Benjamin), 71
"Begriff der Kunstkritik in der deutschen Romantik, Der" (The Concept of Art Criticism in German Romanticism; Benjamin), 70
Begriffsschrift (Conceptual Notation; Frege), 250
Behavior in Public Places (Goffman), 258
Belgian semiotic Groupe (Groupe μ), 295, 324
Belič, A., 520
Bellour, Raymond, 121, 122, 243, 270, 392
Bellugi, Ursula, 580
Belsey, Catherine, 235
Belting, Hans, 261
Belton, John, 122
Benedict, Ruth, 165
Beneke, Friedrich, 465
Benjamin, Jessica, 236
Benjamin, Walter, 29, 59, 60, **70–72,** 390, 482, 541
Bense, Max, 34, 36, 37, **72–74,** 601, 603
Bentham, Jeremy, 162, 249, 356
Benveniste, Émile, 122, 153, 154, 216–217, 244, 301, 322
  critique of Saussure, 332, 537
  notion of *énonciation*, 216–217, 244
Berg, A. I., 423
Berger, Peter, 164
Berger, René, 571
Bergmann, Gustav, 629, 631

Bergson, Henri, 29
Berlin, Brent, 222
Berlin, Sir Isaiah, 627
Berliner Chronik (A Berlin Chronicle; Benjamin), 70
Bernanos, Georges, 272
Bernard, Jeff, *as contributor*, 547–549
Bernstein, Basil, 160, 195, 204, 596, 598
Bernstein, Richard J., 546
Bernštejn, Sergej I., 327, 551
Berr, Henri, 206
Berryman, Robert, 211
Bertin, Jacques, 104
Bertz, Steven H., 113
Bettetini, Gianfranco, 242, 244
Between Signs and Non-Signs (Rossi-Landi), 548
Bhabha, Homi K., 155, 506
Bhartṛhari, **74–76**
Bhāvanā, 96
Bible, 52
  figurative language of, 251
  fourfold intepretation of, 20, 21
Bierman, Arthur, 295, 296
Bierwisch, Manfred, 79
Bi-isotopy, 324
Bīja, 94, 96–97, 383, 384
"*Bildungsroman* and Its Significance in the History of Realism, The" (Bakhtin), 58
Binarism, 42, 43, **76–82,** 111, 152
  and cultural diversity, 155
  distinctive features, 199–201, 351
  in landscapes, 164
  and markedness, 385
  of nature and culture, 165
  opposition between verbal and visual language, 107–108
  and phonological systems, 327, 565
  in pictorial semiotics, 485
  of sex and gender, 89
  in Western thought, 343
Binary code, 457
Binding, chemical, 112–113
Binocular relationships, 488, 633
Biocybernetics, 123
Biogenesis, 339–340
Biological altruism, 407
Biology
  and autopoiesis, 54, 254
  computational, 49
  theoretical, 48–49
Biology of Literature, The (Koch), 339
Biosemiotics, 29, 66–67, **82–84,** 340, 559, 623. *See also* Zoosemiotics
  affordances, 18–19
  artificial life, **48–51**

Biosemiotics, *cont.*
  autopoiesis, **53–55**
  chemical communication, 112–113
  Gaia hypothesis, 253–255
  neurosemiotics, **446–447**
  receptors, 536–537
Biosphere, 376
Biostructuralism, 162
Biota, 253–254
Bipolar cells, 633
Birdwhistell, Ray, 447
Birkhoff, George D., 73
Birmingham Centre for Contemporary Culture Studies, 156, 195, 391
Blache, Vidal de la, 162
Black, Max, 412
Black box, language as, 352
Black Skin, White Masks (Fanon), 505
"Black (W)holes and the Geometry of Black Female Sexuality" (Hammonds), 526
Black women, 526
Blakemore, Colin, 185
Blanchard, Marc Eli, 378
Blanché, Robert, 565
Blason anatomique, 84, 85
Blason poétique, **84–85**
Blasons domestiques (Corrozet), 85
Blazon, 84, **85–86,** 283
Blind Watchmaker, The (Dawkins), 179
Bliss, Charles, 86
Blissymbolics, **86–88,** 297, 299
Blissymbolics Communication Institute, 86
Bloch, Marc, 288
Blocked reflexivity, 202, 203
Bloomfield, Leonard, 188, 328, 386, 533, 598, 617
Bluffing, as a semiotic strategy, 382–383
Blum, Alan, 317–319
Boas, Franz, 638
Boas, George, 28, 133
Body
  adaptors, 372, 450, 585–586
  as basis of social differentiation, 277–278
  idiom, 258
  images of, 205
  memory, 341
  as performative elaboration, 526
  as site of subjectivity, 398
Boethius, 529, 531–532
Bogatyrëv, Pëtr Grigor'evič, **88–89,** 470, 518, 519, 520, 551, 611
Bohr, Niels, 370

Bonamy, Pierre-Nicholas, 149
Bonaparte, Marie, 348
Bond, James, 323
Bonding, 536
Bonfantini, Massimo, 2
Book of Changes (Yi jing), 647
Boole, George, 476, 477, 549
Boolean logic, 46, 136, 227, 320
Boon, James, 289
Booth, Wayne, 122
Bopp, Franz, 541
Bordwell, David, 122
Boudon, Pierre, 34
Bouissac, Paul, *as contributor,* 33–35, 183–184, 323–324, 446–447, 460–461, 481–482, 565–568, 568–571
Boundaries, architectural, 587
Boundaries and regions, systems of, 43, 44
Boundary conditions, 82
  figure-ground, 65
Bourdieu, Pierre, 39, **89–91,** 167, 195
  theory of habitus, 89–90, 277–278, 288, 316, 333
Bourgeois myth, 432–433
Bourgeois peace, 357
Bowie, Malcolm, 348
Bracken, Christopher, *as contributor,* 70–72, 181–183, 505–507, 507–509, 527–528
Bracketing, 220
Bracket syntagma *(syntagme en accolade),* 269, 270
"Brahmakāṇḍa," 74
Brahman, 74
Brāhmī writing system, 385
Braille, 26
Brain models, 135–136
Branches (lines), of diagrams, 190
Brand, 375, 614–616
Branigan, Edward, 122, 243
Braudel, Fernand, 288
Breakpoints, 180
Breathing
  control, 462
  and speech, 588–589
Brecht, Bertolt, 12, 67, 71
Bremond, Claude, 268, 443
Brentano, Franz, 92, 400, 466, 499, 598
Breuer, Josef, 29
Bricolage, 285, 597
Brik, Osip, 551, 644
Brillouin, Léon, 311
Briskin, Linda, 236
British Sign Language, 245, 578
Britton, Karl, 533
Broadbent, Geoffrey, 34

Brög, Hans, 73
Brøndal, Viggo, **91–93,** 147–148, 290, 565
Brown, G. Spencer, 54
Brown, Gillian, 195
Brown, Penelope, 516
Brown, R., 198
Browne, Nick, 121, 122, 243
Brunette, Peter, 121
Brunn, Heinrich von, 645
Brusak, Karel, 611
Bryson, Norman, 261
Buchbinder, David, *as contributor,* 500–502
Buddhism, **93–99,** 650–651
    and Daoism, 175
    Japanese esoteric, 95
    Mahāyāna, 94–95
    mandala, 381–382
    mantras, 383, 384
    philosophy of language, 93–95
    semiotics of, 95–98
    Tantric, 95, 382
Budniakiewicz, Therese, *as contributor,* 5–8, 8–11, 271–274, 347–443, 443–445
Bühler, Karl, 533
    tripartite concept of language functions, 16, 330, 426, 520
Bukharin, Nikolaj I., 553
Bulletin du Cercle Linguistique de Copenhague, 147–148
Bullet theory, 132
Bunn, James, 511
Bunyan, John, 21
Burch, Noel, 121, 122
Burke, Kenneth D., **99–102,** 266–268, 349–350, 627
Burks, Arthur W., 309, 328
Burns, Tom, 258
Bush, Vannevar, 137
Butler, Judith, 525, 526
Butterfly catastrophe, 110, 614
Buyssens, Eric, 533
Bylina, 551
Byron, George Gordon, 505

C

Cahiers du cinéma, 392
Caillois, Roger, 493
Calculi, 1, 456
Calculus, 46, 634
Calculus ratiocinator, 137
California School of Ethnoscience, 222
Calligraphy, 24, 647
Camera Obscura, 122
Camouflage, 418
Canon, The, 497

Canonical tale (narrative schema), 440
Canonization, 501
Cantineau, Jean, 459
Canting arms, 284
Capitalism, 68, 388, 507
    and development of mass media, 389
    expansion of, 508
    imperialist, 507
    multinational, 507
Capital (Marx), 387, 506
Capra, Fritjof, 98
Caracci, Annibale, 294
Carani, Marie, 486
    as contributor, 40–41, 260–261
Cardona, Giorgio Raimondo, 175, 382
Caricature, 107, 260
Carnap, Rudolf, 250, 466, 515, 532, 574, 629, 630, 631
Carnivalesque, 59, 107, 192, 210, 287–288, 527–528
Carol, Noël, 244
Carroll, Lewis, 30, 630
Carse, James, 494
Cartographic semiotics (cartosemiotics), 104
Cartography, **103–106,** 419
Cartoons, **106–108**
    political, 489
Case, Sue-Ellen, 526
Case grammar, 290, 367
Casetti, Francesco, 217, 242, 243, 244
Cassirer, Ernst, **108–110,** 532, 631
Castration complex, 301, 347
Catach, Nina, 113
Catachresis, 489, 506, 543
Catagenesis, 340
Catalyzers, 322
Cataphora, 538
Catastrophe theory (CT), **110–112,** 598, 613
Catch-22 (Heller), 451
Categorial relations, 401, 402, 403
Categorias libri quattuor (Boethius), 401
Catégorie des cas, La (Hjelmslev), 290
Categories (Aristotle), 401
Category affiliation, in diagrams, 190
Catharsis, 534
Caxton, William, 521
Cénème, 113, 481
Center-on/surround-off receptive field, 633
Central-processing unit (CPU), 474
Centre d'Études des Communications de Masse, 322

Centre for Contemporary Cultural Studies, 391
Centre for Theory in the Humanities and Social Sciences, 318
Centripetal and centrifugal forces, in language, 58, 191, 192
Cercle Linguistique de Copenhagen, 147
Cercle Linguistique de Prague, 147
Čerkasskij, M. A., 471
Černov, I., 423
Certainty, On (Wittgenstein), 643
Certeau, Michel de, 333, 588
Červenka, Miroslav, 520
Cestami poetiky a estetiky (Mukařovský), 426
Chagall, Marc, 57
Chambre claire, La (Camera Lucida: Reflections on Photography; Barthes), 61
Champollion, Jean-François, 113
Chan argumentation, 651
Chang, Han-liang, *as contributor,* 113–116
Chaosmosis, 511
Chaos theory, 466, 588, 620
Characters
    in artificial languages, 47
    in Chinese ideograms, 114
    in narrative, 10, 322, 495
Charisma, 604
Charity, principle of, 516
Chart, text as, 99
Chateau, Dominique, 243, 244
Chatman, Seymour, 122, 243
Chaucer, Geoffrey, 352
Checklists, 158, 159
Chemical communication, 83, **112–113,** 311–312, 536–537, 558, 575
Chemical formulas, 23
Chemical signs, 26
"Chemical Theory of Interpenetration, The" (Peirce), 475
Chemoreception, 312
Cherokee Indian ideograms, 298
Chihamba, the White Spirit: A Ritual Drama of the Ndembu (Turner), 620
Child development, linguistic stages in, 314
China, imperial system, 176
Chinese cosmology, 648
Chinese ideograms, **113–116,** 175, 385
Chinese ink landscapes, 651
Chinese logograms, 22, 454–455, 456
Chinese ontological realism, **116–118**
Chinese sign language, 579

Chinese watercolor, 42
Chion, Michel, 122
Chirography, **118–119**
Chodorow, Nancy, 236
Chomsky, Noam, 226, 386, 549, 598
  on childhood language acquisition, 2, 199, 352
  concept of mentalism, 598
  concepts of surface structure and deep structure, 599–600
  notion of competence, 133, 149
  notion of ideal speaker-listener, 353
  phonological theory, 46–47, 78–79, 199, 200, 352
  transformational-generative grammar, 34, 126, 367, 429
Chora, 343
Chorème, 34, 482
Chreod, 598
Christian Doctrine, On (Augustine), 399
Christianity
  and allegory, 20, 21
  symbolism, 569
Christiansen, Broder, 520
"Christmas Tree in Eastern Slovakia, The" (Bogatyrëv), 88
Chroneme, 481
Chronemics, 170, 481
Chronological syntagma, 268–269
Chronotope, 528
Cicero, 568
Cilium, 536
Cinema, 35, **119–123**, 333, 389. *See also* Film Semiotics
  and comics, 131
  as daydream (rêverie), 301
  and "decay of aura," 71
  as discourse, 301
  early studies of, 391–392
  enunciative figures in, 217
  epic, 502
  great syntagmatique system of, 268–270
  metonymy in, 415
  notion of as language, 120
  paradigms of expression in, 120
"Cinematic Apparatus, The" (De Lauretis and Heath), 417
Cinematography, 119
Cinétique, 392
Circle, self-existing, 118
Citizen Kane (film), 270
Citrajñāna, 76
Civ'jan, T. V., 423
Cixous, Hélène, 236
Clark, Eric, 391
Classemes, 323, 324

Classical semiotic aesthetics, 36, 37
Classificatory learning, 142
Classifying messages, 202
Clerc, Laurent, 578
Clichés, 159, 160, 596
Clivage, 301
Closed (external) feedback loop, 232, 337–338
Clothing, 258
  as aniconic visual signs, 26
  codes, 198, 586, 587
  multiple dimensions, 299
  system, 213
Cloud chambers, 257
Cloud seals *(yunzhuan)*, 173, 174, 385
Clynes, Manfred, 18, **123–125**
Coats of arms, 84, 85–86
Code, **125–129**
  in advertising, 13–14
  alphabet as, 22–24
  analogic, 65, 536
  bias in Western conception of, 128
  class-based language, 278–279
  clothing, 60, 198, 586, 587
  cultural, 60, 68, 222
  digital, 65
  duality, 83
  elaborated, 596
  in film semiotics, 120–121
  grammar of, 126
  hermeneutic, 60
  iconic, 65
  in interpersonal behavior, 257–260
  interstratal relationships, 128
  and literary expression, 252
  as meaning-making potential, 126
  military use of, 418–419
  mimetic, 130
  nonspecific, 120
  as open system, 128
  picture, 631
  and pragmatics, 515
  proaïretic, 60
  redundancy relations, 128
  relation between content and expression, 126–127
  restricted vs. elaborated, 160, 204–205, 596
  semic, 60
  as semiotic terminology, 570
  as set of shared rules of interpretation, 125–126
  symbolic, 60
  theory of, 36, 39–40
  traffic-light, 126–128
  as two-dimensional semiotic space, 127–128

Coded iconic (symbolic visual) message, 13–14
Coding, aberrant, 133
Coevolution, **129–130,** 407, 427
  arms race, 129, 180
  and culturgen, 170–171
  and Gaia hypothesis, 255
  manipulation as, 382–383
Cognition
  and language, 118, 369
  simulation of, 135–136
Cognitive-instrumental rationality, 275
Cognitive linguistics, 222
Cognitive Linguistics, 414
Cognitive mapping, 333
Cognitive relativism, 365
Cognitive science, 618
  artificial intelligence as, 45, 97
  connectionist, 97, 111
  ethnoscience, 221, 222
  and knowledge representation, 336
Cognitive universalism, 222
Cognitivism, 97, 98
Cohen, Hermann, 108, 109, 265–266
Cohen, Rina, *as contributor*, 265–266
Cohen, Stanley, 391
Coleridge, Samuel Taylor, 350
Colin, Michel, 121, 244
Collected Papers (Peirce), 37
Collective consciousness, 520
Collective effervescence, 207
Collective representations, 206
Collective unconscious, 251, 420
Colonialism, 155, 192, 286, 505
Colony, 55
Color
  differentiation, 117–118
  in painting, 341, 342
  as a qualisign, 502
  terms, 222
"Colors and Cultures" (Sahlins), 154
Comaroff, Jean, 289
Comaroff, John, 289
Combinatorial semantics, 79
Comedy, 25, 26, 252, 535
Comics, **130–132**, 449, 485, 646
Command, 193, 279
Commemorative stamp, 502, 503, 504
Commentaries (Boethius), 531
Commentary, of emblems, 214
Commodification, 196
Common speech, 548
Communication, 64–67, **132–134,** 516. *See also* Conversation
  animal, 641–642
  axis, 9–10

Communication, *cont.*
  biological, 641
  and coevolution, 129
  competence, 133
  convergence, 243
  cooperation, 243
  and facial expressions, 211–212
  group and grid emphasis in, 204
  intentional model of, 303, 304
  interaction, 243
  intercultural, 651
  as interface, 320
  interpersonal, 257–260
  interspecific, 83, 321–322,
    382–383
  linear models of, 132
  literary, 516–517
  Marxist studies of, 393
  as material process, 134
  mathematical model of, 331
  mechanistic model of, 125–126
  in the military, 418–419
  and natural selection, 641–642
  paradoxical, 201–203
  as process and product, 133–134
  rationalist approach to, 303, 304
  reciprocal and participatory
    models of, 133
  semiotics of, 171
  social processes of, 257–260
  symbolic, 264
  as symbol of social order, 204
  types of, 243
*Communication and the Evolution of
  Society* (Habermas), 276
Communications, 131, 212, 322
Communicative action, theory of,
  275–276, 508
Communicative functions, model
  of, 15
Communicative order of nature, 66
Communicative rationality, 275
Communist Party, 24
Communitas, 621
Community, 133
Commutation test, 429
Comparative philology, 350
Comparative symbology, 620
Compensation, principle of, 93
Competitive learning, 143
Complex isotopy, 324
Complexity, 97
  formal, 422
Compliance/ants, 262, 355
Componential analysis, 79, 200,
  221–222, 324
Computation, 136
  semantics of, 136
  theory of, 490
Computational biology, 49

Computational neuroscience,
  135–136, 141–144
Computational theory, symbol in,
  569
Computer, **136–138,** 171, 407
  abacus as primitive form of, 1
  and artificial life, 48, 49–50
  and commodification of
    knowledge, 508
  debugging, 180–181
  games, 392
  graphics, 119
  icon, 293, 300
  memory, 49
  parallel processing, 466–467
  and pictures, 489–493
  recording, 123
  as semiotic engine, 136–137
  simulation, 491
  systems, 178–179
  virus, 49–50
Computer-mediated
  communication, **138–141,**
    646, 647
  emoticons, 521
  flaming, 246–247
  interface, 319–321
  as performance, 139
  synchronous modes, 138–139
Computer science, 171–172, 603,
    618–619
  algorithms in, 19
  and artificial intelligence, 44–46
  parsing in, 474
  semiography, 559
Computer-supported education,
  490
Conative (appellative) function
  in advertising, 15
  of logo, 375
  of sign, 330, 331
"Concept and Object, On" (Frege),
  251
Conceptual dependence, 559
Conceptualism, theory of, 529
Concretization, 520
Condensation, 99, 166, 345
Condensation/metaphor, 345
*Condition postmoderne, La: Rapport
  sur le savoir* (Lyotard), 377
Cones, 632, 633
Confucianism, 116, 649
Confucius, 648
Conimbricenses, 53, 402, 403, 404
Conjuncts, theory of, 416
Conjuncture, historical, 288
Conklin, Harold, 222
Conklin, William, 363
  as contributor, 356–359, 360–364

Connectionism, 98, 136, **141–144,**
  559
  and error back-propagation, 218
  of knowledge representation, 45,
    337–338
Connotation. *See* Denotation and
  connotation
Connotative logo, 374–375
*Conquest of America, The: The
  Question of the Other* (Todorov),
  157
Conscience collective, La, 206, 207
Consciousness, philosophy of, 275
"Consequences of Literacy, The"
  (Goody), 263–264
Consequences of Pragmatism (Rorty),
  276
Consonants, 23, 386–387
Constable, John, 41, 42
Constatives, 526, 591
Constructivism, 96, 97, 258
Consumerism, 68–69
Consumer research, 15
Consumption, 615
Contagious (metonymic) magic,
  327
Content, 187
  articulation, 43
  plane of, 291, 444, 512, 513, 533,
    537
  substance of, 291
Content analysis, of comics,
  131–132
Content elements (*c*-elements), 471
Context, 603–604
Context markers, 64
Context principle, 250
Contexts (pairings), 310
Contextual approach, to gossip,
  265–266
Contextualization, 192, 304,
  513–514
Contiguity, 307–308, 309, 310, 374,
  415, 416
Contingent scientific discourse, 221
Continuity
  principle of in language, 93
  in relation of subject to world,
    469
Continuous-words association tests
  (CWATs), 560
Contour, 487, 488
Contract, in narrative structure,
  438–440
Contradictories, 566
Contradictory metaterms, 567
Contraries, 566
Contrary metaterms, 567
Contrasts, optic, 487–488
Contre-blason anatomique, 85

Contributions to the Doctrine of Signs (Sebeok), 558

"Contribution to the Aesthetics of the Czech Verse" (Mukařovský), 425

Contrived conversation, 144

Conventionalisation, of iconic signs, 27

Conventional realism, 161

Conventional signs (legisigns), 47, 73, 115, 166, 478, 622
  pictures as, 37, 293–294, 295, 296–297

Convergence, in communication, 243

Convergent (polar) perspective, 488–489

Conversation, **144–147,** 195, 219, 276, 509, 516
  acoustic and visual pauses, 146–147
  analysis of, 195, 219, 592
  computer-mediated, 138–140
  contrived, 144
  correction, 195
  dialectical, 317–319
  Garfinkel's rules for, 219–220
  gaze in, 195
  gesture in, 195
  gossip, 265–266
  implicatures, 302–304
  initial behaviors, 144–145
  interlistener behaviors, 146
  listener's secondary behaviors, 146
  listener's speaker-directed behaviors, 145–146
  natural, 144
  reduced interaction, 144
  secondary turn-change behaviors, 145
  speaker's secondary behaviors, 146
  topic organization, 195
  turn-change behaviors, 145
  turn-taking, 144–145, 195

Conveyable contents, in mapping, 103

Cooccurrence, in diagrams, 190

Cook, David, 507–508

Cook, James, 286

Cooke, Derryck, 430

Coolie, The (Anand), 372

Cool Memories (Baudrillard), 69

Cool Memories II (Baudrillard), 69

Cooperative principle (CP), 243, 302–303, 516

Coordinate transformation, 103

Copenhagen School, **147–148,** 290, 459, 532, 537–538

Coppola, M., 579

Coquet, Jean-Claude, 271, 467, 468

Coreference check, 492

Cornea, 632

Cornell, Drucilla, 363

Cornford, Francis, 26

Corporeal expression, used by actors, 12

Correlation, notion of, 465

Corrozet, Gilles, 85, 215

Corrupt symbol, 68

Cortes, Hernán, 287

Corvin, Michel, 613

Coseriu, Eugen, **148–150,** 151, 196, 482

Cosmogenesis, 339, 340

Cosmology, importance of to literary works, 252

Costume, folk, 89

"Costume as Sign" (Bogatyrëv), 88

Cotext, 184

Coulter, Jeff, 592

Course in General Linguistics (Cours de linguistique générale; Saussure), 32, 91, **150–152,** 299, 555–557, 577, 598, 625
  arbitrary nature of the sign, 153–154
  concept of binary opposition, 76, 81
  distinction between diachronic and synchronic linguistics, 351
  first Russian translation, 335

Courtenay, Jan Baudouin de, 199, 481, 518, 550

Courtés, Joseph, 271, 273, 295, 567

Coward, Rosalind, 235

CPLUS, 47

Cratylus, 149, 328

Creation, poetic, 543

Creolization, 40

Crépeau, Pierre, 471

Crete, 22

Crick, Francis, 224

Critical-discourse analysis, 280

Critical interests, 275

Critical linguistics, 195, 280, 509

Critical semiotics, 509

Criticism, archetypal, 251–252

Critique of Judgment (Kant), 16, 38

Critique of Pure Reason (Kant), 475

Critique of the Political Economy of the Sign, For a (Baudrillard), 68, **152–153**

Croce, Benedetto, 627

Cross-referencing, 179

Crouwel, Wim, 503

Crusaders, 283

Cryptotypes, 639

Crystal, David, 461

Csikszentmihalyi, Mihaly, 494

Cubism, 198

Cued speech, 578

Cuisine, 263

Culler, Jonathan, 151, 533, 534, 556

Cultural adaptations, 165

Cultural anthropology, 158, 204–205, 288–289

Cultural capital, 89–90, 277

Cultural code, 60, 165, 222

Cultural difference, 89–91, **153–157,** 263–265

Cultural Dynamics, 371

Cultural goods, 89–90

Culturalism, 395

Cultural knowledge, 89–90, **157–161,** 264, 277–278, 560–561, 640

Cultural landscape, **161–165,** 419–421, 587–588

Cultural mass production, 332

Cultural models, 158–160, 360

Cultural relativism, 330

Cultural scenarios, 158

Cultural schemata, 165

Cultural scripts, 158

Cultural studies, 156, 186
  approach to mass communication, 391
  on gender and narrative in film, 236
  proverbs as paradigms for, 471
  two paradigms debate, 156

Cultural systems, 169

Culture
  anthropological definition of, 165
  as cognitive structure, 165
  complexity of notion, 153
  effect on display of emotion, 211
  group and grid classifications of, 204–205
  as a knowledge system, 165
  as a semantic system, 185
  symbolic forms of, 165, 263
  traditional definition of, 156

Culture, Media, Language (Hall et al.), 392

Culture, semiotics of, 17, **165–168,** 204–205, 375–377, 624
  cultural knowledge, 157–160
  evolutionary, 339–340
  Koch's sociosemiotic theory, 339
  Leach's model, 360

Culture and Communication (Leach), 360

Culture and Explosion (Lotman), 377

Culture and Imperialism (Said), 505

Cultureme, **168–170,** 277–278, 371, 405

Culturgen, **170–171,** 405, 570

Cusp catastrophe, 110, 111, 614
Cuts, associational, in film, 269
C-VIC, 87
Cybernetics, 54, 65, 72, 125,
    171–172
  approach to cultural analysis, 166
  computational neuroscience,
    135–136
  and concept of parallelism,
    466–467
  feedback and feedforward,
    232–233
  interface, 319–321
  parsing, 474
  terminology of, 570
  theory of, 598
Cyberspace, 138, 492
*Czech and Slovak Folk Theater (Lidové
    divadlo české a slovenské;
    Bogatyrëv), 88

D

Dai Rongzhou, 649
Daisyworld computer model, 254
Daly, Martin, 584
Damisch, Hubert, 35, 539, 541–542
Dance
  as aniconic visual sign, 27
  hierarchies of articulation, 44
  notation, 47–48
Danet, Brenda, *as contributor,*
    138–141, 246–247, 645–647
Danish sign language, 579
Danse macabre (Totentanz), 215
Dante Alighieri, 21, 350
Dao, 173
Daodejing (Tao Te Ching), 173
Daoism, 116, **173–176,** 385, 649
d'Aquili, Eugene, 162–163
Darnton, Robert, 288
Darwin, Charles, **176–178,** 179,
    223, 351, 407, 582
  communication studies, 177–178
  interest in the face as signaling
    system, 229
  natural selection principle,
    176–177, 223, 224, 253
  sexual selection principle,
    177–178, 650
  theory of evolution, 29, 129,
    176–178
Dascal, Marcelo, 516
Dasein, 28
Database, **178–179**
Data glove, 491, 492
David Copperfield (Dickens), 372,
    452
Davidson, David, 516
Davis, Natalie Zemon, 288

Dawkins, Richard, 129, 170,
    179–180, 254, 404, 407, 583
Dayan, Daniel, 122
Deaf, 245–246, 578
Dean, Kenneth, 176
Death, 69
Death in the Family, A (Agee), 451
Deautomatization, 39
Debbèche, Patrick, *as contributor,*
    467–470
de Beauvoir, Simone, 234
Debugging, **180–181**
Decenteredness, 395
Decimal code, 457
Decisive (main) test, 439, 440
Déclaration des droits de la femme (de
    Gouges), 234
*Decline of the West, The (Der
    Untergang des Abendlandes;
    Spengler), 592–593
Decoding channel, 449
Deconstruction, 30, 94–95, 97,
    181–183, 397–398, 497
  Buddhist doctrines of, 94–95, 97
  versus dramatism, 268
  feminist critiques of, 235–236
  of postcolonialism, 506
Decorative art, 261
"Deduction, Induction, and
    Hypothesis" (Peirce), 1
Deductive reasoning, 1–2
Deely, John, 563
  as contributor, 51–53, 399–404,
    498–500, 557–559
Deep structure, 599–600, 602
De Fusco, Renato, 33
Degérando, Joseph-Marie, 295, 299
Degré zéro de l'écriture, Le (Writing
    Degree Zero; Barthes), 59
Deiconization, 27
Deictics, 115, 116, 216, 217, 420,
    448–449
Deixis, **183–184,** 538
De Klerk, F. W., 31
de Lauretis, Teresa, **184–187**
  concept of imaging, 185
  on production and consumption,
    185–186
  theory of female subject of
    semiosis, 185–186, 236, 237
Deledalle, Charles, 603
Deleuze, Gilles, 30, 121, 511
"Delimitation of the Notion of
    Structure in Linguistics and
    Literature, On the" (Lotman),
    376
Delta rule, generalized, 218
De Man, Paul, 182
De Marinis, Marco, 533, 535
Dementia, 447

De Mille, Cecil B., 502
Democratization, 196
De Morgan, Augustus, 476, 477
Demotic script, 456
Denial, 166
Denotation and connotation,
    187–189
  in advertising, 13–14
  Barthes' system of, 60
  Eco's distinction between,
    188–189
  and glossematics, 291, 537–538
  Goodman on, 262
  Hjelmslev's distinction between,
    188
  logical distinction between, 187
  in paraemiology, 471, 472
  and pictures, 540
  stylistic distinction between,
    187–188
  theory of connotation, 36
  theory of denotation and sense,
    250–251
Denotative logo, 374
Deoxyribonucleic acid (DNA), 83,
    223, 224, 253
Depiction, theory of, 487
Depth of sense *(yūgen),* 651
Derivation, 350, 385–386
Derived cultureme, 168, 169
Deroin, Jeanne, 234
Derrida, Jacques, 17, 30, 97, 156,
    181–182, 236, 275, 627
  challenge to intentionality, 315,
    316
  concept of *écriture,* 242
  concept of *logos,* 181
  concept of meaning, 268, 397
  concept of "outside" of language,
    627
  connection between *logos* and
    zoon, 29
  critique of Lacan's notion of
    phallus, 236, 348
  critique of notion of presence,
    315
  and *différance,* 315, 603
  as film semiotician, 121
  on history, 332
  notion of trace, 603, 627
  on signifier-signified distinction,
    151, 182
  on spatial metaphor, 514
"De Saussure's System of
    Linguistics" (Wells), 327
Descartes, René, 399, 404, 499
  essential duality of human and
    animal, 28–29
  theory of passions, 274
  unitary self, 419

Descartes' Critique of Mathematical and Natural Scientific Knowledge (Cassirer), 108
Descent of Man, The (Darwin), 29, 177–178, 582
Descriptive linguistics, 351–352
Descriptive syntagma, 269, 270
Descriptor, 92
Descriptum, 92
Designation, 4
Design configurations, 34
De signis (Bacon), 402
"De Signo" (Conimbricenses), 402
Desire, and relation of subject and object, 8
Desktop publishing, 119
Determination, 4
Determinism, subjective, 395
Deutero-learning, 202
Deuxième sexe, Le (The Second Sex; de Beauvoir), 234
"Development of a Semiotic of film, The" (Worth), 242
Dewey, John, 29, 478
Dharmakāya, 96
Dharmas, linguistic, 93
Dhāraṇī, 94, 95
Dhvani, 74
Diachronic and synchronic linguistics, 48, 149, 150–151, 327, 338–339, 351, 352, 555
Diagrams, 48, **189–191,** 565–566
   Peircean, 293
   synonymy in, 190
Dialectica (Abêlard), 4
Dialectical algorithm, 565
Dialectical conversation, 317–319
Dialectical materialism, aesthetics of, 330
Dialectics, false, 202–203
Dialogism, 58, **191–193,** 195, 317–319, 342, 509
Dialogo dell'imprese militari e amorose (Giovio), 305–306
Dialogue, **193–194**
   of the deaf, 220
   in discourse analysis, 167
   of values in baseball, 63
Diamond Sutra, 94
Dicent indexical sinsign, 503
Dicent sign, 478
Dickens, Charles, 372
Dictionary of American Sign Language, 579–580
Dictionnaire de la langue francaise (Littré), 568
Dictionnaire encyclopédique du théâtre (Corvin), 613
Diderot, Denis, 281–282
Diégèse (diegesis), 120, 122, 130

Diengott, Nilli *as contributor,* 495–498
Différance, 315
Difference, ontological priority over identity, 600
Différend, Le (Lyotard), 377
Differential analyzer, 137
Differentiators (paralinguistic-kinesic constructs), 461, 463
Digital coding, 65, 81, 83, 160
Digital image analysis, 229, 230
Digital representation, 136, 490
Digits, 47
Digraphic calculus, 561
Digraph theory, 560
Dijk, Teun A. van, 196, 242, 391
Dilthey, Wilhelm, 466, 601, 631
Ding, Ersu, *as contributor,* 116–118
Dinnerstein, Dorothy, 236
Diogenes of Sinope, 28
"Direction of the Treatment and the Principles of Its Power, The" (Lacan), 347
DiscAn (discourse analyzer), 561
Discipline and Punish (Foucault), 247
Discours, 217
Discours, figure (Lyotard), 377
Discours de la méthode (Descartes), 28
Discourse
   authoritative, 191–192
   defined, 194
   double-voiced, 58
   ethics, 275, 276–277
   Foucault's notion of, 157, 248
   institutional modes of, 195, 196
   psychotic, 342
   vs. story, 243
Discourse analysis, 132, 133, **194–196,** 596. *See also* Legal discourse
   Althusserian, 24–25
   and apartheid, 31
   critical approaches to, 194–195
   dramatism as, 99–102
   in feminist scholarship, 236
   noncritical approaches to, 195
   stages of development of gossip, 265
   use of theory of implicature, 303
   view of culture, 167
Discourse and Society, 196
Discourse and Text: Linguistic and Intertexual Analysis within Discourse (Fairclough), 195–196
"Discourse in the Novel" (Bakhtin), 191
Discursive formations, 160, 248
Disneyland, 507
Displacement, 25, 37, 99, 345, 543

Displacement/metonymy, 345
Display rules, 212, 230
Dispositif (screening position), 121
Dispositifs pulsionnels, Des (Lyotard), 377
Distance, **196–199.** *See also* Space
Distinction (Bourdieu), 277
Distinctive features, 41, 42, 79, **199–201,** 327, 400, 480, 519, 575
   and language change, 351
   and markedness, 385–387
Distortion, 543
Distributional analysis, 599
Divergent perspective, 488
Divisional (fractional) number code, 456
DNA. *See* Deoxyribonucleic acid (DNA)
Doctrina christiana, De (Augustine of Hippo), 52
Doctrina signorum (doctrine of signs), 399
"Doctrine of Necessity Examined, The" (Peirce), 478
Doing What Comes Naturally (Fish), 356
Dolle, Geneviève, 107
Domestication of the Savage Mind (Goody), 264
Donaldson, Rodney, 67
Donovan, Josephine, 234
Don Quixote (Cervantes), 373
Doolittle, W. Ford, 254
Dostoevskij als Künstler (Trubetzkoy), 618
Dostoyevsky, Fyodor, 58, 342, 528
Dots, in graphs, 190
Double articulation, 33, 41, 42, 484, 537
Double bind, 64, 65, **201–204**
Double-voiced discourse, 58
Douglas, Mary Tew, **204–205,** 207, 360, 569
Douglas, Susan J., 236
Drama, 26
   application of actants to, 7
Dramatism, 99, 266–268
   Burke's, 349, 350
Dramatistic pentad, 99–100, 267
Dramaturgical action, 276
Dramaturgical paradigms, 257, 258
Drawings, 119
Dream, 65
   text as, 99
   as work, 341
Drobisch, Moritz, 476
Droodles, 294
Dry landscape gardens *(kare sansui),* 651

Dual articulation, of boundaries and regions, 43
Dubois, Jacques, 271
Dubois, Philippe, 482, 483
Duchamp, Marcel, 297
Dühring, Eugen K., 465
Duke of Zhou, 648
Dumézil, Georges, 271
Dundes, Alan, 471
Duns Scotus, John, 400, 476, 477
Durdík, Joseph, 425
Dürer, Albrecht, 41
Durham, W. H., 407
Durkheim, Émile, 150, 165, 204, **205–207,** 213, 317, 598
  anticipation of concept of *langue,* 355
  antipsychologism, 206
  concept of collective effervescence, 207
  concept of collective representations, 206
  protostructuralism, 360
  social realism, 359
  sociology, 520
  study of Aboriginal Australians, 364
  on symbolism in primitive cultures, 205, 206
Du sens 2: Essais sémiotiques (Greimas), 271
Dworkin, Ronald, 356
Dyad, 193, 194
Dyer, Gillian, 391
Dynamic functionalism (dynamic structuralism), 500
Dysphoria, 469

E

Eating styles, 277–278
Eccles, John, 466
Echogenesis, 340
Echoics, 449
Eco, Umberto, 33, 41, 51, 108, **209–211,** 392
  on abductive reasoning, 2, 211
  concept of aberrant coding, 133, 210
  concept of iconicity, 295, 296–297
  concept of mapping, 185
  distinction between denotation and connotation, 188–189, 210
  on filmic codes, 241, 299
  five levels of visual codification, 14
  on Goodman, 263
  on the Greek etymology of symbols, 604
  on image of labyrinth, 211

Eco, Umberto, *cont.*
  interest in detective fiction, 211
  on isotopy and topic, 324
  medieval aesthetics, 209
  notion of symbol, 569
  open message, 36, 39, 209–210
  opposition between high and popular culture, 185–186
  on ostension in the theater, 612
  on Piaget's notion of structure, 602
  radical theory of misinterpretation, 535
  reader-response theory, 533, 534–535, 612
  refusal to consider gendered nature of subject, 185, 186, 237
  rhizome, 211
  on sememes, 210, 211
  semiotics of art, 36–37, 299, 484
  semiotic theory, 125–126, 210–211, 378, 558
  on structuralism, 514
  study of carnival, 210
  theory of codes, 14, 39, 210
  theory of sign production, 185, 210
  on use vs. interpretation, 535
  on visual metaphors in comics, 131
Ecological Approach to Visual Perception, The (Gibson), 256
Ecology, 641
  of mind, 67
  of systems thinking, 65
Economic and Philosophical Manuscripts (Marx), 388
Economic-exchange value, 152
Économie libidinale (Libidinal Economy; Lyotard), 377
Economy of signs, 453
Écriture et la différence, L' (Writing and Difference; Derrida), 181, 182
Edelman, Lee, 526
Editing, film, 120
Educational sociology, 89–91
Effet Beaubourg, L' (Baudrillard), 69
Efron, David, 216, 447
Ege, Niels, 537
Egocentric speech, 314
Ego psychology, 345
Egorov, A. G., 423
Egypt, 22
  hieroglyphs, 215, 297
  number representation in, 453–454, 455, 456
Ehrenfels, Christian von, 72
Eikonogenesis, 340

Einbahnstrasse (One-Way Street; Benjamin), 60, 71
"Einige Motive bei Baudelaire, Über" (On Some Motifs in Baudelaire; Benjamin), 71
Einstein, Albert, 109, 629
Eiron, 252
Eisenstein, Sergei, 115, 241, 269, 302
Ejchenbaum, Boris M., 376, 551, 644
Ekman, Paul, **211–212,** 216, 229, 230, 231, 447
Elaborated code, 596
Elaborated speech codes, 160, 204, 205
Electronic mail (e-mail), 138–139, 646
  flaming in, 246
Elementary Forms of the Religious Life, The (Durkheim), 206
Elementary Structures of Kinship, The (Lévi-Strauss), 359, 364
Elements, 43
Elements of Semiology (Eléments de sémiologie; Barthes), 13, 60, 120, 151, **212–214,** 391
Elgin, Catherine, 262, 263
Elias, Norbert, 265, 266
Elicitation, controlled, 221–222
Elision, 351
Elliptic umbilic catastrophe, 110, 614
Ellis, B. J., 164
E-mail. *See* Electronic mail
Emblem, 84, 103, **214–216,** 304, 306, 448
  in cartography, 104
Emblematic (symbolic), 216
Embryology, 223, 422
EMFACS, 231
Emic approach, 429, 618
Emmison, Mike, 107
Emoticons, 139, 246, 521
Emotion
  expression of, 123–125, 448, 450
  facial expressions of, 211–212, 229–230
  "leaking" of suppressed, 230
Emotion dictionary, 232
Emotive signs, 188
Empathy, theory of, 645
Empire des signes, L' (The Empire of Signs; Barthes), 60, 97, 588
Empiricism, 630
  liberal, in mass communication studies, 390, 391
  linguistic, 386
  in scientific discourse, 221
Emprise, 305

Emptiness (*kū*), 97, 98
Encoding somatic channel, 449
Encyclopedia of Unified Science (Carnap), 631
Endosemiotics, 82–83
Engels, Friedrich, 67
Engler, Rudolf, 150
English alphabet, 23
Enigma, 20, 215
Enlightenment, 97, 628
Énoncé, 216
Enonciation impersonnelle ou le site du film, L' (Metz), **216–218,** 244, 417
Ens rationis, 402
Ens reale, 402
Entelechy, 101
Enthousiasme, L': La Critique kantienne de l'histoire (Lyotard), 377
Enthymematic codification, 14
Entropy, negative (negentropy), 311
Entscheidungsproblem (Decision Problem), 619
Enunciation, 184, 185, 186
  allegory as, 21
  Benveniste's notion of, 216–217
  and semiopragmatics of film, 244
Environment, tangible properties of, 282
Epée, Abbé de l', 578
Epic, 25, 501–502
"Epic and Novel: Toward a Methodology for the Study of the Novel" (Bakhtin), 59
Epidemiology, 406
Epigenetic rules, 170, 171
Epigonism, 501
Episodic sequence (*séquence par épisodes*), 269, 270
Epistasis, 407
Episteme, 650–651
Episteme, 247, 287
Epistemogenesis, 340
Epistemology, 262
Epitaph, 329
Epos, 26
Equilibrium, phonological, 351
Equipollent opposition, 459
Equivalence
  of actant and role, 9
  of logic, 296
Erasmus, 305
Erdmann, Karl Otto, 187
Eroticism, 122
Error back-propagation, **218**
Erwartungshorizont (horizon of expectations), 534
Eschbach, A., 612
Esophageal control, 462

Esoteric semiotics, 95
Esoteric tradition, East Asian, 385
Espe, Hartmut, 41, 119, 483
Esperanto, 86, 631
Esposito, Joseph L., *as contributor*, 474–479, 622
Esquisse d'un sémiophysique (Thom), 614
Essai d'analyse structurale du code civil français (An Essay on the Structural Analysis of the French Civil Code; Arnaud), 357
Essais de linguistique générale (Brøndal), 92
Essais linguistiques (Hjelmslev), 148, 291
Essay Concerning Human Understanding (Locke), 399
Esthetic object, 520
"Esthetics and the Theory of Signs" (Morris), 520
Esthétique et psychologie du cinéma (The Aesthetics and Psychology of the Cinema; Mitry), 119, 417
Estrangement, 39
Eternal word, 75
"Ethics of Linguistics, The" (Kristeva), 341
Ethics (Spinoza), 465
Ethnic arts, 330
Ethnic boundaries, 359
Ethnobiology, 222
Ethnobotany, 222
Ethnocentrism, 182, 627
Ethnography, 64, 88, 89, 156, 433
  and rock-art research, 546
  of speaking, 471, 645, 647
  of writing, 645
Ethnomedicine, 222
Ethnomethodology, 195, **218–221**
Ethnomusicology, 430
Ethnoscience, 166–167, **221–222**
Ethnosemantics, 638
Ethology, 37, 82, 641
  and manipulation, 382–383
Etic approach, 618
Etiquette, 198
Etruscans, 23
Eugenesis, 340
Euphoria, 469
Eurasian movement, 617
European Committee for Reception and Audience Research, 535
Europe and Mankind (Europa i čelovečestvo; Trubetzkoy), 617
Evans-Pritchard, E. E., 365
Événementielle, 288
Event tracers, 449
Even-Zohar, Itamar, 500

Evolution, 29, 170–171, 179–180, 212, **223–225,** 616, 641
  of art, 541
  and artificial life, 49, 50–51
  and concept of memes, 405
  cultural, 405
  in Gaian view, 254–255
  at genotype level, 223–224, 405, 406
  and interspecific communication, 321–322
  kin selection, 280
  literary, 552
  and manipulation, 382–383
  of the memes, 180
  and memetics, 405–408
  modern synthetic theory of, 253
  non-Darwinian, 225–226
  organic, 82, 83–84, 223
  at phenotype level, 224–225
  replication, 495–408
  as a semiotic phenomenon, 558
  of sex, 281, 650
  signals, 576
  of social behavior, 582–584
  and *umwelt* theory, 623
Evolutionary Cultural Semiotics (Koch), 339–340
Evolutionary epistemology, 405, 406
"Evolutionary Love" (Peirce), 478
Evolutionary stable strategy (ESS), 179, 583
Evolution of Culture (Koch), 339
Exaptation, **225–226**
Exceptionless sound laws (*ausnahmslosige Lautgesetze*), 351
Exclamation, 32
Exclamation mark, 522, 523
Exclusion, 4
Exegesis for Lines, 648
Exemplification, 38, 262
Exhaustive Capacity of Language, On the (Ouyang Jian), 117–118
Exodus to the East (Iskhod k vostoku), 617
Exosemiotics, 82–83
Exotopy, 287
Expert systems, 45, 179, **226–227,** 320
  dialogue component, 226, 227
  explanation module, 227
  knowledge base, 226
  problem-solving module, 227
  rule-application module, 226, 227
  and symbolic knowledge representation systems, 337
Expiration, 77
Expressibility, 248
Expression, in film, 120

Expression and content, interrelations, 126–129, 213, 291, 537–538

Expression material, in mapping, 103

Expression of the Emotions in Man and Animals, The (Darwin), 178

Expression plane, 107, 291, 444, 512, 513, 533, 537

Expression-relation-content (ERC), 213

Expressive function
in advertising, 15
of art, 38
of logo, 375
of sign, 330, 331

Expressive signs (Husserl), 315

Extended Phenotype, The (Dawkins), 179

Extension, 262, 415

Extensive case, 290

Externalizers, 448, 449–450

Exteroceptive properties, 469

Extradiscursive dependencies, 248

Extrinsic systemic functionalism, 552

Eye contact, 197

F

Fabian, Johannes, 157

Fable, 20, 215

Fabula, 122

Face, **229-231**
dynamic features, 229–230
expression of pain, 230
expressions of emotion in comics, 130
importance of actors' expression in theater, 12
microexpressions, 230
prototypic emotional expressions, 230
as signaling system of emotion, 211–212, 521
spontaneous vs. deliberate expressive systems, 230
static features, 229

Face work, 257, 258

Facial Action Coding System, The (Ekman and Friesen), 212

Facial action coding system (FACS), 212, 229, **231–232**

Fact, Fiction, and Forecast (Goodman), 262

Factorality, 307–308, 309, 310, 311, 415, 416

Fairclough, Norman, 194, 195–196

Fairy tales, 88

Fanon, Frantz, 505

Fanshel, David, 516

Fant, Gunnar, 459

Fantasia, 628

Fantasy narratives, 502

Fascism, 71

"Fashion in 1830, a Study of the Vocabulary of Clothes according to the Journals of the Times" (Greimas), 271

Fashion System, The (Barthes), 213

Fathers and Sons (Turgenev), 372, 373

Faure, Bernard, 95, 651

Faust (Goethe), 502

Feathers, 225

Febvre, Lucien, 288

Fechner, Gustav Theodor, 465

Feedback
closed (external) feedback loop, 232, 337–338
negative processes in Gaia hypothesis, 253
systems, 171

Feedback and feedforward, **232–233**

Feedforward architecture, 142

Feeling and Form (Langer), 38

Feigl, Herbert, 629, 631

Feminine Mystique, The (Friedan), 234

Feminism and feminist theories, 81, 155, 184, 195, **233–237**, 392, 398, 627
and queer theory, 525

Feminist film criticism, 122, 184, 185, 236

Feminist semiotics, 235–236, **237–239**
contributions of Julia Kristeva, 341, 343
contributions to theory of representation and narrative, 238
of law, 363
phases of, 238

Fenollosa, Ernest, 115

Fernandez, Dominique, 121

Fetishism, 122, 301

Fezzan, 546

Fiber tract, 312

Fiction, **239–241**
marker, 239–240
in modern poetics, 496
operator, 240

Fiction and the Reading Public (Leavis, Q. D.), 390

Fiction film *(film de diégèse)*, 300

Fictive representation, 354

Fiedler, Leslie, 507

Field, of a social context, 279

Fielder, John, *as contributor*, 191–193

Figurae, 43, 291, 299, 575

Figurative isotopy, 323

Figurativity, 469, 614

Figure de la bible, 84, 215

Figure-ground boundary, 65

Figurines, 103

Fillmore, Charles, 5

Film as Art (Arnheim), 35

Film de diégèse (fiction film), 300

Film epic, 502

Film semiotics, 184–187, **241–245**, 392, 415, 417. *See also* Cinema
codes, 120, 417
and concept of enunciation, 217
feminist, 122
film as symptom of director's psychoanalytic phenomena, 121
filmic signs, 392
formalist, 417
generative grammar of film, 244
in Germany, 242
humanistic, 119
Marxism in, 122
metaphor and metonymy, 301–302
before Metz, 121
narratology, 122, 242–243
pragmatics, 243–244
psychoanalytic phase of, 121–122, 300, 392, 417
of the 1970s, 392
semiopragmatics, 244
shot in, 120
society-centered, 392
spectator in, 300–302
structural linguistic phase of, 120–121
stylistics, 241
synecdoche, 302
syntax, 241
terminology of, 120
vraisemblance, 417

Film studies, early, 391–392

Film Theory, 242

Finalization, of speech act, 193–194

Finck, Franz N., 150

Fingerspelling, **245–246**, 578, 581

Finite play, 494

Finnegans Wake (Joyce), 564

Fire inscriptions, 646

First International Congress of Linguists, 335, 617

First International Congress of Phonetic Sciences, 1932, 518

First International Congress of Slavicists, 426

Firstness, 294–295

Firth, Raymond, 187, 470–471, 569, 598
Fischer-Jorgensen, Eli, 537
Fish, Stanley, 356, 533, 534, 535
Fisher, David, 343
Fisher, Ronald Aylmer, 281
Fiske, John, 164, 477
Fitch, Brian, 538
Fitzpatrick, Tim, 612
  as contributor, 535–536
"Fixation of Belief, The," 477
Flags, 26
Flaming, 139, **246–247**
Flaubert, Gustave, 505
Fleming, Ian, 209, 211, 323
Floch, Jean-Marie, 14, 485, 644, 645
Flow field, 256–257
Flyting, 246
Focalization, 243, 496
Focal knowledge, 158
Focal level, 428
Focus unit, 104, 105
Fodor, Jerry, 336
Fold catastrophe, 110, 111, 614
Folk arts, 330
Folk classifications, 222
Folk costume, 89
Folklore, 88–89, 560
Folktale, 322, 437, 438–440, 597
  narrative units and functions of, 243
  tests, 439–440
Folk theater, 89
Fondements d'une sémiologie de la musique (Nattiez), 446
Fonseca, Pedro da, 402, 403
Fontanille, Jacques, 274
"Footing" (Goffman), 258
Forager society, 544, 545, 546
Forceville, Charles, as contributor, 411–415
Foregrounding, 39, 520
Formal elements (f-elements), 471
Formalism, 57, 58, 304, 341, 553, 644
Formal Method in Literary Scholarship, The: A Critical Introduction to Sociological Poetics (Bakhtin and Medvedev), 58, 553, 644
Formal sign, 400, 403, 499
"Forms of Time and the Chronotope in the Novel" (Bakhtin), 58
FORTRAN, 47
Fossil record, 223
Foucault, Michel, 69, 167, 195, **247–249**, 275, 392
  concept of archive, 247–248
  concept of episteme, 247, 287

Foucault, Michel, cont.
  concept of power, 196, 248–249, 287
  concept of signifying practices, 247
  critical history of modernity, 248–249
  critique of Lacan, 348
  discourse of science, 207, 287
  "docile bodies," 207
  on history, 332
  notion of discourse, 157, 195, 196, 247–249
  notion of intentionality, 316
  opposition between discursive and nondiscursive, 248
  panopticon, 587
  on sexuality, 525–526
  on space in modernism, 588
  theory of meaning, 398
Foundational knowledge, 157–158
Founding, concept of, 92
Fountain (Duchamp), 297
Fourier, Charles, 61, 234
Fourier analysis, 634
Fovea, 632
Fowler, Roger, 391
Fractal theory, 559.69
Fragments d'un discours amoureux (A Lover's Discourse: Fragments; Barthes), 61
Frame, 259
  in comics, 130
Frame Analysis: An Essay on the Organization of Experience (Goffman), 259–260
Francastel, Pierre, 35
Francis I, 305
Frank, M., 230
Frank, Philipp, 629
Frankfurt School, 332
  and Marxism, 388, 390
Fraser, Nancy, 276
Frazer, James George, 327
Frege, Gottlob, 187, **249–251**, 538, 549, 574
French feminism, 233
French revolution, 234
French semiotics, structuralist movement in, 467
French Sign Language, 578
French structuralism, 495, 598
  challenge to liberal-empiricism, 390–391
  on fictional signs, 240
  on opposition, 460
  and pictorial semiotics, 484
  semiology, 461
French Symbolists, 542
Fresnault-Deruelle, Pierre, 131

Freud, Sigmund, 274, 300, 327
  concept of ego, 346
  concept of subject, 316
  concept of woman, 155
  on condensation and displacement, 99
  on evolutionary thought, 29
  on meanings, 396
  model of language acquistion, 342, 345
  reality principle, 346
  Tel Quel project, 238
  theories of Oedipal complex and castration, 236, 238, 347, 348, 365
  theory of drives, 541
  theory of human sexuality, 347, 348
Freudianism: A Critical Sketch (Voloshinov), 58
Freudianism: A Marxist Critique (Voloshinov), 313
Friedan, Betty, 234
Fries, Jakob, 476
Friesen, Wallace, 211–212, 216, 230, 231, 447
From Morpheme to Texteme (Koch), 339
Frontiers in Semiotics (Deely et al.), 558
Frye, Northrop, 25–26, **251–252,** 495
Fulton, Helen, 389–393
  as contributor, 22–24, 389–393
Function
  aesthetic, 330–331
  communicative, 518
  expressive, 15, 38, 330, 331, 375
  in glossematics, 290
  in narrative unit, 438
  pragmatic, 373
  representative, 373
  in Russian folktales, 6
  as smallest narrative unit, 322
  and structure, 603
Functional analysis, of the utterance, 519
Functional cartography, 103–104
Functionalism, 220, 500, 552
Functional onomatology, 519
Functional structuralism, 88–89, 364, 517
Functional syntax, 519
Functional transformation, 71
"Function and Concept, On" (Frege), 250–251
Functions of Folk Costume in Moravian Slovakia, The (Bogatyrëv), 88
Fundamental norm (Grundnorm), 356

Fung, Richard, 526–527
Fury (film), 269
Fustel de Coulanges, Numa Denis, 206
Futurism, 57
Fu Xi, Emperor, 648
Fuzzy logic, 227
Fuzzy-set methodology, 159, 560

G

Gabelentz, Han Georg Canon von der, 150
Gabora, Liane, *as contributor*, 405–408
Gadamer, Hans-Georg, 358, 534
Gaia hypothesis, **253–256**
Galactogenesis, 339
Galen, 568
Gallaudet, Thomas, 578
Gallop, Jane, 155, 348
Gamberini, Italo, 33
Games, 493–494
Game theory, 257
Ganglion cells, 633
Garber, Marjorie, 526
Gardies, André, 243
Gardiner, Alain, 533
Garfinkel, Harold, 195, 219–221
Garroni, Emilio, 241
Garvin, Paul, 611
Gaudreault, André, 122, 244
Gay and lesbian studies. *See* Queer theory
Gaze, 195
  as secondary distance code, 197
  in semiotics of film, 198
Geckeler, Horst, 482
Geertz, Clifford, 165, 288
Geisteswissenschaften, 601
Gender
  difference, 89
  language bias, 386
  and postcolonialism, 236
  signifiers of in opera, 430, 431
  as signifying practice, 235
  as structure of limitation, 526
"Gender Advertisements" (Goffman), 15
Gender differences, 583–584
Gendered subaltern, 506
Gendered Subjects: The Dynamics of Feminist Teaching (Culley and Portuges), 236
Genealogy, 85
Gene-culture coevolution, 170
Generalized delta rule, 143, 218
General Line, The (film), 121
Generation, 4
Generative aesthetics, 73
Generative metaphor, 433

Generative metrical theories, 367
Generative semantics, 367
Generative-transformational grammar, 34, 46, 126, 147, 195, 351–352, 367, 429
  of film, 244
Genes, 223, 407
Genes, Mind, and Culture: The Coevolutionary Process (Lumsden and Wilson), 170
Genesis, 28
Genes vs. memes (Koch), 339
Genetic adaptations, 165
Genetic algorithms, 49
Genetical Theory of Natural Selection (Fisher), 281
Genetic evolution, 223–224, 405, 406
Genetics, 223, 312
  population, 405, 406
Genette, Gérard, 26, 120, 122, 243, 268, 444
Geneva School, 518
Genosko, Gary, *as contributor,* 59–61, 67–70, 152–153, 209–211, 212–214, 317–319, 322–323, 563–565, 571–572
Geoffroy le Bel, comte d'Anjou (Plantagenet), 283
Geogenesis, 339
Geographic-information system (GIS), 492
Geophysiology, 254
Geopolitical Aesthetic, The (Jameson), 333
German, High and Low, 353
German Ideology, The (Marx), 387
German semiotics, 73
Gestalt degrees, 72–73
Gestalt models, 162–163
Gestalt psychology, 35, 310, 486
"Gestalt Technique of Stem Composition in Shawnee" (Whorf), 639
Gestalt theory, 466, 486, 598, 614
Gestème, 482
Gesture, 27, 195, 447
  articulation, 123–125
  in comics, 130
  emblems, 216
  language of, 149
  used by actors, 12
Ghana, 263
Gibson, Eleanor, 257
Gibson, James J., 41, 118, **256–257,** 261
  on affordances, 18–19
  theory of perception, 18, 256, 282
Giddens, Anthony, 167, 195
Giedion, Sigfried, 162
Gift, 68, 69

Gigi (film), 270
Gilbert, Sandra, 235
Gill, Harjeet Singh, *as contributor,* 3–5, 529–532
Gilman, A., 198
Giovio, Paolo, 305–306
GIS. *See* Geographic-information system
Glacken, Clarence, 161
"Glance at the Development of Semiotics" (Jakobson), 17
Glas (Derrida), 378
Glasgow University Media Group, 391
Global semantic structure, 438
Glorifying test, 439, 440
Glossematics, 36, 60, 147, 148, 289–291, 532, 533, 537–538
Glottogenesis, 340
Gluckman, Max, 266, 620
Glyphs, 27
Godard, Barbara, *as contributor,* 237–239
Gödel, Kurt, 251, 370, 629, 631
Godel, Robert, 150
Godelier, Maurice, 286
Godzich, Wlad, 557
Goethe, J. W. von, 422, 502, 505, 528
Goffman, Erving, 211, **257–260,** 605
Gogol, Nikolai, 376
"Gold Bug, The" (Poe), 378
Golding, Peter, 107
Goldmann, Lucien, 598
Gombrich, Ernst H., 40–41, **260–261,** 263
Gone with the Wind (film), 502
Gongsun Longzi, 116–117
Goodenough, Ward, 221
Goodman, Nelson, **262–263**
  analysis of synonymy and meaning, 262
  argument against iconicity, 295, 296, 299, 354
  concept of compliants, 262, 355
  concept of denotation, 262, 354
  concept of exemplification, 262, 354
  concept of expression, 354
  concept of indirect (mediated) reference, 262–263, 354
  nominalism, 262, 354
  symbol theory of art, 37, 262–263, 354–355
  symptoms of art, 38
  theory of notation, 47–48, 263, 355
Goodrich, Peter, 362
Goodwin, Charles, 249
Goody, John Rankin (Jack), **263–265,** 359, 646

Gordon, David, 516
Gospels, 26
Gossip, **265–266**
Gottdiener, Mark, 164
Goudge, Thomas, 308, 309–310
Gould, Stephen Jay, 223, 225–226, 583–584
Graceful degradation, 142
Gradual opposition, 459
Graffiti, 646, 647
  political, 297
Graham, David, *as contributor*, 84–85, 85–86, 214–216, 283–285, 304–306
"Grain de la voix, Le" ("The Grain of the Voice"; Barthes), 61, 431
Grammar, 74–76, 182
  basic elements for construction of, 92
  dramatistic, 99–100
  generative-transformational, 34, 46, 126, 195, 351–352, 367, 429
  Indian tradition of, 74–76
  modal, 273
  relational, 438
  selection-restriction rules, 597
  of story, 443
  stratificational, 482
  universal, 92–93
  for Whorf, 637–640
Grammar of Motives, A (Burke), 99–102, **266–268**
Grammatical hypercorrection, 597
Grammatical isotopy, 323
Grammatology, 569
Grammatology, Of (Derrida), 151, 181
Gramsci, Antonio, 91, 195
  and Marxism, 388
  notion of hegemony, 395
Grande syntagmatique, La, 121, **268–271**, 417
Grand narrative, 508
Granet, Marcel, 206
Grapard, Allan, 95
Grapes of Wrath, The (Steinbeck), 372, 463
Graphème, 482
Graphemes (strokes), 113–114
Graphical user interface, 178
Graphic art, 487
Graphic strings, 114
Graphogenesis, 340
Graphological language acts, 384
Graphology, and semantics, 427
Graphosyntax, 114, 115, 116
Graphs, 44, 190
Graphs (characters), 114–116
Grathoff, Richard, 603–604
Great Cat Massacre, The (Darnton), 288

Great Code, The (Frye), 251
Great Gatsby, The (Fitzgerald), 452
Greek allegory, 20–21
Greek alphabet, 23
Greek punctuation, 521
Greenberg, Joseph H., 352
Greenlee, Douglas, 296, 308, 309
Gregersen, Frans, 148
Greimas, Algirdas Julien, 34, 42, **271–274**, 598
  actantial model, 5, 6, 8–11, 111, 252, 272, 273
  aspectual syntax, 273–274
  concept of iconicity, 295
  concept of isotopy, 323, 485
  contraries and contradictories, 566
  deep structure vs. surface grammar, 361
  and development of French structuralism, 467
  development of linguistic semiotics, 272–273
  development of sociosemiotics, 273
  differentiation between signification and meaning, 441
  influence of structural linguistics on semiotic theory, 272
  narratology, 243, 272–273, 438, 440–443, 444–445
  notion of "dialectical algorithm," 565
  semiotic analysis of legal discourse, 357, 361
  semiotic dictionary, 271, 273
  semiotics of passions, 274
  semiotic square, 13, 111, 243, 272, 323, 441, 565–568
  structural semantics, 14, 34, 79, 93, 149, 291, 467, 601
  virtual-actual transition, 22
Grice, H. Paul, 258, 302–304, 516
  concept of implicature, 480
Grid and group classifications, 204–205
Griffith, D. W., 502
Grimké, Sarah, 234
Grimm's law, 351
Grosz, Elizabeth, 155
"Grounds of Validity of the Laws of Logic: Further Consequences of Four Incapacities" (Peirce), 477
Groupe 107, 34
"Groupe de recherches sémio-linguistiques" (Semio-Linguistic Research Group), 271, 467
Groupe μ (Liège) School, 415, 416, 485, 486
Group selection, 177, 616

Groves, Peter, *as contributor*, 199–201, 350–354, 366–368, 385–387, 479–481
Growth and Form, On (Thompson), 422
Grundgesetze der Arithmetik (Basic Laws of Arithmetic; Frege), 250
Grundlagen der Arithmetik, Die (The Foundations of Arithmetic; Frege), 250
Grundzüge der Phonologie (Foundations of Phonology; Trubetzkoy), 518, 618
Grzybek, Peter, *as contributor*, 88–89, 335–336, 375–377, 422–425, 427, 470–474, 517–521, 550–553, 617–618
Guatemala, fingerspelling system, 245
Guattari, Félix, 30, 511
Gubar, Susan, 235
Gubern, Roman, 131
  as contributor, 130–132
Guerra, Gustavo, *as contributor*, 627–628
Guerre du golfe n'a pas eu lieu, La (The Gulf War Did Not Take Place; Baudrillard), 69
Guerri, Claudio, 34
Guessing instinct, 2
Guillaume de Champeaux, 529, 530
Guilt, 350
Gurwitsch, Aron, 187
Gustème, 482
Gutenberg, Johannes, 521
Gutenberg Galaxy (McLuhan), 390
Gynocritics, 233

H

Habermas, Jürgen, 133, 195, **275–277**
  ideal speech situation, 276
  and Marxism, 388, 389
  on modernity, 508
  theory of discourse ethics, 276–277
Habit, 186
Habitus, **277–278**, 316, 333
  class differences in, 277–278
  culture, 168–170
  and discourse of schooling, 89–90
  and historical processes, 288
  and language codes, 278–280
  literary texts as sources of data regarding, 371–373
Haeckel, Ernst, 340
Hahn, Hans, 629
Hahn-Neurath, Olga, 629
Haiku, 61
Halbwachs, Maurice, 206

Hall, Edward, 168, 196–197
Hall, Stuart, 155, 156, 389, 391
Halle, Morris, 352, 459
    feature level of language, 79
    mathematical models of
        language, 78–79
    phonological theory, 199, 200
Halliday, Michael A. K., 151,
    278–280, 391, 511, 598
    dynamic model of stratification,
        512–513
    functional systemic linguistics,
        612
    on ideational and interpersonal
        dimensions of communication,
        127
    linguistic theory, 486
    on metalanguage, 411
    on phonetic/kinetic interface,
        512
    social semiotics, 195–303
    speech-act types, 193
Hallucination, 546, 547
Hamilton, William D., 38,
    280–281, 322, 474, 583, 641,
    650
Hamito-Semitic, 350
Hammad, Manar, 34
Hammonds, Evelyn, 526
Hamnet Players, 139
Handelman, Don, *as contributor,*
    603–605, 620–622
Hand-eye-system, 119
Handicap principle, 650
Handshaking, 159, 165, 198
Handwriting, 647
    minuscule and majuscule, 521
Hanna, Barbara, 216
Hanson, Norman R., 2
Hanunoo, 222
Haptics, 256, **281–283,** 540–541
Haraway, Donna, 30
Hard icons, 119
Harkin, Michael, *as contributor,*
    204–205, 205–207, 221–222,
    285–289, 359–360, 364–366
Harland, Richard, 151
Harmonics, as language, 429
Harries-Jones, Peter, *as contributor,*
    64–67, 201–204
Harris, Roy, 150, 556, 576
Harris, William Torrey, 476
Harris, Zellig, 194, 446, 598
Harrison, Jane, 26
Hart, H. L. A., 356
Hartley, John, 391
Hasan, Ruqaiya, 195
Hassan, Ihab, 507
Hatten, Robert, 446
Havelock, Eric, 646

Havercroft, Barbara, *as contributor,*
    539
Havránek, Bohuslav, 517, 519, 520
Hawaii, 286
Hawkes, Terence, 151, 556
Head, C. Grant, 104
Hearing impaired, 245–246, 578
Hearne, Vicki, 30
Heath, Stephen, 121, 184, 392
Hebb, Donald Olding, 142, 143
Hebdige, Dick, 156
Hegel, Georg Wilhelm Friedrich, 17,
    81, 275, 340, 346, 387, 470,
    508
Hegemony, Gramsci's concept of,
    91
Heidegger, Martin, 28, 181, 247,
    318, 508, 627
    discussion of nothing, 630
    phenomenological theory of
        meaning, 396–397
Heidegger et "les juifs" (Lyotard), 377
Height, as motivated sign of power,
    197
Heilbrunn, Benoît, *as contributor,*
    373–375, 614–616
Heisenberg, Werner, 370
Helbo, André, 611
Helmholtz, Hermann von, 109
Helper versus Opponent, 5, 10–11
Hempel, Carl, 629, 631
Henderson, Greig, *as contributor,*
    99–102, 266–268, 349–350
Hendiadys, 489
Heraldry, 84, 85, **283–285**
    and impresa, 304–305
Herbart, Johann Friedrich, 425,
    476, 540
Herder, Johann Gottfried, 109
Heredity, 83, 223, 280
Heritage of Apelles, The (Gombrich),
    261
Hermeneutics, 466, 534
    and allegory, 20–21
    circle, 324
    code, 60
Hermogenes, 149, 328
Hertz, Robert, 109
Hess-Lüttich, Ernst, 244
Heteroglossia, 192, 195, 313
Heterosexism, in feminism, 235
Heterosexuality, discourses of, 526
Hetu (cause), 76
Hexagrams *(gua),* 648, 649
Hexis, 277
Hidden curriculum, 90
Hidden Myth (Langholz-Leymore),
    14
Hidden Persuaders, The (Packard), 391
Hidden units, 141

Hierarchies, of articulation, 44
Hieroglyphs, 241, 453
Hilbert, David, 250
Hildebrand, Adolf von, 540
Hill, Rowland, 503
Hinduism, mantra and, 383
Hippocratic tradition, 568
Hirsch, Eric Donald, 315
Histoire, 217, 301
Historical materialism, 70–72, 275,
    387–388
Historiography
    Annales School of, 286, 288
    double standard in, 235
*Historische Grammatik der Bildende
    Künste* (Riegl), 542
History, **285–289,** 332
    and morphology, 592–593
    and praxis, 286
    privation of, 432
    and structuralism, 286–288
History and Class Consciousness
    (Lukács), 394
*History and Meaning of the Term
    "Phoneme," The* (Jones), 481
History of Sexuality, The, Volume One
    (Foucault), 348, 525
Hitchcock, Alfred, 121, 243, 270
Hitler, Adolph, 101
Hjelmslev, Louis, 34, 79, **289–292,**
    459, 520, 537, 598
    arbitrariness of the sign, 533
    case, 290
    cénème and *plérème,* 113, 481
    concept of *figurae,* 43, 575
    concept of linguistic level, 549
    concept of planes, 127, 213
    content and referent, 187, 210
    and Copenhagen School,
        147–148
    criteria of immanence, 513
    empirical principle, 291
    expression and content, 573
    founding of *Acta Linguistica,* 92
    general grammar, 147, 290
    glossematic theory, 36, 60, 147,
        148, 289–291, 532
    on language as form, 290
    method-oriented formalism, 148
    on morphology, 422
    sign theory, 149, 151, 291
    stratified view of semiosis, 411
    structural semantics, 291
    system and process (text), 126,
        149, 151
    theory of connotation, 13, 188,
        189
    theory of reciprocal relations,
        601–602
Hobo signs, 26, 297

Hochberg, Julian, 297
Hodge, Robert, 195, 196–199, 509, 510
  as contributor, 132–134, 586–588, 596–598
Hodler, Ferdinand, 465
Hodos and Kosmos (Koch), 339
Hoffding, Harald, 91
Hoffmeyer, Jesper, 253
  as contributor, 82–84, 536–537, 624
Hofstadter, Douglas, 97
Hoggart, Richard, 391
Holland, Norman, 533, 535
Holländisches Gruppenporträt (Riegl), 541
Hollerith, Herman, 137
Holmes, Oliver Wendell, 477
Holzrichter, Amanda S., as contributor, 245–246, 578–582
Homeopathic (metaphoric) magic, 327
Homeostasis, 54
Homer, 597
  allegorical readings of, 20, 21
Home signs, 579, 582
Homograph, 298, 526
Homographesis, 526
Homological transcription, 103, 104, 105
Homonyms, 262
Homophonicity, 114, 116, 351
Homosexuality, 525–526
Homosociality, 525
Hone Heke, 286
Hong Kong, fingerspelling system, 245
Honnecourt, Villard de, 40–41
Honzl, Jindřich, 89, 611
hooks, bell, 155
Hopfield learning algorithm, 143
Hopi, 637
Hopkins, John A. F., as contributor, 542–544
Horace, 215
Horapollo, 214
Horizontal cells, 633
Horizontal semiotics, 83
Horkheimer, Max, 390
Hortatory negative, 349
Hoskins, William George, 162
Hosshin seppō, 95
Hostinsky, Otakar, 425
Hour of Decision: Germany and World-Historical Evolution, The (Spengler), 593
How to Do Things with Words (Austin), 591
"How to Make Our Ideas Clear" (Peirce), 477, 550
Huainanzi, 173

Hughes, Everett, 258
Hugo, Victor, 502, 505
Huizinga, Johan, 493, 494
Human geography, 162
Humanism, 248
  and allegory, 21
  scholarship, 120, 367
"Human Rights, Language, and Law" (Conklin), 363
Humboldt, Wilhelm von, 92, 149, 150, 369
Hume, David, 474
Humphrey, Nicholas, 405
Hundun, 173
Hunter, Ian, 249
Hunter-gatherer society, 544
Husserl, Edmund, 108, 250, 310, 358, 469
  concept of founding, 92
  notion of sign, 533, 603
  phenomenological theory of meaning, 396, 520
  on pictorial consciousness, 299
  theory of transcendental intentionality, 187, 314–315
Hussy, Charles, 104
Hutcheon, Linda, 235
Hyenas, exaptation and, 225
Hymenoptera, 280, 583, 641, 642
Hymes, Dell, 133, 366
Hyperbole, 319, 414, 489
Hyperbolic umbilic catastrophe, 110, 614
Hypercode, 185
Hypergram, 116
Hypermedia, 491
Hyperreal, 507
Hypertechnologism, 349
Hypnosis
  and filmic spectator, 302
  in psychoanalysis, 29
Hypogram, 329, 542, 543
Hypo-icon, 293, 295
Hyponoia, 20
Hyponymy, 200
Hypotactic construction, 324
Hypothesis
  generation, 492
  process of adopting, 1, 2
  selection, 492
Hypothetical judgments, 250

I

I Ching. See Yi jing
Icon, 38, 166, **293–294,** 478
  in advertising, 14
  aesthetic, 38
  in Blissymbolics, 87
  computer, 293, 300, 491, 559

Icon, cont.
  hard, 119
  in music, 429
  need of convention to be perceived, 294, 297
  objects as, 294
  photographs as, 482, 483
  pictographs as, 449
  religious, 161, 293, 381
  secondary, 294
  in semiotics, 68, 293–294
  Siddham, 385
  and symbolic type, 605
Iconemes, 299
Iconic codes, 14, 41, 65
Iconic ground, 295, 296, 299, 309
Iconicity, 22, 26, **294–297,** 309
  and Barthes "Rhetoric of the Image," 540
  of chirographs, 119
  degrees of, 295
  Eco's concept of, 295
  Greimas's concept of, 295
  of ideograms, 114–115
  of logos, 373–375
  in mapping, 104, 105
  and nonverbal bodily signs, 449
  of paralanguage alternants, 463–464
  Peircean concept of, 294–295
  of phonograms, 115
  of postage stamp, 502, 503, 504
  of reflectance and shadowing, 487
  of sign languages, 579
  in visual semiotics, 260–261
Iconic sinsign, 504
Iconologia (Ripa), 215
Icotypes, 373
Idealism, dramatism, 267
"Ideas for a Manifesto of Materialistic Semiotics" (Rossi-Landi), 548
Ideational metafunction, of language, 279
Identification, 164
Identifiers, 448, 449
Identity construction, 258, 266
Identity kit, 258
Identity management, 259
Identity narrative, 375
Identity sign, 374
Identity taint, 259
Ideogram (ideograph), 22–23, 26, 86, 241, **297–298,** 449
  aniconic, 297
  Cherokee Indian, 298
  Chinese, 113–116
  in comics, 131
  Fascist, 298

Ideogram (ideograph), *cont.*
  five basic elements of in West, 297
  homographs, 298
  iconic, 297
  pictorial, 297
  synonymous, 297–298
Ideologia, L' (Marxism and Ideology; Rossi-Landi), 548
"Ideological Effects of the Basic Apparatus" (Baudry), 300
Ideological state apparatus (ISA), 24–25, 395
Ideologie, 548
Ideologies of Linguistic Relativity (Rossi-Landi), 548
Idiolect, 314
Idioma de Signos Nicaragüenses (Nicaraguan Sign Language), 579
Illiad (Homer), 20, 501
Illocutionary function, 175, 384, 591
Illuminated manuscripts, 24
Illusionism, 198
  pictorial, 260, 261
Illustrated book, 215
Ilongot, 289
"Image and Code" (Gombrich), 261
Image and picture, **298–300**
  codes, 631
  defined, 486
  Goodman's definition of picture, 262–263, 354–355
  as icons, 293–294, 295, 296, 485
  as identity signs, 296
  Peircean, 293
  plastic function of, 295, 485
  sign, 118–119, 299, 308
  tactile, 488
Image of the City, The (Lynch), 333
Imagery, Frye's classification of, 25–26, 252
Image sign, 374
Imaginary Signifier, The (Le signifiant imaginaire; Metz), **300–302**
Imagination, 3
Imaging, 185
Imaging model, 105
Immanence, 537, 600
Immediate constituents, 367
Imperative, 279
Imperialist semiotics, 505
Impersonal enunciation, 217
Implicature, **302–304,** 480
Imposition, 4
Impresa (personal device), 84, 215, **304–306**
Impression management, 259
Incest taboo, 364
Incidents (Barthes), 61

Inclusion, 190
In-deeperism, 259
Index, 68, 119, 166, 293, **306–308,** 478
  integrational, 322
  performative, 308
  photographs as, 482, 483
  proper, 322
  secondary, 308
  variously defined, 306–307
Indexical-feature transfer, 14
Indexical ground, 307, 308, 309
Indexicality, 87, 183–184, 219–220, **308–311,** 415
  art as, 22, 37, 73
  of chirographic pictures, 118–119
  definitions of, 308–310
  ideograms as, 114–115
  of logos, 373–375
  phonograms as, 115–116
  of postage stamp, 502, 503, 504
  principles of relevance, 415
  protoindex, 311
  secondary, 416
  of sign languages, 579
Indexical semiosis, 14
India, 22
  grammatical tradition, 74–76
  Tantric tradition, 383
Indiana Law Journal, 358
Indicative signs, 315, 316
Indicator, 307
Indifferentist, 530
Indirect (mediated) reference, 262, 543
Individualism, 249
Individual selection, 616
Indo-Arabic, number code, 454, 456–457
Indo-European, 350, 351
Indra's net, 97, 98
Inductive reasoning, 1–2
Industrialization, and development of mass media, 389
Industrial Revolution, 68–69
Infant behavior, 193, 199
Inference programs, 45
Inferences, 256, 257
Inferential walks, 534
Infinite play, 494
Inflection, 385–386
Informant, 322
Information, **311–312**
  aesthetics, 72–73
  indexes, 113
  mathematic theory of, 598
  processing, 320
  systems, 490
  theoretical aesthetics, 36
  theory, 65, 72, 73, 112–113, 125, 311–312, 558, 601

Infra-iconic, 484
Ingarden, Roman, 520, 534
Inglis, Fred, 391
Inner speech, 192, **312–314**
Innis, Harold A., 134, 390
Inoculation, 432
Input units, 141, 143, 218
Inquiry into Meaning and Truth, An (Russell), 550
Inscriptio, 214
Inscriptions, 47, 262
Instance perspective, 607
Instantiation, 178, 179
Institute of Architecture, Buenos Aires, 34
Institut für Umweltforschung, 82
Instrumental sign, 400, 498
Integers, 47
Intellect, 3
Intended allegory, 21
Intension and comprehension, 187, 415
Intensive case, 290
Intentionality, 262, **314–317,** 396, 405, 480, 499
  and legal discourse, 356, 357, 358
Interaction, 243, 372
  group, 259
  ritual, 605
  symbolic, 257–260
Interactional pessimism, 516
Interactionist analysis, **317–319**
Interdiscursive dependencies, 248
Interface, 136, 137, **319–321**
  iconic, 137
  knowledge, 158
  process, 319
  user, 319
Intermediality, in film, 242, 244
Intermediary term, 460
Internal pictures, supporting problem solving, 492–493
International Congress for Linguists, Fourth, 148
International Council of Women, 234
International Episode, An (James), 240
International Journal for the Semiotics of Law, 363
International Linguistic Congress, First, 335, 617
International Philosophical Congress, 426
International Phonological Conference, 1930, 518
Internet, 392
  metaphors of, 413
Internet relay chat (IRC), 139–140, 247
Interoceptive properties, 469

Interpellation, 24, 217, 316
Interpersonal metafunction, of
    language, 279
Interpretant, 134
Interpretation and Overinterpretation
    (Eco), 209
Interrogation mark, 523
Interspecific communication, 83,
    321–322, 382–383
Intersubjectivity, 187, 188, 193,
    276, 341
Intertextuality, 122, 195, 238,
    542–544
    archetypal criticism as, 252
    in film pragmatics, 243, 244
    of Zen gardens, 651
In the Beginning Was Love (Kristeva),
    343
Intichiuma ceremony, 206
Intolerance (film), 502
Intonation, 303, 462
Intradiscursive dependencies, 248
Intrinsic systemic functionalism,
    552
Introduction à la sémiologie
    (Mounin), 612
Introduction to Cybernetics (Ashby),
    570
*Introduction to Mathematical
    Philosophy* (Russell), 549
"Introduction to the Structural
    Analysis of Narratives"
    ("Introduction à l'analyse
    structurale des récits"; Barthes),
    60, **322–323**
Invariance hypothesis, 414
Inverse matrix, 73
Ionians, lexicalized number code,
    455, 456
Irigaray, Luce, 155, 236, 238, 348
Irony, 20, 25, 26, 252, 414
Irreal objective views, 217
Irwin, Anne, *as contributor,* 418–419
Iser, Wolfgang, 533, 534
Ishmael, 21
Isoglosses, 353
Isolates, 168, 169
Isomorphism, 570
Isotopy, **323–324**
ISOTYPE (International System of
    Typographic Picture Education,
    87, 631
*I Think I Am a Verb: More
    Contributions to the Doctrine of
    Signs* (Sebeok), 558
Itō, J., 201
Ivanov, Vjačeslav V., 376, 423, 425,
    446
Izard, Carroll, 211, 229

J

Jackson, Bernard, 357, 361–362,
    363
Jackson, John B., 162
Jackson, John Hughlings, 327
Jacquard, Joseph-Marie, 137
Jaffe, Alexandra, 418
Jakobson, Roman, 92, 315,
    327–330, 335, 500, 520, 565,
    598
    advocacy of Peirce, 327
    on the aesthetic function, 16, 17
    binary model of language, 327,
        335
    code and message, 213
    commentary on *Course in General
        Linguistics,* 154
    concept of binary opposition,
        327, 335, 459–460
    concept of shifter, 183, 309, 328
    critique of Saussure, 327–328
    distinctive features, 575, 618
    on feature level of language, 79
    founding of Prague School, 36,
        517, 518, 519
    on glossematic analysis of
        phonematic structures, 537
    on iconicity of language, 328–329
    on indexicality of language, 309,
        328
    meeting with Moscow linguists,
        423
    on metaphor, 22, 415
    on metonymy and synecdoche,
        415
    model of linguistic
        communication, 16, 33, 153,
        299, **330–332**
    model of six communcative
        functions, 15, 375
    and Moscow Linguistic Circle, 88,
        551
    paradigmatic and syntagmatic
        planes, 596
    phonological theory, 77, 79, 80,
        201
    semiotic poetics, 38, 328–329, 551
    on signifer/signified relation, 328
    as source of film theory, 122
    structural linguistics, 598
    theory of marking, 42
    Trubetzkoy's influence on, 518
Jakubinskij, Lev P., 551
James, Henry, 240
James, William, 466, 477
Jameson, Fredric, **332–334,** 348,
    507–508
Jane Eyre (Brontë), 464
Janlert, Lars-Erik, *as contributor,*
    489–493

Jannello, Cesar, 34
Japan, 60
Japanese esoteric Buddhism, 95
Jarama, El (Ferlosio), 452
Jarry, Alfred, 69
Jauss, Hans Robert, 533, 534
"Jazyce básnickém,O" (On Poetic
    Language), 426
Jefferson, Gail, 195
Jencks, Charles, 162
Jespersen, Otto, 148, 183, 309, 328
Jevons, W. Stanley, 477, 478
Jing (scriptures), 173
Jñāna, 97
Johansen, Svend, 537–538
Johnson, Mark, 163, 222, 412–413
Jokes, 240
Jolivet, Jean, 532
Jones, Daniel, 199, 481
Jones, William, 350
Jordan curves, 487
Jost, François, 122, 243, 244
Journal of Memetics, The, 407
Journal of Speculative Philosophy, The,
    476, 477
Joyce, James, 209, 342, 343, 627
Jude the Obscure (Hardy), 452
Judgments, types of, 250
Judgments for Hexagrams, 648
Jung, Carl G., 251, 420
    concept of synchronicity, 649
Junggrammatiker (Young Turk
    philologists), 350–351, 353
Juridicity, 357

K

Kabuki, 12
Kabyle (Algeria), 89
Kachin, 364
Kafka, Franz, 29, 30
Kagan, M. I., 109
Kakuban, 95
Kalinowski, Georges, 356
Kalāskti, 74
Kamehameha II, 286
Kant, Immanuel, 16, 38, 57, 75,
    206, 404, 600
    biological metaphors, 410
    distinctions among judgments,
        250
Kanthapura (Rao), 372
Kanyó, Zoltán, 473
Kapitzke, Cushla, *as contributor,*
    263–265
Kārakas (actant), 76
Karaṇa (instrument), 76
Karcevskij, Sergej Iosifovic, 77, 327,
    335–336, 518
Kare sansui (dry landscape gardens),
    651

Kariera system, 364
Karma (object or goal), 76, 97
Kartā (actor), 76
Kasher, Asa, 516
Kātyāyana, 74
Katz, David, 282
Katz, Jerold, 79
Kay, Paul, 222
Kaye, K., 193
Keane, Teresa, 271
Keeley, Brian, *as contributor,* 48–51
Keenan, E. O., 303
Kegl, Judy, 579
Kelsen, Hans, 356
Kemp, Wolfgang, 541
Kendon, Adam, 582
Kennedy, John M., *as contributor,*
    18–19, 256–257, 281–283,
    486–489, 631–635
Kerbrat-Orecchioni, Catherine, 189,
    324
Kevelson, Roberta, 357–358,
    360–361
Key exemplars, 159
Key/keyings, 259
Khlebnikov, Velimir, 551
Kiefer, Georg, 73
Kine, 481
Kineme, 481
Kinemics, 481
Kinemorph, 481
Kinephonographs, 449, 464
Kinesics, 169, 170, 372, 481, 585
    developmental, 447
    information, 521
    language markers, 448
    in narrative texts, 451–452
    used by actors, 12
Kinesthetic-image schemata, 158,
    159
Kinetogram, 488
Kinetographs, 449
King Wen, 648
Kin selection, 280, 322, 583
Kinship structures, 263
Kinship studies, 221–222, 359, 364
Kin terms, 166, 167, 221
Kirby, Vicki, *as contributor,* 153–157,
    625–627
Kircher, Athanasius, 29
Kirshenblatt-Gimblett, Barbara, 471
Kissing, 198
Klassische Kunst Die (Classic Art;
    Wölfflin), 644
Klein, Felix, 565
Klein, Melanie, 301
Klein group V4, 565–566
Klima, Edward, 580
Kloepfer, Rolph, 243
Knilli, Friedrich, 242

Knowledge
    authority of, 248
    contextually delimited, 158
    evolution of, 2
    focal, 158
    foundational, 157–158
    as informational commodity, 508
    interface, 158
    manipulation and inference, 45
    in the postmodern condition,
        508
    representation, 45–46
    strategic, 158
    tacit, 158, 159
Knowledge and Human Interests
    (Habermas), 275
Knowledge representation, 142,
    336–338
    connectionist approach, 337–338
    symbol-systems hypothesis,
        336–337
Koch, Walter A., 37, 242, **338–340**
Kohlberg, Lawrence, 276
Köhler, Wolfgang, 35
Kolers, Paul, 569
Kolmogorov, A. A., 423
Konstanz School, 541
Kowzan, Tadeusz, 611
Kozloff, Sarah, 122
Kraft, Victor, 629
Král, Oldrich, *as contributor,*
    647–650
Krampen, Martin, 87, 162
Krebs, John, 130, 180
Kress, Gunther, 195, 509, 510
Krikmann, Arvo, 471
Krimpen, Jan van, 503
Kristeva, Julia, 122, 155, 185, 192,
    340–343, 392
    challenge to Lacan, 342–343
    concept of the abject, 565
    concept of the *chora*, 343
    concept of the semiotic, 341,
        342, 343
    exploration of Bakhtin, 342
    opposition between high and
        popular culture in work,
        185–186
    psychosemiotic theory, 342
    semanalysis, 564
    signifying practice, 341, 342, 343
    spatial metaphors, 342
    speaking subject, 237, 238
    subject in process, 236, 342
    theory of intertextuality, 242
"Kritice strukturalismu v nasí
    literární vede, Ke" ("On the
    Critique of Structuralism in
    Our Literary Studies";
    Mukařovský), 426

"Kritik der Gewalt, Zur" (Critique of
    Violence; Benjamin), 72
Kroker, Arthur, 507–508
Kroker, Marilouise, 507–508
Kručënych, Aleksej, 551
Krull, Ulrich J., *as contributor,*
    112–113, 311–312
Kruszewski, Mikolas, 481
Kubczak, H., 187
Kuhn, Thomas, 46, 287, 405, 461
Kūkai, 95
Kū, 651
Kuleshov, Lev, 241
Kunstbegriffe, 540
Kunstgeschichtliche Grundbegriffe
    (Principles of Art History;
    Wölfflin), 644, 645
"Kunstwerk im Zeitalter seiner
    technischen Reproduzierbarkeit,
    Das" (The Work of Art in the
    Age of Mechanical Reproduction;
    Benjamin), 71
Kuntstwille, 541
Kuntstwollen, 541
Kuntzel, Thierry, 121
Kurkela, Kari, 47
Kuryłowicz, Jerzy, 537

L

Laban, Rudolph, 48
Labial control, 463
Labov, William, 353, 516
Lacan, Jacques, 235, **345–349,** 392,
    415
    algorithm of signifier/signified, 345
    analysis of the production of
        difference, 155
    concept of binary opposition, 327
    concept of
        condensation/metaphor, 345
    concept of
        displacement/metonymy, 345
    feminist critique of, 236, 347–348
    interpretation of "The Purloined
        Letter," 348
    linking of demand, desire, and
        need, 347
    literalization of the subject, 155,
        186
    on mirror phase of infant
        development, 121, 346
    on notion of intentionality, 316
    notion of language, 156
    notion of *points de capiton,*
        345–346
    notion of suture, 186
    notion of symbolic, imaginary, and
        real, 332, 342, 346–347
    patriarchal scheme, 236, 347–348

Lacan, Jacques, *cont.*
  synthesis of Freud and Saussure, 345
  theory of language acquisition, 342
  theory of meaning, 398
  theory of the phallus as signifier, 348
  theory of the semiosis of analysis, 345–349
  theory of the unconscious, 99, 342, 345, 346–348, 398
Ladurie, Emmanuel LeRoy, 288
Lagerwey, John, 175
Lagny, Michèle, 121
Lakoff, George, 163, 222, 412–413, 414, 516
Lakṣaṇa (sign), 76, 96
Lamarck, Jean Baptiste de, 178, 223, 224
Lamb, Sydney M., 151
Lambert, Johann Heinrich, 149
Lambertini, Roberto, 51
Landowski, Eric, 271
Landscape, cultural, 419–421
Landscape gardens, 651
Landscape paintings, 161
Lang, Fritz, 269
Langacker, Ronald, 312, 638
Langage et cinéma (Metz), 417
"Langage et logique" (Brøndal), 92
Langages, 271, 445
Langage sans langue, 241
Langer, Susanne, 17, 38
Langholz-Leymore, Varda, 14
Language
  aesthetic function of, 520
  agonistics of, 377
  analytic philosophy of, 250–251
  apartheid as, 31
  attitudinal function of, 349
  Benjamin on, 71
  Bühler's three functions of, 520
  class-based varieties of, 278–279
  collective action of, 317–319
  community, 133
  as divide between humans and animals, 28
  evolutionary, 29, 584
  games, 508–509
  of gestures, 149
  graphological, 349
  hortatory function of, 349
  ideology in, 386
  of interpretation, 410
  kinesic, 448
  mantras as, 383–384
  markers, 448, 449
  materiality of, 341
  metafunctions of, 279
  moves, 377

Language, *cont.*
  and the negative, 349–350
  neurological basis of, 446–447
  new conception of after Freud, 29
  ordinary, 302
  practical vs. poetic, 519
  as psychoperceptual phenomenon, 312
  and reality, 350
  relation to culture, 153–157
  relation to thought, 92
  in Saussurean sense, 133
  sign, 532–533
  social role of, 350, 353–354
  social semiotics of, 89–91
  structural principles of, 92–93
  as symbolic action, 99–101, 266–268, 349–350
  as system, 410, 640
  theory, 125, 335
  and thought, 313
  transfinite element of, 564
  written, 22–24, 126, 264
Language, philosophy of, 91–93
  Buddhist, 93–95
  Chinese, 116–118
  and knowledge representation, 336
"Language, Mind, and Reality" (Whorf), 640
Language acquisition, 279, 312, 356
  and language change, 352
Language as Articulate Contact (Stewart), 509–510
Language as Ideology (Hodge and Kress), 509
Language as Symbolic Action: Essays on Life, Literature, and Method (Burke), **349–350**
Language change, **350–354,** 387
  emulatory model of, 353, 356
"Language in Relation to Habitual Thought and Behavior" (Whorf), 637–638
Language in the Upper Pleistocene (Koch), 339
Languages of Art: An Approach to a Theory of Symbols (Goodman), 38, 262, **354–355**
Langue and parole, 58, 126, **355–356,** 555, 607, 609
  langue, 32, 77, 151, 194, 368, 625
  parole, 77, 353
Lantern jaw, 590
Laokoon (Lessing), 36
Laozi (Lao Tzu), 173
Larivaille, Paul, 443
Larsen, Svend Erik, *as contributor,* 91–93, 147–148, 289–292, 532–533, 537–538, 624–625

Laryngeal control, 462
Laryngeal vibration, 77
Larynx, communicative functions of, 589
Late Marxism (Jameson), 333
Lateral geniculate nucleus (LGN), 633
Latin, 23
Lattices, 44
Laughlin, Charles, 162–163
Laughter, 463
Laṇkāvatāra Sūtra, 94
Lauretis, Teresa de. *See* de Lauretis, Teresa
Laurette, Pierre, 559
Lausanne school, 150
Lautréamont (Isidore Ducasse), 342
Laver, John, 461
Lavie, Smadar, 605
Law, Fact, and Narrative Coherence (Jackson), 361
Law, semiotics of, **356–359,** 360–364
Law and Semiotics (Kevelson), 363
Law and the Human Sciences (Kevelson), 363
"Law of the Mind, The" (Peirce), 478
Law's Empire (Dworkin), 356
Lazarsfeld, Paul, 390
Leach, Edmund, 288, **359–360**
Learning
  associative, 142
  and dialogue, 193
Learning How to Mean (Halliday), 279
Learning rule, 141–143
Leavis, Frank Raymond, 390
Leavis, Queenie Dorothy, 390
Lechte, John, 343
Lecours, André Roch, 447
Lectures on a Structural Poetics (Lektsii po struktural' noi poetike, vvedenie, teorija stiha; Lotman), 376
"Lectures on Pragmatism" (Peirce), 1–2
Leech, Geoffrey N., 516
Leeuwen, Theo van, *as contributor,* 278–280, 429–432
Lefebvre, Henri, 68
Legacy of Genghis Khan (Nasledie Cingiskhana; Trubetzkoy), 618
Legal discourse, **360–364**
  coherence theory of narrative in, 362
  intentionality in, 356, 357, 358
  Peircean approach to, 357–358, 360–361
  self-referentiality of, 361, 362

Legal discourse, *cont.*
 sexism and racism of, 363
 signifying relations of, 362–363
 structuralist approach to, 356–357, 361
Legal positivism, 356, 357
Légende des siècles, La (Hugo), 502
Legisign, 47, 73, 115, 166, 478, 622
 pictures as, 37, 293–294, 295, 296–297
Leibniz, Gottfried Wilhelm, 92, 137, 149, 274, 649
Lekomeceva, T. V., 423
Lemke, Jay, 512
Leningrad School of Semiotics, 393
Lenneberg, Eric H., 638
Lenticular effect, 561
Leonardo da Vinci, 294
Lesbian and gay studies. *See* Queer theory
Les misérables (Hugo), 502
Lessing, Gotthold E., 36
Les sources manuscrites du cours de linguistique générale de F. de Saussure (Godel), 150
Letters on the Aesthetic Education of Man (Schiller), 475
Letters on the Equality of the Sexes (Grimké), 234
Lettres nouvelles, Les, 59, 432
Levin, J., 266
Levinas, Emmanuel, 182
Levinson, Stephen C., 516
Lévi-Strauss, Claude, 89, 151, 164, 238, 315, **364–366,** 392, 598
 on aboriginal cultures, 364
 analysis of marriage exchange, 364
 approach to folk narratives, 443–444
 arguments on totemism, 364–365
 on cinema, 417
 concept of binary opposition, 264, 285, 327
 concept of bricolage, 597
 concept of mytheme, 80–81
 concept of semantic opposition, 460
 concept of structuralism, 364
 critique of kinship studies, 364
 distinction between language and culture, 165–166
 exploration of nature-culture opposition, 365–366
 history in semiotic model, 285
 on "hot" versus "cold" societies, 285
 influence of Jakobson on, 364
 influence of Saussure on, 364
 model for embodying a structure, 601

Lévi-Strauss, Claude, *cont.*
 myth analysis, 14, 80–81, 272, 285–286, 514, 599
 notational system, 444
 reading of Oedipus myth, 365
 structural anthropology, 42, 154–155, 207, 263, 285, 359, 360, 626
 study of primitive cultures, 365, 602
Lévy-Bruhl, Lucien, 160, 365
Lewin, Kurt Koffka, 35
Lewontin, Richard, 583–584
Lexias, 60, 259
Lexicalized (ionic) number code, 455, 456
Lexical parsing, 474
Lexicogrammar, 279
 and semantics, 427
Lexicology, 271
Lexipictogram, 130
Liberal empiricism, in mass communication studies, 390, 391
Liddell, Scott, 580
Lidov, David, 446
 as contributor, 16–18, 41–44, 48–51, 123–125, 189–191, 330–332, 445–446, 549–550, 561–563, 572–575
Ligand, 112, 312
Light, and vision, 632
"Likeness and Meaning, On" (Goodman), 262
Liminality, theory of, 621
Liminoid, 621
Limits of Interpretation, The (Eco), 209, 210
Lindekens, René, 41, 483, 484, 540
Linearity, **366–368,** 556
Linear models of communication, 132
Linear syntagma, 269, 270
Line of indicativity, 130
Lingis, Alphonso, 378
Lingua franca, 581–582
Lingual control, 463–463
Linguistic alienation, 394
Linguistic capital, 90–91, 394
Linguistic code, 513
Linguistic (Continental) school, 538
Linguistic determinism, 369
Linguistic empiricisim, 386
"Linguistic Factors in the Terminology of Hopi Architecture" (Whorf), 637
Linguistic habitus, 90
Linguistic information, 521
Linguistic market, 90
Linguistic motivation, 32, 114, 117, 153, 197, **368–369**

Linguistic relations, 90–91
Linguistic relativism, 350, **369–371**
Linguistics
 anthropological, 133
 applied, 195
 critical, 195, 280
 descriptive, 351–352
 developmentalism, 354
 diachronic, 327, 339
 of discourse, 60
 generative, 351–352
 historical comparative, 150
 positivist, 370
 Stalinist, 520
 structural, 91–93, 147–148?
 synchronic, 327
 text, 196
Linguistics and Economics (Rossi-Landi), 548
"Linguistics and Semantics" (Coseriu and Geckeler), 482
Linguistic sign, 68, 335
 functional model of, 330
 nature of, 625
 Saussure's theory of, 32, 533, 555–557
Linguistic system
 as meaning potential, 279
 used by actors, 12
Linguistic theory, notion of stratification, 427–429
Linguistic tools, 394
Linguistic turn, 497
Linguistic uncertainty principle, 369–370
Linguistic universality, 117
Linguistic work, 394
"Linguistique structurale" (Brøndal), 92
Linnean classification, 221
Lippit, Akira, *as contributor,* 27–30
LIPS, 227
Lips, communicative functions of, 589–590
Listener feedback, 145–146
Literacy, 263–265
Literariness *(Literaturnost'),* 551
Literary anthropology, **371–373**
Literary device *(priëm),* 551
Literate brokers, 646
Literature, 182
 evolution, 552–553
 history, 25
 importance of cosmology to, 252
 modern poetic theory, 496
 question of reference in, 538–539
 root genres of, 26, 252
 as source of data regarding sign systems of culture, 371–372
 structural theory of, 537

Literature, *cont.*
  study of, 516–517
  symbolic modes of, 25
"Literature and Signification"
  (Barthes), 611–612
Literature of Their Own, A
  (Showalter), 235
Littré, Emile, 568
Liu, Albert, *as contributor,* 421–422,
  592–593, 614, 618–620
Liungman, Carl G., 298
  as contributor, 26–27, 297–298
Liu Xie, 649
Livingston, E., 220–221
Living system, 53–55, 65
Loan signs, fingerspelled, 245
Local syntax, 106
Location of Culture, The (Bhabba),
  506
Lock, Charles, *as contributor,*
  327–330
Locke, John, 399, 557
Locugram (balloon), 131
Locutionary act, 591
LoDagaa, 263
Logic, 264
  equivalence relation of, 296
  formal, 549
  of science, 2
Logica ingredientibus (Logic for
  Beginners; Abélard), 529
Logical atomism, 629
Logical consecution, 4
Logical paradox, 64
Logical positivism (logical
  empiricism), 92, 629, 631
  sign theory of, 532–533
Logical propositions, 642
Logical square, 565
Logical typing, 64
"Logic and Conversation" (Grice),
  302
Logic of science, 2
*Logic of Writing and the Organization
  of Society, The* (Goody), 264
Logique, ou L'art de penser, La (Logic,
  or the Art of Thinking; Arnauld
  and Nicole), 187
Logische Untersuchungen (Husserl), 92
Logo, 297, 298, **373–375,** 615
Logocentrism, 181–182, 236, 237,
  627
Logograms, 22–23
  Chinese, 454–455, 456
Logology, 101
Logonomic system, 510
Logos, 14, 181
  relation to *zoon,* 29
Logothetes, 61
Logotypes, 297, 298, 373
Lomax, Alan, 431

Lombard, Peter, 52–53
London School, 598
Longue durée, 288
Lopez, Donald, 384
Lord, Albert B., 597
Lord of the Rings, The (Tolkien), 502
Lorenz, Konrad, 82, 225
Lotman, Jurij Mikhajlovič, 108,
  121, **375–377,** 423
  analysis of cultural development,
  563
  on filmic language, 241–242
  semantic oppositions, 424–425
  semiotics of culture, 376,
  424–425
  structural theory of literature, 376
  theory of codes, 17, 39–40
Loudness, 462
Louis XII, 305
Louw, Eric, *as contributor,* 24–25,
  30–32, 387–389
Love, 341
Lovelock, James, 253–255
Low mimetic, 25
Loyola, Ignatius, 61
Lucas, George, 502
Luckmann, Thomas, 164
Lucy, John A., 369
Luhmann, Niklas, 275
Lui, Albert, *as contributor*
Lukács, György, 59
  and Marxism, 388
  notions of reification and
  alienation, 394
Luke, Carmen, *as contributor,* 89–91,
  277–278
Lull, Ramón, 137
Lumsden, Charles, 170, 570
Lunačarskij, Anatolij V., 553
Lurija, A. R., 423
Lurz, Meinhold, 644
Lyell, Charles, 351
Lynch, M., 221–222
Lyons, J., 79
Lyotard, Jean-François, **377–379,**
  388
  attack on structuralism and
  Marxism, 377–378
  concept of semiosis, 378
  concept of tensor sign, 378, 511
  on future potential of semiotics,
  510–511
  on postmodernism, 508–509
Lyric, 26
Lyutyy, A. A., 104

M

M (film), 121
Mácha, Karel, 331
Machine, 53–54, 617

Máchův Máj: Estetická studie
  (Mácha's "May": A Study in
  Aesthetics; Mukařovský), 425
Macro nodes, 560
Macular vision, 451
Madame Bovary (Flaubert), 10
Madhyamā[m]
  (mediatory/phonemic), 75
Madwoman in the Attic, The (Gilbert
  and Gubar), 235
Magazines, 389
*Magical Acts, Rituals, and Beliefs in
  Subcarpathian Russia*
  (Bogatyrëv), 88
Magistro, De (Augustine of Hippo),
  52
Magliola, Robert, 97
Magno cells, 633
Magnocellular layers, 633
Maieutics, 318
Majakovskij, Vladimir, 551
Majuscule handwriting, 521
Making News (Tuchman), 219
Making Sense in Law (Jackson),
  361–362
Malayo-Polynesian, 350
Malevich, Casimir, 57
Malinowski, Bronislaw, 127, 128,
  280, 598
Mallarmé, Stéphane, 342
Mallery, G., 294
Mamoulian, Rouben, 269
Man and Technics (Spengler), 593
Manchly, J. W., 137
Maṇḍala, 95, 175, **381–382**
Mandelbrot, Benoit, 69, 422
Mandible, communicative
  functions of, 590
Mandibular control, 463
Manhattan Transfer (Dos Passos),
  462
Manipulation, **382–383**
  signaling as, 180, 321
Manjali, Franson, *as contributor,*
  74–76, 110–112
Mannoni, Octave, 301
Mano-vijñāna, 96
"Man's Glassy Essence" (Peirce),
  478
Mantra, 94–95, **383–385**
Manutius, Aldus, 521
Maori, 286
*Map of the True Form of the Five
  Sacred Mountains,* 175
Mapping, 64, 103–106, 185, 419
  cognitive, 333
  map language (map symbolism),
  104–106
Maranda, Pierre, *as contributor,*
  433–435, 559–561
Marcuse, Herbert, 390

Marcus Vitruvius Pollio, 33
Marey, Etienne-Jules, 30
Margarine, myths of, 432
Marginalist theory of political
    economy, 150
Margulis, Lynn, 54, 253, 254, 255
Marie, Michel, 121, 122, 242–243
Marin, Louis, 539
Marinis, Marco de, 612
Maritain, Jacques, 499
Maritime flag code, 26
Markandaya, Kamala, 372
Markedness, 41, 42, **385–387,** 396,
    401
Markers, 448
Marketing, 15
Markov chains, 560
Marling, Karal Ann, 236
Marmo, Costantino, 51
Marni (film), 270
Marot, Clément, 84
Martha's Vineyard, dialect of, 353,
    578
Martin, James R., 639
Martineau, Harriet, 234
Martinet, André, 42, 213, 351, 537
Marty, Anton, 150
Marty, Robert, 603
Marx, For (Althusser), 24
Marx, Karl, 68, 238, **387–389,** 396,
    627
    Althusser's rereading of, 24–25
    analysis of the value form, 506
    concept of rationality, 275
    concept of social production, 318
    historical materialism, 387–388
    image of inversion, 432
    on meanings, 396
    notion of value, 625
    theory of capitalist economic
        relations, 598
Marxism, 24, 68, 508
    Althusserian, 24–25
    analysis of commodity fetishism,
        152
    approach to mass
        communication studies, 390
    base/superstructure model of
        society, 156, 157
    Benjamin's undialectical version
        of, 71
    and Chinese philosophy of
        language, 118
    and class, 388
    concept of art, 553
    critique of formalism, 553
    and distinctions between high
        and low culture, 500
    influence on mass
        communication studies, 390

Marxism, *cont.*
    model of structure and
        superstructure, 548
    political economy, 152
    semiotics, 342
    structural, 24
    theories of culture, 332
    theory of ideology, 388
Marxism and Form (Jameson), 332
*Marxism and the Philosophy of
    Language: Basic Problems in
    Sociolinguistics* (Voloshinov), 58,
    192, 328
Maser, Siegfried, 73
Massage, 571
Mass communication, 132,
    389–393, 392. *See also* Media
    advertising, 391
    computer-mediated
        communication, 138–140
    popular fiction as a form, 392
    study of, 389–392
Matejka, Ladislav, 611
Material culture studies, 547
    and rock-art research, 546
Materialism
    emphasis on scene in dramatism,
        267
    historical, 387–388
Materialist aesthetics, 376, 541
Materialist determinism, 388
Materialist semiotics, 24–25, 31,
    152–153, 184, 387–389,
    393–396
Materialist structuralism, 24
Maternal feminism, 234
Mathematical communication
    theory, 331
Mathematical logic, 251
Mathematical theory of
    information, 598
Mathematics
    formulas, 23, 293, 295
    realist philosophy of, 250
    set theory, 64
Mathesis matheseos (science of
    science), 422
Mathesius, Vilém, 150–151, 515,
    517, 518, 519, 520
Matilal, Bimal, 75
Matoesian, Gregory, 195
Matrix, 73
Matte Blanco, Ignatio, 98
Maturana, Humberto R., 53–55, 98,
    254, 640
Maugham, W. Somerset, 372
Mauss, Marcel, 68, 204, 206, 360,
    365, 598
Maxims, conversational, 302–303
Maximum transparency, 275

Maxwell, James Clerk, 477, 478
Maya, 456, 637
Mayenowa, Maria Renata, 520
Maze, 211
McAuley, Gay, *as contributor,* 11–13,
    611–613
McCay, Winsor, 131
McClary, Susan, 430
McClelland, J. L., 141
McClelland, John, *as contributor,*
    20–22, 593–596
McHoul, Alec, 107
    as contributor, 591–592, 609–611,
        644
McHugh, Peter, 317, 318
McLuhan, Marshall, 60, 134, 390,
    571, 646
Mead, George Herbert, 258, 603
Mead, Margaret, 64
Meaning, **396–399**
    articulated, 441
    Burke's view of, 251–252
    communication-intention
        theories of, 303, 304
    and contextuality, 192
    correspondence theory of,
        642–643
    in culture, 359–360
    Derrida on, 268, 397
    global system of, 251–252
    Goodman on, 262
    Greimas on, 271, 441
    and legal discourse, 357–358, 361
    of linguistic expression, 384
    methods of linguistic realization
        of, 279
    mimesis theory of, 116
    model of, 614
    phenomenological theory of,
        396, 397
    as process, 289
    realist theory of, 116–117
    as result of text-reader
        interaction, 534
    sentence and word, 75–76
    study of, 515
    of suspicion, 396
    and symbolic-interactionist
        paradigm, 218
    and synonymy, 262
    systems, 640
    truth-conditional theories of,
        303, 304
    and use, 303
    vs. sense, 313
Meaningless utterance, 324
Mechanical Bride, The (McLuhan),
    60
Mechanism, 53–54
Mechelen, Marga van, *as contributor,*
    540–542, 644–645

Media. *See also* Mass
communication
ideological role of, 391
transformations, 242
violence, 391
women in, 236
Medical terminology, 568
Medieval semiotics, 51–53,
399–404
Augustine's definition of sign,
399–400
debate over notion of relative
being, 401–402
definition of relation, 401
Hispanic phase, 402–403, 404
notion of sign, 399
notion of sign as relative being,
400–404
realism and nominalism, 529–532
revision of Augustine's definition
of sign, 400
Medieval theology, allegory in, 20
Mediogenesis, 340
Meditation, 174, 175
Meditations on a Hobby Horse
(Gombrich), 260–261
Medvedev, Pavel Nikolaevich, 57,
644
critique of formalism, 553
critique of material aesthetics, 541
Mega-narrator (*grand imagier*), 243
Meščaninov, I. I., 520
Meier, Richard P., *as contributor,*
245–246, 578–582
Meillet, Antoine, 335
Mein Kampf (Hitler), 101
Meinong, Alexius, 538
Meletinsky, Elizar, 434
Meme, 170, 180, **404–405,**
406–407, 583
Memento mori, 305
Memetics, 404–405, **405–408**
Mémoires: Pour Paul de Man
(Mémoires: For Paul de Man;
Derrida), 181
*Mémoire sur le système primitif des
voyelles dans les langues
indoeuropéennes* (Essay on the
Early System of Vowels in Indo-
European Languages; Saussure),
555
Memorial inscription, 23–24
"Memorial to a Scholarly Mistake,
A" (Šklovskij), 553
Memory, 248
Memory aids, 159
Mendel, Gregor, 223, 253
Menestrier, Claude-François,
214–215, 216
Menger, Karl, 629

Menippean satires, 58
Mentalism, 598
Mentalistes, 288
Mentifacts, 170
Mercer, Kobena, 526
Merleau-Ponty, Maurice, 98, 272,
396, 397, 469
Merrell, Floyd, 54, 98, 511, 563
Mersenne, Marin, 558, 559
Mesmer, Anton Franz, 29
Mesopotamia, 22
Message, 570
"Message photographique, Le"
(Barthes), 539
Mester, R., 201
Metacellulars, 54–55
Metacommunication, 202–203
Metacontext, 64
Metadiscourse, 411
Metagenesis, 340
Metalanguage, 60, 188, 214, 324,
408–411
scientific, 427
second-order, 410
of structuralism, 514
verbal, 427
Metal (heraldry), 284
Metalinguistic function, of sign,
331
in advertising, 15
of logo, 375
Metaphor, 158, 159, **411–415,**
415–416, 560, 605
acts of interpretation as, 628
Bateson on, 66
cross-media, 413
as icon, 20, 115
and implicature, 303
nonverbal, 413, 414
Peircean, 293
shift of focus from verbal to
cognitive level, 413
visual (pictorial), 413
Metaphor and Symbolic Activity, 413
Metaphor and Thought (Ortony),
412, 413
Metaphoric discourse, 240, 327
Metaphoric thought, 163–164
Metaphors We Live By (Lakoff and
Johnson), 412–413
Metaphysical Club, 477
Metaphysics, 181, 182
Metaredundancy, 512–513
Metasemiotic, 291
Metaset, 64
Metathesis, 200
Metodica filosofica e scienza dei segni
(Rossi-Landi), 548
Metonymy, 327, 414, **415–416**
and allegory, 21
and comics, 130

Metonymy, *cont.*
and film, 301–302
and indexicality, 309
and rock art, 547
as secondary indexical sign, 308
Metz, Christian, 122, 392, **417–418**
film as text, 610
initiation of semiotic study of
film, 119–120, 241
la grande syntagmatique, 243,
268–270
le signifiant imaginaire, 300–302
notion of impersonal
enunciation, 216–218, 244, 417
on practices of signification, 242
spectator positioning (*le
dispositif*), 417
Michelet, Jules, 59, 287, 627
Michelet par lui-même (Barthes), 59
Mick, David, 15
Microanalysis, 258
Microexpressions, 230
*Middle Ages of James Joyce, The: The
Aesthetics of Chaosmos* (Eco),
209
Middle English, 352
Middleton, Richard, 430–431
Military, **418–419**
internal communications,
418–419
saluting practices, 418
totemic symbols, 418
use of ritual, 418
Mill, John Stuart, 187, 390
Miller, George A., 414
Milovanovic, Dragan, 362
Mime, 12, 27
Mīmāṃsā, 75
Mimesis, 444, 496, 543
classical theory of, 36, 37, 260
in film studies, 116
theory of meaning, 116
Mimetic codes, 130
Mimicry, 224, 506
Mimicry and Man, Of (Bhabba), 506
Minc, Z. G., 423
*Mind and Nature: Their Necessary
Unity* (Bateson), 65, 66
Mind and Other Matters, Of
(Goodman), 262
Mind reading, 382–383
Mindscape, **419–421**
Minimal signs, 104–106
Minsky, Marvin, 137
Minuscule handwriting, 521
Miroir de la production, Le (The
Mirror of Production;
Baudrillard), 68
"Mirror Stage as Formative of the
Function of the I, The" (Lacan),
346

Misogyny, 85
Misreadings, 209
Mitchell, Juliet, 155
Mitchell, Margaret, 502
Mitry, Jean, 119, 417
Mixed logo, 373
Mnemonic devices, 27
Mobilgrams, 131
Mobility, as motivated sign of
    power, 197
Mock battles, 419
Moctezuma, 287
Modal grammar, 273, 274
Modalities, 273, 274
Modalizers, 538
Mode, of a social context, 279
*Modèles mathématiques de la
    morphogénèse* (Thom), 614
Modeling, 48, 171–172, 183
    in polysystem theory, 501
    systems, 424
Model reader, 209, 534
Model spectator, 535
Modernism, 404
    in art, 588
Modernity, 275, 508
"Modernity versus Post-modernity"
    (Habermas), 508
Modistae, 150
Modular organization, 635
Modus ponens (rule of inference), 2
Moiety system, 364
Molecular biology, 223
Molecular clock, 223
Moles, Abraham, 72, 295
Molino, Jean, 445
Möller-Nass, Karl-Dietmar, 242, 244
Mon, 284–285
Monads, 649
Mona Lisa, 294
Monastic signs, 581
Mondrian, Piet, 42
Monelle, Raymond, 446
Monemes, 105
Monist, The, 478
Monologism, 191
Monoplane systems, 533
Monstration, 122
Montage
    in comics, 131
    in film, 121, 122
    theory of, 241
Montage a/v, 242
Montague, Richard, 309
Montaigne, Michel de, 28
Montspan cave, 545
Monumentality, 543–544
Moore, George E., 643
*Moral Consciousness and
    Communicative Action*
    (Habermas), 276

Morality, 350
Moral reasoning, 276
Morfologi og syntax (Brøndal), 92
Morgan, Lewis Henry, 364, 621
Morpheme, 33, 114, 367, 481
Morphing, 230
Morphogenesis, 110, 614
    chemical, 619
Morphographemes (radicals),
    114–115
"Morphologie" (Goethe), 422
Morphology, 92–93, 421, **421–422,**
    613
    archetypal, 110–111
    chemical, 422
    and historiography, 591–593
"Morphology of History"
    (Spengler), 422
"Morphology of Landscape"
    (Sauer), 422
Morphology of the Folktale (Propp), 6,
    11, 252, 272, 422, 438, 443,
    445, 551
Morphophonemic rules, 352
Morris, Charles, 34, 393, 517, 520,
    548, 557
    definition of pragmatics, 515
    explanation of the sign process,
        574
    notion of sign, 533
    semiosis, 561
    theory of aesthetic iconicity, 36,
        37–38
    and Vienna Circle, 631
Morris, Ray, 107, 265–266
    as contributor, 106–108, 218–221,
        265–266
Morse code, 26
Morton, Henry V., 372
Moscow Linguistic Circle
    (Lingvističeskij Kružok, MLK),
    88, 327, 551, 598
Moscow Symposium on the
    Structural Study of Sign
    Systems, 376
Moscow-Tartu School, **422–425,**
    471, 553
    focus on semiotics of culture,
        424–425
    multidisciplinary approaches to
        language, 423
    natural language as a primary
        modeling system, 424
    notion of secondary modeling
        systems, 424
    notion of text, 424
    orientation toward application,
        424, 425
    semiotics of art, 36
    summer schools, 376, 423

Most Dangerous Game, The (film),
    121
Motherhood, 236
Motion relationships, 488
Motivated signs, 587
Motivation. *See* Linguistic
    Motivation
Mott, Lucretia Coffin, 234
Mounin, Georges, 612
Mouse, 491
Mozi (Mo-tzu), 116
Muel-Dreyfus, Francine, 265, 266
Mühlmann, Wilhelm E., 67–68
Mukařovský, Jan, 16, 33, 36, 39,
    335, **425–427,** 611
    concept of meaning, 397
    description of language function,
        518
    doctrine of the aesthetic norm,
        330–331
    formalistic period, 425
    functional structuralist aesthetics,
        426
    general aesthetics period, 426
    notion of artistic structure, 602
    rejection of Russian formalism,
        426
    review of Šklovskij's *Theory of
        Prose,* 519
Müller, Jürgen E., 244
    as contributor, 216–218, 241–245
Multimedia, 137, 490–491
    semioses, 244
Multimodality, **427–429**
Multiplicative number code,
    454–455, 456
Multiuser dungeons (MUDs), 108
Multivocality (polysemy), 620
Mulvey, Laura, 122, 185
Mumford, Lewis, 162
Münsteraner Arbeitskreis für
    Semiotik, 242
Murdock, Graham, 107
Muriel (film), 121
Murray, Gilbert, 26
"Musement," 2
Music, 42, **429–432**
    in film, 120
    generative analysis, 429
    homophonic, 431
    jazz improvisation, 430
    loudness, 47
    pitches, 44, 47
    popular, 389, 430
    semiotics of, 445
    social meaning, 430–431
    status as sign, 445
    symphonic, 431
    tonal functional, 429, 430, 431
    tonal hierarchy, 44

Musical expression, 123, 125
Musical narration, 430
Musical notation, 47–48, 297
Musical significance vs.
    signification, 431
Musical time, 431
Musical topics, 446
Music and Discourse (Nattiez), 446
Musique en jeu, 445
Mutations, 223, 224
Mutual cooperation coevolution,
    129
Muybridge, Eadweard James, 30
My Antonia (Cather), 452
My Life in the Art World (Arnheim),
    35
Mysticism, 267
Myth, 65, 108, 240, 241, 263,
    433–435, 514, 628
    Amerindian, 286, 365
    in *Anatomy of Criticism* (Frye), 25
    bourgeois, 432–433
    conveyed through codes, 434
    of the dying god, 26
    generative metaphors of, 433–434
    involving twins, 286
    Maori, 286
    as metalanguage, 59–60
    oppositions expressed in, 285
    paradigmatic reading, 365
    polysemy, 434
    relation to advertising, 14
    syntagmatic reading, 365
    transfer of, 365–366
    trickster, 80
Mythemes (*mythèmes*), 80, 366, 444,
    482, 514
Mythogenesis, 340
Mythoi, 25, 252
Mythologies, **432–433**
Mythologies (Barthes), 59–60, 213,
    432
Mythopraxis, 286
"Myth Today" (Barthes), 432

N

Nadin, Mihai, *as contributor*, 72–74,
    108–110, 136–138, 148–150,
    319–321, 467, 601–603
Nāgārjuna, 94
Nagy, Gregory, 482
Nake, Frieder, 73
Namaste, Ki, 527
Name of the Rose, The (Eco), 211
Names, School of, 116–117
Names and Realities, On (Gongsun
    Longzi), 117
Naming, 628
Naming theory (nomenclaturism),
    626

Nāna-rūpa, 94
Napier, John, 137
Narcissism, 341
Narratee, 122
Narration, 496
Narrative
    as a complex sign system, 444
    defined, 437
    emancipation, 508
    enlightenment, 508
    of film as *écriture*, 392
    as final level of discourse, 323
    hierarchies of articulation, 44
    identity, 375
    metalanguage about, 496
    mimetic properties of, 287
    model, 437–438, 440
    propositions, 438
    rock art as, 545
    schema, 272, 440–443
    semantics, 441
    syntagma, 269–270
    units, 438
"Narrative Coherence and the
    Gusies of Legalism"
    (Roermund), 361
Narrative structures, 252, **437–443**
Narratology, 6, 60, 171, **443–445**,
    467–470, 598
    of Barthes, 322–323
    and comics, 130
    of film, 122, 243
    Greimassian, 243, 272–273, 438,
        440–443, **444–445**
    narrative structures, 437–443
    of Paris School of Semiotics,
        272–273
    structural, 6
Nasal resonance, 462
Nasal vibration, 77
Nasca lines, 544
National Councils of Women, 234
National Institution for Deaf-Mutes,
    578
National Organization for Women
    (NOW), 234
National Party of the Republic of
    South Africa, 30, 31
Native American myths, 286, 365
Natkin, Marcel, 629
Natorp, Paul, 631
Nattiez, Jean-Jacques, 429, **445–446**
Natural conversation, 144
Natural language, 46, 291
    in mapping, 104
    semantic syntax of, 110–111
Natural rights, 356
Natural selection, 176–177, 179,
    180, 223–226, 253, 406, 576
    and coevolution, 129–130
    kin selection, 280

Natural selection, *cont.*
    and manipulation, 382–383
    and sex, 281
Natural Symbols (Douglas), 569
Naven (Bateson), 64
Nazism, 101
Ndembu, 620–621
Nectar in a Sieve (Markandaya), 372,
    373
Needham, Joseph, 649
Negative, 349
Negative entropy (negentropy), 311
Negative judgments, 250
Negativity, 341
"Neither-Nor Criticism" (Barthes),
    432
Neoassociationism, 559
Neoclassical poetics, 495
Neocolonialism, 506
Neo-Confucianism, 649
Neogrammmarians, 150, 350–351,
    353, 550, 606
Neo-Kantianism, 57, 108
Neologisms, in semiotic
    terminology, 569–570
Neo-Marxist semiotics, 394
Nervous system, 135
Net graph, 190
"NETtalk," 218
Networking, 136
Neural architecture, 142
Neural computation, 141
Neural nets, 559
Neurath, Otto, 87, 629, 631
Neuroethology, 447
Neurolinguistics, 447
Neurons, 633
Neuroscience, 171
Neurosemiotics, **446–447**
Neutral space, 580
New Criticism, 495, 534
Newell, Allen, 45, 137, 336
New Guinea, 166, 212
New Left Review, 332
News and current-affairs
    broadcasting, 391
New Science, The (Vico), 628
Newspapers, 389
New Yorker speech, 353
Nicene creed, 569
Nicole, Pierre, 187
Nietzsche, Friedrich W., 247, 274,
    275, 396, 398, 508, 593, 627
Nikolaeva, T. M., 423
Nimitta, 96
Noble savage, 545
Nodes, 190, 560, 561
Noëmatique, 482
Noème, 187, 482
Noëtique, 482

Noise, 65, 570
Nomenclature, 221, 222
Nomenclaturism (naming theory), 626
Nominalism, 3, 399, 402, 529. *See also* Realism and nominalism
  in Chinese ontological realism, 116–118
  Goodman and, 47, 262–263
  medieval dispute over, 399
  and realism, **529–532**
  social, 359
Noncoded iconic message, 13
Nondiscursive, 248
Nonspecific codes, 120
Nonverbal bodily sign categories, 168–170, 183, 197–198, 277–278, 372–373, **447–451**
  facial expressions, 211–212, 229–230
  in the military, 418
  sign languages, 578–582
Nonverbal communication in the novel, 371–373, **451–453**
Nonverbal expressions, 183–184
Noologie, 482
Noos, 482
Noosphere, 376
Norm, 149
Norm and Form: Studies in the Art of the Renaissance (Gombrich), 261
Norm-conformative action, 276
North American Indians, manual signs of, 294
North by Northwest (Hitchcock), 121, 243
Nose, communicative functions of, 590
Notational systems, 47–48
  diagrams and, 190
Note and Tone (Kurkela), 47
Nöth, Winfried, *as contributor*, 13–16, 36–40, 338–340
Notificative indication, 306
Nouveau cinéma, 243
Nouveau roman, 243
Novel, 58
  nonverbal communication in, 371–373, **451–453**
  polyphonic, 58
Nuclear bomb impressions, 119
Nuclei, 322
Nucleotides, 406
Number code, 454–457
Number representation, 26, 47, 78, 136, **453–457**
Nunokawa, Jeff, 526
Nursery rhymes, 159

O

Obeyesekere, Gananath, 166
Object
  in actantial model, 8
  adaptors, 372, 450, 586
  relations theory, 236
Objectification, 639
Obnaženie priëma, 552
Occasionalists, 465
Occultation, 15
Occupational activities, 372
Ockham, William of, 402
Octave equivalence, 43
October (film), 121
Ocularization, 243
Odin, Roger, 242–243, 244
Odyssey (Homer), 501
Oedipal complex, 235–236, 347, 444, 599
Offer, 193
Of Human Bondage (Maugham), 372
Ogden, Charles Kay, 187, 532, 533, 572
Olfactory models, 158, 159–160
Oliver Twist (Dickens), 372, 464
Olson, Charles, 507
Ombre des majorités silencieuses, A l' (In the Shadow of the Silent Majorities; Baudrillard), 69
Omkring sprogteoriens grundlaeggelse (Prolegomena to a Theory of Language; Hjelmslev), 147, 148, 151, 290, 513, 573
One-Dimensional Man (Marcuse), 390
One-place predicates, 262
One-step macromutations (saltations), 224
"On Meaning" (Greimas), 271
Onomatopoeiae, 32, 131, 299, 328, 368
On the Road (Kerouac), 464
Ontogeny, 223
  of Gaia, 255
  genesis in, 340
Ontological relations, 402, 403, 404
Ontology, semiotics of, 30
Open message, 36, 39
Opera, 502
  gender signifiers in, 430, 431
Opera aperta (Eco), 39, 209, 210
Opponent, 10–11
Opposition, **459–460**
  abductive, 460
  in absentia, 460
  aesthetic of, 39–40
  equipollent, 459
  gradual, 459
  phonemic, 606

Opposition, *cont.*
  phonological, 460
  in praesentia, 460
  privative, 459
  semantic, 460
  systems of, 43, 44, 76–82
Optical mode, of perception, 541
Optical patterns, 256–257, 634
Optional data-collection protocol, 560
"Optiques cohérentes, Les" (Zemsz), 644
Oral articulation, 77
Oral culture, 138
  in digital communication, 246
  versus literate, 264
  and stereotypes, 597
  verbal dueling, 246
Oral resonance, 462
"Order of Nature, The" (Peirce), 477
Order of Things, The (Foucault), 247
Ordinary People (film), 269
Ordinary sequence, 269, 270
Ordklasserne (Brøndal), 92–93, 147
Organic semiotics, 511
Orientalism, 157, 505–506
Orientalism (Said), 505
Oriental studies, 506
Origin myth, 165
Origin of Species (Darwin), 129, 176–177, 223, 582
Orotundity, 462
Orthography, 351
  fingerspelling, **245–246**
Ortner, Sherry, 288
Ostranenje, 552
Ostwald, Peter, 586
Otherness, 155
Other Worlds, In (Spivak), 155–156
O'Toole, Michael, 486
Oublier Foucault (Forget Foucault; Baudrillard), 69
Oudart, Jean-Pierre, 122
Outcault, Richard F., 131
Outer speech, 312–313
Outline of a Theory of Practice (Bourdieu), 277
Outline of English Structure, An (Trager and Smith), 367
"Outline of the Autonomous Segments in Jacques Rozier's Film Adieu Philippine" (Metz), 268
Outline of the Oldest Period of the Russian Language (Šachmtov), 617
Output units, 141, 143, 218
Outside in the Teaching Machine (Spivak), 506
Ouyang Jian, 117–118

Ouzman, Sven, *as contributor*, 419–421, 544–547
Overcoding, aesthetic, 39
Overdetermination, 395
  hypogrammatic, 543
Ovid, allegorical readings of, 21
OV languages, 352

P

Paásyanti (mental/transcendental), 75
Packard, Vance, 391
"Padakāṇḍa" ("Prakīrṇakāṇḍa"), 74
Painting, 119. *See also* Pictorial semiotics
  abstract, 26
  as autographic work, 47
  bark, 434
  semiotics of, 36
Pairings, 310
Palatalization, 387
Paleography, 23
Panic, 319
Pāṇini, 74
Panofsky, Erwin, 540, 541, 644
Panopticon, 162, 249, 587
Parables, 240
Paraboles et catastrophes (Thom), 614
Parabolic umbilic catastrophe, 110, 614
Paradigm, 415, 416, **460–461**
  approach to gossip, 265–266
  approach to music, 429
Paradigmatic (associative) relations, 415, 555
Paradigmatic axis, in film analysis, 120
Paradoxical injunctions, 201–203
Paradoxical principle, 625
Paralanguage, 372, 448, 450, **461–465**, 585
  features, 303
  information, 521
  in narrative texts, 451
  used by actors, 12
  utterances, 448
Paralinguistics, 588–589
Parallel distributed processing (PDP), 136, 141–144
  description of network, 142
Parallelism, **465–467**
Parallel perspective, 488, 489
Parallel processing, 466
Parallel syntagma, 269
Paralogy, 509
Parā (eternal), 75
Paraphrasis, doctrine of, 356
Parataxis, 328

Paratexts, 375
Pareto, Vilfredo, 150
Paris, nineteenth century, 71
Paris Film Programme, 122
Paris School, 271, 274, 324, **467–470**, 484–485, 612
Parmentier, Richard, 288–289
Parody, 58, 507
Paroemiography, 470
Paroemiology, **470–474**
Parole. *See* Langue and parole
Parry, Milman, 597
Parsing, **474**
Parsons, Talcott, 220, 598
Parvo cells, 633
Pascal, Blaise, 137
Pasolini, Pier Paolo, 241
"Passagen-Werk" (Arcades Project; Benjamin), 71, 72
Passeron, J.-C., 90
Passions, theories of, 274
Passive voice, 519
Pastiche, 507
Pastoralists, 544, 546
Patañjali, 74, 75
Pather Panchali (Banerji), 371, 372, 373
Pathos, 26
Patient, 8
Patriarchy, 122, 525, 526
Patterns,cultural, 168, 169
Paul (saint), 21
Paul, Jeremy, 358
Pavis, Patrice, 611, 612, 613
Paysan de Paris, Le (Aragon), 60
Peano, Giuseppe, 250
Pêcheux, Michel, 133
Peirce, Charles Sanders, 1, 22, 47, 53, 82, 164, 399, **474–479**
  on characterization of photographs, 482
  on computers, 137
  concept of ground, 476
  concept of hypo-icon, 293, 295
  concept of (icon/iconicity), 293–294, 294–295, 328–329
  concept of index/indexicality, 307–308, 309, 310, 328, 329
  concept of influx, 475
  concept of interpretant, 396, 404
  concept of picture sign, 298–299
  concept of plasticity, 475
  concept of regulation, 475
  concept of representation, 476
  concept of semiosis, 134
  concept of semiotic (or semiosic), 563
  concept of subject, 186
  criticism of Descartes' suppression of the animal, 28

Peirce, Charles Sanders, *cont.*
  definition of sign vehicle, 308–309
  doctrine of signs, 396, 478, 533, 557, 572, 574
  on firstness and secondness in sign interpretation, 360
  on formal relations, 475
  and ideas of Bertrand Russell, 550
  introduction of the term *interpretant*, 499
  lectures on the logic of science, 475–476, 477
  legisigns and sinsigns, 622
  logic of triadic relations, 478
  on meaning, 396
  on phenomenology of consciousness, 550
  on positivism, 477
  on pragmatism, 478–479
  relationship with Jakobson, 327–328
  representamen, 574
  on scientific method, 477
  semiotic aesthetics, 17, 36, 37, 73, 210
  semiotic terminology, 570
  shift between nominalism and realism, 603
  study of referential capacity of terms, 476–477
  synechism, 478
  system of categories, 562
  system of phenomenologial and ontological categories, 574
  ten classes of signs, 502–503
  theory of chemical combination, 475
  trichotomy of iconic, indexical, and symbolic signs, 14, 114–116, 166, 296, 307, 328, 404, 476, 478, 574
  trichotomy of qualisign, sinsign, and legisign, 37, 115, 622
  on type-token, 262, 622
Pelham, Judy, *as contributor*, 249–251
Penny black, 503
Pentaculum, 175
Perception
  Gibson's theory of, 18, 256–257
  and indexicality, 310
  traditional theory of, 256
  visual, 260
Perception of the Visual World, The (Gibson), 256
Percheron, Daniel, 122
Peregrinations: Law, Form, Event (Lyotard), 377
Performative index, 308
Performatives, 591
Perfuming, 96–97

Perigram, 131

Peripheral vision, 451

Periphery, concept of in connectionism, 142

Periphrasis, 519

Perkins, David, 107

Perlocutionary function, 175, 384, 591

Permjakov, Grigorii L'vovich, 472–473

Perron, Paul, *as contributor,* 467–470

Personal symbols, 166

Personification, in pictures, 489

Perspective, 257, 634
change of, 492
principles of, 488–489

Perspectivism, 198

Pertinence, 302–303, **479–481**

Peschl, Markus, *as contributor,* 1, 19–20, 44–46, 135–136, 141–144, 171–172, 178–179, 180–181, 218, 226–227, 232–233, 336–338, 474, 681–620

Peter of Ledesma, 403

Peters, Jan Marie Lambert, 241

Petitot-Cocorda, Jean, 110, 111, 598, 600

Petöfi, János, 242

Petroglyphs, 27, 297, 300

Phallocentrism, 236, 627

Phallus, 348

Phaneroscopy, 570

Pharyngeal control, 462

Pharyngeal resonance, 462

Pharynx, communicative functions of, 589

Phatic function, of sign, 153, 331
in advertising, 15
of logo, 375

Phenomenology, 92, 108, 314–315, 317, 520, 534, 598

Phenomenology of Mind (Hegel), 17, 81

Phenotype, 223, 224–225, 639

Pheromones, 575, 641

Philology, 350–354

Philosophical criticism, 70

Philosophical Discourse of Modernity, The (Habermas), 275, 508

Philosophical Investigations (Wittgenstein), 643

Philosophie der Philologie und Semiotik (Koch), 339

Philosophy of Symbolic Forms, The (Cassirer), 108

Philosophy of the Limit, The (Cornell), 363

Phoenician alphabet, 23

Phoneme, 22, 23, 33, 42, **481–482**
and binary oppositions, 76–77, 79, 459, 460, 518, 618
and distinctive features, 199–200
history of definition, 518–519
item-and-arrangement structuralist view of, 367
Saussurean, 76–77
Trubetzkoy's concept of, 77–78

Phonemics, 481

Phonetic alphabet, 47

Phonetic matrices, 78

Phonetic nasalization, 387

Phonetics, 115, 116, 427, 481, 512, 518
and phonology, 77–78, 618

Phonetic writing systems, 26

Phonetization, of the alphabet, 23

Phonocentrism, 182

Phonogram, 115–116

Phonological category, 78

Phonological equilibrium, 351

Phonological rules, 200

"Phonological Theses for the First International Congress of Linguists," 518

Phonological unit, 518

Phonology, 199–201, 427, 429, 512, 618
binary theory of, 328
and semantics
structural, 77–78, 80, 81, 327, 617, 618

Phonosyntaxization, 116

Phonotactics, 387

Phoria, 469

Photogram, 310

Photographic animation, 30

Photography, 48, 71, 249, 389, **482–484**
indexicality, 118, 310, 482, 483
semiotics of, 307
vs. chirography, 119

Photometry, 477

Photons, 632

Phylacteries, 131

Phylogeny, 340

Physical symbol-systems hypothesis, 45, 336–337

Physiologus, 305

Physionotrace, 119

Piaget, Jean, 276, 306–307, 314, 327, 420, 466
Klein group V4, 565–566
notion of structure, 602
theory of cognitive development, 598

Piatigorsky, Alexander, 95

Picasso, Pablo, 294, 545

Pickwick Papers (Dickens), 372, 451

Pictogram, 22, 114, 115, 299

Pictograph, 449

Pictorial metaphors, 413

Pictorial semiotics, 42, 260–261, 298–300, **484–486**, 539–540
aniconic visual signs, 26–27, 85–87
in *Art and Illusion* (Gombrich), 40–41
based upon psychology of perception, 299
comics, 106–108, 130–132
and continuity, 490
emblems, 214–216
iconicity in, 295
logos, 373–375
and picture perception, 486–489
pictures and computers, 489–493
Riegl's theory of intentionality and perception, 540–542
rock art, 544–547
schools of, 484

Pictura, 214

Picture. *See* Image and picture; Pictures and computers

Picture perception, **486–489**

Pictures and computers, **489–493**
external pictures as purpose or condition, 489–491
internal pictures supporting problem solving, 492–493
pictures shared by computer and user in interaction, 491–492

Picture writing, 27

Pike, Kenneth, 598

Pilgrim's Progress (Bunyan), 21

Pillai, K. Raghavan, 74

Pisan, Christine de, 234

Pitch, 462

Plain language movement, 646

Plains Indian Sign Talk (PST), 581–582

Plaisir du texte, Le (The Pleasure of the Text; Barthes), 61

Plan américain, 120

Plan-séquence (sequence shot), 268, 270

Plasticity, of language, 295

Plato, 29, 118, 150, 317, 318, 529, 568
Cratylus, 149, 328
hierarchy of knowledge, 408
on rhetoric, 363
theory of ideas, 603
transcendental realism, 408–409

Play, **493–495,** 514

"Playing the dozens," 246

Play of Musement, The (Sebeok), 26, 37, 558

Plereme (*plérème*), 113, 114, 115, 481

Pleromata, 27, 87
Pliny the Elder, 28
Plot, 438, 440–441, 495
Plot-association tests (PATs), 560
Pluri-isotopy, 324
Plutarch, 28
Poe, Edgar Allen, 348
Poema del Cid, 373, 452
Poetic (aesthetic) function, of sign, 17, 330–331, 520
Poetic characters *(caratteri poetici)*, 628
Poetic communication function
  in advertising, 15
  of logo, 375
Poetic denomination, 335
"Poetic Denomination and the Esthetic Function of Language" (Mukařovský), 519, 520
Poetic logic, 628
Poetics, **495–498**, 542, 628
  allegory, 20–22
  blason poétique, 84–85
  creation, 543
  displacement, 543
  distortion, 543
  fiction, 239–241
  Jakobson's theory of, 328–329
  Koch's theory of, 339
  metaphor, 411–414
  model of poetic signification, 532–544
  poststructuralist, 497–498, 533
  and proverbs, 471
  structuralist, 25–26, 251–252, 496, 533
  vs. interpretation, 495
Poetics (Aristotle), 411, 494, 501, 534
Poetics (journal) 414
Poetic signification, model of, 542–544
Poetics Today, 414, 611
Poetika: Sborniki po teorii poetičeskogo jazyka, 551
Poetry and Science (Koch), 339
Poincaré, Henri, 614
Poinsot, Joannes, 53, 399, 403, 404, **498–500**, 557
Point Counter Point (Huxley), 452
Pointing gestures, 449
Point of view, in film narration, 243
Points de capiton, 345–346
Polákova Vznešenost přírody (Polák's Nature's Sublimity; Mukařovský), 426
Polemic, 58
Politeness principle, 516
Political cartoons, 107, 489
Political economy, and semiology, 152–153
Political liberty, 248–249

Political posters, 646
Political Unconscious, The (Jameson), 332
Politics (Aristotle), 28
"Politics of Legal Semiotics, The" (Paul), 358
Polivanov, Evgenij D., 551
Pollock, Jackson, 42
Poly-dimensional semiotics, 511
Polyfunctionality, 89, 470, 519
Polylogical subject, 564
Polyphonic novel, 58
Polyphony, 58, 431
Polysystem theory, **500–502**
Ponzio, Augusto, 548
Poor theater, 26–27
Popkin, Richard, 559
Poppe, Emile, 243
Popper, Karl, 2, 405, 466
  and Vienna Circle, 629
Popular culture, 156, 391, 392, 597
Popular fiction, 389, 392
Popular Science Monthly, 477
Population genetics, 641
Porphyry, 529, 530
Porter Institute for Poetics and Semiotics, Tel Aviv University, 500
Portrait book, 215
Port Royal Logic, 187
Port Royal School, 92
Positional number code, 454, 455–457
Positivism, 275, 317, 477
  binary logic of, 363
  legal, 356
  linguistics, 370
  logical, 92, 412, 532–533
  Marxist, 388
Posner, Roland, *as contributor*, 453–457, 515–517
Postage stamps, **502–505**
Postcolonialism, 157, 192, 237, **505–507**
  and gender, 236
Postformalists, reception of West European formalism, 644
Postmoderne expliqué aux enfants, Le (Lyotard), 377
Postmodernism, 67–69, 156, **507–509**, 535, 588
  and feminism, 235
  Jameson's characteristics of, 333
  and Marxist theory, 333
  radical critique of modernitiy, 275
  and semiotics of the animal, 30
  theories of meaning, 397–398
Postmodernism, or the Cultural Logic of Late Capitalism (Jameson), 332, 333

Postsemiotics, 509, **509–512**
Poststructuralism, 81, 132, 151, 167, 192, 235–236, **512–515**
  approach to cultural differences, 155–157
  approach to historical discourse, 287
  on the concept of difference as opposition, 626–627
  and discourse of science, 207
  discursively produced subject, 248
  dramatism and, 267
  feminism, 233, 234, 238
  notion of history, 332
  notion of intentionality, 316
  poetics, 497–498, 533
  on Saussurean value, 627
  and semiotics, 258
  and semiotics of the animal, 30
  theories of meaning, 398
Potemkin (film), 302
"Potentiality of the Phenomena of Language, On the" (Mathesius), 150–151, 515
Pot helmets, 283
Potlatch, 68, 69
Pottier, Bernard, 271
Poujade, Pierre, 432
Pouvoir ouvrier, 377
Power, in modernity, 248–249
Power of the Center, The (Arnheim), 35
Powers of Horror, The (Kristeva), 565
Poyatos, Fernando, 168, 448, 461
  as contributor, 144–147, 168–170, 371–373, 447–451, 451–453, 461–465, 521–523, 585–586, 591
Practical interests, 275
Practice of Love, The (de Lauretis), 186
Practice theory, 288
Praepositionernes theori (Brøndal), 92, 93
Pragmatics, 195, 373, **515–517**
  of art, 38–39
  defined, 515
  in dramatism, 267
  empirical, 277
  and implicature, 303, 304
  and metaphor, 412
Prague Linguistic Circle, 17, 88, 92, 327, 330, 335, 425, 495
  Mukařovský's influence on, 426
  study of theater, 611
  Trubetzkoy's activities in, 617
Prague school, 11, 147, **517–521**, 534, 552, 553, 598
  aesthetics, 17, 36
  classical period, 518

Prague school, *cont.*
  concept of dominant function, 330, 331
  functionalism, 330
  impact of Russian formalism on, 518
  influence of on critical linguistics, 195
  markedness concept, 386
  notion of "function," 16, 518
  notion of opposition, 459
  phonology, 364, 518
  relativism, 330
  of the 1960s, 520
  Saussure's influence on, 151
  structural functionalism, 33, 38
  structural-semiotic shift in orientation, 518–520
Prague Spring, 520
Prajñā (bodhi), 97
Prakīrnakānda, 74
Pratibhā, 74
Pratītya-samutpāda, 94
Pravda, Ján, 104, 105
Prayer, text as, 99
"Precession of Simulacra, The" (Baudrillard), 507
Prédire n'est pas expliquer (Thom), 614
Pregnant forms, 614
"Prehistory of the Slavic Languages" (Trubetzkoy), 617, 618
Presemiotic period, 399
Presentational forms, 160
Presentation of Self in Everyday Life (Goffman), 258–259
Press, Charles, 107
Prestructuralism, 91
Presupposition, 324
Preziosi, Donald, 33, 162
Pribram, Karl, 569
Prieto, Louis, 42, 79, 306
Prigogine, Ilya, 422
Primary intersubjectivity, 193
Primary qualities, of paralanguage, 461–462
Primitive Classification (Durkheim and Mauss), 206
Primitive societies, theory of, 68
Primitivist movement, 545
Prince, Gerald, 122
Principes de grammaire générale (Principles of General Grammar; Hjelmslev), 147, 290
Principles of Biological Autonomy (Varela), 55
Principles of Mathematics (Russell), 549
Principles of Phonology (Trubetzkoy), 77, 151
Print, news reporting, 391

Printing press, 389
Prison House of Language, The (Jameson), 332
Privative opposition, 459
Prkachin, Kenneth, *as contributor,* 211–212, 229–231, 231–232
Proaïretic code, 60
Probabilistic grammars, 559
Probabilistic network analysis, 560
"Problem das Stils in der bildende Kunst, Das" (Wölfflin), 644
"Problem of Content, Material, and Form in Verbal Art, The" (Bakhtin), 58, 541
Problem of Russian Self-Awareness, On the (K probleme russkogo samopoznanija; Trubetzkoy), 618
"Problem of Speech Genres, The" (Bakhtin), 59
"Problem of the Text in Linguistics, Philology, and the Human Sciences: An Experiment in Philosophical Analysis, The" (Bakhtin), 59
Problem of Verse Language (Tynjanov), 552
Problems and Projects (Goodman), 262
"Problems in the Study of Literature and Language" (Tynjanov and Jakobson), 518
"Problems in the Typology of Culture" (Lotman), 376
"Problems of Denotation in the Fiction Film" (Metz), 268
Problems of Dostoevsky's Creative Works (Bakhtin), 58
Problems of Dostoevsky's Poetics (Bakhtin), 58
Process and Reality (Whitehead), 422
Process interface, 319
Prodi, Giorgio, 598
"Program of Linguistic Analysis," 518
Projection, 166
Prokaryotic semiosis, 558
Prolegomena to a Theory of Language (Omkring sprogteoriens grundlaeggelse; Hjelmslev), 147, 148, 151, 290, 513, 573
Prolegomenza zu einer Psychologie der Architektur (Wölfflin), 644
Prolepsis, 489
PROLOG, 227
"Promise of Legal Semiotics, The" (Balkin), 358
Proni, Giampaolo, 2
Pronouns
  of address, 198–199
  indexicality, 308, 310
Pronunciation, spelling, 351

Property terms, 262
Propositional negative, 349
Propositions, 591
  logical, 642
"Propositions" (Lotman), 424
Propp, Vladimir A., 6, 7, 10, 88, 422
  algebraic syntax, 434
  approach to folk narratives, 6, 9, 11, 243, 252, 272–273, 437, 438–439, 443–444, 599, 615
  archetypal folktale, 438–439
  spheres of action, 5, 6
Proprioceptive properties, 469
Proscenium-arch theater, 198
Prose, 26
Prosody, 367
Protention, 311
Protoindex, 311
Proto-Indo-European, 350, 351, 568
Protostamp, 502
Prototypes, 158, 159, 166, 460
Proust as Musician (Nattiez), 446
Proverbs, 159
  heuristic model of, 471–472
  study of, 470–474
Proxemics, 12, 169, 170, 197, 448, 481
"Prussianism and Socialism" (Spengler), 593
Psychoanalysis
  and analysis of subject formation, 155
  of culture, 166
  in feminist theory, 195
  and film theory, 119, 121–122, 184, 185, 300, 392, 417
  hypnosis in, 29
  mirror phase, 300
  technique of neutralization, 348
  transference, 346, 348
Psychoanalysis and Cinema (Metz), 392
Psychogenetic symbols, 166
Psychological individuation, 314
Psychology, 65, 248, 249
  ego, 345
  of facial expressions, 211–212
  Gestalt, 35, 310, 486
Psychology of Art (Vygotskij), 551
Psychophysics, 465, 466
Psychopictograms (dream balloons), 131
Psychosomatic medicine, 82, 83
Psychotic discourse, 342
Ptolemy, 477
Pudovkin, Vsevolod, 241
Punctuated equilibria, 223
Punctuation, 26, 64, **521–523**
  codes of in film semiotics, 120
"Purloined Letter, The" (Poe), 348, 378
Purpose, in dramatistic pentad, 267

Q

Qi, 173–174
Quadriller, 249
Quaestiones disputatae de potentia (Aquinas), 402
Qualifiers, 461, 462–463
Qualifying test, 439, 440
Qualisign, 37, 115, 478, 502, 622
Qualitative functions, of punctuation, 522
Quantification, 249
Quantifier, 250, 251
Quantitative functions, of punctuation, 522
Quantum mechanics, 370
Quarrel of universals, 529
Quebec School, 484, 485–486
Queer theory, 186, 237, **525–527**
Quemada, Bernard, 271
Querelle des femmes, 85
"Quest for the Essence of Language" (Jakobson), 328–329
Question, 193
"Question Preliminary to Any Possible Treatment of Psychosis, On a" (Lacan), 347
"Questions Concerning Certain Faculties Claimed for Man" (Peirce), 477
"Questions on Reality" (Peirce), 477
Quine, Willard V. O., 538, 609, 630, 631

R

Rabelais, François, 287, 527
"Rabelais and Gogol" (Bakhtin), 59
Rabelais and His World (Bakhtin), **527–529**
Rabelais in the History of Realism (Bakhtin), 59
Racialized difference, 237
Racial value coding, 505, 506
Racism
  colonial, 505
  in early feminism, 235
Radakovic, Theodor, 629
Radcliffe-Brown, Alfred R., 359, 364, 364
Radicals (morphographemes), 114
Radio, 389
  semiotics of, 242
Radio, an Art of Sound (Arnheim), 35
Radiščev, A. N., 376
RAM, 50
Rambelli, Fabio, *as contributor*, 93–99, 173–176, 381–382, 383–385, 650–652

Rand, Paul, 375
Rao, Raja, 372
Rapoport, Amos, 162
Rappaport, Roy, 166
Rask, Rasmus, 350
Rasmussen, Susan, 266
Rastier, François, 324, 565
Rationality
  cognitive-instrumental, 275
  communicative, 275
  Marx's concept of, 275
  principle of, 516
Rational relations, 402, 403
Ratner, Leonard, 446
Raw and the Cooked, The (Lévi-Strauss), 442
Rawls, John, 276
Ray, Thomas, 50–51
Reactances, 639
Reaction formation, 166
Reactivation, 248
Reader-response theories. *See* Reception and reader-response theories
Reading Capital (Althusser), 24, 25
Reading grid, 324
Realism, 3, 18, 25, 47, 529–530
  in art history, 261
  Chinese ontological, 116–118
  conventional, 161
  emphasis on act in dramatism, 267
  fiction, 505
  theory of meaning, 116–118
  and theory of perception, 256
Realism and nominalism, **529–532**
"Realismus und Positivismus" ("Realism and Positivism"; Schlick), 629
Reality
  in mapping, 103
  and terminology, 350, 370
Realization rule, 352
Reaper, 50
Reasoning
  abductive, **1–3**
  moral, 276
Rebus (syllabic sign), 23, 86, 215
Receiver (R), 125
Recent Theories on the Nature of the Language Sign (Spang-Hanssen), 148, **532–533**
Reception and reader-response theories, 516–517, **533–536**, 612
Receptive fields, retinal, 633
Receptors, 83, 112–113, 311–312, **536–537**, 623
Recherches structurales 1949: Interventions dans le débat glossématique, 148, **537–538**

Recipes, 158, 159
Reciprocal altruism, 321, 582, 583, 616
Reciprocal models of communication, 133
Récit (tale), 120
Reconceptions in Philosophy and Other Arts and Sciences (Goodman), 262
Reconservatism, 508
Recorded voice, in film, 120
Rectification of Names, On the (Xunzi), 117
Recuperative allegory, 21
Recurrence and a Three-Modal Approach to Poetry (Koch), 339
Recurrent architecture, 142
Red Badge of Courage, The (Crane), 464
Redford, Robert, 269
Reduced interaction conversation, 144
Redundancy, 128, 479–480
Reference, **538–539**
  and fiction, 239–241
  indirect (mediated), 262–263, 354
  in literary texts, 538–539
Referent, 187, 294–295, 330, 331
Referential communication function
  in advertising, 15
  of logo, 375
Reflecting barrier, 561
Regenta, La (Alas), 373
Register
  imaginary, 300
  linguistic, 278–279
  semantic, 313
Registers (*lu*), 173, 174
Regression, argument of, 296
Regulators, 448, 450
Reichenbach, Hans, 629, 631
Reid, Thomas, 474
Reidlinger, Albert, 150
Reinach, Salomon, 545
Reinhold, Ernst, 476
Relationes rationis (relations of reason), 401–402, 403
Relation praedicamentalis, 401
Relations, 400–403
  algebra of, 550
  second- and higher-order, 599
Relatio secundum dici, 401, 402
Relatio secundum esse, 402
Relatio transcendentalis, 401
Relative arbitrariness, 368
Relativism, linguistic, 350
Relator, 92
Relatum, 92
Relevance, principle of, 516
Religion, 350
Religious icon, 293
Religious symbols, 297

Renaissance art, 645
Renaissance und Barock (Wölfflin), 644
Repetition, of mantras, 384
Reported speech, 328
Representamen (expression), 37, 47, 48, 115, 134, 294–295, 374
Representation, 183–184, 544
  fictive, 354
  of otherness, 156–157
  semiotics of, 277–278
  styles of in art, 260
  theory of, 238, 248
  vs. signification, 498
Representatives, systems of, 44
Repression, 166
Reproduction, mechanical, 71
Reproduction in Education, Society, and Culture (Bourdieu and Passeron), 90
Republic, The (Plato), 408
Resonance, 462
"Response to a Question Put by the Editorial Board of *Novy Mir*" (Bakhtin), 59
Restricted codes, 160, 204–205, 596
Résumé of a Theory of Language (Hjelmslev), 290
"Resurrection of the Word, The" (Šklovskij), 551
Retention, 311
Retina, 632, 633
Retinotopic maps, 635
Retinotopic principle, 633
Retroductive reasoning, 2
Revesz, Gregor, 281, 282
"Revision of the Dostoevsky Book, On the" (Bakhtin), 59
Revolution, 71–72
Revolutionary language, 342
"Revolution in Poetic Language" (Kristeva), 342
Revzin, I. I., 423
Rey-Debove, Josette, 263
Rhematic iconic legisign, 503
Rhematic indexical sinsign, 502, 503, 504
Rheme, 37, 478
  and theme, 519
Rhetoric, 182, 362–363, 414, 485, 497
  of courtship, 100
  figures of, 20
  of identification, 100, 101
  of objectivity, 646
"Rhetoric of Hitler's 'Battle,' The" (Burke), 101
Rhetoric of Motives, A (Burke), 99
"Rhetoric of the Image"
  ("Rhétorique de l'image";
  Barthes), 13, 416, **539–540,** 615

Rhizome, 211, 511
Rhizomorphous semiotics, 511
Rhoticity, 353
Rhyme, 159
Rhythm, 159
  in language, 341, 342
  ranges, 462
Richards, Ivor Armstrong, 187, 412, 532, 533, 572
Richardson, Alan, *as contributor,* 629–631
Rickert, Heinrich, 631
Ricoeur, Paul, 287, 375, 412
Riddle, 20
Riegl, Alois, **540–542**
Riffaterre, Michael, **542–544**
Ring des Nibelungen, Der (Wagner), 502
Ripa, Cesare, 215
Ritter, Heinrich, 476
Ritual, 160, 240, 241, 366, 372, 605, 620
  communicative, 204–205
  Daoist, 173–176
  interaction, 605
  mantras as, 383, 384
  military use of, 418
  religious, 263
  rite of passage, 621
Ritualization, 576
Ritual Process: Structure and Anti-Structure, The (Turner), 621
Road signs, 297
Robotics, 48, 49, 65
Rock art, 421, **544–547**
  art pour l'art interpretation of, 544–545
  narrative approach, 545
  postmodern approach, 545–547
  sympathetic magic (hunting magic) approach, 545
Rock-music videos, 269, 392
Rodgers, J. L., 407
Rods, 632, 633
Roermund, Bert van, 361
Roland Barthes par Roland Barthes (Roland Barthes on Roland Barthes; Barthes), 61
Role, 603–604
Role of the Reader, The (Eco), 209, 210
Role type, 603
Roman alphabet, 23
Romance, 25, 26, 252
Roman de la rose, 21
Romanian language, 149
Roman punctuation, 521
Roman radiophonique, 35
Romantics, 296
Room of One's Own, A (Woolf), 235

Roots of Literature, The (Koch), 339
Ropars, Marie-Claire, 121, 242
Rorty, Richard, 276
Rosaldo, Renato, 289
Roscelin, 529
Rosch, Eleanor, 413
Rose, Jacqueline, 155, 235
Rossholm, Göran, *as contributor,* 262–263, 354–355
Rossi-Landi, Ferruccio, 24, 33, 393, **547–549**
  on relations between structure and superstructure, 548
  theory of exchange within sign systems, 394
Rousseau, Jean-Jacques, 150, 545
Rowe, R. C., 407
Rozenvejg, V. J., 423
Rubin, Gayle, 525
Ruesch, Jurgen, 65
Rules
  of play, 493–494
  of semiotics, 493–494, 510
Rules of Sociological Method, The (Durkheim), 355
Rumelhart, D. E., 144
Rumsey, Alan, 369, 639
Rural-exterior cultureme, 168
Rural-interior cultureme, 168
Ruse, Michael, *as contributor,* 129–130, 170–171, 176–178, 179–180, 223–225, 225–226, 280–281, 321–322, 382–383, 404–405, 575–576, 582–585, 616–617, 641–642, 650, 652
Russell, Bertrand A., 64, 250, 309, 499, 538, **549–550,** 574, 629
  analysis of the word *the,* 549
  notion of sign, 533
Russell's paradox, 250
Russian folktale, 5, 6–7
Russian formalism, 17, 36, 39, 330, 376, 422, 495, **550–553,** 602
  admiration of Wölfflin, 644
  extrinsic systemic functionalism stage, 552
  intrinsic systemic functionalism stage, 552
  process of interpretation, 533
  reductionist stage, 552
  views on literary evolution, 552–553
Russian revolution, 550
Russischen Dichter des 18. und 19. Jahrhunderts, Die (Trubetzkoy), 618
Ruwet, Nicolas, 429, 446
Ryle, Gilbert, 258, 313, 538, 548
Rypka, Jan, 517
Ryunosuke, Akutagawa, 30

S

Śabdabrama, 74
Šachmtov, A. A., 617
Sacks, Harvey, 195
Sacramental theology, 52–53
Sacred Unity, A: Further Steps to an Ecology of Mind (Bateson), 67
Sade/Fourier/Loyola (Barthes), 61
Sādhana, 76
Sagan, Dorion, 255
Sahlins, Marshall, 154, 286
Said, Edward, 157, 505
Saint Louis Hegelians, 476
Saint-Martin, Fernande, 261, 485–486
 as contributor, 35–36
Śakti, 76
Šākyamuni (Siddhārta Gautama), 95, 381
Salient forms, 614
Saltations, 224
Salthe, Stanley, 598
Salus, M., 42
Salus, P., 42
Saluting, 418
Saṃdhābhāsā (saḍhyābhāsā), 94
Sampradāna (destination), 76
San, 546
Sanskrit, 568
Sanskrit literature, 74
Sapir, Edward, 133, 154, 195, 204, 315, 328, 637
Sapir-Whorf hypothesis, 43, 133, 154, 369, 637
Sarcasm, 302
Sarrasine (Balzac), 60, 315
Sartre, Jean-Paul, 234, 332
Satellite broadcasting, 392
Satire, 26, 107
Sauer, Carol O., 422
Šaumjan, S. K., 423
Saussure, Ferdinand de, 16, 58, 127, 315, **555–557**
 anagrammatic studies, 329
 on arbitrary nature of the sign, 32, 153–154, 368–369, 533, 537, 541, 556, 625–626
 attack on logical positivism and empiricism, 626
 concept of articulation act, 41, 42, 43, 76
 concept of binary opposition, 76–77, 79, 199, 385, 459, 555, 565
 concept of linguistic value, 577, 600, 625–626
 concept of signification, 576, 577, 625
 concept of system, 606
 content and referent, 187

Saussure, Ferdinand de, *cont.*
 diagram of communication, 345
 distinction between diachronic and synchronic linguistics, 351, 605–607
 on extratextual referent, 538
 on grammar, 369
 on language as structure, 601
 langue vs. *parole,* 126, 133, 150, 332, 355–356, 514, 555, 600, 606
 law of value, 68, 77, 79
 linearity principle, 366, 556
 on meaning, 396, 626
 on mime, 27
 on motivated character of pictures and miming, 295
 paradigmatic (associative) relations, 415, 461, 600
 on picture sign, 299
 schema of speech sounds, 77
 semiology, 154, 411, 556–557, 627
 sens and *rôle,* 576–577
 signifier-signified relation, 153, 154, 182, 328, 396, 573, 601, 643
 on sound change, 555
 structural-functional linguistics, 92, 150
 synchronic linguistics, 88, 150, 285, 332, 555
 on syntagmatic relations, 415, 461, 556, 600
 Tel Quel project, 238
Sauter, Willmar, 535, 612
Savage Mind, The (Lévi-Strauss), 365
Savan, David, 309
Scalars, 44
Scene
 in dramatistic pentad, 267
 in great syntagmatic system for film, 269, 270
Scenographic code, 130
Ščerba, L. V., 518
Schaeffer, Jean-Marie, 483
Schapiro, Meyer, 261
Scheffler, Israel, 263
Schegloff, Emanuel, 195
Scheibler,Christoph, 53
Schemata, 27, 87
 radical, 222
Schema theory, 158
Schiller, Friedrich von, 563
Schirato, Tony, *as contributor,* 314–317, 332–334, 396–399
Schism and Continuity in an African Society (Turner), 620
Schismogenesis, 605
Schizophrenia, 65, 66, 201–202
Schleicher, August, 350

Schleiermacher, Friedrich, 465
Schlichtmann, Hansgeorg, 104
 as contributor, 103–106
Schlick, Moritz, 629, 631
Schmalriede, Manfred, 73
Schmidt, S. J., 242
Schoenmakers, Henry, 535, 612
Scholasticism, 92, 465
Schooling, 89–90, 249
School of Names, 116–117
Schramm, Wilbur, 390
Schulz, T. A., 73
Schutz, Alfred, 205, 258
Science, 108
 discourse of, 221
 gossip of, 265–266
 languages of, 629–630
 unification, 548
 unity of, 630
Scientia sexualis (sexual science), 525
Scientism, approach to language, 349
Scienza nuova, La (Vico), 627
Scopophilia, 301
Scotists, 402
Scott, David
 as contributor, 502–505
Screen and Screen Education, 392
Script, 22
Scriptures *(jing),* 173
Seal, 174–175
Searle, John R., 196, 258, 302, 466, 516, 538, 591–592
Sebeok, Thomas A., 26, 37, 82, 83, 253, **557–559**, 652
Sechehaye, Albert, 150, 335, 518
Secondary cultureme, 169
Second International, 387
Sedgewick, Eve Kosofsky, 525
Séduction, De la (Seduction; Baudrillard), 69
Seed syllables *(bīja),* 94, 96–97, 383, 384
Segal, D., 423
Segmentation
 of film, 268–270
 in heraldry, 284
Sein und Zeit (Being and Time; Heidegger), 181
Seitel, Peter, 471–472
Selection-restriction disorders, 596
Self-adaptor activities, 585
Selfish Gene, The (Dawkins), 179, 404–405, 583
Self-production, 254
Self-Reflection in the Arts and Sciences (Blum and McHugh), 319
Self-reflexive text, 122
Sēma, 568, 569
Semanalyse, 569

Semanalysis, 341, 342, 564
Semantic archetypes, 111
Semantic codes, in film semiotics, 120
Semantic differentials, 459
Semantic embedding, 142
Semantic fields, 185
Semantic graphs, 559
Semantic isotopy, 323
Semantic nets, 559
Semantic oppositions, 424–425, 460
Semantics, 22, 515
  of art, 37–38
  combinatorial, 79
  componential analysis, 79, 200
  of computation, 136
  and graphology, 427
  and knowledge representation, 336–338
  and lexicogrammar, 427
  and phonology, 427
  possible-world, 240
  structural, 79
  truth-conditional model of, 304
"Sémantique structurale, Pour une" (Hjelmslev), 291
Sémantique structurale (Greimas), 565
Semantography, 86
Semasiology, 569
Sematology, 569
Seme (*sème*), 79, 323, 324, 482, 566
Sememe (*sémème*), 79, 210, 211, 324, 482, 566
Semic category, 324
Semic code, 60
Sémie, 482
Semiogenesis (Koch), 339, 340
Semiogenetic theory of art, 37
Semiographic cube, 560
Semiography, **559–561**
Semiology, 60, 154, 399, 557
  Barthes on, 151, 212–214, 242
  shift in terminology to *semiotics,* 557, 558
Semiology of Graphics (Bertin), 104
Semionarrative structures, 273, 444
Semiophysics, 614
Semiopragmatics, of film, 244
Semiosis, 73, 82, 543, 558, **561–563**
  critical phenomena of, 562
  defined, 559–560
  indexical, 14
  Lacan's theory of, 345–349
  Lyotard's theory of, 378
  materialist, 395
  multimedia, 244
  Peirce's concept of, 134, 393, 561
  Saussure's concept of, 411

Semiosis, *cont.*
  Saussure's stratified view of, 411
  structured as argumentation, 1
  theory of female subject of, 185–186, 236, 237
  unlimited, 185
  visual, 42
  Voloshinov's theory of, 393, 394
Semiosis (journal), 73, 603
Semiosphere, 82, 377
Semiotica, 445, 558
"Semiotic Analysis of Legal Discourse, The" (Greimas), 361
Semiotic and symbolic, **563–565**
Semiotic calculus, 73
Semiotic engineering, 137
Semiotic function, 307
Semiotic functionalism, 330
Semiotic historiography, 51
Semiotic information, 73
Semioticity, 73
Semiotic matrix, 73
Semiotics, 291
  of allegory, 20–22
  applied, 10
  of architecture, 33–35
  of art, 36–37
  in Buddhism, 97–98
  in contemporary sense, 399
  contextualized theory of, 304
  critical, 509
  cultural, 17, 624
  of cultural codes, 222
  emic approach, 618
  etic approach, 618
  etymology of term, 568
  evolutionary cultural, 339–340
  of fiction, 239–241
  in foundational sense, 399
  growth of as field, 271
  "high," 53
  horizontal, 83
  Kristeva's concept of, 341, 342, 343
  launching as term, 558
  logical-positivist perspective, 466
  marginalizing of feminist theory in, 237
  of music, 429
  notion of dialogue in, 563
  organic, 511
  of passions, 274
  of pictorial art, 539
  polydimensional, 511
  as process, 510–511
  of representation, 277–278
  rhizomorphous, 511
  rules of, 493–494, 510
  scope of, 253
  social, 89–91, 132, 134, 195, 303, 510

Semiotics, *cont.*
  of social reproduction, 548
  survival, 83
  of theater, 533, 535, 611–613
  urban, 587–588, **624–625**
  vertical, 83
  visual, 73
  yogācāra, 96, 98
Semiotics and Language: An Analytical Dictionary (Greimas and Courtés), 271, 273, 323, 467, 468, 482
Semiotics and Legal Theory (Jackson), 357
Semiotics and the Philosophy of Language (Eco), 210–211
Semiotics in the United States (Sebeok), 558
Semiotic Society of America, 558
Semiotics of Cinema (Lotman), 241–242
Semiotics of Passions, The (Greimas and Fontanille), 274, 469, 470
Semiotics of Poetry (Riffaterre), 542
Semiotic square, 21, 324, 441, 467, **565–568**
  Greimasian, 14, 111, 243, 272, 323, 441
Semiotic terminology, 460–461, 481–482, 547, **568–571,** 571, 572–575
Semiotik des Films (Knilli), 242
Sémiotique: Dictionnaire raisonné de la théorie du langage (Greimas and Courtés), 271, 273, 323, 467, 468, 482
Sémiotique des passions (Semiotics of Passions; Greimas and Fontanille), 274, 469, 470
Semiotische ésthetik (Bense), 37
Semitic alphabet, 23
Semiurgy, 152, **571–572**
Semper, Gottfried, 541
Sender (S), 125
Sender versus receiver, 5, 7, 9–10
Sensations, 256
Sense and denotation, theory of, 250–251
"Sense and Meaning, On" (Frege), 251
Sense of Order, The: A Study in the Psychology of Decorative Art (Gombrich), 261
Senses, 3
Senses Considered as Perceptual Systems, The (Gibson), 256
Sense vs. meaning, 313
Sensifics, 569
Sensograms, 131
Sentence meaning, 75–76

Sentences (Lombard), 52–53, 399
Sentence stress, 519
Sentential roles, 8
  equivalence with textual actants, 9
Sentic forms, 123–125
Sentics (Clynes), 125
Sentograph, 123
Sequences, filmic, 268, 269, 270
Sergent, Justine, 447
Sermo (sense), 5
Serpieri, Alessandro, 611
Sets, 168, 169
Set theory, 44, 64, 250, 251
Sex, evolution of, 281
Sexual differences, 89, 233, 234, 235
Sexuality, 347, 525
Sexual science *(scientia sexualis)*, 525
Sexual selection, 177–178, 584, 650
Shaman, 420
Shang, 648
Shannon, Claude, 72, 311, 331, 514, 570
"Shannon information," 576
Shapiro, Meyer, 35
Shapiro, Michael, 42, 352, 446, 563
Shepherd, Walter, 298
Shifters, 122, 183, 307, 309, 328, 329
Shore, Bradd, *as contributor,* 61–64, 157–161, 165–168
Shot, filmic, 120, 241, 243, 301
  autonomous, 268
  as basic element of film semiotics, 241, 242, 268
  point-of-view, 243
Showalter, Elaine, 233, 235
Showdown, 259
Sickel, Theodor, 540
Siddham, 175, 385
Sigmoid function, 143
Sign, **572–575**
  Abélard's concept of, 4
  as active agent, 561
  in advertising, 308
  aesthetic (poetic) function of, 17, 330–331, 520
  algebraic, 328
  alphabet letters as, 23
  arbitrary nature of, 330, 537, 606
  Aristotle's concept of, 150
  art as, 16, 520
  assertive, 250
  astrological, 297
  astronomical, 297
  Augustine's definition of, 51–53, 498
  autonomous, 573

Sign, *cont.*
  Bertrand Russell on, 550
  chemical, 26
  commodity and, 152
  common usage, 572
  conative (appellative), 330, 331, 375
  conventional (legisigns), 166, 293–294, 295, 296–297, 402
  dicent, 478, 503
  economy of, 453
  emotive, 188
  expressive, 315
  fictional, 240
  filmic, 392
  formal, 400, 403, 499
  as form of social interaction, 128
  function, 16, 294, 296, 315, 330–331, 375
  as function of code, 127
  hierarchical range of, 575
  of history, 289
  Hjelmslev on, 149, 151, 291, 533
  hobo, 26, 297
  Husserl on, 533
  identity, 374
  indicative, 315, 316
  instrumental, 400, 498
  as mediating entity, 320
  medieval notion of, 399, 400–404
  metalinguistic function of, 15, 331, 375
  minimal, 104–106
  motivated, 573, 587
  music as, 445
  natural, 402
  notion of substitution, 573
  and parallelism, 466
  Peirce's definition of, 308–309, 396
  phatic function of, 15, 153, 331, 375
  picture, 118–119, 299, 308
  planes of, 533
  political economy of, 68–69
  processes, 466
  punctuation, 26
  referential function of, 330, 331
  relational conception of, 573
  Saussure's concept of, 153–154, 368–369, 533, 555–557
  shift of status in, 504
  social multiaccentuality of, 192
  as symbol, 109
  and symbolic type, 605
  theory of linguistic, 32, 68, 330, 335, 532
  usage in semiotics, 569, 572
  visual signs, 297–298
Signal, **575–576**

Signaling, 224, 229, 641, 650
  facial expression as system of, 211–212, 229–230
  interspecific communication, 321–322
  as manipulation, 180, 321
  and sexuality, 584
  theory of, 180
Sign and Its Masters, The (Sebeok), 558
Signans, 328
Signatum, 328
"Signature événement contexte" ("Signature Event Context; Derrida), 181
Signature of the Visible (Jameson), 333
Signed English, 578
Signed French, 578
Signeme, 481
Signes méthodiques, 578
Sign-exchange value, 152
Signifiant imaginaire, Le (The Imaginary Signifier; Metz), 121, 417
Signific, 115, 116, 569
Significants, 120, 149
Signification, 32, 82, 247, 341, **576–577**
  complex structure of, 567
  cultural systems of, 263–265
  elementary structure of, 567
  indirect, 543
  in medieval semiotics, 403, 404
  musical, 431
  and value, 625
  vs. representation, 498
"Signification of the Phallus, The" (Lacan), 347
Significative indication, 306
Signifié, 120, 149
Signified/signifier relation, 32, 182, 573, 625
  Barthes on, 213
  Karcevskij on, 335
  and language change, 350
Signifier, and markedness, 385, 386
Signifying practice, 341
Sign Is Just a Sign, A (Sebeok), 558
Sign languages, 27, 447, 532–533, **578–582**
  aboriginal, 581
  alternate, 581–582
  American, 578
  British, 578
  Chinese, 579
  Danish, 579
  French, 578
  grammaticized facial expressions, 581

Sign languages, *cont.*
  iconicity and arbitrariness, 579
  internal structure of sign, 579
  monastic, 581
  morphology, 580
  movements and holds, 580
  primary, 578–581
  syntactic structure, 580–581
  use of space in, 580
Sign processes, self-organizing
  nature of, 603
Sign production, in mapping, 103
Signs and Meaning in the Cinema
  (Wollen), 242
Signs of Language, The (Klima and
  Bellugi), 580
Sign space, 580
Sign theory
  dialectic and materialist, 548
  psychological, 533
Sign typologies, 466
Signum, etymology, 568–569
Sign vehicle, 403
  Peirce's definition of, 308–309
  and pragmatics, 515
Silhouettes, 119
Silverstein, Michael, 369–370
Simiand, François, 206
Simile, 20, 413
Simmel, Georg, 109, 317
Simon, Herbert, 45, 137, 320, 336
Simpkins, Scott, *as contributor,*
  257–260, 377–379, 493–495,
  509–512
Simulacra, 68–69
Simulation, 45
Sincronia, diachronia e historia
  (Coseriu), 151
Singhas, A., 579
Singulars, 529, 531
Sinn, 549
Sinn and *Bedeutung,* 187
Sino-Tibetan, 350
Sinsign, 37, 115, 478, 622
Sipek, Borek, 73
Sirk, Douglas, 301
Sister Carrie (Dreiser), 452
Sitwell, O. F. G., 163–164
  as contributor, 161–165
Skaftymov, A. P., 551
Šklovskij, Viktor B., 122, 500, 519,
  551, 552
Skywriting, 646, 647
Slovo a slovesnost (Word and verbal
  art), 519, 520
"Směřuje dnešní teorie uměmi?,
  Kam" (Direction of
  Contemporary Theory of Art;
  Mukařovský), 426
Smith, Dorothy, 195, 219, 220

Smith, H. L., 367
Smith, John Maynard, 179
Smythe, William, 569
Soap operas, 392
So-called objective/subjective views,
  217
Social anthropology, 620
Social class, 249, 277–278, 388
Social contagion, 407
Social contract, 150
Social diffusion, 406
Social drama, 620
Social emancipation, 275
Social engineering, 196
Social epidemics, 406
Socialisme ou barbarie, 377
Social nominalism, 359
Social reproduction, 548
Social sciences, 249
Social Sciences: A Semiotic View
  (Greimas), 271
Social semiotics, 89–91, 132, 133,
  134, 195, 303, 510
Social Semiotics (Hodge and Kress),
  510
Social speech, 314
Societal rationalization, 275, 276
Société de consommation, La (The
  Society of Consumption;
  Baudrillard), 68
Society, 55
Society for the Study of Poetic
  Language (Obščestvo po
  Izučeniju Poètičeskogo Jazyka,
  OPOJAZ), 327, 551
Socioanagogic criticism, 100
Sociobiology, **582–585,** 616,
  641–642
Sociobiology: The New Synthesis
  (Wilson), 583, 641
Sociogenesis, 340
Sociogenetic theory, 313
Sociolect, 543
Sociolinguistics, 195
Sociology, 65, 205–206, 249
  dialogical method in, 317–319
  educational, 89–91
  of literature, 535
  structural-functional, 598
  textualist, 610
  of urbanism, 68
Sociosemiotics, 164, 193, 273, 340
Socrates, 317–318
Socrates (Blum), 318
Sodomy, 525
Sollers, Philippe, 322
Sollertinskij, Ivan Ivanovich, 57
Somatic, random, and emotional
  acts, 372
"Some Consequences of Four
  Incapacities" (Peirce), 477

"Some Reflexions on Practice and
  Theory in Structural Semantics"
  (Hjelmslev), 291
Sonata, 430
Sonesson, Göran, 261, 263
  as contributor, 26–27, 86–88,
  118–119, 187–189, 293–294,
  294–297, 298–300, 306–308,
  308–311, 415–416, 459–460,
  482–484, 484–486, 486,
  539–540
Song dynasty, 651
Sonnet, 329
Sons and Lovers (Lawrence), 451,
  452
Sontag, Susan, 507
Sophist (Plato), 29
Sophists, 150
Sorlin, Pierre, 121
Soteriology, 94, 381, 382
Soto, Domingo de, 400, 498, 499
Sound, in film, 120, 122, 270
Sound change, 351–352
Sound effects, 586
Sound laws, 351
Sounds, **585–586**
  in narrative texts, 452
Source domain (donor domain), 413
Souriau, Etienne, 5, 6–7, 9, 120
South Africa, 30–31
Sovereignty, theory of, 508
Soviet Union, 171
SOV languages, 387
Soweto riots of 1976, 31
Space, 161–164, **586–588.** *See also*
  Distance
  apprehension of, 282
  baseball's organization of, 62–63
  mandalic, 381
Spang-Hanssen, Henning, 148, 188,
  532–533, 537
Sparagmos, 26
Spatial codes, 587
Spatial delimitation, theory of, 34
Spatial semiotics, 624
*Spätrömische Kunstindustrie nach den
  Funden in Österreich-Ungarn*
  (Riegl), 540, 541
Speaking face, 588
Speaking subject, 248, 341, 564,
  606
Species and genres, 529, 531–532
Specific codes, in film, 120
Specifiers, 551
Spectacle *(opsis),* 495
Spectator, 198
  role of, 535
Spectroscopes, 257
Speech, **588–591**
  apocopated, 522
  cued, 578

Speech, *cont.*
egocentric, 314
felicity conditions of, 516
linearity theories of, 366–368
markedness in, 385–386
outer, 312–313
as performance, 647
relative to writing, 646
social, 314
syncopated, 522
transitive, 384
veiled, 418
Speech, Genres, and Other Late Essays (Bakhtin), 58
Speech Acts (Searle), 591
Speech act theory, 59, 133, 183–184, 278–280, 515, 526, **591–592**
and analysis of literature, 538
of Habermas, 275–276
and implicature, 302
and mantras, 383, 384
speech act types, 193
Speech codes, 198
restricted and elaborated, 204–205
Speech sounds, schema of, 77
Speech taboos, 581
Speed lines, 489
Spelling pronunciation, 351
Spencer, Herbert, 176, 223
Spengler, Oswald, 422, **592–593**
Sperber, Dan, 303, 516
Sperry, Roger W., 466
Sphoṭa, 74, 75
Spinoza, Baruch, 267, 274, 465
Spitzer, Leo, 59
Spivak, Gayatri Chakravorty, 155, 236, 506
Spoonerisms, 200
Sport, **593–596**
connotative set, 594
denotative extension, 593–594
distinctive features, 594–595
"Sprache über die Sprache des Menschen, Uber die" ("On Language as Such and on the Language of Man"; Benjamin), 71
S/s, 345
Staal, Frits, 383, 385
Stabilité structurelle et morphogénèse (Thom), 613–614
Stagecoach (film), 121
Stalinist linguistics, 520
Standard Average European (SAE) languages, 637
Stanton, Elizabeth Cady, 234
Star Wars (film), 502
Statement, 193

State transition, 171
Steinbeck, John, 372
Steinberg, Leo, 541
Stencils, 119
Stender-Petersen, Adolf, 537
Stepanov, Yuri, 82
Steps to an Ecology of Mind (Bateson), 65
Stereotype, **596–598**
in comics, 130
and semiology, 560
Stewart, John, 509–510
Stieglitz, Alfred, 644
Stigma: Notes on the Management of Spoiled Identity (Goffman), 259
Stilfragen: Grundlegungen zu einer Geschichte der Ornamentik (Riegl), 540, 541
Stochastic algorithm, 19
Stoics, 568
doctrine of signs, 33, 150
Stokoe, W. C., 579–580
Story and Discourse (Chatman), 243
Story of Lynx (Lévi-Strauss), 285–286
Story vs. discourse, 243
Strand, Paul, 644
Strangers to Ourselves (Kristeva), 343
Strategic knowledge, 158
Stratégies fatales, Les (Fatal Strategies; Baudrillard), 69
"Stratification du langage, La" (Hjelmslev), 291
Strawson, P. F., 538
Street theater, 198
Streit um Spengler, 593
Stress, 303
Strike (film), 269
Stringlets, 50–51
Striptease, myth of, 432
Structural anthropology, 42, 154–155, 263
Leach, 359–360
Lévi-Strauss, 42, 154–155, 207, 263, 285, 359
Structural Anthropology (Lévi-Strauss), 626
Structural asymmetry, of baseball, 62–63
Structural cartography, 104–106
Structural-functional linguistics, 598
Structural hearing, 430
Structuralism, 165–166, **598–601**
basic conceptual features of, 599–600
challenge to notion of intentionality, 315
definitions of narrative unity, 437
diagrammatic model, 563
dynamic models of, 512–515

Structuralism, *cont.*
empiricism, 367
French school of, 240
functional, 517
meaning of in original context, 327
and oppositional relationships, 626
poetics, 25–26, 496, 533
poststructuralist critique of, 512–515
predominance of closed-system models, 514
reactive movement to, 512
in the Soviet Union, 422–425
static functionalism of, 500
study of myth, 365–366
text in, 609
theory of art, 17, 33, 36
view of *langue*, 151
Structuralist linguistics, 33, 43
American, 598
application of to advertising, 13
concept of paradigm, 461
exclusion of gender consideration, 184
"item-and-arrangement" school, 367
"item-and-process" school, 367
and rock art, 547
study of cinema, 119
Structuralist narratology, 443, 444
Structural Marxism, 24–25
Structural opposition, 460
Structural phonology, 77–78, 80, 81, 617, 618
Structural semantics, 79–81, 149
Structural semiotics, 602
"Structural Study of Myth, The" (Lévi-Strauss), 444
Structural syntax, 6, 8
Structure, **601–603**
and function, 602–603
ontology of, 602
Structure of Appearance, The (Goodman), 262
Structure of Scientific Revolutions, The (Kuhn), 461
Structure of the Artistic Text, The (Lotman), 376
Structures intellectuelles (Blanché), 565
Struttura assente (Eco), 14, 39, 299
Studies in Ethnomethodology (Garfinkel), 195
Studies in Logic (Peirce), 478
Studies in Sign Systems (Trudy po znakovym sistemam), 376
Studies on Hysteria (Freud and Breuer), 29

Studie z estetiky (Mukařovský), 426
Stuttgart School of semiotic
    aesthetics, 36, 72
Stylistics, 387
Stylization, 58
Suanpan, 456
Subaltern, gendered, 506
Subculture: The Meaning of Style
    (Hebdige), 156
Subject
    in actantial model, 8
    Burke's view of, 267
    versus object, 5, 7, 8–9
    sentential, 8
    speaking, 248, 341
Subject-centered reason, 275
Subjective determinism, 395
Subjectivism, 393
Subjectivity, 191, 195, 316
    Bakhtin's construction of, 192
    embodied, 236, 237, 238
    gendered, 184–186
    Lacan's model of, 235–236
Subsidiary ideas, 187
Substance, paradox of, 267–268
Substitution of logical equivalents,
    251
*Substrater og Laan i Romansk og
    Germansk* (Brøndal), 91
Subsumation, 324
Subtractive number code, 456
Suicide (Durkheim), 206
Sumerian cuneiform, 22, 23
Sumerian number representation,
    456
Summulae (Poinsot), 498
Suppletion, 386
Supralocal syntax, 106
Surdopedagogy, 423
Surface layout, 488–489
Surface structure, 599–600, 602
Surrealist painting, 308
Survival of the fittest. *See* Natural
    selection
Suspense, 323
Suture, 122, 186
SVO languages, 387
Swallowtail catastrophe, 110, 614
Syllabaries, 23, 26
Syllabic length, 462
Syllogism, 264
Symbiosis, and evolutionary
    change, 255
Symbol, 478
    etymology, 569
    exemplifying, 262, 263
    in knowledge representation
        system, 336
    meanings, 620
    personal, 166

Symbol, *cont.*
    photographs as, 482
    on postage stamps, 502
    psychogenetic, 166
    usage in semiotic literature, 569
Symbolic. *See* Semiotic and
    symbolic
Symbolic action, language as,
    99–101, 266–268, 349–350
Symbolic analysis, 165
Symbolic anthropology, 165,
    359–360
Symbolic code, 60
Symbolic exchange, 68, 69, 152
Symbolic interaction, 218, 257, 275
Symbolic logic, 249–251
Symbolic message, 13
Symbolic motivation, 166
Symbolic power, 89, 90–91
Symbolic representation, in
    artificial intelligence, 45, 336
Symbolic significance, 109
Symbolic signs, in advertising, 14
Symbolic type, **603–604**
Symbolic value, 89
Symbolic violence, 89, 90
Symbolism, 414
Symbolist poetry, 465
Symbolists, 57, 296
Symbolization
    and phonograms, 115–116
    and pictograms, 114
Symbol manipulation, 226–227
Symbols: Public and Private (Firth),
    569
"Symbols, On" (Eco), 569
Symbol strings, 336
Symmetry
    and iconicity, 296
    linguistic, 92, 93
Sympathetic magic (hunting
    magic), 545
Symposium on the Structural Study
    of Sign Systems, 423, 424
Synaptic weights, 141
Synchronic and diachronic, 48,
    149, 150–151, 327, 338–339,
    351, 352, 555, **605–607**
Syncopated speech, 522
Syncretic manifestation, 9
Synecdoche, 309, 415–416
    filmic, 302
    in pictures, 489
    and rock art, 547
    as secondary indexical sign, 308
Synechism, 478
Synesthesia, 452
Synfunction, 552
Synonymic parallelism, 465
Synonymous ideograms, 297–298

Synonymy, 262
Syntactical analysis, 474
Syntactical codes, in film semiotics,
    120
Syntactical functions, of
    punctuation, 522
Syntactic articulation, 47
Syntactic drift, theory of, 352
Syntactic-semantic theory, 9
Syntagm, 115, 415, 416, 461
    as a generative metaphor, 433
    topeme, 105
Syntagmatic approach, to gossip,
    265
Syntagmatic relations, 415, 555,
    596
Syntagmatic solidarities, 368–369
Syntagmatic string, 366, 367
Syntagmatic system, of film
    analysis, 120, 268–270
Syntax
    iconicity, 328–329
    local, 106
    in mapping, 105–106
    semantic, 110–111
Syntaxis, 328
Synthetic parallelism, 465
Synthetic pictures, 119
Syracuse Law Review, 358
Syria, 22
System, 149
Système de la mode (Barthes), 60
Système des objets, Le (The Systems
    of Objects; Baudrillard), 68
System of Logic (Mill), 187
Systems theory, 598
Syuzhet, 122
S/Z (Barthes), 60, 258, 259, 315,
    378, 467, 535

T

Tabarroni, Andrea, 51
Taboo system, 286
Tacit knowledge, 158, 159
Tacsesics, 481
Tactile (haptic) mode of perception,
    540–541
Tactile pictures, 488
Tactile postures, 282
Tagalog, 639
Tagging, 560
Tags, 647
Taine, Hippolyte, 482
Taiwan fingerspelling system, 245
Taking Rights Seriously (Dworkin),
    356
Tales of Love (Kristeva), 343
Talismans *(tianfu, fu),* 173, 174–176,
    381, 385

Talks on Russian Culture (Lotman), 377
Tambiah, Stanley, 95, 384
Tan, Ed, 612
Tantric Buddhism, 95, 382, 384, 385
Taoism. *See* Daoism
Tarasti, Eero, 446
Target domain, 413
Tarski, Alfred, 631
Task-performing activities, 372
Tathatā, 95
Tautology, 302, 432
Taxologie des Englischen (Koch), 339
Taxonomies, 158, 159, 204
  in ethnoscience, 166–167, 221
  of film segments, 268–270
Technical interests, 275
Technographic pictures, 119
Technologization, 196
Teeth, communicative functions of, 589
Teleology, 276, 341
Television, 389
  research on, 391
  violence, 390
Tel Quel group, 238, 340, 392, 395
Temperance, 234
Temperature, and the Gaia hypothesis, 254
Tempo, vocal, 462
Temporal order, 190
Temps modernes, Les, 67
Ten Classes of Signs (Peirce), 502
Tenor
  in metaphor, 413, 415
  of a social context, 279
Tensivity, 469
Tensor sign, 378
Ten Wings, The, 648
Terasaki, A., 592
Tertiary cultureme, 169, 170
Tesnière, Lucien, 5, 6, 438, 617
Tessellation, 42
Tess of the D'Urbervilles (Hardy), 452
Tests, in narrative structure, 438–440
Texas Law Review, 358
Text, 575, **609–611**
  audiovisual, 243, 244
  Barthes on, 60–61, 341, 494
  as chart, 99
  closed, 209
  as dream, 99
  kinesics in, 451–452
  and linguistics, 196
  in modern poetics, 496, 542
  Moscow-Tartu notion of, 424
  open, 209
  paralanguage in, 451

Text, *cont.*
  poetic, 542
  as prayer, 99
  reference in, 538–539
  self-reflexive, 122
  semiotics, 14, 73
  sociolectic, 543
  sounds in, 452
  as source of data regarding habitus, 371–373
  as a system, 552
Textem, Das (Koch), 339
Text linguistics, 196
Text semiotics, 73
  of advertising, 14
Textuality, 544
  Kristeva's concept of, 341
Textual metafunction, of language, 279
Textural coherence, 303
Thai Buddhism, 384
Theaetetus (Plato), 318
Theater, **611–613**
  folk, 89
  poor, 26–27
  semiotics of, 89, 149, 535, 612
  in Western European semiotic theory, 611
Thematic isotopy, 324
Theme and rheme, 519
"Theologisch-politisches Fragment" (Theologisch-political Fragment; Benjamin), 71
Theology, 101
Theoretische ésthetik (Baumgarten), 36
Theories of Symbols (Todorov), 569
Theorizing (Blum), 318
Theory of Communicative Action (Habermas), 275
"Theory of Descriptions" (Russell), 499
Theory of Justice, A (Rawls), 276
Theory of Poetic Language (*Sborniki po teorii poètičeskogo jazyka*), 551
Theory of Prose (Šklovskij), 426, 519
Theory of Semiotics, A (Eco), 39, 210, 391
Theory of Sound Change (Koch), 338–339
"Theory of the Formal Method" (Ejchenbaum), 644
Theriophily, 28
Thermodynamics, 607
Thermograms, 119
Thesaurus, 561
"Theses on the Semiotic Study of Cultures" (Lotman), 376, 424
"Theses Presented to the First Congress of Slavic Philologists in Prague 1929," 518

Thibault, Paul J., *as contributor*, 32–33, 76–82, 125–129, 150–152, 193–194, 275–277, 312–314, 355–356, 368–369, 369–371, 408–411, 427–429, 512–515, 576–577, 598–601, 605–607, 637–641
Thom, René B., 110–111, 307, 422, 570, 598, **613–614**
Thomists, 402
Thompson, D'Arcy W., 422
Thompson, Denys, 390
Thompson, Edward P., 288
Thompson, Evan, *as contributor*, 53–55, 253–256
Thomson, Clive, *as contributor*, 57–59, 527–529
Thomson, William, 476
Thought and Language (Vygotsky), 313
Threadgold, Terry, 238
  as contributor, 184–187, 194–196, 247–249
Throatiness, 462
Through the Lands of the Bible (Morton), 372
Through the Looking Glass (Carroll), 630
Thürlemann, Felix, 485, 645
Thymic component, 469–470
Tianfu (fu; talismans), 173, 174–176, 381, 385
Tierra simulator, 50–51
Timbre, 462
Time, 44, 74–75
  baseball's organization of, 62
  Leach's analysis of, 360
Timpler, Clemens, 53
Tinbergen, Nikolaas, 179, 225
Tincture (heraldry), 284
Tindemans, Carlos, 612
Titunik, Irvin, 611
Todorov, Tzvetan, 26, 157, 268, 287, 443, 569, 598
Token. *See* Type and token
Tolkien, J. R. R., 502
Tolstoy, Leo, 502
Tolton, C. D. E., *as contributor*, 119–123, 268–271, 300–302, 417–418
Toma ševskij, Boris V., 376, 518, 551
Tomkins, Silvan, 211
Toneme, 481
Tongue, communicative functions of, 590
Top down, 474
Topemes, 104–106
Topical codification, 14
Topic change, 303
Topology, 44, 486, 599, 613

Toporov, V. N., 376, 423, 425
Totem, 221
    logo as, 375
    military use of, 418
    poles, 284
Totemism, 206, 364–365
Totentanz (Danse macabre), 84, 215
Touch, as a perceptual system,
    281–282
Touch of Evil (film), 121
Tournament impresa, 305
"Toward a Philosophy of the Act
    [or Deed]" (Bakhtin), 57
"Tower of Babel and the Confusion
    of Tongues, The" (Trubetzkoy),
    618
Trace, 627
"Tracking the Vampire" (Case), 526
Tractatus de signis (Treatise on Signs;
    Poinsot), 53, 399, 498
Tractatus Logico-Philosophicus
    (Wittgenstein), 629, 642, 643
Trademark, **614–616**
Traffic signs, 26
Tragedy, 25, 26, 252, 495, 501
Trager, G. L., 367
"Tragic Misreadings': Queer
    Theory's Erasure of Transgender
    Subjectivity" (Namaste), 527
Transactive criticism, 533, 535
Transcendental relations, 401, 402,
    403
Transcription, 103
Transformation, of a mytheme, 366
Transformational generative (T G)
    grammar, 34, 46, 126, 147,
    195, 351–352, 367, 429
Transformation algorithm, 468
Transformations, 74–75, 467–468
Transforms, 66
Transgendered people, 527
Transition-probability networks,
    561
Transition tables, 171
Transitive speech acts, 384
Transitivity, 8
Translation, 71
Transparence du Mal, La (The
    Transparency of Evil;
    Baudrillard), 68–69
Transparency, principle of, 516
Transtextuality, 122
Travaux du Cercle Linguistique, 519
*Travaux du Cercle Linguistique de
    Copenhague*, 148
Travaux linguistiques de Prague, 520
Travels in Hyperreality (Eco), 209
Traverses, 68
Travesty, 319
Treasure Island (Stevenson), 462

Treatise on Signs (Poinsot), 499
Treatise on the Astrolabe (Chaucer),
    280
Tree graph, 190
Trendelenburg, Friedrich Adolph,
    465, 476
Trevarthen, C., 193
Trickster, 80
Trigrams *(gua)*, 648
Tristan, Flora, 234
Trivers, Robert, 321, **616–617**, 641
Trnka, Bohumil, 517, 519, 520
Trockij, Lev D., 553
Tropes, 414, 415
Tropological codification, 14
Tropological interpretation, of
    Scripture, 21
Tropology, 628
"Trouble with 'Asians,' The" (Fung),
    527
Trubetzkoy, Nikolaj Sergeevič,
    77–78, 151, 335, 459, 518–519,
    565, 598, **617–618**
Trudy po znakovym sistemam
    (Studies on sign systems),
    423–424
"True Real, The" (Kristeva), 342
Truth, 629, 630
Truth and Method (Gadamer), 358
Tsimshian myth of Asdiwal, 365,
    587
Tswana, 31, 289
Tucci, Giuseppe, 381
Tuchman, Gaye, 219
Turing, Alan, 44–45, 422, **618–620**
Turing machine, 19, 44–45, 136,
    618–619
Turkish, 387
Turn-change behaviors, 145
Turner, M., 414
Turner, Victor, 165, 207, 288, 360,
    605, **620–622**
Turn-taking, in conversation,
    144–145, 195
"Two Dogmas of Empiricism"
    (Quine), 630
Two Myths of the New Theatre
    (Barthe), 432
Tynjanov, Jurij N., 122, 376, 500,
    518, 551
Type and token, 47, 262, 480,
    549–550, **622**
Typographics, 119
Typographogenesis, 340
Typology, word-order, 352

U

Ubersfeld, Anne, 611, 612
Uberweb, Friedrich, 476

"Überwindung der Metaphysik durch
    logische Analyse der Sprache"
    ("Overcoming of Metaphysics
    Through Logical Analysis of
    Language"; Carnap), 630
Uexküll, Jakob von, 28, 82, 111, 623
Uexküll, Thure von, 82, 623
Uldall, Jørgen Hans, 537
Ultimate class, 609
Ultrasound, 119
Ulysses (Joyce), 343
Umiker-Sebeok, Jean, 82
Umwelt, 28, 82, 84, 536, **623–624**
Uncarved block image, 173
Unconscious, 28, 29
Underspecification, 200
Understanding Media (McLuhan), 390
Uniformitarianism, 351
United Kingdom, fingerspelling
    system, 245
Unity, of science, 630–631
Universal grammar, 92–93
Universal judgments, 250
Universal language projects, 86
Universal Postal Union, 502
Universals, 529–532
Universe of the Mind (Lotman), 377
Unlimited semiosis, 185
Unsignifying, 173
Upāya, 94, 95
Upper Paleolithic, 545, 546
Urban, Wilbur, 187, 532
Urbancic, Anne, *as contributor*,
    233–237
Urban-exterior cultureme, 168
Urban II, Pope, 283
Urban-interior cultureme, 168
Urban semiotics, 164, 587–588,
    624–625
Urbemes, 33
Urpflanze, 422
Ursprung des deutschen Trauerspiels
    (Origin of the German Tragic
    Drama; Benjamin), 70
Ursus spelaeus (cave bear), 545
User interface, 319
Uses of Literacy, The (Hogart), 391
Use value, 152–153
Uspenskij, B. A., 293, 423
Utopia, 240–241
Utopie, 68
Utterances, 58, 133, 191–192, 424
Uznavanie, 552

V

Vaikharī (phonetic), 75
Vailati, Giovanni, 548
"Vākyakāṇda," 74
Vākyapadīyam (On Sentences and
    Words; Bhartṛhari), 74, 75

Value, 38, 274, 600, **625–627**
Value coding, 505, 506
Van Gennep, Arnold, 621
Van Gogh, Vincent, 42
Vanlier, Henri, 483
Varela, Francisco J., 53–55, 98, 254, 640
"Variability of Vision, The" (Gombrich), 261
Varia semiotica (Koch), 339
Variation, principle of, 93
Vāsanā, 96
Vasarely, Victor, 485
Vasubandhu, 96
Veblen, Thorstein, 478
Vectors, systems of, 44
Vehicle, 47, 412, 413, 415
Veiled speech, 418
Velopharyngeal control, 462
Veltrusky, Jiři, 89
Venn, John, 478
Venn diagrams, 190
Venturi, Robert, 507
Verb, 75, 76
Verbal formulas, 158, 159, 160
Verbal message, 14
Verbal metalanguage, 427
Vereiniging für Ästhetik und Allgemeine Kunstwissenschaft, 644
Verification, 629–630, 631
Verner, Karl, 351
Vertical semiotics, 83
Vertices, 190
Vertiginous play, 493–494
Vertov, Dziga, 241
"*Verum et factum convertuntur*" ("The true is the mark"), 628
Vestème, 482
Vice Versa (Garber), 526
Vico, Giambattista, 109, **627–628**
Videnie, 552
Video, 119
Video conferencing, 138
Vienna circle, **625–631**
Vijñaptimātratā, 96
Vimalakīrta Nirdeśa Sūtra, 94
Vindication of the Rights of Women, A (Wollstonecraft), 234
Vinokur, Grigorij O., 518, 551
Virtual reality, 491–492
Viruses, 224
Vision, 488, 489, **631–635**
   as a computational system, 634, 635
   modular or feature-pathway principle in, 633
   optical patterns, 256–257, 633
   study of, 635
Visual arts, 260–261

Visual illusion, 260
"Visual Image, The" (Gombrich), 261
"Visual Pleasure and Narrative Cinema" (Mulvey), 122
Visual programming, 492
Visual programming languages, 492
Visual semiotics, 35–36, 42, 73, 260–261, 415, 484, 645
Visual signs, 297–298
Visual Thinking (Arnheim), 35
Vitalism, 53–54, 598
Vodička, Felix, 520
Voice, 589
Voice characteristics, 461–462
Voix et le phénomène, La (Speech and Phenomena and Other Essays on Husserl's Theory of Signs; Derrida), 181
VO languages, 352
Volkelt, Johannus, 645
Völkerpsychologie ("folk psychology"; Wundt), 638
Voloshinov, Valentin N., 133, 150, 192, 287, 313, 328
   approach to semiosis, 393, 394
   critique of formalism, 553
   dialogism, 563
   and Marxism, 388
   materialist perspective, 394
   and Peircean pragmatism, 393
   theory of meaning, 397
   theory of signs, 393–394
Von Neumann computer architecture, 19, 466, 619
Voprosy Jazykoznanija, 423
Vowels
   addition of to consonantal alphabet, 23
   articulation, 590
   nasal, 386–387
   oral, 387
   systems, 351
Vox (sound), 5
Voyeurism, 122, 301
Vrba, Elizabeth, 225–226
VSO languages, 387
Vygotsky, Lev, 313, 314, 551

W

Waddington, Conrad H., 598
Wagner, Richard, 502
Wagner Androgyne (Nattiez), 446
Waismann, Friedrich, 629
Wall, Anthony, *as contributor*, 57–59, 239–241, 527–529
Wallace, Alfred Russel, 177
Wallace, Joy, *as contributor*, 340–343, 345–349

Wallis, Mieczyslaw, 87
Walther, Elisabeth, 73
Walzel, Oskar, 644
Wang Bi, 648
Wang Wei, 649
Wantmakers, The (Clark), 391
War and Peace (Tolstoy), 502
Warring States period, 116–117
Watson, Andrew, 254
Watson, J. B., 466
Watson, James, 224
Watt, Ian, 263
Waugh, Linda, 329
Waveforms, 123
Ways of Worldmaking (Goodman), 354
Weaver, Warren, 72, 311, 331, 514, 570
Weber, Ernst Heinrich, 282
Weber, Max, 165, 205, 275, 276, 317, 604
Wechel, Christian, 214
Wechselseitige Erhellung der Künste: Ein Beiträg zur Würdigung kunstgeschichtlicher Begriffe (Walzel), 644
Weiner, Norbert, 166
Weinreich, Ulrich, 196
Weis, Elizabeth, 122
Weiss, Peter, 67
Weissgerber, Leo, 533
Welcome to the Jungle (Mercer), 526
Wellek, René, 520
Welles, Orson, 270
Well of Tears, The (Koch), 339
Wells, Rulon, 327
Wen, King, 648
Wernicke, Carl, 312
Werth, P., 303
Wertheimer, Joseph, 150
Wertheimer, Max, 35
Wertsch, James, 313
Western culture
   closure of metaphysics, 181
   mythological framework of, 252
   philosophy after Hegel, 508
"'What' and the 'How,' The" (Gombrich), 261
"What Are the Signs of What? (A Theory of 'Entitlement')" (Burke), 100
Wheatley, Paul, 162
Wheelock, Wade, 384
Whispering, 523
White, Hayden, 287
Whitehead, Alfred North, 64, 422
Whitman, Walt, 28
Whitney, Hassler, 614
Whitney, William Dwight, 328

Whorf, Benjamin Lee, 43, 195, 328, 329, 588, **637–641**
  linguistic relativism, 133, 154, 369–371
Widrow-Hoff rule, 143
Wiener, Norbert, 137, 570
Wierzbicka, Anna, 201
Wilden, Anthony, 80, 160, 514
Wildgen, Wolfgang, 111
William of Ockham, 477
Williams, Patricia, 363
Williams, Raymond, 153, 390, 395
Williamson, Judith, 391
Wills, David, 121
Wilson, Deirdre, 303, 516
Wilson, Edward O., 170, 570, 583, **641–642**, 652
Wilson, Margo, 584
Wimsatt, William C., 466
Wirth, Uwe, *as contributor,* 1–3
Wissenschaftliche Weltauffassung: Der Wiener Kreis (Scientific World Conception: The Vienna Circle; Neurath et al.), 629
Witchcraft, 205
Wittgenstein, Ludwig, 65, 250, 356, 508, 549, 629, **642–644**
  concept of language use, 548
  correspondence theory of meaning, 384, 642–643
  picture theory of the proposition, 642–643
  theory of language games, 396, 643
  theory of meaning in the *Tractatus,* 642–643
  view of language, 643
Wittig, Monique, 526
Wolff, Christian, 149
Wölfflin, Heinrich, 540, **644–645**
Wollen, Peter, 242, 243
Wollstonecraft, Mary, 234

Women, in the media, 236
Women's Rights Convention, Seneca Falls, 234
Women's suffrage, 234
Woolf, Virginia, 235
Wooten, Sir Henry, 306
"Word, Dialogue, and Novel" (Kristeva), 342
Word processing, 647
Words, 327
  as agents of power, 101
  as basic sign unit, 369
  relationship to reality, 116–118
  as *sermo,* 5
  and things, 3, 4
  as *vox,* 5
Words with Power (Frye), 251
Work of François Rabelais and Popular Culture during the Middle Ages and the Renaissance, The (Bakhtin), 59
Worldview (weltanschauung), 167
World Wide Web, 137, 138
Worth, Sol, 242
Wretched of the Earth, The (Fanon), 505
Wright, Chauncey, 477
Wright, Roger, 352
Writing, 264, 366, 521
  and decontextualization, 646
  ethnography of, 246–247, 521–523, **645–647**
  of mantras, 384–385
  material aspects, 646–647
  as performance, 647
  picture, 24
  relation to speech, 646
Writing Culture (Clifford and Marcus), 156
Wulff, Hans, 242
Wundt, Wilhelm, 369, 465, 638

XYZ
Xianren (Immortal), 174
X-rays, 119
Xunzi, 117
Yamasaki Taikō, 381
Yang, 648
Yell, Susan, *as contributor,* 302–304
"Yellow Kid," 131
Yi jing (I Ching), 74, **647–650**
Yi ming ju shi, 116
Yin, 648
Yinyang, 176
Yoga, 97
Yogācāra semiotics, 96, 98
Young, Jock, 391
Yule, George, 195
Yunzhuan (cloud seals), 173, 174, 385
Zahavi, Amotz, 281, **650**
Zemsz, Abraham, 644, 645
Zen Buddhism, 94, 97–98
Zen discourse, 651
Zen gardens, **650–652**
Zero degree, 60
Zero-order realities, 599
Zhou, Duke of, 648
Zhuangzi (Chuang Tzu), 173
Zhu Xi, 649
Zich, Otakar, 11, 425
Zilsel, Edgar, 629
Žimkin, N. V., 423
Žirmunskij, Viktor, 376
Zoon, 29
Zoosemiotics, 37, 82, 340, 650, **652**
  interspecific communication, 321–322
  introduction of, 558
  and manipulation, 382–383
Zulu, 31